Mala
Singapore
& Brunei

a Lonely Planet travel survival kit

Peter Turner
Chris Taylor
Hugh Finlay

Malaysia, Singapore & Brunei

6th edition

Published by

Lonely Planet Publications

Head Office: PO Box 617, Hawthorn, Vic 3122, Australia

Branches: 155 Filbert St, Suite 251, Oakland, CA 94607, USA

10 Barley Mow Passage, Chiswick, London W4 4PH, UK

71 bis rue du Cardinal Lemoine, 75005 Paris, France

Printed by

Pac-Rim Kwartanusa Printing

Printed in Indonesia

Photographs by

Vicki Beale	Glenn Beanland	Paul Beinssen	Hugh Finlay
Richard I'Anson	Richard Nebesky	Simon Rowe	Paul Steel
Sue Tan	Peter Turner	Tony Wheeler	

Front cover: Boatman on Police Beach, Pulau Gaya, off Kota Kinabalu, Sabah (Simon Rowe)

First Published

May 1982

This Edition

November 1996

Although the authors and publisher have tried to make the information as accurate as possible, they accept no responsibility for any loss, injury or inconvenience sustained by any person using this book.

National Library of Australia Cataloguing in Publication Data

Turner, Peter.
Malaysia, Singapore & Brunei.

6th ed.
Includes index.
ISBN 0 86442 393 4.

1. Malaysia – Guidebooks. 2. Singapore – Guidebooks.
3. Brunei – Guidebooks. I. Taylor, Chris, 1961–. II. Title: Malaysia, Singapore & Brunei.
(Series: Lonely Planet travel survival kit).

915.95

Peter Turner

Peter was born in Melbourne and studied Asian studies, politics and English before setting off on the Asian trail. His long-held interest in South-East Asia has seen him make numerous trips to the region, and he has worked on Lonely Planet's *Singapore city guide, Jakarta city guide, Java, Indonesia, South-East Asia on a shoestring* and *New Zealand*.

Chris Taylor

Chris grew up in England and Australia, and has spent much of his adult life based variously in Melbourne, Tokyo and Taipei. Rescued from a teaching degree by Lonely Planet, he went on to co-author *Japan* and has since worked on *China, Tibet, Tokyo city guide* and *Seoul city guide*, as well as writing Lonely Planet's *Mandarin phrasebook*. Chris is also a frequent contributor to newspapers and magazines. No sooner had he finished *Malaysia, Singapore & Brunei* than he was off to work on a new edition of *Cambodia*. Chris says that if he had the time he would spend it striving for the perfect home-brew cappuccino.

Hugh Finlay

After deciding that there must be more to life than a career in civil engineering, Hugh first hit the road in 1976, on a trail which eventually led him to Africa via Asia, Europe and the Middle East in the early 80s. Since joining Lonely Planet in 1985, Hugh has written Lonely Planet's *Delhi city guide* and *Jordan & Syria*, co-authored *Morocco, Algeria & Tunisia* and contributed to other guides, including *South-East Asia on a shoestring, Africa on a shoestring* and *India*.

From the Authors

Chris Taylor

Thanks to Justin and Alli Hancock of Britain for joining me on what would otherwise have been a dull Tioman expedition. In Sarawak, I owe an enormous debt to Mike Reed, whose expertise on all things Sarawakian changed my outlook on the place and provided me with a rich data base to plagiarise from. Thanks too to Audrey Wan Ullock of the Telang Usan Hotel, and Robert Basiuk and Philip Yong of Borneo Adventure in Kuching. In Brunei, thanks to Chit La Rosa for providing me with last-minute information. In Sabah I am indebted to Florence F Gusti of Tourism Malaysia, who was invariably painstaking and patient with my never-ending inquiries. Thanks also to Wendy Sabah of the Sabah Tourist Promotion Board. Outside Malaysia, as always, a big thank you to Christine Jones of Phoenix Services in Hong Kong, who took care of my travel arrangements. Thanks too to Patrick Hogan in Hong Kong for throwing open the doors of his sprawling Happy Valley apartment. And I'd like to thank all the travellers who commiserated with me on the alcohol-free Perhentian Islands.

This Book

The first edition of this guide was written by Geoff Crowther and Tony and Maureen Wheeler. Research for the second edition was handled by Mark Lightbody. The third edition was the joint effort of Sue Tan and Joe Cummings. Hugh Finlay and Peter Turner updated the fourth and fifth editions. For this sixth edition, Peter Turner covered Singapore and most of Peninsular Malaysia and Chris Taylor covered Sabah, Sarawak and Brunei, as well as the east coast of the peninsula.

From the Publisher

This sixth edition of *Malaysia, Singapore & Brunei* was edited in LP's Melbourne office by Linda Suttie and designed by Adam McCrow. Megan Fraser and Janet Austin assisted with editing and Greg Alford, Kristin Odijk, Mic Looby and David Andrew helped out with proofing. Jon Murray researched and wrote the special section on Places of Worship, with the assistance of Sharan Kaur, who also co-ordinated the colour section on Food in Singapore & Malaysia. Maps were drawn by Adam McCrow and Chris Love and illustrations were done by Adam and Trudi Canavan. Simon Bracken and Adam designed the cover. Kerrie Williams compiled the index.

Thanks to all the travellers who took the time to write to us about their experiences. Their names appear at the back of the book.

Warning & Request

Things change – prices go up, schedules change, good places go bad and bad places go bankrupt – nothing stays the same. So if you find things better or worse, recently opened or long since closed, please write and tell us and help make the next edition better. Your letters will be used to help update future editions and, where possible, important changes will also be included in an Update section in reprints.

We greatly appreciate all information that is sent to us by travellers. Back at Lonely Planet we employ a hard-working readers' letters team to sort through the many letters we receive. The best ones will be rewarded with a free copy of the next edition or another Lonely Planet guide if you prefer. We give away lots of books, but, unfortunately, not every letter/postcard receives one.

Contents

Map Legend

BOUNDARIES

- International Boundary
- Regional Boundary

ROUTES

- Freeway
- Highway
- Major Road
- Unsealed Road or Track
- City Road
- City Street
- Railway
- Underground Railway
- Tram
- Walking Track
- Walking Tour
- Ferry Route
- Cable Car or Chairlift

AREA FEATURES

- Parks
- Built-Up Area
- Pedestrian Mall
- Market
- Cemetery
- Reef
- Beach or Desert
- Rocks

HYDROGRAPHIC FEATURES

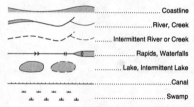

- Coastline
- River, Creek
- Intermittent River or Creek
- Rapids, Waterfalls
- Lake, Intermittent Lake
- Canal
- Swamp

SYMBOLS

- CAPITAL — National Capital
- Capital — Regional Capital
- CITY — Major City
- City — City
- Town — Town
- Village — Village
- Place to Stay, Place to Eat
- Cafe, Pub or Bar
- Post Office, Telephone
- Tourist Information, Bank
- Transport, Parking
- Museum, Youth Hostel
- Caravan Park, Camping Ground
- Church, Cathedral
- Mosque, Sikh Temple
- Temple, Hindu Temple
- Stupa, Metro Station
- Hospital, Police Station
- Embassy, Petrol Station
- Airport, Airfield
- Swimming Pool, Gardens
- Shopping Centre, Zoo
- One Way Street, Route Number (A25)
- Stately Home, Monument
- Castle, Tomb
- Cave, Hut or Shelter
- Mountain or Hill, Lookout
- Lighthouse, Shipwreck
- Pass, Spring
- Golf Course, Bird Sanctuary
- Archaeological Site or Ruins
- Ancient or City Wall
- Cliff or Escarpment, Tunnel
- Railway Station

Note: not all symbols displayed above appear in this book

Introduction

Malaysia, Singapore and Brunei are three independent South-East Asian nations offering the visitor a taste of Asia at its most accessible. These countries are among the richest in Asia, so, as you might expect, they are relatively prosperous and forward-looking. Transport facilities are good, accommodation standards are high and for the visitor there are few problems to be faced.

Yet, despite these high standards, these are not expensive countries to visit. Singapore may be able to offer all the air-conditioned comforts your credit cards can handle, and East Malaysia may at times be a little pricey due to its jungle-frontier situation, but in Peninsular Malaysia the costs can be very cheap if you want them to be.

More important than simple ease of travel, this region offers amazing variety – both geographically and culturally. If you want beaches and tropical islands, it's hard to beat the east coast of the peninsula. If you want mountains, parks and wildlife, you can climb Mt Kinabalu, explore the rivers of Sarawak or trek the trails of the huge Taman Negara National Park on the peninsula. If you want city life, you can try the historic old port of Melaka, the easy-going backstreets of Georgetown in Penang or the modern-as-tomorrow city of Singapore.

When it comes to people, you've got Malays, Chinese, Indians and a whole host of indigenous tribes in Sabah and Sarawak.

Last, but far from least, you've got a choice of food which alone brings people back to the region over and over again; there's no question in many people's minds that Singapore is the food capital of Asia.

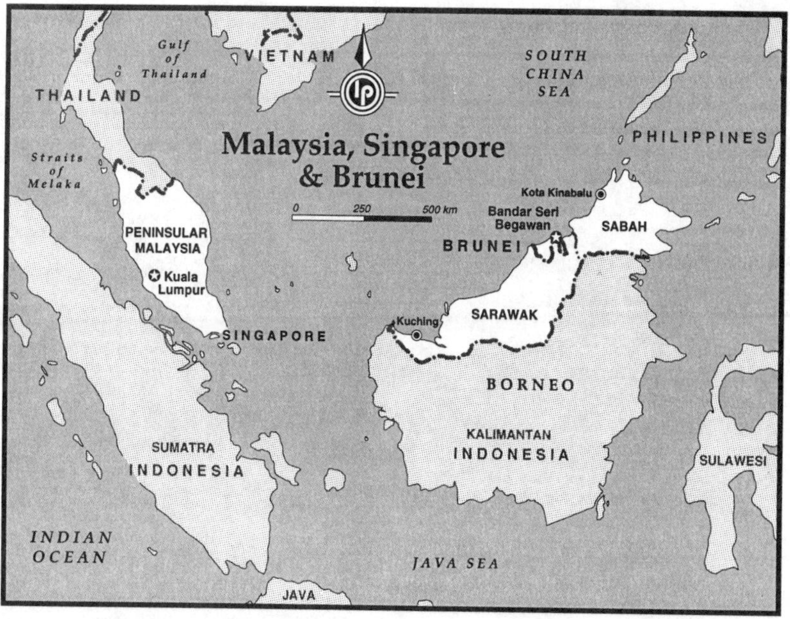

Malaysia

Facts about Malaysia

HISTORY

It is only since WWII that Malaysia, Singapore and Brunei have emerged as three separate, independent countries. Prior to that they were all loosely amalgamated as a British colony, Sarawak excepted, and earlier still they might have been independent Malay kingdoms or part of the greater Majapahit or Sriwijaya empires of what is now Indonesia. In the dim mists of time it's possible that Malaysia was actually the home of the earliest Homo sapiens in Asia. Discoveries have been made in the gigantic Niah Caves of Sarawak which indicate that the Stone Age human was present there, and in other caves of north Borneo and the Malay peninsula, as long ago as 40,000 years.

Early Trade & Empires

Little is known about the Stone Age Malaysians, but around 10,000 years ago the aboriginal Malays – the Orang Asli – began to move down the peninsula from a probable starting point in south-west China. Remote settlements of Orang Asli can still be found in parts of Malaysia, but 4000 years ago they were already being supplanted by the Proto-Malays, ancestors of today's Malays, who at first settled the coastal regions, then moved inland. In the early centuries of the Christian era, Malaya was known as far away as Europe. Ptolemy showed it on his early map with the label 'Golden Chersonese'. It spelt gold not only to the Romans but also to the Indians and Chinese, whose traders arrived not long after in search of that most valuable metal. Hindu mini-states now began to spring up along the great Malay rivers.

The Malay people were basically similar ethnically to the people of Sumatra, Java and even the Philippines, and from time to time various South-East Asian empires extended their control over all or part of the Malay peninsula. Funan, a kingdom based in modern-day Cambodia, at one time controlled the northern part of the peninsula. From the 7th century the great Sumatran-based Sriwijaya empire, with its capital in Palembang, held the whole area and even extended its rule into Thailand. A significant Malay trading kingdom, under the suzerainty of Sriwijaya, became established at the Bujang Valley in today's Perak state. It's Hindu temples remain the most significant reminder of the Hindu-Buddhist period that held sway over much of the peninsula for nearly a millennium.

Sriwijaya eventually fell to the Java-based Majapahit empire, and then in 1403 Parameswara, a Sumatran prince, established himself at Melaka, which soon became the most powerful city-state in the region. At this time the spice trade from the Moluccas was beginning to develop and Melaka, with its strategic position on the straits which separate Sumatra from the Malay peninsula, was a familiar port for ships from the east and west.

In 1405 the Chinese admiral Cheng Ho arrived in Melaka with greetings from the 'Son of Heaven' and, more importantly, the promise of protection from the encroaching Siamese to the north. With this support from China, the power of Melaka extended to include most of the Malay peninsula. At about the same time, Islam arrived in Melaka and soon spread through Malaya.

Portuguese Period

For the next century Melaka's power and wealth expanded to such an extent that the city became one of the wealthiest in the east. So wealthy, in fact, that the Portuguese began to take an active interest in the place. After a preliminary skirmish in 1509, Alfonso de Albuquerque arrived in 1511 with a fleet of 18 ships and overpowered Melaka's 20,000 defenders and their war elephants. The sultan of Melaka fled south with his court to Johor, where the Portuguese were unable to dislodge him. Thus Melaka came to be the centre of European power in the region, while Johor grew to be the main

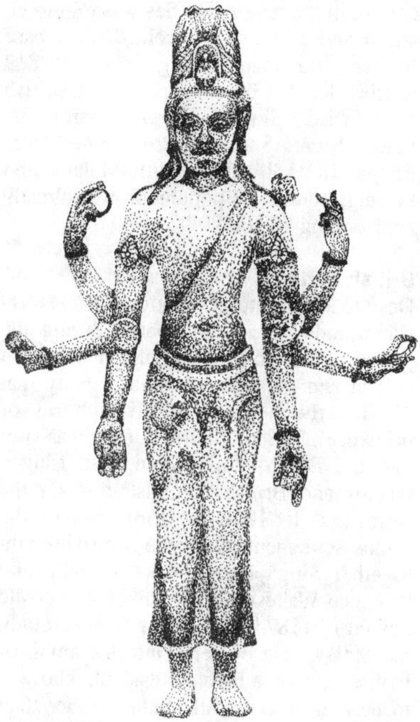

This bronze statue of a Bodhisattva is a relic of the Sumatran-based Sriwijaya empire, which dates back to the 7th century.

Malay city-state, along with other Malay centres at Brunei in north Borneo and Acheh in the north of Sumatra.

The Portuguese were to hold Melaka for over 100 years, although they were never able to capitalise on the city's fabulous wealth and superb position. Portuguese trading power and strength was never great enough to take full advantage of the volume of trade that used to flow through Melaka, but, more importantly, the Portuguese did not develop the complex pattern of influence and patronage upon which Melaka had based its power and control. Worse, the Portuguese reputation for narrow-mindedness and cruelty had preceded them, and they gained few converts to Christianity and little support for their rule.

Thus the other Malay states were able to grow into the vacuum created by the Portuguese takeover of Melaka, and while they squabbled and fought among themselves, they also had the strength to make attacks on Melaka. Gradually Portuguese power declined, and after long skirmishes with the Dutch, who supported the rulers of Johor, Melaka eventually fell to the Dutch, after a long and bitter siege, in 1641.

Dutch Period

Like the Portuguese, the Dutch were to rule Melaka for over a century but, also like the Portuguese, the Dutch failed to recognise that Melaka's greatest importance was as a centre for entrepôt trade. To an even greater extent than their predecessors, the Dutch tried to keep Melaka's trade totally to themselves, and as a result Melaka continued to decline. Also, the greatest Dutch interest was reserved for Batavia, modern-day Jakarta, so Melaka was always the poor sister to the more important Javan port.

British Arrive

By the late 18th century the British began to eye Malaysia, having previously been tied up with their Indian possessions. In 1786 Captain Francis Light docked at Penang and occupied it. Light followed a free-trade policy at Penang, a clear contrast to the monopolistic intentions of the Portuguese and then the Dutch in Melaka. Penang soon became a thriving port, and by 1800 the population of the island, virtually uninhabited when Light took over, had reached 10,000.

Meanwhile, events far away in Europe were conspiring to consolidate British influence on the Malay peninsula. When Napoleon overran the Netherlands in 1795, the British East India Company took over the administration of Melaka and other Dutch possessions in the region. In 1814, with Napoleon defeated, an agreement was reached on the return of these possessions, and by 1818 Melaka and Java had been returned to Dutch control.

Nevertheless, Britain's brief spell at the helm prompted some British figures to argue for more influence on the peninsula, particularly given that Malaysian ports of call made access to major trading destinations such as China easier. The calls of Sir Thomas Stamford Raffles to supplant the Dutch in Malaya had largely fallen on deaf ears. But in 1818, with the re-establishment of Dutch control in the region, Raffles was told to go ahead and establish a second British base further south than Penang. In early 1819 Raffles decided on Singapore as a British base. In 1826 Singapore became part of the British Straits Settlements, governed from Bengal in India along with Melaka and Penang; by then its population was already approaching 100,000.

This Dutch tombstone is one of many at St Paul's Church in Melaka. The Dutch ruled Melaka for over a century, from 1641.

British Period

Despite local cultural traditions, the Malaysia of today came into being during the period of British rule. Initially in 1824 the British and the Dutch signed a treaty that divided the peninsula into 'spheres of influence'. The kingdom of Johor was split into the Dutch-administered Riau Lingga Islands and British administration on the peninsula. In 1826 the formation of the Straits Settlements under the British brought together Singapore, Melaka, Penang and Province Wellesley (the mainland opposite Penang). In 1874 the Pangkor Treaty brought the Malay state of Perak into the ambit of British rule via a British Resident, who was to be consulted on all matters 'other than those touching upon Malay religion and custom'.

As was the case in India, the British Residential system allowed colonial influence to prosper without ever having to go to war. The system preserved the prestige of local rulers while at the same time providing the British with indirect control over matters – chiefly economic – that interested them most. In 1896 the states of Perak, Selangor, Negeri Sembilan and Pahang became the Federated Malay States (FMS), each governed indirectly by a British Resident. Johor held out until 1913, while Kelantan, Terengganu, Perlis and Kedah were controlled by the Thais until 1909, when they became known as the Unfederated Malay States (UMS), again under the British Residential system.

British influence in Malaya brought enormous economic and social changes. A communications infrastructure was established to allow the smooth transport of the produce of rubber estates and tin mines to ports. A

In 1819 Stamford Raffles established a British base in Singapore, which later became part of the British Straits Settlements.

colonial legal and administrative system was put in place, providing an environment in which free enterprise could flourish. But it was on the social front that the British administration was to have the greatest long-term effects.

Raffles, and later other British administrators, argued for an ethnic division of labour. A British-educated Malay elite should have a place in the administration system, while ordinary Malays should continue fishing and farming. Chinese immigrants from the coastal provinces of Fujian (Hokkien) and Guangdong were imported as traders and workers in tin mines. And finally Indians were brought over to work in the bureaucracy, on the rubber estates and as labourers in public works. By the turn of the 19th century, Malaya's economy had been revolutionised, but then so had its social makeup. The once predominantly Malay peninsula was emerging as an ethnic melting pot.

Meanwhile in Borneo

Across the South China Sea, in the steamy jungles of North Borneo, events were unfolding with all the implausibility of high Victorian melodrama. In 1838 James Brooke, a British adventurer, arrived in Borneo with his armed sloop to find the Brunei aristocracy facing rebellion from dissatisfied inland tribes. He quelled the rebellion and in gratitude was given power over part of what is today Sarawak. Appointing himself 'Raja Brooke', he successfully tamed the fractious tribes, suppressed head-hunting, eliminated the dreaded Borneo pirates and founded a personal dynasty that was to last for over 100 years. The Brooke family of 'white rajas' were still empire building, bringing more and more of Borneo under their power, when the Japanese arrived during WWII.

The extension of British influence into Sabah took a less romantic complexion. In 1865 the American consul to Brunei managed to acquire a lease for most of what is now Sabah. He sold it in Hong Kong, after which it was sold again to the Austrian consul there, Count Von Overbeck. Overbeck had no success interesting his government in a new territory, and finally Sabah ended up in the hands of Alfred Dent, an

James Brooke, the first of the Brooke family of 'white rajas', became raja of Sarawak in 1842.

Englishman. Dent established the British North Borneo Company, and from 1881 the land the company governed became British North Borneo.

WWII Period

By 1913 all of Peninsular Malaysia and north-west Borneo was united in a loose federation known as British Malaya. The colony prospered, though overwhelmingly the economy was dependent on tin and rubber – by the time WWII broke out in Europe, Malaya supplied nearly 40% of the world's rubber and 60% of its tin.

At the same time, Chinese and Indian immigrants arrived in such numbers that they eventually outnumbered the indigenous Malays. A 1931 census revealed that Chinese alone numbered over 1.7 million as opposed to 1.6 million Malays.

The arrival of WWII, however, was sudden and devastating. A few hours before the first Japanese aircraft was sighted over Pearl Harbor, the Japanese landed at Kota Bharu in the north of Malaya and started their lightning dash down the peninsula. British confidence that they were more than a match for the Japanese soon proved to be sadly misplaced, and it took the Japanese little over a month to take Kuala Lumpur and a month more to reach the doorstep of Singapore. North Borneo had fallen to the Japanese with even greater speed.

The Japanese were unable to form a cohesive policy in Malaya, since there was not a well-organised Malay independence movement which they could harness to their goals. Furthermore, many Chinese were bitterly opposed to the Japanese, who had invaded China in the 1930s. Remnants of the British forces continued a guerrilla struggle against the Japanese throughout the war, and the Communist Malayan People's Anti-Japanese Army (predominantly Chinese) also continued the struggle against the Japanese.

Postwar & the Emergency

When the Japanese surrendered on 15 August 1945, the British inherited a troubled country. The ethnic divide between indigenous Malays and the Chinese had polarised around the issue of Japanese resistance and around the future of Malaya. The mainly Chinese Malayan Communist Party (MCP) for its part maintained that many Malays and their leaders had capitulated to and cooperated with the Japanese occupation, and in some cases the MCP meted out punishment to the guilty parties.

The British response was a plan to form a Malayan Union under the sovereignty of the British crown, in which citizenship was to be extended to all with equal rights. There was an outcry from native Malays, and in March 1946 the United Malays National Organisation (UMNO) formed to fight the proposal. The British backed off, and in February 1948 they formed the Federation of Malaya. The sultans maintained their sovereignty and Malays were granted special privileges denied to the non-native inhabitants of Malaya – the Indians and Chinese.

Meanwhile the MCP, which had fought against the Japanese throughout the war, launched a guerrilla struggle to end British colonial rule. In 1950 the British declared the Emergency and put the country on a war footing. The Communist threat was eventually declared over in 1960, although there were sporadic outbreaks of violence until 1989. The Communists never enjoyed a broad spectrum of support. They were always predominantly a Chinese grouping, and while the Malays might have wanted independence from Britain they certainly did not want rule by the Chinese. Nor were all Chinese in favour of the party; it was mainly an uprising of the peasantry and lower classes.

Despite the diminished threat of Communist takeover, guerrillas were still resident in the jungle around the Thai border until the last remaining faithful accepted the government's long-standing amnesty in 1989.

Independence

In 1955 Britain agreed that Malaya would become fully independent within two years. Elections held in 1955 swept the Alliance

Party, a union of the Malayan Indian Congress (MIC), UMNO and the Malayan Chinese Association (MCA), into power. Nevertheless, when Malaya achieved *merdeka* (independence) on 15 August 1957, the resulting Merdeka Constitution enshrined special privileges for the indigenous Malays, while at the same time offering citizenship to all. Conflicting interpretations of these twin aims were to bedevil the country in years to come. Tunku Abdul Rahman was the leader of the new nation, which came into existence with remarkably few problems.

In Singapore things went nowhere near as smoothly and politics became increasingly radical. The election in 1959 swept Lee Kuan Yew's People's Action Party (PAP) into power, but they faced a whole series of major problems. When the Federation of Malaya was formed in 1948, the Malay leaders were strongly opposed to including Singapore because this would have tipped the racial balance from a Malay majority to a Chinese one. Furthermore, while politics in Malaya was orderly, upper class and gentlemanly, in Singapore it was anything but.

Nevertheless, to Singapore, merger with Malaya seemed to be the only answer to high unemployment, a soaring birth rate and the loss of its traditional trading role with the growth of independent South-East Asian nations. Malaya was none too keen to inherit this little parcel of problems, but when it seemed possible that the moderate PAP might be toppled by its own left wing, the thought of a moderate Singapore within Malaysia became less off-putting than the thought of a Communist Singapore outside it. Accordingly in 1961 Tunku Abdul Rahman agreed to work towards the creation of a Malaysia which would include Singapore. To balance the addition of Singapore, discussion also commenced on adding Sarawak, Sabah and Brunei to the union. This proposal was welcomed by Britain, which had been facing the problem of exactly what to do with its North Borneo possessions.

Confrontation

Accordingly in 1963 Malaysia came into existence, although at the last moment Brunei, afraid of losing its oil wealth, refused to join. No sooner had Malaysia been created than problems arose. First of all the Philippines laid claim to Sabah, which had been known as North Borneo prior to the union. More seriously, Indonesia laid claim to the whole island, and Sukarno, now in the final phase of his megalomania, commenced his ill-starred 'Confrontation'. Indonesian guerrilla forces crossed the borders from Kalimantan (Indonesian Borneo) into Sabah and Sarawak, and landings were made in Peninsular Malaysia and even in Singapore. British troops, having finally quelled the Emergency only four years earlier, now found themselves back in the jungle once again.

Singapore Departs

At the same time, relations between Malaya and Singapore soured almost as soon as Malaysia was formed. The principal stumbling block to a happy union lay in Singapore's refusal to extend constitutional Malay privileges to Malays in Singapore. In August 1965, exactly two years after Malaysia was created, Singapore was kicked out.

Malays, Malaya & Malaysia

Malays are the indigenous people of Malaysia, although they are not the original inhabitants. Malaya is the old name for the country which, prior to 1963, consisted only of the states on the peninsula. With the amalgamation of Malaya, Sarawak and Sabah, the title Malaysia was coined for the new nation, and the peninsula is now referred to as Peninsular Malaysia, while Sarawak and Sabah are referred to as East Malaysia. ■

Racial Problems

Singapore and Brunei had jumped ship, but at least Malaysia was now an independent country. One niggling problem that remained, however, was that the country was far from integrated. Naturally, the Alliance Party looked to education and language as the cornerstones of national identity. But what they had not counted on was the fierce opposition of other ethnic groups to what many saw as the extension of Malay privileges into the education system.

Privileges or no, Malays had a very weak hold on the economy. In 1969 only 1.5% of company assets in Malaysia were owned by Malays and per capita income among Malays was less than 50% of that of non-Malays. But attempts to make Bahasa Malaysia the one national language, along with the privileges Malays had in land ownership, business licences, educational opportunities and government positions, resulted in resentment from non-Malays. Their opposition to such moves resulted in the Alliance Party losing its two-thirds majority in the May 1969 federal elections. Victorious opposition parties took to the streets in celebration. The next day, on 13 May, a UMNO rally took to the streets in Kuala Lumpur and intercommunal riots broke out. Hundreds of people were killed.

Following these riots the government moved to improve the position of Malays in Malaysia with greater speed. The title bumiputra, or sons of the soil, was created to denote the indigenous Malay people: this meant not only Malays but also the aboriginal inhabitants and the indigenous peoples of Sarawak and Sabah. New guidelines were instituted stipulating how much of a company's share must be held by bumiputras and in other ways enforcing a Malay share in the nation's wealth.

Although many Chinese realised that Malaysia could never attain real stability without an equitable distribution of the country's wealth, there was also much resentment, and many talented people either left the country or simply withdrew their abilities and capital. Fortunately, Malaysia's natural wealth enabled it to absorb this flight of talent and wealth, but the problem of bringing the Malays to an equal position in the nation, economically as well as politically, is one that is still not fully resolved.

After 1969 government policy aimed to integrate economic development and ethnic policy. A series of five-year plans have been undertaken, with the ultimate objective of transforming Malaysia into a developed country in which race no longer has any bearing on economic function. On the political front, the Alliance Party expanded, drawing in other parties, to become the National Front, though this party is dominated by the UMNO.

Malaysia & Islam

While promotion of Bahasa Malaysia has been the main focus of the drive to forge a national identity, Islam has also been an important rallying point. The Malaysian Islamic Youth Movement was formed in 1971 with the aim of promoting Islamic values and even implementing Islamic law *(sharia)* in Malaysia. In November 1993 the most Islamic of Malaysia's states, Kelantan, attempted to do just that. The new laws would have required federal constitutional changes, and among other things required that thieves have their right hands amputated and that adulterers be stoned to death.

Islam presents the national government with a prickly problem. On the one hand, UMNO is bound to represent Malay and Islamic interests. On the other, a full-blown Islamic revival would run counter to the government's economic aims. Kelantan, for example, remains a poor state, a quarter of its population lives below the poverty line, and local policies have caused foreign investment to dwindle.

The other issue to consider is that an Islamic resurgence is potentially even more destabilising to ethnic unity than the problems associated with promotion of Bahasa Malaysia and with Malay domination of politics. Efforts by Islamic groups to outlaw alcohol, lotteries, unisex hairdressers and even to enforce conservative Islamic dress standards go down badly with Malaysia's pork-eating, gambling-mad ethnic Chinese.

Malaysia Today

By any standards Malaysia has put in an impressive performance over the last decade. In 1995 the country was registering growth of 9.5%, the eighth time in consecutive years that growth rates of over 8% had been recorded. In large part this can be attributed to the government's economic planning, diversifying an economy that was once reliant almost entirely on rubber, tin and logging.

Politically, UMNO, by far the majority faction of the National Front coalition, has marched from strength to strength, virtually annihilating the opposition. Elections in mid-1995 gave the Front its greatest victory since independence in 1957. It now controls 161 of the 192 parliamentary seats and all but one (Kelantan) of the state assemblies.

UMNO's success can be attributed in large part to Prime Minister Datuk Seri Mahathir Mohamad. Dr Mahathir, a man of strong opinions and near-visionary ambitions on Malaysia's part, has become the country's longest serving prime minister and has guided the country to prosperity. He is also known for his confrontationalist politics. Since coming to power in 1981 he has presided over a split in his own party, detained 107 people without trial in 1987, and dismissed six judges in 1988. He has also taken on the sultans, theoretically revoking their immunity from the law, presided over clashes with the Parti Islam se-Malaysia (PAS) government in Kelantan over the PAS push to create an Islamic state, and carried out a long-running campaign against the Sabah state government, which placed a ban on logging exports in 1993 but had to back down after federal intervention.

Dr Mahathir has also been keen to exert his profile on the world stage as a pan-Asia leader. He fulminates regularly on the subject of western colonialist attitudes and decadence, and promotes 'Asian Values' as a means to economic prosperity without any of what he maintains are its nasty side-effects – notably single-parent families, homosexuality and drugs. He advocates an East Asian Economic Caucus (EAEC), an Asia-only

Asian Values

If you have not heard of Asian Values it is probably because you are an illiterate product of western degeneracy, no doubt reared in a single-parent family, most likely gay, possibly a victim (or perpetrator) of incest and an odds on favourite for alcohol and drug addiction. As Dr Mahathir puts it in his recent book *The Voice of Asia*, 'Western societies are riddled with single-parent families, which foster incest, with homosexuality, with cohabitation, with unrestrained avarice, with disrespect for others and, of course, rejection of religious teachings and values'.

Overall this is slightly depressing news for those of us unfortunate enough to have grown up in the west. But then the pundits of Asian Values are not ones to pull their punches. The west, they maintain, has had its day. The next century will belong to Asia.

As cash registers tinkle ever louder across the region, Asian Values have emerged as the home-grown theoretical arm of the 'Asian miracle.' Not that anyone can much agree on what they are.

Dr Mahathir, head of an Islamic Malay state and very much an Asian Values man, is uncomfortable about equating Asian Values with neo-Confucianism, even if it *is* neo-Confucian Chinese who are making most of his money. Lee Kuan Yew, on the other hand, a pioneer of Asian Values and former head of a Chinese state, has no problems with neo-Confucianism.

Elsewhere around the region, the Japanese, still recovering from subway gas attacks and a long-term economic downturn, are not too sure that simply being Asian is a ticket to the good life. The South Koreans have two former presidents facing charges of massive corruption. China is socialist and keeps muttering about invading Taiwan (Asians are peaceful people and don't invade each other, according to Dr Mahathir). The Thais are too enamoured of having a good time. And countries like the Philippines, Myanmar and North Korea should probably be disqualified as Asians – they can't even figure out how to make money.

Still, despite problems finding a model for Asian Values, the gist of the matter is that Asian people are hard-working, politically quiescent (read obedient) family types who are good at making money. Westerners are...well, the opposite.

Chris Taylor

counterpart to the Asia-Pacific Economic Cooperation (APEC), which he claims to be controlled by US and Australian interests.

There has been much conjecture that Dr Mahathir, already 70 years old, is in for the long haul. After all, Asia is a region where political longevity is the norm. However, in late 1995 he announced that he would be stepping down some time in the 'near future' for his successor, Deputy Prime Minister Anwar Ibrahim, who is seen as staunchly Malay but less anti-western and more a man of the people.

GEOGRAPHY

Malaysia consists of two distinct parts. Peninsular Malaysia is the long finger of land extending down from Asia as if pointing towards Indonesia and Australia. Much of the peninsula is covered by dense jungle, particularly in its northern half where there are also high mountains, and the central area is very lightly populated. While on the western side of the peninsula there is a long fertile plain running down to the sea, the mountains descend more steeply on the eastern side, where there are also many more beaches.

The other part of the country, comprising more than 50% of its area, is East Malaysia – the northern part of the island of Borneo (the larger, southern part is the Indonesian state of Kalimantan). East Malaysia is divided between Sarawak and Sabah, with Brunei a small enclave between them. Both parts are covered by dense jungle with many large river systems, particularly in Sarawak. Mt Kinabalu in Sabah is the highest mountain in South-East Asia between the Himalayas and New Guinea, at 4101 metres.

CLIMATE

Malaysia has a typically tropical climate – it's hot and humid year-round. The temperature rarely drops below 20°C even at night and usually climbs to 30°C or more during the day. The tropics can take some adjusting to. Take it easy when you first arrive and try to avoid running around in the heat of the midday sun.

Rain tends to arrive in brief torrential downpours and is soon replaced by more of that everpresent sunshine. At certain times of the year it may rain every day, but it's rare that it rains all day. Although the region is monsoonal, it's only the east coast of Peninsular Malaysia that has a real rainy season – elsewhere it's just a time of year when the average rainfall is heavier than at other times of year.

Throughout the region the humidity tends to hover around the 90% mark, but on the peninsula you can always escape from heat and humidity by retreating to the delightfully cool hill stations.

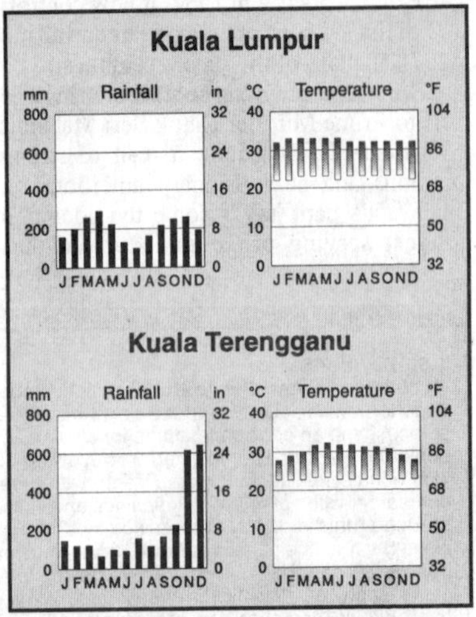

Peninsular Malaysia

The peninsula is affected by the monsoon winds blowing from the north-east between October and May, and from the south-west the rest of the year.

The October-May monsoon brings rain to most of the peninsula, but the east coast bears the full brunt, with the heaviest rain falling from November to February. For the rest of the year the east coast is relatively dry.

Rainfall on the west coast is much more

variable and comes throughout the year. Much of the west coast is sheltered by the central mountains from the worst of the October-May rains, but it also gets some rain from the less pronounced May-October monsoon.

The flat south of the peninsula around Johor and Singapore gets rainfall all year, slightly more from November to February. Further north rainfall is fairly even year-round, with January-February and especially June-July being the drier months. The north-west around Alor Setar and Langkawi receives less rainfall and has a more distinct wet season from April to October, and the rest of the year is quite dry. Penang seasons are similar but not as pronounced and it gets high rainfall in September-October.

East Malaysia

East Malaysia also gets the north-east and south-west monsoons. Sarawak has high rainfall year-round, especially round Kuching, with October to March being the wettest months, peaking in December-January. Sabah also gets high rainfall on the north-east coast at this time, while the west coast of Sabah gets most of its rainfall from May to November. Sabah receives less rainfall than Sarawak.

ECOLOGY & ENVIRONMENT

Malaysia attracts more than its fair share of criticism on the environmental front, and it is an issue that the government is particularly sensitive about. Dr Mahathir, Malaysia's long-serving prime minister, and his government maintain the line that western concern about environmental issues in developing countries is a form of hypocrisy. And there is some truth in this. After all, logging (and this is where foreign criticism is loudest) began in earnest in Sabah and Sarawak during the 1930s by the British Borneo Timber Company. There is also the fact that logging has decimated rainforests in the nearby countries of Thailand, Indonesia, Myanmar and Cambodia, countries where other issues tend to dominate the western consciousness.

That said, preserving something of Malaysia's environmental heritage before it is all shipped overseas as logs is of utmost importance. Probably more than 60% of Peninsular Malaysia's rainforests have been logged, and similar figures apply to East Malaysia. Government initiatives and the formation of national parks has slowed down logging on the peninsula, but it continues at heavy rates in Sabah and Sarawak.

It is unrealistic to expect developing nations such as Malaysia to stop logging altogether. The easiest route to limiting the damage is for Malaysia to keep developing, diversifying its economy into value-added goods so that it has more money to spend on protecting what is left of the rainforests. In the meantime, both the states and federal governments are making some effort towards ensuring that harvesting of logs is undertaken with more care, that it is restricted to certain areas and that reforesting programmes are undertaken.

FLORA & FAUNA

Malaysia is home to some of the most diverse systems of flora and fauna in the world. Its ancient rainforests have, in some cases, remained virtually unchanged for many millions of years. The area's climatic stability, plentiful rainfall and tropical greenhouse heat have endowed Malaysia with a cornucopia of bizarre life forms. In fact, scientists are still far from knowing even a significant percentage of the mysteries concealed in Malaysia's forests.

In Peninsular Malaysia alone there are over 8000 species of flowering plants, including 2000 trees, 800 orchids and 200 palms. Here is found the world's tallest tropical tree species, the *tualang*, reaching a height of 80 metres, with a base diameter of over three metres. The rafflesia is the world's largest flower, measuring up to one metre across and weighing up to nine kg.

There are over 200 species of mammals, 450 of birds, 250 of reptiles (including 100 snakes, 14 tortoises and turtles and three crocodiles), 90 frogs and 150,000 insects (including the giant birdwing butterflies and

MALAYSIAN WILDLIFE

Malaysia's forests and well-run national parks offer some of the best opportunities to see wildlife in South-East Asia. Wildlife spotting is never easy. It requires patience, and the ability to train your eyes and especially your ears to the sounds and movements of the jungle. The common Malay name for the following animals is given in brackets after the common English name.

Primates

Orang-utan (Orang Hutan) These magnificent long-haired red apes are native only to Borneo and northern Sumatra. Males are up to 1.5 metres tall and can weigh 100 kg, while the females are much smaller and rarely exceed 50 kg. Orang-utans are active during the day and they eat mainly fruit, leaves and insects. Unlike most monkeys and apes, they make nests from branches and are solitary animals, but the young stay with their mothers for the first five years of their lives. Orang-utans are most common in lowland forest and are widespread in Sabah and Sarawak, though their numbers have decreased due to hunting and loss of forests. The easiest places to see them are at the Sepilok Orang-utan Rehabilitation Centre in Sabah or the Semenggok Wildlife Rehabilitation Centre in Sarawak.

Orang-utans

Monkey (Monyet) Malaysia has 10 species of monkey, defined in two groups: the langurs (including the proboscis monkey) and the macaques. The langurs (or leaf monkeys) are mostly tree-dwelling and generally have black palms and soles and grey faces. The macaques are partly terrestrial, have pale palms and soles and brown or red faces. Monkeys usually live in groups of eight to 10, but sometimes form troupes of 50 or more.

The banded langur (cenaka) is found throughout the peninsula and in Sarawak, and is usually black or dark grey with a lighter underside. The spectacled langur (cenkung) has white 'spectacle' rings around the eyes, and is found mainly in the inland forest areas of the peninsula and the islands of Langkawi, Penang and Perhentian Besar. The most common langur in East Malaysia is the maroon langur (kelasi), which has a long tail and colouring similar to the orang-utan.

The proboscis monkey (monyet belanda) is easily identified by its large pendulous nose. These Jimmy Durantes of the jungle are generally a greyish-yellow colour with light underparts and reddish colouring on the head. They are active in the day, especially in the early morning and late afternoon, and are most commonly found in coastal and riverine swamp forests. They are found only in Borneo. There are colonies in Brunei at the mouth of the river, in eastern Sabah on the Kinabatang River and at Bako National Park in Sarawak.

The most common monkey of all is the long-tailed macaque (kera), found throughout Malaysia. They form large groups, are found in urban areas and are known to raid plantations and orchards. The long-tailed macaque is generally a dull brown colour with lighter underparts, and the face is naked pinkish-brown skin with long cheek whiskers. The pig-tailed macaque (beruk) and the stump-tailed macaque are less common in the wild, but are easily identified by their short tails. The beruks are often trained to pick coconuts.

Proboscis monkeys

Gibbon (Ungka) The gibbon is distinguished from the monkey by the absence of a tail. These slender, graceful animals only inhabit forest areas and they use their long arms to move swiftly through the forest canopy. It is rare to see one in the wild, and they are protected by law. The white-handed gibbon (ungka tangan putih) is usually black with a white face, hands and feet. The agile gibbon (ungka tangan hitam) is usually grey or grey-brown with a white band around the face, and black feet and hands.

Slow Loris (Kongkang) Though classified as a primate, the cute loris looks something like a small tree-dwelling badger. This nocturnal animal has large eyes surrounded by dark rings, thick fur, a stumpy tail and grasping hand-like feet. Widespread in Peninsular Malaysia and East Malaysia, they are also found on the islands of Pangkor, Penang and Tioman, as well as Singapore. They are forest dwellers but are also found in plantations and even in suburban gardens.

Slow loris

Sun Bear (Beruang)
Malaysia's only bear is found throughout South-East Asia. It is not common but can be found on the peninsula and in Sabah and Sarawak. Relatively small – it is one to 1.5 metres long from head to the base of the tail and weighs 50 to 60 kg – the Sun Bear is black with pale chest markings.

The Sun Bear's diet consists of bees' nests, termites, small animals, fruit and vegetation. A largely nocturnal forest animal, the Sun Bear has been known to enter plantation areas and can be dangerous.

Cats

Tiger (Harimau) This endangered species was once common throughout Asia from Iran through Siberia to Java and Bali. It is estimated that only 6000 of these magnificent creatures exist today, mostly in India, and their numbers are ever decreasing. Hunting has decimated their population and poachers are attracted by the high prices they can ask for tiger bones, which are prized as a traditional Chinese medicine. Tigers were once common in Peninsular Malaysia but are now rare, though they can still be sighted at Taman Negara. Tigers are mostly nocturnal and solitary creatures, feeding on wild pig, other small animals, frogs and fish. Sightings have been reported in Malaysia of tigers of three metres in length from head to tail, and an adult male tiger can weigh over 200 kg.

Leopard (Harimau Bintang) The leopard, or panther, is not common in Malaysia but reportedly still exists in the forests of the peninsula. Leopards are found from Africa to India and through to Java. In Malaysia the black panther is more common than the brown spotted leopard. Leopards are solitary creatures and, unlike tigers, frequently inhabit trees.

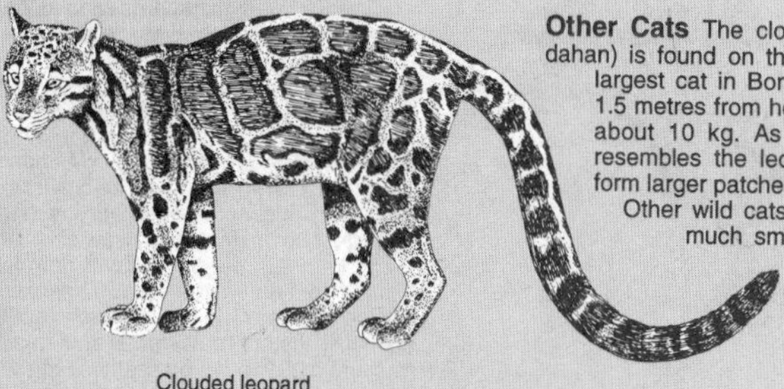

Clouded leopard

Other Cats The clouded leopard (harimau dahan) is found on the peninsula and is the largest cat in Borneo, measuring around 1.5 metres from head to tail and weighing about 10 kg. As its name suggests, it resembles the leopard, though its spots form larger patches.

Other wild cats found in Malaysia are much smaller, about the size of large domestic cats. Most are widespread in Asia, though not common in Malaysia and difficult to see in the wild. The marbled cat (kucing dahan) and the leopard cat (kucing batu) are both similar to the clouded leopard but smaller. The flat-headed cat (kucing hutan) is similar to the domesticated Burmese cat. The bay cat (kucing hutan) is red or grey and unique to Borneo. It has been reported around Kuching and the Baram River.

Civet (Musang)
Malaysia has a number of species of civet cat, medium-sized animals with long noses and tails. Civets look something like a cross between a large possum and a cat. Nocturnal and usually solitary, they are carnivorous, feeding on insects, small reptiles and mammals, but also eat fruit. The common palm civet (musang pulut) is found throughout Malaysia, and also Singapore, frequently in inhabited areas. The head and body is up to half a metre long, with a tail almost the same length. The Malay civet (tangalung) is larger and has distinctive rings around the tail and neck, with a spotted or striped coat.

The binturong (binturong) is the largest of the civets and can be almost two metres long from head to tail and weigh in excess of 10 kg. It has a black shaggy coat and long tufts of hair on the ears. It is omnivorous and is at home on the ground and in trees. Also known as the bearcat, it is more reminiscent of the Sun Bear than of a civet.

Masked palm civet

Asian Elephant (Gajah)
The Asian elephant was once widespread throughout Asia but is today restricted mainly to reserves in India and South-East Asia. Adult males grow to 2.5 metres tall and can weigh up to 3000 kg, with tusks up to 1.5 metres in length. Female elephants are slightly smaller and have only small tusks or none. The gestation period for the elephant is 21 months, and elephants have been known to live for over 50 years. Adult males can be solitary, but elephants usually form small herds, which can come together to form groups of 50 to 100. Although their numbers are low, elephants are still found on Peninsular Malaysia and in eastern Sabah.

Tapir (Tapir or Tenuk)
The Malayan tapir is a large herbivorous animal, looking something like a cross between a wild pig and a hippo. They are up to two metres in length, have stumpy tails and can weigh well over 300 kg. The young are striped and adults have white lower backs and hindquarters. They have been known to exist from northern Thailand through to Sumatra but are now very rare in the wild.

Malayan tapir

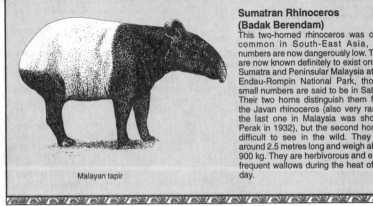

Sumatran Rhinoceros (Badak Berendam)
This two-horned rhinoceros was once common in South-East Asia, but numbers are now dangerously low. They are now known definitely to exist only in Sumatra and Peninsular Malaysia at the Endau-Rompin National Park, though small numbers are said to be in Sabah. Their two horns distinguish them from the Javan rhinoceros (also very rare – the last one in Malaysia was shot in Perak in 1932), but the second horn is difficult to see in the wild. They are around 2.5 metres long and weigh about 900 kg. They are herbivorous and enjoy frequent wallows during the heat of the day.

Pangolin (Tenggiling)

The pangolin, or scaly anteater, is a distinctive mammal covered in scales. Almost a metre long from head to tail, it weighs up to seven kg and has a long tapering head and tail. They are found from Burma to Java and are widespread on the peninsula, Penang and Borneo, and have also been recorded in Singapore. They are nocturnal forest animals, but are also found in plantations and gardens. They feed on termite and ant burrows, which they dig up with their powerful front claws.

Pangolin

Squirrel (Tupai)

Malaysia has over 20 species of squirrel, of which 11 species are unique to Borneo. Most are similar in appearance, and it is difficult to distinguish between the species, except for the giant squirrel (kerawak), which is the largest and is found on the peninsula, Borneo and Singapore. It is up to 800 mm from the head to the tip of the long, bushy tail. Two common species are the plantain squirrel (tupai pinang), a red-bellied squirrel with black and brown side stripes, and Prevost's squirrel (tupai gading), a brightly coloured, red-bellied squirrel, usually with white on the legs.

Flying squirrels (tupai terbang) are nocturnal and most species are rare, but you may spot them at dusk as they spread all four limbs, joined by their 'wing' flaps, and glide (they can't fly as such) from the trees. Horsefield's flying squirrel (tupai terbang ekor merah), one of the largest and most common flying squirrels, is found throughout Malaysia and in Singapore.

Bat (Kelawar)

The bat is the only mammal that can truly fly, and Malaysia has over 100 species of bat, classified into fruit bats and the other families of bats. Most of the fruit bats rely on sight and smell and don't have well-developed sonar capabilities like the other bats. Fruit bats can congregate in hundreds, making them a pest in orchard areas. The largest of the fruit bats is the Malayan flying fox (keluang), which is the world's largest bat. It has a wing span of up to 1.5 metres and is common in Taman Negara National Park. Other bats feed primarily on insects, and there are two species of false vampire bat that eat small vertebrates, such as other bats and birds.

Other Mammals

Malaysia has a number of species of native rats and mice (tikus), as well as moles, shrews (cencurut) and gymnures, which are often mistaken for rats. The moonrat (tikus ambing bulan) is a gymnure that looks like a giant white rat with a large rounded body and a long tapering snout. Adults are around half a metre long, from the head to the tip of the tail, and are mostly white with sparse black hair. You can't miss it if you see one, but if you're still in doubt, sniff the air – they stink.

Malaysia has a number of species of treeshrew, which are difficult to distinguish from squirrels. The carnivorous mongooses (bambun) are related to the civets but look more like small otters. Otters (berang-berang), martens (mengkira), weasels (pulasan) and badgers (teludu) are also found in Malaysia.

Wild pig (babi hutan) are found in forest areas on the peninsula. Deer, including the barking deer (kijang) and sambar (rusa), are found on the peninsula and in Borneo, as are mouse deer (pelanduk, kancil). The kancil is noted in Malay folklore as a particularly clever animal.

Gaur (seladang) are huge native cattle, standing almost two metres at the shoulder and weighing around 900 kg. They are an endangered species and are now rare.

Domesticated Animals

The water buffalo (kerbau) is the workhorse of Asian rural life. These huge, slow beasts are native to India and South-East Asia.

Domestic Asian cattle (lembu) are similar to wild native cattle, such as the banteng, which has a slight shoulder hump and large horns that curve in towards each other. The domesticated form, known as Bali cattle and found throughout South-East Asia, are smaller and have shorter horns.

The domestic pig (babi) is black and only about half a metre tall, and is a variant of the wild pig. The domestic goat is also a cross with the native goat, or serow (kambing gurun).

The domesticated cat (kucing) in Malaysia is usually white with orange patches. The often-bent tail is short. Dogs (anjing) are considered unclean animals by Muslims and are not as prolific as in the west. Some domesticated dogs have interbred with the wild red dog (serigala), which is found throughout much of Asia. ■

the Atlas moth). There are snakes, lizards and frogs that can 'fly', spiders that eat birds, giant (as well as flying) squirrels and many smaller creatures which, nevertheless, in Malaysia come in 'giant' models. Even the leeches can seem huge.

Mammals include elephants, rhinos (very rare now), tapirs, tigers, leopards, honey bears, several kinds of deer, tempadau (forest cattle), various gibbons and monkeys (including in Borneo the orang-utan and the bizarre proboscis monkey), scaly anteaters (pangolins) and porcupines, to name a few.

The bird life features spectacular pheasants, hornbills (including the rare helmeted hornbill, prized for its 'ivory' – actually the base of its 'horn', or casque) and such colourful birds as kingfishers, sunbirds, pittas, woodpeckers, trogons and barbets. Snakes include cobras (notably the spitting cobra, which shoots venom into the eyes of its prey), vipers (the kind seen in snake temples), pythons (including the reticulated python, the world's longest snake, which can grow to over 10 metres) and colourful tree snakes (most are harmless to humans).

National Parks

The British established the first national park in Malaysia in 1938 and it is now included in Taman Negara, Malaysia's major national park. East Malaysia has several national parks, forming a valuable and growing network. Though much of the rainforest remains threatened, there is a gathering tide of environmental awareness in Malaysia, aided by the fact that there is money to be made out of national parks through tourism.

The greatest concern today is to see more areas protected in Peninsular Malaysia, because the diversity of the flora and fauna here is the richest, containing much that does not extend to Borneo. Many areas have been proposed for protection, with the most important area being the lowland forests of Endau-Rompin (perhaps the last refuge for the Sumatran rhinoceros, photographed in the wild only in December 1983), straddling the borders of Pahang and Johor. In the 1970s the region of Gunung Mulu, in east Sarawak, was the centre of what became the most intensively studied tropical forest area in the world, leading to the establishment of a major national park there.

For those who wish to experience the primeval world of the ancient rainforests, Taman Negara offers a spectacular introduction, but there are other places which can be visited in Peninsular Malaysia, and a visit to East Malaysia is recommended, if only to see (and perhaps climb) Mt Kinabalu. Details are provided below for the main national parks and several other places.

Accommodation is not a problem when visiting most national parks. Various categories, from hostel to chalet, are available. Transport and accommodation operations are increasingly being handled by private tour companies, and you have to book in advance and pay a deposit. The best times to visit are June to September (east coast, including Taman Negara) or October through March (west coast).

In Sabah, contact the Sabah Parks office (☎ 088-211585), Box 10626, Kota Kinabalu. It's in Block K of the Sinsuran Kompleks on Jalan Tun Fuad Stephens, opposite the waterfront. In Sarawak, contact the National

Parks & Wildlife office (☎ 082-248088), on the 7th floor of the Satok building on Jalan Satok, about a km west of the centre of Kuching. It is always advisable to settle all arrangements and fees in advance. The best time to visit is April to the end of October. Basic information is available in all areas and may be found in tourist offices also.

Taman Negara National Park A scenic region of forested plateau, hills and mountains covering 4343 sq km, the national park ranges in altitude from 120 to 2150 metres (the summit of Gunung Tahan, the highest mountain in Peninsular Malaysia). It is traversed by several rivers. Of these, the Tembeling provides access to the park headquarters. From Kuala Lumpur take a bus or taxi to Kuala Tembeling via Jerantut. Here you meet the park boat for the 60 km trip into the park, taking three to four hours. Around the headquarters are several trails, and a number of observation hides can be visited. For the adventurous, it's a nine-day return trip to Gunung Tahan; otherwise there is much to do walking the trails, watching at the hides or arranging a river trip.

Endau-Rompin National Park This wildlife reserve is the last refuge in Malaysia of the Sumatran rhinoceros. The park is on the east coast of the peninsula, on the border between Johor and Pahang, and is accessible by car along a rough road from Kahang on the Keluang-Mersing road. It is also possible to reach the park by boat along the Endau River. There is a camping ground, but the park is not well developed for visitors.

Entry permits can be obtained from the State Security Council (☎ 07-223 1033), 1st floor, Bangunan Sultan Ibrahim, Johor Bahru).

Gunung Mulu National Park This is Sarawak's largest national park, covering an area of 544 sq km. The park contains Sarawak's second-highest peak, Gunung Mulu, 2376 metres of sandstone, and also Gunung Api, 1750 metres of limestone. The surrounding vegetation varies from peat swamp to limestone and forest terrain.

This national park contains about 1500 species of flowering plants, including 10 species of the famous pitcher plant. Removing these plants from the national park, or from the country, is strictly prohibited – there is a smuggling network.

Gunung Mulu National Park also has an extensive underground cave system, one of the largest in the world. The Deer Cave runs through an entire mountain, and the Clearwater Cave is the longest cave in South-East Asia, with a length of 51.5 km. Other caves in the park can be visited for adventure caving.

Gunung Mulu is a popular destination in Sarawak, though it is an expensive place to visit, and recent moves have tried to force visitors to go with tour groups.

Bako National Park A small park of 26 sq km in west Sarawak, the Bako National Park is on the peninsula at the mouth of the Bako River. It features sandstone cliffs and sandy bays, with a range of forest types, including mangroves. It is about a 30-minute bus ride from Kuching to Kampung Bako, from where you take a boat into the park. The park has beach areas and a network of paths. There is good hostel accommodation and a restaurant. It's a pleasant place to spend a few days. There are good walks, and the wildlife includes proboscis monkeys.

Kubah National Park Opened in 1995, Kubah National Park (22 sq km) is an easy day trip from Kuching. There is no accommodation at the park yet, but there are several trails for walking. Kubah represents a good opportunity to see the wildlife and rainforest vegetation of Sarawak for those who are on just a flying visit and don't have time to make a longer trip to Bako or Gunung Mulu national parks. Also at Kubah is the Matang Wildlife Centre, which when it is fully operational will rehabilitate animals that have been captured or separated from their native environments.

Gunung Gading National Park This 54 sq km park is at the western tip of Sarawak and was opened to the public in mid-1994. The main attraction here is the rafflesia, the world's largest flowering plant. Plankways have been laid down, providing access to the areas in which the rafflesia is most likely to be found. The rafflesia has no distinct flowering season, so visitors are advised to ring ahead to the park headquarters and find out if any are in bloom before setting out to the park.

Batang Ai National Park Batang Ai is north of the Batang Ai reservoir, around four hours east of Kuching. With the exception of a Hilton hotel development, this park is still very undeveloped and you will have to join a tour from Kuching to explore it.

Niah National Park This 31 sq km park was originally established to protect the valuable Niah Caves, made famous by the discoveries of traces of early humans dating back 40,000 years. The caves are also remarkable for the millions of bats and swiftlets which roost there. The swiftlets are famous, as their nests made of saliva are collected for bird's-nest soup. Other examples of cave life can be seen, and if you are lucky you may see the black-and-white bat hawk at the entrance waiting to pounce on a bat or swiftlet.

The park, in east Sarawak, is easily accessible from Bintulu or Miri via nearby Batu Niah. Cheap hostel space or more expensive resthouses are readily available. The walk from the park headquarters to the caves includes the famous three km plank trail, which takes 45 minutes to one hour. There are other trails in the park and a longhouse nearby. It's one of the most popular destinations in Sarawak.

Simalajau National Park Another recently opened national park in Sarawak, Simalajau (75 sq km) is relatively untouristed and has some good sandy beaches, where green turtles sometimes come ashore to lay their eggs. The inland dipterocarp forest area is home to 24 species of mammals and 185 species of birds. Accommodation is available at the park.

Lambir Hills National Park This park, in north-eastern Sarawak between Miri and Niah National Park, encompasses sandstone hills and covers an area of 6952 hectares. It is a popular weekend spot, with waterfalls and picnic facilities, but it also has good walks through rich dipterocarp forest. The park headquarters are only 32 km from Miri, and Lambir Hills can be done as a day trip, but good accommodation is also available at the park for those who want to explore the jungle at a more leisurely pace.

Tunku Abdul Rahman National Park This park covers five islands off Kota Kinabalu, Sabah, and has an area of about 49 sq km. The feature attractions are coral reefs and beaches that can be visited only by making arrangements with private boat operators, which is good if you can organise a small group. Park headquarters are on Pulau Manukan, the second-largest island. There are visitor facilities on this island (chalets) and on Pulau Sapi (day-use facilities, walking trails, good beaches), Pulau Gaya (walking trails) and Pulau Mamutik (resthouse).

This park partly developed from the notion that protecting offshore islands also protected the flora and fauna of Sabah, until it was demonstrated that most of it is not found off the mainland. Fortunately, it led to the establishment of the first valuable marine park, and the hope that Malaysia will protect more of its marine resources.

Kinabalu National Park This magnificent park of about 750 sq km was established in 1964 to protect the massif of Mt Kinabalu and its environs. The region has been a focal point of exploration and scientific investigation in Borneo for over a century. Today the focus has shifted more towards tourism, as the climb to the summit offers an exciting enticement to the visitor.

The park headquarters (1560 metres) are about 85 km (two hours' travel) from Kota

Kinabalu. It is advisable to book ahead for accommodation at the headquarters and the mountain huts. Ascent of the mountain is normally done in two days with an overnight stay on the mountain near the summit. The trail is well marked, with steeper sections graded and other aids provided nearer the top. You'll need to carry some good cold-weather gear, as it gets cold up at the huts at night. Guides are compulsory for all visitors. Around the headquarters there are several shorter trails, and a day or overnight trip can be made to the Poring Hot Springs, about 20 km by road on the other side of Ranau.

Other Parks & Reserves

Malaysia has a number of other state forest parks and reserves. Close to Kuala Lumpur is Templer Park, a protected forest area, and the Forestry Research Institute of Malaysia (FRIM) maintains a jungle park at Sungei Buloh, only 15 km north-west of the city centre. Both provide good opportunities for seeing the jungle if you won't be venturing further afield.

Taman Alam Kuala Selangor, north-west of KL just outside Kuala Selangor, is a 290 hectare nature park of mangroves and some secondary forest, noted for its birdlife. Accommodation is available at the park.

Kenong Rimba is a state park bordering Taman Negara and is becoming increasing popular for jungle walks organised out of Kuala Lipis.

In Sabah, the Sepilok Orang-Utan Rehabilitation Centre outside of Sandakan is an area of lowland forest for seeing orang-utans. The Danum Valley Conservation Area in eastern Sabah has been established by the Sabah Foundation and timber companies as an area in which to study the effects of logging on the forest. There are numerous jungle trails, along which you can spot a wide variety of birds and animals. Accommodation is available at a luxury resort.

The Semenggok Wildlife Rehabilitation Centre is Sarawak's equivalent of the Sepilok centre in Sabah. It is, however, a much less interesting place to visit, simply because there are very few animals here, but it's still worth visiting if you can't make it to Sepilok.

GOVERNMENT

Malaysia is a confederation of 13 states and the federal districts of Kuala Lumpur and Labuan Island. It is a constitutional monarchy and the head of state is the *yang di-pertuan agong*, or 'king', elected every five years by the sultans who head nine of the peninsular states.

The country has two houses of parliament. The lower house is the Dewan Rakyat (People's Council), consisting of 180 members elected every five years, and it is this house that forms the government and holds the real power. The senate, or Dewan Negara (States' Council), consists of 70 members, 40 of whom are appointed by the yang di-pertuan agong on the basis of their experience or wisdom or to represent interest groups or minorities. The remaining 30 are elected by the state legislatures.

Each state has its own government, and members are elected to the unicameral state legislatures every five years. States have wide powers to pass laws. Each state also has a head of state, and in the case of the peninsula the hereditary sultans, who exist in all states except Melaka and Penang, are appointed. The states of Sabah and Sarawak in East Malaysia are rather different from the Peninsular Malaysian states, since they were separate colonies, not parts of Malaya, prior to independence. The four states without sultans have a *yang di-pertuan negeri*, or governor, appointed by the federal government for four years.

The judiciary is composed of the Supreme Court, High Courts and magistrates courts. Penghulus courts were set up to try disputes at a village level, but they can only try disputes worth no more than RM50, so cases are very rarely heard. The *penghulu* (village chief) acts on an informal level. In Sabah and Sarawak native courts exist to try breaches of native law or custom, acting in much the same way as Islamic courts, which are there to try breaches of Islamic *syariah* law among Muslims.

Sultans

The sultans' positions are enshrined in the constitution, but their power is largely ceremonial. The yang di-pertuan agong must approve all acts of parliament and can refuse the appointment of a prime minister, but he acts on the advice of parliament and the cabinet. The same is true of the sultans as heads of their respective states.

The political process is very similar to the institutions of governors and governor-generals as found in British Commonwealth countries.

The first great sultanate was that of Melaka, which rose to prominence in the 15th century. It began life as a Hindu kingdom, but with the conversion to Islam the raja, or king, took on the title of sultan. Hindu traditions and court customs continued in the courts of the sultans despite the rise of Islam and are still evident today. After European intervention and the defeat of Melaka, the peninsula fragmented into a number of small sultanates and by the 19th century the Malay sultanates were in disarray, many of them involved in internal wars, while the Siamese controlled the north of the peninsula.

The British stepped in, using military force to resolve some disputes and appointing Residents to the sultans as 'advisers'. The British exerted their influence by shoring up the sultanates, which may well have disappeared otherwise. The British increasingly assumed power from the traditional monarchs but maintained the sultanate system and the rights and privileges of the sultans, which were enshrined in the constitution come independence.

For Malays, the sultans are the upholders of Malay tradition and the symbolic heads of Islam. They command great respect, especially in rural areas and east-coast states. The royal families have emerged as a modern elite and are very active in government and business. Scandals involving assault, abuse of privilege and corruption have helped to undermine their position, but they still exert a great deal of influence in modern Malaysia.

Sultans, Fast Cars & the Law

Like England, Malaysia has royalty and nobility – but there are nine royal families, not just one. Like Britain's House of Windsor, they come in for plenty of criticism – but you don't hear it, because criticising Malaysia's royalty can put you in prison on a charge of sedition. In part this relates back to Malaysia's early history as an independent state, when politicians often had royal connections, the first prime minister, Tunku Abdul Rahman, in particular.

Nine of the states of Malaysia are ruled by sultans, who are totally exempt from the law. They take it in turn to assume the title of yang di-pertuan agong, effectively the 'king' of Malaysia. Although they're not inclined towards prancing around half-naked or indulging in anguished marital separations, the Malaysian nobility does produce its own colourful scandals.

The funniest in recent years has been the sultan of Kelantan and his penchant for expensive toys. Each sultan is allowed to own seven imported cars without paying import duties and taxes. This rule has customarily been treated with some flexibility, ie 10 is near enough to seven if your maths isn't too good. Unfortunately for the sultan of Kelantan, it was finally decided that 20 was definitely more than seven, and when a brand-new Lamborghini Diablo arrived in an air-freight consignment at Kuala Lumpur airport the sultan was informed he would have to pay import duties before he was allowed to take it home. 'Let me at least sit in my new toy,' implored the sultan, who then proceeded to screech out of the hangar and burn rubber all the way back to the palace in Kelantan!

More serious than mere evasion of customs duty are outright cases of law breaking. In 1976 one member of the Johor royal family was actually convicted of manslaughter, then pardoned by his father, the sultan at the time. The Malaysian parliament was informed that the sultan of Johor and his son had been involved in 23 cases of assault.

Although the Malaysian government would quite like to bring the sultans to heel, their popularity in rural areas and their image as protectors of Malay culture and history make the government reluctant to meddle with the status quo. The Malaysian constitution also makes it difficult to institute changes, as it specifically states that no alteration can be made to the sultans' 'privileges, position, honours or dignities' without their agreement!

Tony Wheeler

Reaching for the Sky

We now know that the world's highest flagpole erected in Kuala Lumpur was just a warm-up. In late 1995 the finishing touches were being put to Kuala Lumpur's Petronas Towers, currently the tallest building in the world. At 450 metres it outdoes its nearest contender (and former world champion), the US Sears Tower, by seven metres.

Dr Mahathir, visionary leader of Malaysia, is in a building kind of mood. A new US$3.5 billion airport is slated for KL, the Bakun Dam in Sarawak will be the world's tallest dam, and best of all plans are afoot to build a new capital city from scratch. A former rubber plantation 25 km south of KL has been chosen as the site of the latter. Dr Mahathir, ever one to lead by example, has announced he will move his office there by 1998.

Malaysia's new capital will be called Putrajaya. Judging by the promotional blurbs, it sounds like the kind of place a robot might be quite happy to live in: an 'environmentally benign' 'information hub' linked to KL and the rest of the world by a 'multimedia super-corridor'. Wow. As yet there is no word about performance facilities for tourist-pleasers like kite flying and top spinning, but no doubt these are in the works.

The bill for Putrajaya alone is estimated at US$8 billion. Budgeting for the dams, new airports and super-tall buildings brings the total bill for Malaysia's current construction binge up to approximately US$60 billion. Some economists wonder whether Malaysia can afford it; others warn it may breed inflation and derail the economy. Then again, if the economy gets derailed at least Malaysians will be the first to hear about it thanks to that 'multimedia super-corridor'. And there will always be that shiny new airport to make a quick exit from.

Chris Taylor

ECONOMY

Malaysia is an Asian economic boom country, riding on the back of over a decade of high growth averaging 8% per year. Since independence it has moved away from its reliance on tin and rubber and diversified its economy by aggressively attracting investment, both foreign and domestic. After Singapore and Brunei, it is the most developed country in South-East Asia with the highest standard of living.

Malaysia's push to become a manufacturing centre has seen it become a major supplier of electronic components and equipment, and along with others, such as textiles and footwear, manufactured goods now count for over half of all exports. Important primary exports are petroleum and petroleum products, logs and timber, and palm oil. Rubber now accounts for less than 2% of exports, tin barely half of 1%. Major imports are machinery and equipment, chemicals, food and petroleum products. Major trading partner are Japan, the USA and Singapore.

Malaysia's rapid increase in manufacturing has been achieved by modernising the country's transport, communications and energy infrastructure, developing industrial zones and offering substantial tax breaks for investors in export-oriented industries.

The government has promoted a relatively open, market-oriented economy and instituted major reforms by dismantling many state-run enterprises and encouraging private enterprise to undertake many of the country's development projects. Though promoting a free market in some areas, the government is also an investor in the economy (usually as a minority partner) and controls prices on some key commodities such as fuel and rice.

Some economists have dubbed Malaysia (along with other booming Asian countries) an 'economy on steroids', arguing that large foreign investment and government development projects produce high but unsustainable growth rates and inefficient economies. Maybe, but the steroids seem to be doing the trick for Malaysia, with growing exports and development, rapidly improving standards of living and virtually no unemployment. Malaysia has to import labour from Indonesia, Thailand, the Philippines, Bangladesh and elsewhere, and it also has a substantial illegal workforce.

However, some are starting wonder if the craving for development is overextending the country's resources. Major projects under construction are the new high-tech capital city of Putrajaya (US$8 billion), the Bakun Dam (US$6 billion), new airport and freeway links (US$7.6 billion), the city of Gelang Patah in Johor (US$12.8 billion), Kuala Lumpur's LRT (US$2 billion), power plants (US$4.8)...the list goes on. Imports are rising and the country can never get enough cement. Foreign debt is also increasing and overheating threatens to push inflation higher than the officially admitted 3%.

The government is worried about inflation and has instituted a national 'zero inflation' campaign, but it is unlikely that the government will pull back from its aggressive development push. Malaysia is well on the way to achieving the national goals of the Wawasan 2020 programme, Prime Minister Mahathir's '20-20 Vision', which aims for Malaysia to reach developed-nation status by the year 2020.

POPULATION

Malaysia's population is currently around 19.5 million, but the Wawasan 2020 programme, which is the government's plan for taking Malaysia into the next century, gives a target population of 70 million by 2020!

PEOPLE

The people of Malaysia come from a number of different ethnic groups – Malay, Chinese, Indian, indigenous Orang Asli and the various tribes of Sarawak and Sabah. Approximately 85% of the population lives in Peninsular Malaysia and the remaining 15% in the much more lightly populated states of Sabah and Sarawak.

It's reasonable to say that political power is controlled by the Malays, while the Chinese have their fingers on the economic pulse. The old images of Malays being a rural, traditional people and Chinese being an urban, capitalist class can still be applied, but the stereotypes are slowly breaking down. Malays dominate the countryside, but the large proportion of urban Malays is growing, attracted by the new wealth and jobs of the cities.

The Indians, the next largest group, is less easy to categorise and is divided by religion and linguistic background. A small, English-educated Indian elite has always played a prominent role in Malaysian society, and a significant merchant class exists, but a large percentage of Indians, imported as indentured labourers by the British, remain a disadvantaged labouring class.

Malaysia is very much a multiracial society, something that has figured prominently and not always happily in its development. From the ashes of the communal riots of 1969, when distrust between the Malays and Chinese peaked, the country has managed to forge a much more tolerant, multicultural society. Though communal loyalties remain strong, the emergence of a single 'Malaysian' identity is now a much discussed and lauded concept, even if not yet really embraced.

Much of the improvement in race relations is due, paradoxically, to the government's bumiputra policy. This policy of positive discrimination in favour of the Malays, largely responsible for events in 1969, was accelerated after the riots to concentrate on Malay economic advancement. Through awarding government contracts to bumiputra groups, requiring bumiputra involvement in economic projects and targeting Malay areas for economic development, the government has increased Malay involvement in the economy, albeit largely for an elite, and helped defuse Malay fears and resentment of Chinese economic dominance.

A widespread backlash from the Chinese community has not emerged, because the government has given the country a booming economy, benefiting Chinese entrepreneurs and delivering jobs to Chinese and Malays alike. Dr Mahathir's government is also careful to show even-handedness in cultural issues and keep the Chinese community on side. Though Dr Mahathir expresses Asian chauvinism in his anti-west speeches, in itself a unifying populist issue at home, his government is keen to avoid Malay chauvinism. The Chinese remain excluded from political control, and are disadvantaged by bumiputra policies, but the government has indicated that the races will compete on equal footing when the development goals of Wawasan 2020 are achieved.

The once bitter issue of the promotion of Bahasa Malaysia, the national language, has also ultimately helped unify the country as the proficiency and use of the language has spread among all races. The government has also allayed Chinese and Indian concerns at attempts to introduce it as the sole language of instruction in all levels of education and is again promoting English, for business as well as communal reasons.

Malaysia has made enormous strides in promoting racial harmony, but old divisions still exist. Moves such as those by the Kelantan government to introduce Islamic law that applies to all its citizens, including the Chinese, has the potential to open old wounds, but the federal government is keen to put a lid on any threats to the largely peaceful multicultural balance in today's Malaysia.

Peninsular Malaysia

Malays The Malays are the majority indigenous people of the region, although they were preceded by aboriginal people, small pockets of whom still survive. The Malays are Muslim and, despite major changes in recent decades, are still to some extent 'country' rather than 'city' people.

Despite the fact that they account for only 55% of the population of Peninsular Malaysia (much less in Borneo), they are largely responsible for the political fortunes of the country.

Chinese The Chinese were later arrivals. Although some have been there since the time of Admiral Cheng Ho's visit to Melaka in 1405, the vast majority of the region's Chinese settlers have arrived since the beginning of the 19th century.

The majority arrived here from southern provinces of China but belong to different dialect groups, the major ones being Hakkas, Hokkiens, Teochews, Cantonese and Hainanese. Although all Chinese use the same written language, the dialects are not mutually comprehensible. Most Malaysian Chinese nowadays speak Mandarin; if they don't, a Hokkien and a Hakka speaker may well have to resort to English or Malay to communicate.

The Baba Chinese, or Peranakans, of Melaka speak a Malay dialect but are still culturally Chinese.

The Chinese comprise about 35% of the population in Peninsular Malaysia, 30% in Sarawak and 16% in Sabah. They are generally traders and merchants.

Indians The region's Indian population arrived later still and in a more organised fashion. Whereas the Chinese flooded in of their own volition, the Indians were mainly brought in to provide plantation labour for the British colonists. Usually landless labourers, they were enticed under indentured labour schemes of three to five years, though later arrivals were free labourers who paid their own passage. The majority of the Indian population are Tamils, while the rest are mainly Malayalis from the other southern state of Kerala, with a smattering of Punjabis, Gujeratis, Telugus and Bengalis. They account for 10% of the population on the peninsula, and are mainly concentrated in the larger towns of the west coast.

Orang Asli There are still small scattered groups of Orang Asli, 'Original People', in Peninsular Malaysia. They number over 80,000 according to the latest census, and are the descendants of the people who inhabited the peninsula before the Malays arrived. Although most have given up their nomadic or shifting-agriculture techniques and some have been absorbed into modern Malaysian society, there are still a number of Orang Asli settlements in the forests and rural areas of the interior. There are many Orang Asli tribes, but the three main racial groups are the Negritos, the Senoi and the Proto-Malays.

The Negritos are thought to be the oldest inhabitants of the Malay peninsula and are the smallest group of Orang Asli people, numbering less than 3000. They resemble Melanesians but are small in stature and have intermarried with other Orang Asli such as the Senoi. Some suggest that they are more closely related to the tribal people of India and the Andaman Islands. Traditionally nomadic hunters, the Negritos inhabit the inland forest areas of the peninsula, primarily in Kelantan and Perak. The largest tribes are the Jahai and the Batek.

The Senoi are the most numerous Orang Asli (46,000), and were the second wave of immigrants to inhabit Peninsular Malaysia. Their language is related to the Mon-Khmer hill tribes of Cambodia, and for the most part they resemble Malays. Traditionally they are shifting agriculturalists, forming permanent settlements, but today many Senoi have integrated into modern Malaysian society. Senoi villages are found mostly in Perak, Pahang and Kelantan, and the largest tribes are the Semai and the Temiar.

The Proto-Malays (population 35,000) are the third group of immigrants to the peninsula. It is thought that they came from Sumatra and the Riau Archipelago of Indonesia; they closely resemble the Malays and nowadays speak Malay. Proto-Malays are most numerous in Pahang, but are found throughout Johor, Negeri Sembilan and Selangor. The largest tribes are the Jakun, who can be visited at Tasik Cini; the Temuan; and the Semelai, centred mostly on Tasik Bera in Pahang.

Although some Orang Asli are Muslim (most notably the Proto-Malay Orang Laut of south-west coastal Johor), the majority have resisted conversion and retain their animist religions. Orang Asli are classified as bumiputra and therefore are eligible for the same economic advantages as the Malay, but they are still the most economically disadvantaged group. While wage-earners do contribute to village economies, many Orang Asli communities still rely on traditional crops and hunting, and some still live a traditional, nomadic life in the jungles. The government is keen to promote development but also to foster Islam in some areas.

East Malaysia

The population make-up of the east Malaysian states of Sabah and Sarawak is far more complex than in Peninsular Malaysia, with around 25 ethnic groups in the two states.

Malays The indigenous Malays, who make up around 20% of the population, are descended from local people who converted to Islam and adopted Malay customs around 400 years ago.

The Melanie, who number around 100,000 in Sarawak, are also native Malays but are ethnically different from the Malays in that they have different physical characteristics and speak different dialects. Most of the Melanie are followers of Islam, while the rest have converted to Christianity.

Chinese The Chinese minority in the east Malaysian states is less significant than on

Minangkabaus

The Minangkabau people from Sumatra migrated to Peninsular Malaysia in quite large numbers from the 17th century. They were attracted by the rich tin mines of the peninsula, and many also became successful merchants and farmers, particularly in the sparsely settled interior. The Malay sultans had no objections to the large numbers of Minangkabau immigrants, as they brought Islam with them to the interior and also went a long way towards off-setting the large influxes of Chinese.

Although the Minangkabau people were related ethnically and linguistically to Malays on the peninsula, there was a marked difference in their social organisation in that it was matrilineal – ie descent and inheritance are traced through the female line.

While property is vested in the clan, or *suku*, ownership of it passes from mother to daughter. On marriage the husband enters his new wife's suku. Traditionally the husband would continue to live with his mother after marriage and only visit his wife in her suku! ■

the mainland but is no less important, as they are basically the merchants and have a large influence on the economy.

Dayaks Dayak is the term used to cover the non-Muslim people of Borneo. These people migrated to Borneo at times and along routes which are not clearly defined. It is estimated that there are more than 200 Dayak tribes in Borneo.

Ethnic Groups in Sarawak The most important ethnic group in Sarawak is the Iban, numbering around 395,000. The early Europeans in the area named them Sea Dayaks, as they used to make forays down the rivers and out to sea. They were fierce headhunters and gave the Europeans a bad time along the coasts. Today the Iban are largely longhouse dwellers who live along the Rejang and Baram rivers in Sarawak.

The Bidayuh, who number around 107,000 in Sarawak, are another important group. They live along the rivers in Sarawak's First Division, the area around Kuching including the Skrang River.

The other, much smaller, tribes, including the Kenyah, Kayan, Kelabit, Lun Bawang, Kajang, Kedayan, Bisaya and Punan, constitute around 5% of Sarawak's total population. It's these small tribal communities of Sarawak that are worst hit by the logging which is currently destroying the rainforests at an incredible rate. The Penan (Punan) are particularly hard hit, as they lead a purely hunter-gatherer existence, relying totally on the forest for food and shelter. The other communities practise the much-maligned (by the government) slash-and-burn agriculture and so, while they are less devastated by the loss of forest, still find their land, lifestyle and customs under siege from the disruption.

Ethnic Groups in Sabah The people of Sabah are different again. While there are significant minorities of Chinese (16%) and Bajaus (10%), the major ethnic group is the Kadazans, who account for around 25%. Other smaller groups include the Murut (5%), Malays, Orang Sungai (river people), Sulu, Tidong and Bisaya. There are also significant numbers of refugees/immigrants from both the Philippines and Indonesia, residing mostly in the eastern towns of Sandakan, Lahad Datu and Tawau.

The Kadazans are traditionally agriculturalists and longhouse dwellers who live mainly in the west of the state. These days there have been large-scale conversions to Christianity and Islam, and many Kadazans have moved to the cities.

The Bajau live mainly in the north-west of the state, and around Semporna in the south-east. They were originally Sulu Sea pirates but these days pursue the much more prosaic practices of agriculture and animal husbandry.

The only other group of any size is the Murut, who number around 40,000 and live in the south-west in the Tenom area. They are agriculturalists who used to occupy a much larger area of Sabah but were pushed south by the migrating Kadazans.

ARTS

It's along the east coast of Peninsular Malaysia, the predominantly Malay part of Malaysia, that you'll find Malay arts and crafts, culture and games at their liveliest and most widely practised. However, the Kelantan government has sought to ban dancing and other un-Islamic folk performances in its push for religious purity.

Dance

There are a variety of dances and dance dramas performed in Malaysia. Though disco dancing is the most popular dance form these days, traditional dance troupes perform for special occasions.

Menora is a dance drama of Thai origin performed by an all-male cast dressed in grotesque masks.

Mak yong is a similar traditional form of theatre, but the participants are all females. These performances often take place at Puja Keteks, Buddhist festivals held at temples in Kelantan, near the Thai border.

The *joget* is an upbeat dance with Portuguese origins. It is danced by couples who have to move quickly although they never touch. It is the most popular traditional dance in Malaysia today and is often performed at Malay weddings by professional dancers. In Melaka it is better known as *chakunchak*.

Rebana kercing is a dance performed by young men to the accompaniment of tambourines. Other dances, not all of which are from the east coast, include the *tari piring, hadrah* and *zapin*.

The *rodat* is a dance from Terengganu and is accompanied by the *tar* drum.

Berdikir barat is a comparatively recent activity – a sort of poetic debating contest where two teams have to ridicule and argue with each other in instantaneously composed verse!

The *joget* is the most popular traditional dance in Malaysia.

Music

Musical Instruments Traditional Malay music is based largely on the *gendang* (drum), of which there are more than a dozen types. The four most commonly used are:

rebana besar – used at major festivals and on religious occasions
rebana ubi – the long drums of Kelantan, made from hollowed-out logs
kompang or *rebana kercing* – used widely at official functions
tar – used as an accompaniment to the rodat dance

Other percussion instruments include the *gong, cerucap* (made of shells), *raurau* (coconut shells), *kertuk* and *pertuang* (both made from bamboo), and the wooden *celampang*.

Wind instruments include a number of types of flute (such as the *seruling* and *serunai)* and the trumpet-like *nafiri*.

Stringed instruments are also an important component of a traditional ensemble. Instruments include the *biola, gambus* and *sundatang*.

The *nobat* is an exclusive royal orchestra of four or five players using drums, flute, trumpet and gong. They play only on ceremonial occasions and are only found these days in the states of Kedah, Terengganu, Johor and Perak.

The *gamelan*, a traditional Indonesian gong orchestra, is also found in the state of Kelantan, where a typical ensemble will comprise four different gongs, two xylophones and a large drum.

Music Types Much Malay music has heavy Islamic and Chinese influences and takes different forms. The major types include:

hadrah – Islamic chants, sometimes accompanied by dance and music
ghazal – female singers with orchestra, mainly in Johor
dondang sayang – Chinese-influenced romantic songs accompanied by an orchestra, mainly in Melaka
zikir – a type of religious singing

Silat

Also known as *bersilat*, this is the Malay martial art which originated in Melaka in the 15th century. Today it is a highly refined and stylised activity. Demonstrations are often performed at ceremonies and weddings, accompanied by music from drums and gongs.

Wayang Kulit

Similar to the shadow-puppet performances of other South-East Asian countries, in particular Java in Indonesia, the *wayang kulit* (shadow play) retells tales from the Hindu epic the *Ramayana*.

The Tok Dalang, or 'Father of the Mysteries', sits behind a semi-transparent screen and manipulates the buffalo-hide puppets whose images are thrown onto the screen. Characters include heroes, demons, kings, animals and, ever favourites, clowns.

Performances can last for many hours and throughout that time the puppeteer has to move the figures, sing all the voice parts and conduct the orchestra – it's a feat of some endurance. There are two forms of wayang kulit – the *wayang siam* and *wayang melayu*. Performances often take place at weddings or after the harvest.

The wayang kulit used to be an immensely popular form of entertainment, but it was all but killed off with the advent of the all-conquering TV. Fifty years ago there were well over 100 wayang kulit masters; these days there are less than half a dozen. The tourist industry has been something of a saviour for the wayang kulit performers, and the art form is unlikely to disappear completely.

Wayang kulit uses the shadows of puppets to tell the stories of the Hindu *Ramayana*.

Crafts

Batik Originally an Indonesian craft, batik has made itself equally at home in Malaysia. You'll find it in Penang on the west coast, but Kelantan is its true home.

The refined Malay martial art of *silat* is performed at ceremonies accompanied by music.

Batik cloth is produced by drawing out a pattern with wax and then dyeing the material. The wax is then melted away by boiling the cloth, and a second wax design is drawn in. After repeated waxing, dyeing and boiling processes, an intricate and beautifully coloured design is produced.

Batik can be found as clothes, cushion covers, tablecloths, placemats or simply as works of art. Malay designs are usually less traditional than those found in neighbouring Indonesia. The wax designs can either be drawn out on a one-off basis or printed on with a stencil.

Kain Songket & Other Weaving A speciality of Kelantan and Terengganu, *kain songket* is a handwoven fabric with gold and silver threads woven into the material. Clothes made from this beautiful fabric are usually reserved for the most important festivals and occasions. *Mengkuang* is a far more prosaic form of weaving using pandanus leaves and strips of bamboo to make baskets, bags and mats.

Silver & Brasswork Kelantan is famed for its silversmiths, who work in a variety of ways and specialise in filigree and repoussé work. In the latter, designs are hammered through the silver from the underside. Kampung Sireh at Kota Bharu is a centre for silverwork. Brasswork is an equally traditional skill in Kuala Terengganu.

SOCIETY & CONDUCT

Malay Customs

That Malays are Muslim is a tautology. Most follow Islam devoutly, and Islam provides the social fabric of Malay society. When Islam came to Malaysia it supplanted existing spiritual beliefs and systems of social law, or *adat*; however, conversion to Islam did not mean a total abolition of existing customs and beliefs. Many aspects of adat are still a part of everyday life in the *kampung* (village), or indeed in the suburbs of the cities. Though Islam and modern life have seen the passing of many older beliefs and customs, they have shaped Malay society.

Adat, with its roots in the Hindu period and earlier, is customary law that places great emphasis on collective rather than individual responsibility. It is very much a village-based social system and its principles still affect everyday life for many Malays. *Adat temenggong* defines the authoritarian, patriarchal system of the sultans and still influences court ritual in some areas. It owes its existence to the Hindu state, with ultimate power placed in the hands of the raja, or king.

The kampung and its obligations of kinship are at the heart of the Malay world. It is mutually supportive and places great emphasis on maintaining harmony. In principle, villagers are of equal status, though a headman is appointed on the basis of his wealth, greater experience or spiritual knowledge. Traditionally the founder of the village was appointed village leader (*ketua kampung* or penghulu), and often members of the same family would also become leaders. A penghulu is usually a *haji*, one who has made the pilgrimage to Mecca – a position of great importance.

As a religious leader, the *imam* as the keeper of Islamic knowledge and the leader of prayer also holds a position of great importance in the community. The *pawang* and the *bomoh* are keepers of a spiritual knowledge that is part of an older tradition. A pawang possesses skills and esoteric knowledge about such things as the rice harvest, rain making, fishing etc and knows the rituals needed to ensure their success and appease the necessary spirits. The bomoh is a spiritual healer who has not only learned the knowledge of curative plants but can contact the spirit world and harness its power. The bomoh's chants, or *mantra*, may contain Sanskrit words but will more often contain passages from the Koran and invoke the power of Allah. The bomohs, or at least their imitators, can still occasionally be seen in the markets as they put on their magic shows and then bring out their cure-all medicines for sale. Though the bomoh is a dying tradition that flies in the face of orthodox Islam, it is widely held that prominent members of UMNO (the ruling government party) consult bomohs for political guidance.

Islamic fundamentalism and western rationalism have both helped to undermine the role of the pawang and the bomoh, but spirits, magic and such things as *keramat* (saint) worship still survive in the village despite such ideas being at odds with Islamic teachings. Many traditional beliefs and adat customs have adapted to Islam, rather than having been destroyed by it.

Ceremonies Adat is most noticeable in the important ceremonies of birth, circumcision and marriage. Customs of everyday life are known as *adat resam*, while customs and traditions relating to the courts of the sultans are known as *adat istiadat diraja*.

Traditionally in a birth attended by the midwife, the baby is spat on to protect it from the spirits of disease and the Muslim call to prayer is whispered in the baby's ear. On the seventh day the baby's first hair-cutting *(bercukur)* is performed and the baby is named. If it is later decided that the name doesn't suit the baby or is hampering its development, the name can be changed.

The circumcision of boys *(bersunat)* is a major event and usually occurs around the ages of eight to 12 years. The boy will be dressed in finery and seated on a dais. After feasting, passages from the Koran are read and the boy will repeat verses read by the imam. The circumcision occurs the next morning, when traditionally the boy would sit astride a banana trunk and the *mudin*, or circumciser, performs the operation. Modern medical practices are now largely employed.

The Malay wedding tradition is quite involved and there are a number of rituals to be observed. The prospective husband despatches an uncle or aunt to his wife-to-be's house to get the family's permission to marry *(hantar tanda)*. Once this is given, the couple are engaged *(bertunang)*, and then the ceremony *(akad nikah)* takes place.

The bride and groom, dressed in traditional kain songket – silk with gold thread – have henna applied to their palms and fingertips *(berinai)* and then, in a ceremony with significant Hindu influence *(bersanding)*, they 'sit in state' on a dais and are surrounded by both modern gifts and traditional offerings, such as a bouquet of folded paper flowers in a vase made of bath towels, ringed by quail eggs in satin ribbons. The couple are showered with *bunga rampai* (flower petals and thinly shredded pandan leaves) and sprinkled with *air mawar* (rose water).

Important ceremonies in family life are accompanied by a feast known as *kenduri*. Guests can number in the hundreds and preparations take days, as many traditional dishes such as *nasi minyak* (spicy rice) and *pulut kuning* (sticky saffron rice) have to be prepared. The cost of these feasts can be a burden on poorer families.

The bride and groom, dressed in *songket*, perform the wedding dance at a traditional Malay wedding.

The most important festival is Hari Raya Puasa, the end of the fasting month. New clothes are bought, families are reunited and, of course, there is much feasting in the style of the kenduri when an 'open house' is offered for family, friends and neighbours and everyone goes visiting.

Traditional Pastimes Top spinning (*main gasing*) may not seem like an activity for grown-ups to engage in, but *gasing*, Malaysian tops, are not child's play. A top can weigh up to seven kg and it takes a good deal of strength to whip the five metre cord back and spin the top competitively. The top is hurled on to a polished mud slab, then scooped up with a thin wooden bat and placed to spin on a small, metal-tipped wooden post.

Top-spinning contests are held in east-coast villages during the slack time of year while the rice is ripening. Contests are usually between teams of fighting tops, where the attackers attempt to dislodge the defenders from a prearranged pattern, or there are contests for length of spin. The record spinning time approaches two hours!

Flying kites is another child's game that takes on adult-size proportions on the east coast. Kite-flying contests include events for greatest height reached and also competitions between fighting kites.

The kites, which can be up to 2.5 metres wide, are real works of art. There are cat kites, bird kites and, most popular, the *wau bulan*, or moon kite. An attachment to the front of the kite makes a humming noise and in favourable conditions a kite may be left flying, humming pleasantly, all night. Kites are popular souvenirs of Malaysia, and a stylised Kelantan kite is the symbol of Malaysia Airlines.

Sepak raga is one of the most popular kampung games. The equipment needed to play the game is simplicity itself – a lightweight ball made of strips of rotan. Drawn up in a circle, the opposing teams must keep the ball continuously in the air, using legs, head and shoulders. Points are scored for each time a team member hits the ball.

Sepak takraw is a version of the same game where the players hit the ball back and forth over a net, as in volleyball – but again without using hands. It's a popular sport in a number of South-East Asian countries and the Thais are the champions.

Bird-singing competitions are a very popular pastime, particularly on the east coast. The *merbuk* and *tekukur* dove birds are suspended in highly decorative cages from eight-metre-high poles, supposedly because this is the height at which the birds feel most relaxed. Apparently each bird has its own unique song.

It's all taken very seriously and competition is fierce – at a large contest there may be as many as 300 birds, and champion tweeters can be worth anything up to RM50,000! Kota Bharu is one of the best places to see a bird-singing contest as they take place every Friday morning. Larger local and national competitions are also held annually.

Chinese Customs

The Chinese are born into a very different cultural tradition from that of the Malays. Chinese culture has evolved over 3,000 years, and for much of that time it was the centre of Asia; indeed, as far as the Chinese themselves were concerned, the whole world. It's not surprising that the Chinese are proud of such a distinguished past, and most Malaysian Chinese can tell you the village, town or at least province in China from which their ancestors emigrated.

At the heart of the Chinese sense of cultural continuity is the family. Most Chinese families and family businesses will have a small family shrine adorned with photographs of grandparents and usually plaques engraved with the names of ancestors stretching as far back as it is possible to trace them. Even distant ancestors, long removed from the petty troubles of everyday life, take a keen interest in their family's daily tribulations. It is important to pay respect to them by lighting incense and bowing with the hands clasped in prayer *(bai-bai)* at least once a day, and particularly when making decisions that may affect family fortunes.

Chinese families are patrilineal. Only male children are able to continue the family name – and it is the name that is all important in one's connection with one's ancestors. Women traditionally had very low status in the Chinese familial scheme of things. Married off at a young age, girls were considered a drain on family resources. Such attitudes are much less common nowadays, though boys are still coveted by Chinese parents.

The theoretical and ethical backbone of Chinese family relationships can be found in the teachings of China's most famous sage, Confucius. Confucianism (much vaunted nowadays as the source of a conservative work ethic that will catapult Asia into dazzling economic prosperity) provides a hierarchical structure of respect within the family that extends into society as a whole. It also places great emphasis on scholarship. Most Chinese parents will spare nothing to ensure their children get a good education.

Many Chinese customs are undergoing great changes nowadays. Marriages, for example, are rarely arranged by matchmakers or by agreements between families, as they were in the past. An astrologer may be consulted, however, to determine an auspicious date for the wedding. As is the case in China and Taiwan, most Chinese opt for a white wedding. Red was the traditional colour; white is the colour of death and funerals.

Funerals remain much more traditional, elaborate affairs. The body is dressed in best clothes and sealed in the coffin along with a few valuables. The coffin is placed in front of the ancestral altar in the house, and joss-sticks and candles are burnt. Mourning and prayers may go on for three days before the funeral, which is an expensive affair involving the hire of professional mourners and musicians who clash cymbals and gongs to drive away the evil spirits. Food and drink are provided to all those who visit the house to pay their respects.

Traditionally children would mourn the death of a father for three years and white would be worn, but modern life has seen the mourning period greatly reduced. Whatever changes in tradition have occurred, the importance of the grave and its upkeep remains, and most Chinese will pay their respects to the elders on All Souls Day (also known as Tomb-Sweeping Day).

Chinese New Year is the major festival, and even Chinese who profess no religion will celebrate it with gusto. It is a time for clearing out the old and bringing in the new. The house is given a spring clean and all business affairs and debts brought up to date before the new year. It is a time for family, friends and feasting, and *ang pow*, red envelopes of money, are given to children. Chap Goh Meh is the last day of the Chinese New Year and is the peak of celebrations.

Indian Customs

The majority of Malaysian Indians are Hindus and come from southern India and so the customs and festivals that are more important in the south of India, especially Madras, are the most popular in Malaysia.

Traditionally, the *namakarana*, or name-giving ceremony, is held about 10 days after the birth of a baby. An astrologer will be called upon to give an auspicious name, often the name of a god. Boys are very much favoured, as only males can perform certain family rituals and the dowry system in India can mean financial ruin for a family with too many daughters.

The major ceremony in the life of a boy of higher caste, especially for the highest caste Brahmans, is the initiation involving receiving the sacred threads. The boy is bathed, blessed by priests and showered with rice by guests. Then three strands of thread, representing Brahma, Vishnu and Shiva, are draped around the boy's left shoulder and knotted underneath the right arm, and the boy has officially been initiated into his caste.

Arranged marriages are still common, though the bride and groom have an increasing say in the choice of their intended partner. The day, hour and minute of the wedding are also the preserve of the astrologer. The marriage is usually held at the house of the bride's family. The couple are seated on a dais and a sacred flame is place in the centre of the room. The final ceremony involves the bridegroom placing the *thali* necklace around the bride's neck, and then the couple proceed around the fire seven times.

Deepavali, or the Festival of Lights, is the major Indian festival in Malaysia, when homes are decorated with oil lamps to signify the victory of light over darkness. The spectacular Thaipusam is the most exciting festival, when pilgrims perform masochistic feats at temples across the country. A major Indian festival is Ponggal, which is the harvest festival in Tamil Nadu in India, though in Malaysia it does not coincide with the harvest and is of less importance.

Avoiding Offence

As in many Muslim countries, Islam in Malaysia has seen a significant revival over the past 10 years or so. It's wise for visitors to be appropriately discreet in dress and behaviour, particularly on the more strictly Muslim east coast of the peninsula.

For women, topless bathing is definitely not acceptable, and away from the beaches you should cover as much as possible. Don't take your cue from fellow travellers but from Malaysian women. For men, shorts are considered odd attire for adults but they are not offensive. Bare torsos are not considered acceptable in the villages and towns.

Unfortunately, women may encounter unwanted attention from Malaysian men who consider western women to be of loose morals. Dressing conservatively will help to alleviate any problems.

As in most Asian countries, it is very impolite to use the left hand to give or receive something, as the left hand is used for washing after going to the toilet. Pointing or beckoning with the forefinger is considered rude, and Malaysians will motion towards something with the thumb atop a loose fist, while hailing someone will be done by waving the fingers downwards from an open hand. Shoes must be removed before entering a mosque and are also usually removed before entering someone's house.

For etiquette in a Dayak longhouse, see the Rejang River section in the Sarawak chapter.

RELIGION

The variety of religions found in Malaysia is a direct reflection of the diversity of races living there. Although Islam is the state religion of Malaysia, freedom of religion is guaranteed.

The Malays are almost all Muslims. The Chinese embrace an eclectic brew of Taoism, Buddhism and ancestor worship, though some are Christians. The majority of the region's Indian population come from south India and are mainly Hindu, though some are Muslims or Sikhs.

Although Christianity has made no great inroads into Peninsular Malaysia it has had a much greater impact upon East Malaysia, where many of the indigenous people have converted to Christianity, although others still follow their animist traditions.

Islam

In the early 7th century in Mecca, Mohammed received the word of Allah (God) and called on the people to turn away from pagan worship and submit to the one true God. His teachings appealed to the poorer levels of society and angered the wealthy merchant class. By 622 life had become sufficiently unpleasant to force Mohammed and his followers to migrate to Medina, an oasis town some 300 km to the north. This migration – the *hijrah* – marks the beginning of the Islamic calendar, year 1 AH, or 622 AD. By 630 AD Mohammed had gained a sufficient following to return and take Mecca.

With boundless zeal the followers of Mohammed spread the word, using force where necessary, and by 644 the Islamic state covered Syria, Persia, Mesopotamia, Egypt and North Africa; in following decades its influence would extend from the Atlantic to the Indian Ocean.

Islam is the Arabic word for submission, and it is the duty of all Muslims to submit themselves to Allah. This profession of faith (the *Shahada)* is the first of the Five Pillars of Islam, the five tenets in the Koran which guide Muslims in their daily life:

Shahada 'There is no God but Allah and Mohammed is his prophet.' This profession of faith is the fundamental tenet of Islam. It is to Islam what the Lord's Prayer is to Christianity, and it is often quoted (eg to greet the newborn and farewell the dead).

Salah The call to prayer. Five times a day – at dawn, midday, mid-afternoon, sunset and nightfall – Muslims must face Mecca and recite the prescribed prayer. *Kiblat*, the Malay word for the direction of Mecca, accompanies an arrow in many hotel rooms.

Zakat This was originally the act of giving alms to the poor and needy. The amount was fixed at 5% of one's income. It has been developed by some modern states into an obligatory land tax which goes to help the poor.

Ramadan This is the ninth month of the Muslim calendar, when all Muslims must abstain from eating, drinking, smoking and sex from dawn to dusk. It commemorates the month when Mohammed had the Koran revealed to him; the purpose of the physical deprivation is to strengthen the will and forfeit the body to the spirit.

Hajj The pilgrimage to Mecca, the holiest place in Islam. It is the duty of every Muslim who is fit and can afford it to make the pilgrimage at least once in their life. On the pilgrimage, the pilgrim *(haji)* wears two plain white sheets and walks around the *kabbah*, the black stone in the centre of the mosque, seven times. Other ceremonies, such as sacrificing an animal and shaving the pilgrim's head, also take place.

According to Muslim belief, Allah is the same as the God worshipped by Christians and Jews. Adam, Abraham, Noah, Moses, David, Jacob, Joseph, Job and Jesus are all recognised as prophets by Islam. Jesus is not, however, recognised as the son of God. According to Islam, all these prophets partly received the word of God but only Mohammed received the complete revelation.

In its early days Islam suffered a major schism that divided the faith into two streams: the Sunnis (or Sunnites) and the Shi'ites. The prophet's son-in-law, Ali, became the fourth caliph following the murder of Mohammed's third successor, and he in turn was assassinated in 661 by the governor of Syria, who set himself up as caliph. The Sunnis, who comprise the majority of Muslims today, including the Malays, are followers of the succession from this caliph, while the Shi'ites follow the descendants of Ali. The Shi'ites are mostly distributed in Iran, Iraq, Syria, India and Yemen. The Malaysian government actively discourages Shi'ite sects, which it regards as extremist.

Islam in Malaysia Islam came to Malaysia with the Indian traders from south India and was not of the more orthodox Islamic tradition of Arabia. Islam was adopted peacefully by the coastal trading ports of Malaysia and Indonesia, absorbing rather than conquering existing beliefs.

Islam was established in northern Sumatra by the end of the 13th century, but didn't become dominant until the third ruler of Melaka adopted it in the mid-14th century. Melaka's political dominance in the region saw the religion spread throughout Malaysia and Indonesia. By the time the Portuguese arrived in the 16th century, Islam was firmly established and conversion to Christianity was difficult.

Islamic sultanates replaced Hindu kingdoms, though the Hindu idea of kings remained. The traditions of adat (customary law) continued, but Islamic law dominated, while the caste system, never as entrenched as in India, had no place in the more egalitarian Islamic society. Women exerted a great deal of influence in pre-Islamic Malay society. There were examples of women leaders in Malay societies, and the descendants of the Sumatran Minangkabau in Negeri Sembilan have a matriarchal society. The arrival of Islam weakened the position of women. Nonetheless, women were not cloistered or forced to wear full purdah as in the Middle East, and Malay women today still enjoy more freedom than in many other Muslim societies.

Malay ceremonies and beliefs still exhibit pre-Islamic traditions, but most Malays are ardent Muslims and to suggest otherwise to a Malay would cause great offence. With the rise of Islamic fundamentalism, the calls to introduce Islamic law and purify the practices of Islam have increased, but while the government is keen to espouse Muslim ideals, it is wary of religious extremism. Islamic law (syariah) is the preserve of state governments, as is the establishment of Muslim courts, which since 1988 cannot be overruled by secular courts. Only Muslims are tried in Islamic courts. Kelantan state is the country's hotbed of Islamic fervour, and the state government is keen to apply syariah to all of its citizens, as it has shown by outlawing alcohol in restaurants and nightclubs and banning snooker halls. The government there has also renamed the Beach of Passionate Love (Pantai Cinta Berahi) Moonlight Beach (Pantai Cahaya Bulan).

The Koran is the main source of religious law for Malays, and though few are proficient in Arabic, all Malay children are sent to learn to read the Koran. Malaysia has an annual Koran-reading competition, and passages of the Koran are read in Arabic at many Malay ceremonies. However, the main medium of religious instruction is Jawi, the Malay language written in the Arabic script. Kitab Jawi (Jawi books written by Malay religious scholars) are widely read in the mosques and *pondok* (religious schools). For centuries these books have been the main source of Islamic thought for Malays, and while they express the same beliefs and tenets held by Muslims worldwide, they do so with a Malay perspective.

There is no Malaysia-wide head of Islam. The sultans of the various states are also the Islamic heads of their respective states, while the yang di-pertuan agong is head of Islam in his own state and in Melaka, Penang, Sabah and Sarawak.

Chinese Religion

It is slightly misleading to talk about Chinese religion in the sense of an overarching set of beliefs that regulate daily life. Most Chinese, if asked, will profess to be Buddhist if anything. In reality, however, the Chinese spiritual life is made up of Taoism, Confucianism, Buddhism, folklore and animist *fengshui*, or divination. Taoism is far too complex to discuss in any detail, but it has influenced much of the deep structure of the Chinese world view and given rise to such enduring concepts as *yin* and *yang*. Its influence can be seen in such things as Chinese medicine, tai-chi and the Chinese martial arts. Taoist sages also figure prominently in the rich Chinese pantheon of gods.

Chinese Buddhism, on the other hand, has adapted so thoroughly to the indigenous beliefs of China that it little resembles the Buddhism of the popular western imagination. Even Chinese Buddhist images are usually jovial well-fed fellows, apparently enjoying the fruits of a prosperous life – a far cry from the emaciated other-worldliness of the Thai Buddhas. For the average Chinese believer Buddhism provides succour, and just as importantly can be called on for good fortune in exams and business ventures.

If Taoism and Buddhism converge as a spiritual focus for the Chinese, it is Confucianism that provides the ethical bedrock of Chinese society. In brief it defines relationships and the responsibilities that go with them.

Taoism, Buddhism and Confucianism are just part of the story. Fengshui, the animist (and essentially Taoist) belief that lines of energy (often identified as dragons) run through the earth and animate it, is another factor. Ancestor worship is another, as is Chinese mythology, with its god-like heroes.

Overall, however, Chinese religion is ultimately a pragmatic affair, and in this the Chinese differ drastically from Malay followers of Islam. The Chinese burn paper money for their gods (to enrich them) and provide them with feasts and performances. The gods of popular Chinese religion are not above a shrewd investment if it happens along but also like to unwind and have a good time.

In the practical world of popular religion, *fu* (fortune) is the key word. The Chinese will go to great lengths to convince the spirit world to help them get it. Gods have to be appeased, bad spirits blown away and sleeping dragons soothed to ensure fortune comes along.

The most popular gods and local deities, or *shen*, in Malaysia are Kuan Yin, the goddess of mercy, and Toh Peh Kong, found only outside China and representing the spirit of the pioneers. Kuan Ti, the god of war, is also very popular and is nowadays regarded as the god of wealth. Sam Po Shan, the spirit of the Chinese Admiral Cheng Ho, who visited Melaka in the 15th century, is worshipped as the patron saint of travellers. Offerings of joss sticks and fruit are made at temples, household altars and at the sides of roads throughout the country. While ancestor worship plays an important role, it is not practised as extensively as it is in China, where many generations of ancestors may be worshipped. The Chinese immigrants to Malaysia generally only honour the ancestors of a few generations.

Hinduism

On first appearances, Hinduism is a complex religion. Its basic premise is simple enough though: we all go through a series of rebirths and reincarnations that eventually lead to *moksha*, the spiritual salvation which frees one from the cycle of rebirths. With each rebirth you can move closer to or further from eventual moksha; the deciding factor is your *karma*, which is literally a law of cause and effect. Bad actions during your life result in bad karma, which ends in lower reincarnation. Conversely, if your deeds and actions have been good you will reincarnate on a higher level and be a step closer to eventual freedom from rebirth. *Dharma*, or the natural law, defines the total social, ethical and spiritual harmony of your life.

Hinduism has three basic practices: *puja*, or worship; the cremation of the dead; and the rules and regulations of the caste system. Although still very strong in India, the caste system was never significant in Malaysia, mainly because the labourers brought here from India were generally from the lower classes.

Westerners often have trouble understanding Hinduism, principally because of its vast pantheon of gods. In fact, you can look upon all these different gods simply as pictorial representations of the many attributes of a god. The one omnipresent god usually has three physical representations: Brahma, the creator; Vishnu, the preserver; and Shiva, the destroyer or reproducer. All three gods are usually shown with four arms, but Brahma has the added advantage of four heads to represent his all-seeing presence. The four *Vedas*, the books of 'divine knowledge' which are the foundation of Hindu philosophy, are supposed to have emanated from his mouths.

Hinduism is not a proselytising religion, since you cannot be converted. You're either born a Hindu or you are not; you can never become one.

Hinduism in Malaysia dates back at least 1500 years and there are Hindu influences in cultural traditions, such as the wayang kulit (see Arts, above) and the wedding ceremony (see Society & Culture, above). However, it is only in the last 100 or so years, following the influx of Indian contract labourers and settlers, that it has again become widely practised.

LANGUAGE

The official language is Bahasa Malaysia, also referred to as Bahasa Melayu, language of the Malays. You can get along quite happily with English throughout Malaysia and, although it is not the official language, it is often still the linking language between the various ethnic groups, especially for the middle classes. When a Tamil wants to speak to a Chinese or a Chinese to a Malay, it's likely they'll speak English.

Other everyday languages include the Chinese dialects like Cantonese, Hakka and Hokkien. The majority of the region's Indians speak Tamil, although there are also groups who speak Malayalam, Hindi or another Indian language. Many different dialects are spoken by the Dayak peoples of Sabah and Sarawak in East Malaysia. See the Rejang River section in the Sarawak chapter for Iban words and phrases.

Malay is virtually the same as Indonesian, but there are a number of different words. Many of the differences are in the loan words – English-based for Malay and Dutch-based for Indonesian. If you are coming from Indonesia and have developed a proficiency in the language, you may initially be confused by the pronunciation. Because Bahasa Indonesia is a second language for most people in Indonesia, its pronunciation is taught in schools and is fairly standard. In Malaysia, however, it is subject to greater regional variances in pronunciation and slang – so much so that a Malaysian from Negeri Sembilan may have difficulty understanding someone from Kelantan.

Malay is, at least in its most basic form, very simple. There are no tense changes. You indicate the tense by using words such as yesterday or tomorrow or you just add *sudah* (already) to make anything past tense. Many nouns are pluralised simply by saying them twice – thus *buku* is 'book', *buku-buku* is 'books'. Or *anak* is 'child', *anak-anak* is 'children'. Other language simplifications include the omission of the articles 'the', 'a' or 'an'. Thus you just say *buku baik* rather than 'a good book' or 'the good book'. The verb 'to be' is also omitted, so again it would be *buku baik* rather than 'the book is good'. Malay is also a very musical and evocative language – 'the sun', for example, is *matahari*, or 'the eye of the day'.

Just as many Hindi words have found their way into Indian-English, many Malay terms are used in everyday English. You'll often read in the papers or see ads with the word *bumiputra*, which literally means 'sons of the soil' but is used to specify that the job or whatever is open only to Malay Malaysians, not Indian Malaysians or Chinese Malaysians. Papers occasionally complain about *jaga keretas*, the people who operate car-parking rackets – pay them to 'protect' your car while it's parked or you'll wish you had. Or you may hear of a couple being accused of *khalwat* – literally 'close proximity' and something unmarried Muslims should not be suspected of!

Lonely Planet publishes the *Malay phrasebook*, which is a handy pocket-sized introduction to the Malay language.

New Spelling

The new spelling system of Bahasa Malaysia brings it into line with Indonesian. However, many of the old spellings are still in use for place names and people's names. The main changes are that 'c' is used instead of 'ch' and is pronounced as in the English word 'church', and 'o' often becomes 'u' when it is the final syllable, eg *kampung* not *kampong*, *teluk* not *telok*.

Pronunciation

Most sounds are the same as in English, although a few vowels and consonants differ.

a	as in 'hut'
e	like the 'e' in 'earn' when unstressed, as in *besar* (big); and sometimes hardly pronounced at all, as in the greeting *selamat*, which sounds like 'slamat' when spoken quickly. When stressed it is like the 'a' in 'may', as in *meja* (table). There is no rule as to when the 'e' is stressed or unstressed.
i	as in 'hit'
o	like the 'oa' in 'boat'
u	like the 'u' in 'flute'
ai	like the 'i' in 'line'
au	like a drawn out 'ow', as in 'cow'
ua	each vowel is pronounced

The pronunciation of consonants is very straightforward. Most sound like English consonants, except:

c	like the 'ch' in 'chair'
g	always hard, like the 'g' in 'garden'
ng	like the 'ng' in 'singer'
ngg	like the 'ng' in 'anger'
j	like the 'j' in 'join'
r	pronounced clearly and distinctly
h	like the English 'h' but a bit stronger (as if you were sighing), though almost silent at the end of a word
k	like the English 'k' except when it is at the end of the word, in which case you just stop short of actually saying the 'k'
ny	a single sound; like the 'n' and 'y' in 'can you' run together

Stress

There is no strong stress in Malay, and nearly all syllables have equal emphasis, but a good approximation is to stress the second-last syllable. The main exception to the rule is the unstressed 'e' in words such as *besar* (big), pronounced be-SAR.

Basics

Yes.	*Ya.*
No.	*Tidak.*
Thank you (very much).	*Terima kasih (banyak).*
You're welcome.	*Sama-sama.*
Please.	*Tolong/Silakan.*
Sorry/Pardon?	*Maaf.*
Excuse me.	*Maafkan saya.*

Greetings

Good morning.
Selamat pagi.
Good day. (around midday)
Selamat tengah hari.
Good afternoon.
Selamat petang.
Good night.
Selamat malam.
Goodbye. (to person staying)
Selamat tinggal.
Goodbye. (to person going)
Selamat jalan.

Small Talk

How are you?
Apa khabar?
Fine thanks.
Khabar baik.
What is your name?
Siapa nama kamu?
My name is ...
Nama saya ...
Where are you from?
Dari mana asal saudara?
I'm from ...
Saya dari ...
How old are you?
Berapa umur saudara?
I am ...
Umur saya ...

Good/Very nice.	*Bagus.*
No good.	*Tidak baik.*
All right/Good/Fine.	*Baik.*

Language Difficulties

Do you speak English?
Bolehkah anda berbicara bahasa Inggeris?
I (don't) understand.
Saya (tidak) faham.
Please write that word down.
Tolong tuliskan perkataan.
Please repeat it.
Tolong ulangi.

Getting Around

How can I get to ...
Bagaimana saya pergi ke ... ?
How many km?
Berapa kilometre?
Where is ...?
Di mana ...?

What time does the ... leave?	*Pukul berapakah ... berangkat?*
bus	*bas*
train	*keretapi*
ship	*kapal*
boat	*bot*
rickshaw/trishaw	*beca*

Where can I hire a bicycle?
Di mana tempat sewa basikal?
Where can I rent a car?
Di manakah saya boleh menyewa kereta?
Please give me two tickets.
Tolong berikan saya dua tiket.

ticket window	*tempat tikit/kaunter*
1st class	*kelas satu*
economy class	*kelas ekonomi*

Directions

Which way?	*Ke mana?*
Go straight ahead!	*Jalan terus!*
Turn left.	*Belok kiri.*
Turn right.	*Belok kanan.*
at the T-junction	*di pertigaan*
at the traffic lights	*di lampu lalu lintas*
in front of	*di hadapan*
next to	*di samping/ di sebelah*
behind	*di belakang*
opposite	*berhadapan dengan*
here/there	*di sini/di sana*
north	*utara*
south	*selatan*
east	*timur*
west	*barat*

Around Town

Where is a/the ...?	*Di mana ada ...?*
bank	*bank*
embassy	*kedutaan besar*
hospital	*hospital*
hotel	*hotel*
museum	*musium*
police station	*stesen polis*
post office	*pejabat pos*
public telephone	*telepon umum*
public toilet	*tandas awam*
tourist office	*pejabat pelancong*
town square	*dewan perbandaran*

When does it open?
Bila buka?
When does it close?
Bila tutup?
I want to call ...
Saya mahu menelefon ...
I want to change a travellers' cheque.
Saya mau menukar cek pengembaraan.

Useful Signs

ENTRANCE	*MASUK*
EXIT	*KELUAR*
HOT/COLD	*PANAS/SEJUK*
NO SMOKING	*DI LARANG MEROKOK*
OPEN/CLOSED	*BUKA/TUTUP*
TELEPHONE	*TELEPON*
TOILETS	*TANDAS*
MEN	*LELAKI*
WOMEN	*PEREMPUAN*

Accommodation

hotel	*hotel*
losmen	*losmen*
cheap hotel	*hotel yang murah*
nice hotel	*hotel yang bagus*
inexpensive hotel	*hotel yang murah*

Is there a room available?
Ada bilik kosong?
I'd like a room for one/two people.
Saya perlu bilik untuk satu/dua orang.
with a bathroom
dengan bilik mandi
with a fan
dengan kipas angin
How much for one night/person?
Berapa harga satu malam/orang?
Can I see the room?
Boleh saya lihat biliknya?
I don't like this room.
Saya tidak suka bilik ini.

sleep	*tidur*
bed	*tempat tidur*
room	*bilik*
soap	*sabun*
dirty	*kotor*
expensive	*mahal*

Food

fried rice	*nasi goreng*
boiled rice	*nasi putih*
rice with odds & ends	*nasi campur*
fried noodles	*mee goreng*
noodle soup	*mee kuah*
soup	*sup*
fried vegetables	*cap cai*
with crispy noodles	*tami*
sweet & sour omelette	*fu yung hai*
fish	*ikan*
chicken	*ayam*
egg	*telur*
pork	*babi*
frog	*kodok*
crab	*ketam*
beef	*daging lembu*
prawns	*udang*
potatoes	*kentang*
vegetables	*sayur-sayuran*

Drinks

drinks	*minum-minum*
drinking water	*air minum*
orange juice	*air jeruk/air oren*
coffee	*kopi*
tea	*teh*
sugar	*gula*
milk	*susu*

Description

sweet	*manis*
steaming hot	*panas*
spicy hot	*pedas*
cold	*sejuk*
delicious	*enak*
special	*istimewa*

Finally, for vegetarians, *Saya tidak mau ikan, ayam atau daging* means 'I don't want fish, chicken or meat'.

Shopping

How much?
Berapa?
Can you lower the price?
Boleh kurang?

barber	*tukang cukur*
bookshop	*kedai buku*
chemist	*farmasi*
grocery	*kedai makanan*
market	*pasar*
night market	*pasar malam*
shopping centre	*pusat membeli-belah*
shop	*kedai*
this/that	*ini/itu*
big/small	*besar/kecil*

Health & Emergencies

Where is a ...	*Di mana ada ...*
dentist	*doktor gigi*
doctor	*doktor*
hospital	*hospital*
medicine	*ubat*
pharmacy	*apotik/farmasi*

I'm allergic to penicillin/antibiotics.
Saya alergik kepada penisilin/antibiotik.
I'm pregnant.
Saya hamil.

antibiotics	*antibiotik*
antiseptic	*antiseptik*
aspirin	*aspirin*
penicillin	*penisilin*
quinine	*kina*
sleeping pills	*pil tidur*
tablet/pill	*pil*
vitamins	*vitamin*

Emergencies

Help!
Tolong!
It's an emergency!
Keadaan darurat!
Stop!
Berhenti!
Go away!
Pergi!
There's been an accident!
Ada kemalangan!
Call a doctor!
Panggil doktor!
Call an ambulance!
Panggil ambulans!
I've been robbed!
Saya dirompak!
I am lost.
Saya sesat.

Time

What is the time?	*Pukul berapa?*
7 o'clock	*pukul tujuh*
hour	*jam*
week	*minggu*
year	*tahun*
When?	*Bila?*
How long?	*Berapa lama?*
tomorrow	*besok*
yesterday	*kelmarin*

Days of the Week

Monday	*hari Isnin*
Tuesday	*hari Selasa*
Wednesday	*hari Rabu*
Thursday	*hari Kamis*
Friday	*hari Jumaat*
Saturday	*hari Sabtu*
Sunday	*hari Minggu*

Numbers

1	*satu*
2	*dua*
3	*tiga*
4	*empat*
5	*lima*
6	*enam*
7	*tujuh*
8	*delapan/lapan*
9	*sembilan*
10	*sepuluh*
11	*sebelas*
12	*dua belas*
20	*dua puluh*
21	*dua puluh satu*
30	*tiga puluh*
53	*lima puluh tiga*
100	*seratus*
1000	*seribu*
½	*setengah*

Places of Worship

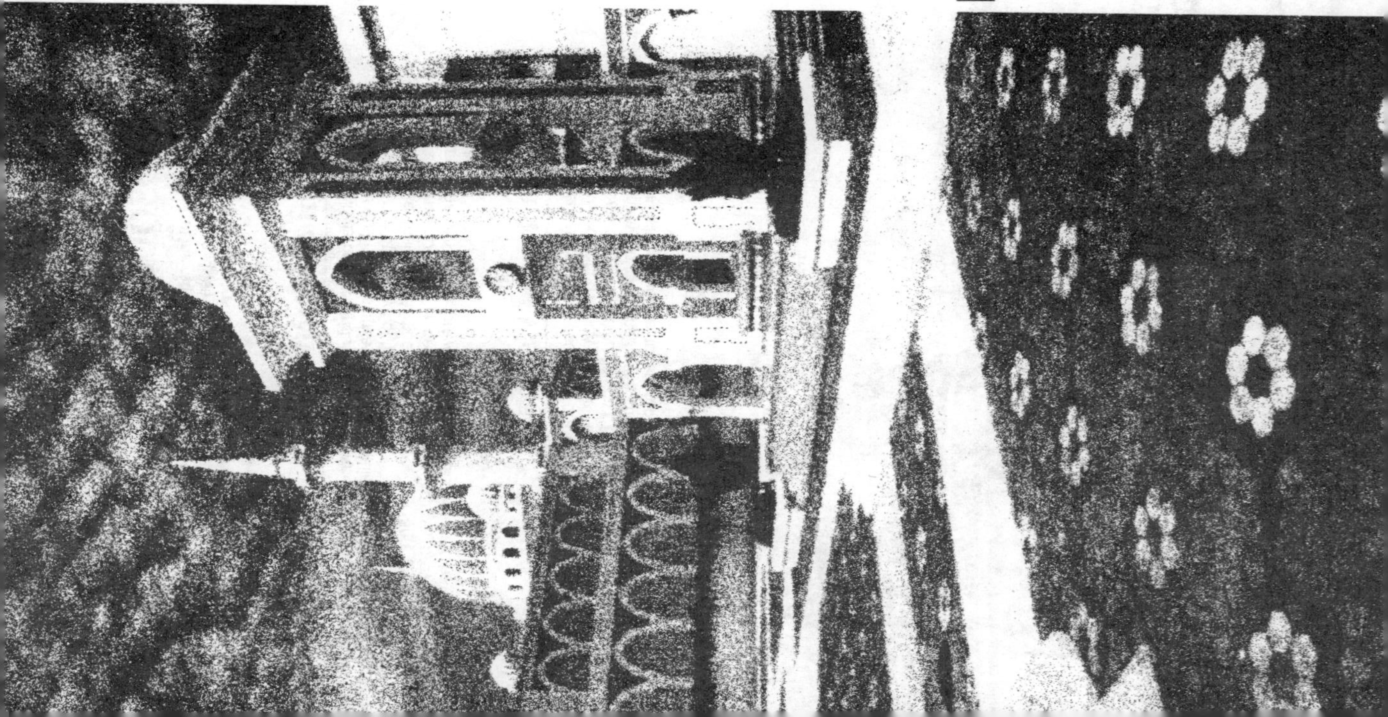

MOSQUES

While much of the region's public architecture has Indian roots, and many of the older mosques follow Indian styles (rather than Middle Eastern styles), some newer mosques are modern showpieces of extraordinary design.

Design & Function

The Masjid Jamek, or 'Friday Mosque', is where the community gathers for prayer on Friday (Islam's holy day). Smaller, local mosques are used for prayer on other days of the week.

Despite their sometimes astounding beauty and great variety of design, mosques are essentially simple buildings, providing a large space for communal prayer. Larger mosques may have a school attached.

Etiquette for Visitors

You must remove your shoes before entering a mosque. Find out if visitors are permitted at prayer times – often they are not. Many mosques admit women visitors, but some don't. Both men and women must dress appropriately, covering their arms and legs. A few larger mosques have robes for visitors who are not appropriately dressed.

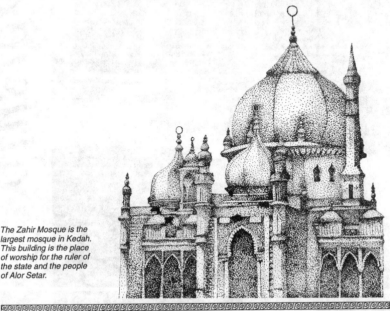

The Zahir Mosque is the largest mosque in Kedah. This building is the place of worship for the ruler of the state and the people of Alor Setar.

Examples of Mosques

One of the oldest surviving mosques in Kuala Lumpur is the picturesque Masjid Jamek overlooking Merdeka Square. In contrast, Kuala Lumpur's enormous Masjid Negara ('National Mosque') is an example of modernistic design. Singapore's large Sultan Mosque is the focus for the Muslim community, and Brunei's Omar Ali Saifuddin Mosque is a stunning modern structure.

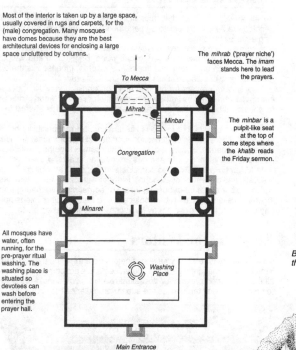

Most of the interior is taken up by a large space, usually covered in rugs and carpets, for the (male) congregation. Many mosques have domes because they are the best architectural devices for enclosing a large space uncluttered by columns.

The *mihrab* ('prayer niche') faces Mecca. The *imam* stands here to lead the prayers.

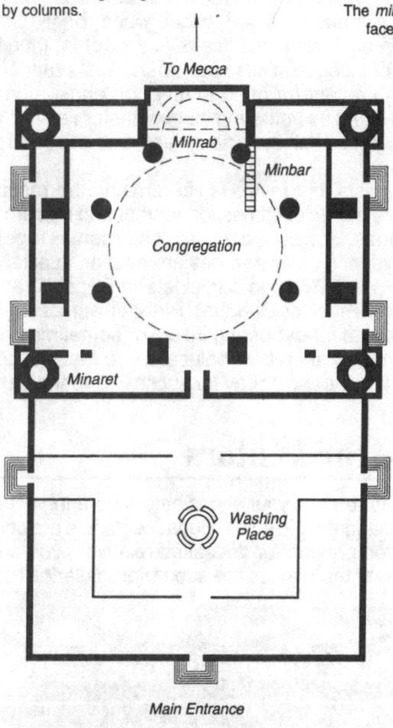

The *minbar* is a pulpit-like seat at the top of some steps where the *khatib* reads the Friday sermon.

All mosques have water, often running, for the pre-prayer ritual washing. The washing place is situated so devotees can wash before entering the prayer hall.

Most mosques have a minaret, usually a tower, which the *muezzin* climbs five times a day to call the faithful to prayer. Increasingly, the muezzin's call is tape-recorded and booms out over loudspeakers. Most older Malaysian mosques are based on Indian designs, so there is usually one minaret rather than several.

Below: A Muslim reads the Koran.

CHINESE TEMPLES

Taoism, Buddhism and Confucianism have blended in Chinese religion, and while many temples are theoretically Buddhist or Taoist, it takes a sharp eye to determine which is which. You'll often find statues of the Buddha side by side with statues of Taoist deities. You may also see a statue of Confucius, but a temple devoted entirely to Confucius will be a much quieter and less colourfully decorated place than the usual Chinese temple.

Design & Function

An elaborate 'Chinese'-style roof distinguishes most temples. Some temples are built to a multistorey pagoda design, but many are simpler single-storey buildings.

A screen often separates the main entrance from the main hall of the temple, which is a riot of carved, gilded wood, bright cloth and various antiquities such as ceremonial chairs and swords. Incense fills the air, as the lighting of incense sticks accompanies all prayer.

People burn prayers for good fortune, or 'ghost money' to appease evil spirits who might be bothering them or their relatives. Food is offered to ghosts, although after they have tasted it, the food is shared in a communal feast.

There are priests, but religious life remains the responsibility of the individual. There are no set times for prayers and no communal services except for funerals. However, the community comes together to observe popular holidays, and noisy parades are held on special occasions.

In Malaysia many Chinese participate in Buddhist as well as Taoist festivals, and days such as Buddha's Birthday attract crowds to temples. Noise, colour and a lot of burning incense (sometimes emanating from incense sticks bigger than baseball bats) are features of religious holidays. At other times people pray for success and the basics of life.

Etiquette for Visitors

It is customary to remove your shoes before entering a temple, although it might not be mandatory in some. Because people are coming and going all the time, often praying for deceased relatives, you should resist the temptation to treat temples as the superb art galleries they often are.

The Chinese Temple in Bandar Seri Begawan, Brunei, features colourful tilework and carved, gilded wood.

Examples of Chinese Temples

In Kuala Lumpur you'll find many Chinese temples, such as the ornate Chan See Shu Yuen Temple. The Kuan Yin Teng Temple in Georgetown on Penang Island is especially popular among devotees, as is Singapore's Kuan Yin Temple.

In the north of Peninsular Malaysia there are some Buddhist temples (such as Wat Chayamangkalaram on Penang) that are Thai-style temples devoted to Theravada Buddhism rather than Chinese temples. The Temple of 1000 Lights in Singapore is a Thai-style temple, but with technicolour Chinese decorations.

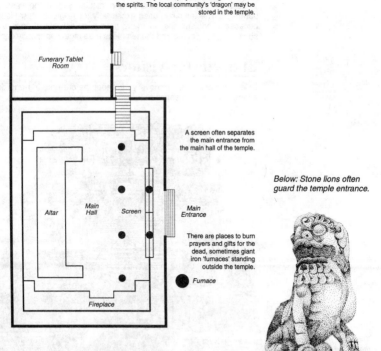

There is sometimes a separate room where the funerary tablets (small blocks of wood inscribed with characters) of deceased members of the community are displayed. Offerings are left for the spirits. The local community's 'dragon' may be stored in the temple.

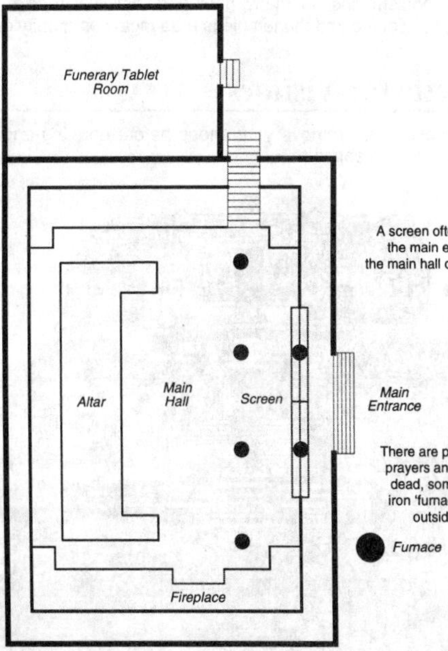

A screen often separates the main entrance from the main hall of the temple.

There are places to burn prayers and gifts for the dead, sometimes giant iron 'furnaces' standing outside the temple.

At the back of the hall is a large and elaborately decorated altar, usually containing an image of the deity (or person) to whom the temple is dedicated. In front of the altar is some sort of bench or table where devotees light their incense and pray.

Below: Stone lions often guard the temple entrance.

HINDU TEMPLES

As most of the region's Hindus are of south Indian descent, it isn't surprising that Hindu temples here adopt design elements from south Indian temples.

Design & Function

For Hindus, the square is the perfect shape (a circle isn't perfect because it implies motion), so temples are always based on a square ground plan. Extremely complex rules govern the siting, design and building of each individual temple, based on numerology, astronomy, astrology and religious law. These are so complicated and so important that it's customary for each temple to harbour its own particular set of calculations as though they were religious texts.

Each temple is dedicated to a particular god in the vast Hindu pantheon. The temple is used exclusively for religious rites. However, because Hinduism has so many rites and festivals, there's always something happening and the temple is a de facto community centre.

Etiquette for Visitors

Dress conservatively, remove your shoes before entering and do not attempt to enter the sanctum.

The south Indian Hindu temple Sri Mahamariamman in Kuala Lumpur plays a major part in the Thaipusam festival.

Examples of Hindu Temples

The Sri Mahamariamman Temple in Kuala Lumpur dates from 1873 and is large and ornate, as is the Sri Mariamman Temple in Singapore. In Georgetown on Penang Island, there's another Sri Mariamman Temple, also elaborately sculptured and painted.

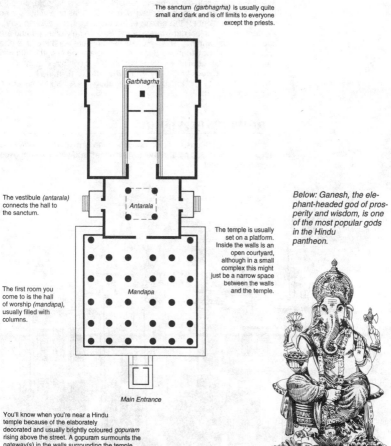

The sanctum *(garbhagrha)* is usually quite small and dark and is off limits to everyone except the priests.

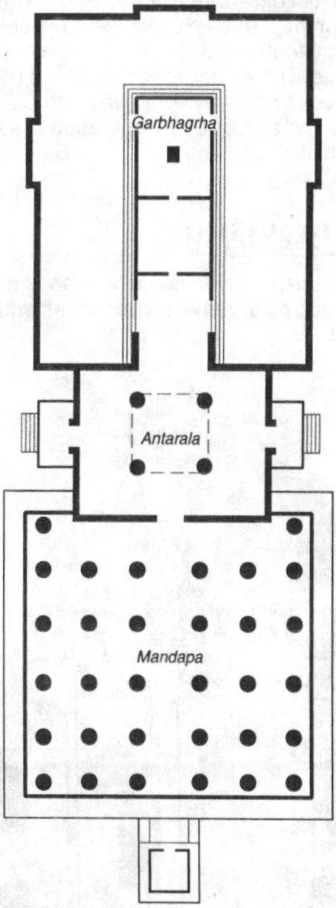

The vestibule *(antarala)* connects the hall to the sanctum.

The temple is usually set on a platform. Inside the walls is an open courtyard, although in a small complex this might just be a narrow space between the walls and the temple.

The first room you come to is the hall of worship *(mandapa)*, usually filled with columns.

You'll know when you're near a Hindu temple because of the elaborately decorated and usually brightly coloured *gopuram* rising above the street. A gopuram surmounts the gateway(s) in the walls surrounding the temple.

Below: Ganesh, the elephant-headed god of prosperity and wisdom, is one of the most popular gods in the Hindu pantheon.

SIKH TEMPLES

Sikhism doesn't recognise caste or class, so everyone becomes involved in ceremonies. Communal meals are a feature of temple activities.

Design & Function

A Sikh temple is called a *gurdwara*. Outside there is a flagpole, called a *nishan sahib*, flying a triangular flag with the Sikh insignia. There is no special requirement for the design of the building, but most use some elements from Punjabi gurdwaras. Sikhs worship only one god and are opposed to idol worship. You'll probably see pictures of the Gurus (the spiritual leaders who founded Sikhism), especially the first, the fifth and the 10th (last) Gurus. The wisdom of the Gurus is contained in the *Guru Granth Sahib*, a book written by Arjun, the fifth Guru, in the early 17th century. It has become an object of veneration in itself and is regarded as the 'living' Guru.

Etiquette for Visitors

Sikhism is an egalitarian religion and everyone is welcome to enter the temple. However, you must remove your shoes and you are supposed to cover your head.

The Gurdwara Sahib Yishun is an elegant new Sikh temple in Singapore.

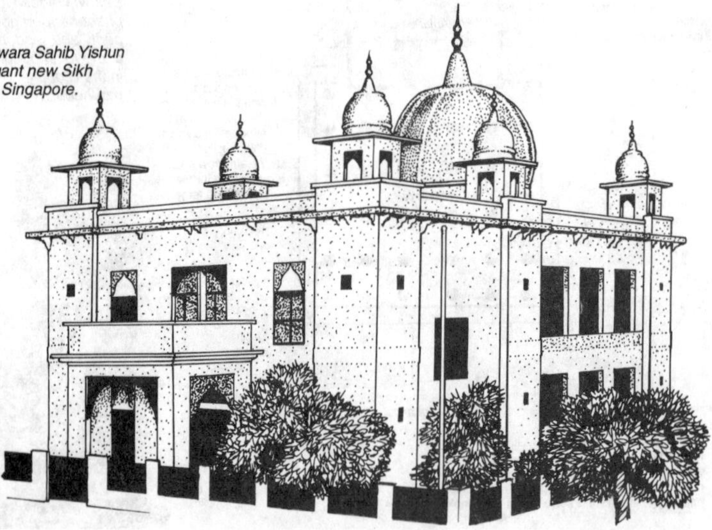

Examples of Sikh Temples

In general, Sikh temples in this region have until recently been quite modest buildings, such as the Sri Guru Singh Sabha on Wilkie Rd in Singapore. Unlike almost all other religions, there was little attempt to reproduce the architectural styles of the religion's birthplace. However, the increasing wealth of the Sikh community has seen some impressive new temples built, such as the Gurdwara Sahib Yishun, also in Singapore.

Sikhism differs from Hinduism in that there are no caste-related taboos in the preparation and cooking of food. This is an important community ritual, and every gurdwara has a large and cheerful kitchen.

Food prepared in the temple is eaten as a communal meal in the dining hall.

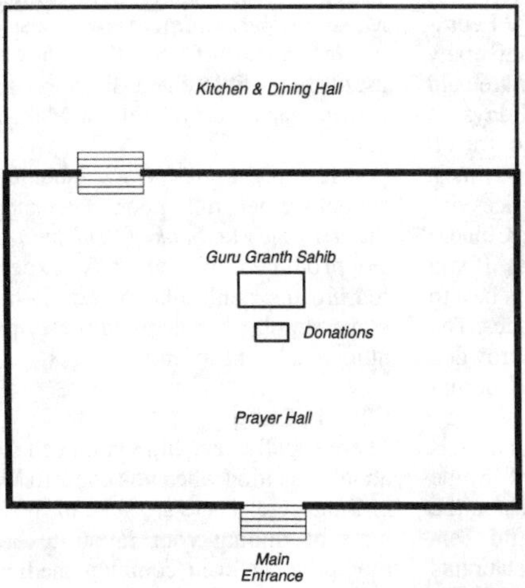

The *Guru Granth Sahib*, the holy book, is 'woken' in the morning and 'draped' in robes. In the evening it is put to bed. It is the centrepiece of ceremonies.

The temple is always entered by the main door. Sikhs approach the *Guru Granth Sahib* and bow. Money for the upkeep of the temple is usually placed in a box in front of the holy book.

Below: The holy book of the Sikhs, the Guru Granth Sahib, contains writings from Sikh Gurus, Muslim fakirs and Hindu saints. There is one in every gurdwara.

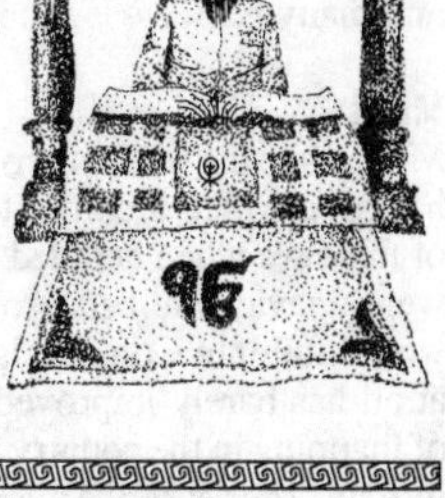

Facts for the Visitor

PLANNING

When to Go

Rain occurs fairly evenly throughout the year in Malaysia and the differences between the main October-April rainy season and the rest of the year are not that marked, so travel is possible year-round. The exception is the east coast of the peninsula, which receives heavy rain from November to January. During these months many east coast resorts close down and boat services drop off or stop altogether. Travel through the west coast is not affected. The states of Sabah and Sarawak receive high rainfall throughout the year, but it is heaviest from October to April.

Malaysia has many colourful festivals, such as Thaipusam around January/ February, and with such a wide ethnic diversity celebrations of one kind or another are held throughout the year. Public holidays in Malaysia are not a good time to travel. Malaysians like to get away at these times, so transport is crowded and hotel prices rise in the resorts. The peak times are Chinese New Year, Hari Raya and Christmas. If you are in the country at these times, it is best to stay put until the holiday rush subsides. The main beach and hill resorts also get crowded on weekends but are often deserted during the week.

The Muslim fasting month of Ramadan is generally not a problem for travel. Some services may be cut back, especially in the east coast states of Kelantan and Terengganu, but transport, hotels, restaurants and many businesses function as normal.

Maps

Malaysia still suffers from an Emergency hangover when it comes to maps, a product of the days when detailed maps of Malaysia were unavailable because of fears that they would fall into Communist hands. The situation has barely improved and the standard of mapping in the country is one of the worst in Asia. Tourist office maps are available for the main destinations but are usually little more than sketch maps. In smaller cities and towns maps are simply unavailable unless you have government contacts. The other problem is that with so much development maps date very quickly and new roads and buildings are not shown.

Good maps can be found for Kuala Lumpur, Penang, Melaka and some other cities. The best are foreign produced. *Periplus* produces an excellent series of city and regional maps, including maps of Malaysia, Johor, Kuala Lumpur, Melaka, Penang, Sabah and Sarawak. Another good overall map is the *Malaysia* map produced by Nelles Verlag. It has a scale of 1:1.5 million for all Malaysia; *West Malaysia* covers just the peninsula at a scale of 1:650,000. They are very useful but a little dated. Both Periplus and Nelles maps are available in Malaysia and abroad.

A few map atlases are available in Malaysia but are generally poor. One exception is the *Heritage Mapbook of Peninsular Malaysia* produced by Petronas, excellent if touring the peninsula by car. It has strip maps, simple town maps and descriptions of numerous points of interest.

What to Bring

There's really very little you need to worry about forgetting when you come to Malaysia or Singapore. There are none of those problems of finding your favourite brand of toothpaste or even common medicines. If you want film for your camera it will be cheaper here than at home.

Clothes are readily available and very reasonably priced. The best advice is to bring as little with you as possible; travelling light is the only way to go. In any case, you don't need too much to start with, as the weather is perpetually of the short-sleeve variety. However, if you're planning to head up to the hill stations, you may appreciate a sweater or light jacket in the evenings.

Dress is casual throughout the region – budget travellers may find a set of 'dress up' gear sensible for dealing with officialdom, but you're highly unlikely to need formal clothing too often.

Sensible accessories include sunglasses, a hat, a water bottle/canteen, a pocket knife, a day pack, a basic first-aid kit and a money belt or pouch.

HIGHLIGHTS & PLANNING AN ITINERARY

Travel in Malaysia is easily divided between the peninsula and the Borneo states of Sabah and Sarawak. To get a good look at both halves of Malaysia will take at least a couple of months, but most visitors only go to the peninsula. Borneo is almost another country, for Malaysians as well as foreign tourists.

Travel around Peninsular Malaysia is easy, so you can see a lot in a relatively short time without being hampered or exhausted by transport connections. Travel in Sarawak and Sabah is more time-consuming and requires more planning.

A personal itinerary depends very much on personal interests and budget. The following outlines the major routes and main destinations to help in planning, but you'll find many more places of interest in the book.

Peninsular Malaysia

Travel on the peninsula is often divided into west and east coasts, and you can do a tour down one side and up the other for an overall look. The mountainous jungle area of the centre, containing Taman Negara National Park, is usually included in the east coast but many visit it as a diversion from the west coast.

If time is limited to a week or two, it is best to concentrate on just one coast. The west coast has the main historical and cultural attractions, while the east coast is mainly for beaches. In three or four weeks you can sample both sides, and in two months you can explore all the peninsula in depth.

The well-worn tourist route, starting from Singapore, is up the west coast via Melaka, KL and the Cameron Highlands to Penang. Then over to Kota Bharu and down the east coast via Kuala Terengganu and Kuantan to the beach resorts of the Perhentian Islands, Tioman Island and others in between. Then it's back to Taman Negara and KL or Singapore. Of course there are numerous variations and a number of other places to visit, but surprisingly few visitors venture away from this route.

The main travel routes for each coast are listed below.

West Coast The west coast is the dominant half of the peninsula, containing the major cities and industry of Malaysia. Historically it is the most interesting and has the greatest colonial influence. Culturally the west coast is also the more diverse, and the cities are a vibrant Chinese/Malay/Indian mix. The west coast is more modern than the east, both in economic development and outlook.

The main highlights of the west coast, contained on almost everyone's itinerary, are the cities of Kuala Lumpur, Penang and Melaka, and the hill station of the Cameron Highlands. The west also has a couple of decent beach resorts, as well as other hill stations and interesting cities.

The following outlines the main tourist destinations through the west coast from south to north:

Melaka – Malaysia's most historic city, showcasing Portuguese, Dutch, British and Baba-Nyonya heritage

Kuala Lumpur – the busy capital, with good shopping, eating, nightlife and a few attractions and side trips

Fraser's Hill (Selangor) – a less visited but attractive, old-fashioned hill station

Cameron Highlands (Perak) – Malaysia's premier hill station, a break from the heat with jungle walks, tea plantations and gardens

Pulau Pangkor (Perak) – a smaller resort island with some of the west coast's best beaches

Taiping & Maxwell Hill (Perak) – a seldom visited historic town but a good side trip and a base for visiting Maxwell Hill, the smallest and quietest hill station

Penang – the first British settlement, with a host of attractions, including the interesting city of Georgetown and beach resorts

Langkawi (Kedah) – a major resort island with good beaches and a profusion of luxury hotels

In one week, Melaka-KL-Cameron Highlands-Penang is possible but rushed, unless you drop one destination or just transit through KL. Two weeks is more comfortable and you could also include another destination or three: Pulau Pangkor, Langkawi, Taiping, Kuala Kangsar, Fraser's Hill or Maxwell Hill. Fraser's Hill or Maxwell Hill could be substituted for the Cameron Highlands if you prefer a less developed hill station. In three weeks you could conceivably do the lot, though a month allows a more relaxing pace.

East Coast The less-developed states of Kelantan, Terengganu and Pahang are a Malay stronghold, with much less Chinese and Indian influence. The cities are bustling but small, and it is still primarily a rural area. The east coast provides a glimpse into Malay culture, and Kota Bharu promotes itself as a sort of Malay culturefest, but the main attractions are the beach resorts found right along the coast. The waters on the east coast are clearer than on the west and the offshore islands have the best beaches in Malaysia.

Inland in Pahang state is the Taman Negara National Park, Malaysia's most visited and extensive area of protected rainforest.

Moving from north to south, the highlights of the east coast are:

Kota Bharu (Kelantan) – the capital of Malaysia's most Islamic state, Kota Bharu has some low-key historical attractions, an excellent night market and regular Malay cultural performances – a well established fixture on the overland trail

Perhentian Islands (Terengganu) – something of a diving and snorkelling paradise, the Perhentian Islands are deservedly popular; the lack of alcohol and psychotropic substances makes these islands a good alternative to the party-party islands of Thailand – the perfect place to watch the sun going down sipping a lemonade

Marang (Terengganu) – a beach paradise that nearly happened; Marang is developing into a blot on the landscape very quickly

Cherating (Pahang) – *kampung*-style travellers' hangout with a reasonable beach and the only nightlife on the east coast

Tioman Island (Pahang) – the east coast's most famous attraction, a stunning island with a good range of accommodation, cross-island walks, snorkelling and diving

Taman Negara (Pahang) – Malaysia's premier and most visited national park, with magnificent jungle and good walks, but wrongly billed as a wildlife park

In a week you could take in a couple of beaches, though with limited time many people prefer to choose just one and take it easy. Tioman is a popular destination if coming from KL or Singapore. From Thailand, you could head to Kota Bharu for a couple of days and then the Perhentian Islands. In a couple of weeks you can go right along the coast, though three weeks or more is preferable if you want to take in all the beaches and relax.

Taman Negara requires at least four or five days. You really need three days in the park to do it justice, and from KL or Kuantan getting in and out of the park will take the best part of a day's travel in each direction, usually with an overnight stop in Jerantut. To do one of the longer walks, count on at least a week, closer to two if you tackle Gunung Tahan.

East Malaysia

Sarawak Sarawak is one of the least visited parts of Malaysia, and this is a pity. The longhouse experience is off limits to all but the most determined (or affluent) travellers nowadays, but Kuching is a real treat. Sarawak also has some of the best national parks in all of Malaysia.

Kuching – one of the most pleasant cities in Malaysia with enough in the way of sights to keep you busy for a few days; good food too

Kubah National Park – place to see the rafflesia, the world's largest flower, with easy access from Kuching

Bako National Park – 30 km of jungle trails

Rejang River – a muddy logging conduit for the most part, but for the traveller with time a possibility to visit upriver longhouses

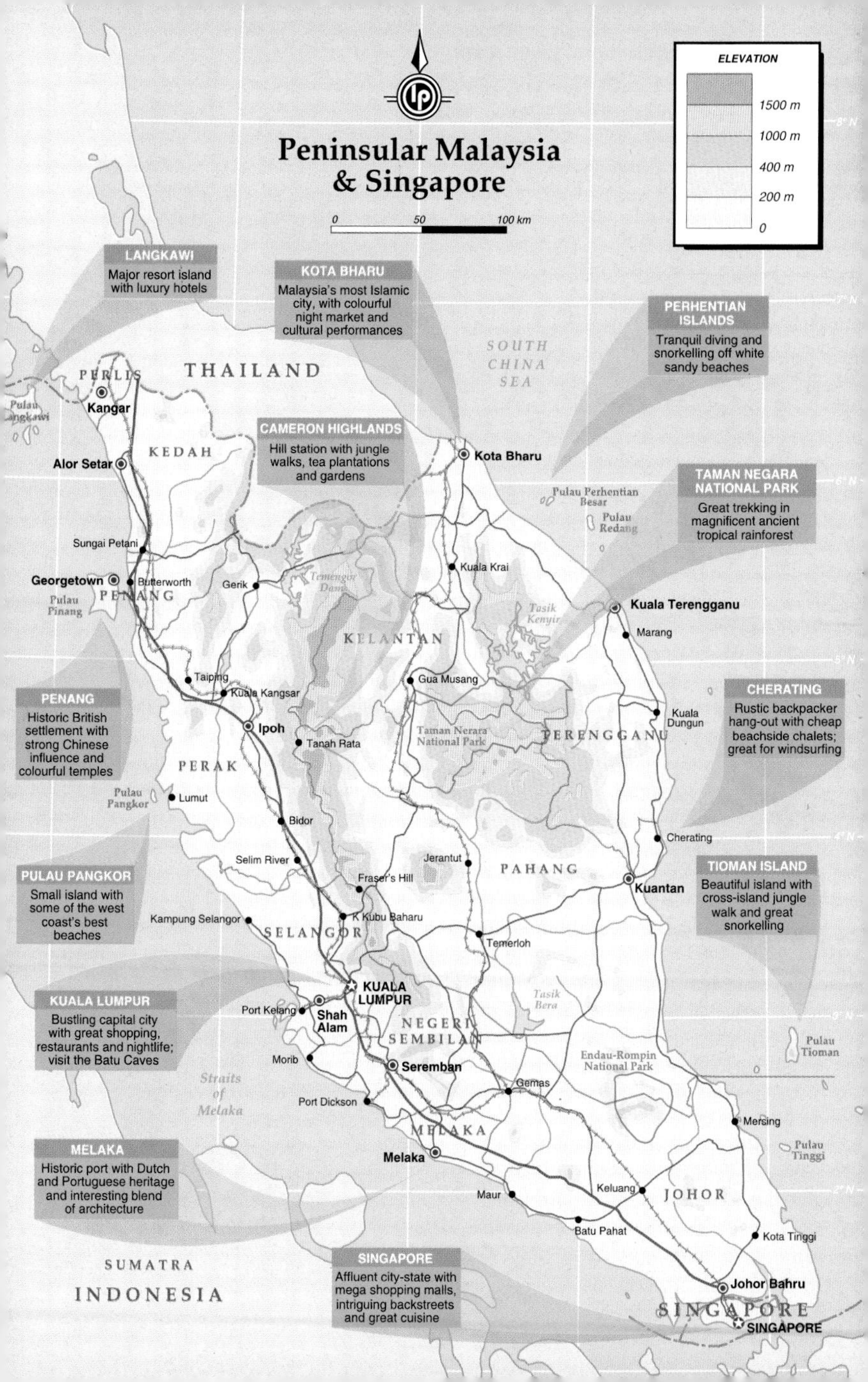

Peninsular Malaysia & Singapore
ELEVATION
1500 m
1000 m
400 m
200 m
0
0
50
100 km
LANGKAWI
Major resort island with luxury hotels
KOTA BHARU
Malaysia's most Islamic city, with colourful night market and cultural performances
PERHENTIAN ISLANDS
Tranquil diving and snorkelling off white sandy beaches
CAMERON HIGHLANDS
Hill station with jungle walks, tea plantations and gardens
TAMAN NEGARA NATIONAL PARK
Great trekking in magnificent ancient tropical rainforest
PENANG
Historic British settlement with strong Chinese influence and colourful temples
CHERATING
Rustic backpacker hang-out with cheap beachside chalets; great for windsurfing
PULAU PANGKOR
Small island with some of the west coast's best beaches
TIOMAN ISLAND
Beautiful island with cross-island jungle walk and great snorkelling
KUALA LUMPUR
Bustling capital city with great shopping, restaurants and nightlife; visit the Batu Caves
MELAKA
Historic port with Dutch and Portuguese heritage and interesting blend of architecture
SINGAPORE
Affluent city-state with mega shopping malls, intriguing backstreets and great cuisine
THAILAND
SOUTH CHINA SEA
PERLIS
Kangar
KEDAH
Alor Setar
Kota Bharu
Pulau Perhentian Besar
Pulau Redang
Sungai Petani
Georgetown
Butterworth
PENANG
Pulau Pinang
Gerik
Temengor Dam
Kuala Krai
Kuala Terengganu
Marang
KELANTAN
Tasik Kenyir
Taiping
Kuala Kangsar
Gua Musang
Ipoh
Tanah Rata
Taman Negara National Park
TERENGGANU
Kuala Dungun
PERAK
Pulau Pangkor
Lumut
Bidor
Cherating
Selim River
Jerantut
PAHANG
Fraser's Hill
Kuantan
Kampung Selangor
K Kubu Baharu
SELANGOR
Temerloh
KUALA LUMPUR
Tasik Bera
Port Kelang
Shah Alam
NEGERI SEMBILAN
Pulau Tioman
Morib
Seremban
Endau-Rompin National Park
Straits of Melaka
Gemas
Port Dickson
Mersing
MELAKA
Pulau Tinggi
Melaka
Keluang
JOHOR
Maur
Batu Pahat
Kota Tinggi
SUMATRA
INDONESIA
Johor Bahru
SINGAPORE
SINGAPORE

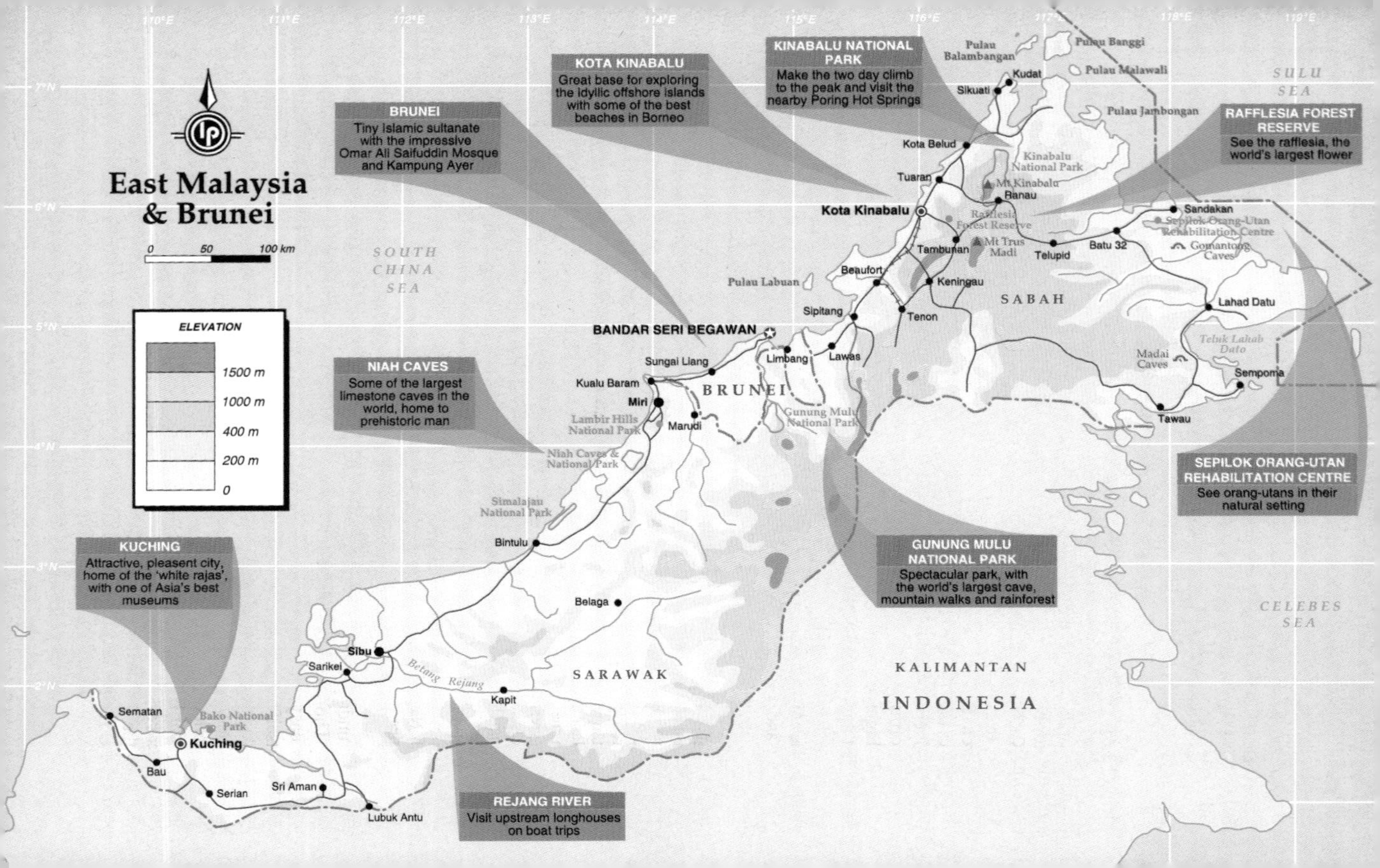

East Malaysia & Brunei
0 50 100 km
ELEVATION
1500 m
1000 m
400 m
200 m
0
BRUNEI
Tiny Islamic sultanate with the impressive Omar Ali Saifuddin Mosque and Kampung Ayer
KOTA KINABALU
Great base for exploring the idyllic offshore islands with some of the best beaches in Borneo
KINABALU NATIONAL PARK
Make the two day climb to the peak and visit the nearby Poring Hot Springs
RAFFLESIA FOREST RESERVE
See the rafflesia, the world's largest flower
SEPILOK ORANG-UTAN REHABILITATION CENTRE
See orang-utans in their natural setting
GUNUNG MULU NATIONAL PARK
Spectacular park, with the world's largest cave, mountain walks and rainforest
NIAH CAVES
Some of the largest limestone caves in the world, home to prehistoric man
KUCHING
Attractive, pleasent city, home of the 'white rajas', with one of Asia's best museums
REJANG RIVER
Visit upstream longhouses on boat trips
110°E
111°E
112°E
113°E
114°E
115°E
116°E
117°E
118°E
119°E
7°N
6°N
5°N
4°N
3°N
2°N
SOUTH CHINA SEA
SULU SEA
CELEBES SEA
KALIMANTAN
INDONESIA
SABAH
SARAWAK
BRUNEI
Pulau Balambangan
Pulau Banggi
Pulau Malawali
Pulau Jambongan
Pulau Labuan
Kudat
Sikuati
Kota Belud
Tuaran
Kota Kinabalu
Kinabalu National Park
Mt Kinabalu
Ranau
Rafflesia Forest Reserve
Mt Trus Madi
Tambunan
Telupid
Batu 32
Sandakan
Sepilok Orang-Utan Rehabilitation Centre
Gomantong Caves
Beaufort
Keningau
Tenon
Sipitang
Lawas
Limbang
BANDAR SERI BEGAWAN
Sungai Liang
Kualu Baram
Miri
Marudi
Lambir Hills National Park
Gunung Mulu National Park
Niah Caves & National Park
Simalajau National Park
Bintulu
Belaga
Lahad Datu
Teluk Lahab Dato
Madai Caves
Sempoma
Tawau
Sibu
Sarikei
Betang Rejang
Kapit
Sematan
Bako National Park
Kuching
Bau
Serian
Sri Aman
Lubuk Antu

Niah Caves – some of the largest caves in the world, with access via fantastic three km plankwalk through the rainforest
Gunung Mulu National Park – the most spectacular of Sarawak's national parks, with caves, mountain walks and forests; unfortunately many budget travellers are put off by the costs

In a week you could fly in to Kuching, make a day trip to Kubah, spend two or three days in Bako or take a longhouse tour out of Kuching for two or three days.

From Kuching, Niah Caves is at least a three-day excursion on the way through to Sabah. Even if you fly into Mulu, at least four or five days should be allowed. A trip up the Rejang River requires a week or more to make it worthwhile.

All the highlights could be visited in three weeks, but a month is preferable.

Sabah The chief attractions of Sabah are Mt Kinabalu and the Turtle Islands National Park.

Kota Kinabalu – more a base to prepare your assault on the rest of Sabah than a place to linger, but the islands and beaches of the Tunku Abdul Rahman National Park make a good side trip
Rafflesia Forest Reserve – Sabah's reserve for searching out the world's largest flower
Kinabalu National Park – the highest mountain between the Himalayas and the peaks of New Guinea; great walks in the park, and the climb to the peak is not as difficult as you might imagine
Sepilok Orang-Utan Rehabilitation Centre – one of only a few orang-utan centres, and one of the easiest places to see orang-utans in their natural setting
Turtle Islands National Park – popular island retreat with turtles

In a week, undoubtedly the place to go is Mt Kinabalu. Though the climb is only overnight, it is easy to spend a few more days at the park itself and visit nearby Poring Hot Springs. Access is via Kota Kinabalu, from where nearby Tunku Abdul Rahman National Park can be visited as a day trip, or longer if your budget allows. In two weeks, you can cover all of western Sabah, also taking in the Rafflesia Forest Reserve and perhaps the Tenom-Beaufort jungle train.

Eastern Sabah has the Sepilok Orang-Utan Rehabilitation Centre, which is a day trip from Sandakan, and Turtle Islands National Park, usually a three-day trip. So the main highlights of Sabah, west and east, can be seen comfortably in three weeks. The other attractions of note in eastern Sabah are Danum Valley, and Sipadan Island for diving, both expensive destinations – count on another week or more for these two.

TOURIST OFFICES

Malaysia has an efficient national tourist body, Tourism Malaysia (Malaysia Tourism Promotion Board). It produces a large number of glossy brochures and other literature, most of it fairly useful.

There are also a number of state tourist promotion organisations, such as the Penang Tourist Association, which will often have more detailed information on the area, while Tourism Malaysia can provide brochures and information for all parts of Malaysia.

Tourism Malaysia and state tourism offices are listed under each city with representation. The head office of Tourism Malaysia (☎ 03-293 5188; fax 03-293 5884) is on the 24th to 27th floors, Menara Dato Onn, Putra World Trade Centre, 45 Jalan Tun Ismail 50480, Kuala Lumpur.

Tourist Offices Abroad

Tourism Malaysia also maintains the following offices overseas. They are good places for information before you leave.

Australia
Ground floor, 65 York St, Sydney 2000, NSW (☎ (02) 9299-4441)
56 William St, Perth 6000, WA (☎ (09) 481-0400)
Canada
830 Burrard St, Vancouver, BC V6Z 2K4 (☎ (604) 689-8899)
France
29 Rue des Pyramides, 75001 Paris (☎ (01) 42 97 41 71)
Germany
Rossmarkt 11, 60311 Frankfurt-am-Main (☎ (069) 28 37 82)

Hong Kong
    Ground floor, Malaysia Building, 47-50 Gloucester Rd (☎ 2528-5810)
Italy
    2nd floor, Piazza San Babila, 20122 Milan (☎ (02) 796-702)
Japan
    2nd floor, Nichiginmae Kyodo Building, 3-2-4 Nihombashi-Hongokucho Chuo-ku, Tokyo 103 (☎ (03) 3279-3081)
Singapore
    10 Collyer Quay, 01-06 Ocean Building, Singapore 0104 (☎ 02-532 6321)
South Africa
    1st floor, Hutton Court, Cnr Jan Smuts Ave & Summit Rd, 2196 Johannesburg (☎ (011) 327 0400)
Sweden
    Ground floor, Sveavagen 18, 10386 Stockholm (☎ (08) 249-900)
Thailand
    315 Silom Rd, Bangkok 10500 (☎ (02) 236-7606)
UK
    57 Trafalgar Square, London WC2N 5DU (☎ (0171) 930 7932)
USA
    818 West 7th St, Suite 804, Los Angeles, CA 90017 (☎ (213) 689-9702)
    595 Madison Ave, Suite 1800, New York, NY 10022 (☎ (212) 754-1113)

VISAS & DOCUMENTS

Passport

Visitors must be in possession of a valid passport or internationally recognised travel document valid for at least six months beyond the date of entry into Malaysia.

Visas

Malaysian Visas Commonwealth citizens (except those from India, Bangladesh, Sri Lanka and Pakistan), citizens of the Republic of Ireland, Switzerland, the Netherlands, San Marino and Liechtenstein do not require a visa to visit Malaysia.

Citizens of Austria, Belgium, Czech Republic, Denmark, Finland, Hungary, Germany, Iceland, Italy, Japan, Luxembourg, Norway, Slovak Republic, South Korea, Sweden, the USA and most Arab countries do not require a visa for a visit not exceeding three months.

Citizens of France, Greece, Poland, South Africa and many South American and African countries do not require a visa for a visit not exceeding one month. Most other nationalities are given a shorter stay period or require a visa. Citizens of Israel cannot enter Malaysia, but with thawing relations between the two countries this may soon change.

Most nationalities are given a 30 or 60 day visa on arrival, depending on the expected length of stay. As a general rule, if you arrive by air you will be given 60 days automatically, though coming overland you may be given 30 days unless you specifically ask for a 60 day permit. It's then possible to get an extension at an immigration office in the country for up to three months total stay. This is a straightforward procedure which can be done in major cities.

Sabah and Sarawak are treated in some ways like separate countries. Your passport will be checked again on arrival in each state and a new stay permit issued. You are usually issued with a 30 day permit on arrival in Sarawak or Sabah. Travelling directly from either Sabah or Sarawak back to Peninsular Malaysia, however, there are no formalities and you do not start a new entry period, so your 30 day permit from Sabah or Sarawak remains valid. You can then extend your initial 30 day permit, though it can be difficult to get an extension in Sarawak.

Thai Visas You can get Thai visas from the embassies in Singapore or Kuala Lumpur or the consulates in Penang or Kota Bharu. The consulates are quick and convenient.

There are two main types of Thai visa: if you have an onward air ticket and will not be staying in Thailand for more than four weeks, you do not need to prearrange a visa and can get a free entry permit (not extendible) on arrival by air or land; otherwise a two-month tourist visa from a Thai consulate or embassy costs RM33. Two photos are required.

Indonesian Visas For most western nationalities no visa is required on arrival in Indonesia, as long as you have a ticket out (not always rigidly enforced) and do not intend to stay more than 60 days. The only catch is that the 'no visa' entry only applies if you both enter and leave Indonesia through certain recognised gateways. These entry and exit points include all the usual airports and seaports, but there are some places, such as Jayapura in Irian Jaya, not on the list. If you intend to arrive or leave Indonesia through one of the oddball places, then you have to get a visa in advance.

Travel Insurance

A travel insurance policy to cover theft, loss and medical problems is strongly recommended. Though Malaysia is generally a healthy and safe country to travel in, sickness, accidents and theft do happen. There are a wide variety of policies and travel agents have recommendations. Check the small print to see if it covers potentially dangerous sporting activities you may do, such as diving or trekking, and make sure that it adequately covers your valuables. A few credit cards offer limited, sometimes full, travel insurance to the holder.

Documents

Major Malaysian car hire agencies will rent a car on the production of a valid home licence with a photo and don't also require an International Driving Permit. Though not required, an International Driving Permit is good to have if stopped by overly officious police looking for any dubious reason to extract 'fines' – a rare occurrence but it happens. International Driving Permits can be obtained through motoring associations in your home country. Bring your home driver's licence even if you don't intend to drive – you might decide to use it, and it can occasionally be good for identification purposes.

A YHA card is of limited use in Malaysia, as only KL, Melaka and Port Dickson have YHA hostels, though it can also be used to waive the small initial membership fee at some YMCAs and YWCAs. Bring it if you have one.

An ISIC international student card is also of limited use but worth bringing. Most student discounts, such as on the trains, are only available for Malaysian students, but it can also be useful at hostels and flashing it occasionally brings discounts.

An International Health Card is not necessary to enter Malaysia except to show vaccination against yellow fever if travelling from South America. If you do get vaccinations, though, it is a good idea to have them recorded on a International Health Card, for your own record if nothing else (see the Health section for more information).

EMBASSIES

Malaysian Embassies

Visas can be obtained at Malaysian diplomatic missions overseas, including:

Australia
: 7 Perth Ave, Yarralumla, Canberra ACT 2600 (☎ (06) 273-1543)

Brunei
: 473 Kampung Pelambayan, Jalan Kota Baru, Bandar Seri Begawan (☎ 02-228410)

Canada
: 60 Boteler St, Ottawa, Ontario K1N 8Y7 (☎ (613) 237-5182)

China
: 13 Dhongzhimenwai Dajie, Sanlitun, Beijing (☎ (010) 532-2531)

France
: 2, bis rue Benouville, Paris 75116 (☎ (01) 45.53.11.83)

Germany
: Mittelstrasse 43, 5300 Bonn 2 (☎ (0228) 37 68 03 06)

Hong Kong
: 25th floor, Malaysia Building, 50 Gloucester Rd, Wanchai (☎ 2527-0921)

India
: 50M Satya Marg, Chanakyapuri, New Delhi 110021 (☎ (011) 601-291)
: Consulate: 287 TTK Rd, Madras 600018 (☎ (044) 453-580)

Indonesia
: Jalan Rasuna Said Kav X/6, Kuningan, Jakarta (☎ (021) 522-4947)
: Consulates: 11 Jalan Diponegoro, Medan (☎ (061) 25313)
: 32 Jalan Diponegoro, Pekanbaru (☎ 23913)
: 42 Jalan A Yani, Pontianak, Kalimantan (☎ 32986)

Japan
: 20-16, Nanpeidai-cho, Shibuya-ku, Tokyo 150 (☎ (03) 3476-3840)

Myanmar (Burma)
82 Diplomatic Quarters, Pyidaungsu Yeikhta Rd, Yangon (Rangoon)(☎ (01) 220248)
Netherlands
Rustenburgweg, 22517 KE, The Hague (☎ (070) 350-6506)
New Zealand
10 Washington Ave, Brooklyn, Wellington (☎ (04) 385-2439)
Pakistan
224 Nazimuddin Rd, F-7/4, Islamabad (☎ (051) 821-0147)
Papua New Guinea
Unit 1, 2nd floor, Pacific View Apartments, Pruth St, Korobosea, Port Moresby (☎ 252-076)
Philippines
107 Tordesillas St, Salcedo Village, Makati, Metro Manila (☎ (02) 817-4581)
Singapore
301 Jervois Rd, Singapore 1024 (☎ 02-235 0111)
Sri Lanka
47/1 Jawatta Rd, Colombo 7 (☎ (01) 502-858)
Thailand
35 South Sathorn Rd, Bangkok 10120 (☎ (02) 286-1390)
Consulate: 4 Sukhom Rd, Songkhla (☎ 311-062)
UK
45 Belgrave Square, London SW1X 8QT (☎ (0171) 235-8033)
USA
2401 Massachusetts Ave NW, Washington DC 20008 (☎ (202) 328-2700)
Vietnam
Block A-3 Van Phuc, Hanoi (☎ (04) 53371)

Foreign Embassies in Malaysia

Countries with diplomatic representation in Malaysia include (all in Kuala Lumpur unless otherwise noted):

Australia
6 Jalan Yap Kwan Sweng (☎ 03-242 3122)
Brunei
MBF Plaza, 172 Jalan Ampang (☎ 03-261 2800)
Canada
MBF Plaza, 172 Jalan Ampang (☎ 03-261 2000)
China
229 Jalan Ampang (☎ 03-242 8495)
Denmark
Angkasa Raya Building, 123 Jalan Ampang (☎ 03-202 2001)
France
192 Jalan Ampang (☎ 03-249 4122)
Consulate: Wisma Rajab, 82 Bishop St, Penang (☎ 04-262 8816)
Germany
3 Jalan U Thant (☎ 03-242 9666)
India
Jalan Taman Duta (☎ 03-253 3510)
Indonesia
233 Jalan Tun Razak (☎ 03-984 2011)
Consulates: 467 Jalan Burma, Penang (☎ 04-282 4686)
5A Pisang Rd, Kuching, Sarawak (☎ 082-241734)
Jalan Karamunsing, Kota Kinabalu, Sabah (☎ 088-219110)
Jalan Apas, Tawau, Sabah (☎ 089-772052)
Japan
11 Pertiaran Stonor (☎ 03-242 7044)
Consulates: 2 Jalan Biggs, Penang (☎ 04-229 8222)
Wisma Yakin, Jalan Datuk Salleh Sulong, Kota Kinabalu, Sabah (☎ 088-254695)
Myanmar (Burma)
5 Jalan Taman U Thant (☎ 03-242 3863)
New Zealand
Menara IMC, Jalan Tun Razak (☎ 03-238 2533)
Pakistan
132 Jalan Ampang (☎ 03-241 8877)
Papua New Guinea
5 Jalan U Thant (☎ 03-245 5145)
Philippines
1 Jalan Changkat Kia Peng (☎ 03-248 4233)
Singapore
209 Jalan Tun Razak (☎ 03-261 6277)
Sri Lanka
2A Jalan Ampang Hilir (☎ 03-456 0917)
Sweden
6th floor, Angkasa Raya Building, 123 Jalan Ampang (☎ 03-248 5981)
Switzerland
16 Persiaran Madge (☎ 03-248 0622)
Thailand
206 Jalan Ampang (☎ 03-248 8222)
Consulates: 1 Jalan Tunku Abdul Rahman, Penang (☎ 04-282 8029)
4426 Jalan Pengkalan Chepa, Kota Bharu (☎ 09-744 0867)
UK
185 Jalan Ampang (☎ 03-248 2122)
USA
376 Jalan Tun Razak (☎ 03-248 9011)
Vietnam
Vietnam House, 4 Persiaran Stonor (☎ 03-248 4036)

CUSTOMS

The following dutiable items can be brought into Malaysia free of duty: one litre of alcohol, 225 grams of tobacco (200 cigarettes) and souvenirs and gifts not exceeding RM200. Cameras, portable radios, perfume, cosmetics and watches do not attract duty.

The list of prohibited items is longer and includes, among others: counterfeit currency, weapons (including imitations), 'obscene and prejudicial articles', fire crackers and drugs.

MONEY

Costs

Though one of the more expensive countries in South-East Asia, Malaysia is still cheap by world standards and caters well to all budgets. You can easily find a spartan double room in an old hotel for as little as US$5, but if you want to spend US$100 a night that's no problem either. Though still plentiful, the older cheap hotels are diminishing in number, but new travellers' guesthouses are springing up in the tourist centres and offer dormitory beds for around US$2.50, as well as cheap rooms. The mid-range is well catered for and hotel rooms with air-con and attached bathroom start at around US$12. Large hotels and resort apartments are springing up everywhere, and the imminent glut augers well for price cutting in many areas.

Food is a delight, and an economical delight at that. There's an incredible variety of restaurants offering excellent food at amazingly cheap prices. You'll wonder if anyone ever eats at home when you can get a meal in a small restaurant for not much over US$1. Chicken-rice with soup, a soft drink, a cup of coffee and a couple of varieties of tropical fruit to finish up with will set you back less than US$3 in any food centre. At the other end of the scale, the fancy hotels and restaurants in the main cities offer French cuisine at Parisian prices.

It's the same story when it comes to getting around. If you want to travel by chauffeur-driven air-conditioned car you can, but there are lots of cheaper and quite comfortable means of getting around. There are plenty of reasonably priced trishaws and taxis for local travel – the drivers are reasonably honest, so there's no need to get into the frantic bargaining sessions or fear the subsequent arguments that taxi travel in some Asian countries entails. For long distance, Malaysia has excellent buses, trains and taxis, all at very reasonable prices.

On top of these travel essentials – accommodation, food and transport – you'll also find nonessentials and luxuries are moderately priced, even downright cheap.

Carrying Money

Travellers' Cheques & Cash Travellers' cheques are always the safest way to carry money, though it doesn't hurt to have some cash (say US$100 to US$200) carried separately from your travellers' cheques for emergencies if your cheques are stolen or you have to change money after hours at a moneychanger or large hotel.

All major brands of travellers' cheques are acceptable in Malaysia. Cash in major currencies is also readily exchanged, though like everywhere else in the world the US$ has a slight edge.

Credit Cards & ATMs Credit cards are also a viable and very convenient way to carry money if you use them correctly. They are readily acceptable for purchases in many establishments – airline offices, car hire agencies, major hotels, better restaurants, large shops etc. MasterCard and Visa are widely accepted and the best to carry.

Banks all over the country also accept credit cards for over-the-counter cash advances, or through automatic teller machines (ATMs) if your card has a personal identification number attached. With this facility you can get cash quickly any time of the night or day, you don't pay commission charges and the interbank exchange rates are often better than those offered for cash or travellers' cheques. The disadvantages are that interest is charged unless your account always has a positive balance to draw on – pay extra money into your credit card account before you leave or get someone at home to ensure that is always in the black. Other disadvantages are that things can go wrong with credit cards. If an ATM refuses to accept your card and your bank is 10,000 km away, it is difficult to clear up any problems. Some banks also charge penalties for overseas cash advances and have minimum withdrawal amounts, so check before you leave. Don't rely totally on a credit card – also take some travellers' cheques or cash, and a second credit card is also good insurance.

Maybank, Malaysia's biggest bank with branches everywhere, accepts both Visa and MasterCard at its ATMs. The Hongkong Bank accepts Visa and the Standard Chartered Bank accepts MasterCard through ATMs. Other bank ATMs that accept credit cards display the relevant symbols. Some banks in Malaysia are also linked to international banking networks such as Cirrus (the most common), Maestro and Plus, allowing withdrawals from overseas savings accounts. Check with your bank at home to see if you can use this facility in Malaysia.

Currency

The local currency is the Malaysian ringgit (RM), which is divided into 100 sen. It is a strong, stable currency and is slowly rising in value against most other world currencies.

Notes in circulation are RM5, RM10, RM20, RM50, RM100, RM500 and RM1000; the coins in use are 1, 5, 10, 20 and 50 sen, and RM1. Old RM1 notes are occasionally seen and new RM2 notes have just been introduced, the first of a new series of notes that will include a RM15 note.

Banks are efficient and there are also plenty of moneychangers. Banks usually charge commission, typically around RM5 per transaction, whereas the moneychangers have no charges but their rates vary more – so know what the current rate is before dealing with moneychangers. For cash you'll generally get a better rate at a moneychanger than in a bank – it's usually quicker too. Away from the tourist centres, moneychangers' rates are often poorer and they may not change travellers' cheques.

Currency Exchange

The following table shows the exchange rates:

Australia	A$1	=	RM1.97
Canada	C$1	=	RM1.84
France	FF10	=	RM4.83
Germany	DM1	=	RM1.63
Hong Kong	HK$10	=	RM3.23
Indonesia	Rp 1000	=	RM1.07
Japan	¥100	=	RM2.30
New Zealand	NZ$1	=	RM1.68
Singapore	S$1	=	RM1.78
Thailand	Baht 100	=	RM9.91
UK	UK£1	=	RM3.84
USA	US$1	=	RM2.50

Tipping & Bargaining

Tipping is not normally done in Malaysia. The more expensive hotels and restaurants have a 10% service charge, while at the cheaper places tipping is not expected. Taxi and rickshaw drivers will naturally not knock back a tip should you decide to give one but it's not expected as a matter of course.

Bargaining is not usually required for everyday goods, unlike in some Asian countries. Always bargain for souvenirs, antiques and other tourist items, even if prices are displayed. Prices are rarely fixed in tourist outlets and can be grossly inflated. Other major purchases, such as cameras and electronics, also usually require bargaining except in department stores. Bargaining should be conducted with equanimity – aggression will only force the trader to lose face, pushing prices up.

Transport prices are fixed but negotiation is required for trishaws and unmetered taxis around town or for charter. Hotels may be willing to bend their prices, especially if business is slack. Expensive hotels are most likely to drop prices, and you should always inquire about the discount rates, which will often bring an immediate reduction.

POST & COMMUNICATIONS

Malaysia has an efficient postal system with good poste restantes at the major post offices. Post offices are open daily from 8 am to 5 pm and closed on Sunday and public holidays (closed on Friday and public holidays in Kedah, Kelantan and Terengganu). The GPO in Kuala Lumpur is also open Sunday morning.

Postal Rates

Aerograms and postcards cost RM0.50 to any destination. Letters to Australia cost RM0.55 per 10 grams, letters to the UK and Europe cost RM0.90 and letters to the USA cost RM1.10.

It's easy to send parcels from any major post office although the rates are fairly high, from around RM20 to RM35 for a one kg parcel depending on the destination.

Telephone

Local Calls There are good telephone communications throughout the country. You can direct-dial long-distance calls between all major towns in Malaysia. Local calls cost 10 sen for three minutes.

All over the country you'll come across card telephones (Kadfon), operated by Telekom Malaysia and a private communications company, Uniphone. These telephones take coins or plastic cards and are convenient, except you need different cards for each company. Uniphone cards can be bought from 7-Eleven outlets and some other shops. They come in denominations of RM3, RM5, RM10, RM30 and RM50 (international calls only). Telekom cards are available from Telekom offices, post offices and some shops.

Calls to Singapore are STD (long-distance) rather than international calls. Area codes for Malaysia include:

Town	*Area Code*
Cameron Highlands	05
Ipoh	05
Johor Bahru	07
Kota Bharu	09
Kota Kinabalu	088
Kuala Lumpur	03
Kuala Terengganu	09
Kuantan	09
Kuching	082
Labuan	087
Langkawi	04
Melaka	06
Miri	085
Penang	04
Sandakan	089
Singapore	02

International Calls

Country	*Number*
Australia – Telstra	8000061
– Optus	8000068
Canada	8000017
Hong Kong	8000085
Italy	8000039
Japan	8000081
Netherlands	8000031
New Zealand	8000064
South Korea	8000082
Taiwan	8000088
UK – BT	8000044
– Mercury	8000048
USA – AT&T	8000011
– MCI	8000012
– Sprint	8000016

International Calls International calls can be direct-dialled from private phones, from some public phone booths using a phone card and from Telekom offices. Calls can be made at Uniphone booths that accept international calls; these are orange (rather than yellow) booths. Telekom booths that accept internal calls are marked 'IDD-Domestik'. There are also phones in most major towns, usually at the Telekom office, the airport or a major hotel, which accept credit cards for international calls. These are the Malaysia Telekom phones where you have to swipe your card down a slot on the right-hand side of the phone. Some Uniphone phones also accept credit cards. The access code for making international calls from Malaysia is 007.

For calls via the operator you have to go to a Telekom office, found in all major cities, or ring ☎ 108 from a private phone. A minimum charge of around RM1 applies for the connection, even if the connection is busy. For international call inquiries (rates, country codes) dial ☎ 103.

For calls to a number of countries, it's possible to make collect (reverse charge) calls from any phone in the country. If you are at a public phone it's the same cost as a local call (10 sen for three minutes); from private phones there is no charge. You get connected direct to the operator in the home country. The list on the previous page includes the countries hooked up to this service and the numbers to dial.

To call Malaysia from outside the country, the country code is 60. Drop the 0 before the area code (eg 3 instead of 03 for Kuala Lumpur) when calling from outside Malaysia.

BOOKS

A wide variety of books are available in Malaysia, and there are a number of good bookshops in which to find them.

Lonely Planet

South-East Asia on a shoestring is our overall guidebook to the region. For those travelling further afield, there are other LP guides to most South-East and North-East Asian countries. Lonely Planet's *Singapore city guide* is available for travellers just going to Singapore. LP also publishes the *Malay phrasebook*, an introduction to the Malay language.

People & Society

Kampong Boy by Lat (Straits Times Publishing) provides a delightful introduction to Malay life. It's a humorous autobiographical cartoon series on growing up in a village (kampung) and then moving to the town of Ipoh. Lat has many other excellent cartoon collections in print.

Culture Shock Malaysia (1994) by JoAnn Craig explains the customs, cultures and lifestyles of Malaysia's polyglot population to expatriates working there.

An Analysis of Malay Magic (1991) by KM Endicott is a scholarly look at Malay folk religion and the importance of spirits and magic in the world view of Malays.

Chinese Beliefs & Practices in South-East Asia edited by Cheu Hock Tong is an excellent introduction to Chinese religion and society, with special reference to variations from mainland Chinese customs.

The Prime Minister, Dr Mahathir Mohamad, is a prolific writer and has written a number of books interesting for their insight into his thinking. What they lack in scholarship is made up for by Dr Mahathir's lively, controversial style. *The Malay Dilemma* (1970), written before he became prime minister, is an interesting polemic of racial stereotyping and calls for the Malays to take control of their own destiny. It was banned for a number of years. His latest offering, *The Voice of Asia* (1995), co-authored with Japan's Ishihara Shintaro, outlines his notions of Asian Values, stressing the need for Asia to assert its own identity in the face of western arrogance and decadence.

Ian Buruma's *God's Dust* looks critically at the 'westernisation' of Asia, and in a long chapter on Malaysia and Singapore searchingly examines the idea of Asian Values. It is a fascinating read by the writer of *Japanese Mirror*, already established as something of a classic.

History

A Short History of Malaysia, Singapore & Brunei by C Mary Turnbull is straightforward and a good introductory volume on Malaysia's long history, from early civilisation to modern politics. *A History of Malaya* by R Winstedt is a standard history with a colonial perspective.

A History of Malaysia by Barbara Andaya and Leonard Watson is one of the best histories with a post-independence slant.

A number of books deal with the fall of Malaysia and Singapore and the subsequent Japanese occupation, and the internal and external struggles of the 50s and 60s. *The Jungle is Neutral* by F Spencer Chapman recounts the hardships and adventures of a British guerrilla force that fought on in the jungles of Malaya for the rest of the war. *The War of the Running Dogs – Malaya 1948-1960* by Noel Barber recounts the events of the long-running Communist insurrection.

The Undeclared War – The Story of the Indonesian Confrontation by Harold James and Denis Sheil-Small tells the story of the strange and disorganised confrontation with Indonesia which arose immediately after the Communist struggle.

Fiction

Singapore and Malaysia have always provided

a fertile setting for novelists, and Joseph Conrad's *The Shadow Line* and *Lord Jim* both use the region as a setting. Somerset Maugham also set many of his classic short stories in Malaya – look for the *Borneo Stories*.

The Long Day Wanes is a reissue in one volume of Anthony Burgess' classic *Malayan Trilogy*. It's well worth picking up a copy – it has some of the finest English-language fiction set in South-East Asia. Burgess' depiction of a variously alcoholic, set-upon, bewildered and valiant collection of Brits attempting to carry the flickering torch of empire against a backdrop of Malay nationalism bristles with superbly realised characters and fascinating insights.

The Consul's File by Paul Theroux is a very readable collection of short stories set in, of all places, Ayer Hitam near Kuala Lumpur. Theroux's *Saint Jack* is set in Singapore.

Turtle Beach by Blanche d'Alpuget (1981) is an Australian novel set during the racial tensions of 1969 and focuses on the plight of Vietnamese boat people. The subsequent film, and its portrayal of Malay racial hatred, outraged Malaysia, and both the book and the film have been banned.

Borneo

Nineteenth Century Borneo – A Study in Diplomatic Rivalry by Graham Irwin is a good book on the fascinating history of Sarawak, Sabah and Brunei.

Rajah Charles Brooke – Monarch of all He Surveyed by Colin N Criswell tells more about the white rajas, as does *The White Rajahs of Sarawak* by Robert Payne.

Vanishing World, the Ibans of Borneo by Leigh Wright has some beautiful colour photographs.

A Stroll Through Borneo by James Barclay (1980) is a delightful tale of a long walk and river trip through Sarawak, Sabah and Indonesian Kalimantan. The contrasts between Malaysian bureaucracy and the Indonesian variety are enlightening, with the Malaysians coming off distinctly second best.

Into the Heart of Borneo by Redmond O'Hanlon (1984) is the humorous, classic adventure of two foreigners as they journey by foot and boat into Borneo.

Another good read is *Stranger in the Forest* by Eric Hansen, about the author's experiences trekking right across Sarawak and Kalimantan. Or try *The Day Nothing Happened* by Terence Clarke, an entertaining novel about an American engineer who comes to Sarawak to build a road through the jungle.

Sarawak Crafts: Methods, Material and Motifs by Heidi Munan is a good introduction, but if you can afford it buy *Hornbill and Dragon* by Bernard Sellato, a superbly illustrated large-format bible of Borneo crafts.

For wildlife, *A Field Guide to the Mammals of Borneo* by Junaidi Payne, Charles M Francis and Karen Phillipps is a must. The illustrations are excellent. The definitive guide to birds is Smythies' *Birds of Borneo*, but the World Wide Fund for Nature (WWF) and the Sabah Foundation have condensed this weighty volume into the *Pocket Guide to the Birds of Borneo*, which is brilliantly illustrated and ideal for the field.

Travel

Mountains of Malaysia – a Practical Guide and Manual by John Briggs is essential reading for anyone intending to do a lot of mountain walking in Malaysia. The coverage ranges from fairly easy walks to technical climbs, mostly in Sabah and Sarawak, but Peninsular Malaysia is not forgotten and Taman Negara, the Cameron Highlands, Gunung Jerai and others are included.

Tales from the South China Seas, edited by Charles Allen, is the South-East Asian version of *Plain Tales from the Raj*. It recounts the stories of the British colonial experience, mostly in Malaya.

A Malaysian Journey (1993) by Rehman Rashad is an excellent introduction to Malaysia. Written by an expatriate Malaysian journalist who returns to travel right around his home county, it is peppered with affectionate and critical insights and touches on Malaysia's history and current issues.

Bookshops

The best bookshop chains are MPH, Times and Berita.

In Kuala Lumpur the best bookshops are on Jalan Bukit Bintang. The Bukit Bintang Plaza has MPH and Berita bookstores. The Central Market also has a Berita bookshop. In the Weld Supermarket building on Jalan Raja Chulan there's a big branch of Times bookshops.

In Penang there are several good bookshops along Beach Rd (Jalan Pantai) and the E&O Hotel also has a good bookshop. Major hotels often have bookstalls, but on the east coast the selection of bookshops is not as good as elsewhere.

ONLINE SERVICES

The Lonely Planet World Wide Web site has up-to-the-minute travel information, including reports from our researchers and other travellers and an interactive forum called the Thorn Tree. There are also links to other useful sites. The Internet address is: http://www.lonelyplanet.com.

NEWSPAPERS & MAGAZINES

Malaysia has newspapers in Malay, English, Chinese and Tamil. Malay newspapers account for just over 50% of all newspaper sales, English just under 30%, Chinese around 20% and Tamil about 3%. The *New Straits Times* is the main offering in English. It is a broadsheet paper with good coverage of local and overseas events. Other English-language papers include the *The Star* and the *Malay Mail*, while in East Malaysia there are locals such as the *Borneo Post* and the *Sarawak Tribune*.

In Bahasa Malaysia the main paper, and the one with the highest circulation of any paper, is the *Berita Harian*, while a second-string paper is the *Utusan Malaysia*.

Newspapers tend to follow the government line, but criticism of the government is tolerated to a degree and the press is much less strictly controlled than in Singapore. Strict laws to control the press are in force but are rarely invoked.

Though 'anti-Malaysian' stories in the foreign press occasionally provoke the ire of the government, Asian and western magazines are readily available in Malaysia.

RADIO & TV

Radio and TV are equally cosmopolitan in their languages and programming. Malaysia has two government TV channels, RTM 1 and 2, and two commercial stations. Programmes range from local productions in the various languages to imports from the USA and UK. Television censorship is strict. Kissing and other western decadence that threatens to undermine Asian Values is cut, though commercial stations are somewhat more liberal.

Radio Malaysia runs six domestic channels broadcasting in all the major languages and there are a number of commercial stations.

PHOTOGRAPHY & VIDEO

Photography

Malaysia is a delightful country to photograph. There's a lot of natural colour and activity and the people usually have no antipathy to being photographed. However, it is, of course, polite to ask permission before photographing people or taking pictures in mosques or temples. There is usually no objection to taking photographs in places of worship: in Chinese temples, virtually anything goes.

The usual rules for tropical photography apply: try to take photographs early in the morning or late in the afternoon. By 10 am the sun will already be high in the sky and colours are easily washed out. A polarising filter can help to keep down the tropical haze. Try to keep your camera and film in a good environment – don't leave your camera out in direct sunlight, try to keep film as cool as possible and have it developed as soon as possible after use.

Colour film can be developed quickly, cheaply and competently, but Kodachrome colour slides are usually sent to Australia for developing. Ektachrome, however, can be developed locally.

Film is cheap and readily available in Malaysia, including slide film, except in small towns. Processing is also reasonably priced, as are cameras and accessories.

Video

Properly used, a video camera can give a fascinating record of your holiday. As well as videoing the obvious things – sunsets, spectacular views – remember to record some of the ordinary everyday details of life in the country. Often the most interesting things occur when you're actually intent on filming something else. Remember too that, unlike still photography, video 'flows' – so, for example, you can shoot scenes of countryside rolling past the train window.

Video cameras these days have amazingly sensitive microphones, and you might be surprised how much sound will be picked up. This can also be a problem if there is a lot of ambient noise – filming by the side of a busy road might seem OK when you do it, but viewing it back home might simply give you a deafening cacophony of traffic noise. One good rule to follow for beginners is to try to film in long takes, and don't move the camera around too much. Otherwise, your video could well make your viewers seasick! If your camera has a stabiliser, you can use it to obtain good footage while travelling on various means of transport, even on bumpy roads.

Finally, remember to follow the same rules regarding people's sensitivities as for still photography – having a video camera shoved in their face is probably even more annoying and offensive for locals than a still camera. Always ask permission first.

TIME

Malaysia is 16 hours ahead of US Pacific Standard Time (San Francisco and Los Angeles), 13 hours ahead of US Eastern Standard Time (New York), eight hours ahead of GMT/UTC (London) and two hours behind Australian Eastern Standard Time (Sydney and Melbourne). Thus, when it is noon in Kuala Lumpur, it is 8 pm in Los Angeles and 11 pm in New York (the previous day), 4 am in London and 2 pm in Sydney and Melbourne.

ELECTRICITY

Electricity supplies are dependable throughout Malaysia. Supply is 220-240V, 50 cycles. Power sockets are almost always of the three-square-pin type found in the UK, although some older places have the three-round-pin sockets, also as in the UK.

WEIGHTS & MEASURES

Malaysia uses the metric system. For readers more familiar with the imperial system, there's a conversion table at the back of this book.

Some addresses refer to *batu* (literally stone), the mileposts that are still found on a few roads. So an address might be 'Batu 10, Jalan Ipoh', which means at the 10 mile mark on the Ipoh Rd, even though the 10 mile marker may have long been replaced by a 16 km post. You may come across other ancient measurements such as the *kati* (about 600 grams), but these are rare.

Fruit may be sold by the biji, eg 'three biji RM1', but the biji is not a unit of weight, as one bewildered reader thought, but a classifier for fruit and roughly translates as 'piece'. In Malay, it is poor usage to say 'tiga rambutan' (three rambutan) and the proper usage is 'tiga biji rambutan' (three 'pieces' of rambutan), just as in English 'three pieces of paper' is correct, not 'three papers'.

HEALTH

Malaysia enjoys a good standard of health and cleanliness. It is one of the healthiest countries in South-East Asia, but the usual rules for healthy living in a tropical environment apply. Ensure that you do not become dehydrated, particularly before you have acquired some acclimatisation, by keeping your liquid intake up. Wear cool, lightweight clothes and avoid prolonged exposure to the sun. Treat cuts and scratches with care, since they can easily become infected.

In Malaysia, government hospitals are free or make a nominal charge. Medical staff and most of the senior nursing staff speak good English. In the cities queues can be long but you usually won't have to wait long in smaller towns. Private clinics also exist, especially in KL, and there are many private practitioners, who invariably speak English.

Travel health depends on your predeparture preparations, your day-to-day health care while travelling and how you handle any medical problem or emergency that does develop. While the list of potential dangers can seem quite frightening, the chance of contracting any major disease in Malaysia is very small, and with some basic precautions and adequate information few travellers experience more than upset stomachs.

Travel Health Guides

There are a number of books on travel health:

- *Staying Healthy in Asia, Africa & Latin America* by Dirk Schroeder, Moon Publications, 1995. Probably the best all-round guide to carry, as it's compact but very detailed and well organised.
- *Travellers' Health* by Dr Richard Dawood, Oxford University Press, 1995. Comprehensive, easy to read, authoritative and also highly recommended, although it's rather large to lug around.
- *Where There Is No Doctor* by David Werner, Macmillan, 1994. A very detailed guide intended for someone, like a Peace Corps worker, going to work in an underdeveloped country rather than for the average traveller.
- *Travel with Children* by Maureen Wheeler, Lonely Planet Publications, 1995. Includes basic advice on travel health for younger children.

Predeparture Planning

Health Insurance A travel insurance policy to cover theft, loss and medical problems is a good idea. There is a wide variety of policies available and your travel agent will be able to make recommendations. Some policies offer lower and higher medical-expense options but the higher ones are chiefly for countries such as the USA which have extremely high medical costs. Check the small print:

- Some policies specifically exclude 'dangerous activities', which can include scuba diving, motorcycling, even trekking. If such activities are on your agenda, you don't want that sort of policy. A locally acquired motorcycle licence may not be valid under your policy.
- You may prefer a policy which pays doctors or hospitals direct rather than you having to pay on the spot and claim later. If you have to claim later make sure you keep all documentation. Some policies ask you to call back (reverse charges) to a centre in your home country where an immediate assessment of your problem is made.
- Check that the policy covers ambulances or an emergency flight home. If you have to stretch out you will need two seats and somebody has to pay for them!

Medical Kit It's wise to carry a small, straightforward medical kit. The kit should include:

- Aspirin or paracetamol (acetaminophen in the USA) – for pain or fever.
- Antihistamine (such as Benadryl) – useful as a decongestant for colds and allergies, to ease the itch from insect bites or stings and to help prevent motion sickness. There are several antihistamines on the market, all with different pros and cons (eg a tendency to cause drowsiness), so it's worth discussing your requirements with a pharmacist or doctor. Antihistamines may cause sedation and interact with alcohol, so care should be taken when using them.
- Antibiotics – useful if you're travelling well off the beaten track, but they must be prescribed and you should carry the prescription with you. Some individuals are allergic to commonly prescribed antibiotics such as penicillin or sulpha drugs. It would be sensible to always carry this information when travelling.
- Loperamide (eg Imodium) or Lomotil – for diarrhoea; prochlorperazine (eg Stemetil) or metaclopramide (eg Maxalon) for nausea and vomiting. Antidiarrhoea medication should not be given to children under the age of 12.
- Rehydration mixture – for treatment of severe diarrhoea. This is particularly important if travelling with children but is recommended for everyone.
- Antiseptic such as povidone-iodine (eg Betadine), which comes as a solution, ointment, powder and impregnated swabs – for cuts and grazes.
- Calamine lotion or Stingose spray – to ease irritation from bites or stings.
- Bandages and Band-aids – for minor injuries.
- Scissors, tweezers and a thermometer (note that mercury thermometers are prohibited by airlines).
- Insect repellent, sunscreen, suntan lotion, Chap Stick and water-purification tablets.

Ideally antibiotics should be administered only under medical supervision and should never be taken indiscriminately. Take only the recommended dose at the prescribed intervals and continue using the antibiotic for the prescribed period, even if the illness seems to be cured earlier. Antibiotics are quite specific to the infections they can treat. Stop immediately if there are any serious reactions and don't use the antibiotic at all if you are unsure that you have the correct one.

Health Preparations Make sure you're healthy before you start travelling. If you are embarking on a long trip make sure your teeth are OK; there are lots of places where a visit to the dentist would be the last thing you'd want.

If you wear glasses take a spare pair and your prescription. Losing your glasses can be a real problem, though in Malaysia it is relatively easy and cheap to get glasses replaced.

If you require a particular medication take an adequate supply, as it may not be available locally. Take the prescription or, better still, part of the packaging showing the generic rather than the brand name (which may not be locally available), as it will make getting replacements easier. It's wise to have a legible prescription or a letter from your doctor with you to show that you legally use the medication – it's surprising how often over-the-counter drugs from one place are illegal without a prescription or even banned in another.

Immunisations Vaccinations provide protection against diseases you might meet along the way. The only vaccination required to enter Malaysia is yellow fever if coming from an infected area (parts of Africa and South America). However, other vaccines are recommended for travel in certain areas even though not required by law.

All vaccinations should be recorded on an International Health Certificate, which is available from your physician or government health department.

Plan ahead for getting your vaccinations: some of them require an initial shot followed by a booster, while some vaccinations should not be given together. It is recommended you seek medical advice at least six weeks prior to travel.

Most travellers from western countries will have been immunised against various diseases during childhood but your doctor may still recommend booster shots against measles or polio, diseases still prevalent in many developing countries. The period of protection offered by vaccinations differs widely and some are contraindicated if you are pregnant.

The following vaccinations are applicable to Malaysia. Though the chances of contracting the diseases are small they will provide more complete health protection. Vaccinations include:

- *Tetanus & Diphtheria* Boosters are necessary every 10 years and protection is highly recommended.
- *Polio* A booster of either the oral or injected vaccine is required every 10 years to maintain our immunity from childhood vaccination. Polio is a very serious, easily transmitted disease which is still prevalent in many developing countries.
- *Typhoid* Available either as an injection or oral capsules. Protection lasts from one to five years depending on the vaccine and is useful if you are travelling for long in rural, tropical areas. You may get some side effects such as pain at the injection site, fever, headache and a general unwell feeling. A new single-dose injectable vaccine, which appears to have few side effects, is now available but is more expensive. Side effects are unusual with the oral form but occasionally an individual will have stomach cramps.
- *Cholera* Cholera vaccinations are not normally recommended and are contraindicated during pregnancy, but there have been periodic outbreaks of cholera in Malaysia, such as the one in Penang in mid-1996. The cholera vaccine is not very effective but should still be considered if you are going into an infected area because it may reduce the severity of the disease. The vaccination protects only 50% of recipients and is good for only four to six months. This is a disease of insanitation, so if there have been reports of cholera be especially careful about what you eat, drink and brush your teeth with. Symptoms include a sudden onset of acute diarrhoea with 'rice water' stools, vomiting, muscular cramps and extreme weakness. You need medical help – but treat for dehydration, which can be extreme.
- *Hepatitis A* The most common travel-acquired illness which can be prevented by vaccination.

Protection can be provided in two ways – either with the antibody gamma globulin or with a new vaccine called Havrix.

Havrix provides long term immunity (possibly more than 10 years) after an initial course of two injections and a booster at one year. It may be more expensive than gamma globulin but certainly has many advantages, including length of protection and ease of administration. It is important to know that being a vaccine it will take about three weeks to provide satisfactory protection.

Gamma globulin is not a vaccination but a ready-made antibody which reduces the chances of hepatitis infection. It should be given as close as possible to departure because it is at its most effective in the first few weeks after administration and the effectiveness tapers off gradually between three and six months.

Hepatitis B Travellers at risk of contact (see the Infectious Diseases section) are strongly advised to be vaccinated, especially if they are children or will have close contact with children. The vaccination course comprises three injections given over a six-month period, then boosters every three to five years. The initial course of injections can be given over as short a period as 28 days, then boosted after 12 months if more rapid protection is required.

Basic Rules

Care in what you eat and drink is the most important health rule; stomach upsets are the most likely travel health problem but the majority of these upsets will be relatively minor. Malaysia is one of the healthiest countries in Asia to travel in, but diarrhoea is always a potential problem. Don't become paranoid; trying the local food is part of the experience of travel, after all.

Water In the major towns and cities in Malaysia you can drink tap water, but it is still wise to ensure that water has been boiled in kampungs or off the beaten track. If you don't know for certain that the water is safe, always assume the worst. A wide variety of bottled water is available in Malaysia, even though a health survey a few years ago revealed that many brands were prepared in unhygienic conditions and not purified. Don't let this worry you though – at least they do check and attempt to enforce health standards in Malaysia.

If you will be going on extended walks in remote areas, you will have to rely on stream water and this should be purified. The simplest way of purifying water is to boil it thoroughly. Vigorously boiling for five minutes should be satisfactory; longer at high altitudes. If you cannot boil water it should be treated chemically. Chlorine tablets (Puritabs, Steritabs or other brand names) will kill many pathogens, but not the pathogens causing giardia and amoebic cysts. Iodine is very effective in purifying water and is available in tablet form (such as Potable Aqua), but follow the directions carefully and remember that too much iodine can be harmful.

Food Standards of food preparation in Malaysia are high and subject to government health controls, but that doesn't mean that standards of hygiene are always acceptable. Food stalls are generally safe places to eat but some are definitely on the grotty side. If a place looks clean and well run and the vendor looks clean and healthy, the food is probably safe. In general, places that are packed with travellers or locals will be fine, while empty restaurants are questionable.

Salads and fruit should be washed with purified water or peeled where possible before being eaten. Ice cream is usually OK if it is a reputable brand name. Thoroughly cooked food is safest, but not if it has been left to cool or has been reheated.

Nutrition Finding good food in Malaysia is not a problem; the problem is deciding what to eat from all the delicious varieties. Make sure your diet is well balanced. There is plenty of variety and healthy food.

In such a hot climate make sure you drink enough – don't rely on feeling thirsty to indicate when you should drink. Not needing to urinate or very dark yellow urine is a danger sign. Always carry a water bottle with you on long trips, and when walking, even on short walks. Excessive sweating can lead to loss of salt and therefore muscle cramping. Salt tablets are not a good idea as a preventative, but in places where salt is not used much adding salt to food can help.

Everyday Health Normal body temperature is 98.6°F or 37°C; more than 2°C (4°F) higher indicates a high fever. The normal adult pulse rate is 60 to 100 per minute (children 80 to 100, babies 100 to 140). You should know how to take a temperature and a pulse rate. As a general rule the pulse increases about 20 beats per minute for each °C (2°F) rise in fever.

Respiration (breathing) rate is also an indicator of illness. Count the number of breaths per minute: between 12 and 20 is normal for adults and older children (up to 30 for younger children, 40 for babies). People with a high fever or serious respiratory illness (like pneumonia) breathe more quickly than normal. More than 40 shallow breaths a minute may indicate pneumonia.

Many health problems can be avoided by taking care of yourself. Wash your hands frequently – it's quite easy to contaminate your own food. Avoid climatic extremes: keep out of the sun when it's hot, dress warmly when it's cold. Avoid potential diseases by dressing sensibly. You can get worm infections by walking barefoot. Avoid insect bites by covering bare skin when insects are around, by screening windows or beds or by using insect repellents.

Environmental Hazards

Sunburn You can get sunburnt in Malaysia, so use a sunscreen and take extra care to cover areas which don't normally see the sun, such as your feet. A hat provides added protection, and you should also use zinc cream or some other barrier cream for your nose and lips. Calamine lotion is good for mild sunburn.

Prickly Heat Prickly heat is an itchy rash caused by excessive perspiration trapped under the skin. It usually strikes people who have just arrived in a hot climate and whose pores have not yet opened sufficiently to cope with greater sweating. Keeping cool but bathing often, using a mild talcum powder or even resorting to air-conditioning may help until you acclimatise.

Heat Exhaustion Dehydration or salt deficiency can cause heat exhaustion. Take time to acclimatise to high temperatures and make sure you get sufficient liquids. Wear loose clothing and a broad-brimmed hat. Do not do anything too physically demanding.

Salt deficiency is characterised by fatigue, lethargy, headaches, giddiness and muscle cramps and in this case salt tablets may help. Vomiting or diarrhoea can deplete your liquid and salt levels. Anhydrotic heat exhaustion, caused by an inability to sweat, is quite rare. Unlike the other forms of heat exhaustion, it is likely to strike people who have been in a hot climate for some time rather than newcomers.

Heat Stroke This serious, sometimes fatal, condition can occur if the body's heat-regulating mechanism breaks down and the body temperature rises to dangerous levels. Long, continuous periods of exposure to high temperatures can leave you vulnerable to heat stroke. You should avoid excessive alcohol or strenuous activity when you first arrive in a hot climate.

The symptoms are feeling unwell, not sweating very much or at all and a high body temperature (39°C to 41°C). Where sweating has ceased the skin becomes flushed and red. Severe, throbbing headaches and lack of coordination will also occur, and the sufferer may be confused or aggressive. Eventually the victim will become delirious or convulse. Hospitalisation is essential, but meanwhile get victims out of the sun, remove their clothing, cover them with a wet sheet or towel and then fan continually.

Fungal Infections Hot weather fungal infections are most likely to occur on the scalp, between the toes or fingers (athlete's foot), in the groin (jock itch or crotch rot) and on the body (ringworm). You get ringworm (which is a fungal infection, not a worm) from infected animals or by walking on damp areas, such as shower floors.

To prevent fungal infections wear loose, comfortable clothes, avoid artificial fibres, wash frequently and dry carefully. If you do get an infection, wash the infected area daily with a disinfectant or medicated soap and water, and rinse and dry well. Apply an antifungal powder like the widely available Tinaderm. Try to expose the infected area to air or sunlight as much as possible and wash all towels and underwear in hot water as well as changing them often.

Altitude Sickness Acute Mountain Sickness, or AMS, occurs at high altitude and can be fatal. In Malaysia the only place you're likely to get it is on Mt Kinabalu in Sabah. Symptoms usually develop during the first 24 hours at altitude but may be delayed. Symptoms of benign AMS include headache, lethargy, dizziness, difficulty sleeping and loss of appetite. Malignant AMS may develop from benign AMS or without warning and can be fatal. These symptoms include breathlessness, dry cough, severe headache, lack of coordination and balance, confusion, irrational behaviour, vomiting, drowsiness and unconsciousness.

It is compulsory to take a guide up Mt Kinabalu. If you develop symptoms, they are most likely benign, but tell your guide.

Motion Sickness Eating lightly before and during a trip will reduce the chances of motion sickness. If you are prone to motion sickness try to find a place that minimises disturbance – near the wing on aircraft, close to midships on boats, near the centre on buses. Fresh air usually helps; reading and cigarette smoke don't. Commercial motion-sickness preparations, which can cause drowsiness, have to be taken before the trip commences; when you're feeling sick it's too late. Ginger (available in capsule form) and peppermint (including mint-flavoured sweets) are natural preventatives.

Jet Lag Jet lag is experienced when a person travels by air across more than three time zones (each time zone usually represents a one-hour time difference). It occurs because many of the functions of the human body (such as temperature, pulse rate and emptying of the bladder and bowels) are regulated by internal 24-hour cycles called circadian rhythms. When we travel long distances rapidly, our bodies take time to adjust to the 'new time' of our destination, and we may experience fatigue, disorientation, insomnia, anxiety, impaired concentration and loss of appetite. These effects will usually be gone within three days of arrival, but there are ways of minimising the impact of jet lag:

- Rest for a couple of days prior to departure; try to avoid late nights and last-minute dashes for travellers' cheques, passport etc.
- Try to select flight schedules that minimise sleep deprivation; arriving late in the day means you can go to sleep soon after you arrive. For very long flights, try to organise a stopover.
- Avoid excessive eating (which bloats the stomach) and alcohol (which causes dehydration) during the flight. Instead, drink plenty of non-carbonated, non-alcoholic drinks such as fruit juice or water.
- Avoid smoking, as this reduces the amount of oxygen in the aeroplane cabin even further and causes greater fatigue.
- Make yourself comfortable by wearing loose-fitting clothes and perhaps bringing an eye mask and ear plugs to help you sleep.

Infectious Diseases

Diarrhoea A change of water, food or climate can all cause the runs; diarrhoea caused by contaminated food or water is more serious. Despite all your precautions you may still get a mild bout of travellers' diarrhoea but a few rushed toilet trips with no other symptoms is not indicative of a serious problem. Moderate diarrhoea, involving half a dozen loose movements in a day, is more of a nuisance. Dehydration is the main danger with any diarrhoea, particularly for children, where dehydration can occur quite quickly. Fluid replacement remains the mainstay of management. Weak black tea with a little sugar, soda water or soft drinks allowed to go flat and diluted 50% with water are all good. With severe diarrhoea a rehydrating solution is necessary to replace minerals and salts. Commercially available oral rehydration salts are very useful; add the contents of one sachet to a litre of boiled or bottled water. In an emergency you can make up a solution of eight teaspoons of sugar to a litre of boiled water and provide salted cracker biscuits at the same time. You should stick to a bland diet as you recover.

Lomotil or Imodium can be used to bring relief from the symptoms, although they do not actually cure the problem. Only use these drugs if absolutely necessary – eg if you *must* travel. For children under 12 years Lomotil and Imodium are not recommended. Under all circumstances fluid replacement is the most important thing to remember. Do not use these drugs if the person has a high fever or is severely dehydrated.

In certain situations antibiotics (consult a doctor) may be indicated:

- Watery diarrhoea with blood and mucous. (Gut-paralysing drugs like Imodium or Lomotil should be avoided in this situation.)
- Watery diarrhoea with fever and lethargy.
- Persistent diarrhoea not improving after 48 hours.
- Severe diarrhoea, if it is logistically difficult to stay in one place.

Giardiasis The parasite causing this intestinal disorder is present in contaminated water. The symptoms are stomach cramps, nausea, a bloated stomach, watery, foul-smelling diarrhoea and frequent gas. Giardiasis can appear several weeks after you have been exposed to the parasite. The symptoms may disappear for a few days and then return; this can go on for several weeks. Tinidazole (Fasigyn) or metronidazole (Flagyl) is the recommended drug for treatment. Either can be used in a single treatment dose. Antibiotics are of no use.

Dysentery This serious illness is caused by contaminated food or water and is characterised by severe diarrhoea, often with blood or mucus in the stool. There are two kinds of dysentery. Bacillary dysentery is characterised by a high fever and rapid onset; headache, vomiting and stomach pains are also symptoms. It generally does not last longer than a week, but it is highly contagious. Amoebic dysentery is often more gradual in the onset of symptoms, with cramping abdominal pain and vomiting less likely; fever may not be present. It is not a self-limiting disease: it will persist until treated and can recur and cause long-term health problems.

A stool test is necessary to diagnose which kind of dysentery you have, so you should seek medical help urgently.

Viral Gastroenteritis This is caused not by bacteria but, as the name suggests, by a virus. It is characterised by stomach cramps, diarrhoea, and sometimes by vomiting and/or a slight fever. All you can do is rest and drink lots of fluids.

Hepatitis Hepatitis is a general term for inflammation of the liver. There are many causes of this condition: drugs, alcohol and infections are but a few. Hepatitis is not a major problem in Malaysia compared with some other Asian countries.

Hepatitis A The symptoms are fever, chills, headache, fatigue, weakness and aches and pains. This is followed by loss of appetite, nausea, vomiting, abdominal pain, dark urine, light-coloured faeces and jaundiced skin and the whites of the eyes may turn yellow. You should seek medical advice, but in general there is not much you can do apart from resting, drinking lots of fluids, eating lightly and avoiding fatty foods. People who have had hepatitis must forego alcohol for six months after the illness, as hepatitis attacks the liver and it needs that amount of time to recover.

The routes of transmission are via contaminated water, shellfish contaminated by sewerage, or foodstuffs sold by food handlers with poor standards of hygiene.

Taking care with what you eat and drink can go a long way towards preventing this disease. But this is a very infectious virus, so if there is any risk of exposure, additional cover is highly recommended. This cover comes in two forms: gamma globulin and Havrix (see the Immunisations section above).

Hepatitis B This is also a very common disease, spread through contact with infected blood, blood products or bodily fluids – for example, through sexual contact, unsterilised needles, blood transfusions or small breaks in the skin. Other risks include having a shave or tattoo in a local shop and having your body pierced. The symptoms of type B are much the same as type A except that they are more severe and may lead to irreparable liver damage or even liver cancer. Although there is no treatment for hepatitis B, a cheap and effective vaccine is available; the only problem is that for long-lasting cover you need a six-month course. Persons who should receive a hepatitis B vaccination include anyone who anticipates contact with blood or other bodily secretions, either as a health-care worker or through sexual contact with the local population, particularly those who intend to stay in the country for a long period of time.

Typhoid Typhoid fever is another gut infection that travels the faecal-oral route – ie contaminated water and food are responsible. Vaccination against typhoid is not totally effective and it is one of the most dangerous infections, so medical help must be sought. Typhoid outbreaks have occasionally occurred in remote rural areas of Malaysia but are rare and are widely reported in the local press, so you can avoid infected areas.

Worms These parasites are most common in rural, tropical areas and a stool test when you return home is not a bad idea. They can be present on unwashed vegetables or in undercooked meat and you can pick them up through your skin by walking in bare feet. Infestations may not show up for some time, and although they are generally not serious, if left untreated they can cause severe health problems. A stool test is necessary to pinpoint the problem and medication is often available over the counter.

Tetanus This potentially fatal disease is found worldwide, occurring more commonly in undeveloped tropical areas. It is difficult to treat but is preventable with immunisation. Tetanus occurs when a wound becomes infected by a germ which lives in soil and in the faeces of horses and other animals, so clean all cuts, punctures or animal bites. Tetanus is also known as lockjaw, and the first symptom may be discomfort in swallowing or stiffening of the jaw and neck; this is followed by painful convulsions of the jaw and whole body.

Sexually Transmitted Diseases Sexual contact with an infected sexual partner spreads these diseases. While abstinence is the only 100% preventative, using condoms is also effective. Gonorrhoea, herpes and syphilis are the most common of these diseases; sores, blisters or rashes around the genitals, discharges or pain when urinating are common symptoms. Symptoms may be less marked or not observed at all in women. Syphilis symptoms eventually disappear completely but the disease continues and can cause severe problems in later years. The treatment of gonorrhoea and syphilis is with antibiotics.

There are numerous other sexually transmitted diseases, for most of which effective treatment is available. However, there is no cure for herpes and there is also currently no cure for AIDS.

HIV/AIDS HIV, the human immunodeficiency virus, may develop into AIDS, acquired immune deficiency syndrome. HIV is a major problem in many countries. Any exposure to blood, blood products or bodily fluids may put the individual at risk. In many developing countries transmission is predominantly through heterosexual sexual activity. This is quite different from industrialised countries, where transmission is mostly through contact between homosexual or bisexual males, or via contaminated needles shared by IV drug users. Apart from abstinence, the most effective preventative is always to practise safe sex using condoms. It is impossible to detect the HIV-positive status of an otherwise healthy-looking person without a blood test.

HIV/AIDS can also be spread through infected blood transfusions; some developing countries cannot afford to screen blood for transfusions. It can also be spread by dirty needles – vaccinations, acupuncture, tattooing and ear or nose piercing can be potentially as dangerous as intravenous drug use if the equipment is not clean. If you do need an injection, ask to see the syringe unwrapped in front of you, or better still, take a needle and syringe pack with you overseas – it is a cheap insurance package against infection with HIV.

Fear of HIV infection should never preclude treatment for serious medical conditions. Although there may be a risk of infection, it is very small indeed.

Insect-Borne Diseases

Malaria This serious disease is spread by mosquitoes. It is endemic in East Malaysia, but apart from occasional, isolated outbreaks, it is not found in Peninsular Malaysia. It crops up every now and again in the Cameron Highlands, but the risk is low. Unless you are planning on spending extended periods in the Cameron Highlands, malarial prophylactics are unnecessary. For Sabah and Sarawak they are recommended.

Antimalarial drugs do not prevent you from being infected but kill the parasites during a stage in their development.

There are a number of different types of malaria. The one of most concern is *falciparum* malaria. This is responsible for the very serious cerebral malaria. Falciparum is the predominant form in many malaria-prone areas of the world.

The problem in recent years has been the emergence of increasing resistance to commonly used antimalarials such as chloroquine, maloprim and proguanil. Newer drugs such as mefloquine (Lariam) and doxycycline (Vibramycin, Doryx) are often recommended for chloroquine and multidrug-resistant areas. Expert advice should be sought, as there are many factors to consider when deciding on the type of antimalarial medication, including the area to be visited, the risk of exposure to malaria-carrying mosquitoes, your medical history, and your age and pregnancy status. It is also important to discuss the side-effect profile of the medication, so you can work out some level of risk-versus-benefit ratio. It is also very important to be sure of the correct dosage of the medication prescribed to you. Some people have inadvertently taken weekly medication (chloroquine) on a daily basis, with disastrous effects. While discussing dosages for prevention of malaria, it is often advisable to include the dosages required for treatment, especially if your trip is through a high-risk area that would isolate you from medical care.

The main messages are:

- Primary prevention must always be in the form of mosquito-avoidance measures. The mosquitoes that transmit malaria bite from dusk to dawn and during this period travellers are advised to:
  1. wear light-coloured clothing
  2. wear long pants and long-sleeved shirts
  3. use mosquito repellents containing the compound DEET on exposed areas (overuse of DEET may be harmful, especially to children, but its use is considered preferable to being bitten by disease-transmitting mosquitoes)
  4. avoid highly scented perfumes or aftershave
  5. use a mosquito net – it may be worth taking your own
- While no antimalarial is 100% effective, taking the most appropriate drug significantly reduces the risk of contracting the disease.
- No one should ever die from malaria. It can be diagnosed by a simple blood test. Symptoms range from fever, chills and sweating, headache and abdominal pains to a vague feeling of ill-health, so seek examination immediately if there is any suggestion of malaria.

Contrary to popular belief, once a traveller contracts malaria he/she does not have it for life. Two species of the parasite may lie dormant in the liver but they can also be eradicated using a specific medication. Malaria is curable, as long as the traveller seeks medical help when symptoms occur.

Dengue Fever There is no prophylactic available for this mosquito-spread disease; the main preventative measure is to avoid mosquito bites. A sudden onset of fever, headaches and severe joint and muscle pains are the first signs before a rash starts on the trunk of the body and spreads to the limbs and face. After a further few days, the fever will subside and recovery will begin. Serious complications are not common but full recovery can take up to a month or more.

Cuts, Bites & Stings

Cuts & Scratches Skin punctures can easily become infected in hot climates and may be difficult to heal. Treat any cut with an antiseptic such as povidone-iodine. Where possible avoid bandages and Band-aids, which can keep wounds wet. Coral cuts are notoriously slow to heal, and if they are not adequately cleaned small pieces of coral can become embedded in the wound. Avoid coral cuts by wearing shoes when walking on reefs, and clean any cut thoroughly with sodium peroxide if available.

Bites & Stings Bee and wasp stings are usually painful rather than dangerous. Calamine lotion or Stingose spray will give relief and ice packs will reduce the pain and swelling.

Snakes To minimise your chances of being bitten always wear boots, socks and long trousers when walking through undergrowth where snakes may be present. Don't put your hands into holes and crevices, and be careful when collecting firewood.

Snake bites do not cause instantaneous death and antivenenes are usually available. Keep the victim calm and still, wrap the bitten limb tightly, as you would for a sprained ankle, and then attach a splint to immobilise it. Then seek medical help, if possible with the dead snake for identification. Don't attempt to catch the snake if there is even a remote possibility of being bitten. Tourniquets and sucking out the poison are now comprehensively discredited.

Jellyfish Local advice is the best way of avoiding contact with these sea creatures with stinging tentacles. The box jellyfish is found in some in-shore waters around Sabah and can be potentially fatal, but stings from most jellyfish are simply rather painful. Dousing in vinegar will de-activate any stingers which have not 'fired'. Calamine lotion, antihistamines and analgesics may reduce the reaction and relieve the pain.

Bedbugs & Lice Bedbugs live in various places, but particularly in dirty mattresses and bedding. Spots of blood on bedclothes or on the wall around the bed can be read as a suggestion to find another hotel. Bedbugs leave itchy bites in neat rows. Calamine lotion or Stingose spray may help.

All lice cause itching and discomfort. They make themselves at home in your hair (head lice), your clothing (body lice) or in your pubic hair (crabs). You catch lice through direct contact with infected people or by sharing combs, clothing and the like. Powder or shampoo treatment will kill the lice and infected clothing should then be washed in very hot water.

Leeches Leeches may be present in damp rainforest conditions; they attach themselves to your skin to suck your blood. Trekkers often get them on their legs or in their boots. Salt or a lighted cigarette end will make them fall off. If you pull them off, the bite is more likely to become infected. Spraying boots and socks with insect repellent may keep them away.

Women's Health

Gynaecological Problems Poor diet, lowered resistance due to the use of antibiotics for stomach upsets and even contraceptive pills can lead to vaginal infections when travelling in hot climates. Maintaining good personal hygiene and wearing skirts or loose-fitting trousers and cotton underwear will help to prevent infections.

Yeast infections, characterised by a rash, itch and discharge, can be treated with a vinegar or lemon-juice douche or with yoghurt. Nystatin, miconazole or clotrimazole suppositories are the usual medical prescription. Trichomoniasis and gardnerella are more serious infections; symptoms are a smelly discharge and sometimes a burning sensation when urinating. Male sexual partners must also be treated, and if a vinegar-water douche is not effective medical attention should be sought. Metronidazole (Flagyl) is the prescribed drug.

Pregnancy Most miscarriages occur during the first three months of pregnancy, so this is the most risky time to travel as far as your own health is concerned. Miscarriage is not uncommon, and can occasionally lead to severe bleeding. The last three months should also be spent within reasonable distance of good medical care. A baby born as early as 24 weeks stands a chance of survival, but only in a good modern hospital. Pregnant women should avoid all unnecessary medication, but vaccinations and malarial prophylactics should still be taken where possible. Additional care should be taken to prevent illness and particular attention should be paid to diet and nutrition. Alcohol and nicotine, for example, should be avoided.

WOMEN TRAVELLERS

Foreign women travelling in Malaysia face no particular problems. The main point to bear in mind is that Malaysia is a Muslim country and modesty in dress is important. While many female travellers wear fairly skimpy gear without a hassle, it would be prudent to keep the shoulders and thighs covered. At the beach, Malaysian women and families would be embarrassed to find women bathing topless – cover up.

Other precautions apply as much to men as to women. Though Malaysia is generally a very safe country, don't walk alone at night on empty beaches or poorly lit streets.

Many travellers – not just women – have reported the existence of small peep-holes in the walls and doors of cheap hotels. Plug them up with tissue paper, ask for another room or move to another hotel. Remember that in some places cheap hotels are in fact brothels.

Tampons can be found in supermarkets in the main cities if you hunt around, but pads are more commonly available, so if you use tampons bring your own.

It also pays to treat overly friendly strangers, both male and female, with a good deal of caution.

GAY & LESBIAN TRAVELLERS

Gay issues are swept under the carpet in Malaysia. Just as the government denied for many years that AIDS was a problem, the official attitude seems to be that, as a strongly Muslim country steeped in Asian Values, homosexuality in Malaysia doesn't exist and it is a western aberration. This is of course nonsense and Malaysia has always had a substantial gay community. Indeed it tends to celebrate its transvestite community, much as in Singapore's Bugis St of old, and government and public attitudes are best defined as disinterested tolerance rather than hostility.

Though the country has started to give AIDS programmes prominence after it realised the growth of the problem in the heterosexual sex industry and among drug users, you'll find little discussion of gay issues in the media or community at large. Gay groups and venues are thin on the ground, with the exception of the more cosmopolitan and liberal-minded KL.

DANGERS & ANNOYANCES

Theft

Malaysia is not a theft-prone country – in fact, compared with Indonesia or Thailand it is an extremely safe country to travel in. Nevertheless, it pays to keep a close eye on your belongings, especially your travel documents (passport, travellers' cheques etc). These items should be kept with you at all times.

A small, sturdy padlock is well worth carrying, especially if you are going to be staying at any of the cheap chalets found on Malaysia's beaches, where flimsy padlocks (with God knows how many duplicate keys) are the norm.

Drugs

In Malaysia, the answer is simple – don't. Drug trafficking carries a mandatory death penalty. In almost every village in Malaysia you will see anti-*dadah* (drugs) signs portraying a skull and cross-bones and a noose. No one can say they haven't been warned!

Under Malaysian law all drug offenders are considered equal, and being a foreigner will not save you from the gallows. A number of foreigners have been executed in Malaysia, some of them for possession of amazingly small quantities of heroin.

The penalties are severe and the authorities seem to catch a steady stream of unsuccessful peddlers, smugglers and users. Mere possession can bring down a lengthy jail sentence and a beating with the rotan.

BUSINESS HOURS

Government offices are usually open Monday to Friday from 8 am to 4.15 pm. Most close for lunch from 12.45 to 2 pm, and on Friday the lunch break is from 12.15 to 2.45 pm for Friday prayers at the mosque. On Saturday the offices are open from 8 am to 12.45 pm.

Bank hours are generally 10 am to 3 pm on weekdays and 9.30 to 11.30 am on Saturday. Shop hours are variable, although Monday to Saturday from 9 am to 6 pm is a good rule of thumb for small shops. Major department stores, shopping malls, Chinese emporiums and some large stores are open from around 10 am until 9 or 10 pm seven days a week.

Most of Malaysia follows this working week – Monday to Friday with Saturday a half day. But in the more Islamic-minded states of Kedah, Perlis, Kelantan and Terengganu government offices, banks and many shops are closed on Friday and on Saturday afternoon. They have declared Friday the holiday, and their working week is from Sunday to Thursday with Saturday a half day. However, federal government offices follow the same hours as the rest of the country. Kelantan has announced a five-day week from Sunday to Thursday but the federal government is trying to block it.

PUBLIC HOLIDAYS & SPECIAL EVENTS

With so many cultures and religions in Malaysia, there is quite an amazing number of occasions to celebrate. Although some of them have a fixed date each year, the Hindus, Muslims and Chinese all follow a lunar calendar, so the dates for many events vary each year. Tourism Malaysia puts out bi-annual *Calendar of Events* sheets with specific dates and venues of various festivals and parades, but state tourist offices have more detailed listings.

Public Holidays

In addition to the national public holidays, each state has its own holidays, usually asso-

Drugs in Malaysia

Visitors to Malaysia are greeted by skull & crossbones emblems and warnings that the penalty for trafficking drugs is death. It's a sobering start to a holiday and a good reason to leave your stash at home.

The penalty imposed on local drug users is less final but also fairly sobering. Anyone suspected of using drugs in Malaysia can be stopped and required to provide a urine sample for testing. If drugs are detected – any drug, including marijuana – it's off to a 'rehabilitation centre' for one to three years.

As you might expect, Malaysian drug rehabilitation centres are not pleasant places. According to *The Economist*, there are 21 of them scattered around the country, housing around 10,000 drug users. Inmates first spend some time in a 'detoxification cell' before graduating to a regime of exercise and religious education. For good behaviour they are hired out to local factories for a very minimum wage. Anyone not keen on the idea of one to three years of detoxification and hard labour is advised to give drugs a miss while in Malaysia.

Chris Taylor

Malaysia – the Holiday Country

With so many religions that require ritual celebration, and strong state loyalties that also need appeasement, Malaysia has a mind-boggling 44 days of public holidays each year, not including any special holidays proclaimed from time to time. That, however, is in a good year. Most holidays are based on the Muslim lunar calendar, which is 10 or 11 days shorter than the Gregorian calendar, or the Hindu and Chinese calendars, based on lunar and solar cycles, so holiday dates vary each year and a few usually overlap, reducing the number.

A major combination of holidays occurred in 1996, when Hari Raya, the most important Muslim celebration, and Chinese New Year, the most important Chinese celebration, coincided. The combination produced chaos across the nation as everyone went on holiday and there was plenty of self-congratulatory reflection on how the races get along so well in today's multicultural Malaysia. The two are set to coincide again in 1997.

Malaysia's massive number of holidays are not celebrated nationwide, because holidays vary from state to state. No one gets all those holidays, except perhaps a crafty travelling salesperson who can carefully arrange their itinerary. So which state is the big winner of all those days off?

Every state gets at least 11 national holidays and most get another five or six state holidays, but Sabah is the party state, topping the rankings with 18 holidays per year. And who is the big loser? Well, you – if you happen to hit Malaysia when the calendars align and inadvertently cross borders just in time to catch a few sultans' birthdays. Then you may find yourself constantly looking around for a bank that isn't closed, a bus that isn't full and a hotel that hasn't raised its prices. The compensation is that you may see some spectacular events and street parades or be invited to an 'open house', for hospitable Malaysians will always entertain family, friends, neighbours and perhaps even passers-by at the times of major celebrations. ■

ciated with the sultan's birthday or a Muslim celebration. Muslim holidays move back 10 or 11 days each year. Approximate dates are given for 1997 and 1998 but may vary by one day. Hindu and Chinese holiday dates also vary but stay roughly within the designated months. Malaysia's mind-boggling number of public holidays are:

January-February

New Year's Day
1 January (National except Johor, Kedah, Kelantan, Perlis, Terengganu)

Sultan of Kedah's Birthday
2nd Sunday of January (Kedah)

Awal Ramadan (Beginning of Ramadan)
Variable (10 January 1997, 31 December 1998) (Johor, Melaka)

Nuzul Al-Quran
Variable (26 January 1997, 15 January 1998) (Kelantan, Pahang, Perak, Perlis, Selangor, Terengganu)

Federal Territory Day
1 February (KL, Labuan)

**Chinese New Year*
Variable, two days (one day only in Kelantan, Terengganu)

Thaipusam
Variable (Johor, Negeri Sembilan, Perak, Penang, Selangor)

**Hari Raya Puasa*
Variable (9 & 10 February 1997, 30 & 31 January 1998)

March

Sultan of Selangor's Birthday
2nd Saturday of March (Selangor)

Anniversary of Installation of Sultan of Terengganu
21 March (Terengganu)

Sultan of Kelantan's Birthday
30 & 31 March (Kelantan)

April

Good Friday
Variable (Sarawak, Sabah)

Sultan of Johor's Birthday
8 April (Johor)

Melaka Historical City Day
15 April (Melaka)

**Hari Raya Haji*
Variable (17 April 1997, 7 April 1998) (the following day is also a holiday in Kedah, Kelantan, Perlis & Terengganu)

Sultan of Perak's Birthday
19 April (Perak)

Sultan of Terengganu's Birthday
29 April (Terengganu)

May

**Worker's Day*
1 May

Hol Day
7 May (Pahang)
**Awal Muharram (Muslim New Year)*
Variable (9 May 1997, 28 April 1998)
Harvest Festival
30 & 31 May (Sabah, Labuan)
**Wesak Day*
Variable

June
**Yang di-Pertuan Agong's (King's) Birthday*
1st Saturday in June
Dayak Festival
1 & 2 June (Sarawak)
Raja of Perlis' Birthday
Variable (Perlis)

July
Governor of Penang's Birthday
2nd Saturday in July (Penang)
**Prophet's Birthday*
Variable (18 July 1997, 7 July 1998)
Governor of Negeri Sembilan's Birthday
19 July (Negeri Sembilan)

August
**National Day*
31 August

September
Malaysia Day
16 September (Sabah)

October-November
Governor of Melaka's Birthday
2nd Saturday in October (Melaka)
Sultan of Pahang's Birthday
24 October (Pahang)
Deepavali
Variable (National except Sarawak & Labuan)
Hol Day (Sultan Ismail)
Variable (10 November 1997, 31 October 1998) (Johor)
Israk & Mikraj
Variable (29 November 1997, 18 November 1998) (Kedah, Negeri Sembilan)

December
**Christmas Day*
25 December

* National Holiday

Festivals & Events

The public holidays mark many of the major festivals, but numerous other events are celebrated with temple offerings or chanting from the Koran.

The major Islamic events each year are connected with Ramadan, the month during which Muslims cannot eat or drink from sunrise to sunset.

Fifteen days before the commencement of Ramadan the souls of the dead are supposed to visit their homes on Nisfu Night. During Ramadan Lailatul Qadar, the 'Night of Grandeur', Muslims celebrate the arrival of the Koran on earth from heaven before its revelation by Mohammed. A Koran-reading competition is held in Kuala Lumpur (and extensively televised) during Ramadan.

Hari Raya Puasa marks the end of the month-long fast with two days of joyful celebration. This is the major holiday of the Muslim calendar and it can be difficult to find accommodation in Malaysia, particularly on the east coast. During this time everyone wears new clothes, homes are cleaned and redecorated and everyone seems to visit everyone else.

Hari Raya Haji is the day when pilgrims mark the successful completion of the *hajj* (pilgrimage to Mecca). It is a two-day holiday in many of the peninsula states and is marked by the consumption of large amounts of cakes and sweets.

The major Chinese event is Chinese New Year, and the major Indian celebration is Deepavali, though Thaipusam is the most spectacular, celebrated with masochistic spectacle in some states of the peninsula.

Various other special events are held in Malaysia, covering everything from fun runs and Grand Prix events to kite flying and fishing competitions. Tourism Malaysia puts out pamphlets.

January-February

Thai Pongal A Hindu harvest festival marking the beginning of the Hindu month of Thai, considered the luckiest month of the year. Celebrated among Tamils.

Chinese New Year Dragon dances and pedestrian parades mark the start of the new year. Families hold open house, unmarried relatives (especially children) receive *ang pows* (money in red packets), businesses traditionally clear their debts and everybody wishes you a Kong Hee Fatt Choy (a happy and prosperous New Year).

Birthday of the Jade Emperor Nine days after New Year, a Chinese festival honours Yu Huang, the supreme ruler of heaven, with offerings at temples.

Ban Hood Huat Hoay A 12-day celebration for the Day of Ten Thousand Buddhas is held at the Kek Lok Si Temple in Penang.

Chap Goh Meh On the 15th day after Chinese New Year, the celebrations officially end.

Chingay In Johor Bahru, processions of Chinese flagbearers balancing bamboo flagpoles six to 12 metres long can be seen on the 22nd day after New Year.

Thaipusam One of the most dramatic Hindu festivals (now banned in India), in which devotees honour Lord Subramaniam with acts of amazing masochism. In Kuala Lumpur they march in a procession to the Batu Caves carrying *kavadis*, heavy metal frames decorated with peacock feathers, fruit and flowers. The kavadis are hung from their bodies with metal hooks and spikes driven into the flesh. Other devotees pierce their cheeks and tongues with metal skewers, or walk on sandals of nails. Along the procession route, the kavadi carriers dance to the drum beat while spectators urge them on with shouts of 'Vel, Vel'. In the evening the procession continues with an image of Subramaniam in a temple car. On Penang Island, Thaipusam is celebrated at the Waterfall Temple.

Late February

Kwong Teck Sun Ong's Birthday Celebration of the birthday of a child deity at the Chinese temple in Kuching.

March-April

Tua Peck Kong Paper money and paper models of useful things to have with you in the afterlife are burnt at the Sia Sen Temple in Kuching.

Easter On Palm Sunday a candlelight procession is held at St Peter's in Melaka. Good Friday and Easter Monday also witness colourful celebrations at St Peter's and other Melaka churches.

Panguni Uttiram On the full-moon day of the Tamil month of Panguni, the marriage of Siva to Shakti and of Lord Subramaniam to Theivani is celebrated.

Birthday of the Goddess of Mercy Offerings are made to the very popular Kuan Yin at her temples in Penang and Kuala Lumpur.

Cheng Ming On Cheng Ming, Chinese traditionally visit the tombs of their ancestors to clean and repair them and make offerings.

Sri Rama Navami A nine-day festival held by the Brahman caste to honour the Hindu hero of the Ramayana, Sri Rama.

Birthday of the Monkey God The birthday of T'se Tien Tai Seng Yeh is celebrated twice a year. Mediums pierce their cheeks and tongues with skewers and go into trances during which they write special charms in blood.

April-May

Songkran Festival A traditional Thai Buddhist New Year in which Buddha images are bathed.

Chithirai Vishu Start of the Hindu New Year.

Puja Pantai A large three-day Hindu-inspired Malay festival held five km south of Kuala Terengganu.

Birthday of the Queen of Heaven Ma Cho Po, the queen of heaven and goddess of the sea, is honoured at her temples.

Wesak Day Buddha's birth, enlightenment and death are celebrated by various events, including the release of caged birds to symbolise the setting free of captive souls.

May

The turtle season starts in May, and from then through to September giant turtles come ashore each night to lay their eggs along the beach at Rantau Abang on the east coast of the peninsula.

June

Gawai Dayak Annual Sarawak Dayak Festival on 1 & 2 June to mark the end of the rice season. War dances, cockfights and blowpipe events all take place.

Festa de San Pedro Christian celebration in honour of the patron saint of the fishing community on 29 June, particularly celebrated by the Eurasian-Portuguese community of Melaka.

Birthday of the God of War Kuan Ti, who has the ability to avert war and to protect people during war, is honoured on his birthday.

June-August

Dragon Boat Festival Commemorating the death of a Chinese saint who drowned himself. In an attempt to save him, the local fishing community paddled out to sea, beating drums to scare away any fish that might attack him. To mark the anniversary, this festival is celebrated with boat races in Penang and other places.

July

Birthday of Kuan Yin The goddess of mercy has another birthday!

Feast of St Anne A Roman Catholic festival celebrated at St Anne's Church in Penang.

Prophet Mohammed's Birthday Muslims pray and religious leaders recite verses from the Koran.

July-August

Sri Krishna Jayanti A 10-day Hindu festival celebrating popular events in Krishna's life is highlighted on day eight by celebrations of his birthday. The Laxmi Narayan Temple in Kuala Lumpur is a particular focus.

Lumut Sea Carnival At Lumut, the port for Pangkor Island, boat races, swimming races and many other events are held.

August

Festival of the Seven Sisters Chinese girls pray to the weaving maid for good husbands.

Festival of the Hungry Ghosts The souls of the dead are released for one day of feasting and entertainment on earth. Chinese operas and other events are laid on for them and food is put out. The ghosts eat the spirit of the food, but thoughtfully leave the substance for mortal celebrants. Mainly in Penang.

National Day (Hari Kebangsaan) Malaysia celebrates Malaysia's independence on 31 August with events all over the country, but particularly in Kuala Lumpur, where there are parades and a variety of performances in the Lake Gardens.

August-September

Vinayagar Chathuri During the Tamil month of Avani, prayers are offered to Vinayagar, another name for the extremely popular elephant-headed god Ganesh.

September

Feast of Santa Cruz A month-long pilgrimage season in September at the Church of Santa Cruz at Malim, Melaka.

Papar Tamu Besar This annual market festival is held from 15 to 20 September in an area of Sabah renowned for its beautiful Kadazan girls.

Moon Cake Festival The overthrow of the Mongol warlords in ancient China is celebrated by eating moon cakes and lighting colourful paper lanterns. Moon cakes are made with bean paste, lotus seeds and sometimes a duck egg.

September-October

Thimithi (Fire-Walking Ceremony) Hindu devotees prove their faith by walking across glowing coals at the Gajah Berang Temple in Melaka.

Navarathri In the Tamil month of Purattasi the Hindu festival of 'Nine Nights' is dedicated to the wives of Siva, Vishnu and Brahma. Young girls are dressed as the goddess Kali.

Festival of the Nine Emperor Gods Nine days of Chinese operas, processions and other events honour the nine emperor gods. At the Kau Ong Yah Temples in Kuala Lumpur and Penang fire-walking ceremonies are held on the evening of the ninth day.

October

Puja Ketek Offerings are brought to Buddhist shrines, or *keteks*, in the state of Kelantan. Traditional dances are often performed.

October-November

Kantha Shashithi Subramaniam, a great fighter against the forces of evil, is honoured during the Hindu month of Aipasi.

Deepavali Later in the same month, Rama's victory over the demon King Ravana is celebrated with the 'Festival of Lights', when tiny oil-lamps are lit outside Hindu homes, as it's believed that Lakshmi, the goddess of wealth, will not enter an unlit home. For businesspeople, it is time to start a new financial year, and for the family a pre-dawn oil bath, new clothes and lots of sweets are called for. It's bad luck to sweep the house, as this would sweep away good fortune, and it's also bad luck to break anything on this day.

Birthday of Kuan Yin The birthday of the popular goddess of mercy is celebrated yet again.

Kartikai Deepam Huge bonfires are lit to commemorate Siva's appearance as a pillar of fire following an argument with Vishnu and Brahma. The Thandayuthapani Temple in Muar is a major site for this festival.

Guru Nanak's Birthday The birthday of Guru Nanak, founder of the Sikh religion, is celebrated on 22 November.

December

Pesta Pulau Penang Two-month carnival on Penang Island in November and December featuring many water events, including dragon-boat races towards the end of the festival.

Winter Solstice Festival Chinese festival to offer thanks for a good harvest.

Christmas Day On 25 December

ACCOMMODATION

Malaysia has a very wide range of accommodation possibilities – you can still find places to stay for US$5 per person per night, while at the other end of the scale more luxurious 'international standard' hotels can be well over US$100 a night for a room. Accommodation possibilities include the following options.

International Hotels

There are modern, multistorey, air-con, swimming pool, all mod-cons hotels of the major international chains (Hyatt, Holiday Inn, Hilton) and of many local chains such as the Merlin hotels, all over Malaysia. In these hotels, nightly costs are generally from RM200 and up for a double. Malaysia has not suffered the price hikes of neighbouring Singapore, but Kuala Lumpur and Penang have seen climbing occupancy rates and higher prices.

Traditional Chinese Hotels

At the other end of the price scale are the traditional Chinese hotels found in great numbers all over Malaysia. They're the mainstay of budget travellers and backpackers, and in Malaysia you can generally find a good room for RM12 to RM25. Chinese hotels are generally fairly spartan – bare floors and just a bed, a couple of chairs and a table, a wardrobe and a sink. The showers and toilets (which will almost inevitably be Asian squat style) will generally be down the corridor. A point to watch for: couples can sometimes economise by asking for a single, since in Chinese hotel language single means one double bed, while double means two beds. Don't think this is being tight; in Chinese hotels you can pack as many into one room as you wish.

The main catch with these hotels is that they can sometimes be terribly noisy. They're often on main streets, and the bottom rung of the Chinese hotel ladder has a serious design problem – the walls rarely reach the ceiling. The top is simply meshed or barred in. This is great for ventilation but terrible for acoustics. Every noise carries throughout the hotel and Chinese hotels all awake to a terrible dawn chorus of hawking, coughing and spitting.

That aside, these hotels are delightfully traditional in style (all swishing ceiling fans and old furniture), are almost always spotlessly clean (there are exceptions) and are great fun to stay in. They're very often built on top of coffee bars or restaurants, so food is never more than a few steps away. And they're cheap.

There are also many older-style Chinese places a notch up from the most basic places, where RM12 to RM25 will get you a fan-cooled room with common facilities. For RM25 to RM40 you can often find air-conditioned rooms with attached bathroom – but still basically Chinese in their spartan style.

Other Possibilities

There are also a number of alternatives to the cheap hotels in Malaysia. For a start, some of the old British-developed resthouses are still in operation. These were set up during the colonial era to provide accommodation for travelling officials and later provided excellent shelter for all types of travellers. Many of the resthouses are still government owned but are now privately operated. Some have been turned into mid-range resorts, but many retain traditional style, often at pleasantly low prices.

There are a number of YMCAs and YWCAs around Malaysia, which are often mid-range rather than budget.

Malaysia also has a number of cheap local accommodation possibilities, usually at beach centres and in the major tourist cities. These may be huts on the beach or guesthouses – private homes or rented houses divided by partition walls into a number of rooms. Dormitory accommodation is available. Rooms are usually spartan, but this is the cheapest accommodation around and often the nicest, with a real family atmosphere. These places often cater only to foreign travellers and offer their customers lots of little extras to outdo the competition, such as free tea and coffee, bicycles, transport and even haircuts. A dorm bed will cost RM6 to RM8, and rooms will cost from RM12 right up to RM40 for a hotel-style room with air-con.

Taxes & Service Charges

In Malaysia there's a 5% government tax that applies to all hotel rooms. On top of this there's a 10% service charge in the more expensive places. You are not expected to tip in addition to this. Expensive places almost always quote prices exclusive of tax and service charge – this is represented as ++ (called plus-plus), eg $120++ for a double. Nett means that tax and service charges are included. Tax and service charges are also applied to food, drinks and services in the more expensive hotels and restaurants.

Cheap Malaysian hotels, however, generally quote a price inclusive of the 5% government tax.

FOOD

While travelling around some parts of Asia is as good as a session with Weight Watchers, Singapore and Malaysia are quite the opposite. The food is simply terrific, the variety unbeatable and the costs pleasantly low. Whether you're looking for Chinese food, Malay food, Indian food, Indonesian food or even a Big Mac, you'll find happiness! For a complete description, see the colour section Food in Singapore & Malaysia in this chapter.

Tropical Fruit

Once you've tried rambutans, mangosteens, jackfruit and durians, how can you ever go back to boring old apples and oranges? If you're already addicted to tropical fruit, Singapore and Malaysia are great places to indulge the passion. If you've not yet been initiated, there could hardly be a better place in the world to develop a taste for these exotic flavours.

For an easy introduction, head for the fruit stalls, which you'll find in food centres or even just on the streets. Slices of a whole variety of fruits (including those dull old apples and oranges) are laid out on ice in a colourful and mouth-watering display from which you can make a selection for just 30 sen and up. You can also have a fruit salad made up on the spot from as many fruits as you care to choose. Some tastes to sample include:

Rambutan (Nephelium lappaceum) The Malay name means 'spiny' and that's just what they are. Rambutans are the size of a large walnut or small tangerine and they're covered in soft red spines. You peel the skin away to reveal a very close cousin to the lychee, with cool and mouth-watering flesh around a central stone. The main rambutan season is from June to September.

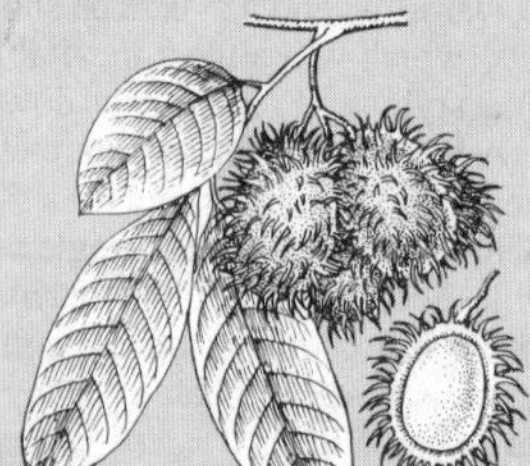

Rambutan *(Nephelium lappaceum)*

Pineapple (Ananas comosus) Probably the most popular tropical fruit, a slice of pineapple is always a delicious thirst quencher. You've not really tasted pineapple until you're handed a whole one, skin sliced away and with the central stem to hold it by while the juice runs down your arm!

Mangosteen *(Gancinia mangostana)*

Mangosteen (Garcinia mangostana) One of the finest tropical fruits, the mangosteen is about the size of a small orange or apple. The dark purple outer skin breaks open to reveal pure white segments shaped like orange segments – but with a sweet-sour flavour which has been compared to a combination of strawberries and grapes. Queen Victoria, so the story goes, offered a considerable prize to anybody able to bring a mangosteen back intact from the east for her to try. The main season is from June to September.

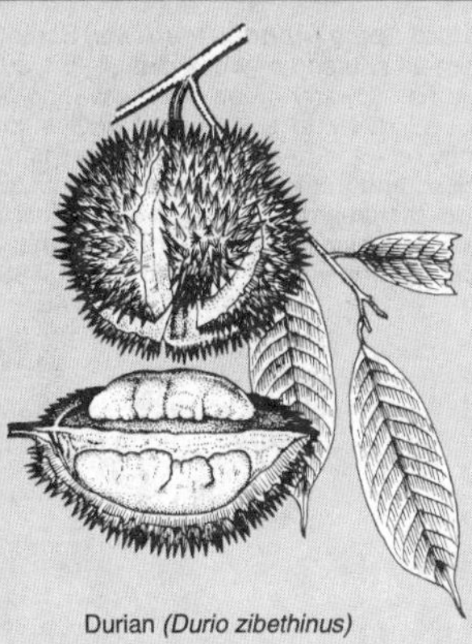

Durian *(Durio zibethinus)*

Durian (Durio zibethinus) The region's most infamous fruit, the durian is a large oval fruit about 20 to 25 cm long, although it may often grow much larger. The durian is renowned for its phenomenal smell, a stink so powerful that first-timers are often forced to hold their noses while they taste. In fact durians emanate a stench so redolent of open sewers that in season you'll see signs in hotels all over Malaysia warning that durians are expressly forbidden entry. It's definitely an acquired taste – the nearest approximation is onion-flavoured ice cream. There are two seasons: from June to August and again from November to February.

When the hardy, spiny shell is cracked open, pale white-green segments are revealed with a taste as distinctive as their smell. Durians are so highly esteemed that great care is taken over their selection and you'll see gourmets feeling them carefully, sniffing them reverently and finally demanding a preliminary taste before purchasing.

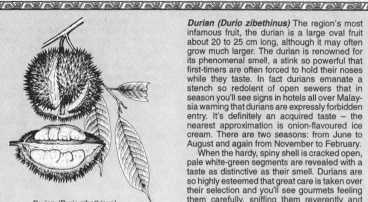

Durians are also expensive and, unlike other fruits which are generally yin (cooling), durians are yang (heaty) – so much so that the durian is said to be a powerful aphrodisiac. It's no wonder that durians are reputed to be the only fruit which a tiger craves!

Jackfruit (nangka; Artocarpus heterophyllus) This enormous watermelon-sized fruit hangs from trees and, when opened, breaks up into a large number of bright orange-yellow segments with a slightly rubbery texture. The nangka is covered by a green pimply skin, but it's too big and too messy to clean to make buying a whole one worthwhile. From street fruit-stalls you can often buy several nangka segments skewered on a stick. Nangka is available all year round, but is most prolific from June to December.

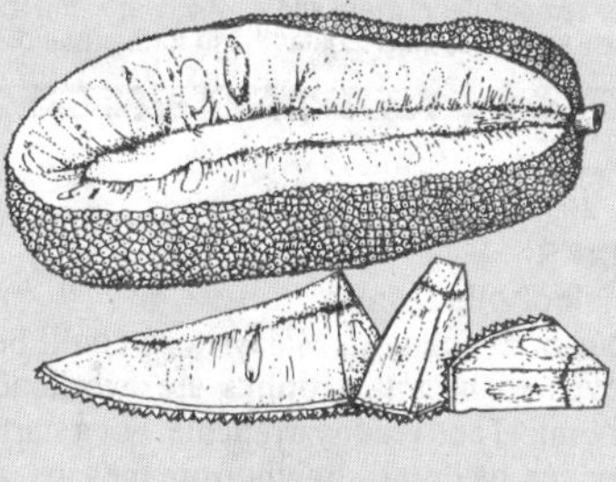

Jackfruit *(Artocarpus hetero-phyllus)*

Papaya (Carica papaya) The papaya, or pawpaw, originated in Central America but is now quite common throughout South-East Asia and is very popular at breakfast time: a slice of papaya served with a dash of lemon juice is the perfect way to start the day. The papaya is about 30 cm or so in length and the bright orange flesh is somewhat similar in texture and appearance to pumpkin but related in taste to a melon. The numerous black seeds in the centre of a papaya are said to have a contraceptive effect if eaten by women. The fruit is available year-round.

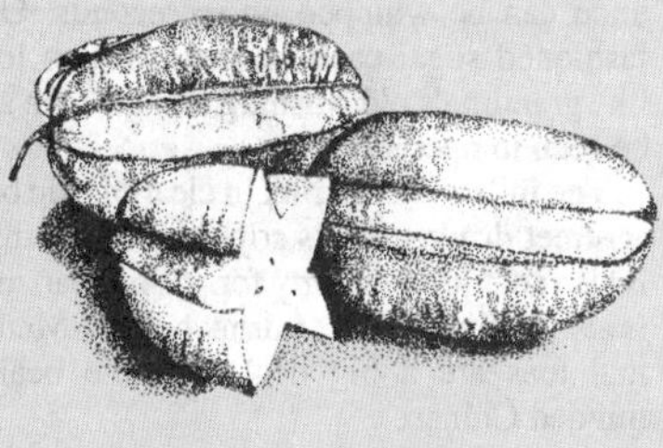

Starfruit *(Averrhoa carambola)*

Starfruit (carambola, belembing; Averrhoa carambola) The starfruit takes its name from its cross-sectional star shape. A translucent green-yellow in colour, starfruit has a crisp, cool, watery taste. It is available year-round.

Banana (pisang; Musa) Malaysia is a major producer of bananas and more than 40 varieties are known to grow here. Some, such as the *pisang embun* and *pisang mas*, are grown specifically for eating raw, while others, such as the *pisang abu* (or plantain) and *pisang awak*, must be cooked before eating.

Custard apple *(Annona muricata)*

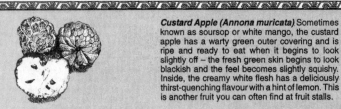

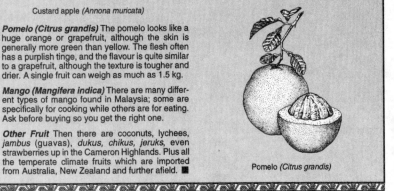

Custard Apple (Annona muricata) Sometimes known as soursop or white mango, the custard apple has a warty green outer covering and is ripe and ready to eat when it begins to look slightly off – the fresh green skin begins to look blackish and the feel becomes slightly squishy. Inside, the creamy white flesh has a deliciously thirst-quenching flavour with a hint of lemon. This is another fruit you can often find at fruit stalls.

Pomelo (Citrus grandis) The pomelo looks like a huge orange or grapefruit, although the skin is generally more green than yellow. The flesh often has a purplish tinge, and the flavour is quite similar to a grapefruit, although the texture is tougher and drier. A single fruit can weigh as much as 1.5 kg.

Mango (Mangifera indica) There are many different types of mango found in Malaysia; some are specifically for cooking while others are for eating. Ask before buying so you get the right one.

Other Fruit Then there are coconuts, lychees, *jambus* (guavas), *dukus, chikus, jeruks,* even strawberries up in the Cameron Highlands. Plus all the temperate climate fruits which are imported from Australia, New Zealand and further afield. ■

Pomelo *(Citrus grandis)*

DRINKS

Nonalcoholic Drinks

Life can be thirsty in Malaysia so you'll be relieved to hear that drinks are excellent, economical and readily available. For a start, water can be drunk straight from the taps in most larger Malaysian cities (which is a far cry from many other Asian countries, where drinking water without elaborate sterilising preparations is foolhardy).

Secondly there is a wide variety of soft drinks, from Coca-Cola, Pepsi, 7-Up and Fanta to a variety of F&N flavours including sarsaparilla (for root beer fans). Soft drinks generally cost around RM1.

You can also find those fruit-juice-in-a-box drinks all over the region with both normal fruit flavours and also oddities like chrysanthemum tea.

Sipping a coffee or tea in a Chinese coffee shop or restaurant is a time-honoured pursuit at any time of day or night. If you want your tea, which the Chinese and Malays make very well, without the added thickening of condensed milk, then ask for *teh-o*. Shout it out – it's one of those words which cannot be said quietly. If you don't want sugar either, you have to ask for *teh kosong*, but you're unlikely to get it – they simply cannot believe anyone would drink their tea that way!

Fruit juices are very popular and very good. With the aid of a blender and crushed ice, delicious concoctions like watermelon juice can be whipped up in seconds. Old-fashioned sugar-cane crushers, which look like grandma's old washing mangle, can still be seen in operation.

The milky white drink in clear plastic bins at street drink-stalls is soybean milk, which is also sold in a yoghurty form. Soybean milk is also available in soft-drink bottles. Medicinal teas are a big deal with the health-minded Chinese.

Alcoholic Drinks

Beer drinkers will probably find Anchor,

Samsu

Drinkers will find Malaysia an expensive country for a beer, with a large bottle costing at least RM8, usually more, and in some states a beer is hard to find. For really cheap alcohol the only answer is the dreaded *samsu*. Sold in small bottles of around 150 ml and costing only RM2, this firewater has an alcohol content from 20 to 70%. Some claim tonic properties, curing everything from rheumatism to indigestion, but make no mistake: this is cheap, deadly booze.

Or at least it used to be deadly, especially in the Indian plantation areas where contaminated, home-distilled samsu regularly killed half a village. Though illegal distilling still goes on, many brands of samsu are legally manufactured under brand names such as Three Snakes, Horse Brand, Tiger and other descriptive labels. Many are also named after Indian warriors, for samsu is typically a product of the South Indian brewing tradition, where villages produce a variety of 'toddy' from fermented coconut and stronger rice-wine brews.

Samsu drinking is a problem not just among the poor, rural Indian community but also in the cities and among Malays and foreign workers. Though only licensed outlets are allowed to sell it, most of it is sold under the counter through general shops and private houses. ■

Tiger or Carlsberg beer to their taste, although the minimum price for a large bottle of beer is at least RM8. Irish travellers may be surprised to find that Guinness has a considerable following in Malaysia – in part because the Chinese believe that it has a strong medicinal value. ABC Stout is a cheaper local equivalent of the dark black brew.

ENTERTAINMENT

Entertainment in Malaysia is much the same as in western countries, though Asian Values apply. The traditional pastimes of wayang puppet theatre and traditional dance have all but disappeared, except for special occasions or tourist recreations. The main cities have discos, clubs, pubs and bars, usually fairly tame with high bar prices. KL has a very lively and extensive nightlife scene – if you are looking for a place to rage this is it. Almost every town has a karaoke bar if you are desperate for something to do, and large hotels usually have something happening.

Cinemas generally show B-grade adventure movies and Hong Kong kungfu flicks, either dubbed or with multiple subtitles covering all the major languages. The latest Hollywood blockbusters are occasionally shown, though movies are heavily censored. You occasionally come across surprises – on our last trip, a small tin-shed cinema out in the back blocks was screening *Once Were Warriors*, a recent, award-winning New Zealand movie. The various cultural organisations in KL and Penang, such as Alliance Française and the Goethe Institut, have regular screenings of their foreign-language films.

THINGS TO BUY

Every tourist centre has a selection of shops and stalls selling souvenirs but because of high wages handicrafts are not a big item in Malaysia. Many of the 'Malay' handicrafts on sale are imported from Indonesia and elsewhere. Nevertheless many attractive souvenirs and handicrafts can be found, but you should always bargain hard for tourist-oriented items.

Malaysian kites *(wau)* are readily available and are a colourful and typical souvenir from Malaysia – Kota Bharu is a good place to find them. The distinctive Kedah pottery – hand-painted, bulb-shaped pots with long necks – is another Malaysian craft, as are pewterware, most of which comes from Selangor, and wavy-bladed *kris* knives, many of which come from Indonesia. Some fine Dayak weavings and wood carvings can be found in Sarawak, but prices are very high. The east coast of the peninsula has attractive *songket* (weaving with gold thread) and Malaysia also produces batik, usually with floral motifs though the work is not always that fine.

FOOD IN SINGAPORE & MALAYSIA

Chinese Food

When people in the west speak of Chinese food, they probably mean Cantonese food. It's the best known and most popular variety of Chinese cooking – even in Singapore, where the majority of Chinese are not Cantonese. Cantonese food is noted for the variety and freshness of its ingredients. The food is usually stir-fried with just a touch of oil to ensure that the result is crisp and fresh. All those best-known 'western Chinese' dishes fit into this category – sweet & sour dishes, won ton soup, chow mein, spring rolls.

With Cantonese food, the more people you can muster for the meal the better, because dishes are traditionally shared so that everyone manages to sample the greatest variety. A corollary of this is that Cantonese food should be balanced: traditionally, all foods are said to be either *yin* – 'cooling' – like vegetables, most fruits and clear soups, or *yang* – 'heaty' – like starchy foods and meat. A 'cooling' dish should be balanced by a 'heaty' dish: too much of one or the other is not good for you.

Another Cantonese speciality is dim sum, or 'little heart'. Dim sum is usually eaten at lunch time or as a Sunday brunch. Dim sum restaurants are usually large, noisy affairs and the dim sum, little snacks that come in small bowls, are whisked around the tables on individual trolleys or carts. As they come by, you simply ask for a plate of this or a bowl of that. At the end of the meal your bill is toted up from the number of empty containers on your table.

Cantonese cuisine can also offer real extremes – shark's-fin soup or bird's-nest soup are expensive delicacies from one end of the scale; *mee* (noodles) or *congee* (rice porridge) are cheap basics from the other end.

Far less familiar than the dishes of Canton are the cuisines from the north and west of China – Sichuan, Shanghai and Beijing. Sichuan (or Szechuan) food is the fiery food of China, where peppers really get into the act. Whereas the tastes of Cantonese food are delicate and understated, in Sichuan food the flavours are strong and dramatic – garlic and chillies play their part in dishes like diced chicken or hot & sour soup.

Beijing food is, of course, best known for the famous Beijing duck, where the specially fattened ducks are basted in syrup and roasted on a revolving spit. The duck skin is served as a separate first course. Like the other northern cuisines, Beijing food is less subtle than Cantonese food. Although Beijing food is usually eaten with noodles or steamed buns in China, because rice does not grow in the cold northern Beijing region, in Singapore and Malaysia it's equally likely to come with rice.

Food from Shanghai is to some extent a cross between northern and Cantonese cuisines – combining the strong flavours of the north with the ingredients of Canton. It is not easy to find, however, in Singapore and Malaysia.

Although Cantonese is the best known southern Chinese cuisine, it is quite easy to find a number of other regional styles – particularly since so many of the region's Chinese are Hokkiens or Hakkas. One of the best known of these southern dishes comes from the island of Hainan. Throughout Malaysia one of the most widespread and economical meals is Hainanese chicken-rice. It's one of those dishes whose very simplicity ensures its quality. Chicken-rice is simply steamed chicken, rice boiled or steamed in the chicken stock, a clear soup and slices of cucumber. Flavour this delicate dish with soy or chilli sauce and you've got a delicious meal for around RM3. The Hainanese also produce steamboat, a sort of Oriental variation of a Swiss fondue, where you have a boiling stockpot in the middle of the table, into which you dip pieces of meat, seafood or vegetables.

The Hokkiens come from the Fujian province in China and make up the largest dialect group in Singapore. Although Hokkien food is rated way down the Chinese gastronomic scale, it has provided the unofficial national dish of Singapore – Hokkien fried mee, or Singapore noodles. It's made of thick egg noodles cooked with pork, seafood and vegetables and a rich sauce. Hokkien *popiah* spring rolls are also delicious.

Teochew food, from the area around Swatow in China, is another style noted for its delicacy and natural flavour. Teochew food is also famous for seafood, and a popular food-centre dish is *char kway teow* – broad noodles, clams and eggs fried in chilli and black bean sauce.

Hakka food is noted for its simple ingredients and the best known Hakka dish, again easily found in food centres, is *yong tau foo* – bean curd stuffed with minced meat.

Indian Food

Indian food is one of the region's greatest delights. Indeed, it's easier to find really good Indian food in Singapore or Malaysia than in India! Very approximately, you can divide Indian food into southern, Muslim and northern – food from southern India tends to be hotter, with the emphasis on vegetarian

ALL PHOTOS BY GLENN BEANLAND

Chinese Food

Top: Beijing duck, served with pancakes and plum sauce, is a well-known dish from north China.
Middle: Shark's-fin soup is an expensive Cantonese delicacy.
Bottom: *Gongbao jiding*, chicken with peanuts and chilli pepper, is a popular Sichuan dish.

ALL PHOTOS BY GLENN BEANLAND

Indian Food

Top: Spices used in Indian cooking include ginger, cumin, garlic, chillies (fresh and dried), cardamoms, cloves, mustard seeds, anise, coriander seeds and curry leaves.

Middle: Tandoori chicken is a north Indian dish cooked in a tandoori oven after an overnight marinade.

Bottom: *Baingan bharta* (an eggplant dish) served with yoghurt and chapatis makes a nice meal.

ALL PHOTOS BY GLENN BEANLAND

Malay Food

Top: The Indonesian dish *gado-gado*, vegetables with peanut sauce, is also found in Malaysia.
Middle: One of the better-known Malay dishes is *sambal udang*, fiery curry prawns.
Bottom: *Nasi lemak* is a popular Malay dish consisting of coconut rice served with fried anchovies, peanuts, sliced egg and cucumber, *sambal* (a fiery chilli dish) and a curry.

ALL PHOTOS BY GLENN BEANLAND

Malay & Nyonya Food

Top: *Tofu goreng* is fried bean curd, often stuffed with vegetables and served with peanut sauce.
Middle: Pickled cucumber with sliced pork is a simple Nyonya side dish.
Bottom: Fresh coriander leaves, lengkuas, lemon juice, dried chillies, coconut milk and dried prawns are frequently used in Malay cooking.

food, while Muslim food tends to be more subtle in its spicing and uses more meat. Muslim food is a mixture of southern and northern Indian influences and has developed a distinctly Malaysian style. The rich Mogul dishes of northern India are not so common and are generally only found in more expensive restaurants. Common to all Indian food are the spices or *masala*, the lentil soup known as *dhal*, the yoghurt and water drink known as *lassi* and the sauces or condiments known as chutneys.

The typical south Indian dish is a rice plate. If you ask for one in a vegetarian restaurant you won't get a plate at all but a large *daun pisang* (banana leaf). On this a large mound of rice is placed, then scoops of a variety of vegetable curries and a couple of papadums are tossed in for good measure. With your right hand (south Indian vegetarian food is never eaten with utensils), you then knead the curries into the rice and eat away. When your banana leaf starts to get empty you'll suddenly find it refilled – for the rice plate is always an 'as much as you can eat' meal. When you've finished, fold the banana leaf in two, with the fold towards you, to indicate that you've had enough.

Other vegetarian dishes include the popular *masala dosai*, a thin pancake which, when rolled around the masala (spiced vegetables) with some *rasam* (spicy soup) on the side, provides about the cheapest light meal you could ask for. An equivalent snack meal in Indian Muslim restaurants is *murtabak*, made from paper-thin dough filled with egg and minced mutton and lightly grilled with oil. A *roti canai* – made from murtabak dough – which you dip into a bowl of dhal or curry is a very popular and filling breakfast throughout the region. A *samosa* is roughly the Indian equivalent of a Chinese spring roll.

A favourite Indian Muslim dish, and one which is cheap, easy to find and of excellent standard, is *biryani*. Served with a chicken or mutton curry, the dish takes its name from the saffron-coloured rice it is usually served with.

A particular favourite is the north Indian *tandoori* food, which takes its name from the clay tandoor oven in which meat is cooked after an overnight marinade in a complex yoghurt and spice mixture. Tandoori chicken is the best known tandoori dish. Although rice is also eaten in north India, it is not so much the ever-present staple it is in the south. North Indian food makes wide use of the delicious Indian breads like *naan, chapatis, parathas* and *rotis*.

Malay, Indonesian & Nyonya Food

Surprisingly, Malay food is not as easily found in Malaysia as Chinese or Indian food, although many Malay dishes, like *satay*, are everywhere. Satay is delicious tiny kebabs of chicken, mutton or beef dipped in a spicy peanut sauce. Some Malay dishes you may have a chance to try include *tahu goreng* – fried soybean curd and bean sprouts in a peanut sauce; *ikan bilis* (anchovies) – tiny fish fried whole; *ikan assam* – fried fish in a sour tamarind curry; *sambal udang* – fiery curry prawns. *Ayam goreng* is fried chicken and *rendang* is a sort of spiced curried meat in coconut marinade. *Nasi goreng* (or fried rice – 'nasi' is rice and 'goreng' is fried) is widely available, but it is as much a Chinese and Indian dish as Malay, and each style has its own flavours. *Nasi lemak* is coconut rice served with fried ikan bilis, peanuts and a curry dish.

Indonesian food is very similar to Malay, and you'll find Malaysian regional dishes that have been influenced by Indonesian cuisine, as well as a number of Indonesian restaurants scattered around. In Sumatra the Indonesian food bends much more towards curries and chillies. The popular Sumatran food is *nasi padang*, from the Minangkabau region of West Sumatra, and consists of a wide variety of hot curries served with rice. The Malaysian equivalent is found in the state of Negeri Sembilan, originally peopled by Minangkabau settlers from Sumatra. *Mie rebus*, noodles in a rich soy-based sauce, is a Javanese dish that has been adopted as a local favourite in Johor.

Nyonya cooking is a local variation on Chinese and Malay food – it uses Chinese ingredients but with local spices like lemon grass and coconut cream. Nyonya cooking is essentially a home skill rather than a restaurant one, but a number of Nyonya restaurants can be found. *Laksa lemak*, a spicy coconut-based noodle soup, is a classic Nyonya dish that has been adopted by all Malaysians and found everywhere. *Laksa Penang* is the more sour variety from Penang that uses fish paste for the stock.

Desserts

Although desserts are not a really big deal in the region, you can find some interesting after-dinner snacks, such as *pisang goreng* (banana fritters) or *ais kacang* and *cendol*. Halfway between a drink and a dessert, ais kacang is rather like an old-fashioned sno-cone, but the shaved ice is topped with syrups and condensed milk and it's all piled on top of a foundation of beans and jellies! It sounds gross and looks lurid but tastes terrific! Cendol is similar – it consists of coconut milk with brown sugar syrup and greenish noodle-like things topped with shaved ice (it also tastes terrific). ■

Antiques are readily available in Melaka and to a lesser extent Penang. Everything from lion-head door knockers to marble-topped tables are on sale, but prices are often very high and hard bargaining is required. Chinese pottery and jewellery is available everywhere.

Malaysia is reasonably priced for electronics, though the range is not great and prices are slightly higher than in Singapore, which has a much better range. Portable radios and cameras are duty-free in Malaysia. Cameras and accessories in particular are a good buy.

Copies of brand-name goods can be found – you can outfit yourself with Nike, Lacoste and Rolex for a fraction of the cost of the real thing – or the real thing is also on sale in profusion.

Depending on your country of origin you may find clothes and shoes a reasonable buy. The range and styles are good, and larger sizes are available. Cheap cotton beachwear can be found at the beach centres.

Getting There & Away

AIR

Kuala Lumpur is the major gateway to Malaysia, handling almost all international flights except for a few regional flights from Asia, which come via Penang, Kota Kinabalu and a few other cities. Many airlines service Malaysia, but the country's international carrier, Malaysia Airlines (MAS), is the major carrier.

KL and Penang are good places for buying tickets for onward travel, though prices fluctuate and good deals available one year may not be available the next. In the past, many shady fly-by-night travel operators were in existence. Though this isn't such a problem now, it pays to be wary and deal with the more established agents.

The air fares quoted here give an indication of deals available at the time of research, but air fares can vary substantially from season to season, even month to month. They reflect the cheapest fares on offer, which may rise, but keep an eye out for special promotional offers.

USA

It's possible to find fares from the US west coast to Malaysia for around US$830 return, with MAS being one of the cheapest. Virgin has a route-sharing deal with MAS and also has cheap fares. It is only marginally more expensive to KL than to Singapore. From New York, fares start at US$1050. Some cheap fares may include a stopover in Hong Kong. There are also budget and super Apex fares available out of the west coast. Similar deals from the east coast can be found in the Sunday papers there.

The *New York Times*, the *Los Angeles Times*, the *Chicago Tribune* and the *San Francisco Examiner* all produce weekly travel sections in which you'll find any number of travel agents' ads. Council Travel and STA Travel have offices in major cities nationwide.

The magazine *Travel Unlimited* (PO Box 1058, Allston, MA 02134) publishes details of the cheapest air fares and courier possibilities for destinations all over the world from the USA.

Australia

Malaysia Airlines is the main carrier between Australia and Kuala Lumpur. Qantas and Ansett also fly to KL. MAS used to offer good deals to KL but prices have risen. Fares are usually lower from Australia to Singapore as there is much more competition.

Discounted fares from Melbourne/Sydney to Kuala Lumpur cost around A$980 return in the low season, rising to A$1100 in the high season (December to February). Flying from Brisbane is about A$100 cheaper, from Perth A$200 cheaper.

STA Travel and Flight Centres International are major dealers in cheap air fares. Also check the travel agents' ads in the travel sections of newspapers and ring around.

New Zealand

Malaysia Airlines and Air New Zealand fly between Auckland and Kuala Lumpur. Discounted economy fares start at around NZ$830/1200 one-way/return, but flights to Singapore are considerably cheaper. STA Travel and Flight Centre are large air ticket discounters with offices all over the country.

UK

London has the best deals for flights to Malaysia and Singapore. You can take your pick of a wide range of carriers, but the cheapest (book as far ahead as possible) is Aeroflot for UK£400 return to Kuala Lumpur. Other possibilities include Pakistan International Airlines (UK£440) and Air Lanka (UK£490).

Other airlines such as Lufthansa, Virgin and MAS have return prices from around UK£550, but there are seasonal fluctuations of around UK£100. One-way flights start at around UK£235. Bear in mind that all flights out of the UK now carry a UK£10 departure tax and this is added to the cost of your ticket.

For information on travel agents and special deals, check the Sunday papers and weekly listings magazines such as *Time Out*. London's 'bucket' shops can offer some great deals, but some of these places are fly-by-night operations. Most British agents are registered with the Association of British Travel Agents (ABTA), which guarantees tickets booked with member agents.

Popular and reliable British agents include Campus Travel (☎ (0171) 730-8111), with 41 branches nationwide; STA Travel (☎ (0171) 361-6262); Trailfinders (☎ (0171) 938-3366), with branches in London, Birmingham, Bristol, Glasgow and Manchester; and Crusader Travel (☎ (0181) 744-0474).

Continental Europe

Special round-trip fares to Kuala Lumpur from Amsterdam have recently ranged from Dfl 2409 to Dfl 7486 and from Paris from FF 9085 to FF 14,155.

Asia

Hong Kong Hong Kong is no longer the discount centre it once was. The cheapest one-way flights to Malaysia cost around US$200. Philippine Airlines have flights to Kuala Lumpur and Kota Kinabalu via Manila for HK$1420/1620 one-way and HK$2620/2820 return respectively.

Dragonair and MAS also have flights to Kota Kinabalu, but they are expensive: HK$2990 one-way and HK$3220 return.

MAS has direct flights to Kuala Lumpur for HK$2720 one-way, HK$3500 return. It may work out cheaper to fly to Singapore rather than Kuala Lumpur. Garuda has once-weekly flights to Singapore for HK$1670 one-way, HK$2220 return, though you will need to book well ahead to get a seat. United Airlines has late-night flights to Singapore at HK$2070/2820 one-way/return. Philippine Airlines flights go to Singapore via Manila and cost HK$1520/2620.

Tsimshatsui is Hong Kong's budget travel agency centre. Most of the operators nowadays are reliable. One of the best around is Phoenix Services (☎ 2722-7378) at 6F, Milton Mansion, 96 Nathan Rd, Tsimshatsui.

Japan Return flights from Japan to Singapore and Kuala Lumpur or Penang cost between ¥50,000 and ¥60,000. One-way tickets are expensive, averaging around ¥50,000. The best agency to deal with is STA Travel, which has branches in Tokyo (☎ (03) 5485-8380) and in Osaka (☎ (06) 262-7066). A'Cross Travel is another reliable agency that is used to dealing with foreigners; it has branches in Tokyo (☎ (03) 3378-7421), Osaka (☎ (06) 364-3048) and Kyoto (☎ (075) 255-3559).

For information on the latest discount prices Tokyo residents should pick up a copy of *Tokyo Journal*, while residents of the Kansai region should get hold of *Kansai Time Out*.

Thailand The place to buy tickets to Malaysia and Singapore in Bangkok is Khao San Rd. The agents here deal in discounted tickets; rip-offs do occur from time to time, so take care. The STA Travel agent in Bangkok is Tour Centre (☎ 281-5314) at the Thai Hotel, 78 Prachatipatai Rd. One-way flights to Penang are inexpensive, but it is also worth considering flying to Hat Yai and then travelling overland to Penang: flights to Penang are around US$150, slightly more to KL; flights to Hat Yai cost only around US$85.

Indonesia There are several interesting variations from Indonesia to Malaysia. The short hop from Medan in Sumatra to Penang costs around US$60; from Penang it's RM140. There are also weekly flights between Kuching in Sarawak and Pontianak in Kalimantan, the Indonesian part of the island of Borneo, for RM177. Similarly, at the eastern end of Borneo there is a weekly connection between Tawau in Sabah and Tarakan in Kalimantan. For Java, the cheapest connections are from Singapore for as little as US$70, though MAS has competitively priced flights from Johor Bahru to Jakarta.

India & Other Places in Asia Although Indonesia and Thailand are the two 'normal' places to travel to or from, there are plenty of other possibilities, including India, Sri Lanka, Myanmar and the Philippines. For details on cheap air fares refer to the Getting There & Away sections in Singapore and Penang – these are the two airline ticket centres.

Departure Tax

Malaysia levies airport taxes on all its flights. It's RM40 on international flights, RM20 to Singapore and Brunei. If you buy your tickets in Malaysia, the departure tax is included in the price.

LAND

Thailand

You can cross the border by land at Padang Besar (road or rail), Bukit Kayu Hitam (road) or Keroh-Betong (road) in the west, or at Rantau Panjang-Sungai Golok or Pengkalan Kubor in the east. For information on Thai visas, refer to the Visas & Documents section in the Malaysia – Facts for the Visitor chapter.

Road – West Coast Although there are border points at Padang Besar and Keroh, the majority of travellers cross by road at Bukit Kayu Hitam on the main North-South Highway for Hat Yai. The easiest way to cross this border is to take a bus from Georgetown (see Penang) right through to Hat Yai for around RM20. Buses also run from Alor Setar to the large border post complex at Bukit Kayu Hitam, from where you walk a few hundred metres to the Thai checkpost. On the other side buses and taxis run to Sadao and Hat Yai. From Hat Yai there are plenty of buses and trains to Phuket, Bangkok and other places.

The other alternative is to cross at Padang Besar, where it is an easy walk across. The only reason to go this way by road is if you're heading to/from Langkawi. Buses run from Kuala Perlis to Padang Besar via Kangar. The train from Alor Setar all the way to Hat Yai is the easiest way to cross this border.

Road – East Coast The Thai border is at Rantau Panjang (Sungai Golok on the Thai side), 1½ hours by bus from Kota Bharu. From Rantau Panjang walk across the border, and then it's about one km to the station, from where trains go to Hat Yai, Surathani and Bangkok. See Kota Bharu in the Kelantan chapter for more details.

An alternative route into Thailand is via Pengkalan Kubor on the coast. It's more time-consuming and very few travellers go this way. See Around Kota Bharu for more details.

Train The rail route into Thailand is on the Butterworth-Alor Setar-Hat Yai route, which crosses into Thailand at Padang Besar. You can take the International Express (all 2nd class) from Butterworth all the way to Bangkok with connections from Singapore and Kuala Lumpur. From Hat Yai there are frequent train and bus connections to other parts of Thailand (see the table on the next page for train fares and schedules). One train a day also goes from Alor Setar to Hat Yai (see Alor Setar in the Kedah & Perlis chapter for details).

A variation on the International Express is the Eastern & Oriental Express, which runs once a week and caters to the well-heeled. The train is done out in antique opulence and is South-East Asia's answer to the Orient Express. It takes 42 hours to do the 2000 km journey from Singapore to Bangkok. Don your linen suit, sip a gin & tonic and dig deep for the fare – around US$1200.

Singapore

The Causeway, the bridge that links Johor Bahru with Singapore, handles the overwhelming bulk of traffic between the countries. Trains and buses run from all over Malaysia straight through to Singapore, or you can take a bus to Johor Bahru and get a taxi or one of the frequent buses from JB to Singapore. The JB buses will drop you at the border posts and don't wait long, but you simply keep your ticket and get on the next bus that comes along. Some travellers who have taken the through express buses from

International Express

Fares (2nd class):

	Singapore	Kuala Lumpur	Butterworth
Hat Yai	S$64.20	RM38.80	RM14.80
Bangkok	S$91.70	RM66.30	RM42.30

Schedule:

Train No 48 (International Express from Butterworth – runs daily)		Train No 49 (International Express from Bangkok – runs daily)
13:40	Butterworth	12:40
15:32	Alor Setar	10:52
16:40*	Hat Yai	7:20*
8:35*	Bangkok	15:15*

* Thai time is one hour behind Malaysian time.

In addition, there is an express surcharge on the International Express (RM13.60 air-con, or RM8.10 non-air-con). Additional cost for a berth ranges from RM11.80 to RM29, depending on whether you want a 2nd class upper, 2nd class lower, air-con or non-air-con.

elsewhere in Malaysia have reported that they have been left stranded at the border after delays at immigration. These buses should (and usually do) wait – complain to the bus company if this happens.

See the Singapore – Getting There & Away chapter and Johor Bahru in the Johor chapter for more details.

Indonesia

It is easy to cross the land border between Malaysia and Indonesia, between Pontianak in Kalimantan and Kuching in Sarawak. A daily express bus (10 hours) runs between Pontianak and Kuching. The bus crosses at the Tebedu/Entikong border, which is now a visa-free entry point into Indonesia.

SEA

Thailand

Regular daily boats run between Langkawi and Satun in Thailand. There are customs and immigration posts here, so you can cross quite legally, although it's an unusual and rarely used entry/exit point. Make sure you get your passport stamped on entry.

In the main tourist season (around Christmas) yachts also operate irregularly between Langkawi and Phuket in Thailand, taking in Thai islands on the way for around US$200 per person. See Langkawi in the Kedah & Perlis chapter for more details.

Singapore

There are a number of possible crossings across the Straits of Johor, but the vast majority of people cross on the Causeway, either by train or by road.

The main ferry crossing is between Changi Village (Singapore) and Tanjung Belungkor (Malaysia), and exists mainly for Singaporeans holidaying in Desaru on the Malaysian coast. Small boats also ply between Pengerang in Johor and Changi Village in Singapore.

The Singapore – Getting There & Away chapter has full details.

Indonesia

There are three regular services between Malaysia and Indonesia – Penang-Medan and Melaka-Dumai connecting Peninsular Malaysia with Sumatra, and Tawau-Tarakan connecting Sabah with Kalimantan in Borneo.

The very popular crossing between Penang

and Medan is handled by two companies that between them have services most days of the week. The journey takes 4½ hours and costs RM110/90 in 1st/2nd class. The boats actually land in Belawan in Sumatra, and the journey to Medan is completed by bus (included in the price). See the Penang chapter for details.

Twice daily high-speed ferries operate between Melaka and Dumai (RM80, 2½ hours) in Sumatra. Dumai is now a visa-free entry port into Indonesia for most nationalities. This is becoming a more popular connection, but there is nothing in Dumai – take a bus out to other parts of Sumatra.

Boats also operate most days from Tawau in Sabah to Nunukan in Kalimantan and then on to Tarakan in Kalimantan (see under Tawau in the Sabah chapter for details). This is not a recognised border crossing for visa-free entry so an Indonesian visa must be obtained in advance if entering or exiting through this way.

Yet another possibility is to take a boat from Pasir Gudang, about 30 km from Johor Bahru. Boats go direct to Batam and Bintang in Indonesia's Riau Archipelago, and to Surabaya in Java. SS Holidays in Pasir Gudang is the main agent. A new duty-free complex and ferry terminal is under construction in Johor Bahru and when completed will have ferries to the Riau Archipelago. See Johor Bahru in the Johor chapter for details on all these boats.

Getting Around

AIR

Malaysia Airlines (MAS) is the country's main domestic operator. The Malaysian Air Fares chart below details some of the main regional routes and the standard one-way fares in Malaysian ringgit. MAS has many other regional routes in Sarawak and Sabah. It operates Airbuses, Boeing 737s and Fokker F50s on its domestic routes, plus 12-seater Twin Otters on most of the more remote Sarawak and Sabah routes.

In East Malaysia, where many communities rely on air transport as the only quick way in or out, many local flights operate. These flights are very much dependent on the vagaries of the weather. In the wet season, places like Bario in Sarawak can be isolated for days at a time, so don't venture into this area if you have a very tight schedule. During school holidays these flights are completely booked. At other times it's easier to get a seat at a few days' notice, but always book as far in advance as possible.

The other domestic carrier is Pelangi Air. It offers far fewer flights but covers a few destinations that MAS doesn't, notably Tioman Island and some routes to Ipoh and Langkawi.

Malaysia Airlines Discounts & Special Flights

A variety of worthwhile discounts are available, especially for groups and for travel between Peninsular Malaysia and East Malaysia. Student discounts are only available for students enrolled in Malaysian institutions.

The following discounts apply for families or groups (a group must comprise at least three people) on regular MAS return economy air fares. Maximum stay is 30 days, and tickets must be booked and paid for at least seven days in advance.

- 50% between Peninsular and East Malaysia, and between Sabah and Sarawak
- 25% within Peninsular Malaysia, Sabah or Sarawak

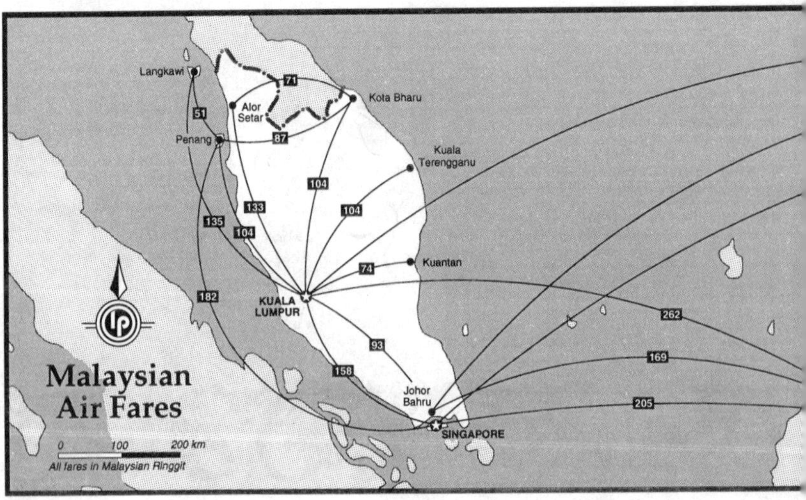

- 25% anywhere in Malaysia for families (a couple with or without children), provided one spouse pays full fare. Children receive a discount on the applicable child's fare.

Other discounts include travel for groups of 10 or more between Malaysia and Singapore or Brunei, and for escorted disabled passengers (50% discount and 25% for the escort).

MAS also has a number of special night flights and advance purchase fares (restrictions apply). Seven-day advance purchase one-way tickets/Apex 30-day return tickets are available for the following flights from Johor Bahru or Kuala Lumpur:

Destination	*Fare (RM)*
JB to Kuching	144/305
JB to Kota Kinabalu	295/624
JB to Penang	150/318
KL to Kuching	227/425
KL to Kota Kinabalu	372/689
KL to Miri	359/679
KL to Labuan	372/656

There are also a few economy night flights between Kuala Lumpur and Kota Kinabalu (RM306), Kuching (RM187), Alor Setar (RM74) and Penang (RM73), and between JB and KK (RM260).

Flying from Malaysia vs Singapore

You can save quite a few dollars if you are flying to Sarawak or Sabah by flying from Johor Bahru rather than Kuala Lumpur or Singapore. The regular economy fare is RM205 from Johor Bahru to Kuching against RM262 from KL and S$193 from Singapore. To Kota Kinabalu, the respective fares are RM347, RM437 and S$391. To persuade travellers to take advantage of these lower fares, MAS offers a bus service directly from its office at the Novotel Orchid Hotel in Singapore to the Johor Bahru airport, for S$10.

It is worth bearing in mind that fares on flights between Singapore and Malaysia cost almost the same in ringgit/dollar terms whether bought in Malaysia or Singapore. Thus a Penang-Singapore ticket costs RM182 in Malaysia, while a Singapore-Penang ticket costs S$170 in Singapore, making the Singapore ticket much more expensive when the exchange rate is taken into account.

BUS

Malaysia has an excellent bus system. There are public buses on local runs and a variety

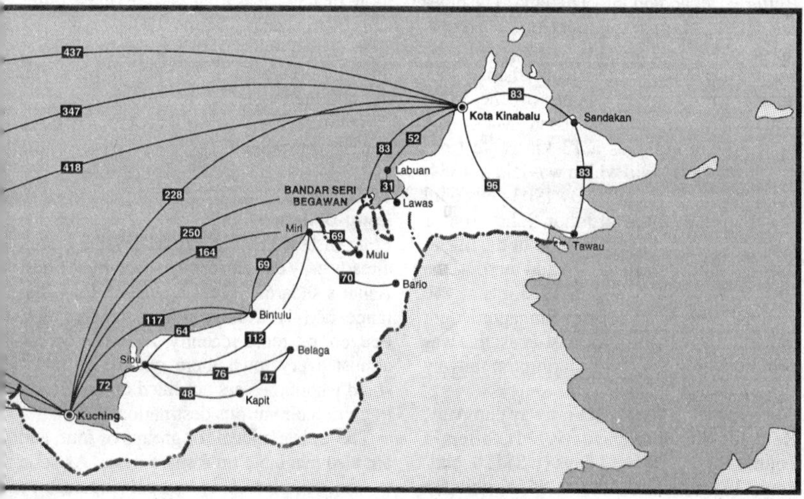

of privately operated buses on the longer trips, as well as the big fleet of Ekspres Nasional express buses. In larger towns there may be a number of bus stops – a main station or two, plus some of the private companies may operate directly from their own offices.

Buses are fast, economical and comfortable and seats can be reserved. On major runs so many buses go that you can often just turn up and get a seat on the next bus. On the main routes most buses are air-conditioned and cost only a few ringgit more than the regular buses. They make mid-day travel a sweat-free activity, but beware – as one traveller put it, 'Malaysian air-conditioned buses are really meat lockers on wheels with just two settings: cold and suspended animation'.

Getting off the beaten track is a little more difficult. Small towns and *kampungs* all over the country are serviced by public buses, but these are usually non-air-con rattlers and services are a lot less frequent. In these cases is often better to get a taxi rather than wait.

TRAIN

Malaysia has a modern, comfortable and economical railway service, although there are basically only two railway lines. One runs from Singapore to Kuala Lumpur, Butterworth and on into Thailand. The other branches off from this line at Gemas and runs through Kuala Lipis up to the north-east corner of the country near Kota Bharu. Other lines are just minor branches off these two routes and are not much used. Malaysia's first railway line was a 13 km route from Taiping to Port Weld which was laid in 1884, but it is no longer in use. By 1903 you could travel all the way from Johor Bahru to near Butterworth, and the extension of the line to the Thai border in 1918 and across the Causeway to Singapore in 1923 meant you could travel by train from Singapore right into Thailand. In 1931 the east-coast line was completed, effectively bringing the railway system to its present state.

The privatised national railway company, Keretapi Tanah Melayu (KTM), offers a Tourist Railpass for 30 days (US$120, children US$60) or 10 days (US$55, children US$28). This pass entitles the holder to unlimited travel on any class of train but does not include sleeping berth charges. Railpasses are available only to foreigners and can be purchased at a number of main railway stations. You have to do a lot of train travel to make them worthwhile.

Malaysia basically has three types of rail services – express, limited express and local trains. Express trains are air-con and generally 1st and 2nd class only, and on night trains there's a choice of sleepers or seats. Limited express trains may have 2nd and 3rd class only but some have 1st, 2nd and 3rd class with overnight sleepers. Local trains are usually 3rd class non-air-con only, but some have 2nd class (see the tables on the next page for train fares and schedules).

The express trains stop only at main stations. Limited express trains stop at a few more stations but still provide a quick service. These two options are much faster than the local trains, and in most respects are definitely the ones to take. The local services that operate, mostly on the Tumpat-Singapore line, are colourful experiences for short journeys. They stop everywhere, including out in the middle of the jungle to let passengers and their goods on and off, but they take more than twice as long as the express trains and run to erratic schedules.

In Sabah there's also a small narrow-gauge railway line which can take you through the Pegas River gorge from Tenom to Beaufort. The trip is a great experience and is well worth doing.

TAXI

Long-Distance Taxis

Long-distance taxis make Malaysian travel, already easy and convenient even by the best Asian standards, a real breeze. A long-distance taxi is usually a diesel Mercedes, Peugeot or, more recently, Japanese car. In almost every town there will be a 'teksi' stand where the cars are lined up and ready to go to their various destinations.

The taxis are ideal for groups of four, and are also available on a share basis. As soon as a full complement of four passengers turns up, off you go. Between major towns you have a reasonable chance of finding other passengers to share without having to wait too long, but otherwise you will have to charter a whole taxi, which is four times the single fare rate (quoted throughout this book). As Malaysia becomes increasingly wealthy, and people can afford to hire a whole taxi, the share system is becoming less reliable. Early in the morning is the best time to find other people to share a taxi, or you can inquire at the taxi stand the day before to see when is the best time.

Taxi rates are fixed by the government and posted at the taxi stands; usually the rate for a whole taxi is listed. To have the air-con switched on costs a little extra. Taxi fares generally work out at about twice the comparable bus fares. If you want to charter a taxi to an obscure destination or by the hour, some negotiation is usually called for.

Taxi drivers often drive at frightening speed. They don't have as many head-on collisions as you might expect, but closing your eyes at times of high stress certainly helps.

CAR

Rental

Rent-a-car operations are well established in Malaysia. Major rental operators in Malaysia include Avis, Budget, Hertz, National and Thrifty, although there are numerous others including many local operators only found in one city. Unlimited distance rates are posted at around RM150 per day or RM900 per week, including insurance and collision damage waiver. This is for a 1.3 litre Proton Saga, the cheapest and most popular car in Malaysia; the Proton Wira is a step up in standard and slightly more expensive. The Proton is basically a Mitsubishi assembled under licence in Malaysia. Charges for a Ford Laser are around RM200 per day or RM1200 per week.

These are the standard rates from the major car hire companies but you can often get better deals, either through smaller local companies or when the major companies offer special deals. Rates drop substantially for longer rentals and you can get a Proton Saga for as little as RM2000 per month, including unlimited km and insurance, if you shop around by phone. The main advantage of dealing with a large company is that it has offices all over the country, giving better backup if something goes wrong and allowing you to pick up in one city and drop off in another (typically for a RM50 surcharge).

KL is the best place to look for car hire and Penang is also good (see those sections for more details). In Sabah and Sarawak there is less competition and rates are higher, partly because of the condition of the roads.

A valid overseas licence is needed to rent a car. An International Driving Permit is usually not required by local car hire companies but it is recommended to bring one (see Documents in the Malaysia – Facts for the Visitor chapter). Age limits apply, and most companies require that drivers are at least 23 years old.

Driving

In many Asian countries driving is either a fraught experience (ever seen the rush hour in Bangkok or Jakarta?), full of local dangers (I'd hate to think what would happen if you collided with a cow in India), the roads are terrible, cars are unavailable, or for some other reason driving yourself is not really possible. None of these drawbacks apply in Malaysia. The roads are generally of a high standard, there are plenty of new cars available and driving standards are not too hair-raising.

The Lebuh Raya, or North-South Highway, is a new six-lane expressway which runs virtually the whole length of the peninsula from the Thai border in the north to Johor Bahru in the south. There are toll charges for using the expressway, and these vary according to the distance travelled. It's not all that cheap, the result being that the normal highways remain crowded while traffic on the expressway is light. As an example, a 50 km journey costs around RM5. Many other highways are in excellent condition and many others are in process of construction.

Driving in the big cities, especially KL, is confusing, chaotic and not much fun, but once out in the countryside driving is relatively easy and a car gives you a great deal of flexibility.

Basically, driving in Malaysia follows

Train Fares from Butterworth (RM)

	Express			*Limited Express*		
Class	*1st*	*2nd*	*3rd*	*1st*	*2nd*	*3rd*
Padang Besar	34	20	11	25.50	11.10	6.30
Taiping	23	15	8	14.40	6.30	3.60
Ipoh	36	21	11	27.80	12.10	6.90
Tapah Road	44	24	13	36.00	15.60	8.90
Kuala Lumpur	67	34	19	58.50	25.40	14.40
Tampin	85	42	23	76.50	33.20	18.90
Johor Bahru	122	58	33	114.00	49.40	28.10
Singapore	127	60	34	118.50	51.40	29.90

Train Fares from Kuala Lumpur (RM)

	Express			*Limited Express*		
Class	*1st*	*2nd*	*3rd*	*1st*	*2nd*	*3rd*
Padang Besar	89	44	24	81.00	35.10	20.00
Butterworth	67	34	19	58.50	25.40	14.40
Taiping	53	28	16	45.00	19.50	11.10
Ipoh	40	22	12	31.50	13.70	7.80
Tapah Road	32	19	10	23.30	10.10	5.80
Tampin	27	17	9	18.80	8.20	4.70
Johor Bahru	64	33	18	55.50	24.10	13.70
Singapore	68	34	19	60.00	26.00	14.80
Jerantut	–	–	–	52.50	33.80	13.00
Kuala Lipis	–	–	–	61.50	26.70	15.20
Wakaf Bahru	–	–	–	103.50	44.90	25.50
Tumpat	–	–	–	106.50	46.20	26.20

Train Fares from Singapore (S$)

	Express			*Limited Express*		
Class	*1st*	*2nd*	*3rd*	*1st*	*2nd*	*3rd*
Padang Besar	148	69	38	139.50	60.50	34.40
Butterworth	127	60	34	118.50	51.40	29.20
Taiping	112	53	30	103.50	44.90	25.50
Ipoh	100	48	27	91.50	39.70	22.60
Tapah Road	92	45	25	84.00	36.40	20.70
Kuala Lumpur	68	34	19	60.00	26.00	14.80
Tampin	50	27	15	42.00	18.20	10.40
Johor Bahru	13	10	6	4.20	1.90	1.10
Kuala Lipis	76	38	21	–	29.30	16.70
Wakaf Bahru	119	57	32	–	48.10	27.40
Tumpat	121	57	32	–	48.80	27.70

Supplementary berth charges are as follows: RM30 for 1st class; RM20 for 2nd class air-con lower berth; RM14 for 2nd class air-con upper berth; RM11.50 for 2nd class non-air-con lower berth; and RM11.50 for 2nd class non-air-con upper berth.

much the same rules as in Britain or Australia – cars are right-hand drive and you drive on the left side of the road. The only additional precaution you need to take is to remain constantly aware of the possible additional road hazards of stray animals and the large

Timetables for Main West Coast Services

Train/No	*ER/1*	*ESP/3*	*EL/7*	*SM/9*	*EM/53*
Hat Yai	–	–	1550	–	–
Alor Setar	–	–	1915	–	–
Butterworth	0730	1435	–	2200	2255
Taiping	0900	1600	2315	2347	0021
Ipoh	1033	1732	0105	0146	0235
Kuala Lumpur	1410	2115	0545	0625	0720

Train/No	*XSP/4*	*ER/2*	*EL/8*	*SM/10*	*EM/54*
Kuala Lumpur	0730	1415	2030	2200	2230
Ipoh	1040	1736	0028	0123	0234
Taiping	1218	1913	0231	0340	0503
Butterworth	1410	2110	–	0555	0720
Alor Setar	–	–	0619	–	–
Hat Yai	–	–	0915	–	–

Train/No	*XSP/5*	*ES/57*	*ER/1*	*EM/59*	*SM/11*
Kuala Lumpur	0725	–	1430	2100	2225
Tampin	0916	–	1629	2332	0057
Gemas	1003	1400	1719	0043	0210
Johor Bahru	1250	1735	2011	0455	0550
Singapore	1600	1850	2235	0705	–

Train/No	*ER/2*	*ES/58*	*XSP/6*	*EM/60*	*SM/12*
Singapore	0730	0830	1425	2000	2230
Johor Bahru	0754	0856	1448	2027	2255
Gemas	1055	1305	1747	0110	0220
Tampin	1141	–	1840	0207	0327
Kuala Lumpur	1350	–	2005	0510	0605

ES & EM trains are limited express services, all others express.

Timetables for Main East Coast Service

Train/No	*81*	*XST/15*
Tumpat	1500	1930
Wakaf Baru	1512	1940
Kuala Lipis	2004	2358
Jerantut	0535	0102
Gemas	0220	0350
Johor Bahru	–	0655
Singapore	–	0805

	82	*XST/14*
Singapore	–	2130
Johor Bahru	–	2155
Gemas	0220	0111
Jerantut	0535	0406
Kuala Lipis	0646	0506
Wakaf Baru	1154	0934
Tumpat	1220	1000

* Train XST/15 operates on Wednesday, Friday and Sunday. Train XST/14 on Tuesday, Thursday and Saturday.

XST trains are express services, 82 & 81 limited express.

number of motorcyclists. Take it easy on the back roads through the kampungs.

Although most drivers in Malaysia are relatively sane, safe and slow, there are also a fair few who specialise in overtaking on blind corners and otherwise trusting in divine intervention. Long-distance taxi drivers are particular specialists in these activities. Malaysian drivers also operate a curious signalling system where a left flashing indicator means 'you are safe to overtake', or 'I'm about to turn off', or 'I've forgotten to turn my indicator off', or 'look out, I'm about to do something totally unpredictable'.

Petrol is inexpensive at around RM1.15 a litre; diesel fuel costs RM0.65 per litre. Remember that wearing safety belts *is* compulsory, although these are fitted to the front seats only. Parking regulations are a little

By Bicycle – Peninsular Malaysia & Singapore

Bicycle touring from Singapore, around Malaysia and on to Thailand is an increasingly popular activity.

Equipment A well-maintained bike with good tyres is essential. Road conditions are good enough for touring bikes.

Essential tools include: Allen keys, spoke key, tyre levers and a small Swiss army knife.

Accessories include: helmet, gloves, panniers, front pack with map-holder, rear-view mirror that attaches to the right handlebar, sunglasses, spare tube and patch kit, pump, bungee cord, two large water bottles, insect repellent and sunscreen.

Pack lightly, with everything in waterproof plastic bags. Warm weather clothes, pullover (for high altitudes) and a rain shell are recommended.

Shipping Bikes are carried free in lieu of luggage on most scheduled international flights. Charter carriers have their own rules. You can purchase a box from the airlines or supply your own. When boxes are unavailable, handlers are often more careful with the unboxed bikes. Take the pedals off (tape them to the back rack), secure the pump with tape and turn the handlebars. Place your panniers in the dead space of the shipping box to protect the gears.

Planning The Tourist Board map (scale 1:1,000,000) is adequate, but Nelles' map of *West Malaysia* (scale 1:650,000) is better. Weather and wind will hasten or slow your progress, so a flexible overall plan is best. The equatorial climate has high temperatures, and it's wet all year round. The winds are north-east from November to February and south-west from April to September. March and October are the changeover months when winds are light and variable. Due to the seasonal headwinds, ride north on the west coast from November to February and south on the east coast from April to September. There are no organised bicycle tours to Singapore/Malaysia.

Road Rules *Ride on the left.* Third world rules apply: the right of way belongs to the larger vehicle. Use a rear-view mirror.

Practical Information The main road system is well engineered with good surfaces. The secondary road system is limited. In high traffic areas, road safety is a problem because of narrow roads with no shoulders (especially within 50 km around KL).

Singapore has many bicycle shops. Throughout Malaysia minor repairs can be handled but major repairs on foreign bikes can be made in KL at Triathlon Sports Center (☎ 03-982-6633).

A major concern when riding in a tropical climate is dehydration. Drink at least half a litre of water before riding and keep drinking fluids all day. Drink *before* you feel thirsty.

Alternative Transport In general, buses do not take bicycles, although some express buses might if their luggage compartment is empty – good luck! Trains take bikes, but they must be shipped ahead with freight. Hitching in small trucks is always an excellent option, but rides are tougher to get here than in the rest of Asia. Pick-up trucks are best. Keep the panniers on the bike to protect the gears when putting bikes in trucks.

curious – though most cities have parking meters, in some places they have a strange human parking-meter system where your car collects a stack of little tickets under its wiper and you then have to find somebody to give the money to, at so many sen per ticket.

The Automobile Association of Malaysia will let you join its organisation if you have a letter of introduction from your own automobile association.

HITCHING

Malaysia has long had a reputation for being an excellent place for hitchhiking and it's generally still true, though with the ease of the buses most travellers don't bother.

You'll get picked up both by expats and by Malaysians and Singaporeans, but it's strictly an activity for foreigners – a hitchhiking Malaysian would probably just get left by the roadside! So the first rule of thumb

Routes

Changi Airport to Singapore (25 km) There is no way to take your bike on public transport. You must ride, but it's illegal on the East Coast Parkway. Take the East Coast Parkway to the East Coast Parkway Service Rd. Turn left onto the East Coast Parkway Service Rd and follow this to the 13 km road marker, then turn right onto Fort Rd. Turn left onto Mountbatten Rd, pass Stadium Rd and then turn left onto Nicoll Highway into the city.

Singapore to Johor Bahru (27 km) There are multiple options on city streets through Singapore to the bridge to Johor Bahru. The most direct route is along Bukit Timah Rd to Woodlands Rd to the bridge. It is also possible to take bicycles on the ferries that leave from Changi Village, going to Pengerang for Desaru in Johor state.

West Coast Peninsular Malaysia This route is through rolling hills and flat country, with interesting cities to visit. From Johor Bahru follow the coast west to Highway 1 (four lanes with shoulder) and turn on to a secondary road to Pontian Kecil (61 km) on the coast. Follow Highway 5 along the coast to Batu Pahat (73 km), then Muar (53 km) and Melaka (45 km). There are some views of the Straits of Melaka from the road. Port Dickson is another 94 km and from there to Banting it's 83 km.

After Banting the traffic becomes treacherous on this narrow highway to Kelang (32 km) where there is a turn-off to KL (32 km). There are some designated bicycle lanes in KL.

From Kuala Lumpur to Butterworth, the best route is via the coast and inland roads to Taiping, and then secondary roads to Butterworth.

From Butterworth, take the ferry to Penang Island (bikes are not allowed on the bridge). There is some good riding on the island along the beaches.

Cross-Peninsula Route This route has very light traffic. From Butterworth (Penang) to Baling (91 km) there are multiple routes with few signposts. Ask for Baling or Gerik. There are hills from Baling to Gerik (62 km). Gerik has facilities and hotels, and you can also stay at Pulau Banding. Highway 4 is a well engineered road with good surfaces. There are some long climbs through the interior mountains; facilities are sparse with no hotels. Gerik to Jeli is 124 km, and Jeli to the crossroads of Highway 4 and 3 is 97 km. Expect rain.

East Coast Peninsular Malaysia This is the most popular route for cycling through the peninsula. Although like on all highways traffic is increasing, there is less traffic on this route than on the west-coast route, and it's flat and follows the coast for long stretches.

Highway 3 from Kota Bharu (168 km) south to Kuala Terengganu has light traffic but fast-moving buses and trucks. About 80 km before Kuala Terengganu you can cut into the beach (14 km) and enjoy a quiet coastal ride into the city. Highway 3 runs along the coast to Kuala Dungun (78 km). From Kuala Dungun to Kuantan (131 km) there are many beach hotels (most are closed in the off season)

Take the passenger ferry across the river from Kuantan and follow another quiet coastal road south to Pekan (47 km). Continue from Pekan to Mersing back on Highway 3 (144 km). Follow Highway 3 to Kota Tinggi (92 km). The highway is wider from here to Johor Bahru (41 km), with heavy traffic.

Peter & Sally Blommer,
Cycle Singapore/Malaysia – Blommer

in Malaysia is to look foreign. Look neat and tidy too (a worldwide rule for successful hitching), but make sure your backpack is in view and you look like someone on their way around the country.

On the west coast of Malaysia, hitching is generally quite easy but it is not possible on the main Lebuh Raya expressway. On the east coast, traffic is lighter and there may be long waits between rides. Hitching in East Malaysia also depends on the traffic, although it's quite possible.

Keep in mind that hitching is never entirely safe in any country in the world, and we don't recommend it. Travellers who decide to hitch should understand that they are taking a small but potentially serious risk. People who do choose to hitch will be safer if they travel in pairs and let someone know where they are planning to go.

BOAT

There are no services connecting the peninsula with East Malaysia. On a local level, there are boats between the peninsula and offshore islands, and along the rivers of Sabah and Sarawak – see the relevant sections for full details.

LOCAL TRANSPORT

Local transport varies widely from place to place. Large cities have city taxis (as opposed to long-distance taxis), and usually these have meters, though in some cases (notably Kuala Lumpur) drivers may be unwilling to use them. In major cities there are buses – in Kuala Lumpur the government buses are backed up by private operators. KL also has new commuter trains and the LRT (Light Rail Transit).

In many towns there are also bicycle rickshaws. While they have died out in Kuala Lumpur and have become principally a tourist gimmick in many Malaysian cities, they are still a viable form of transport. Indeed, in places like Georgetown, with its convoluted and narrow streets, a bicycle rickshaw is probably the best way of getting around. See the relevant city sections for more details on local transport.

Kuala Lumpur

In 130 years, Kuala Lumpur has grown from nothing to a modern, bustling city of over one million people. The city's skyline these days is a reflection of the booming Malaysian economy – there's a host of gleaming skyscrapers, and many more are under construction, including the KL City Centre (Petronas Towers), the world's tallest building.

KL (as it's almost universally known) is a federal territory, directly under the control of the central government. The city's urban sprawl extends well beyond the boundaries of the territory into surrounding Selangor state, particularly along the Kelang Valley to Petaling Jaya, Shah Alam and Kelang, where much of the city's workforce and industry is located.

Greater KL, with a population closer to two million, forms the powerhouse of the Malaysian economy. KL is the place to do deals and make it rich, and is the recipient of many of the country's extravagant development schemes. As well as the KL City Centre, the LRT (Light Rail Transit) may help alleviate the choking traffic, a new US$3.5 billion international airport is being built at Sepang, 33 km south of the city, and nearby, construction has started on the city of Putrajaya. This US$8 billion project will be the new capital, housing the government administration, including 76,000 public servants, in a high-tech wonderland of the future.

Despite all the recent developments, however, KL retains plenty of character – old colonial buildings still stand out proudly right in the centre of town, and Chinatown, with its street vendors and night markets in the heart of the city, is as vibrant as any you'll encounter. To complete the cultural mix, there's a bustling Little India and the sprawling Malay-dominated Chow Kit Market north of the centre.

On first impressions, many visitors find KL to be just another busy and noisy Asian city, but it more than repays any time spent if you're prepared to delve a bit deeper. It still has the colour that has been so effectively wiped out in Singapore, yet lacks the pollution and congestion of Bangkok. KL certainly has plenty of traffic problems though, despite the numerous multi-lane highways and flyovers.

Full Name: Federal Territory of Kuala Lumpur
Area: 243 sq km
Population: 1.1 million

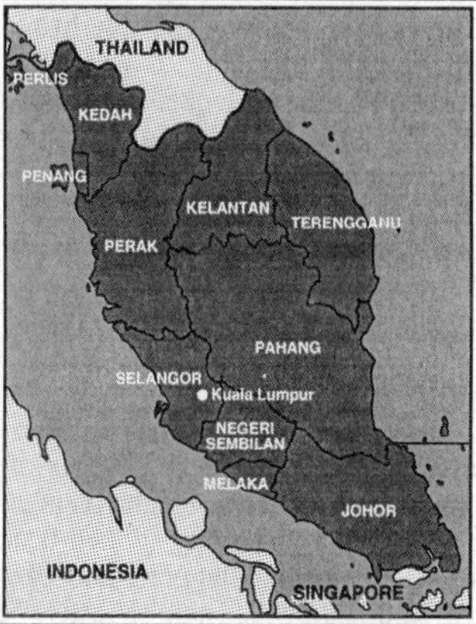

History

Kuala Lumpur came into being in the 1860s when a band of prospectors in search of tin landed at the meeting point of the Kelang and Gombak rivers and imaginatively named the place Kuala Lumpur – 'Muddy Confluence'. More than half of those first arrivals were to die of malaria and other tropical diseases, but the tin they discovered in Ampang attracted more miners and KL quickly became a brawling, noisy, violent boom town.

As in other parts of Malaysia, the local

sultan appointed a 'Kapitan China' to bring the unruly Chinese fortune-seekers into line – a problem which Yap Ah Loy jumped at with such ruthless relish that he became known as the founder of KL.

In the 1880s successful miners and merchants began to build fine homes along Jalan Ampang, the British Resident Frank Swettenham pushed through a far-reaching new town plan, and in 1886 a railway line linked KL to Port Kelang.

The town has never looked back, and now it's not only the business and commercial capital of Malaysia, but also the political capital. It is also the largest city in Malaysia.

Kuala Lumpur has the status of a Federal Territory located within Selangor state. The area was ceded by Selangor in 1974.

Orientation

The traditional heart of KL is Merdeka Square, not far from the confluence of the two muddy rivers from which KL takes its name. The square is easily spotted because of its 95-metre-high flagpole, and parades and ceremonies are held here on festive occasions. Just to the south-east of this square across the river, the banking district merges into the older Chinatown, a bustling area with a wide range of accommodation.

The GPO is just south of Merdeka Square. A little further on is the national mosque and the KL railway station, and beyond them is KL's green belt, where you can find the Lake Gardens, National Museum and Monument and the Malaysian Parliament.

Heading east from the Merdeka Square area is Jalan Tun Perak, a major trunk road which leads to the transport hub of the country, the Puduraya bus and taxi station on the eastern edge of the central district.

To the north-east of Puduraya, around Jalan Ampang and Jalan Sultan Ismail, the Golden Triangle is the modern development centre, crammed with luxury hotels, shopping centres and office towers. This is the real heart of the new, booming KL.

Running north from Merdeka Square is Jalan Tuanku Abdul Rahman. It runs one-way north-south, through Little India and Chow Kit. A few of KL's cheaper hotels are found there. Jalan Raja Laut runs almost parallel to Jalan Tuanku Abdul Rahman and takes the northbound traffic. Both roads are horrendously noisy during peak hours.

KL is a relatively easy city to find your way around, although getting from place to place on foot around the city can be frustrating as the new six-lane roads and flyovers divide the area up into sections which are not connected by footpaths.

Information

Tourist Offices KL is well endowed with tourist offices.

The biggest and most useful is the Malaysia Tourist Information Centre (☎ 03-264 3929), 109 Jalan Ampang, north-east of the city centre. Housed in the former mansion of a Malaysian planter and tin miner (later the British, and then the Japanese, army headquarters), it is almost a tourist attraction in its own right. As well as a tourist information counter (open 9 am to 9 pm daily), there's a moneychanger, MAS counter, Ekspres Nasional bus booking counter, a national parks information counter and a Telekom office (open office hours). Cultural performances are also held here including dances (see Entertainment) and the 10-minute *Know Malaysia* audiovisual show. The centre also has an expensive restaurant and a souvenir shop. This is the best place to come for information on other states, as there are push-button maps and video presentations on each state in the Federation.

More conveniently located, the KL Visitors Centre (☎ 03-293 6661) is in the centre, at the junction of Jalan Raja Laut and Jalan Parliamen. Though not as well set up for information, it is housed in a wonderful Malay-style building. There's also a tourist office (☎ 03-274 6063) at the railway station, and both these offices are open from 9 am to 9 pm daily. There's also a counter in the arrivals hall at the international terminal at the airport (☎ 03-746 5707).

Tourism Malaysia has its head office at the Putra World Trade Centre on Jalan Tun Ismail in the north of KL. It also has a tourist information counter (☎ 03-441 1295) on level two of the same building, open Monday to Friday from 8.30 am to 4.45 pm and Saturday from 8 am to 12.45 pm.

Kuala Lumpur Now! is a good, widely available tourist publication. It is produced monthly but is not always updated.

Immigration Office The immigration office (☎ 03-255 5077) is at Block 1, Pusat Bandar Damansara, about one km west of the Lake Gardens. Take a Sri Jaya bus No 250 from the Jalan Sultan Mohammed bus stand.

Money Banks can be found throughout the central area of KL. The biggest concentration is on and around Jalan Silang at the northern edge of Chinatown. In this area, banks include the Hongkong Bank and Maybank for changing cash and travellers' cheques and for withdrawals through ATMs. Maybank also has a convenient branch on Jalan Bukit Bintang in the Golden Triangle district. Banks are open from 10 am to 4 pm, Monday to Friday, and 10 am to 12.30 pm on Saturdays.

Moneychangers are also in plentiful supply; try Jalan Sultan near the Kelang bus station, Jalan Ampang or Jalan Tuanku Abdul Rahman near Little India. Most shopping centres have moneychangers.

Post & Communications The huge GPO building is across the Kelang River from the central district. It is open Monday to Saturday from 8 am to 6 pm, and 10 am to 12.45 pm on Sunday. The poste restante mail is held at the information desk.

For international calls in business hours, the best place to head for is the previously mentioned Malaysia Tourist Information Centre. At other times, the Telekom office just off Jalan Raja Chulan, close to the centre, is open 24 hours a day.

There are credit-card phones at both centres, on the 1st floor of Central Market and at the GPO. There's also a Home Country Direct phone at the railway station, and on this you can make direct collect (reverse charge) calls to a number of countries. For sending faxes there's a credit-card fax machine at the GPO.

Travel Agencies MSL (☎ 03-442 4722), 66 Jalan Putra, is a long-running student travel agency. This is a reliable company and it often has some interesting deals on offer.

Other big, established agents for airline tickets and tours include: Mayflower (☎ 03-248 6700), with a branch in Sogo department store (☎ 03-294 0933) on Jalan Tuanku Abdul Rahman; and Enesty Travel (☎ 03-273 2525) at the KL railway station.

Bookshops The two best bookstore chains, Times and MPH, are well represented in KL. Times has branches in The Weld shopping centre on the corner of Jalan P Ramlee and Jalan Raja Chulan, at the Star Hill shopping centre on Jalan Bukit Bintang and at the Sungei Wang Plaza on Jalan Sultan Ismail. MPH has a cramped but good bookstore in the Bukit Bintang Plaza on Jalan Bukit Bintang, where the Berita Bookstore also has a good range. All are in the Golden Triangle.

Cultural Centres & Libraries The following libraries are maintained in KL:

Alliance Française
  15 Lorong Gurney (☎ 03-292 5929)
Australian Information Library
  Jalan Yap Kwan Seng (☎ 03-242 3122)
British Council
  Jalan Bukit Aman (☎ 03-298 7555)
Goethe Institut
  1 Langgak Golf (☎ 03-242 2011)
Japan Cultural Centre
  Wisma Nusantara, Jalan Puncak
  (☎ 03-230 6630)
Lincoln Resource Center
  376 Jalan Tun Razak (☎ 03-242 0291)
National Library
  Jalan Tun Razak (☎ 03-292 7686)
New Zealand Library
  193 Jalan Tun Razak (☎ 03-248 6422)

Merdeka Square

Merdeka Square, at the heart of colonial KL, was part of the open field formerly known as the Padang. It was here during the colonial days that Malaysia's administrators engaged

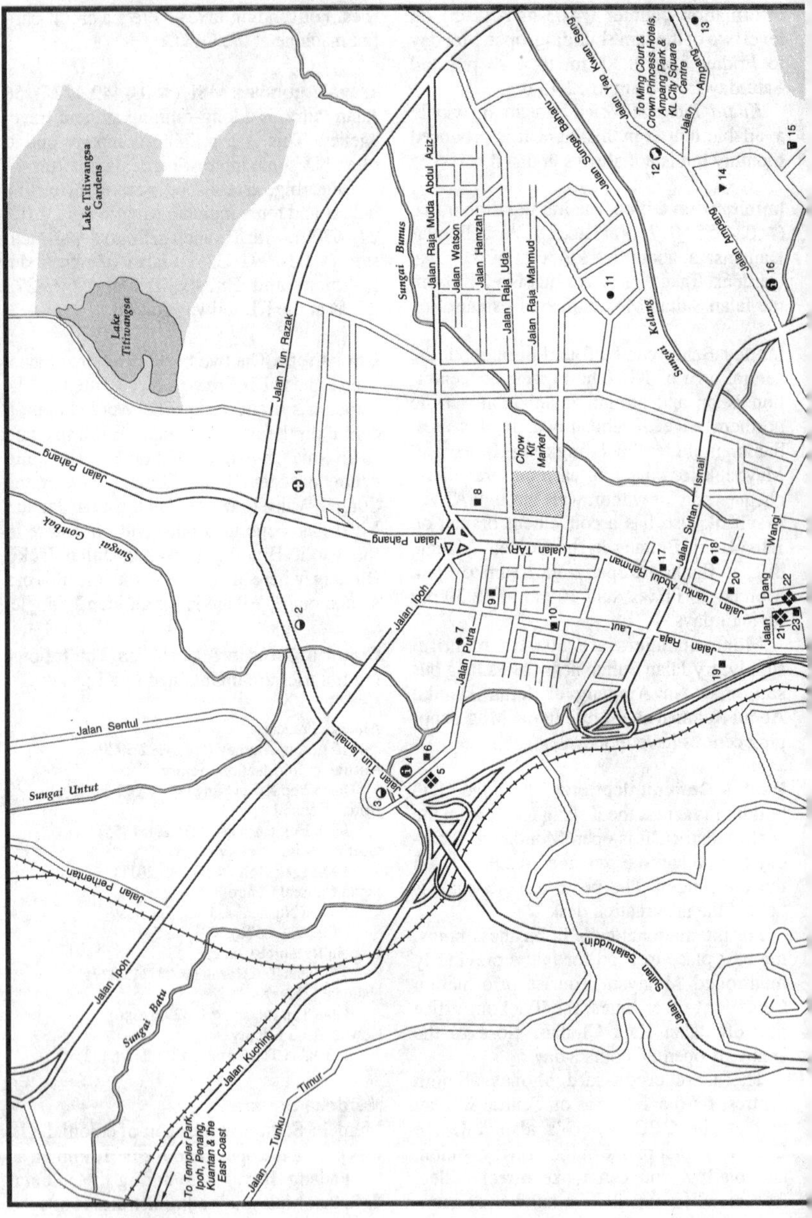
Lake Titiwangsa Gardens
Lake Titiwangsa
Jalan Tun Razak
Jalan Pahang
Sungai Gombak
Jalan Sentul
Sungai Untut
Jalan Perhentian
Jalan Ipoh
Sungai Batu
Jalan Kuching
To Templer Park, Ipoh, Penang, Kuantan & the East Coast
Jalan Tunku Timur
Jalan Tun Ismail
Jalan Ipoh
Jalan Putra
Sungai Bunus
Jalan Raja Muda Abdul Aziz
Jalan Watson
Jalan Hamzah
Jalan Raja Uda
Jalan Raja Mahmud
Chow Kit Market
Jalan TAR
(Jalan Tuanku Abdul Rahman)
Jalan Sultan Ismail
Jalan Raja Laut
Jalan Dang Wangi
Jalan Sungai Baharu
Jalan Yap Kwan Seng
To Ming Court & Crown Princess Hotels, Ampang Park & KL City Square Centre
Jalan Ampang
Sungai Kelang
Jalan Sultan Salahuddin
1
2
3
4
5
6
7
8
9
10
11
12
13
14
15
16
17
18
19
20
21
22
23

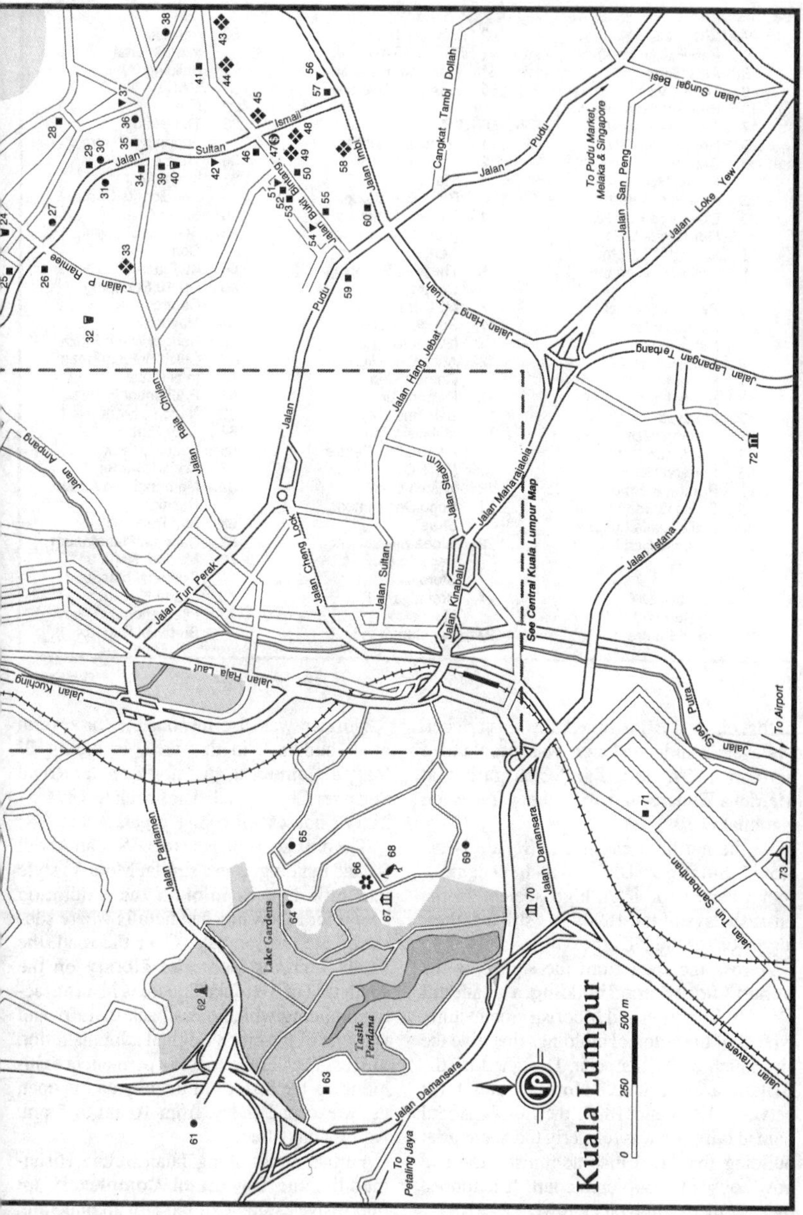
Kuala Lumpur
0
250
500 m
Jalan Sultan Ismail
Jalan P Ramlee
Jalan Bukit Bintang
Jalan Imbi
Jalan Pudu
Cangkat Tambi Dollah
Jalan Sungai Besi
To Pudu Market, Melaka & Singapore
Jalan San Peng
Jalan Loke Yew
Jalan Hang Tuah
Jalan Hang Jebat
Jalan Lapangan Terbang
Jalan Raja Chulan
Jalan Ampang
Jalan Stadium
Jalan Maharajalela
See Central Kuala Lumpur Map
Jalan Cheng Lock
Jalan Tun Perak
Jalan Sultan
Jalan Kinabalu
Jalan Istana
Jalan Raja Laut
Jalan Kuching
Jalan Syed Putra
To Airport
Jalan Parliamen
Lake Gardens
Tasik Perdana
Jalan Damansara
Jalan Tun Sambanthan
Jalan Travers
To Petaling Jaya

PLACES TO STAY

6 Pan Pacific Hotel
8 Asia Hotel
9 Transit Villa
10 Ben Soo Homestay
17 Paradise Lodge
19 Holiday Inn City Centre
20 Shiraz Hotel
23 Kowloon Hotel
25 Concorde Hotel & Hard Rock Cafe
26 Shangri-La Hotel
28 Holiday Inn on the Park
29 Equatorial Hotel
34 Lodge Hotel
35 Hilton Hotel
39 Hotel Istana
41 Regent Hotel
46 Agora Hotel
50 Malaysia Hotel
52 Bintang Warisan Hotel
53 Cardogan Hotel
55 Federal Hotel
57 Parkroyal Hotel
59 Swiss Garden Hotel
60 Melia Kuala Lumpur
63 Carcosa Seri Negara
71 YMCA

PLACES TO EAT

14 Le Coq D'Or
37 Food Centre
42 Edo Sushi
51 Tamnak Thai
54 Restoran Ramzan
56 Restoran Oversea

OTHER

1 General Hospital
2 Pekeliling Bus Station
3 Putra Bus Station
4 Tourism Malaysia (Putra World Trade Centre)
5 The Mall Shopping Centre
7 MSL Travel
11 Sunday Market (Pasar Minggu)
12 Australian High Commission
13 Pelangi Air
15 Betelnut
16 Malaysia Tourist Information Centre (MATIC)
18 Wisma Loke
21 Sogo Department Store
22 Globe Silk Department Store
24 Brannigans & Modesto's
27 Life Centre
30 Pernas International Building
31 MAS
32 Fire
33 The Weld Shopping Centre
36 Wisma Stephens
38 Karyaneka Handicrafts Centre
40 Shark Club
43 Star Hill Shopping Centre
44 KL Plaza
45 Lot 10 Shopping Centre
47 Maybank
48 Sungei Wang Plaza
49 Bukit Bintang Plaza
58 Imbi Plaza
61 Parliament House
62 National Monument
64 Deer Park
65 Butterfly Park
66 Orchid Garden
67 Memorial Tun Abdul Razak
68 Bird Park
69 National Planetarium
70 Muzium Negara (National Museum)
72 Istana Negara
73 International Buddhist Pagoda

in that curious British rite known as cricket. Malaysia's independence was proclaimed here in 1957, and dignitaries gather at Merdeka Square to watch the parades on National Day.

At the northern end of the Square is the **Royal Selangor Club**, which became a social centre for KL's high society in the tin-rush days of the 1890s. It's still a gathering place for the KL elite.

Across the road from the square is the **Sultan Abdul Samad building**, a wonderful blend of Victorian and Moorish architecture, typical of the colonial buildings that give the city much of its character. Designed by the British architect AC Norman and built between 1894 and 1897, the Sultan Abdul Samad building was formerly the Secretariat building for the British administration and now houses the supreme court. It is topped by a 43-metre-high clock tower.

Norman was also responsible for several other buildings in this area, including **St Mary's Cathedral**, just north of the Royal Selangor Club, which dates back to 1894. St Mary's houses a fine pipe organ.

The old City Hall, next to the Sultan Abdul Samad building, is in a similar Moorish style and now houses **Infokraf**, an exhibition centre for Malaysian handicrafts where souvenirs are also on sale. Over the road, the **Kuala Lumpur Memorial Library** on the south side of Merdeka Square is in an attractive building which dates back to 1909 and was one of the city's original administration offices. The library houses a permanent exhibition on the history of the city and is open daily, except Sunday, from 10 am to 5 pm. Admission is free.

Further south along Jalan Sultan Hishamuddin, the **Dayabumi Complex** is an impressive example of modern architecture, using Islamic arches and motifs in a multi-sided high-rise tower.

Masjid Jamek

The most delightful of all KL's mosques, the 'Friday Mosque' is at the confluence of the Kelang and Gombak rivers and lies behind the Sultan Abdul Samad building. This was the place where KL's founders first set foot in the town and where supplies were landed for the tin mines.

Set in a grove of palm trees, the mosque is a picturesque structure with onion domes and minarets striped in red and white. It was built in 1907 and is at its best when viewed at sunset and early evening from Jalan Benteng across the river. There is a new mirror-glass office building there which gives excellent reflections of the mosque.

Chinatown

South of the Masjid Jamek are the teeming streets of KL's Chinatown. Bounded by Jalan Sultan, Jalan Cheng Lock and Jalan Sultan Mohammed, this crowded, colourful area is the usual melange of signs, shops, activity and noise. The central section of **Jalan Petaling** is closed to traffic and is a frantically busy market, at its most colourful at night when brightly lit.

There are many historic Chinese shops still standing in KL's Chinatown, and local conservation groups are making efforts to protect them from city development and to restore them to their former glory.

Central Market Previously the city's produce market, this Art Deco building has been refurbished to become a centre for handicraft, antique and art sales, and it is surrounded by pedestrian areas, a welcome break from Chinatown's choking traffic. There are shops on two levels, hawker centres, restaurants, fast-food outlets, bars and a cinema complex in the annex on the northern side.

It is easy to spend an hour or more wandering around the various crafts outlets, which sell everything from cheap souvenirs and jewellery to very expensive Asian artefacts and antiques. As a general rule, the higher the price the more you should bargain. Shops also stock clothes, music tapes and other goods. Various rotating exhibits are on display and cultural shows are staged in the evenings. Or get your palm read for fortune, fame and happiness from Master Chin upstairs on the 2nd level.

Temples The small **Sze Yah Temple**, hidden behind some shops at 14A Lebuh Pudu near the Central Market, is one of the oldest in KL. 'Kapitan China' Yap Ah Loy himself organised its construction, and there's a photograph of him on an altar in the back of the temple.

Built in 1906, the typically ornate **Chan See Shu Yuen Temple** stands at the end of Jalan Petaling and is one of the largest in KL.

The **Khoon Yam Temple** is a Hokkien Chinese temple dating back to the turn of the century and is just across Jalan Stadium from the Chan See Shu Yuen Temple.

Dating from 1873, the **Sri Mahamariamman Temple** is a large and ornate south Indian Hindu temple. It's also in Chinatown at 163 Jalan Tun HS Lee. The temple was refurbished in 1985 and houses a large silver chariot dedicated to Lord Muruga. During the Thaipusam festival this chariot is a central part of a long procession to Batu Caves.

Railway Station

KL's magnificent railway station, close to the national mosque, is a building full of eastern promise. Built in 1911, this delightful example of British colonial humour is a Moorish fantasy of spires, minarets, towers, cupolas and arches. It couldn't look any better if it had been built as a set for some whimsical Hollywood extravaganza.

Across from this superb railway station is the equally wonderful Malayan Railway Administration building.

National Art Gallery

This art gallery (Balai Seni Lukis Negara) is housed in the former Majestic Hotel, opposite the railway station. It has permanent exhibitions of modern paintings by Malaysian artists and rotating exhibitions that include art from around the world. It's not worth a special trip, but if you're in the vicinity (say, waiting for a train), you could while away half an hour or so there.

Admission is free and the hours are 10 am to 6 pm daily.

Masjid Negara

Situated in five hectares of landscaped gardens, the modernistic National Mosque is one of the largest in South-East Asia. A 73-metre-high minaret stands in the centre of a pool, and the main dome of the mosque is in the form of an 18-pointed star which represents the 13 states of Malaysia and the five pillars of Islam. Forty-eight smaller domes cover the courtyard; their design is said to be inspired by the Grand Mosque in Mecca. The mosque, which is close to the railway station, can accommodate 8000 people.

Visitors must remove their shoes upon entry and be 'properly' attired – they'll lend you a robe if your own clothing is not suitable. It's open for non-Muslims outside of prayer times, which are around 8 to 9 am, 1 to 2 pm, 4 to 5 pm and 7 to 8 pm. Women must use a separate entrance.

Muzium Negara

At the southern end of the Lake Gardens and less than a km along Jalan Damansara from the railway station, the National Museum was built on the site of the old Selangor Museum, which was destroyed during WWII. The museum was opened in 1963, and its design and construction is a mixture of Malay architectural styles and crafts. It houses a varied collection on Malaysia's history, arts, crafts, cultures and people.

There are interesting sections on the history of KL, Chinese traditions, the Orang Asli and the country's economy. An unusual exhibit is the skull of an elephant which derailed a train. It's doubtful that the elephant actually charged the ironclad monster which was invading its jungle domain.

Another strange exhibit is an 'amok catcher', an ugly barbed device used to catch and hold a person who has run amok. There are frequent art exhibitions held at the museum, and outside there are railway engines, an aircraft and other larger items.

Admission to the museum is RM1 and it is open daily from 9 am to 6 pm except on Friday, when it closes between noon and 2.45 pm. Minibus No 33, 35 or 38 from Jalan Tuanku Abdul Rahman will take you to the museum.

Lake Gardens

The 92 hectare gardens, established in 1888, form the green belt of KL. As in many planned colonial cities in Malaysia, the garden district lies at the edge of the central city area, typically around landscaped hills, and the British elite built their residences nearby away from the hurly burly of downtown commerce and other races. The British Resident, Frank Swettenham, built his official residence overlooking the gardens, and it is now the Carcosa Seri Negara, Malaysia's most expensive hotel.

The central focus of the gardens is Tasik Perdana, the 'Premier Lake', which was once known as Sydney Lake. On weekends you can rent boats for a leisurely paddle around the lake.

The gardens contain a host of other attractions, open from 9 am to 6 pm. You can take a leisurely, if sweaty, stroll to them, or a shuttle bus (50 sen) does a loop of the main attractions from 9 am to 7 pm daily, except Friday, when it ceases operation from noon to 3 pm. Minibus No 18, 21, 46 or 48 from Jalan Tun Perak or Sri Jaya bus No 244 or 250 from the Sultan Mohammed bus stand will take you to the gardens.

One of the highlights of the gardens is the large **Bird Park**, with its attractive gardens and a large variety of South-East Asian and other birds. Entry is RM5. Just north is the **Orchid Garden**, with over 800 species of orchids, and the adjoining **Hibiscus Garden**. Entry is free. The **Memorial Tun Abdul Razak** opposite the Bird Park is dedicated to Malaysia's second prime minister and displays the Tun's memorabilia. Nearby, the **Deer Park** has a number of tame deer, including the tiny kancil.

The **Butterfly Park** claims to be the largest in South-East Asia and has a number of species in its landscaped enclosure. There is also a butterfly museum and a cafe. Entry is RM5.

The massive **National Monument** overlooks the Lake Gardens from a hillside at their northern end. Sculpted in bronze in 1966 by Felix de Weldon, the creator of the Iwo Jima monument in Washington DC, the monument commemorates the successful defeat of the Communist terrorists during the Emergency.

Overlooking the Lake Gardens from the north-west, Malaysia's **Parliament House** is dominated by an 18 storey office block. Prior permission must be obtained to visit parliament.

Also at the Lake Gardens is the **National Planetarium**, which resembles a futuristic mosque. It has a space science exhibition and puts on astronomy shows. The planetarium is closed on Monday.

Jalan Tuanku Abdul Rahman

North from the city centre, Jalan Tuanku Abdul Rahman leads through an old section of the city, passing Little India. The main street of **Little India** is Jalan Masjid India, crammed with Indian shops and restaurants. This is place to buy saris, batik or Muslim religious paraphernalia. Centred on the mosque, Little India has all the feel of a Middle Eastern bazaar.

Heading further north along Jalan Tuanku Abdul Rahman, many of the buildings are modern, but one surviving colonial relic is the **Coliseum Hotel**. Enter through the saloon doors to the bar, where you can relax in a planter's chair and sip a drink; waiters in starched linen jackets serve grills in the adjoining restaurant. The Coliseum hasn't changed in decades because, in Chinese tradition it is said, the wealthy owner began his business empire here and has retained it in its original form for good luck.

Jalan Tuanku Abdul Rahman is good for shopping during the day, and you can browse in the Globe Silk department store for cheap clothes or in Sogo department store, the country's biggest. Further north you enter the Chow Kit area, once a famed red-light district and hang-out for transvestites, though it has largely been cleaned out now. The **Chow Kit Market** is a Malay market, with a gaggle of roadside vendors lining the main street. All manner of goods are on sale – cheap clothes, basketware and leather goods are good buys if you bargain hard. The area around the Asia Hotel is crammed with hawker stalls, good for satay or nasi lemak.

On Saturday night Jalan Tuanku Abdul Rahman is closed to traffic and hosts the liveliest night market in the city. Stalls line the street as far as the Sogo department store, and buskers play.

Golden Triangle

The Golden Triangle is the showpiece of Malaysia's economic boom. Crammed with multistorey high-rises, including the world's tallest building, the KL City Centre, it is the place to shop, or dine and drink until the wee hours of the morning. Jalan Sultan Ismail is the main drag, with most of the luxury hotels and nightspots spaced out along its length. The most lively area, with the biggest concentration of shopping malls, is near the intersection of Jalan Sultan Ismail and Jalan Bukit Bintang. This is the best area to shop in KL, and you can also visit the **Karyaneka Handicrafts Centre**, nearby on Jalan Raja Chulan.

Just behind Jalan Bukit Bintang, **Jalan Alor** is the best of KL's various venues for hawker food. It gets going around 7 pm and stays open late. The backstreets leading off from Jalan Alor form a lively red-light district.

At the northern edge of the Golden Triangle, **Jalan Ampang** was built up by the early tin millionaires and is lined with impressive mansions. Today many of the fine buildings have become embassies and consulates, so the street is KL's 'Ambassador's Row'. One of these fine stately homes has been converted into a luxurious restaurant, Le Coq d'Or, while another has become the previously

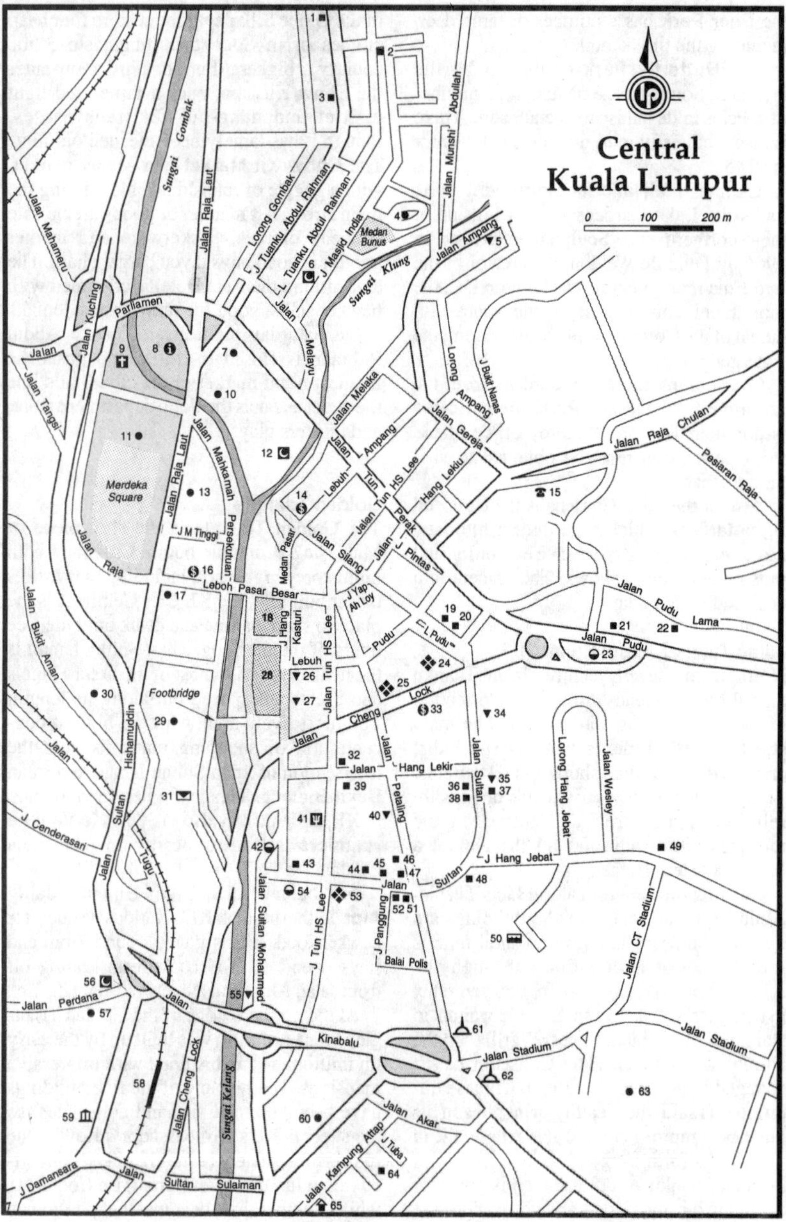
Central
Kuala Lumpur
0
100
200 m
Sungai Gombak
Sungai Klung
Sungai Kelang
Jalan Raja Laut
Lorong Gombak
J Tuanku Abdul Rahman
L. Tuanku Abdul Rahman
J Masjid India
Jalan Munshi Abdullah
Medan Bunus
Jalan Ampang
Jalan Maharajalela
Jalan Kuching
Parliamen
Jalan
Jalan Tangsi
Jalan Melayu
Jalan Melaka
Lorong Ampang
J Bukit Nanas
Jalan Gereja
Jalan Raja Chulan
Pesiaran Raja
Jalan Mahkamah Persekutuan
Merdeka Square
Jalan Raja
Jalan Tun Perak
Lebuh Ampang
Jalan Tun HS Lee
Hang Lekiu
J M Tinggi
Medan Pasar
Jalan Silang
J Pintas
Leboh Pasar Besar
J Yap Ah Loy
J Hang Kasturi
Lebuh Pudu
L. Pudu
Jalan Pudu Lama
Jalan Pudu
Jalan Bukit Aman
Footbridge
Jalan Cheng Lock
Jalan Sultan Hishamuddin
Jalan Hang Lekir
Jalan Petaling
Jalan Sultan
Lorong Hang Jebat
Jalan Wesley
J Cenderasari
Jalan Tugu
J Hang Jebat
Jalan Sultan Mohammed
J Tun HS Lee
J Panggung
Balai Polis
Jalan CT Stadium
Jalan Stadium
Jalan Perdana
Jalan Kinabalu
Jalan Cheng Lock
Jalan Akar
Jalan Kampung Attap
J Tuba
J Damansara
Jalan Sultan Sulaiman
1
2
3
4
5
6
7
8
9
10
11
12
13
14
15
16
17
18
19
20
21
22
23
24
25
26
27
28
29
30
31
32
33
34
35
36
37
38
39
40
41
42
43
44
45
46
47
48
49
50
51
52
53
54
55
56
57
58
59
60
61
62
63
64
65

mentioned Malaysia Tourist Information Centre.

Other Attractions

Museums Museums are scattered around the city, though most visitors only bother taking in the Muzium Negara and the rest are for those with special interests.

The **Numismatic Museum** houses an interesting collection of coins and notes. It's in the Maybank building at 100 Jalan Tun Perak, near the Puduraya bus and taxi station. It is open daily from 10 am to 6 pm and admission is free.

Five km north of the city on Jalan Padang Tembak, the **Armed Forces Museum** has a collection of weapons, paintings, uniforms and other military paraphernalia inside, and cannons and tanks outside. The museum is open Saturday to Thursday from 10 am to 6 pm, and admission is free. In the same area is the **Police Museum** on Jalan Semarak, which is open daily from 8 am to 3.15 pm, except Saturday and Sunday, when it closes at noon. Both of these museums can be reached on a No 19 or 20 minibus from Jalan Tun HS Lee in Chinatown. At the Malaysian Air Force Base six km from the city centre, the **Air Force Museum** is just a hangar with a few light planes and air force memorabilia. You can get there on a Sri Jaya bus No 13 from Jalan Hang Jebat.

International Buddhist Pagoda This modern pagoda is in the south of KL, off Jalan Tun Sambanthan in the Brickfields area. On the same site is a Bodhi tree and a Buddhist shrine dating back to late last century, built by Sinhalese Buddhists. Minibus No 12 from Kelang bus station will take you there.

Markets

KL's lively streets are host to busy **pasar malam** (night markets), where hawker food stalls set up and a variety of goods are on sale. The Saturday night market along Jalan Tuanku Abdul Rahman is one of the best in the city, and Jalan Petaling in Chinatown is

PLACES TO STAY

1 Rex Hotel
2 TI Lodge
3 Coliseum Hotel
19 Travellers' Moon Lodge
20 Travellers' Home
21 KL City Lodge
22 Kawana Tourist Inn
32 Backpackers Travellers Lodge
36 Colonial Hotel
37 Hotel Furama
38 Backpackers Travellers Inn
39 Hotel Malaya
43 Starlight Hotel
44 Mandarin Hotel
45 Wan Kow Hotel
46 CT Guest House
47 Lee Mun Travellers Inn
48 Swiss Inn
49 YWCA
51 Hotel Lok Ann
52 Hotel City Inn
64 Riverside Lodge
65 KL International Youth Hostel

PLACES TO EAT

5 Kapitan's Club
26 McDonald's
27 Restoran Yusoof
34 KFC
35 Angel Cake House
40 Food Centre
55 Food Stalls

OTHER

4 Little India Night Market
6 Masjid Little India
7 City Hall
8 Kuala Lumpur Visitors Centre
9 St Mary's Cathedral
10 High Court
11 Royal Selangor Club
12 Masjid Jamek
13 Sultan Abdul Samad Building
14 Hongkong Bank
15 Telekom Building
16 Standard Chartered Bank
17 Infokraf Handicrafts Centre
18 Central Market Annex
23 Puduraya Bus & Taxi Station
24 Kota Raya
25 S&M Shopping Arcade
28 Central Market
29 Dayabumi Complex
30 British Council
31 GPO
33 Standard Chartered Bank
41 Sri Mahamariamman Temple
42 Jalan Sultan Mohammed Bus Stand (Airport Buses)
50 Swimming Pool
53 UDA Ocean Plaza
54 Kelang Bus Stand
56 Masjid Negara (National Mosque)
57 Islamic Centre
58 KL Railway Station
59 National Art Gallery
60 UMBC Building
61 Chan See Shu Yuen Temple
62 Khoon Yam Temple
63 Stadium Merdeka

an incredibly busy market, open day and night, and an excellent place to have a Chinese *al fresco* meal or snack or pick up some cheap clothes or a kg of lychees or mangoes – well worth a visit.

In the Kampung Bahru area north-east of the city centre is the site, each Saturday night along Jalan Raja Muda, for KL's **Sunday Market (Pasar Minggu)**, so-called because it continues through into Sunday morning. It's a food and produce market, a handicrafts market and a place to sample a wide variety of Malay foods. Also in the north of town is the **Chow Kit Market**, which lines Jalan Tuanku Abdul Rahman and the backstreets around the Asia Hotel (not on the nearby Jalan Chow Kit). This is an incredibly busy place from early morning until late at night. During the day the stalls sell all manner of bits and pieces while after 6 pm the food stalls take over.

Another huge market is the **Pudu Market**, on Jalan Pudu about three km south-east of the city centre in the area around Jalan Pasar Baru, near the intersection of Jalan Pudu and Jalan Tun Razak. This is predominantly a Chinese-run wet (produce) market, but it's very colourful and well worth a visit. It's definitely a *wet* market – it's a good idea to wear shoes rather than thongs or sandals. At the market stalls you can get every imaginable type of fruit, vegetable, fish and meat – everything from a chicken's foot (from a chicken slaughtered and butchered on the spot) to a stingray fillet or a pig's penis. Minibus No 25 from Jalan Simpang near Chinatown runs close by.

Swimming Pool

There's a public swimming pool next to the Chinwoo Stadium, on the rise just off Jalan Hang Jebat, just a couple of minutes' walk from Chinatown.

Places to Stay

The main area for cheap accommodation is Chinatown, near the Puduraya bus and taxi station. Chinatown is noisy, traffic-clogged and grotty, but very central, always lively

Hash House Harriers

The internationally known Hash House Harriers was first established in KL in 1938 by a group of British colonials who found themselves drinking too much and needing exercise. 'Hash house' was the nickname for the dining room of the Selangor Club Chambers, a social centre of the times. The harrier idea of a group of runners chasing papers along trails set by an appointed member (the 'hare') was not altogether new – previous groups had existed in KL, Ipoh, Johor Bahru and Melaka in colonial Malaya. In Shanghai and Kuching the sport was carried out on horseback. However, it was the original Hash House Harriers (HHHs) that institutionalised the chase to such a degree that it became an expat tradition all over Asia.

Until 1961 there was only the KL Hash, but in the following year a second chapter opened in Singapore, followed by Brunei, Kuching, Kota Kinabalu, Ipoh and Penang. Eventually the first group outside Singapore/Malaysia was opened in Perth in 1967. There are now around 500 HHHs in 70 countries and there are annual interhash meetings held at a different place each year.

A few hours in advance of a hash run, the hare goes to the run site – which changes with each run – and lays an irregular trail (sometimes including false trails) using paper markers. The point is to allow faster runners to scout for the next bit of trail while slower harriers catch up. The run begins with a call of 'on, on' – the slogan of all HHHs – and when looking for paper markers runners shout out 'are you?', to which runners ahead reply 'checking' to help in trail-finding. A typical run lasts one to 1½ hours and is followed by beer drinking at the end of the trail and a meal at a local restaurant. In KL the meals are usually at a Chinese restaurant and each runner contributes about RM8 to cover costs.

There are several branches in the KL area, including one for men only (the original tradition) and one for women only (the Hash House Harriettes). The rest are mixed. Most of the larger Malaysian towns have their own branches. All Malaysian hash clubs have locals among their membership.

The hash welcomes guest participants. For those so inclined, a hash run would be an interesting way to meet both locals and expats while seeing a bit of the Malaysian countryside (runs tend to be held in secondary jungle areas, or on rubber or palm-oil estates). For information, write to the Kuala Lumpur Hash House Harriers, PO Box 10182, Kuala Lumpur. ■

and interesting to wander around. Most of KL's backpackers' guesthouses are found here, and Chinatown also has a good selection of mid-range hotels.

The Jalan Tuanku Abdul Rahman area also has a few cheap and mid-range hotels and a couple of guesthouses. Though not quite as convenient as Chinatown, it is still central and lively during the day. Since the red-light district around here has been cleaned out, it tends to be quiet at night, except Saturday night when the city's best night market is held along Jalan Tuanku Abdul Rahman.

The main area for mid-range and top end hotels is the Golden Triangle district, to the east of the downtown area, where you'll find most of KL's shopping malls and nightlife. Lively Jalan Bukit Bintang is a good hunting ground for mid-range hotels and a large number of luxury hotels are scattered around nearby.

Places to Stay – bottom end

Bottom-end accommodation in KL consists of a variety of ever-dwindling Chinese hotels and a choice of guesthouses. Many of the cheap hotels are very seedy and run-down, and their days are numbered. As a rule, hotels with signs written only in Malay, 'Rumah Tumpangan', are long-term boarding houses or offer more than just rooms.

Guesthouses KL has a number of guesthouses which cater almost exclusively to budget travellers. They typically have partitioned rooms in city buildings, so rooms with a window are rare. Accommodation in general is expensive in KL, so you don't get a lot for your money. Most travellers doing it on the cheap find these places ideal for a few days, though some of these guesthouses are overdue for an overhaul. They all offer similar services: dorm beds as well as rooms, washing facilities and a noticeboard and they will book buses. The better places fill up quickly and it can be difficult to find a cheap room if you arrive in the evening.

Right on the edge of Chinatown and only a few minutes' walk from the Puduraya bus and taxi station is the *Travellers' Moon Lodge* (☎ 03-230 6601) at 36C Jalan Silang. It is crammed with hot, little plywood-walled rooms for RM20, but the hallway dorm on the top floor next to the rooftop breakfast area is at least cooler and costs RM8.50. Plenty of travellers seem to find it just fine, for it is always packed. A breakfast of toast, tea and coffee is included. Just a few doors along, and run by the same people, is the *Travellers Home* (☎ 03-230 6601) at 46C Jalan Silang. It is smaller and quieter with larger, better rooms for RM23, but breakfast is not included.

Also in Chinatown, at 60 Jalan Sultan, is the *Backpackers Travellers Inn* (☎ 03-238 2473). This is another popular place, and though a little cramped with typically small and windowless rooms, it's clean and well run. Dorm beds cost RM8, or RM10 with air-con. A variety of singles/doubles range from RM22/25 with fan up to RM40/50 with air-con.

Their offshoot, the more spacious *Backpackers Travellers Lodge* (☎ 03-201 0889), 158 Jalan TN HS Lee, is one of the better guesthouses. Clean rooms start at RM25 with fan and range up to RM50 with air-con and attached bathroom. Dorm beds cost RM8. There's a good, if spartan, TV lounge and the usual variety of services are offered.

Close by at Wisma BWT, 103 Jalan Petaling, is the *CT Guest House* (☎ 03-232 0417). It's a little scruffy but quite acceptable place smack in the middle of Chinatown, and the street outside at night is a busy market. Dorm beds cost RM9 in four-bed rooms, while most rooms are RM24 single or double with breakfast.

Also in Chinatown is the *Lee Mun Travellers Inn* on the 5th floor of the Bangunan Luen Seng Bersaudara on the corner of Jalan Sultan and Jalan Petaling. Double rooms for RM20 are large and the dorm costs RM10, but this place needs a good scrub. Consider it if the other places are full.

The *KL City Lodge* (☎ 03-230 5275) at 16 Jalan Pudu is right opposite the bus station. This is more a regular, scruffy hotel but still draws a few travellers. Dorm beds cost RM8 or RM10 with air-con, while rooms are RM20/25 for singles/doubles or RM35 with air-con. In the same area, the quiet *Kawana Tourist Inn* (☎ 03-238 6714) at 68 Jalan Pudu Lama is well kept with good rooms, but the dorms are tiny and the place lacks atmosphere. Dorm beds cost RM12, while double rooms cost RM30 with fan up to RM50 with air-con.

North of the centre, just off Jalan Raja Laut, is the very friendly, family-run *Ben Soo Homestay* (☎ 03-291 8096) at 61B Jalan Tiong Nam, near the Sentosa Hotel. Dorm beds in this small homestay are RM10 and double rooms with fan are RM25 up to RM35, all including breakfast. Dorms have only four beds and all rooms have windows and are light and airy. If you ring Ben Soo on his mobile phone (☎ 010-332 7013) from the bus or railway station, he will come and pick you up.

Further north, between Jalan Raja Laut and Jalan Tuanku Abdul Rahman, is the *Transit Villa* (☎ 03-441 0443) at 36-2 Jalan Chow Kit, near the 7-Eleven store at the northern end of Jalan Raja Laut. Dorm beds cost RM12, while rooms cost RM22/29. It's a reasonable place but not popular with travellers.

Also in this area, at 319-1 Jalan Tuanku Abdul Rahman, you'll find the *Paradise Lodge* (☎ 03-292 2872), a more expensive bed & breakfast. Singles/doubles cost RM25/35, or RM35/45 with air-con. A basic breakfast is also included.

Similar but a little better is the friendly *TI Lodge* (☎ 03-293 0261), in the heart of Little India at 20 Lorong Bunus Enam. Good rooms, most newly painted, cost RM40 with fan, RM45 with air-con and RM55 with air-con and attached bath. Breakfast is included.

Another place worthy of mention is the *Riverside Lodge* (☎ 03-201 1210) in a quiet area at 80A Jalan Rotan, a small street off Jalan Kampung Attap just south of Chinatown. It's very close to the brown landmark UMBC building. It's a friendly little place with dorm beds for RM8 and large, clean rooms for RM20, RM23 and RM25. Though a fair way from the action, it is close to the railway station.

Nearby, the *KL International Youth Hostel* (☎ 03-230 6870) is at 21 Jalan Kampung Attap, about five minutes' walk south of Chinatown. Beds cost RM15 for the first night, RM12 on subsequent nights. It is fully air-con and only a short walk from the railway station.

At the top of the guesthouse range is the *Bonanza Hotel* (☎ 03-244 8053) on Jalan Bukit Bintang at No 72 next to the Bintang Warisan Hotel. This place offers a bit more space than the Chinatown guesthouses but is also more expensive because of its location. A dorm bed costs RM20 and there are rooms for RM30/45 (RM40/60 with air-con).

Finally, there are the Ys. The *YMCA* (☎ 03-274 1439) at 95 Jalan Padang Belia, south of the centre off Jalan Tun Sambanthan, has good if slightly expensive accommodation. Its distance from the centre makes it an unattractive option, unless you have your own transport. Rooms cost RM38/50 and range up to RM75 for four-bed rooms. Take minibus No 12 and ask for the Lido Cinema.

The *YWCA* (☎ 03-283 225) is much more central at 12 Jalan Hang Jebat. It has plain but acceptable rooms for women at RM30/50 and for couples from RM50, and family rooms are also available.

Hotels – Jalan Tuanku Abdul Rahman

Moving up Jalan Tuanku Abdul Rahman from its junction with Jalan Tun Perak, there's the *Coliseum Hotel* (☎ 03-292 6270) at No 100 with its famous old planters' restaurant and bar downstairs. All rooms share common bath facilities and cost RM22 with fan, RM30 for a double with air-con. The rooms are a little run-down but large and quiet and the location is very good. It's a very good deal for KL; consequently it is often full.

Jalan Tuanku Abdul Rahman also has a couple of other basic but cheap hotels. At No 136 the *Tivoli Hotel* (☎ 03-292 4108) is a reasonable Chinese cheapie which charges RM25 for rooms with fan and common bath. The *Rex Hotel* nearby at No 132 is similar.

Hotels – Chinatown Cheapest of the Chinese cheapies is the well-camouflaged *Wan Kow Hotel* at 16 Jalan Sultan. Very basic rooms with fan and common bath cost RM25.

Also very cheap is the *Colonial Hotel* (☎ 03-238 0336) at 39 Jalan Sultan, where singles/doubles go for RM24/30, or RM34 with air-con. This hotel is more geared towards travellers, but the noisy, wire-topped rooms are run-down. Check for peep-holes. There are many more cheap hotels in Chinatown, most of them short-time places.

More expensive is the *Starlight Hotel* (☎ 03-238 9811) at 90 Jalan Hang Kasturi, right opposite the Kelang bus station. It has doubles with bath and air-con from RM55/70. The rooms are large although sparsely furnished, and some cop the noise from the bus station across the road.

Places to Stay – middle

KL has a good selection of mid-range hotels, but prices are higher than elsewhere in Malaysia. In the past few years new mid-range hotels have cropped up and more are being built, so increased competition means that discounts are often offered, especially in the more expensive hotels. Air-conditioning, attached bathroom and TV are standard facilities at these hotels.

Chinatown On Jalan Sultan near Jalan Tun HS Lee is the quiet *Hotel City Inn* (☎ 03-238 9190). The rooms are comfortable but small. It's central and reasonable value at RM69/80. Just a few doors along is the comfortable *Hotel Lok Ann* (☎ 03-238 9544) at 113A Jalan Petaling, where you'll pay RM60/74 for a single/double. The only problem here is that all the rooms overlook the noisy Jalan Sultan, although things usually quieten down by about 11 pm.

Chinatown has a number of more luxurious hotels in this range. The *Hotel Malaya* (☎ 03-232 7722; fax 03-230 0980), on the corner of Jalan Tun HS Lee and Jalan Hang Lekir, has good double rooms for RM140 and RM160, before discount. There's also a good restaurant and coffee shop here.

Also worth trying is the *Hotel Furama* (☎ 03-230 1777; fax 03-230 2110) in the Kompleks Selangor on Jalan Sultan. Rooms in this relatively modern high-rise cost RM128/148. The *Mandarin Hotel* (☎ 03-230 3000; fax 03-230 4363), 2-8 Jalan Sultan, is a smaller but similar hotel with rooms from RM115/126.

The *Swiss Inn* (☎ 03-232 3333; fax 03-201 6699), 62 Jalan Sultan, is a very popular, new hotel right in the heart of Chinatown. Comfortable, spotless rooms cost RM136 to RM159 and the hotel has a lounge bar with live music and a good coffee shop that is popular for its cheap buffet breakfasts. Widely advertised rates of RM100 are only for certain rooms and often not available.

The *Hotel Puduraya* (☎ 03-232 1000; fax 03-230 5567) is on top of the Puduraya bus and taxi station. This large high-rise is a little faded but has well-appointed rooms for RM104/115. The hotel has a good coffee shop and a couple of bars. It may be ideal if you are overnighting for bus or taxi connections, but the hot and chaotic bus station downstairs does not offer a welcoming face to KL for longer stays.

Jalan Tuanku Abdul Rahman The *Shiraz Hotel* (☎ 03-292 2625) at 1 Jalan Medan Tuanku on the corner of Jalan Tuanku Abdul Rahman is an unremarkable place at the bottom of this range and has rooms for RM70.

The *Kowloon Hotel* (☎ 03-293 4246; fax 03-292 6548) at 142 Jalan Tuanku Abdul Rahman is one of the older breed of modern hotels. It has an infamous reputation because of its health club on the 2nd floor, but guests are not disturbed. Rooms costing from RM85/103 could do with an upgrade but are clean, large and well appointed.

At the top end of Jalan Tuanku Abdul Rahman is the *Asia Hotel* (☎ 03-292 6077; fax 03-292 27734) at 69 Jalan Haji Hussein. This long-running place is quite popular and upgraded rooms are of a high standard. Rooms start at RM156 for standard double rooms, but large discounts are often available.

Jalan Bukit Bintang Jalan Bukit Bintang, just to the east of the city centre at the edge of the Golden Triangle, has a large selection of mid-range hotels and the competition means that discounts are often available. It's a lively street good for shopping, eating and nightlife.

The *Malaysia Hotel* (☎ 03-242 8033; fax 03-242 8033) at 67 Jalan Bukit Bintang is looking a little down at heel but provides comfortable accommodation. It costs RM118/128 for twin/double rooms, including breakfast.

Across the street, the *Cardogan Hotel* (☎ 03-244 4856; fax 03-244 4865) at No 64 is similar but a touch better appointed. Standard rooms cost RM128 and deluxe rooms are RM160, plus 15%. All rooms have minibar as well as the usual facilities.

At No 106, the *Agora Hotel* (☎ 03-242 8133; fax 03-245 8133) is an old hotel that has undergone a major facelift. Good singles/doubles cost RM117/135.

The *Bintang Warisan Hotel* (☎ 03-248 8111; fax 03-248 2333) at No 68 is a larger, new hotel and the best of all the mid-range Bukit Bintang hotels. Singles/doubles start at RM120/140, plus 15%.

Not far from Jalan Bukit Bintang is the small *Lodge Hotel* (☎ 03-242 0122; fax 03-241 6819) on Jalan Sultan Ismail. This older motel-style place has a small swimming pool next to its Indian restaurant. Musty rooms for RM92 in the 'annex' building have seen better days, but rooms in the main building are more comfortable and cost RM115 and RM138.

Railway Station The *Heritage Hotel* (☎ 03-273 5588; fax 03-273 2842), housed in KL's magnificent colonial railway station, is open again after renovations. The hotel has some fine old touches but most rooms have modern decor. Rooms cost RM180 and RM230, plus 15%, but expect substantial discounts. Suite rooms are still being refurbished in grander colonial style.

Places to Stay – top end

Kuala Lumpur has a profusion of luxury hotels, and many of the cranes that dot the skyline are working on new additions to the KL hotel scene. They cater primarily to business travellers, and despite the huge number of luxury hotel rooms, occupancy rates are high. All of these hotels have a swimming pool and a host of restaurants and bars. Many offer discounts on the regular rates quoted here, but advance bookings through travel agents will reap a better deal. All add 5% tax and 10% service charge to the rates.

Most luxury hotels are found in the Golden Triangle commercial district. Jalan Sultan Ismail has the biggest collection, including the ever-popular *Hilton*, the huge *Shangri-La* and the recently overhauled *Concorde*, which is home to the very popular Hard Rock Cafe. The older *Equatorial* has also been recently renovated. The *Istana* on the corner with Raja Jalan Chulan has one of the most impressive lobbies and is favoured by visiting dignitaries. At the bottom end of Jalan Sultan Ismail, the *Parkroyal* is next to Lot 10 and handy for other shopping plazas. Just around the corner on Jalan Imbi, the *Melia Kuala Lumpur* has all the facilities though is not quite up with the best.

Set among the mid-range hotels on Jalan Bukit Bintang, the *Federal* was the first modern luxury hotel in KL, dating from independence, and it is smaller and slightly cheaper than the new hotels. Nearby on Jalan Pudu the *Swiss Garden* is on a busy, dead stretch of the street but close enough to the action. At the northern end of Jalan Bukit Bintang, the impressive *Regent* is well located and in the superluxury category.

The eastern end of Jalan Ampang also has a few top end hotels, and more are being built. The *Ming Court* is close to shopping possibilities. Nearby on Jalan Tun Razak is the *Crown Princess*, while a few hundred metres south, *Mi Casa* is an apartment hotel with suite-style rooms.

The Holiday Inn chain has two hotels in KL. The *Holiday Inn on the Park* is on Jalan Pinang in the Golden Triangle, while the older *Holiday Inn City Centre* is indeed in the city centre, on Jalan Raja Laut. Further north are the *Pan Pacific* at the Putra World Trade Centre, and across the road is the new *Legend* in The Mall.

For colonial style, the *Carcosa Seri Negara* comprises two magnificent colonial mansions in tranquil gardens at the western edge of the Lake Gardens. Carcosa was the residence of

Thaipusam

Each year in the Hindu month of Thai (January/February), when the constellation of Pusam is in its ascendancy, up to a million devotees and onlookers flock to the Batu Caves to honour Lord Subramaniam (sometimes called Muruga). His chariot takes pride of place and is attended by thousands of devotees as it makes its way from KL's Sri Mahamariamman Temple to the Batu Caves.

The greatest spectacle is the *kavadi* carriers, the devotees who subject themselves to masochistic acts as fulfilment for answered prayers. Many of the devotees carry offerings of milk in *paal kudam*, or milk pots, often connected to the skin by hooks. Others pierce their tongues and cheeks with hooks, skewers and tridents. Couples whose prayers for children have been answered carry their babies in saffron cradles made of sugar cane stalks.

Most spectacular are the vel kavadis, great cages of spikes that pierce the skin of the carrier and are decorated with peacock feathers, pictures of deities and flowers. To the beating of drums and chants of 'Vel, Vel' the devotees form a constant procession to the caves and up the 272 steps to the main shrine.

Originating in Tamil Nadu and now banned in India, this is the most spectacular Hindu festival in Malaysia, celebrated with the greatest gusto in Kuala Lumpur. It is also celebrated in Penang at the Nattukotai Chettiar Temple and the Arulmigu Balathandayuthapani Temple, and in Johor Bahru at the Sri Thandayuthabani Temple. Ipoh also attracts a large number of devotees, who follow the procession from the Sri Mariamar Temple in Buntong to the Sri Subramaniar Temple in Gunung Cheroh. In Singapore the procession goes from the Sri Srinivasa Perumal Temple to the Chettiar Hindu Temple.

Below: A devotee carries a vel kavadi to the Batu Caves during the Thaipusam festival in KL.

PAUL BEINSSEN

Top: Devotees must make their way up the 272 steps to the Batu Caves.

Bottom Left: Her cheeks and tongue pierced with skewers, an entranced woman takes part in the procession in Singapore.

Bottom Right: In Singapore a penitent proceeds to the sound of drums to the Chettiar Hindu Temple.

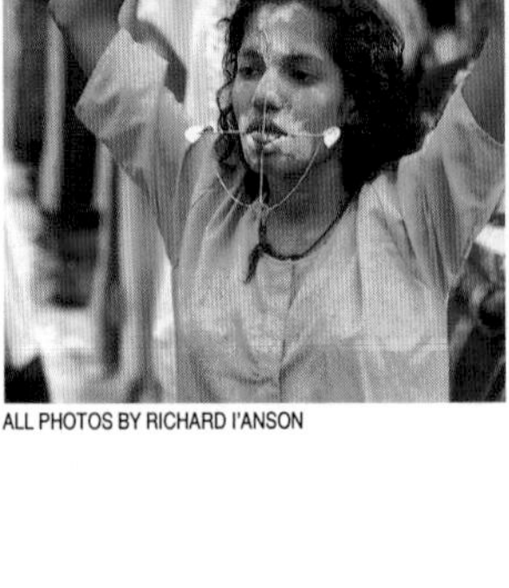

ALL PHOTOS BY RICHARD I'ANSON

Sir Frank Swettenham, the British Resident, and Seri Negara was the official guesthouse. They now house 14 luxury suites.

Carcosa Seri Negara, Taman Tasik Perdana
(☎ 03-282 188; fax 03-282 7888). Suites RM950 to RM2600.
Concorde Hotel, 2 Jalan Sultan
(☎ 03-244 2200; fax 03-244 1628). Rooms from RM220.
Crown Princess Hotel, City Square Centre, Jalan Tun Razak
(☎ 03-262 5522; fax 03-262 4492). Rooms from RM360.
Equatorial Hotel, Jalan Sultan Ismail
(☎ 03-261 7777; fax 03-261 9020). Rooms from RM280/300.
Federal Hotel, 35 Jalan Bukit Bintang
(☎ 03-248 9166; fax 03-248 2877). Rooms from RM245/265.
Hilton Hotel, Jalan Sultan Ismail
(☎ 03-242 2222; fax 03-292 9069). Rooms from RM370/400.
Holiday Inn City Centre, Jalan Raja Laut
(☎ 03-293 9233; fax 03-293 9634). Rooms from RM280/310.
Holiday Inn on the Park, Jalan Pinang
(☎ 03-248 1066; fax 03-293 3964). Rooms from RM310/330.
Hotel Istana, 73 Jalan Raja Chulan
(☎ 03-241 9988; fax 03-244 0111). Rooms from RM390/420.
Legend Hotel, 100 Jalan Putra
(☎ 03-442 9888; fax 03-443 0700). Rooms from RM300/320.
Melia Kuala Lumpur, 16 Jalan Imbi
(☎ 03-242 8333; fax 03-273 1569). Rooms from RM250.
Mi Casa Hotel Apartments, 386B Jalan Tun Razak
(☎ 03-261 8833; fax 03-261 1186). Suites from RM290 to RM760.
Ming Court Hotel, Jalan Ampang
(☎ 03-261 8888; fax 03-262 3428). Rooms from RM340/370.
Pan Pacific Hotel, Jalan Putra
(☎ 03-442 5555; fax 03-441 7236). Rooms from RM350/380.
Parkroyal Hotel, Jalan Sultan Ismail
(☎ 03-242 5588; fax 03-241 4281). Rooms from RM340/370.
Regent Hotel, 160 Jalan Bukit Bintang
(☎ 03-241 8000; fax 03-242 1441). Rooms from RM490.
Shangri-La Hotel, 11 Jalan Sultan Ismail
(☎ 03-232 2388; fax 03-230 1514). Rooms from RM440.
Swiss Garden Hotel, 117 Jalan Pudu
(☎ 03-241 3333; fax 03-241 5555). Rooms from RM300.

Places to Eat

Hawker Food KL is well endowed with hawker venues, dotted all around the city.

In Chinatown, *Jalan Petaling* is closed to traffic between Jalan Cheng Lock and Jalan Sultan and tables are set up in the evenings outside the Chinese restaurants, which are on Jalan Hang Lekir between Jalan Petaling and Jalan Sultan. The stall on the corner of Jalan Sultan and Jalan Hang Lekir does steamboat. The food is on skewers and is all laid out on the table, so you just cook what you want and then pay at the end based on the number of empty skewers you have. There are also stalls in this area selling peanut pancakes, sweets, drinks and fruit.

The *Central Market* in Chinatown also has a good selection of hawker food, upstairs on the 2nd level and in the covered rooftop Taman Selera.

Other night markets with good food include the *Sunday Market* out at Kampung Bahru and the *Chow Kit Market*, just off Jalan Tuanku Abdul Rahman close to the Asia Hotel. Both are good places for Malay food, and night owls head to Chow Kit for the all-night nasi lemak stalls.

The Saturday night market on *Jalan Tuanku Abdul Rahman* has a large collection of food vendors and a great atmosphere. Most stalls sell snacks for take-aways, but a few also set up tables for eating there. Jalan Masjid India in Little India is good for both Indian and non-Indian food in the evenings.

Jalan Alor, one street west of Jalan Bukit Bintang in the Golden Triangle district, is a pleasant place to dine at open-air tables in the evening. Food stalls and coffee shops serve some of the best Chinese hawker fare in KL, and the ikan bakar (grilled fish) is superb. *Jalan Raja Chulan* in the Golden Triangle has another hawker centre just past Wisma Stephens on the left-hand side. The food here is mainly Indian and Malay.

Most shopping malls have food courts for slightly more expensive hawker food in air-con surrounds. One of the best is in The Mall shopping centre, opposite the Putra World Trade Centre on Jalan Putra. The *Medan Hang Tuah* on the top floor is a re-creation of an old city street, complete with mock shophouses, and has an excellent selection of Malay, Chinese and Indian favourites at cheap prices.

Shopping malls in the Golden Triangle also have hawker food. For something a little different, the *Chilli Food Court* in the basement of the Isetan department store in Lot 10 has a wide range of Asian food including Korean, Japanese and Vietnamese. American is also featured – a steak costs around RM15.

Indian Little India is a good hunting ground for Indian food. Plenty of coffee shops can be found in the *Jalan Masjid India/Jalan Tuanku Abdul Rahman* area, and food stalls also specialise in Indian food. It's about the cheapest Indian food around, and they serve tandoori chicken, naan, dosas and chapatis.

For something more upmarket, *Bangles*, upstairs at 60A Jalan Tuanku Abdul Rahman, is an Indian restaurant with a good reputation. Further along, the *Shiraz Hotel* on the corner of Jalan Tuanku Abdul Rahman and Jalan Medan Tuanku has a reasonable Pakistani restaurant. Some prefer the similar *Omar Khayyam* next door.

The *Bilal* restaurant at 33 Jalan Ampang is a KL institution for north Indian food at reasonable prices. Tandoori chicken and breads are featured.

In Chinatown's Central Market, *Hameed's* is a thriving, cafeteria-style restaurant with Indian noodles and curries, including fish-head curry, at low prices. Facing the market on the Jalan Hang Kasturi pedestrian mall, *Restoran Yusoof* at No 36 is another popular place for roti, biryani and other Indian Muslim fare. The original coffee shop restaurant is complemented by a slightly trendier offshoot a couple of doors along.

On Jalan Bukit Bintang the *Restoran Ramzan* has an excellent range of murtabak, biryani and curry at cheap prices.

For south Indian food, head to the Brickfields area, a couple of km south of the city centre, where there are four or five daun pisang (banana leaf) restaurants serving rice with vegetarian, fish, chicken and mutton curries. One of the best is *Devi's*.

Chinese Chinese restaurants can be found everywhere, but particularly around Chinatown and along Jalan Bukit Bintang, which is off Jalan Pudu past the Puduraya bus and taxi station.

In the Sungei Wang Plaza on Jalan Sultan Ismail near Jalan Bukit Bintang is the *Esquire Kitchen Restoran*, which is very popular for lunch, mainly because it does a RM5 set meal of soup, a Chinese dish and unlimited rice, and tea or coffee. At the entrance to this plaza is the *Super Noodle House*, which is cheap and popular. The *Mayblossom* at No 1/F inside the plaza is more upmarket, but the set meals are good value for superior Cantonese fare.

In The Mall shopping centre in the north of the city there's the Chinese fast-food answer to McDonald's. It's called *Little Eat of China*, and instead of burgers they serve noodles, dumplings, pancakes and porridge.

A local speciality in KL is bah kut teh, which is supposed to have originated in Kelang. It's pork ribs with white rice and Chinese tea and is a very popular breakfast meal. There are stalls in the Chinatown night market selling this dish.

Restoran Oversea, 88 Jalan Imbi, is a large, very popular Cantonese restaurant, with banquet-style meals for groups. All the Chinese favourites from shark's fin to belachan are served, and though moderately priced it's easy to order up big.

Malay There are Malay *warungs* (small eating stalls) and *kedai kopis* (coffee shops) throughout KL, but especially along and just off Jalan Tuanku Abdul Rahman. Several of those in the vicinity of the Coliseum Hotel are excellent and cheap; look for nasi lemak in the early mornings. The *Restoran Imaf*, just down from the Minerva Bookshop, is a good bet.

The *Kapitan's Club*, 35 Jalan Ampang, has a mixed menu that includes some Chinese and western dishes, though the food is primarily Peranakan. Curry Kapitan is a speciality, as are the savoury Peranakan pastries. Housed in a semi-restored shophouse, it has a good atmosphere and moderate prices –

you can eat well for less than RM20 per person.

Dondang Sayang in the Life Centre on Jalan Sultan Ismail is a classy restaurant, with Nyonya specialities and moderately high prices.

In the Bukit Bintang Plaza on Jalan Bukit Bintang there are a couple of Malay restaurants – the *Rasa Utara* (☎ 03-248 8369), which specialises in food from Kedah state, and the *Satay Anika*, which is more of a satay fast-food restaurant.

The *Nelayan Floating Restaurant* (☎ 03-422 8600), at Taman Tasik Titiwangsa off Jalan Kuantan in north KL, is an amazing place. Huts are built over the lake and the daily-changing menu features six cuisines. It's one of the best 'splurge' restaurants for Malay food.

Thai Thai food possibilities range from tom yam soup at food centres to some expensive Thai restaurants in the big hotels.

A cheaper restaurant is the *Thai Kitchen* (☎ 03-274 4303) in the Central Market on Jalan Hang Kasturi. Decor amounts to air-conditioning and not much else, but the food is tasty and reasonably priced.

The *Tamnak Thai* (☎ 03-245 5191), 74 Jalan Bukit Bintang, has a bit more atmosphere and an extensive menu of classic Thai dishes. Prices are very reasonable, with most mains around RM8, and an excellent meal for two without drinks will cost around RM40.

The more expensive *Barn Thai* at 370B Jalan Tun Razak is as popular for the live music as for the Thai food. *Mekong* (☎ 03-262 5522) in the Crown Princess Hotel on Jalan Tun Razak serves Vietnamese as well as Thai dishes in very stylish surrounds.

Japanese As usual, Japanese food is expensive. *Edo Sushi*, 39 Jalan Sultan Ismail, is more reasonably priced for sushi served on the conveyor belt bar. Set meals for around RM20 are good value. The *Edo Kirin* in the Regent Hotel on Jalan Bukit Bintang has excellent Japanese food at suitably breathtaking prices. The *Kampachi* in the Hotel Equatorial on Jalan Sultan Ismail is also good and expensive, but cheaper set meals are available.

Western KL has a surprising variety of western restaurants. Not to be missed is the restaurant in the *Coliseum Hotel* on Jalan Tuanku Abdul Rahman, which has excellent steaks. When they say it's served on a sizzle plate they really mean it; the waiters zip up behind you and whip a bib around your neck to protect your clothes from the sizzle. For around RM20 you can get a great steak and salad, and it also does roast chicken and grilled fillet of sole with chips. The place is quite a colonial experience and has scarcely changed over the years.

American fast-food outlets abound, including, at the bottom of Jalan Tuanku Abdul Rahman, *KFC* and *A&W* takeaways. *McDonald's* are ubiquitous, and outlets can be found opposite the Central Market and on Jalan Bukit Bintang.

Cal's Diner in the basement of the Lot 10 shopping centre on Jalan Sultan Ismail recreates an American diner and has burgers, dogs and American breakfasts. Also in the basement, *Kafe El Pama* is a pleasant little Mediterranean cafe with fare ranging from spaghetti to felafel and shawarma (RM6.50).

In Chinatown, the *Angel Cake House* on Jalan Sultan is a good bakery. They offer all kinds of buns and rolls stuffed with chicken curry or cheeses and fresh from the oven. Also available are pizza, macaroni, fruit tarts and chocolate cakes.

The *Delifrance* chain is good for pastries and coffee. Branches can be found at The Mall on Jalan Putra and Lot 10 on Jalan Sultan Ismail, while the Star Hill shopping mall on Jalan Bukit Bintang has the more upmarket, bistro-style *La Brasserie de Delifrance*.

Le Coq d'Or (☎ 03-261 9732), a restaurant in a fine turn-of-the-century mansion at 121 Jalan Ampang, is not quite as expensive as the elegant surroundings might indicate. Western food is served in the dark, cavernous interior, which has faded touches of the raj. Expect to pay around RM80 for two at dinner, or the set lunch with a main of fish, lamb chops etc is excellent value for RM9 plus 15%. It's open daily from noon to 2.30 pm and 7 to 10 pm.

Cafe Le Parc (☎ 03-264 8289), 3rd floor, City Square Centre, Jalan Tun Razak, has superb Italian food, with authentic and innovative dishes. Meat dishes such as scaloppine cost around RM35, while pastas are around RM20. With the expensive drinks the bill soon mounts, but the set lunch for only RM20 is good value.

American grills are easy enough to find. *TGIF* (Thank God It's Friday) in the Life Centre on Jalan Sultan Ismail is very popular, especially on Fridays, for steaks (RM35), or pizzas and pasta cost around RM22. Over the road is *Bierkeller* in the Menara Haw Par, for bratwurst washed down with German beer. Many of the bars and nightspots around town are popular dining spots for grills, such as the *Hard Rock Cafe*. Get there early before the music starts, the crowds queue and service becomes difficult.

Self-Catering For self-catering, you can find supermarkets in Chinatown at the S&M Shopping Arcade on Jalan Chen Lock and at the UDA Ocean Plaza on the corner of Jalan Sultan and Jalan Tun HS Lee. On Jalan Tuanku Abdul Rahman, Sogo department store has a well-stocked supermarket. Many of the shopping malls and department stores in the Golden Triangle have supermarkets, including one in the basement of the Isetan department store in Lot 10 on Jalan Sultan Ismail.

Entertainment

Bars, Discos & Live Music KL's burgeoning nightlife is mostly found in the Golden Triangle. Jalan Sultan Ismael is the centre of the universe for KL's middle class, while bored youth who can't afford the prices at the fashionable bars and clubs hang out in front of McDonald's on a Friday and Saturday night. Wannabe Hell's Angels compare 100cc sports bikes and conduct impromptu drag races along Sultan Ismail. The roar is deafening, and heaven help you if you are caught in the middle of the street when the traffic lights change.

The *Hard Rock Cafe* in the Concorde Hotel on Jalan Sultan Ismail is still the hottest spot in town. It has the usual food-and-rock memorabilia blend. Bands play from 11 pm, interspersed with disco music for dancing. Like most night spots, it is open until 2 am every night, except Friday and Saturday, when it rocks until 3 am and the queues stretch down the street. There's no cover charge, although you do have to order and pay for one drink to get in the door.

For a change of pace, *Bierkeller* in the Menara Haw Par opposite the Hard Rock Cafe has an older clientele of expats and tourists in search of German food, German magazines and a large selection of brews.

A short stroll behind the Hard Rock Cafe, *Brannigans* and *Modesto's* are next to each other on Lorong Perak, an alleyway that runs into Jalan P Ramlee. Long-running Brannigans has a reputation as a pick-up spot, which means that it is packed with men. Modesto's is currently a very popular club, with the latest pop music and lots of trendy KL-ites. Drinks are cheaper on Tuesday, Wednesday is ladies' night and Italian food is served throughout the week.

The Shangri-La Hotel on Jalan Sultan Ismail is home to *Club Oz*, an upmarket disco with dance music and occasional bands. A two-drink cover charge of RM30 applies and dress is designer label.

Around the corner from the Shangri-La, *Fire* in the Menara Sabre on Lorong P Ramlee is a techno disco popular with teenyboppers.

The *Shark Club* on Sultan Ismail near the Hotel Istana is open 24 hours and packs in the crowds. On weekends a band plays downstairs next to the open-air BBQ area, while the upstairs bar has darts, backgammon and 'fun pub' activities like arm wrestling, though drinking is the favourite pastime. There's no cover charge.

Kafe Blues in the Lot 10 shopping centre on the corner of Jalan Sultan Ismail and Jalan Bukit Bintang features local jazz and blues musicians. The bar is small and the volume is cranked up high; the open-air terrace facing the street offers a respite and serves grills.

Nearby in the Parkroyal Hotel, *Karrumba* is a world music bar playing everything from reggae to cha cha cha, with a fair smattering of pop. Cover charges vary with the band, and the crowd is moneyed.

Other popular discos in the Golden Triangle include *Betelnut* on Jalan Penang near the Holiday Inn on the Park. On Jalan Tun Razak, about half a km east of Jalan Imbi, *The Jump* is a well-patronised club in the Wisma Inai. At 370B Jalan Tun Razak, *Barn Thai* is a Thai restaurant and long-running jazz/rock joint with a good atmosphere – bands play from around 11 pm to 3 am on weekends.

Chinatown is quiet in the evenings, but the Central Market has a few places for a drink. Well off the yuppie circuit, they are not particularly lively but cheaper and down to earth. Facing the river on the western side of the market, the *Riverbank* has the occasional jazz band or guitar strummer. You can also sit outside for a break from the smoky interior. Tuesday, Thursday and Sunday are all-night happy hours. A few doors away, the *Bull's Head* is an English-style pub. Despite the decor, it's Eagles on the jukebox and Anchor on tap, but the beer is cheap, conversation is audible and you can sit outside and snack on curries and breads from a tandoori hawker.

Or step back in time to the bar at the *Coliseum Hotel* on Jalan Tuanku Abdul Rahman, where you can sip a beer and chat to the regulars.

Cultural Shows The *Malaysian Tourist Information Centre* (☎ 03-264 3929) on Jalan Ampang has traditional dance performances (RM2) at 3.30 pm on Tuesday, Thursday, Saturday and Sunday, and other special events, usually in the evening. The centre produces monthly brochures listing events in the city, or ring for details.

The *Central Market* (☎ 03-274 6542) has a regular program of events ranging from Indian dancing and *pencak silat* martial arts performances to Malay comedy nights. Free performances are held at 7.45 pm on Friday, Saturday and Sunday. Pick up a copy of their monthly calendar from the tourist offices.

Hotels and restaurants also have dinner cultural shows. Regular venues include the *Restoran Seri Melayu* (☎ 03-245 1833), I Jalan Conlay, behind the Karyaneka Handicraft Centre, which serves Malay food and stages mostly Malay and Indian dances for RM45 plus taxes. *Titiwangsa Seafood Village* (☎ 03-421 8585), Jalan Temerluh at Taman Tasik Titiwangsa, and the rather exclusive *Eden Village Restaurant* (☎ 03-241 1093), 260 Jalan Raja Chulan, also have dance performances.

Cinemas There are plenty of cinemas in the central area. Check the *New Straits Times* or other dailies for listings. Kungfu extravaganzas, Indian musicals and B-grade American adventure movies are the norm, but the occasional Hollywood blockbuster gets shown without being dubbed. The various cultural centres sometimes show films.

Things to Buy

KL promotes itself as a shopping haven, and certainly the city has plenty of shopping malls to cater to increasingly affluent Malaysians. Clothes and shoes are reasonably priced, and though not as cheap as the neighbouring countries of Thailand and Indonesia, the range is better. Electronics are reasonably priced, but Singapore has a much wider range at lower prices. KL is very competitively priced for camera gear and film.

KL is the best place to buy handicrafts in Malaysia, but high wages mean that Malaysia produces very few handicrafts these days. Traditional Malay pottery and kites can be found, but almost everything else is imported from Indonesia, Thailand or elsewhere. However, attractive jewellery, wood carvings, lacquerware, *kris* knives etc can be found.

Shops & Markets The Central Market complex, housed in a cavernous Art Deco building (formerly a wet market) in Chinatown, is a fun place to shop and offers a large

The *kris*, an ornate wavy-bladed knife, is a popular souvenir.

range of souvenirs, antiques, art, clothes and more. Some of the antique shops are interesting for old bric-a-brac, and Wan Tradisi at shop M51 has a good collection of Malaysian kites. Stalls sell cheap jewellery, while the art shops can be very expensive. Bargain.

Jalan Petaling in the heart of Chinatown is one of the most colourful shopping streets in KL, particularly at night. This roadside market has a some craftwork, cheap clothes and copy watches. Hard bargaining is definitely in order.

The Karyaneka Handicraft Centre, out past the Hilton on Jalan Raja Chulan, displays a wide variety of local craftwork in quasi-traditional settings. Hours are from 9 am to 6 pm.

Jalan Tuanku Abdul Rahman has a variety of shops selling goods including local crafts along the arcade known as Aked Ibu Kota, opposite the Coliseum Hotel. Further north, stalls along the street at the Chow Kit Market sell cheap clothes and leather goods. Jalan Masjid India is the place to shop for saris, Indian silks and other textiles. Jalan Melayu has Indonesian religious goods and also local batik and other art.

Pewterware, made from high-quality Malaysian tin, is an important local craft. Royal Selangor Pewter is the main manufacturer and its pewter is available all over town in department stores and shops. Its factory is at 4 Jalan Usahawan, eight km north-east of central KL. It is open Monday to Saturday from 8.30 am to 4.45 pm, and 9 am to 4 pm on Sunday.

Shopping Malls KL's many shopping malls are the place to go for clothes, shoes, electronics, cameras and everyday goods. The Golden Triangle has the biggest selection. Shopping malls are generally open from 10 am to 10 pm, but smaller shops in the malls start closing around 9 pm.

Sungei Wang Plaza on Jalan Sultan Ismail and the BB Plaza on Jalan Bukit Bintang adjoin each other to form one of the biggest and best complexes. The Metrojaya and Parkson Grand department stores combine with hundreds of small shops to sell just about everything, but these malls are particularly good for clothes, shoes, books and camera gear. Two other nearby malls are Lot 10 and Star Hill, both on Jalan Bukit Bintang. These new, upmarket malls sell designer labels, and Star Hill also features children's wear, toy shops and a playground on the top floor.

Imbi Plaza, around the corner on Jalan Imbi, is a small complex specialising in computers. It's a good place to pick up dirt-cheap software and CD-ROMs.

The large Weld shopping centre, with the Weld Supermarket and a number of other shops in the same complex, is on Jalan Raja Chulan.

On Jalan Ampang, Ampang Park includes the Hankyu department store and some jewellery shops. It is linked by a pedestrian bridge to Central Square on Jalan Tun Razak, which has clothes shops and interesting interior design and furniture stores.

On Jalan Tuanku Abdul Rahman, Globe Silk is a KL institution. This long-running, smaller department store has cosmetics, textiles, clothes etc at some of the cheapest prices in town. In contrast, Sogo, further north, is a huge, new department store for designer clothes, household goods and a few electronics.

For genuine designer-label clothes, shoes

and perfume, The Mall shopping centre on Jalan Putra opposite the Pan Pacific Hotel is a good place to look. The Yaohan department store here has a reasonable selection of electronics in the basement – good for getting an idea of prices. Most of the shopping malls have small electronics shops, where bargaining is often required.

Chinatown also has a few busy shopping centres, including the cramped S&M Shopping Arcade on Jalan Chen Lock and the more upmarket Kota Raya nearby for clothes, shoes and a reasonable selection of music tapes and CDs.

Getting There & Away

Kuala Lumpur is Malaysia's principal international arrival gateway and a central crossroads for bus, train or taxi travel.

Air Kuala Lumpur is well served by international airlines and there are flights to and from Australia, Singapore, Indonesia, Thailand, India, the Philippines, Hong Kong and various destinations in Europe. You should always reconfirm international flights out of KL.

Some of the airline offices in KL include:

Aeroflot
  Wisma Tong Ah, 1 Jalan Perak (☎ 03-261 3231)
Air India
  Angkasa Raya building, Jalan Ampang (☎ 03-242 0166)
Air Lanka
  Wisma KWSG, Jalan Kampung Attap (☎ 03-274 0211)
British Airways
  Plaza See Hoy Chan, Jalan Raja Chulan (☎ 03-232 5797)
Cathay Pacific Airways
  UBN Tower, 10 Jalan P Ramlee (☎ 03-238 3377)
China Airlines
  Amoda building, 22 Jalan Imbi (☎ 03-242 7344)
Garuda Airways
  3rd floor, City Square Centre, Jalan Tun Razak (☎ 03-262 2811)
Japan Airlines
  KL Airport (☎ 03-261 1722)
Malaysia Airlines
  MAS building, Jalan Sultan Ismail (☎ 03-261 0555); 24-hour reservations (☎ 03-746 3000)
Pelangi Air
  18th floor, Menara TR, 161B Jalan Ampang (☎ 03-262 4446)
Philippine Airlines
  Wisma Stephens, Jalan Raja Chulan (☎ 03-242 9040)
Pakistan International Airlines
  Angkasa Raya building, Jalan Ampang (☎ 03-242 5444)
Qantas
  UBN Tower, 10 Jalan P Ramlee (☎ 03-238 9133)
Royal Brunei Airlines
  UBN Tower, 10 Jalan P Ramlee (☎ 03-230 7166)
Royal Jordanian
  MUI Plaza, Jalan P Ramlee (☎ 03-248 5362)
Singapore Airlines
  Wisma SIA, 2 Jalan Dang Wangi (☎ 03-292 3122)
Thai Airways International
  Wisma Gold Hill, 67 Jalan Raja Laut (☎ 03-201 1900)

On the domestic network, KL is the hub of MAS services and there are nonstop flights to:

Destination	*Flights daily*	*Fare (RM)*
Alor Setar	5	113*
Ipoh	3	66
Johor Bahru	8	93
Kota Bharu	8	104*
Kota Kinabalu	6	437*
Kuala Terengganu	3	104
Kuantan	5	74
Kuching	6	262*
Labuan	2	437
Langkawi	6	135
Miri	2	422
Penang	16	104*
Singapore	15	147

* Cheaper night fares and advance purchase fares are applicable on some flights on these routes.

MAS and Singapore Airlines also operate a joint shuttle service between KL and Singapore. Tickets cost RM111 and are sold on a stand-by basis. Simply turn up at the shuttle counter at the airport, take a number and wait for the next available flight. So many flights operate that you shouldn't have to wait more than an hour.

Pelangi Air has nonstop flights to Tioman Island (twice daily, RM141), Ipoh (daily, RM66), Johor Bahru (daily, RM91), Pangkor (twice daily, RM120), Kerteh (twice daily, RM125) and Kuala Terengganu (three times weekly, RM104).

Bus KL's main bus station is Puduraya, just east of Chinatown. From here buses go all over Peninsular Malaysia, including the east coast, and to Singapore and Thailand. The Pekeliling and the Putra bus stations to the north of the city handle a greater number of services to the east coast, but most visitors to KL find Puduraya more convenient for east coast services. The other bus station is Kelang in Chinatown, which has buses to Shah Alam and Kelang, which are now virtually suburbs of KL.

The only long-distance destinations that Puduraya doesn't handle are Kuala Lipis and Jerantut, the jumping off point for Taman Negara National Park. These buses leave only from the Pekeliling bus station. The Taman Negara Resort at the Hotel Istana also has a shuttle service operated by Reliance Travel for RM25 that takes you all the way to the Kuala Tembeling jetty. Guesthouses in KL can also arrange a shuttle service for the same price which picks you up at the guesthouse and drops you off at Kuala Tembeling.

Most guesthouses and some hotels can arrange bus bookings, a handy service, and there is an office of Ekspres Nasional (☎ 03-262 7682), one of the largest bus companies, at the Malaysia Tourist Information Centre on Jalan Ampang. Otherwise bookings can be made directly at the bus company booths at the bus stations.

Puduraya Bus Station This hot, confusing, clamorous bus and taxi station is centrally located on Jalan Pudu. Inside the station there are dozens of bus company ticket windows, so it's just a matter of checking them out and finding one with a departure time that suits you. Right at the main entrance is a Tourist Police Office and, opposite, an Information Counter (Kaunter Pertanyaan; ☎ 03-230 0145). It pays to ask at one of these first, and they can direct you to the appropriate window for buying a ticket. Buses leave from the various numbered platforms in the basement, which are designated by bus company rather than destination.

There are departures to most places throughout the day, and at night to main towns. On the main runs services are so numerous that you can sometimes just turn up and get a seat on the next bus, but tickets should preferably be booked at least the day before, a few days before during peak holiday periods.

Ekspres Nasional has the largest office inside the terminal. They have buses to most major destinations, including an 8.30 am bus to the Cameron Highlands. Outside the station on Jalan Pudu there are at least another dozen companies that handle the buses to Thailand.

There's a left-luggage office in the Puduraya bus and taxi station. It is open daily from 8 am to 10 pm and the charge is RM1.50 per item per day.

Typical fares and journey times from KL follow. Only limited daily services run to the Cameron Highlands and east coast destinations, but there are frequent departures to the other destinations listed.

Destination	*Fare (RM)*	*Duration (hours)*
Alor Setar	25	9
Butterworth	17.50	7
Cameron Highlands	10	5
Ipoh	10	4
Johor Bahru	16.50	6
Kota Bharu	25	10
Kuala Terengganu	22	7
Kuantan	12.50	5
Lumut	15	4
Melaka	6.50	3½
Mersing	16.50	6½
Penang	19	7½
Singapore	18	7
Taiping	13.50	6

Kelang Bus Station Buses to Kelang and Port Kelang (No 793) and Shah Alam (No 337, 338) leave from the Kelang bus station at the end of Jalan Hang Kasturi in Chinatown. The left-luggage office here costs RM2 and is open from 7 am to 10 pm.

Putra Bus Station Though Puduraya handles buses to the east coast, Putra bus station (☎ 03-442 9530), opposite the Putra

World Trade Centre, also has a number of the large coach services. Most buses leave in the morning around 8 to 10 am and then in the evening from 8 to 10 pm. Buses go to Kuantan, Kuala Terengganu and Kota Bharu.

Pekeliling Bus Station Buses for Jerantut (for Taman Negara) and Kuala Lipis operate only from the Pekeliling bus station (☎ 03-442 1256) in the north of the city, just off Jalan Tun Razak. To Kuala Lipis (RM8, four hours) there are at least four departures daily. Currently, only one company, Syarikat Kumpulan Udara Perwira, has buses to Jerantut (RM9, 3½ hours) via Temerloh at 8.45 and 10.45 am and 1.45 and 6.15 pm. Alternatively, buses run to Temerloh at least every hour between 7 am and 6 pm, and from Temerloh regular buses run to Jerantut.

From Pekeliling, buses also go every half hour to Raub, and hourly to Kuantan from 8 am to 6.30 pm. Buses run every half hour to the Genting Highlands

Train Kuala Lumpur is also the hub of the KTM national railway system and there are daily departures for Butterworth, Wakaf Baru (for Kota Bharu), Johor Bahru and Singapore. This well-organised station has an information office (☎ 03-274 7435) at platform 1, which can advise on schedules and check seat availability. On most express services seats can be booked up to 30 days in advance. See the Malaysia Getting Around chapter for full fare and schedule information. City Trains also link KL with Shah Alam and Kelang in Selangor, and Seremban in Negeri Sembilan (see the Getting Around section below).

In the Golden Triangle district there is a KTM ticket booth (☎ 03-245 6902) on the concourse level of the Sungei Wang Plaza on Jalan Sultan Ismail, at the Parkson Grand department store entrance. It is open daily from 10 am to 7 pm, except Sunday, when it closes at 6 pm.

Taxi While the buses depart from downstairs in the Puduraya bus and taxi station, the long-distance taxis are upstairs on the 1st floor. If you want to share a taxi, it is best to turn up early in the morning. Chances are reasonable of finding other passengers waiting to share on the main runs to Johor Bahru, Melaka, Ipoh and Penang, but as always it is a matter of luck and it can sometimes take a long wait to get a full complement of four passengers. Otherwise you will have to take a whole taxi, which is four times the per person rate.

There are lots of taxis, and per person fares include Melaka (RM13), Johor Bahru (RM31), Singapore (RM36), Ipoh (RM22), Lumut (RM32), Cameron Highlands (RM32), Penang (RM50), Genting Highlands (RM10), Fraser's Hill (RM18), Jerantut (RM17), Kuala Lipis (RM15), Kuantan (RM25), Kuala Terengganu (RM35) and Kota Bharu (RM35). Prices are for non-air-con. Add about RM2 to RM10 for air-con, depending on the distance. Prices should include toll charges, but some taxi drivers, especially those on the Johor Bahru run, insist on charging extra.

Car Driving around the city has little to recommend it, but KL is the best place to hire a car for touring the peninsula. Rates start at around RM150 a day for a recent model small car. The best deals are for rentals of one month or more – as low as RM2000 for one month hire, including insurance and unlimited km. Shop around by phone. As well as the major companies, dozens of small hire companies are listed in the Yellow Pages.

All the major companies have offices at the airport as well as the following city offices:

Avis
  40 Jalan Sultan Ismail (☎ 03-241 7144)
Budget
  Wisma MCA, 163 Jalan Ampang (☎ 03-262 4119)
Hertz
  214A Kompleks Antarabangsa, Jalan Sultan Ismail (☎ 03-242 1014)
National
  G47, Wisma HLA, Jalan Sultan Ismail (☎ 03-248 0522)

Getting Around

The Airport KL's Subang airport is 20 km west of the city centre. Terminal 1 is the international terminal. Terminal 2 handles flights to Singapore and a few other regional routes. Terminal 3 is the domestic terminal. Terminals 2 and 3 are linked by footbridge, while a free shuttle bus runs the 1.5 km to Terminal 1.

Airport departure tax is RM40 on international flights, RM20 to Singapore and Brunei and RM5 on domestic flights.

Subang is looking a little tatty, and the facilities are not what you'd expect from the international gateway to a country with such grandiose ambitions as Malaysia. Duty-free stores sell alcohol, perfume and cigarettes and some department-store-style shops sell a hodgepodge of goods at inflated prices. Eating and drinking outlets are limited, dull and expensive. Try not to get stuck in transit here.

All this will change with when the new mega airport at Sepang is completed, but it is unlikely to be in operation before 1998.

Special airport taxis from KL's airport operate on a coupon system, and the fare is RM22 to Chinatown and RM26 to the Golden Triangle area (more from midnight to 6 am). Purchase a coupon from a booth to the right of the terminal as you leave the arrivals hall and use it to pay the driver. The price does not include the freeway toll of 70 sen. The system has been designed to eliminate fare cheating from the airport. Ignore drivers that come up to you offering a ride.

Going to the airport, take any city taxi – count on paying RM25 to RM30.

You can also go by bus – Indrakota air-con buses (RM1.90) and Sri Jaya No 47 (RM1.60) operate every 20 minutes from the Jalan Sultan Mohammed bus stand, opposite the Kelang bus station, from 6.30 am to 10.30pm. The trip takes 45 minutes, though it's a good idea to allow more time since traffic can be bad.

Bus Getting around KL by bus is a pain, simply because there's at least half a dozen private bus companies operating, as well as hundreds of pink minibuses. They operate from different stations and there's a lot of duplication of routes. The government's plan to amalgamate bus services was announced a couple of years ago but has still not been implemented.

The main city bus companies include Sri Jaya (dark blue with white stripes), Len Seng (beige with red stripes), Len (red), Foh Hup (green) and Toong Foong (white with blue stripes). The new Intrakota buses (grey with blue stripes) are air-conditioned and provide the best service. The fares on the buses are 20 sen for the first two km and go up five sen each additional km. Air-con services are 50 sen for the first two km and then five sen per km. The minibuses operate on a fixed fare of 60 sen anywhere along their route. Whenever possible, have correct change ready when boarding the buses, particularly during rush hours. There are a number of bus stands around the city, including the huge Puduraya bus and taxi station on Jalan Pudu, the Kelang bus station on Jalan Sultan Mohammed, the Jalan Sultan Mohammed bus stand opposite the Kelang bus station, and by the Central Market.

The bus system is fairly baffling, and unless you're going to be in KL for some time there's little point in trying to come to grips with it, especially as the taxi fares are so cheap. The central area is pretty compact and you really only need public transport for trips out of the city and to the airport.

City Trains One of the initiatives to ease traffic congestion in the city is the new KTM Komuter service, which runs along the existing long-distance railway lines, stopping at city stations. The main north-south line runs from Sentul, just north of the city centre, to Port Kelang via Shah Ahlam and Kelang. The other line runs north-west from Rawang to the south-east at Kajang and on to Seremban, 66 km south of KL. All trains pass through the KL railway station.

The service does not connect central KL with any of the city's attractions and is primarily designed for those who commute to KL from the vast, outlying urban sprawl.

Though of limited use to visitors, it is an easy way to get to Shah Alam and Kelang in Selangor, or Seremban in Negeri Sembilan. If you are bored, you can always take one of the trains out and back to experience suburban KL.

Services operate from around 6 am to 11.30 pm. Trains run every hour, every half hour during peak periods. Ticket dispensing machines are installed at stations – select your destination and the price is displayed. To Kelang costs RM3.10, to Seremban RM5.70.

LRT KL's new pride and joy is the Light Rail Transit system, the city's main answer to alleviate KL's horrendous traffic snarls.

System I, beginning operations in 1996, runs from Ampang to Pudu station next to the Puduraya bus and taxi station, then through the city centre to Jalan Sultan Ismail, near the corner of Jalan Raja Laut. Phase 2 of this line will extend it north.

In the central city, the line runs above ground on massive flyovers. Stations are fitted with electronic turnstiles and ticketing devices. Fares range from 75 sen to RM2.90.

The system should be a boon to travellers to the city, especially when System II is completed in 1998. It will link the KL railway station and the Central Market in Chinatown with Ampang, via Jalan Ampang.

Taxi KL has plenty of taxis and fares start at RM1.50 for the first two km, with an additional 10 sen for each 200 metres. From midnight to 6 am there's a 50% supplement on top of the meter fare, and extra passengers (more than two) are charged 20 sen each. RM1 is charged for luggage placed in the boot. Meters do not have time charges when stationary in traffic.

At these rates taxis are very cheap, perhaps too cheap as the taxis drivers claim. With KL's traffic problems, many drivers don't want to sit in a traffic snarl for just a couple of ringgit or are unwilling to go to out-of-the-way destinations from where it is hard to get a fare back. In these cases they are sometimes unwilling to use the meter. Get out and hail another, or if you have to bargain, short fares around town will cost around RM3 and it should cost no more than RM6 to go right across the central city area. The government is talking about reviewing the fare structure, so if the rates increase taxis may be more willing to use meters.

Taxis at bus stations don't use the meter and prey on new arrivals to the city. They will ask at least double the going rate. It is better to go out to the street and hail a taxi from there. At the railway station, taxis operate on the coupon system from outside platform 4 (the river side of the station). It costs RM3 to Chinatown, RM5 to the Golden Triangle.

When you do finally get a taxi, it may seem to head in the opposite direction to what you'd expect, simply because in KL the quickest route between two points is not necessarily the most direct one, or the system of one-way streets makes direct travel impossible.

AROUND KUALA LUMPUR

A number of attractions lie just outside the city boundaries in Selangor state, though they are within the urban bounds of Greater KL. The Batu Caves are the premier attraction, and the zoo also makes a pleasant escape from the city. Many of the attractions further afield in Selangor can also be visited as day trips from KL (see the Selangor chapter).

Batu Caves

The huge Batu Caves are the best-known attraction in the vicinity of KL. They are just 13 km north of the capital, a short distance off the Ipoh road. The caves are in a towering limestone formation and were little known until about 100 years ago. Later a small Hindu shrine was built in the major cave, and it became a pilgrimage centre during the annual Thaipusam festival. Each year in February, thousands of pilgrims flock to the caves to engage in or watch the spectacularly masochistic feats of Thaipusam devotees.

The major cave, a vast open space known as the Temple Cave, is reached by a straight flight of 272 steps. Beyond the stairs is the main temple. There are a number of other caves in the same formation, including a small cave at the base of the outcrop which has been made into a museum, with figures of the various Hindu gods. Lord Subramaniam, an aspect of Shiva, takes centre stage as the dancing Shiva, and other deities such as the fearsome Durga, Shiva's female half, are on display.

Getting There & Away To reach the caves, take minibus No 11 from the Central Market or Len bus No 70 from outside the Bangkok Bank bus stand on Jalan Tun HS Lee in Chinatown. The bus trip takes about 30 minutes and it's wise to tell the driver you're going all the way to the caves; if there aren't many people the minibuses sometimes stop earlier.

During the Thaipusam festival special trains also run to the caves.

National Zoo & Aquarium

East of KL on the road to Ulu Kelang, about 13 km out, is the 62 hectare site of the National Zoo & Aquarium. Laid out around a central lake, the zoo collection emphasises the wildlife found in Malaysia. There are elephant rides and other amusements for children. A shuttle bus runs around the spacious, landscaped grounds. Though a good zoo by Asian standards, some of the animal enclosures are still cramped despite all the open space.

The zoo is open daily from 9 am to 5 pm and admission is RM5. To get there, take a Len Seng bus No 170 or 177 from Lebuh Ampang, or you can take minibus No 17 also from Lebuh Ampang.

Forestry Research Institute & Museum

The Forestry Research Institute of Malaysia (FRIM) maintains this jungle park at Sungei Buloh, 15 km north-west of the city centre. This area of jungle is the centre of FRIM studies into forest regeneration. The museum here outlines the work done by FRIM and explains the rainforest habitat and its renewal. Various arboretums display the flora of Malaysia's rainforests.

The main interest is the jungle trails, the closest to KL. The park is popular for picnics on weekends but also has a variety of walks, from short strolls to the more strenuous walk up to the waterfall. There is also a canopy walkway that allows closer inspection of the rainforest canopy.

The park is reached via the suburb of Kepang and is open from 8 am to 6 pm. Take minibus No 31 from the corner of Jalan Ampang and Jalan Gereja, just to the north of Chinatown.

Templer Park

Beside the Ipoh road, 22 km north of KL past the Batu Caves, Templer Park was established during the colonial period by the British high commissioner Sir Gerald Templer. The 500 hectare park is a tract of primary jungle, preserved within easy reach of the city. There are a number of marked jungle paths, swimming lagoons and several waterfalls within the park boundaries.

Just north of the park is a 350-metre-high limestone formation known as Bukit Takun, and close by is the smaller Anak Takun, which has many caves.

Getting There & Away To get to Templer Park, take bus No 66 from the Puduraya bus and taxi station. The trip takes about one hour.

Selangor

Selangor state surrounds the Federal Territory of Kuala Lumpur city. Its focus is the busy Kelang Valley, which runs from KL down to the coast at Port Kelang, the nation's busiest port. The valley forms almost an urban extension of KL and contains much of Malaysia's industry. Shah Alam has modern glories, such as its huge mosque, and you can also pay a visit to the nearby agricultural park. Further towards the coast, Kelang has a few reminders of the old sultanate, but it is not until you reach Kuala Selangor, further north on the coast, that you finally leave the traffic and urban sprawl behind.

Many of the state's attractions – such as the Batu Caves, National Zoo and Templer Park on the northern outskirts of KL – are best visited in day trips from KL and so are included in the KL chapter. However, further north from KL are a number of other places of interest. The main attractions are the hill stations of Genting Highlands and Fraser's Hill, which both straddle the state border with Pahang.

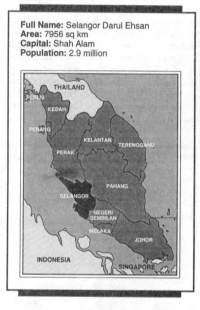

Full Name: Selangor Darul Ehsan
Area: 7956 sq km
Capital: Shah Alam
Population: 2.9 million

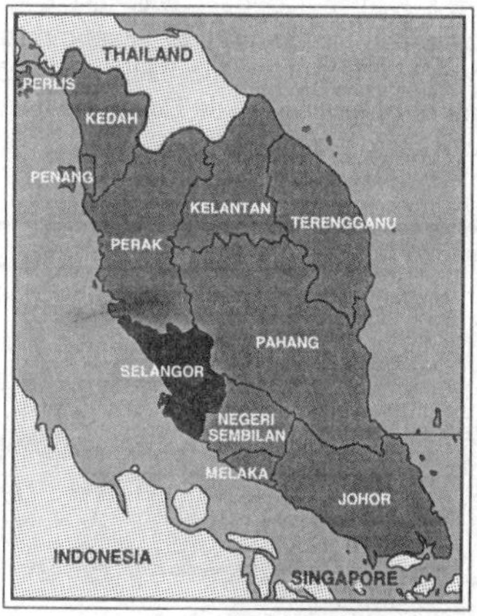

PENINSULAR MALAYSIA

History

In the 15th century, Selangor was under the control of Tun Perak, the great *bendahara* (chief minister) of Melaka. Once Melaka fell to the Portuguese, control of Selangor was hotly contested, partly because of its rich tin reserves. The Minangkabau settlers, who had started to migrate to the area from Sumatra only about 100 years earlier, were themselves displaced by Buginese immigrants from Celebes (present-day Sulawesi). The Dutch, meanwhile, made some fairly ineffective moves to establish control over the tin trade by building forts at Kuala Linggi and Kuala Selangor.

By the middle of the 18th century, the Buginese had established the current sultanate, based at Kuala Selangor, and their sphere of influence spread as far as western Sumatra and the Riau Archipelago. The 19th century saw an influx of Chinese merchants and miners, drawn by the rapidly growing and lucrative tin trade, and many attained powerful positions – in 1857 two merchants went into partnership with two Selangor chiefs to open tin mines at Ampang, out of which grew the city of Kuala Lumpur.

The success of the tin trade and the growing wealth of the Chinese communities led to conflicts among the Selangor chiefs and between the miners. The outcome was a prolonged civil war, initially only between the chiefs, but before long the Chinese miners were also dragged into the conflict. The miners fought not only against the chiefs but also among themselves, as they belonged to different secret societies and allied themselves with different chiefs. In 1872 KL, which up until then had been controlled by the 'Kapitan China' (Chinese leader appointed by the miners) Yap Ah Loy, was captured and razed to the ground, although it was retaken in 1873, which brought about an end to the civil war.

By this time the British were keen to impose some order on the chaos, especially as tin production had dropped to a fraction of what it had been, and this at a time when industrialisation in Europe meant high demand – and prices – for raw materials. In 1874 a British Resident was installed at Kelang, and for the next 25 years the state prospered, largely on the back of another boom in tin prices. Kuala Lumpur was resurrected from the wreckage of the 1871 attack and by the turn of the century was a well-ordered and prosperous place.

In 1896 Selangor was one of four states which formed the Federated Malay States, which were centrally administered from Kuala Lumpur. This in turn led to the Federation of Malaya in 1948 and finally the Federation of Malaysia in 1963. In 1974 Kuala Lumpur city was ceded by the sultan of Selangor and became the Federal Territory.

KELANG VALLEY

Heading south-west of KL along the Kelang Highway, you pass under the Kota Darul

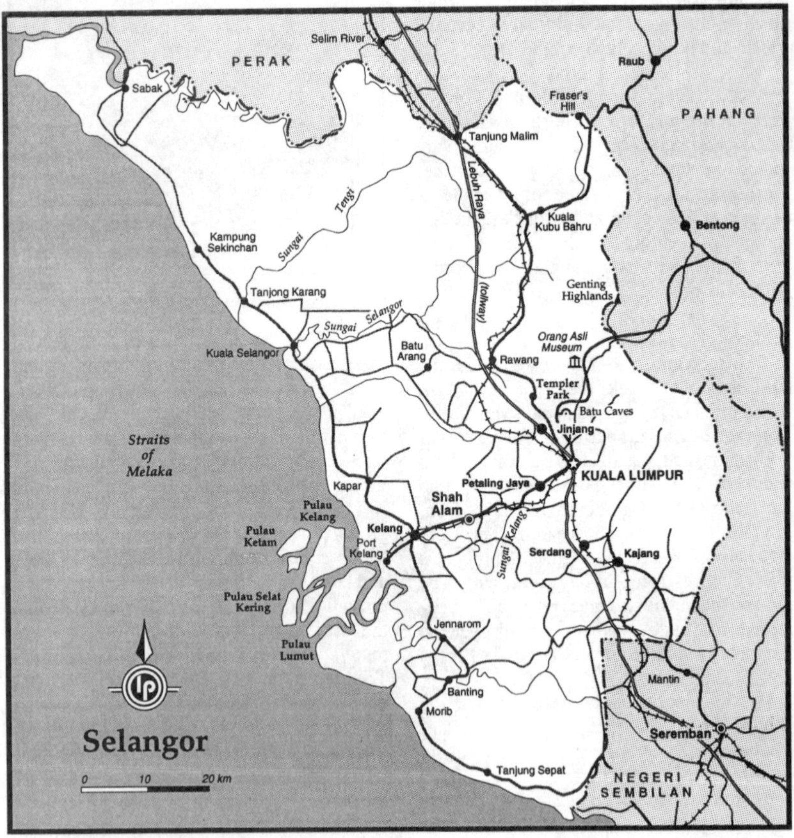

Ehsan ceremonial archway marking the boundary between KL and Selangor. Apart from the archway, little else distinguishes the expanse of housing estates and industrial parks. Just over the boundary is Petaling Jaya, for all intents and purposes a suburb of KL. Petaling Jaya blends into Shah Alam, the state capital, which bends into Kelang, the old royal capital.

Petaling Jaya

Petaling Jaya is a modern suburb of KL, just 11 km south-west of the city centre. Originally developed as a dormitory town to the capital, PJ has grown so rapidly and successfully that it has become a major industrial centre in its own right. Many engineering and high-tech industries, such as Motorola, have huge industrial installations here. PJ, including the surrounding districts, has a population of 500,000, and its neat, planned housing estates are favourites of the middle classes. PJ has grown so rapidly that this satellite town now has its own satellite, Subang Jaya. The University of Malaya is en route to PJ.

PJ is well supplied with shopping malls, gourmet restaurants and good nightlife, popular with well-to-do KL residents. **Sunway Lagoon** is a huge, new waterpark with swimming pools and enormous waterslides. Admission is RM15 for adults, RM10 for children.

In Petaling Jaya, sections are numbered (eg SS2); SS means 'sub-section'.

Places to Stay The cheapest place is the *South Pacific Hotel* (☎ 03-756 9922) at 7 Jalan 52/16, which is off Jalan Yong Shook Lin. It has rooms from RM78. Next up the scale is *Shah's Village Hotel* (☎ 03-756 9322), 3 Lorong Sultan, Peti Surat 115, where rooms start at RM140.

The main business hotel is the *Petaling Jaya Hilton* (☎ 03-755 9122) at 2 Jalan Barat, with rooms from RM300. Further out near the airport is the *Hyatt Regency Saujana* (☎ 03-746 1234) on the Subang Airport Highway and the *Merlin Subang* (☎ 03-733 5211) at Jalan SS 12/1 Subang Jaya.

Places to Eat Petaling Jaya's countless restaurants include Baba-Nyonya cuisine, banana-leaf Indian, Malay, Chinese and Thai.

The food at *Thai Kitchen* in PJ's SS2 district has long been held in high regard. *Sri Saigon* (☎ 03-775 3681), 53 Jalan SS2/30, is an excellent Vietnamese restaurant where you can eat well for around RM30.

Out of Africa (☎ 03-755 3432), 1 Jalan Sultan, not far from the Hilton, is a very popular and moderately priced South African restaurant, serving everything from venison pie to Malay 'Cape' curries.

Kelana Seafood Centre (☎ 03-703 8188) on Jalan Perbandaran in the SS7 district is a PJ institution. In a lakeside setting west of PJ centre, it is lit up like a Christmas tree at night and serves excellent seafood. The set meals are reasonably priced.

Entertainment PJ was once the centre of KL's nightlife, in the days when KL closed down early and only the streetwalkers and seedy bars provided any life. These days, with so much happening in the Golden Triangle, PJ's nightlife caters primarily to local residents. Most of the nightlife is in the Damansara Utama district. Of note is *Piccadilly* in the Kimisawa complex, KL's number one underground venue. Alternative bands promote 'anti-social' tendencies and have raised the eyebrows of the authorities.

Getting There & Away Buses to PJ run regularly from the Kelang bus station in KL. A taxi from KL will cost around RM12.

Shah Alam

The newly established capital of Selangor state is just an hour's drive west of KL. Only 20 years ago it was just a rubber and palm-oil plantation, but in 1978 a massive building programme was undertaken and the city now boasts a well-developed infrastructure, some enormous public buildings and a rapidly growing population. Shah Alam is home to many industrial complexes, including the Proton Saga plant.

Like many planned cities, Shah Alam has

very wide streets, an artificial lake and great distances between parts of the city, making it very difficult to get around. It is, however, quite an attractive city, with the centrepiece being the lake and the impressive **Sultan Salahuddin Abdul Aziz Shah Mosque**. This huge, gleaming mosque accommodates up to 24,000 worshippers and is the largest in Malaysia.

Millions of ringgit have been lavished on the **State Museum**, a short walk from the mosque around the lake. It's a very impressive structure, both inside and out, and the range of displays and the depth of labelling are creditable. After a couple of hours here you'll know everything there is to know about Selangor and the sultan.

Shah Alam is also the venue for the 500cc Malaysian Motorcycling Grand Prix, held in April every year.

Places to Stay & Eat The cheapest option is *7A Lodge* (☎ 03-559 2763), 7A Jalan Sukun 4/7, one km west of the mosque. Simple air-con rooms with attached bath cost RM40. The *ITM Hotel* (☎ 03-559 2078), part of the Institut Teknologi MARA, is a very comfortable hotel with well-appointed rooms for RM106/135 including breakfast and taxes.

The luxurious *Holiday Inn* (☎ 03-550 3696) is housed in the tower of the Plaza Perangsang, one of the two towers near the state mosque. Rooms cost RM280/320 including taxes.

The PKNS Plaza, next to the towering Holiday Inn, is Shah Alam's shopping mall and one of the few places to eat. On the ground floor there are a number of fast-food places, including a *KFC* outlet. On the lake near the Holiday Inn, the *Lake View Restaurant* is an expensive 'floating' restaurant.

Getting There & Away Catch a Kelang bus No 222 from the Kelang bus station in KL.

Bukit Cahaya Seri Alam

This 'agroforestry theme park' is a popular family escape for KL residents on weekends. It's a curious blend of landscaped gardens and forest areas, designed to stress ecological values along with the need for agriculture and to keep the kids amused. The park has attractive lakes, formal and agricultural gardens, arboretums, animal enclosures, an aviary and forest walks. There's also a flying fox and a canopy walkway of sorts.

The park is open from 9 am to 5 pm daily, except Monday. It is four km north-west of the state mosque, reached by bus from the Shah Alam bus station.

Kelang

Kelang is the former capital of Selangor and the old royal capital where the British installed their first Resident in Selangor in 1874. The main attractions are in the old city, south of the bus station and across the river near the train station.

The **Gedung Raja Abdullah** is an old warehouse, one of the oldest Malay buildings in the country, once used by the sultan to store tin from the rich mines in the area. It now houses a tin museum, with displays on local history and the ore that was so important to Selangor and Malaysia. The museum is only a few hundred metres from the railway station, next to the bridge by the river. It is open 9 am to 5 pm, closed Friday from noon to 2.45 pm.

One km south of the railway station along Jalan Raya Timur, the **Sultan Sulaiman Mosque** blends Art Deco with Middle Eastern influences. Behind the mosque is the **Istana Alam Shah**, once the main palace of the sultan before Shah Alam became the capital.

Kelang can easily be visited as a day trip from KL, or as a stopover on the way north along the coast. Kelang has a few mid-range hotels, such as the *Prima Hotel* (☎ 03-342 9066) on the highway near the bus station.

Getting There & Away Kelang's huge bus station is right in the centre of town opposite the Orchard Square shopping centre. Buses go to all major destinations on the west coast, including Melaka, Johor Bahru, Ipoh and Kuala Lumpur. The taxi station is behind the bus station, one street east. The No 225 express bus from the Kelang bus station in KL to Port Kelang also stops in Kelang.

To visit Kelang on a day trip from KL, the Komuter trains from KL's railway station provide a handy service as the Kelang station is in the old city close to the museum and mosque.

Port Kelang

Thirty km south-west of KL, eight km past Kelang, Port Kelang is the major seaport for KL. It's not a particularly attractive place, but it is famous for its excellent seafood, particularly chilli crabs. Port Kelang also has a number of cheap and mid-range hotels, but since the ferry to Sumatra stopped running, few travellers bother to visit, let alone stay in, Port Kelang.

The half-hour ferry trip to **Pulau Ketam** is a popular excursion on weekends with KL residents. The island has a stilt fishing village and Chinese seafood restaurants. Public ferries leave every couple of hours from the wharf at the end of Jalan Raja Muda.

Morib, south of Port Kelang and 64 km from KL, is a popular weekend escape and beach resort, although the beach itself is definitely nothing special.

Getting There & Away Buses from KL's Kelang bus station run to Port Kelang, and Komuter trains also run to/from the capital.

KUALA SELANGOR

This small town is on the coast where the Selangor River meets the sea. Though well off the beaten tourist track, it has a few notable points of interest for those venturing along this back route to Perak state and Pulau Pangkor.

Bukit Melawati

The flat coastal plain along this stretch of the coast is broken by Bukit Melawati, the hill overlooking the town. It provided an ideal site for monitoring shipping in the Straits of Melaka, first by the sultans of Selangor, then by the Dutch and British. The hill once contained two forts, though the only remains of note are some sections of wall and restored cannons under the lighthouse on top of the hill.

It is a pleasant walk through the landscaped parklands and forest to the top with views across the mangrove coastline. Further down the hill is the Makam Di-Raja Kuala Selangor, the mausoleum of the local rajas, and some fine colonial bungalows, now the preserve of government officials.

The road up Bukit Melawati starts just one block behind the shops facing the bus station. The road does a clockwise loop of the hill and you can walk up and around in about an hour.

Taman Alam Kuala Selangor

This 290 hectare nature park is on the estuary of the Selangor River, two km from town below Bukit Melawati. The turn-off to the park is a few hundred metres from the bus station, at the archway over the road to Bukit Melawati. This park of mangroves and some secondary forest is noted for its birdlife, especially waders in the mangroves. Around 150 species have been sighted, including 100 local species, the rest migratory. The definite 26 sightings of waders include the rare spoonbilled sandpiper. The park is also home to many leaf monkeys, and you may be lucky and spot otters, nocturnal leopard cats and civets.

To aid in bird spotting, two watchtowers and hides have been constructed, and two boardwalks lead through the mangroves to the sea. Nature trails, which take anything from 25 minutes to 2½ hours to complete, radiate from the visitors' centre. The main trails are dirt roads but the side trails are more interesting. Don't expect great jungle walks – the birdlife is the main attraction. The visitors' centre at the park is open daily and rents binoculars. The park also has good accommodation. Entry costs RM1.

Fireflies

Of the 130-odd species of firefly, those of South-East Asia are the most spectacular, noted for their displays of synchronised flashing. The folded-wing fireflies *(Pteroptyx tener)* gather in favourite berembang trees along the banks of the Sungai Selangor, and when large numbers form (sometimes in their thousands) their flashing becomes synchronised at about three flashes per second.

This natural light show can be seen at Kuala Kuantan, 10 km from Kuala Selangor. Take the turn-off to Batang Berjuntai, two km south of Kuala Selangor. Wooden boats oar out on the river to the show trees and their dazzling display. Boats take four people at RM6 each for the 40 minute trip, and go on demand throughout the evening from around 8 until 11 pm. This is a very popular excursion for tour groups and KL residents – the large car park fills on weekends – but it is much quieter during the week. Bookings can be made on ☎ 03-889 2403. The trips are not recommended on full moon and rainy nights, when the fireflies are not at their luminous best. Take mosquito repellent.

A taxi from Kuala Selangor costs RM20 for the return trip and it will wait for you. Various tours run from KL but tend to cater for large groups. Operators include Exciting Outing Travel (☎ 03-238 1131), Asean Overland (☎ 03-292 5622) and Reliance Sightseeing (☎ 03-248 0111).

Places to Stay

Kuala Selangor is just one long block of shops next to the bus station. Directly opposite the bus station is *Hotel Kuala Selangor* (☎ 03-889 2709), 90B Jalan Stesen, with spotless rooms for RM22.50 with fan, RM 33.50 with air-con and RM37.50 with air-con and attached bathroom. One street back, the *Melawati Ria Hotel* (☎ 03-889 2190), 15 Jalan Raja Jalil, is an older hotel with air-con rooms for RM40 and RM45.

The most attractive option, but a long walk from town, is right in the nature park. *Taman Alam Kuala Selangor* (☎ 03-889 2294) has small, simple A-frames for RM18, or larger chalets with attached bathrooms for RM38 and RM42. The chalets sleep four. A kitchen is available for guests' use and kitchen utensils can be hired for RM5.

Another good option is the *Bukit Melawati Rest House* (☎ 03-889 1357) on the hill. If you can find the caretaker, a double costs RM40 and meals are available.

Getting There & Away

From KL, air-con buses (RM3.90, one hour) leave from platform 24 of the Puduraya bus and taxi station for Kuala Selangor. Buses also run between Kuala Selangor and Kelang (RM2.70 air-con). Heading north from Kuala Selangor to Perak state, first take one of the old rattlers to Tanjong Karang (RM1), where air-con services connect to Telok Intan, but chances are you will have to take another local bus to Sabak Bernam on the state border, where more frequent buses operate throughout Perak.

Taxis from the bus station include Kuala Lumpur (RM8), Kelang (RM4) and Teluk Intan (RM10).

TANJONG KARANG

This unprepossessing town on the highway 18 km north of Kuala Selangor is at the heart of the state's premier rice-growing district. The only real attraction of the area is the chance to stay in a *kampung* in the rice fields at nearby Sungei Sireh.

Sungai Sireh Agrotourism/Homestay (☎ 03-879 8004) places visitors in family homes, allowing a good opportunity to experience kampung life. Accommodation is in a kampung house – simple but comfortable and you share facilities with the family. The cost is RM35 per day, including breakfast and lunch. The office for this programme is five km north of the highway from Tanjung Karang, and then eight km to the end of Sungei Sirih Rd, directly opposite the large water purification plant. It is best to book, and the company can arrange transport from Tanjong Karang.

KAJANG

This town, about 20 km south of KL on the KL-Seremban route, is said to have the best satay in all of Malaysia. If your meal time is approaching, it's worth stopping.

ORANG ASLI MUSEUM

This very informative museum is 24 km north of Kuala Lumpur on the way to the Genting Highlands. Though small, it houses a large number of exhibits and gives some good insights into the life and culture of Peninsular Malaysia's 80,000 indigenous inhabitants. It's well worth a look.

It is open from Saturday to Thursday from 9.30 am to 5.30 pm; admission is free. The museum is on the Old Pahang Rd, one km past the now-defunct Mimaland amusement park.

GENTING HIGHLANDS

While the style of other Malaysian hill stations is Old English, in the Genting Highlands it's modern skyscrapers; where the entertainment at the older stations is jungle walks, here it's a casino; instead of waterfalls and mountain views, Genting has an artificial lake and a cable car. If that does not sound to your taste, then drive straight by, for the Genting Highlands is a thoroughly modern hill station designed to cater for the affluent citizens of KL, just an hour to the south.

The first stage of the Genting Highlands was opened in the early 70s and three concrete hotels dominate the landscape. These include Malaysia's only casino, in the 18 storey Genting Hotel, with all the usual western games of chance and eastern favourites like keno and *tai sai*. Patrons must be at least 21 years old. There is a sign denying Muslims entrance.

Then there's the four-hectare artificial lake with boating facilities, which is encircled by a miniature railway for children. Naturally there's a golf course 700 metres down from the hotels, reached by a cable car. Forgetting nothing, the resort also has a bowling alley and a cave temple, the Chin Swee Temple, on the road up to the resort. Of course Genting has cooler weather like any other hill station; the main part of the resort is at a little over 1700 metres altitude.

Places to Stay

The emphasis is on international standards but there is one place offering if not cheap at least economy accommodation. The 820 room *Resort Hotel* (☎ 03-211 1118) has rooms from RM80. At the top there's the 635 room *Genting Hotel* (☎ 03-211 1118) with rooms from RM130 up to RM290 and every mod con imaginable, from saunas and swimming pool to tennis courts and a 'revolving disco restaurant'! The *Genting View Resort* (☎ 03-211 1877) has 220 rooms from RM240.

The *Awana Golf & Country Club* (☎ 03-211 3015) at the 12th Km charges RM220 for doubles and offers recreational activities such as swimming, tennis, squash, golf and horse riding.

Getting There & Away

There is a regular RM4.50 bus service between the Puduraya bus and taxi station in KL and the Genting Hotel. There are about nine services daily on weekdays, more on weekends. More frequent buses also run from the Pekeliling bus station in KL.

You can also get there by share-taxi from Puduraya for RM10 in around an hour, but count on having to hire a whole taxi for RM40. It's about 50 km from KL.

FRASER'S HILL

Fraser's Hill takes its name from Louis James Fraser, a reclusive ore-trader who lived here around the turn of the century. It's said he ran a remote and illegal gambling and opium den, but he was long gone when the area's potential as a hill station was recognised in 1910. The station, set at a cool 1524 metres altitude, is quiet and relatively undeveloped. Of all the hill stations it retains the most colonial charm, though its character is threatened by a new road and plans for more high-rise condominiums.

The bungalows, private and public, are haunts of the KL elite who flock here in expensive cars on weekends and holidays. Though a family destination, it also has a reputation as a resort for illicit liaisons, but old-fashioned service prevails at Fraser's and discretion is assured.

Compared with the Cameron Highlands, there is relatively little to do at Fraser's Hill besides relax in the cool and take in a stroll and the views. On weekdays it is almost deserted, and everyone is in bed by 10 pm.

Information

The Fraser's Hill Development Corporation (FHDC) information office (☎ 09-362 2201) is between the golf club and the Merlin Fraser's Hill hotel, near the post office. It can supply maps and information brochures and will book most of the accommodation in Fraser's Hill. The office is open daily from 8 am to 7 pm. It also contains a small museum with old photos of the resort. Bicycles can be hired for RM4 per hour and a Home Direct Phone is outside for international calls.

A small branch of the Maybank is at the Merlin, open Monday to Friday from 9.30 am to 4 pm, and Saturday from 9.30 to 11 am. Outside these hours, change money at the Merlin itself.

Like Genting Highlands, Fraser's Hill is right on the Selangor-Pahang state border. Though usually claimed by Pahang, almost all visitors come via Selangor, and the state border actually cuts right through the town.

Things to See & Do

As in the Cameron Highlands, there are many beautiful gardens around the town, and also many wild flowers. The dense jungle and towering trees are impressive, but walks are mostly limited to strolls around the paved but quiet roads. The only real trail of note is the three hour walk that runs from the children's playground and comes out near the Corona Nursery. It is strenuous and muddy in parts.

Fraser's Hill is a favourite with bird-watchers, with 265 species sighted, included 100 resident birds. Endemic species include the Mountain Peacock Pheasant, Malaysian Whistling-Thrush and the rare cutia and Rusty Naped-Pitta.

The picturesque golf course, where banded leaf monkeys wander, forms the real 'centre' of Fraser's Hill. A game costs RM40 on weekends or you could take in a spot of tennis or horse riding. Paddle boats can be hired at Allan's Waters, a small lake/stagnant pond next to the flower nursery.

About five km from the information office is the Jeriau Waterfall with a swimming pool

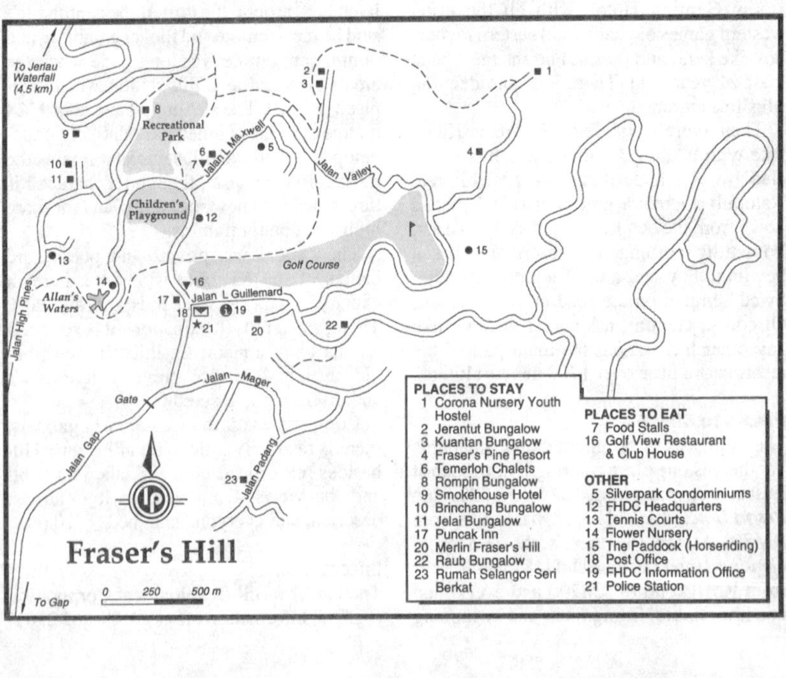

fed from the falls. Unfortunately the walking path leading to the falls is closed, but it can be reached by the road.

Places to Stay – bottom end

Fraser's is not a budget resort. The only cheap option is the *Corona Nursery Youth Hostel* (☎ 09-362 2225) at the isolated flower nursery, a long 40 minute walk from the information office. It's run by a friendly Indian family, but the rooms for RM10 are very basic and it also serves as a boarding house. There is a lounge and kitchen for guests' use.

A 'budget' hotel is being built about 100 metres south of Allan's Waters and may be open when you visit, but rooms are unlikely to be less than RM40.

Places to Stay – middle

Most of the accommodation is run by the FHDC, a government-contracted *bumiputra* organisation. Dozens of other bungalows are scattered around Fraser's Hill, but most are corporate or government bungalows closed to the public.

Rates at FHDC lodgings are slightly lower during the week, while the 'peak season' is on weekends and public holidays, when bookings are strongly recommended. All rooms have attached bathrooms with hot showers and 5% tax is added to the rates.

Most visitors end up staying at the *Puncak Inn*, because the bus stops outside and it is central. It is right above the little shopping centre and has doubles from RM58.50 to RM85.50 (or RM65 to RM95 in peak season). It looks inviting from the outside, but the rooms are ordinary and expensive.

The *Temerloh Chalets*, one km away, are modern-styled octagonal chalets divided into two rooms costing RM 67.50 (RM75 peak) each. The rooms are run-down but large with fine views. The chalets have a restaurant and hawker stalls are next door.

The FHDC also has bungalows, well worth the extra money. They are stone buildings with pleasant gardens, good views, large lounge areas and plenty of colonial grace, but they can be musty because of the high rainfall at Fraser's.

The bungalows are a fair way from the bus stop, but once you get your gear there it is a pleasant walk around the roads. All the bungalows cost RM89.10 (RM99 peak) for large rooms, and food is provided if there is enough demand. The bungalows are the *Jerantut*, *Kuantan*, *Rompin*, *Raub* and *Brinchang*. The Raub is the most central, while the Kuantan and Jerantut have pleasant hillside aspects but are almost three km from the centre. The Rompin and the Brinchang are only one km from the centre. The Brinchang, in a secluded position with inspiring views across the mountains, is the pick of all the bungalows.

Another option is the *Rumah Selangor Seri Berkat*, the Selangor government rest-house, across the state line on the south side of Fraser's Hill. Book through the District Office (☎ 03-804 1026) in Kuala Kubu Bahru. Though the view is over the football field, this two-storey colonial edifice built in 1926 has large rooms with towering ceilings for RM60. Even larger VIP rooms cost RM80. It's near the sultan's palace.

The Selangor government also runs the wonderfully old-fashioned *Rumah Rehat Gap* right at the Gap turn-off on the main road eight km below Fraser's itself. This is a fine place if you get stuck. Capacious rooms cost RM40 and RM60 with bath, big enough for three people with room to spare. It's in a pretty setting and has a comfortable lounge, a good restaurant and bathtubs with real hot water (if the generator is up to it!).

Places to Stay – top end

At the top end of the scale there's the *Merlin Fraser's Hill* (☎ 09-362 2300), a modern resort but the rooms are long overdue for an upgrade. Rooms cost RM200, but substantial discounts are available. The hotel overlooks the golf course.

The *Fraser's Pine Resort* (☎ 09-362 2122) has bright, better one/two/three bedroom apartments for RM264/330/396 at peak holiday periods, 30% less on weekdays.

The *Smokehouse Hotel* (☎ 09-362 2226), just up from the Puncak Inn, is a mock-Tudor building in the same style as the Smokehouse in the Cameron Highlands. With its exposed beams, log fires, stained armchairs and the lingering smell of roasts, it has a dilapidated charm but imminent renovations will turn it into the most exclusive of resorts.

Other bungalows and a set of condominiums on Fraser's are privately owned by corporations or by time-share owners in KL. It is sometimes possible to rent a room, but advance bookings are necessary. The FHDC can help.

Places to Eat

The small shopping centre at the Puncak Inn is the model of ethnicity with Malay, Chinese, and Indian restaurants all represented. At one end is the Chinese *Hill View* with simple meals and snacks, while at the other is the Malay *Arzed*. Between the two is the *Restoran Puncak* serving roti canai any time of day.

Across the road, the *Golf View Restaurant* at the golf club is a little more upmarket. The western/Malaysian food is more varied and moderately priced. The restaurant terrace overlooking the golf course is a great spot for breakfast. In the evening, they turn up the music and it becomes the town's disco/karaoke lounge, the only nightlife apart from schmaltzy organ music at the Merlin lounge.

The *Steak House* at the Temerloh Chalets is dingy but the steaks are cheap enough at around RM10. Next door is a small gathering of food stalls serving basic hawker fare, but a feed costs only RM2. At the top end there's the expensive Merlin, with one restaurant and a coffee house.

A Devonshire tea in the drawing room of the *Smokehouse Hotel* is a pleasant experience for RM9.

Getting There & Away

Fraser's Hill is 103 km north of KL and 240 km from Kuantan on the east coast. The usual access is via Kuala Kubu Bahru (KKB), 62 km north of KL, just off the KL-Butterworth road and the KL-Butterworth railway line.

From KL, take a Tanjung Malim bus, No 66 or 100, from platform 18 at the Puduraya bus and taxi station. You must take either the 6 or 9 am bus to ensure connections. These buses take the old Ipoh road (not the freeway) and will drop you at KKB (RM3.80, two to three hours), from where buses depart for Fraser's Hill (RM2.30, two hours) at 8 am and 12.30 pm.

Leaving Fraser's Hill, buses to KKB depart at 10 am and 2 pm. If you are heading east, these buses can drop you on the main road to meet the Kuala Lipis buses at 10.30 am or 3.30 pm. The Kuala Lipis bus goes via Raub for connections to Jerantut and Kuantan. For the Cameron Highlands, from KKB take a bus to Tapah and then another to the Cameron Highlands.

A taxi from KKB to Fraser's Hill is RM45 for the whole taxi. A taxi from KL's Puduraya bus and taxi station is around RM70.

If you're driving, be warned that there's no fuel station in Fraser's; the nearest places with fuel are Raub and KKB.

The last eight km up to Fraser's Hill is on a steep, winding, one-way section. At the Gap you leave the KKB-Raub road to make this final ascent. Traffic is permitted uphill and downhill at the following times:

Up to Fraser's Hill from the Gap

7	to	7.40 am
9	to	9.40 am
11	to	11.40 am
1	to	1.40 pm
3	to	3.40 pm
5	to	5.40 pm
7	to	7.40 pm

Down from Fraser's Hill

8	to	8.40 am
10	to	10.40 am
Noon	to	12.40 pm
2	to	2.40 pm
4	to	4.40 pm
6	to	6.40 pm

From 7.40 pm to 7 am the road is open both ways and you take your chances! The logic is that you can see the headlights of any vehicle coming the other way. A road is under construction that will allow cars to go up one-way and down the other, but completion is still a long way off.

Perak

Perak is one of the largest states on the peninsula and has a population of about two million. For many years the state was famous for its rich tin deposits; in fact, it gained its name from the ore (*perak* means 'silver' in Malay). Perak also gave birth to another mainstay of the Malaysian economy – the rubber industry.

For the visitor, the main attractions of Perak are the island of Pangkor, which lies just off the southern coast; the capital city of Ipoh with its cave temples; and the historic town of Kuala Kangsar. Perak is also the access point for the Cameron Highlands, Malaysia's premier hill station and one of the country's most popular tourist destinations. Taiping and nearby Maxwell Hill also make an interesting detour.

Full Name: Perak Darul Ridzuan
Area: 21,000 sq km
Capital: Ipoh
Population: 2 million

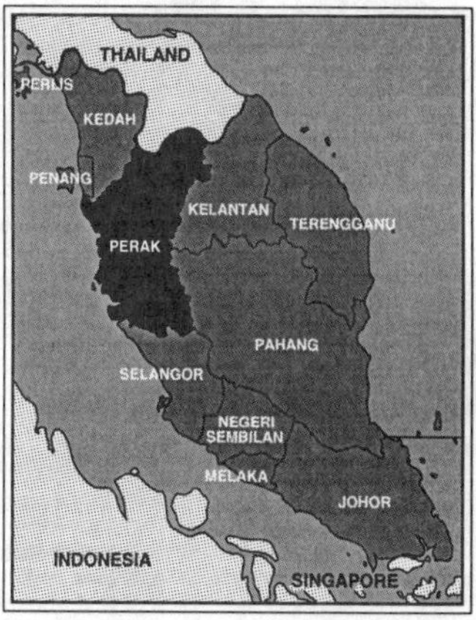

History

The current sultanate of Perak dates back to the early 16th century, when the eldest son of the last sultan of Melaka, Sultan Muzaffar, established the dynasty on the banks of the Perak River. Being so rich in tin, the state was regularly threatened. Dutch efforts in the 17th century to monopolise the tin trade came to little, and remains of their forts can still be seen on Pangkor and at the mouth of the Perak River.

The Bugis in the south and the Thais in the north both made concerted attempts to dominate Perak in the 18th century, and but for British assistance in the 1820s the state would have come under Thai influence.

The British remained reluctant to intervene in the peninsula, but growing investment from the Straits Settlements saw the government petitioned to assume control. The rich tin mines of Perak attracted British interests, especially when the canning industry boomed in Europe in the 1860s. The mines also attracted a great influx of Chinese miners, who formed rival clan groups that battled to control the mines, with Malay chiefs taking sides. British interests in the tin trade were threatened, and so in 1874 they decided to step in, marking the first real colonial incursion on the peninsula.

The Perak sultanate was in disarray, and fighting among the successors to the throne gave the British their opportunity. In 1874 the governor, Sir Andrew Clarke, convened a meeting at Pangkor in which Sultan Abdullah was installed on the throne in preference to Raja Ismail, the other main contender. The Pangkor Treaty that ensued also required that the sultan accept a British Resident, who was to be consulted on all issues other than those relating to religion and Malay custom.

Though the Resident had no executive authority, this foot in the door soon saw an escalation of British rule. In 1875, only one year after the Pangkor Treaty, Sultan Abdullah was forced under threat of deposition to accept an administration of British officials

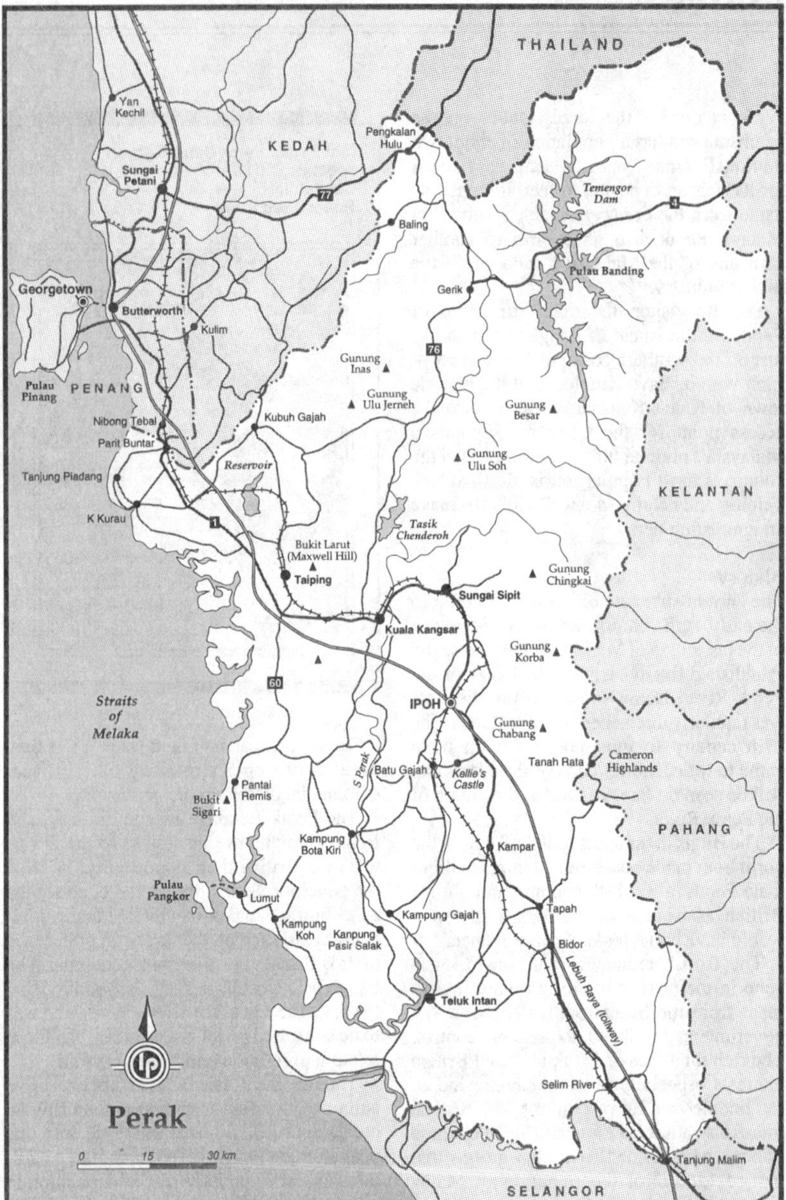
THAILAND
KEDAH
Yan Kechil
Sungai Petani
Pengkalan Hulu
77
Temengor Dam
4
Baling
Pulau Banding
Georgetown
Butterworth
Kulim
Gerik
76
Gunung Inas
Pulau Pinang
PENANG
Gunung Ulu Jerneh
Gunung Besar
Nibong Tebal
Kubuh Gajah
Parit Buntar
Gunung Ulu Soh
Reservoir
Tanjung Piadang
KELANTAN
K Kurau
1
Tasik Chenderoh
Bukit Larut (Maxwell Hill)
Gunung Chingkai
Taiping
Sungai Sipit
Kuala Kangsar
Gunung Korba
60
Straits of Melaka
IPOH
Gunung Chabang
Cameron Highlands
Tanah Rata
S Perak
Batu Gajah
Kellie's Castle
Pantai Remis
Bukit Sigari
PAHANG
Kampung Bota Kiri
Kampar
Pulau Pangkor
Lumut
Tapah
Kampung Gajah
Kampung Koh
Kanpung Pasir Salak
Bidor
Lebuh Raya (tollway)
Teluk Intan
Selim River
Perak
0
15
30 km
Tanjung Malim
SELANGOR

that would govern Perak for the sultan. The various Perak chiefs were united in their desire to get rid of the Resident, JWW Birch, who was promptly assassinated at Pasir Salak in November 1875. Troops were called in to fight what proved to be a shortlived war, Sultan Abdullah was exiled to the Seychelles and a new British-sanctioned sultan was installed.

Hugh Low, well versed in Malay affairs and language, then became Resident in Kuala Kangsar and proved to be a much more able administrator. He assumed control of taxes from the tin mines and greater control in state affairs, while the sultans maintained their status but were increasingly effete figureheads bought out with stipends. The first railway in the state from Taiping to Port Weld was built in 1885, and the wealth of tin saw rapid development in Taiping and Ipoh.

In 1896 Perak, along with Selangor, Pahang and Negeri Sembilan, became part of the Federated Malay States, which in 1948 became the Federation of Malaya.

TANJUNG MALIM TO IPOH

The road north from KL crosses the border from Selangor into Perak at Tanjung Malim. If you have your own transport, you can get off the main North-South Highway and take the old highway through a number of interesting towns. The first point of interest is the town of Selim River, where during WWII the British forces made an unsuccessful last-ditch attempt to halt the Japanese advance. Selim River has a good resthouse.

The first main town is Bidor, where you can turn off for Teluk Intan, 42 km to the west. Pasir Salak, 25 km north of Teluk Intan, is a small village of some interest, and from there you can follow the Perak River Valley to Kampung Bota Kiri. The river valley along here was the original home of the Perak sultanate and is dotted with many royal graves. From Kampung Bota Kiri you can take the road to Lumut and head north through the *kampungs* to Ipoh.

On the highway north of Bidor is Tapah, the gateway to the Cameron Highlands. Further north is Kampar, famous for its pomelo orchards, and many pomelo stalls line the highway.

Teluk Intan

There is no pressing reason to visit Teluk Intan – its only gazetted tourist attraction is its leaning clock tower, but it's a pleasant, lazy town at the junction of the Perak and Bidor rivers. Once known as the Teluk Anson, after the name of an early colonial administrator, the government renamed the town after independence.

The town's impressive pagoda-style **clock tower** is seven storeys high and is the town's answer to the Leaning Tower of Pisa. Local lore has it that it was built, in the manner of the Taj Mahal, by a mourning Chinese merchant in 1885 as a memorial to his wife. Officially closed, if you seek out the caretaker he will show you around for a few ringgit.

An interesting old-style covered market is next to the tower, and a good, new food-stall centre is opposite. Teluk Intan also has a few fine colonial buildings and old Chinese shop houses. The Istana Raja Muda Perak is the crumbling palace of the next in line to the sultanate of Perak.

Places to Stay The bus station is right near the clock tower. One block from the bus station away from the tower, *Hotel Kok Min* (☎ 05-622 1529), 1605A Jalan Sekolah, is a well-kept old villa with rooms from RM20. Next door the similar *Kum Ah Hotel* (☎ 05-622 1407) is more run-down but has a good restaurant with tables out front for al fresco dining. A little further along, the *Anson Hotel* (☎ 05-622 6166) is the best in the town centre with air-con rooms from RM44.

Pasir Salak

This sleepy village is best known as the place where the first British Resident of Perak, James WW Birch, was slain in 1875 while bathing at a rafthouse on the river. Birch is widely characterised as an intolerant man, insensitive to Malay customs and known to lecture Sultan Abdullah in public. However, his murder was as much a reaction to the colonial government's decision to assume direct control in Perak as it was to any shortcomings in Birch's personality. His executioners, Maharaja Lela, a local chief, Dato Sagar and Pandak Indut were arrested by British troops and later hanged. They have since been enshrined as national heroes.

A memorial to Birch marks the spot, but of more interest are the three restored traditional houses, *rumah kutai*, that are the main feature of the historical complex at Pasir Salak. They show the features of Perak houses, with carved eaves, shuttered windows and walls of wood and woven bamboo to allow breezes to enter the house. One functions as a VIP guesthouse, while another, reputed to be 120 years old, describes the events of 1875 and features a few paintings, kris and other old weapons. The third house has traditional customs and other memorabilia.

The historical complex is open 10 am to 6 pm on weekends, 10 am to 12.45 pm from Monday to Thursday.

Getting There & Away Pasir Salak is a few km from Kampung Gajah, which is connected by infrequent buses to Teluk Intan and Ipoh. A chartered taxi to Kampung Gajah from Teluk Intan costs RM12, or from Ipoh RM24. Taxis from Kampung Gajah to Pasir Salak cost RM4.

Tapah

The small town of Tapah has no attractions but is the main transit point for bus connections to and from the Cameron Highlands.

Places to Stay If you get stuck, Tapah has good, cheap hotels only two minutes' walk from the bus station.

As you come out of the bus station, the *Hotel Bunga Raya* (☎ 05-401 1436) is to your right on the corner of Jalan Raja and Main Rd above the KFC restaurant. Clean fan rooms with attached bathroom cost RM16 but are a little noisy.

For something better, take the street directly opposite the bus station two short blocks to Jalan Setesen. Right near the corner, the *Hotel Utara* (☎ 05-401 2299) at No 35 has rooms with bath for RM18, or RM24 with air-con. One block down at No 23, the *Hotel Timuran* (☎ 05-401 1092) is similar but also has a Chinese coffee shop downstairs. Fan rooms with bath cost RM18 and good air-con rooms are RM30.

Getting There & Away The bus station on Jalan Raja is central, only 250 metres from the main road. Local buses to the Cameron Highlands leave roughly every hour from 8.15 am to 6.15 pm. The winding journey to Tanah Rata takes two hours and costs RM3.50. Taxis to Tanah Rata (RM6) leave from the taxi station on Jalan Raja, 100 metres from the bus station and they also hang out at the Restoran Caspian on the main road. In the afternoon it is more difficult to get a share taxi, and you may have to charter a whole cab (RM24).

From the bus station a few departures go to KL and Penang, but most express services for long-distance destinations leave from the Restoran Caspian (☎ 05-401 1193), 9 Main Rd. Turn right as you come out of the bus station, then left at Main Rd, and the Restoran Caspian is just four shops down from KFC. They also have a sub-agent, the Kah Mee Agency, directly opposite the bus station.

From the Restoran Caspian buses go to: KL (RM10, three hours) roughly every half hour from 8.30 am to 6.30 pm; Penang (RM10, four hours) at 10 and 11 am and noon; to Singapore (RM36 and RM43, eight hours) at 10 am, 9 and 9.30 pm; Melaka (RM19, six hours) at 10 and 11.45 am; Lumut (RM10, three hours) at 11.30 am; Kuantan (RM23, eight hours) at 9.30 am and 10 pm; and Hat Yai (RM32, 10 hours) at 11.30 pm. These buses can also be booked at CS Travel & Tours in Tanah Rata.

Regular air-con buses to Ipoh (RM4, 1½ hours) leave from the next street north. From the bus station turn right and follow Jalan Raja over Main Rd, then turn right at the next street – the depot is just around the corner.

The railway station, known as Tapah Rd Station, is nine km from town. Tapah Rd buses run every half hour from the bus station between 7 am and 7 pm. To Butterworth, day trains leave at 9.50 am and 4.40 pm, to KL at 11.35 am and 6.30 pm. Other services leave in the middle of the night.

CAMERON HIGHLANDS

Malaysia's most extensive hill station, about 60 km off the main KL-Ipoh-Butterworth road at Tapah, is at an altitude of 1300 to 1800 metres. The Cameron Highlands encompasses a large area stretching along the road from the town of Ringlet through the main towns of Tanah Rata, Brinchang and beyond.

The Cameron Highlands takes its name from William Cameron, the surveyor who mapped the area in 1885. He was soon followed by tea planters, Chinese vegetable farmers and finally by those seeking a cool escape from the heat of the lowlands.

The temperature rarely drops below 8°C or climbs above 24°C, and the area is fairly fertile. Vegetables grow in profusion, flowers are cultivated for sale all over Malaysia, it's the centre of Malaysian tea production and wild flowers bloom everywhere.

The cool weather tempts visitors to exertions normally forgotten at sea level – there's an excellent golf course, a network of jungle trails, waterfalls and mountains, and less taxing points of interest such as a colourful Buddhist temple and a number of tea plantations where visitors are welcome.

Up until a few years ago, development here was fairly limited, but construction of large apartment blocks is changing the old-fashioned, English atmosphere of the Cameron Highlands. A new road is being pushed through to link up with the North-South Highway, which will make the Highlands much more accessible and speed development, but mercifully that is still a few years away. Until then, the ugly, new intrusions are relatively few and the Cameron Highlands is still a relaxing destination.

Orientation

Though the Cameron Highlands lies just over the Perak state border in Pahang state, it can be accessed only from Perak and so is included in this chapter for convenience.

From the turn-off at Tapah it's 46 km up to Ringlet, the first village of the Highlands. Ringlet is primarily a Malay town and not particularly interesting. Although it has a few places to stay most visitors press on higher up. Soon after Ringlet you skirt the lake created by Sultan Abu Bakar Dam.

About 14 km past Ringlet you reach Tanah Rata, the main town of the Highlands. As you enter, the new apartment blocks towering above town give way to the busy Main Rd lined with restaurants and old-fashioned shops. Tanah Rata has a large Indian population, descendants of the Indian workers brought here to pick tea. It is the most central town with the widest range of accommodation. Most visitors stay in Tanah Rata.

Only a few km further brings you up to the golf course, around which you'll find many of the Highlands' more expensive hotels. Continue on beyond the golf course, and at around the 65 km peg you reach the other main Highlands town, Brinchang, a more modern, Chinese town. Though Brinchang has a good range of facilities and is close enough to many of the attractions, it has less character than Tanah Rata and is more isolated if you are dependant on public transport.

The road continues up beyond Brinchang to grungy Kampung Raja, a tea estate village, and the Blue Valley Tea Estate at 90 km. You can also turn off to the top of Gunung Brinchang at 80 km, to the north-west.

Information

Tanah Rata has a small tourist office on the main street. It is open Monday to Friday from 8 am to 4.15 pm (closed Friday 12.15 to 2.45 pm) and Saturday from 8 am to 12.45 pm. They have a number of local maps for sale, including a reasonable colour sketch map, and book half-day tours of the Highlands for RM15. The tourist office also has a small museum exhibiting cultural artefacts. The post office, banks, hospital and bus station are also on the main street in Tanah Rata.

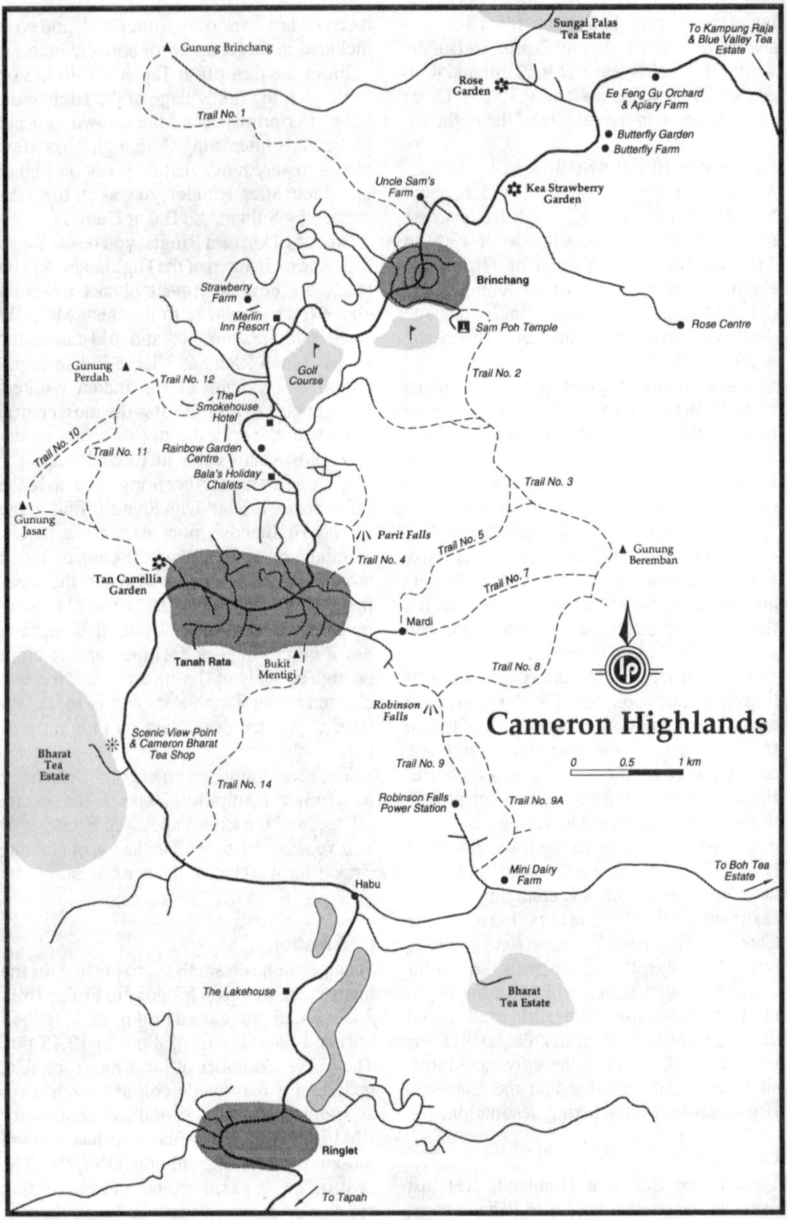
Cameron Highlands
Gunung Brinchang
Sungai Palas Tea Estate
To Kampung Raja & Blue Valley Tea Estate
Rose Garden
Ee Feng Gu Orchard & Apiary Farm
Butterfly Garden
Butterfly Farm
Trail No. 1
Uncle Sam's Farm
Kea Strawberry Garden
Brinchang
Strawberry Farm
Merlin Inn Resort
Sam Poh Temple
Rose Centre
Golf Course
Gunung Perdah
Trail No. 12
Trail No. 2
The Smokehouse Hotel
Trail No. 10
Trail No. 11
Rainbow Garden Centre
Bala's Holiday Chalets
Trail No. 3
Gunung Jasar
Parit Falls
Trail No. 5
Gunung Beremban
Trail No. 4
Tan Camellia Garden
Trail No. 7
Mardi
Tanah Rata
Bukit Mentigi
Trail No. 8
Robinson Falls
Scenic View Point & Cameron Bharat Tea Shop
Bharat Tea Estate
Trail No. 9
0
0.5
1 km
Trail No. 14
Robinson Falls Power Station
Trail No. 9A
Mini Dairy Farm
To Boh Tea Estate
Habu
The Lakehouse
Bharat Tea Estate
Ringlet
To Tapah

Things to See

The **Sam Poh Temple**, just below Brinchang and about one km off the road, is a typically Chinese kaleidoscope of colours with Buddha statues, stone lions and incense burners. It is signposted as the 'Tokong Temple' from the main road. **Mardi** is an agricultural research station in Tanah Rata – tours must be arranged in advance.

There are a number of **flower nurseries, vegetable farms** and **strawberry farms** in the Highlands. The main season for strawberries is January. There is an **Orang Asli settlement** near Brinchang, but there's little reason to visit it.

About 10 km beyond Brinchang is the **Butterfly Garden**, where over 300 varieties flutter around, as well as an impressive collection of enormous rhinoceros beetles and scorpions. In true Asian style, where vendors of the same product cluster together, the **Butterfly Farm** is a virtually identical, competing attraction next door. Both are open 9 am to 6 pm and charge RM3 entry. The bus tours call in here.

Gunung Brinchang (2032 metres) is the highest point reached by surfaced road on the peninsula. It's a long slog on foot but if you are driving it's a must. The seven km road is narrow and incredibly steep in places but the views from the top are superb.

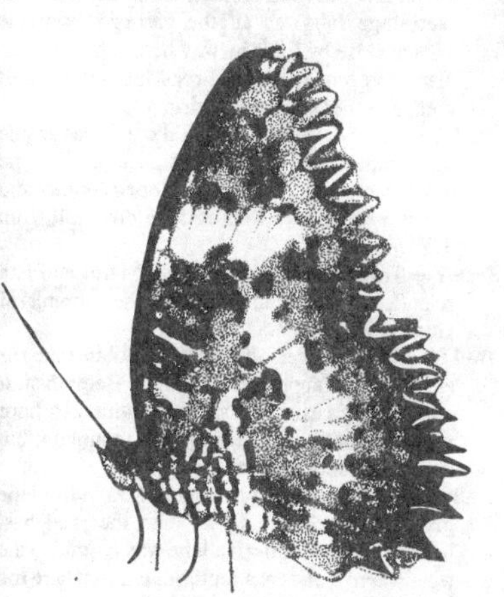

Over 300 varieties of butterfly can be found at the Butterfly Garden near Brinchang.

Tea Plantations A visit to a tea plantation is a popular Highlands activity. The first tea was planted in 1926. The main company is the Boh Tea Estate, and their brands dominate the market for Cameron Highlands tea.

The easiest estate to visit is Boh's Sungai Palas Estate, north of Brinchang off the road to Gunung Brinchang. It is well set up with an attractive visitors centre where you can buy tea and tea sets in the gift shop, or sample the brew of your choice in the tea rooms. Free tours showing the tea process are conducted on demand from 8 am to 3 pm, except Monday, when the estate is closed. Sunday is the pickers' day off, but the processing factory remains open.

The tea is still cured with wood fires, which apparently imparts some flavour to the finished product. It is almost all mechanised these days, including the picking, and the tea is mechanically sifted into the various grades from dust to choice leaf.

Most tours include the Sungai Palas Estate. Or it can easily be reached by public bus from Tanah Rata leaving at 9.30 and 11.45 am and 1.45 pm, returning at 12.10 and 2.30 pm. You can also visit other tea estates, but guided tours are usually given only for organised groups.

Activities

Walks There are a variety of walks around the Highlands, many leading to waterfalls, mountain peaks and other scenic spots. The walks can sometimes can be difficult to follow and no high-quality maps are available.

The start of the trails are marked with large but sometimes obscured signboards. The popular tracks are reasonably well maintained and periodically cleared with brush cutters, but it doesn't take long for them to become overgrown, especially the less popular trails. There is little or no signposting of side trails, and you occasionally come across false trails that go nowhere. The

Tea Processing

Tea bushes are plucked every seven to eight days, and though once done by hand it is now almost all mechanised in Malaysia. It takes five kg of leaves to make one kg of tea. The collected leaves are weighed and 'withered' – a drying process in which air is blown across troughs by fans in order to reduce the moisture content by about 50%. The dried leaves are then rolled, to twist, break and rupture the leaf cells and release the juices for fermentation. The finer leaves are then separated out and the larger ones are rolled once again.

Fermentation, which is really oxidisation of the leaf enzymes, has to be critically controlled to develop the characteristic flavour and aroma of the tea. The fermented leaves are then 'fired', a process in which excess moisture is driven off in a drying machine. It is at this time that the leaves become black. Finally the tea is sorted into grades, and stalks and fibres are removed before it is stored in bins to mature. ■

guesthouses in Tanah Rata all have books with comments from guests who have walked the trails. They are a good source of information for the latest track conditions.

You should take care not to get lost, and always bring water, some food and rain gear for the unpredictable weather. Trails 4 and 9 (as far as Robinson Falls) are easy walks taking an hour or less. Trail 14 is an easy longer walk, while a combination of Trails 11 and 12 is slightly more challenging. The rest may be 'tough going', depending on your level of fitness.

The walks are generally interesting, as they pass through relatively unspoiled jungle, and the cool weather makes walking a pleasure. Trail 12 is particularly good for wild flowers – the Cameron Highlands is famed for its orchids.

Although the walks around the Highlands are all relatively short, there is obviously great potential for longer walks from there. A glance at the map will indicate what a short, straight-line distance it is from the Highlands down to Ipoh or the main road. For any walk outside the immediate area, however, the local authorities have to be notified and a guide is necessary.

Trail 1 – This trail leads from around the side of the transmitter station on top of Gunung Brinchang down to the army camp just north of Brinchang. It is a steep, muddy, overgrown trail and should only be tackled from the top down by experienced hikers. Take the seven km paved road to Gunung Brinchang through the tea plantations – pleasant enough to start, but dull after a while so try hitching. The trail down takes about 1½ hours, unless you get lost and wander through the jungle for a couple of days, as did two foreigners recently.

Trail 2 – Starting just before the Sam Poh Temple outside Brinchang, this steep, strenuous hike follows a thin, slippery track for 1½ hours before it eventually joins Trail 3.

Trail 3 – This starts at Arcadia Cottage behind the golf course and climbs towards Gunung Beremban (1841 metres), getting progressively steeper near the summit. It is a strenuous three hour walk all the way to the mountain or an easier walk if you only go as far as Trail 5 and take it back to Mardi.

Trail 4 – Trail 4 starts next to the river just past the New Garden Inn in Tanah Rata. It leads to the Parit Falls, but unfortunately these are more like 'sewerage falls' as all the garbage from the village close by finds its way here. The falls can also be reached from the road around the golf course. Either walk is less than a km.

Trail 5 – Trail 5 starts at Mardi. Take the road inside the complex and follow the sign around to the left. It's a 1½ hour walk though open country and forest, and an easy walk if done downhill from Trail 3.

Trail 7 – This one also starts inside Mardi and is a relentless three hour climb to the summit of Gunung Beremban.

Trail 8 – This branches off Trail 9 at Robinson Falls and is a steep approach to Gunung Beremban. It is a slightly easier but still strenuous 2½ hour walk if done in reverse from the mountain, but the trail is harder to find.

Trails 9 & 9A – Popular Trail 9 starts 1.5 km from the main road in Tanah Rata. Take the road past Mardi and then follow it all the way around to the right where it ends at a footbridge. From here the trail leads downhill past Robinson Falls to a metal gate, about 15 minutes away. Trail 9 leads through the gate and follows the water pipeline down a very steep, sometimes slippery incline through the jungle to the power station, less than one hour away. From the power station you can walk to the Boh Rd and back to the main road or take the more gradual Trail 9A back up to the waterfall, a less taxing walk.

Trails 10, 11 & 12 – Gunung Jasar (1696 metres) is a fairly strenuous walk reached by Trail 10, starting behind the Oly Apartments near the digital clock in Tanah Rata. Go through the Tan Camellia Garden and uphill to the left. You can bypass the summit and take Trail 11, which joins Trail 12 and emerges at the Hilltop Bungalow, a moderately easy two hour walk. Trail 12 also leads to Gunung Perdah (1576 metres), a moderate one hour climb from the Hilltop Bungalow.

Trails 13 & 14 – Trail 14 takes three hours and starts on Jalan Dayang Endah in Tanah Rata, just to the side of the big milk bottle at the Pusat Pengumpulan Susu. This pleasant, moderately easy trail winds gradually downhill, most of the way through thick jungle, before it reaches vegetable gardens near the main road halfway between Tanah Rata and Ringlet. After about 10 minutes from the start of the trail it forks – take the left for Trail 14, while the right fork is Trail 13, a short side trail that comes out behind the tourist office.

Golf & Tennis If you want a game of golf you'll need to be suitably dressed, as regulations prohibit singlets and 'revealing' shorts. Green fees are RM42 for a whole day (RM63 on weekends), or RM32 after 4 pm. Club, shoe and ball hire will cost around RM35 more.

Across the road from the golf shop there are a couple of tennis courts for hire. Inquire at the golf shop.

Organised Tours

Titiwangsa (☎ 05-491 2169) and Bala's Holiday Chalets both run popular half-day tours of the area for RM15, leaving around 9 am and 2 pm. Bookings can be made at the tourist office and travel agents in Tanah Rata. These can be a good way of seeing all the various attractions, which are well spread out and either difficult or impossible to reach by public transport. Places visited include the butterfly farm (RM3 entry fee not included), a rose garden and a tea estate.

Places to Stay

The Highlands can be very busy in April, August and December during the school holidays, when many families go there for vacations. At these times it is a good idea to book accommodation. Prices in the more expensive places vary with demand and have high-season rates in holiday periods and substantially cheaper rates in quiet periods. Accommodation is generally expensive.

Fortunately Tanah Rata has a good selection of travellers' guesthouses for cheap accommodation, as well as more expensive hotels. There are a couple of places in Ringlet, but there's little reason to stay here as it's 14 km from Tanah Rata. Brinchang, the secondary Highlands town a few km beyond Tanah Rata, also has a selection of hotels and prices are a bit cheaper than at Tanah Rata, but there is little reason to stay here, especially if you are dependent on public transport.

Many middle and top-end hotels are scattered around the Highlands, mostly between Tanah Rata and Brinchang.

Places to Stay – bottom end

Tanah Rata One of the most popular travellers' places is the friendly *Twin Pines Chalet* (☎ 05-491 2169), just a short walk from the centre of Tanah Rata. The communal veranda is a good gathering place for tuning into the travellers' grapevine, with a good noticeboard and notebooks full of info. Breakfast and drinks (including beer) are available. The only drawback is that it can be cramped, and unfortunately the new shopping development out front has spoilt the view and the peace and quiet. Dorm beds cost RM7, or doubles/triples are RM20/26.

Just behind the Twin Pines, the *Papillon Guest House* (☎ 05-491 4069) is a very congenial, new place in a family house with a kitchen, laundry and good, central sitting room. It is quite spacious with rooms ranging from RM20 for those facing the sitting room up to RM35 with attached bath. Dorm beds cost RM6.

On the same road as the Twin Pines but quieter, the good *Cameronian Inn* (☎ 05-491 1327) is another converted suburban house, complete with an expanse of lawn. Facilities are similar to those at the other guesthouses, including a small restaurant and a TV/video room, but the rooms are bigger and carpeted. Rooms from RM16 are internal-facing and dark, but others with attached shower from RM25 are very good value. Dorm beds are available for RM6, but this place is more popular with couples.

Also close to the centre of Tanah Rata is *Father's Guest House* (☎ 05-491 2484). It's up a long flight of stone steps, a bit of a grunt with a heavy backpack, or the longer road access is more gradual. The old, bunker-style Nissen huts don't look much on first sighting, but they are very clean and comfortable inside. This very well run guesthouse has a communal kitchen and TV area with an extensive video collection. Dorm beds cost RM6, and double rooms are RM16. A few rooms for RM25 are also available in the seminary house nearby on the hill. These rooms have a small bathroom cubicle and French doors leading onto the garden.

About two km from town along the road to Brinchang is *Bala's Holiday Chalets* (☎ 05-491 1660). The dorm beds for RM7 are very basic, as are the cheaper rooms for RM16 to RM25. The rooms with attached bath for RM40 to RM60 are better but expensive. The

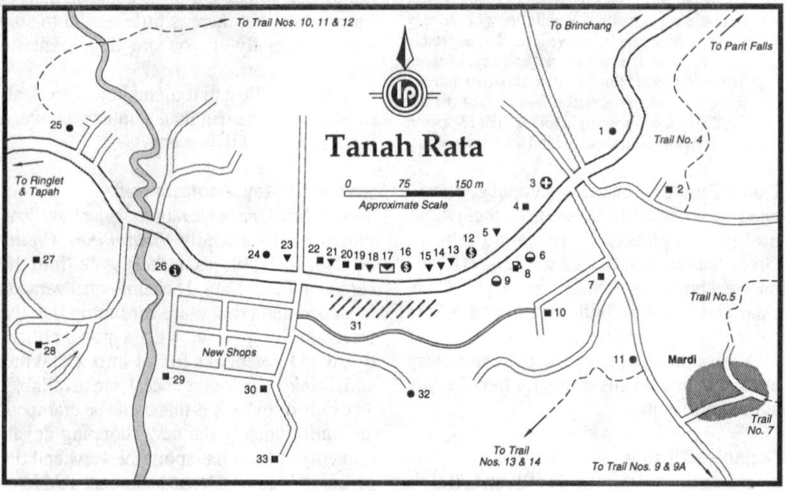

PLACES TO STAY

2 New Garden Inn
4 Highlands Lodge
7 Tanah Rata Rest House
10 Cool Point Hotel
19 Seah Meng Hotel
20 Downtown Hotel
22 Federal Hotel
27 Heritage Hotel
28 Father's Guest House
29 Cameronian Inn
30 Twin Pines Chalet
33 Papillon Guest House

PLACES TO EAT

5 Restoran No 14
13 Mayflower Restaurant
14 Restoran Thanam
15 Restaurant Kumar
18 Orient Restaurant
21 Roselane Coffee House
23 Jasmine Restaurant
31 Malay Food Stalls

OTHER

1 District Office
3 Hospital
6 Taxi Station
8 Shell Station
9 Bus Station
11 'Big Milk Bottle'
12 Maybank
16 Hongkong Bank
17 Post Office
24 CS Travel & Tours
25 Oly Apartments
26 Tourist Office
32 Council Offices

ALL PHOTOS BY RICHARD I'ANSON

Kuala Lumpur

Top: A view of central Kuala Lumpur

Middle: Drum festival in KL: traditional Malay music is based largely on the drum, or *gendang*.

Bottom: KL's Islamic Centre is near the modernistic National Mosque.

RICHARD I'ANSON

Peninsular Malaysia

Travellers can visit tea plantations in the Cameron Highlands and see how tea is harvested and processed and sample the brew.

pluses are the restaurant and views from the pretty garden. The distance from the centre is a drawback if you don't have transport.

Tanah Rata also has plenty of hotels on the main street. One of the best is the friendly *Seah Meng Hotel* (☎ 05-491 1618) at 39 Main Rd. It's a very clean hotel that has had a facelift. Doubles with common bath cost RM25, or rooms with attached bath are RM35 and RM40.

Right at the end of the strip is the *Highlands Lodge* (☎ 05-491 1922) at 4 Main Rd. It's clean but the rooms are very spartan. Doubles cost RM20 or RM28 with attached bath.

Others include the *Downtown Hotel* (☎ 05-491 2868) at No 41, with rooms from RM20 up to RM40 with attached bathroom. The *Federal Hotel* (☎ 05-491 1777) at No 44 is similar.

Brinchang All Brinchang's hotels are around the central square. The *Hotel Sentosa* (☎ 05-491 1907) is about the cheapest habitable place, with rooms from RM20 with common bath. Right next door is the *Plastro Hotel* (☎ 05-491 1387), which looks dingy from the outside but has good-sized double rooms with common bath for RM25. The *Silverstar Hotel* (☎ 05-491 1387) is basic but the cheapest around with rooms from RM14.

The *Hotel Highlands* (☎ 05-491 1588) is edging towards the mid-range and has rooms with bathroom from RM37 rising to RM53 in the high season.

Places to Stay – middle

Tanah Rata You don't get a lot for your money in the mid-range, and prices are much higher than elsewhere in Malaysia.

The cavernous *Tanah Rata Rest House* (☎ 05-491 1254) has plenty of colonial style, though it has seen better days. Large rooms with bathroom go for RM60 and range up to RM100 for huge, suite rooms. It's popular with families and often booked out, especially on weekends and school holidays.

The *New Garden Inn* (☎ 05-491 5170) is just the other side of the kids' playground in Tanah Rata. It has blocks of modern rooms in the large grounds from RM115, dropping to RM81 in quiet periods. The rooms in the main building have a more old-fashioned character. It is comfortable but nothing special.

The *Cool Point Hotel* (☎ 05-491 4914) is a new, modern hotel in the centre of town providing higher standards for a few ringgit more. Rooms cost RM125 and RM180, dropping to RM90 and RM140 in the off-season.

Private apartments can be rented and are worth considering for longer stays. Check with the shops on Main Rd displaying 'apartment for rent' signs, or the Seah Meng Hotel also rents a couple of moderately priced apartments on the hill behind the shops.

Brinchang Brinchang also has a few mid-range hotels. At the bottom of this range, the *Hill Garden Lodge* (☎ 05-491 2988) is on the western side of the town square and has neat and tidy rooms with bathroom from RM58, rising to a steep RM98 during holidays. The *Parkland Hotel* (☎ 05-491 1299), on the eastern side of the square, is a mini-high-rise and the best mid-range option. Double rooms are RM98 in peak periods or RM68 otherwise, presenting good value. Larger, more expensive rooms are also available.

Places to Stay – top end

The 'olde worlde' *Lakehouse* (☎ 05-495 6152) overlooks the lake near Ringlet and is very upmarket. Rooms cost RM220/250 with breakfast, and there are two-bedroom family suites for RM420. It is one of the most delightful hotels in the Highlands, and reasonable value for the high standards on offer, but you really need your own transport to stay here.

In Tanah Rata, the new *Heritage Hotel* (☎ 05-491 3888) is part of the huge apartment complex dominating the southern edge of town. It has 170 rooms from RM180 to RM280, plus 15%, but substantial discounts are often on offer. The private apartments surrounding the hotel start at a mere RM250,000 to buy, and are typical of the holiday apartments springing up willy-nilly across the country. They are the result of generous tax breaks allowed for anything vaguely related to the tourist industry, short-sighted planning regulations and a policy of development at any cost.

Back by the golf course on the other side of Tanah Rata, *The Smokehouse Hotel* (☎ 05-491 1214) is a copy of an old English country pub and looks the part, with exposed beams, low ceilings, open fireplaces and a suitably genteel atmosphere. It has been totally renovated and has suites for around RM400.

Overlooking the northern end of the golf course is the large *Merlin Inn Resort* (☎ 05-491 1205), which has rather ordinary double rooms from RM260 plus taxes. Off-season rates from RM158 are more palatable.

A km or so past the golf course, at the top of a windy side road, is the *Strawberry Park Resort* (☎ 05-491 1166). It's a huge new apartment-type set-up and is popular among Singaporeans on package holidays. The room rates are RM220, or RM250 to RM800 for an apartment.

In Brinchang, the huge new *Rosa Pasadena Hotel* (☎ 05-491 2288) is in the centre of town one street west of the main square. It's something of an eyesore and seems totally out of place in a town so small. Rooms start at RM130/160 plus taxes, and suites cost from RM650.

Places to Eat

Tanah Rata The cheapest food in Tanah Rata is to be found at the row of Malay food stalls along the main street. One stall, called the *Excellent Food Centre*, has an extensive menu and good food. On Saturday nights it becomes a 'sizzler' restaurant and is a cheap place to have a steak. Adjoining this stall is the *Fresh Milk Corner*, which, as you may have guessed, sells fresh pasteurised milk, yoghurt and lassis. Other stalls have Chinese food, satay and all the usual Malay dishes – just wander along until you see something attractive.

The other side of the road is Tanah Rata's lively restaurant scene. A host of cheap and moderately priced restaurants line the wide pavement perched above the street and many set up tables outside. Two of the most popular are the *Restaurant Kumar* and adjacent *Restoran Thanam*. Both serve Indian food and spruik out front for the travellers' trade. They also do western breakfasts, juices, lassis and Chinese food, including good claypot rice meals in the evening, all at low prices.

The best Indian food at even lower prices is at *Restoran No 14* next to the Maybank. They offer big thali meals and the popular masala dosa. It is so popular that they can run out of food, so don't leave your dining here too late.

Steamboat in the Highlands is a traditional taste treat. It's the Chinese equivalent of a Swiss fondue, where you get plates of meat, shrimp, vegetables and eggs and brew your soup over a burner on the table. You need at least two people, but the more the better. Try the set lunch or dinner at the *Orient Restaurant*, also in the main street. It's a traditional steamboat meal and is very good value at RM12 per person (minimum of two people).

Further along Main Rd is the Chinese *Jasmine Restaurant*, which has a good value, set four-course meal. At the *Roselane Coffee House* they serve good, cheap breakfasts,

Jim Thompson

The Cameron Highlands' most famous jungle walker was the man who never came back from his walk. American Jim Thompson is credited with founding the Thai silk industry after WWII. He made a personal fortune, and his beautiful, antique-packed house beside a *khlong* (canal) in Bangkok is a major tourist attraction today. On 26 March 1967, while holidaying in the Highlands, Jim Thompson left his villa for a pre-dinner stroll – never to be seen again. Despite extensive searches, the mystery of his disappearance has never been explained. Kidnapped? Taken by a tiger? Or simply a planned disappearance or suicide? Nobody knows. ■

and at lunch and dinner they have a set meal of soup, main course and ice cream for RM7.50.

Out at *Bala's Holiday Chalets*, they have an extensive menu, and excellent scones with jam and cream.

In addition to these places, all the middle and top-end hotels have their own expensive restaurants. *The Smokehouse Hotel* is 'ideal for homesick Brits' – you can get expensive tea and scones, sandwiches with the crusts cut off, and fairly pricey meals.

Brinchang Brinchang has a good night market, which sets up in the main square in the late afternoon, so you can eat for just a couple of ringgit then. A permanent food-stall centre is at the southern end of the square.

Brinchang has excellent Chinese food, and steamboat also features widely. For cheap, no-frills coffee shop fare, the *Kwan Kee* on the western side of the square is the most popular in town. Slightly more up-market places can be found on the street behind the Kwan Kee, near the Rosa Pasadena Hotel. Right at the entrance to the hotel, the *Palm Leaf Garden* has pleasing decor and moderate prices for good Malaysian and Thai food.

The restaurant on the ground floor of the *Parkland Hotel* has western food, with steaks from RM18, and other Chinese and Malay dishes, including steamboat for RM12 per person.

Ringlet There are a number of Chinese *kedai kopis* in Ringlet, or you can have a banana-leaf meal at the *Sri Melor Restoran*.

Getting There & Away

Bus It's a long, gradual and often scenic climb from Tapah in Perak state to the Highlands, with plenty of corners on the way. From the Golf Course Inn down to the main road junction, one visitor reported counting 653! The road passes a number of dirt poor Orang Asli settlements and roadside shanties where the Orang Asli sell their produce.

Buses from Tapah to Tanah Rata (RM3.50, two hours) run roughly every hour from 8.15 am to 6.15 pm and continue on to Brinchang. From Tanah Rata to Tapah there are buses on the hour from 8 am to 5 pm. The bus drivers on this route seem to be frustrated racing drivers, and everyone seems to overtake on blind corners.

Most long-distance buses leave from Tapah, but direct services go from Tanah Rata to KL (RM10, five hours) at 8.30 am and 1.30 pm, and to Penang (RM14.10, six hours) at 9.30 am and 2.30 pm. Book at the bus station. Express National has a bus to KL at 2.30 pm – book at the Downtown Hotel.

Many more services leave from Tapah and can be booked at any of the backpacker places, or at CS Travel & Tours (☎ 05-491 1200), 47 Main Rd, Tanah Rata. See under Tapah for full details of these buses.

Taxi There are regular taxis from the taxi stand (☎ 05-491 1234) on the main street in Tanah Rata. Things are much busier in the morning, so it's best to go then if you are looking for someone to share. The fares are RM6 to Tapah, RM20 to Ipoh and RM30 to KL.

Getting Around

Bus Most of the buses coming up from Tapah to Tanah Rata continue on to Brinchang, so getting between those two places is not a problem between 9 am and 8 pm.

From Tanah Rata to Kampung Raja, 25 km away across the Highlands, there are five buses daily. It's quite a scenic trip, and you can use these buses to get to the butterfly farm past Brinchang.

Taxi For touring around, a cab costs RM15 per hour, or you can go up to Gunung Brinchang and back for RM50.

The trip from Tanah Rata to Ringlet costs RM8, Brinchang costs RM2.50, and to Boh Tea Estates costs RM12.

IPOH

The 'city of millionaires' made its fortune from the rich tin mines of the Kinta Valley. The elegant mansions of Ipoh testify to the many successful Chinese miners, and some of the mines around Ipoh are still producing today. With a population of 390,000 people, over 500,000 including the surrounding districts, Ipoh is Malaysia's third largest city, but development fever is less rabid in this Chinese-dominated city than in other parts of Malaysia. As a result it is not as hurried as its size indicates and has retained many of its historic buildings.

For the visitor, Ipoh is mainly a transit town, a place where you change buses if you're heading for Pangkor Island, or where you pause to sample what is reputed to be some of the finest Chinese food in Malaysia. It's worth a longer visit to explore the Buddhist temples cut into the limestone outcrops north and south of the town.

'Old Town' Ipoh is centred on the Kinta River between Jalan Sultan Idris Shah and Jalan Sultan Iskandar and is worth a wander for the old Chinese and British architecture. The grand civic buildings close to and including the railway station give some idea of just how prosperous this city must have once been.

When the city expanded at the turn of the century, it extended east over the river to the 'New Town', also a repository of fine colonial shophouses, and now the more lively part of town. While the city centre remains largely preserved and free from development, it is also dead in the evenings, when most Ipohites gravitate to the shopping centres such as Plaza Ocean on Jalan Dato Onn Jaafar or the large Ipoh Parade on Jalan Abdul Adil.

Information

Ipoh has three tourist offices that can give you a brochure with a good map of Ipoh, but don't expect much else. The most convenient is that run by the Ipoh City Council (☎ 05-241 3733) on Jalan Abdul Adil. It is open Monday to Friday from 8 am to 4.15 pm, closed for lunch from 12.45 to 2 pm (12.15 to 2.45 on Friday), and also opens on Saturday morning from 8 am to 12.45 pm. The Perak Tourist Information Centre is to the north of town in the State Secretariat building on Jalan Panglima Bukit Gantang Wahab, and the Perak Tourist Association is to the east of town in the Casuarina Hotel on Jalan Gopeng.

Banks include the Hongkong and Standard Chartered banks on Jalan Dato Maharajah Lela near the clock tower, and the Maybank on Jalan Bandar Timah.

Many of Ipoh's main streets have been renamed in recent years, and while the street signs give the new (and often overly lengthy) names, the streets are often still known by the old names. The main ones include Jalan Chamberlain (now Jalan CM Yussuf), Jalan Leech (Jalan Bandar Timah), Jalan Station (Jalan Dato Maharajah Lela), Jalan Post Office (Jalan Dato Sagor) and Jalan Kelab (Jalan Panglima Bukit Gantang Wahab!).

Listen to Ipoh's traffic lights as they change to walk – they provide a gracious touch, striking up a chorus of Beethoven's *Ode to Joy*.

Colonial Architecture

Ipoh's grand colonial architecture is found in the Old Town. The **railway station** is a blend of Moorish and Victorian architecture, similar to the KL railway station, and houses the wonderfully old-fashioned Majestic Hotel. Directly opposite, the **Dewan Bandaran** (City Hall) is a dazzling white neo-classical building of grand proportions. A short walk away on Jalan Dato Sagor, the **Birch Memorial Clocktower** was erected to the memory of JWW Birch, Perak's first British Resident, who was murdered at Pasir Salak. Birch was a tactless 'adviser' who quickly assumed the role of colonial ruler, and the Perak chiefs were united in their effort to get rid of him. The friezes on the clock tower try to show more cultural sensitivity by depicting the growth of civilisation, including Asian civilisation.

The mock-Tudor **Royal Ipoh Club** overlooks the playing fields of the Padang and is still a centre of exclusivity. To the north of the Padang, **St Michael's Institution** is the most imposing of all colonial buildings, a grand three storey building with arched verandas.

The Old Town also features many rows of colonial shops, though those in the city area east of the river are generally in better condition and form one of the most extensive areas of later shophouse architecture in Malaysia.

Cave Temples

Ipoh is set among jungle-clad limestone hills that jut out spectacularly from the valley. The hills are riddled with caves that are a great source of mystic power, and over the years favourite meditational grottoes have became large scale temples. There are cave temples both south and north of the town – the most important being the Perak Tong Temple about six km north of town and the Sam Poh Temple a few km south of town. Both are right on the main road and easy to get to. Less impressive, but the closest to town, is the Gunung Cheroh Hindu Temple on Jalan Raja Musa Aziz, just a short walk from the YMCA. It comes alive during the spectacularly masochistic Thaipusam festival in February.

Perak Tong Temple The main feature of this large and impressive complex of caverns and grottoes is the paintings on the interior walls, done by artists from all over South-East Asia. There are various figures of the Buddha and a huge bell in the main chamber which is rung every time someone makes a donation.

A winding series of 300-odd steps leads up through the cave and outside to the balconied areas above, which have good views of the surrounding countryside – it's just a pity that Ipoh's factories clutter the immediate area.

The temple can be reached by city bus No 3 or any Kuala Kangsar-bound bus from the local bus station.

Sam Poh Tong Temple This temple to the south of town is very popular with people passing by, and the main attraction seems to be the tortoise pond in a small natural courtyard created ages ago when the roof of a cave collapsed. There are literally dozens of tortoises swimming in the thick green water. The tortoises are 'released' into the pond by locals, as it is apparently good luck to do so. As you enter the temple you'll be accosted by kids trying to sell you bunches of greenery to feed the tortoises.

Inside the temple itself there's a huge cavern with a small reclining Buddha, and various other smaller caverns. There's a vegetarian restaurant to the right of the temple entrance.

The ornamental garden in front of the temple is quite scenic and is a popular spot to have your photo taken.

The temple is open daily from 7.30 am to 6 pm and can be reached by a Kampar bus No 66.

Mekprasit Temple The Mekprasit Temple is a Thai Buddhist temple about three km north of town at 102-A Kuala Kangsar Rd, the main Taiping road. The main feature of the temple is the 24-metre-long reclining Buddha, one of the largest in Malaysia.

Geological Museum

Rock hounds might enjoy a visit to the geological museum, five km east of the railway station on Jalan Sultan Azlan Shah. Hundreds of mineral samples and fossils are on display, including exhibits relating to tin. It is open Monday to Friday from 8 am to 4.15 pm and Saturday from 8 am to 12.45 pm.

Places to Stay – bottom end

The main hotel area is around Jalan CM Yussuf, south of the main drag, Jalan Sultan Iskandar. As most roads around here are busy, rooms overlooking the street are affected by traffic noise, so ask for a room at the back. Though mid-range hotels are in abundance, cheap hotels are harder to find.

Bottom of the barrel is the *Cathay Hotel* (☎ 05-241 3322) at No 88, but what it lacks in ambience is more than made up for by the price and the friendly manager. Large, scruffy rooms cost RM19, RM21 with attached bathroom or RM32 with air-con and bath.

Of a slightly better standard is the *Embassy Hotel* (☎ 05-254 9496) at 35 Jalan CM Yussuf, where rooms with fan and bath

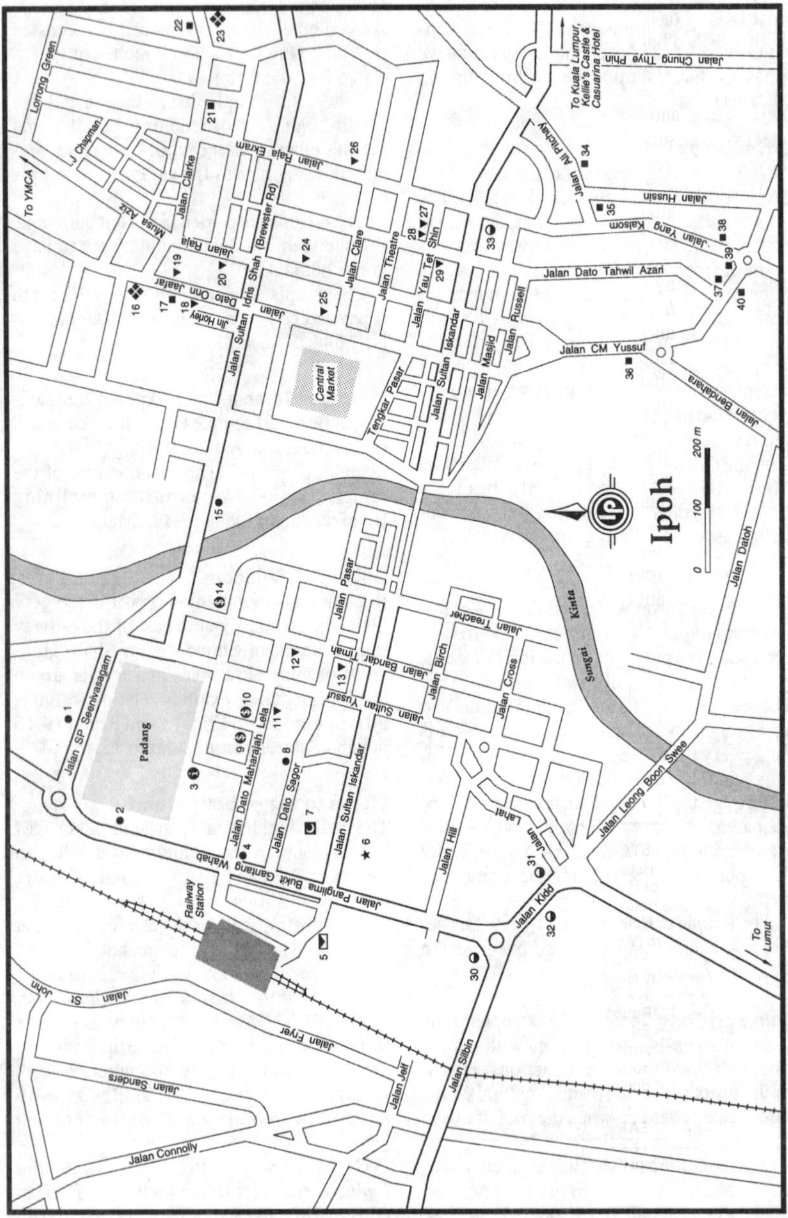
Ipoh
0
100
200 m
Sungai Kinta
Central Market
Padang
Railway Station
To YMCA
To Kuala Lumpur, Kellie's Castle & Casuarina Hotel
To Lumut
Lorrong Green
J Chapman
Musa Aziz
Jalan Clarke
Jalan Raja
Jalan Raja Ekram
Jalan Dato Onn Jaafar
Jln Horley
Jalan Sultan Idris Shah (Brewster Rd)
Jalan Clare
Jalan Theatre
Jalan Yau Tet Shin
Jalan Sultan Iskandar
Jalan Russell
Jalan Masjid
Tengkar Pasar
Jalan Chung Thye Phin
Jalan Ali Pitchay
Jalan Hussin
Jalan Yang Kalsom
Jalan Dato Tahwil Azar
Jalan CM Yussuf
Jalan Bendahara
Jalan Datoh
Jalan Leong Boon Swee
Jalan Treacher
Jalan Pasar
Jalan Bandar Timah
Jalan Birch
Jalan Cross
Jalan Sultan Yussuf
Jalan Lahat
Jalan Hill
Jalan Kidd
Jalan SP Seenivasagam
Jalan Dato Maharajah Lela
Jalan Dato Sagor
Jalan Sultan Iskandar
Jalan Panglima Bukit Gantang Wahab
Jalan Silibin
Jalan St John
Jalan Fryer
Jalan Sanders
Jalan Jelf
Jalan Connolly
1
2
3
4
5
6
7
8
9
10
11
12
13
14
15
16
17
18
19
20
21
22
23
24
25
26
27
28
29
30
31
32
33
34
35
36
37
38
39
40

cost RM28, or RM35 for an air-con double with attached bath.

The *New Hollywood Hotel* (☎ 05-241 5322) at No 72 Jalan CM Yussuf has rooms with air-con and bath for RM33/40. It's very clean but not such a great deal, though it does have a good restaurant, the Pinang, on the ground floor.

The mid-range *YMCA* (see below) also has dorm beds.

Places to Stay – middle

The *Wanwah (Winner) Hotel* (☎ 05-241 5177), 32 Jalan Ali Pitchay, is a large, spotless hotel – all tiles and polish. The fan rooms with attached bath for RM30 are very good value, and rooms with air-con, TV and hot water cost RM49.

A few doors away, the *Central Hotel* (☎ 05-241 0142), 20 Jalan Ali Pitchay, is a notch up in quality and also good value. Air-con rooms with shower but not toilet cost RM32, RM46 with bathroom and TV, or the large balcony rooms at front for RM57 are the most pleasant but noisy.

The *French Hotel* (☎ 05-253 3111), 60 Jalan Dato Onn Jaafar, is in a livelier part of town near the central market. This is a former top hotel that has lost some of its shine, but it has well-appointed rooms for RM75 and RM85 and suites for RM115.

The *YMCA* (☎ 05-254 0809), 211 Jalan Raja Musa Aziz, is very good value but inconveniently located two km north of the central market. Good, modern rooms with private facilities and hot water range from RM43/51 to RM53/61 for deluxe singles/doubles with balconies. The large but usually empty 20-bed dorm costs RM12, or smaller dorms are RM13 and RM15. The Y has large grounds, tennis courts, a pool table and a cafeteria. Take any Ipoh Garden bus to the Jalan Hospital intersection and then walk five minutes along Jalan Raja Musa Aziz.

Places to Stay – top end

Discounts of 20% or more off the published rates quoted here are readily available for the asking.

For style, but not service, the pick of Ipoh's hotels is undoubtedly the *Majestic Hotel* (☎ 05-255 5605) at the railway station. This magnificent colonial edifice has been restored, and even if not particularly well, it has at least maintained its character from the days when it was the preferred British hotel. Rooms costing RM100/120 on the 2nd floor face a courtyard and are comfortable but look like motel rooms. Go for the RM150 deluxe rooms on the 3rd floor, which have parquetry floors, high ceilings and planter's chairs outside on the wide, arched veranda. Discounts of up to 30% are available on all rooms.

PLACES TO STAY

17 French Hotel
21 Excelsior Hotel
22 Syuen Hotel
34 Central Hotel
35 Wanwah (Winner) Hotel
36 Embassy Hotel
37 New Hollywood Hotel & Rahman Restaurant
38 Ritz Kowloon
39 Cathay Hotel
40 Ritz Garden Hotel

PLACES TO EAT

11 Restoran Kari Shal's
12 Kedai Kopi Kong Heng
13 Restoran Chui Kah
18 Blue Window Cafe
19 KFC
20 Cafe Deliparis
24 Medan Selera Dato Tawhil Azar
25 McDonald's
26 French & Noor Jahan Bakeries
27 Hup Kee
28 Restoran Wong
29 Restoran Onn Kee

OTHER

1 St Michael's Institution
2 Royal Ipoh Club
3 Perak Tourist Information Centre
4 Dewan Bandaran
5 Post Office
6 Police
7 Mosque
8 Birch Memorial Clocktower
9 Hong Kong Bank
10 Standard Chartered Bank
14 Maybank
15 MAS
16 Plaza Ocean
23 Ipoh Parade
30 City Buses
31 Lumut Buses
32 Long-Distance Bus Station
33 Hosni Express Buses

The *Ritz Garden Hotel* (☎ 05-254 7777), 79 Jalan CM Yussuf, is a somewhat characterless hotel straddling the middle and top end but has very well appointed rooms with all the trimmings for RM118. Its sister hotel, the *Ritz Kowloon* (☎ 05-254 7778), 92 Jalan Yang Kalsom, has slightly smaller but virtually identical rooms for only RM88 (after discount).

Ipoh's best hotels, all adding 15% tax and service to their rates, in ascending order are: the older *Excelsior Hotel* (☎ 05-253 6666), 43 Jalan Clarke, with rooms from RM189; the *Casuarina Hotel* (☎ 05-255 5555) on Jalan Gopeng (the KL road), a true international-standard hotel with large grounds and rooms from RM220; and the more central *Syuen Hotel* (☎ 05-252 8889), 88 Jalan Sultan Abdul Jalil, with rooms from RM230.

Places to Eat

Ipoh has plenty of restaurants and is the home of the rice noodle dish known as kway teow. Ipoh's kway teow is reputed to be the best in Malaysia. The city's best-known place for kway teow is *Kedai Kopi Kong Heng* on Jalan Bandar Timah between Jalan Pasar (Market Rd) and Jalan Dato Maharajah Lela, a bustling restaurant serving a bit of everything. The kway teow soup has tender strips of chicken and prawns. They also have good roast chicken and popiah. Kong Heng is one of the oldest Chinese restaurants in the city, but there are several others like it on and off Jalan Bandar Timah which bustle during the day.

In the same area, the *Restoran Chui Kah* on the corner of Jalan Bandar Timah and Jalan Pasar is an upmarket Chinese restaurant which specialises in steamboat.

Ipoh has plenty of food-stall centres. On Jalan Raja Musa Aziz, the large *Medan Selera Dato Tawhil Azar*, better known as the Children's Playground, has stalls arranged around a small square. It's a very popular place for Malay food in the evening and is open late. During the day there's a small food centre next to the Birch Memorial Clocktower, while at night the *Pusat Makanan Majestic* on Jalan Raja Musa Aziz is sometimes lively when night market stalls set up on the streets out front. Ipoh's most renowned hawker centre is *Glutton Square* at Ipoh Garden, but it is six km north-east of the city centre.

At night, many of the restaurants in the Old Town are closed, so a good place to head for is Jalan Yau Tet Shin in the New Town. On opposite corners, the *Restoran Wong* and *Restoran Onn Kee* specialise in tauge ayam (chicken and bean sprouts) and kway teow. These very popular coffee shop restaurants set up tables on the pavement that spill onto the street as diners flock in the evening. A little further down the street is the slightly more upmarket *Hup Kee* for seafood.

For Indian food, the *Rahman Restaurant* on Jalan CM Yussuf is very clean and has a wide range of dishes. It also has an air-con room upstairs. A good air-con Indian restaurant is the *Restoran Kari Shal's* on Jalan Dato Maharajah Lela, where prices are very reasonable.

The central market is huge and has a wide range of fruit and vegies, a great place to come if you are putting your own meals together. Jalan Raja Ekram has a couple of good bakeries, the *French* and *Noor Jahan*, for breads and pastries. *Café Déliparis* on Jalan Raja Musa Aziz is a copy of the Delifrance chain and not as good but has reasonable pastries and coffee.

For something more familiar, *McDonald's* is on Jalan Clare near the central market. The *Blue Window Cafe*, 56 Jalan Dato Onn Jaafar, is a chic, air-con restaurant for steaks, New Zealand lamb and grilled prawns. Prices are high but the food is innovative, and cheaper Asian dishes are also offered.

The Majestic Hotel's *Locomotive Restaurant* on the ground floor at the railway station has magnificent pillars and gigantic ceilings – great atmosphere even if the buffet meals are only average.

Entertainment

During the Emergency in the 1950s, Ipoh's tag as the 'City of Tin' was replaced with 'City of Girls' due to the number of bars and bordellos catering to British troops. The troops have gone, but Ipoh still has an inordinate number of seedy karaoke lounges, bars and 'health clubs', mostly on and around Jalan Yang Kalsom, where girls and clients drink in dingy cubicles.

The less-seedy *Make a Lot* karaoke lounge next to the Winner Hotel on Jalan Ali Pitchay is at least lively and thoughtfully offers a home delivery service for those who have drunk too much to drive home. On the outskirts of town around the Parkson Ria department store on Jalan Sultan Azlan Shah at Ipoh Garden, you'll find a number of bars that are lively on the weekend.

Otherwise, Ipoh's nightlife is thin on the ground and is mostly confined to the big hotels such as the *Excelsior, Casuarina* and *Syuen*.

Getting There & Away

Air Pelangi Air (☎ 05-312 4770) flies to Kuala Lumpur (daily, RM66), Melaka (daily, RM120), Langkawi (four times weekly, RM107) and Medan (Tuesday and Saturday, RM198) in Sumatra. MAS has four departures daily to KL (RM66).

Bus Ipoh is on the main KL-Butterworth road; 219 km north of KL, 173 km south of Butterworth. The long-distance bus station is in the south-east corner of the city centre, a taxi ride from the main hotel area. There are numerous companies here, with departures at varying times. The touts are fairly vigorous, so there's no danger of not being able to find a bus. Many of the air-con departures to places outside the immediate Ipoh area leave at night.

Only one bus to Lumut goes from the long-distance bus station at 5 pm – the main service is offered by Syarikat Perak Roadway, whose buses leave from their station across Jalan Tun Abdul Rasak. Departures go roughly every hour, and though some are air-con, most are not.

The city bus station also handles buses to the outlying regions close to Ipoh, such as Kangar, Batu Gajah and Gopeng, and local services to Kuala Kangsar.

Destinations and fares include Kuala Kangsar (RM3), Butterworth (RM8), Tapah (RM4.50), KL (RM9.50), Lumut (RM3.50), Melaka (RM16), Johor Bahru (RM26), Alor Setar (RM13), Kuantan (RM23) and Hat Yai (RM28) in Thailand. Tickets should be booked in advance if possible.

Hozni Express Buses on Jalan Yang Kalsom also handles a few services, mostly to the east coast.

Train Ipoh is on the main railway line between Singapore and Butterworth and all trains stop at Ipoh. The 10.40 am and 5.36 pm express trains north also stop at Kuala Kangsar (50 minutes) and Taiping (1½ hours) before continuing on to Butterworth (3½ hours).

Taxi Long-distance taxis leave from beside the bus station, and there is also another rank directly across the road. Destinations include Kuala Kangsar (RM5), Taiping (RM8), Butterworth (RM16), Lumut (RM7) and KL (RM22). A taxi to Tapah, for the Cameron Highlands, costs RM8 per person, but departures are not frequent and chances are you'll have to take a whole taxi. A taxi all the way to the Cameron Highlands costs RM80.

AROUND IPOH

Kellie's Castle

This amazing leftover from colonial times is set by a small river about 30 km south-west of Ipoh. The castle referred to is in fact an old unfinished mansion. It was to be one in the mould of great colonial houses, complete with Moorish-style windows and even a lift. A wealthy British plantation owner, William Kellie Smith, who lived in a splendid mansion in this area early this century, commissioned the building of the 'castle', which was to be the home of his (as yet unborn) son. Seventy Hindu artisans were brought in from Madras to work on the mansion. Smith died in Lisbon in 1926 on a trip home to England, and the house was never finished. The jungle has reclaimed some of the building, entwined with vines and massive trees, but the well-tended site is now a popular tourist spot, open 8.30 am to 7.30 pm (admission 50 sen).

Close by is a Hindu temple, built for the artisans by Smith when a mysterious illness decimated the workforce and the remaining workers believed that a temple was needed to appease the gods. To show their gratitude to Smith, the workers placed a statue of him, complete with white suit and topee, among the Hindu deities on the temple roof. The temple is about 500 metres from the 'castle'.

Kellie's castle is inconvenient to reach without your own transport. The easiest way is to take a bus to Batu Gajah or Gopeng from Ipoh's local bus station. A bus service runs approximately every hour between Batu Gajah and Gopeng, passing right out front of Kellie's castle.

LUMUT

Despite attempts to promote Lumut as a tourist destination in its own right, the town is little more than the departure point for Pangkor Island. Lumut is another go-ahead area. It's port has been developed to service the nearby industrial estates, and the town itself has had a pleasing facelift. Country clubs and luxury hotels are springing up everywhere, but Lumut has little to offer apart from some souvenir shops selling shells and some reasonable beaches outside town.

The Malaysian Navy has its principal base just outside town, and some 25,000 sailors make up the overwhelming majority of the towns inhabitants. You'll see the huge, Singapore-like apartment complexes of the naval quarters as you go out on the Dindings River to Pangkor. At the base is the **Royal Malaysian Navy Museum**, open daily except Friday. The sailors frequent **Teluk Batik** beach, a good beach seven km from town. Teluk Batik is also the site for the Pesta Lumut sea carnival in August each year.

Information

The Tourism Malaysia office (☎ 05-683 4057) is on the other side of the clock tower from the jetty. Motorists on their way to Pangkor can find a 24 hour long-term car park behind the Shell petrol station. Cars are guarded, and the charge is RM5 per day.

Places to Stay

If you get marooned on the way to Pangkor, Lumut has a reasonable choice of hotels and plenty of restaurants.

The *Phin Lum Hooi Hotel* (☎ 05-683 5641), 93 Jalan Titi Panjang, is about half a km from the bus stand not far from the ferry jetty. It charges RM18 for a single and is clean and friendly and has a restaurant downstairs.

The most convenient hotels are those on the main street, Jalan Iskandar Shah, right near the ferry jetty. *Hotel Indah* (☎ 05-683 5064) at No 208 is a good mid-range hotel with spotless air-con singles/doubles with hot water for RM40/50. Next door, the *Hotel Manjung Permai* (☎ 05-683 4934) at No 212 is a more upmarket high-rise with rooms from RM80.

The *Orient Star* (☎ 05-683 4199), one km further out along Jalan Iskandar Shah towards the navy base, is typical of the new developments. This international-class hotel is on the waterfront but has no beach and seems over the top for Lumut. Rooms start at RM220/240 plus 15%.

Getting There & Away

Bus Lumut is 206 km south of Butterworth and 101 km south-west of Ipoh, the main turn-off for Lumut on the KL-Butterworth road. The bus station is near the centre of town, a five minute walk to the ferry jetty. Lumut is well connected with other destinations on the peninsula. On Pangkor, bus agents in Pangkor town, such as the Chuan Full Hotel, handle bookings for the express buses.

The easiest connection is on the new highway to/from Ipoh via Batu Gajah. Ipoh-Lumut buses run hourly and cost RM3.50. Direct buses from KL to Lumut (RM13, five hours) run several times per day. There are daily buses from Butterworth to Lumut for RM8.50, or alternatively take one of the frequent buses from Butterworth to Taiping, then another bus on to Lumut from there. Other destinations served by buses from Lumut include Johor Bahru (RM29), Singapore (RM33), Melaka (RM21) and Tapah (RM8.50) for the Cameron Highlands.

Taxi Long-distance taxis are RM27.50 per person for Butterworth-Lumut or RM10 for Ipoh-Lumut. To KL it's RM30 air-con.

Boat Kuala Perlis Langkawi Ferry Service (☎ 05-683 4258) at the ferry jetty has a high-speed service from Lumut to Belawan in Sumatra. It leaves Lumut on Thursday at 10 am, and leaves Belawan on Wednesday at 11 am. The trip takes 3½ hours and costs RM110/90 one-way in 1st class/economy. The price includes the bus ride between Belawan and Medan. In Medan contact Trophy Tours (☎ 061-514888) at Jalan Brigadier Jend Katamso 33-D.

PULAU PANGKOR

The island of Pangkor is close to the coast off Lumut – easily accessible via Ipoh. It's a popular resort island noted for its fine beaches, which can be visited by the road that rings the island, while the jungle-clad hills of the interior are virtually untouched.

At eight square km and with a population of 25,000, Pangkor is a relatively small island, but that hasn't stopped the government trying to promote and develop it as one of Malaysia's main tourist destinations. This means that Pangkor's laid-back, kampung feel is disappearing, though development is still relatively low key. Pasir Bogak is the most developed beach, consisting of a string of mid-range hotels, a few restaurants and not much else. Teluk Nipah, probably the best beach on the island, is in transition from a small kampung to another Pasir Bogak as new mid-range hotels spring up around the local guesthouses. The only other developments on Pangkor are the three mega-resorts on isolated beaches.

Pangkor is a popular local resort, only a 30 minute ferry ride from the mainland and close to large population centres, so crowds are inevitable. It is very popular on weekends and holidays, but during the week the beaches are almost empty. A visit to the island is still principally a 'laze on the beach' operation, but there are also a few interesting things to do.

Before tourism took off, Pangkor relied on fishing. Fishing and dried fish products are still a major industry for the island, particularly on the east coast. Pangkor was also a bit player in the battle to control trade in the Straits of Melaka. In the 17th century the Dutch built a fort on the island in their bid to monopolise the Perak tin trade, but were less than keen to defend Perak against Achehnese and Siamese incursions. They were driven out by a local ruler before returning briefly some 50 years later. In 1874 it was the setting for the signing of the Pangkor Treaty, when a contender to the Perak throne sought British backing. As a result, a British Resident was installed in Perak and the colonial era on the peninsula began.

Orientation

Finding things on Pangkor is very simple. On the east coast of the island, facing the mainland, there's a continuous village strip comprising Sungai Pinang Kecil (SPK), Sungai Pinang Besar (SPB) and Pangkor town.

The ferry from Lumut stops at SPK before Pangkor town, the main town. The road which runs along the coast on this side turns west at Pangkor town and runs directly across the island, only two km wide at this point, to Pasir Bogak, the most developed beach on the island. From there it runs north to the village of Teluk Nipah, which is the focus of the budget accommodation, and on to the northern end of the island, past the new airstrip, reaching Pangkor's other flash hotels at Teluk Belanga and Teluk Dalam in the north. The road from there back to the eastern side of the island is winding and very steep in parts but paved all the way.

Information

The Maybank in Pangkor town is open the usual hours, and also has an ATM for credit-card withdrawals. The moneychanger in the Wonderful shop on the road to Pasir Bogak changes cash and travellers' cheques at lower rates but is open until 9 pm.

Beaches

The beach at **Pasir Bogak** is OK for swimming but during holidays it's crowded, at least by Malaysia's 'empty beach' standards. It's a lovely white sand beach but quite narrow. **Teluk Nipah** further north is a wider, better beach. The best beach on this side is at **Coral Bay**, about a 20 minute bicycle ride from Pasir Bogak. The water is a clear emerald-green due to the presence of limestone, and usually the beach is quite clean and pretty.

Turtles come in to lay their eggs at night on **Teluk Ketapang** beach, only a short walk north of Pasir Bogak. May, June and July are the main months, and June is usually best of all if you want to go midnight turtle-spotting. Sightings are becoming increasingly rare these days.

Teluk Belanga (Golden Sands Beach) at the northern end of the island is pleasant. Access is restricted to Pan-Pacific Pangkor Resort guests, though day-trippers can visit for a ridiculous RM40. In between there are a number of virtually deserted beaches which you can reach by boat, by motorcycle or on foot.

Emerald Bay on nearby Pulau Pangkor Laut is a beautiful little horseshoe-shaped bay with clear water, fine coral and a gently sloping beach. The entire island of Pangkor

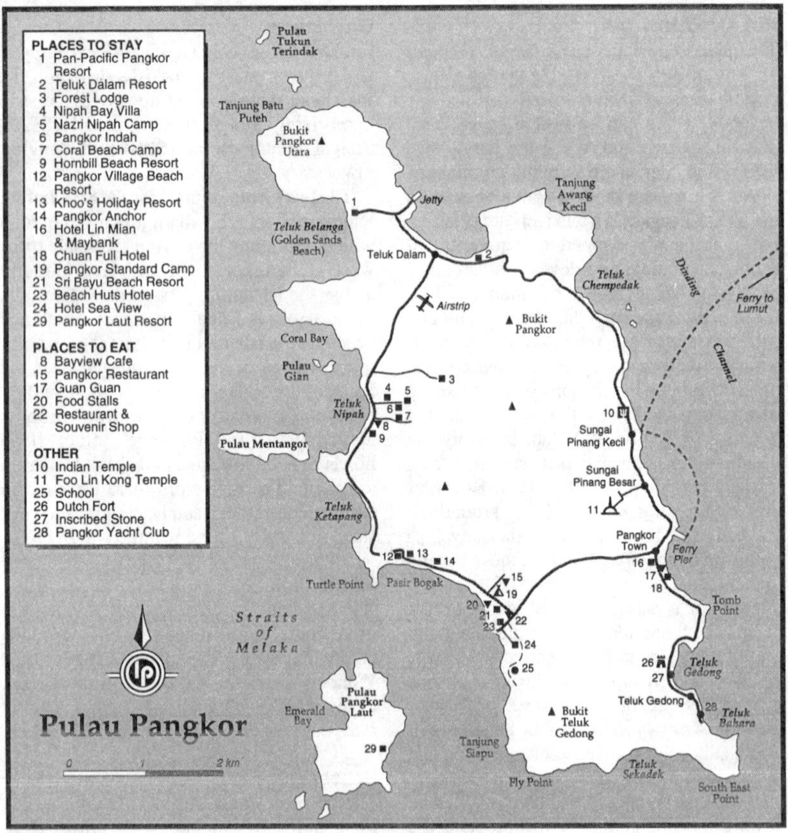

Laut has been taken over by a hotel conglomerate, but some of the boat tours stop at the beach.

Pangkor sometimes suffers the usual blight of Malaysian beach resorts, litter, especially after a long weekend.

Exploring the Island

The island lends itself well to exploration by motorcycle, by bicycle or on foot. Spend a day doing a loop of the island, following the paved road all the way around. By motorcycle it takes about three or four hours with stops, around six or seven hours by bicycle, or you could even walk it in a long day.

The western side has a few deserted beaches to stop off at before the road heads inland past the airstrip to Kampung Teluk Dalam, a straggling fishing village. Unless you can talk your way in for nothing, there's not much point in forking out RM40 to visit the Pan-Pacific at Teluk Belanga, so keep heading east along the new road over the headland. This is a steep and twisting road through some superb jungle.

On the eastern side, from SPK it's a continuous village strip on to Pangkor town – messy but full of interest. There's lots to look at: boat building, fish being dried or frozen and a colourful south Indian temple. This is principally the Chinese and Indian part of the island.

In SPB the **Foo Lin Kong Temple** is worth a quick look. Located on the side of the hill, the main 'attraction' is a mini Great Wall of China! It also has some tacky rock paintings and other features of dubious artistic merit. The animal cages are downright depressing. The temple is signposted from the main road.

Pangkor's one bit of history is three km south of Pangkor town at Teluk Gedong. There the **Dutch Fort** was built in 1670, after the Dutch had been given the boot from Lower Perak. In 1690 they rebuilt the wooden fort in brick, but lost it soon afterwards. The Dutch retook the fort in 1693 but, despite frequent visits, did not reoccupy it until 1745; only three years later they abandoned it for good. The old fort was totally swallowed by the jungle until 1973, when it was rebuilt as far as the remaining bricks would allow.

On the waterfront 50 metres beyond the fort is a huge **inscribed stone**, carved with the symbol of the Dutch East India Company (VOC) and other ancient graffiti, including a faint carving which supposedly depicts a tiger stealing a child. This is said to relate to an incident when a child of a local European dignitary disappeared while playing near the rock. The Dutch liked the idea of the tiger story; the more likely explanation is that the boy was abducted by some of the disenchanted locals.

The road ends just past the fishing village of Teluk Gedong at the Pangkor Yacht Club, a small marina and club house that fails to attract interest, let alone yachts.

Other Activities

Snorkelling gear, boats, canoes and even jet skis can be hired through hotels or on the beach at Pasir Bogak and Teluk Nipah. Speed boats will take you for a blast, or you can go water skiing. A small boat to take you snorkelling to some of the small nearby islands or less accessible beaches starts at around RM50. Round-the-island boat trips start at around RM150 for three to four people but a boat can cost up to RM250. It pays to negotiate.

Boats can also be hired to go to Pulau Sembilan, a group of nine islands popular for sports fishing, about 1½ hours south-west from Pangkor by boat. An annual fishing event is held at the islands, which also have deserted white-sand beaches.

A jungle trail crosses the island from Teluk Nipah and comes out near the Foo Lin Kong Temple, while another trail lead from Pasir Bogak to Bukit Pangkor before joining the east coast road. Walking trails are lightly used and often overgrown – take a guide and *parang*.

Places to Stay

Pasir Bogak has most of the larger mid-range resorts and, while it's not the Costa Brava, it does get crowded and is pressing to be a real resort beach. Though it has a souvenir shop, a few restaurants and weekend crowds, there is no nightlife to speak of and no resort scene. As Pasir Bogak is already quite cramped, a number of new places have sprung up at the next bay to the north, Teluk Nipah. Teluk Nipah has a better beach, and while development is taking over, it still clings to its kampung atmosphere.

Teluk Nipah The hotels here are at the mercy of the taxi mafia, which not only get the high taxi fare but also extract RM10 commission from hotel owners for every guest they deliver. Consequently this is added to the hotel rates, but if you are staying more than a couple of nights you may be able to negotiate a discount.

The most popular travellers-only place is *Joe Fisherman Village* (☎ 05-685 2389). Accommodation consists of the usual A-frame 'chalets' found at beach resorts throughout the country. While very basic, most people find them quite adequate. The cost is RM20 for two, or slightly more substantial cottages cost RM30. Good basic meals are available, and there are motorbikes and bicycles for rent.

Right next door is *Nazri Nipah Camp* (☎ 05-685 2014), a friendly place that has a variety of accommodation and meals. A-frames cost RM20, rooms with bathroom cost RM40 and larger A-frame chalets around the garden cost RM50.

Further towards the beach accommodation is mid-range. *Pangkor Indah* (☎ 05-685 2017) is a small, new place with a good cafe. Attractive air-con chalets for RM80 are one of the best deals around. Next along is another new construction, the *Pangkor Bayview* (☎ 05-685 3540). The rooms are comfortable, but the building is a large intrusion. Opposite, the very pleasant *Nipah Bay Villa* (☎ 06-685 2198) is one of the best in Teluk Nipah, with a large grassed area and quite luxurious air-con chalets for RM145 a double, including meals. Children below 12 years pay RM15.

Nearer the beach, the *Ombak Inn* and *Lyana Villa* are less inspiring with rooms from RM50.

The *Hornbill Beach Resort* (☎ 05-685 2005) has the best position, directly opposite the beach. Its charming hosts offer high standards of accommodation and service. Attractive air-con rooms, some of the best in Teluk Nipah, face the beach or the jungle behind and cost RM130.

The street behind the main accommodation area also has an increasing number of places to stay. The *Coral Beach Camp* (☎ 05-685 2711) is a long-running budget place with A-frame huts for RM25, or double rooms for RM50. It lacks atmosphere but will arrange reasonably priced boat trips. The *Suka Suka Beach Resort* (☎ 05-685 2494) has pleasant gardens and attractive but fairly spartan bamboo chalets with attached bathroom for RM65. The *Seagull Beach Resort* (☎ 6852878) is neat and new, but no bargain. Simple chalets with mattresses on the floor cost RM30/40 for singles/doubles or good air-con double rooms are RM110.

The *Forest Lodge* (☎ 05-685 2005) is to the north of the village and a couple of km inland. Surrounded by jungle but a long walk from the beach, it caters mostly to groups. Large dorms cost RM8 and chalets are being built.

Pasir Bogak The rest of Pangkor's accommodation possibilities are grouped at each end of the beach at Pasir Bogak. The accommodation here is mainly aimed at the upper end of the market, although there are a couple of cheaper options. Prices quoted are weekend rates but discounts apply during the week.

Starting at the western end, there's the *Pangkor Village Beach Resort* (☎ 05-685 2227), which is mainly tented accommodation costing RM14 per person, the main drawback being that the tents get intolerably hot in the afternoon. Small, air-con chalets along the beach front cost RM130 a double and basic huts are RM43, including dinner and breakfast.

Next up is *Khoo's Holiday Resort* (☎ 05-685 1164). The main building is a rather ugly concrete conglomeration, but the wooden chalets on the hill behind are a good option.

The chalets with attached bathroom are fairly simple but have great views across the ocean. They cost RM54.60 and RM78.75 with discounts of around 20% during the week.

The cheapest option is the *Pangkor Anchor* (☎ 05-685 1363), a short distance along from Khoo's. Small, ageing A-frame huts with a mattress on the floor cost RM8.50 per person, but they are in a shady grove and so remain fairly cool.

At the other end of the beach, where the road from Pangkor town crosses the island, are the other hotels. The *Hotel Sea View* (☎ 05-685 1605) has very average air-con doubles for RM115 with bath, and better family rooms or chalets for RM161, all including breakfast. Various packages and off-season discounts are offered.

The *Beach Huts Hotel* (☎ 05-685 1159) has ageing double rooms at RM69, or with air-con at RM80. Double chalets with attached bath, air-con, TV and fridge cost RM138, and these are set in the garden just back from the beach.

On the other side of the road behind the beach is the *Pangkor Standard Camp* (☎ 05-685 1878), a reasonable cheaper option. Cramped A-frame huts cost RM21/31 for a double/triple, or chalets are RM42 a double. They rent bicycles and motorbikes.

Right behind the Beach Huts Hotel is the sprawling *Sri Bayu Beach Resort* (☎ 05-685 1929). This well-conceived place has all the facilities of a top-end resort, including swimming pool, tennis courts and a choice of eating options. Chalets cost RM320 a double including breakfast and dinner, plus taxes, but discounts of around 30% apply in quiet periods.

Elsewhere Apart from Pasir Bogak, there is also the *Pan-Pacific Pangkor Resort* (☎ 05-685 1399) at Teluk Belanga (Golden Sands Beach) at the northern end of the island. The Pan-Pacific has rooms starting at RM260 plus 15% and go up to RM550 for a bungalow. Sporting and recreational facilities include a nine-hole golf course, and the hotel is on a very pleasant stretch of beach, nicely isolated from the development elsewhere. The beach here is restricted to hotel guests only, but if you want to pay RM40 you can use the pool and beach (not the golf course) and get a lunch included.

A couple of km away, the new *Teluk Dalam Resort* is almost finished and has individual luxury bungalows. The beach is OK, but the resort is not as well sited as the Pan-Pacific.

Pulau Pangkor Laut, the island opposite Pasir Bogak, is totally in the grasp of the *Pangkor Laut Resort* (☎ 05-699 1100). It is certainly exclusive and does its best to shun locals, day-trippers and other riff raff. There is a small swimming pool, tennis courts, two restaurants, a disco, and three or four private beaches around the island, including the picturesque Emerald Bay on the side facing away from Pangkor. Rates start at RM400 for a double including meals and range up to RM10,000 for a luxury yacht. There's a reservation office at Lumut, which arranges transport to the island.

Pangkor Town As the whole attraction of Pangkor is the beaches, there is little point in staying in Pangkor town, but if you get stuck there are a couple of cheap Chinese hotels.

The *Hotel Lin Mian* (☎ 05-685 1123), right near the Maybank, is very tidy but unwelcoming. Air-con rooms start at RM40. Head further down to the exceptionally friendly *Chuan Full Hotel* (☎ 05-685 1123), 60-62 Main Rd, a rickety old wooden hotel but immaculately kept with a veranda at back overlooking the waterfront. Singles/doubles cost RM15/20 with bathroom or RM30 a double with air-con, and you can book buses from Lumut here.

Places to Eat

Teluk Nipah Many guests tend to dine at their accommodation, which nearly all serve food, but Teluk Nipah does have some basic food stalls at the beach and a couple of restaurants. The *Bayview Cafe* is a good spot for a meal, either inside or opposite at tables overlooking the beach. Down the street next to the Bayview Cafe, the *Restoran Takana*

Juo is tucked away back from the beach, but it's a pleasant, cheap restaurant serving Malay food.

Pasir Bogak All the hotels have restaurants and there are a few other places as well. There's a small food centre near Khoo's, and another further along the beach near the Sri Bayu.

Tucked away along a small dirt road which runs alongside the Pangkor Standard Camp is the *Pangkor Restaurant*, a cheap seafood and Chinese food restaurant which is popular with the locals.

More upmarket is the *Restoran Number One*, an excellent seafood restaurant where a good meal of prawns, fish or crab will cost around RM20 per person, much more for lobster.

The restaurant in the *Hotel Sea View* is outdoors, right by the beach. While the food is only mediocre, it's an excellent place to watch the sunset from. The restaurant in the *Beach Huts Hotel* is reasonable.

Pangkor Town Pangkor town has a proliferation of cheap, Chinese kedai kopis, some of which serve excellent seafood. On Main Rd, the *Guan Guan* is an old favourite for seafood and *Restoran Fook Hang* is also popular. The *Restoran Kasim Selamat* does good roti canai and murtabak.

Getting There & Away

Air Pelangi Air flies to/from KL (RM120) and Singapore's Seletar airport (RM204, S$190 from Singapore).

Boat Pan Silver Ferry has departures between Lumut and Pangkor town every 20 minutes from 6.45 am to 8 pm and then at 9 pm, and from 6.30 am to 8 pm from Pangkor. The fare is RM2 each way. Ferries also stop at Sungai Pinang Kecil between Lumut and Pangkor town.

From Lumut six ferries daily also go to the northern end of the island across the isthmus from the Pan-Pacific Pangkor Resort, the first at 8.30 am, the last at 6.30 pm. The other ferry service connects Lumut with the Pangkor Laut Resort on Pulau Pangkor Laut, leaving Lumut at 10.30 am, 1.30 and 4.15 pm.

Getting Around

Bus Buses run every hour or so from Pangkor town across the island to the far end of the beach at Pasir Bogak (RM1) and back again. Two buses a day go to Teluk Nipah, but these are for locals only, forcing you to take the taxis.

Taxi Pangkor has plenty of minibus taxis. From the jetty in Pangkor town, the standard fares are: Pasir Bogak (RM4), Teluk Nipah (RM10), Pan-Pacific Pangkor Resort (RM18) or RM30 for an around-the-island trip.

Motorcycle & Bicycle The ideal way to see the island is by motorcycle or bicycle. There are a number of places at Pangkor town, Pasir Bogak and Teluk Nipah that rent them out for around RM25 to RM30 per day for a motorcycle, and RM10 per day for a bicycle.

KUALA KANGSAR

Beside the highway, north-west of Ipoh, Kuala Kangsar has been the royal town of Perak state since the sultan moved his capital here in the 18th century. It was also the first foothold for the British as they moved to control the peninsula by installing Residents at the royal courts in the 1870s. By the 1890s the rapid growth of the tin towns of Ipoh and Taiping overshadowed Kuala Kangsar, and the town remains a quiet backwater steeped in Malay tradition.

This small town has a split personality. The small central business area bustles like any town, but to the east overlooking the Perak River, the royal district is spacious and quiet and the most attractive of all Malaysia's royal cities. Kuala Kangsar's main sights are quite impressive though few, and the whole town can easily be explored in a morning or afternoon.

Things to See

Heading out on Jalan Istana past the wide Perak River, the first striking example of the wealth of the sultanate is the small but magnificent **Ubadiah Mosque** with its fine golden onion-dome. It's probably the finest mosque in Malaysia, although it looks almost as if it's viewed through a distorting mirror, since its minarets are squeezed up tightly against the dome. It was completed in 1917 after delays due to WWI and rampant elephants that destroyed the marble tiles.

Overlooking the river, **Istana Iskandariah** is a suitably opulent palace built in 1933. It is best viewed from the riverside to appreciate the original palace, which mixes Art Deco with Islamic motifs. The later annex on the southern side dating from 1984 is less striking. The palace is not open to visitors on a casual basis, but permission for visits can be obtained by writing to the Sultan's Office, Setiausaha Sulit, DYMM Sultan Perak, 33007 Kuala Kangsar.

There is also an earlier wooden *istana*, **Istana Kenangan**, which was built in 1926 without the use of nails, and served as the royal quarters until the Istana Iskandariah was completed. This earlier istana houses the Royal Museum, with displays relevant to the state and the Perak royal family. The museum is open daily from 9.30 am to 5 pm, but is closed on Thursday afternoon and Friday.

Closer to town on Jalan Istana near the Ubudiah Mosque, the **Istana Hulu** is another substantial palace inspired by Victorian architecture. Built in 1903, it is now the Raja Perempuan Mazwin School.

Kuala Kangsar was the birthplace of Malaysia's great **rubber industry**. A number of rubber trees had been planted by Hugh Low in his residency gardens, from seed stock smuggled from Brazil, but it was not until the invention of the pneumatic tyre in 1888, and then the popularity of the motor car at the turn of the century, that rubber suddenly came into demand and rubber plantations sprang up across the country. All of the trees in the new plantations are descended

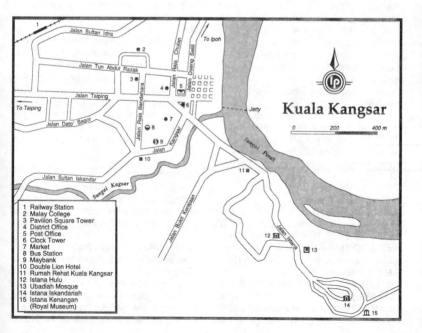

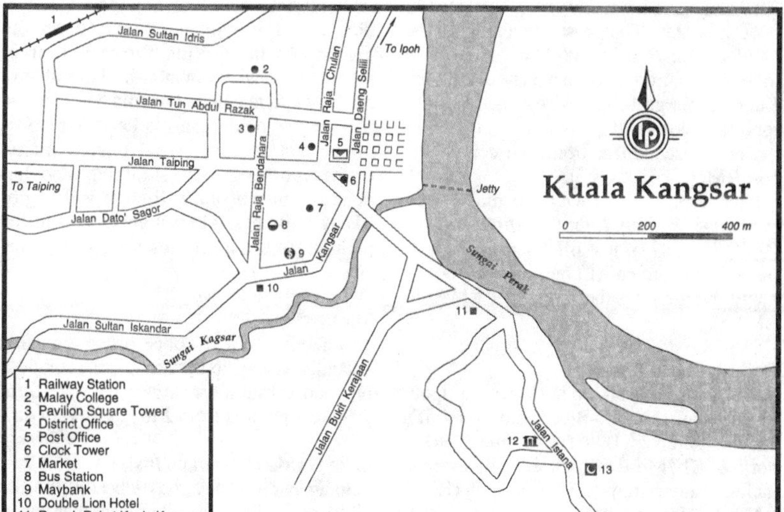

from the original rubber trees planted in Kuala Kangsar or the Singapore Botanical Gardens. You can still see one of those first trees in the district office compound.

As in many Malaysian cities with a colonial past, the **Malay College** to the north of town is the most impressive colonial building. Established in 1905, it was the first and one of the only Malay schools to provide English education with the purpose of training the Malay elite for the civil service. It not only provided clerical workers for the British administration but nationalist leaders who formed the more conservative 'Malaya for Malays' faction.

Opposite the Malay College, the **Pavilion Square Tower** is a delightful folly overlooking the surrounding parkland and playing fields. Built in 1930, this small, three storey sports pavilion of Malay and colonial design allowed the royalty and VIPs to view polo matches in comfort.

Places to Stay

Kuala Kangsar has a few cheap hotels for an overnight stay. The most convenient is the *Double Lion Hotel* (☎ 05-776 1010), close to the bus station above a bakery at 74 Jalan Kangsar. Large rooms with attached bathroom are clean and good value at RM18 in the newer section at front. Air-con rooms cost RM30.

The best place in town is the modernised resthouse *Rumah Rehat Kuala Kangsar* (☎ 05-776 3872), just off Jalan Istana near the kris monument. Large, air-con rooms, many overlooking the river, cost RM60 to RM100.

Getting There & Away

Kuala Kangsar is 50 km north-west of Ipoh, just off the main KL-Butterworth road. It's 123 km south of Butterworth and 269 km north of KL. More frequent bus connections include Butterworth (RM5.60), Ipoh (RM3, RM1.50 non-air-con), KL (RM11.70), Lumut (RM5.10) and Taiping. For the east coast, the only connection is to Kota Bharu (RM14.50) at 9.45 am; one morning and one afternoon bus go as far as Gerik (RM4.85).

Taxis leave from next to the bus station, with regular departures to Butterworth (RM11), KL (RM24), Ipoh (RM4.50) and Taiping (RM3).

The train station is less conveniently located to the north-east of town. All KL-Butterworth trains stop in Kuala Kangsar.

TAIPING

The 'town of everlasting peace' hardly started out that way. A century ago, when it was known as Larut, the town was a raucous, rough-and-tumble tin-mining centre – the oldest one in Malaysia. Bitter feuds broke out three times between rival Chinese secret societies, with injury, torture and death taking place on all sides. When colonial administrators finally brought the bloody mayhem under control in 1874, they took the prudent step of renaming the town. Though it was then the largest and most important town in Perak, by 1890 the Kinta Valley around Ipoh had already begun to overshadow Taiping as the centre of the tin industry.

Taiping is now a low-key town, and any new developments are centred on the highway on the outskirts. The central part of town is somewhat down-at-heel but always lively, while in contrast the old colonial district centred on the famous Lake Gardens is green and tranquil. Apart from misty, Chinese-looking views, Taiping also has quite a number of old, well-preserved Anglo-Malay buildings. There's good food in the night market, a great museum and no tourists.

Information

The helpful Tourist Police office, on Jalan Iskandar at the taxi station, can provide a map and answer most queries. It is open from 9 am to 1 pm and from 2 to 5 pm every day.

Lake Gardens (Taman Tasik)

Taiping is renowned for its beautiful Lake Gardens, built on the site of an abandoned tin mine right beside the town in 1890. The well-kept gardens owe some of their lush greenery to the fact that Taiping has one of the highest annual rainfalls in Peninsular

Malaysia. In the hills which rise above the gardens is Bukit Larut (formerly Maxwell Hill), the oldest hill station in Malaysia.

The Lake Gardens also contains the small, pleasantly landscaped **Taiping Zoo**, open 8.30 am to 6.30 pm. Admission is RM2 plus a small camera fee.

Muzium Perak

At the far end of the gardens, the state museum is open from 9 am to 5 pm daily, but closed from 12.15 to 2.45 pm on Friday. Housed in a fine colonial building, it's the oldest and one of the best museums in Malaysia. Its contents include interesting exhibits on the Orang Asli, as well as craft and historical exhibits.

The motley collection of stuffed animals, reptiles and birds is slightly repugnant but highly educational, representing as it does

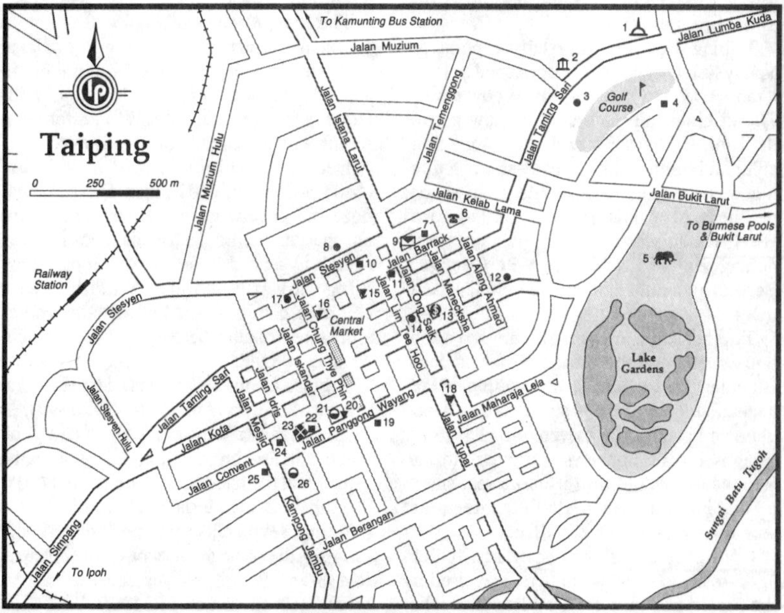

PLACES TO STAY
- 4 New Rest House
- 7 Hotel Fuliyean
- 10 Town Rest House
- 11 Hong Kong Hotel
- 19 Swiss Hotel
- 22 Peace Hotel
- 24 Peking Hotel
- 25 Legend Inn

PLACES TO EAT
- 15 Restoran Tom Yam Taiping
- 16 Bismillah Restoran
- 18 Pusat Penjaja Taiping
- 20 Food Centre

OTHER
- 1 Ling Nam Temple
- 2 Muzium Perak
- 3 Prison
- 5 Taiping Zoo
- 6 Telekom
- 8 King Edward School
- 9 Post Office
- 12 District Office
- 13 Standard Chartered Bank
- 14 Jam Besar (Clock Tower)
- 17 St George's School
- 21 Taxi Station
- 23 The Store (Department Store & Supermarket)
- 26 Local Bus Station

almost all mammals found in Malaysia and a wide cross-section of birdlife.

Historic Buildings

A wander around town will turn up some reminders of Taiping's former glory. The neo-classical **District Office** on Jalan Kota lies at the edge of Taiping's central Chinatown and at the start of the colonial district around today's Lake Gardens. Closer to town on Jalan Kota, the **Jam Besar** (clock tower) was built in 1890 and once functioned as the fire station.

Taiping was also the starting point for Malaysia's first railway line; opened in 1885, it ran 13.5 km to Port Weld but is now closed. The original railway station is now part of the **King Edward School**, itself a gracious colonial building. The railway station building is just to the west of the main school building. Also on Jalan Stesyen, the **Town Rest House** was once the governor's residence, built in 1885, and **St George's School** is another imposing colonial landmark.

Taiping has a number of fine old shophouses, such as the **Peace Hotel** on Jalan Iskandar. This magnificent example of Peranakan architecture has stucco tiles, stained glass and beautifully carved bird and flower designs on the upper wall dividers inside. Renovation would turn it into a real showpiece, but until then don't contemplate staying here – it's a seedy dive.

Opposite the museum, the **prison**, built in 1885 to house lawless miners, was used by the Japanese during the war, later as a rehabilitation centre for captured Communists during the Emergency and then for housing political detainees under the ISA (Internal Security Act) ruling.

Near the museum, the **Ling Nam Temple** is the oldest Chinese temple in Perak and has a boat figure dedicated to the Chinese emperor who built the first canal in China.

Other Attractions

Taiping has an **Allied War Cemetery**, just east of the Lake Gardens, with row upon row of headstones for the British, Australian and Indian troops killed during WWII. Further past the cemetery down a side road, the **Burmese Pools** are a popular bathing spot by the river.

Places to Stay

Taiping has an excellent selection of moderately priced accommodation. Most of the cheap hotels are scattered in the streets around the central market, the liveliest but noisiest part of town. The better choices are a few streets away.

The *Hong Kong Hotel* (☎ 05-807 3824) at 79 Jalan Barrack (the entrance is on Jalan Lim Tee Hooi) is close to everything but in a quiet side street. This welcoming, well-kept hotel is a bargain at RM16/22 for large rooms with attached bath and air-con.

Nearby, the historic *Town Rest House* (☎ 05-808 8482), 101 Jalan Stesyen, was once the governor's residence. The rooms are spartan, but this place has loads of character and a good little cafe overlooking the King Edward School. A double with common bath costs RM20, or large rooms with three double beds and attached bathroom cost RM35.

Right in the thick of things near the central market, the *Swiss Hotel* (☎ 05-807 4899), 37 Jalan Panggong Wayang, is clean and good value with air-con rooms from RM24. In the same area, the friendly *Peking Hotel* (☎ 05-807 2975), 2 Jalan Idris, is a fine old colonial building set back from the street. Quiet rooms at the back are very basic but cheap at RM18 and RM22. Newer and better front rooms with air-con cost RM30.

The *Hotel Fuliyean* (☎ 05-806 8648), 14 Jalan Barrack, is a newer mid-range hotel with dazzling tile work everywhere. Immaculate rooms with bathroom, hot water, TV and phone are RM50.

The *New Rest House (Rumah Rehat Baru)* (☎ 05-807 2044) in Taman Tasik (Lake Gardens) is approached through the pillars of what once the Resident's house – you can drive through the remains of Hugh Low's living room. The resthouse itself is a large, modern concrete place that is showing signs of decay, but it overlooks the Lake Gardens, has a good terrace restaurant, and is very good value at RM31.50 for huge doubles with bathroom, fan and balcony, RM35 with air-con. Though close to Taiping's main attractions it is well out of the city, so you'll need a taxi to get there.

Taiping's best hotel is the *Legend Inn* (☎ 05-806 0000), a three-star hotel with rooms for RM120 and RM160, less after discount. Rooms have all the trimmings and the hotel has a good lobby coffee shop, but this new hotel is already looking a little spotty.

Places to Eat

Taiping has a good array of food centres. The one next to the taxi station is very clean and has a wide variety. The biggest, the *Pusat Penjaja Taiping*, takes up a whole block on Jalan Sultan Abdullah and serves mostly Chinese food with a Malay section at one end. Taiping's large night market has many open-air eating stalls – murtabak and delicious ayam percik (marinated chicken on skewers) are specialities.

Taiping also has a host of coffee shops serving economical food. One of the oldest and most venerable is the *Bismillah Restoran* for roti and biryani.

Restoran Tom Yam Taiping at 120 Jalan Taming Sari is an excellent little restaurant with seductive air-con and a huge range of dishes at cheap prices. As well as tom yam, many Malay dishes are featured as well as more expensive seafood and western dishes such as steak or lamb grills.

The *New Rest House* does a good stab at western food, such as chicken cutlets, and has fine views of the mountains and the Lake Gardens from the terrace.

Getting There & Away

Taiping is several km off the main KL-Butterworth road. It's 88 km south of Butterworth and 304 km north of KL. The express bus station is out in the sticks at Kamunting near the highway, seven km from town. There are no hotels nearby or any reason to stay in Kamunting – take a bus (60 sen) or taxi (RM3.50) to the centre. If you just want to visit Taiping for the day, the left luggage counter at the bus station, open 9 am to 11 pm, costs RM1 per bag per day. Frequent buses go to Butterworth (RM1.90, RM3.80 air-con), Ipoh (RM3.80) and KL (RM13.20), with less-frequent connections to other destinations, including Lumut and 9 pm buses to Kuantan.

The local bus station in the centre of town near the market has non-air-con buses to the surrounding towns and further afield to Kuala Kangsar, Ipoh and Grik.

The taxi station is near the central market. Regular taxis operate to Butterworth (RM8.50), Ipoh (RM8) and Kuala Kangsar (RM4).

All KL-Butterworth trains stop at Taiping's railway station, half a km east of the town centre.

BUKIT LARUT (MAXWELL HILL)

The oldest hill station in Malaysia is 12 km from Taiping, at an altitude of 1019 metres. It was formerly a tea estate that has now been closed, and this quiet little station is simply a cool and peaceful place to be. There are no golf courses, fancy restaurants or other hill-station trappings – let alone casinos. Few people visit Maxwell Hill, renamed Bukit Larut but still more commonly known by its original name. In fact, the bungalows there only accommodate a total of 66 visitors. During the school holidays all are full. Even if you don't stay, Maxwell Hill makes an excellent day trip.

Getting up to Maxwell Hill is half the fun, and once there you've got fine views down over Taiping and the Lake Gardens far below. From the road towards the top you can see the coast all the way from Penang to Pangkor on a clear day.

Exploring the Hill

Most visitors go up and back by Land Rover, though the hill is also a favourite with local walkers who go up in about three to four hours. The walk along the road through the jungle is pleasant but taxing, or you can take a Land Rover up and walk down.

The first stop is at the Tea Gardens checkpoint at the Batu 3.5 (5.5 km) mark, where a ramshackle guesthouse and a few exotic trees are the only reminder of the former tea estate. Next up at Batu 6 (9.5 km) is the main post at Maxwell Hill, where you'll find the Bukit Larut Guesthouse, Bungalow Beringin, Rumah Angkasa and a *kantin* for meals. The Land Rovers stop at the main administration office, where you book for the return journey – very advisable on weekends. There are some pleasant strolls through the nearby gardens from here.

The Land Rovers will continue one km up the hill to Gunung Hijau Rest House. Nearby are the Cendana, Tempinis and Sri Kanangan bungalows. From here it is a half-hour walk along the road, noted for its profusion of butterflies, to the transmitter station at the top of the hill.

The jungle on the hill is superb, but the only real trail for exploring it leads off the main road before the transmitter station. It follows a water pipe to Gunung Hijau (1448 metres) and an abandoned guesthouse. You can follow the leech-ridden path for only about 15 minutes to an old pumping station, now curiously functioning as a small Shiva shrine, but even this short walk allows a good chance of seeing monkeys and numerous birds. Beyond the shrine, the trail is overgrown and should only be undertaken with a guide.

Walking back down the road, it takes half an hour from Gunung Hijau Rest House to the Bukit Larut Guesthouse, another one hour to the Tea Gardens checkpoint, then another 1½ hours to the Land Rover station at the bottom of the hill.

Places to Stay & Eat

You can book space in one of the bungalows by ringing ☎ 05-807 7241 or by writing to the Officer in Charge, Bukit Larut Hill Resort, Taiping. If you've not booked earlier, you can ring from the Land Rover station at the bottom of the hill.

There are two resthouse bungalows – *Bukit Larut Guesthouse* (four double rooms) and the *Gunung Hijau Rest House* (three double rooms), with rooms for RM15. The bungalows *Beringin*, *Cendana* and *Tempinis* are equipped with kitchens, so you need to come with provisions. Beringin accommodates up to six people and costs RM30, while Cendana has three double rooms, accommodating up to eight people, and costs RM100. Tempinis can accommodate 10 people and costs RM100. The *Rumah Angkasa* and *Sri Kayangan* are more luxurious and cost RM150 and RM200, but are normally available only for VIPs. The *Tea Gardens Guesthouse* has long been closed but plans are afoot to renovate and reopen it. Meals are available at the bungalows but should be ordered in advance.

Day-trippers can get basic rice or noodle meals at the *Surau Kanteen* near the main office, or the nearby *Bukit Larut Guesthouse* is usually open for meals and has great views.

Getting There & Away

Prior to WWII, you had a choice of walking, riding a pony or being carried up in a sedan chair, as there was no road to the station. Japanese POWs were put to work building a road at the close of the war, and it was opened in 1948.

Private cars are not allowed on the road, which is only open to government Land Rovers that run a regular service from the station at the foot of the hill, just above the Taiping Lake Gardens. They operate every hour on the hour from 8 am to 6 pm and the trip takes about 40 minutes.

The winding road negotiates 72 hairpin bends on the steep ascent, and traffic is strictly one way. You can glimpse superb views through the trees on the way up. The up and down Land Rovers meet at Tea Gardens, the midway point. Fares from the bottom cost RM2 to the administration office and RM2.50 to Gunung Hijau Rest House. Alternatively, you can walk to the top in about three or four hours.

To book a seat on a Land Rover (which is advisable), ring the station at the bottom of the hill (☎ 05-807 7243). A taxi from central Taiping to this station, about two km east of the Lake Gardens, should cost around RM4.

GERIK

Gerik, in the isolated north-east of Perak, was once just a logging 'cowboy town', but the East-West Highway and the huge Temengor Dam hydroelectric scheme have put it on the map. For WWII buffs, the area has many associations with the exploits of Force 136.

Lying as it does at the edge of the some of most extensive and untamed jungle in Malaysia, this small, grotty town still has something of a frontier feel, with a very mixed population of Chinese merchants, Malay and Indian logging workers and a noticeable presence of negrito Orang Asli.

Places to Stay

Gerik has a number of basic hotels. A short walk from the bus station down Jalan Takong Datuk, the *Friendly Park Hotel* (☎ 05-791 2378) at No 60 is one of the better choices. Clean, comfortable rooms with attached bathroom cost RM32 or RM40 with air-con and hot water. Further along the *Great Wall Hotel* at No 20 is the best budget option. Clean, basic rooms with shared bathroom cost RM15.

The *Rest House (Rumah Rehat Gerik)* (☎ 05-791 1454), 682 Jalan Haji Meor Yahya, is the best. It is in the only attractive part of town, surrounded by gardens, 1.5 km west of the centre. Large, modern rooms cost RM45 or RM60 with air-con.

Getting There & Away

Though it is a central point between the east and west coasts, Gerik is not well connected for buses. An 8.45 am express bus runs to Butterworth; otherwise catch a local bus to Baling first. For Kota Bharu, first catch a bus to Tanah Merah. Buses to Ipoh (RM6) leave at 11 am and 4 pm, and buses to Kuala Kangsar and Taiping leave at 7.45 am and 3.30 pm. The bus to KL (RM16.60) leaves at 10 am. The taxi station is opposite the bus station; fairly regular share taxis go to Butterworth (RM15), Kuala Kangsar (RM10) and Ipoh (RM15) in the morning.

A few buses throughout the day go to Pulau Banding for RM5, or Tanah Merah buses also go via Pulau Banding. A chartered taxi to Pulau Banding costs RM20, or RM30 return.

TASIK TEMENGOR

This huge lake, formed by damming the upper reaches of the Perak River, is now one of Malaysia's largest lakes. It is at the centre of the most undeveloped region of the peninsula, surrounded by dense jungle, home to the negrito tribes of the Kintak and Jahai people.

The main focus of tourist interest is **Pulau Banding**, a small island in the middle of the lake, straddled by the East-West Highway. The highway actually connects the island to the shore, with bridges over the lake on either side. A few resorts cater to anglers attracted by the many fish in the lake, the largest variety being the tomak (giant snakefish) weighing in at around five kg.

The climate is appreciably cooler than on the coast, and though the dead trees poking out of the lake detract from the beauty, the expanses of water and surrounding jungle-clad hills are very scenic. Boat and fishing trips can be organised, as well as trips to Orang Asli villages on the edge of the lake.

Places to Stay & Eat

The *Banding Island Resort* (☎ 05-791 2076) is on the western side of the island, 35 km from Gerik. It's an old-fashioned hotel with a good dining room and wonderful views of the lake. Large rooms are very comfortable and well maintained but a little expensive at RM75 to RM99. Budget accommodation is advertised for RM20 but often seems to be unavailable. A basic but cheap food centre is nearby. Boat tours are offered, including a round-island trip for RM45 per person (minimum four), a rainforest and bird-watching trip for RM60 and a visit to an Orang Asli village for RM99.

Aman Resort (☎ 05-791 1005) on the eastern side of the island is better value for accommodation and tours, though somewhat dull. Accommodation is in floating chalets on the lake for RM35, and there is a restaurant.

Similar accommodation is available at *Mohammed Shah Resort* (☎ 05-791 2885) across the bridge on the mainland.

Getting There & Away

Pulau Banding can make a good overnight stop on the East-West Highway if you have a car, but bus connections are more difficult. Butterworth-Kota Bharu buses will drop you off if you pay for the whole trip, but they are usually full when passing through and won't pick up. The easiest access is from Gerik, or coming from Kelantan, take a Gerik bus from Tanah Merah.

Penang

Penang state, or Pulau Pinang, is made up of the island of Penang and a narrow strip of land on the mainland coast known as Sebarang Prai (or Province Wellesley). While there is little to see on the coastal strip, the island itself is a major tourist attraction and has been on the travellers' overland trail for years.

Full Name: Pulau Pinang Mutiara Timur
Area: 1031 sq km
Capital: Georgetown
Population: 1.1 million

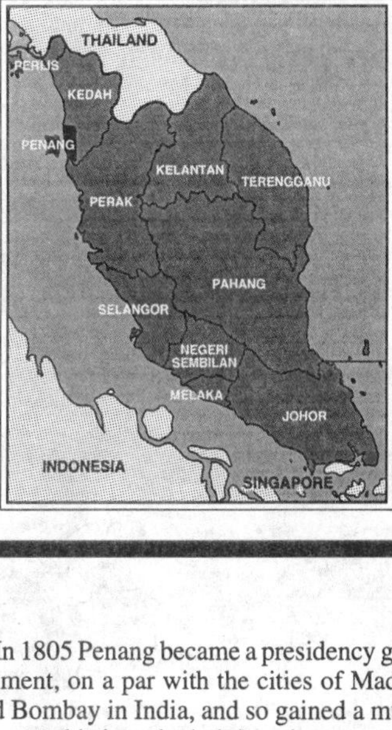

History

In 1786 Captain Francis Light, on behalf of the East India Company, acquired possession of Penang (Betelnut) Island from the local sultan in return for protection. He renamed the island Prince of Wales Island, as the acquisition date happened to fall on the Prince's birthday. It's said that Light loaded his ship's cannons with silver dollars and fired them into the jungle to encourage his labourers to hack back the undergrowth. Whatever the truth of the tale, he soon established the small town of Georgetown, named after the Prince of Wales, who later became King George IV, with Lebuh Light, Chulia, Pitt and Bishop as its boundaries. Founding towns must have been a Light family tradition – his son is credited with the founding of Adelaide in Australia, which is today a sister city to Georgetown. Light also negotiated with the sultan for a strip of land on the mainland adjacent to the island, and this became known as Province Wellesley.

To encourage settlers, Light permitted new arrivals to claim as much land as they could clear, and this, coupled with the duty-free port which Light had declared, quickly attracted settlers from all over Asia. Although it was virtually uninhabited in 1786, by the turn of the century Penang was home to over 10,000 people.

The local economy was slow to develop, as mainly European planters set up pepper and spice plantations, all of which were slow-growing crops and required a high initial outlay, and they were hindered by a limited labour force.

In 1805 Penang became a presidency government, on a par with the cities of Madras and Bombay in India, and so gained a much more sophisticated administrative structure.

In 1816 the first English-language school in South-East Asia was opened in Georgetown. Penang has always been a cosmopolitan place and has attracted dreamers, artists, intellectuals and dissidents.

Sebarang Prai

BUTTERWORTH

There's little reason to pause in Butterworth; it's just a port for ferries to Penang Island, and the site of a large air force base. The only point of interest is the **Penang Bird Park**, 12 km east of the ferry terminal across the river. This large landscaped park has over 800 species of birds, most from South-East Asia. It is open from 9 am to 7 pm; entry is RM4. Take bus No 65 from the Butterworth bus terminal, or a Juara bus from the Komtar centre in Georgetown.

Most of the land transport (buses, trains, taxis) between Penang and other places in Peninsular Malaysia and in Thailand actually leaves from Butterworth, right next to the ferry terminal for ferries to and from Georgetown.

Places to Stay

Butterworth has a number of hotels, if for some reason you want to stop. *G-Seven Transit* (☎ 04-331 2662), 4832 Jalan Pantai, is only a five minute walk north of the bus station past the Esso oil terminal. It's a plain but clean guesthouse with partitioned rooms for RM15/25; air-con rooms are RM25/35, RM45 with attached bathroom. The *Hotel Sri Pantai* is another budget hotel a few doors along.

Plenty of other hotels can be found a couple of km further north in the centre of the town. The *Ambassadress Hotel* (☎ 04-

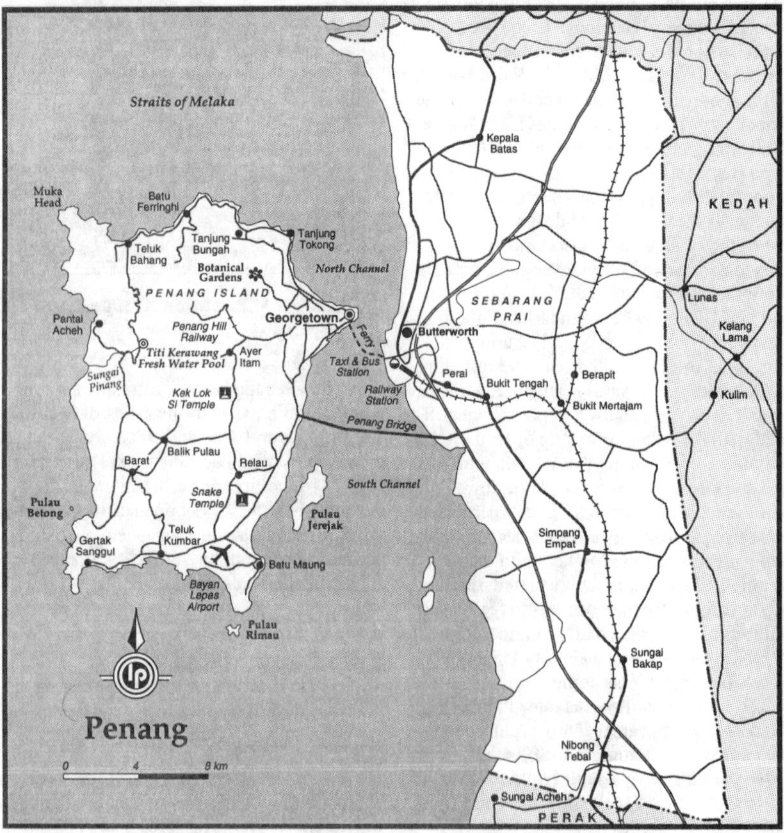

332 7788) at 4425 Jalan Bagan Luar has air-con rooms from RM53. The *Travel Lodge* (☎ 04-333 3399) at 1 Lorong Bagan Luar is at the top of the range and has rooms from RM130.

Getting There & Away

See the Getting There & Away and Getting Around sections at the end of this chapter for all transport-related options to and from Butterworth.

Penang Island

Penang is the oldest British settlement in Malaysia, predating both Singapore and Melaka. It is also one of Malaysia's major tourist attractions. This is hardly surprising, for the 285 sq km Penang Island has popular beach resorts and an intriguing and historically interesting town which is also noted for its superb food.

Penang's major city, Georgetown, is often referred to as Penang, although correctly that is the name of the island (the actual Malay spelling is Pinang). Central Georgetown is a sprawling, somewhat grotty Chinese city, steeped in history and with plenty of old character that is fast disappearing elsewhere. If you walk from the ferry to Chinatown, the main tourist centre around Lebuh Chulia, it would seem that Penang missed the development boom sweeping the rest of the country. However, high-rise apartments and industrial areas crowd the outskirts of expanding Georgetown, especially south towards the bridge and airport, and west to the beaches.

Penang's beaches are touted as a big drawcard for visitors. The main resort of Batu Ferringhi has its appeal, but the beaches are not as spectacular as the tourist literature would make out. Beaches close to the city suffer to some extent from pollution. The beaches along the north coast are the most visited and easily accessible, while those around the south of the island are undeveloped and difficult to reach.

GEORGETOWN

Georgetown is a real Chinatown, with far more Chinese flavour than Singapore or Hong Kong. Those larger cities have had their Chinese flavour submerged under a gleaming concrete, glass and chrome confusion, but in the older parts of Georgetown the clock seems to have stopped 50 years ago. It's an easy-going, colourful city full of crumbling old shophouses, bicycle rickshaws and ancient trades.

The city has plenty of reminders of colonial rule, and its winding streets and old temples are always fascinating to wander around. Most visitors to the island stay in Georgetown, which is well supplied with hotels, restaurants and all the facilities of a major city.

Orientation

The old city of Georgetown has a population of 220,000, and the greater urban area has a population of 400,000 out of a total of just over half a million for the whole island. Georgetown is in the north-east of the island, where the straits between the island and the mainland are at their narrowest.

A vehicle and passenger ferry service operates 24 hours a day across the three-km-wide channel between Georgetown and Butterworth on the mainland. South of the ferry crossing is the Penang Bridge – the longest in South-East Asia – which links the island with Malaysia's North-South Highway (Lebuh Raya).

Georgetown is a compact city and most places can easily be reached on foot or by bicycle rickshaw. The old colonial part of town centres on Fort Cornwallis. Lebuh Pantai is the main street of the 'city', the financial district crammed with banks and stately buildings that once housed the colonial administration.

You'll find most of Georgetown's popular cheap hotels along Lebuh Chulia in Chinatown. Jalan Penang is a main thoroughfare and a popular shopping street. In this area you'll find a number of the more expensive hotels, including, at the waterfront end of Jalan Penang, the venerable Eastern & Oriental Hotel.

If you follow Jalan Penang south you'll pass the modern multistorey Kompleks Tun Abdul Razak (Komtar), where the MAS office is located, and eventually leave town and continue towards the Bayan Lepas Airport. If you turn west at the waterfront end of Jalan Penang, you follow the coastline and eventually come to the northern beaches, including Batu Ferringhi. This road runs right around the island and eventually brings you back into town, via the airport.

Finding your way around Georgetown is slightly complicated by the street names. Jalan Penang may also be referred to as Jalan Pinang or as Penang Rd – but there's also a Penang St, which may also be referred to as Lebuh Pinang! Similarly, Pitt St is sometimes called Lebuh Pitt, and Chulia St is Lebuh Chulia. The old spelling for Lebuh is Leboh and some of the street signs still use this spelling.

Information

Tourist Offices The Penang Tourist Association (☎ 04-281 6665) is on Jalan Tun Syed Sheh Barakbah, close to Fort Cornwallis in the centre of Georgetown. It is a useful source of information and the office is open from 8.30 am to 1 pm and 2 to 4.30 pm Monday to Thursday, from 8.30 am to 12.30 pm and 2.30 to 4.30 pm on Friday and from 8.30 am to 1 pm on Saturday.

The central government tourist body, Tourism Malaysia, also has an office (☎ 04-262 0066) just a few doors along in the same building with all the usual Tourism Malaysia literature, although it has nothing really specific for Penang. It is open similar hours.

The best of the tourist offices is the Penang Tourist Guides Association office (☎ 04-261 4461) on the 3rd floor of the Komtar centre on Jalan Penang. It is open Monday to Saturday from 10 am to 6 pm and Sunday from 11 am to 7 pm. It is staffed by volunteer guides who really know their stuff and are extremely helpful with specific inquiries.

Foreign Consulates Medan, the entry point from Penang to the Indonesian island of Sumatra, is counted as one of the 'usual' entry points where most nationalities are issued an entry permit on arrival for 60 days.

Visas are not required to visit Thailand for a stay of up to four weeks. For longer stays, apply for a visa at the Thai Consulate, open 9 am to noon and 2 to 4 pm, Monday to Friday. It has a reputation for being difficult with long-term stayers coming down to renew their visas, but bona fide tourists shouldn't have problems. Tourist visas cost RM33 for two months; lots of travel agencies up and down Lebuh Chulia will obtain the visa for you for an additional RM10.

Some foreign consulates in Georgetown include:

France
  Wisma Rajab, 82 Lebuh Bishop (☎ 04-262 9707)
Indonesia
  467 Jalan Burma (☎ 04-282 4686)
Japan
  2 Jalan Biggs (☎ 04-229 8222)
Thailand
  1 Jalan Tunku Abdul Rahman (☎ 04-282 8029)

Immigration The immigration office (☎ 04-261 5122) is at 29A Lebuh Pantai in the centre of town.

Money There are branches of the major banks on Lebuh Pantai near the GPO. At the northern end of Lebuh Chulia there are numerous moneychangers, who are open longer hours than the banks and have competitive rates.

The American Express office (☎ 04-228 2690) is at 22 Lebuh Victoria.

Post & Communications The GPO is in the centre of town on Lebuh Downing. It is open Monday to Saturday from 8.30 am to 4.30 pm. The poste restante counter is open Monday to Saturday from 8 am to 6 pm. There are also post offices on the ground floor of the Komtar centre, and on Lebuh Buckingham near Lebuh Pitt.

If you need a parcel wrapped for posting, MS Ally, a stationers on Lebuh Pantai near the GPO, provides this service for around RM3.

The Telekom office is on Jalan Burma, a

15 minute walk from Lebuh Chulia. It is open 24 hours a day and calls can be made quickly and easily. There is also a phone here which you can use to get through instantly to the operator in your home country and make reverse charge (collect) calls. There's another telephone office at the GPO, also open 24 hours.

Travel Agencies Penang has many travel agents, mostly at the northern end of Lebuh Chulia, offering excellent bargains in discounted airline tickets. Although most of them are fine there are some who are not totally trustworthy.

Silver-Econ Travel (☎ 04-262 9882) at 436 Lebuh Chulia; MSL (☎ 04-261 6154) in the Ming Court Hotel on Jalan Macalister near Jalan Rangoon; and Happy Holidays (☎ 04-262 9222) at 442 Lebuh Chulia are all reliable operators, which many travellers use. See the Getting There & Away section at the end of this chapter for more on airline ticket discounters.

Bookshops There are several fairly good bookshops along Lebuh Pantai, as well as a good one in the E&O Hotel. The Popular Bookshop in the Komtar centre is a large shop with cheap novels, a good travel book section and a reasonable selection of books on Malaysia and Penang. Times has the best English bookshop in town – in Penang Plaza and a smaller branch in the Yaohan department store in the Komtar centre.

For second-hand books, check out the numerous small shops along Lebuh Chulia between the Swiss Hotel and Jalan Penang or browse through the huge selection of second-hand books in the stalls on the 2nd floor of the Chowrasta Bazaar on Jalan Penang.

Libraries The Penang Library is on the 1st floor of the Dewan Sri Pinang on Lebuh Duke. It has a large collection of books of local interest and is open from 9 am to 5 pm Tuesday to Saturday and from 9.30 am to 1 pm on Sunday.

The British Council Library (☎ 04-263 0332) is at 43 Green Hall and is open Tuesday and Wednesday from 10 am to 8 pm, Thursday and Friday from 10 am to 6 pm and Saturday from 10 am to 4 pm.

The Alliance Française (☎ 04-281 6008) at 8 Jalan Yeoh Guan Seok has a library which is open from 10 am to noon and 3.30 to 6.30 pm on weekdays only. The Malaysian German Society Library (☎ 04-281 6853) at 250B Jalan Air Itam is open 9.30 am to 1 pm and 2.30 to 6 pm on weekdays.

Medical Services Outpatient medical care is generally inexpensive in Malaysia. The following hospitals are recommended for travellers. Dial ☎ 999 for ambulance service.

General Hospital
Jalan Residensi (☎ 04-229 3333)
Penang Adventist Hospital
465 Jalan Burma (☎ 04-226 1133)

Dangers & Annoyances Georgetown still bears traces of its seamier past, and though the opium dens have gone, heroin is a large problem. Beware of those trishaw riders offering drugs and remember that Malaysia's penalties for drug use are very severe (death for possession of more than 15 grams of any contraband). Prostitution is also big in Penang, and trishaw drivers will try to push girls as much as drugs to unaccompanied male travellers.

Colonial District

As the oldest British settlement in Malaysia, many grand colonial buildings can still be found in Penang. Francis Light first stepped ashore in 1786 on the site of Fort Cornwallis, which is the main attraction and a good place to start a tour of the colonial district around the waterfront. Many of the buildings in the area are marked with signboards outlining their history and significance. They are included in a numbered walking tour that also takes in the temples and mosques of old Chinatown further inland. This good walking tour is outlined in the *American Express Heritage Trail* pamphlet, which is

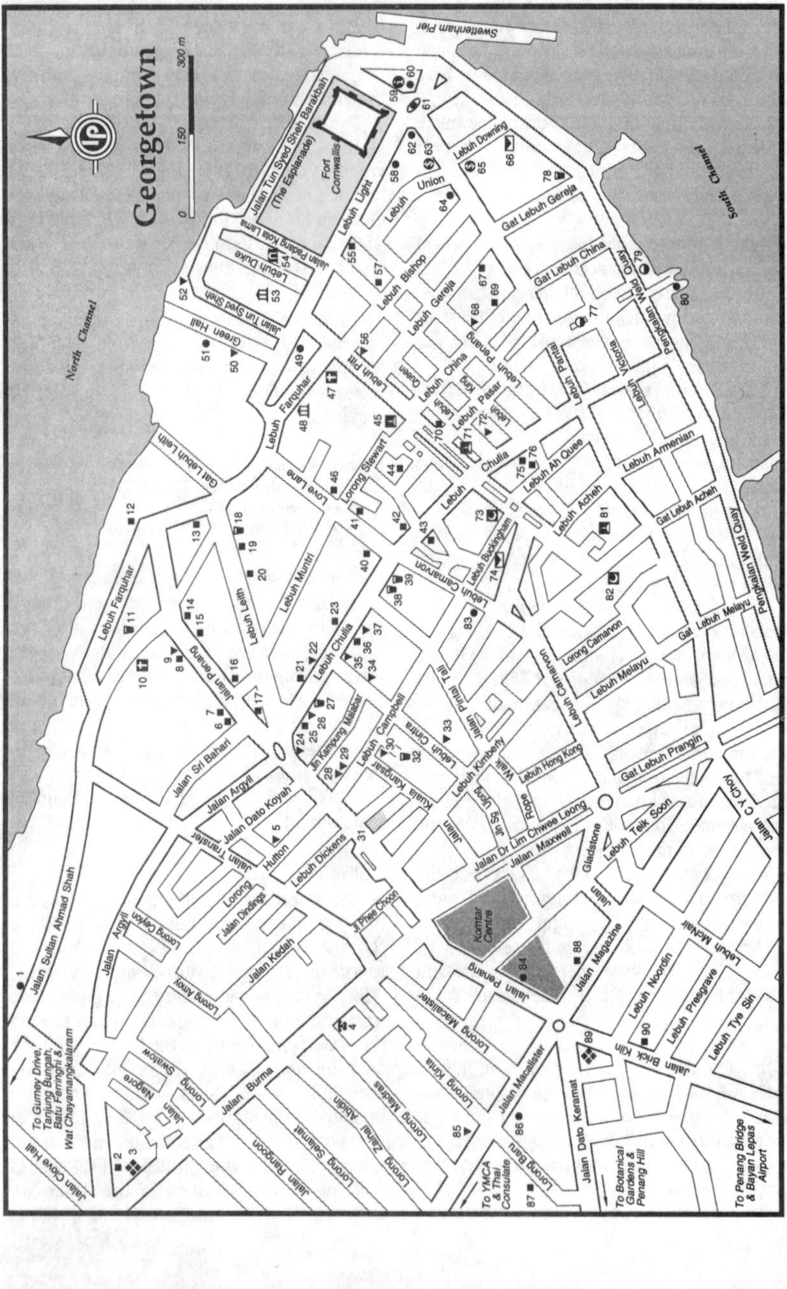
Georgetown
0
150
300 m
North Channel
South Channel
Swettenham Pier
Fort Cornwallis
Jalan Tun Syed Sheh Barakbah (The Esplanade)
Jalan Padang Kota Lama
Lebuh Duke
Jalan Tun Syed Sheh
Green Hall
Lebuh Light
Lebuh Union
Lebuh Downing
Lebuh Bishop
Lebuh Gereja
Gat Lebuh Gereja
Gat Lebuh China
Pengkalan Weld Quay
Lebuh Farquhar
Lebuh Pitt
Queen
Lebuh China
King
Lebuh Penang
Lebuh Pasar
Lebuh Pantai
Lebuh Victoria
Gat Lebuh Leith
Love Lane
Lorong Stewart
Lebuh Chulia
Lebuh Ah Quee
Lebuh Armenian
Lebuh Acheh
Gat Lebuh Acheh
Lebuh Buckingham
Lebuh Carnarvon
Lebuh Muntri
Lebuh Leith
Jalan Penang
Jalan Sri Bahari
Jalan Argyll
Jln Kampung Malabar
Lebuh Campbell
Lebuh Cintra
Jalan Pintal Tali
Lorong Carnarvon
Lebuh Melayu
Gat Lebuh Melayu
Pengkalan Weld Quay
Lebuh Hong Kong
Gat Lebuh Prangin
Lebuh Kimberly
Rope Walk
Jln Sg Ujong
Kuala Kangsar
Jalan Dato Koyah
Jalan Transfer
Hutton
Lebuh Dickens
Lorong Hutton
Jalan Dindings
Lorong Ceylon
Jl Phee Choon
Jalan Dr Lim Chwee Leong
Jalan Maxwell
Gladstone
Lebuh Teik Soon
Jalan C Y Choy
Jalan Gladstone
Komtar Centre
Jalan Penang
Jalan Magazine
Lebuh Noordin
Lebuh McNair
Lebuh Presgrave
Lebuh Tye Sin
Jalan Brick Kiln
Jalan Sultan Ahmad Shah
Jalan Argyll
Lorong Amoy
Jalan Kedah
Lorong Macalister
Jalan Macalister
Lorong Kinta
Lorong Madras
Lorong Zainal Abidin
Lorong Selamat
Jalan Rangoon
Jalan Burma
Lorong Swatow
Jalan Nagore
Jalan Clove Hall
Lorong Baru
Jalan Dato Keramat
To Gurney Drive, Tanjung Bungah, Batu Ferringhi & Wat Chayamangkalaram
To YMCA & Thai Consulate
To Botanical Gardens & Penang Hill
To Penang Bridge & Bayan Lepas Airport

well worth picking up at the tourist office (if they have a copy) and some hotels.

Opposite the south-east corner of Fort Cornwallis is the **Victoria Memorial Clocktower**, a gleaming white tower topped by a Moorish dome. Donated by a local Chinese millionaire to honour Queen Victoria's Diamond Jubilee in 1897, it stands 60 feet tall – one foot for every year of her reign. Lebuh Pantai to the south is the main street of the 'city', the financial district crammed with banks and stately buildings that once housed the colonial administration.

Another typical feature of a Malaysian colonial city is the Padang, the open playing field that serves as a green, central square ringed by public buildings. Georgetown's Padang stretches west from Fort Cornwallis to the **City Hall** (Dewan Bandaran), one of Penang's most imposing buildings with fine porticos. The Public Library behind is not architecturally interesting, but it houses the city's **Art Gallery**, featuring rotating exhibits on the 3rd floor.

On the southern side is the neo-classical **State Assembly Building** (Dewan Undangan Negeri), and further north along Lebuh Light is the equally impressive **Supreme Court**.

Behind the Supreme Court, **St George's Church** on Lebuh Farquhar was built in 1818 and is the oldest Anglican church in South-East Asia. This gracefully proportioned building with its marble floor and towering spire was built by convict labour.

PLACES TO STAY

2 Sheraton Inn
6 White House Hotel
7 Towne House Hotel
8 Peking Hotel
12 Eastern & Oriental (E&O) Hotel
13 Hotel City Bayview
14 Hotel Continental
15 Malaysia Hotel
16 Merchant Hotel
17 Oriental Hotel
19 Waldorf Hotel
20 Cathay Hotel
21 Lum Thean Hotel
23 Eng Aun Hotel
25 Hang Chow Hotel
36 Swiss Hotel
40 Pin Seng Hotel
41 Wan Hai Hotel
42 Tye Ann Hotel
43 Honpin Hotel
44 Hotel Noble
46 Tiong Wah Hotel
55 New Pathe Hotel
57 Hotel Rio
67 D'Budget Hostel
69 GT Guest House
70 Broadway Hostel
75 Paradise Bed & Breakfast
76 Plaza Hostel
87 Sunway Hotel
88 Shangri-La
90 Hotel Grand Continental

PLACES TO EAT

5 Tandoori House
9 Polar Cafe
22 Sin Hin Cafe
24 Yasmeen Restaurant
26 Tai Wah Coffee Shop & Bar
28 Taj Restaurant
29 Hameediyah Restaurant
30 Diner's Bakery
33 Green Planet
34 Hong Kong Restaurant
35 Sin Kuan Hwa Cafe
37 Eng Thai Cafe
50 Geethanjali
52 Esplanade Food Centre
56 Dragon King
68 Kaliaman Restaurant
72 Dawood
85 Oriental Restaurant

OTHER

1 Singapore Airlines
3 Penang Plaza
4 Telekom
10 St Georges Church & Cemetery
11 Hippodrome Disco
18 20 Lebuh Leith
27 Reggae Club
31 Chowrasta Bazaar
32 Rock Garden Disco
38 Hong Kong Bar
39 Hot Life Cafe
45 Kuan Yin Teng Temple
47 St George's Church
48 Penang Museum
49 Supreme Court
51 British Council
53 Penang Library & Art Gallery
54 City Hall
58 State Assembly Building
59 Penang Tourist Association & Tourism Malaysia
60 Medan Ferry Offices
61 Victoria Memorial Clocktower
62 Immigration
63 Standard Chartered Bank
64 MS Alley
65 Hongkong Bank
66 GPO
71 Sri Mariamman Temple
73 Kapitan Kling Mosque
74 Post Office
77 City Bus Terminal
78 Sol Fun Disco
79 Round Island Buses
80 Railway Booking Office
81 Khoo Kongsi
82 Aacheen St Mosque
83 Market
84 MAS
86 Thai International
89 Gama Department Store

Also on Lebuh Farquhar is the double-spired **Cathedral of the Assumption**.

Fort Cornwallis The timeworn walls of Fort Cornwallis in the centre of town are one of Penang's oldest sights. It was here that Captain Light first set foot on the virtually uninhabited island and established the free port where trade would, he hoped, be attracted from Britain's Dutch rivals. At first a wooden fort was built, but between 1808 and 1810 convict labour was used to replace it with the present stone structure.

Today only the outer walls of the fort stand. The area within has been made into a park, with souvenir shops and a couple of food outlets. You can walk around the battlements, liberally studded with old cannons. Many of these were retrieved from local pirates, although they were originally cast by the Dutch. Seri Rambai, the most important and largest cannon, faces the north coast and dates back to 1603. It has a chequered history, having been given by the Dutch to the sultan of Johor. There it fell into the hands of the Achehnese and was taken by pirates before ending up at the fort. It's famed for its procreative powers, and childless women are recommended to place flowers in the barrel of 'the big one' and offer special prayers.

Underneath the cannon in an old gunpowder magazine is a small, interesting museum chronicling the history of the fort and Penang.

The fort is open daily from 8 am to 7 pm and entry is RM1.

Penang Museum From the town's foundation site it's only a short stroll to the museum on Lebuh Farquhar. In front is a statue of Captain Light, which was removed by the Japanese during WWII but retrieved and re-erected, minus its sword, after the war. The small museum has lots of old photos and documents, furniture, costumes, the medal collection of Tunku Abdul Rahman and numerous other memorabilia. One of the original Penang Hill funicular railcars is displayed outside the museum.

An interesting section recounts the bloody nine days of rioting between Chinese secret societies in 1867, attributed by bewildered British authorities to a rambutan-throwing incident. Georgetown suffered a near civil war before the administrators took a firm hand. The societies were heavily fined and the proceeds used to build police stations which subsequently kept the peace.

Due to structural damage, the museum has been closed for well over a year, but may be open again by the time you read this.

Chinatown

Inland from the former administration centre of the British lies the twisting streets of the old city, dotted with temples, mosques and traditional businesses. The large Chinatown from Lebuh Pantai to Jalan Penang is centred on Lebuh Chulia, still the lively heart of Georgetown, but pockets of Indian and Malay areas remain within and around it.

Georgetown is a delight to wander around at any time of day. Set off in any direction and you're certain to find plenty of interest, whether it's the beautiful old Chinese shophouses, an early-morning vegetable market, a temple ceremony, the crowded shops or a late *pasar malam* (night market).

Jalan Penang and Jalan Campbell are the main shopping streets with modern air-conditioned shops, but it's along the more old-fashioned streets like Lebuh Chulia or Rope Walk (Jalan Pintal Tali) that you'll find the unusual bargains – like a 'Beware of the Dog' sign that adds the warning in Malay (*'Awas – Ada Anjing'*) and in Chinese characters. At the Lebuh Farquhar end of Jalan Penang there is a string of handicraft and antique shops.

Trishaws are the ideal way of getting around Georgetown, particularly at night when trishaw travel takes on an almost magical quality.

All the usual Chinese events are likely to be taking place at any time: a funeral procession with what looks like a run-down Dixieland jazz band leading the mourners, colourful parades at festival times and ancient grandmas pushing out their stalls to set up for a day's business. All around you'll

ALL PHOTOS BY RICHARD I'ANSON

Peninsular Malaysia

Top: Georgetown is a fascinating city full of winding streets and crumbling old shophouses.

Middle: Chinese lanterns at Penang's Kek Lok Si, the largest Buddhist temple in Malaysia

Bottom: The ornate Cheng Hoon Temple in Melaka was founded in 1646.

ALL PHOTOS BY TONY WHEELER

Peninsular Malaysia

Top: Penang's Khoo Khongsi, clan house of the Khoos, is part temple, part meeting hall.
Middle: Khoo Khongsi is a colourful mix of dragons, statues, paintings, tiles and carvings.
Bottom: Penang's brightly painted Thai temple, Wat Chayamangkalaran, houses a huge reclining Buddha.

hear those distinctively Chinese noises: the clatter of mahjong tiles from inside houses, the trilling of caged songbirds and everywhere loud arguments and conversations.

Nor can you miss Georgetown's other inhabitants. Tamils from the south of India cool boiled milk by nonchalantly hurling it through the air from one cup to another. Money changing is almost exclusively an Indian enterprise, and stocky Sikhs with antique-looking guns can be seen guarding many banks and jewellery shops. Little India, with its spice and sari shops, Indian temples and restaurants, is centred on the Sri Mariamman Temple on Lebuh Queen, between Lebuh Chulia and Lebuh Pasar.

Altogether, Georgetown is a place where there's always something of interest to see. For an excellent view over this whole sprawling scene, there's a viewing gallery on the 59th floor of the Komtar centre. Admission costs RM5, although this can be credited towards any of the (overpriced) souvenirs available in the huge shop on the same floor. Buy tickets from the counter of the Penang Tourist Guides Association on the 3rd floor.

Kuan Yin Teng Temple On Lebuh Pitt, just round the corner from the museum, is the temple of Kuan Yin, the goddess of mercy. The temple was built in the 1800s by the first Chinese settlers in Penang. It's not a terribly impressive or interesting temple, but it's right in the centre of the old part of Georgetown and is the most popular Chinese temple in the city. Perhaps it's Kuan Yin's own reputation as a goddess on the lookout for everyone's well-being, or possibly it's the presence of other well-known gods, like the god of prosperity, that accounts for this temple's popularity.

Whatever the reasons, there's often something going on: worshippers burning paper money at the furnaces in front of the temple, a night-time puppet or Chinese theatre performance, or devotees simply offering joss sticks inside the temple.

Kapitan Kling Mosque At the time when Kuan Yin's temple was being constructed, Penang's first Indian Muslim settlers (East India Company troops) set to and built this mosque at the junction of Lebuh Pitt and Lebuh Buckingham. The mosque is yellow, in a typically Indian-influenced Islamic style, and has a single minaret.

Khoo Kongsi The Khoo Kongsi is in Cannon Square close to the end of Lebuh Pitt. A *kongsi* is a clan house, a building which is partly a temple and partly a meeting hall for Chinese of the same clan or surname.

Penang has many kongsis, but this one, the clan house of the Khoos, is by far the finest. Its construction was first considered around 1853, but it was not built until 1898. The completed building was so magnificent and elaborate that nobody was surprised when the roof caught fire on the very night it was completed! That misfortune was simply interpreted as a message from above that they'd really been overdoing things, so the Khoos rebuilt it in a marginally less grandiose style.

The present kongsi, dating from 1906 and extensively renovated in the 1950s, is also known as the 'Dragon Mountain Hall'. It is a colourful mix of dragons, statues, paintings, lamps, coloured tiles and carvings, and is one part of Penang which definitely should not be missed.

Although the Khoo Kongsi is far and away the most well known kongsi in Georgetown, there are a number of others, including the modern Lee Kongsi on Jalan Burma, the combined kongsi of the Chuah, Sin and Quah clans at the corner of Jalan Burma and Codrington Ave, the Khaw Kongsi on Jalan Burma and the Yap Kongsi on Lebuh Armenian.

Acheen St Mosque A short walk from the Khoo Kongsi, this Malay mosque on Lebuh Acheh is unusual for its Egyptian-style minaret – most Malay mosques have Moorish minarets. Built in 1808 by a wealthy Arab trader, the mosque was the focal point for the Malay and Arab traders in this quarter, which is the oldest Malay kampung in Georgetown.

Sri Mariamman Temple Lebuh Queen runs parallel to Lebuh Pitt, and about midway between the Kuan Yin Teng Temple and the Kapitan Kling Mosque you'll find this Hindu temple, another example of Penang's religious diversity.

The Sri Mariamman Temple is a typical south Indian temple with its elaborately sculptured and painted *gopuram* towering over the entrance. Built in 1883, it's the oldest Hindu temple in Georgetown and is testimony to the strong Indian influence you'll also find in this most Chinese of towns.

Wat Chayamangkalaram

At Lorong Burma just off the road to Batu Ferringhi is a major Thai temple – Temple of the Reclining Buddha. This brightly painted temple houses a 32-metre-long reclining Buddha, loudly proclaimed in Penang as the third longest in the world – you can take that claim with a pinch of salt since there's at least one other in Malaysia that is larger, plus one in Thailand (at least) and two in Myanmar (Burma). Nevertheless, it's a colourful and picturesque temple.

The **Dhammikarama Burmese Buddhist Temple** is directly across the road from it, with two large stone elephants flanking the gates. The first Buddhist temple on Penang, it was built in 1805 and has had many later additions.

Penang Buddhist Association

Completed in 1931, this is a most unusual Chinese Buddhist temple. Instead of the usual gaudy and colourful design of most Chinese temples it is quiet, tasteful and refined. The Buddha statues are carved from Italian marble, and glass chandeliers, made in Penang, hang from above. Housed in a large building showing Art Deco influences, Buddhist devotees flock here on Wesak Day. It's on Jalan Anson.

Other Mosques, Churches & Temples

The **Shiva Temple** on Jalan Dato Keramat is hidden behind a high wall. The **Nattukotai Temple** on Waterfall Rd is the largest Hindu temple in Penang and is dedicated to Bala Subramaniam.

Out at Tanjung Tokong the **Tua Pek Kong Temple** is dedicated to the God of Prosperity and dates from 1837. Finally the glossy, modern **Penang State Mosque** at Ayer Itam has good views from the 50-metre-high minaret.

Organised Tours

The big hotels and travel agents all book tours. Georgetown Tour & Travels (☎ 04-261 4461) is one of the major companies offering 3½ to four-hour tours for RM20. They pick up from hotels (RM5 extra from Batu Ferringhi) and offer a Round Island Tour, Hill & Temple Tour and City Tour. Their Nite Tour (RM25) is a conspicuous parade through the streets by trishaw.

Festivals

All the usual festivals are celebrated in Penang, but some are celebrated with extra special energy. In November and December the annual **Pesta Pulau Penang**, or Penang Islands Festival, has various cultural events, parades, carnivals and all the fun that usually accompanies such occasions.

The masochistic Hindu festival of **Thaipusam** is celebrated in Penang with a fervour to rival Singapore and KL, but without quite the same crowds. The Nattukotai Temple on Waterfall Rd is the main centre in Penang for the activities.

Chinese New Year is celebrated with particular gusto in Penang. The Khoo Kongsi gets done up for the event and dance troupes perform all over the city.

Pick up a copy of the annual *Penang Calendar of Events* from the tourist offices.

Places to Stay – bottom end

Hostels A number of new travellers' hostels are springing up in Penang. They are relatively new and clean and offer good travel information, but they tend to be insular and characterless compared with the hotels. Rooms are partitioned and spartan – you usually get a bed and that's about it, but they are clean and well set up for travellers.

The *Plaza Hostel* (☎ 04-263 0560), 32 Lebuh Ah Quee, is very popular and has an air-con lounge. Beds in the large dorm cost RM7, or small rooms start at RM14/18 and go up to RM35 with air-con, all with common bath. Safe lockers are available, and there are motorcycles for rent.

Another favourite is *D'Budget Hostel* (☎ 04-263 4794), 9 Lebuh Gereja, close to the ferry terminal and buses. A dorm bed in seven-bed dorms costs RM7, or the four-bed share rooms are RM8. Small rooms cost RM15/20, and larger, more expensive rooms are available. This hostel is big on security and the 5th floor rooftop sitting area is a winner.

Around the corner the *Paradise Bed & Breakfast* (☎ 04-262 8439) at 99 Chulia St has singles/doubles for RM15/18 or larger rooms for RM29/35, all including breakfast. Rooms are clean and tidy but vary from small windowless boxes to lighter, better rooms.

The *Broadway Hostel* (☎ 04-262 8550), 35F Jalan Masjid Kapitan Keling, is less popular with travellers but has good rooms, many with windows, for RM15/25 up to RM40 with air-con. Dorm beds cost RM7.

GT Guest House (☎ 04-262 5833), 14 Lebuh China, has large dorms with beds for RM8 and small partitioned rooms for RM15/18. It is friendly enough but less appealing than some of the others.

The *YMCA* (☎ 04-228 2211) at 211 Jalan Macalister is at the top of this range. Simple but very comfortable singles/doubles cost RM33/35 or RM43/45 with air-con, and good mid-range rooms with hot water and TV cost RM60 to RM80. All rooms have attached showers. There's a RM2 temporary membership charge for non-members of the YMCA, but this can be waived if you're a YHA member or have a student card. The YMCA also has a TV lounge and cafeteria. To get there, take a No 7 bus.

Hotels Georgetown has a great number of cheap hotels with lots of character but some are long overdue for an overhaul. Stroll down Lebuh Chulia, Lebuh Leith or Love Lane and you'll come across them. Remember that in virtually all the places listed here, two people can share a bed and just take a single room, while double usually means two double beds.

Two popular travellers' places are the *Swiss Hotel* (☎ 04-262 0133) at 431F Lebuh Chulia and the *Eng Aun* (☎ 04-261 2333) directly across the road at No 380. Both of these hotels attract lots of travellers, have travellers' cafes and are well positioned on Lebuh Chulia, but far enough back from the street with car parks in front to insulate them from street noise. The well-run, if sometimes over-run, Swiss Hotel has tidy singles/doubles with fan and common bath for RM17.60/21. The Eng Aun has an excellent cafe and a variety of rooms starting at RM14.70 for a single with common facilities, while large doubles with attached showers (toilets shared) range from RM19 to RM24. It's cheap and very popular, but the decrepit rooms are long overdue for maintenance and would benefit from a good scrub.

At 282 Lebuh Chulia, the *Tye Ann Hotel* (☎ 04-261 4875) is very popular, particularly for its breakfasts downstairs in the restaurant. Rooms are small but private and cost RM16 single or double and there are also RM6 dorm beds. This is another place so busy that it doesn't worry about upkeep, and a good fumigation of the beds wouldn't go astray.

In the streets just off Lebuh Chulia there are a number of other popular places. At 35 Love Lane, the *Wan Hai Hotel* (☎ 04-261 6853) has dorm beds for RM6 and rooms for RM16 with common bath. It's a friendly, well-run place in a classic Chinese hotel. Rooms are basic and a little noisy but have some style.

The *Tiong Wah Hotel* (☎ 04-262 2057), close by at 23 Love Lane, is a typical older-style Chinese place in a very quiet area. Rooms with common bath are available for RM18/22.

Also on Love Lane, at No 82 and very close to Lebuh Chulia, is the friendly *Pin Seng Hotel* (☎ 04-261 9004). It's actually tucked down a little alley and so is well insulated from any street noise. Rooms vary from the crumbling to the presentable, so it pays to check out a few. Rooms with common bath start at RM17.70, with shower (but no toilet) from RM20.80.

The *White House Hotel* (☎ 04-263 2385) at 72 Jalan Penang is a definite notch up in quality, with large spotless rooms for RM27.50 or RM38.50 with air-con. Those which overlook Jalan Penang are noisy – try to get one at the rear.

At 36 Lorong Pasar, just one small block in from Lebuh Chulia, the *Hotel Noble* (☎ 04-261 2372) is a quiet place with rooms for RM14. Larger RM18 rooms have showers but shared toilets.

Back on Lebuh Chulia near the junction with Jalan Penang, there are a few more places if none of the above appeal. At 511 Lebuh Chulia is the *Hang Chow Hotel* (☎ 04-261 0810), a rickety old wooden hotel typical of many with rooms for RM18, but it's well run and has an excellent coffee shop downstairs popular for breakfast. The *Eastern Hotel* (☎ 04-261 4597) next door at 509 Lebuh Chulia has slightly better rooms, but the mosque next door is a deterrent.

The *Lum Thean Hotel* (☎ 04-261 4117) at 422 Lebuh Chulia is not too promising with its modern facade, but behind it you'll find a typical Chinese hotel with some magnificent wood carvings at the back of the lobby. Rooms with fan and shower range from RM16 to RM25, with shower and toilet for RM29.

In Little India at 64-1 Lebuh Bishop, the *Hotel Rio* (☎ 04-265 0010) has rooms for RM25/30 with common bath. While nothing special, it is close to the ferry terminal.

The *Polar Cafe* (☎ 04-262 2054), 48A Jalan Penang, is also a bed & breakfast with average rooms but the cafe is good. Rooms with fan are RM20, or RM40 with air-con, attached bath and hot water, including breakfast.

During peak travel times it can be difficult to find a room, but there are many more cheap Chinese hotels on Lebuh Chulia, Lebuh Campbell and the small connecting streets – a quick wander around will turn up any number of them.

Places to Stay – middle

The wonderful-looking *Cathay Hotel* (☎ 04-262 6271) at 22 Lebuh Leith is a grand colonial hotel and one of Penang's few well-maintained old hotels. The cavernous lobby nearly equals the exterior. Prices for the huge spotless rooms are RM46 with fan and bath, RM58 with air-con and attached bath. The hotel also has a 'health club', but patrons use the rear entrance and guests are not disturbed.

If the Cathay is full, right next door at 13 Lebuh Leith is the *Waldorf Hotel* (☎ 04-262 6140). It's a characterless concrete box but has reasonable rooms (all air-con) for RM46/69 with bath attached.

At 273B Lebuh Chulia, opposite the Tye Ann, the *Honpin Hotel* (☎ 04-262 5243) is another more modern place right in the thick of things with an excellent cafe downstairs and reasonable rooms from RM46 with air-con and bath.

On Lebuh Light there's the *New Pathe Hotel* (☎ 04-262 0195), an older place right opposite the Padang. It has good-sized rooms for RM36/44 with air-con and bath. It's just a pity that all the rooms have frosted glass so you can't take advantage of the view.

While Lebuh Chulia is the main street in Georgetown for cheap hotels, around the corner Jalan Penang has a string of mid-range hotels. They range from large three-star hotels that have seen better days to smaller, fully air-con hotels. Though it's central, Jalan Penang is still a very busy road.

The cheaper options are on the western side of the street. The *Peking Hotel* (☎ 04-263 6191) at 50A Jalan Penang is good value in this range, with rooms for RM52/64 with air-con, attached bath and TV. The *Towne House Hotel* (☎ 04-263 8621), 70 Penang Rd, is similar but more expensive at RM76.

The bigger high-rises on the eastern side of Jalan Penang are all of a similar standard and have coffee shops, car parking and room service. Rooms are well appointed with air-con, bath, TV and phone but are worn. Competition is stiff so discounts are readily offered. The *Oriental Hotel* (☎ 04-263 4211), on the corner of Jalan Penang and

Lebuh Chulia, has good-sized rooms for RM90. The *Merchant Hotel* (☎ 04-263 2828) costs RM125/140 before the substantial discounts. The *Malaysia Hotel* (☎ 04-263 3311) at 7 Jalan Penang has rooms from RM96. The adjacent *Hotel Continental* (☎ 04-263 6388) at No 5 wins by a nose among this bunch, and has rooms for RM110, dropping to RM92 after discount.

Places to Stay – top end

Penang's biggest hotels, of the resort variety, are out at Batu Ferringhi and Tanjong Bunga, but Georgetown has a few luxury hotels. All have swimming pools and add 15% tax and service to the rates.

Grandest (and oldest) is the fine old *Eastern & Oriental Hotel* (☎ 04-263 0630), 10 Farquhar St, one of those superb, stylish old establishments in the Raffles manner – indeed it was built by the Sarkies brothers, who also constructed the Raffles in Singapore and the Strand in Yangon (Rangoon). It has featured in several Somerset Maugham stories. The E&O Hotel was built in 1885, is right on the waterfront and has beautiful gardens right down to the water. Singles/doubles in the newer wing cost RM118/128, but are nothing special. Go for the huge rooms in the old part of the hotel for RM158/178 or try the suites, which start at RM210, plus taxes. Stay there while you can – a new 13 storey annex and renovations of the old wing are planned for late 1996.

Across the road from the E&O at the top of Jalan Penang is the multistorey *City Bayview Hotel* (☎ 04-263 3161), 25A Farquhar St, topped by a revolving restaurant with great views over Georgetown. Rooms are very comfortable with all the trimmings but are looking a little tired. Rates start at RM190/210. The *Hotel Grand Continental* (☎ 04-263 6688), 68 Jalan Brick Kiln, is similar but better value with rooms from RM150/170.

The *Sheraton Inn* (☎ 04-229 6166) on Jalan Burma is another of Penang's top-class places, though not quite up there with the best. Rooms start at RM295, but are normally reduced.

The *Sunway Hotel* (☎ 04-229 9988), 33 Lorong Baru, off Jalan Macalister, is a new hotel with well-appointed rooms for RM200/230 – one of the best for the money in this range.

The *Shangri-La* (☎ 04-262 2622) is next to the Komtar centre on Jalan Magazine. This is Georgetown's most luxurious hotel with a host of bars and restaurants. Rooms start at RM330.

Places to Eat

Penang is another of the region's delightful food experiences, with a wide variety of restaurants and many local specialities to tempt you.

For a start, laksa is particularly associated with Penang. *Laksa assam*, or simply Penang laksa, is a fish soup with a sour taste from the tamarind, or assam paste; it is served with special white laksa noodles. Originally a Thai dish, *laksa lemak* has also been adopted by Penang. It's basically similar to laksa assam, except coconut milk is substituted for the tamarind.

Seafood is, of course, very popular in Penang and there are many restaurants that specialise in fresh fish, crabs and prawns – particularly along the northern beach fringe.

Despite its Chinese character, Penang also has a strong Indian presence and there are some popular specialities to savour. Curry Kapitan is a Penang chicken curry which supposedly takes its name from a Dutch sea captain asking his Indonesian mess boy what was on that night. The answer was 'curry, Kapitan', and it's been on the menu ever since.

Murtabak (a thin roti canai pastry stuffed with egg, vegetables and meat), while not actually a Penang speciality, is done with particular flair on the island.

Hawker Food Georgetown has a big selection of street stalls, with nightly gatherings at places like the seafront *Esplanade Food Centre* behind the Penang Library. This is one of the best hawker centres, as much for the delightful sea breezes as the food. The wide range of Malay stalls are good for trying local Penang specialities. The more restaurant-like Chinese section features seafood and icy cold beer.

Gurney Drive, three km further along the coast on the way to Tanjung Bunga, is another popular seafront hawker venue. Hawker-style restaurants here, including the one at the far end of Gurney Drive, are noted for their seafood.

Lorong Baru, just off Jalan Macalister, is another lively location where food stalls set up in the evenings. Another market good for Malay food springs up every night along Lebuh Kimberley on the corner of Lebuh Cintra, not far from the Komtar centre. Two other hawker areas can be found near the Komtar centre just off Jalan Burma on Lorong Selamat and Lorong Swatow. Lorong Swatow is good for laksa, rojak (green fruit salad in a spicy sauce) and ice kacang, the shaved-ice desert.

Lebuh Chulia is a great place for noodles at night. After 9 pm, small Chinese stalls set up tables underneath the shop verandas and the street is always a lively procession. Most stalls are found along the street around the Honpin Hotel at No 273.

The big pasar malam changes venue every three weeks, so check at the tourist office for its current location (usually some distance from the centre of town). It's mainly for clothes and household goods, but there are a few hawker stalls. It doesn't really get going until around 8 pm.

Indian Penang's Little India is along Lebuh Pasar between Lebuh Penang and Lebuh Pitt and along the side streets between. Several small restaurants and stalls in this area offer cheap north (Muslim) and south (vegetarian) Indian food.

Among the more popular Indian restaurants is *Dawood* at 63 Lebuh Queen, opposite the Sri Mariamman Temple. Curry Kapitan is just one of the many curry dishes at this reasonably priced restaurant. Beer is not available (since it's run by Indian Muslims), but the lime juice is excellent and so is the ice cream.

Between Lebuh Queen and Lebuh King on Lebuh Pasar is the easy-to-miss *Krishna Vilas*, good for south Indian breakfasts – idli (steamed rice flour cakes) and dosai – and very cheap.

In Chinatown on Lebuh Campbell, the *Taj Restaurant* at 166 and the *Hameediyah Restaurant* at 164A are two Indian Muslim coffee shops with pre-war decor, good curries and murtabak at very cheap prices. The Taj also has an upstairs, air-con section, which is amazingly dowdy.

The *Yasmeen Restaurant* at 177 Jalan Penang, near the corner of Lebuh Chulia, is another place for murtabak, biryani or a quick snack of roti canai with dhal dip – a cheap meal at any time of the day.

For something slightly more upmarket, try the *Kaliaman Restaurant* on Lebuh Penang. This air-con place has south Indian banana-leaf meals at lunchtime for RM3, or RM4 for non-vegetarian, and does excellent north Indian food in the evening.

For good north Indian curries and tandoori food in modern, air-con surroundings, try *Tandoori House* on Lorong Hutton, which has a number of mid-range restaurants. You can eat well for around RM20 per person.

Chinese There are so many Chinese restaurants in Penang that making any specific recommendations is really rather meaningless. Here are a few, however.

At 29 Lebuh Cintra, the *Hong Kong Restaurant* is good, cheap and varied and has a menu in English. One of Georgetown's 'excellent Hainanese chicken-rice' purveyors is the *Sin Kuan Hwa Cafe*, on the corner of Lebuh Chulia and Lebuh Cintra.

One of the most popular outdoor Chinese places is *Hsiang Yang Cafe*, across the street from the Tye Ann Hotel on Lebuh Chulia. It's really a hawker centre, with a cheap and good Chinese buffet, plus noodles, satay and popiah vendors.

Nyonya Penang, like Melaka and Singapore, was the home of the Straits-born Chinese, or Babas and Nyonyas. They combined Chinese and Malay traditions, which is very evident in their cuisine. The *Dragon King* on the corner of Lebuh Bishop and Lebuh Pitt specialises in traditional Nyonya wedding cuisine and is definitely worth a try. Expect to pay around RM30 for two.

Geethanjali, 31 Green Hall, has stylish decor and a variety of Penang hawker favourites, including Nyonya dishes. Prices are very reasonable, allowing you to try a number of dishes in air-con comfort.

Seafood Penang has a number of seafood restaurants, and Gurney Drive has a good selection of restaurants for dining by the sea. Housed in the old villas facing the foreshore are a number of very popular restaurants with outdoor tables, each with a selection of hawkers providing seafood and other fare. The *Public Cafe* is recommended and, as well as seafood, does great crispy chicken. The *Carnation* and *Restoran New Zealand* are two other very popular venues.

The *Oriental*, 42 Tanjong Tokong, on the water at the north-west end of Gurney Drive is an upmarket restaurant with excellent seafood. Their branch at 62 Jalan Macalister is cheaper and favoured by locals for reasonably priced seafood.

Breakfast & Western Lebuh Chulia has some delightfully old-fashioned coffee shops for a leisurely, cheap breakfast at marble-topped tables while you browse the *New Straits Times*. As well as the coffee, tea and toast served at coffee shops everywhere, those on Lebuh Chulia have much more extensive western breakfast menus that include muesli, porridge, toast and marmalade and other favourites. Popular travellers' hang-outs include the quirky little cafe at the *Tye Ann Hotel* and the tiny *Eng Thai Cafe* at 417B Lebuh Chulia, not far from the Eng Aun and Swiss hotels. Other small Chinese cafes with western breakfast menus include the excellent coffee shop at the *Hang Chow Hotel* at 511 and the popular little *Sin Hin Cafe* at 402. At 487 Lebuh Chulia, the very popular *Tai Wah Coffee Shop & Bar* buzzes with activity all day long until late at night. Western breakfasts are also available at the *Eng Aun*, *Swiss* and *Cathay* hotels.

The *Green Planet* at 63 Lebuh Cintra is a popular travellers' restaurant where you can read (and add to) the travel-tips notebooks they have on India, Thailand, Africa and elsewhere. It has a very stylish decor for a travellers' restaurant and, while certainly not the cheapest place in town, has a varied menu of mostly western dishes. The music is also good and the atmosphere relaxed. Services provided include international phone calls, bus ticket sales and motorcycle rental.

For a splurge, the *E&O Hotel* has good value lunch buffets, although you have to sit inside. The Friday buffet for RM19.50 is a particularly good deal.

The Komtar centre has a supermarket and is a good hunting ground for fast food. On the 1st to 3rd floors you'll find *KFC, McDonald's, Pizza Hut* and *A&W*. On the 5th floor there's a pleasant hawker centre with all the usual Chinese and local dishes.

Diner's Bakery on Lebuh Campbell has great baked goodies ranging from cheesecake to wholemeal bread, although there are cheaper bakeries around.

For a meal with a view, there's the *Musical Coffee Lounge* on the 58th floor of the Komtar centre. At lunchtimes they have a reasonably priced buffet of western food.

Entertainment

Lebuh Chulia is a good place to wander for a beer, with a good selection of street-side cafes popular with travellers. The *Reggae Club* at No 483 is a popular little bar where the music is stuck on Bob Marley and the beers are reasonably priced at under RM5. The *Hot Life Cafe* at No 363 is a slightly fancier clone but less lively. A couple of doors from the Reggae Club, the *Tai Wah Coffee Shop & Bar* at No 487 is a long-running favourite with cheap beers. This standard coffee shop attracts patrons until the early hours. The *Coco Island Pub & Cafe* under the Honpin Hotel at No 273 is surrounded by hawker carts in the evening and the tables scattered over the pavement are great for taking in the street life. Last, and least, the *Hong Kong* at No 371 is an air-con bar with grimy Emergency decor popular with expat armed forces personnel.

Around the corner from Lebuh Chulia near the Cathay Hotel, *20 Lebuh Leith* is a new breed of Penang pub. Housed in a wonderfully restored Chinese shophouse, it's the happening place for the more moneyed (beers at RM8), with a deejay, a variety of bar areas and tables out front. It's open until 2 am during the week, 3 am on weekends. This stretch is set to become a lively area with another bar due to open next door. The magnificent Chong Fatt Tze Mansion over the road is undergoing restoration with plans to become an entertainment venue.

Georgetown also has discos open until around 3 am. The *Rock Garden*, set back from Lebuh Campbell, gets lively on weekends and features Hong Kong bands. Admission is RM25, including the first drink. *Sol Fun Disco*, on the corner of Pengkalan Weld and Gat Lebuh Gereja, is a breezier place with different level bars and deejay music and is better value at RM16 entry (including two drinks). The *Hippodrome* on Jalan Sultan Ahmad Shah is another long-running venue but less lively.

Things to Buy

Even though Penang lost its duty-free status to Langkawi back in the 80s, it is still a good place to shop. KL has a bigger range, but Penang has good antique and curio shops and plenty of outlets for cameras, electronics, clothes and shoes at competitive prices. Copies of brand name goods are cheap. Bargaining is usually required, except in department stores.

Jalan Penang is the best shopping street in Georgetown. Start at the Komtar centre for clothes, shoes, electronics and everyday goods. Dozens of shops small and large sell just about everything. Opposite Komtar on Jalan Penang is a collection of small shops good for pewter, jewellery, basketware and other handicrafts. Camera specialists are also here, and a recommended camera repair shop is Soon Camera Clinic around the corner at 2-04 Wisma Central, 41 Jalan Macalister. Further south on Jalan Penang, the Gama department store is good for cheap clothes and household goods. The Penang Plaza on Jalan Burma near the Sheraton is another central shopping mall.

A number of interesting shops sell arts, antiques and curios. At the top end of Jalan Penang near the E&O Hotel is a string of half a dozen art shops such as Peking Arts & Craft at No 3B and Asia Handicraft at No 3I. A wander along Lebuh Chulia will also turn up a selection, such as Oriental Arts & Antiques at No 440A. Prices range from the reasonable to the ridiculous. Bargain hard.

Lebuh Campbell is also a good shopping street, and stalls on the corner with Jalan Penang have a large range of leather and rattan goods. Further south, Rope Walk has small shops selling old bric-a-brac and antiques. Over towards the waterfront, Lebuh Bishop also has a few antique shops.

If you need camping, fishing or other sporting equipment try China Emporium at 18 Lebuh Pantai or LE Chong at 435 Lebuh Pantai. Hua Heng Huat at 28 Lebuh Gereja is another.

Batu Ferringhi shopping possibilities range from the large and expensive Yahyong Gallery for Asian art to the night market selling all sorts of souvenirs, copy watches and the like. Cheap beachwear and light cotton clothes can be found at the souvenir centre on the beach near the guesthouse strip.

Getting There & Away

See the Getting There & Away and Getting Around sections at the end of this chapter for all transport-related options to and from Georgetown.

AROUND GEORGETOWN

Penang Hill

Rising 830 metres above Georgetown, the top of Penang Hill provides a cool retreat from the sticky heat below – it's generally about 5°C cooler than at sea level. From the summit you've got a spectacular view over the island and across to the mainland. There are pleasant gardens, an old-fashioned kiosk, a restaurant and a hotel, as well as a Hindu temple and a Muslim mosque on the top.

Penang Hill is particularly pleasant at dusk as Georgetown, far below, starts to light up.

Penang Hill was first cleared by Francis Light soon after settlement to grow strawberries; the hill was originally known as Strawberry Hill. A trail to the top was cleared from the Botanical Gardens waterfall and access was by foot or packhorse, or sedan chair for the wealthy. In 1890 the famous hoteliers, the Sarkies brothers, opened the Crag Hotel, which is now a Public Works Department building. The official name of the hill was Flag Hill (now translated as Bukit Bendera), but it is universally known as Penang Hill.

Attempts to make it a popular hill resort were thwarted by difficult access, and the first attempt at a mountain railway proved to be a dismal failure. In 1923 a Swiss-built funicular railway system was completed, and the tiny cable-pulled cars have trundled up and down ever since. The trip takes a crawling half an hour with a change of train at the halfway point. On the way you pass the bungalows originally built for British officials and other wealthy citizens. A few years ago the original funicular cars were replaced by more modern ones, but the queues on weekends and public holidays can still be as long as ever.

A number of roads and walking trails traverse the hill. You can walk all the way to the Botanical Gardens in about three hours from the trail near the Viaduct railway station or via the jeep track from the top. Take water and food on longer walks. The Bellevue Hotel has a good map in the lobby showing trails. The hotel also has a small aviary garden featuring exotic birds. It's open from 9 am to 6 pm; admission is RM2.

Places to Stay On top of Penang Hill, the small *Bellevue Hotel* (☎ 04-829 9500) is quiet with a delightful garden, a good restaurant and the best views in town. Though a historic building, later remodelling has destroyed most of its architectural features, but the rooms retain some character and are large and comfortable. Buckminster Fuller was a regular guest here and photos and commentaries in the lobby commemorate him. A retreat here will cost RM88/110 for singles/doubles. Access is via the funicular railway and then it's a five minute walk. Alternatively, ring to arrange a 4WD pick-up (RM40) from the Botanical Gardens.

Getting There & Away Take Juara bus No 1, Lim Seng bus No 91 or minibus No 21 from Pengkalan Weld or Lebuh Chulia to Ayer Itam (every five minutes), then MPPP bus No 8 to the funicular railway station. The ascent of the hill costs RM3/4 for the one-way/round trip. Departures go every 15 to 30 minutes from 6.30 am to 9.15 pm from the bottom, until 11.45 pm on weekends. The queues here are often horrendous – waits of half an hour and more are not uncommon on weekends.

The energetic can get to the top by an interesting six km hike starting from the Moon Gate at the Botanical Gardens. The hike takes nearly three hours, so be sure to bring along a water bottle. The easier jeep trail to the top starts beyond the Moon Gate and is closed to private vehicles. Both routes meet near a small tea kiosk.

Kek Lok Si Temple

On a hilltop at Ayer Itam, close to the funicular station for Penang Hill, stands the largest Buddhist temple in Malaysia. Construction commenced in 1890 and took more than 20 years to complete.

The entrance is reached through arcades of souvenir stalls, past a tightly packed turtle pond and murky fish ponds until you reach the Ban Po Thar, or Ten Thousand Buddhas Pagoda.

A 'voluntary' contribution is the price to climb to the top of the seven-tier, 30-metre-high tower, which is said to be Burmese at the top, Chinese at the bottom and Thai in between. In the other three-storey shrine there is a large Thai Buddha image that was donated by King Bhumibol of Thailand. Standing high above all the temple structures is a striking white figure of Kuan Yin, the goddess of mercy.

It's an impressive temple, though crowded with tourists as much as worshippers. You must take off your shoes to enter the temple, but beware of the 'one-shoe bandits', local pranksters who steal just one shoe.

Getting There & Away To get there from Georgetown, take a Juara bus No 1 or Lim Seng bus No 91 from Lebuh Chulia or minibus No 21 to the Ayer Itam terminal.

Ayer Itam Dam

Ayer Itam Dam, three km from Kek Lok Si, has an 18 hectare lake. It's one of several reservoirs on the island. Penang's largest Hindu temple, the Nattukotai Chettiar, is on top of a hill beyond the dam. There's a good view from the top, 233 metres above sea level. This is the most important site in Penang for ceremonies during the Thaipusam festival.

Botanical Gardens

Penang's 30 hectare Botanical Gardens are off Waterfall Rd and are also known as the Waterfall Gardens after the stream that cascades through them down from Penang Hill. They've also been dubbed the Monkey Gardens, due to the many monkeys that appear on the lawn for a feed early each morning and late each afternoon. The gardens also have a small zoo and from there a path leads up Penang Hill. The gardens are open from 7 am to 7 pm.

Getting There & Away Take a Juara bus No 7 from Lebuh Chulia.

AROUND THE ISLAND

You can make an interesting circuit of the island either in your own car, on a motorcycle or (at a push) bicycle, on a tour, or by public transport. On a motorcycle or by car, figure on about five hours with plenty of sightseeing and refreshment stops. If you are on a bicycle, allow all day. It's 70 km all the way round, but it's only along the north coast that the road runs right on the coast, so you're not beside the beaches all the way. The following route takes you from Georgetown in a clockwise direction around the island. The road to Bayan Lepas (where the airport is located) is traffic clogged and built up all the way, but further around it is much quieter.

Snake Temple

At the 15 km marker, a couple of km before the airport, you reach Penang's Snake Temple, or the Temple of the Azure Cloud. The temple was built in 1850 and is dedicated to Chor Soo Kong. The snakes are venomous Wagler's pit vipers and are said to be slightly 'doped' by the incense smoke which drifts around the temple. Though a famous attraction for many years, it has become run-down and the snakes almost nonexistent – easily missed. Admission is free, although 'donations' are requested.

Getting There & Away Take a Yellow Bus No 66 from Lebuh Chulia.

Batu Maung

After the snake temple you soon reach a turn-off to the Chinese fishing village of Batu Maung, about three km away. There's an expensive seafood restaurant built on stilts over the water. It's an excellent place for a meal at sunset.

Getting There & Away Catch a Yellow Bus No 68 from Lebuh Chulia.

Bayan Lepas

Next up is the village of Bayan Lepas and Penang's international airport. Just beyond Bayan Lepas, a renovated temple has a shrine dedicated to the legendary Admiral Cheng Ho (see the Melaka chapter). The temple sanctifies a huge 'footprint' on the rock which is said to belong to the famous eunuch.

Getting There & Away Yellow Bus No 66 goes through Bayan Lepas.

Teluk Kumbar

Back on the main road you climb up, then drop down to Teluk Kumbar, from where you can detour to the fishing village of Gertak Sanggul. You'll pass some beaches, including Pantai Asam, on the way. Although scenic, these beaches are not all that good for swimming.

Balik Pulau
A little further north you reach Balik Pulau, the main town on the island circuit. There are a number of restaurants and cafes here, but no accommodation – going around the island has to be a one-day operation, unless you bring camping gear. Balik Pulau is a good place to have lunch though, and the local speciality, *laksa balik pulau*, is a must. It's a tasty rice-noodle concoction with a thick fish broth, mint leaves, pineapple slivers, onions and fresh chillies.

The Holy Name of Jesus Church was built in 1854 and its twin spires stand out impressively from the jungle behind.

Between Balik Pulau and Sungai Pinang you pass through an area of Malay kampungs – if you're on a bicycle or motorcycle (the side roads aren't quite wide enough for cars), turn off at Jalan P Pasir and tour the picture-perfect village there, with carefully kept traditional Malay houses, flower gardens and coconut groves that look like they've been neatly swept.

Getting There & Away Balik Pulau is the terminus of the Yellow Bus No 66 from Georgetown. It can also be reached on bus No 85, which takes the inland route.

Sungai Pinang & Pantai Acheh
Next is Sungai Pinang, a busy Chinese village built along a stagnant river – the antithesis of the preceding Malay village, but worth a peek nonetheless. Further on, another road turns off to Pantai Acheh, another small fishing village with very little of interest.

Two km north, at the 14 km marker on the road to Teluk Bahang, is a trail to the Penang Organic Farm (☎ 04-657 5591). By motorbike it is a 10 minute ride along the track, or a 30 minute walk. Interested visitors can stay in return for help on the farm (though you need to ring ahead).

Getting There & Away Yellow Bus Nos 75 and 76 run infrequently between Balik Pulau and Teluk Bahang.

Titi Kerawang
From the turn-off to Pantai Acheh, the road starts to climb and twist, offering glimpses of the coast and the sea far below. The jungle becomes denser and before long you reach Titi Kerawang, a waterfall just off the road with a natural swimming pool. During durian season, there are stalls set up along the road selling the spiky orbs, and you can also see the trees themselves, with nets strung below the trees to protect the precious fruit when they fall.

Forest Recreation Park
After the descent down towards the north coast you come to the Forest Recreation Park not far from Teluk Bahang, which has a forestry museum and trails through the park. The park is open during the day but closed Monday.

Butterfly Farm
A short distance closer to the coast is the Butterfly Farm. It has 3000 live butterflies representing over 50 species, and it also has a mounted insect display and a huge (and expensive) souvenir shop. It's open from 9 am to 5 pm daily (to 6 pm on weekends). Admission is RM4.

Getting There & Away The Butterfly Farm is a one km walk from the bus stop in Teluk Bahang.

Teluk Bahang
Finally you get back to the coast at Teluk Bahang, the village which marks the western end of the northern beach strip. It is a laid-back, overgrown fishing village, but the huge Penang Mutiara Resort at the eastern end of the bay, and ugly multistorey tenement housing at the western end, point to the future. The effluent from the many fishing boats and refuse washed down the river make this a dirty beach, but the stretch in front of the hotel is good. The main reason to visit Teluk Bahang is for the excellent seafood and the walks around the headland.

Teluk Bahang has a couple of **batik factories** where you can see batik being made and buy a wide variety of batik articles at quite high prices.

From Teluk Bahang you can also trek down the beach to **Muka Head**, the isolated rocky promontory marked by a lighthouse at the extreme north-western corner of the island. The trail passes the University of Malaysia marine research station and the privately owned Teluk Duyong, one of the best beaches on the island. South of Muka Head is Keracut Beach, also called Monkey Beach, where there are shelters, pit toilets and lots of bird and monkey life – camping is possible. Refer to the map for hiking trails.

The **Penang Cultural Centre**, next to The Catch restaurant in the Penang Mutiara Resort, has a traditionally styled *balai* (meeting house) and Borneo longhouse, where exhibitions of local crafts and pastimes are displayed for tourist groups, coinciding with a dance performance. It is open 9 am to 5 pm, but not much happens until the tourist buses arrive for the 45 minute shows at 10.15 am, noon and 3.15 pm. Packages including transport are organised from all the major hotels for RM28.

Places to Stay Although few travellers bother staying in Teluk Bahang, it has some relaxed and cheap family homestays and a luxury resort. Take the beachward road from the roundabout, follow it round to just before the Balai Polis, and on the right at No 365, Mk 2, is *Rama's* (☎ 04-881 1179), with dorm beds for RM6, or double rooms for RM12. It's a very friendly, well-kept place run by a Hindu family, and they also have a quite luxurious, self-contained flat for RM50.

Miss Loh's is a guesthouse off the main road towards the Butterfly Farm. Miss Loh can be contacted at the Kwong Tuck Hing shop on the main road. It's a comfortable place to stay, set in a large garden. Dorm beds are RM7, doubles RM15 to RM30.

Fisherman Village Guest House (☎ 04-885 2936) is down a small lane, signposted off the road leading to the End of the World Restoran. It's in Kampong Nelayan, the Malay fishing kampung, and offers simple, tidy rooms for RM18.

The *Penang Mutiara Beach Resort* (☎ 04-885 2828) is a top-class hotel, one of the best on the island. It's raked and netted beach is kept spotlessly clean, and it has a range of water sport activities. Rooms range from RM350 to RM420 and a variety of suites are on offer.

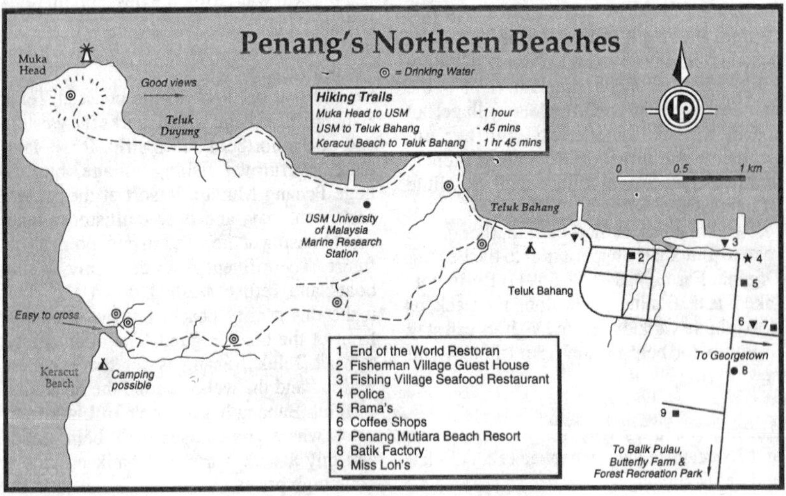

Places to Eat With all those fishing boats in the harbour, excellent, fresh seafood is guaranteed. The *End of the World Restoran* at the other end of the village is renown for its reasonably priced seafood and attracts crowds of diners in the evening clamouring for the huge prawns, whole fish and crabs. Hidden away but just as good is the *Fishing Village Seafood Restaurant*, which also serves excellent, fresh seafood dishes.

The shopping area in the main street also has a few coffee shops, offering Chinese dishes and seafood and a couple of good Indian places do murtabak, south Indian dishes like dosai, and milk shakes.

Getting There & Away The Hin Bus No 93 runs from Georgetown all the way along the north coast of the island as far as Teluk Bahang. You can catch it from Lebuh Chulia.

Batu Ferringhi

A little further along the coast towards Georgetown, Batu Ferringhi (Foreigner's Rock) is a resort strip lined with big hotels, tourist shops, restaurants and car and motorcycle rental offices. There are also plenty of moneychangers to welcome you.

The beach itself is quite good, though not up there with Malaysia's best and the water is not of the tropically clear variety you might expect. The beach is kept clean, even on weekends when hordes of day-trippers visit.

Batu Ferringhi has the drawbacks of a large resort (it can be crowded and much of the greenery has been replaced by concrete), but also the advantages (plenty of restaurants, watering holes and recreation facilities). It has quite a lively resort feel, and there is a good night market on the main road selling trinkets. The big hotels offer good deals at times and cheaper accommodation is available if you want a few days by the beach.

Although Georgetown is only half an hour away by bus, by public transport Batu Ferringhi is inconvenient if you want to explore the city in any depth. The road from Batu Ferringhi to Teluk Bahang is a picturesque stretch with small coves and more beaches.

Places to Stay – bottom end Back in the 70s when the grass was green and the living cheap and easy, Batu Ferringhi, along with Teluk Bahang, was a favourite on the travellers' trail and Malaysian immigration used to periodically round up any 'Suspected Hippy In Transit' and deport them. Batu Ferringhi is much more upmarket these days, and immigration less fervent, and only a few travellers stay at the cheaper guesthouses right opposite the beach.

As you take the road down the main beach and then right at Guan Guan Cafe, the *Baba Guest House* (☎ 04-881 1686) is the first place you come across. This very tidy family home has rooms for RM25. The RM50 air-con rooms with bath are quite luxurious.

Next door *Shalini's Guest House* (☎ 04-881 1859) is an old, two storey wooden house. Rooms are spartan, but cheap for Batu Ferringhi at RM20. Rooms with two beds cost RM30 or RM60 with air-con and bath. Meals are available and the balcony is a nice place to relax.

Right next door is the long-running *Ali's Guest House* (☎ 04-881 1316), which has a shady jungle of a garden. The rooms at back for RM25 are dank, but the new front rooms with bath for RM45 are much better.

Next along, *Ah Beng* (☎ 04-881 1036) is similar to Shalini's – an almost identical two storey house with an upstairs balcony and similar prices. However, it is better maintained and this is the pick of the crop for a cheap room.

Places to Stay – middle The only place in this category is the *Lone Pine Hotel* (☎ 04-881 1511). It's an older low-rise hotel with a small swimming pool, quite comfortable but overpriced unless you can get a hefty discount, which are offered outside the holiday periods. Rooms at the side are shabby for RM132, but those with sea views for RM142 plus 15% are better.

Places to Stay – top end Batu Ferringhi's 'international standard' hotels, almost all of which are right on the beach, are strung out along more than one km of coastline. Although the Batu Ferringhi is not one of the best in Malaysia, these beachfront hotels are relaxed places for a family vacation. There are facilities along the beach for a variety of water sport activities, including boat tours, windsurfing and paraflying, offered either by the hotels or by independent operators. These hotels have air-con and all have swimming pools. Prices vary depending on whether or not you're facing the beach.

Starting from the eastern (Georgetown) end of the beach there's the *Ferringhi Beach Hotel*, which has the best sea view of all – it's right on a jutting point before Batu Ferringhi proper. Despite its being a couple of km out of Batu Ferringhi and across the road from the beach (reached by overhead walkway), it is very luxurious and often offers considerable discounts.

Next comes *Rasa Sayang Resort* – the largest and most expensive of them all. Its design is an exotic interpretation of traditional Malay styles and it's the one place at Batu Ferringhi with real local character.

Opposite the Rasa Sayang, the *Merit Sri Sayang Resort Apartments* has suites with kitchenettes and balconies. These are holiday apartments (so they're more cheaply fitted and without all the facilities of a hotel), but the multistorey complex does have a pool, laundry facilities, a gymnasium etc. Good mid-week discounts are available.

Beside the Rasa Sayang is the smaller, older and quite reasonably priced *Palm Beach Hotel*. The large *Golden Sands Hotel* is next to that. The Palm Beach, Rasa Sayang and Golden Sands are all under the same management, and if you stay at one you can use the facilities of all three.

Further along are the *Holiday Inn Penang*, the *Penang Parkroyal Hotel* and the older *Casuarina Beach Hotel*. The newly renovated and extended *Bayview Pacific Beach Hotel* is at the far end of the beach. The beach

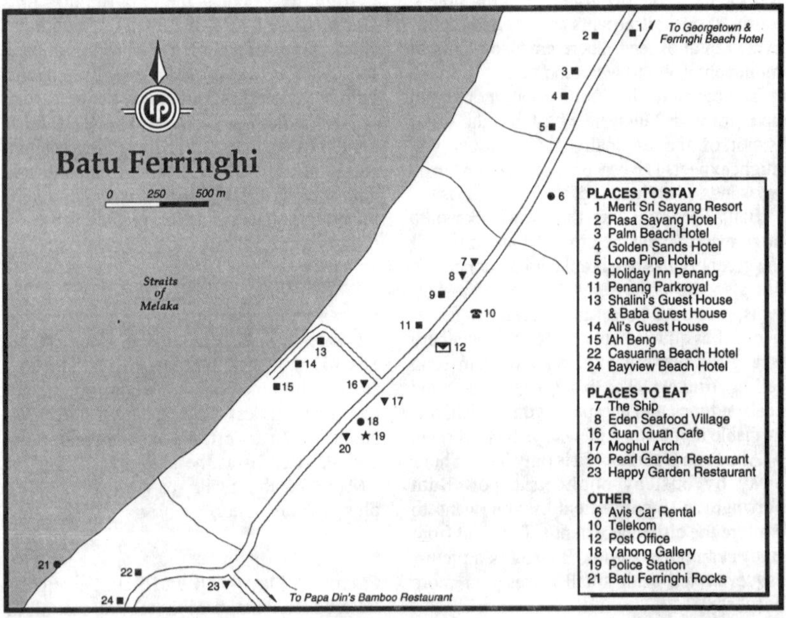

slopes into the water a little more gradually here, so the swimming is better at this end.

Details of the hotels follow. As well as rooms, all the hotels have suites. All add 15% tax and service charge to the rates.

Bayview Pacific Beach Hotel (☎ 04-881 2123);
400 rooms, singles/doubles from RM150/180 to RM275/300.
Casuarina Beach Hotel (☎ 04-881 1711);
180 rooms, singles/doubles for RM230/250.
Ferringhi Beach Hotel (☎ 04-890 5999);
350 rooms, singles/doubles RM200/225 to 225/250.
Golden Sands Hotel (☎ 04-881 1911);
400 rooms, doubles RM255 to RM360.
Holiday Inn Penang (☎ 04-881 1601);
350 rooms, doubles RM300 to RM350.
Merit Sri Sayang Resort Apartments (☎ 04-881 1113);
180 one/two/three bedroom suites for RM190/290/380.
Palm Beach Hotel (☎ 04-881 1621);
145 rooms, doubles from RM155 to RM205.
Penang Parkroyal Hotel (☎ 04-881 1133);
330 rooms, doubles from RM300 to RM400.
Rasa Sayang Resort (☎ 04-881 1811);
510 rooms, doubles from RM340.

Places to Eat All the big hotels have restaurants. The Rasa Sayang has a positive plethora of them, from a Japanese restaurant to a 'British grill room'. There's also the *Eden Seafood Village* on the main road, which has typical Chinese food with an accent on seafood, and night-time entertainment. *The Ship* next door is a galleon-styled monstrosity with a steak restaurant (steaks around RM20) on the top deck and the Captain's Cabin bar downstairs for happy hours' beer (RM3.50) for a pre-dinner drink.

Further along the road in the main group of shops, there are a couple of cheap restaurants. The *Guan Guan Cafe* has mostly Chinese food but you can also get everything from steak and chips to seafood. You can get a good meal for just a couple of dollars.

Almost opposite, the very fancy *Pearl Garden Restaurant* has terraced dining areas and Chinese food for around RM20 a main meal, or the *Moghul Arch* has more moderately priced north Indian food.

A short distance towards Teluk Bahang there is the *Happy Garden Restaurant*, a pleasant outdoor place serving western and Chinese meals. Alongside the Happy Garden there's a side road which leads to *Papa Din's Bamboo Restaurant*, which is run by an interesting and friendly old gentleman and has excellent, inexpensive Malaysian food.

The big hotels are well stocked with excellent, expensive restaurants. *Tiffins* in the Penang Parkroyal Hotel is worth it for the stylish Asian decor and the rijsttafel banquets for RM35 – ten courses of Dutch/Indonesian food served to the beating of gongs. The more expensive à la carte menu has a mixture of western and Asian dishes.

Tanjung Bungah

When heading west from Georgetown, Tanjung Bungah (Cape of Flowers) is the first real beach, but it's not attractive for swimming. Although Tanjung Bungah has also experienced a building boom with big hotels and apartment blocks cropping up everywhere, Batu Ferringhi is a better option.

Places to Stay – bottom end A good budget offering here is the *Lost Paradise* (☎ 04-890 7641), at the western end of town, just past the Mar Vista Resort. It's set right on the beach and consists of Penang bungalows that are somewhat run-down but have plenty of character. A good restaurant in a garden setting overlooks the beach and Georgetown. Singles/doubles cost RM20/30 with common bath.

The nearby *Mar Vista* (☎ 04-890 3388) is typical of the newer developments: a large high-rise with a swimming pool. Apartments with kitchenettes cost RM220/320/420 for one/two/three bedrooms. You'll need to factor in a 15% tax, though larger discounts are usually available. Other top-end places include the *Crown Prince Hotel* (☎ 04-890 4111) and the *Novotel Penang* (☎ 04-890 3303).

GETTING THERE & AWAY

Air

International MAS flies to Medan in Sumatra,

a very popular route. MAS and Singapore Airlines have regular flights to Singapore. MAS and Thai Airways International fly between Penang and Hat Yai, Phuket and Bangkok. Other international connections include direct flights to Hong Kong with MAS or Cathay Pacific or to Madras in India with MAS. Pelangi also has direct flights to Banda Aceh in Sumatra three times a week.

Penang is a major centre for cheap airline tickets, and, overall, a good place for buying tickets. In the past there have been numerous cut-and-run merchants at work, and though less common now it pays to ask around and be careful. Long-running, reliable agents are listed under Information earlier in this chapter.

Fares tend to vary with the airline; the cheapest tickets to London, for example, are with Aeroflot or Bangladesh Biman, but some typical one-way tickets on offer in Penang are listed below.

You could take the Pacific route (Singapore, Jakarta, Denpasar, Sydney, Auckland, Fiji, Papeete, Los Angeles) with a combined Garuda/Air New Zealand ticket for RM2500.

Multi-stop fares to Europe or through Asia are not so easy, but you could go from Singapore, KL or Bangkok to Delhi and on to London with Air India for RM1200.

Domestic Penang is well served on the MAS domestic network:

Destination	*Frequency*	*Fare (RM)*
Johor Bahru	daily	178
Kota Bharu	daily	87
KL	17 daily	104
Langkawi	four daily	51
Singapore	five daily	182

Pelangi Air flies three times weekly to KL (RM96) and Kuala Terengganu (RM151).

Airline Offices Some of the airline offices located in Penang include:

Cathay Pacific
  Menara PSCI, Jalan Sultan Ahmad Shah (☎ 04-226 0411)
Malaysia Airlines
  Komtar Centre, Jalan Penang (☎ 04-262 0011)
Pelangi Air
  3rd floor, Komtar centre, Jalan Penang (☎ 04-644 6869)
Singapore Airlines
  Wisma Penang Gardens, Jalan Sultan Ahmad Shah (☎ 04-228 3201)
Thai Airways International
  Wisma Central, 41 Jalan Macalister (☎ 04-226 6000)

The MAS office in the Komtar centre is open from 8.30 am to 6 pm Monday to Saturday, and from 8.30 am to 1 pm on Sunday.

Typical one-way tickets on offer in Penang

Destination	*Fare (RM)*	*Airline*	*Departs from*
Medan	140	Sempati, MAS	Penang
Banda Aceh	220	Pelangi	Penang
Madras	610	Air India	Penang
Phuket	170	Thai	Penang
Bangkok	350	Thai	Penang
Hong Kong	610	China Airlines, MAS	Penang
London	830	Aeroflot	KL
USA (west)	1050	China Airlines	KL
Australia (east)	800	China Airlines	Bangkok
	960	Alitalia, Gulf Air	Singapore
	1090	MAS	KL
Australia (west)	900	MAS	KL
Jakarta	180	Air France	Singapore

Bus

The main bus terminal is beside the ferry terminal in Butterworth. Butterworth has many more buses than Penang, but a number of services also leave from Georgetown.

In Georgetown, most buses depart from the basement of the Komtar centre, where the bus companies have ticket offices. Much easier are the travel agents on Lebuh Chulia (several are near the Eng Aun and Swiss hotels, for example) and hotels also sell bus tickets. Some long-distance buses leave from other parts of Georgetown: New SIA Tours & Travel (☎ 04-262 2951), 35 Pengkalan Weld, is a major agent and buses stop at their office.

Only four buses a day go to Kota Bharu from the Komtar centre at 9 am and 9 pm – book well in advance. Other east coast buses leave from Butterworth. Only two buses per day go to the Cameron Highlands from Georgetown; if full, first take a bus to Tapah.

Most of the long-distance departures are at night. Typical fares are:

Destination	*Fare (RM)*
Alor Setar	5
Kota Bharu	20
Kuala Terengganu	24
Kuala Perlis	7
Kuantan	26
Taiping	4
Ipoh	8
Tapah	10
Cameron Highlands	14
Lumut	9
KL	19
Melaka	24
Johor Bahru	35
Singapore	30 to 40

There are also bus and minibus services out of Malaysia to Hat Yai (RM20), Phuket (RM40), Surat Thani (RM40) and Bangkok (RM65). Many hotels or travel agents can arrange tickets.

Train

The railway station, like the bus and taxi stations, is right by the ferry terminal at Butterworth.

The Malaysia – Getting There & Away and Getting Around chapters have full details on fares and schedules for the Butterworth, KL and Singapore services and the train services to Hat Yai and Bangkok in Thailand.

You can make reservations at the station (☎ 04-334 7962) in Butterworth or at the railway booking office (☎ 04-261 0290) at the ferry terminal on Pengkalan Weld in Georgetown. There's a good left-luggage facility at the station in Butterworth, open 6 am to 9 pm daily.

Taxi

The long-distance taxis also operate from a depot beside the Butterworth ferry terminal. It's also possible to book them at some of the hot-spot backpacker hotels or directly with drivers. Typical fares for non-air-con/air-con taxis include:

Destination	*Fare (RM)*
Alor Setar	9/12
Ipoh	15/20
KL	35/41
Kuala Perlis	14
Kota Bharu	40
Lumut	16/21
Taiping	9/12

Car

Penang Bridge, completed in 1985, is the longest bridge in Asia and is said to be the third longest in the world. If you drive across, there is a RM7 toll at the toll plaza on the mainland, but there is no charge going back the other way.

Rental Penang is a good place to rent a car. Good deals can be found at the smaller agents, especially those at Batu Ferringhi, though the main companies are also worth trying for special deals. Rates start at around RM90 per day including insurance but drop considerably for longer rentals. Two cheaper agents are Ruhanmas (☎ 04-881 1760) at the Penang Parkroyal Hotel in Batu Ferringhi and Bob Rent-A-Car (☎ 04-229 1111), 11 Gottlieb Rd near the Botanical Gardens. The major companies with offices in Penang are:

Avis
388 Batu Ferringhi (☎ 04-881 1522)
Budget
Insight Travel, 105A, Oriental Hotel Building, Jalan Penang, Georgetown (☎ 04-263 1240)
Hertz
38 Farquhar St, Georgetown (☎ 04-263 5914)
National
1 Pengkalan Weld, Georgetown (☎ 04-262 9404)

Boat

Sumatra There are two companies operating boats to Medan in Sumatra. The Kuala Perlis Langkawi Ferry Service Co (☎ 04-262 5630) has its office near the tourist office. Ferries leave Penang on Tuesday and Saturday at 10 am. The journey takes 4½ hours and costs RM110/90 in 1st/2nd class. The boats actually land in Belawan in Sumatra, and the journey to Medan is completed by bus (45 minutes, included in the price). Departures from Belawan are at 11 am on Friday and Sunday. The Medan agent is Trophy Tours (☎ 061-514888), 33D Jalan Brigadier Jend Katamso.

The second company is Ekspres Bahagia (☎ 04-263 1943). They have departures from Penang on Monday, Wednesday, and Friday at 10 am. These boats also go to Belawan, and the fare is also RM110/90 in 1st/2nd class. Departures from Belawan are on Tuesday, Thursday and Saturday at 11 pm.

Both these companies have changing schedules, but between them they will have a departure most days of the week throughout the year.

Kuala Perlis Langkawi Ferry Service also has an on-again, off-again service to Langkawi for RM45, depending on demand and the season. Don't count on it.

GETTING AROUND

The Airport

Penang's Bayan Lepas Airport, with its Minangkabau-style terminal, is 18 km south of Georgetown. A coupon system operates for taxis from the airport. The fare to Georgetown is RM19.

You can get a Yellow Bus No 83 to the airport from stops along Pengkalan Weld or Lebuh Chulia – they operate hourly on this route from 6 am to 9 pm. Taxis take about 45 minutes from the centre of town, while the bus takes at least an hour.

Around the Island

Getting around the island by road is easiest with your own transport, particularly since the road does not actually run along the coast except on the northern side, and you have to leave the main road to get out to the small fishing villages and isolated beaches.

Bus There are three main bus departure points in Georgetown, and five bus companies. The city buses (Juara Buses) all depart from the terminal at Lebuh Victoria, which is directly in front of the ferry terminal. Most of these buses also go along Lebuh Chulia, so you can pick them up at the stops along that street.

The other main stand is at Pengkalan Weld, next to the ferry terminal, where the other bus companies operate from – Yellow Bus, Hin Bus, Sri Negara Transport and Lim Seng Bus Co. The new Orient Minibus service has good buses and fares cost a fixed 70 sen anywhere around town. Some handy routes, as well as the operators, route numbers and pick-up points, are listed in the table below.

For around RM5 you can make the circuit by public transport. Start with a Yellow Bus No 66 and hop off at the Snake Temple. This Yellow Bus No 66 will take you all the way to Balik Pulau, from where you have to change to another Yellow Bus, a No 76 for Teluk Bahang. There are only a few per day, roughly every 2¼ hours from 7.30 am to 7.15 pm, so it's wise to leave Georgetown early and check the departure times when you reach Balik Pulau. At Teluk Bahang you're on the northern beach strip and you simply take a blue Hin Bus No 93 to Georgetown.

Destination	*Operator & Route No*	*Pick-Up*
Ayer Itam	LS 91, Juara 1	Lebuh Chulia
Bayan Lepas Airport	YB 83	Lebuh Chulia
Batu Ferringhi	HB 93	Lebuh Chulia
Botanical Gardens	Juara 7	Lebuh Chulia
Gurney Drive	SN 136, HC 93 or 94	Lebuh Chulia
Penang Hill Railway from Ayer Itam	Juara 8	Ayer Itam
Snake Temple	YB 66	Lebuh Chulia
Teluk Bahang	HB 93	Lebuh Chulia
Thai Consulate	SN 136 or 137	Lebuh Chulia

Taxi Penang's taxis are all metered, but getting the drivers to use the meters is virtually impossible, so it's a matter of negotiating the fare before you set off. Some sample fares from Georgetown are: Batu Ferringhi RM14, Botanical Gardens RM8 to RM10, Penang Hill/Kek Lok Si Temple RM8, Snake Temple RM15 and Bayan Lepas Airport RM15.

Trishaw Bicycle rickshaws are an ideal way to negotiate Georgetown's backstreets and cost around RM1 per km – but, as with the taxis, agree on the fare before departure.

If you come across to Penang Island from Butterworth on the ferry, grab a trishaw to the cheap hotel area around Lebuh Chulia for RM3 – or, alternatively, you can walk there in five or 10 minutes. The riders will know plenty of other hotels if the one you select is full. For touring around, the rate is around RM10 an hour.

Motorcycle & Bicycle You can hire bicycles from any number of places, including hotels catering to travellers and shops along Lebuh Chulia. Bicycles cost RM8, and motorcycles cost from RM20 to RM25. Just remember that if you don't have a motorcycle licence your travel insurance probably won't cover you in the case of an accident.

Ferry There's a 24 hour ferry service between Georgetown and Butterworth on the mainland. Ferries take passengers and cars every eight minutes from 6.30 am to 9.30 pm, then roughly every 15 minutes to an hour. Fares are charged only from Butterworth to Penang; the other direction is free. The adult fare is 40 sen; cars cost around RM7 depending on the size.

Kedah & Perlis

On the north-western corner of the peninsula, the picturesque states of Kedah and Perlis are the rice bowls of Malaysia, producing over half of the country's domestic supplies. A green sea of rice paddies stretches away from the road for much of the distance through the area. Perlis, once part of Kedah, is also the smallest state in Malaysia, with an area of 795 sq km, and both states are important gateways into Thailand.

This corner of Peninsular Malaysia sees very few tourists, although there are a number of attractions in the area worth visiting. The main attraction is the island of Langkawi.

Kedah
Full Name: Kedah Darulaman
Area: 9426 sq km
Capital: Alor Setar
Population: 1.3 million

Perlis
Full Name: Perlis Indera Kayangan
Area: 795 sq km
Capital: Kangar
Population: 185,000

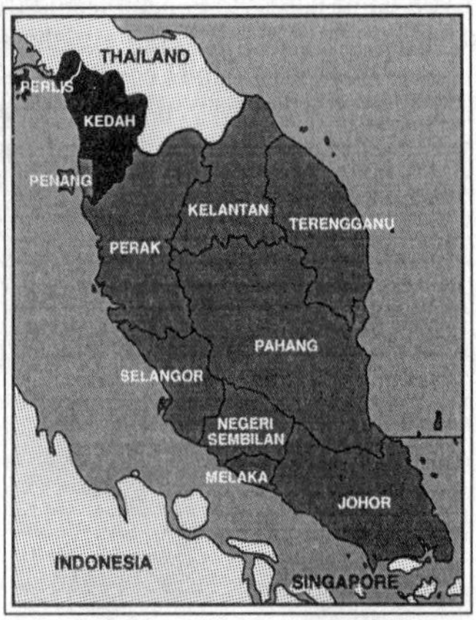

Kedah

Kedah is very much a Malay state. It was controlled or influenced by the Thais for much of the 19th century, and the British did not gain a foothold until well after they had established themselves in most other parts of Malaysia. With miles of flat rice-paddy plains, it has a rural feel, though development is increasing at a rapid pace in the capital, Alor Setar, and on the resort island of Langkawi.

For travellers, the most important towns in the state are Alor Setar and the small fishing ports of Kuala Kedah and Kuala Perlis, from where ferries operate to Langkawi. The small hill station of Gunung Jerai and the archaeological remains of Lembah Bujang, the cradle of Hindu-Buddhism in Malaysia, are interesting side trips for those with time to spare.

Kedah state has different business hours to most of the peninsula. Banks and government offices are closed on Friday. Saturday is a half-day and Sunday is a normal business day.

History

Settlement in Kedah goes right back to the Stone Age; some of the earliest archaeological sites in the country are found near Gunung Jerai. More recent finds in the Bujang Valley date back to the Hindu-Buddhist period, and the current royal family can trace its line back directly to this time. Finds in the Bujang Valley show that it was the cradle of Hindu-Buddhist civilisation on the peninsula and one of the first places to come into contact with Indian traders.

During the 7th and 8th centuries Kedah paid tribute to the Sriwijaya Sumatran empire, but later fell under the influence of the Thais until the 15th century, when the rise of Melaka led to the Islamisation of the area.

In the 17th century Kedah was attacked by the Portuguese, after their conquest of Melaka, and by the Achehnese, who saw Kedah as a threat to their own spice production.

After the handover of Penang to the British in the late 18th century, Kedah once again came under Thai control early in the 19th century. It remained under Thai control, either directly or as a vassal, until early in the 20th century when the Thais passed control to the British.

After WWII, during which Kedah (along with Kelantan) was the first part of Malaya to be invaded by the Japanese, Kedah became part of the Federation of Malaya in 1948.

SUNGAI PETANI

Known locally as SP, the acronym gives Sungai Petani an air of importance it doesn't deserve. The only reason to stop at this unremarkable town on the highway between Butterworth and Alor Setar is for transport connections to Gunung Jerai or the archaeology museum at Lembah Bujang.

If you get stuck, cheap hotels are within walking distance of the bus station. The

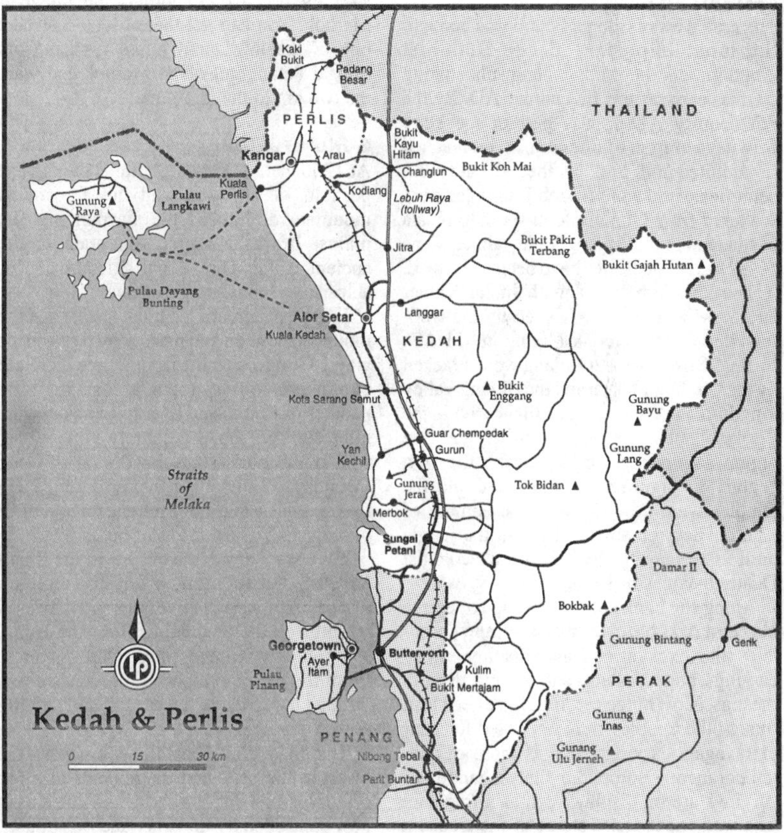

Hotel Duta (☎ 04-421 6424), 7 Jalan Petri, is one of the best options with singles/doubles from RM19/23. Top of the heap by far is the *Sungai Petani Inn* (☎ 04-421 3411), 427 Jalan Kolam Air, which has a swimming pool and rooms for RM92/110. One good reason to stop in SP is the *Restoran Seri Petani*, an excellent South Indian restaurant on the main street, Jalan Tunku Ibrahim, opposite the Hongkong Bank near the clock tower.

Sungai Petani is on the main rail line, and the bus station and taxi stand is one block from the main street near the centre of town.

LEMBAH BUJANG

The area west of Sungei Petani was home to the most important Hindu-Buddhist kingdom on the Malay peninsula, dating from as early as the 5th century AD. By the 7th century AD it was part of the large Sriwijaya empire of Sumatra, and it reached its architectural peak in the 9th and 10th centuries. Hindu and Buddhist temples were scattered from Gunung Jerai south to Kuala Muda, and in the Bujang Valley alone, some 53 archaeological sites have been excavated.

The kingdom traded with India, Khmer and Sriwijaya and was visited by the well-travelled Chinese monk I-Tsing in 671 AD. In 1025 Sriwijaya and Bujang were attacked by the Cholas of India, and the Bujang Valley kingdom later forged an alliance with the Cholas against the waning Sriwijaya. The region continued to trade, but by the 14th century its significance had faded and the temples were deserted with the coming of Islam. They remained buried in the jungle until first excavated by British archaeologist Quatrich-Wales in 1936.

Along the banks of the Bujang River, the **Muzium Arkeologi Lembah Bujang** chronicles the excavations and displays stone carvings, pottery chards and other finds from the digs. Most of the carvings have been lost, though the temples were not noted for their extravagant carvings such as those of contemporaneous Borobudur. Only a handful of carvings are on display, such as a fragment of a wall frieze and a statue of the elephant god Ganesha. Most numerous are the Shivaite *yoni* fertility stones.

Though of enormous archaeological significance, the exhibits are neither breathtaking nor well labelled – most labels are in Malay, but even they are not particularly enlightening. The main interest are the temples *(candi)* behind the museum, relocated and reconstructed at Lembah Bujang. They are small, unadorned temples and only the bases remain. The most significant and largest is that of 1000-year-old Candi Bukit Batu Pahat.

The museum is open 9 am to 4 pm daily, except Friday, when it closes from 12.15 to 2.45 pm. It is two km north of the village of Merbok. You can get there by taxi, or take one of the infrequent buses to Yan from Sungai Petani, get off at Merbok and walk the two km to the museum.

GUNUNG JERAI

At 1206 metres, Gunung Jerai is the highest peak in Kedah state, and this forest-clad mountain dominates the surrounding flat plains. It was a sacred mountain in the ancient Hindu period and a landmark for ships from India and Indonesia.

From the recreation park at the base of the mountain, a steep and narrow road snakes its way 13 km to a resort from where there are expansive views north across the rice paddies of Kedah and over to Langkawi. As hill resorts go, this is definitely a minor one, well off the tourist route, but during the week (Monday to Thursday) it's often deserted and makes a pleasant, cool retreat for a day or two. Bring a lover or lots of books.

Two km before the resort is the small **Muzium Perhutanan**, a forestry museum that has exhibits on native trees and their uses but little on the mountain's flora and fauna. The highlight is the fossilised elephant turds. From the museum a paved trail leads down through the forest to a waterfall and bathing pools.

The road continues three km past the resort to the peak and the remains of a 6th century Hindu bathing shrine, but the area is now controlled by the army and off limits.

Places to Stay

Peringan Gunung Jerai (☎ 04-422 3345) is a low-key resort with an old, converted villa housing a moderately priced restaurant. Accommodation is in modern but worn chalets. Standard rooms with private balconies, hot water showers and towering ceilings cost RM92 a double; more luxurious deluxe rooms are RM115. Chalets sleeping six cost RM172.50. At those rates it is overpriced but 40% discounts usually apply during the week. Tents can also be hired for camping.

Getting There & Away

Gunung Jerai is 60 km north of Butterworth, four km north of Gurun just before Guar Chempedak. From the car park on the highway at the bottom of the mountain, jeeps go to the resort from 8 am to 5 pm for RM5 per person, but other passengers to share are scarce during the week. Private vehicles can also use the road.

Some buses between Butterworth and Alor Setar pass right by the car park, but not the express services that use the North-South Highway. From Sungai Petani take a taxi or the Guar Chempedak bus to the car park.

ALOR SETAR

The capital of Kedah state is on the mainland north of Penang, on the main road to the Thai border. Few visitors stop in Alor Setar, the turn-off point for Kuala Perlis, from where ferries run to Pulau Langkawi, but it does have a few notable points of interest.

Alor Setar's long association with Thailand is evident in the Thai temples around the city, but the main points of interest lie around the Padang, where some grand reminders of the sultanate are worth seeing, especially the Zahir Mosque and the Balai Besar audience hall.

Alor Setar came under Thai suzerainty until the Bangkok Treaty of 1909 transferred rights to the British. The city and the state therefore had less colonial influence, and Alor Setar is very much a Malay city, with fewer Chinese and Indians than in other west coast cities.

It has the feel of a large village being dragged towards development, with the building of wide-paved roads, shopping plazas and the futuristic Telekom tower dominating the city. The tallest building is still the UMNO centre, not surprisingly as Alor Setar is a stronghold of the ruling Malay party, having provided its two greatest prime ministers, Tunku Abdul Rahman and Mahathir Mohammed.

Information

The state tourist office (☎ 04-730 1957) is upstairs in the State Secretariat Building on Jalan Sultan Badlishah. It has a few brochures.

The Padang

The large, open town square has a number of interesting buildings around its perimeter. The open-sided **Balai Besar**, or Big Hall, was built in 1898 and is still used by the sultan of Kedah for ceremonial functions. Supported on tall pillars topped with Victorian iron lacework, it also shows Thai influences in its decoration.

Around the side of the Balai Besar is the **Muzium Di Raja**, which served as the royal palace for the sultan and other members of the family from 1856. It has the usual royal family regalia and the Dewan Astaka room is lined with hunting trophies. Tunku Abdul Rahman, a prince of the Kedah royal family and the first prime minister of Malaysia, is honoured with his own displays. Of note is a picture of the Tunku and his wife with Queen Elizabeth and Prince Philip, who looks very chic in a stockinged outfit. The museum is open daily from 10 am to 6 pm, closed Friday from noon to 3 pm.

At the southern edge of the square is the **Balai Seni Negeri**, the state art gallery, which is housed in a fine colonial building but the collection of paintings inside is easily forgotten. It is open the same hours as the Muzium Di Raja.

On the other side of the square is the **Zahir Mosque**, the state mosque completed in 1912. It is one the largest and grandest mosques in Malaysia. Topped with domes,

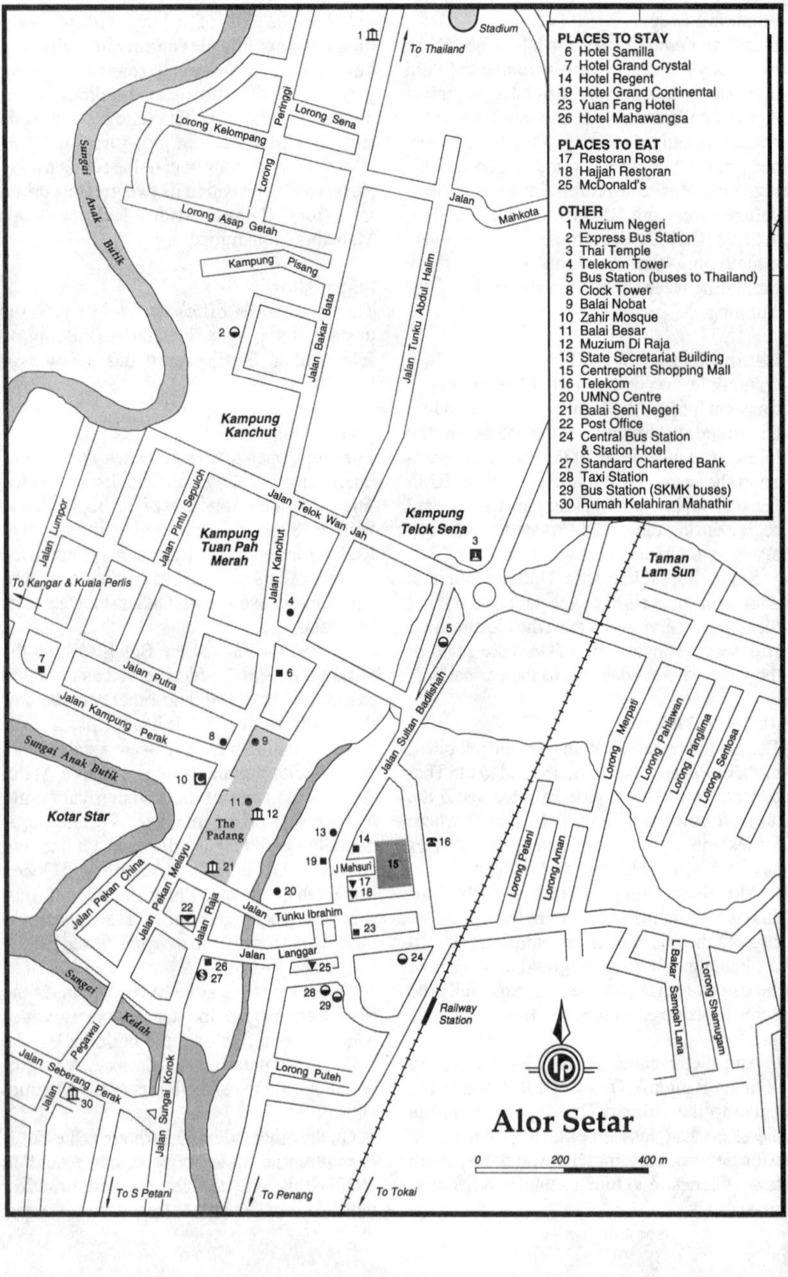
PLACES TO STAY
6 Hotel Samilla
7 Hotel Grand Crystal
14 Hotel Regent
19 Hotel Grand Continental
23 Yuan Fang Hotel
26 Hotel Mahawangsa
PLACES TO EAT
17 Restoran Rose
18 Hajjah Restoran
25 McDonald's
OTHER
1 Muzium Negeri
2 Express Bus Station
3 Thai Temple
4 Telekom Tower
5 Bus Station (buses to Thailand)
8 Clock Tower
9 Balai Nobat
10 Zahir Mosque
11 Balai Besar
12 Muzium Di Raja
13 State Secretariat Building
15 Centrepoint Shopping Mall
16 Telekom
20 UMNO Centre
21 Balai Seni Negeri
22 Post Office
24 Central Bus Station & Station Hotel
27 Standard Chartered Bank
28 Taxi Station
29 Bus Station (SKMK buses)
30 Rumah Kelahiran Mahathir
Stadium
To Thailand
Lorong Kelompang
Lorong Peringgi
Lorong Sena
Lorong Asap Getah
Kampung Pisang
Jalan Mahkota
Sungai Anak Butik
Jalan Bakar Bata
Jalan Tunku Abdul Halim
Kampung Kanchut
Jalan Telok Wan Jah
Kampung Telok Sena
Kampung Tuan Pah Merah
Jalan Lumpor
Jalan Pintu Sepuloh
Jalan Kanchut
Taman Lam Sun
To Kangar & Kuala Perlis
Jalan Putra
Jalan Kampung Perak
Jalan Sultan Badlishah
Lorong Merpati
Lorong Pahlawan
Lorong Panglima
Lorong Sentosa
Kotar Star
The Padang
J Mahsuri
Lorong Petani
Lorong Aman
Jalan Pekan China
Jalan Pekan Melayu
Jalan Raja
Jalan Tunku Ibrahim
Jalan Langgar
Sungai Kedah
L Bakar Sampah Lana
Lorong Shamugam
Railway Station
Jalan Pegawai
Jalan Seberang Perak
Jalan Sungai Korok
Lorong Puteh
Alor Setar
0
200
400 m
To S Petani
To Penang
To Tokai

and medieval and Mogul spires, it looks more like an eastern potentate's castle.

The **Balai Nobat**, a small octagonal building topped by an onion-shaped dome, houses the *nobat*, or royal orchestra. A nobat is principally composed of percussion instruments, and the drums in this orchestra are said to have been a gift from the sultan of Melaka in the 15th century. It is not open to the public and the instruments are only resurrected on special occasions.

The **clock tower** is another architectural whimsy of a type found in many Malaysian cities.

Muzium Negeri

On the main road, two km north of the Padang, the State Museum is built in a style similar to that of the Balai Besar. The museum has a good collection of early Chinese porcelain and a few artefacts from the archaeological excavations made at the Bujang Valley. The Bunga Emas exhibited at the museum entrance is a fabulous 'gold tree' produced by court artisans and given triennially in tribute to the Thais right up until 1909, when the British formally assumed power in Kedah. Next to the museum is the royal boathouse, where royal barges and boats will be housed when construction is finished.

The museum is open 10 am to 6 pm daily (closed Friday noon to 2.30 pm).

Rumah Kelahiran Mahathir

This *kampung* house at 18 Lorong Kilang Ais is the family home and birthplace of the current prime minister. It has been turned into a museum which, though not particularly interesting, manages to avoid sycophancy. It provides a good history of Dr Mahathir, the son of a teacher, who became a doctor in Alor Setar before venturing into politics. Most interesting are his articles on Malay themes, published in the *Straits Times* in the late 40s under a pseudonym, providing an interesting insight into the man's thinking and political development.

Places to Stay

Cheap hotels are scarce but can be found on Jalan Langgar near the bus station in the centre of town. They are noisy but OK for one night. The *Station Hotel* (☎ 04-733 3786) at 74 Jalan Langgar, right above the bus station, is one of the cheapest in town, with rooms from RM17. The *Yuan Fang Hotel* (☎ 04-733 1376) on Jalan Langgar is similarly priced.

Good mid-range hotels abound. The *Hotel Mahawangsa* (☎ 04-733 1433) at 449 Jalan Raja, diagonally opposite the GPO, has air-con rooms at RM49. A step up the scale is the *Hotel Regent* (☎ 04-731 1900), 1536-G Jalan Sultan Badlishah, with air-con rooms for RM55 and RM66. The *Hotel Samila* (☎ 04-731 8888) at 27 Jalan Kanchut is another 70s hotel with rooms that have all the trimmings for RM70, and it also has a good restaurant and MTV lounge.

At the top is the *Hotel Grand Continental* (☎ 04-733 5917), in the centre of town at 134 Jalan Sultan Badlishah, with singles/doubles from RM143/156 including taxes, but substantial discounts are often offered. Better value is its smaller sister hotel, the *Hotel Grand Crystal* (☎ 04-731 3333) at 40 Jalan Kampung Perak, which has a swimming pool and rooms from RM110/120, but discounts can make it almost as cheap as the mid-range hotels.

Places to Eat

On Jalan Sultan Badlishah, south of the Hotel Grand Continental, is a popular Thai Muslim place, *Hajjah Restoran*. The *Restoran Rose* nearby is also popular for Indian food.

Along Jalan Langgar near the local bus terminal are several coffee shops serving inexpensive Malay and Chinese food and a *McDonald's*.

Getting There & Away

Alor Setar is 91 km north of Butterworth and 48 km from the Thai border at Bukit Kayu Hitam. Only a few buses go from Alor Setar all the way to Hat Yai in Thailand. More frequent buses run to the border, from where Thai buses go Hat Yai (see under Bukit Kayu

Hitam for this border crossing). The train is slower but easier and more interesting.

Air The airport is 11 km north of town just off the North-South Highway. MAS has daily flights to KL (RM71) and Kota Bharu (RM74).

Bus Alor Setar has a confusing array of bus stations. The main central bus station on Jalan Langgar handles local services to destinations south and west, and to Butterworth. Buses to Butterworth (RM4.25, 1½ hours) leave every half hour between 7 am and 8 pm. Most take the quick North-South Highway, but not all. Buses to Kuala Kedah (80 sen, half an hour) also leave from here. From the port of Kuala Kedah ferries run to Langkawi.

Another smaller station, nearby behind the taxi station, also handles local services and the SKMK express buses to Kota Bharu at 9 am and 9 pm.

The small station north of the centre on Jalan Sultan Badlishah has a few local services to the north of the state including buses to Bukit Kayu Hitam. Ekspres Tanjung (☎ 04-731 3329) has two buses daily to Hat Yai for RM10.

The main express bus station is two km to the north-east of the centre. Bus ticket offices line the streets nearby and handle a large number of long-distance coach buses to KL, Melaka, Johor Bahru, Singapore etc and to the east coast destinations of Kuantan, Kuala Terengganu and Kota Bharu.

Train The railway from Butterworth to Bangkok runs through Alor Setar and the border town of Padang Besar in Perlis. The *International Express* to Hat Yai and Bangkok comes through at 3.30 pm but you'll need to book well in advance. Alternatively, take the 6 am train to Hat Yai (RM8, three hours), a more scenic alternative to the buses. Check at the station the day before, but seats are almost always available on the morning of departure. From Hat Yai the train departs to Alor Setar at 3.50 pm.

Taxi Taxis from the taxi station include Kuala Kedah (RM1.50), Bukit Kayu Hitam (RM5), Kangar (RM3.50), Padang Besar (RM6) and Butterworth (RM9).

KUALA KEDAH

This busy fishing village 12 km from Alor Setar is the gateway to Langkawi if coming from the south. The **Kota Kuala Kedah** is a fort on the opposite bank of the Kedah River from the town. Built around 1770 to protect the main port of the sultanate, it fell to the Thais in 1821. The walls, cannons and gateway of this partially restored fort can be inspected.

There is little else to detain you from catching a ferry straight to Langkawi. Ferries leave approximately every 1½ hours from 8 am to 6.30 pm and cost RM13.

LANGKAWI

The 104 islands of the Langkawi group are 30 km off the coast from Kuala Perlis, at the northern end of Peninsular Malaysia bordering Thailand. They're accessible by boat from Kuala Perlis, Kuala Kedah and Thailand; or by air from Penang, 112 km south, and KL.

The islands, strategically situated where the Indian Ocean narrows down into the Straits of Melaka, were once a haven for pirates and could easily have become the site for the first British foothold in Malaya instead of Penang. Earlier they were charted by Admiral Cheng Ho on his visit to Melaka in 1405, and for centuries they came under Thai suzerainty.

The only island with any real settlement is the main island of Pulau Langkawi, a large island of 478.5 sq km, with jungle-clad hills in the interior and good beaches scattered around the coast. It is almost as big as Singapore Island, and like Singapore it is growing through land reclamation.

Langkawi is a go-ahead area, targeted by the government for development as the country's premier tourist resort. The island is very much a symbol of the new Malaysia and a showcase for advancement of the *bumiputra* Malays. Its development is backed enthusiastically by the prime minister, Dr Mahathir, who worked as a doctor on the island in the 50s before entering parliament.

Tourism took off in 1986 when Chinese-dominated Penang lost its duty-free status to the then Malay backwater of Langkawi. Billions of ringgit have since poured in to develop the island, which has excellent roads, impressive resort hotels, burgeoning shopping centres and a new international airport.

For the visitor, the island is in danger of becoming overdeveloped. Building sites work 24 hours a day on new hotels and shopping centres, but most of the development is in the main town, Kuah, and in isolated beach resorts around the coast. Away from the built-up areas, Langkawi is still a rural Malay island of small villages, rice paddies and water buffalo.

It is an island steeped in legends, and the favourite legend is of Mahsuri, who was wrongly accused of infidelity and before being killed for her crime put a curse on the island for seven generations. The curse has now expired it seems and the island's 50,000 inhabitants are enjoying the growing wealth of the tourism developments.

Langkawi certainly has its natural attractions, though the atmosphere and beaches of Peninsular Malaysia's east coast attract more travellers and Langkawi still caters primarily to Malaysians, Singaporeans and the growing east Asian tourism market. Yet it has some good beaches and excellent resorts for a luxury holiday. Cheaper accommodation exists and it makes an interesting exit or entry point to or from Thailand.

The wet season in Langkawi is around April to October, and the dry is much drier compared with most of the peninsula.

Orientation

Kuah, in the south-east corner of the island is the main town and the arrival point for the ferries. New hotels and shopping centres are popping up everywhere, but the beaches are elsewhere on the island.

Pantai Cenang and Pantai Kok are on the south-western coast of the island and are the best places to stay. Pantai Cenang is the more developed and popular of the two, although the water here is fairly murky at times. The less-developed beach at Pantai Kok is much better, but it is set to be turned into a golf course in the near future. Pantai Tengah is another beach, almost a southerly continuation of Pantai Cenang.

The airport is on the west of the island, and a few resorts are found nearby at Kuala Muda, but the beach is one of the worst on Langkawi.

Along the north coast of the island the only accommodation is in resorts at Teluk Datai in the west and Tanjung Rhu in the east. The latter has one of the better beaches on the island. In between the two is the island's port, Teluk Ewa, although the ferries dock at Kuah. Teluk Ewa handles cargo vessels and is dominated by a huge cement factory nearby.

Information

Tourism Malaysia (☎ 04-966 7789) has an information booth at the jetty in Kuah, and the main office is one km towards town on the foreshore near the mosque. Both are open daily from 9 am to 1 pm and 2 to 6 pm.

Langkawi is part of Kedah state, so banks and government offices are closed on Friday and Saturday afternoon, but open Sunday. The only banks on the island are at Kuah. Elsewhere you'll have to rely on the resort hotels, and they may not change money for non-guests.

You can make international telephone calls at the Telekom office in Kuah, and some resorts have phones in the lobby that allow international calls using a phone card.

Kuah

The once small fishing village of Kuah is the island's main town. Though still small, it is a hive of activity and new industry, and the island taxi drivers even complain about the afternoon rush hour. New resort hotels are being built at a frantic pace – goodness knows why, as there is no beach. The only 'sight' in town is the picturesque waterside mosque with its golden dome and Moorish arches and minarets rising above the palm trees.

Kuah is the main place to shop on Langkawi, but despite all the promotion as a duty-free shopping paradise, the range of goods is disappointing and the prices much the same as elsewhere in Malaysia. Banks, duty-free shops and small emporiums are found in the main centre of town, just over a km from the jetty. Duty-free cigarettes and liquor, including Malaysian beer, are cheap. Even Japanese motorcycles are duty-free in Kuah, but they can't be taken off the island.

The new northern section of town is becoming the more interesting shopping area, and though still lacklustre, things will improve when the new market-style shopping complex next to the Tiara Hotel is finished.

Mahsuri's Tomb & Padang Masirat

These sites are a few km west of Kuah, on the road which leads to the west-coast beaches and to the airport. Mahsuri was a legendary 10th century Malay princess unjustly accused of adultery and sentenced to death. All attempts to execute her failed until the indignant Mahsuri *agreed* to die, but not before issuing the curse that 'there shall

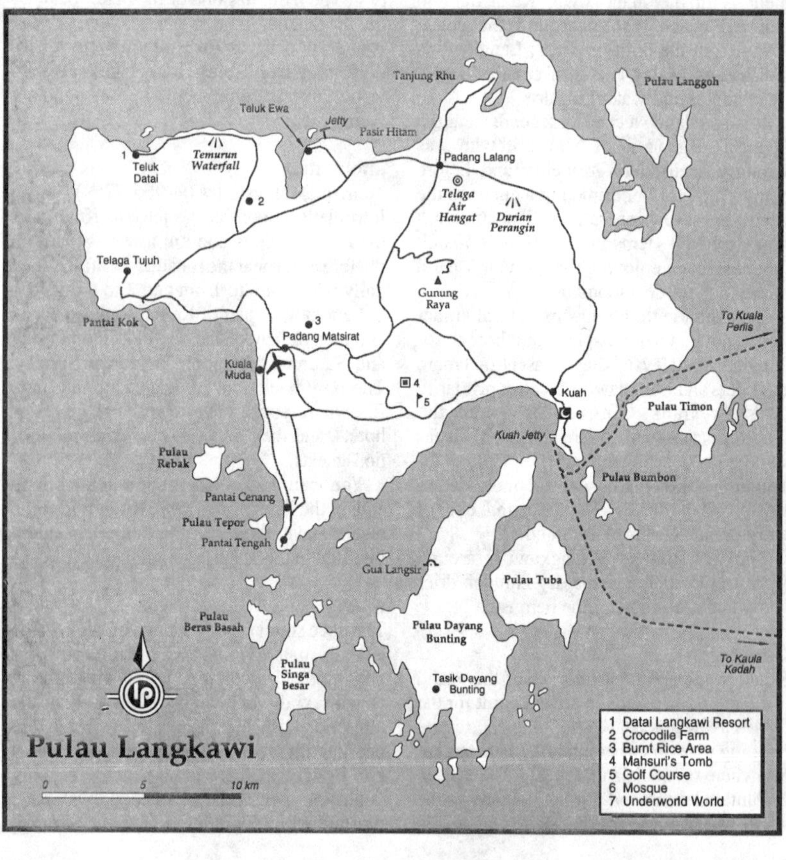

be no peace or prosperity on this island for a period of seven generations'.

A result of that curse can still sometimes be seen at nearby Padang Matsirat, the 'field of burnt rice'. There, villagers once burnt their rice fields rather than allow them to fall into the hands of Siamese invaders. It is said that heavy rain still sometimes brings traces of burnt rice to the surface.

Pantai Cenang

This two km strip of good beach lies at the south-west corner of Langkawi, 25 km from Kuah.

A sandbar appears at low tide where you can inspect the local sea life. Between November and January, you can walk across this sandbar to the nearby island of Pulau Rebak, but only for two hours around low tide. Another nearby island is Pulau Tepor, which can be reached by a hired boat from Cenang Beach.

Pantai Cenang is where most of the local beach chalet development has occurred. Unfortunately, because the blocks of land are long and narrow, the beach frontage is minimal and so some of the chalets only have a view of the chalet in front. During the season it seems all these places fill up, but at any other time most are virtually empty, especially at the southern end of the beach and at Pantai Tengah.

Pantai Cenang is lively in the main tourist season, and it has good restaurants and a few bars. The beer is cheap, and at least it has beer, in comparison with the 'dry' resorts of the east coast of Peninsular Malaysia.

At the southern end of Pantai Cenang near Pantai Tengah, the Zon is a large duty-free shopping complex. It also includes **Underwater World**, a large aquarium with a walk-through tunnel to view the many fish up close. It is open 10 am to 7.30 pm, and entry is RM10 (RM6 for children).

Pantai Tengah

Pantai Tengah is a smaller, quieter beach just south of Pantai Cenang over a small rocky point and very similar to Pantai Cenang. Development is going ahead here too, with two huge new resorts, another being built, and a few low-key places with chalet accommodation.

Pantai Kok

On the western part of the island, 12 km north of Pantai Cenang, Kok Beach fronts a beautiful bay surrounded by limestone mountains and jungle. The water is a bit clearer here than at any of the other beaches.

Pantai Kok is flanked by three large but unobtrusive resorts, and it has a number of low-key chalets that are destined for demolition to make way for a golf course.

Telaga Tujuh

Telaga Tujuh is only a 2.5 km walk from Pantai Kok. Water cascades nearly 100 metres down a hillside through a series of seven *(tujuh)* wells *(telaga)*. You can slide down from one of these shallow pools to another near the top of the falls – the stone channels are very smooth.

To get there, you'll have to take a bus to Pantai Kok from Kuah (RM1.60), or a taxi from Pantai Cenang (RM10), and then walk 2.5 km, or go by motorcycle, in which case you drive to the end of the road about one km past Pantai Kok, and turn along the road to the right, away from the Burau Bay Resort.

Teluk Datai

Teluk Datai is some distance off the main road round the island. It is the site for a mega-resort, the most exclusive on the island, and upmarket golf course. The beach is good at the resort, but it is only for guests. The road continues past the resort to a headland where a short trail will take you through the jungle down to the sea – a pleasant spot but there is no beach to speak of.

On the way to Teluk Datai is the **Crocodile Farm**, a manufactured tourist attraction where you can view crocodiles and see them put through their paces in shows at 11.15 am and 2.45 pm. It is open from 9 am to 6 pm and entry is RM6. The cafe here serves lousy food made even less palatable by the drone of Muzak.

The **Temurun Waterfall** is halfway between

the Crocodile Farm and the resort. The high falls are worth a look and marked by a huge concrete archway spanning the road.

Pasir Hitam

A couple of km west of Tanjung Rhu, this beach is noted for its black sand, although it's not a real black-sand beach – simply streaks of black through the sand caused by a spring that deposits mineral oxides. It's really a very contrived attraction, as the beach is only a couple of metres wide and is at the foot of a five-metre drop, so you can't even walk along it. There is a large souvenir market next to it, selling cheap beachwear and tourist tat.

The waters off Pasir Hitam are dotted with huge boulders.

Tanjung Rhu

Just beyond Pasir Hitam at the village of Padang Lalang there's a roundabout with a turn-off to the north to Tanjung Rhu, while the main road continues on back to Kuah.

Tanjung Rhu has one of Langkawi's better beaches. The water is shallow and at low tide you can walk across the sandbank to the neighbouring island, except during monsoon season. The water swirls across the bank as the tide comes in.

Around the promontory, accessible by boat, is the Gua Cherita cave. Along the coast for a couple of km before the beach, the tiny fish known as ikan bilis (anchovies) are spread out on mats to dry in the sun.

Gunung Raya

The tallest mountain on the island at 881 metres can be reached by a snaking, paved road through the jungle. It is a spectacular drive to the top with views across the island and over to Thailand. At the top is a VIP bungalow, a sort of Camp David for government ministers, which when in use means the road is closed.

Telaga Air Hangat

These hot springs are towards the north of the island, not far from the turn-off to Tanjung Rhu. Like so many places in Malaysia, they are associated with an intriguing legend:

Langkawi Island's two most powerful families, so the story goes, became involved in a bitter argument over a marriage proposal. A fight broke out and all the kitchen utensils were used as missiles. The gravy *(kuah)* was spilt at (yes!) Kuah and seeped into the ground at Kisap (seep). A pot landed at Belanga Perak (broken pot) and finally the saucepan of hot water *(air panas)* came to land here.

The fathers of these two families got their comeuppance for causing all this mayhem – they are now the island's two major mountain peaks. The hot springs themselves, although unimpressive, have become the centre of a major tourist trap. This is development gone mad. As the tourist literature puts it, 'the mythical hot springs are now celebrated by a sprawling hotspringscape housed within in a most colourful Cultural Theme Park'! What more is there to say?

Durian Perangin

Fifteen km north of Kuah is the turn-off to this waterfall. There's a small sign by the shop there and a larger sign by a second turn-off a bit further on.

The falls are three km off the road, along a rough track. In the dry season there's very little to see. The falls are best seen at the end of the monsoon season – late September, early October.

Nearby Islands

Pulau Dayang Bunting Tasik Dayang Bunting, or the Lake of the Pregnant Maiden, is located on the island of the same name, south of Langkawi itself. It is a freshwater lake and is good for swimming.

A legend states that a childless couple, after 19 years of unsuccessful efforts, had a baby girl after drinking from this lake. Since then it has been a popular pilgrimage centre for those hoping for children! Legend also says that the lake is inhabited by a large white crocodile.

On the same island is Gua Langsir, or the Cave of the Banshee, which is inhabited by thousands of bats. Marble is quarried on the island and shipped to the mainland for processing. To get to this island you must hire a boat from the Kuah jetty or Pantai Cenang.

Boat trips to Pulau Dayang Bunting usually add in a stop at Pulau Singa Besar, where there is reasonable snorkelling. During the monsoon season, July to mid-September, the seas are usually too rough and unpredictable for boat trips to Dayang Bunting. From Cenang boats can be hired for about RM15 per person, eight to a boat. The large hotels and travel agents in Kuah also organise trips.

Pulau Bumbon Only 10 minutes from the Kuah jetty, this island has a floating restaurant and bungalows. There's a pleasant beach nearby and another one 15 minutes' walk over the hill. Le Bumbon Island Resort (☎ 010-3332979) is a simple, mid-range resort catering mostly for package tours and it also runs day trips from Kuah for RM20.

Pulau Payar Marine Park This marine park 30 km south of Langkawi incorporates a number of islands, the largest being Pulau Payar. A large floating platform is moored off the island and includes a bar/restaurant and underwater observation chamber to view the reef. From here, you can go snorkelling and diving or rent glass-bottom boats. This upmarket marine tourism venture is reached on day tours from the Kuah jetty for RM180. Hotels and travel agents take bookings, or phone Sriwani at ☎ 04-966 7318.

Places to Stay

Budget accommodation is becoming increasingly rare on Langkawi. Even then it starts at around RM30 a night for a simple room or beach chalet. The resorts range from small mid-range chalets to five-star luxury. Prices drop in the off season but some of the large resorts hold their prices. Mid-range options are expensive compared with elsewhere in Malaysia. Package deals through travel agents are usually the cheapest way to enjoy Langkawi's beaches in luxury.

Although during school holidays and at the peak time of November to February Langkawi gets very crowded, at other times of the year supply far outstrips demand and the prices come down considerably.

Kuah Kuah has seen the greatest tourist development is recent years, which is hard to understand given its lack of beaches. It has a big selection of hotels, but it is much better to head for Pantai Kok or Pantai Cenang.

A short ride by share-taxi will take you from the pier to any of Kuah's cheaper accommodation, all of which are strung out along the waterfront around the bay.

On past the mosque, about a km from the pier, you'll come to two vaguely budget hotels. The *Asia Hotel* (☎ 04-966 6216) has reasonable air-con rooms with TV and attached bathroom for RM50, or RM60 with hot showers. A few doors down at the *Hotel Langkawi* (☎ 04-966 6248), rooms cost RM20 for a small windowless box with fan and common bath, RM40 with air-con, TV and bath.

Better value is the slightly grander *Region Hotel* (☎ 04-966 7719), Jalan Persiaran Putra. This three-storey hotel has air-con rooms with bath and TV for RM50. It is back from the main road – take the street near the mosque. About a km north of the centre of town in the new area is the *Malaysia Hotel & Restaurant* (☎ 04-966 8087), 39 Pusat Mas. Small singles/doubles with air-con, TV, minibar and attached bath cost RM65/75. Dorm beds are available for RM20. Similar mid-range hotels can be found nearby.

Top-end hotels include the *Sheraton Perdana Resort* (☎ 04-966 2020), a couple of km south of the jetty away from the town. Rooms cost RM350, before discount. The huge *Tiara Hotel*, nearing completion at the northern end of town, looks set to be the mother of all resorts on the island. Styled after a medieval castle, complete with moat, it has its own large shopping centre and a decent beach manufactured from imported sand.

Pantai Cenang Pantai Cenang is the liveliest beach strip with accommodation ranging from budget to the international standard

Pelangi Beach Resort. They all straggle along the two km of beach between the turn-off to Kuah at the northern end and Pantai Tengah to the south.

Most accommodation is mid-range. Even at the budget places you pay around RM30 for a chalet with bath attached.

At the southern end of the beach, near the Zon shopping centre, the *Langkapuri Beach Resort* (☎ 04-955 1202) has small, comfortable cottages for RM95 to RM160.

Directly opposite across the road from the beach is *2020 Chalets* (☎ 04-955 2806), a reasonable budget place with chalets for RM30 and larger chalets for RM70 with air-con. Further north again are the *Suria* (☎ 04-955 1776) and *Samila* (☎ 04-955 1964), two basic and cramped places with fairly unattractive chalets from RM35 with bath.

The *AB Motel* (☎ 04-955 1300) is next. It is one of the older places on Pantai Cenang, and though dowdy and not overly welcoming, it is cheap and faces the beach. Big chalets around a lawn cost RM30 or RM50 with air-con. It has a decent restaurant.

Next door to the AB is the *Sandy Beach Motel* (☎ 04-955 1308), probably the most popular place but it can get very crowded. The A-frame chalets near the beach are quite good, but towards the road they are packed a bit too tightly together. They cost RM35 for a double with fan and bath, and there are air-con rooms in a new three-storey block for RM80.

Right across the road is the *Beach View Motel* (☎ 04-955 1186), which has a view of nothing at all. Small chalets with fan and attached bath go for RM35. There's a small shop here which sells basic items, and it has motorcycles for rent. There's also a laundry next door.

Next door to the Sandy Beach is a good mid-range place, the *Semarak Beach Resort* (☎ 04-955 1377), which has pleasant chalets and lawns facing the beach, and an excellent, if slightly expensive, restaurant. The spacious chalets go for RM78 with fan and bath, or RM110 with air-con.

After a gap of a couple of hundred metres there's another group of places, including the very pleasant *Beach Garden & Bistro* (☎ 04-955 1363), run by a German couple. It has a swimming pool and just a dozen rooms which cost RM90/110 with air-con and bath, rising to RM125/145 in the high season, plus 10% tax. The restaurant here is excellent.

The most northerly place on this beach, the first you come to when coming from Kuah or the airport, is the very flash Singapore-owned *Pelangi Beach Resort* (☎ 04-955 1001), with every luxury including island swimming pool, sports facilities, restaurant and even electric buggies to take you to your room. No expense has been spared on this place, and the prices reflect this – RM286/308 and up.

Pantai Tengah There is a lot less development here, although there are still a couple of large resorts.

Just after the headland which separates the two beaches is a cluster of three budget places all charging RM35 for basic chalets – *Green Hill Beach Motel* (☎ 04-955 1935), the *Sugary Sands* (☎ 04-955 1317) and the *Tanjung Mali* (☎ 04-955 1891). The Green Hill and Sugary Sands are pretty basic and little thought has gone into the siting of the chalets. The Tanjung Mali is marginally better and also has more comfortable air-con bungalows for RM65 and RM85.

Next along is probably the best value place on this beach – the mid-range *Sunset Beach Resort* (☎ 04-955 2285). Although the chalets run in a line back from the beach and so have no views, the restaurant and bar are right on the beach. The facilities are good, but it is a simple resort. All cottages are air-con and cost RM55 at the rear of the block and RM100 closest to the beach.

After a gap of undeveloped land there is another place right on the beach. The *Charlie Motel* (☎ 04-955 1200) has been around for some years, although the chalets are quite new. Simple but pleasant air-con chalets cost RM55 for a double with bath, and RM85 for those facing the beach. The restaurant on the beach is good.

Finally there are the resorts. The *Langkawi Village Resort* (☎ 04-955 1511) has individual two-storey chalets dotted around the main building. It has a pool and a couple of places to eat and is popular among European tour groups. The rack rates are RM170 for a room including taxes.

At the end of the road is the other resort, the *Langkawi Holiday Villa Beach Resort* (☎ 04-955 1701). This is a superb place with every imaginable facility, including a pool, a couple of restaurants and bars. Accommodation is in rooms rather than chalets, and the design is such that all rooms have sea views. Rooms start at RM220.

Pantai Kok Pantai Kok is the cheapest, most laid back beach on the island, but plans to redevelop the whole area as a golf course means its days are numbered. The developments are set to happen over the life of this book, so it pays to ring first.

The best place is *The Last Resort* (☎ 04-955 1046), run by an expatriate Englishman and his Malay wife. There's a choice of rooms with bathroom in a 'longhouse' for RM35, or chalets with air-con go for RM50. The atmosphere here is good, with an interesting mix of people and an attractive restaurant.

Next door, *Inapan Mama* (☎ 04-955 1352) is a positive eyesore – fibrocement blockhouses with about as much aesthetic appeal as a bus shelter for RM50, and cheaper sweat boxes across the road. However Mama is something of a character and the restaurant is reasonable.

On the other side of The Last Resort, *Coral Beach Resort* (☎ 04-955 1000) has better than average little chalets for RM35 with fan and bathroom or RM60 with air-con, but better value is the *Kok Bay Motel* (☎ 04-955 1407) directly next door again. Almost identical chalets here cost only RM30.

Further on, the *Country Beach Motel* (☎ 04-955 1212) has basic rooms for RM18, and better chalets from RM30 to RM65, but they already seem to be resigned to redevelopment and can't be bothered.

Further east opposite the turn-off to Teluk Datai, the *Mila Beach Motel* (☎ 04-955 1049) has a few good chalets for RM50 and the scruffy but pleasant *Jungle Bar* right on the beach to hang out for a meal or a drink.

Next along are two characterless places, the *Dayang Beach Resort* (☎ 04-955 1058) and the *Pantai Kok Motel* (☎ 04-959 2541), which was run-down when they built it. Rooms and chalets start at RM30 at both places. Across the road away from the beach are the *Tropica* (☎ 04-955 2312) and *Memories* (☎ 04-955 1118) motels. Tropica has uninspiring chalets with bathroom for RM25. They also rent motorbikes for RM25 per day, which like their chalets are poorly maintained, so try before you rent. Memories has a shanty at the back with rooms for RM15, but mostly chalets for RM35.

A notch up is the *Idaman Bay Resort* (☎ 04-955 1212), well back from the beach down a dirt road, but with attractive chalets for RM55 built on stilts around a pond. Best of all is its excellent restaurant.

Pantai Kok is flanked by large resorts. Just around the headland at the western end of the beach, right by the track leading to Telaga Tujuh, is the *Burau Bay Beach Resort* (☎ 04-959 1061). Although owned by the same people who have the Pelangi at Pantai Cenang, it's certainly not in the same class. The buildings are all made from steel rather than wood, and the effect is nowhere near as good. Nevertheless, it has good facilities, and costs RM190/220 including taxes and breakfast.

Further on is the big *Berjaya Langkawi Beach Resort* (☎ 04-959 1888), one of the best on the island. Luxury chalets cost RM280 to RM350 and suites are available. It has an excellent range of sporting facilities, which one day will include a golf course that threatens to swallow the rest of Pantai Kok.

At the opposite end of the beach, a couple of km back towards Pantai Cenang, is the sparkling *Sheraton Langkawi Resort* (☎ 04-955 1901), with over 200 rooms arranged around a shady headland and a small beach. Rates range from RM180 for a standard room in the low season up to RM285 for a deluxe room in the high season, plus taxes.

Teluk Datai The *Datai Langkawi* (☎ 04-959 2500) is the island's most exclusive and isolated beach resort, with a huge golf course attached. Attractive chalets, many built on stilts over the water, are scattered around the large grounds and cost RM460 to RM700. Guests are shuttled around by golf buggies.

Tanjung Rhu There are two places here: a small low-key place and a high-rise (well, it's four storeys) monster. The former is the *Mutiara Beach Hotel* (☎ 04-955 6488) with swimming pool and restaurant. The room rates are RM150/180 including taxes.

Right next door is the *Radisson Tanjung Rhu* (☎ 04-959 1091), with its buildings arranged around a central courtyard. It is undergoing a massive renovation which will make it one of the best hotels on the island.

Kuala Muda Kuala Muda is the beach directly opposite the airport runway, north of Pantai Cenang. It has a reasonable stretch of sand for sunbathing, but step into the shallow water and you'll find yourself ankle deep in mud.

The *Delima Resort* (☎ 04-955 1801) is a huge resort with 1500 rooms, a massive swimming pool and its own shopping centre. It looks very flash from the road, but it is mostly a mid-range resort. The cheaper rooms are already looking the worst for wear but are good value at RM60 and RM83 with balcony. More luxurious rooms are RM110, and one/two-bedroom suites cost RM275/550. The resort also has an excellent, cheap hawkers night market.

The *Lankasuka Resort* (☎ 04-955 6888) is more upmarket and has a large aquarium/tourist complex still under construction. Rooms cost RM150 and suites are RM250 and RM300. Like the Delima, rates are lower than elsewhere on the island.

Places to Eat

Kuah A good collection of food stalls sets up from 6 pm in the backstreets behind the Region Hotel and stay open late. In the streets behind the Langkawi Duty Free you'll find good, inexpensive Chinese coffee shops.

Kuah has some good restaurants overlooking the waterfront in the centre of town, such as the open-air *Rahim Cafe*. Seafood is featured. Two km from town, but worth the effort to get there, *Restoran Sangkor Ikan* is a fish farm restaurant on stilts at the sea's edge. Excellent seafood will set you back around RM30 per person. To get there take the main back road, Jalan Penarak, behind the mosque south and follow the Beringin Beach Resort signs.

All the big hotels have their own restaurants.

Pantai Cenang The *Hot Wok Cafe*, opposite the Semarak Beach Resort, has very good Chinese and western food, and seafood is featured. The prices are reasonable and it's a very popular place in the evenings.

Champor-Champor is a stylish restaurant offering a mixture of western and Asian cuisines. The food is excellent and it has a good little bar for a drink, but prices are high with mains around RM15 to RM20.

Backhofen has beer, bratwurst and other German fare. It comes alive around Christmas, the main German tourist season, but is quiet other times of the year.

Many of the hotels at Pantai Cenang have restaurants. The one at the *Sandy Beach Motel* is cheap and popular, and the food is quite good. The *Semarak* next door serves very good food.

If you feel like a splurge, there are a couple of places to try. The *Beach Garden & Bistro* has a restaurant right on the beach and serves excellent western food.

The *Pelangi* resort has a sumptuous dining room with good buffet meals, including a breakfast buffet for RM19.

Pantai Tengah Though not as well supplied with restaurants as Pantai Cenang, Pantai Tengah has a few decent places. The *Charlie Motel* is good for a cheap meal. The restaurant overlooks the beach and does a good job of Thai and Malaysian food, even if the service is very slow.

The *White Sand Seafood Restaurant* is a moderately priced Chinese restaurant with an extensive menu. It's good for banquets.

The *Safari Bar & Restaurant* is a happening place in the main tourist season. Chinese, Thai and Malaysian dishes cost around RM5 to RM10 or a steak is RM20. It's an attractive bamboo and thatch place, popular for the drinking as much as the food, and it has cheap happy hours in the early evening.

The *Oasis Beach Pub* is another sometimes lively bar for drinking, but food is also available.

Pantai Kok The only restaurants are found in the places to stay. The *Idaman Bay Resort* serves excellent Thai food and is the liveliest and most popular restaurant around. The others serve uninspiring fair at higher than average prices. *The Last Resort* has an attractive restaurant and a bar, or the *Inapan Mama* and the *Jungle Bar* are also reasonable places to hang out if you tire of Idaman Bay.

Things to Buy

Despite its duty-free status, Langkawi's shopping is disappointing. Apart from cheap cigarettes and alcohol, shopping is either geared to domestic visitors with oddities like kitchen utensils on offer, or the Japanese market with imported designer-name T-shirts and fashion accessories at inflated prices. Electronics are no bargain and the range is poor. You'll find a much bigger range of goods and the same or cheaper prices in Kuala Lumpur and Penang. Handicrafts are limited to Kedah pottery or a few marble souvenirs made locally.

More shopping centres are being built and the competition may improve the range and bring prices down. Kuah is the main shopping area with a handful of duty-free shops, which are only really worth browsing for cigarettes and alcohol; a growing number of smaller shops have clothes, shoes and a few electronics and even Harley-Davidson has opened an outlet. Duty-free shops can also be found at the ferry terminal, the airport and the Zon shopping centre on the border of Pantai Cenang and Pantai Tengah, and some resorts also have small shopping plazas.

Getting There & Away

Air MAS (☎ 04-966 6622) has direct daily flights between Langkawi and KL (RM134), Penang (RM51) and Singapore (RM200). MAS plans to introduce direct international flights when the runway extension is completed. Pelangi (☎ 04-955 2261) has direct flights to Ipoh (RM107) four times a week.

The island's new international terminal is an impressive structure with a number of shops. A large duty-free complex and a convention centre is a few hundred metres from the terminal. It hosts the huge LIMA aerospace exhibition held annually around November.

Boat Ferries between Kuala Perlis and Langkawi leave hourly in either direction between 8 am and 6 pm, and the trip takes around one hour and costs RM10. Fares depend on demand and can vary depending on the tourist season.

There are also regular ferries between Langkawi and the small port town of Kuala Kedah, not far from Alor Setar. Ferries go every 1½ hours from 8 am to 6.30 pm and cost RM13.

Kuala Perlis Langkawi Ferry Service (☎ 04-966 7876) also has an irregular ferry service to Penang for RM45. It has stopped operation but may start up again.

Thailand Small ferries operate to Satun on the Thai coast from the Kuah jetty daily at 8.45 am and 12.30 and 3.30 pm. They cost RM15 and from Satun buses and taxis go to Hat Yai. During the main tourist season from mid-November until the end of March private yachts operate between Langkawi and Phuket. They run round-trip package trips from Pantai Kok for US$250 for six days all-inclusive, but you can also arrange to be dropped off in Phuket. The best place to organise a trip is at The Last Resort at Pantai Kok.

Getting Around

The Airport Taxis from the airport cost RM12 to the jetty and RM10 to Pantai Kok or Pantai Cenang. Buy a coupon at the desk before leaving the airport terminal.

Bus The bus station in Kuah is opposite the hospital, in the centre of town, but services are not that frequent and are limited in scope. Infrequent buses go from the jetty to the centre of Kuah for 60 sen.

From Kuah there are buses to Pantai Cenang (RM1.30) hourly from 7 am to 6 pm. To Pantai Kok (RM1.70) there are just four departures daily, at 8 and 10.30 am and 2 and 4.30 pm. The only other service is to Ewa, with departures hourly from 8 am to 6 pm.

Taxi Taxis are the main way of getting around. Fares are fixed and high. From the Kuah jetty fares are: Kuah town (RM4), airport (RM12), Pantai Cenang/ Pantai Tengah (RM12) and Pantai Kok (RM16).

Car Cars can be rented cheaply. Touts at the ferry terminal will assail you on arrival, or they can be rented at any of the beach resorts. The going rate is RM80 per day.

Motorcycle & Bicycle The easiest way to get around is to hire a motorcycle (usually Honda 70cc step-thrus) for the day. You can do a very leisurely circuit of the island (70 km) in a day. The roads are excellent and though traffic on the island is increasing, outside of Kuah it's very pleasant and easy riding. Motorbikes can be hired at stands all over the island, and none seem too fussed about whether you have a licence or not. The charge is usually RM25 per day.

Most of the places with motorcycles also have bikes for rent. Mountain bikes cost RM12 per day.

BUKIT KAYU HITAM

This is the main border crossing between Malaysia and Thailand, 48 km north of Alor Setar. With the completion of the North-South Highway, this route handles the vast majority of road traffic between the two countries and all the buses to Hat Yai come this way.

At the border post are a few restaurants, private car parking facilities and a Tourism Malaysia office. The easiest way to cross the border is to take a through bus all the way to Hat Yai, or buses and taxis from Alor Setar run right up to the Malaysian customs post. From here walk a few hundred metres past the big duty-free shopping complex to the Thai checkpost. Taxis and buses on the other side run to Sadao and Hat Yai.

Arriving from Thailand, you'll find regular buses and taxis that go to Alor Setar, from where frequent buses go to Butterworth and Kuala Kedah for Langkawi. Kuala Perlis, the other departure point for Langkawi, is more difficult to reach – first take a bus to Changlun, another to Kangar and then another to Kuala Perlis.

Perlis

The tiny state of Perlis, tucked away in the far north-east corner of Malaysia on the Thai border, tends to be the forgotten state of Malaysia. Apart from a sugar refinery and cement factory, its economy is still dominated by agriculture.

Its tourist attractions are few, and Perlis is primarily a state to transit through. Kuala Perlis is one of the access ports for Langkawi, and Padang Besar is the main border town if arriving by train from Thailand.

History

Perlis was originally part of Kedah, though it variously came under Thai and Achehnese sovereignty. After the Thais conquered Kedah in 1821, the sultan of Kedah made unsuccessful attempts to regain his territory by force until in 1842 he agreed to accept Siamese terms. The Siamese reinstalled the sultan but made Perlis into a separate vassal principality with its own raja.

As was the case in Kedah, power was transferred from the Thais to the British in 1909 under the Treaty of Bangkok and the

British installed a Resident at Arau. During the Japanese occupation, Perlis was returned to Thailand. After the war it became part of the Malayan Union and then the Federation of Malaysia.

KANGAR

Kangar, 56 km north-west of Alor Setar, is the main town in the state of Perlis. It's a low-lying, modern town surrounded by rice paddies but has little of interest for travellers. If you're stuck for something to do you can see the state mosque on Jalan Besar out towards the Pens Travelodge.

Places to Stay

Kangar has a few hotels, including the *Federal Hotel* (☎ 04-976 6288) at 104 Jalan Kangar. Head down the side street opposite the eastern side of the bus station and it is just one block away. This reasonable mid-range hotel has fan-cooled rooms for RM35 and air-con rooms from RM55. The Chinese restaurant downstairs is good.

The cheapest in town is the basic *Hotel Ban Cheong* (☎ 04-976 1184) at 76 Jalan Kangar, half a block from the Federal. This typical old Chinese hotel has rooms from RM18.

Top of the pile is the *Pens Travelodge* (☎ 04-976 7755), 135 Jalan Besar, on the road to Arau. This international hotel is about the biggest thing in Kangar and has a swimming pool, restaurants and a bar. Rooms cost RM160/210 plus 15%.

Getting There & Away

The bus station is central and has buses to KL, Butterworth and Alor Setar. Regular buses run to Kuala Perlis (85 sen) and Padang Besar (RM2.05). A taxi to Kuala Perlis costs RM1.50 per person.

KUALA PERLIS

This small port town in the extreme north-west of the peninsula is visited mainly as the departure point for Langkawi. It is the closest access port to the island if coming from Thailand.

The main part of Kuala Perlis is just a couple of streets with plenty of restaurants and shops and a bank. Kangar is only 11 km away if you need to get access to more facilities. The older part of town has interesting houses and mosques built on stilts over the water around the mangrove swamps. The flash, new ferry terminal is less than one km from the centre of town.

Places to Stay

On the main street in the centre of town, the *Pens Hotel* (☎ 04-985 4122) is a good mid-range hotel with singles/doubles for RM63/75. The much more basic *Asia Hotel* (☎ 04-985 5392) is on the outskirts, 1½ km from the ferry terminal on the road out of town. Rooms cost RM22.

Getting There & Away

Buses and taxis go from the ferry terminal. Most services go to Kangar, but there are also direct buses to Butterworth, Alor Setar, KL and Padang Besar (for Thailand). The short taxi ride into Kangar costs RM1.50, or RM5 to Padang Besar.

The new ferry terminal has a number of companies operating ferries to Langkawi and touts selling accommodation on the island. Ferries leave at least every hour from 8 am to 6 pm and cost RM10. If you are driving, private car parks near the ferry will look after your car for RM5 per day.

ARAU

The royal capital of Perlis is 10 km east of Kangar. It has an *istana* (palace), looking almost Dutch colonial in design, though it is nowhere as grand as that of other states. Opposite is the royal mosque.

Arau is on the railway line north to Padang Besar and connected by bus to Kangar.

PADANG BESAR

This border town to Thailand is 50 km north of Kangar. It's popular for Malaysians because of the duty-free market that operates in the neutral territory between the two countries. This area is a prime smuggling route for both Malaysians and Thais. Malaysia's Anti-Smuggling Unit occasionally makes an arrest, but the overall trade is hardly affected.

The town itself is nothing special. The bus station is on the outskirts about a km from the large border crossing complex. Regular buses run to Kangar, and there are bus connections on the Thai side for Hat Yai and other destinations. The train is a better bet, but the only train to Hat Yai from Padang Besar leaves at 7.45 am.

GUA KELAM

Near Kaki Bukit in the extreme north-west corner of the state, this limestone cave is the state's premier tourist attraction, which says little for tourism in Perlis. The cave is interesting enough, but difficult to reach.

The cave is the only access to the village of Wang Kelian, an area of high-quality tin ore and in 1970 a suspension boardwalk was installed right through the 400-metre-long cavern. A river runs through the cave and emerges in a cascade, a popular swimming spot. On the other side of cave is a landscaped park with walks. It's a pleasant picnic spot and the tin mine is a short distance from the far end of the cavern. Be warned that motorcycles also use the boardwalk, so you need to keep an ear open.

The cave is a one km walk from the small village of Kaki Bukit, which is 35 km from Kangar, but bus connections are very infrequent.

Negeri Sembilan

The small state of Negeri Sembilan ('Nine States') is one of the most unusual states historically, and a centre for the Minangkabau people, who originally came from Sumatra. Negeri Sembilan's main tourist destination is the beach resort of Port Dickson, popular with KL residents, but Malaysia has many other better beaches. Few international visitors include Negeri Sembilan in their itinerary, but the area around Seremban has a few points of interest for those interested in the Minangkabau and their distinctive architecture.

Full Name: Negeri Sembilan Darul Khusus
Area: 6643 sq km
Capital: Seremban
Population: 702,000

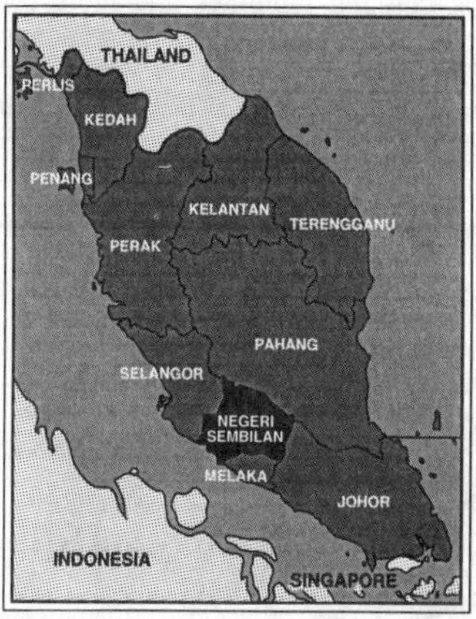

History

During the Melaka sultanate of the 15th century, many Minangkabau people from Sumatra settled in the Melaka area. They lived under the protection of the Melaka rulers initially, but with the fall of Melaka to the Portuguese the Minangkabaus sought protection from the sultans of Johor.

With the increasing power of the Bugis in Selangor, the Minangkabaus felt increasingly insecure and so sought protection from the royal house of Sumatra. Raja Melewar, a Minangkabau prince, was appointed the first *yang di-pertuan besar* (head of state) of Negeri Sembilan in 1773, by the *undang* (territorial chiefs) of the districts of Sungei Ujong, Jelebu, Johol and Rembau. The confederacy of Negeri Sembilan was never anything more formal than a loose union of nine Minangkabau states, or *luaks*, and there's even some confusion as to the make-up of that union.

The royal capital of Negeri Sembilan was established at Sri Menanti, and Raja Melewar indulged himself here. He had very little real power and was virtually confined to ceremonial duties.

Like Selangor to the north, Negeri Sembilan was rich in tin, and so suffered unrest and political instability in the 17th century. After Raja Melewar's death, the post of yang di-pertuan was filled by a succession of Sumatran chiefs, until a series of protracted tin-related wars from 1824 to 1832 led to the severance of political ties with Sumatra.

The second half of the 19th century saw the civil disturbances continue, particularly in the northern state of Sungei Ujong. There was also much interstate rivalry between the yang di-pertuan besar, the undang and the *dato klana* (the ruler of Sungei Ujong). In the 1880s the British gradually increased their influence in the area, and the territories of Sri Menanti, Tampin, Rembau and Jelebu were united in a new confederacy controlled by a British Resident. In 1895 Sungei Ujong was added to the union, and it is this union of five districts that makes up the current state of Negeri Sembilan.

SEREMBAN

South of KL, Seremban is a modern city of 270,000 people founded during the tin boom of the late 19th century. The downtown area is a grid of constant traffic, a few colonial shophouses and modern shopping centres. This central area is noisy and devoid of interest.

Heading east to the hills bordering downtown, Seremban takes on a different personality. The Lake Gardens are a pleasant respite from the traffic and further into the hills is the old colonial district, dotted with bungalows, colonial buildings and more parks favoured by joggers and tai-chi proponents.

Though not brimming over with tourist interest, as the capital of Negeri Sembilan, Seremban is a centre for Minangkabau culture. Buffalo horn roofs adorn many of the new buildings, but the only real access to Minangkabau culture is at the good museum on the outskirts of town.

State Museum

The State Museum (Muzium Negeri) is built in the style of a Minangkabau palace and includes good craft and historical exhibits. The Emergency is covered, complete with photographs of the Communist leaders, including some gruesome post-capture portraits reminiscent of those of the bullet-ridden Che Guevara.

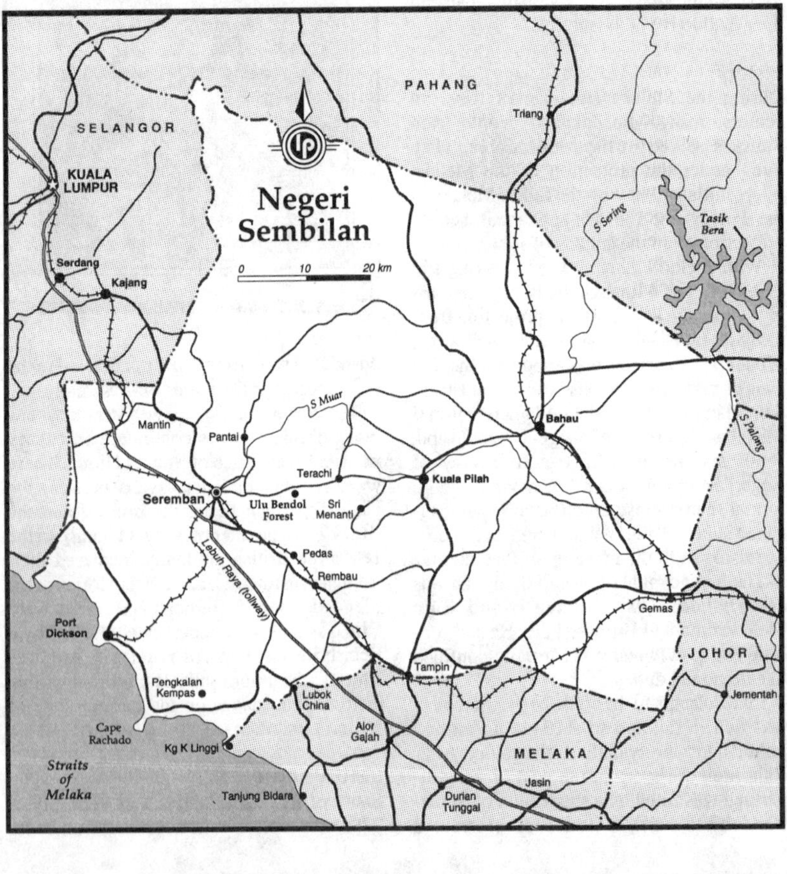

The main interest lies in the two traditional Minangkabau houses in the grounds next to the museum. The **Istana Ampang Tinggi** was constructed in the 1860s near Sri Menanti, a gift from the sultan to his daughter. Though small, it shows the intricate carving of palace architecture and traditional thatch roof. Minangkabau houses were built entirely without nails, though this is now a lost art it seems, for nails were used when the palace was reconstructed on this site. Next to the palace, the **Rumah Minangkabau** is a much plainer traditional house with a shingle roof, but it exhibits the hallmark curved roof style based on the buffalo horn.

The buffalo plays a leading role in Minangkabau tradition, and the word Minangkabau comes from *minang* (to win) and *kerbau* (water buffalo), a reference to the legend surrounding their origins that highlights Minangkabau ingenuity. When the Javanese came to the Minangkabau homelands in Sumatra to assume suzerainty, the Minangkabau were prepared to go to war, but to avoid bloodshed they instead proposed a bullfight. The Minangkabau dispatched a tiny calf to fight the enormous Javanese bull – a ruse which stunned both the bull and onlookers. The calf, separated from its mother several days before the fight and with sharp metal spears attached to its horns, went straight for the bull's belly in search of milk. The gored and bleeding bull took to its heels and the crowd shouted 'minangkabau, minangkabau!'

The museum is in the grounds of the Taman Seni Budaya Negeri (Arts & Cultural Park), which also includes a *gasing* pavilion and a craft shop. Top-spinning events are only held on special occasions and the selection of crafts is unexciting. The museum is three km west of the bus station on the road to Kuala Lumpur. It is open 10 am to 6 pm, except Monday (closed), Thursday (open 8.15 am to 1 pm) and Friday (closed 12.15 to 2.45 pm).

Lake Gardens

The attractive Lake Gardens are a popular recreation reserve and the place for courting couples to commit *khalwat* in the evenings. Paddle boats can be hired, a small aviary is on the western side and cultural events are sometimes staged at the park's open pavilion. The gardens are at the edge of the green and tranquil colonial district, now mostly housing government quarters. There are many other parkland areas to the east of the Lake Gardens, including the **Hutan Rekreasi**, a small jungle park in the city.

Architecture

No new building in Seremban is complete without a Minangkabau curved roof, but the only really fine welding of modern and traditional architecture is the **State Secretariat building**. The wonderful multiple points of the roof are a central landmark for Seremban. Opposite is the **Istana Besar**, home of the sultan of Negeri Sembilan, but it is closed to the public. Directly south is the neo-classical **State Library**, Seremban's most imposing colonial building and once the centre for the colonial administration.

Lower down towards the town is the **State Mosque**, with its nine pillars symbolising the nine original states of Negeri Sembilan. This modern, futuristic mosque is relatively restrained compared with some other mosques erected to the glory of Islam in Malaysia.

In the downtown area, colonial architecture includes the **Catholic Church** (Gereja Katolik Visitation) with its Gothic spires and the more sober **Methodist Church** built in 1920. The **King George V School** on Jalan Za'aba was the premier colonial school for Seremban's elite and still functions as a high school. It is one of the largest and most impressive colonial buildings.

Places to Stay

Seremban has a collection of seedy and dirty hotels in the downtown area. Many function as boarding houses or bordellos, and the halfway decent cheap hotels are some of the most overpriced in Malaysia. The *Hotel Nam Yong* (☎ 06-762 0155), 5 Jalan Tuanku Munawir, is more dirty than seedy. The desperately impecunious can get a room for

RM18. The *Oriental Hotel* (☎ 06-763 0119) at 11 Jalan Tuanku Munawir is at least a little cleaner and has rooms for RM28. The *Happy Hotel* (☎ 06-763 0172), 35 Jalan Tunku Hassan, is slightly better again and has clean rooms with bathroom for RM35 but many are windowless.

The mid-range hotels are preferable, but none are bargains. The *Carlton Star Hotel* (☎ 06-762 5336) at 47 Jalan Dato Sheikh Ahmad has a flash lobby and coffee shop but is just a better class of seedy. Air-con rooms are nothing special at RM60/80 for singles/doubles. Cheaper and plainer is the *Hotel Nam Keow* (☎ 06-763 5578), 61-62 Jalan Dato Bandar Tunggal, where partitioned rooms with attached bathroom cost RM50/60. It's clean and friendly.

Top-end hotels are more reasonably priced for the facilities on offer. The *Tasik Hotel* (☎ 06-763 0994) on Jalan Tetamu is central and overlooks the Lake Gardens. With a distinctive Minangkabau-style roof, it has a swimming pool and a good coffee shop. Though service and maintenance may be lacking, very good motel-style rooms cost RM100. The new *Seri Malaysia Hotel* (☎ 06-764 4181), Jalan Sungei Ujong, also

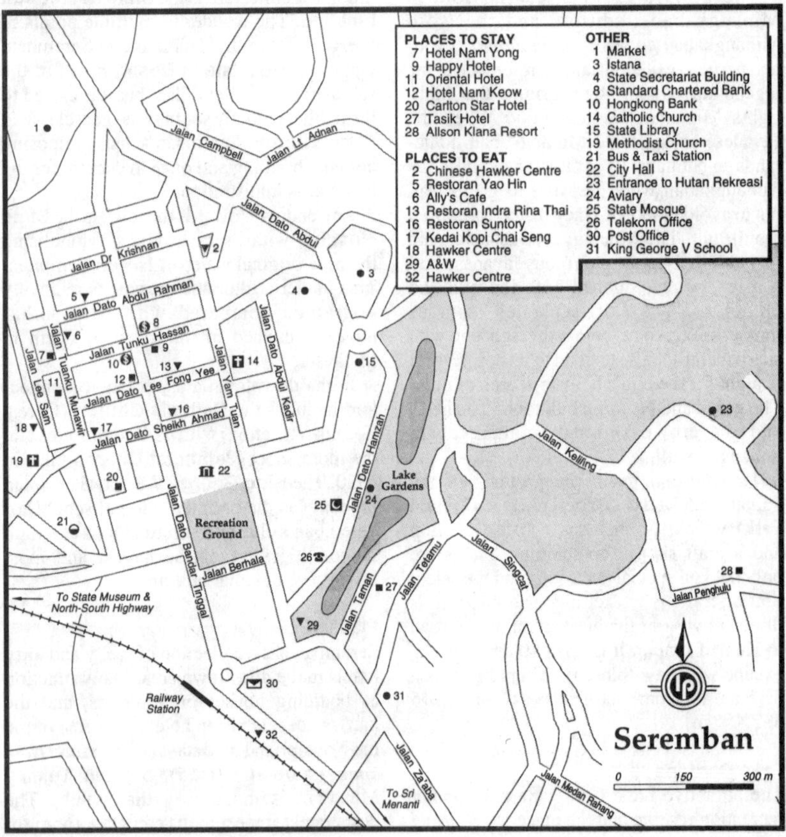

offers well-appointed rooms for RM100, but it is less conveniently located one km west of the bus station on the road to the museum.

The top hotel by far is the *Allson Klana Resort* (☎ 06-762 9600), Jalan Penghulu Cantik, on a hill to the east of the Lake Gardens. Set in large grounds, it has all the facilities of an international-class hotel. Rooms start at RM280/300 before discount.

Places to Eat

Seremban has a good selection of hawker centres for cheap eats. Food stalls, serving mostly Malay dishes and some spicy Minangkabau fare, can be found at the railway station and at the modern, upstairs hawker centre on Jalan Lee Sam. Jalan Lee Sam also hosts the lively Saturday night market, which has plenty of food stalls. The best place for Chinese favourites in an al fresco setting is on the corner of Jalan Yam Tuan and Jalan Dr Krishnan, where hawkers set up in the car park on fine evenings.

Of Seremban's many coffee shops, *Ally's Cafe* on Jalan Tuanku Munawir has roti and curries, while the popular *Kedai Kopi Chai Seng* on Jalan Dato Sheikh Ahmad specialises not in Chinese dishes but satay. Jalan Dato Abdul Rahman has the pick of the Chinese coffee shops, including *Restoran Yao Hin* with dumplings and dim sum for breakfast and claypot dishes such as fish head curry for dinner.

For good value, air-con dining, *Restoran Suntory* on Jalan Dato Lee Fong Yee has an extensive Chinese menu at moderate prices, and western dishes such as lamb chops and fish & chips for RM6.50. *A&W*, right at the Lake Gardens, is a favourite with Seremban's middle classes for western food.

Thai food in Malaysia is usually tom yam and not much else, but *Restoran Indra Rina Thai*, 4 Jalan Dato Lee Fong Yee, is an excellent Thai restaurant with a huge range of authentic Thai dishes. Small mains cost around RM6 – the red curry and squid salad are recommended.

Getting There & Away

Seremban is 62 km south of KL, less than an hour on the Lebuh Raya. The city is a major travel hub and the new bus station on Jalan Sungei Ujong has frequent departures to KL, Melaka, Port Dickson, Johor Bahru and other destinations throughout the peninsula. The bus station has an information booth and left-luggage facilities, and long-distance taxis operate from upstairs.

Seremban is on the main north-south rail line. KTM Komuter trains, part of KL's city rail network, also run to/from KL's central railway station every hour. The trip to KL takes just over one hour and costs RM5.70.

SEREMBAN TO KUALA PILAH

Heading east from Seremban the road meanders through the hills to the town of Kuala Pilah, passing points of interest on the way. This is the heartland of Minangkabau culture, centred on the old royal town of Sri Menanti.

Along the main road to Kuala Pilah are a number of **Minangkabau houses**, though the traditional thatch of the buffalo horn roofs have been replaced by more utilitarian corrugated iron. The village of Terachi, 27 km

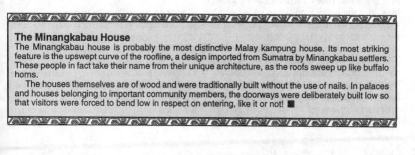

The Minangkabau House

The Minangkabau house is probably the most distinctive Malay kampung house. Its most striking feature is the upswept curve of the roofline, a design imported from Sumatra by Minangkabau settlers. These people in fact take their name from their unique architecture, as the roofs sweep up like buffalo horns.

The houses themselves are of wood and were traditionally built without the use of nails. In palaces and houses belonging to important community members, the doorways were deliberately built low so that visitors were forced to bend low in respect on entering, like it or not! ■

from Seremban at the turn-off to Sri Menanti, has some particularly fine traditional houses as does Sri Menanti itself. Pantai and Nilai, a short distance north-east of Seremban, also have Minangkabau houses.

Hutan Lipur Ulu Bendol
This dense forest park makes a good day trip from Seremban, only 20 km away, and the primary dipterocarp rainforest has some excellent short walks. The well-maintained main trail from the park headquarters follows the Batang Terachi river and passes small cascading waterfalls before rising more sharply to the summit of Gunung Angsi (825 metres) with fine views across Seremban and out to the Straits of Melaka. The steeper sections can be taxing but this is a relatively easy 4.5 km walk taking around four hours return. Shorter self-guided trails with plaques identifying the trees branch out around the park headquarters. The park is very popular on weekends.

Though usually done as a day trip, the park also has accommodation in attractive but unfurnished cabins and chalets costing RM10 and RM30 per night. Bookings must be made in advance at the District Forest Office (Pejabat Hutan Daerah) (☎ 06-481 1036) in Kuala Pilah. The park headquarters is less than one km behind the restaurant and food stalls on the main road, where Seremban-Kuala Pilah buses will drop you off.

Sri Menanti
Sri Menanti, just off the Seremban to Kuala Pilah road, is the old royal capital first settled over 400 years ago by the Minangkabau from Sumatra. This sleepy hamlet is nestled in a highland valley surrounding by green hills, and the manicured lawns are as much a product of the straggling sheep that wander the town as the royal gardeners.

Things to See The centre of town is just a row of ramshackle shops and a few houses, but just past the Sri Menanti's own small Lake Gardens is the **Istana Besar**, the impressive palace of the sultan of Negeri Sembilan. Built in the 1930s, it has a new addition featuring the obligatory Minangkabau roof done in blue tiles, but it is not open to the public.

The main interest lies just beyond the Istana Besar at the **Istana Lama** (Old Palace), now a museum. Built in 1908 as a replacement for an older palace that burnt down, the three-storey palace is raised off the ground on pillars, many of them carved, and is topped by a tower that once served as the royal treasury. Though not particularly Minangkabau, it is a good example of court architecture typical of early 20th century palaces. It now houses the Muzium Diraja, dedicated to Negeri Sembilan's royalty, with costumes, weapons and preserved royal bedrooms. Memorabilia of the sultans feature prominently, especially that of Tuanku Abdul Rahman, the first yang di-pertuan agong, or king of Malaysia, at the time of independence in 1957. Both Abdul Rahman and his son, Tuanku Ja'afar, who was appointed yang di-pertuan agong in 1994, were noted sports fanatics and Sri Menanti even has a royal golf course just beyond the museum.

The museum is open 10 am to 6 pm, except Monday (closed), Thursday (open 8.15 am to 1 pm) and Friday (closed 12.15 to 2.45 pm). Over the road from the museum is one of the finest Minangkabau houses you'll see in Negeri Sembilan, though this former palace is falling into disrepair.

Also of note in Sri Menanti is the **Makam Diraja**, the royal graves in the compound next to the mosque. The graveyard has a Victorian/Moorish pavilion and the grave of Tuanku Abdul Rahman takes prominent place directly inside the gates.

Places to Stay Though you can easily see all of the sights in an hour or two, Sri Menanti is a very quiet, pleasant spot for an overnight stay. The new *Sri Menanti Resort* (☎ 06-497 6200), right next to the Istana Lama, has a swimming pool, restaurant and well-appointed singles/doubles for RM75/95 or attractive chalets with sitting rooms for RM110/130. It's often empty, so discounts may be available.

Getting There & Away From Seremban, first take a bus to Kuala Pilah from where three buses a day go to Sri Menanti. Rather than wait for a bus, you can take a whole taxi from Kuala Pilah for only RM4.

Kuala Pilah

Kuala Pilah, 40 km east of Seremban, is the main town of this strongly Minangkabau region. It is mostly a place for transport connections, though it's a pleasant valley town and the interesting old Sim Tong Chinese temple, on the main street of town towards Bahau, is worth a look. Opposite is a Chinese-style arch dedicated to Martin Lister, the first British Resident of Negeri Sembilan.

Kuala Pilah has cheap Chinese hotels and, on a hill overlooking the town, a pleasant resthouse, *Rumah Persinggahan* (☎ 06-481 4146) on Jalan Bukit. Kuala Pilah is also a good place to try Minangkabau food such as *rendang*, a fiery meat curry.

Getting There & Away From Seremban, blue-and-yellow KBS buses leave from the eastern side of the bus station roughly every hour throughout the day and evening. From Kuala Pilah it is also possible to get connections north to Temerloh and east all the way to Kuantan, but usually you will first have to take another local bus to Bahau, on the highway 20 km to the east.

PORT DICKSON

Port Dickson is just a small port town of no interest, but it is the gateway to the stretch of beach extending 16 km south to Cape Rachado. This beach is very popular with KL residents on weekends, and a string of mostly upmarket hotels are spread out all the way to Cape Rachado. Despite its popularity, the beaches are not great. The sands vary from red to grey-white. The water, like elsewhere along the Straits of Melaka, is murky and very shallow for swimming. Occasional oil spills from passing tankers don't help. If you are desperate for a quick escape to the beach from KL, or just want to live it up in a resort, Port Dickson is OK for a couple of days, but Malaysia has better beaches.

Originally built by the Portuguese in the 16th century, the **Cape Rachado** lighthouse offers fine views. On a clear day you can see Sumatra, 38 km away across the Straits of Melaka. The turn-off to the lighthouse is near Km 13. Head down the road for two km and then through the forest reserve for another km to the lighthouse.

Port Dickson's tourist office is on the beach, four km from town.

Places to Stay

The attraction is the beach, so don't bother with the hotels in Port Dickson town. The best beaches start from around the Km 8 peg. Most hotels are upmarket, and new resorts and condominiums are sprouting everywhere. On weekends many hotels are fully booked, especially the cheaper places (apart from the youth hostel), but discounts often apply during the week.

The *Port Dickson Youth Hostel* (☎ 06-647 2188) is back from the road in spacious grounds at Km 6.5, but it attracts few visitors. It costs just RM11 for the first night for clean and modern dorms, RM8 for subsequent nights. Older dorms are RM9 for the first night, then RM6. Four-bed chalets are also available for RM50. Non-YHA (Hostelling International) members pay an extra one-off fee of RM5. There are shops and warungs in front of the hostel on the main road.

Just before the Youth Hostel is the *Seri Malaysia Hotel* (☎ 06-647 6070), part of a new chain that offers quality rooms for only RM100 single or double. It is a very popular Malay hotel.

At Km 7, the *Bayu Beach Resort* (☎ 06-647 3703) is a big hotel with a pool, bar and restaurants. Rooms for RM140 on weekdays are good value, but rates rise to RM200 on weekends. Apartments range from RM154 to RM400 (RM200 to RM450 on weekends).

At Km 8 is another collection of big hotels, the best being the Minangkabau-styled *Regency* (☎ 06-647 4090) with a pool, tennis and squash courts. Rooms cost RM210 and RM250, before discount.

Next along is the *Si-Rusa Inn* (☎ 06-662 5233) at Km 12. This older mid-range resort has rooms for RM80, or RM92 with hot water in the bathrooms, while chalets with fridge and TV cost RM120 and RM140. It is back from the road and right on the beach.

A selection of budget places can be found at Km 13. The *Hotel Selat* (☎ 06-662 5109) is a standard mid-range place near the main road with air-con rooms from RM55. Past the Hotel Selat is the red sand beach, but it is well away from the main road and quiet, with water deep enough for swimming and a boat shed with canoes for hire. Run by a friendly Chinese couple, the *Kong Ming Hotel* (☎ 06-662 5683) is right by the beach and good value at RM25 for rooms with or without bath (the rooms without bath face the sea). Nearby, the very run-down *Lido Hotel* (☎ 06-662 5273) has doubles from RM35.

Finally, on the turn-off road to Cape Rachado one km before the lighthouse, the new *Ilham Resort* (☎ 06-662 6800) has three-bedroom apartments for RM350 and four-bedroom apartments for RM450. It is one of the best resorts on the coast, but the shallow beach is no better than elsewhere.

Getting There & Away

Port Dickson is 94 km south of KL, 34 km south of Seremban and 90 km north of Melaka. The bus and taxi stations are next to each other in the centre of the town. By bus it's RM3.80 from Melaka, and RM5 from KL's Puduraya bus and taxi station. A taxi costs RM11.50 to KL or RM10.20 to Melaka.

From Port Dickson town there are buses which will drop you off wherever you like along the beach.

PEDAS HOT SPRINGS

Heading south of Seremban along the old highway is the Pedas Hot Springs, one km before the small town of Pedas. You can soak in the somewhat run-down private baths.

PENGKALAN KEMPAS

About 50 km north of Melaka is the small town of Pengkalan Kempas. Just a short distance on the Lubok China or Melaka side of town, a 'Kompleks Sejarah Pengkalan Kempas' sign indicates the grave of Sheikh Ahmad Majnun, about 100 metres off the road. This local hero died in 1467 and beside his grave, which is sheltered by a structure in the final stages of complete collapse, are three two-metre-high stones standing upright in the ground.

These mysterious stones, known as the sword, the spoon and the rudder, are thought to be older than the grave itself. Immediately in front of the grave is another stone with a hole through it. The circular opening is said to tighten up on the arm of any liar foolish enough to thrust it through.

Melaka

The small state of Melaka (Malacca), centred on the historically important port of Melaka, is one of the most interesting on the peninsula. In the 15th century Melaka rose to become the greatest trading port in South-East Asia and attracted waves of conquering Europeans. Though Melaka's importance has long since declined, it retains reminders of its rich history and its fascinating mixture of Chinese and European culture.

Full Name: Melaka Bandaraya Bersejarah
Area: 1650 sq km
Capital: Melaka
Population: 505,000

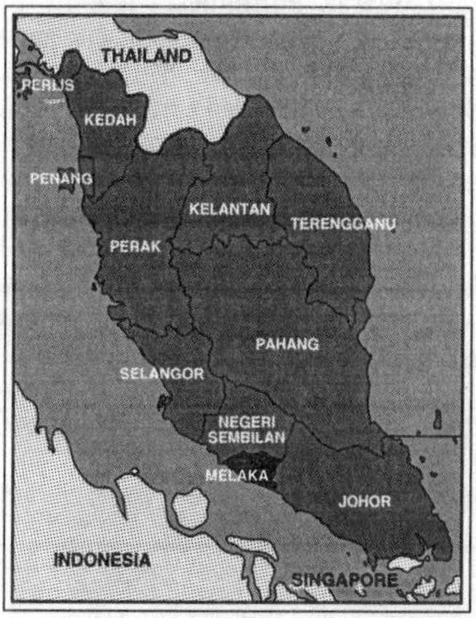

History

Under the Melaka sultanates the city was a wealthy centre of trade with China, India, Siam and Indonesia, due to its strategic position on the Straits of Melaka. The Melaka sultanates were the beginning of what is today Malaysia, and some Malaysians say this city is where you find the soul of Malaysia.

Melaka was just another fishing village until it attracted the attentions of Parameswara, a Hindu prince from Sumatra. Parameswara had thrown off allegiance to the Majapahit empire and fled to Temasek (modern-day Singapore), where his piracy and other exploits brought Siamese attack in 1398, forcing him to flee again to Melaka, where he set up his headquarters.

Melaka under Parameswara soon became a favoured port for resupplying trading ships plying the strategic Straits of Melaka. Halfway between China and India, and with easy access to the spice islands of Indonesia, Melaka attracted merchants from all over the east.

In 1405 Admiral Cheng Ho, the 'three-jewelled eunuch prince', arrived in Melaka bearing gifts from the Ming emperor and the promise of protection from archenemies, the Siamese. From these early contacts with China, Chinese settlers followed and came to be known as the Babas and Nyonyas, or Straits Chinese. They are the longest-settled Chinese people in Malaysia and infused many Malay customs with their Chinese heritage.

Despite internal squabbles and intrigues, by the time of Parameswara's death in 1414, Melaka was already a powerful trading state. As a cosmopolitan centre, it also came in contact with Islam, brought by traders from India. The third ruler of Melaka, Maharaja Mohammed Shah (1424-44), converted to Islam, and his son, Mudzaffar Shah, took the title of sultan and made Islam the state religion.

Under the banner of Islam, Melaka became the major entrepôt port in South-East Asia, attracting Muslim Indian merchants away from competing Sumatran ports. Melaka became a centre for Islam, disseminating the religion throughout the Indonesian archipelago. The Melaka sultans ruled over the greatest empire in Malaysia's history, and successfully repulsed Siamese attacks. The Malay language became the lingua franca of trade in the region, and

Melaka produced the first major piece of Malay literature, the *Sejarah Melayu* (or *Malay Annals)*, a history of the sultanate.

In 1509 the Portuguese arrived at Melaka seeking the wealth of the spice and China trades, but after an initially friendly reception, the Melakans attacked the Portuguese fleet and took a number of prisoners.

This action was the pretext for an outright assault by the Portuguese, and in 1511 Alfonso d'Albuquerque took the city and the sultan fled to Johor, where he re-established his kingdom. Under the Portuguese, the fortress of A'Famosa was constructed, and missionaries like the famous Francis Xavier strove to implant Christianity. Melaka continued to be an important trading post, but while Portuguese canons could easily conquer Melaka, they could not force the Muslim merchants from Arabia and India to trade there. Other trading ports in the area, such as Islamic Demak on Java, grew to overshadow Melaka.

The Portuguese left behind their language and Catholicism, both still practised among Melaka's Portuguese Eurasians, but the period of Portuguese strength in the east was short-lived. Melaka suffered harrying attacks from the rulers of neighbouring Johor and Negeri Sembilan, as well as from the Islamic power of Acheh in Sumatra. As Dutch influence in Indonesia grew, Batavia (modern-day Jakarta) developed as the principal European port of the region and Melaka declined further. Finally, the Dutch attacked the city and in 1641 it passed into their hands after a siege lasting eight months.

The Dutch built fine public buildings and churches, which today are the most solid reminders of the European presence in the city. Melaka became the centre for peninsular trade, but it was only a minor part of a greater empire, and the Dutch directed their energies into their possessions in Indonesia. Like their Portuguese predecessors, the Dutch ruled Melaka for only about 150 years.

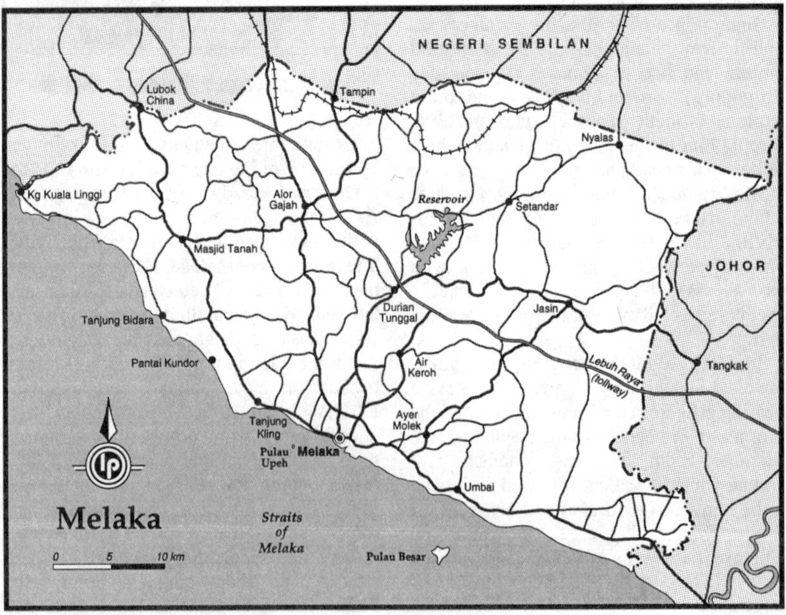

When the French occupied Holland in 1795, the British, allies of the Dutch, temporarily took over administration of the Dutch colonies. The British administrators, essentially traders, were opposed to the Dutch policy of trade monopoly and clearly saw that the Dutch and themselves would be bitter rivals in Malaysia when and if Melaka was returned. Accordingly in 1807 they started to demolish the fortress and forcibly move the population to Penang, to ensure that if Melaka was restored to the Dutch it would be no rival to the British Malayan centres.

Fortunately Stamford Raffles, the far-sighted founder of Singapore, stepped in before these destructive policies could go too far, and in 1824 Melaka was permanently ceded to the British in exchange for the Sumatran port of Bencoolen (Bengkulu today).

Melaka, together with Penang and Singapore, formed the Straits Settlements, the three British territories that were the centres for later expansion into the peninsula. However, under British rule Melaka was always the lesser light of the Straits Settlements, and Melaka was soon superseded by the rapidly growing commercial importance of Singapore. Apart from a brief revival of its fortunes in the early 20th century when rubber was an important crop, Melaka once again became a quiet backwater.

MELAKA

Malaysia's most historically interesting city, Melaka was the greatest trading state in South-East Asia under the Melaka sultanates. The complete series of European incursions in Malaysia – Portuguese, Dutch and British – were played out here, and Melaka still bears testament to their presence. In the centre of town, much of the old Dutch city remains, and Medan Portugis is still home to Portuguese Eurasians. Of all Melaka's mixed traditions, perhaps the most interesting are the Babas and Nyonyas, the offspring of the original Chinese settlers who intermarried and adopted many Malay customs.

Melaka is a place of intriguing Chinese streets and antique shops, old Chinese temples and cemeteries and nostalgic reminders of the now-departed European colonial powers. The traditional Malay *kampung* house in the Melaka area, with its distinctive colourful tiled entrance steps, can be seen along the river in east Melaka or in the Tanjung Kling district north of the city.

For long a sleepy backwater town living on memories of past glories, Melaka is starting to experience the economic boom sweeping the rest of the country. Massive land reclamation has seen the historic waterfront retreat inland, and a huge shopping mall and new apartment blocks now enjoy Melaka's sea views. Despite the modernisation, Chinatown and the old city area are still delightfully old-fashioned, and Melaka remains one of Malaysia's premier tourist destinations.

Orientation

Melaka is a small town – easy to find your way around and compact enough to explore on foot, bicycle or trishaw. Jalan Munshi Abdullah is the main road through the city.

The Melaka House

While following the standard kampung house pattern of a wooden structure on short stilts, the Melaka kampung house is easily identifiable by its tiled front stairway. This leads up to the front veranda and is the formal entrance to the house. This entrance is the one used by guests, and the front veranda itself is the formal entertainment area.

The middle *(tengah)* section is the living area, and the steps at the side of the house here are those used by the family and friends. It would be inappropriate for guests to enter here.

At the rear of the house is the kitchen and eating area *(dapur)*. The steps here are used only by the women of the house. ■

The interesting and older parts of Melaka are mainly near the river and the ever-receding waterfront, particularly around the old Dutch-built Stadthuys (town hall), where you'll also find the tourist office, Christ Church, St Paul's Church, Porta de Santiago and the Cultural Museum. Across the river, Chinatown also has many points of interest. Further afield within the city are more historic attractions such as Bukit China, St John's Fort and Medan Portugis. Well outside the town, Melaka state has a few beaches, offshore islands and the theme park area of Air Keroh out near the North-South Highway (Lebuh Raya). (See Around Melaka later in this chapter.)

Information

The local tourist office (☎ 06-283 6538) is right in the heart of the city, almost opposite Christ Church. Staffed by very helpful people, it is open every day from 8.45 am to 5 pm, closed Friday lunchtime from 12.15 to 2.45 pm. On the opposite corner, with a good map of Melaka and its attractions out front, is the office of the Malacca Tourist Police (☎ 06-282 2222), which can answer basic queries.

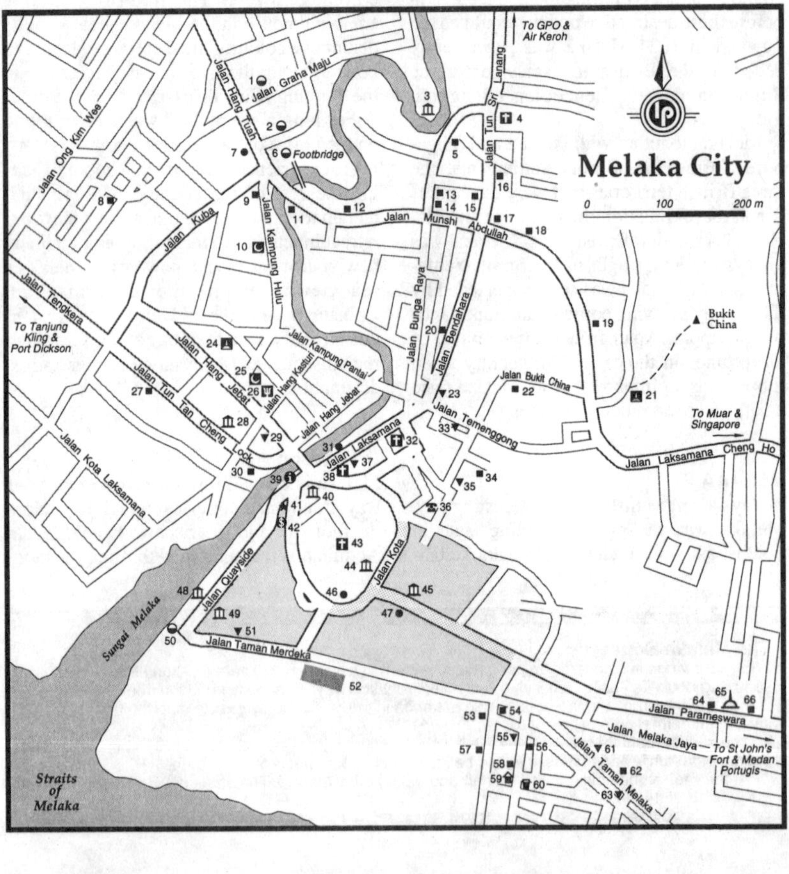

The main post office is three km north of central Melaka on Jalan Bukit Baru at the corner of Jalan Panglima Awang. To get there, take bus No 19 from the bus terminal. There is also a post office shop right next to the Malaysian Youth Museum on Jalan Laksamana in the centre of town.

For visa extensions, the immigration office (☎ 06-282 4955) is at Wisma Persekutuan on Jalan Hang Tuah. There is another post at the ferry dock to handle departure and entry to/from Dumai in Indonesia.

Melaka has plenty of banks for changing money. The Hongkong Bank near the Stadthuys is convenient but charges RM5 per transaction to change cash and travellers' cheques.

Town Square & St Paul's Hill

The main area of interest in Melaka is the old city on the eastern side of the river. In front of the tourist office is Town Square, also known as Dutch Square, where the Stadthuys and Christ Church are solid reminders of the Dutch presence.

Rising above Town Square is St Paul's Hill (Bukit St Paul), site of the original Portuguese fort of A'Famosa. The ruins of St Paul's Church and the Porta de Santiago are the only remains of the Portuguese presence. Nearby are the Cultural Museum and Proclamation of Independence Hall, while back on the river is the Maritime Museum.

All the historical points of interest are included as a signposted 'Heritage Trail', an excellent self-guided walk that also takes in parts of Chinatown.

Stadthuys The most imposing relic of the Dutch period in Melaka is the massive red town hall, built between 1641 and 1660 and believed to be the oldest Dutch building in the east. It displays all the typical features of Dutch colonial architecture, including substantial solid doors and louvred windows. The other buildings around the Town Square, including the old clock tower, follow the same red theme.

Today the Stadthuys houses the excellent

PLACES TO STAY

5 Majestic Hotel
8 Malacca Town Holiday Lodge 2
9 Visma Hotel
11 Plaza Inn
12 May Chiang Hotel
13 Hong Kong Hotel
14 Ng Fook Hotel
15 Ramada Renaissance Hotel
16 City Bayview Hotel
17 Hotel Accordian
18 Emperor Hotel
19 Palace Hotel
20 Central Hotel
22 Eastern Heritage Guest House
27 The Baba House
30 Heeren House
34 Apple Guest House
53 Robin's Nest
54 Amy Home Stay
56 Sunny's Inn
57 Travellers' Lodge
58 SD Rest House
59 Melaka Youth Hostel
62 Malacca Town Holiday Lodge
64 Kancil Guest House
66 My Place Guest House

PLACES TO EAT

23 Sri Lakshmi Vilas
29 Jonkers Melaka Restoran
33 Restoran Veni
35 UE Tea House
37 Restaurant Kim Swee Huat
51 Glutton's Corner
55 New Golden Dragon
61 Nyonya Makka
63 Ole Sayang

OTHER

1 Local Bus Station
2 Taxi Station
3 Villa Formosa
4 Church of St Peter
6 Express Bus Terminal
7 Immigration
10 Kampung Hulu Mosque
21 Sam Po Kong Temple & Hang Li Poh Well
24 Cheng Hoon Teng Temple
25 Kampung Kling Mosque
26 Sri Pogyatha Vinoyagar Moorthi Temple
28 Baba-Nonya Heritage Museum
31 Karyaneka Handicrafts Emporium
32 Church of St Francis
36 Telekom
38 Christ Church
39 Tourist Office
40 Stadthuys
41 Tourist Police
42 Hongkong Bank
43 St Paul's Church
44 Cultural Museum
45 Proclamation of Independence Hall
46 Porta de Santiago
47 Sound & Light Show
48 Maritime Museum
49 Royal Malaysian Navy Museum
50 Ferries to Dumai
52 Mahkota Parade
60 Orchid Pub
65 Buddhist Temple

historical, ethnographic and literature museums, where a couple of fruitful hours can be spent. The **History Museum** gives a detailed explanation of Melaka's history through old maps, lithographs, oil paintings and photographs. Unlike most museums in Malaysia that give little or no explanation, here it would take a couple of hours to read your way through the labels alone. The **Ethnographic Museum** has displays on many aspects of local culture and traditions, including good displays of the marriage ceremonies of the various ethnic communities found in Melaka. The less-interesting **Literature Museum** is housed in a separate building behind. The Stadthuys and its museums are open from 9 am to 6 pm daily, except Friday lunchtime from 12.15 to 2.45 pm; entry is RM2.

Christ Church Nearby, facing one end of the main square, is the bright red Christ Church. The pink bricks were brought out from Zeeland in Holland and faced with local red laterite when the church was constructed in 1753. Under the British this Dutch Reform church was converted for Anglican use, and the weathercock and bell tower were added, but it still has its old Dutch tombstones laid in the floor. Its massive 15-metre-long ceiling beams were each cut from a single tree.

Malaysian Youth Museum Next to Christ Church on Jalan Laksamana, the Malaysian Youth Museum (Muzium Belia Malaysia) was formerly the general post office and is a good example of British colonial architecture. The museum itself displays the workings of the Malaysian Youth Council and other bodies – even Malaysians find this one boring.

St Paul's Church From the Stadthuys, steps lead up to the top of St Paul's Hill, topped by the ruins of St Paul's Church. Originally built by the Portuguese in 1521 as the small 'Our Lady of the Hill' chapel, it was regularly visited by Francis Xavier. Following his death in China, the saint's body was brought here and buried for nine months before being transferred to Goa in India, where it remains today. A marble statue of Francis Xavier commemorates his interment here over 400 years ago.

In 1556 the church was enlarged to two storeys and a tower was added to the front in 1590. The church was renamed following the Dutch takeover, but when the Dutch completed their own Christ Church at the base of the hill it fell into disuse. Under the British it lost its tower, although a lighthouse was built in front of it, and it eventually ended up as a storehouse for gunpowder. The church has been in ruins now for more than 150 years, but the setting is beautiful, the walls are imposing and fine old Dutch tombstones stand around the interior.

Porta de Santiago There are steps from St Paul's Church down the hill to the Porta de Santiago, once the main gate, and all that remains, of the Portuguese fortress of A'Famosa, originally constructed by Alfonso d'Albuquerque in 1512. Stamford Raffles may have stepped in before the complete destruction of the old fortress, but it was a near thing. Curiously, this sole surviving relic of the old fort bears the Dutch East India Company's coat of arms: this was part of the fort which the Dutch reconstructed in 1607, following their takeover.

Nearby is a small grandstand, used as the venue for the Sound & Light Show each evening (see Entertainment).

Cultural Museum Just along from the Porta de Santiago at the base of St Paul's Hill is a wooden replica of a Melaka sultan's palace which contains the Cultural Museum (Muzium Budaya). This new building is based on the original 15th century palace, supposedly from descriptions provided in the *Malay Annals*. Although the exhibits concentrate on traditional Melakan culture, there are also exhibits from other parts of Malaysia. Included are apparel, games, weaponry, musical instruments, stone inscriptions and photographic exhibits, as well as a diorama of the sultan's court, with

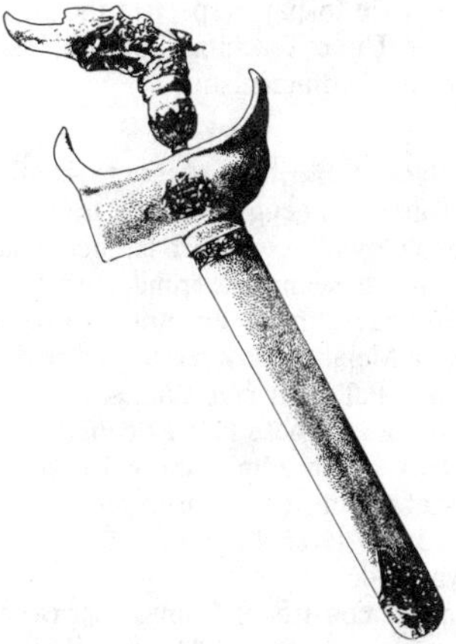

The *kris* is a traditional Malay weapon.

costumed mannequins representing the various positions held within the hierarchy. Admission to this interesting building costs RM1.50, and it is open from 9 am to 6 pm.

Proclamation of Independence Hall
Housed in a British villa dating from 1912, this museum (Memorial Pergistiharan Kemerdekaan) is dedicated to events leading up to independence in 1957. Ironically, it was once the Melaka Club, a bastion of colonialism. The grand building features the architectural whimsies of the day and is topped by Mogul-inspired domes. Inside, the historical displays are a bit dry but are still good for an insight into the political history of Malaysia, even if the mood tends to be ultra-nationalistic and the role of the Communists is ignored. Many will find the 1957 Chevy outside, used on the hustings by Tunku Abdul Rahman, of equal interest.

The museum is open from 9 am to 6 pm, but closed on Friday from noon to 3 pm and all day Monday. Entry is free.

Maritime Museum This huge re-creation of a Portuguese ship, the *Flora de la Mar*, is next to the river near the tourist office. It houses yet more detailed descriptions of Melaka's history, as well as ship models, dioramas and an interesting map room featuring charts dating back to Portuguese times.

The museum is open from 9 am to 9 pm (closed Friday from 12.15 to 2.45 pm) and entry is RM2. The price includes entry to the **Royal Malaysian Navy Museum** across the street, which has navy memorabilia and salvaged remnants from the *Diana*, sunk off Melaka in 1817 while voyaging from Guangzhou (Canton) to Madras. A major salvage operation in 1993 recovered the ship and its cargo of tea, sugar and over 18 tons of chinaware. New technology has made salvage expeditions in the Straits of Melaka a viable business, and the waters potentially hold a trove of ancient treasures. There is a concern that Melaka's land reclamation is burying forever historical artefacts, and that any new reclamation should only proceed after detailed archaeological studies of the shoreline.

Chinatown
Melaka's Chinatown, west of the river, is a fascinating area to wander around. With its twisting streets, Peranakan (Straits Chinese) shophouses, ancient temples and mosques, its history of settlement and trade is equally as fascinating as the reminders of colonial rule, and still current.

Although Melaka has long lost its importance as a port, ancient-looking Sumatran schooners still sail up the river and moor at the banks. Today, however, their cargo is not the varied treasures of the east, but charcoal for the cooking fires of the city or lumber from Indonesia. There's a good view of the river and boats from the bridge beside the tourist office, and you can also take a river boat tour (see Organised Tours).

Crossing over the bridge you enter **Jalan Hang Jebat**, formerly known as Jonkers St, or Junk St. Melaka is famed for its antique shops and you may still find some of the treasures of the east in the antique shops scattered along this street. You can easily spend an hour or more browsing, but don't expect to find any bargains. There's an assortment of interesting shops and the odd Chinese or Hindu temple or mosque squeezed into this intriguing old street. The most notable temple is the Cheng Hoon Teng Temple (see below).

Jalan Tun Tan Cheng Lock, running parallel to Jalan Hang Jebat, is also worth a stroll. This narrow street, now a one-way thoroughfare with disturbingly fast moving traffic, was the preferred address for wealthy Baba traders who were most active during the short-lived rubber boom of the early 20th century. These typical Peranakan houses with their intricate tiles and plasterwork exhibit Chinese, Dutch and British influences. The Baba-Nyonya Heritage Museum (see below) is the main highlight, and stop to look at the fine Chee Mansion set back from the street at No 117.

Other points of interest in Chinatown are the **Sri Pogyatha Vinoyagar Moorthi Temple**, dating from 1781 and dedicated to the Hindu deity Vinayagar, and the **Kampung Kling Mosque**. This ancient mosque has a multi-tiered *meru* roof, which owes its inspiration to Hindu temples, and a watch-tower minaret typical of early mosques in Sumatra and Java. In the same style further north, the **Kampung Hulu Mosque** dates from 1728 and is the oldest in Malaysia.

Cheng Hoon Teng Temple This fascinating temple in the old part of the city is the oldest Chinese temple in Malaysia and has an inscription commemorating Admiral Cheng Ho's epochal visit to Melaka. The brightly coloured roof bears the usual assortment of mythical Chinese creatures. Entered through massive hardwood doors, the temple is equally colourful and ornate inside. The temple's ceremonial mast rises above the old houses in this part of Melaka.

The name literally means 'Temple of the Evergreen Clouds'. The temple was founded in 1646 by Kapitan China Lee Wei King, a native of Amoy in China. All materials used in building the original temple were imported from China, as were the artisans who designed and built it in the southern Chinese style to pay respect to the San Y Chiao, or Three Teachings, of Buddhism, Taoism and Confucianism.

Baba-Nyonya Heritage Museum At 48-50 Jalan Tun Tan Cheng Lock is a traditional Peranakan townhouse which has been made into a small museum. The architecture of this type of house, many examples of which survive in Melaka today, has been described as 'Chinese Palladian' and 'Chinese Baroque'. The interiors of these houses contain open courtyards which admit sun and rain. The interior of the museum is arranged so that it looks like a typical 19th century Baba-Nyonya residence.

Furniture consists of Chinese hardwoods fashioned in a mixture of Chinese, Victorian and Dutch designs with mother-of-pearl inlay. There are also displays of 'Nyonya ware', multicoloured ceramic designs from Jiangxi and Guangdong provinces in China, made specifically for Straits Chinese. Nyonya ceramics and tilework are usually a blend of pinks, yellows, dark blues and greens.

The museum (☎ 06-283 1273) is open from 10 am to 12.30 pm and 2 to 4.30 pm. Admission is RM7, which includes a good 45 minute tour of the house conducted by the Baba family who own the house – well worth it if you have an interest in Peranakan culture.

Bukit China

In the middle of the 15th century the sultan of Melaka's ambassador to China returned with the Ming emperor's daughter to wed the sultan and thus seal relations between the two countries. She brought with her a vast retinue, including 500 handmaidens, and Bukit China (China Hill) was established as their residence. It has been a Chinese area ever since and, together with two adjoining hills, forms a Chinese graveyard covering over 25 hectares. With over 12,000 graves, this is said to be the largest in the world outside China itself. Some of the ornate graves date back to the Ming dynasty, but unhappily most of them are now in a sorry state.

Chinese graveyards are often built on hillsides because the bulk of the hill shields the graves from evil winds, while at the same time the spirits get a good view of what their descendants are up to down below. In our more space-conscious modern world, Chinese graves are gradually losing their spacious and expansive traditional design.

Sam Po Kong Temple & Hang Li Poh Well

Apart from his real-life role as an admiral and ambassador, Cheng Ho is also religiously venerated, and this temple is dedicated to him. Built in 1795, it's at the foot of Bukit China.

Next to the temple is the Hang Li Poh Well, built in the 15th century by Sultan Mansor Shah for his Chinese wife, Princess Hang Li Poh. It was an important source of water for Melaka and a prime target for opposition forces wanting to take the city. Johor forces poisoned it in 1551, killing 200 Portuguese. The Dutch in 1606 and the Achehnese in 1628 subsequently employed the same tactic. The Dutch eventually built the fortifications that surround the well, but it has long since fallen into ruin. Taking a drink from the well was said to ensure a visitor's return to the city. Today the water is visibly impure, and tossing a coin into the well is the recommended way of ensuring a return trip.

Church of St Peter

This unexceptional church on Jalan Bendahara was built in 1710 by descendants of the early Portuguese settlers. It has some interesting stained-glass windows and old tombstones. It does not get much use for most of the year, but it comes alive on Good Friday when Melakans flock here. Many of them make the occasion an excuse for an annual trip home from other parts of the country. The church is still associated with the Portuguese church in Macau.

Villa Sentosa

While not an official museum as such, this 1920s Malay kampung house, just across the river from the Majestic Hotel in Kampung Morten, is open to the public. The family still lives here and one of the family members will show you around. Though not exactly full of collectibles and history, it provides a good opportunity to poke around a kampung house and meet the family. A donation is expected at the end. Villa Sentosa is open to visitors daily from 9 am to 1 pm and 2 to 5 pm, except Friday, when it is open from 2.45 to 5 pm.

After you've finished you can wander around Kampung Morten, where there are a number of more traditional kampung houses. The one right next to Villa Sentosa is very typical.

Medan Portugis

Three km east of the city centre on the coast is the area known as Medan Portugis, or Portuguese Square. In this small kampung there are about 500 descendants of marriages which took place between the colonial Portuguese and Malays 400 years ago. The kampung is centred on the square, styled after a typical Portuguese *mercado*, but it was only built in the late 1980s, after Prime Minister Mahathir visited and promised to build a cultural focus for the settlement. The kampung itself is unexceptional, and there's little of interest for the visitor, except for the restaurants and cultural shows on Saturday nights, when Portuguese-Malay and Malay cultural ensembles perform for RM2.

Fort St John

Although the British demolished most of Porta de Santiago, they left the small Dutch fort of St John untouched. The fort was originally a Portuguese chapel dedicated to St John the Baptist until it was rebuilt by the Dutch in the 18th century. It stands on a hilltop to the east of town just before the turn-off to Medan Portugis – heading east along Jalan Parameswara, turn left into Jalan Bukit Senjuang. There are fine views from the top of the hill, but only a few walls and cannon emplacements of the fort remain.

Masjid Tengkera
This 150 year old mosque, two km along the road towards Port Dickson, is of typical Sumatran design, featuring a square, multi-tiered roof. In its graveyard is the tomb of Sultan Hussein of Johor, who in 1819 signed over the island of Singapore to Stamford Raffles. The sultan later retired to Melaka, where he died in 1853. Get there on bus No 18 from Jalan Kubu.

Organised Tours
Boat Trips Daily river-boat tours of Melaka leave from the quay behind the tourist office, where bookings can also be made. The trip takes 45 minutes, costs RM6 (children RM3) and passes through the downtown area and old godowns, riverside fish markets and on to Kampung Morten, where the Villa Sentosa is located. On the way back it takes in the wharves further down river. Tours are dependent on interest but usually depart at 10 and 11 am, noon, and 1 and 2 pm. There has to be at least six passengers before the tour will operate, or you can pay RM25 for the whole boat. It's an interesting, relaxing tour.

Boat trips can also be made to the offshore islands in the Straits of Melaka (see Around Melaka).

Festivals
Major festivals in Melaka include the Good Friday and Easter Sunday processions at St Peter's, and the feast in June in honour of the patron saint of the fishing community, also held at St Peters.

The nationwide bathing festival known as Mandi Safar is exuberantly celebrated in the Tanjung Kling district during the Muslim month of Safar.

Places to Stay – bottom end
Guesthouses Melaka has some excellent traveller-oriented guesthouses. Most of them are in the area known as Taman Melaka Raya, the reclaimed land just south of Jalan Taman Merdeka. They are virtually all on the 2nd and 3rd floors of some new and rather characterless blocks of buildings, but offer good facilities: common room with books, TVs and noticeboards, small kitchens and a variety of rooms. Though few rooms have windows some do have skylights. The interior walls are often only plywood.

The atmosphere in all of these places is generally good, and there's lots of competition so they provide good value for money. Prices are typically RM7 for a dorm, though some are still charging the 'old' RM6 price, and rooms start at RM12/15 for singles/doubles and range up to RM25 or more for larger rooms with air-con. The very cheapest rooms are in short supply and usually full. Breakfast is often included in the price. There's also quite a turnover in the guesthouse business and many tend to move around the area in search of cheaper rents.

To get to Taman Melaka Raya, take bus No 17 from the bus terminal for 40 sen and get off just past the huge Mahkota Parade shopping mall. Alternatively, a taxi or trishaw will cost RM5. The streets in this area are unnamed and all places just give a building number as the address – and I defy anyone to crack the code that was used to number the buildings!

In the street directly south of the roundabout, you'll find two of the most popular guesthouses. *Robin's Nest* (☎ 06-282 9142) at No 205B is very clean and well run with a good atmosphere. Rooms range from RM15 up to RM25 and dorm beds are RM6.

Further down the same street is the similarly priced *Travellers' Lodge* at 214B. This popular, long-running place has a large and welcoming common room and a rooftop garden.

One street east is the *Melaka Youth Hostel* (Asrama Belia) (☎ 06-282 7915). This spotless, well-run hostel has a large TV/sitting/dining area with a small kitchen, but like many places it's not really set up for cooking. The dormitory rooms are larger and quieter than most and lockers are provided. A dorm bed costs RM10 for the first night, RM7 for each additional night, or the air-con dorms cost RM14, then RM10 for subsequent nights.

In the same street, the *SD Rest House* (☎ 06-284 7080) at No 258B is a slightly more upmarket guesthouse, with good rooms and higher prices, but it's not as popular with travellers. Fan rooms start at RM15, and air-con rooms range from RM25 to RM35.

Close by, at 270A-B, is *Sunny's Inn* (☎ 06-283 7990), a family-run place with a variety of rooms. Dorm beds are RM7, a tiny single costs RM12, but most rooms range from RM15 up to RM30 with air-con.

On Jalan Taman Merdeka, the main thoroughfare in this area, *Amy Home Stay* at 156B is another place popular with travellers. The atmosphere is good and the place is well maintained. Dorm beds cost RM7, and rooms range from RM15.

Also on Jalan Taman Melaka is the *Malacca Town Holiday Lodge* (☎ 06-284 8830) at 148B. Although it doesn't have the decorated common room of many of the other hostels, this place is kept squeaky clean and is well run. There's no dorm, and singles/doubles start at RM12/15. Some of the rooms look onto a balcony with lots of greenery.

Away from Taman Melaka Raya there are a number of other guesthouses dotted around. One of the best is the popular *Eastern Heritage Guest House* (☎ 06-283 3026) at 8 Jalan Bukit China, well located just a short walk from the centre of town. It is housed in a superb old Melaka building dating from 1918, which has Peranakan tiling and impressive carved panelling in the main part of the house. It has loads of character but the rooms are just typical guesthouse rooms, costing from RM12/15 up to RM30 for more expensive rooms with balconies, or RM6 for dorm beds. Downstairs is a common room, and a kitchen which provides meals.

Nearby, the *Apple Guest House* (☎ 010-667 8744) at 24-1 Lorong Banda Kaba is in a much newer house with reasonably clean rooms and has a good atmosphere. Rooms start at RM15/18 and dorms are RM6.

Two more guesthouses can be found further out of town near the Chinese temple on Jalan Parameswara. The *Kancil Guest House* at No 177 is clean, quiet and secure with a small garden out the back, but tends to be too strictly run and has dropped off in popularity. Rooms start at RM15 though most are around RM25.

Also close to the Chinese temple is *My Place Guest House* at No 205 Jalan Parameswara. Run by friendly Indian hosts it is very popular despite being a little cramped. Standard plywood partitioned rooms start at RM12/15 and the dorm costs RM6.

Also north of the river is the *Malacca Town Holiday Lodge 2* (☎ 06-284 6905) at 52 Kampung Empat. It's run by the same people who have the lodge of the same name in Taman Melaka Raya. The location is somewhat inconvenient as it's a bit of a walk to the historical sites, but, like their other guesthouse, it is impeccably clean. They have a good variety of rooms (no dorms) from RM15 a double. Large rooms with attached bath cost RM25 to RM35, or quite palatial rooms with air-con and bath cost RM36 to RM45.

Hotels Melaka is also well endowed with hotels in all price ranges.

Cheapest of all is the very basic *Central Hotel* (☎ 06-282 2984) in a very good location at 31 Jalan Bendahara. Rooms with fan cost RM14/18 for singles/doubles, RM25 with bath. Though shabby, at these prices it's hard to beat.

The rambling old *Majestic Hotel* (☎ 06-282 2455) at 188 Jalan Bunga Raya is a classic old hotel reminiscent of the Cathay Hotel in Penang. High ceilings and swishing fans add to the cool lazy atmosphere, and there's a bar and car park. Though it could do with a good scrub, it is reasonable value at RM15 for a small fan room, ranging up to RM42 for a large room with air-con and bathroom.

Many cheap hotels are found along or just off Jalan Munshi Abdullah near the bus terminal. The *Ng Fook* (☎ 06-282 8055) at 154 Jalan Bunga Raya, just north of Jalan Munshi Abdullah, is basic but OK, with double rooms for RM23, RM28 with bath or up to RM39 with air-con and bath. A few doors away the slightly cheaper *Hong Kong Hotel* (☎ 06-282 3392) costs RM20 for a double, RM26 with attached bath and RM28 with air-con. At No 100 Jalan Munshi Abdullah the *New Cathay Hotel* (☎ 06-282 3744) has seen better days but is not bad value. The front rooms should be avoided, as the road is noisy as hell. Rooms cost RM20 with fan, RM26 with fan and bath and RM38 with bath and air-con.

In the old part of town, the *Chong Hoe Hotel* (☎ 06-282 6102) at 26 Jalan Tukang Emas is well located and good value at RM18 with fan and common bath, RM24 with fan and bath and RM30 to RM40 with air-con and attached bath.

Places to Stay – middle

Most of the mid-range hotels are in the northern part of town, and the central Chinatown area has a couple of good options.

At the bottom end of this range, the *May Chiang Hotel* (☎ 06-283 9535) at 52 Jalan Munshi Abdullah is just a few minutes' walk from the bus and taxi stations. Rooms in this very friendly and immaculately clean place cost RM40 with air-con and bath.

The more modern *Visma Hotel* (☎ 06-283 8799) at 111 Jalan Kampung Hulu is close to the bridge and Jalan Munshi Abdullah. Air-con, carpeted rooms with attached bath are very good value at RM38 and RM45. Nearby, the *Plaza Inn* (☎ 06-284 0881) at 2 Jalan Munshi Abdullah is a much larger, fancier hotel that has fallen from grace. Discounted rooms at RM98 are good value, but a complete overhaul is planned and prices will rise.

Further east along Jalan Munshi Abdullah is the small *Hotel Accordian* (☎ 06-282 1911). Rooms are comfortable, if a little faded and small, for RM75/85. 'Executive' doubles cost RM120. The *Palace Hotel* (☎ 06-282 5355) at No 201 Jalan Munshi Abdullah is similar and has rooms for RM75/85 and larger deluxe rooms for RM100/120 plus 15% taxes, but discounts are normally available.

Melaka's crumbling Chinatown has managed to avoid demolition – and wholesale renovation – but two new hotels have set up shop in restored buildings. *The Baba House* (☎ 06-281 1216), 125 Jalan Tun Tan Cheng Lock, with its tilework, carved panels and cool, interior courtyard downstairs, has loads of style. Rooms with attached bath are very comfortable and cost RM60, RM85 and RM95. The only drawback is that the cheaper rooms in this row of former shophouses are internal facing and don't have windows.

For position and style it's hard to beat *Heeren House* (☎ 06-281 4241), 1 Jalan Tun Tan Cheng Lock, right in the heart of town. Immaculate rooms in this former godown all overlook the river and have polished floorboards, a few pieces of antique furniture and all mod-cons for RM99, or RM119 on weekends. This small, six-roomed guesthouse also has a good cafe downstairs serving Peranakan and Portuguese food.

Places to Stay – top end

Melaka has a couple of older high-rise hotels that are no longer up with the best but offer all facilities and substantial discounts. The *City Bayview Hotel* (☎ 06-283 9888) on Jalan Bendahara has a swimming pool, a health centre and a number of eating and drinking venues. Room rates start at RM260 plus 15%, before discount.

Not quite as luxurious is the *Emperor Hotel* (☎ 06-284 0777), in the same area at 123 Jalan Munshi Abdullah. It also has a pool, restaurants and bars. The room rate here is RM140 after discount, though more expensive rooms and suites are available.

On Jalan Bendahara, the *Ramada Renaissance Hotel* (☎ 06-284 8888) is the most luxurious hotel in town. Facilities include tennis and squash courts, a swimming pool and a disco. Rooms start at RM300, plus taxes.

Places to Eat

Melaka's food reflects its history. It is the home of Nyonya cuisine and Portuguese Eurasian food. The classic Nyonya dish, laksa soup, is the best in Malaysia – the rich coconut base makes it tastier than the sour Penang variety. Medan Portugis is the place to try Portuguese-influenced dishes – mostly seafood, though the fiery 'devil curry' is also worth a try.

Despite its culinary reputation, Melaka is not overly endowed with food venues and for the most part you'll find standard fare at Chinese, Indian and Malay coffee shops. In the evenings the centre of town is very quiet. The Taman Raya Melaka area has more life and restaurants that stay open late.

One good place to eat is along Jalan Taman Merdeka, on what used to be the waterfront. The permanent stalls here, known locally as *Glutton's Corner*, serve all the usual food centre specialities, though at higher prices. The land reclamation has spoilt the sea views, but the food is still good. Just walk along and see what attracts you – the *Bunga Raya* at No 40 has excellent steamed crabs.

The *Mahkota Parade shopping mall* nearby is mostly a centre for western fast food, though the food court on the 1st floor serves the usual hawker favourites. You'll find a supermarket in the basement for self-catering.

Right in the centre of town, at 38 Jalan Laksamana, the *Restaurant Kim Swee Huat* has an impressive menu and caters to western tastes: for breakfast you can get muesli, porridge or toast. Also very central is the *Restoran Pandan* behind the tourist office, an outdoor place with umbrellas. The western and Malay food, however, is bland and overpriced.

Good, if slightly expensive, daytime cafes for Nyonya dishes can be found in restored Peranakan houses in Chinatown. The cafe within the *Heerin House* guesthouse has a delightful atmosphere and is a good place for cakes and Peranakan and Portuguese food. It also serves western breakfasts. The *Jonkers Melaka Restoran*, 17 Jalan Hang Jebat, is a craft shop with a few tables which serve Nyonya dishes – a good place for a snack or a Nyonya set lunch.

The *UE Tea House*, 20 Lorong Bukit China, is a small Chinese coffee shop and the place for a dim sum breakfast. The much grander *Emperor Hotel* on Jalan Munshi Abdullah does a good dim sum buffet for RM9 from 7 am to 2 pm, Monday to Saturday.

For Indian food head to Little India, the area around the corner of Jalan Temenggong and Jalan Bendahara. The *Sri Lakshmi Vilas*, 2 Jalan Bendahara, is typical and has cheap roti canai and murtabak. The *Sri Krishna Bavan* right next door is very similar. Around the corner at 34 Jalan Temenggong, the *Restoran Veni* has cheap vegetarian and non-vegetarian set meals and roti canai breakfasts.

Taman Melaka Raya, where many of the travellers' guesthouses are located, has a good range of eateries. A food-stall centre is on Jalan Parameswara opposite the entrance to the Sound & Light Show. For duck rice, noodles and other Chinese hawker fare, the *New Golden Dragon* is a good coffee shop with tables outside on the pavement. Other cheap Chinese and Indian coffee shops can be found along Jalan Taman Melaka, or for excellent Nyonya fare head to the *Ole Sayang* at No 198 or the *Nyonya Makka* at No 123. Both these air-conditioned restaurants serve a variety of Nyonya specialities for around RM8 per dish.

It's well worth making the trip out to Medan Portugis, where you can sample Malay-Portuguese cuisine at outdoor tables facing the sea. Take bus No 17 from the local bus station, or a taxi which will cost RM5. Inside the square, *Restoran de Lisbon* is the most popular, as much for the entertainment as the food. Bands play most nights of the week, though the big night is Saturday, when cultural shows are held. The seafood is superb – chilli crabs cost around RM15, or the devil curry is RM8. The other popular place in the square is *Restoran D'Nolasco*. With side dishes and drinks the bill soon mounts at these restaurants. You could try the slightly cheaper seafood-stalls which front the sea next to the square. The two most popular with tables overlooking the sea are the *Sea Terrace* and *V&J*. Finally, *San Pedro* on Jalan Albuquerque, one street back from the sea outside the square, is a more stylish and intimate place for Malay-Portuguese meals or a drink.

Also a long way from town, but worth it

for the atmosphere, is the *Restoran Peranakan* at 317 Jalan Klebang Besar. It's located four km west of town on the coast road to Tanjung Kling. Authentic Peranakan food is served in a magnificent Peranakan villa.

Entertainment

The *Sound & Light Show*, held near the Porta de Santiago, is Melaka's most popular form of evening entertainment. The sound system booms and the ruins are lit up to explain Melaka's history with a shamefully political bent. It's quite good theatre and the one-hour shows are held each evening at 8 pm in Malay and at 9.30 pm in English. During Ramadan there are English shows only, held at 8.30 pm. Entry is RM5 (children RM3).

Portuguese cultural shows are held at the restaurants at *Medan Portugis* every Saturday night from around 8 pm (entry RM2). Dance groups perform Portuguese and Malay dances to a traditional band and make for a lively night. Pop bands play during the week, when it is quieter. The music is so-so but it's a pleasant spot next to the sea for meal or a drink.

Melaka's nightlife is otherwise unexciting. *Sparks Disco* on the top floor of Mahkota Parade is the current favourite and features Filipina bands. A first-drink cover charge of RM15 applies (RM20 on Saturday nights), and it is open until 2 am. *Mega Disco* in the City Bayview Hotel is popular with young Chinese. Taman Melaka Raya has a number of karaoke lounges – the *Orchid* near the YHA Hostel is a sometimes lively pub featuring Indonesian *dangdut* music, if you are desperate for something to do.

Things to Buy

You can easily spend a couple of hours strolling through the many antique shops along Jalan Hang Jebat (Jonkers St) and Jalan Tun Tan Cheng Lock in the old part of town. Here you'll find Malaysia's best range of antiques, but not all of it is old and not all of it from Malaysia. Prices are very high and haggling is essential.

Shops are stocked with an impressive range of antique furniture, porcelain, old lamps, coins, *songket* material, assorted bric-a-brac and crafts. Silver Galore at 27 Lorong Hang Jebat has an interesting collection of trinkets, gem stones and jewellery. For something different, Wah Aik at 92 Jalan Hang Jebat crafts doll-like shoes for bound feet, once the height of gruesome fashion for well-to-do Chinese women in Melaka. The bound shoes cost RM75; or, if you can wait a few weeks, you can order some magnificent, custom-made Peranakan slippers from Mr Yeo.

Souvenir stalls selling cheap trinkets (mostly from Indonesia) can be found at the Cultural Museum, next to Christ Church near the tourist office. Across from Christ Church on Jalan Laksamana are a few galleries and upmarket shops. Karyaneka Handicrafts Emporium is good for traditional pottery. Dulukala at No 9 is the most interesting, with Indonesian crafts, primitive art and some fine modern pottery tea sets.

Getting There & Away

Melaka is 149 km from KL, 216 km from Johor Bahru and just 90 km from Port Dickson. Melaka's local bus station, express bus terminal and taxi station are all in the same area beside Jalan Hang Tuah.

Air Pelangi Air (☎ 06-385 1175) at the airport has daily services between Melaka and Singapore (RM118, S$110) or Ipoh (RM120). It also flies to Medan (RM258) and Pekanbaru (RM145) in Sumatra on Tuesdays and Saturdays. The MAS office (☎ 06-283 5722) is in the City Bayview Hotel (although the national carrier doesn't service Melaka).

Bus Most of the bus companies have their offices in the buildings near the express bus terminal. It pays to book the day before for any destination other than KL: there are so many buses to KL that you can usually just turn up and get on the next departure. Half a dozen companies have air-con buses to KL (RM6.50, 3½ hours) throughout the day from 7 am to 7 pm.

To Singapore (RM11.50, five hours), express buses leave hourly from 8 am to 6 pm, and it's advisable to book in advance. Buses to Johor Bahru (RM10, 3½ hours) leave roughly every half hour. To Muar (RM2.50, one hour) buses depart every half hour throughout the day.

There are also buses for Butterworth and Penang (RM26) at 8.30 pm, Lumut (RM21) at 9.30 pm and Ipoh (RM16). To the east coast, two buses per day go to Kuantan (RM14) at 2 pm, and evening buses go to Kuala Terengganu (RM22) and Kota Bharu (RM24).

Train The nearest railway station is on the main north-south line at Tampin, 38 km north of Melaka. Check schedules at the Melaka railway office (☎ 06-282 3091). Taxis and buses run between Melaka and Tampin.

Taxi Taxis leave from the taxi station just opposite the local bus station and operate to Port Dickson (RM10), Johor Bahru (RM23), Seremban (RM10), Mersing (RM12) and KL (RM13).

Car If you are driving your own vehicle, Melaka's one-way traffic system will probably frustrate you at every turn.

If you want to rent a vehicle, the following companies have offices in Melaka:

Avis
  124 Jalan Bendahara (☎ 06-284 6710)
Hertz
  City Bayview Hotel (☎ 06-282 8862)

Boat Daily high-speed ferries (RM80, 2½ hours) operate between Melaka and Dumai in Sumatra. Two buses leave at 10 am and one at 2 pm from the river wharf just past the Museum Samudra. Boats are operated by Madai Shipping (☎ 06-284 0671), Tunas Rupat Utama (☎ 06-283 2506) and Masamas (☎ 06-281 8200), which all have booths at the wharf in Melaka. Buy your ticket the day before departure. Dumai is now a visa-free entry port into Indonesia for most nationalities.

Getting Around

Melaka's airport is 9.5 km from the centre of town. Local Batang bus No 65 runs from the local bus station for 80 sen.

Melaka is easily explored on foot, but one useful service is the No 17 town bus from the local bus station, which runs to Taman Melaka Raya and on to Medan Portugis. To get out to Tanjung Kling take Patt Hup bus No 51 from the local bus station. Bus No 19 goes to Air Keroh.

The Historical Melaka Shuttle (☎ 06-283 6538) is a tourist shuttle bus that loops from the tourist office through Chinatown, on to the Malacca Renaissance and other top-end hotels, then out to Air Keroh. It returns via Bukit China and Mahkota Parade. A ticket valid for the whole day costs RM5 and allows three stops. Buses leave hourly from 9.30 am to 4.30 pm.

You can rent a bicycle from one of the guesthouses for RM5 a day. A bicycle rickshaw is another ideal way of getting around compact and slow-moving Melaka. By the hour they should cost about RM15, or RM5 for any one-way trip within the town, but you'll have to bargain. Taxis are unmetered, and similarly charge a rather steep RM5 for a trip anywhere around town.

AROUND MELAKA

Air Keroh

About 15 km north of Melaka right at the Melaka turn-off on the North-South Highway, Air Keroh is home to a number of manufactured tourist attractions popular with Malaysian and Singaporean families on weekends. Compared with the sights of the city, it is all very plastic but worth a stop if you have your own vehicle and are passing by. Air Keroh can also be reached by a No 19 town bus from the local bus station in Melaka; alternatively, the tourist shuttle bus stops outside most of the attractions. All attractions are open from 9 am to 6 pm daily.

Heading north from Melaka, the first point of interest is the **Melaka Zoo**, a small but well-landscaped zoo. Entry is RM3 (RM1 for children). Behind the zoo is the Air Keroh

Country Club & Golf Course and an artificial lake where paddle boats can be hired.

Next along on the main road, **Taman Buaya Melaka** (Melaka Crocodile Farm) has crocs in tanks, as well as a ghost house and fairground rides – family entertainment at its tackiest. Entry is RM3 (RM1 for children).

Nearby, the **Air Keroh Recreational Forest** is part secondary jungle/part landscaped park with paved trails, picnic areas and a forestry museum. The Orang Asli Village inside the park has a few scruffy grass huts, ostensibly to give some insight into the lifestyle of Malaysia's Orang Asli tribes. The forest is a pleasant enough place for a stroll and entry is free, but it certainly ain't Taman Negara.

A few hundred metres further north, **Taman Mini Malaysia/Mini ASEAN** is the main attraction at Air Keroh. This large theme park has examples of traditional houses from all 13 Malaysian states, as well as from other ASEAN countries. Each house contains a few handicrafts and wax dummies in traditional dress representing the region. Though a lot of the houses tend to look the same, it's quite educational and good value at RM4 (RM2 children). On weekends, fairly predictable cultural shows are held at 11.30 am and 2.30 pm.

Finally there's the **Butterfly Farm**, which has a pleasantly landscaped butterfly enclosure, though the butterflies are not all that numerous. More impressive is the collection of snakes, scorpions and enormous spiders. Entry is RM4 (children RM2).

Places to Stay Air Keroh has some pleasant accommodation, but few visitors bother staying this far out. The *Air Keroh Recreational Forest* (☎ 06-232 8401) has camp sites for 50 sen per person, four-bed hostel units for RM40 and more comfortable chalets for RM50 a double. It has been primarily set up for school groups.

Near Mini Malaysia, the *Air Keroh Country Resort* (☎ 06-232 5211) is an older-style resort with a swimming pool and tennis courts. Motel rooms start at RM110 and chalets at RM180. Behind the zoo near the lake, the similar *Air Keroh D'Village* (☎ 06-232 8000) has rooms for RM120/150 and the more upmarket *Malacca Village Paradise Resort* (☎ 06-232 3600) costs RM250.

Islands

A couple of islands off the coast of Melaka have resorts, and they make popular day trips.

The small island of **Pulau Besar**, a little south of Melaka and five km off the coast, is a popular weekend joy-ride, reached by boat from Umbai, 10 km south-east of Melaka. The island has a few historic graves and reminders of the Japanese occupation, but the main reason to come here is for the pleasant beaches. The water here is a little clearer than on the mainland and the hilly island is cloaked in greenery.

The much smaller **Pulau Upeh** is closer to Melaka, and while it can make a good retreat from the city, it is less interesting than Pulau Besar. Boats leave from the jetty near the tourist office in town, but day-trippers will have to arrange a visit with the resort (see below).

Places to Stay On Pulau Besar, the *Samudera Resort* (☎ 06-281 4001) has a variety of chalet accommodation ranging from RM70 to RM150. The chalets over the water are very attractive and there is also a restaurant. The new *Pandanusa Resort* is nearing completion and will also offer luxury accommodation for around RM150.

On Pulau Upeh, the *Upeh Island Resort* (☎ 06-232 8061) also has luxury chalets from RM155 to RM250.

Getting There & Away Boats go from Umbai to Pulau Besar on demand and cost RM10 return. On weekends there are plenty of boats, but during the week you may have to hire a whole boat for RM80 for a speed boat or RM50 for a fishing boat.

Ring the resort for transport to Palau Upeh. Charter tours that take in Upeh can also be arranged – the tourist office has details of operators.

Tanjung Kling/Pantai Kundor

This area about 10 km north-west of Melaka

used to be a mildly popular retreat from the city, but these days, with the polluted waters and lack of budget accommodation, few travellers make it out here.

Tanjung Kling is almost a suburb of Melaka on the main road to Port Dickson, while Pantai Kundor is right on the water a couple of km further from town. Tanjung Kling is a go-ahead area, with condominiums and top-end hotels sprouting all along the coast, which is hard to understand given the rather ordinary beach. Pantai Kundor is quieter and the beach is a decent enough stretch of whitish sand, but with all the shipping traffic in the Straits of Melaka, it is not exactly a tropical paradise.

Places to Stay & Eat One of the first places of interest, nine km from Melaka, is *Klebang Beach Resort* (☎ 06-315588), on the beach and fronting the main road. This new, mid-range hotel has a pool, restaurant and well-appointed rooms for RM138 and RM155. The accommodation is very good but the beach here is just a tiny strip of sand. A few hundred metres further along is the very pleasant *Shah's Beach Resort* (☎ 06-542990). This Mediterranean-style resort is well set out and has a swimming pool, tennis courts, bar and restaurant. Accommodation is in chalet-type rooms which cost RM126 by the pool, RM110 by the beach and RM92 near the road, but discounts are regularly offered.

Past Tanjung Kling is the turn-off to Pantai Kundor, where the beach is better and not as heavily trafficked. The first place you come to is the *Motel Tanjung Kling* (☎ 06-515749), a run-down hotel with a pleasant location right by the water. The gloomy rooms with fan for RM48 are poor value; the better renovated rooms with bath and air-con cost RM78.

A better bet for mid-range accommodation at Pantai Kundor is the *Straitsview Lodge* (☎ 06-514627), two km or so further on. A variety of comfortable but quite basic chalets with air-con and bath cost RM60 and RM70. It's a very pleasant place with a good seafood restaurant.

Right next door, the *Mutiara Malacca Beach Resort* (☎ 06-518518) is a luxury high-rise hotel with a pool, tennis courts and one of the best stretches of beach out front over the road. Rooms start at RM185 and two-bedroom suites cost from RM270, all plus 15%. Some good discounts are offered at times, making it an attractive option for a luxury break from Melaka.

Getting There & Away Catch the Patt Hup bus No 51 from the local bus station. They go every half hour or so. A share-taxi to Tanjung Kling costs around RM2 per person, or RM8 for the whole vehicle.

Tanjung Bidara

About 20 km north-west of Melaka on the way to Port Dickson is Tanjung Bidara, one of the better beach areas along this stretch of coast. It is quiet and well away from the main road, and though the water is murky, the sandy beaches are pleasant and greenery is reasonably prolific. The main beach is at the Tanjung Bidara Beach Resort, where there is also a public beach area with food stalls.

Places to Stay The *Tanjung Bidara Beach Resort* (☎ 06-542990) is a quiet, relaxing resort with a swimming pool and restaurant. It is looking a little worn but provides very comfortable accommodation in rooms for RM115 and in more luxurious chalets costing from RM200 to RM280. However, discounts are sometimes available.

Good, cheaper accommodation can also be found at the beach a few km away at Kampung Pasir Gembur. *Bidara Beach Lodge* (☎ 06-543340), 78 Lorong Haji Abdullah, has double rooms for RM36 or RM79 with air-con and attached bathroom. A 10% service charge applies on the rooms and at the lodge's restaurant.

Getting There & Away Buses from Melaka run to Masjid Tanah, from where a taxi to Tanjung Bidara Beach Resort or Kampung Pasir Gembur costs RM4. Infrequent buses also run to the army base at Tanjung Bidara, from where it is a short walk to the beach.

Johor

The state of Johor occupies the southernmost tip of the Malay peninsula and is connected to the island of Singapore by a causeway. Economically it is one of the most important states in the country, with huge rubber, palm oil and pineapple plantations, and a growing industrial base. It is also the most populated and Johor Bahru with a population of over 700,000 people is the second-largest city in Malaysia.

Johor emerged as the successor to Melaka and the sultanate was the most powerful and important in Malaysia. The royal family enjoys something of a notorious reputation. The sultan has accumulated an army of bodyguards and after an incident in which the Johor sultan allegedly beat a hockey coach, the prime minister stepped in to curtail the powers and privileges of the sultans, which include immunity from prosecution.

Few visitors stop in Johor, although many visit Mersing on the east coast, simply because it is the access point for the beautiful island of Tioman (itself in Pahang state).

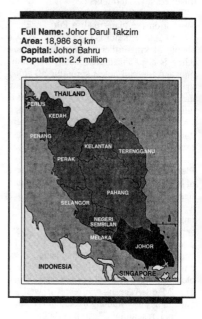

Full Name: Johor Darul Takzim
Area: 18,986 sq km
Capital: Johor Bahru
Population: 2.4 million

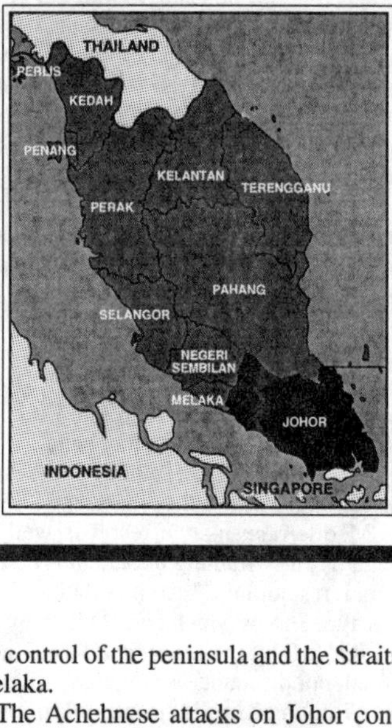

History

Johor's history is really a continuation of Melaka's. When the latter fell to the Portuguese in the 16th century, Johor became the pre-eminent Malay state and its rulers (the first of whom was the son of the last sultan of Melaka) were seen as the protectors of the western Malay states. Early on the Portuguese attacked Johor on a number of occasions but eventually were more or less content to let them rule from their capital on the Johor River, even though they were something of an impediment to trade in the area.

The kingdom of Acheh on the northern tip of Sumatra also had ambitions in the area, and so for the entire second half of the 16th century Johor was under constant threat. It was a period which saw a triangular struggle between the Portuguese, Johor and Acheh for control of the peninsula and the Straits of Melaka.

The Achehnese attacks on Johor continued well into the 17th century, and for a period from 1623 the kingdom's rulers had no fixed address, as their capital on the island of Lingga in the Johor River had been razed.

Johor's fortunes took a decided turn for the better with the coming of the Dutch, who allied themselves with Johor for a combined (and ultimately successful) attack against the Portuguese at Melaka in 1641. In return for co-operation in helping to defeat the Portuguese, Johor was freed from virtually all the tariffs and trading restrictions imposed on other states by the Dutch. Johor also overcame threats from the Minangkabaus and managed to ride out some domestic squabbling from within. By the end of the 17th century it was among the strongest Asian powers in the region.

A war with the Bugis in 1716 left Johor weakened and further political instability followed when a Minangkabau, Raja Kecil of Siak, claimed the throne and overthrew the weak sultan in 1719. His control lasted for just two years and was never secure, and he was soon toppled by the Buginese. At this time Sulaiman, the son of the former sultan Abdul Jalil, was installed on the throne by the Buginese, and his descendants were to rule the state until it eventually disappeared in the early years of the 20th century. Throughout the 18th century the Bugis influence within the state grew, until the Dutch East India Company wrested control of Riau-Johor in 1784, marking the end of Bugis domination of western Malaya.

In 1819, with the court of the Johor sultan split by Malay and Bugis factions, Stamford Raffles was able to bring about the cession of Singapore to the British and the pensioning off of the sultans, while actual power went to the *temenggong* (Malay minister in charge of defence and justice). The temenggongs continued to rule the state very ably, the most notable among them being the

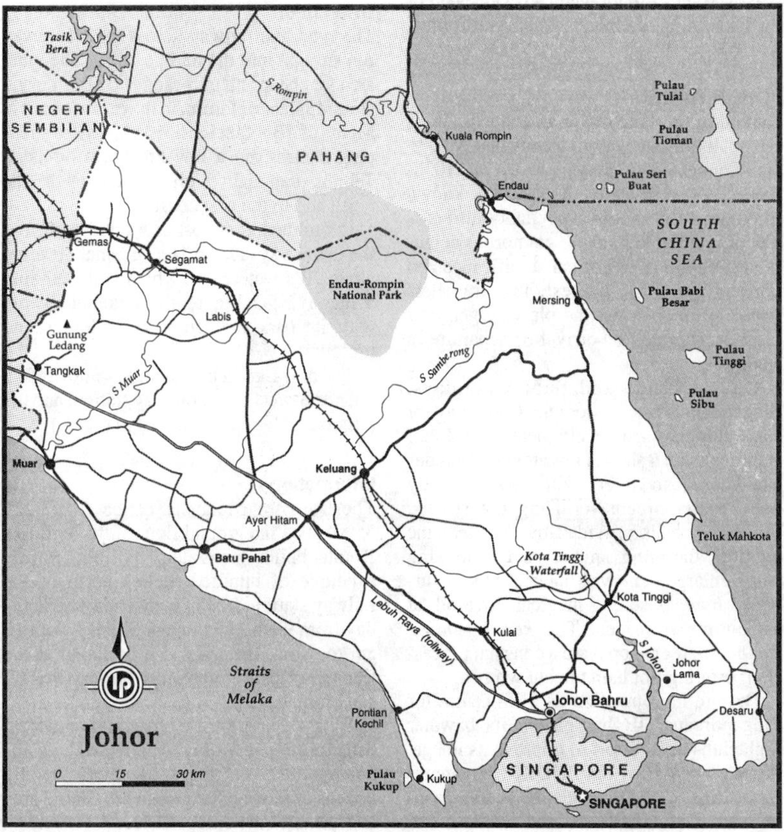

flamboyant Abu Bakar, who elevated himself to the position of sultan of Johor in 1886. Through his contacts with people in high places in London and Singapore he was able to resist the British desire to bring Johor closer under its control. He also undertook an ambitious modernisation programme for the state, while continuing to live the high life. Today he is fondly remembered as the Father of Johor.

Abu Bakar's successor and son, Ibrahim, was less powerful and in 1914 was forced by the British to accept a 'general adviser' who had powers similar to those exercised by the Residents in other states. Sultan Ibrahim was still the ruler of Johor when it became part of the Federation of Malaya, which was formed in 1948.

JOHOR BAHRU

Capital of the state of Johor, Johor Bahru is the southern gateway to Peninsular Malaysia. Connected to Singapore by the 1038-metre-long Causeway, JB (as it is known throughout the country) inevitably suffers as a poor relation to its more glamorous neighbour. Despite its historical significance and various points of interest, few travellers pause in JB; it's just the place to get your passport stamped on arrival or departure in Malaysia.

On weekends and public holidays, Singaporeans flock across the Causeway for sex, shopping and excitement, and Johor Bahru puts on a show. Downtown JB exudes a real border-town feel, with crowds, mostly male Singaporeans, cruising the streets. Street theatre is provided by the medicine vendors dangling snakes and promising penis enlargement with their elixirs or turbaned *bomohs* selling magical 'love oil' at astronomical prices. The *kedai gunting rambut* (barber shops) are a constant procession, offering not haircuts but women.

Despite its reputation as a sin centre for Singaporeans, JB has closed its bawdier nightclubs in an effort to improve its image. A major centre of the SIJORI (Singapore-Johor-Riau) growth triangle, JB is a burgeoning centre of investment and construction. New roads, industrial estates, shopping centres and hotels are changing the face of the city. Despite all this, JB is still chaotic and fairly tatty. It is both a breath of fresh air and a bad aroma as you arrive from squeaky-clean and sterile Singapore.

It's possible to spend an enjoyable day or two in JB, as it has an excellent museum to visit by day and a thriving night market. In the business centre of town you still get the pavement hawkers and other colourful stalls which are so much a part of Asia – and which, to a great extent, the Singaporeans have so effectively killed off.

Orientation

The road and railway across the Causeway run straight into the middle of JB. The main area for cheap and mid-range hotels is on and around Jalan Meldrum, in the centre of town. Many of JB's fancier hotels and new shopping centres are a few km north on Jalan Tebrau, the main highway leading to the north and to the east coast.

Off to the left almost as soon as you cross the Causeway is Jalan Tun Dr Ismail, leading along JB's waterfront, which is undergoing a massive facelift, to the colonial district with its parkland, colonial buildings and museum.

The new Larkin bus and taxi station is five km north-west of the railway station, and the airport is 32 km from the city centre.

Information

The Tourism Malaysia office (☎ 07-222 3590) is on the ground floor of the high-rise Komtar building on Jalan Tun Abdul Razak, a couple of hundred metres north of the railway station. It is open Monday to Saturday from 9 am to 5 pm and Sunday from 10 am to 4 pm. Branches can be found at the Causeway just before you go through Malaysian immigration.

With so many people crossing to and from Singapore every day (many Malaysians commute to work there), there are literally dozens of moneychangers in the central area and the rates are competitive.

The immigration office (☎ 07-224 4253) is on the 1st floor, Blok B, Wisma Persekutuan, Jalan Air Molek.

For international calls, there's the Telekom building opposite the Puteri Pan Pacific Hotel in the centre, where it's possible to make credit-card calls at any time, or calls through the operator during business hours. There are more credit-card phones in the lobby of the Tropical Inn.

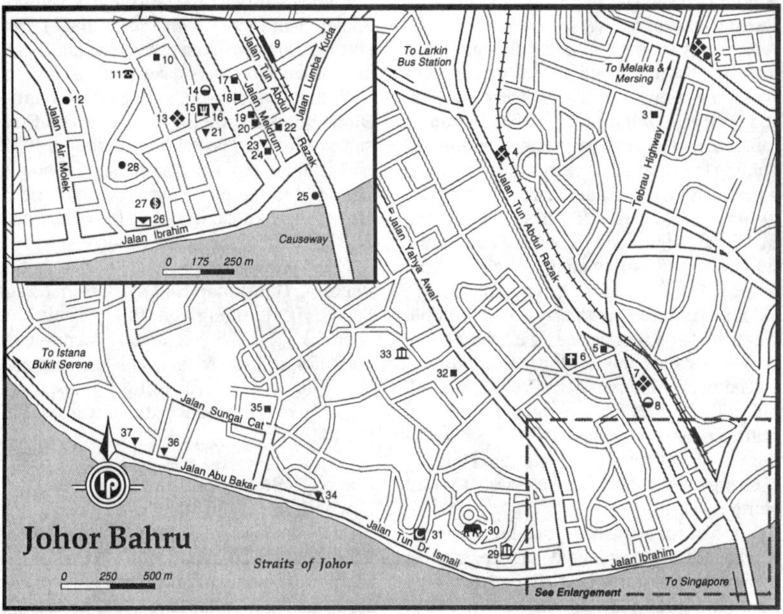

PLACES TO STAY
- 3 Hotel Grand Continental
- 5 Tropical Inn
- 10 Puteri Pan Pacific Hotel
- 17 City View Hotel
- 18 Hotel JB
- 19 Hotel New Chuan Seng
- 20 Hawaii Hotel
- 22 Causeway Inn
- 24 Top Hotel
- 32 Footloose Homestay
- 35 Hyatt Regency

PLACES TO EAT
- 16 Pasar Malam
- 21 Restoran Nilla
- 23 Restoran Medina
- 34 Tepian Tebrau Food Centre
- 36 Selera Sungei Chat Food Centre
- 37 Marina Seafood Village

OTHER
- 1 Plaza Pelangi
- 2 Menara Pelangi
- 4 Best World
- 6 Church of the Immaculate Conception
- 7 Komtar Building
- 8 Singapore Taxi Station
- 9 Railway Station
- 11 Telekom
- 12 Immigration Office
- 13 Plaza Kota Raya
- 14 Taxi Station
- 15 Sri Mariamman Temple
- 25 Immigration Check Point
- 26 Post Office
- 27 Hongkong Bank
- 28 Bangunan Sultan Ibrahim
- 29 Royal Abu Bakar Museum
- 30 Zoo
- 31 Sultan Abu Bakar Mosque
- 33 Johor Art Gallery

Royal Abu Bakar Museum (Muzium Diraja Abu Bakar)

Overlooking the Straits of Johor, the Istana Besar was once the main palace of the Johor royal family. It was built in Victorian style by Anglophile sultan Abu Bakar in 1866 and is now open to the public as a Royal Abu Bakar Museum.

Every state with a sultan has a similar museum, but this is undoubtedly the finest in Malaysia, conveying like no other the wealth and privilege of the sultans. The museum is full of the sultan's possessions, furniture and hunting trophies and is set out much as it was when in use as the palace. The superb exhibits include Chinese, Japanese, Indian and Malay carved wooden pieces, and an amazing full-size crystal-glass table and chairs from France. The hunting room has some bizarre exhibits from the pukka days when wildlife was there to be shot, including elephant's-foot umbrella stands and antelope-leg ashtrays!

The palace is open daily from 9 am to 6 pm, although there's no entry after 5 pm. Entrance for foreigners is a hefty US$7 (children US$3), payable in ringgit at lousy exchange rates. Despite the price, it's well worth a visit.

The 53 hectare palace grounds (free entry) are beautifully manicured and are a great breathing space in this fairly cramped city. There are good views across the Straits of Johor, although Singapore's industrial backside is not terribly picturesque.

Other Attractions

Further west from the museum is the most attractive part of Johor Bahru, the old colonial/royal district of greenery and fine buildings. The whole waterfront opposite is being redeveloped and may be a pleasant place to stroll when finished, but until then the high-speed traffic along the main road and the distance between sights make for a hot, dusty walk.

Behind the Royal Abu Bakar Museum and approached through the palace gardens is a small **zoo**, once the private zoo of the sultan.

The magnificent **Sultan Abu Bakar Mosque,** built from 1892 to 1900, is a mixture of architectural styles, principally Victorian. The minarets look like British clock towers, and this mosque is difficult to distinguish from a colonial administrative building. The large mosque can accommodate 2000 people.

Further north is the **Johor Art Gallery** (Galeri Seni Johor), with a collection of kris, pottery, traditional clothing etc. The fine building housing the gallery dates from 1910.

With a 32-metre-high stone tower, **Istana Bukit Serene** is the actual residence of the sultan of Johor. The palace was built in 1932 and features Art Deco influences. Though not open to the public, you can glimpse it along Jalan Skudai. It is along the waterfront, five km west of the Istana Besar.

One building that is hard to miss is the imposing **Bangunan Sultan Ibrahim** (State Secretariat building) on Bukit Timbalan, overlooking the city centre. This city landmark has a 64-metre-high square tower, and looks like a medieval fortress transported from Turkey or Mogul India. It was built in the 1940s.

Places to Stay – bottom end

Few visitors stay in JB; it's too close to the greater attractions of Singapore. On the other hand, Johor is an important business centre, so there are plenty of hotels, although prices are generally high for Peninsular Malaysia.

Far and away the best place to stay in JB is the *Footloose Homestay* (☎ 07-224 2881) at 4H Jalan Ismail, just off Jalan Gertak Merah in a quiet suburban area. It's a 15 minute walk from the train station but relaxing and friendly. There's one double room for RM24, or just six dorm beds for RM12 per person, all including breakfast. Dinner is available for RM4 and there is a laundry service. As there are only eight beds, it's wise to phone ahead.

Good, cheap hotels are difficult to find in the centre of town. The cheapest is the *Hotel New Chuan Seng* at 35 Jalan Meldrum, a very basic Chinese hotel with typical partitioned rooms with wire-mesh-topped walls, fan and basin. It costs RM25 for a room with one double bed, RM30 for two beds. The beds at least are clean and it's good value for expensive JB. Entry is through the coffee shop downstairs.

Places to Stay – middle

The best value is probably the *Hotel JB* (☎ 07-223 4788) at 80A Jalan Wong Ah Fook. Fan rooms go for RM40, RM49 with fan and bath, and start at RM59 with air-con and bath. The rooms here are very clean and not as box-like as some other places. The *Hawaii Hotel* (☎ 07-224 0633) at 21 Jalan Meldrum is reasonable value for carpeted rooms with air-con and bath. Double rooms start at RM44.

Also good value is the *Top Hotel* (☎ 07-224 4755) at 12 Jalan Meldrum. All rooms have air-con and attached bath and cost RM55, RM10 more with TV. Just around the corner at 2 Jalan Siew Niam, the *Hotel Le Tian* (☎ 07-224 8151) next to the Restoran Medina costs the same but is shabbier.

Jalan Meldrum also has a selection of better mid-range hotels approaching three-star standard, such as the *City View Hotel* (☎ 07-224 9291) at 16 Jalan Station on the corner of Jalan Meldrum. Doubles cost RM100, including breakfast. The *Causeway Inn* (☎ 07-224 8811) at 6A Jalan Meldrum is good value for well-appointed rooms with air-con, TV and attached bath. A few internal-facing rooms with no view cost RM66, though most have views, some across the Straits of Johor, and cost RM82 and RM100 a double.

Places to Stay – top end

Big hotels are sprouting up everywhere in JB, primarily to cater to business travellers. The government keeps talking about a tourist boom, but hotels are often quiet and big discounts are readily available on published rates.

The older *Tropical Inn* (☎ 07-224 7888) at 15 Jalan Gereja has rooms from RM160/180. The hotel has a restaurant and coffee house as well as a bar and health centre, but no swimming pool.

The *Holiday Inn* (☎ 07-332 3800) is a couple of km north of the centre in Century Gardens on Jalan Dato Sulaiman. Rooms cost from RM290/320. There is a swimming pool, health club, restaurant and 24 hour coffee lounge.

The *Puteri Pan Pacific Hotel* (☎ 07-223 3333), right in the centre of town and easy to spot, has an impressive range of features including a swimming pool, fitness centre, business centre and four restaurants. Rooms start at RM280/310.

Competing with the Pan Pacific to be JB's best is the *Hyatt Regency* (☎ 07-222 1234) on Jalan Sungai Chat, 2.5 km west of the city centre past the Sultan Abu Bakar Mosque. Rooms start at RM330.

Places to Eat

Johor Bahru is a good place for food, especially seafood. JB also has good hawker venues, the best being the very active *pasar malam* (night market) outside the Hindu temple on Jalan Wong Ah Fook. Divided into three sections – Chinese, Malay and Indian – it has a great selection of dishes. Local specialities to look out for include *laksa Johor*, relying heavily on coconut, and *mee rebus*, noodles in a thick sauce, showing the Javanese influence in Johor.

Another night market can be found near the Komtar building between Jalan Wong Ah Fook and Jalan Tun Abdul Razak. Air-con food centres can be found inside the Komtar centre and at the Plaza Kota Raya, which has a selection of western fast food and a supermarket on the 2nd level. The fancier *East & West* on the 5th floor of Plaza Kota Raya is a notable little restaurant serving local favourites for around RM5, or good western meals such as fish & chips (RM10) and steaks (RM20).

JB has some good Indian restaurants, including the ever busy *Restoran Medina* on the corner of Jalan Meldrum and Jalan Siew Niam. It serves excellent murtabak, biryani and curries. Right opposite the Sri Mariamman Temple, *Restoran Nilla* at 3 Jalan Ungku Puan specialises in south Indian banana leaf set meals. Most meals are vegetarian, but fish-head curry is also featured.

Singaporeans come across the Causeway

in the evenings just to eat cheap seafood. The main venues are along the waterfront to the west of the city centre. The food is great but the sea aspect is spoiled by the very busy road. The *Tepian Tebrau* food centre on Jalan Abu Bakar is famous for its excellent seafood. One km further west on the corner of Jalan Sungei Chat is the *Selera Sungei Chat*, another well-patronised seafood centre specialising in ikan bakar (grilled fish). Nearby at the New Straits Hotel on Jalan Skudai, *Marina Seafood Village* has superb seafood dishes at moderate prices, though you can run up quite a bill with drinks and all the extras that get tacked on. The restaurant is three km from the centre of town but worth the trip.

Things to Buy

JB promotes itself as a major shopping destination and new shopping centres are being built at a frantic pace. Singaporeans do come across to JB to do their shopping – petrol and groceries – but for most goods Singapore has better prices and a far better range. Major shopping centres in central JB are the older Komtar centre or the much flasher Plaza Kota Raya. Other large new malls to the north of the city centre include the Plaza Pelangi on Jalan Tebrau and Best World on Jalan Tun Abdul Razak.

A duty-free shopping complex is under construction on the waterfront, two km east of the Causeway.

Getting There & Away

Air The MAS office (☎ 07-334 1001) is on the 1st floor of the Menara Pelangi building on Jalan Kuning at Taman Pelangi, 2.5 km from the centre of town. JB is well served by MAS flights and, as an incentive to fly from JB rather than Singapore, fares from here to other places in Malaysia are much cheaper than from Singapore. There are direct flights from JB to Kota Kinabalu (daily, RM347), KL (nine daily, RM93), Kuching (twice daily, RM169) and Penang (daily, RM178). MAS also has direct international flights to Jakarta, Surabaya and Denpasar in Indonesia.

Pelangi Air (☎ 07-332 4366) has direct flights to Kuala Lumpur (daily, RM91) with connections further afield. Pelangi also has international flights to Padang (three times weekly, RM260) and Palembang (four times weekly, RM280) in Sumatra. International tickets are cheaper if purchased through a travel agent.

Bus Due to the hassles of crossing the Causeway – customs, immigration and so on – there's a much wider selection of buses and long-distance taxis to other towns in Peninsular Malaysia from JB than from Singapore.

Frequent buses operate between Singapore's Ban San terminal on Queen St and JB's bus station. The most convenient service is the air-con Singapore-Johor Bahru Express, which operates roughly every 15 minutes from 6.30 am until midnight and costs RM1.80. Alternatively, regular SBS bus No 170 costs RM1. Tickets should be bought from the respective booths at the JB bus station before boarding. (See the Singapore – Getting There & Away chapter for more details on this crossing.)

JB's new Larkin bus station is inconveniently located five km north of town, but the buses from Singapore all run from the Causeway to the bus station, or a taxi from the centre of town should cost RM3. At this busy bus station at least a dozen companies have offices, and there are departures throughout the day for all the major towns in Peninsular Malaysia. Destinations include: Melaka (hourly, RM10), KL (RM16.50), Lumut (RM27), Ipoh (RM26) and Butterworth (RM35). Most buses to Melaka come through from Singapore, so it pays to book in advance. To the east coast there are departures to Mersing (RM8), Kuantan (RM16), Kuala Terengganu (RM23) and Kota Bharu (RM29). For Kota Tinggi (RM2) take a Transit Link bus No 41 from the bus station.

Train There are daily trains from JB to KL and Butterworth, and these can be used to get to most places on the west coast. The line passes through Tampin (for Melaka), Seremban,

KL, Tapah Road (for Cameron Highlands), Ipoh and Taiping. The booking office is open from 9 am to 6 pm daily. There are also trains to Singapore, but it's more convenient to take a bus or taxi. See the Malaysia – Getting Around chapter for full schedule and fare information.

Taxi The new long-distance taxi station is at the Larkin bus terminal, but the old terminals in the centre of town are still operating. From the main JB taxi station on Jalan Wong Ah Fook there are regular taxis to Kota Tinggi (RM4), Mersing (RM12), Kuantan (RM36), Melaka (RM23) and KL (RM36).

Registered taxis to Singapore only leave from the terminal further north on Jalan Wong Ah Fook, on the 1st level of the car park next to the Komtar centre. A taxi across the Causeway to the Queen St terminal in Singapore should cost RM25 for the whole vehicle. From Singapore to JB the fare is S$24. Other taxis and private cars around town will also offer their services, but bargaining is required. You can negotiate to get dropped off at a hotel in Singapore – RM30 to RM40 depending on where you want to go.

Car The main car rental companies include:

Avis
  Tropical Inn Hotel, 15 Jalan Gereja (☎ 07-224 4824)
Budget
  2nd Floor, Orchid Plaza, Jalan Wong Ah Fook (☎ 07-224 3951)
Hertz
  Room 646, Puteri Pan Pacific Hotel, Jalan Salim (☎ 07-223 7520)
National
  Sultan Ismail Airport, Senai (☎ 07-599 4532)

Boat Boats operate from Pasir Gudang, about 30 km from Johor Bahru, direct to Surabaya in Java and to the islands of Batam and Bintang in Indonesia's Riau Archipelago. SS Holidays (☎ 07-251 1577), Level 3, 12-13, Kompleks Pusat Bandar, Pasir Gudang, has a ship to Surabaya once every two weeks (ring for departure days). Fares range from RM200 in an eight berth economy cabin to RM280 in a two berth 1st class cabin and the journey takes 60 hours. It also has daily boats to Batam (RM30, 1½ hours) at 9 am and 2 pm and Bintang (RM50, three hours) at 10 am, but these may stop when JB's new ferry terminal is completed. A taxi to the harbour at Pasir Gudang costs around RM25, or you can take the red bus No 224 to Pusat Bandar for RM1.20 and then a taxi to the harbour.

JB's new duty-free ferry terminal at Bebas Cukai, two km east of the Causeway, is nearing completion. When finished it will have regular ferry services to Changi Point and possibly the World Trade Centre in Singapore, as well as Tanjung Belungkor and Mersing in Johor, and Batam in Indonesia.

Palm Oil

The oil palm *(Elaeis guineensis)* is probably the most common tree in Peninsular Malaysia today. When travelling along the main roads of the peninsula, particularly in Johor and Pahang, and in Sabah, you come across seas of oil-palm trees which seem to stretch on endlessly.

The oil palm was first introduced in the 1860s from seeds brought from Sri Lanka (although the tree itself is a native of West Africa), but it was not until 1917 that the first oil-palm plantation was established. Since WWII Malaysia has been the world's top producer of palm oil, with current annual production running at around 7.2 million tonnes.

The oil is extracted from the orange-coloured fruit, which grows in bunches just below the fronds. It is used primarily for cooking, although research is under way to find other uses, such as an engine fuel.

Malaysia has invested heavily in palm oil, and it is one of the country's major primary industry exports. Unfavourable assessments of palm oil as an edible oil by the US Food & Drug Administration has caused an uproar in Malaysia, which blames it on the US sunflower oil industry lobby. ■

Getting Around

The Airport JB's airport is 32 km out of town at Senai on the road to Melaka and KL.

The SPS Coach Service (☎ 07-334 1001) to the airport leaves from the Puteri Pan Pacific Hotel and costs RM4. It meets all incoming and outgoing flights between 5 am and 7 pm. This is the same bus that comes through from Singapore's Novotel Orchid Hotel – it costs S$10 from Singapore to the JB airport, or RM10 from JB to Singapore.

Alternatively, take local bus No 207, but departures are infrequent.

Taxi Taxis around town have meters, but drivers are not always willing to use them. If you bargain, you can go almost anywhere around JB for RM3, or taxis can be hired at around RM20 per hour for sightseeing.

AROUND JOHOR BAHRU

Kukup

About 40 km south-west of JB on the Straits of Melaka, across from Sumatra, is the fishing village of Kukup. The village is famous throughout Malaysia and Singapore for its seafood, especially prawns, and for its open-air restaurants, most of which are built on stilts over the water. Singaporeans, who are obsessed with the loss of their own *kampung* life, flock to this village on weekends, mostly for the seafood. A boat trip to a *kelong* (fishing trap built on stilts) is included in the many day trip packages that run to Kukup from Singapore.

Next to Kukup is Kampung Air Masin (Salt Water Village), renowned for its top quality *belacan* (shrimp paste). Both villages are largely inhabited by Hokkien Chinese.

Kukup's large new jetty points to things to come, and a ferry service to Tuas in Singapore is planned. By road, Kukup is reached by taking a bus or taxi from JB to Pontian Kecil and then another to Kukup. A shared taxi from JB to Pontian Kecil costs RM5, and then another to Kukup costs RM3. A chartered taxi all the way from JB costs RM40.

JOHOR BAHRU TO MELAKA

The main road north from JB runs to KL and Melaka. It's a productive region of palm oil, rubber and pineapple plantations.

Ayer Hitam

Ayer Hitam, 80 km north-west of JB, is an important crossroads. Here you can turn left to go to Batu Pahat, Muar and Melaka; you can continue straight on for Segamat, Seremban and KL or alternatively for Segamat and Temerloh; or you can turn right for Kluang and Mersing on the east coast. Ayer Hitam is a popular rest stop for buses, taxis and motorists, so there are lots of small restaurants. **Kampung Macap**, south of Ayer Hitam, is well known for its Aw Pottery works.

Batu Pahat

The riverine town of Batu Pahat is famed for its Chinese cuisine, although it also has a minor reputation as a 'sin city' for jaded Singaporeans. It has a few buildings of note, such as the town's Art Deco mosque and the Chinese Chamber of Commerce building.

Places to Stay Accommodation can be hard to find on weekends. The *Batu Pahat Rest House (Rumah Persinggahan)* (☎ 07-434 1181) at 870 Jalan Tasek has large air-con doubles for RM52 and RM63. It's just by the roundabout in the south of town, where the roads from Ayer Hitam and Kukup meet. At the more basic *Fairyland Hotel* (☎ 07-434 1777) on Jalan Rahmat you can get a large double room with fan for RM25. Or for some luxury the *Hotel Carnival* (☎ 07-431 5122) at 2 Jalan Fatimah in the centre of town has a few standard rooms for RM60 and deluxe rooms for RM110, including taxes.

Muar

Also known as Bandar Maharani, this riverside town was once an important commercial centre. It is noted for its traditional Malay culture, including *ghazal* music and the *kuda kepang* (horse trance) dance, originally from Java.

It's a typical Malaysian town with a bustling Chinatown of restaurants and hotels, but further along the river is the graceful colonial district with its government offices, court house, customs house and school. Further along Jalan Petri by the river, Masjid Jamek is a Victorian fantasy of a mosque, in much the same style as JB's Sultan Abu Bakar Mosque.

Though Muar sees few tourists, it is worth a stop on the trip to or from Melaka. Between Muar and Melaka there are a number of kampungs with traditional-style Melaka houses.

Places to Stay The very good *Muar Rest House (Rumah Persinggahan)* (☎ 07-952 7744) at 2222 Jalan Sultanah has huge air-con doubles for RM70; it has a restaurant overlooking the river. Muar has plenty of cheaper hotels, including the *Hotel Lee Wa* (☎ 06-951 5995), 75 Jalan Arab, with spartan but clean rooms with attached bath for RM26. The modern-style *Kingdom Hotel* (☎ 06-952 1921), a short walk from the bus station at 158 Jalan Meriam, charges RM28/35 for clean singles/doubles. The rooms for RM50 at the *Park View Hotel* (☎ 06-951 6655) on Jalan Petrie are a little larger but not much better, but it is in a good position overlooking the river.

Gunung Ledang

The highest mountain in Johor, Gunung Ledang (formerly Mt Ophir), is noted for its series of waterfalls and pools for swimming. The 'falls are a lot nicer than those at Kota Tinggi and they stretch along the mountain-side for a longer way', reported one visitor, and they are a popular weekend day trip for locals. From the falls longer, rugged trails lead to the summit. To get there, take a Muar-Segamat bus and get out at Sagil; ask the conductor. It's then a one km-plus walk through the plantation to the bottom of the falls.

JOHOR BAHRU TO MERSING

Kota Tinggi

The small town of Kota Tinggi is 42 km from JB on the road to Mersing. The town itself is of little interest but the waterfalls at **Lumbong**, 15 km north-west of the town, are a very popular weekend retreat.

The falls, at the base of 624-metre-high **Gunung Muntahak**, leap down 36 metres and then flow through a series of pools which are ideal for a cooling dip. The smaller pools are shallow enough for safe use by children. Entry to the falls is RM1 per person, plus RM2 per car.

A couple of km from Kota Tinggi town is **Kampung Kelantan**, where the sultans of Johor have their mausoleums.

Places to Stay & Eat At the falls you can stay at the *Kota Tinggi Waterfall Resort* (☎ 07-833 1146), a recently renovated place where air-con chalets cost RM150 on weekends and RM110 on weekdays. Weekend bookings are heavy.

It is more economical to stay in Kota Tinggi itself. One of the best options is the *Sin May Chun Hotel* (☎ 07-833 3573) at 26 Jalan Tambatan, where clean, spacious rooms cost RM28/38. The *Hotel Bunga Raya* (☎ 07-833 3023) at 12 Jalan Jaafar, opposite the bus station, is another good place, with doubles from RM27. The more upmarket *Nasha Hotel* (07-833 8000) at 40 Jalan Tambatan is not a bargain, with ordinary air-con doubles at RM60.

Getting There & Away Regular buses (No 41, RM2) and taxis (RM4) go from JB to Kota Tinggi. From Kota Tinggi to the waterfalls, take bus No 43.

Johor Lama

Following the fall of Melaka to the Portuguese, the Malay kingdom was transferred to Johor Lama, about 30 km down the Johor River from Kota Tinggi. The town was built as a fortified capital between 1547 and 1587, but was later abandoned as JB rose in prominence. There were a number of skirmishes between Malay and Portuguese fleets along the Johor River, and on two occasions the town was sacked and burnt.

Today the old fort of Kota Batu, overlooking the river, has been restored, but getting to Johor Lama is a major pain. If you have transport, you can drive there. The turn-off is 26 km from Kota Tinggi on the Desaru road, and from there it's 13 km – seven of which are along a dirt road which becomes treacherous after rain. The alternative is to arrange a boat for the downriver trip.

Jason's Bay (Teluk Mahkota)

A turn-off 13 km north of Kota Tinggi leads down 24 km of rather rough road to the sheltered waters of Jason's Bay. There are 10 km of sandy beach but few facilities at this relatively isolated spot.

Places to Stay The *Jason's Bay Beach Resort* (☎ 07-881 8077) has dorm beds for RM15 (RM20 on weekends) and chalets with fan and bath for RM60 (RM80) or with air-con for RM100 (RM120). It's also possible to camp here.

Desaru

On a 20 km stretch of beach at Tanjung Penawar, 88 km east of JB and also reached via Kota Tinggi, this resort area is a popular weekend escape for Singaporeans. The beach is quite good, but it's not particularly interesting for other international visitors to Malaysia.

Places to Stay & Eat Accommodation at Desaru is provided by expensive resorts. The *Desaru Garden Beach Resort* (☎ 07-822 1101) does, however, have a camping ground at RM5 per head and dorm beds at RM12 per head. Unless you cook your own food, you will have to eat in the resort restaurants. The Desaru Garden Beach Resort, like its companion, the *Desaru View* (☎ 07-822 1221), also has top-end accommodation with the full range of amenities from S$180. Prices rise significantly on weekends.

At Batu Layar, 16 km south of Desaru, the *Batu Layar Beach Resort* (☎ 07-822 1835) is a new place with garishly painted A-frame chalets from RM65 (more on weekends).

Getting There & Away Buses (RM3.50) and taxis operate from Kota Tinggi. A popular way for Singaporeans to reach Desaru is to take the ferry to Belungkur from North Changi for S$4, and from there take a taxi to Desaru for RM30.

MERSING

Mersing is a small fishing village on the east coast of Peninsular Malaysia. It's the departure point for the boats which travel between the mainland and the beautiful islands lying just off the coast in the South China Sea. The river bustles with fishing boats, and there's an impressive-looking mosque on a hill above the town. Mersing also has some good beaches, such as Sri Pantai and Sekakap – six and 13 km south; and Ayer Papan and Panyabong – 10 and 50 km to the north.

Orientation

As you enter town and cross over the bridge to the roundabout, Jalan Abu Bakar is the main street leading to the boat dock. Jalan Ismail also meets the roundabout and runs roughly parallel to Jalan Abu Bakar.

Information

The new Mersing Tourist Information Centre (☎ 07-799 5212) is a good place to get information on sailing times for the islands and on accommodation around town. It's around five minutes' walk from the jetty.

At the Plaza R&R centre next door to the ferry jetty, the office of the Mersing Tourist Boat Hire Association (☎ 07-799 1222) is another good source of information on sailing times. There's also a credit-card phone in this shopping centre and a number of travel agents.

Travellers' cheques can be changed at the Bank Bumiputra Malaysia Berhad on Jalan Ismail or at the licensed moneychanger in the goldsmith shop on Jalan Abu Bakar.

Places to Stay

Sheikh Tourist Agency (☎ 07-799 3767) at 1B Jalan Abu Bakar is the travellers' place with dorm beds for RM5, and the travel agency downstairs provides good information. It's opposite the post office, a few hundred metres before the boat dock. Right next door is *Omar's Backpackers Hostel*, which is less popular but offers near-identical accommodation at RM6, or RM14 for a double room.

The *Farm Guest House* (07-799 3767) is

a rustic retreat a few km from town, where dorm accommodation and all meals costs RM15. Phone them to be picked up from Mersing. *Kali's Guest House* (☎ 07-799 3613) is another popular place with similar rates (without the meals). The attached pizzeria serves up some very good fare.

There are a couple of Chinese cheapies on Jalan Abu Bakar. The *East Coast Hotel* (☎ 07-799 1337) at 43A Jalan Abu Bakar has clean, large rooms from RM14. Next door at 44A is the *Syuan Koong Hotel* (☎ 07-799 1498) with rooms from RM15 to RM28.

Up the scale a bit is the popular *Hotel Embassy* (☎ 07-799 1301) on Jalan Ismail near the roundabout, where clean, comfortable rooms with attached bath, hot water and fan cost RM25, or RM35 with air-con. Of a similar standard, but not as good, is the *Golden City Hotel* (☎ 07-799 1325) near the bus station, with rooms for RM16/25, or RM32 with air-con. Another in this range is the *Mersing Hotel* (☎ 07-796 1004) between Jalan Ismail and Jalan Abu Bakar, with rooms for RM20 with fan and RM35 with air-con, all with attached bath.

For something a little more salubrious there's the *Country Hotel* (☎ 07-799 1799), right at the bus station. Rooms in this recently renovated hotel cost RM45/50 with air-con and bath.

At the top of the scale is the *Mersing Merlin Inn* (☎ 07-799 1312), two km from town on the Endau road. It's not exactly international standard, but it is fully air-conditioned and has a swimming pool. Singles/doubles are RM105/115, including breakfast and taxes.

Places to Eat

For a roti telur and coffee breakfast, try the *Restoran Keluarga* on Jalan Ismail, or the *E&W Cafe* just around the corner from the Hotel Embassy. For a good selection of fresh cakes and bread, try the *Sri Mersing Cafe* on Jalan Sulaiman.

For cheap Chinese food, there are lots of cafes on Jalan Sulaiman or Jalan Abu Bakar. For cheap, tasty Indian food, try the *Restoran Zam Zam*, next door to Sheikh Tourist agency, and the *Sri Laxmi Restoran* at 30 Jalan Dato Mohammed Ali. For Padang food, there's the restaurant next to the moneychanger on Jalan Abu Bakar.

You can get good seafood in Mersing. The Chinese *Golden Dragon Restaurant* in the

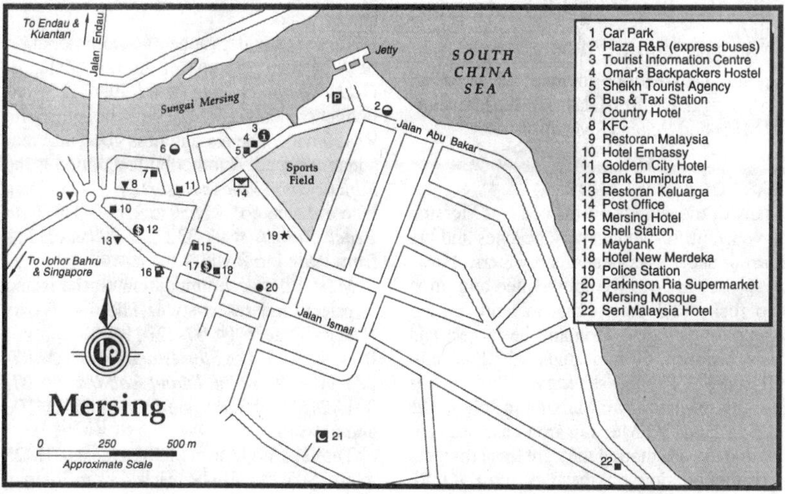

Hotel Embassy is good, and you can try curried wild-boar meat here. There are some more-expensive Chinese places on the Endau road.

The new *Plaza R&R* centre down by the jetty has a number of stalls selling various foods. There's little to choose between them and all make for a decent lunch.

Getting There & Away

Mersing is 133 km north of JB and 189 km south of Kuantan. The local bus and taxi station is opposite the Country Hotel on Jalan Sulaiman near the river. Long-distance buses for Singapore (RM11), JB (RM7.60), KL (RM16.50), Penang (RM26.50), Ipoh (RM36.50), Melaka (RM11.20) and other destinations start and terminate at the Plaza R&R opposite the jetty. The ticket booths are at the back of the plaza and are run by various long-distance bus companies depending on the destination.

Other long-distance buses stop at the Restoran Malaysia on the roundabout. You can buy tickets at the restaurant, but in peak travel periods it is sometimes difficult to get a seat. Destinations served from Mersing include: JB (three daily), Kota Tinggi (hourly), Kuantan (four daily), Kuala Terengganu (two daily), Kota Bharu (one daily) and KL (two daily).

The taxi station is right next to the bus station. Destinations include: JB (RM12), Kota Tinggi (RM8), Melaka (RM25), Kuantan (RM15) and Pekan (RM12).

EAST COAST ISLANDS

Many of the islands off the coast of Mersing have beautiful white sandy beaches and are surrounded by crystal-clear waters. However, they are mostly uninhabited and often too rocky and precipitous to land on. An exception is Pulau Tioman, the largest and most beautiful of the islands, which is actually part of Pahang state, even though it is usually reached from Mersing in Johor. The other islands off Mersing aren't as spectacular as Tioman, though they are less crowded. Accommodation on these is mostly mid-range chalets, and the prices tend to be higher than at Tioman.

Pulau Tioman

Tioman has beautiful beaches, clear water and coral for snorkelling or diving enthusiasts. For more information, see the Pahang chapter.

Pulau Rawa

This tiny island is 16 km from Mersing. The beach is superb and you can snorkel or dive in the crystal-clear waters, though much of the coral around the island itself is dead.

The *Rawa Safaris Island Resort* (☎ 07-799 1204) is the only place to stay. There is a bewildering range of choices, starting at basic but comfortable bungalows for RM110 to beachfront rooms for RM184 including taxes. The restaurant has a bar, and facilities include windsurfing, canoeing, scuba diving and snorkelling. The resort has its own boat, and the booking office is in Mersing, next to the jetty. The round-trip fare is RM25.

Pulau Sibu

Sibu is one of the largest and most popular islands. The beaches are beautiful and good for snorkelling, and there are jungle treks across the island. Windsurfers and canoes can be hired.

There is a wider range of accommodation on Sibu than on most of the other islands. *O&H Kampung Huts* (☎ 07-799 3125) has budget chalets for RM20 without bathroom, RM50 with. The restaurant is good and reasonably priced. Another budget option is the *Sibu Coconut Village Resort* (☎ 07-553552), where chalets cost RM50 to RM80. The *Twin Beach Resort* (☎ 07-332 2122) has chalets from RM45 to RM80.

Most other accommodation on the island is pricey and resort-style. The *Sea Gypsy Village Resort* (☎ 07-223 1493) charges from RM175. The *Sibu Island Resort* (☎ 07-223 1188) and *Sibu Island Cabanas* (☎ 07-331 7216) both have rates of around RM100 and upwards.

The 2½ hour trip to Sibu costs RM25 return. Sibu can also be reached from Tanjong

Leman (RM3 per person by taxi from Kota Tinggi). From Sedili, boats leave at 10 am and 4.30 pm and cost RM26 return for the 2½ hour trip.

Pulau Babi Besar

This island is one of the closest to the peninsula. Boats take about an hour to reach the island from Mersing and cost RM15 one way. Accommodation is mostly more expensive chalets.

There are some inexpensive chalet operations on Babi Besar with prices from RM10 to RM20, but it would be a good idea to ask around in Mersing as to whether they are still running before heading over to the island.

The *Sun Dancer* (☎ 07-799 4995) is one of the less expensive options, with chalets starting at RM30 (though the deluxe chalets are RM140). The *White Sand Beach Resort* (☎ 07-799 4995) is another outfit with cheaper accommodation (from RM40).

The *Radin Island Resort* (☎ 07-799 4152) has chalets from RM140 to RM195. The *Hillside Chalet Island Resort* (☎ 07-799 4831) has similar rates. Charges are about 20% higher on weekends.

Pulau Tengah

Near Pulau Babi Besar, Tengah is 16 km off the coast and takes 1½ hours by boat (RM15 one way). Once a Vietnamese refugee camp, it is now gazetted as a marine park, and leatherback turtles come here to lay their eggs in July.

The *Pirate Bay Island Resort* is an expensive resort operation with a members-only golf course, among other amenities.

Pulau Hujung & Pulau Aur

These remote islands not that long ago had no facilities to offer, but are being developed. Ask around in Mersing for the latest on getting there and what is available in the way of accommodation. At the time of writing, Pulau Aur had a small number of resorts and chalets, including the *Blue Water Resort* (☎ 07-799 4072), the *Friendly Waters Chalet* (☎ 07-447 2108) and *Mahmood's Chalet* (☎ 07-799 4217).

Hujung is closer to the mainland and boats to the other islands may be able to drop you off. Pulau Aur is the most remote island – the boat trip takes at least four hours.

Pulau Tinggi

Tinggi is probably the most impressive island when seen from a distance, as it's an extinct volcano (*tinggi* means 'tall' in Bahasa Malaysia). Boats from Mersing take about two hours and cost RM50 return.

Accommodation is in resorts, though some locals reportedly supply budget accommodation. The *Tinggi Island Resort* (☎ 07-7994451) has chalets from RM110 including breakfast. Facilities available include fishing, boating, snorkelling and windsurfing. At the *Apil Beauty Island* (☎ 07-799 4355) there are chalets ranging from RM80 to RM120. The top spot on the island is *Nadia's Inn Tropical Resort* (☎ 07-799 5582), where luxury accommodation costs from RM220 to RM550.

Pahang

By far the largest state in Peninsular Malaysia, Pahang has plenty to offer the visitor. The east coast has some beautiful beaches, and the tropical paradise of Tioman Island lies just off the south coast, but the interior, with its pristine rainforests is equally alluring. Taman Negara National Park, which is accessible only by boat, is the usual place to get right into the rainforest, but places like Kuala Lipis are also gaining in popularity.

For those who want to get right off the beaten track, the beautiful Tasik Chini lake, close to the huge Pahang River in the centre of the state, is worth exploring, and even more remote is the Endau-Rompin National Park, one of Malaysia's newest and least visited national parks.

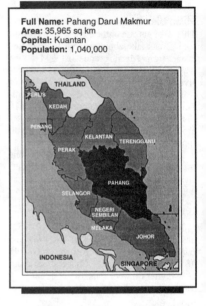

Full Name: Pahang Darul Makmur
Area: 35,965 sq km
Capital: Kuantan
Population: 1,040,000

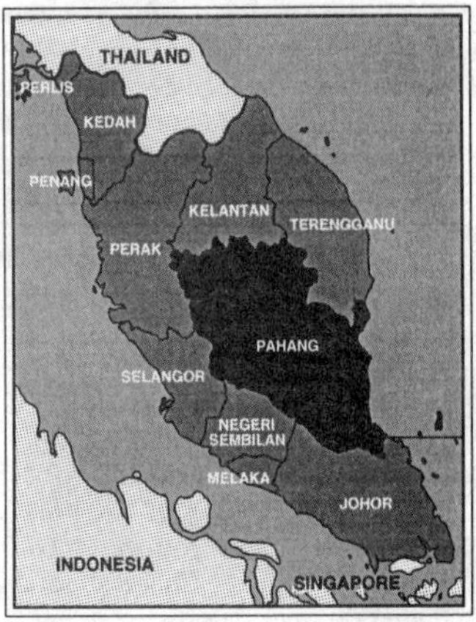

History

Important archaeological finds dating back to Neolithic times have been made along the Pahang's Tembeling River. By the 8th century the Sumatran Sriwijaya empire held sway along the coast, until its collapse in the 14th century, after which Pahang became a Siamese dependency.

Pahang only really emerged as a separate political entity when the Melaka sultanate launched an attack against the Siamese in the middle of the 15th century and installed Muhammad, the eldest son of the Melaka sultan, as ruler.

In the 16th century the state became a pawn in the four-way struggle for ascendancy between Johor, Acheh, the Dutch and the Portuguese. In a period of 30 years it was sacked many times, its rich mineral-based economy was ruined, its rulers were killed or abducted and much of its population was murdered or enslaved. After the decline of the Achehnese empire in the mid-17th century, Pahang was ruled by Johor for the next 200 years.

From 1858 until 1863 Pahang suffered a protracted civil war brought about by a leadership struggle between two brothers, Wan Ahmad and Mutahir, on the death of their father, the sultan. Wan Ahmad finally won, and in 1887 he became sultan. His role from then on was largely symbolic, as the British, who had great interest in the state's commercial potential and were worried about Ahmad's autocratic style and the way he was dishing out large concessions to other foreign speculators, had forced him to sign a treaty bringing the state under the control of a British Resident.

In 1896 Pahang was one of the four states which became the Federated Malay States (the others were Perak, Selangor and Negeri Sembilan), which in turn became the Federation of Malaya in 1948 and then the Federation of Malaysia in 1963.

Tioman Island

Turtle-shaped Tioman Island is the largest and most spectacular of the east coast islands. It may not be the isolated paradise it once was, but its sheer size (39 km long and 12 km wide) packs in the multiple attractions of laze-away-the-day beaches and crystal clear water thick with coral and fish, as well as jungle-clad mountains complete with waterfalls and fast-flowing streams. Back in the late 1950s Hollywood got wind of Tioman and famously made it the setting for the mythical Bali Hai in the film *South Pacific*. The crowds have been pouring in for a first-hand taste of paradise ever since; an airport has materialised, sandwiched between vertiginous mountains and the sea; and express boat services to the mainland have multiplied.

It comes as no surprise that Tioman today is geared almost entirely to tourism. The permanent population is low, with just a handful of small *kampungs* dotted around the coast; the mountainous jungle of the interior is home only to monkeys and other wildlife. Visitors usually outnumber villagers, and at

certain times of the year Tioman can get quite crowded, especially in Salang and Air Batang. If you want to get away from it all, head for the less accessible Juara on the other side of the island.

Tioman is undoubtedly the most popular destination on the east coast, and while some travellers give the place a miss precisely for this reason, it's worth bearing in mind that the island is big enough to allow you to get away from it all with a bit of effort. With just one short stretch of paved road (from the telecommunications tower one km south of the Berjaya Tioman Beach Resort to the airstrip at Tekek, about two km north), transportation around the island is still by creaky fishing boats or via an arduous slog over the waist of the island.

On an incidental note, Tioman has been blessed with some delightful place names. The highest peak, Gunung Kajang, is 'Palm-Frond Hill', and Gunung Chula Naga is 'Dragon-Horn Hill'. The villages are equally imaginatively named. There's Kampung Tekek ('Lizard Village'), Kampung Salang ('Elephant Village'), Kampung Juara ('Catfish Village') and even Kampung Mukut ('Village of Doubt').

Orientation & Information

The island is wilder and more mountainous at the southern end. The single strip of road, the resort and most of the smaller, cheaper places are along the west coast. There's a good trail across the island to Juara on the east coast, where there is also cheap accommodation.

You can cash travellers' cheques at the Berjaya Tioman Beach Resort and at the moneychanger next to the ferry pier at Tekek. There are also moneychangers at Air Batang and Salang, although their rates are nothing to sing about – generally around 10% less than you'd get at a bank on the mainland.

There are numerous public phones at Tekek, Air Batang and at Salang, but at the time of writing most of them were still unconnected. Only Telekom cards can be used for calls and these are on sale at shops around the island – though they frequently sell out. A number of the guesthouses have mobile phones, and they will often let you make calls – usually at prohibitive rates.

Bear in mind that everything stocked in shops on Tioman is shipped over from the mainland and tends to be expensive – stock up on essentials before you arrive.

Wildlife

Tioman is of great interest to biologists because of its relative isolation from the similarly forested terrain of the peninsula. Some animals common on the peninsula are completely missing from the island, while others are present in unexpectedly large numbers.

Tioman has a very large mouse-deer population, for example, and also has a wide variety of lizards in larger than usual numbers. You've got a good chance of seeing some wildlife while you are on Tioman – particularly bats, which come out in force each evening.

The waters around Tioman shelter the usual technicolour schools of exotic fish and a surprising number of turtles. At Nipah, Juara and Pulau Tulai (Coral Island) you have a good chance of seeing turtles come ashore to lay their eggs.

Activities

Cross-Island Walk The most popular walk is the cross-island trek from Tekek to Juara. The trail is easy to follow, and most of the way is through shady jungle. The walk starts about one km north of the jetty in Tekek, and the trail starts to climb when you pass the mosque on your left. Take some bottled water with you. At the halfway point is a small drink stand selling Coke and mineral water.

It's a relatively steep climb through dense jungle following the course of the Besar River to the highest point. The steepest sections have concrete steps, but plans to concrete the whole path have as yet come to nothing. You pass a small waterfall around halfway up the hill, but swimming here is prohibited. Once over the top of the range, the trail slopes down more gradually and soon leaves the damp, dark jungle for the cooler and brighter area of a rubber plantation and then coconut palms as you reach the coast. The walk across the island to Juara takes 1½ to three hours. If you don't want to walk back, the Sea Bus leaves Juara for Salang, Air Batang and Tekek (RM15) at 3 pm.

Other Walks You can also walk along much of the west coast, but the trails are often difficult to follow and you should take water.

From Tekek you can walk south to the resort in about 30 minutes either by the road (it's steep) or by rock-hopping around the headland. From there you can walk through the golf course, and just before the telecommunications tower there is a trail to the beautiful, deserted beach of Bunut. From the end of the beach the sometimes faint trail continues over the headland to a couple of rickety bridges across the mangroves just before Paya. From Paya you can walk south to Genting – the trail is easy to follow and there are houses along the way where you can ask directions.

Heading north from Tekek, you cross the small headland to Air Batang, and from ABC

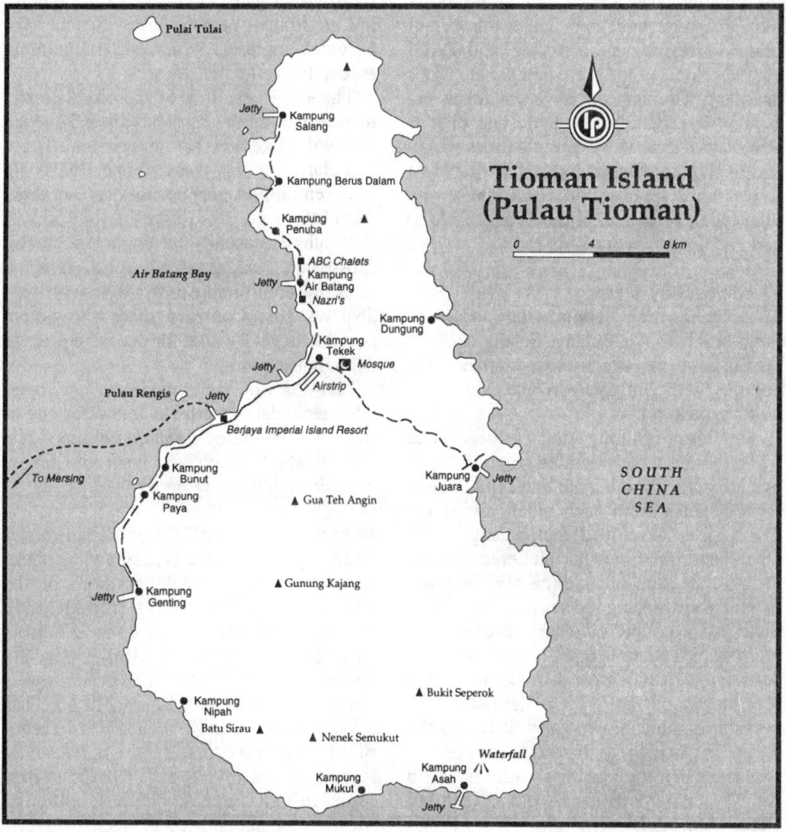

Huts at the other end of the bay it's a 10 minute climb over the headland to Penuba Bay and Monkey Beach. The trail then goes through the rainforest to a deserted yellow-sand beach, where the trail continues at the other end over the next headland to a white-sand beach. At the end of this is a rotten, washed-out bridge where the trail starts the long, steep climb over the headland to Salang. The trail is not well marked here, but the undergrowth is not thick if you lose the trail. It takes about three hours from Air Batang to Salang.

Scuba Diving & Snorkelling Virtually all the travellers' places have snorkelling equipment for hire, and there are a number of places offering scuba diving and PADI courses. Some of the more popular are Ben's at Salang, Tioman Reef Divers at Tekek and Ianz at Air Batang. At Ianz, one dive is RM79, two dives RM99, night dives RM59 and PADI certificate courses RM629. At Ben's, two dives cost RM110, or RM90 with your own equipment, night dives are RM80 and PADI courses are RM625.

Places to Stay & Eat

Most foreign travellers gravitate to one of three beaches: Air Batang, Salang or Juara (Tekek has a poor beach and tends to be more popular with Singaporean and Malaysian holiday-makers).

Air Batang is a long stretch of beach, and while there is a considerable range of chalet operations to choose from they tend to keep their distance from each other, giving the beach a less 'developed' feel. Salang, on the other hand, is somewhat cluttered, though the beach is excellent and it is also the place to be if you want a good selection of restaurants and a couple of places to enjoy late night drinks. Juara is a get-away-from-it-all destination. It has a good beach and just a few chalet outfits with restaurants, and everything winds down early. It is also the cheapest place to be based. From June to August, when the island is swarming with people, accommodation becomes tight, but either side of these months it's a buyer's market. During the heavy November to January monsoon the island is almost deserted.

Apart from the international-standard Berjaya Tioman Beach Resort, accommodation is mostly in the form of small and often ridiculously cramped wooden chalets and longhouse rooms. Chalets generally cost from RM20 to RM50, depending on facilities. For RM20 you'll get a small chalet with a double bed and attached bath. Once you start paying over RM25 you should get a mosquito net and fan as well. Over RM30 the only difference usually is that the chalets are bigger. It is not easy to find places with two single rather than one double bed, and families or groups wanting larger chalets have very few options. It's worth bargaining, especially for longer stays.

There are very few of the old A-frame, *atap*-roof huts left – most have been knocked down to make way for new chalets. Those that linger on cost from around RM10 (no bath, no fan, no net, no light) up to about RM15.

Rooms are usually in longhouse blocks. Mostly they are cheap plywood constructions, but comfortable motel-style rooms are also available. Compare prices – it is often possible to get a chalet for the same price as a longhouse room.

Long lists of accommodation are somewhat redundant as most places offer one or more of about three standard options – just choose which beach you want and take a wander from the jetty on arrival.

Resort The *Berjaya Tioman Beach Resort* (☎ 09-414 5445), a massive sprawling place, is the only international-class hotel on the island. It has 375 rooms from RM260 upwards, with discounts of up to 25% from November to February. Most rooms are chalet-style with air-con. The beach here is probably the best on the island. The hotel has a very impressive range of facilities – a beautiful 18 hole golf course, tennis, horse riding, jet-skis, scuba diving etc. There's even a room full of poker machines, although Muslims are not allowed to enter.

This hotel can be heavily booked, particularly during school holidays. The four restaurants are all very good, but, as you might expect, they're by no means cheap.

Kampung Tekek Tekek is the largest village on the island and is the administrative centre. The airport is here and there are a few well-stocked shops. Tekek's beach is not among the best on the island. The cheaper accommodation is north of the jetty. The area south of the jetty, not far from the resort, has a good stretch of beach, but the chalets are bit pricey.

The southern places are a 10 minute walk along the airport road (walking along the beach involves fording a stream). The first place you come to is the *Mastura Chalets*, which has a dive shop, followed by the *Tekek Inn*, which has rooms and huts from RM15. Next door is the *Sri Tioman*, where small huts with mattresses on the floor and mosquito nets cost RM20. Chalets cost RM30. Behind Sri Tioman, next to the road, is *Persona Island Resort*, with upmarket longhouse rooms and chalets from RM80 to RM100 – they are not particularly good value for money. The *Coral Reef*, back on the beach, has chalets for RM30.

Towards the end of the beach, and right next to each other, are two more-upmarket places. *Babura* has a block of very good rooms with baths, mosquito nets and fans for RM30, and a cluster of beachside chalets for RM35, RM90 with air-con. Its restaurant is one of the more popular on this end of the beach and there's a small bar serving cold beer. *Swiss Cottages* has basic chalets from RM30 and air-con chalets from RM90 – it's not a bargain and the restaurant here is apathetically run.

Accommodation north of the jetty is generally fairly grim, often located away from the beach and with little to recommend it. If you are looking for budget accommodation, you are probably better off heading for Air Batang or Juara. *Ramli's*, a few minutes' walk along from the '7 till 7' corner store, is one of the better options, with chalets from RM15. The most popular place is *Mango Grove*, which is a further 10 minutes' walk, next door to the new Marine Centre. Chalets here cost from RM20, the restaurant is not bad, and it often stays open late – the only drawback is that it is sited on a rocky outcrop and you have to walk a fair way to the beach.

Besides all the chalet restaurants, there are several places to eat out on the airport road. The most popular is the *Liza Restaurant*. It's a little expensive, the food is average, and they don't serve drinks – the only thing that can really be said in its favour is that the surroundings are pleasant.

Air Batang Usually referred to as ABC, Air Batang is a popular beach just over the headland to the north of Tekek. Along with Salang, it's the main travellers' centre, with a lazy string of chalet operations connected by a concrete path that runs the length of the beach. There's a small information office at the jetty, roughly in the middle of the beach, where you can buy boat tickets and find out sailing times. ABC is a more relaxing place to be than Tekek and there's more greenery. Some sections of the beach, however, are rocky and poor for swimming.

Just north of the jetty is *Aris Huts*, a grotty little place where chalets cost RM25. Close by, over a creek, is the pleasant *South Pacific Chalets*. There are a few chalets right on the beach for RM15 and others on the other side of the path for RM20 to RM30. The restaurant here is quite popular – the cheese and pineapple jaffles are excellent. *Johan's House* is not far away and not a bad place to stay. It has chalets dotted around a lawn on the hill. They range from RM25 to RM100 with air-con.

Across another small creek is *CT's Cottages*. This place charges RM30 for larger than usual chalets with bath, fan and net, and there's one large family chalet with a kitchen, right on the beach, for RM80. Next door is *Tioman House*, which has some small chalets for RM15 and larger ones for RM25. The shop sells basic supplies, and the *Sri Nelayan Restaurant* next door has a few basic chalets for RM10.

Next along is *Kartini's Place*, one of the most basic places on this beach. The huts have no bath, electricity or mosquito net, but are undeniably cheap at RM7.

After the next creek is the *Coconut Cafe* and another small shop, followed by the friendly *Rinda Cafe*, where simple but clean chalets cost from RM15. There's a pleasant lawn area, though note the sign – 'No alcohol here, please'.

The next place is *Nazri's Beach Cabins*, a beautiful place to be based, with chalets from RM40 to RM80. It has a well-tended lawn and a very pleasant elevated restaurant.

Lastly, right at the end of the beach, is *ABC Chalets*, probably the most popular place with travellers. This is the place to meet other travellers, not to get away from it all. Accommodation ranges from RM15 for huts with just a mattress on the floor to RM30 for chalets with all the usual facilities and RM40 for the chalets built right out over the rocks at the end of the beach. The restaurant is one of the best in Air Batang, but when the place is full it can take some time for orders to arrive. They also have a laundry service (not just for guests), and snorkelling gear for hire.

Immediately south of the jetty are a couple of small outfits with basic rooms or chalets from RM10 to RM15, but they are close to Air Batang's generator and tend to be noisy. A little further on and a better choice is the *Mawar Beach Chalets*, with a row of chalets right on the concrete path for RM15.

TC Chalets a bit further along is a small and friendly place with just six fairly cramped chalets for RM25 with bath, fan and net. There's a restaurant open during the day.

Zahara's (My Friend's Place) is next and has a popular restaurant and a few standard chalets, some of them uncomfortably close to the restaurant. At *Mokhtar's Place Chalets* next door, the chalets are well spaced in a large garden. It's a good place, with standard chalets for RM25. Also here is Ianz Dive Shop (see Activities).

Much further along, at the end of the beach, is *Nazri's*, another popular travellers' hang-out. It has some very shabby old chalets and A-frames, which cost RM15, and a variety of newer chalets, which cost up to RM85.

Penuba Bay Over the headland from ABC, the *Penuba Bay Cafe* has a few huts for RM15 and some chalets on the hill. It's certainly peaceful, but accommodation is limited, so it's worth checking to see if there's room before lugging your gear over the headland, although it's not a long walk.

Salang If you stopped at Tekek or Air Batang on the way, the small bay at Salang is likely to come as a surprise. The beach is beautiful, but the waterfront area is the most congested on the island. In terms of swimming and easy access to a variety of restaurants and activities, however, Salang is probably Tioman's best place to be based. It is also popular with divers. Ben's Diving Centre, run by a Malay guy who lived in Germany for several years and efficiently staffed by foreign instructors, is popular. The beach is about 700 metres long, and the jetty is towards the southern end.

The main places of interest to travellers are south of the jetty. *Khalid's Place* is a popular option. It's set back from the beach and has a nice garden, although it does get a bit of noise from the generator shed. Standard chalets cost RM25, or there are four-bed chalets for RM60, RM100 with air-con.

Across the small creek is another cluster of chalet outfits. *Nora's Chalets* has its reception and restaurant on the beach, but the chalets are actually back across the creek. Next along is the *Salang Inn*, with a row of rooms right along the path. They all have attached bath and cost RM25. Lastly there's *Zaid's*, which is one of the most popular with travellers. There are dorm beds in large A-frame chalets, as well as longhouse rooms. Prices range from RM20 to RM60.

The *Indah Salang* is the second place north of the jetty, and it sprawls along the beach for some distance. It has a big restaurant, bar and shop, and is pressing for resort status. There's a wide variety of accommodation, from basic bungalows for RM20 to RM30, four-bed chalets for RM30 to RM50, and four-bed air-con chalets for RM120.

The *Salang Beach Resort* is another resort-style operation with a Chinese restaurant and pricey chalets – RM40 with fan, or RM110 and upwards with air-con. In front of the resort is *Sunset Boulevard*, a restaurant/bar built on stilts over the water – it is the only bar on the island, apart from those at the resort.

At the end of the beach is *Ella's Hut* and *Salang Hut*, which both have restaurants and basic huts from RM25.

Juara Juara is less developed and quieter than most of the other beaches around Tioman. The beach is excellent, though the sea is very rough in the monsoon season. You can also arrange river trips and excursions to the nearby rubber plantation.

There are at least half a dozen places to stay, but even though costs are lower than elsewhere most of the old A-frames have been demolished to make way for basic chalets. Most chalets here average between RM15 and RM20, and some come with an attached bathroom.

Happy Cafe, right by the jetty, is a clean and tidy little establishment with A-frames and chalets. The cafe is good and there is a library for guests.

Atan's Cafe is similar, while the *Juara Mutiara Cafe* has some old longhouse rooms as well as chalets. Further south are older places such as *Din's*, *Sunrise Place* and *Rainbow Chalet*, the last of these being one of the cheaper options.

Paradise Point, just north of the jetty, is another good place. It has a good restaurant and new chalets.

Paya Paya is a few km south of the Berjaya Tioman Beach Resort. The beach is OK but nothing special. Most of the people coming to this beach are on package holidays, and costs are higher than elsewhere. The *Paya Beach Resort* (☎ 07-799 1432) has air-con rooms for RM90/110. A cheaper option is the *Paya Holiday Resort* with rooms from RM35. There are other accommodation options at the *Paya Village* and the upmarket *Paya Tioman Resort*.

Genting Very few travellers make it to Genting, and with good reason. There's little in the way of transport to other parts of the island, the beach is poor and tourist developments are aimed at attracting free-spending Singaporeans. There is some reasonably inexpensive accommodation about, but most of it is resort-style, complete with karaoke entertainment. Boats go to Genting from Mersing.

Nipah This is the place to stay if you really want to get away from it all. The beach is superb, with good snorkelling, and, apart from a couple of longhouse blocks that are only open during the holiday periods, there's only one place to stay.

It would be sensible to ring ahead to the *Nipah Beach Resort* (☎ 07-799 1012) if you want to stay at Nipah. Prices start at around RM30, but you may be able to bargain for something cheaper. Only the boats to and from Mersing stop here, by arrangement, and there are no trails to Nipah.

Getting There & Away

Air Silk Air and Pelangi Air have daily flights to/from Singapore for RM132 (S$99). Pelangi also flies daily to KL (four daily, RM125) and to Kuantan (daily, RM77). Berjaya is another small feeder airline, with daily flights to KL for the same price. The booking office for all air tickets is at the Berjaya Tioman Beach Resort.

Boat There are two east-coast entrances to Tioman. Most travellers get to Tioman from Mersing, but for those travelling south down the coast it is easier to get there from Tanjong Gemok, on the border of Pahang and Johor states, 38 km north of Mersing.

From Tanjong Gemok boats leave twice daily during peak season, at 9 am and 2 pm. The cost is RM25. Theoretically, the boat takes 1½ hours, but by the time it gets to Tekek (the terminus), after having docked at the resort and disgorged half the passengers, it is more likely to have taken two to 2½ hours. Boats from Tioman back to Tanjong Gemok leave at 11.30 am and 4.30 pm.

From Mersing there are a variety of services to Tioman, though sailing times vary according to the tide. Most boats nowadays are express services, taking around 1½ hours and costing RM25. They normally stop at Genting, Paya, the resort, Tekek, Air Batang (ABC) and Salang. Return tickets provide a RM5 discount.

The Mersing jetty is five minutes' walk from the town centre and you'll find the offices for boats to all the islands in this area.

Singapore There's a daily high-speed catamaran service between Singapore and Tioman. It departs from Singapore's World Trade Centre daily at 7.55 am, and from the Berjaya Tioman Beach Resort jetty at 1.30 pm. The trip takes 4½ hours and costs S$79/140 one-way/round-trip. Bookings can be made at the desk in the lobby of the Berjaya Tioman Beach Resort. In Singapore the office for bookings is Kalpin Tours (☎ 02-271 4866), 02-40 World Trade Centre. There are usually no sailings in the monsoon season, from October/November to 1 March.

Getting Around

Boat The Sea Bus service operates regular boats between the resort, Tekek, Air Batang and Salang. About five boats per day go in both directions. For example, boats leave Air Batang for Salang at 9.30, 10 and 11.30 am and 2.30 and 4.30 pm. Services are less frequent during the monsoon season. Tekek to Air Batang (or ABC as it appears on the schedules) or the resort is RM3, to Salang it's RM6. Air Batang to Salang is also RM6. Boats may leave up to 20 minutes before or after advertised, so it's a good idea to get to the ferry pier early. Tickets are available from agents at the jetties, or in restaurants. You can also pay on the boat, but don't expect them to change a RM50 note.

The Sea Bus also has a few other services: there's an around-the-island trip for RM30 and a Pulau Tulai (Coral Island) trip for RM20. The around-the-island trip leaves around 9 am and stops at most of the beaches and Kampung Asah, from where it is a 10 minute walk to the waterfall. It then goes on to Juara for lunch and then snorkelling at Teluk Dalum on the north-east side of the island. You can take this boat to travel between the beaches of the west coast of the island and Juara for RM15. The Coral Island boat drops you off in the morning and picks you up in the afternoon – bring your own snorkelling gear on either trip and a packed lunch for the Coral Island trip.

If you want to get to the southern beaches, ask the captain of the round-island boat to drop you off. But if you want to return you'll have to wait for one of the infrequent boats from Mersing, which may well mean staying overnight or longer.

Boat charter is expensive, costing between RM300 and RM400 per day.

The Coast

ENDAU TO KUANTAN

Endau

There's little of interest in Endau itself, but you can hire boats to make trips up the remote Endau River to the Endau-Rompin National Park and Orang Asli settlements in the interior.

It is possible to get about 110 km upriver in fair-sized boats, almost to Kampung Patah, which is the last village up the river. From there, smaller boats are required to negotiate the rapids into Orang Asli country. Smaller boats can be hired at Kampung Punan, about 100 km from Endau.

Boats to Tioman Island leave from the jetty on the north side of the river, which is known as Tanjong Gemok. See the Tioman Island Getting There & Away section above for more details.

Endau-Rompin National Park

At 870 sq km, Endau-Rompin is one of the largest national parks on the peninsula. It is Malaysia's last refuge of the Sumatran rhinoceros, though they only roam remote areas that are off limits to visitors. The park's lowland forests are among the only ones remaining in Malaysia and have been determined to harbour unique varieties of plant life.

There has been little development of tourist facilities at Endau-Rompin, which means that visiting the park on a budget and as an independent traveller is not easy. You will need to organise an entry permit, which can be obtained from the State Security Council, 2nd floor, Bangunan Sultan Ibrahim, Bukit Timbalan, Johor Bahru, and which costs RM20. It is also worth asking the tourist office in Kuantan about organising a permit in Kuantan.

Access to the park is via base camp, which is around 26 km from Felda Semendang. The latter can be reached by bus from Kuantan. Accommodation at base camp is provided by the Forestry Department. Maps are available at base camp, but officials here generally require that you hire a guide to explore the park.

The chief attractions of the park are the flora and fauna, river trips and some magnificent waterfalls. Rare animals in the forest include tigers, elephants and tapir. There are also various kinds of hornbills, as well as unique plant life such as the walking stick palm *(Phycorapis syngaporensis)* and the climbing bamboo *(Rhopa loblaste)*.

Getting There & Away Boats can be hired in Endau for around RM380 for a two to three day round-trip up the Endau River to the park. The park can also be reached by a rough road from Kahang on the Keluang-Mersing road, but a 4WD is necessary for the later sections of the road.

Currently, the easiest way to see the park is to take an organised trip. There are numerous agencies in Johor Bahru offering trips to the park, and the tourist information office in Kuantan also has tours for RM350 for two people, three days and two nights. The Watering Hole Bungalows in Kuala Rompin also have economical tours to Endau-Rompin. They cost RM280 per person all-inclusive for a five-day trip (minimum of four people; RM380 per person for three or less). They leave on Thursdays from the Watering Hole Bungalows in Kuala Rompin, but you need to get there a few days before so they can organise permits (photocopy of passport and three photos needed).

Kuala Rompin & Nenasi

Again there is nothing to see or do in Kuala Rompin, but with a 4WD vehicle you can go inland to Iban (10 km) and a further 25 km to Kampung Aur, where there are Orang Asli settlements. There's also a good place to stay close to town.

At Nenasi boats can be hired and you can go upriver to the Orang Asli village of Kampung Ulu Serai.

Places to Stay Three km south of town and two km off the main road is the very pleasant *Watering Hole Bungalows* (☎ 011-411894). It's a very quiet and isolated place – perfect if you want to do nothing for a few days. It's run by a Swiss-Malaysian couple and is kept very clean and neat. The beach here is nothing special but is perfectly OK for swimming. A-frame huts cost RM14 per person and there are small bungalows at RM20 per person, or with bath attached for RM30 per person. Dinner and breakfast are included in the price. The easiest way to get there is to wait at the Kuala Rompin bus station; they pick up from there daily at 2.30 and 5 pm (no need to ring).

Pekan

The royal town of Pahang state has a couple of well-built white-marble mosques and the sultan's palace, the modern and downright ugly **Istana Abu Bakar**. The *istana* is on the Kuantan edge of town.

Much more interesting is the **Museum Sultan Abu Bakar**, the state museum housed in a building built by the Brits for the local Resident. It has a wide variety of exhibits, although unfortunately much of the labelling is in Bahasa Malaysia only. Much of the museum is dedicated to the lives of the Pahang royal family, but there are also natural history, ceramics and tin-mining displays. In the shady garden there's a depressing mini-zoo, the sultan's old Cadillac, a 'traditional' kampung house (complete with non-traditional items such as a wind-up gramophone and a treadle sewing machine) and a houseboat once used on the river. The museum is open daily from 9.30 am to 5 pm, except Monday (closed) and Friday (9.30 am to 12.15 pm). Entry is RM1.

The **Pahang River**, crossed at this town by a lengthy bridge, is the longest river in Malaysia and was the last east-coast river to be bridged. At the river mouth on the other side is the small fishing village of Kuala Pahang.

A road follows the Pahang River to Chini, from where you can reach **Tasik Chini** (see the Around Kuantan section). Buses run along this road.

Silk weaving can be seen at **Kampung Pulau Keladi**, only about five km out of Pekan along the road to Tasik Chini. Silk is for sale at the centre, but it's by no means cheap. In the same area is the birthplace of Sultan Tun Abdul Razak (Tempat Lahir TAR), but the house is only a reconstruction of the original and is not all that interesting.

Places to Stay There's not much in the way of accommodation in Pekan, and most travellers visit as a day trip from Kuantan. The *Pekan Hotel*, close to the bus station at 60 Jalan Tengku Arif Bendahara, is a typical Chinese hotel with spartan rooms for RM15. The *Deyza Hotel* next door is similar.

Getting There & Away The bus station is right in the centre of town and buses run regularly between Kuantan and Pekan. Bus No 31 leaves approximately every 45 minutes from Kuantan. The taxi station is across the road on the bank of the river; destinations include Kuantan (RM5), Kuala Rompin (RM6), Mersing (RM12) and Chini (RM5.50).

KUANTAN

About midway up the east coast from Singapore to Kota Bharu, Kuantan is the capital of the state of Pahang and the start of the east-coast beach strip which extends all the way to Kota Bharu.

Kuantan is a well-organised, bustling city and a major stopover point when you are travelling north, south or across the peninsula. There's little of interest in Kuantan itself, but it's one of the more pleasant east-coast cities and there are a number of interesting places nearby.

Information

The tourist office (☎ 09-513 3026) is by the taxi station, opposite the Kompleks Terantum, Kuantan's biggest shopping complex and 22 storey office block.

The post office, Telekom office and most of the banks are on Jalan Mahkota near the huge and soaring Sultan Ahmed I mosque. The bookshop at 23 Jalan Mahkota is a licensed moneychanger and also has some English-language books. The immigration office (☎ 09-514 2155) is at Wisma Persekutuan on Jalan Gambut.

Mr Dobi is a laundromat at 128 Jalan Telok Sisek, near the Hotel New Meriah, and charges RM5 for a full-load wash and dry (they do the work).

Things to See

Take a stroll along the riverbank and watch the activity on the wide **Kuantan River**. From the jetty at the end of Jalan Masjid you can get a ferry across the river for about 50 sen to the small fishing village of **Kampung Tanjung Lumpur**.

The Kuantan area produces some good **handicrafts**, and there is a batik factory a few km from the town centre on the road to the airport. On Jalan Besar near the Samudra River View Hotel there are a number of shops selling local trinkets and craftwork. Bargain hard. For antiquities from China and South-East Asia, take your credit card to Golden Light Antiques, E-1486 Jalan Dato Wong Ah Jang.

The main **market** is held on Saturday, on the main road to the airport near the turn-off to Mersing, about four km from town.

Kuantan's major attraction is **Teluk Chempedak beach**, about four km from town. See the Around Kuantan section for details.

Places to Stay

Kuantan has dozens of cheap Chinese hotels and a few upmarket places, but the big international hotels are a few km out of town at Teluk Chempedak.

Places to Stay – bottom end

On Jalan Mahkota near the taxi station, the *Min Heng Hotel* (☎ 09-513 5885) is the cheapest in town at RM12/14 for singles/doubles. It's a classic Chinese cheapie – bare floorboards, wire-topped walls, *pintu pagar* (saloon doors) on the outside of the rooms and very basic.

The *Tong Nam Ah Hotel* (☎ 09-513 5204) on Jalan Besar near the taxi station is a good, cheap hotel with rooms for around RM15. Not far away, the *Hotel Baru Raya* (☎ 09-513 5334) is better but overpriced at RM29 for a room with fan, or RM39/49 with air-con. It is open 24 hours, which is convenient if you arrive on a night bus.

On Jalan Telok Sisek, between Jalan Merdeka and Jalan Bank, there are a number of cheap hotels. The *Hotel Moonlight* (☎ 09-554220), 50-52 Jalan Telok Sisek, has good balcony rooms with attached bath for RM15 and more expensive rooms with bath and

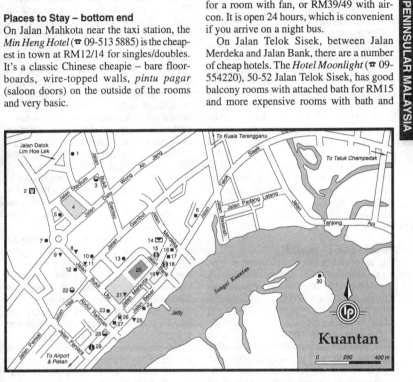

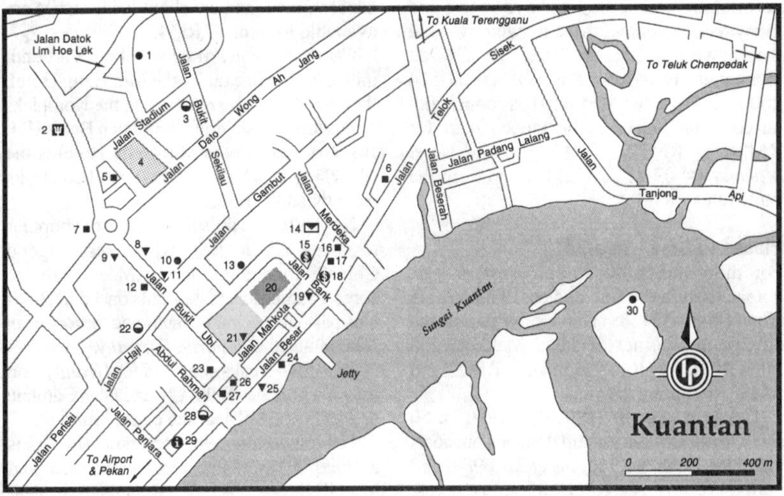

PLACES TO STAY
- 5 Hotel Makmur
- 6 Hotel New Meriah
- 7 Hotel Pacific
- 12 New Capitol Hotel
- 16 Suraya Hotel
- 17 Hotel Embassy
- 23 Min Heng Hotel
- 24 Samudra River View Hotel
- 26 Tong Nam Ah Hotel
- 27 Hotel Baru Raya

PLACES TO EAT
- 4 Central Market
- 8 Restoran Biryani
- 9 Restoran Parvathy
- 11 Grandy's
- 19 Tiki's Restoran
- 21 Food Stalls
- 25 Outdoor Food Stalls

OTHER
- 1 Stadium
- 2 Hindu Temple
- 3 Long-Distance Bus Station
- 10 MAS
- 13 Immigration
- 14 Post Office
- 15 Maybank
- 18 Standard Chartered Bank
- 20 Mosque Sultan Ahmed I
- 22 Local Bus Station
- 28 Taxi Station
- 29 Tourist Office
- 30 Kampung Tanjung Lumpur

air-con for RM30. A few doors along, the *Mei Lai Hotel* is noisy but clean and a good buy at RM12/14 for singles/doubles.

For a room with attached bath, the *New Capitol Hotel* (☎ 09-513 5222), 55 Jalan Bukit Ubi, is a good choice. It has spotless rooms for RM18, or RM30 with air-con.

The *Hotel New Meriah* (☎ 09-525 433) at 142 Jalan Telok Sisek is a good place in this range, with carpeted rooms with attached bath and occasional hot water for RM21/24. Rooms with air-con cost RM28/31 – it's good value.

Near the central market are two quite good hotels. They are cheaply put together by partitioning off the floors above shops, and many have no outward-facing windows, but their newness means they are clean and well appointed. The *Hotel Sri Intan* (☎ 09-514 2000), 13-15 Jalan Stadium, has rooms with air-con that works and attached bath for RM26 to RM32. Next door, the *Hotel Makmur* (☎ 09-514 1363) has rooms at the same rates.

Places to Stay – middle

For three-star, fully air-con western-style hotels, there are a few choices. The *Suraya Hotel* (☎ 09-554268) is in a busy part of the city, on the corner of Jalan Mahkota and Jalan Merdeka. It has rooms for RM75 and RM85, including taxes.

The *Hotel Pacific* (☎ 09-514 1980) at 60 Jalan Bukit Ubi is a step up the scale but costs much the same, with rooms at RM69/79 and deluxe rooms for RM79/85, plus taxes. Better again is the *Samudra River View Hotel* (☎ 09-555333), well located by the river on Jalan Besar. Standard rooms, all with air-con, bath, phone and TV, cost RM80, while deluxe rooms are RM100, plus taxes. Next door is the *Hotel Classic* (☎ 09-554599), with pleasantly decorated rooms from RM75 to RM105, including taxes.

Places to Eat

Kuantan has a good selection of eating places. The small Muslim food stalls dotted along the riverbank, across from the Hotel Baru Raya, are a great place to sit and watch the boats pass by. The seafood is particularly good and the prawns are huge, although expensive at RM8 each for the largest ones. Another good area for evening food stalls is Jalan Mahkota, not far from the mosque. There are more food stalls set up near the central market, with serve-yourself nasi padang places, and good Chinese seafood hotpot – select what you want and cook it in the vats of boiling water.

For breakfast, try *Tiki's Restoran* up the far end of Jalan Mahkota. It's only open during the day, and the two ever-busy brothers who run this place really welcome travellers. Western-style breakfasts, including a newspaper to read, and excellent local dishes are available for around RM4.

There are plenty of good bakeries around, including the one under the Min Heng Hotel, the *Terantum Bakery & Cafe* in the Kompleks Terantum, and several along Jalan Bukit Ubi. Just next door to the Min Heng Hotel is the *Min Heng Steakhouse*, where not bad steaks can be had for RM13 and up.

Not far from Tiki's Restoran is the popular *Restoran Cheun Kee*, which serves good Chinese food for around RM3. There are some good Indian restaurants on Jalan Bukit Ubi, past Jalan Gambut, including the *Restoran Biryani* and the *Restoran Parvathy*.

Fast-food freaks can head for *Grandy's* on the corner of Jalan Bukit Ubi and Jalan Gambut, or *KFC* or *A&W* near the central market.

For something more upmarket, *The Ark* is a floating restaurant serving western and local dishes, and is moored on the river near the end of Jalan Penjara.

Getting There & Away

Air Malaysia Airlines (☎ 09-515 7055) has direct flights to Singapore (four weekly, RM146), Kuching (weekly, RM233) and KL (five daily, RM74).

Pelangi Air (☎ 09-538 1177) has flights to Tioman Island (daily, RM77).

Bus All the bus companies have their offices on the 2nd floor of the enormous new express bus station on Jalan Stadium. Many operate the same routes, so it's usually simply a question of choosing the time that suits you.

Buses to KL (RM12.10, five hours) leave at least hourly from 7.30 am until 1 am. Buses to Mersing (RM11, three hours), Johor Bahru (RM16, five hours) and Singapore (RM16.50, seven hours) leave between 9 am and 1 pm, and then at 11 pm.

For Cherating, take the No 27 Kemaman bus from the local bus station for RM2.50. The trip takes about one hour. Buses go throughout the day to Kuala Terengganu (RM8, four hours) and Kota Bharu (RM16, six hours), and there are a couple of late-night buses. For Taman Negara, direct buses to Jerantut (RM8.50, three hours) leave between 9 am and 3 pm. Buses to Melaka (RM17.60, four hours) leave around 8 am and 2 pm. For Penang (RM26, 12 hours) there are two departures in the evening.

Taxi Taxis cost RM5 to Pekan, RM15 to Mersing and RM30 to Johor Bahru. Heading north it's RM6 to Kemaman or Cherating. To Kuala Terengganu it's RM15, or RM25 to Kota Bharu. Across the peninsula it's RM10 to Temerloh, RM15 to Jerantut, RM18 to Raub and RM20/25 to KL.

Car All the major car rental companies have offices in Kuantan.

Avis
  102 Jalan Telok Sisek (☎ 09-523666)
Budget
  59 Jalan Haji Abdul Aziz (☎ 09-526370)
Hertz
  Samudra Riverview Hotel, Jalan Besar
  (☎ 09-528041)
National
  49 Jalan Telok Sisek (☎ 09-527863)

AROUND KUANTAN

Teluk Chempedak

Kuantan's beach, bound by rocky headlands at each end, is quite pleasant, but there are better beaches on the peninsula. There are a number of walking tracks in the park area on the promontory.

Teluk Chempedak, which was a quiet little place until the early 70s, now has two international hotels and a row of bars, clubs and restaurants. The foreshore is paved and lined with shops, restaurants and food stalls. It's a popular promenade and meeting place in the evening and has the feel of a built-up European resort. On the Hyatt's beachfront is a small wooden junk which carried 162 Vietnamese boat people on their hazardous voyage to the west – it's now the Sampan Bar, where you can pay over the odds for a beer or Coke.

Places to Stay Teluk Chempedak is an upmarket accommodation alternative to Kuantan. There are no real budget hotels.

In the street behind the Hillview Hotel, the *Sri Pantai Bungalows* (☎ 09-525 250) has good, clean, carpeted rooms with fan for RM25, or with air-con for RM60; self-contained apartments cost RM80, and discounts are available off-season. There are plenty of other places in this street charging from RM20 for a room, but some are in a pretty dire state – just ask at a 'room to let' sign if you're interested.

Right behind the Hyatt is the ugly *Hotel Kuantan* (☎ 09-513 0026) with good fan-cooled rooms for RM44 and air-con rooms for RM66/77. Round on the main road there's the musty and ridiculously over-priced *Hillview Hotel* (☎ 09-521 555) with rooms for RM80.

The *Samudra Beach Resort* (☎ 09-513 5933) is a long walk around the promontory back towards Kuantan from the main beach, and at low tide the beach out the front is very shallow and sometimes dirty. Nonetheless, the motel rooms are very well appointed and it's the best mid-range accommodation in Teluk Chempedak. Rooms cost from RM65 and there's a restaurant.

The two top places are the *Hyatt Kuantan* (☎ 09-513 1234) and the adjacent *Merlin Kuantan* (☎ 09-514 1388), which together take up most of the beachfront. The Hyatt is suffering from a dose of concrete fade, but it has a far more impressive list of facilities than the Merlin. Most Hyatt rooms cost from RM245 to RM345, while the Merlin costs from RM210 upwards, all including taxes.

Places to Eat Food is one of Teluk Chempedak's main attractions – in fact it's about the only attraction. Apart from the food stalls at the end of the beach there's not much in the way of cheap eats. However, the beachfront restaurants are not as expensive as they look, and the food is generally excellent.

On the foreshore, *Pataya* and *Restoran Massafalah* are pleasant, open-air places specialising in seafood, though the air-con places on the main road are generally better value. Among these is the restaurant at the *Hillview Hotel*, which specialises in steamboat meals. The other air-con restaurants serve mostly Chinese seafood and Malay specialities. Dishes start from RM5 and go up to RM35 for a whole lobster.

Also worth checking out are the two pubs across the road from the Hilton on the road coming into the beach: *Checkers Pub* and *Country Ranch*. Both serve reasonably priced northern Indian cuisine, draft beer and other drinks. Checkers is the better of the two – Country Ranch is more about drinking than eating.

Getting There & Away The No 39 bus from Kuantan takes you to Teluk Chempedak for 60 sen. You can catch it at the local bus station or at the M3 bus stand on the corner of Jalan Mahkota and Jalan Masjid. In theory the buses are supposed to pull in to the stand facing Jalan Masjid, but in practice you have to stand on Jalan Mahkota and hail them down, 20 metres past the M2 bus stand. A taxi out to Teluk costs RM5.

Beserah

Just 10 km from Kuantan, the small fishing village of Beserah is a centre for handicrafts as well as a quiet place to kick back and relax for a few days. Crafts include batik, carvings and shell items from the village of Sungai Karang, a little further north. Kite flying, top spinning and other east-coast activities can occasionally be seen there. Batu Hitam is a good beach just north of Beserah.

Places to Stay & Eat A number of guesthouse operations have sprung up in recent years, though it is unlikely Beserah will ever be swarming with foreign visitors. A popular place to stay is *La Chaumiere* (09-544 7662). It has French management, is close to the beach and costs RM15 for bed and breakfast. If you are travelling by bus, get off at the Kampung Pantai Beserah stop, cross the road and go down the side street towards Kampung Pelidong, a distance of around 1.3 km. Alternatively, take a taxi from Kuantan for RM6.

At the other end of the beach is the *Beserah Beach Resthouse* (09-544 7492), which has similar rates to La Chaumiere but which is a much less pleasant place to be based. *Jaafar's Place* is a kampung house about half a km off the road on the inland side. A sign points it out and bus drivers know it. Accommodation costs RM8 a night, or RM15 including all meals. Facilities are very basic. Reactions to this place are varied – some travellers feel it's restful, easy-going and friendly, while others claim it's a 'pack-them-in rip-off' with 'bad food and zero facilities'. There's no denying that the places at Cherating, 40 km north, offer better value for money.

Getting There & Away Buses to Kemaman (No 27), Balok (No 30) and Sungai Karang (No 28) all pass through Beserah. They leave from the main bus station in Kuantan and the fare is 60 sen. Taxis from Kuantan cost RM6.

Berkelah Falls

The Berkelah Falls are about 50 km from Kuantan. The final six km of the trip involves a jungle trek from the main road. The falls come down a hillside in a series of eight cascades. The Marathandhavar Temple is the venue for a major Hindu festival in March or April each year.

Getting There & Away Catch a bus to Maran from the main bus station for RM3.35. At Maran, you'll see a bridge by the river. This is where the walk to the falls begins (there is a sign indicating the direction). The jungle track is overgrown due to lack of use and maintenance. The walk takes about three hours.

Gua Charas (Charas Caves)

Twenty-six km north of Kuantan at Panching, the limestone outcrop containing the Charas (also spelt Charah) caves rises sheer from the surrounding palm plantations. The caves owe their fame to a Thai Buddhist monk who came to meditate here about 50 years ago. There's a monk in residence, and the caretaker's wife can tell you about the caves.

It's a steep climb up an external stairway to the caves' entrance. In the more enclosed cave there's a nine-metre-long reclining Buddha carved from solid rock, and other Buddhist statuary. Once a year in July, sunlight penetrates the cave and illuminates the head of the reclining Buddha.

Admission is RM1. The caves are lit, but bring a torch to explore the side caverns, or you can hire one for RM2.

Three km before Panching is a turn-off that leads to the airport and the Pandan waterfalls, five km from the main road.

Getting There & Away Take the Sungai Lembing bus (No 48) from the main bus station in Kuantan and get off at the small village of Panching. From the bus stop in town it's a hot four km walk each way, but there's usually someone visiting the caves who will stop and offer you a lift. Traffic is heaviest on Sunday. The alternative is to hire someone in Panching to give you a lift on the back of their motorcycle for around RM2.

Sungai Lembing

This old tin-mining town boasted the world's longest underground tin mine until it went into receivership after the collapse of tin prices in the late 80s. There's talk of opening the mine as a tourist attraction, but at the moment it is still closed. There are a few old colonial buildings, but otherwise there's not really much to see. Sungai Lembing is about 25 km past Panching and can be reached by bus No 48.

If you have your own 4WD vehicle, you can make a 16 km side trip from Sungai Lembing to **Gunung Tapis Park**. This park is noted for its rapids, hot springs and fishing. The park is not developed, but there are plenty of good spots for camping. Arrangements can be made through the tourist information office in Kuantan.

Tasik Chini

Turn south from the Temerloh road 56 km west of Kuantan, and 12 km from the turn-off is Kampung Belimbing, the main access point for Tasik Chini. From there you can hire a boat to cross the Pahang River and go through the jungle up the Chini River to the lotus-covered expanse of Tasik Chini.

The lake is in fact a series of 12 lakes, and around its shores live the Jakun people, an Orang Asli tribe of Melayu Asli origin. The Jakun believe that the spirit of the lake is the serpent Naga Seri Gumum, which translates in the tourist literature as 'Loch Ness monster'.

Although getting to Tasik Chini is not that easy, it's well worth the effort. It's a beautiful area and you can walk for miles in jungle territory. There is a very low-key resort, or you can stay at the nearby Orang Asli village of Kampung Gumum and use it as a base from which to make jungle treks.

Places to Stay & Eat The *Lake Cini Resort* (09-456 7897), on the southern shore of the lake, has good cabins with attached bathroom from RM77 for doubles. Some cabins are also set aside for dormitory accommodation – a bed in a 10 bed cabin costs RM18.50. Outside school holidays you may well have a dormitory to yourself.

The restaurant at the resort serves simple food for RM4 to RM6 per dish. Accommodation, food and equipment rental are subject to a 10% service charge.

A much cheaper option is *Rajan Jones Guest House* in the Orang Asli settlement of Kampung Gumum, a two minute boat ride from the resort or a 30 minute walk. Rajan is in fact of Indian descent (making him Indian Jones?), but he speaks excellent English and is knowledgeable about the Orang Asli. Accommodation is extremely basic – there's no electricity or running water in the village – but it's a rare opportunity to stay near the jungle and make expeditions into it. The cost is RM15 per person including dinner and breakfast. Rajan organises overnight jungle treks, canoeing, fishing and night hikes. There's also a chance of seeing a traditional 'healing ceremony', in which the local witch doctor does his stuff. These ceremonies are still practised – they are not just for the tourists' benefit.

Getting There & Away Tasik Chini can be reached by boat from Belimbing or by road from Pekan, but both ways are difficult by public transport.

The tourist information stand in Kuantan can arrange day trips to Tasik Chini for RM50 per person, but the cheapest tours are from Cherating at RM35 per person.

From Kuantan you can catch a bus to Maran and get off at the Tasik Chini turn-off, from where it's 12 km to Kampung Belimbing. You will have to hitch or walk, as bus services to Belimbing no longer operate. Traffic on this road is light.

From Belimbing you can hire a boat to Tasik Chini. The cost is RM40 per boat for a two hour trip, including a tour of the lakes and a visit to an Orang Asli village. The price is the same if you just want to be dropped at the resort or Kampung Gumum. A boat can take four people.

The alternative is to take a bus to Felda Chini, south of the lake, from Kuantan or Pekan. The Mara No 121 buses marked 'Cini' leave Kuantan's bus station five times daily, cost RM5.70 and take two hours. It's two km from Felda Chini to the palm-oil factory, and a further 11 km (although the sign says eight) from the intersection there to the resort, on a sealed road. Without a car, the only way to get to the resort or Kampung Gumum is by hiring someone with a motorcycle to take you there for about RM5, or by walking or hitching (very little traffic). If you stay at the resort, they can drop you at Kampung Chini when you leave.

For a group of four, a taxi from Kuantan is another option. The cost is RM60 to the resort or Kampung Gumum. If you want the latter, tell the taxi driver you want to go to the Tasik Chini Orang Asli kampung. A taxi from Kuala Rompin costs RM80.

BESERAH TO CHERATING

There are small resorts along this stretch of coast offering good mid to upper-range accommodation. The sheltered beaches are quite good but the water is very shallow when the tide is out.

North of Beserah, the small island of Ular, 'Snake Island', is only a short distance offshore and easily reached by a local fishing boat. It's then only a couple of km north to the kampung of Cherating, a very popular backpackers' centre.

Places to Stay

The *Gloria Maris Resort* (☎ 09-544 7788) is 9.5 km from Kuantan, one km past Beserah. Chalets on the beach cost from RM70. Further along, 14 km from Kuantan, is the village of Balok and *Le Village* (☎ 09-544 7900), a new, small resort. Good chalets with bath and air-con cost from RM90 including taxes. If you want a beach view, the cheapest chalets are RM130. There is a pool and a good restaurant, and they rent bicycles.

Further out, 16 km from Kuantan, is the large *Coral Beach Resort* (☎ 09-544 7544). It is approaching international standard and costs RM190/220 for internal-facing rooms and RM230/250 for rooms facing the beach, all including taxes.

CHERATING

Along with Tioman and the Perhentian islands, Cherating is one of the most popular pit stops on the east coast. A travellers' kampung, complete with budget shacks by the sea, a handful of bars, some good restaurants with banana-pancake breakfasts and a reasonable beach with windsurfer breezes, Cherating is as close as the east coast gets to southern Thailand.

Many people visiting Cherating settle down and stay for weeks. Cherating has a long stretch of beach, which is not exactly pristine but is good for swimming. There are also the secluded bays just to the north, and at certain times of the year turtles come ashore to lay their eggs at Chendor Beach, right by Club Mediterranée. You cannot walk along the beach to Chendor, due to the rocky headland, but word spreads quickly if the turtles come ashore and you may be able to arrange a lift.

Cherating is a good base from which to explore the surrounding area. You can arrange mini-treks and river trips, and most of the places to stay can arrange tours to Tasik Chini (RM35); Gua Charas, Sungai Lembing and Pandan Falls (RM30); and Pulau Ular.

Information

There's no bank in Cherating, but you can change money (at a poor rate) and also make international phone calls at the Checkpoint Cherating shop on the beach road.

Places to Stay

Accommodation ranges from basic A-frame huts, each with a double mattress and light, but no fan, to more comfortable 'chalets' with bathrooms. Most of the A-frame huts cost around RM10 and sleep two people; the chalets range from RM15 to RM50. Most of

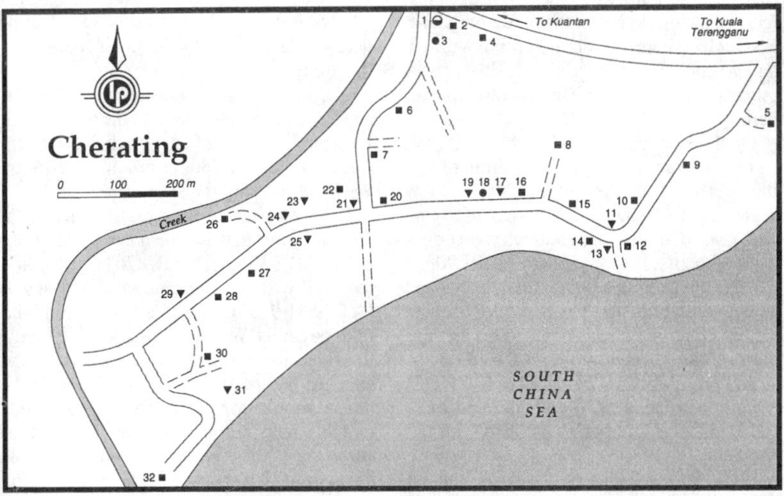

PLACES TO STAY		
2	Mak Long Teh's Homestay	
4	Mak De's Homestay	
5	The Moon	
6	Maznah's Guest House	
7	Matahari Chalets	
8	Sunshine Resort	
9	Residence Inn Cherating	
10	Spag'n Resort	
12	Duyong Beach Resort	
14	Cherating Mini Motel	
15	Cherating Inn Chalets	
16	Ranting Holiday Resort	
20	Cherating Cottage	
22	Riverside Beach Huts	
26	Green Leaves Inn	
27	Coconut Inn	
28	Tanjung Inn	
30	Kampung Inn	
32	Cherating Bayview Resort	

PLACES TO EAT

- 11 B&R Restaurant
- 13 Pop In Steakhouse & Pub
- 17 Mimi's
- 19 Lianee Cafe
- 21 Restoran Riverside
- 23 Payung Cafe
- 24 Blue Lagoon Restoran
- 25 Evening Food Stalls
- 29 Sayang Restaurant
- 31 Driftwood Restaurant

OTHER

- 1 Bus Stop
- 3 Handicraft Centre
- 18 Checkpoint Cherating

the places have their own restaurants and you can easily spend a few days in Cherating and not sample them all.

On the main road are two of the longest-running homestays – *Mak Long Teh's* and *Mak De's*. Mak De's charges RM7, while Mak Teh's charges RM12 per person for accommodation, breakfast and dinner. Both places are less popular than they once were, which is hardly surprising given their proximity to the busy main road.

One of the best places for an extended stay is the *Matahari Chalets* (09-581 9126) on the road between the beachfront and the main road. Large rooms with balcony, fridge (yes, fridge), mosquito net and fan are a bargain at RM12/15. There's a common room with TV and a kitchen for guests' use. It's a very relaxed place and you can do batik courses here.

On the other side of the beach road there's a group of three places, all with similar facilities and all good. The *Coconut Inn* has a few basic A-frame chalets for RM15 with fan, and RM25/30 with fan and bath. Next door is the attractive *Tanjung Inn* (☎ 09-581 9081). Chalets are sited in a pleasant lawn area and chalets with bath and fan cost RM40; there are also family chalets for RM60. The third place is the *Kampung Inn* (☎ 09-439 344), set in a pretty coconut grove. The chalets cost RM15 with fan, RM20 with fan and bath, and RM30 for a larger room, also with fan and bath.

Right on the banks of the river, and set right in among low trees, is the cosy and rustic *Green Leaves Inn*. The few chalets here are very small and the facilities quite basic, but it's still popular. There's also a small restaurant.

On the same side of the road is the *Payung Cafe*, also on the riverbank. There are a few chalets around a large lawn, and these are quite good at RM15.

Next along on the same side of the road is the *Riverside Beach Huts*. It's a friendly place and has chalets with fan for RM20, and with air-con for RM60.

The *Cherating Cottage* was expanding its operations at the time of writing and, as well as basic rooms for RM15 (shared bath) and chalets with bath for RM25, it plans to offer air-con chalets for RM60.

Towards the northern end of the beach road is the *Ranting Holiday Resort* (☎ 09-581 9068). This place is geared more towards Singaporean and Malaysian holiday-makers than to foreign travellers; chalets range from RM50 with fan to RM70 with air-con. The *Sunshine Resort*, along a dirt track next to the Ranting, is uninspired and best avoided.

A better choice is the *Cherating Inn Chalets* (☎ 010-987-9734), which has basic single chalets with fan for RM30 and RM50 with two beds. Across the road is the *Cherating Mini Motel*. It's in a fairly sad state of decay and not worth the RM35 it charges for the grotty chalets.

The mid-range *Duyong Beach Resort* (☎ 09-581 9335) is the last place on the beach road. It's a bit of a resort affair, with chalets ranging from RM40 to RM80; prices go up 10% on weekends and holidays.

If you continue up the road from here, past the monstrous new *Residence Inn Cherating* (☎ 09-581 9333 – from RM201), you come to a trail with a sign pointing to *The Moon* (☎ 09-581 9186). This place is set amid the trees on a hill ('We look down on Club Med', the flyer announces), and has chalets with attached bathroom for RM30/35 and longhouse rooms for RM10/20; weekly and monthly rates are also available. The main attraction is the *Deadly Nightshade Bar & Restaurant*, which usually has a couple of foreigners working in it. It's a unique place.

One of the better mid-range places is at the opposite (southern) end of the beach. The *Cherating Bayview Resort* (☎ 09-581 9248) has good chalets for RM70 on weekdays and RM80 on weekends, and air-con chalets back from the beach a bit for RM100 and RM120 respectively.

To the north of Cherating is the large (325 rooms) and securely guarded *Club Mediterranée* (☎ 09-591 131). This was the first Club Med holiday resort in Asia, and the majority of people who stay there come to Malaysia from Europe or Australia on all-inclusive package deals. However, if you've always wanted to try a Club Med there are often short-stay packages offered in Malaysia. Regular cost? Over RM1000 a week.

There are also a couple of new resorts just a few km south of Cherating and 38 km north of Kuantan. The *Cherating Holiday Villa Beach Resort* (☎ 09-581 9500) has its rooms arranged around a small pool set back a short distance from the beach. All rooms have air-con, in-house videos, IDD phones and minibars. Deluxe rooms are the cheapest and cost RM165/185, and there are suites from RM220, including taxes.

Just a km or so away is the *Palm Grove Beach Resort* (☎ 09-581 9439), with rooms from RM240/280 including taxes. All rooms have beach views, but the place lacks any local character as the design is pretty uninspiring.

Places to Eat

Most guesthouses have their own restaurants, but there are also a few other restaurants in Cherating, all within easy walking distance of each other. The *Sayang Restaurant* does good Indian food, and *Mimi's*, at the opposite end of the beach, is a popular place. The *Payung Cafe* is a good place for spaghetti and goulash in the evening.

For Chinese and Malay food, there are the *Lianee Cafe*, the *Restoran Riverside*, the *Blue Lagoon Restoran* and the *Moonlight Lagoon* restaurants on the beach road. All four of them offer similar dishes and prices.

The *Driftwood Restaurant* on the beachfront near the Kampung Inn is a good place for both a beer and a meal. If some travellers find dishes like the lasagne and pizza a little overpriced, there's still no denying that it's the best western food in town. Driftwood is open only in the evening. Another evening eating option is the food stalls which are set up beside the road opposite the Payung Cafe.

Getting There & Away

To get to Cherating, catch a bus marked 'Kemaman' from the main bus station in Kuantan. Buses leave every hour, the fare is RM2.50 and the journey takes one hour. When coming from the north, any bus going to Kuantan will drop you on the main road. From Cherating to Kuantan, wave down a bus to Kuantan from the bus stop outside Mak Long Teh's.

Central Pahang

TAMAN NEGARA NATIONAL PARK

Peninsular Malaysia's great national park covers 4343 sq km and sprawls across the states of Pahang, Kelantan and Terengganu. The part of the park most visited is in Pahang.

Taman Negara is billed, perhaps wrongly, as a wildlife park. Certainly this magnificent wilderness area is a haven for endangered species such as elephants, tigers, panthers and rhinos, but numbers are low and sightings of anything more exotic than snakes, lizards, monkeys, small deer and perhaps tapir are rare. The birdlife is prolific, however, and chances are you'll see more insects – many at extremely close quarters – than you've ever seen in your life.

Taman Negara is not wide open savanna as in African game parks, and the jungle is so dense that you could pass within metres of an animal and never know it. Chances of spotting wildlife are greatest if you do an extended trek away from the heavily trafficked park headquarters, but sightings are never guaranteed.

For this reason, many travellers come away disappointed, but the greatest reward of a visit to Taman Negara is simply the chance to get out into one of the most pristine primary rainforests still existing in the world. The jungle here is claimed to be the oldest in the world, having existed largely as is for the past 130 million years. None of the ice ages affected this part of the world, and it has also been free of volcanic activity and other geological upheavals.

The 60 km boat trip from Kuala Tembeling to Kuala Tahan (park HQ) takes two to three hours, depending on the level of the river. You reach the park boundary near Kuala Atok, 35 km from Kuala Tembeling.

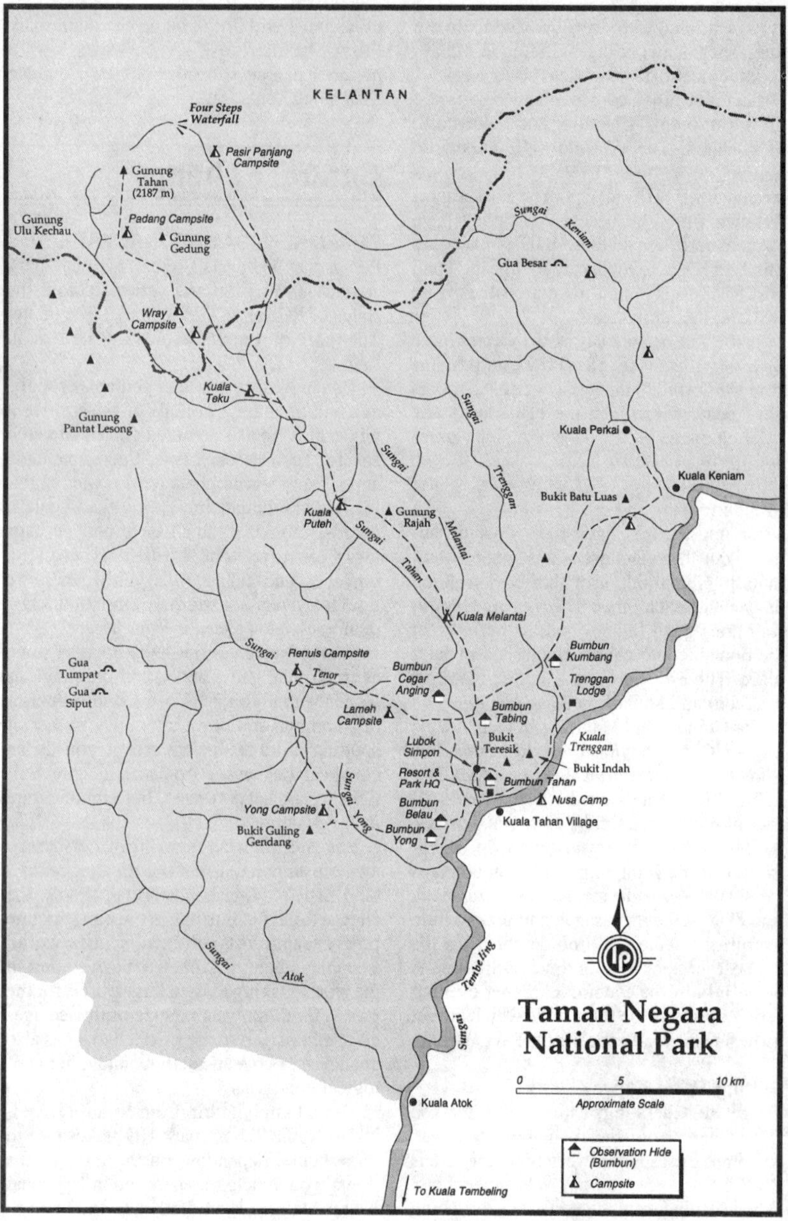

KELANTAN
Four Steps Waterfall
Pasir Panjang Campsite
Gunung Tahan (2187 m)
Padang Campsite
Gunung Ulu Kechau
Gunung Gedung
Wray Campsite
Kuala Teku
Gunung Pantat Lesong
Sungai Keniam
Gua Besar
Sungai Trenggan
Kuala Perkai
Kuala Keniam
Bukit Batu Luas
Sungai Tahan
Kuala Puteh
Gunung Rajah
Sungai Melantai
Kuala Melantai
Sungai Tenor
Renuis Campsite
Gua Tumpat
Gua Siput
Bumbun Cegar Anging
Bumbun Kumbang
Trenggan Lodge
Lameh Campsite
Bumbun Tabing
Kuala Trenggan
Lubok Simpon
Bukit Teresik
Bukit Indah
Resort & Park HQ
Bumbun Tahan
Nusa Camp
Sungai Yong
Yong Campsite
Bumbun Belau
Kuala Tahan Village
Bukit Guling Gendang
Bumbun Yong
Sungai Atok
Sungai Tembeling
Taman Negara National Park
0 5 10 km
Approximate Scale
Kuala Atok
Observation Hide (Bumbun)
Campsite
To Kuala Tembeling

Along the river, you'll see several Orang Asli kampungs, domestic water buffalo and the local fishing people. You might also see monkeys, otters, kingfishers and hornbills from the boat. It's a beautiful journey.

The best time to visit the park is in the dry season between February and September, though the park is now open during the rainy season, when it doesn't always rain and the number of visitors drops dramatically. The peak season for visitors is from April to August.

Entrance to the park costs RM1, and a camera permit is RM5. A fishing licence costs RM10. These you get at the office at the Kuala Tembeling jetty. If you are driving there's a free undercover car park here too.

Orientation & Information

The park headquarters and the privately run Taman Negara Resort are at Kuala Tahan. The Wildlife Department and the resort jointly operate a counter at the resort's reception area, open 8 am to 10 pm. On arrival, you must register at this counter before heading off into the park or to other accommodation outside the park. You can get a sketch map of the park and information here, or at the Department of Wildlife office next door.

Facilities at Kuala Tahan include chalets, a hostel, a campground, a restaurant, a cafeteria and a shop selling a range of tinned foods, toiletries, batteries and snacks – all at inflated prices. Camping, hiking and fishing gear can be hired from the campground office past the shop.

Every night at 8.45 pm a free slide show is held in the Interpretive Centre near the cafeteria. Boats or a guide for trekking can be arranged at the Wildlife Department office or at the resort, which also offers activities such as a night jungle walk (RM15), cave trip (RM35), rapid shooting (RM25) and a 'kampung experience' (RM35). At the resort you can also change money (lousy rate) and make phone calls (expensive).

The kampung of Kuala Tahan, directly across the Tembeling River from the park HQ, also has a couple of cheaper shops, cafes moored on the river and a selection of budget accommodation. The only other places with organised accommodation (other than the hides, see below) are Nusa Camp, about 15 minutes by boat up the Tembeling River from the park HQ, and lodges at Kuala Trenggan, Kuala Keniam and Kuala Perkai.

Although everyday clothes are quite suitable around Kuala Tahan, be well prepared if heading further afield. Lightweight cotton clothing is ideal. Loose-fitting, long trousers are better than shorts and protect legs against scratches and insect bites. Whatever you wear, you will soon be drenched in sweat and covered in mud. Take a water bottle, even on short walks, and on longer walks take water purifying tablets to sterilise stream water.

Good boots are essential. Lightweight, canvas jungle boots cost RM2.50 per day from the campground office and lace up high to help keep out leeches. Sleeping bags, tents, cooking gear, flashlights etc can also be hired for trekking or overnighting in a hide.

River travel in the early morning hours can be surprisingly cold. Mosquitoes can be annoying, but you can buy repellent at the park shop.

Leeches are generally not a major problem, although they can be a real nuisance after heavy rain. There are many ways to keep these little blood-suckers at bay – mosquito repellent, tobacco, salt, toothpaste and soap can all be used, with varying degrees of success. A liberal coating of insect spray over shoes and socks works best.

The Department of Wildlife puts out an excellent booklet entitled *An Illustrated Guide in the Kuala Tahan Region of Taman Negara*. Though a little dated, it gives a good overview of flora and fauna of the park, and includes detailed trail descriptions. It is available only at the registration office at Kuala Tembeling – if they get around to printing more.

A much more comprehensive description of the park (complete with trail maps) appears in the book *Parks of Malaysia* by John Briggs (1991), available in some bookshops in Malaysia.

Hides & Salt Licks

Taman Negara has several readily accessible hides *(bumbun)*, many close to Kuala Tahan and Kuala Trenggan. All hides are built overlooking salt licks and grassy clearings, which attract feeding nocturnal animals. There's a chance of spotting tapir, wild boar or deer, but sightings of elephant and other large game are extremely rare. Chances of seeing wildlife will increase if you head for the hides furthest from park HQ. If you're staying overnight, you need to take your food and a sleeping bag. Hides are very rustic with pit toilets. They cost RM5 per person per night and sleep seven or eight people. It pays to book at the Wildlife office the day before. Tabing and Kumbang are the most popular hides with the highest chances of seeing wildlife.

Even if you're not lucky enough to see any wildlife, the fantastic sounds of the jungle are well worth the time and effort taken to reach the hides. The 'symphony' is at its best at dusk and dawn.

A powerful torch is necessary to see any animals that wander into the salt-lick area. It's best to arrange shifts where one person stays awake, searching the clearing with a torch every 10 to 15 minutes, while everyone else sleeps until it's their turn to take over.

Rats can be a problem at some of the hides. They search for food during the night and have been known to move whole bottles of cooking oil (one of their favourite treats) from hides to their nests. Either hang food high out of reach, or, as one traveller suggested, leave some in the centre of the floor so you can see them – some of the rats are gigantic.

Bumbun Tahan This is an artificial salt lick less than five minutes' walk from the reception building. It's a clearing which has been planted with pasture grass and there's a waterhole nearby. This close to the resort, there's little chance of seeing any animals apart from monkeys.

Bumbun Belau & Bumbun Yong These hides on the Yong River sleep eight people and have water nearby. It takes about 1½ hours to walk to Bumbun Belau from the park HQ, and you can visit Gua Telinga (see below) along the way. From Belau it's less than half an hour to Bumbun Yong. Both can also be reached by the riverboat service.

Bumbun Tabing The hide at this natural salt lick is about a one hour walk from Kuala Tahan, and is equipped with a toilet and *tempat mandi* (bathing area). Nearby, there's a river with fairly clean water (though it should be boiled before drinking).

Bumbun Kumbang You can either walk to Bumbun Kumbang (about seven hours from Kuala Tahan) or take the riverboat service up the Tembeling River to Kuala Trenggan. The boat journey from Kuala Tahan takes about 35 minutes, and then it's a 45 minute walk to the hide. The animals seen there most commonly are tapir, rats, monkeys and gibbons, but the odd elephant has also been seen.

Bumbun Cegar Anjing Once an airstrip, this is now an artificial salt lick established to attract wild cattle and deer. A nice clear river runs a few metres from the hide. Bumbun Cegar Anjing is 1½ hours' walk from Kuala Tahan, but after rains it may only be accessible by boat.

Mountains & Walks

The major activity at Taman Negara is walking through the magnificent jungle. There's a wide variety of walking and trekking possibilities – from an hour's stroll to nine arduous days.

The trails around the park headquarters allow quick access to the jungle but are heavily trafficked. However, relatively few visitors venture far beyond the headquarters, and the longer walks are far less trammelled. A long day-walk will take you away from the madding crowd. Getting well away from it all requires a few days' trekking and/or expensive trips upriver by boat.

Short Walks from Kuala Tahan Trails around park HQ are easy to follow. They are signposted and have approximate walking times marked clearly along the way. If you're interested in birdlife, it's best to start walking before 8 am.

Heading out past the chalets and cafeteria, the Bukit Indah trail leads along the Tembeling River to the **Canopy Walkway**, suspended 25 metres above the ground between massive trees and allowing closer inspection of the higher reaches of the forest. It is open daily except Fridays from 11 am to 3 pm and costs RM2.

From behind the canopy walkway a trail leads to **Bukit Teresik**, from the top of which are fine views across the forest. The trail is steep and slippery in parts but quite easily negotiated and takes about an hour up and back. You can descend back down this trail to the resort or, back near the Canopy Walkway, a branch trail leads across to **Lubok Simpon**, a swimming area on the Tahan River, from where it is an easy stroll back to park HQ. The entire loop can easily be done in three hours.

Past the Canopy Walkway, another branch off the main trail leads to **Bukit Indah**, another steep but rewarding hill with fine views across the forest and the rapids in the Tembeling River.

The well-marked main trail along the bank of the Tembeling River leads nine km to **Kuala Trenggan**. This is a popular trail for those heading to the Bumbun Kumbang hide. You need to set out early and allow five hours. Though generally flat, it traverses a few small hills before reaching the Trenggan

The Future of Taman Negara

First established as a preservation area in 1937, Taman Negara is Malaysia's oldest and most prestigious national park. However, the largest protected area of primary rainforest on the peninsula is coming under increasing scrutiny. Promoted internationally as a wildlife haven and *the* place to experience the jungle in Malaysia, many doubt that the park can withstand the onslaught.

Since the park accommodation was privatised in 1991 and facilities upgraded, visitor numbers have more than doubled to over 40,000 per year. The effects are very noticeable. Where once large animals roamed right up to park headquarters, sightings are now rare and the effective animal-habitat area of the park has decreased. Trails around park HQ are up to four metres wide and suffer from erosion due to the number of walkers.

With all the increased traffic putting strains on the park, there has been much talk of how to best preserve Taman Negara and cater to increasing visitor interest.

The uneasy mix of privatisation and government control has been blamed for many of the problems, but it is only one of many factors affecting Taman Negara. Improved facilities and easier access has attracted many more visitors, but only a small percentage venture far beyond park HQ or the Tembeling River. The resort also provides needed local employment, and increased wealth from tourism in the area, along with stiff government penalties, has helped eliminate poaching by villagers.

Lack of government funding and understaffing means that the remoter parts of the park are largely beyond the control of the Wildlife Department. Taman Negara is home to perhaps 600 elephants and a high percentage of Malaysia's estimated 300 tigers, which are increasingly being pushed towards the Kelantan and Terengganu borders, but no one really knows because there is little or no monitoring of wildlife numbers or movement in the park.

Poachers, attracted by the illicit trade in rare species and the high price of ivory and tiger bones, enter the park from the north. Poaching is largely blamed on Thais, but policing is difficult and few poachers are caught. The Orang Asli who live within the park are also allowed to hunt and continue their traditional nomadic lifestyle, but their impact is relatively low.

Problems not only exist within the park but also outside it. Once animals would roam beyond the park boundaries into neighbouring districts, but increasing settlement along the park boundaries is eliminating this buffer zone, driving the animals further into the interior.

Answers to the park's problems are not easy to find, and solutions even harder to implement. At a recent conference, one suggestion was to completely privatise the park, though it was probably designed to highlight the problems facing the Wildlife Department and spur the government to allocate more resources. Restricting access, by introducing quotas or raising prices, also seems unpalatable. Taman Negara is one of Malaysia's major tourist attractions. Not only does it provide foreign income but it is an important educational resource for Malaysians increasingly aware of the ecology and natural beauty of their own wilderness areas. ■

River, where Trenggan Lodge lies on the other side. From the lodge boats go back to Nusa Camp and Kuala Tahan, or it's a further two km walk to **Bumbun Kumbang**. An alternative, longer trail leads inland back across the Trenggan River from Bumbun Kumbang to the campsite at Lubuk Lesong on the Tahan River and then back to park HQ. This trail is flat most the way and crosses many small streams. Count on six hours from the hide. Check with park HQ for river levels – the Trenggan River can only be forded when levels are low.

Gua Telinga is a cave south-west of the park HQ, and it takes about 1½ hours to walk there, after first crossing the Tahan River by sampan. There is a stream through the cave and a rope to guide you for the 80 metres (bring a torch). It's a strenuous half-hour walk – and crawl – through the cave, and there's plenty of bat shit which can't be avoided! You can either return to the main path through the cave, or take the path around the rocky outcrop at the far end of the cave. Once back at the main path, it's a further 15 minutes' walk to the Bumbun Belau hide, where you can spend the night, or walk directly back to Kuala Tahan.

Heading north through the campground at Kuala Tahan, the trail leads all the way to Gunung Tahan, but you can do an easy day walk to **Lata Berkoh**, the cascading rapids on the Tahan River. The trail passes Lubok Simpon swimming hole and Bumbun Tabing, 1¼ hours from Kuala Tahan. About 15 minutes further is the turn-off to Lata Berkoh. Frequent boats also run to just below the cascades.

Short Walks from Nusa Camp If you are staying at Nusa Camp there's a couple of interesting walks in the vicinity, outside the park. Abai Waterfall is only an hour's walk along a clear trail, and it's a great spot for a swim.

Gunung Warisan is a small peak devoid of trees a couple of hours' walk from the camp. It's an excellent walk in the very early morning, but it gets hot in the afternoon as there is no shade.

Longer Treks The shortest of the longer treks is **Rentis Tenor** (Tenor Trail), which takes three days from Kuala Tahan. It's quite popular, but the trail is not always clear and a guide is needed. The first day involves getting a boat across the Tahan River at park HQ and then taking the trail to Gua Telinga and beyond for about seven hours to Yong campsite. The second day is a six hour walk to the Renuis campsite. On the third day you have to cross the Tahan River (up to waist deep) to get back to Kuala Tahan. It's about a six hour walk. Or you can stop for another night at the Lameh campsite, about half way.

Another popular walk is the trail from Kuala Trenggan to **Kuala Keniam**. It is normally done by chartering a boat to Kuala Keniam and then walking back to Kuala Trenggan. Taking at least six hours, the trail is quite taxing and hilly in parts, and passes a series of limestone caves. This walk can be combined with one of the Kuala Tahan-Kuala Trenggan trails to form a two day trip, overnighting in the Trenggan Lodge or Bumbun Kumbang. It is also possible to walk from Kuala Keniam to the lodge at Kuala Perkai, an easy two hour walk.

The trek for the really adventurous is the ascent of **Gunung Tahan** (2187 metres, the highest peak in Peninsular Malaysia), 55 km from park HQ. It takes nine days at a steady pace, although it can be done in seven. A guide is compulsory and the resort organises trips for eight people costing RM638, or RM680 for 12 people. This trek is certainly no picnic, but those who do it say it is well worth the effort. Guides and equipment can be arranged at park HQ, although it is generally better to organise this trek in advance so you don't have to hang around park HQ for a couple of days, which is often the case. There are no shelters along the way, so you have to be fully equipped. For camping near the summit of Tahan you'll need a lightweight sleeping bag, blanket or tracksuit to sleep in.

Fishing

Anglers will find the park a real paradise. Fish found in the park rivers include the superb fighting fish known in India as the mahseer but here as the kelasa.

Popular fishing rivers include the Tahan River, the Keniam River (above Kuala Trenggan) and the remote Sepia River. The best fishing months are February, March, July and August. A fishing permit costs RM10 and hiring a rod costs RM5 per day.

Boat Trips

The easiest and least expensive way of getting around the park by river is the river-bus service, which has scheduled departures to Kuala Trenggan, Bumbun Belau and Bumbun Yong from Kuala Tahan and Nusa Camp (see Getting Around below for details). Otherwise boats can be chartered from park HQ or Kuala Tahan village.

Boat charter can be very expensive unless you can organise a group. Book a boat at park HQ at least the day before and they may be able to combine individuals. Boat trips to Lata Berkoh rapids, Kuala Trenggan and Kuala Keniam are all popular and can be combined with walks, short or long. Prices for four/12-seater boats include:

Lata Berkoh	RM80
Kuala Trenggan	RM70/90
Kuala Keniam	RM140/160
Kuala Perkai	RM180

Places to Stay & Eat

Kuala Tahan All accommodation at park HQ is operated by the privately run *Taman Negara Resort* (☎ 09-266 3500; fax 09-266 1500). Bookings can also be made through its Kuala Lumpur Sales Office (☎ 03-245 5585) on the 2nd floor of the Hotel Istana, 73 Jalan Raja Chulan. A 15% tax and service charge is added to all the rates quoted here.

You can camp at park HQ for RM2 per person per night. Two/four person tents can be hired for RM8/14. Other camp sites with minimal facilities are scattered throughout Taman Negara.

The hostel part of the resort has nine rooms, each clean and comfortable with four bunk beds, overhead fans and personal lockers. Men and women share the dormitory rooms, but there are separate toilets and showers. The hostel costs RM18 per person.

Rooms in the brick guesthouse, the old park accommodation centre, cost RM120/150 for comfortable rooms with air-con and hot water. More attractive and luxurious wooden chalets, 85 in all, cost RM170/200, or RM260/290 for larger chalet suites. Top of the range are the two-bedroom VIP bungalows for RM520.

The pleasant *Teresek Cafeteria* at the resort serves fried rice, noodles, spaghetti and the like for around RM5. The chic *Tahan Restaurant* has surprisingly high standards of food and service out here in the jungle. You can dine à la carte or the more popular buffet meals range from RM22 at breakfast to RM32 for dinner.

Significantly cheaper meals can be found at the floating *KT Restoran* moored on the riverbank just along from the park HQ jetty. Excellent Malaysian and western meals are served.

Kampung Kuala Tahan The village of Kuala Tahan directly across the river from park HQ is slightly less convenient but much cheaper for accommodation and food. Crossing the river is easy – simply go down to the park HQ jetty, wave to the restaurants moored on the other bank and a motorised sampan will come and pick you up. Sampans go on demand throughout the day and evening, and are free if you eat at the restaurants or stay in the village.

Past the floating restaurants, high on the bank overlooking the river, the first place you come to is the friendly *Liang Hostel*, which has basic plywood-walled rooms, each with four beds costing RM10 per person. Nearby, the thatch-roofed *Tembeling Hostel* is even more basic, but it has a pleasant lawn area and provides good information on the park. Each room has two single beds with mosquito nets for RM10 per person.

Further in the village, *Pakwarin Chalets* has more comfortable accommodation in simple A-frames for RM30. *Teresek View Village* (☎ 09-266 3065) has large dorms for RM10, small A-frame huts for RM30 and new, mid-range chalets with fan and bath for RM50 and RM60. This is the closest thing to a tourist resort in the village, and it also has a mini-mart and large restaurant overlooking the river.

Floating barge restaurants line the sandbar (more a rockbar) opposite park HQ, all selling basic noodle and rice meals for as little as RM2. The *Restaurant Terapong* is one of the most popular with a slightly more varied menu, and the *Family* and *Ria* restaurants are also good places to dine over the river.

Nusa Camp Quieter and away from park HQ, *Nusa Camp* is 15 minutes up the Tembeling River from Kuala Tahan. It's much more of a 'jungle camp' than anything at park HQ. Dorm beds cost RM9, A-frames are RM45 a double and slightly more sophisticated cottages with attached bath are RM60 to RM80. The restaurant serves good but unexciting food for RM6 for breakfast, RM8 for lunch and RM8.50 for dinner.

Bookings can be made in KL at the Nusa Camp desk at the tourist centre on Jalan Ampang (☎ 03-242 3929, ext 112), or at their Jerantut office (☎ 09-266 2369) at the bus station. They run their own boat from Kuala Tembeling, and their riverbus service between Nusa Camp and the Kuala Tahan runs approximately every two hours up to 6 pm.

Kuala Trenggan & Kuala Keniam About 35 minutes upstream from Kuala Tahan at Kuala Trenggan is the quite luxurious *Trenggan Lodge* and further upriver is the *Keniam Lodge*. These are the places to get right away from it all, but they are both run by the resort, so creature comforts are well catered for. Each has a restaurant and 10 rooms with attached bath at RM110 and RM120 respectively.

Kuala Perkai The Wildlife Department has a basic, isolated lodge at Kuala Perkai, two hours' walk past Kuala Keniam It costs RM8 per person and you must take all bedding and cooking equipment with you. It is popular with fishing enthusiasts. Check for availability at park HQ.

Getting There & Away

The main way to get to Taman Negara is to take a bus or train to Jerantut, the gateway town to the park, then a bus or taxi to Kuala Tembeling, from where two boats per day go to park HQ.

Air Pelangi Air has discontinued scheduled flights to the airfield at Kuala Tiang, about halfway between Kuala Tembeling and Kuala Tahan, and is unlikely to resume them in the near future.

Land See Jerantut, below, for details of buses and taxis to Kuala Tembeling. Kuala Tembeling can also be reached by train, but it is less certain. If you make prior arrangements, the jungle trains between Jerantut and Kuala Lipis will let you off at the trackside stop of Tembeling Halt, a 2.5 km walk from the jetty. Trains do not usually pick up from there, and the nearest station is at Mela, 20 minutes by bus from the jetty. From Mela a 1 pm jungle train goes north to Tumpat and a 5.30 pm train goes to Kuala Lipis only. Heading south, go to Jerantut and catch a train from there.

From the resort's office at the Hotel Istana in Kuala Lumpur, Reliance Travel has a daily shuttle bus all the way to Kuala Tembeling, leaving at 8 am and costing RM25. Other small operators also offer this service. Most of the travellers' guesthouses in KL can arrange pick up and drop off at Kuala Tembeling for the same price.

A rough road now goes all the way from Jerantut to Kuala Tahan village. The road is unsealed much of the way, and though negotiable by car when dry, it is recommended only for 4WD vehicles. The Jerantut Resthouse and the Green Park Guest House (see Jerantut) can organise transport to the park this way. Places to stay in the village can arrange a trip out on a local minibus (RM18, two hours) that goes to Jerantut most mornings. Though slightly quicker than the boat, the road is less interesting.

You can walk into the park from Merapoh, at the Pahang/Kuantan border. The trail from Merapoh joins the Gunung Tahan trail, adding another two days to the Gunung Tahan trek. Guides are compulsory and can be hired in Kuala Lipis to take you in, but it is easier to arrange a guide at the park for the walk out. It is also possible to take a boat to the upper reaches of the park and walk out to Terengganu state.

Boat The main entry point into the park is by river boat from Kuala Tembeling, 18 km from Jerantut. Boats leave from the jetty, 500 metres west of the turn-off to the small village of Kuala Tembeling.

There are two daily departures, at 9 am and 2 pm (2.30 pm on Fridays). Boats are operated by the resort and Nusa Camp, whose boats also stop at park HQ before continuing to Nusa Camp, so you can take either service regardless of where you stay. You can make reservations with the resort's office in KL or the Nusa Camp office in KL or Jerantut, but bookings are not essential, except perhaps during holiday periods.

It's a 2½ to three hour boat trip from Kuala Tembeling to park HQ at Kuala Tahan, depending on how swiftly the river is flowing. The trip costs RM18 one-way. Boats depart at 9 am and 2 pm and take two to 2½ hours for the trip to from Kuala Tahan to Kuala Tembeling.

Getting Around

Nusa Camp has a riverboat service from Kuala Tahan to Nusa Camp (RM5, RM2 for Nusa Camp guests) at 10 am and 12.30, 3 and 6 pm. In the opposite direction there are departures from Nusa Camp at 8.15, 10.15, 11.15 am and 2.15, 3.15, 3.45 and 6 pm. To Kuala Trenggan boats from Kuala Tahan via Nusa Camp leave at 10 am and 3.15 pm and cost RM10 from Kuala Tahan, RM5 from Nusa Camp. The return boats leave at 11 am and 3.30 pm.

The other service is from Kuala Tahan to Bumbun Belau and Bumbun Yong at 8.30 am and 5.30 pm. While they keep pretty much to schedule during peak periods, in the wet season they drop services or stop all together. In Kuala Tahan, the Restaurant Terapong has the latest information on these boats.

For charter boats, the Wildlife office is helpful in trying to arrange groups for those who want to share costs. Charter boats can also be arranged in Kuala Tahan village for the same price.

JERANTUT

The small town of Jerantut is the gateway to Taman Negara National Park. Most visitors to the park spend at least one night here, but the town itself has no real attractions.

Information

Nusa Camp (☎ 09-266 2369) has an office at the bus station, open 8 am to 6 pm, for bookings at their Taman Negara camp. They also change travellers' cheques and cash, but banks have better rates. The travel agent at the railway station has general information and books the Taman Negara Resort.

You can stock up on supplies at the Jaya emporium on the main road towards Temerloh, or at the Pasar Ya Milliondon Supermarket near the market. Fruit stalls line the road opposite the Jaya emporium.

There is a good Chinese laundry on the main road a few doors north of the Hotel Jerantut. It provides quick service for the inevitably stinking trekkers coming out of Taman Negara.

Places to Stay

Jerantut has plenty of hotels, but the popular places can get very busy during the peak periods for visiting Taman Negara.

A couple of new guesthouses have sprung up in Jerantut. The small, friendly *Green Park Guest House* (☎ 09-266 3884) on Jalan Besar has four-bed dorms for RM8 and singles/doubles/triples for RM12/20/27. Accommodation is simple, but snacks are served and the owner, a former guide in Taman Negara, is an excellent source of information and arranges transport to the park. The less-inspiring *Friendly Hostel*

(☎ 010-987 9086) opposite the railway station has large dorms for RM8.

The cheapest hotels can be found on the main road south of the railway station. The best of a bad bunch is the *Hotel Jerantut* (☎ 09-266 5568), 36 Jalan Besar. Rooms with tiny shower cubicles (toilets are shared) cost RM13. Opposite the bus station, the *Hotel Chett Fatt* (☎ 09-266 5805) is a reasonable place if you can't be bothered walking further. It costs RM15 for a fan room, RM20 to RM28 with air-con.

The *Jerantut Resthouse* (☎ 09-266 4488), across the railway line on the way to Kuala Lipis, is deservedly the most popular place in town. Pleasant motel-style doubles/triples cost RM20/25 with fan and bath or air-con doubles cost RM44 to RM60. Dorm beds for RM7 are available in the hall at the back. The restaurant here is excellent, transport and tours to Taman Negara are offered and every evening an informative briefing is given on the park. The resthouse is about 10 minutes' walk from the railway station; about 20 from the bus station.

The resthouse also runs the large, slightly fancier *Sri Emas Hotel* (☎ 09-266 4499). Dorm beds cost RM7, rooms with fan and hot shower are RM25 and air-con rooms range from RM46 up to the RM100 suites. It offers the same services as the resthouse.

Places to Eat

The food-stall centre between the market and railway station is surprisingly good and offers Thai dishes and seafood as well as the usual favourites. Cheap coffee-shops can be found along the main road near the bus station, or the restaurant at the *Jerantut Resthouse* has a varied menu and attracts hordes of travellers. The best Chinese restaurants are on the road to Taman Negara past the emporium. *Restaurant Sun Tien Loy* has good food and is reasonably priced, and a few doors along the air-con *Restoran Pau Lou* is one of the fanciest in town.

Getting There & Away

Train Jerantut is on the Tumpat-Gemas railway line. The express train to Singapore (seven hours) leaves at 1 am on Wednesday, Friday and Sunday or the daily 9.20 pm to Gemas connects with another train to Singapore (nine hours in total).

To Wakaf Bahru (the nearest station to Kota Bharu on the Tumpat line) express

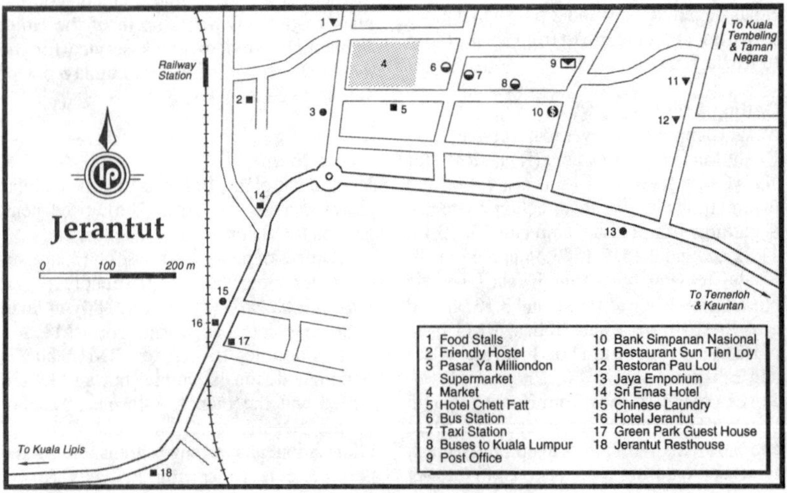

trains take six hours and leave at 4 or 5.40 am; otherwise the stopping-all-stations jungle train leaves at 12.30 pm and takes about 12 hours. All northbound trains go via Kuala Lipis, and a Kuala Lipis-only train leaves at 4.40 pm.

Bus & Taxi The bus and taxi station is in the centre of town. Buses to KL leave from the ticket offices on the other side of the taxi station from the main bus station.

At present only one company operates four buses a day to KL's Pekeliling bus station (RM9, 3½ hours) going via Temerloh. The last bus leaves around 4.30 pm, but schedules vary. If you miss the bus to KL, buses go every half-hour to Temerloh (RM2.40, one hour), from where more-numerous connections go to KL and other destinations.

Two companies have buses to Kuantan (RM8.40, three hours), with seven departures up until 3 pm.

The buses coming through from KL continue on to Kuala Lipis; otherwise first take a bus to Benta (hourly from 7 am to 6 pm), and then another to Kuala Lipis.

Taxis cost RM4 to Kuala Tembeling, RM6 to Temerloh, RM17 to KL and RM15 to Kuantan.

Kuala Tembeling & Taman Negara Buses to Kuala Tembeling (RM1.20, 45 minutes), for Taman Negara, leave at 8.15 and 11 am and 1.30 and 5.15 pm, but schedules are unreliable and seem designed to just miss the Taman Negara boats. The buses will drop you at the jetty, 500 metres past the township, but the 8.15 am bus is not guaranteed to make the 9 am boat to Taman Negara. From the jetty, buses to Jerantut come by at around 12.30 and 4 pm, but don't count on it.

The best bet is to take a taxi between Jerantut and Kuala Tembeling. A whole taxi costs RM15, but chances of finding other passengers to share are good.

The Jerantut Resthouse and the Green Park Guest House also arrange minibuses to Kuala Tembeling for RM4 per person. They can also arrange transport by road all the way to Kuala Tahan. If there is enough demand, the Jerantut Resthouse runs good tours to Kuala Tahan for RM20, visiting cocoa, rubber and palm oil plantations on the way. Most visitors prefer to take the scenic river trip, but you can go by road one way and return by boat.

KEMAHANG BIRD SANCTUARY

This attractive, 300 hectare recreation park is 58 km from Jerantut on the way to Kuala Lipis. From the landscaped picnic area around the waterfall, paths lead off into the dense jungle. The main trail is a rugged three hour walk above the waterfall and involves plenty of scrambling over rocks. Of note for its birdlife, including jungle fowl and hornbills, the jungle is also home to kijang deer and tapir. The sanctuary attracts local picnickers on weekends but otherwise gets few visitors, and it is difficult to reach.

From Jerantut take a Benta bus to the 36 mile marker and then it is a two km walk along the paved road through the cocoa plantations. Spartan A-frame huts are available for RM10 or you can camp, and the on-site caretaker runs a food stall. Bookings can be made through the resthouse in Kuala Lipis.

KUALA LIPIS

At the confluence of the Lipis and Jelai rivers, Kuala Lipis is a small town with a colonial past. The centre of town, with fine rows of shophouses down the main street, is the busy Chinese commercial district. Further south on the hilly outskirts, Kuala Lipis has a few colonial reminders from the days when it was the most important town in Pahang.

Kuala Lipis was a gold-mining centre long before the British arrived in 1887, but its heyday dates from 1898 when it became the capital of Pahang. Grand colonial buildings date from this period and trade increased when the railway came through in 1924.

In 1955 the capital shifted to Kuantan and Kuala Lipis declined. It is a sleepy town, but new construction and the delights of a shopping mall are signs of new wealth. The long-since-closed gold mines have been reopened with the help of foreign technology.

Kuala Lipis makes a pleasant enough overnight stop, but the main reason to visit is to a make a jungle trek in the nearby Kenong Rimba State Park. Two popular budget hotel operators and two travel agents arrange these treks (see Kenong Rimba State Park below for details).

Information

The so-called Tourist Information Centre at the railway station is a private travel agent selling its own trips to Kenong Rimba, but you can get a map of the town and basic queries answered.

Things to See

Colonial architecture buffs will appreciate the imposing **District Offices** on a hill one km south from the centre of town. The offices overlook the exclusive **Clifford School**, another grand public building that began life as the Anglo-Chinese School in 1913, before it was renamed after Sir Hugh Clifford, the second British Resident of Pahang.

The road next to the school leads up the hill to the **Pahang Club**, a sprawling wooden bungalow with wide, open verandas. With its planter's chairs and hunting trophies, it clings to its colonial club traditions in the face of decay.

The **Rest House** on another hill facing the District Offices is a large, gracious building, once the British Resident's residence. It houses a small museum in the foyer chronicling the town's history.

Places to Stay

The two most popular travellers' hotels, which both organise treks to Kenong Rimba, are on the main street, only 100 metres from the bus station and 200 metres from the train station.

Behind the Sports Toto lottery counter, the *Gin Loke Hotel* (☎ 09-312 1388) at 64 Jalan Besar has cheap plywood-partitioned rooms and is run by a friendly Chinese family. The cost is RM12 with fan and common bath. Right next door at No 63 is the ever-popular *Appu's Guest House* (☎ 09-312 3142), which has similar rooms and lots of travel information. Rooms cost RM12 and RM15 or air-con rooms cost RM30 and RM35.

Kuala Lipis has other cheap hotels on Jalan Besar, including the *Hotel Tong Kok* (☎ 09-312 1027), where rooms cost RM14. The *Hotel Jelai* (☎ 09-312 1562), 44 Jalan Jelai, on the riverfront road parallel with the main street, is a very clean hotel with a variety of rooms from RM19, or RM30 with air-con. Some have balconies overlooking the river.

In the mid-range, the spic-and-span *Hotel Sri Pahang* (☎ 09-312 2445), 1st floor Bangunan UMNO, is good value at RM30 for rooms with attached bathroom, RM38 with air-con. It's across the railway line, a 10 minute walk from the train station.

For something different, *De' Rakit Chalet* (☎ 09-312 3963) is a floating hotel and restaurant moored on the river on Jalan Jelai right in the centre of town. Good self-contained chalets with balconies for RM45 are the most peaceful in Kuala Lipis.

The *Rest House (Rumah Persinggahan Bukit Residensi)* (☎ 09-312 2599) is a fair hike from the centre on a hill overlooking the town but it has loads of colonial style. Large rooms (some with balcony) with air-con and attached bath cost RM40 and RM50, or small, uninspiring rooms in the back section cost RM35. It has a good restaurant.

The top-ranking hotel is the three-star *Taipan Hotel* (☎ 09-312 2555) on Jalan Lipis Benta, still under construction but due to open soon. It is near the Rest House, at the bottom of the hill.

Getting There & Away

There is an express train to Singapore (eight hours) at midnight on Wednesday, Friday and Sunday, or the daily 8 pm train to Gemas also connects to Singapore. Slow jungle trains to Gemas leave at 7 am and 3.15 pm. All southbound trains stop at Jerantut, and if you want to go to Taman Negara, you can take the 7 am train to Tembeling Halt, a 2.5 km walk from Kuala Tembeling; but schedules are unreliable and you must request in advance for the train to stop.

Express trains to Tumpat (five hours) leave at 5.10 or 6.50 am and stop at Wakaf Bharu (the closest station to Kota Bharu). Slow but interesting jungle trains (11 hours) depart at 2.10 and 6.15 pm.

Five buses per day run between Kuala Lipis and KL's Pekeliling bus station from 8 am to 6 pm. Buses go to Kuantan at 8 am and 2.30 pm and to Gua Musang at 8 am and 1 pm. Marzin Express has a bus to Kota Bharu at 2 pm. Taxis leave from the bus station to Kota Bharu (RM20), KL (RM18) and other destinations.

KENONG RIMBA STATE PARK

This 120 sq km forest park is a sprawling area of lowland forest rising to the limestone foothills bordering Taman Negara. The park can be explored on good three or four-day jungle treks organised out of Kuala Lipis. The loop trail through the park provides an excellent opportunity to experience the jungle at close hand, and at cheap prices. Kenong Rimba is attracting an increasing number of visitors, but the trail is still relatively untrammelled.

Despite fanciful local claims that the park is a haven for elephants, tigers and rhinos escaping from over-touristed Taman Negara, big mammals are rare. Monkeys, wild pigs, squirrels, civets and possibly nocturnal tapir are all you should expect to see.

A permit from the District Forest Office is not required, contrary to what you may be told in Kuala Lipis, but you must be accompanied by a registered guide.

Walking the Trail

Access is from Kuala Lipis on the jungle train to Batu Sembilan (Mile 9), a 20 minute trip. From Batu Sembilan, boats are hired for RM15 per person to Jeti Tanjung Kiara, just across the river from Kampung Kuala Kenong. From the jetty it is a 30 minute walk to the park entrance along the road through Kampung Dusun, which is just a scattering of a few houses with one small shop. Further on from the shop, past the house with the 'souvenirs' sign, a side trail to the right leads to three caves – Gua Batu Tangga, Gua Batu Tangkup and Gua Batu Telahup. A number of confusing trails go through the swampy forest here. The guided trips include an exploration of the caves. The main trail eventually rejoins the road right at the entrance to the park where there is a gate and a footbridge over a stream.

The trail into the park leads another 30 minutes to Gunung Kesong, a large limestone outcrop. The forest department has a hut here, and 200 metres further on is the Persona Chalets. Sheltered by the hill, some of the trees here are enormous. Gunung Kesong contains a number of caves, the most impressive being Gunung Hijau, the 'Bat Cave', on a side trail around to the right (east) across two bridges. It is a large cavern where hundreds of small bats hang from the ceiling.

From Gunung Kesong the trail leads north through lowland forest to the waterfall of Lata Kenong, better known as the 'Seven Steps'. It is a three to four hour walk following the Kenong River and crossing small streams. About an hour before the falls is the first of the log bridges across the river that require something of a balancing act to negotiate, or the less sure-footed can straddle their way across. The trail then negotiates the mountain foothills to the huts at the Kenong campsite just before the falls, a series of cascades.

From Lata Kenong, the trail continues up and down more hills with other river crossings to Gunung Putih. Though no mountain climbing is involved this is the most strenuous part of the trek, taking about five hours and passing through some impressive forest. Gunung Putih is another rocky, cave-ridden outcrop that can be climbed via a side trail.

The main trail continues on past Gunung Putih through the foothills back to the lowland forest. Another side trail leads to a nearby Orang Asli village, home of the Batek people. The main trail leads back to Gunung Kesong, about four hours all up from Gunung Putih.

Other side trips can be made in the park, including a visit to the Lata Babi waterfall, and to Gua Batu Tinggi, across the river from Kampung Dusun.

PENINSULAR MALAYSIA

Organised Tours

Guides are compulsory for entry to the park and can be arranged in Kuala Lipis. The cheapest and most popular are those organised at Appu's Guest House and the Gin Loke Hotel, which are usually four-day/three-night treks.

Appu has been taking trips to Kenong Rimba for years and gets good reviews from travellers. His trips cost RM35 per day and guests are escorted from Kuala Lipis. Mr & Mrs Tan at the Gin Loke also run popular trips costing RM30 per day – they put you on the train and a local guide meets you at Batu Sembilan. The boat ride (RM30 return) is extra. Prices for both include food, guide and all expenses in the park. These are no-frills jungle experiences – you camp in the park but all equipment and cooking is provided. Trips go when enough people are interested, usually every two or three days, or ring to make a booking.

Upstairs in the Medan Stesyen, the new building in front of the Kuala Lipis railway station, Pan Holiday (☎ 09-312 3598) runs a variety of treks from one day for RM50 per person (minimum four) to four days for RM180. They own the only chalets in the park, so they provide more comfort, but treks only go as far as Lata Kenong. The affiliated, privately run Tourist Information Centre (☎ 09-312 3277) also has an office in the Medan Stesyen and at the railway station itself. They have exactly the same treks and use the Persona Chalets. Other activities offered are river rafting for RM100 and a five day trek to Gunung Tahan via Merapoh (RM350) on the western edge of the Taman Negara.

Places to Stay

The only real accommodation in the park is the *Persona Chalets* at Gunung Kesong. These spartan but comfortable huts each have four bunk beds and cost RM40.

The *Kenong campsite* near the Lata Kenong waterfall consists of open-sided huts on stilts and a campfire for cooking. The jungle treks camp at this site, and also at caves and rock overhangs at Gunung Kesong and Gunung Putih.

RAUB

You may find yourself in this large, crossroads town getting transport connections to Fraser's Hill or Kuala Lipis. From Raub (pronounced 'Rob'), frequent buses also go to KL's Pekeliling bus station.

Raub has a few cheap hotels on the main road including the very basic *Hotel Raub*, 57 Jalan Kuala Lipis, and a few doors along the *Hotel Fee Chui* (☎ 09-355 1327), where singles/doubles cost RM14/25. The more gracious *Rest House (Rumah Persinggahan)* (☎ 09-355 5230) has rooms for RM50.

TEMERLOH

Temerloh is an old town on the banks of the enormous Pahang River. It has a hint of colonial style and a colourful Saturday market. New industrial estates on the outskirts point to the future, and Temerloh is pressing to supersede Kuantan as the state capital. As the main city of central Pahang, it is a transport hub, the only real reason to visit.

The railway station is 12 km away at **Mentakab**, a thriving satellite of Temerloh that has little of interest for the visitor.

Places to Stay & Eat

From the bus station head away from the river along the main street past the new shops. At the T-junction take the laneway up the steps almost opposite. This will bring you to the *Hotel Bersih* and the *Hong Fong Hotel*, both dives. On the corner opposite, the *Hotel Isis* (☎ 09-296 3136), 12 Jalan Tengku Bakar, is much better and has rooms for RM10/16 or RM24 with air-con and bath. Further along at No 40, the *New Ban Hin Hotel* (☎ 09-296 2331) is similar.

One km from the bus station past the mosque, the old *Temerloh Rest House (Rumah Persinggahan)* (☎ 09-296 3254) on Jalan Datok Hamzah has large, well-appointed rooms for RM60. It has a wonderful restaurant on the lawns overlooking the river. Next door, the *Seri Malaysia Hotel* (☎ 03-296 5776) is a new, more luxurious hotel with rooms from RM90.

The new food-stall centre next to the bus

station overlooks the river. The satay here is superb.

Getting There & Away

Temerloh's bus station is central, about 400 metres from the cheap-hotel area. Buses go to all parts of the peninsula, including Melaka (RM8.50) at 8.30 and 10.15 am and 5 pm, Penang (RM22) at 6.30, 8 and 10.30 pm and Kota Bharu (RM23) at 10 pm. Buses to Jerantut leave every half-hour between 6 am and 6.45 pm. Buses to KL's Pekeliling bus station leave at least every hour between 7 am and 6 pm, and there are frequent buses to Kuantan.

Taxis at the bus station go to Mentakab (RM1), Jerantut (RM6), Kuantan (RM10) and KL (RM12).

TASIK BERA

Tasik Bera is the largest natural lake in Malaysia, and around its shores are Orang Asli kampungs. The main kampung is Kota Iskandar, at the southern end of the lake. The lake is surrounded by ugly Felda (Federal Land Development Authority) palm oil plantations, developed to promote local industry among the Orang Asli. The lake itself has been invaded and choked by tall rasau grass. All in all, Tasik Bera is an ecological disaster area and only worth visiting by those with a strong interest in the settlements of the Semelai Orang Asli.

There is no public transport to the lake, and a chartered taxi from Temerloh costs around RM60 return with negotiation. By car from Temerloh, head south to Bahau and turn-off at Kerayang. It is then 19 km along the main road, then a further 11 km through the plantations, following the 'Tasik Bera' signs all the way to a lone kampung house. The family here rents motorboats to go cruising through the grass on the lake to other settlements. The asking rate is RM100 for a couple of hours, less with bargaining.

Access by car from the south is easier. From Bahau head north to Keratong Junction and then take Highway 11 for 30 km to the turn-off to Kota Iskandar, a straggling settlement where there's a government resthouse. Keratong Junction is also reached by a good road from Kuala Pilah in Negeri Sembilan.

Terengganu

The small east coast state of Terengganu is, along with Kelantan to the north, one of the states richest in Malay culture. Until the completion of the roads to KL and the west coast, this part of Malaysia was fairly isolated from the rest of the country and didn't receive many Indian and Chinese immigrants. Consequently, cultural influences came much more from the north. Traditional activities such as kite flying, top spinning, *songket* weaving and batik printing are all alive and well in Terengganu.

If you are seeking a beach to laze around on for a few days, Terengganu has arguably the best in the country. The Perhentian Islands are far less developed than Tioman, and the water is crystal-clear blue. The state is also famous for the leatherback turtles which come ashore from May to September at Rantau Abang.

Like its northern neighbour, Terengganu is a very conservative Muslim state, so you should dress and behave accordingly. If knocking back a few beers in the evening is an essential part of your travel routine, it is also worth bearing in mind that alcohol – while not impossible to get hold of – is not widely available in Terengganu.

Full Name: Terengganu Darul Iman
Area: 12,955 sq km
Capital: Kuala Terengganu
Population: one million (approximately)

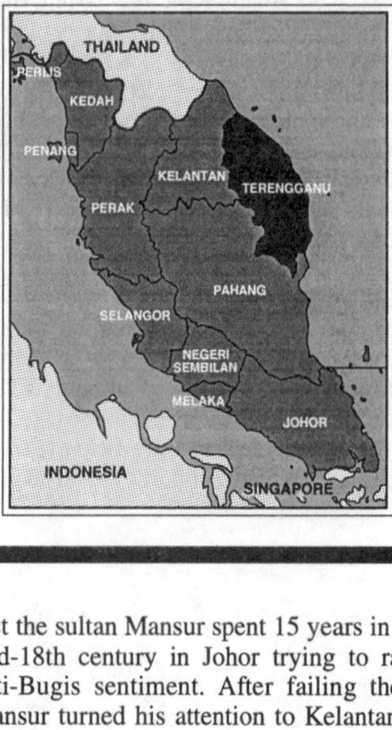

History

When the Melaka sultanate was established in the 14th century, Terengganu was already paying tribute to the Siamese in the north, although a 1303 inscription found at Kuala Brang establishes that an Islamic state was already in existence here at that time. It wasn't long before Terengganu became a vassal of Melaka, but it managed to retain a large degree of independence during the time of the Riau-Johor ascendancy, and was trading with Siam and China.

Terengganu was formally established as a state in 1724. The first sultan was Tun Zainal Abidin, a young brother of one of the former Johor sultans. The close association with Johor was to continue for some years, and in fact the sultan Mansur spent 15 years in the mid-18th century in Johor trying to rally anti-Bugis sentiment. After failing there, Mansur turned his attention to Kelantan to the north and, after some fighting and shrewd manoeuvring, had his son installed as the ruler of Kelantan. The main legacy of Mansur's reign was that Terengganu became a vassal of the Siamese.

Terengganu was controlled by the Siamese for the duration of the 19th century. However, the Terengganu sultan, Baginda Omar, a man renowned for his intelligence and energy, kept the Siamese at arm's length and the state flourished under his rule.

In 1909 an Anglo-Siamese treaty saw power pass to the British. It was an unpopular move locally, and in 1928 a short-lived peasant uprising erupted. It was put down and the British went about consolidating

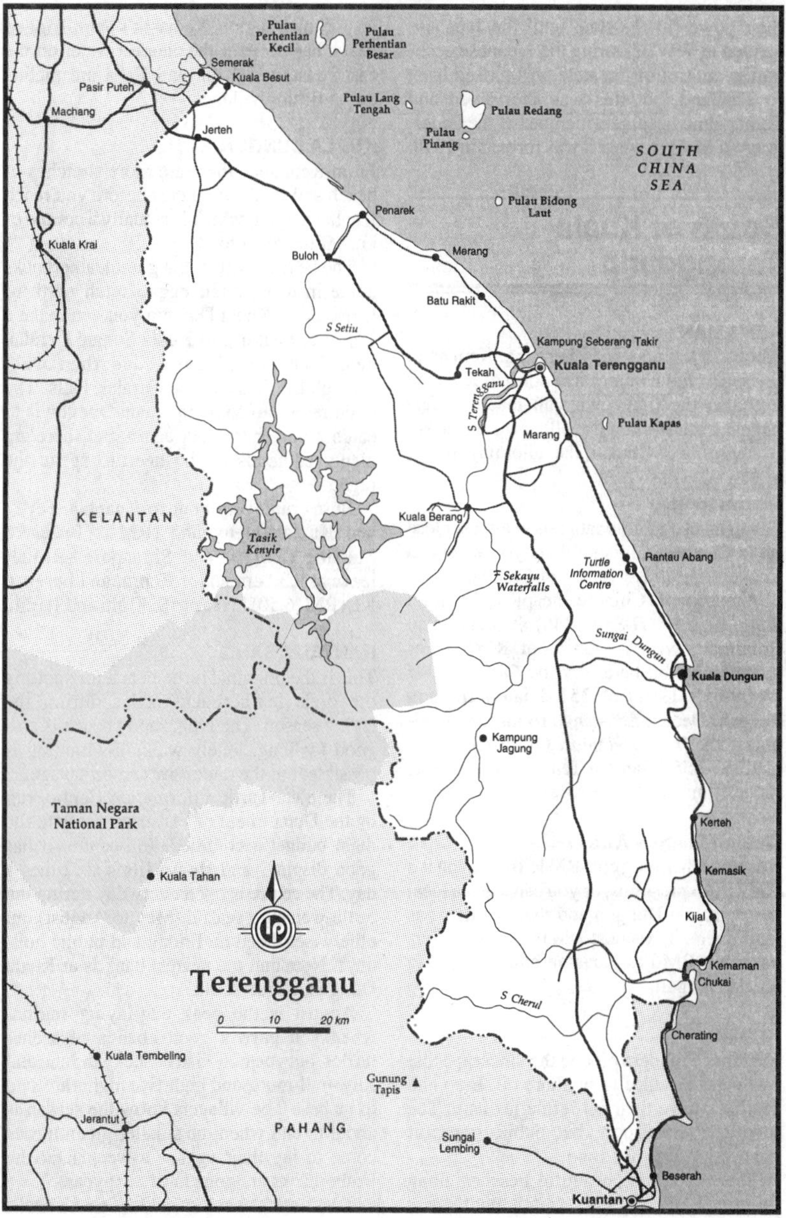

Pulau Perhentian Kecil
Pulau Perhentian Besar
Semerak
Kuala Besut
Pasir Puteh
Machang
Pulau Lang Tengah
Pulau Redang
Pulau Pinang
Jerteh
SOUTH CHINA SEA
Pulau Bidong Laut
Penarek
Kuala Krai
Buloh
Merang
Batu Rakit
S Setiu
Kampung Seberang Takir
Kuala Terengganu
Tekah
S Terengganu
Pulau Kapas
Marang
KELANTAN
Kuala Berang
Tasik Kenyir
Rantau Abang
Turtle Information Centre
Sekayu Waterfalls
Sungai Dungun
Kuala Dungun
Kampung Jagung
Taman Negara National Park
Kerteh
Kemasik
Kuala Tahan
Kijal
Kemaman
Chukai
Terengganu
S Cherul
0
10
20 km
Cherating
Kuala Tembeling
Gunung Tapis
Jerantut
PAHANG
Sungai Lembing
Beserah
Kuantan

their power in the state until the Japanese arrived in WWII. During the Japanese occupation control of the state was passed back to Thailand, but this was short-lived and Terengganu became a member of the Federation of Malaya when it was formed in 1948.

South of Kuala Terengganu

KEMAMAN

About 25 km north of Cherating, Kemaman is the first town of any size north of Kuantan and also the first town you reach in Terengganu state when travelling up the coast. It merges with Chukai, the adjoining town.

Places to Stay

Given that accommodation is available close by in Cherating, it is unlikely you will need to overnight in Kemaman or Chukai.

A reasonable Chinese cheapie is the *Hotel Tong Juan* (☎ 09-859 1346) at K117 Jalan Sulaiman, with rooms from RM15. For something a bit better try the *Cathay Hotel* (☎ 09-859 1901) at 351 Jalan Kampung Tengah. Decent mid-range rooms are available at the *Hotel Delamore* (☎ 09-859 1802) at K353-355 Jalan Kg Tengah, where costs range from RM40 to RM60.

Getting There & Away

Buses to Cherating cost RM1. To Marang it's RM7 by express bus, or you can catch a local bus to Kuala Dungun and then another bus from there. Taxis cost RM13 to Kuala Terengganu, RM6 to Kuantan and RM6.50 to Kuala Dungun.

KERTEH

Kerteh is a modern blot on the landscape that owes its existence to offshore oil. Esso and Petronas have their oil refineries here. The town has an airport, but public transport connections are not good.

There are some beautiful beaches along the stretch of coast near Kerteh, but there is no accommodation. Kemasik's palm-fringed beach has some of the clearest water on the east coast, and Kijal and Paka are picturesque fishing villages.

KUALA DUNGUN

From Kemaman there are more stretches of beach and small *kampungs* before you reach Kuala Dungun, which is actually a couple of km off the main road.

The beaches where the giant leatherbacks come in to lay their eggs stretch north of there. From Kuala Dungun you can make a 1½-hour boat trip to Kuala Sungai Ceralak near Kampung Jagung, and then walk through the forest to the Ceralak Falls. The main reason to come to Kuala Dungun is to catch a bus or taxi out again, but there are plenty of hotels if you need to spend the night.

Buses run every hour to Kuantan (RM8) and Kuala Terengganu (RM4). Buses to Mersing (RM16) and Singapore (RM23) leave at 9.30 am and 9.30 pm, and buses to KL (RM16.50) leave at 10.30 am and 10 pm.

RANTAU ABANG

This is the principal turtle beach for spotting the great leatherback turtles during the laying season. The long, sandy beach is also good for long, lonely walks. Swimming is possible, but the undertow can be savage.

There's a Turtle Information Centre, run by the Department of Fisheries, close to the main budget accommodation centre. It has good displays and shows films six times a day. The centre is open every day during the turtle-watching season (May to August) but otherwise closed on Friday and public holidays. Note that the nearest bank is at Kuala Dungun, 22 km south.

August is the peak egg-laying season, when you have a good chance of seeing turtles, but you may also be lucky in June and July. Full-moon and high-tide nights are said to be best. The villagers know the season is about to end when the smaller green turtles come to lay their eggs – a week later the leatherbacks are gone until next year.

The turtles were once the east coast's

primary tourist attraction, which contributed to the decline of turtle numbers. Now fewer and fewer turtles attract fewer and fewer tourists. The government has made a concerted, if not always well policed, effort to preserve the turtles and their egg-laying habitat. They introduced heavy fines and tried to stamp out the gross behaviour of the past – pulling the turtles' flippers, shining lights in their eyes, taking the eggs and even riding on the turtles' backs. Flash photography and shining torches on the turtles are prohibited, and you must keep a reasonable distance.

The beach is now divided into three sections during the season – prohibited, semi-public (where you have to buy tickets) and free access – in an attempt to control the 'hang gang, the turtles are up' mentality.

Places to Stay & Eat

Right on the beach in front of the Turtle Information Centre are two travellers' places. *Awang's* (☎ 09-844 3500) is the more popular of the two. Rooms with fan and bath go for RM15/20; there are also air-con family rooms (two double beds and one

The Turtle

Four species of turtle visit the east coast, in an area ranging from 35 to 150 km north of Kuantan: the leatherback *(Dermochelys coriacea)*, the hawksbill *(Eretmochelys imbricata)*, the green turtle *(Chelonia mydas)* and the olive ridley *(Lepidochelys oliveacea)*.

The villagers believe that the giant leatherback turtles are attracted to Rantau Abang every year because of a large black stone resembling a turtle in the river. A more mundane explanation is that the sharp drop-off at the beach means that the turtles' laborious climb onto land is made considerably easier. At other times of the year the leatherbacks can wander as far away as the Atlantic Ocean, but each year between June and September they return to the Malaysian coast to lay their eggs. Or at least they used to. Sightings of leatherback turtles numbered almost 1000 back in the 1984 season; numbers have now dropped to less than 100 per year. No one knows what has happened to the turtles, but certainly visitor interest hasn't helped. Hopefully they have found another secluded breeding ground.

If you do get to see a turtle, the egg-laying process is an awesome one, for the female leatherback can weigh up to 750 kg and reach over three metres in length. After crawling laboriously up the beach, well above the high-tide line, each female digs a deep hole in the sand for her eggs. Usually she digs a false decoy hole first and fills it in again before digging the real hole.

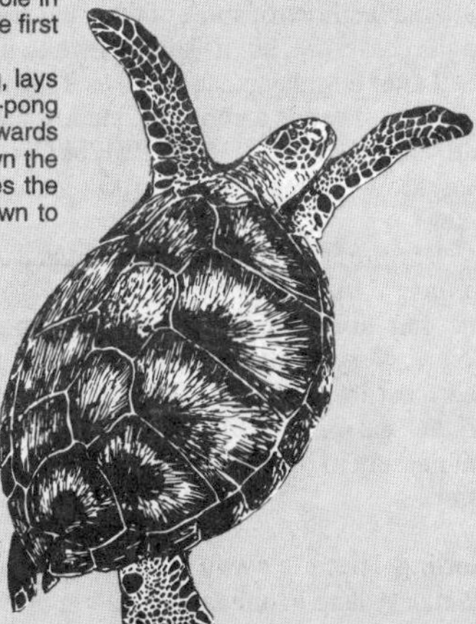

Into this cavity the turtle, with much huffing and puffing, lays between 50 and 140 eggs which look rather like large ping-pong balls. Having covered the eggs, she then heads back towards the water, leaving tracks as if a tank had just driven down the beach. It all takes an enormous effort, and several times the turtle will pause to catch her breath as 'tears' trickle down to keep sand out of her eyes.

Finally the giant turtle reaches the water and an amazing transformation takes place. The heavy, ungainly, cumbersome creature is suddenly back in its element and glides off silently into the night.

The whole process can take two or more hours from start to finish, and in each laying season an individual turtle may make several trips to the beach before disappearing until the next year.

The eggs take about 55 days to hatch. It's a fraught process, for many eggs are taken by crabs and other predators. Newly hatched young turtles weigh only about 35g and are around six cm long. They are easy prey for birds during their perilous crawl to the sea, and for fish and other creatures when they reach the water. It's a long time before they rival their parents in size. ■

single) available. Awang's has a good restaurant and it is right on the beach.

The *Ismail Beach Resort* (☎ 09-844 1054) next door has similar rooms for RM10 for a double with common bath, RM20 with bath and fan and RM30 for a large double room with bath and fan. It's worth having a quick look at both places before making a decision on which to stay at. Both Awang's and Ismail offer discount rates off season.

Dahimah's Guest House (☎ 010-983 5057) is about one km south towards Kuala Dungun and is a popular mid-range option. Rooms with bath and fan are RM30, and RM50 with air-con and bath. It has a good restaurant and arranges trips in the area.

The *Merantau Inn* (☎ 09-844 1131) is a mid-range motel-style place at Kuala Abang, roughly midway between Dungun and Rantau Abang. Chalets cost from RM42 with bath and fan and RM65 with air-con. There are also family rooms for RM80 with fan and RM120 with air-con. If you have your own camping equipment, you can camp here for RM5 per tent.

Nine km north of Kuala Dungun, the elegant *Tanjung Jara Beach Hotel* (☎ 09-844 1801) is a 100 room beach resort set on a beautiful beach. It may not have the international facilities of some of the other resorts on the east coast, but its superb layout, modelled after a Malay palace, makes it the most beautiful. There's a pool, bar and restaurant, and singles/doubles cost RM260/290, or bungalow suites are RM500, including taxes.

The resort also operates the *Rantau Abang Tanjung Jara Visitor Centre* (09-844 1533), one km north of the Turtle Information Centre. Very comfortable chalets with four beds cost from RM70 to RM120 depending on the season, or RM100/150 with air-con, making them good value for groups and families.

Getting There & Away

Rantau Abang is only about 22 km north of Kuala Dungun, which in turn is 80 km south of Kuala Terengganu and 138 km north of Kuantan. The nearest airport is at Kerteh, where there are flights to Kuantan, Kuala Terengganu and KL.

Dungun-Kuala Terengganu buses run in both directions every hour and there's a bus stop right near the Turtle Information Centre. Rantau Abang to Kuala Terengganu costs RM4 and to Dungun costs RM1.50. Heading south you can try to hail a long-distance bus, or take the bus to Kuala Dungun, from where hourly buses go to Kuantan, as well as to Mersing, Singapore and KL.

MARANG

Marang, a picturesque fishing village on the mouth of the Marang River, has long been a favourite stopover for travellers making their way along the east coast. Nowadays, however, it is a town on the move. A civic beautification job is rapidly modernising the town proper and at least one travellers' guesthouse has been swept away in its wake.

Marang is still worth a visit. The river is dotted with brightly painted boats, the water is crystal clear and thick with fish and there are good beaches in the south of town, where you will find a couple of budget resort outfits. It is also the departure point for Kapas Island. Marang is a conservative village, however, especially across the river from the main town, and reserve in dress and behaviour is recommended.

On Sunday nights there's an active night market selling food, clothes and lots of useless knick-knacks.

Places to Stay & Eat

There are a number of travellers' places, mostly on the northern side of the river or close to town, and a couple of mid-range places stretch south of Marang around the town of Rhu Muda.

Most of the guesthouses close to town are on the lagoon, a stone's throw from the beach. *Kamal's Guest House* (☎ 09-618 2181) is the longest running and one of the best. It's a friendly place with a pleasant garden setting. Dorm beds are RM5, rooms are RM10 and chalets are RM12. The restaurant is deservedly popular. The *Island View Resort* (☎ 09-618 2006) is also good, has free bicycles for guests and charges RM18 for rooms with fan and bathroom and RM35 and upwards for air-con rooms. On the hill behind Kamal's is the *Marang Guesthouse*. It's a notch up from the other guesthouses and has its own restaurant. A dorm bed is RM6, while rooms with fan are RM18. Air-con rooms are available from RM45.

Sandwiched between Kamal's Guesthouse and the Island View Resort is the *Hotel Seri Malaysia* (☎ 09-618 2889), an upmarket chain hotel, where air-con doubles range from RM90. This modern hotel development is probably a sign of things to come in Marang.

The best of the resort outfits south of the river is the *Bell Kiss Swiss Resort* (☎ 09-618 1579), formerly known as the Mare Nostrum. It has friendly Swiss management and the restaurant is good, stays open late and serves beer (something of rarity in this neck of the woods). Simple A-frame chalets are RM20 with common bath, and more luxurious chalets with bath are RM50.

Nearby, the *Angullia Beach House Resort* (☎ 09-618 2403) is the most attractive place in Marang. It's right on a beautiful stretch of beach in a lovely garden setting, but it's overpriced at RM50 for rooms with fan and RM65 upwards for air-con. The restaurant is aimed at free-spending Singaporeans and makes few concessions to budget travellers – you are better off eating at the nearby Bell Kiss Swiss Resort.

Further south are more places to stay, but they are a long way from anywhere and see very few foreign guests. The *Rhu Muda Motel* (☎ 09-618 2328), between the main road and the beach, is well kept and costs RM25 for A-frames and RM80 for rooms with air-con and bath. The restaurant is good.

PENINSULAR MALAYSIA

Getting There & Away

Marang is 30 minutes south of Kuala Terengganu, and regular buses run to and from Kuala Dungun and Kuala Terengganu. Hail

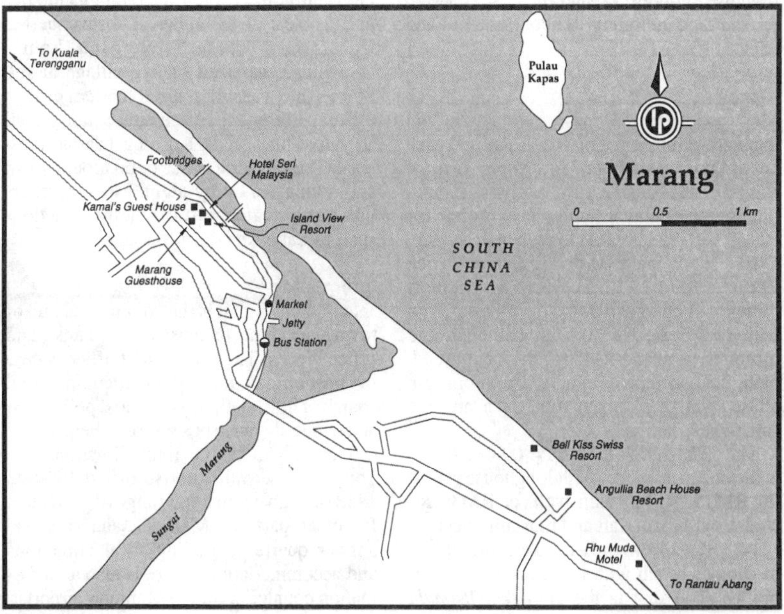

any bus, as the express buses also stop sometimes. The fare is RM1 to Kuala Terengganu.

PULAU KAPAS

Six km offshore from Marang is the beautiful small island of Kapas, with clear water and beaches of powdery white sand. All the accommodation is clustered together on two small beaches in the centre of the island, but you can walk around the headlands to quieter beaches and there is also a rough track across the island. Kapas is best avoided during holidays and long weekends, when it is overrun with day-trippers.

Diving & Snorkelling

Kapas is billed as a snorkellers' paradise, though coral is scarce on the most accessible beaches facing the coast. Pulau Raja, the tiny island just off Kapas, has good snorkelling.

The Kapas Garden Resort has scuba gear and a boat, and the charge is RM135 for two dives.

Any of the budget places in town can organise snorkelling, and the cost is RM15 for the day, including the boat ride out and back to Kapas.

Places to Stay & Eat

Most people visit Kapas on a day trip, but there are a number of places to stay and each has its own restaurant. The *Kapas Garden Resort* (☎ 011-987 1305), run by a hospitable Dutch-Malay couple, has rooms for RM45 with bath, or RM55 with bath and fan.

Next door is the *Mak Cik Gemuk Beach Resort* (☎ 09-618 1221), which has the most rooms and charges RM18 for a basic room with two beds; RM40 with bath, fan and mosquito nets; and RM50 with a double bed, bath, fan and mosquito nets. The rooms are all set well back from the beach and are somewhat cramped.

The *Zaki Beach Chalet* (☎ 09-612 0258) is the cheapest place, with longhouse rooms for RM15, RM20 with bath, or RM30 for chalets with bath, fan and mosquito nets.

A short walk around a headland brings you to another beach with a couple more possibilities. The first is the upmarket *Primula Kapas Island Village Resort*, complete with swimming pool, where chalets start at RM110/130. The second place, at the far end of the beach, is the *Sri Kapas Lodge* (09-618 1529). Basic rooms cost from RM50.

It is also possible to camp on the beach between the two accommodation areas, but bring your own food and water.

Getting There & Away

There's no problem getting a boat to Kapas – most of the places to stay in Marang can arrange it for you, or there are booking offices on the main street. Boats shuttle backwards and forwards throughout the day, and the cost is RM7.50 one way.

Kuala Terengganu

Standing on a promontory formed by the South China Sea on one side and the wide Terengganu River on the other, Kuala Terengganu is the capital of Terengganu state and the seat of the sultan. Oil revenue has transformed Kuala Terengganu from a sprawling, oversized fishing village of stilt houses into a medium-sized modern city.

Kuala Terengganu remains a fairly conservative place with a strong Islamic presence. There is little to see or do around town and nothing to do by night. Most travellers use it as a staging post to nearby attractions such as Lake Kenyir or Marang.

Information

Jalan Sultan Ismail is the commercial hub of town and home to most of the banks and office blocks. The state tourist office is near the post office but is not a particularly good source of information. The tourist police post at the long-distance bus station is helpful and can point you in the right direction. The Tourism Malaysia tourist office (09-622 1433) can give you a full range of brochures for other parts of Malaysia and can also answer queries regarding local attractions and accommodation. There is also an information counter at Sultan Mahmud airport.

The immigration office (☎ 09-622 1424) is at Wisma Persekutuan on Jalan Sultan Ismail. Dobi Ria is a laundromat at 9 Jalan Kampung Dalam; there's another next door to the Seaview Hotel.

Things to See

Kuala Terengganu's compact Chinatown can be found on **Jalan Bandar**. It comprises the usual array of hole-in-the-wall Chinese shops, hairdressing salons and restaurants, as well as a sleepy Chinese temple and some narrow alleys leading to jetties on the waterfront.

The **central market** is a lively, colourful spot, with fruit and foods of all types on sale. When they say the fish is fresh, they really mean it – the fishing boats dock right outside. The floor above the fish section has a good collection of batik and songket.

Across the road from the market and next door to the state tourist office, look for the flight of stairs leading up to **Bukit Puteri**, a 200 metre hill with good views of the city. The hill is also home to the remains of a 19th century fort (the legacy of inter-sultanate warfare), some cannons and a bell. It is a minor attraction.

Continuing past the market, you come to the **Istana Maziah**, the sultan's palace, on your right. The palace is closed to the public, except for some ceremonial occasions. Near the *istana* is the gleaming **Zainal Abidin Mosque**.

Pantai Batu Buruk is the city beach and a popular place to stroll in the evening when the food stalls open up. It is a pleasant stretch of sand, but swimming can be dangerous here. Across the road, the **Cultural Centre** sometimes stages *pencak silat* and wayang shows on Friday between 5 and 6.30 pm. Check with the tourist office.

The **Istana Tengku Long Museum** is housed in the old sultan's palace at Losong, a few km from town on the bank of the river. The wooden palace buildings are set in attractive gardens, and there's a boat museum. Apart from the occasional exhibition, it's not really worth visiting until the state museum moves there from Bukit Kecil.

The jetty is the place for a 40 sen ferry ride to **Pulau Duyung**, the largest island in the estuary. Fishing boats are built there using age-old techniques and tools; it's worth a wander around.

A boat from beside the market will take you across to Kampung Seberang Takir, a fishing village on the other side of the river mouth. Five km upriver is **Kampung Pulau Rusa**, which has a number of interesting old traditional houses. Ferries and buses go there. You can also hire a boat on an hourly or daily basis to explore further upriver.

Places to Stay – bottom end

Ping Anchorage (☎ 09-622 0851), upstairs at 77A Jalan Dato Isaac, is the No 1 travellers' place. It has a rooftop restaurant and bar and also organises tours to Kapas, Sekayu Falls, Kenyir Lake etc. Dorm beds are RM5 and rooms are RM12 to RM15, RM20 with attached bath. The rooms are good, but most have wire-topped walls and can be noisy.

Another good option, though less popular, is the *Triple A Guesthouse* (☎ 09-622 7372). Dorm beds range from RM5 to RM8, while single/doubles are RM12/15. It's conveniently located close to the state tourist office and the central market. Call them from the airport or bus station and the owners will pick you up.

Awi's Yellow House is a unique guesthouse built on stilts over the river. It's in the boat-building village on Pulau Duyung, a 15 minute ferry ride across the river. A bed with mosquito net costs RM5 per night in the open dorm, or the small thatched rooms are RM16. Tea and coffee are free and most people cook their own food, but there is a small restaurant next door. It's a beautiful, relaxed place and highly recommended. The catch is getting over there – boats can be infrequent during the day (outside of peak hours).

Places to Stay – middle

The best mid-range value for money is probably the *Seaview Hotel* (☎ 09-622 1911) at 18A Jalan Masjid Abidin, close to the istana. Rooms with fan and common bath cost RM18/28, doubles with attached bath are

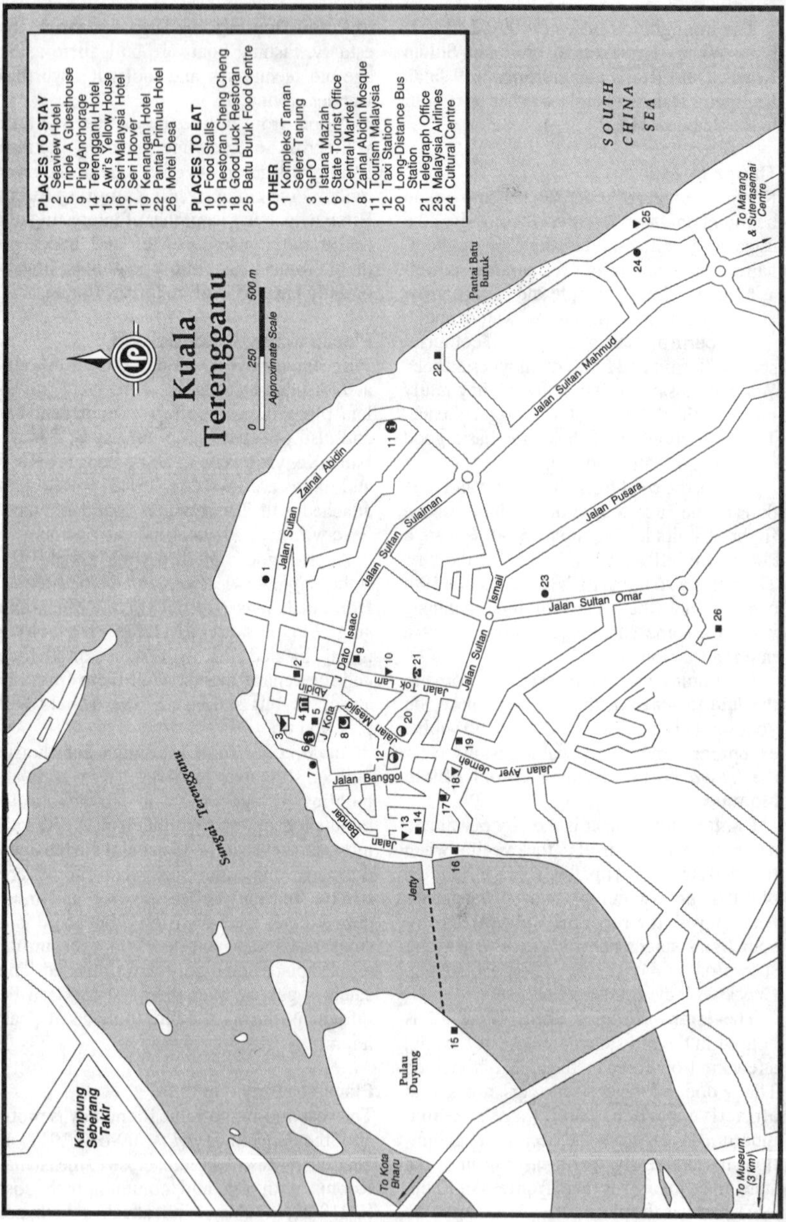
Kuala Terengganu
0
250
500 m
Approximate Scale
PLACES TO STAY
2 Seaview Hotel
5 Triple A Guesthouse
9 Ping Anchorage
14 Terengganu Hotel
15 Awi's Yellow House
16 Seri Malaysia Hotel
17 Seri Hoover
19 Kenangan Hotel
22 Pantai Primula Hotel
26 Motel Desa
PLACES TO EAT
10 Food Stalls
13 Restoran Cheng Cheng
18 Good Luck Restoran
25 Batu Buruk Food Centre
OTHER
1 Kompleks Taman Selera Tanjung
3 GPO
4 Istana Maziah
6 State Tourist Office
7 Central Market
8 Zainal Abidin Mosque
11 Tourism Malaysia
12 Taxi Station
20 Long-Distance Bus Station
21 Telegraph Office
23 Malaysia Airlines
24 Cultural Centre
SOUTH CHINA SEA
Pantai Batu Buruk
Jalan Sultan Mahmud
Jalan Pusara
Jalan Sultan Zainal Abidin
Jalan Sultan Sulaiman
Jalan Sultan Ismail
Jalan Sultan Omar
J Dato Isaac
Jalan Tok Lam
Abidin
J Kota
Jalan Masjid
Jalan Banggol
Jalan Bandar
Jalan Ayer Jemeh
Sungai Terengganu
Jetty
Pulau Duyung
Kampung Seberang Takir
To Kota Bharu
To Museum (3 km)
To Marang & Suterasemai Centre

RM32 and singles/doubles with air-con and bath are RM56/66.

Most mid-range accommodation is on Jalan Sultan Ismail. The *Terengganu Hotel* (☎ 09-622 2900), at the western end of Jalan Sultan Ismail, is one of the cheaper options, with rooms at RM33 with fan or RM55 with air-con and attached bath. It's seen better days and is not particularly friendly.

The *Hotel KT Mutiara* (☎ 09-622 2655), 67 Jalan Sultan Ismail, is a recently refurbished hotel that offers good mid-range comforts at RM55 to RM85. A couple of doors along is the *Kenangan Hotel* (☎ 09-622 2688), a slightly shabby establishment with air-con singles/doubles at RM48/73. The *Seri Hoover* (☎ 09-623 3833), at 49 Jalan Sultan Ismail, offers similar standards, with rooms at RM58/79.

Places to Stay – top end

For top-end luxury at affordable prices, the *Seri Malaysia Hotel* (☎ 09-623 6454), at the southern end of Jalan Bandar, is a good option. Singles/doubles cost RM100, and spacious family rooms are RM120.

The *Motel Desa* (☎ 09-622 3033) is in a beautiful garden setting on the top of Bukit Pak Api, but unless you have your own transport it's a very inconvenient place to stay. Singles/doubles cost RM120/140; it has a good restaurant and a swimming pool.

The *Pantai Primula Hotel* (☎ 09-622 2100) provides international-class accommodation, and due to low occupancy rates often sports generous 'promotional discounts'. Posted rates are RM160 for standard rooms, RM241 and upwards for deluxe rooms, inclusive of tax. The hotel has a swimming pool, three restaurants and other services you would expect.

Places to Eat

There is a string of good food stalls on Jalan Tok Lam near the telegraph office, and this is one of the best places to seek out an evening meal. The *Batu Buruk Food Centre* on the beachfront and the 2nd floor of the *Kompleks Taman Selera Tanjung* are also good places to seek out inexpensive Malay and Chinese food.

For Indian food, look out for the *Restoran Thaofiq*, a few doors away from the Seaview Hotel on Jalan Masjid Abidin. It is possible to put together a good meal here for just a few ringgits.

The *Restoran Cheng Cheng* at 224 Jalan Bandar has average buffet-style Chinese at affordable prices. Meals are priced using a colour-coded peg system – when you've finished eating, take the plate with peg to the counter and pay.

One of the best areas for Chinese food is at the southern end of Jalan Banggol around the Plaza Perdana. Among the restaurants here are the *Chuan Kee* on Jalan Banggol, which has good chicken-rice and fruit juices, and the *Good Luck Restoran* around the corner on Jalan Engku Sar. The Good Luck is a bit more expensive, but it has an extensive menu and you can sit at tables on the pavement and watch life roll by.

If you feel like a minor extravagance, the *Pantai Primula Hotel* sometimes puts on an excellent smorgasbord of Malay food. There are also some upmarket seafood restaurants at Batu Buruk.

Things to Buy

Kuala Terengganu is a good place to buy batik and songket, the intricate weaving using gold and silver threads. You can see silk-weaving at the Suterasemai Centre, a few km from town on the road to Marang. The handicraft centre is 10 km from town at Rhusila, not far from Marang, but the best place to buy handicrafts is upstairs at the central market.

Getting There & Away

Air Malaysia Airlines (☎ 09-622 1415), 13 Jalan Sultan Omar, services Kuala Terengganu. There are direct flights to/from KL (twice daily, RM104). A taxi to the airport costs RM15.

Bus Kuala Terengganu has a new bus station on Jalan Masjid Abidin which serves as a terminus for both long-distance and local buses. Heading south, there are regular buses to Marang (RM1), Rantau Abang (RM3), Kuantan (RM9), Mersing (RM18), Johor Bahru (RM22.10) and Singapore (RM23.10). To Kuala Lumpur the fare is RM21.70, and to Melaka RM24.

Buses to Kota Bharu (RM7.40) leave every 1½ to two hours from 8.30 am to 7 pm. There are also buses to Butterworth (RM24).

Taxi The main taxi stand is next to the bus station. It costs RM2.50 to Marang, RM8 to Jerteh (for Kuala Besut), RM6 to Rantau Abang, RM12 to Kota Bharu, RM15 to Kuantan and RM35/45 to KL.

Getting Around

Bus There are regular regional buses from the bus station. For the museum take a Losong bus; for the handicraft and silk-weaving centres take a Marang or Medan Jaya bus.

Taxi Taxis around town cost a minimum of RM5, but there are not many of them about. Try the taxi area next to the bus station.

Trishaw Kuala Terengganu was once the trishaw capital of Malaysia, and while their numbers have dropped, they are still the main form of intra-city transport and cost roughly RM1 per km.

AROUND KUALA TERENGGANU

Sekayu Waterfalls

The Sekayu Waterfalls are 56 km south-west of Kuala Terengganu. You can catch a bus to Kuala Berang, and from there it is about 15 km to the falls, where there are pleasant natural swimming pools. A taxi out to the falls costs RM5. Ping Anchorage does day trips out to the falls for RM35. There is a resthouse and chalets, costing around RM40 per night. Phone the District Office in Kuala Berang (☎ 09-681 1259) for bookings.

Lake Kenyir

Lake Kenyir is being developed as a massive 'eco-tourist' destination by local tourist authorities (eco-tourism equals eco-dollars). Access roads are being laid down and a host of new accommodation options and other tourist facilities are either on the drawing board or under construction. Despite the 'eco-tourism' sloganeering, the lake was formed by the construction of Kenyir Dam in 1985. The chief attraction of the finished tourist package will probably be water sports, though the lake – covering over 38,000 hectares and containing 340 islands – is not without its attractions. Kenyir will also in future provide an interesting alternative route into Taman Negara National Park.

The lake is 15 km from Kuala Berang and 55 km from Kuala Terengganu, and can be combined with a trip to the Sekayu Waterfalls. At the time of writing, the main access point was Pengkalan Gawi, a nondescript place with a tourist information office. Operations will shift to Penkalan Utama when a five km access road from Gawi is completed.

Waterfalls are high on the list of Kenyir's attractions. Lasir Waterfall, around 16 km south of Pengkalan Gawi, is the most impressive, and can be reached by boat – a resthouse, camping facilities and jungle treks are planned for the area. Saok Waterfall, on the other side of the lake from Pengkalan Gawi, is a picturesque spot that is popular with local picnickers. Batu Biwa and Batu Taat limestone caves border the lake and are actually inside Taman Negara National Park. It takes around two hours by boat to reach them from Pengkalan Gawi.

Places to Stay Most of the accommodation is in resort chalets or longhouse-style structures built over the lake. There is nothing in the way of budget options, but camping facilities are being developed. The resorts generally offer packages inclusive of meals and boat transport from Pengkawan Gawi. Ping Anchorage in Kuala Terengganu offers some competitively priced packages.

One of the cheaper possibilities is *Kenyir Woods* (☎ 09-623 8188), across the lake from Pengkawan Gawi. Comfortable chalets built on a slope overlooking the lake cost from RM50. A two-day/one-night package costs RM120.

The *Primula Kenyir Lake Resort* (☎ 09-622 2100) is on Poh Island, just three minutes by speedboat from Pengkalan Gawi. Chalets range from RM100 to RM150 – the more expensive ones are built on stilts over the water.

South of Penankan Gawi (around 30 minutes by boat) is the *Muping Island Resort* (☎ 09-681 2197), a longhouse village built over the lake. Rates start at RM130 for two days and one night. Not far away is *Uncle John's Resort* (☎ 09-622 9564), where rates start at RM135 for two days and one night. Access to Uncle John's is via the main dam at Jenagor.

Getting There & Away You can reach Kuala Berang by bus or taxi from Kuala Terengganu, but from Kuala Berang to the lake you'll have to hire a taxi or private car for around RM20. You can arrange day trips or accommodation at the state tourist office in Kuala Terengganu, and the Ping Anchorage in Kuala Terengganu does a three-day 'houseboat adventure' for RM190.

Getting Around The chief impediment to doing Lake Kenyir solo is the prohibitive cost of getting around by boat. From Pengkawan Gawi most destinations are RM200 and upwards. There are plans to build a road encircling the lake.

North of Kuala Terengganu

North of Kuala Terengganu the main road leaves the coast and runs inland to Kota Bharu, 165 km north, via Jerteh. The quiet coastal backroad from Kuala Terengganu to Penarek runs along a beautiful stretch of coast, and there are other turn-offs from the main road to fishing villages and quiet beaches. For cyclists there is also a backroad along the coast from Penarek to Kuala Besut.

The final stretch into Kota Bharu runs through fertile rice-growing areas, mirroring the similar area in Kedah and Perlis at the northern end of the peninsula on the western side.

BATU RAKIT

Twenty-four km north of Kuala Terengganu is the small village of Batu Rakit. The beach is quite good, though not as good as those further north. You can stay at the *Pantai Batu Rakit Guest House* for RM26 a night. Take the Batu Rakit bus from Kuala Terengganu for RM1.30, and from the bus station walk down to the beach and turn left to get to the guesthouse.

MERANG

The sleepy little fishing village of Merang (not to be confused with Marang) is 14 km north of Batu Rakit. There's nothing to do here, but the beautiful beach is lined with coconut palms and lapped by clear water. It is one of the few remaining villages of its kind where development hasn't gone ahead in leaps and bounds. Further north are more beautiful beaches, at Bari and Penarek, but there is no cheap accommodation.

Places to Stay & Eat

The easygoing *Naughty Dragon's Green Planet Homestay* right in the centre of the village is a place where it's easy to spend a few relaxing days. Unfortunately this place was set to change hands some time in late 1996, and its fate is uncertain. Accommodation is basic but comfortable and the cost is RM15 for a double, or RM7 in one of the three-bed dorms. Kitchen facilities are available if you want to do your own cooking, but there are only a couple of tiny shops in the village. There are a couple of basic *kedai kopis* in the village also.

Another option is *Razak's Kampung House*, also in the centre of the village. Here the cost is RM15 per person.

There is also resort accommodation not far away at the *Sutra Beach Resort* (☎ 011-623 3718). Room prices start at RM120.

Getting There & Away

Don't go to Merang if you're in a hurry. Buses are infrequent and hitching is slow.

From Kuala Terengganu take one of the three daily Penarek buses (noon and 4 and 5 pm, RM2.20) or one of the more frequent minibus vans (RM3) from in front of the bookstore on Jalan Masjid. A taxi from Kuala Terengganu costs RM3 per person.

If you're coming from the north, get off at Permaisuri on the main highway and then take one of the hourly buses to Penarek. From Penarek there are occasional buses to Merang, but don't bother waiting – take a share-taxi (RM2) or Econovan, or hitch.

PULAU REDANG

One of the largest and most inaccessible of the east coast islands, Pulau Redang was for a long time the secret of divers. Naturally the inevitable happened, and it's now home to an exclusive resort and a nine hole golf course.

Despite the development, Redang is one of nine islands that together form a protected marine park and offers excellent diving and snorkelling. Siltation from the resort construction is said to have resulted in some coral damage, but concerted efforts are being made to prevent further damage – even snorkelling is restricted to certain areas. To the south of the island are the beautiful bays of Teluk Dalam, Teluk Kalong and Pasir Panjang.

Nearby Islands

Pulau Lang Tengah is an uninhabited island about 10 km from Redang and has excellent snorkelling. Pulau Pinang is the small island opposite the fishing village, and other nearby islands include Pulau Tenggol, Pulau Ekor Tebu and Pulau Ling. Pulau Lima, a group of five islands two hours by boat from Redang, also has good snorkelling.

Places to Stay

Accommodation on Pulau Redang is best organised as a package in Kuala Terengganu. Ping Anchorage in Kuala Terengganu has the cheapest deal at RM240 for two nights, three days with camping equipment and meals provided. The other option is very upmarket resort accommodation at *Redang Lagoon* (☎ 09-827 2116).

Getting There & Away

To hire a boat from Merang costs around RM350 return. It is very difficult to get a boat to Redang in the monsoon.

KUALA BESUT

Kuala Besut, on the coast south of Kota Bharu, has a reasonably pleasant beach and is an interesting, though grubby, fishing village. A visit to this town is usually just a preliminary to a trip to the Perhentian Islands.

A few km south of Kuala Besut is Bukit Keluang, an attractive beach with small caves reached by a wooden walkway. Bukit Belatan waterfall, in the Gunung Tebu Forest Reserve, is 11 km from Jerteh.

Places to Stay

There is a surprisingly large number of places to choose from in Besut. The cheapest option around is the *Coco Hut Chalet* (☎ 09-687 2085). It has very basic rooms for RM10 and RM15. If you want a little more comfort, the *Nan Hotel* is just down the road from the Perhentian Islands ferry pier and has singles/doubles with attached bathroom and ceiling fan for RM35 and air-con doubles for RM45.

The *Primula Beach Resort* (☎ 09-687 6322) is an uninspiring beachside concrete block one km south of town over the bridge at Pantai Air Tawar. Rooms cost RM100/120 and up. Take any southbound bus or a trishaw.

Getting There & Away

From the south, take a bus to Jerteh on the main highway, from where buses go every 40 minutes to Kuala Besut. From Kota Bharu it's easier to get off at Pasir Puteh and take a bus from there. A share-taxi from Jerteh or Pasir Puteh to Kuala Besut costs RM1.50. Taxis from Kuala Terengganu cost RM10, from Kota Bharu RM5.

PERHENTIAN ISLANDS

A 1½ hour boat trip from Kuala Besut will take you to the beautiful islands of Perhentian Besar and Perhentian Kecil, just 21 km off the coast. These are arguably the most beautiful islands in Malaysia.

A narrow strait separates the 'besar', or big island, from the 'kecil', or small island. Pulau Perhentian Besar has more accommodation, but the places on Pulau Perhentian Kecil are better, as are the beaches. Most of the beaches on both islands have a lot of dead coral on them, but Pasir Panjang (Long Beach) on Perhentian Kecil is a beautiful long white sandy beach and has good accommodation. Perhentian Kecil is also the administrative centre and has a fair-sized village with a few kedai kopis and shops.

As far as things to 'see and do' go, it's simply a case of lazing around and watching the coconuts fall. There are beautiful beaches and excellent snorkelling and scuba diving. Bring plenty of books and suntan lotion.

Tourist development has been slow to reach these quiet islands – this isn't Langkawi, fortunately. There's just one mid-range resort and a couple of dozen places with basic chalets.

Information

The only place to change money is at the Perhentian Island Resort on Perhentian Besar, but the rate is about 10% less than you'll get in a bank. You can also make telephone calls from here – again, at exorbitant rates. A couple of the chalet operations around the islands also offer telephone services on their mobiles.

Diving & Snorkelling

There are excellent coral reefs off both islands, but for land-based snorkelling the best bet is the northern end of Long Beach on Kecil. Most of the chalets organise boating trips for snorkelling, and these are well worth the RM13 or so per person. All places also rent out mask, snorkel and flippers for RM10.

For scuba divers there are several operations on Perhentian Besar. At the Perhentian Island Resort it costs RM165 for two boat-based dives including all equipment, or

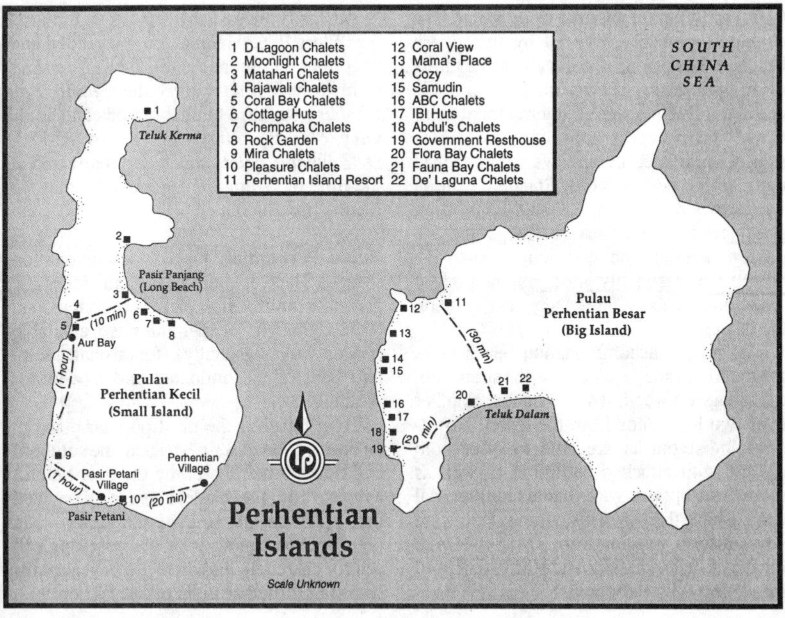

RM130 with just air and tanks; for one dive it's RM110/85. Night dives are also popular, and these cost RM90 including all equipment. PADI dive courses are held here, and these cost RM700 and take four to five days. The resort also hires out windsurfers for RM15 per hour, sailboats for RM30 per hour and kayaks for RM7 per hour.

Both Coral View and Mama's Place also offer diving courses at rates slightly cheaper than those at the resort. It would be sensible to check out all three places before making a decision. Over on Perhentian Kecil is the Turtle Island Dive centre, next door to Matahari Chalets.

Whichever way you dive, there's a good chance of seeing turtles and stingrays in addition to a wide variety of fish, and reef sharks (supposedly harmless) are also common.

Places to Stay & Eat

Pulau Perhentian Besar There are two basic choices: the resort or the 'budget-accommodation beach'.

The *Perhentian Island Resort* (☎ 010-901 0100) is 'Where reality is like a dream'. The slogan is probably inspired by the superb beach and its beautiful coral and has nothing to do with drugs. The resort is comfortable and attractive but not of international standard. The cheapest accommodation is in roomy fan-cooled bungalows with attached bath, which cost RM120. Standard air-con bungalows range from RM160. Everything is subject to a 10% service charge and 5% government tax. The restaurant is expensive but does a reasonably good job and does at least serve drinks – unlike anywhere else on the island.

The budget accommodation beach faces the mainland and is just across the strait from the village on Kecil. It's a 20 minute clamber over two headlands from the resort. Nowadays, most outfits are able to offer both chalets with attached bathroom as well as more basic options with shared facilities. All chalets have their own restaurants. Prices are very uniform, ranging from RM15 to RM20 for the no-frills versions and RM30 to RM40 for chalets with bathrooms.

At the northern end of the beach is *Coral View*, with a number of closely bunched chalets, each with attached bath. Close by is *Mama's Place*, a more basic operation with cheaper prices. Next along is *Cozy*, one of the cheaper set-ups around. On the downside, this place is built on a rocky headland and access to some of the chalets is difficult, if not dangerous – not a good place to bring young kids.

Coco Hut and *Samudin*, the next two, are unremarkable, while next south is *ABC Chalets,* which is well set up with cheap, basic huts right on the beach under the trees. *IBI Huts* and *Abdul's Chalets* are both very popular and have good restaurants.

You can also find yourself a quiet place to camp beyond the *Government Resthouse* (reserved for those with the right connections), although this area is far from quiet on long weekends (notably the end of April, when the Sultan's Birthday and Worker's Day coincide), when the place becomes packed with Malaysian families camping out.

An easily missed track leads to the next bay, Flora Bay, which is more secluded and becoming more popular. The *Flora Bay Chalets* and (inevitably) the *Fauna Bay Chalets* both have budget options and some very classy chalets for up to RM70. *De'Laguna Chalets* was being renovated at the time of writing and the results may be worth checking out.

Pulau Perhentian Kecil Accommodation over on Kecil is more basic and prices are generally lower – most places hover at around RM20, though cheaper rates are available (prices vary seasonally), for a chalet with two beds, a mosquito net and a well for washing.

Long Beach is the most popular place to be based. *Chempaka Chalets*, at the southern end of the beach, is run by the ever-helpful Musky, and the chalets are well spaced across a slope and so have sea views – and breezes. You can do your own cooking (50 sen for charcoal), and there are pancakes for breakfast (order the night before). There's no electricity here, but kerosene lamps are provided in the evenings, and there's free tea and biscuits all day.

Next along is the *Cottage Huts*. The popularity of this place stems largely from its restaurant right on the beach, although you don't have to stay here to eat here. Many of the chalets are cramped together and, although quite OK, are not as good as others. There's electricity until 11 pm.

Matahari Chalets is one of the most popular places, not least due to its restaurant, which has some of the best cooking around.

Right at the northern end of the beach is the *Moonlight Chalets*, with just a few chalets tucked into the corner of the bay. It's well set up and a good place to stay.

If you really want to get away from it all, this island is perfect. There are a number of small bays around the island, each with just one set of chalets, and often the only access is by boat. *D Lagoon Chalets* is on Teluk Kerma, a small bay on the western side of the island. The beach here has quite a bit of dead coral. In addition to chalets there are a number of rooms in a 'longhouse' for the same price. There's a small restaurant, and tracks lead to a couple of very remote beaches in the north-west corner of the island. It is one of the few places on the island that has chalets with attached bathroom.

On the western side of the island, *Coral Bay Chalets*, the pioneer on this bay, has been joined by a couple of other chalet operations: *Rajawali* and *Aur Bay*. It's worth taking a look at all three – Rajawali is more upmarket, with prices from RM35. The bay is quiet and gets good sunsets, and the feeding of the huge monitor lizards late every afternoon shouldn't be missed. It's just a short walk across the 'waist' of the island to Long Beach, although, as is the case with all places, the boats from the mainland will drop you anywhere.

Further south on the west coast is the *Mira Chalets*. This is another beautiful little beach and there are only a few chalets. The elevated restaurant has great views out over the water and is a popular place. Walking tracks lead through the rainforest to Pasir Petani (half an hour) or north to Coral Bay (one hour).

On the south coast at Pasir Petani, there are a couple of choices. The cheaper of the two is *Pleasure Chalets*, just a few chalets by the beach. Next door is the more upmarket *Pasir Petani Village*, which has pleasant chalets, each with attached bath and fan, for RM45.

Getting There & Away

The one-way trip from Kuala Besut to Perhentian costs RM15. Most boats leave Perhentian early in the morning and return late morning and throughout the afternoon. The boats will drop you off at any of the beaches. When you want to leave it's a good idea to let the owner of your chalets know the day before.

Small boats ply between the two islands for RM3 per person, but you may have to wait for a while.

Kelantan

Kelantan is Malaysia at its most Malayan – a centre for Malay culture, crafts and religion. It's the place to see kite-flying contests, watch batik being made, admire traditional woodcarving techniques, photograph colourful marketplaces and marvel at the skills of *songket* weavers and silversmiths.

While the capital, Kota Bharu, is a good place to sample traditional Malay culture, the true Malay spirit is found in the villages of Kelantan, and Kota Bharu makes a good base from which travellers can explore the surrounding countryside. Much of Kelantan's character can be attributed to the fact that it was one of the last states to come under British rule.

Kelantan is the most conservative state in Peninsular Malaysia. It's the last bastion of opposition rule in Malaysia, and the government – an alliance of Semangat '46 and PAS, an Islamic party – is set on protecting its constituents from rampant development and corruption. As a result, with the exception of Sabah, Kelantan is Malaysia's poorest state. Fortunately, local government attempts to ban the public consumption of alcohol and introduce stoning for adultery have been thwarted by local interest groups and the federal government so far. But even so, Kelantan is a world apart from the go-go western states of Peninsular Malaysia.

The Kelantan state economy is driven by the production of rice, based mainly on the fertile plain of the Kelantan River, which flows due north through the state, finding the sea just north of Kota Bharu. Fishing and tobacco growing are other important activities.

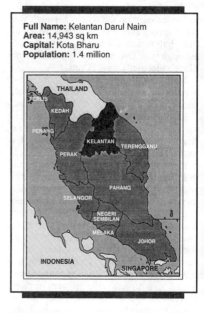

Full Name: Kelantan Darul Naim
Area: 14,943 sq km
Capital: Kota Bharu
Population: 1.4 million

History

Archaeological finds at Gua Musang and Gua Cha have turned up evidence of human settlements dating back to prehistoric times.

In later times (early Christian era), Kelantan was influenced by the Indianised Funan kingdom on the Mekong River. Farming methods used in Kelantan are based on Funan practices, and the *wayang kulit* shadow play and weaving methods are also thought to have come from Funan.

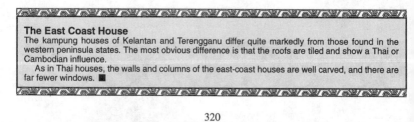

The East Coast House

The kampung houses of Kelantan and Terengganu differ quite markedly from those found in the western peninsula states. The most obvious difference is that the roofs are tiled and show a Thai or Cambodian influence.

As in Thai houses, the walls and columns of the east-coast houses are well carved, and there are far fewer windows. ■

PETER TURNER

VICKI BEALE

Peninsular Malaysia

Top: The Zahir Mosque in Alor Setar, Kedah, is one of the grandest in Malaysia.

Bottom: The picturesque fishing village of Marang in Terengganu is a favourite stopover for travellers.

HUGH FINLAY

TONY WHEELER

PAUL STEEL

HUGH FINLAY

Peninsular Malaysia

Top: Ferry to Pangkor, a resort island with fine beaches and jungle-clad hills
Middle Left: Boats off Langkawi Island in Kedah
Middle Right: A mosque near Melaka
Bottom: A colonial building in Pahang

After being a vassal of first the Sumatran Sriwijaya empire and then the Siamese, Kelantan then came under the sway of the new Melaka sultanate in the 15th century, and on Melaka's demise was ruled by Johor in the 17th century and then by Terengganu in the 18th century.

By the 1820s Kelantan was the most populous and one of the most prosperous states on the peninsula. As was the case in Terengganu, Kelantan escaped the ravages of the disputes which plagued the west-coast states, and so experienced largely unimpeded development. Also like Terengganu, Kelantan had strong ties with Siam throughout the 19th century, before control was passed to the British following the signing of an Anglo-Siamese treaty in 1909. The biggest upheaval for the state came in the late 18th century when it was hit by a spate of natural disasters – hurricanes, famine and cattle plagues – and many of its residents migrated to Kedah.

During WWII, Kelantan was the first place in Malaya to be invaded by Japanese troops. During the Japanese occupation, control of the state was passed to Thailand, but in 1948 Kelantan became a member of the Federation of Malaya.

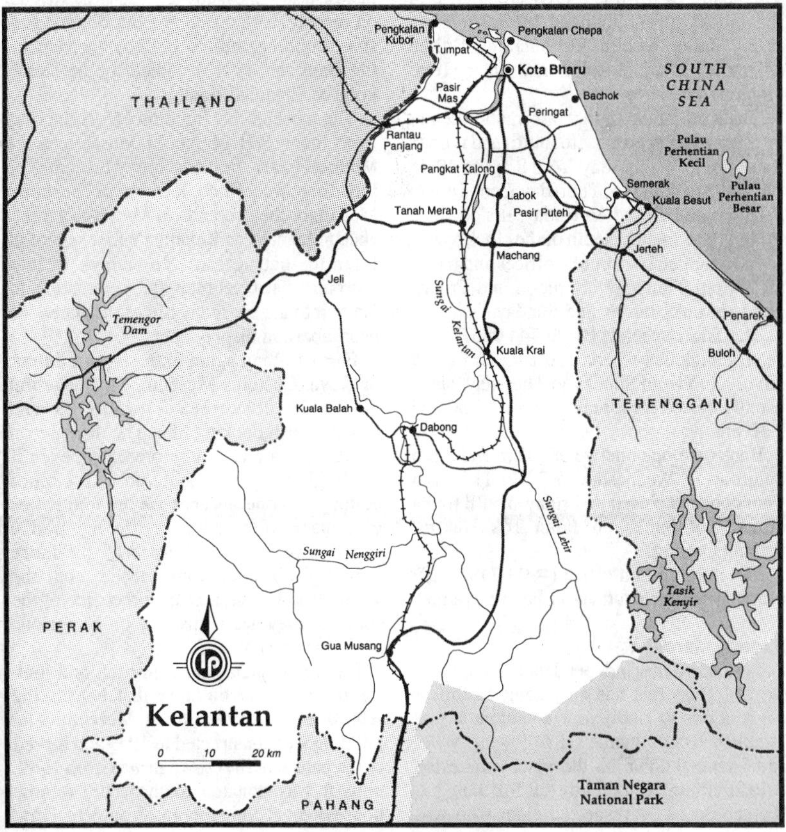

KOTA BHARU

In the north-east corner of the peninsula, Kota Bharu is the termination of the east-coast road and a gateway to Thailand.

At first glance, Kota Bharu is much like the other east-coast cities – a modern, architecturally uninspired town set on the banks of a wide river. But if you scratch the surface, Kota Bharu has a number of attractions and is a good base for exploring the surrounding region. Many travellers plan an overnight stop here en route to or from Thailand. Many end up staying much longer.

Orientation & Information

The centre of town is a busy area, north of the clock tower, bounded by Jalan Pintu Pong, Jalan Kebun Sultan/Jalan Sultan Mahmud, Jalan Hospital and Jalan Temenggong.

The Kota Bharu tourist information centre (☎ 09-748 5534) is a useful outfit and is open Saturday to Wednesday from 8 am to 12.45 pm and 2 to 4.30 pm, Thursday from 8 am to 1.15 pm and closed on Friday. It's on Jalan Sultan Ibrahim, just south of the clock tower.

In Kelantan, state public offices and banks are closed Thursday afternoon and Friday, but open on Saturday and Sunday.

The Thai consulate (☎ 09-744 0867) is on Jalan Pengkalan Chepa and is open from 9 am to 4 pm from Sunday to Thursday, but is usually closed for lunch between 12.30 and 2.30 pm.

Banks are open between 10 am and 3 pm Saturday to Wednesday, 9.30 to 11.30 am Thursday and closed on Friday. You'll find a number of banks on Jalan Tok Hakim/Padang Garong.

The immigration office (☎ 09-748 2120) is at Wisma Persekutuan on Jalan Bayam.

Padang Merdeka

Padang Merdeka (Independence Square) is a strip of grass that has only some historical associations to claim your attention. It was established as a memorial following WWI and is best known as the place where the British exhibited the body of Tok Janggut, 'Father Beard', a respected elder who was killed at Pasir Puteh in 1915 after leading a 2000-strong uprising against British imperialism (more specifically, British land taxes).

Padang Merdeka Museums

The real attraction of the Padang Merdeka area is the cluster of museums close by. They are all open from 10 am to 6 pm, closed on Friday, and charge RM2 or RM3 entry.

Starting closest to the river, the first museum you come to is the **Bank Kerapu**, or WWII Memorial Museum. It's basically a collection of photographic memorabilia illustrating the perfidy of the Japanese, but there is also some hardware (Japanese swords) on display. It's housed in Kota Bharu's first stone building, built in 1912 by the Mercantile Bank and later occupied by the Hongkong & Shanghai Bank.

The mosque-like building across the road from the WWII Memorial Museum is the **Muzium Islam**, or the Islamic Museum. The building was once known as Serambi Mekah, or the 'Veranda to Mecca' – a reference to its days as Kelantan's first school of Islamic instruction. Nowadays it is a museum that celebrates the percolation of Islam into the everyday life of the state – no beer labels on display here.

Further along again is the **Istana Jahar**, or Royal Customs Museum. This beautiful old wooden structure dates back to 1887 and is well worth ducking into. The displays on courtly life are tastefully presented, even if the English captions could do with a bit of editing – in one instance we are told it was customary for the sultan to offer his 'brid' a 'goft' after which there was no more 'wailing' for invitations. Inside, note the wrought-iron staircases on either side of the room – they lead upstairs to a glorious wooden veranda.

From the Istana Jahar, turn left and look for the sky-blue building that houses the **Istana Batu**, or the Royal Museum. The building was constructed in 1939 and served as the palace of the crown prince from 1969, until it was donated to the state. It now houses a royal dining room, an opulent living room, replicas of the crown jewels and other royal bric-a-brac.

Finally, across the road is the **Kampung Kraftangan**, or the Handicraft Village. This is a touristy *kampung* idyll (all arts and crafts, no toiling in the fields) and features a museum with displays of silver smithing, batik making and other cultural activities. There are performances on Sunday from 3 pm to 6 pm, and there are also souvenirs for sale and an upmarket seafood restaurant (Rhong Sree Seafood Garden) to relax in.

Surrounded by walls and closed to the public is the **Istana Balai Besar**, or the Palace of the Large Audience Hall.

Markets

The central market is one of the most colourful and active in Malaysia. It is in a modern octagonal building with traders selling fresh produce on the ground floor, and stalls on the floors above selling spices, basketware and other goods. Near the market is the Bazaar Buluh Kubu, a good place to buy handicrafts.

The old central market consists of a complete block of food stalls on the ground floor, and the stalls on the 1st floor have a good selection of batik, songket and clothes.

Cultural Centre (Gelanggang Seni)

Kota Bharu provides an opportunity to see top spinning, traditional dance dramas, wayang kulit and other traditional activities. The place to go is Gelanggang Seni, across the road from the Hotel Perdana on Jalan Sultan Mahmud. Performances of one kind or another are held from February to October, except during Ramadan. Free afternoon and evening sessions are held on Saturday, Sunday, Monday and Wednesday. Check with the tourist information centre for more details.

State Museum

The State Museum is opposite the clock tower, next to the tourist information centre. It brings together an eclectic array of artefacts, crafts, paintings and photographic displays, all connected in some way or another with Kelantan state. There's some excellent Ming and Qing dynasty porcelain downstairs and kites upstairs. The downstairs local art exhibit is given over to nostalgic celebrations of kampung life – everyone is spinning tops, flying kites, dancing and basically having so much cultural fun you'd think there were tourists paying them to do it. It is open from 10.30 am to 5.45 pm, closed on Friday; entry is RM2.

Events

Each year around August, Kota Bharu has a **bird-singing contest** when you can see the prized merbok or ketitir birds perform. On Friday mornings there's also a bird-singing contest out near Johnty's Guesthouse. Here the locals hang their decorative birdcages up on long poles, then sit back and listen. It seems to happen to a lesser extent on other days as well.

The spectacular **kite festival** is usually held in May, the **drum festival** in July and the **top-spinning contest** in September. The **Sultan's Birthday** celebration involves a week of cultural events. The dates vary, so check with the tourist information centre or get hold of Tourism Malaysia's *Calendar of Events* brochure.

The traditional Malay pastime of kite flying is especially popular in Kota Bharu.

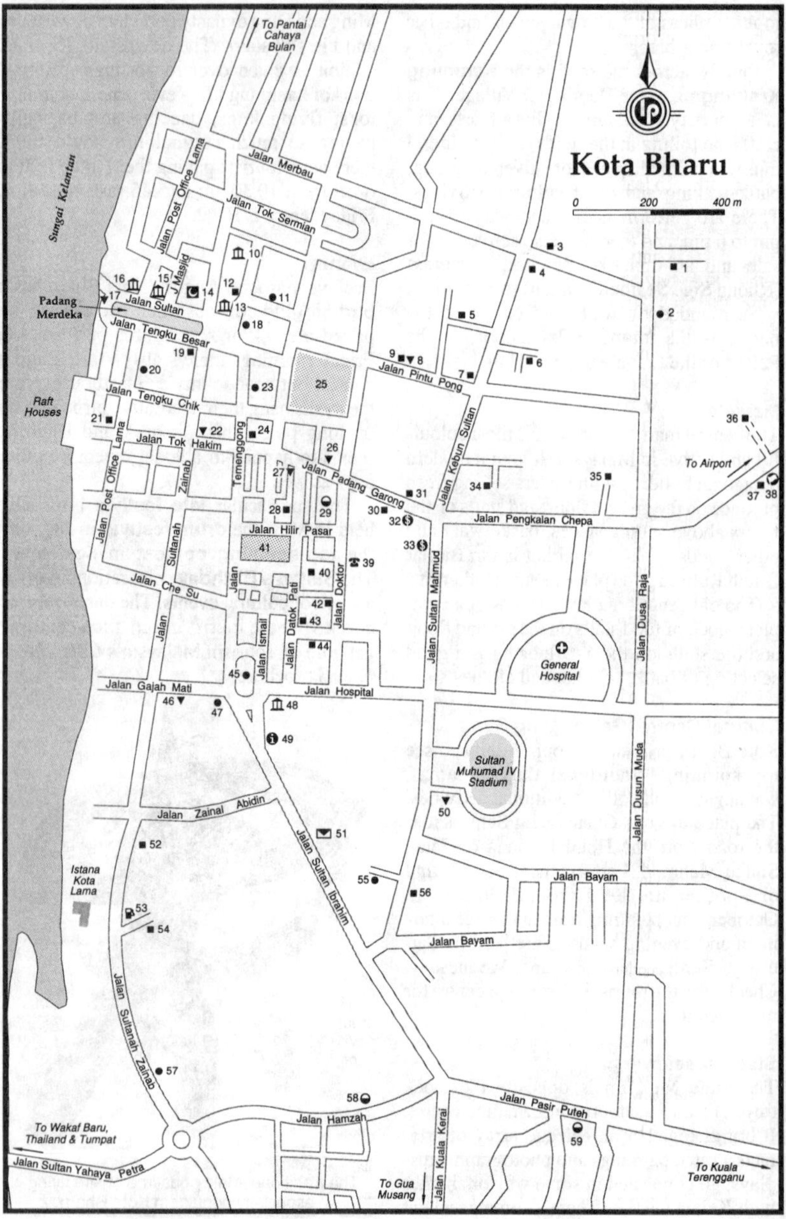
Kota Bharu
0
200
400 m
To Pantai Cahaya Bulan
Sungai Kelantan
Jalan Merbau
Jalan Tok Semian
Jalan Post Office Lama
J Masjid
Padang Merdeka
Jalan Sultan
Jalan Tengku Besar
Raft Houses
Jalan Tengku Chik
Jalan Tok Hakim
Jalan Post Office Lama
Jalan Zainab
Jalan Temenggong
Jalan Sultanah
Jalan Che Su
Jalan
Jalan Ismail
Jalan Datok Pati
Jalan Doktor
Jalan Hilir Pasar
Jalan Padang Garong
Jalan Pintu Pong
Jalan Kebun Sultan
Jalan Pengkalan Chepa
Jalan Sultan Mahmud
Jalan Dusa Raja
To Airport
General Hospital
Jalan Gajah Mati
Jalan Hospital
Sultan Muhumad IV Stadium
Jalan Dusun Muda
Jalan Zainal Abidin
Jalan Sultan Ibrahim
Istana Kota Lama
Jalan Bayam
Jalan Bayam
Jalan Sultanah Zainab
Jalan Pasir Puteh
Jalan Hamzah
Jalan Kuala Kerai
To Wakaf Baru, Thailand & Tumpat
Jalan Sultan Yahaya Petra
To Gua Musang
To Kuala Terengganu
1
2
3
4
5
6
7
8
9
10
11
12
13
14
15
16
17
18
19
20
21
22
23
24
25
26
27
28
29
30
31
32
33
34
35
36
37
38
39
40
41
42
43
44
45
46
47
48
49
50
51
52
53
54
55
56
57
58
59

Organised Tours

The tourist information centre has expensive but rewarding tours: a morning craft tour (RM35), a river safari and jungle-trekking tour (RM60) and a three day 'kampung experience', 'home-stay' programme (RM160), where you stay with a family and get the opportunity to learn local crafts. The latter is very popular.

Some of the guesthouses around town also run tours. Johnty's Guesthouse has a two-night/three-day package out to the Jelawang Jungle for RM130 that gets good reviews from travellers. Other travel agents around town provide the same service at higher rates.

Places to Stay – bottom end

Locals count upwards of 60 guesthouse outfits in Kota Bharu, and there will probably be more by the time you have this book in your hands – the place is swarming with them. Prices vary only marginally, hovering around RM6 for a dorm bed, RM8/10 for a single/double and RM12 to 15 for a room with attached bathroom. Most have bicycles and cooking facilities.

For anyone spending more than a couple of days in Kota Bharu, the best places to be based in are the 'home-stays' on the outskirts of town. The guesthouses in the centre of town are generally noisy and slightly claustrophobic (coffin-size rooms divided by paper-thin wooden panelling), though few of them are wanting for a smile or useful travelling tips.

Johnty's Guesthouse (☎ 09-747 8677) deserves a plug. It's a friendly place run by a couple of young Malay guys. There's a garden and a comfortable living room, and a basic breakfast is included. There are also cooking facilities and the occasional evening barbecue. It's around 15 minutes' walk from the centre of town and is very quiet. When Johnty's is full, many travellers head over to *Zeck Traveller's Inn* (☎ 09-747 3423), around five minutes' walk way.

On an alley off Jalan Pengkalan Chepa, near the Thai consulate, is the popular *Mummy's Hitec Hostel* in a funky old house with a large garden. Sadly Mummy herself – a legendary pioneer on the Kota Bharu guesthouse scene – passed away recently, but the

PLACES TO STAY

1 Johnty's Guest House
3 KB Garden Hostel
4 Star Hostel
5 Ideal Travellers' Guest House
6 Hostel Pantai
7 Juita Inn
9 City Guest House
12 Safar Inn
19 Hotel Indah
21 Hotel North Malaysia & Restoran Donald Duck
24 Temenggong Hotel
28 Thye Ann Hotel
30 Yee Guest House
31 Kencana Inn
34 Friendly Guest House
35 Zeck Traveller's Inn
36 Mummy's Hitec Hostel
37 Rainbow Inn Guest House
40 Hitech Hostel & Taxis
42 Kencana Inn City Centre
43 Hotel Murni
44 Hotel Ansar
52 Menora Guest House
54 Rebana House
56 Hotel Perdana

PLACES TO EAT

8 KFC
17 Food Stalls
22 McDonald's
26 Night Market Food Stalls
27 Razak Restoran
46 Meena Curry House
50 Food Stalls

OTHER

2 Bird-Singing Place
10 Royal Museum
11 Handicraft Village
13 Royal Customs Museum
14 State Mosque
15 Islamic Museum
16 WWII Memorial Museum
18 Istana Balai Besar
20 Antique Shop
23 Bazaar Buluh Kubu
25 Central Market
29 Central Bus & Taxi Station
32 Hongkong Bank
33 Maybank
38 Thai Consulate
39 Telekom
41 Old Central Market
45 Clock Tower
47 MAS
48 State Museum
49 Tourist Information Centre
51 Post Office
53 Caltex Station
55 Gelanggang Seni (Cultural Centre)
57 Silversmith
58 External (Jalan Hamzah) Bus Station
59 Langgar Bus Station

show goes on all the same. All beds here have mosquito nets, which is an important consideration in Kota Bharu, and there's a kitchen if you want to do your own cooking. Back down on Jalan Pengkalan Chepa is the *Rainbow Inn Guest House* (☎ 09-747 2708). This house has a pleasant garden and some great artwork on the walls, courtesy of inspired travellers – the drawback is the noise from the traffic on the main road.

Back towards town and also on Jalan Pengkalan Chepa is the popular *Town Guest House* (☎ 09-748 5192). The big plus is the rooftop restaurant with good cheap food. Opposite here is the *Windmill Hostel*, another popular place.

If you want to be more centrally located yet insulated from the traffic noise, the *Ideal Travellers' Guest House* (☎ 09-744 2246), in a private house down an alley off Jalan Pintu Pong, is a good choice. It's quiet and has a pleasant garden, but it's often full. Apart from the standard rates, it has rooms with attached bath for RM25. It also runs the *Friendly Guest House*, a few hundred metres away, just off Jalan Kebun Sultan. It's not as attractive, but is also quiet and has good rooms, some with attached bath for RM15 – it's a second best.

Of the places in the centre of town, the *KB Inn* (☎ 09-744 1786) and *Yee Guest House* (☎ 09-744 1944) are popular options. They are virtually next door to each other on Jalan Padang Garong, not far from the bus station. Both are friendly places, but the KB is the more popular of the two – it has a good common-room and the ever-fussing Nasron to look after you.

At 3338-D Jalan Sultanah Zainab is the *Menora Guest House* (☎ 09-748 1669). There's a variety of accommodation, from dorm beds for RM5 up to large double rooms for RM18. Although on a busy road it's fairly quiet and the rooftop terrace is popular.

Not far south of the Menora is *Rebana House* – look for the faded sign pointing up an alley next to Caltex station. It's a lovely house, decorated Malay-style with lots of artwork around. There's a variety of rooms available, ranging from the RM6 dorm and pokey RM8 singles to some beautiful old rooms and chalets in the garden for RM10 to RM15.

Apart from the guesthouses, which cater almost exclusively to westerners, there are the *asramas*, which are guesthouses catering almost exclusively to Malaysians. They generally charge RM5 in large dorms and RM12 and upwards for rooms. Another option, if you are desperate, is one of the old Chinese hotels around the bus station – they are usually noisy, seedy but relatively inexpensive with rooms at around RM15. Possibilities include the *Thye Ann Hotel* and the *Hotel North Malaysia* (see the map for locations).

Places to Stay – middle

Kota Bharu's mid-range accommodation has been steadily improving in recent years, and there are now a number of good-value options to choose from. All offer air-con rooms, 24 hour hot water, TV and all the other services you'd expect.

Nestled away in a quiet part of town between the Royal Customs Museum and the Royal Museum is the *Safar Inn* (☎ 09-747 8000; fax 09-747 9000), where singles/doubles start at RM52/69. The *Hotel Ansar* (☎ 09-747 4000; fax 09-746 1150) offers very similar standards at slightly higher rates – RM70 for a standard double. It advertises itself as an Islamic hotel, which as far as we can tell means no beer for sale in the lobby coffee shop.

The *Kencana Inn* (☎ 09-744 7994), Jalan Padang Garong, is fully air-con and at the top of this range, with rooms for RM68/80 and upwards. They also have a cheaper place on Jalan Doktor, the *Kencana Inn City Centre* (☎ 09-744 0944), which is a few steps down in quality and charges RM63/73 for standard singles/doubles. Both the Kencana Inn hotels often offer substantial discounts.

The *Hotel Indah* (☎ 09-748 5081; fax 748-2788), opposite Padang Merdeka on Jalan Tengku Besar, is a long-runner but offers value for money at RM57.50/66.70 for its single/double rooms.

The *Temenggong Hotel* (☎ 09-744 1481) on Jalan Tok Hakim is a nondescript mid-range hotel with rates starting at RM70/80 for singles/doubles.

Finally the *Hotel Tokyo Baru* (☎ 09-744 9488) on Jalan Tok Hakim near the Temenggong Hotel charges excessively high rates for its basic air-con rooms, though the staff are friendly and provide useful travel services. Rooms start at RM56.

Places to Stay – top end

Right in the centre on Jalan Datok Pati, the *Hotel Murni* (☎ 09-748 2399; fax 09-744 7255) has seen better days but still tends to be popular with businesspeople. Singles/doubles cost RM92/104 to RM250, plus taxes. The *Juita Inn* (☎ 09-744 6888; fax 09-744 5777) is probably a better bet – it's newer and friendlier. Rooms start at RM95/110 for singles/doubles.

The top hotel is undoubtedly the 136 room *Hotel Perdana* (☎ 09-748 5000) on Jalan Sultan Mahmud. Superior rooms cost RM190/210 and deluxe rooms are also available. It's the biggest hotel in Kota Bharu, fully air-con, with swimming pool, bowling alley and squash and tennis courts.

Places to Eat

The best and cheapest Malay food in Kota Bharu is found at the *night market*, opposite the central bus station. The food stalls are set up in the evenings and there's a wide variety of delicious, cheap Malay food. Just bear in mind the whole thing closes down for evening prayers between 7 and 7.45 pm.

Most of the stalls at the night market deal in variations on the nasi goreng theme, but Thai-style tom yam soups are also popular. More offbeat possibilities include the blue rice, hard-boiled quail eggs or that old favourite, barbecued stingray.

It's also a good place to snack-track and then buy rice wrapped in banana leaf from one of the rice stalls. You can then sit at any of the tables, eat your meal and order a drink (nothing alcoholic). Traditionally you eat with the right hand – each table has a jug of water and a roll of tissue paper to clean your fingers – but forks and spoons are readily available. Local specialities include: ayam percik (marinated chicken enclosed between bamboo skewers) and nasi kerabu (rice with coconut, fish and spices). Some locals reckon that the best ayam percik comes from the *Yati* stall, in the corner of the market near the traffic lights.

It's easy to write off the rest of Kota Bharu after the night market, but there's a surprising amount of very good food around town. More good food stalls are next to the river opposite the Padang Merdeka, and at the stadium, which has a number of stalls selling ABC (ais batu kacang – the shaved ice dessert). The *Razak Restoran*, on the corner of Jalan Datok Pati and Jalan Padang Garong, is cheap and has excellent Indian Muslim food. For an excellent lunchtime Malay curry on a banana leaf, try the *Meena Curry House* on Jalan Gajah Mati. For breakfast, roti canai and coffee are best at the cafe next door to the Hotel Tokyo Baru on Jalan Tok Hakim. Patrons get to sit around a 'bar' and can play with the cigarette lighters dangling from rubber straps.

There are plenty of Chinese restaurants around town, including good chicken-rice places on Jalan Padang Garong near the Kencana Inn. The *Restoran Vegetarian*, on Jalan Post Office Lama, has good Chinese vegetarian food. The *Restoran Donald Duck* cooks up a very good Cantonese-style duck and rice, and the beer comes in chilled glasses so cold that a block of ice forms in the glass before you can finish the drink.

At the Hotel Murni, the *Selandang Coffee House* does extremely good Chinese and passable generic western dishes at affordable mid-range prices – draught beer is also available. The *Juita Inn* has a good mid-range Thai restaurant. Head over to the *Rhong Sree Seafood Garden* for a kampung-style seafood experience.

Things to Buy

Kota Bharu is a centre for Malay crafts. Batik, songket, silverware, woodcarving and kite-making factories and shops are dotted around town.

One of the best places to see handicrafts is on the road north to Pantai Cahaya Bulan (PCB). There are a number of workshops representing most crafts stretched out along the road all the way to the beach. Just out of town the road turns to the right, at Kampung Penambang, and close to each other you'll find a batik and songket centre, a kite maker and a woodcarver. Past the Km 9 marker at Kampung Badang is a good silversmith and a handicraft centre. Further on at Kampung Kemumin is the workshop of master kite maker Yasok Haji Umat. There are plenty of other craft places, open every day except Friday. You can take bus No 10 to get to them, but the best way is by car or bicycle, as they are spread out over a six km stretch.

There are also silversmiths on Jalan Sultanah Zainab, and the Semasa Batik Factory is on the road to Gua Musang, down the road beside Lee's garage, which you reach on bus No 5. The markets are as good a place as any to buy handicrafts, if you know the prices and bargain hard. For batik, you can also try Wisma Batik, on Jalan Che Su, just around the corner from the Hotel Murni.

Getting There & Away

Air The Malaysia Airlines office (☎ 09-744 7000) is opposite the clock tower on Jalan Gajah Mati. Direct flights go to Penang (RM87), Alor Setar (RM71) and KL (RM104).

Bus The state-run SKMK is the largest bus company, and runs all the city and regional buses, as well as most of the long-distance buses. It operates from the central bus station (city and regional buses) and the Langgar bus station (long-distance buses). All the other long-distance bus companies operate from the Jalan Hamzah external bus station. On arrival in Kota Bharu some of the buses will drop you at the central bus station, but they don't depart from there.

SKMK is the easiest to deal with, as it has ticket offices at all the bus stations. Long-distance departures are from the Langgar bus station but, just to make things confusing, a few evening buses also go from the central bus station. Ask which station your bus departs from when you buy your ticket, and book as far ahead as possible, especially for the Butterworth and Penang buses.

SKMK has regular buses to Kuala Terengganu (RM7.50, three hours) and Kuantan (RM16, six hours). Buses to Johor Bahru (RM29 air-con, 10 hours), Singapore (RM30, 12 hours) and KL (RM25, 10 hours) leave at 8 pm (also 9 pm to KL). The buses to Butterworth (RM20, eight hours) and Penang leave in the morning at 10 am and in the evening. There is a bus to Jerantut (RM18) at 8.30 am. Other destinations are Alor Setar, Gerik, Kuala Dungun, Kuala Lipis, Melaka, Mersing and Temerloh.

The other companies cover many of the same routes and are worth trying if the SKMK buses are full. Buy your tickets at the Jalan Hamzah external bus station, or some of the companies have agents at the Bazaar Buluh Kubu. Bumi Express is the only company with buses to Melaka.

All regional buses leave from the central bus station. Destinations include: Wakaf Baru (Nos 19, 27, 27a, 43), Rantau Panjang (Nos 29, 29a, 36), Tumpat (No 19), Bachok (Nos 2, 23, 29), Pasir Puteh (Nos 3, 3a), Jerteh (No 3a), Kuala Krai (Nos 5, 57) and Gua Musang (No 57).

Train The jungle railway starts at Tumpat and goes through Kuala Krai, Gua Musang, Kuala Lipis and Jerantut (for Taman Negara National Park) and eventually meets the Singapore-KL line at Gemas. Travel is slow but the scenery is certainly worth it. The nearest station to Kota Bharu is at Wakaf Baru, a 80 sen trip on bus No 19 or 27.

The fastest train leaves Wakaf Baru at 7.40 pm on Wednesday, Friday and Sunday and goes right through to Singapore. If you're heading for Kuala Lipis and Jerantut, the 3.10 pm train to Gemas is probably the best one to take – it is a limited express allowing you to see some of the jungle during daylight hours. There's also a daily local train at 6 am – it takes twice as long (count on 12 hours to Jerantut) but is a colourful jungle train experience. Both 2nd and 3rd class are comfortable – the only difference between the two is that 3rd class gets more crowded, but you'll usually have no problems getting a seat at Wakaf Baru. Refer to the introductory

Getting Around chapter for the train timetable and fare details on express trains.

Taxi The taxi station is on the southern side of the central bus station, and there is an overflow station during the day at the site of the night market.

Main taxi destinations and costs are: Kuala Terengganu (RM12), Kuantan (RM25), KL (RM35/45), Butterworth (RM38) and Kuala Lipis (RM35).

Car Avis has an office (☎ 09-748 4457) in the Hotel Perdana on Jalan Sultan Mahmud.

Thailand The Thai border is at Rantau Panjang (Sungai Golok on the Thai side), 1½ hours by bus from Kota Bharu. Bus No 29B departs on the hour from the central bus station and costs RM2.60. From Rantau Panjang walk across the border; it's about one km to the station – a trishaw costs RM3. Malaysian currency is accepted in Sungai Golok. Share-taxis from Kota Bharu to Rantau Panjang cost RM3.50 and take 45 minutes.

From Sungai Golok there is a train to Surathani at 6 am, one to Bangkok at 10.05 am and an express train to Bangkok at 10.55 am. All stop at Hat Yai and Surathani. Buses to Hat Yai leave from the Valentine Hotel in Sungai Golok until 3 pm, and there are taxis to Yala and Narathiwat town.

An alternative route into Thailand is via Pengkalan Kubor on the coast. It's more time-consuming and very few travellers go this way. See the Around Kota Bharu section below for more details.

Getting Around

Kota Bharu itself is fairly compact, and it is possible to get almost everywhere on foot.

The Airport The airport is eight km from town – take bus No 9 from the old central market. A taxi costs RM11.

Bus Most of the city buses leave from the middle of the old central market, on the Jalan Hilir Pasar side, or from opposite the Bazaar Buluh Kubu. To Pantai Cahaya Bulan (PCB) take bus No 10. It leaves from the Bazaar Buluh Kubu or you can catch it at the bus stand in front of the Kencana Inn.

Trishaw Trishaws still linger on, though most people nowadays get around on motorbikes. A short journey up to a km costs RM1.

AROUND KOTA BHARU

Masjid Kampung Laut

Reputed to be the oldest mosque in Peninsular Malaysia, this mosque was built about 300 years ago by Javanese Muslims as thanks for a narrow escape from pirates.

It originally stood at Kampung Laut, just across the river from Kota Bharu, but each year the monsoon floods (November to January) caused considerable damage to the wooden mosque and in 1968 it was moved to a safer location. It now stands about 10 km inland at Kampung Nilam Puri, a local centre for religious study.

Pantai Cahaya Bulan (PCB)

PCB is a Malay acronym that sounds far more appealing translated into English – the 'Beach of Passionate Love'. At least that is what it was once called. Pantai Cinta Berahi is now known as Pantai Cahaya Bulan – 'Moonlight Beach' – in keeping with Islamic sensitivities. Fortunately the same acronym applies and everyone refers to it as PCB.

PCB is 10 km north of the town, only 30 minutes by bus from Kota Bharu. It's a good day-trip option on a sunny day, but hardly the kind of place you'd want to retire to. Accommodation is provided by shabby resorts and even the beach looks a little tired.

Places to Stay The only budget accommodation is at the *Long House Beach Motel* (☎ 09-773 1090). It's a vaguely depressing place, but basic A-frames (fan-cooled) are available at RM20. There are also five-bed air-con rooms available for RM69. Just across the road is the *Resort Pantai Cinta Berahi* (☎ 09-773 2307), which has a number of cottages dotted among the trees. Room rates start at RM150 for a double, including taxes. It also has a swimming pool.

PENINSULAR MALAYSIA

The *HB Village* (☎ 09-773 4993), two km from the village, is more of a budget option. Fan-cooled chalets cost RM50, air-con RM60 – all have attached bathrooms.

The *Perdana Resort* (☎ 09-773 3000) has a swimming pool, tennis courts, a restaurant, and even a five hole golf course. Bungalows cost RM120 to RM210, including taxes.

Getting There & Away The No 10 bus from Kota Bharu stops at the Perdana Resort and terminates close to the Long House Beach Motel. A taxi from Kota Bharu costs RM12.

Pantai Irama

Pantai Irama ('Beach of Melody') at Bachok has landscaped gardens along the foreshore and is popular with day-trippers. Like most of the beaches around Kota Bharu, it's pleasant but nothing special. Bus Nos 2A and 2B run out to the beach.

Places to Stay There is mid-range accommodation at the *Motel Bachok* (☎ 09-778 8462).

Other Beaches

Pantai Dasar Sabak, 13 km from Kota Bharu and three km beyond the Pengkalan Chepa airport, is a beach with a history. On 7 December 1941, the Pacific Theatre of WWII commenced there on the beach when Japanese troops stormed ashore, a full hour and a half before the rising sun rose over Pearl Harbor.

Other beaches close to Kota Bharu include **Pantai Dalam Rhu** near the fishing village of Semerak, 19 km from Pasir Puteh, not far from the Terengganu state border. It's sometimes known as Pantai Bisikan Bayu, the 'Beach of Whispering Breeze'. North of Kota Bharu there's **Pantai Kuda** ('Horse Beach'), 25 km away in the Tumpat area, and **Pantai Seri Tujuh** (see the following Tumpat District section).

Tumpat District

Tumpat district is a major agricultural area bordering Thailand, and the Thai influence is very noticeable. Small villages are scattered among the picturesque rice fields, and there are a number of interesting Thai Buddhist temples, such as Wat Phothivihan. Other places of interest include the beach resort at Pantai Seri Tujuh, and Pengkalan Kubor is an exit point for Thailand. Tumpat town is at the end of the railway line, but it has no hotels.

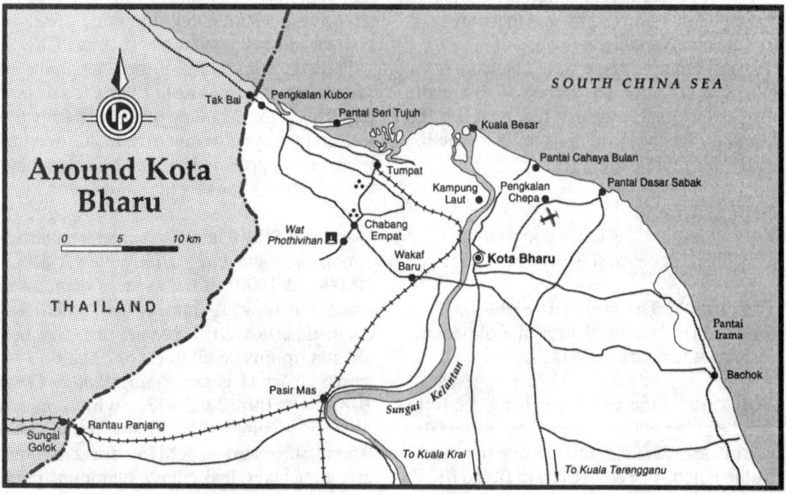

Temples Wat Phothivihan, a Buddhist temple with a 40-metre-long reclining Buddha statue, is claimed to be one of the largest in South-East Asia. It was built in 1973. There is a resthouse available for use by sincere devotees, for a donation.

To get to Wat Phothivihan, take bus No 19 or 27 to Chabang Empat. Get off at the crossroads and turn left. Walk 3.5 km along this road, through interesting villages and paddy fields, until you reach Kampung Jambu and the reclining Buddha (it takes about one hour).

The region is dotted with Thai-influenced temples, or wats, and the Wesak Festival (usually held in August) is a particularly good time to visit them. At Chabang Empat, if you take the turn to the right past the police station there is another wat one km away. There are wats on the main road two km south of Tumpat; continue past Chabang Empat on bus No 19 to reach Wat Phikulthong.

Pantai Seri Tujuh Resort This down-market beach resort is on a long spit of land, with a sweeping stretch of beach facing the sea and a quiet bay behind. It is popular during holidays, but otherwise very quiet. The resort is government-run, and rooms cost from RM25 up to RM80 for chalets with air-con. Phone 09-725 7285 for bookings.

Pengkalan Kubor Right on the Thai border, Pengkalan Kubor is the immigration checkpoint for this little-used back route into Thailand. During the day a large car-ferry crosses the river over to busy Tak Bai in Thailand. From Kota Bharu, take bus No 27, 27A or 43.

Don't take the small long-propeller boats that cross in the evening. These cater to Malaysians looking for Thai girls.

Waterfalls

There are a number of waterfalls in the Pasir Puteh area. Jeram Pasu is the most popular; to reach it you have to follow an eight km path from Kampung Padang Pak Amat, about 35 km south of Kota Bharu en route to Pasir Puteh. Other falls in this area include Jeram Tapeh, Cherang Tuli and Jeram Lenang.

River Trips

You can make a number of river trips from Kota Bharu. A short trip takes you downstream to the river mouth at Kuala Besar and you can then return on bus No 28. Longer trips can be made from Kuala Krai.

From Kota Bharu, take bus No 5 to Kuala Krai at 7.45 am and then a boat from Kuala Krai to Kuala Balah (RM5.80) at 10.30 am – no boat on Fridays. It's a two hour trip through dense jungle.

From Kuala Balah you can hitch or pay for a ride (around RM5) to Jeli, near the Thai border, then take a bus from there back to Kota Bharu (approximately RM2). Buses on the new East-West Highway also pass through Jeli.

It's worth staying in Kuala Balah overnight, so you have time to look around. You can catch a boat back to Kuala Krai very early the next morning. Another alternative is to get off the boat at Dabong, before you reach Kuala Balah. Dabong is on the railway line and you can get a train back to Kota Bharu at around 1.45 pm. The train takes three long hours to reach Kuala Krai and a further two hours from there to Wakaf Baru. From Wakaf Baru, take bus No 19 or 27 into Kota Bharu. However, it's much easier to leave the train at Kuala Krai and to catch a taxi from there to Kota Bharu for RM6 – the taxi trip takes about one hour.

From Dabong, it's a one hour walk to the caves at Gua Ikan. Ask locals for directions to the caves and to the waterfall, which is in the same area (maybe 30 minutes further on). It's also possible to combine this trip with a visit to the Jelawang Jungle (see below).

Places to Stay Kuala Balah has been rebuilt a km or so away from its previous flood-prone site. You can stay at the *Rest House*. There are also a couple of basic rooms available for rent in Dabong.

Jelawang Jungle

Unless you have camping equipment it is difficult to explore the forest around here. What's more, given that the bungalow operation in the Jelawang Jungle has shut down, transport (a combination of boat and taxi) to the Jelawang Jungle is also touch and go. Johnty's Guesthouse in Kota Bharu offers economical tours out to Jelawang, and this is probably the best way to visit the place. The chief attraction is the Seven-Step Waterfall, but the forest is also rich in wildlife.

COAST TO COAST

The East-West Highway starts near Kota Bharu and runs roughly parallel to the Thai border, eventually meeting the little-used road north from Kuala Kangsar to Keroh on the Thai border at Gerik. It's something of an engineering masterpiece, and the views from the highway are often superb. However, the road is subject to closure during the monsoon.

The East-West Highway was a massive undertaking, hindered by the harsh jungle terrain, monsoon washouts and regular attacks by Communist guerrillas. The last remnants of the guerrillas have long emerged from the jungle in surrender, but the road still has its hazards and travel on the road is restricted to daylight hours.

JUNGLE RAILWAY

The central railway line goes largely through aboriginal territory. It's an area of dense jungle offering magnificent views.

Commencing near Kota Bharu, the line runs to Kuala Krai, Gua Musang, Kuala Lipis and Jerantut (access point for the Taman Negara National Park) and eventually meets the Singapore-KL railway line at Gemas. Unless you have managed to book a sleeping berth right through, you'll probably find yourself sharing a seat with vast quantities of agricultural produce and babies. Allow for at least a couple of hours' delay.

The line's days are probably numbered, as roads are being pushed through. The road now goes all the way from Singapore through Kuala Lipis to Kota Bharu. The train is a lot slower but definitely more interesting.

See the Kota Bharu and the introductory Getting Around section for timetable and fares on the jungle train. Taxis from Kota Bharu to Gua Musang cost RM14, from Kuala Krai RM12.

Kuala Krai

Kuala Krai, 65 km south of Kota Bharu, is not an attraction in itself, and about the only thing to do is to visit the small zoo specialising in local wildlife, including native bears and musang (civet cats). It's open every day except Friday from 9 am to 6.30 pm, closed from 12.30 to 2 pm.

Places to Stay The *Hotel Keow Sin* is on the main road 50 metres from the railway station. Basic rooms cost from RM10. Further along the street, the *Hotel Joo Mui* is similar. The *Hotel Krai* has better rooms from RM15 – you may need to bargain.

Gua Musang

This former logging camp is now rapidly expanding, and planners see it as the centre of a huge new development area carved from the jungle. Logging is still a major industry, and the town has a frontier feel to it, but the massive new administrative buildings on the outskirts of town point to its future.

Gua Musang (Musang Cave) owes its name to the caves in the limestone outcrop that towers above the railway station. The musang is a native civet cat that looks like a cross between a large cat and a possum, with long fur and a long curling tail, but unfortunately hunters have killed off these former inhabitants of the caves.

It is possible to explore the caves, but it is a very steep, hazardous climb to the entrance. The entrance is above the kampung next to the railway line, a few hundred metres from the station. Take a torch. A guide is recommended.

Places to Stay The *Rest House* is a rundown, rambling old place that costs RM16 for a room with shared bathroom. There are also a number of economical Chinese hotels on Jalan Besar. Good options are the *Hotel Alishan* and the *Hotel Merling* (☎ 09-912 1813), both of which have rooms from RM25 to RM40. The top place is the *Kesedar Inn* (☎ 09-912 1229) just outside town. Rooms here cost RM35/42 with fan, RM50/57 with air-con.

Sarawak

Approximately the same size as Peninsular Malaysia, yet with only around one-10th of its population, Sarawak is probably the least visited of all Malaysia's states. This is a shame. Sarawak has some excellent national parks, Kuching is one of the most pleasant cities in all of Asia and upriver (if one travels far enough) is untouched jungle. The politics of logging have injured the state's international reputation to be sure, but there remains much that is worthwhile.

Many of the tribes who live upstream of the major rivers of Sarawak (the Rejang, Balleh, Belaga, Balui, Baram and Skrang) live in longhouses – 'villages' where the entire population lives under one roof with separate rooms leading on to one long communal veranda. Hospitality to visitors is a way of life in the longhouses, and some travellers in Sarawak will stay overnight at one during their travels. Sarawak has a good system of national parks: Bako, Niah, Lambir Hills and Gunung Mulu are popular destinations that offer visitors a good chance to explore the jungle.

Full Name: Sarawak Bumi Kenyalang
Area: 124,967 sq km
Capital: Kuching
Population: 1.8 million

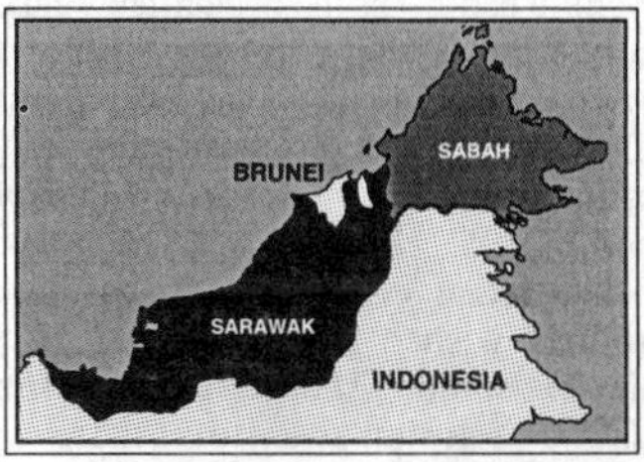

History

From the 15th until the early 19th century Sarawak was under the loose control of the sultanate of Brunei. It was only with the arrival of Sir James Brooke, the first of the 'white rajas', that it became a separate political region.

James Brooke, invalided from the British East India Company, set off on a journey of discovery armed with a sizeable inheritance and a well-armed ship. He arrived in Sarawak in 1839 only to find the local viceroy, Prince Makota, under siege from rebellious Bidayuh and Malays of the Sarawak River. Brooke's fortuitous arrival put him in the perfect position to ingratiate himself with the local leaders. He put down the rebellion, and by way of reward was installed as raja of Sarawak on 18 September 1842.

When James Brooke died in 1868 he was succeeded by his nephew, Charles Brooke. Through a policy of divide-and-rule among the local tribes, and sometimes ruthless punishment of those that challenged his authority, he extended his control and the extents of his kingdom during his long reign until his death in 1917.

The third white raja was Charles Vyner Brooke, second son of Charles Brooke, who was to be last in this Boy's Own dynasty of white potentates.

Sarawak's period as the personal kingdom of the Brooke family ended with the arrival of the Japanese in WWII. When the Japanese forces capitulated in August 1945, Sarawak was placed under an Australian military administration until April 1946, when Charles Vyner Brooke, who had fled to Sydney during the war, made it known that he wanted to cede Sarawak to the British. The Bill of Cession was debated in the State Council (Council Negeri) and was finally passed in May 1946. On July 1 Sarawak officially became a British Crown Colony, thus putting Britain in the curious position of acquiring a new colony at a time when it was shedding others. Cession was followed by a brief but bloody anti-cession movement supported chiefly by Anthony Brooke, Charles Vyner Brooke's nephew and heir apparent to the white raja title, and about 300 government officers who had resigned in protest at being excluded from the political process. The conflict climaxed in late 1949 when the governor of Sarawak, Duncan Stewart, was murdered by a Malay student. By 1951 the movement had lost its momentum and Anthony Brooke urged its supporters to give it up.

Along with Sabah (then North Borneo) and Brunei, Sarawak remained under British control when Malaya gained its independence in 1957. In 1962 a British inquiry concluded that the people of the Borneo territories wished to become part of the Malay Federation. At the last minute Brunei pulled out, as it didn't want to see the revenue from its vast oil reserves channelled to the peninsula. At the same time Malaya also had to convince the UN that Filipino claims to North Borneo were unfounded, as were Indonesia's claims that the formation of Malaysia was a British neo-colonialist plot. The agreement was finally hammered out in July 1963, and in September of the same year the Federation of Malaysia was born. The so-called Confrontation with Indonesia continued right up until 1966 and at its height 50,000 British, Australian and New Zealand forces were deployed in the Malaysian-Indonesian border area.

Although the Emergency over the Communist insurgency on the peninsula was declared over in 1960, things were still on the boil in Sarawak. The state had a large population of impoverished Chinese peasant farmers and labourers, and it was these people who found appeal in the North Kalimantan Communist Party, which supported guerrilla activity. Communist aspirations in Borneo were killed off, however, after the collapse of the Indonesian Communist Party in 1965, after which time the Indonesians and Malaysians combined forces to drive them out of their bases in Sarawak.

Today, Sarawak is doing better than its northern neighbour Sabah. Kuching has an air of easy affluence, and the state economy is growing at over 10% annually. Oil and timber are the mainstays of the economy, though the state gets a mere 5% of oil revenues – the rest goes to the federal government.

Logging in Sarawak

Sarawak has long been a favourite target of conservationists' ire, and with good reason. Extensive logging has done irreparable damage to the rainforests and displaced the indigenous peoples who lived there. Nevertheless, before leaping to the moral high ground and indulging in a tirade against unscrupulous authorities and greedy developers, it is also worth considering the record of other countries in the region, or those in the west for that matter. Most authorities on the subject agree that the Sarawak state government has done a better job of restraining loggers than neighbouring countries such as Indonesia, Thailand and the Philippines.

Currently, Sarawak still has 60% forest cover, although much of this forest has been selectively logged at least once in the last 20 years. On the surface, the state government appears to be keeping its word on forest conservation. Timber quotas have been reduced, making 30,000 people jobless, the export of whole logs has been banned, and the current slump in world timber prices has cut production even further. The laws may be in place, but enforcement, particularly in remote areas (ie most of Sarawak), is weak. Unemployed timber workers return to shifting cultivation, putting further pressure on the forest. Meanwhile new jobs in downstream timber-processing plants are reserved for Indonesian migrant labourers, who are prepared to work for wages the poorest Sarawakian would deem an insult.

Selective logging and helicopter logging are being portrayed as eco-friendly, but no matter how much care is taken they still involve the construction of logging roads and holding areas. These roads, bulldozed across bare earth, cause massive soil erosion, leading to river silting and the destruction of fish populations, an important protein source

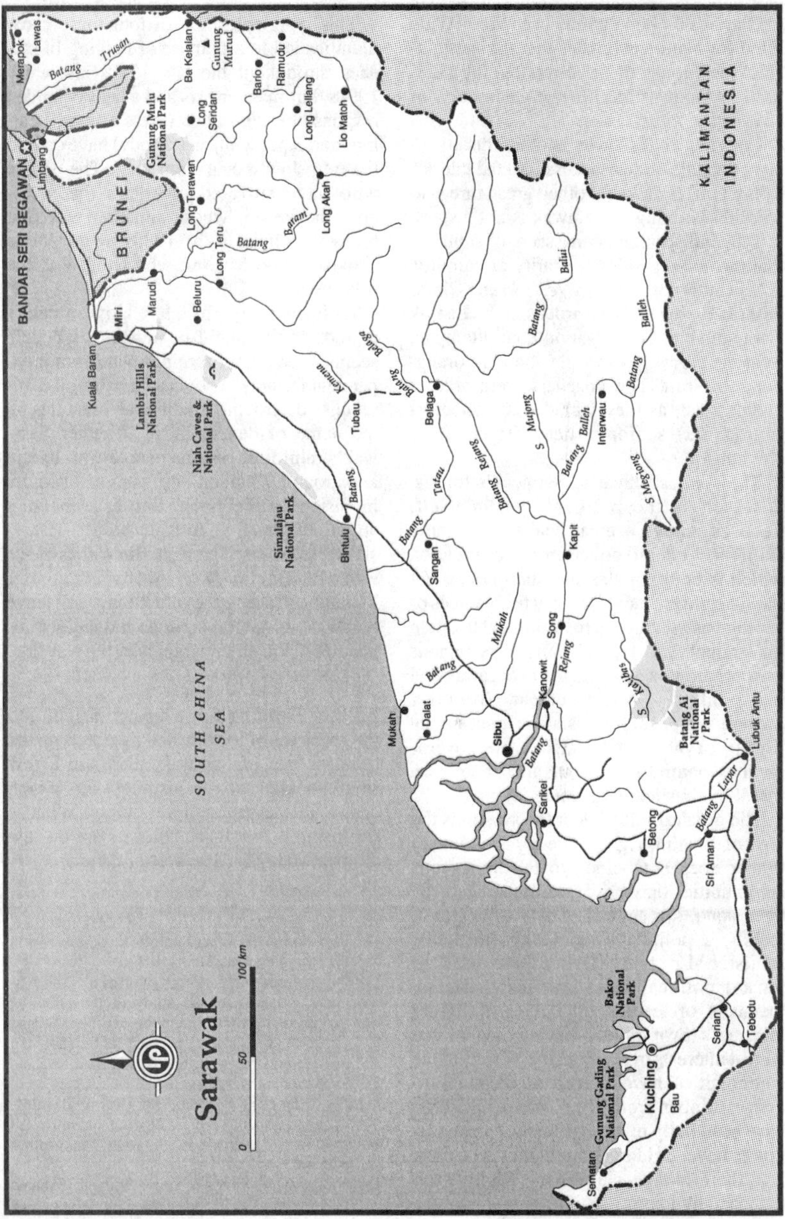
Sarawak
0
50
100 km
SOUTH CHINA SEA
BANDAR SERI BEGAWAN
BRUNEI
Limbang
Merapok
Lawas
Batang
Trusan
Ba Kelalan
Gunung Murud
Gunung Mulu National Park
Long Seridan
Bario
Ramudu
Long Lellang
Lio Matoh
Long Terawan
Long Akah
Long Teru
Batang
Baram
Marudi
Beluru
Miri
Kuala Baram
Lambir Hills National Park
Niah Caves & National Park
Tubau
Kemena
Batang
Belaga
Batang
Belaga
Batang
Balui
Batang
Balleh
Interwau
S Mujong
Batang
Balleh
S Mengiong
Batang
Rejang
Tatau
Batang
Bintulu
Simalajau National Park
Batang
Sangan
Kapit
Mukah
Song
Rejang
Kanowit
S Katibas
Batang
Mukah
Dalat
Sibu
Batang
Sarikei
Betong
Batang Ai National Park
Lubuk Antu
Lupar
Batang
Sri Aman
Bako National Park
Kuching
Serian
Tebedu
Bau
Gunung Gading National Park
Sematan
KALIMANTAN
INDONESIA

for Sarawak's population. The World Wide Fund for Nature estimates that the 'sustainable' techniques of selective logging practised in Sarawak lead to the destruction of 46% of the forest cover.

Logging roads have another disadvantage; they allow easy access into the interior to hunters, Sarawak's other great threat to wildlife. Hunting in Sarawak is not a sport. It is the indiscriminate massacre of anything that moves, regardless of rarity or edibility. A recent report in the *New Straits Times* described how native wardens in the Lanjuk Entimau Total Conservation Zone attempted to arrest a group of people shooting orang-utans for fun. The poachers were able to avoid arrest, as they included a number of (un-named) senior police officers from Kuching!

The greatest threat to Sarawak's forests, however, is the political system itself. Sarawak enjoys a great deal of autonomy from the federal government, a situation which is both popular and appropriate. Yet the state government has very few sources of revenue as oil and gas royalties and taxation go straight into federal coffers. A famous cartoon shows a cow grazing in Sarawak and being milked in Kuala Lumpur. Given that the only major source of state revenues is the royalty payable on logs, the state government is naturally reluctant to cut its own throat by drastically reducing logging.

The greatest injustice of the system is the area of logging rights. The right to extract timber does not belong to the indigenous communities on whose traditional lands the trees stand. It is controlled by the director of forests, a political appointee of the chief minister. Logging licences are used to reward political allies and enrich family members of leading politicians, the chief minister's own family having one of the largest interests in the industry. Where native communities have lodged applications to extract timber from their own land, these have been flatly rejected. Finally, compensation is never paid to communities who have had their Native Customary Rights land damaged by logging activities.

This marginalisation of longhouse communities led to a number of logging blockades throughout the late 1980s and early 1990s, but mass arrests and a heavy-handed response by the police (mass arrests, beatings and rapes while in custody) have caused these to slowly fade from view. The people who have suffered most are the semi-nomadic Penan, whose situation was first brought to light in the 1980s by the Swiss activist Bruno Manser, who lived with the tribespeople.

Unfortunately the state government's attitude to the plight of indigenous people seems to be one of turning them from independent farmers to coolies on palm-oil plantations, destroying traditional lifestyles in the name of development. Whether Sarawak's rainforest and the people who live in and around it will end up winners or losers in Vision 2020 (Prime Minister Mahathir's ambitious plan for a fully developed Malaysia) still remains to be seen. But with projects like the Bakun Dam going ahead, Dr Mahathir's race to the future may well leave Sarawak, its natural heritage and indigenous peoples licking their wounds by the wayside.

Further Reading For a deeper insight into the problems of logging and its effects on the tribal people of Sarawak, there are a few small booklets by various publishers which deal with the problem admirably. What is surprising is that these booklets are on sale all over Malaysia. The best of them are:

The Battle for Sarawak's Forests (SAM, Penang). A large-format paperback chronicling the events in the struggle up until early 1989.

Logging against the Natives of Sarawak (INSAN, Petaling Jaya). A case study of the effect of logging on longhouse communities in the Belaga district, as well as some accounts of the shocking injuries and paltry compensation paid to some local logging workers.

Pirates, Squatters & Poachers (Survival International, London). This is an excellent introduction to the subject, with good background material.

Solving Sarawak's Forest & Native Problem (Sahabat Alam Malaysia, Penang). As the title suggests,

EAST MALAYSIA

some proposals for a solution to the problems in Sarawak, including a draft of the UN Universal Declaration on Rights of Indigenous Peoples, which is to be presented to the UN General Assembly for discussion and, hopefully, adoption.

Visas & Permits

Even though Sarawak is part of Malaysia, it has its own immigration controls, which are designed, mainly, to protect the indigenous tribal people from being swamped by migrants from the peninsula and elsewhere. They also conspire to restrict the access of foreigners to the same tribal people – the last thing the government wants is another Bruno Manser alerting the world to the shoddy treatment these people are receiving as logging continues. If you're entering Sarawak from the peninsula or Sabah you will have to go through immigration again, even though you are already in Malaysia.

On arrival, most nationalities will be granted a one-month stay. In theory this can be extended at immigration offices in Kuching or Miri, but in practice extensions are rarely given. The Sarawak state government is very touchy about unannounced researchers, journalists, photographers and the like – so remember, you're a tourist, nothing more.

For travel into many parts of the interior, foreigners are supposed to obtain permits from the nearest District Office. The government has stated that it wants to cut down on logging and promote tourism as an alternative source of income, yet its time-consuming, frustrating permit system suggests the opposite. Many travellers simply don't bother getting permits at all and just go where they want. It is very rare to be asked to show a permit.

National-park permits are also required but these are largely a formality. They are generally issued as a matter of course when you check in at the park HQ, so there's little point in trying to get one in advance. Bear in mind that the penalty for visiting national parks without a permit is a fine of RM1000 *and* six months in prison (at least it's not death), so always check in at the park HQ before going any further. Permits are required for the Semenggok Wildlife Rehabilitation Centre, but these are issued instantly (along with permits for Bako National Park) at the Sarawak tourist information centre in Kuching.

If you plan to visit any of the longhouses above Kapit on the Rejang or Balleh rivers you will need a permit, which can be obtained in Kapit without fuss or fee. It can be trickier getting a permit for travel in the interior of the north-east. This is the scene of most logging and where the Dayaks are most active against the government. Permits are required from the District Office in Miri or Marudi for travel to Gunung Mulu, Bario and the upper reaches of the Baram River. It is a time-consuming process, and you will be interviewed to determine your real reason for travelling to the interior, but most travellers don't have any problems, as long as they have absolutely nothing to do with journalism. Tell them you are a carpenter if you think your profession may be a problem.

National Parks

The Malaysian jungles contain some of the oldest undisturbed areas of rainforest in the world. It's estimated that they've existed for about 100 million years, since they remained largely unaffected by the far-reaching climatic changes brought on elsewhere by the Ice Ages. In recent years, however, vast areas of this virgin forest – particularly in Sarawak and Sabah – have been devastated by the uncontrolled and thoughtless activities of timber and mineral concerns.

Fortunately, quite large areas of some of the best and most spectacular of these rainforests have been made into national parks, in which all commercial activities are banned. These parks are, in effect, the essence of a trip to Borneo, other than visits to longhouses. A lot of effort goes into maintaining them and making them accessible to visitors, and you cannot help but be captivated by the astonishing variety of plant and animal life to be found. In Sarawak itself at present there are nine such parks:

Bako National Park – north of Kuching (27 sq km)
Batang Ai National Park – 250 km south-east of Kuching
Gunung Gading National Park – on Sarawak's extreme western tip near Sematan (54 sq km)
Gunung Mulu National Park – east of Marudi near the Brunei border (529 sq km)
Kubah National Park – just 20 km west of Kuching (22 sq km)
Lambir Hills National Park – just south of Miri (69 sq km)
Niah National Park – of Niah Caves fame, about halfway between Bintulu and Miri (31 sq km)
Simalajau National Park – on the coast, north-east of Bintulu (75 sq km)
Tanjung Datu National Park – next to Gunung Gading National Park; recently gazetted and as yet not open to public

Tanjung Datu, Kubah and Simalajau do not have accommodation and visitor facilities, but these are planned and may open in the near future.

Costs Charges and accommodation for national parks have been standardised throughout Sarawak. Most of the incidental charges are small, but they can mount up. First of all, there is a 10% nonrefundable reservation charge for accommodation bookings, or the full amount if the total is less than RM10 – in other words, if you book a room in a chalet for one night at RM120, you will end up spending RM132. Secondly, all national parks have a park entrance fee of RM3, RM1 if you are under 18. There are also fees for cameras and video cameras brought into the parks: RM5 per camera; RM10 per video camera. Professional filming of the parks will cost RM200.

Getting Around

Air Malaysia Airlines has a comprehensive network of domestic flights served by its fleet of 12-seater Twin Otter aircraft. Fortunately domestic flights are a real bargain, which is just as well, as often the only viable way into the interior is by plane. If you have plans to visit places such as Bario and Long Lellang in the highlands, then chances are you'll be going at least one way by plane. Kuching and Miri are connected to each other and to Sabah by regular flights on 120-seater 737s, while Sibu and Bintulu are served by 50-seater Fokker F50s.

Places in Sarawak served by MAS flights are Ba Kelalan, Bario, Belaga, Bintulu, Kapit, Kuching, Lawas, Limbang, Long Lellang, Long Semado, Long Seridan, Marudi, Miri, Mukah, Mulu and Sibu.

The hassle with taking the Twin Otter flights in the interior is that they are very much subject to the vagaries of the weather. In the dry season (April to September) this is usually not a problem, but in the wet season, especially in Bario, it can rain continuously for a few days at a time. If you are relying on these flights, make sure you have some time up your sleeve to allow for delays. Overbooking is another problem, and during school holidays (mid-May to mid-June, late October to early December) it is virtually impossible to get a seat on *any* Twin Otter flight into the interior at short notice. The only hope is to turn up at the airport and hope for a cancellation.

The free baggage allowance on the Twin Otters is only 10 kg per person, but excess baggage only costs from 40 sen to RM1.30 per kg, depending on the distance flown.

With the cost of accommodation in Brunei so high, many people find themselves flying straight over that country, although it is possible to transit overland in a day without having to stay overnight. The cheapest and most convenient option is the flight from Miri to Labuan (RM66), a duty-free island off the coast of Sabah, from where there are plane and boat connections with the mainland and Kota Kinabalu. It's also possible to fly from Miri to Sandakan (RM152), Tawau (RM167) or direct to Kota Kinabalu (RM104).

Road Travel by road in Sarawak is improving rapidly, as the trunk road from Kuching to the Brunei border is well on the way to being surfaced all the way. There may still be some sections of dirt between Sibu and Miri, and if that's the case you'll get a taste of what travel in Sarawak used to be like – roads that are rough and dusty beyond belief in the dry season, and rough and treacherously slippery in the wet season.

Between Sibu, Bintulu and Miri there are plenty of buses daily in each direction. At the moment Sibu to Bintulu takes three hours, Bintulu to Niah Caves takes two hours, Niah Caves to Miri is two hours and Miri to Kuala Baram (the Brunei border) is one hour. The road between Kuching and Sibu is completed, but the high-speed passenger launches, which do the trip in a very smart 3½ hours, are still the best way to travel. Buses take around seven hours and are no cheaper.

There are also buses heading west from Kuching to Bau, Lundu and Sematan, and north to Bako (for Bako National Park).

Hitching is possible in Sarawak, although traffic is usually light. In this chapter we've indicated where hitching is feasible. However, hitching is never entirely safe and travellers who decide to hitch should understand that they are taking a small but potentially serious risk. People who do choose to hitch will be safer if they travel in pairs and let someone know where they are planning to go.

Boat Sarawak is the home of incredibly fast passenger launches known by the generic term *ekspres*. These are long, narrow river boats which carry around 100 people in aircraft-type seats. All the boats have air-con, video screens showing kungfu movies and karaoke videos, and powered turbo-charged V12 diesel engines which generate speeds of up to 60 km/h! The newest boats are very sleek and streamlined, looking very much like aircraft in fact. Unfortunately, these boats are a disaster waiting to happen, as the windows are all sealed and the only exits may be obstructed by baggage. All new boats now have to be fitted with proper emergency exits, but there will still be boats which don't have them. The other problem is overcrowding when the roof fills up with passengers. Riding at 60 km/h in a boat weighed down with produce and passengers as it dodges the debris of logging can be disconcerting (to say the least), but accidents are rare.

The river boats provide regular connections between Sibu and Kapit (two to three hours, RM15), and Kuala Baram and Marudi (two hours, RM15). In the wet season, when there is more water in the rivers, there are also services from Kapit to Belaga (six hours, RM20), Marudi to Kuala Apoh (two hours, RM10) and from Kuala Apoh to Long Terawan (RM8).

As well as the river ekspres boats, there are sea/river services between Kuching and Sibu (four hours, RM29). These are larger, ocean-going versions of the river ekspres boats – still with the aircraft seats, air-con and violent videos.

South-West Sarawak

KUCHING

Kuching is without a doubt the most pleasant and interesting city in Borneo. Indeed, for quality of life, lack of traffic congestion and pollution, it's one of the most attractive cities in all South-East Asia. It's easy to spend a few days exploring the place and visiting nearby attractions.

Built principally on the southern bank of the Sarawak River, Kuching was known as 'Sarawak' in the 19th century. Prior to James Brooke settling in the city, the country's capital had been variously at Lidah Tanah and Santubong. Kuching was given its name by the second white raja in 1872. The name means 'cat' in Malay, and there is much speculation as to how the city got its name. Two of the more likely theories are that it was named after the Kuching River, which in turn was named after the fruit tree *mata kuching*, or that it was so called because of the many wild cats found along its banks in the time of the white rajas.

Although Kuching is quite a large city, the centre is very compact and seems isolated from the suburbs by its river and parks. The city contains many beautifully landscaped parks and gardens, historic buildings, an interesting waterfront, colourful markets, one of Asia's best museums and a collection

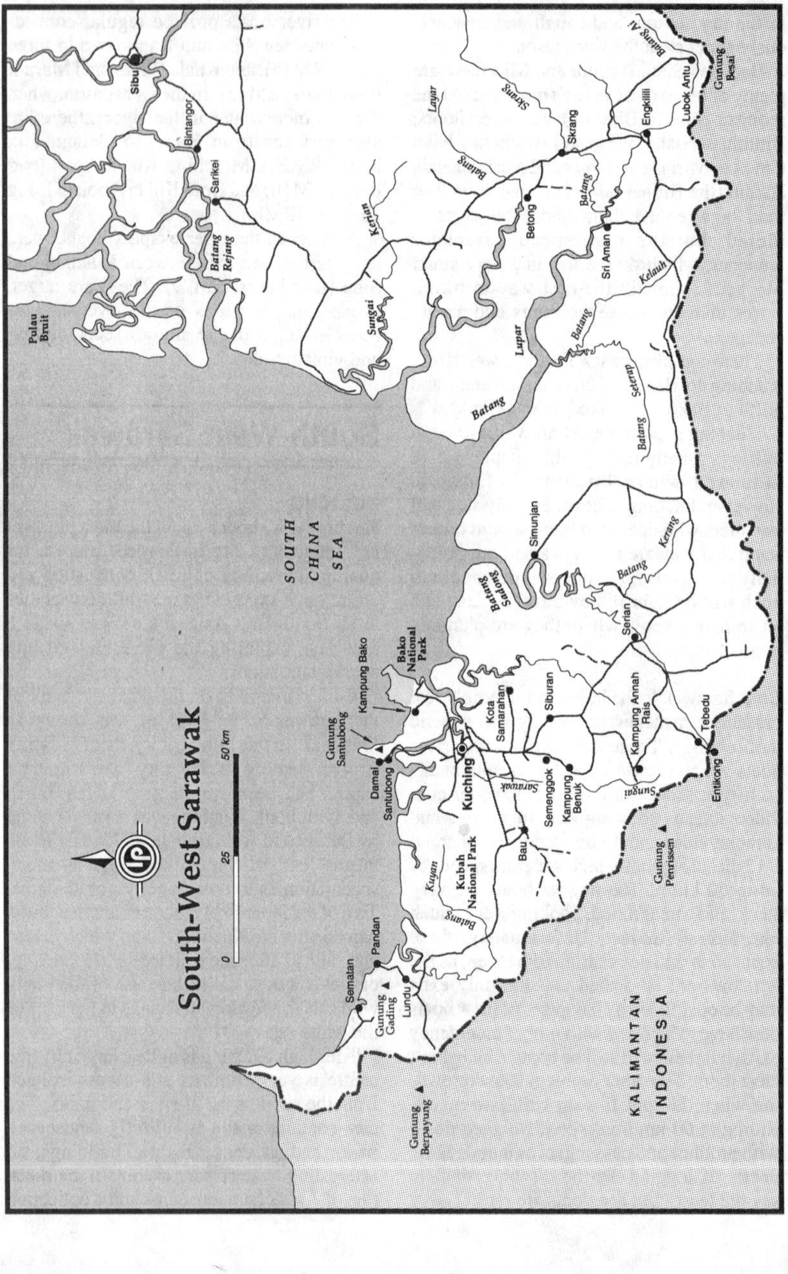
South-West Sarawak
0
25
50 km
SOUTH
CHINA
SEA
Pulau
Bruit
Sibu
Bintangor
Sarikei
Batang
Rejang
Sungai
Kerian
Batang
Lupar
Batang
Layar
Skrang
Batang Ai
Skrang
Engkilili
Lubok Antu
Gunung
Besai
Betong
Batang
Sri Aman
Kelauh
Batang
Seterap
Batang
Simunjan
Batang
Sadong
Batang
Kerang
Serian
Tebedu
Entikong
Kampung Annah
Rais
Siburan
Kota
Samarahan
Kampung Bako
Bako
National
Park
Gunung
Santubong
Damai
Santubong
Kuching
Sarawak
Semenggok
Kampung
Benuk
Sungai
Bau
Kubah
National Park
Kuyan
Batang
Gunung
Penrissen
Pandan
Sematan
Gunung
Gading
Lundu
Gunung
Berpayung
KALIMANTAN
INDONESIA

of Chinese temples, Christian churches and the striking State Mosque. Kuching is also graced by an outrageously futuristic civic centre – it bears more resemblance to some type of spacecraft, and with a price tag of 35 million ringgit one can only wonder at the folly of the state's planners – how many longhouses in the interior still don't have a reliable water supply? The waterfront between the market and the Holiday Inn has undergone a massive, landscaped face-lift and is a good place to stroll in the evenings.

There's plenty in and around Kuching to keep you busy for a few days, and it makes an ideal base from which to visit Bako National Park.

Orientation

By comparison with the state capitals of Peninsular Malaysia, the centre of Kuching is small and compact and almost all places of interest or importance to travellers are within easy walking distance of each other.

You should only need to use public buses or taxis when travelling to and from the airport (about 12 km) or to the wharfs at Pending for boats to Sibu (about six km).

Information

Tourist Information The Sarawak Tourist Association (STA) office (☎ 082-240620) is on Main Bazaar, in a new octagonal building on the waterfront. It is a helpful office, and is the place to go with specific queries. The office is open Monday to Thursday from 8 am to 12.45 pm and 2 to 4.15 pm, Friday from 8 to 11.30 am and 2.30 to 4.15 pm, and Saturday from 8 am to 12.45 pm. The staff can arrange bookings and permits for the national parks and for Semenggok, and they have the latest details on all the bus and boat schedules. There is also an STA office at the airport that has a limited range of brochures.

Another useful office is the Sarawak Tourist Information Centre (☎ 082-410942) on Padang Merdeka. In the same building is the National Parks & Wildlife booking office (☎ 082-248088), which can arrange permits and accommodation for Bako, Gunung Gading and Semenggok.

Those arriving by air at Kuching should look out for the *Official Kuching Guide*, an excellent locally produced publication on Kuching and surrounding sights. It is available in the arrivals hall and should also be stocked at tourist offices around town.

Visas The immigration office (☎ 082-245661) is in the state government offices on Jalan Simpang Tiga, about three km south of the centre on the way to the airport. To get there, catch a CCL bus No 6 or 17 from near the State Mosque.

For Indonesian visas, take a CLL bus No 6 from near the State Mosque to the Indonesian Consulate (☎ 082-241734) at 5A Jalan Pisang. It is open Monday to Friday from 8 am to noon and from 2 to 4 pm. Visas are not required for most nationalities for entry by air to Pontianak or by land at Entikong, where two-month entry permits are issued. You need a visa if exiting through Indonesia via a non-recognised crossing. Visas cost RM10. Four colour photos are required, and if you drop off your passport before 9.30 am, you can collect the visa in the afternoon.

Money For changing money (travellers' cheques) the best place to go is the Hongkong Bank on Jalan Tun Haji Openg near the junction with Main Bazaar. It has a dedicated Bureau de Change on the 1st floor, and transactions are completed with the minimum of fuss. Banking hours are 9.30 am to 3 pm on weekdays and 9.30 to 11 am on Saturday. Other banks with exchange services include the Standard Chartered Bank and the Bank of Commerce.

Mohamed Yahia & Sons, the bookshop in the basement of the Sarawak Plaza, is a licensed moneychanger that changes cash and travellers' cheques and is open every day from 10 am to 9 pm, but closed on Friday from noon to 2 pm.

American Express American Express (☎ 082-252600) has an office on the 3rd floor of the MAS building on Jalan Song Thian Cheok.

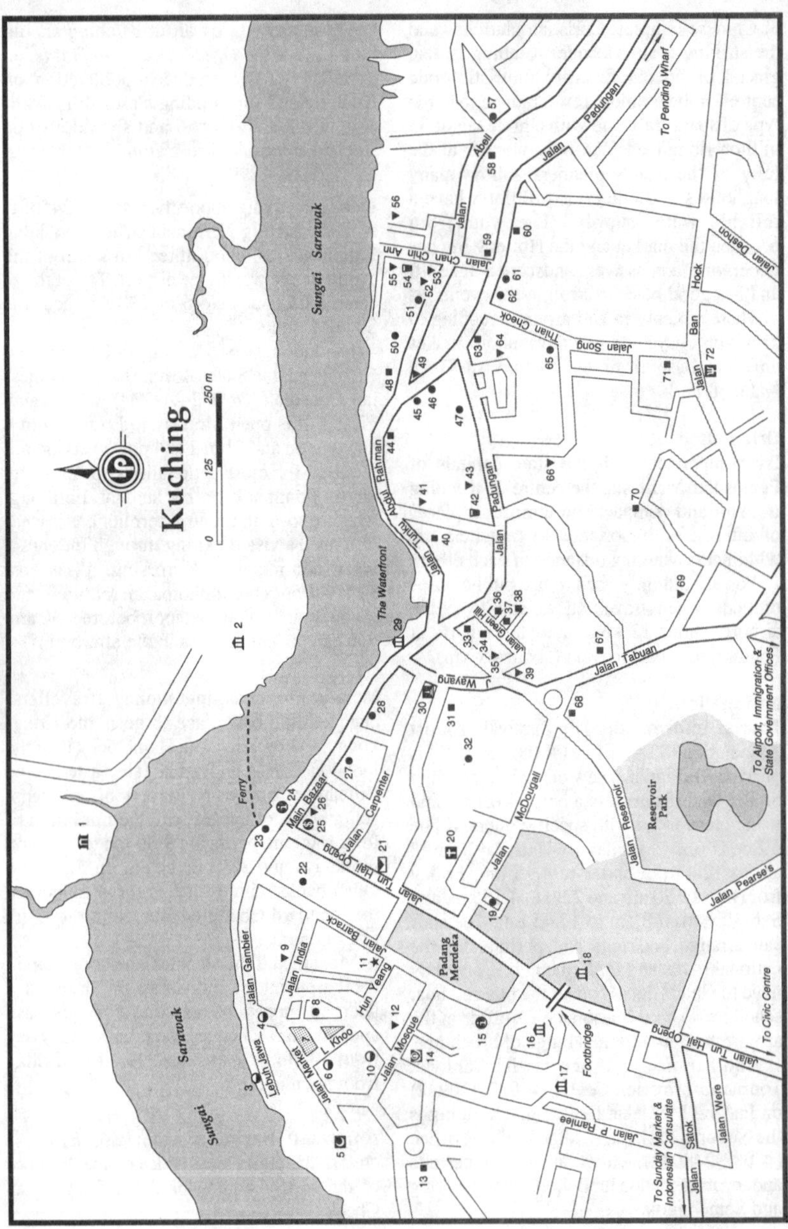
Kuching
0
125
250 m
Sungai Sarawak
Sungai Sarawak
Ferry
The Waterfront
Main Bazaar
Jalan Tunku Abdul Rahman
Jalan Padungan
Jalan Abell
Jalan Padungan
To Pending Wharf
Jalan Chan Chin Ann
Jalan Song
Jalan Ban Hock
Jalan Deshon
Jalan Tabuan
To Airport, Immigration & State Government Offices
Reservoir Park
Jalan Reservoir
Jalan Pearse's
Jalan McDougall
J. Wayang
Jalan Green Hill
Jalan Carpenter
Jalan Tun Haji Openg
Jalan Barrack
Jalan India
Jalan Gambier
Lebuh Jawa
Jalan Market
L. Khoo
Hun Yeang
Jalan Mosque
Padang Merdeka
Footbridge
Jalan Tun Haji Openg
To Civic Centre
To Sunday Market & Indonesian Consulate
Jalan P Ramlee
Jalan Satok
Jalan Were

Post The GPO is right in the centre on Jalan Tun Haji Openg. It is open from 8 am to 4 pm Monday to Friday, 8 am to 6.30 pm on Saturday and 9 am to 4 pm on Sunday.

Travel Agencies There is an incredible array of travel agents and tour operators in town. Ask the tourist office for recommendations for travel agents; if you want to visit a longhouse, they often know when tours are going and will help put you on to an agent. All the agents offer city tours and tours to the national parks and main points of interest around Sarawak, as well as longhouse tours.

Borneo Adventure (☎ 082-245175; fax 082-422626), at 55 Main Bazaar, rarely has room on its tours for people who pop into the office, but it is an excellent choice for those who plan ahead. Special interests such as bird-watching, photography, natural history and textiles (crafts) are catered for. This Canadian-Malaysian-run company has been awarded prizes for its eco-tourist projects involving the indigenous peoples of Sarawak.

Interworld Travel (☎ 082-252344) at 85 Jalan Rambutan has longhouse day trips, as well as longer Skrang River trips. CPH (☎ 082-426981), 70 Jalan Padungan, has Skrang and Lemanak River safaris. Borneo Interland Travel (☎ 082-413595), 1st floor, 63 Main Bazaar, is a general agency that offers a wide variety of tours. Borneo Excursion Travel (☎ 082-418318), A65 Level 2, Sarawak Mall, is good for booking longhouse tours. See also the section on Organised Tours, below.

Books & Maps The Mohamed Yahia & Sons bookshop in the basement of the Sarawak Plaza has the best range of books on Borneo and Malaysia, including a large stock of the scholarly *Sarawak Museum Journal*, as well as a collection of cheap novels. The owners also have a bookstore in the Holiday Inn, which has good maps. The Star Bookshop,

PLACES TO STAY

13 Arif Hotel
31 Anglican Diocesan Resthouse
33 Kuching Hotel
34 Metropole Inn & Concorde Marine Office
36 Goodwood Inn
37 Mandarin Lodging House
38 Orchid Inn
40 Hilton Hotel
44 Riverside Majestic
48 Holiday Inn
58 Longhouse Hotel
59 Kapit Hotel
60 Ching Hin Hotel
63 Ban Hua Hin
67 Borneo Hotel
68 Fata Hotel
70 Telang Usan Hotel
71 Liwah Hotel

PLACES TO EAT

7 Food Centre
9 Jubilee Restaurant
12 Saujana Food Centre
26 Green Vegetarian Restaurant
35 Green Hill Corner
39 Tiger Garden
41 Koreana
43 Stamang BBQ
49 McDonald's
52 Suan Chicken Rice
53 Pizza Hut
55 Kuching Food Centre
56 KTS Seafood Canteen
64 Top Spot Food Court
66 See Good Seafood Restaurant
69 San Francisco Grill & Mariner's Pub

OTHER

1 Istana
2 Fort Margherita
3 STC Buses
4 Taxi Station
5 Masjid Negeri (State Mosque)
6 Petra Jaya Buses
8 Electra House
10 Chin Lian Long Buses
11 Central Police Station
14 Sikh Temple
15 Sarawak Tourist Information Centre
16 Sarawak Museum (New Building)
17 Muzium Islam Sarawak
18 Sarawak Museum (Old Building)
19 Kuching Plaza
20 Anglican Cathedral
21 GPO
22 Court House
23 Square Tower
24 Sarawak Tourist Association Office
25 Hongkong Bank
27 Star Bookshop
28 Borneo Adventure
29 Chinese History Museum
30 Hong San Temple
32 Bishop's House
42 De Tavern
45 Singapore Airlines
46 Dragonair
47 Borneo Excursion Travel
50 Sarawak Plaza
51 Eeze Trading
54 Cat City
57 British Council
61 Tan Brothers
62 Ekspres Bahagia
65 MAS
72 Hindu Temple

30 Main Bazaar, has good books on Borneo, as does the bookshop at the Sarawak Museum, which also has a decent selection of maps.

For novels and general reading to replenish your stash, the best bookshop in town is Times Books, which is downstairs in the Riverside Shopping Complex, next door to the Riverside Majestic Hotel. It has a surprisingly wide and up-to-date range of paperbacks.

Periplus produces *Sarawak & Kuching* as part of its Malaysia Regional Maps series. It is an excellent fold-out colour production, with Sarawak at a scale of 1:1000,000 and the Kuching area at 1:350,000. It also has detailed maps of Kuching, Bintulu, Miri, Sibu and Kapit, as well as Gunung Muru National Park. The map is available in bookshops in Kuching.

For more detailed sectional maps, you can try the Lands & Survey Department (Jabatan Tanah dan Ukar) in the state government offices near the end of Jalan Simpang Tiga. Excellent large-scale maps – 1:1,000,000 and 1:500,000 maps of the whole of Sarawak, plus 1:50,000 of various parts of the state – are available, but you need security clearance from the police HQ in the centre of town for the sectional maps. It is possible to get it, but very difficult.

The British Council Library (☎ 082-256044) is at 142 Jalan Abell in the Bangunan WSK. It has recent issues of the *Independent* and other British dailies, if you're starved for news.

EAST MALAYSIA

Istana

This shingle-roofed palace, set amid rolling lawns on the northern bank of the Sarawak River, was built by the second white raja, Charles Brooke, in 1870. During the Japanese occupation, prisoners were interned in the basement of the building. It's no longer open to the public, as it's now the governor of Sarawak's residence. It looks very grand, especially when lit up at night, and is plainly visible from the waterfront on the opposite side of the river.

Fort Margherita

Built by Charles Brooke in 1879 and named after his wife, Ranee Margaret, the fort was designed to guard the entrance to Kuching in the days when piracy was commonplace. It is now a police museum (Muzium Polis) which houses a collection of weapons, uniformed dummies and memorabilia of the Japanese occupation and the Communist insurgency, as well as currency-forging equipment seized at various times.

It's well worth a visit and is open every day, except Monday and public holidays, from 10 am to 6 pm. There's no entry charge but you have to produce your passport at the guard's room at the entrance.

To get there take one of the small *tambangs* (ferry boats) which ply back and forth all day until late evening between the landing stage behind the Square Tower and the bus stop below the fort. The fare is 20 sen each way, and you should leave the exact change on the seat as you leave the boat – an unusual local custom. If you want to hire a tambang to take you up or down the river for a cruise, the fare is RM15 for 1½ hours.

Sarawak Museum

This is one of the best museums in Asia and should not be missed. It consists of two sections, old and new, connected by a footbridge over Jalan Tun Haji Openg. Both are worth a visit.

Built in the style of a Normandy townhouse, the old wing was opened in 1891 under the direction of the anthropologist Alfred Wallace, a contemporary of Darwin, who spent two years in Kuching at the invitation of Charles Brooke. The new wing is modern and air-conditioned. Together they house a fascinating collection of tribal artefacts, stuffed animals and birds from the Borneo jungles, a shell collection, a re-creation of a longhouse complete with headhunting skulls, wild photographs of even wilder tribal people from the beginning of the century, and a whole section on the exploration and processing of oil.

Also included are ceramics, brassware, Chinese jars and furniture and a great section on the culture and lifestyle of some of the country's many tribal peoples. There's a cave replica and a description of gathering birds' nests for soup. Through the day, various video and slide shows are offered in the new section. There's also a souvenir and gift shop, a good place to pick up books and postcards.

The museum is open from 9 am to 6 pm; it's closed on Friday. Entry is free.

Islamic Museum

The Muzium Islam Sarawak is adjacent to the new wing of the Sarawak Museum. Set in the tastefully renovated Maderasah Malayu building, the exhibits on the Malay Islamic heritage are presented in seven galleries that face onto a courtyard garden. Opening hours are the same as those for the Sarawak Museum.

Chinese History Museum

A new addition to Kuching's cultural attractions, the Chinese History Museum is part of the waterfront development. It has interesting exhibits on the Chinese diaspora, the routes taken, trading associations formed and so on. The museum is open from 10 am to 6 pm; closed on Friday. Entry is free.

Court House & Brooke Memorial

The Court House was opened in 1874 (the clock tower was added in 1883). It was the third to be built on this site, and in its time was the centre of operations for the entire government. State magistrate councils were held here until 1973, when the new government complex on Jalan Tun Haji Openg opened. Today it is the magistrate's court. Also at the Court House is a memorial to Charles Brooke, the second white raja.

Temples, Mosques & Churches

As Chinese temples go, Kuching's are modest affairs. Historically, the most important is the **Tua Pek Kong**, just down the road from the Hilton. Officially it is dated at 1876, but written sources mention it as long ago as 1846, which would make it the oldest building in Kuching. The **Hong San Temple**, at the junction of Jalan Carpenter and Jalan Wayang, dates back to 1897, and is also worth a look if you are in the area.

On Jalan Ban Hock there is a Hindu temple, and off Jalan Mosque there's a Sikh temple. The **Indian Mosque** has been through many transformations (records date back to the 1850s), and can be found down an obscure passageway between 37 and 39 Jalan India.

The **Masjid Negeri** (State Mosque), completed in 1968, is visually impressive, particularly from across the river, but otherwise uninteresting. There is no admission for non-Muslims from Thursday 3 pm to Friday 3 pm, Saturday from 4 to 6 pm and Sunday from 2 to 5 pm.

Of the Christian churches, perhaps the most interesting is the futuristic, single-roofed **Roman Catholic Cathedral**, past the Sarawak Museum on Jalan Tun Haji Openg.

Other Interesting Buildings

Kuching has many other buildings worthy of note. The **Square Tower** on Main Bazaar, opposite the end of Jalan Tun Haji Openg, was built in 1879 as a prison. On Jalan Tun Haji Openg near the GPO is the curious three-storey building known as the **Pavilion**. Built in 1907, it has been home to various government bodies including the general hospital and the education department (the present occupant). The **GPO** itself is an unusual sight with its Corinthian columns in the facade.

At the top of the hill is the **Bishop's House**, the oldest dwelling in Sarawak. It was built in 1849 and was occupied by Dr McDougall, the first Anglican Bishop of Borneo.

Imagine a huge mechanical quadruped topped with a half-furled umbrella, and you've got Kuching's futuristic **Civic Centre**. It is about one km south of the city centre along Jalan Tun Haji Openg. It has, among other things, a planetarium which has shows in English at 3 pm daily, with an extra show at 7.30 pm on Tuesday and Thursday. The viewing platform provides good panoramic views of the city and environs. Entry to the centre costs RM2.

Cat Statues

Definitely minor attractions, but wonderfully kitschy and photogenic, Kuching's cat statues can be seen opposite the Holiday Inn and at the intersection of Jalan Padungan and Jalan Central.

Markets

Kuching's open-air market is along the waterfront on Jalan Gambier. It's small and not particularly interesting, unless you hit a good day and some villagers are in town. At the waterfront, there is an outdoor area and a clothes and hawker centre in a large white building. Along Jalan Gambier there are open-air food stalls, and fresh vegetables and foodstuffs can also be bought there.

The Sunday morning market is sometimes very busy and can be well worth the walk. It's along Jalan Satok; turn away from the museum at the corner of Jalan Satok and Jalan Tun Haji Openg. The villagers bring all their produce and livestock to this area late on Saturday afternoon – so the Sunday market actually begins on Saturday night. The villagers sleep at their stalls overnight and resume trading around 5 am on Sunday. You may see all manner of food, including some vegetables and herbs you haven't seen before. Wild boars are butchered, and chopped-up turtles are on display. You may also see fantastic orchids, live fish hanging in plastic bags of water, bats, cassowaries, monkeys, lizards – you name it, it's for sale. There are live birds, plastic toys, clothes and other odds and ends usually reserved for Woolworth's.

Jalan Carpenter

This narrow street lined with old Chinese shophouses (signposted as Jalan Ewe Hai at its eastern end) is interesting to wander through, with its little shops, businesses and laneways. It burned down in the Great Fire of Kuching in 1884, and rows of brick terraces replaced the old thatched buildings. There are also a couple of restaurants and a bakery. On Sundays the streets are remarkably quiet – good for strolling and taking pictures. It seems a day for those eternal Chinese pastimes – mahjong and card playing.

Basket sellers are found at Kuching's open-air market along the waterfront.

Organised Tours

Besides the usual day trips in and around Kuching town, many travel agents offer longer trips out to national parks or to longhouses along the Skrang and Rejang rivers. Expect to pay at least RM220 for a two-day (one night) longhouse trip for a minimum of four people, while half-day city tours are around RM40. See also the section on Travel Agencies, above.

The MV *Equatorial* is a cruise boat that plies the Sarawak River in the evenings. A two-hour sunset cruise costs RM25 or RM35 with dinner. Departures are from the wharf behind Sarawak Plaza at 5.30 pm but are somewhat haphazard – contact Leisure Holidays (☎ 082-240566), 37 Jalan Padungan.

Places to Stay – bottom end

Kuching has only one fully fledged budget hostel, and this is the *B&B Inn* (☎ 082-237366), at 30 Jalan Tabuan, next door to the Borneo Hotel. It's a great place to be based, clean and friendly, with good travel informa-

EAST MALAYSIA

tion available. Costs – including breakfast – are RM14 in a six-bed dorm, RM22 for a single, RM30 for doubles/twins.

The *Anglican Diocesan Rest House* (☎ 082-414027), on the hill at the back of St Thomas' church, is strictly speaking reserved for those on Church business and does not always have rooms available. Nevertheless, it's worth a try if the B&B is full. Rooms with fan and shared bath cost RM18 to RM25, while large fan-cooled flats with attached bathroom cost RM30 to RM35. The easiest access is up the steps from the link road next to the Hong San temple. Access by car is from Jalan McDougall.

In general, hotel prices start at around RM25 to RM30 for a single, but there are a couple of cheaper alternatives around town. The cheapest is the basic *Kuching Hotel* (☎ 082-413985) on Jalan Temple. Rooms are equipped with fans and sinks, and cost from RM18 to RM23. The communal bathrooms and toilets are clean, and the manager and staff are very helpful.

The *Arif Hotel* is not far from the State Mosque. It's a reasonable place, and fan rooms cost RM24 to RM28 with bath. Air-con rooms cost RM40 to RM45, but the mid-range places offer better value for these prices.

Places to Stay – middle

Kuching has dozens of mid-range places and competition is fierce, so they are reasonably priced for what you get. All of these hotels have air-con, attached bathrooms, carpeting, TV and telephones in the rooms.

On Jalan Green Hill there's a whole group of mid-range 'lodging houses', many of which cater to long-term residents. There's little to choose between them – they are all quite acceptable and cost roughly the same. The *Green Mountain Lodging House* (☎ 082-416320) at No 1 has rooms from RM40, and the *Mandarin Lodging House* (☎ 082-418269) at No 6 has rooms from RM35 to RM45. The *Orchid Inn* (☎ 082-411417), at No 2, and the *Goodwood Inn* (☎ 082-244862), at No 16, both have rooms between RM35 and RM45.

Also on Jalan Green Hill is the *Metropole Inn Hotel* (☎ 082-412561) at No 22. This is a much larger hotel with rooms for RM40/60. The *Kapit Hotel* (☎ 082-244179) at 59 Jalan Padungan has rooms from RM36 to RM46. The rooms are definitely on the small side and you get more for your money elsewhere. Across the road, the *Ching Hin Hotel* (☎ 082-244662), 74 Jalan Padungan, is much better for just a few extra dollars. Singles/doubles cost RM40/50.

At the end of Jalan McDougall is the *Fata Hotel* (☎ 082-248111), a more upmarket place with better rooms at RM60 to RM80. The *Hotel Longhouse* (☎ 082-419333), at 101 Jalan Abell, offers similar standards from RM40 for an economy single, RM50 for a standard double and RM60 for deluxe rooms. The *Liwah Hotel* (☎ 082-429222), on Jalan Song Thian Cheok, looks impressive from the lobby, but the rooms are overpriced at RM72/82 to RM88/97 for singles/doubles.

There are some good upper mid-range hotels in Kuching that provide reasonably priced alternatives to the top-end hotels. Top of the list in this category is the *Telang Usan Hotel* (☎ 082-415588; fax 082-425316), Jalan Ban Hock. It is Sarawak's only Orang Ulu-owned and managed hotel, and the Kenyah decor inside is just one of the touches that makes the place stand out. The Dulit Coffee Shop has some of the best western and local cuisine in town. Good doubles range from RM90 to RM200, but discounts are sometimes available upon polite request.

The *Borneo Hotel* (☎ 082-244122; fax 082-245848), 30 Jalan Tabuan, is also recommended. Kuching's longest-running hotel, it has very large rooms from RM110/190, though again discounts are often available.

Places to Stay – top end

During quieter periods, many of Kuching's top-end hotels reduce rates drastically, sometimes by as much as 40%, to attract customers. All of these hotels have pools, restaurants, bars and discos. Add 10% service charge and 5% tax to the room rates.

The *Kuching Hilton Hotel* (☎ 082-248200; fax 082-428984) is the best in town and provides the full complement of services, a popular disco and some very good restaurants. Standard rooms start at RM325/380 and suites are from RM670 to RM2100. Discounts are often available.

On Jalan Tunku Abdul Rahman, right on the river, is the *Holiday Inn* (☎ 082-423111; fax 082-426169), with standard rooms ranging from RM240 to RM300 and suites from RM520 to RM1500.

The *Riverside Majestic* (☎ 082-247777), across from the Holiday Inn, has standard rooms ranging from RM250 to RM350, and suites from RM485 to RM2750 for those on the 19th floor. The Riverside Complex also houses a modern shopping centre, Cineplex and bowling alley.

Places to Eat

Kuching has the best food in Sarawak, arguably in all of Borneo. Along with a wide selection of excellent restaurants, Kuching is home to a large number of hawker centres and small food stalls.

Food Centres The so-called Open Air Market (it's covered) on Jalan Market next to the taxi stand is one of the largest and most popular food centres. One section serves mostly Muslim food and the other has mostly Chinese. There is also a small Chinese food centre opposite the Hong San Temple on Jalan Wayang.

Take the lift to the 5th floor of the Saujana car park for the *Saujana Food Centre*. This Muslim food centre has mostly Malay stalls, but it includes *Pizza Ria*, which sells pizzas with a difference. Try the beef rendang pizza.

The *Top Spot Food Court*, off Jalan Padungan behind the MAS building, is a popular food-stall centre, once again on top of a car park. It is more classy than the Saujana.

Chinese Just along from the Top Spot is *See Good*, a Chinese seafood restaurant where English is spoken and you can try local Sarawak specialities – order some midin (crispy jungle fern) or the ambol, which looks like a long fleshy worm steamed in bamboo and is also known locally as monyet punya – literally 'monkey's got one'.

For Chinese with a view, head over to the *Beijing Riverbank* opposite the Riverside Majestic Hotel and overlooking the river. Upstairs is a Chinese Muslim restaurant (exceedingly rare outside China), while downstairs has a 24 hour cafe serving snacks and light meals. The best Chinese fare in town is probably at the *Tsui Hua Lau*, a Chinese banquet-style restaurant around the corner from the Telang Usan Hotel.

For something less expensive, there are two decent places opposite the Rex Cinema near Jalan Green Hill: the *Green Hill Corner*, which has a good selection of Malaysian Chinese standards, and the *Tiger Garden*, which has outdoor seating and is a good place to knock back a couple of beers and enjoy a leisurely meal.

The *Singapore Fried Rice* chain has a few branches around town, including one on Jalan Green Hill, next door to the Metropole Inn. The advantage of these places is that vegetable dishes are also available along with the standards like steamed chicken and rice.

Fast Food For fast food, check out the area around the Holiday Inn, particularly Sarawak Plaza, where there are branches of *KFC*, *McDonald's*, *Pizza Hut* and local permutations like *Sugar Bun* and *Hertz Chicken*.

Malay Jalan India has three long-runners: the *Jubilee, Madinah* and *Malaya*, all very close to each other on the same side of the street. They all serve inexpensive Malay curries of the kind widely available in Peninsular Malaysia. Not far away on Jalan Carpenter is the *National Islamic Cafe*, which serves tasty, cheap Malay food, and has excellent rotis and murtabak.

Seafood Kuching has excellent seafood. The local speciality is steamed pomfret fish, but the sambal prawns are also a favourite. The *See Good* restaurant (mentioned in the Chinese entry above) is a good place to sample Kuching seafood prepared at its best. The friendly staff will help you make economical choices.

Elsewhere around town, the *KTS Seafood Canteen* sets up tables and chairs on the waterfront in the evening and has some of the best seafood in town. Young women representing the major beer labels keep the drinks coming.

Thai If you take a stroll along the Kuching waterfront, look out for the *Steamship Restaurant*, a new place that serves Thai, Chinese and Singaporean cuisine.

Western The best western cuisine is provided by the international hotels, notably the *Steak House* in the Hilton. For something more economical, the *Dulit Coffee House* at the Telang Usan Hotel is a good bet. The food here is excellent. The *San Francisco Grill*, just up the road from the Borneo Hotel, tries hard with its steaks and is popular with expat residents, but somebody should shoot the piano player.

Vegetarian Look out for the *Green Vegetarian Restaurant* on Main Bazaar, across the road from the Kuching waterfront. The decor is basic, but with bargain prices like the RM2.50 set lunch, who's complaining? Southern Indian curries are served here, and it is open from 8 am to 8 pm.

Entertainment

Unlike the east coast of Peninsular Malaysia (and much of the west coast too), Sarawak has a strong drinking culture. Kuching has a large number of bars, karaoke lounges and discos, and it's worth getting out in the evening at least once. You are much more likely to meet people – and possibly get some useful upriver contacts – in a bar than you are at a cheap hawker stall or a restaurant.

Opposite the Hilton car park, look out for *De Tavern*. This extremely friendly place is Kayan-run and frequented by an interesting mix of Malays, Chinese, Indians, Ibans, Kayans and western expats – a couple of nights in here and you'll be on a first name basis with half of Kuching. First-time visitors are usually treated to a free tipple of *tuak* – Iban rice wine. Upstairs and a few doors down from De Tavern is the *Fisherman's Pub* – a low-key karaoke bar with psychedelic fish decor.

For late-night action, there are a number of venues. *Cat City* has live music, but doesn't really get going until around 11 pm. *Peppers*, in the Hilton, is probably the most popular disco in town, particularly on 'ladies night' – Wednesday and Friday. *Mariner's Fun Pub & Disco* is just up the road from the Borneo Hotel and is another popular late-night haunt. There is live music until 2 am, when the deejay takes over. This place gets packed with everyone from logging barons to transvestites on the weekends – great people-watching, good party atmosphere.

Things to Buy

Kuching is probably the best place in Borneo for buying tribal artefacts. Shops selling arts and crafts are scattered around the city, notably along Main Bazaar. Don't expect anything in the way of bargains.

Hog charm sticks go for RM80 to RM100, and you can also buy larger, crudely carved totems for RM400 to RM1000 and intricately patterned baskets for up to RM800 depending on quality, source and age. Also very fine are the woven textiles, especially the Iban *pua kumbu*, starting at around RM200. Jewellery is likewise expensive. It's best to spend some time browsing before you commit yourself to a purchase, and be prepared to bargain hard. Sibu is in fact a cheaper place to buy artefacts, but the range there is far smaller and the quality is generally inferior.

The best area to start browsing is along Main Bazaar, where every second shop seems to be a gallery-style craft centre. Even if you are not in the market for any purchases, it is well worth ducking into some of these places. Some are piled higgledy-piggledy with all manner of bric-a-brac, others are presented like studios – it all makes for fascinating browsing, and the shopkeepers are generally very laid back.

Shops along here with a good selection include Unika Sarawak at No 78 and Native Arts at No 92. Sarakraf, at No 14, was set up by the Sarawak Economic Development Corporation, and is a good place for quality items.

On Jalan Tunku Abdul Rahman just past the Holiday Inn is Eeze Trading (☎ 082-254941), which has a whole stack of birds' nests and mounted scorpions, spiders and other insects, but little else. In the same area is Tan Brothers on Jalan Padungan. The range here is good and the prices are quite reasonable.

Getting There & Away

Air The MAS office (☎ 082-244144) is on Jalan Song Thian Cheok. It is open Monday to Friday from 8 am to 5 pm, Saturday from 8 am to 4.30 pm and Sunday from 8 am to 4 pm. Singapore Airlines (☎ 082-240266) is in the Ang Chang building on Jalan Tunku Abdul Rahman.

Singapore & Peninsular Malaysia The regular MAS fare between KL and Kuching is RM262. There are early-morning flights for RM187 (economy fare). Charter flights between KL and Kuching are also operated five times weekly by Transmile Air (TA) for RM177 one way, RM350 return. Tickets can be booked with Reliance Travel in KL (03-248 6022) or in Kuching (082-253404).

From Singapore to Kuching the fare is S$193, but in the opposite direction it's only RM205. Singapore Airlines also does this route for RM205.

Skipping over to Johor Bahru from Singapore drops the fare to RM169. You can buy the ticket in Singapore at the MAS office for the Singapore dollar equivalent. To encourage people to fly from Johor Bahru, MAS has a direct bus service from its office at the Novotel Orchid Hotel to the Johor Bahru airport for S$10. The absurd aspect of this arrangement is that you have to go through Malaysian immigration when entering from Singapore, and again a couple of hours later when entering Sarawak from the peninsula! MAS also has a 14-day (sometimes more) advance-purchase fare which can lower prices even further.

From Kuching the economy fare to Bandar Seri Begawan is RM250.

Indonesia MAS operates two flights per week, on Monday and Wednesday, from Kuching to Pontianak (Kalimantan). The cost is RM177 plus RM20 departure tax. Pontianak is a 'visa free' entry point to Indonesia, so most nationalities do not require visas.

Around Sarawak & Sabah Although MAS has a very extensive provincial network, none of the flights to the interior operate out of Kuching. You have to go to Sibu or Miri for those. From Kuching there are numerous daily flights to Sibu (RM72), Bintulu (RM117), Miri (RM164) and Kota Kinabalu (three flights daily, RM228), and one flight per day to Labuan (RM199).

Bus At first, bus transport from Kuching may seem chaotic, as there's no bus terminal. The main bus station area is near the market.

The main long-distance Sarawak Transport Company (STC) (☎ 082-242967) has green and yellow buses that depart from the terminus on Lebuh Jawa, which is a continuation of Jalan Gambier. They service the towns of south-west Sarawak around Kuching and are generally beat-up old tanks, which is a reflection of the roads. However, they do have a few air-con express buses to Sarikei and Sri Aman.

The Petra Jaya buses (☎ 082-429418) (yellow with red and black stripes) leave from Lebuh Khoo Hun Yeang near Electra House, and these are the buses for Bako National Park and Damai/Santubong. The blue and white Chin Lian Long Company buses leave from Lebuh Gartak near Jalan Mosque and have city buses for the airport and wharf (see Getting Around). Other long-distance buses for Sarikei, Bintulu and Miri leave from the Regional Express Bus Terminal on Jalan Penrissen, five km from town. Tickets can be bought at the Biaramas Express booking office (☎ 082-429418) on Jalan Khoo Hun Yeang, near Electra House.

For Semenggok take STC bus No 6, which departs approximately hourly and costs RM1.50. Other destinations and fares are listed in the table below.

Petra Jaya bus No 6 goes to Kampung Bako, from where boats go to the national park. Buses leave approximately hourly between 6.40 am and 6 pm and cost RM2.10. Petra Jaya bus No 2B goes to Santubong about every 45 minutes between 6.40 am and 6 pm, and costs RM2.30. Some of these buses continue on to Damai and the Sarawak Cultural Village. These cost RM2.80. There are six daily and they start running at 7.30 am. The last bus back from Damai is at 5.40 pm but, be warned, it sometimes fails to turn up.

Very few travellers bother with buses to Bintulu and Miri given that it is faster to travel by boat via Sibu. Generally it is necessary to change buses at Sarikei, which is the main bus junction for points further north. From here buses continue on to Bintulu, though a few buses from Kuching go straight through.

The main long-distance bus companies are on Jalan Penrissen, five km from town. Borneo Highway Express (☎ 084-427035), PB Bas Ekspres (☎ 082-461277) and Biaramas Express (☎ 082-452139) all have buses to Sarikei (RM28) with connections from Sarikei to Bintulu (RM24), and Biaramas will sell a through ticket to Miri (RM70). The buses are modern with air-con and kungfu movies. Most of the long-distance bus companies have ticket offices at or near the Petra Jaya bus station on Lebuh Khoo Hun Yeang.

Indonesia Biaramas Express (☎ 082-452139), 3½ mile, Jalan Penrissen, has a bus to Pontianak in Indonesia leaving at 7.30 am; it takes approximately 10 hours and costs RM34.50. The bus crosses at the Tebedu/Entikong border. This is now a visa-free entry point into Indonesia for most nationalities – check with the Indonesian embassy first. It is a slow haul from Serian to Tebedu on the Sarawak side, but the Indonesians have built a good highway from Entikong to Pontianak.

Boat – Kuching-Sarikei-Sibu There are three express boats between Kuching and Sibu. There is little to choose between them, although departure times differ. They all take around four hours; a change of boat (from a sea-going boat to a smaller river boat) is required at Sarikei; and of course they have violent videos laid on for your entertainment. Ekspres Pertama and Concorde Marine charge RM29 (RM35 1st class), while Ekspres Bahagia charges RM33 (RM38 1st class). Concorde is perhaps the best of the three, as you can sit outside on the ocean leg of the trip. All boats should be booked at least a day in advance to be on the safe side.

All boats leave from one of the wharfs in the horribly industrial suburb of Pending, about six km east of the city centre. Catch bus No 17 or 19 from outside the market on Main Bazaar and tell the driver which boat you are catching. A taxi costs RM10.

The addresses of boat operators and the departure times from Kuching are as follows:

Concorde Marine, Metropole Inn Hotel (☎ 082-412551), Jalan Green Hill; 8.30 am
Ekspres Bahagia (☎ 082-421948), 50 Jalan Padungan; 1 pm
Ekspres Pertama (☎ 082-414735), 196 Jalan Padungan; 8.30 am

STC Buses from Kuching

Destination	*Fare (RM)*	*Frequency*	*Bus No*	*Distance*
Bau	3	every 20 minutes	2	35 km
Lundu	6.60	3 times daily	2B	98 km
Serian	4.60	every 20 minutes	3, 3A	65 km
Sri Aman	15	3 times daily	15	195 km
Airport	0.90	every 50 minutes	12A	11 km

EAST MALAYSIA

Getting Around

The Airport A taxi between Kuching airport and the city centre costs RM13 (50% more after midnight). Buses are available between the airport and the centre of town for 90 sen, and they operate every 50 minutes from 6.30 am to 6 pm. The only bus going to the airport is STC green and yellow bus No 12A; No 12 goes to the *old* airport.

Bus City routes are mostly covered by the blue and white Chin Lian Long buses, which leave from Lebuh Gartak, near Jalan Mosque, and can be caught at other bus stops around town. The tourist office can supply details of routes. The two main services are bus No 6 to the Indonesian Consulate, and bus No 17 or 19 to the express boat wharf.

Taxi Taxis wait around the market and the area where long-distance buses drop passengers. There is usually no problem flagging down a taxi on the street, and charges start at RM5, though the taxis are unmetered.

Car Car rental costs in Sarawak are higher than in Peninsular Malaysia, starting at around RM130 per day for a Proton Saga. Pronto Car Rental (082-236889) has an office at 98 Jalan Padungan, and is a reliable operator with a large fleet of vehicles. Mayflower Car Rental (☎ 082-410110) is the other option. It has an office at 4.24A, 4th floor, Bangunan Satok, Jalan Satok, but the branch at the airport (☎ 082-575233) is easier to find.

Boat Small boats and express boats ply the Sarawak River, connecting the small villages around Kuching. You can also charter boats for RM15-20 per hour. Make sure you agree on the fare before you take the ride.

BAKO NATIONAL PARK

This park is at the mouth of the Bako River, north of Kuching, and contains some 27 sq km of unspoilt tropical rainforest. The coastline has many beaches, rocky headlands and mangrove swamps, while the interior features seven distinctive types of vegetation. Due to the different vegetation types, many animals – notably the rare and protected species of hornbill and the proboscis monkey – have made their homes in this park.

It's a very beautiful area and is well worth a visit. Walkers will not be disappointed, but don't expect too much of the beaches. Bako is near the mouth of the Sarawak River, which disgorges its muddy contents into the South China Sea. As is the case with all Sarawak's beaches, crystal-clear water and white sand are not to be found.

Over 30 km of well-marked trails have been laid through the park to make it accessible, and all of them are colour-coded with a paint-mark on trees adjacent to the path. On some of the longer walks you should plan your route before leaving, and aim to be back at the hostels at Telok Assam before dark at 6.45 pm. Although you may be told that a guide is necessary, it's easy to find your way around without one.

If you're thinking of walking to the end of the longest trail (Jalan Telok Limau), you may need to camp out or arrange transport to collect you, since it's impossible to do the return trip on foot in one day. Transport can be arranged with the park warden. Listed in the table below are the main trails in the park, and the times given are those recommended by the national park (fast walkers can almost halve them).

A permit is needed to visit the park, and this, along with accommodation bookings, can be obtained in advance at the Sarawak Tourist Information Centre (☎ 082-248088) in Kuching. Telephone bookings are accepted but must be confirmed and paid for at least three days before your intended departure. A permit is not necessary for day trips, but if you're planning to stay overnight you should book ahead and arrange a permit. It's best to avoid weekends if possible, as the park gets more crowded then.

Park HQ

On arrival at the park HQ it is necessary to register. There is an RM3 entry fee, plus RM5 per camera and RM10 per video camera.

SIMON ROWE

HUGH FINLAY

SIMON ROWE

Sarawak
Top: Bako National Park comprises coastal beaches, mangrove swamps and tropical rainforest.
Middle: Logging barges are a common sight on Sarawak's rivers.
Bottom: A boat transports woven thatch for roofs to villages along the Rejang River.

GLENN BEANLAND

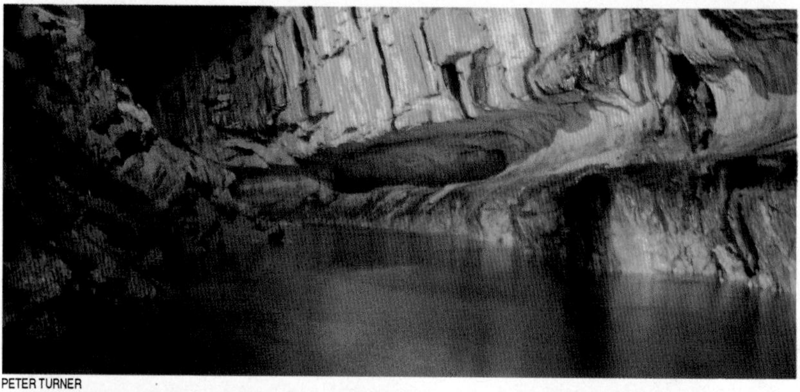

PETER TURNER

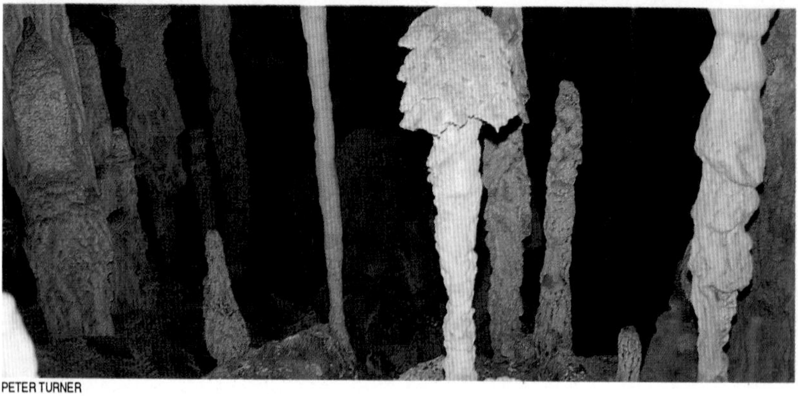

PETER TURNER

Sarawak

Top: The Niah Caves once were home to prehistoric humans.
Middle: The 51-km-long Clearwater Cave in Gunung Mulu National Park
Bottom: Gunung Mulu National Park is noted for its many underground caves.

Places to Stay & Eat

There are resthouses, hostels and a camping site at the park. Resthouses include fridges, gas burners, all utensils and bed linen. It costs RM80 per resthouse, or RM40 per double room. Hostel cabins sleep four to a room and beds cost RM10 per person. Linen, cooking utensils and a few cups and plates are provided. The standard of accommodation is very good, and the hostel is one of the

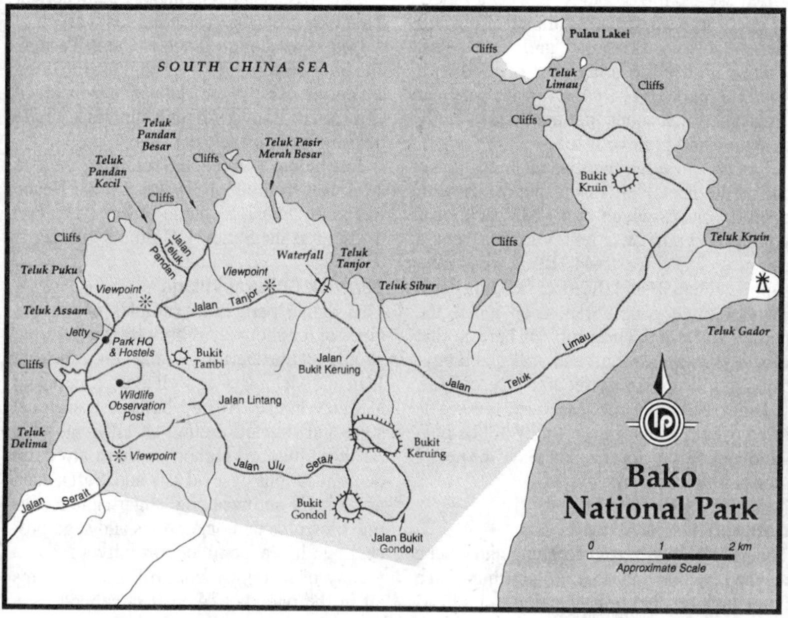

Walking Trails – Bako National Park

Name of Path	*Destination*	*Time Required*
Jalan Lintang	circular path	3-4 hours
Jalan Tanjung Sapi	cliffs/viewpoint	½ hour
Jalan Telok Delima	mangroves	¾ hour
Jalan Telok Pandan	cove beaches	1½ hours
Jalan Telok Paku	cove beach	¾ hour
Jalan Serait	park boundary	1½ hours
Jalan Tanjor	waterfalls	2 hours
Jalan Tanjung Rhu	cliffs/viewpoint	2½ hours
Jalan Bukit Keruing/ Jalan Bukit Gondol	mountain path	7 hours
Jalan Ulu Serait/ Jalan Telok Limau	Pulau Lakei (island)	8 hours

best in Sarawak – certainly better than that at Niah Caves. Accommodation bookings are essential for the resthouses and advisable for the hostel rooms, though you should be able to get a bed if you just front up.

The park canteen sells cheap, basic meals – fried rice and fried noodles – and has a variety of goods for sale (mainly tinned food) but there is also fresh bread and vegetables. There's no need to bring a lot of food with you. The park HQ is home to wild pigs and long-tailed macaques that are always ready to swoop and grab your food!

Lastly, there are permanent tents (basically fly sheets) on raised platforms with open fireplaces which cost RM8 each, or if you have your own tent you can rent a camping space for RM4. Bring your own supplies/utensils and sheets or sleeping bags. Two or three people can sleep under the permanent tents. The problem here is that monkeys prowl around and will pinch anything that is not firmly secured – be careful.

From November to February the sea is often rough, and at times it may not be possible for boats to approach or leave the hostel area at Telok Assam.

Getting There & Away

The park is 37 km from Kuching and can be reached by bus and boat. To get there, take Petra Jaya bus No 6 in Kuching; the fare is RM2.10 one way (RM3 for a return ticket, valid for a week). The trip to Kampung Bako takes about 45 minutes and buses depart hourly from 6.40 am to 6 pm. The last bus back from Bako to Kuching departs at 5 pm.

From Kampung Bako, you must charter a private boat to the national park for about RM25 for up to 10 people, or RM3 per person if there are more than 10. Bako is a very popular park, especially on weekends, and chances are that a few people on the bus will be looking to share a boat. The journey takes about 30 minutes.

SANTUBONG & DAMAI

The small fishing village of Santubong, 32 km north of Kuching, has the nearest beach to Kuching, other than the beaches in the nearby Bako National Park, and is very popular with local people on the weekends. The beach isn't great and the sight of semi-naked foreigners may cause a stir, but it is a picturesque spot at the mouth of a river, with Gunung Santubong towering dramatically nearby. At Sungai Jaong, about 1.5 km upriver from the coast, rock carvings can be seen.

Near Santubong village is Camp Permai, one of those paramilitary, potential-fulfilling adventure camps – a Malaysian version of Outward Bound – with rock climbing, jungle trekking and obstacle courses.

Just before you reach Santubong there is a turn-off to the Holiday Inn Damai Beach Resort at Damai, a couple of km away, and next to it is the Sarawak Cultural Village.

Sarawak Cultural Village

This theme park has examples of various types of longhouses, as built by the different peoples of the interior – Orang Ulu, Bidayuh, Iban and Melanau – as well as a Chinese and a Malay house. All are built in traditional style and situated around an artificial lake. At the different longhouses there are daily demonstrations of local arts and crafts, such as basketry and weaving, sugar-cane crushing, blowpipe demonstrations and sago processing. It's a good opportunity to see a variety of activities from different cultures all in the one spot. A visit is capped by a choreographed one-hour dance performance at 11.30 am and 4.30 pm. It is all very touristy, as you would expect, but well done.

The village has a morning programme (9 am to 12.30 pm) and an afternoon programme (2 to 5.30 pm). Be sure to get there at 9 am or 2 pm to see all the attractions and get your money's worth, as entry is a hefty RM45 (RM22.50 for children). For more information phone ☎ 082-422411.

Places to Stay

Accommodation in Santubong and Damai is resort style and definitely not for travellers on a budget. The *Holiday Inn Damai Beach Resort* (☎ 082-846999; fax 082-846777) has standard rooms from RM218 to RM290, although discounts are offered. It has a pleasant, small beach, even if it is manufactured from imported sand.

The *Damai Lagoon Resort* (☎ 082-234900; fax 082-234901) is twinned with the Riverside Majestic Hotel in Kuching. Standard rooms are RM276 to RM330, while suites are RM600 to RM2250.

The *Santubong Kuching Resort* (☎ 082-238888; fax 082-236666) is the least expensive of the resorts, and provides a wide range of services and activities (tennis and basketball courts, watersports, nearby golf course, mountain biking etc) for RM110 for standard rooms; suites cost RM190 to RM330.

Camp Permai caters mostly for school groups but accommodation is available – there are often substantially discounted rates for 'tree-top cabins' on weekdays. Ring Camp Permai Sarawak (☎ 082-255393) in Kuching for details.

Getting There & Away

Petra Jaya bus No 2B goes to Santubong and Damai (for the Sarawak Cultural Village); see the Kuching Getting There & Away section for details. The Holiday Inn in Kuching also has shuttle buses to Damai for a steep RM12.

KUBAH NATIONAL PARK

Just 20 km west of Kuching, and opened in 1995, Kubah National park is an easy day trip from Kuching. Park facilities are still being developed. As yet there is nowhere to stay and there are just three jungle trails. Plans are afoot to improve the trails by adding plankwalks and bridges, and these should be in place by the time you have this book in your hands. There is also a path to the summit of Gunung Serapi, which takes around two or three hours.

While Kubah is rich in wildlife, there is less chance of encountering it than in Bako. Kubah does, however, have a wide variety of palms and orchids, and it also has waterfalls with bathing pools. The most popular trail starts on the Gunung Serapi trail at around 900 metres and descends through rainforest into a swampy area before ending at a stream and picnic area beside the Matang Wildlife Centre (see below).

Matang Wildlife Centre

Part of Kubah National Park, the Matang Wildlife Centre will perform a similar function to Semenggok when completed. It includes wildlife conservation areas in the rainforest, and will also rehabilitate animals that have been captured or separated from their native environments. The centre itself is already open to visitors (mainly as a popular weekend swimming area), but work on the rainforest enclosures will not begin until some time in 1996.

Getting There & Away

The Matang Bus Company's yellow and orange buses leave from outside the Saujana car park in Kuching. Take bus No 18, which costs RM3 and takes around 50 minutes. Buses leave approximately every 1½ hours between 6 and 10 am and 1 and 5 pm, though services are likely to become more frequent as facilities at the park improve.

SEMENGGOK WILDLIFE REHABILITATION CENTRE

This is where you'll find Sarawak's answer to the orang-utan sanctuary at Sepilok in Sabah. The Semenggok (also spelt Semenggoh, Semengok and Semengoh!) sanctuary, 32 km south of Kuching, is a rehabilitation centre for orang-utans, monkeys, honey bears and hornbills which have been either orphaned or kept illegally by locals.

This is a working field-station and is not really set up for tourism, making it less of a zoo than the Sepilok Orang-Utan Rehabilitation Centre in Sabah. The semi-wild orang-utans are fed at 8.30 to 9 am and again at 3 pm to 3.15 pm, so it's best to time your visit to coincide with one of these feeding sessions. The centre is open every day from 8 am to 12.45 pm and from 2 to 4.15 pm.

The centre is reached from the Forest Department Nursery along a plankwalk through the forest – a very pleasant walk. There are also a couple of signposted jungle trails behind the nursery – the Southern Trail can be used as an alternative to the plankwalk but is slippery and muddy in the wet season.

A permit is required in order to visit the

sanctuary and can be arranged, free of charge, at the Sarawak Tourist Information Centre.

Getting There & Away

To get to the centre and Forest Department Nursery, take STC Penrissen bus No 6 from Kuching. The trip takes about 40 minutes, costs RM1.50 and there are departures hourly. The bus will drop you at the Forest Department Nursery. If you are driving, there is a road through the forest to the rehabilitation centre from the Botanical Research Station, 500 metres before the Forest Department Nursery.

BIDAYUH LONGHOUSES

As you might expect, the most interesting and unspoilt longhouses are found furthest from the main urban centres, particularly along the upper reaches of the Skrang, Rejang, Balleh, Belaga, Balui and Baram rivers.

If you're not planning on going that far, or would like a preview, then the nearest longhouses to Kuching are the Bidayuh longhouses to the south of the city.

Kampung Benuk, which is a 35 km bus ride south of the city, followed by a short walk, is only a few km past Semenggok on the same road. Don't expect too much of this place – all the package tours include it on their itinerary, so it's very commercialised.

Kampung Annah Rais is one of the best known of the 'tourist' longhouses. This impressive longhouse of over 100 doors has preserved its traditional look, largely because the deal with the tour agencies doesn't allow the use of nontraditional materials (corrugated iron is bad for tourism). The villagers must also keep the tour operators informed of any special festivities that will be happening in the village.

Kampung Gayu is another place that is visited by tour groups, though there are many others in this area.

It is possible to climb **Gunung Penrissen** on the Sarawak/Kalimantan border. The two to three day trek is only for experienced, well-equipped climbers. Guides need to be hired – in Kampung Annah Rais or nearby Kampung Padawan.

JONG'S CROCODILE FARM

This crocodile farm is 29 km south of Kuching, just off the Serian highway at

EAST MALAYSIA

The Bidayuh

When you're totally outnumbered by warlike Ibans who want your head and your farmland, life can get a little difficult. That Sarawak's 90,000 Bidayuh survived at all is tribute to their legendary toughness, adaptability and good humour.

The Bidayuh responded to the Iban threat by building fortified longhouses far inland, leading early European travellers to call them 'Land Dayaks', to distinguish them from the Iban 'Sea Dayaks'. They also built imposing octagonal skull houses (*baruk*) to house their enemies' heads.

In their remote hill farms, the Bidayuh grow hill rice, maize and sugar cane as staples, and pepper, cocoa and rubber for cash. They have developed superb handicrafts: their basketry is every bit as fine as that of the Penan, although subtly different, and they are splendid craftsmen in bamboo – whole longhouses were built of this tough, durable material, and water supplies are delivered from remote mountain springs through complex arrays of bamboo plumbing.

The Bidayuhs were James and Charles Brooke's favourite people. This may have something to do with their legendary honesty, their love of music and dance and their physical beauty.

Aesthetics aside, one of the best reasons to spend time with the Bidayuh is because they are Borneo's master wine makers. Their *tuak*, or rice wine, is comparable to that of the Iban, and they produce liquid masterpieces from anything that contains carbohydrates. *Tuak tebu* (sugar-cane wine), *tuak tampui* (mangosteen tuak) and *tuak appel* (cider) can enliven an evening spent in a kampung or longhouse beyond your wildest expectations.

Don't bother learning the language, though. When Bidayuhs are introduced they speak in Malay or English, because if they're not from the same village they probably can't understand each other's dialect. Maybe that's why they became such good brewers – to overcome the language barrier.

Mike Reed

Siburan. If crocodiles in concrete tanks are your thing, it is open daily and entry is RM5 for adults (RM3 on Sunday) and RM1 for children. There is also a mini-zoo.

STC bus No 3, 3A or 9 will drop you at the signposted turn-off on the highway, from where it is a short walk to the farm.

BAU & SEMATAN

Bau, an old gold-mining town, is en route to Sematan and Gunung Gading National Park, though most travellers give it a miss. Chinese miners and Raja Brooke were first attracted to Bau by gold, but nowadays its main claim to fame is the limestone Fairy Caves, a popular weekend picnic spot around 10 km outside town. You will have to hitch or take a taxi to get out there.

Sematan is a tiny coastal village near the extreme western end of Sarawak. The beach is clean and deserted, though the very shallow water doesn't make for good swimming. This is a real get-away-from-it-all kind of destination, but all things considered it is a rough journey to a so-so beach. The area around here is popular with well-to-do Kuching residents who have beach bungalows, some of which can be rented.

Places to Stay & Eat

In Sematan, the *Thomas Lai Bungalows* are a number of large two and three-bedroom bungalows in a coconut palm grove next to the sea. These spartan wooden bungalows with *mandi*, basic kitchen facilities and veranda are very run-down and overpriced at RM80 to RM120 for better bungalows right on the beach. Try bargaining for mid-week specials. You can telephone ☎ 082-332098 in Kuching, or see the caretaker in Sematan. Sematan has other private bungalows – ask around. In the centre of the village is the *Sematan Hotel* (☎ 082-711162), which is reasonably priced and has fan rooms for RM20 to RM28 and better air-con rooms for RM45 and RM50. Sematan has a couple of Chinese coffee-shops, and food stalls at the small market.

Getting There & Away

Direct transport to Bau is via STC bus No 2. The journey takes around one hour and costs RM3. Buses leave every 20 minutes between 6 am and 6 pm.

To get to Sematan, you will have to take a bus to the village of Lundu, which is also the exit point for Gunung Gading National Park, and change there. STC bus No 2B costs RM6.60 or RM7.80 (air-con) and takes around two hours to Lundu. Departures are at 8 and 11.30 am, and 12.45, 2.15 and 4 pm. From Lundu there are 10 daily STC buses to Sematan (route No 17); it's a one hour journey on a very rough road at a cost of RM2.

GUNUNG GADING NATIONAL PARK

Gazetted as a national park in 1984, it was not until mid-1994 that the park was opened to the public. In terms of tourism, the park is still in its infancy, which for some visitors will no doubt be a drawcard in itself. The chief attraction, however, is the rafflesia, the world's largest flowering plant. Plankways have been laid down, providing access to the areas in which the rafflesia is most likely to be found. Bear in mind though that the flower has no specific flowering season, and it is a good idea to check whether any are in bloom before heading out there. Ring the park HQ (☎ 082-735714) or the National Parks & Wildlife booking office (☎ 082-248088) in Kuching.

Tourism-impact studies have been undertaken on the park and there are now plans to develop further jungle trails like those at Bako. Among the trails planned is one to the summit of Gunung Gading (906 metres).

Places to Stay

It is still early days and undoubtedly more accommodation will spring up, but at the time of writing the park HQ provided accommodation in two chalets, each with two double rooms. Chalets cost RM126 and sleep four people. Hostel accommodation is also available at RM10.50 per person.

In Lundu there are a couple of hotels. The *Cheng Hak Boarding House* (082-735018) has rooms from RM12 to RM40, but it's a grotty kind of place. The *Lundu Gading Hotel* (☎ 082-735299) has air-con rooms at RM60.

Getting There & Away

See the Bau & Sematan Getting There & Away entry for information on getting to Lundu from Kuching. From Lundu it is only around a five minute drive to Gunung Gading. Take a Pandan bus (ask to be dropped off at the park) or hitch.

SERIAN

Serian is a very small town 65 km south-east of Kuching. On weekends it's a popular destination for Kuching residents, who come to picnic at Taman Danu, a landscaped park built around a lake, or to visit the pleasant Taman Rekreasi Ranchan, about five km from town, where there are small waterfalls. The other attraction is a bustling local market, where unusual produce for sale includes snake meat and sago worms.

Places to Stay

If you want to stay overnight, the *Kota Semarahan Serian Hotel* (☎ 082-874118) has rooms from RM20.

Getting There & Away

From Kuching take an STC express bus No 3 or 3A to Serian; the journey takes about an hour and the fare is RM4.60 or RM5 (air-con). Buses leave every half-hour (approximately) between 6.30 am and 6 pm. Taman Danu is on the outskirts of town towards Sri Aman, while the Ranchan Waterfalls are further out of town up a side road off the road to Sri Aman. If you go on a weekend, try hitching, as there's lots of traffic.

SRI AMAN

On the Lupar River, halfway between Kuching and Sarikei, Sri Aman is a sleepy town with a bustling market. Right in town, looking across the river, is Fort Alice, one of Raja Brooke's old forts dating from 1864. Apart from this, Sri Aman doesn't have much to offer, but some travellers stop over and use Sri Aman as a base to explore the surrounding area and its longhouses. The Skrang, Lemanak and Ai rivers flow into the Lupar, and many of the tours organised out of Kuching bring their groups to the longhouses along these tributaries. Many of the tour operators have built their own accommodation facilities outside the longhouses.

There isn't a lot of river traffic at Sri Aman itself, and while it is close to the confluence of the Skrang River, most boats to the longhouses go from Kampung Skrang, further north, where the highway crosses the Skrang River. Similarly, most boats to the Lemanak and Ai rivers leave from Engkilili, or on the highway outside town where the road crosses the Lupar River.

Places to Stay

The basic *Sun Sun Hotel*, opposite the market near the waterfront, has large, clean singles/doubles with fans for RM20/25. It is very spartan but quite acceptable. The newer *Alishan Hotel* (☎ 083-322578) is a better bet for a cheap room. It mostly has air-con singles/doubles for RM35/40, but the RM22 fan rooms are better than those at the Sun Sun.

The *Taiwan Hotel* (☎ 083-322493) is similar to the Alishan and has air-con rooms for RM32 to RM34 and rooms with fans for RM28. The mid-range *Hoover Hotel* (☎ 083-321985) is the best place in town and has rooms with air-con, attached bathroom and TV from RM30 to RM70.

Getting There & Away

STC has eight buses a day from 8 am to 6 pm from Kuching to Sri Aman (RM12.20). Frequent buses go between Sri Aman and Sarikei (RM12.20), from where bus connections further north are possible and boats go up the Rejang to Sibu. The quickest way to get to Sibu is to take an express bus to Bintangor (RM16.50), but tell the driver you want to catch the ferry to Sibu and you will be let off a few km before Bintangor. From here a local bus will take you to the Rejang River, from where a ferry (RM1) does the short trip to Sibu.

From Sri Aman STC buses go to the surrounding villages of Skrang (RM3.60), Batu Lintang (RM2.50), Engkilili (RM2.50) and Lubok Antu (RM5.20).

BATANG AI NATIONAL PARK

Gazetted in 1991, Batang Ai is north of the Batang Ai reservoir (which was formed by a hydroelectric scheme), around four hours east of Kuching. The park is home to orang-utans, hornbills and gibbons, as well as to dipterocarp forest. As yet there is no visitors' centre and no accommodation in the park, though some travel agencies in Kuching can arrange for longhouse accommodation on the fringes of the park. The *Hilton Batang Ai Longhouse Resort* (☎ 083-584338; fax 083-584339) is a unique experiment: a luxury longhouse resort which allows guests to enjoy jungle adventure by day and upmarket comforts by night. Although this place is out in the middle of nowhere, the rooms are all air-con and have IDD phone, and the hotel has a swimming pool, bar, restaurant with cultural performances and seminar facilities. Standard rooms cost RM170 to RM190, and suites cost from RM230.

Up the Rejang River

The mighty Rejang River is the stuff of 'into the heart of Borneo' fantasy. It is the main artery of trade with the interior for all of central and southern Sarawak, and scattered along its banks, and those of its tributaries, particularly the upper reaches, are the longhouses of the Iban and other tribes. Travellers who view the Rejang as a ticket to longhouse retreats and tribal innocence, however, are likely to be disappointed.

For a start, the Rejang is the main trading conduit for logs from the forests in the upper reaches of the river (and its tributaries the Balleh, Belaga and Balui rivers). The number of log-laden barges on the river is astounding. Before the loggers arrived, the river was a clear green; these days it's a muddy brown from all the topsoil which has washed out of the forests. What's more, a massive hydroelectric dam project to the north of Belaga at Bakun will bring with it roads, labourers and far-reaching change to the area.

The best time for a trip up the Rejang is in late May and early June, as this is the time of Gawai, the Dayak harvest festival, when there is plenty of movement on the rivers and the longhouses welcome visitors. There are also plenty of celebrations, which usually involve the consumption of copious quantities of *arak* and *tuak* (rice wine).

On the river there is hotel accommodation only in Song, Kanowit, Kapit and Belaga.

Visiting a Longhouse

Most people head off up the river with the intention of visiting a longhouse, and certainly this is well worth doing. However, there is no guarantee that you will succeed, as while the hospitality of the longhouse tribes is famous, it cannot be relied on for unannounced visits. It's not just a matter of rolling up on the doorstep of a longhouse and expecting to be welcomed with open arms. Without an introduction, the Orang Ulu are not going to invite you into their homes – turning up unannounced is not just bad manners, in certain circumstances it can be a minor catastrophe, particularly if there has been a recent death or certain rituals are under way. Without an invitation, there is little point in making this often expensive and arduous journey upriver.

Longhouses can be found all the way along the Rejang, and while most visitors head for Kapit and beyond, there are plenty of longhouses further downriver around Kanowit and Song. As you go further upriver, the longhouses will not necessarily be more traditional. Most longhouses are made from modern building materials, and in fact many longhouse communities are moving towards individual houses, which fare much better if there is a fire. Similarly, amulets and head feathers are reserved for ceremonial occasions; jeans, shorts and T-shirts are the preferred everyday longhouse attire. Traditional customs, beliefs and festivals are still practised, but the jungle *is* part of the 20th century – you may spend days getting to a longhouse only to find everyone sitting around watching CNN on satellite TV.

To arrange a visit, the most important

commodity you need is time. If you are short of it, take a tour. Most travellers head for Kapit, a small administrative town upriver. It's the last big settlement on the river, and it's here that the longhouse people come in for supplies. The best strategy for finding someone to take you to a longhouse is to make yourself known around the town – sit in the cafes and get talking to people. If you are not the sociable type, it's unlikely that anyone is going to want to invite you to their home – unless you have a couple of bottles of Henessy XO.

Before heading upriver from Kapit, you need to get a permit from the state office. This only takes a few minutes, but permits are not available on Saturday afternoon or Sunday. The permit is merely a formality, and chances are you'll never be asked for it. On the top floor of the same building is the Lands & Surveys Department office. They have excellent maps of Sarawak, and for a small charge will photocopy sections of the most detailed ones. These give good detail of the Rejang and Balleh rivers, including many longhouse names.

Many travellers head for the stretch of the Rejang River between Kapit and Belaga. This area is easily accessible as there are express boats operating between the two towns, in the wet season at least. Perhaps a more interesting river is the Balleh River, which branches off to the east a short distance upstream from Kapit. Both these rivers have dozens of small tributaries, and it's up these that you really want to go. At Belaga the Balui and Belaga rivers merge and become the Rejang River. To travel up either of these rivers from Belaga requires permission from the Resident in Belaga, and this is generally not given, although it seems there's little to stop you if you are determined. The Katibas River, which joins the Rejang at Song (between Sibu and Kapit), is also a good river to explore, and no permits are required.

Some people have reported that some of the longhouse inhabitants between Kapit and Belaga are decidedly unfriendly towards visitors. No doubt they're sick to death of strangers turning up out of the blue and expecting to be welcomed with open arms,

The Bakun Dam

In 1995, after 15 years on the drawing boards, the Bakun Dam project finally got the official go-ahead. Ekran, the company building the dam, can start lopping down trees – around 700 sq km of them (an area roughly the size of Singapore). The logs cleared will be worth at least US$200 million to Ekran. Two of Sarawak's chief minister's sons are major company shareholders.

That's the gist of the story – environmental destruction, big bucks, a whiff of nepotism. Interesting sub-plots involve the displacement of indigenous inhabitants, seismic activity in the Bakun area (which might bring the whole thing toppling down) and overall feasibility worries. All up, it amounts to a very controversial subject.

Bakun is for the most part an area of untouched rainforest in the upper reaches of the Rejang river, past Belaga. The dam project is going to be a big one. Its hydroelectric capacity will rival that of the Aswan Dam in Egypt. Sarawak does not need that much electricity, so the plan is to divert it to Peninsular Malaysia via a 650 km deep-sea cable system. At this point, sceptics raise their eyebrows. As of late 1995, plans for the cable had not been approved, despite the fact that forest clearance had.

Anyone would think that a controversial project like the Bakun Dam would be the last thing either the federal or the Sarawak governments need. But there is big money at stake. So much money apparently that the government is prepared to ride roughshod over its own legal processes. Environmental assessments of projects like the Bakun Dam should legally be published. The 250 page assessment of the environmental impact of the Bakun project has – via some clever manoeuvring by the federal government – been withheld from the public. It is reported to warn of dire environmental consequences, not just to the immediate Bakun area but to the whole Rejang River system.

Environmental groups argue it is too soon to start logging. Financing for the RM15 billion dam project is uncertain, the environmental impact of the project is unknown, tribal residents of the area will have to be relocated, and the exact details of how to carry electricity across 650 km of ocean remain hazy. It seems, though, that whether the dam gets built or not the area will be logged – Ekran and its shareholders will make their money.

Chris Taylor

fed and entertained. One traveller was stuck for words when an old Iban lady asked: 'Where in Europe can I go and be welcomed into a stranger's house?' Don't let this put you off, as generally the Iban are very friendly, hospitable people who welcome foreigners and are pleased to invite you into their homes. Staying at a longhouse is one of the highlights of any trip to Sarawak.

Having found someone to take you, you'll need to stock up with gifts with which to 'pay' for your visit. Forget any qualms you may have about giving people things that might be bad for them – cigarettes and alcohol are the gifts most appreciated. A carton of cigarettes and a few bottles of whisky will go down well. Sweets are always popular too, and not just with the kids. Of course if you can give something original, especially from your own country, it will be well received.

On arrival at the longhouse ask for the *tuai rumah* (chief). You'll then probably be offered a place to stay for the night and be invited to join them for a meal.

Longhouse Etiquette Longhouse etiquette is fairly formal, and there are a number of important customs you need to be aware of so you don't make a fool of yourself or cause offence. Firstly, never enter a longhouse without permission; always wait to be invited. If there is a *pemali* (ritual prohibition) in force (usually after a death or some misfortune), indicated by a bunch of branches tied to the rail at the bottom of the ladder or by a white flag near the entrance, you won't be invited in – find another longhouse.

Once inside, always remove your shoes; it's extremely bad form to wear footwear inside a longhouse. Chances are you'll be given a welcome drink of *tuak*; drink it, or at least some of it. Accept food and drinks with both hands rather than just one.

Meals are usually taken with the tuai rumah and are served on the floor and eaten with both hands. Don't stretch your legs when sitting on the mat; this applies at any time, not just during meals. Don't spit or blow your nose during a meal. Chances are the food will be fairly bland and uninteresting but, again, eat some of it, or at the very least

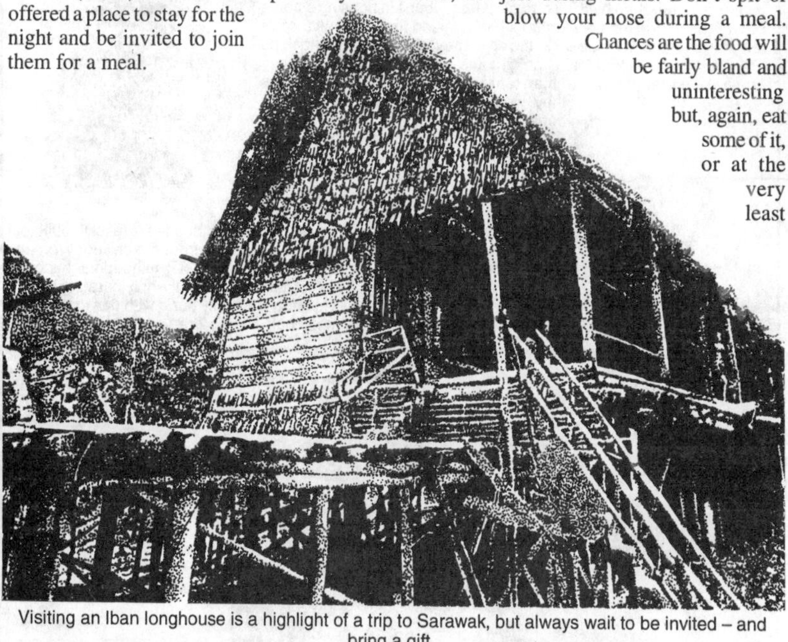

Visiting an Iban longhouse is a highlight of a trip to Sarawak, but always wait to be invited – and bring a gift.

touch the food and then touch your mouth. Vegetarians may find it difficult, as meat is usually used in local cooking. It's not a bad idea to take along some food of your own, but bear in mind you will have to offer to share it.

When washing or bathing in the river, men are expected to wear at least underpants while women should stay covered with a sarung. Nudity is not on – this is not Europe.

In the evenings there'll probably be a lot of tuak drinking, and you may well be expected to sing and dance. Join in and don't be afraid to make an idiot of yourself – the locals will love it! Tuak usually tastes weak but it is pretty potent stuff, and although it doesn't usually result in a hangover it is a fairly safe bet that you'll find yourself going to the toilet frequently the following day. The accepted way to drink it is from the glass in a single shot.

Make an effort to speak at least a few words of Iban. Although there's always someone

The Iban

The Iban are likely to come as a shock to anyone who imagines these people as happy natives marooned from the 20th century deep in the jungles of Borneo. Sarawak's most adaptable and resourceful ethnic group are far too savvy to turn a blind eye to the convenience of a Land Cruiser or the pleasure afforded by satellite TV. Those who shake their heads in disappointment, however, should look again. The Iban manage to maintain a tribal culture that is every bit as rich in a Kuching housing estate as it is in the rural longhouse of tradition.

For most Ibans, however, the longhouse is still their first choice of dwelling, even when built of concrete. Urban Ibans in housing estates buy terraced houses adjacent to each other, so that a semblance of longhouse life is maintained in the city. They enjoy close friendships with their Chinese and Malay neighbours across the street, but they generally prefer to have an Iban family living either side of them, as they would in their grandparents' longhouse.

But the majority of Sarawak's 550,000 Ibans (the largest single ethnic group) still live in the countryside, growing hill rice, breeding pigs and chickens, and supplementing their income with pepper, rubber, oil palm and cocoa. Most longhouses are still built of ironwood, with ancient skulls still hanging from the ceiling. Women still weave the fabulous *pua kumbu* blankets, although lighting is supplied nowadays by a generator rather than a paraffin lamp. Cooking is usually done with gas instead of charcoal. The children all go to school, but they can still perform the Ngajat dance to alarming effect. And although most Ibans are nowadays Christian, impressive feasts are still held for the dead (Gawai Antu), and for the great bird of omen, the hornbill (Gawai Kenyalang). And the rice wine (*tuak*) is as potent as it ever was.

Economic development has not dragged the Iban reluctantly into the late 20th century. Rather, the Iban have seized the 20th century by the scruff of the neck and dragged it kicking and screaming into the longhouse.

Mike Reed

who speaks Malay, any attempt at communication in the local lingo is warmly appreciated. Your conversations will be limited if you speak only English.

What to Take Apart from gifts, other indispensable items include a torch, mosquito repellent and a medical kit with plenty of aspirin or Panadol and Lomotil, Imodium or other anti-diarrhoeal.

Some Iban Words & Phrases

I	*aku*
you	*nuan*
drink	*ngirup*
eat	*makai*
thank you	*terima kasih*
day	*hari*
night	*malam*
where	*dini*
what	*nama*
good	*manah*
not good	*jai also enda manah*
I'm sorry.	*Aku minta ampun.*
go	*bejalai*
today	*saharitu*
tomorrow	*pegilah*

Good morning.
Salamat pagi.
Good afternoon.
Salamat tengah-hari.
Good night.
Salamat malam.
Good bye.
Salamat tinggal.
How are you?
Gerai nuan?
Pleased to meet you.
Rindu amat betemu enggau nuan.
See you again.
Arap ke betemu baru.
Who is the chief?
Sapa tuai rumah kita ditu?
What is your name?
Sapa nama nuan?
Where do we bathe/wash?
Dini endor kitai mandi?
Can I take a photograph of you?
Tau aku ngambi gambar nuan?

SIBU

Sibu is the main port city on the Rejang River and will probably be your first stop on the river. Situated 60 km upstream from the ocean, its bustling waterfront sports all manner of craft, from motorised dugouts to ocean-going cargo boats. It's here that the raw materials of the interior – logs, gravel, minerals and agricultural produce – are brought for transhipment and export. Manufactured goods from Peninsular Malaysia and abroad also arrive here for distribution to the interior.

There's not a great deal to do in Sibu unless you like hanging around on waterfronts or at vegetable markets, and although both of these are quite entertaining, most travellers only stay overnight in Sibu and head off up the Rejang the next day.

It's worth climbing the tower of the Chinese temple, as there are great views of the river from the top of the tower.

At the other end of the waterfront, just past the bus station, there is a clock tower, donated by the Orient Clock Co, complete with a clock that plays different tunes on the hour – very tacky!

Information

The GPO is right in the centre of town, as are the major banks. The MAS office (☎ 083-326166) is at 61 Jalan Tunku Osman, a few minutes' walk from the centre of town. It is open Monday to Friday from 8 am to 5 pm, Saturday from 8 am to 4 pm and Sunday from 8 am to 12.30 pm.

There is an excellent swimming pool about a 30 minute bus ride from the centre. Take bus No 10 from the bus station. The pool is open Monday to Thursday from 2 to 6 pm, Friday from 2 to 5 and 7 to 9 pm, Saturday from 9 to 11 am and 2 to 5 pm, and Sunday from 9 to 11 am and 2 to 5 and 7 to 9 pm; entry is RM1.

The express boat wharf is right in the centre of town, just near the Chinese temple, and the bus station is also on the waterfront. Everything in Sibu (apart from the swimming pool and airport) is located within walking distance of the boat wharf and the bus station.

Places to Stay – bottom end

Sibu has dozens of budget hotels. Many of them, however, are seedy places, especially those displaying signs saying *bilik untuk sewa* (or variations), which means 'rooms for rent'. These places house long-term residents.

The best place to stay is the Methodist guesthouse, *Hoover House* (☎ 084-332973), next to the church on Jalan Pulau. It's excellent value at RM10 per person for clean, well-kept rooms with polished wooden floors, fans and attached western-style bathrooms, but it is very hard to get a room here – it is usually full. Check with the caretaker around the back.

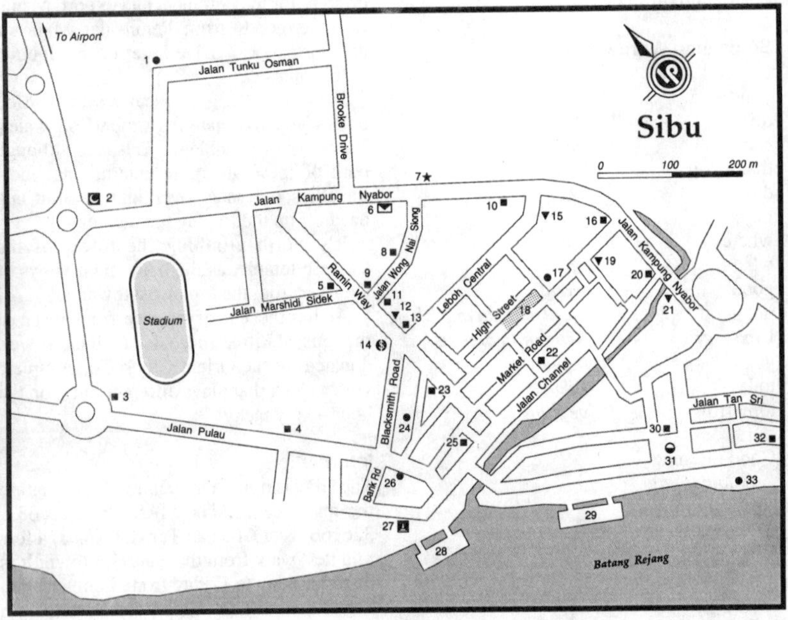

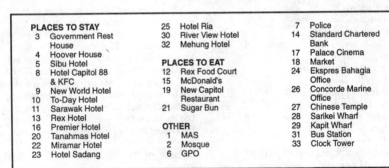

PLACES TO STAY
- 3 Government Rest House
- 4 Hoover House
- 5 Sibu Hotel
- 8 Hotel Capitol 88 & KFC
- 9 New World Hotel
- 10 To-Day Hotel
- 11 Sarawak Hotel
- 13 Rex Hotel
- 16 Premier Hotel
- 20 Tanahmas Hotel
- 22 Miramar Hotel
- 23 Hotel Sadang
- 25 Hotel Ria
- 30 River View Hotel
- 32 Mehung Hotel

PLACES TO EAT
- 12 Rex Food Court
- 15 McDonald's
- 19 New Capitol Restaurant
- 21 Sugar Bun

OTHER
- 1 MAS
- 2 Mosque
- 6 GPO
- 7 Police
- 14 Standard Chartered Bank
- 17 Palace Cinema
- 18 Market
- 24 Ekspres Bahagia Office
- 26 Concorde Marine Office
- 27 Chinese Temple
- 28 Sarikei Wharf
- 29 Kapit Wharf
- 31 Bus Station
- 33 Clock Tower

If you can't get into Hoover House, check around the bus station for budget accommodation. It's a squalid part of town, but despite appearances it's safe. The *Mehung Hotel* (☎ 084-324852), at 17 Maju Rd, has small rooms from RM15, and decent rooms with fan and tiny bathroom from RM20 (single or double) or RM30 with air-con. On the street behind this hotel are a couple of grotty hostels with rooms from RM12. The *New Park Hostel* and the *Holiday Hotel* are two of them – not recommended, but OK to crash out in for a night.

The town centre has better hotels, though naturally prices are higher. The *Sibu Hotel* (☎ 084-330784) on Jalan Marshidi Sidek is good for the price and recommended. The rooms cost RM16 with fan, RM20 with fan and bath or RM28 with air-con, bath and TV. The *To-Day Hotel* (☎ 084-336499), at 40 Jalan Kampung Nyabor, is a well-run place and also home to 'Yeo's Tattoo Artist'. Clean air-con rooms with bath and TV cost RM25/30.

Places to Stay – middle

Right beside the bus station is the *River View Hotel* (☎ 084-334419), 65 Mission Rd. Spotlessly clean and comfortable rooms with TV, attached bathroom, telephone and carpet cost from RM30/36 for singles/doubles up to RM50 for very large rooms. The chief drawback here is the noisy karaoke parlour next door to the upstairs reception.

Similar and also recommended is the *Sarawak Hotel* (☎ 084-333455), 34 Jalan Cross on the corner of Jalan Wong Nai Siong. Newly renovated singles/doubles cost from RM30/36. Opposite is the *New World Hotel* (☎ 084-310311), 1 Jalan Wong Nai Siong, which has rooms from RM30/36, but the Sarawak is slightly better value. *Hotel Capitol 88* (☎ 084-336444), 19 Jalan Wong Nai Siong, has good rooms for RM30/48.

The *Li Hua Hotel* (☎ 084-324000) is at the Longbridge Commercial Centre about 300 metres along the river from the bus station, past the Mehung Hotel. It is fully air-conditioned and has a good coffee shop. Standard singles/doubles cost from RM66/105. It is a good hotel for the price and popular with local businesspeople.

Places to Stay – top end

The two best hotels are near each other on Jalan Kampung Nyabor. Add 10% service charge and 5% tax to the prices, but you can normally get a discount of around 20%. Rooms at the *Premier Hotel* (☎ 084-323222) cost from RM110/130, RM160/180 for deluxe. If you get a discount (very likely) it's a good deal, given that these rates include breakfast and the rooms have minibars, IDD phones and in-house movies.

The *Tanahmas Hotel* (☎ 084-333188) is newer and offers very much the same standards as the Premier but at higher rates. Singles/doubles cost RM165/185 and those facing the river are RM185/205.

Places to Eat

The best cheap food in Sibu is found at the various hawker centres and food stalls. There's a small two storey food centre at the end of Market Rd, at the rear of the Palace Cinema, which has stalls selling Malay curries, roti and laksa as well as Chinese food and ais kacang. There are also food stalls on the 2nd floor of the market.

Rex Food Court is a small air-con food centre with a selection of Chinese and western food, including the *Good Morning Sibu* breakfast stall, which does a reasonable job of western breakfasts.

In the late afternoon, stalls are set up near the market, mainly outside the Miramar Hotel, and these are great for picking up snack foods such as pau (steamed dumplings), barbecued chicken wings and all manner of sweets.

For western fast food, *Sugar Bun* and *McDonald's* are on Jalan Kampung Nyabor, and there's a *KFC* outlet on Jalan Wong Nai Siong.

The riverfront area near the Mehung Hotel has a number of Chinese restaurants. One of the best for an inexpensive chicken and rice plate is *Sarawak Chicken Rice*. Close by is the more upmarket *Haibin Restaurant*.

For a full-on sit-down Chinese meal at a

proper restaurant, try the *New Capitol Restaurant* adjacent to the Premier Hotel. It's expensive, but the food is reportedly the best in Sibu. The *Premier Hotel* itself does good all-you-can-eat buffet dinners for RM16, and there are other cheaper buffets during the day. The *Li Hua Hotel* has good food in its coffee shop/restaurant and is moderately priced.

Getting There & Away

Air If you're travelling by boat from Sibu to Kapit and Belaga and want to fly back, book your flight as far in advance as possible because the Sibu-Kapit-Belaga (and return) sector is only covered twice a week, on Thursday and Sunday, by a 12-seater Twin Otter. The fare is RM48 to Kapit, RM76 to Belaga. There are also Twin Otter flights to Marudi three times a week (RM100).

To Kuching there are flights throughout the day (RM72) and to Bintulu seven daily for RM64. Some of these flights go on to Miri (RM112) and five daily flights go direct. You can also fly to Kota Kinabalu (RM180) via Bintulu or Miri.

EAST MALAYSIA

Bus – Bintulu & Miri The 220 km road from Sibu to Bintulu is sealed all the way. Syarikat Bus Express has air-con buses to Bintulu at 6.15, 9 and 10.30 am and 12.15, 2 and 4.30 pm for RM18. There are also two departures for the 7½ hour trip to Miri, at 6.45 and 9.30 am. The buses are air-con and the fare is RM34. Ideally, bus tickets should be bought half a day or more in advance, though turning up an hour or so before departure is usually fairly safe.

The Lanang Bus Co has five buses a day to Bintulu between 6 am and 2 pm. The fare is RM16.50 and the trip takes around four hours. The buses are air-conditioned but much older than the Syarikat buses, and they pick up and put down passengers on the way. Buy your ticket on the bus, and get there before the scheduled departure if you want a seat.

Bus – Kuching See the Kuching Getting There & Away section for details about road transport between Kuching and Sibu. Sarikei, further down the Rejang River, is the main connection point for buses to Kuching. Direct buses from Kapit take seven hours and cost RM32 – boats do the trip in half the time for around the same price.

Boat – Sarikei & Kuching All express boats to Sarikei and Kuching (change at Sarikei) leave from the Sarikei Wharf in front of the Chinese temple. There are three boats operating to Kuching; the trip takes around four hours and costs RM29 to RM33 depending on the company. The trip involves changing from smaller river boats to larger sea-going vessels at Sarikei.

Although it's best to buy tickets in advance, especially during holiday periods, you should have no difficulty getting one on the boat. Ticket outlets and departure times from Sibu are:

Concorde Marine (☎ 084-331593), 1 Bank Rd; 11.30 am
Ekspres Bahagia (☎ 084-319228), 20 Jalan Tukang Besi; 6.45 am; 11.45 am
Ekspres Pertama (☎ 084-335055), 14 Khoo Peng Loong Rd; 7 am

Boat – Kapit-Belaga Getting to Kapit is the first leg of the journey up the Rejang River. The ekspres launches which do this trip cover the 130 km or so from Sibu to Kapit in a shade over two hours! The first launch from Sibu leaves at 5.45 am, and when there's enough water in the river this boat goes on to Belaga. Other launches leave approximately hourly up until noon or sometimes later. Just go down to the Kapit Wharf and ask which is the next boat. People are very helpful and the boats usually have a 'clock' displaying intended departure time. The fare to Kapit is RM15.

All launches call at Kanowit and Song, and may stop at smaller settlements and logging camps en route.

Getting Around

If you arrive in Sibu by launch (from Kuching or Sarikei) or by cargo/passenger boat (from Kuching, Sarikei, Bintulu or Miri), then you will dock at Sarikei or Kapit wharves, which are both only a few minutes' walk from all the main hotels and restaurants.

If you arrive by air, take either a taxi or bus No 1 to the bus station in the centre of town. This is also where the Bintulu and Miri buses leave from.

KAPIT

This small town on the south-eastern bank of the Rejang River dates from the days of the white rajas and still sports an old wooden fort built by Charles Brooke. To travellers it's just a sleepy riverside town tucked into the rainforest, but to upriver people it's the 'big city' to which they come to buy, sell and exchange goods, as well as for entertainment – there are pool halls, and a few of the cafes have video machines.

The bank of the river here is quite steep, so in the dry season when the water level falls it's quite a drop to the river. For an idea of how high the water can get, check out the flood markers on the front of the old fort.

If you are looking for a lift and introduction to a longhouse, ask at the Petronas or Shell fuel barges.

There are two longhouses about seven km from town along Jalan Selerik, but they're thoroughly urbanised.

Information

If you need to change money (ie travellers' cheques), there are three banks in town – try the Kong Ming Bank in the same block as the Kapit Longhouse Hotel overlooking New Bazaar, or the Malayan Bank next door to the Hotel Meligai. You can get good maps of the area at the Lands & Survey Department office on the top floor of the State Government Complex. The MAS agent is Hua Chiong Co (☎ 084-796988), located one block back from the waterfront.

Permits for Travel Beyond Kapit Go to the Pejabat Am office on the 1st floor of the State Government Complex and collect the

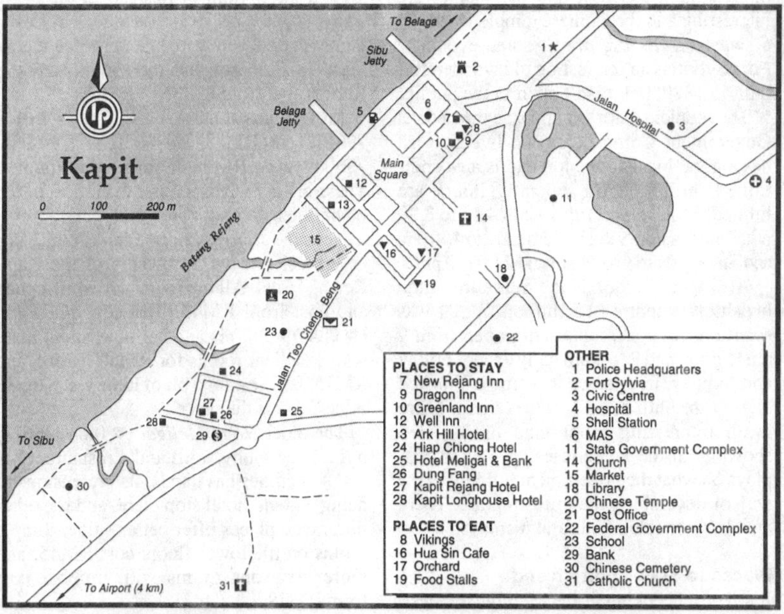

necessary forms. Fill them in and take them next door to the Resident's Office, and the permit will be issued in a couple of minutes. One question in the form asks when your cholera vaccination expires, but this is not checked. The permit is valid for either five or 10 days, depending on which you specify, and is valid for travel up the Rejang as far as Belaga and up the Balleh River for an unspecified distance. If you get up the river and find your permit is going to expire, don't lose any sleep – it seems the only people who want to have anything to do with the permits are the people at the office that issues them. Upon arrival in Belaga, you are supposed to report to police, who can issue another permit to go further upriver.

These government offices are only open normal office hours, so if you arrive on a weekend you'll have to wait until Monday morning for them to open.

EAST MALAYSIA

Things to See

There isn't a great deal to do or see in Kapit, though the waterfront and the market are interesting and the Chinese temple works up a sweat on the big drums some evenings. **Fort Sylvia** is an interesting old wooden fort built in 1880, but it isn't open to the public.

The municipal **library** opposite the Federal Government Complex on the bypass road has a good local collection and is air-conditioned, although the opening hours are limited: Monday to Friday from 4.15 to 8.30 pm; Saturday from 9 to 11.15 am and 2 to 4.30 pm; and Sunday from 9 to 11 am and 2 to 6.30 pm.

Also worth a look is the **museum** in the lavish civic centre (2.5 million ringgit was spent on this). It's supposedly open from 9 am to noon and 2 to 4 pm daily except Friday and Sunday. In practice it seems it's locked all the time until a visitor comes along. There is an interesting relief map of the area showing all the longhouses, as well as displays on what the government is doing in the way of developing the infrastructure. There are also a couple of cultural displays.

Places to Stay – bottom end

It's worth checking at the *Methodist Guesthouse* to see if there are any vacancies. As is the case in Sibu, this place is normally reserved for those on church business, but there may be budget accommodation available. Otherwise, the place to head for is the *Kapit Rejang Hotel* (☎ 084-796709), which has good, cheap singles/doubles with fan on the top floor for RM16/20, or RM22/26 on the lower floors with bath and air-con. The management is helpful and welcomes travellers.

The other two cheap hotels are very seedy, not particularly pleasant places to stay, and you won't be welcomed. If you have no option, the *Kapit Longhouse Hotel* (☎ 084-796415) has singles/doubles with fan and bath for RM22/26, or RM30 with air-con and bath. The *Hiap Chiong Hotel* is a real dive, but you can get a fan room for RM20.

Places to Stay – middle

Kapit has experienced a minor hotel boom and has a glut of good mid-range hotels. All have rooms with air-con, attached bath and TV. At the bottom of this range, the *Dung Fang* (☎ 084-797778) has an unfortunate name (in case you were wondering, it means 'east' in Chinese), but the rooms are new. Rooms cost from RM35 to RM50.

Most rooms at the *Ark Hill Hotel* (☎ 084-796168) cost RM38, and the *Well Inn* (☎ 084-796009) costs RM35/38 for singles/doubles. These are a few years older than most of the other hotels but both are good.

The *New Rejang Inn* (☎ 084-796600) is a new hotel run by the owners of the Kapit Rejang Hotel. All the rooms are immaculate and cost from RM45. The *Greenland Inn* (☎ 084-796388) is another new, small hotel with excellent rooms for RM50, RM65 and RM75. If you want a bit of luxury at bargain prices, this is the place.

The older *Hotel Meligai* (☎ 084-796611) has a large lobby, a lift and a restaurant/bar that sometimes has bands. Its pretensions to being a grand hotel stop there, and the other mid-range places offer better value. Simple rooms on the lower floors cost RM45, and more luxurious rooms with minibar cost from RM78.

Places to Eat

Food stalls set up in the evening at the night market. The *River View (Ming Hock) Restaurant* on the top floor of the market building is good.

Kapit has a number of good Chinese coffee shops serving the usual Chinese dishes. The *Hua Sin Cafe* serves reasonably priced food, as well as more expensive seafood. The popular *Kah Ping Cafe* on the main square has good pork dishes.

Just because you are out in the middle of the jungle doesn't mean you can't have pizza and hamburgers. *Vikings* restaurant has fried chicken and other western fast food, while the *Frosty Boy* under the Greenland Inn has pizzas and ice cream.

The *Orchard* is an expensive, air-con Cantonese restaurant. It is banquet-style, so it is good for groups.

Getting There & Away

Air When the river is really low you will not be able to get a launch or boat to Belaga, so if this is your intended destination the only way of getting there is to fly. MAS flies Sibu-Kapit-Belaga and back on Thursday and Sunday. The fare is RM47 to Belaga and RM48 to Sibu.

Taxi The only local road transport is taxis, and there are very few of these. It isn't surprising, since there's hardly anywhere you can go by road. If you arrive by air you'll have to take a taxi the two km into town.

Boat – Sibu Ekspres launch departures to Sibu are from 8 am until around 3 pm. Just go down to the jetty when you're ready and hop on. The Kapit to Sibu fare is RM15 and the journey takes from 2½ to 3 hours, depending on the number of stops made.

Boat – Belaga During the wet season, ekspres launches leave for Belaga daily from the main jetty. The trip takes up to six hours and costs RM20. During the dry season when the river is low, the ekspres boats can't get through the Pelagus Rapids, about an hour

The Orang Ulu

If you don't fancy the idea of having your face smeared with greasy soot and being dumped unceremoniously in the river, then perhaps you should steer well clear of the Kayan and Kenyah tribes. But if you do you'll miss out on one of the best travel experiences in Borneo.

The two tribes are numbered among the Orang Ulu (a general term literally meaning 'upriver people' which covers a host of different inland tribes). The Kayan and Kenyah tribes are the people you're most likely to meet when travelling on the Upper Rejang or Upper Baram rivers.

Both tribes are originally from Central Kalimantan, and have been gradually expanding downriver into Sarawak for centuries, fighting fierce territorial wars with the Iban that were not finally ended until 1923. They have different languages but very similar cultures, based on settled dry rice farming. Sarawak's most artistic peoples, the Kayan and Kenyah build ornate and imposing longhouses, decorated with exquisite woodcarvings and bizarre 'tree of life' paintings. And like all Sarawakians, they take hospitality very seriously.

If you visit a longhouse around Belaga or the Upper Baram, you won't find a boisterous Iban-style welcome, but appearances can be deceptive. The Kayan and Kenyah are more reserved and refined than the Iban, but if you spend a day or two with them they will start to let their hair down. At sunset, huge glasses of *borak* (sour, very potent rice wine) are handed out and downed to a chorus of '*duiiiii...*', the local drinking song. Cigarettes made from fierce local tobacco are passed around. Sape players weave complex and haunting melodies on their mandolin-like instrument, and long-eared, tattooed ladies sing praise songs to the guests between chews of betelnut.

You may be treated to warrior dances from the men and fan dances from the young women, and even a display of traditional wrestling. And if you're lucky, the festivities will last to sun-up, when the soot-smearing and dunking take place. It's the traditional Orang Ulu sense-of-humour test, given only to true friends. And after such a memorable night you're probably in need of a bath anyway.

Mike Reed

upstream of Kapit. This is mainly because there is no protection for the propeller and, at RM2000 each for new propellers, the boat owners are, not surprisingly, unwilling to risk damage. Small cargo boats still do the run, however. They are uncomfortable, take around eight hours and charge RM50. If you catch one of these boats, make sure you wear clothes that give you protection from the sun, as there may be no shade.

There are also boats heading up the Balleh River on a daily basis as far as Interwau – ask at the fuel barges in Kapit.

If you want to charter a longboat to take you upriver you're looking at around RM150 per day, excluding fuel – so the all-up charge is around RM200. This includes the services of the operator and someone who keeps an eye out for obstructions, especially when the river is low.

PELAGUS RESORT

Around one hour upriver from Kapit is the new *Pelagus Resort* (☎ 082-238033; fax 082-238050). It's easy to be cynical about developments such as these, but for those with the money to spend Pelagus offers an ideal opportunity to visit nearby Iban and other Orang Ulu longhouses, as well as the rainforest in a part of Sarawak that would otherwise be inaccessible. Room rates are from RM140 to RM175 (with air-con) plus taxes, and the resort has a restaurant and swimming pool.

BELAGA

Belaga is just a small village and government administration centre on the upper reaches of the Rejang, where the river divides into the Belaga and Balui rivers. Belaga is a base to explore the interior, and along these rivers there are many interesting Kayan and Kenyah longhouses. If you start talking to a friendly local on the boat, you might be invited to stay at their longhouse. Don't forget to offer food, cigarettes or some small gift as a contribution towards your keep. Otherwise, chances are you will find someone in Belaga (or they will find you) with suggestions of longhouses to visit, or offers to guide you. A few operators have jungle treks at reasonable rates – from RM150 for three days/two nights, and longer treks are available.

Permits are required for travel beyond Belaga. This requires police and District Office clearance. It is usually not a problem to get a permit, though it may be restricted to travel as far as the Bakun Rapids, one hour upstream from Belaga. This may well be because of the dangers of upriver travel during the dry season, or because the Penan live beyond the Bakun Rapids. Some travellers have been issued permits for unrestricted travel with no fuss at all, while others have simply gone ahead without permits – although if you do this it might be an idea to let someone else know where you are heading, in case any problems arise. Permits are not required to use the logging road to Tubau.

Upriver from Belaga

The easiest way to head upriver is to take the ekspres boat that goes up the Balui River as far as Long Pangai, a Lahanan longhouse past the Linau River.

The nearest longhouses to Belaga, such as Uma Aging and Uma Kahei, are mostly Kayan, but Uma Neh is a Kejaman longhouse and Long Semiang is a Lahanan longhouse within half an hour by boat. The Kenyah also live along the Balui, such as at Uma Baudang before the Bakun Rapids, and much further up the river beyond Long Panai at Long Bulan, Long Jawi and Long Busang. Other peoples along the upper reaches of the Balui include the Punan at Long Belangan and the Ukit at Uma Ukit.

Do not turn up unannounced. Get an invitation to a longhouse from someone in town.

Places to Stay

The *Belaga Hotel* (☎ 084-461244) is good value and the most popular place with travellers. A double room with attached bathroom is RM15 with fan or RM25 to RM40 with air-con. Next door, the *Bee Lian Hotel* (☎ 084-461416) is a little newer but otherwise of the same standard. Air-con rooms cost RM25. There's also the *Huan Kilah Lodging House* (☎ 084-461259), a basic hotel with cheap fan rooms for RM15, if the Belaga is out of cheap rooms.

Getting There & Away

The Belaga transport situation is set to change in big ways if the Bakun Dam project goes ahead. Road links will probably be established with other parts of Sarawak. At present there is much uncertainty about what will happen.

From Belaga, ekspres boats go upriver as far as Long Pangai.

In the dry season it's possible to travel overland between Belaga and Bintulu. The journey is not easy; nor is it cheap, unless you get the right connections at the right time. It is possible to do the journey in one day, but allow two in case you get stuck along the way. The first step is to take a boat up the Belaga River to the logging camp, just past Long Mitik. It is possible to get an ekspres boat from Belaga for RM5, when there is enough demand; otherwise, to hire a longboat costs about RM90. From the camp, a regular Land Cruiser does the run to Tubau. The best time to get a Land Cruiser is around 8 am, when there is likely to be more traffic and more people to share the cost of RM150 per vehicle (for six people the cost is only RM25 per person). It takes about three hours to Tubau. From Tubau there are ekspres boats to Bintulu (the last leaves at noon) which cost RM14 and take about 3½ hours. If you are stuck in Tubau, there is accommodation for RM10.

There are variations on this route, depending on who you meet on your journey. It may be possible to get a lift with logging trucks. Land Cruisers also go to a logging camp (known as Centre Camp), from where another Land Cruiser or a boat can take you to Tubau.

The trip is just as viable in the opposite direction.

North-East Sarawak

BINTULU

Bintulu is a modern, air-conditioned boom town which it is best to pass through as quickly as possible – it is a dull place with little going for it. Bintulu is mostly a bus transit town, and with the transport connections there's generally no need to stay overnight. If you are heading for Niah Caves, Bintulu is a good place to stock up with provisions, although the little town of Batu Niah near the national park has an adequate selection.

Bintulu is also the jumping-off point for Simalajau National Park, 20 km north-east of the town. There is accommodation at the park, and in time the long sandy beaches and interesting flora and fauna (especially birdlife) will probably make this a popular park.

Information

The Bintulu Welcome Centre (☎ 086-332277), BDA building, Jalan Somerville, is designed to welcome new business opportunities rather than travellers, but they will try to help you with any queries and give you a brochure.

The MAS office (☎ 086-331554) is on Jalan Masjid and is open Monday to Friday from 8.30 am to 4.30 pm, Saturday from 8.30 am to 3.30 pm and Sunday from 8.30 am to 12.30 pm.

Places to Stay – bottom end

Bintulu is swarming with hotels, but most of them are air-con mid-range places. If you're on a budget, Bintulu is not a very good place to overnight – the cheap hotels tend to be seedy.

The *Capital Hotel* (☎ 086-334667) has a few scruffy rooms with fan for RM15, and a variety of air-con rooms with bath for RM20 to RM45. It's a big anonymous place.

Two better places are near the Plaza Hotel. The *Duong Hing* (☎ 086-336698) is at 20 New Commercial Centre just around the corner from Jalan Abang Galau. It is a small, friendly place, and rooms with bath and fan are quite good for RM10/20, while air-con singles/doubles cost RM25/28. The *Dragon Inn* (☎ 086-334223) mostly has air-con rooms with bath and TV for RM30, but also has a couple of cheaper fan rooms with bath for RM20.

Places to Stay – middle

Most of the hotels in Bintulu are fairly new mid-range hotels with good air-con rooms with TV, phone and attached bathroom. They are all of a similar standard and there is little to choose between them. *Ung Ping Inn* (☎ 086-337373), 127 Jalan Masjid, is one of the better places. All rooms cost RM40. *Fata Inn* (☎ 086-332998), 113 Jalan Masjid, is no better though a little more expensive at RM40/48 for singles/doubles. Also on Jalan Masjid at No 161 is *My House Inn* (☎ 086-336399), which has good rooms for RM40/45. Going up in quality, at No 149 Jalan Masjid, is the *City Inn* (☎ 086-337711), which costs RM43/47. The *Kamena Hotel* (☎ 086-331533), at the back of 78 Jalan Keppel, is on a quiet backstreet and has been completely refurbished. Rooms cost RM55/58.

For slightly upmarket mid-range accommodation, the *Sunlight Hotel* (☎ 086-332577), on the corner of Jalan Abang Galau and Jalan Pedada, is a reasonable choice at RM50/55. Next door is the *Royal Hotel* (☎ 086-332166), a better choice and this is reflected in the room rates: RM69/79. For this money you may as well spend a few more dollars and stay at the Hoover (see below), which is much better.

Places to Stay – top end

The *Plaza Hotel* (☎ 086-335111) is the top hotel in Bintulu and the place where all the expat oil industry workers stay. It has a rooftop swimming pool, restaurants, bars and all the other mod-cons you'd expect for RM157/1179 for a standard room, or

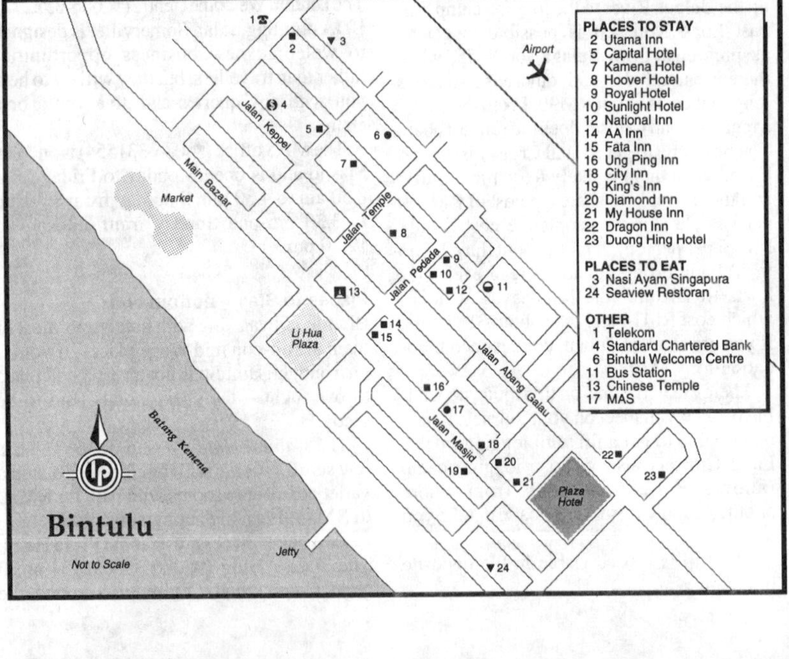

RM178/200 for deluxe rooms. Add 15% for tax and service charge, but you should be able to get a 20% discount on the published rates.

The *Hoover Hotel* (☎ 086-337166) is a smaller hotel without the facilities of the Plaza, but its well-appointed rooms are a cheaper alternative. Rooms cost RM75/86 including tax, and it has a cafe and bar.

Places to Eat

The top floor of the new market is the place to go for hawker food. It has dozens of food stalls, and you can sit and look across the river. The night market at the bus station is good for take-away snacks such as satay, grilled chicken and fish. By the waterfront, the *Seaview Restoran* has standard Chinese food, and they do good toasted sandwiches and coffee at breakfast. *Nasi Ayam Singapura* is a good, air-con stop for lunch. There are literally dozens of Chinese kopi kedais on Jalan Masjid, all offering very similar fare.

The Li Hua Plaza has a *Sugar Bun* for western fast food, or you can try the *Plaza Hotel* for decidedly better and more expensive western food.

Entertainment

There is no shortage of places to drink in Bintulu – what else is there to do? With the exception of the bar in the Plaza Hotel (which has live bands on the weekend), however, entertainment in Bintulu is for the most part restricted to karaoke bars. The disco next door to the City Inn is popular but will probably be empty before midnight. If you need a night on the town, save your energy for Miri or Kuching.

Getting There & Away

Air MAS has seven flights daily to Sibu (RM64), six daily to Kuching (RM117), five daily to Miri (RM69) and one daily to Kota Kinabalu (RM127). The airport is smack in the middle of town.

Bus – Batu Niah & Miri Bintulu's well-organised bus station is close to the centre of town. Syarikat Bas Suria (☎ 086-335489) is the main operator for buses to Batu Niah and Miri. There are 16 daily buses to Miri and half of these stop at Batu Niah en route. Buses run approximately every 40 minutes between 6 am and 6 pm. To Batu Niah it costs RM10 (with or without air-con), and the trip takes about two hours. Buses to Miri take around four hours and cost RM18 air-con, RM16.80 non-air-con.

Bus – Sibu & Kuching Syarikat Bas Suria has buses to Sibu at 6.15 and 9 am, noon, 2 and 4.30 pm for RM18. There are also other bus companies with services to Sibu.

Rejang Transport (☎ 086-338518) has air-con buses to Sarikei at 6 am and 1 pm, and these link up with buses to Kuching. The cost is RM24 to Sarikei, RM52 to Kuching. Borneo Highway Express (☎ 086-339855) has Sarikei-Kuching buses at 6 am and 6 pm for the same price. Biaramas Express also has buses to Sarikei and Miri at 6 and 11.30 am for the same price.

Boat If you're trying to get to Belaga there are ekspres launches that go up the Kemena River as far as Tubau. The journey takes about 3½ hours and costs RM14. Boats leave from the jetty, just a few minutes' walk from the bus station, generally between 9 am and noon.

SIMALAJAU NATIONAL PARK

Facilities have only recently been developed at Simalajau National Park, and it is relatively untouristed. It has some excellent deserted sandy beaches, where green turtles sometimes come ashore to lay their eggs. The forest area is home to 24 species of mammals and 185 species of birds.

There are five chalet units at the park with two rooms in each. Each room has four beds, and the cost per room is RM60. The hostel has four-bed dorms at RM10 per bed. Bookings can be made through the national parks booking office (☎ 085-331117 ext 50) in Bintulu. You will also need to get a permit at the same office.

NIAH NATIONAL PARK & NIAH CAVES

A visit to the Niah Caves is one of the most memorable experiences in East Malaysia. The Great Cave, one of the largest in the world, is in the centre of the Niah National Park, which is dominated by the 394-metre-high limestone massif of Gunung Subis, visible from far away.

Since 1958, when archaeologists discovered evidence that humans have been living in and around the caves for some 40,000 years, they have been under the protection of the Sarawak Museum.

The rock paintings found in the Painted Cave were the only ones known to exist in Borneo at the time and were associated with several small canoe-like boats which were used as coffins, indicating that this part of the caves was used as a burial ground. A reconstruction of this cave, together with some of the remains found there, can be seen in the Sarawak Museum in Kuching.

Pangkalan Lubang

The park HQ and hostel resthouses are on the Niah River at Pangkalan Lubang, about four km from Batu Niah. The park HQ Visitors' Centre has some interesting and informative displays on the geology, archaeology and other aspects of the caves.

The area around the HQ itself is not without interest. While you're relaxing in the cane chairs on the hostel veranda, keep an eye on the river. The river level can change by over a metre depending on the strength of the tides out to sea, 17 km away, and the current varies from static to quite strong. You may also see large, log-laden barges chug their way downstream. These barges are almost as wide as the river. At the river-mouth, the logs are loaded onto ships and exported to Japan, South Korea, Taiwan and the Philippines.

Wildlife occasionally seen in the river includes monitor lizards (up to two metres long), crocodiles and snakes, but they're all

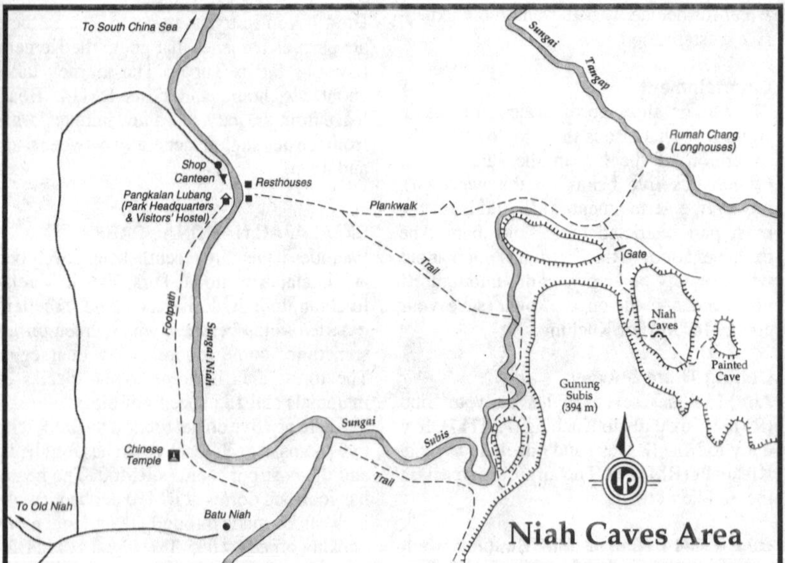

Niah Caves Area

extremely shy and, for the benefit of those who are thinking of swimming in the river, rarely seen around the park HQ.

The Caves

To get to the caves from the hostel and HQ you first have to take the longboat across the Niah River. The standard charge is 50 sen per person.

Once across the river there's a three-km-long plankwalk to the caves. It is made of Belian wood, which is very durable and so heavy that it cannot be transported by water, since it doesn't float. This plankwalk passes through very pretty primary rainforest all the way to the caves. If you do the trip in the rainy season, take care – the plankwalk gets very slippery.

Unfortunately, most visitors are so intent on reaching the caves that they miss out on the life in the forest around them. If you break your trek and spend some time just watching and listening, you may be lucky enough to see such animals as the long-tailed macaque monkeys, hornbills, squirrels and flying lizards, as well as the many hundreds of species of butterflies which inhabit this forest. Even if you don't, you'll certainly hear much more than you see.

Shortly before you reach the cave entrance the plankwalk forks; the right fork goes to the caves, while the left fork goes to the village of Rumah Chang, where there are a couple of longhouses. There's also a store selling cold beer and soft drinks!

Inside the huge Great Cave the plankwalk continues, so navigation is easy. The white handrails are usually visible from a short distance, but where the cave narrows and leads to the Painted Cave it's pitch black – you'll need a torch. Because of the plankwalks there's no need to hire a guide – it's all very straightforward.

In addition to the plankwalk there are a number of vague trails through the jungle which will take you to the summit of Gunung Subis. They're supposed to be marked with blue and white paint strips on the trunks of trees, but these are not at all obvious. Other walks in the area are also worth investigating.

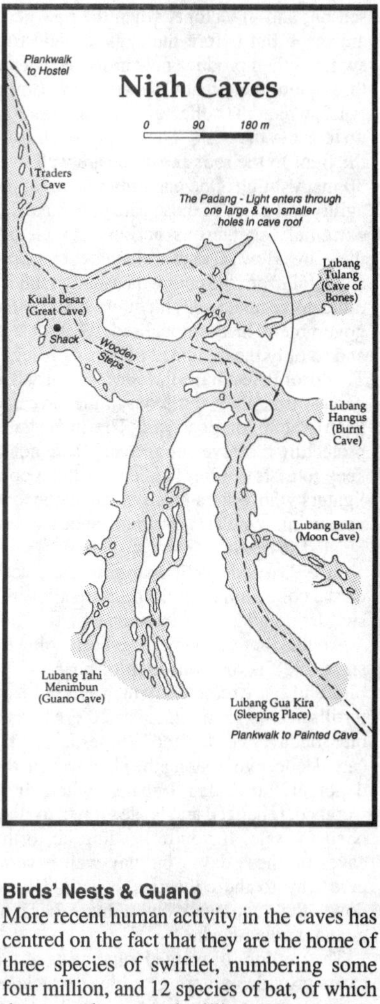

Birds' Nests & Guano

More recent human activity in the caves has centred on the fact that they are the home of three species of swiftlet, numbering some four million, and 12 species of bat, of which there are also several million.

The swiftlets construct their nests in crevices in the roof of the Great Cave, and it's these nests which are used in the preparation of that famous Chinese dish, bird's-nest soup.

The collection of these nests, which are sold for RM700 or more a kg, is limited to two seasons: May-June, after the breeding season; and in October when the new nests are made but before the eggs are laid (the swiftlets then produce new nests). Scattered throughout the Great Cave are many flimsy poles, which the collectors have to scramble up to get to the nests. The poles stretch from the floor to the roof and some are well over 30 metres high. One can only marvel at the agility and nerve of those who undertake this extremely dangerous activity. Inevitably there are a few serious accidents each year – and a fall from the ceiling is usually fatal. In order to regulate this lucrative market, the government has nationalised the industry, and so only the regulated collecting is legal. The local Penan have the concession, and at harvest time they camp out in the cave and keep watch for poachers. The huge gates protecting the cave entrance are there not to keep tourists out but to keep out the moonlighters who want a piece of the action, and who want to gather nests outside of the designated season.

In 1993 a two year moratorium was placed on the collection of birds' nests, to allow the swiftlet population to increase.

Another activity which has been going on since 1928 is the collection of guano – the bird and bat excrement which is used as a fertiliser. The guano is collected each week on Monday, Tuesday and Wednesday, and is carted laboriously along the plankwalk to the depot at Pangkalan Lubang, where it is weighed, rebagged and boated down to Batu Niah for sale. If you're heading up to the caves on these days you may well have to give way to the collectors sweating it out down the plankwalk, with huge bags of guano on their backs.

The millions of winged inhabitants of the caves provide an unforgettable spectacle as evening comes along. Swiftlets are day fliers and bats are nocturnal animals, so if you arrange to be at the mouth of the cave around 6 pm you can watch the shift change as the swiftlets return home and the bats go out for the night. You might even be lucky enough to see one of the large predatory birds, such as the bat hawks, swoop into the cave for a meal.

If you go up to the caves at this time, be sure to bring a strong torch for the return trip. It's an exciting night-time jungle experience, but made easy by the plankwalk. Though you are certain to hear and see plenty on the way, you'll probably remember most the many luminous mushrooms that grow beside the plankwalk.

Permits & Information

Officially a permit is needed to visit Niah, and this is issued as a matter of course when you check in at the park HQ at Pangkalan Lubang.

You can book accommodation for Niah at the national parks offices in Miri or Kuching, but make sure you get a receipt to show you've paid, as the information doesn't necessarily get passed on to the park HQ. Bookings are advisable for the hostel, and essential for the resthouses. For the hostel, it's usually not a problem to just turn up at the caves without a booking, especially during the week. If your luck is out and there's no accommodation, the worst you'd have to do is sleep on the office floor or head back the four km to Batu Niah, where there are a few hotels.

Signs at the park state that it is necessary for visitors to the caves to have a guide, but this is optional and very few people go with a guide.

Places to Stay

Pangkalan Lubang The *Visitors' Hostel* at the park HQ is a great place to stay. Standards have improved in the last few years, although there has also been a corresponding price hike. Comfortable four-bed dorms cost RM10 per bed. Also available are four-bed rooms in chalets for RM60. Air-con two-bed VIP chalets are another option at RM200.

On checking in you are issued with a sheet and a blanket, and eating utensils are provided if you want to cook. The park has a canteen that serves good meals, or you can buy provisions at a store just outside the park next to the canteen. It sells only basic provisions – mostly canned goods – so if you are going to cook your own food it is wise to bring some with you. In the dry season the rainwater tanks often run out, so the water is drawn from the river and must be boiled before drinking.

Batu Niah If for some reason you don't want to stay at the Visitors' Hostel or your time of arrival prevents you from getting there that night, there are four hotels in Batu Niah. The *Niah Caves Hotel* (☎ 085-737726) is clean and costs RM22/26 for a single/double. All rooms are air-con and have common bath, and there's a restaurant downstairs.

The *Hock Seng Hotel* (☎ 085-737740) mostly has air-con rooms for RM30 with bath, but it also has some cheaper fan rooms.

The *Park View Hotel* (☎ 085-737021) is a good mid-range choice, with rooms at RM100/110 plus taxes for singles/doubles – discounts of 30-50% are available upon request. The *Niah Caves Inn* (☎ 085-737333) is the newest hotel in town and probably the best. Rooms cost from RM58 to RM63.

Getting There & Away

Batu Niah to Pangkalan Lubang Whether you come from Bintulu or Miri you will end up at Batu Niah, the nearest town to the park. Transport to the park HQ is by taxi or by boat. Boats cost RM2 per person if there are five or more of you, or RM10 per boat. Taxis also cost RM10. Boats do most of their business in the morning, and after midday it is often much less time-consuming to get a taxi, a few of which are always waiting next to the bus stand. The boat is more fun, however – an exhilarating trip of just a few minutes through the jungle.

Lastly, you can walk along the track by the river, but this takes about an hour.

On arrival at the park, check in at the park HQ.

Bus – Bintulu There are eight direct buses daily from Bintulu to Batu Niah, from approximately 6 am until 6 pm. The fare is RM10 and the journey takes about two hours. The direct Bintulu-Miri buses bypass Batu Niah – if you take one of these you will have to walk or hitch eight km to Batu Niah. From Batu Niah to Bintulu, buses leave at 6, 7 and 10 am, noon and 1.30 and 3 pm (check with locals to be sure the times haven't changed). Buses leave from the bus stand in the centre of town, and there is no ticket agency – pay as you board the bus.

Bus – Miri There are six daily buses from Miri direct to Batu Niah. They depart approximately on the hour between 6.45 am and 4 pm, cost RM9 and the trip takes about two hours. From Batu Niah to Miri there are departures at 6.45, 7.45, 8 and 11 am and 1 and 3.30 pm. Catch these same buses for Lambir Hills National Park, 32 km from Miri. The fare to Lambir Hills is RM6.

LAMBIR HILLS NATIONAL PARK

Lambir Hills is a chain of sandstone hills which reaches a peak of 465 metres at Bukit Lambir. The national park encompassing the hills covers an area of 6952 hectares and at its closest is only 20 km from Miri. It is a popular weekend spot, and Miri residents come by the carload to take the 15 minute walk to the pretty waterfalls near the park HQ. The waterfall cascades into a good swimming hole, and there are picnic areas along the river.

Lambir Hills is worth visiting for more than weekend picnics, however. It offers fine rainforest walks through rich dipterocarp forest containing many species of flora, including a large variety of palms. Among the wildlife found here are Bornean gibbons, tarsiers, pangolins and barking deer, though your chances of seeing them are slim. The park is also home to many species of birds.

Lambir Hills is a good day trip from Miri, and since accommodation has been built, visitors can now spend a few days enjoying the forest and exploring some of the longer walks without having to hurry. While it doesn't have the spectacular scenery of Niah and Mulu, or the diversity of Bako, Lambir Hills is an excellent park for short jungle walks.

The park headquarters are 32 km from Miri. Here you'll find the park office (☎ 085-

36637) and information centre, a canteen and accommodation.

Walks

The most popular walk is that to the waterfalls. It is an easy 15 minute stroll from the park HQ, and the trail passes two waterfalls before reaching the main Latak waterfall. At Latak there are shelters, changing sheds and a large clear pool, ideal for swimming. This walk is much quieter on weekdays.

From Latak Falls the main trail heads off to Bukit Pantu and Bukit Lambir. Just above the falls at the start of the trail is the 40 metre tree tower. From the top you get views of the forest canopy and it is a good spot for bird-watching.

The main trail goes all the way to Bukit Lambir, from where there are fine views. Off the main trail there are many worthwhile diversions. Nibong, Pantu, Pancur, Dinding and Tengkorong waterfalls can be visited, and Bukit Pantu is the nearest peak to the park HQ. The trail is steep and slippery in places, but the walks are not overly strenuous. Bukit Pantu is a straightforward climb, though the stretch to Bukit Lambir can be tiring, especially in the humid, tropical conditions.

Below are the walking times as posted at the park HQ. They are conservative, and you can halve them if you are very fit and in a hurry. It is possible to arrive at the park in the morning, walk to Bukit Lambir and back, and then be on your way to Miri or Niah National Park, but this doesn't leave much time for appreciating the jungle or looking out for wildlife along the way. Register your name at the booth at the start of the trail before you head off.

Trail	*One way from Park HQ*
Latak	30 min
Nibong	1 hour 50 min
Bukit Pantu	1 hour 35 min
Pantu waterfall	1 hour 10 min
Bukit Lambir	3½ hours
Tengkorong	2 hours
Pancur	2½ hours

Places to Stay & Eat

The new accommodation facilities are very comfortable. The only drawback is that the accommodation at the park HQ is only a few hundred metres from the main highway, and you don't get the feeling of being in the middle of the jungle. The park insists on advance bookings, though you are unlikely

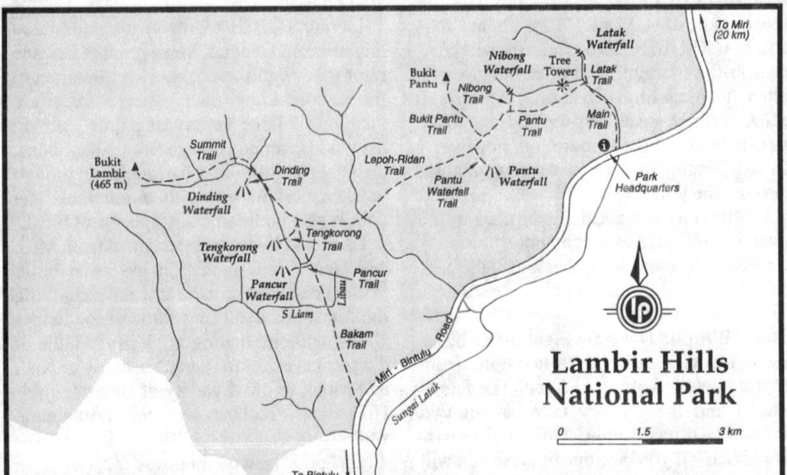

to be turned away if you don't have one. Bookings can be made at the national parks office in Miri, or at the office at Niah National Park.

The hostel costs RM10 per person in a four-bed room. Standard resthouses cost RM40 per room, while deluxe two-bedroom chalets cost RM60 per room or RM120 per chalet. Camping facilities are also available for RM4 per person. The park has a canteen serving fried rice or variations thereof, and the hostel and resthouses have their own cooking facilities. The canteen sells basic provisions, but it is best to bring some fresh food if you will be cooking.

Getting There & Away

Lambir Hills is on the main highway and easily reached by bus from Miri. Take the Batu Niah bus for RM2.40, or any non-express bus going to Bintulu. From Niah National Park, the buses from Batu Niah to Miri pass Lambir Hills and cost RM6.

From the park you have to stand out the front and hail the buses. The national park staff can tell you when buses are due. Heading south, the last buses to Batu Niah and Bintulu pass at around 3.15 pm. Heading north to Miri, the last buses go at around 4.30 pm. The express buses might stop for you, but don't count on it.

MIRI

Miri is a rapidly expanding commercial centre and R&R retreat for oil workers. It is by no means an unpleasant place but there is little to hold the average traveller. Nevertheless, for those who have been slogging through the rainforest and are yearning for the bright lights, Miri has plenty of good restaurants and probably the most lively nightlife scene in all of Borneo. It doesn't deserve the bad rap it gets from most quarters.

Most travellers just overnight in Miri en route to Brunei, to the Niah Caves, to Gunung Mulu or to Bario.

Orientation & Information

Everything in Miri is within easy walking distance of everywhere else, so there's no need to take taxis or local buses to get anywhere, except to the airport. Wisma Pelita Tunku is Miri's main shopping mall and office complex, and the Oil Town is another new shopping complex. The MAS office (☎ 085-411444) is on Jalan Yu Seng Selatan, about 10 minutes' walk from the centre. It is open Monday to Friday from 8.30 am to 4.30 pm, Saturday from 8.30 am to 4 pm and Sunday from 8.30 am to 12.30 pm. The post office is about 15 minutes' walk from the town centre along Jalan Sylvia, which continues on from Jalan Brooke.

National Parks Permits & Bookings The National Parks office (☎ 085-436637) is in the government office complex on Jalan Raja. Opening hours are 8 am to 12.45 pm and 2 to 4.15 pm Monday to Friday, and 8 am to 12.45 pm on Saturday. They don't really want to know you here, but you can book accommodation for Niah and Lambir Hills national parks. For a permit and accommodation for Gunung Mulu, the official line is that individual travel is not possible and all visitors must go through a travel agent. If pressed, they may issue a permit and book accommodation for you, if you first get a permit from the Resident's Office on Jalan Raja.

That's where it gets tricky. A permit for visits to Gunung Mulu, or to Bario and the interior, first involves picking up the form from the Resident's Office and then taking it, with a photocopy of your passport and your immigration departure card, to the police station for their approval. They will grill you here. Remember, logging is good for the economy and the environment, and your occupation must not be remotely connected to journalism. Once you obtain police clearance (it takes up to a day), you have to go back to the Resident's Office for the permit. Once you have this permit, you have to go to the national parks office to obtain *their* permit. Is it any wonder, with all this rigmarole and deliberate bureaucratic obstruction, that many travellers just head off and don't worry about permits at all? If you have problems with the Resident's

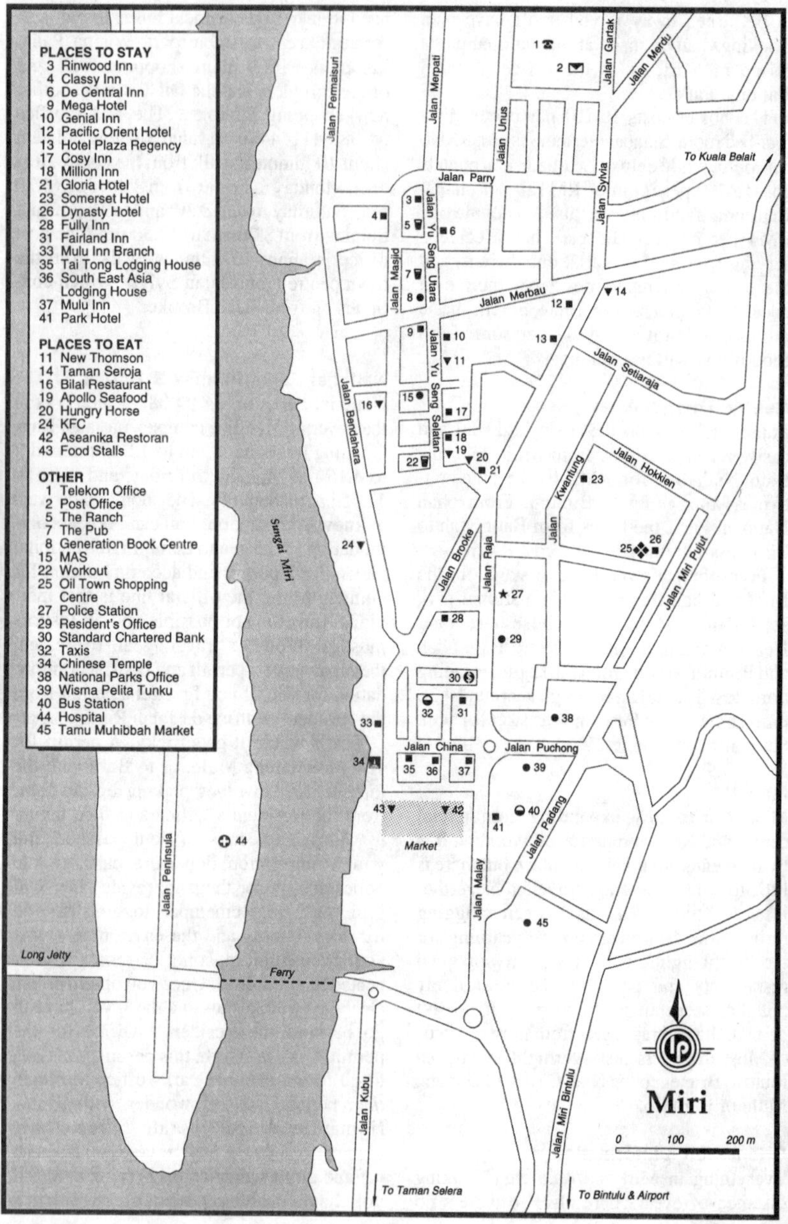
PLACES TO STAY
3 Rinwood Inn
4 Classy Inn
6 De Central Inn
9 Mega Hotel
10 Genial Inn
12 Pacific Orient Hotel
13 Hotel Plaza Regency
17 Cosy Inn
18 Million Inn
21 Gloria Hotel
23 Somerset Hotel
26 Dynasty Hotel
28 Fully Inn
31 Fairland Inn
33 Mulu Inn Branch
35 Tai Tong Lodging House
36 South East Asia Lodging House
37 Mulu Inn
41 Park Hotel
PLACES TO EAT
11 New Thomson
14 Taman Seroja
16 Bilal Restaurant
19 Apollo Seafood
20 Hungry Horse
24 KFC
42 Aseanika Restoran
43 Food Stalls
OTHER
1 Telekom Office
2 Post Office
5 The Ranch
7 The Pub
8 Generation Book Centre
15 MAS
22 Workout
25 Oil Town Shopping Centre
27 Police Station
29 Resident's Office
30 Standard Chartered Bank
32 Taxis
34 Chinese Temple
38 National Parks Office
39 Wisma Pelita Tunku
40 Bus Station
44 Hospital
45 Tamu Muhibbah Market
Jalan Permaisuri
Jalan Merpati
Jalan Unus
Jalan Gartak
Jalan Merdu
To Kuala Belait
Jalan Sylvia
Jalan Parry
Jalan Yu Seng Utara
Jalan Masjid
Jalan Merbau
Jalan Setiaraja
Jalan Yu Seng Selatan
Jalan Bendahara
Jalan Kwantung
Jalan Hokkien
Sungai Miri
Jalan Brooke
Jalan Raja
Jalan Miri Pujut
Jalan China
Jalan Puchong
Market
Jalan Padang
Jalan Malay
Jalan Peninsula
Long Jetty
Ferry
Jalan Kubu
Jalan Miri Bintulu
Miri
0 100 200 m
To Taman Selera
To Bintulu & Airport

EAST MALAYSIA

Office you can try the District Officer in Marudi.

Money The Standard Chartered Bank on Jalan Raja is best equipped for changing travellers' cheques, but they charge a hefty RM14 per transaction. There are money-changers on and around Jalan China which are open longer hours, but they only change cash.

Travel Agencies If you want to organise a trip to Gunung Mulu or elsewhere in the interior, there are plenty of travel agents in Miri. Borneo Adventure (☎ 085-414935), Pacific Orient Hotel, 49 Jalan Brooke, is a long-established and reliable operator. Tropical Adventure (☎ 085-419337), 228 Jalan Maju near the MAS office, is one of the largest agencies, with an interesting range of tours. There are also travel agencies in Wisma Pelita Tunku, such as Transworld Travel Services (☎ 085-422277) on the 2nd floor.

Bookshops On the 1st floor of Wisma Pelita Tunku is the Pelita Book Centre, which has quite a good local collection as well as English novels and other publications. In the Oil Town, the Bookshop has a good selection, or try the Generation Book Centre on Jalan Yu Seng Utara.

Things to See

Miri has a passable **beach** at Taman Selera, three km south of town. Closer beaches are on the spit of land next to the long jetty, where the oil-rig boats pull in – take the free ferry across the river – but the beaches here are very littered.

Miri's **markets** are lively and the old part of town is home to various market blocks. The Tamu Muhibbah is a new market complex where local Dayaks come down to Miri to sell vegetables.

Places to Stay – bottom end

Miri has little in the way of budget accommodation. The cheaper hotels are in the bus station/market area; they tend to be noisy and seedy. Mid-range hotels represent much better value for money.

The only remotely cheap option is the dorms in a couple of the Chinese hotels, although these have little privacy and no security. The *Tai Tong Lodging House* (☎ 085-411072), at 26 Jalan China, has dorm beds in the lobby for RM8, although the noise and cigarette smoke can make for a restless stay. Other basic but clean rooms in this Chinese cheapie go for RM27/35 with fan and common bath, or RM42 for a double with bath and air-con. The dorm is very insecure and the hotel advises that you check your bags in for safekeeping – this costs RM5 per bag.

The *South East Asia Lodging House* (☎ 085-415488), on the taxi stand square behind the Cathay Cinema, has rooms at RM28 with fan, RM38 with air-con (all with common bath).

For a private room, the *Fairland Inn* (☎ 085-4138981), also on the square behind the Cathay Cinema, is much better. This friendly hotel has small, clean rooms with windows, air-con, attached bath and TV for RM30/35.

Places to Stay – middle

The *Mulu Inn* has air-con rooms with attached bathroom for RM25/35. It is right by the bus station, and if you are only overnighting for bus connections it is convenient.

The main area for mid-range hotels is the new part of town around Jalan Yu Seng Utara and Jalan Yu Seng Selatan, which has most of the nightlife and some good restaurants. It is a bit of a hike from the bus station, but a good area to stay in. The *Genial Inn* (☎ 085-410966) is an excellent place to be based. The manager is friendly, and clean air-con rooms are RM40/45 for singles/doubles.

Miri has plenty of other good places with rooms starting at RM50 to RM60. *De Central Inn* (☎ 085-412518), 14 Jalan Yu Seng Utara, is one of the better options. It has good rooms with fridge for RM50/60, and is popular with expat oil workers. It has a lively bar/coffee shop at the back (avoid the rooms next to it). On Jalan Masjid, the *Classy Inn* (☎ 085-425793) has good rooms starting at

RM59/66. The *Million Inn* (☎ 085-415085), 6 Jalan Yu Seng Selatan, is similar and costs RM68/75.

Places to Stay – top end

Most of the big hotels in Miri are getting old and are not that much more expensive, or better, than the better mid-range places. You will usually be offered the discount rates as a matter of course. If not, ask, and tell them you're from Shell. The prices quoted here are the discount rates, and include service charge and tax.

At 27 Jalan Brooke is the *Gloria Hotel* (☎ 085-416699), which has windowless economy rooms for RM72 or better rooms for RM96 to RM130. Further along Jalan Brooke at No 47 is the *Hotel Plaza Regency* (☎ 085-413113) with some economy rooms at RM50, but with most rooms ranging from RM80 to RM100. Next to it is the *Pacific Orient Hotel* (☎ 085-313333) with rooms from RM110/145.

The *Park Hotel* (☎ 085-414555), on Jalan Malay, is one of the better places in Miri and has a wide range of rooms from RM60 for a budget single to RM242 for a suite. The *Rinwood Inn* (☎ 085-415888), at Lot 579 Jalan Yu Seng Utara, is a smaller place with room rates ranging from RM120.

The *Mega Hotel* (☎ 085-432432; fax 085-427373) is a new addition to the Miri skyline and located right in the newer part of town. It has 280 rooms and rates for standard doubles start at RM220.

After the Holiday Inn, the top hotel in town is the *Dynasty Hotel* (☎ 085-421111; fax 085-422222), on Jalan Pujut Lutong. It has all the services you would expect, plus Thai and Chinese restaurants, a health centre and karaoke entertainment. Standard rooms cost from RM190 to RM240.

The *Holiday Inn Miri* (☎ 085-418888; fax 085-419999) is around four km out of town on the beach. It has won Holiday Inn Group prizes, has an international-standard fitness centre and a jacuzzi with swim-up bar, not to mention Clippers, an English-style pub with live music that attracts many Miri locals on the weekends. Rates start at RM230/260 or RM250/280 with a sea view.

Places to Eat

Other than hotel restaurants there are plenty of good food places in Miri, especially in the new blocks between Jalan Brooke and the waterfront.

For hawker food there's a small food centre near the Chinese temple where you can choose between Malay food and the usual Chinese dishes. There's also a small fruit and vegetable market here. On the other side of this market is the *Aseanika Restoran*, which does superb rotis and also serves Indonesian food. The Tamu Muhibbah market also has food stalls open during the day.

Out on the beach, the *Taman Selera* food centre has the best setting. On Jalan Brooke, the *Taman Seroja* is a very pleasant open-air food-stall centre where you can get good satay, more expensive seafood and other dishes. In the Oil Town shopping centre, the *Food Stall* is a small air-con food centre.

For good curries and excellent rotis, *Bilal Restaurant* is one of the better Indian restaurants you'll find in Sarawak. It is on Jalan Persiaran Kabor, a pedestrian mall, and in the evenings the restaurant sets up tables on the pavement.

On Jalan Yu Seng Selatan there are quite a few more upmarket and fast-food places. One of the best restaurants in Miri is the open-air *Apollo Seafood*, which serves superb Chinese food, steamboat and of course seafood. Prices are surprisingly reasonable but you need to get here early in the evening to get a table – it's a very popular place, both with locals and expatriates. Another good seafood place on Jalan Yu Seng Selatan is *Sin Mui Pin*, near the Cosy Inn; it's a big coffee shop that serves delicious fish grilled in banana leaves. A few doors away is the *New Thomson*, a good place for greasy steaks, grills and fish & chips at moderate prices. On the same street is the *Danish Hot Bread Bakery* with a good selection of cakes and pastries.

In Wisma Pelita Tunku there is a branch of the local *Sugar Bun* fast-food chain, where you'll find a selection of pastries, cakes and buns, plus the usual fast-food hamburger and fried-chicken section. In the same building is the Pelita Supermarket, where you can stock up with supplies before heading for Niah Caves. Miri also has a *Hungry Horse* and a *KFC*.

Entertainment

Miri's large expat population and its proximity to deadly dull Brunei has endowed it with the liveliest nightlife scene in Sarawak. There are pubs with bands and discos packed with people even in the middle of the week. The only problem is that things really don't get going until around 11 pm. There are no cover charges, but like elsewhere in Sabah and Sarawak beers usually cost around RM9.

A good place to start the evening is the *Pub*, on Jalan Yu Seng Utara, which is basically just a friendly watering hole until 11.30 pm, when the deejay turns up. The *Ranch* is just down the road and has live music from around 10.30 pm. It gets packed by around 1 am. *Clippers*, out at the Holiday Inn, is a popular spot, but inconvenient to get to. *Follow Me* and *Workout* are other lively discos. There are dozens more.

Things to Buy

Miri has a few arts and crafts stores, but the range is nowhere near as good as in Kuching. The Wisma Pelita Tunku is the handiest place to look: try Longhouse Handicraft Centre on the 3rd floor, and Miri Antiques & Arts Centre on the 4th floor. Syarikat Unique Arts & Handicraft Centre is at the 2½ Mile, Airport Rd, but the selection is no better than in town.

Getting There & Away

Air MAS has Twin Otter services to Marudi (twice daily, RM29), Bario (daily, RM82), Long Lellang (twice weekly, RM66), Long Seridan (weekly, RM57), Limbang (seven daily, RM45), Lawas (four daily, RM59), Labuan (twice daily, RM57) and Mulu (three daily, RM69).

Bigger aircraft fly to Bintulu (four daily, RM69), Kota Kinabalu (six daily, RM95), Kuching (15 daily, RM164) and Sibu (eight daily, RM112).

Bus All buses leave from the bus station next to Wisma Pelita Tunku.

Bintulu, Batu Niah & Lambir Hills Syarikat Bas Suria (☎ 085-34317) operates buses to Bintulu at 6.30, 7 (air-con), 7.30, 8, 9 (air-con) and 10.30 am (air-con), noon (air-con), 12.30, 1.30 (air-con) and 2 pm. The trip takes about 4½ hours and the fare is RM16.80 (non-air-con) or RM18 (air-con).

Syarikat Bas Suria also has buses from Miri direct to Batu Niah. They depart approximately hourly between 6.45 am and 4 pm. The trip costs RM9 and takes about two hours. The Batu Niah buses, and other buses heading south past Km 32, all pass Lambir Hills on the highway. The cost is RM2.40 from Miri.

Sibu There are three buses daily, two departing at 6.45 am and one at 9.30 am, going all the way to Sibu. The trip takes eight hours and costs RM29 or RM35 (air-con).

Brunei To get to Brunei, you can take a bus to Kuala Belait, then another bus to Seria, then another bus to Bandar Seri Begawan, Brunei's capital. The alternative to all this bus-hopping is to take one of the private minibus services which go all the way to Bandar Seri Begawan for RM30. Miri-Sibu Express (☎ 085-433898), at the back of the Park Hotel at the bus station, has minibuses leaving Miri at 11 am and 2 pm.

The Miri Belait Transport Company (☎ 085-419129) has its office at the bus station and operates five buses daily to Kuala Belait – the first town in Brunei – at 7, 9 and 10.30 am, 1 and 3.30 pm. The fare is RM12.20 and the trip takes about 2½ hours. The road is sealed from Miri to Kuala Baram, where a river crossing is made. Vehicles often have to queue for some time before reaching the ferry, so most passengers get out and wait for their bus/car by the edge of the water. You can leave your bags on the bus.

Just across the river you go through the Malaysian immigration checkpoint and reboard the same bus for the two minute ride to the Brunei immigration checkpoint. You must take all your belongings off the bus and go through passport control and customs.

Once through customs, you board a Brunei bus which takes you to the Belait River for another ferry crossing. The queues here are often horrendous, but this is not a problem if you are travelling by bus, as the driver and passengers leave the bus on one side, cross on the ferry (free), then board another bus parked on the other side. Your ticket from Miri takes you all the way to Kuala Belait.

At Kuala Belait you are dropped at the Belait United Traction Company bus stand, from where you can take another bus to Seria. This is preferable to staying in Kuala Belait overnight, as the cheapest hotel in Kuala Belait charges around B$100 for a single room!

Buses depart Kuala Belait for Seria frequently throughout the day and cost B$1. The last bus goes at 6.30 pm and shared taxis cost B$4. The journey takes about 30 minutes.

If you need to change money – no one is interested in the Malaysian ringgit – the Hongkong Bank is opposite the bus stand in Kuala Belait. It is also possible to change ringgits into Brunei currency (and vice versa) on the ferry across the Belait River with the ferry hands. It's a good idea to know the rates of exchange beforehand if you do this.

From Seria, you must take another bus to Bandar Seri Begawan. Several bus companies do the run and there are several buses daily until 2.30 pm. The fare is B$4 and the journey takes about two hours. It's a good sealed road all the way. From Kuala Belait or Seria to Bandar Seri Begawan it's also easy to hitch.

Early in the morning, you can also get taxis from the bus station in Miri to Kuala Belait for RM25 per person. Share taxis are available direct to Bandar Seri Begawan for RM40, but there is no fixed timetable. Ask at your hotel – most can organise for the taxis to pick you up.

Marudi Miri Belait Transport Company has buses to Kuala Baram every half-hour or so between 6 and 11 am, then roughly every hour until 9 pm. The fare is RM2.20 and the journey takes 45 minutes. From Kuala Baram, express boats to Marudi cost RM15 and leave at 7.15, 7.40, 8.15, 9 and 11 am, noon, 1, 2 and 3 pm.

Taxi Long-distance taxis operate from the bus station, but, like elsewhere in Sarawak, you will normally have a long wait to get other passengers to share a ride. The price to charter a taxi to Lambir Hills is RM20 or to Batu Niah RM60.

Getting Around

Bus No 7 runs between Miri and the airport from 6.15 am and 8 pm. It costs RM1. Taxis to and from the airport cost RM12.

Miri itself is easy to get around. It is a small place and everything around town can be reached on foot. For Taman Selera, take bus No 1, 5 or 11; the cost is 40 sen.

MARUDI

Marudi is devoid of attractions, but you will probably find yourself coming through here on your way to or from the interior, and unless you fly from Miri to Bario, you need to get a permit from the District Office here to head further upstream or to Mulu.

There are good views of the river from the hilltop Fort Hose, built in 1901. There are two banks for changing foreign currency.

There is a road network around Marudi and you can visit longhouses at Long Selaban and Long Moh – you can either hitch or take a taxi.

Places to Stay & Eat

The popular *Grand Hotel* (☎ 085-755711), Marudi Bazaar, is a good place four or five blocks from where the ekspres launches dock. The cheapest single room is RM16 with fan, but most rooms are air-con and cost RM34 to RM55. The *Alisan* (☎ 085-755911) also has a few cheap fan rooms for RM17/35, but they are small and windowless. Rooms with air-con and TV cost RM36/42.

The *Hotel Zola* (☎ 085-755311) is a notch better and has air-con rooms from RM36 to

RM58. The *Victoria Hotel* (☎ 085-756067), near the Alisan on Maidan Queen, is new and has very good doubles for RM55.

Ah Jong's is a good place for breakfast as it has fresh bread and doughnuts. For Chinese food the *Rose Garden* has been recommended.

Getting There & Away

Air MAS operates daily Twin Otter flights to Miri (RM29) and Bario (RM55), three flights weekly to Sibu (RM100), twice-weekly flights to Long Lellang (RM46), weekly flights to Long Seridan (RM42) and flights on Monday and Thursday to Mulu (RM40). The airstrip is within walking distance of town.

Boat The ekspres boats from Kuala Baram to Marudi operate every hour or so. The trip costs RM15, and there's no extra charge for the kungfu or American wrestling videos.

See under Gunung Mulu National Park for full details of getting to the park. Heading upriver, ekspres boats to Kuala Apoh or Long Terawan (depending on the water level) leave when they have enough passengers for RM20. The trip takes about three to 3½ hours.

Heading up the Baram River, express boats go to Long Lama and Long Miri.

BARAM RIVER

The mighty Baram River is the main artery of north-east Sarawak. From Marudi it runs deep into the interior through Kayan and Kenyah territory, and even continues, via its tributary the Dapur, right up into the Kelabit Highlands around Bario. Its upper reaches are also home to the Penan, the semi-nomadic hunter-gatherers who have become symbolic of a disappearing way of life for the Dayak peoples of Sarawak. The Baram region is also one of the remaining major areas of primary forest in Borneo, and one of the most heavily logged. The north-east is the centre of disputes between the government, logging companies and the local tribes.

The logging roads in the Baram region have been the subject of many blockades and arrests of activists, including Australian activists recently. For this reason, the government is wary of any individual travellers venturing along the Baram. Permits must be obtained in Miri or Marudi, but Miri travel agents can arrange tours along the Baram.

Getting There & Away

Doing it alone is not easy, or cheap, assuming you can get a permit. From Marudi, express boats go as far as Long Lama, and from there it is possible to go by regular boat to Long Miri. From Long Miri travel is by smaller longboat, which must be chartered (at least RM150 per day plus fuel). It is a full day's travel by boat to Long Akah, and then a day or more to Long Matoh.

The other alternative is by road, which involves expensive Land Cruiser hire. From the main highway south of Miri it is possible to go by a good logging road to Long Miri and all the way to Long Akah. This road is being pushed further into the jungle towards Long Lellang and beyond.

GUNUNG MULU NATIONAL PARK

Gunung Mulu National Park is one of the most popular travel destinations in Sarawak, and the most spectacular of Sarawak's national parks. Unfortunately, it's also one of the most expensive places to visit, and recent moves to discourage individual travellers means that it is largely the preserve of tour groups, which come to Gunung Mulu in big numbers. It is possible to go to Gunung Mulu on your own, but it involves expense and effort. Reports from travellers vary; some feel the expense is worthwhile, others don't.

Gunung Mulu is Sarawak's largest national park, covering 529 sq km of peat-swamp, sandstone, limestone and montane forests. The two major mountains are Gunung Mulu (2377 metres of sandstone) and Gunung Api (1750 metres of limestone).

The park contains hundreds of species of flowering plants, fungi, mosses and ferns. It has around 10 different species of pitcher plants, which attract botanists and scientists from around the world.

Gunung Mulu has a variety of mammals,

Eight different types of hornbill can be found in the Gunung Mulu National Park.

birds (eight different types of hornbill), frogs, fish and insects, but it's not the place to head for if you want to see loads of exotic wild animals.

The park is noted for its many underground caves. Cave explorers recently discovered the largest cave chamber in the world, the Sarawak Chamber, and the 51-km-long Clearwater Cave is one of the longest in the world. The Deer Cave, Lang Cave, Clearwater Cave and Wind Cave are all lit and easily accessible via plankwalks. The other caves are closed to the public, but adventure caving trips can be arranged.

Many of the caves closed to the public are inaccessible or considered dangerous, while some contain fragile formations that park authorities want to preserve and protect from further deterioration.

Gunung Mulu is being developed in a big way as a major tourist attraction in Sarawak. First the airstrip and then the huge, Japanese-run Royal Mulu Resort were built. Now there are plans to build a golf course opposite the park. This novel approach to eco-tourism will involve the demolition of village houses and the acquisition of land claimed by the local Berawan people, who are understandably very upset at the government's actions and the lack of consultation about the park's development.

Permits & Bookings

If you take a tour you will have all the paperwork done for you. Independent travellers, on the other hand, should put aside a day in Miri to organise it themselves.

First go to the National Parks & Wildlife Office (085-436637) in Miri, where you will be asked to fill in a form to obtain a permit. This permit should then be photocopied along with the information page of your passport and taken to the Resident's Office (085-433202) on Jalan Raja. Fill in another form and hand over the photocopies. Now it is time to obtain police clearance at the Police HQ (☎ 085-432533) on Jalan Pujut. Clearance granted? You can now book accommodation at the national park office.

It's time-consuming but not as bad as it sounds. And bear in mind, if you foolishly forget to organise your permit in Miri, the parks office in Mulu can issue one on the spot when you arrive. You do, however, run the risk of finding all the accommodation booked out if you do it this way.

Guides & Fees

Gunung Mulu is an expensive park to visit because you have to hire a guide to go anywhere, and to get there often requires expensive boat-hire costs. Unless you go with a group, or form a group once you are at the park, costs are prohibitive.

Guides should be waiting for visitors at the entrances to the caves. Costs vary depending on the cave. For Clearwater and Wind caves, guides cost RM40 per group; for Deer and Lang's caves, guides cost RM20 per group. A guide for trekking costs around RM35 per day. Boat hire costs from RM85 for a visit to Clearwater Cave to RM350 for the Pinnacles trek. For example, to visit Clearwater Cave and Wind Cave costs RM85 for the boat and RM40 for a guide, making it RM125. This is a hefty price for an individual, but among a group of five the price is a reasonable RM28. The only

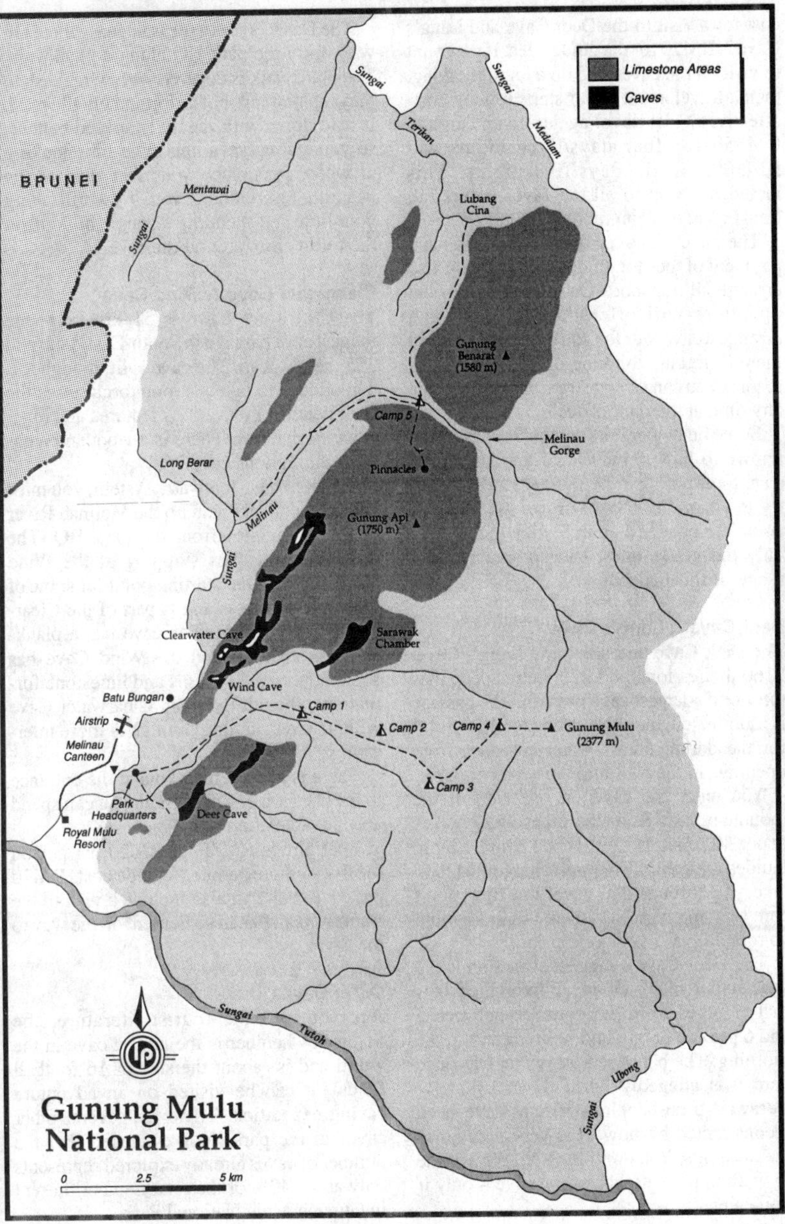
Limestone Areas
Caves
BRUNEI
Sungai Terikan
Sungai Medalam
Sungai Mentawai
Lubang Cina
Gunung Benarat (1580 m)
Camp 5
Melinau Gorge
Pinnacles
Long Berar
Sungai Melinau
Gunung Api (1750 m)
Clearwater Cave
Sarawak Chamber
Wind Cave
Batu Bungan
Camp 1
Airstrip
Camp 2
Camp 4
Gunung Mulu (2377 m)
Melinau Canteen
Camp 3
Park Headquarters
Deer Cave
Royal Mulu Resort
Sungai Tutoh
Sungai Ubong
Gunung Mulu National Park
0
2.5
5 km

cost for a visit to the Deer Cave and Lang's Cave is RM20 for the guide's fee. If you want to visit all the caves and do a lot of trekking, then a travel agent's tour starts to look cost-effective. Most travel agents charge around RM350 for four days/three nights and RM500 for six days/five nights. This includes a visit to all the caves, a trek, all transfers and accommodation.

The park office handles all bookings and payment of fees for guides, and they can also arrange all transport. On arrival, some boat operators will offer their services and arrange a cave tour for you on the spot. Avoid them if you are thinking of finding a group to join. You can arrange transport and a guide any time at the park office.

Some boat operators and guides have been known to line up individual travellers for a cave tour, put them all in one boat and then try to charge each of them for the hire of a complete boat and an individual guide. Pay only the group rates, and complain to the ranger if this happens.

Deer Cave & Lang's Cave

The Deer Cave and adjoining Lang's Cave, 2160 metres long and 220 metres deep, has the world's largest cave passage. The passage is illuminated, though a strong torch is useful for the darker areas. Water cascades from openings in the roof after very heavy rain.

You enter the cave on one side of the mountain, exit from the other and it takes about 30 minutes to walk the entire length. Guides are compulsory and charge RM20 to take you through the cave, but they don't care how many people there are in a group, so round up as many as you can.

The Deer Cave's biggest attraction is the spectacular black cloud of free-tailed bats that emerges from the entrance between 5 and 6 pm each night and returns early in the morning. The bat observatory that was once here was allegedly burnt down by angry Berawan tribespeople – it may have been reconstructed by now. It is very popular in the evenings. You don't have to take a guide to walk to the entrance of the cave – only if you enter.

The Deer Cave is a pleasant, easy three km walk from the park HQ along a plankwalk. The plankwalk is covered with wire mesh to prevent slipping, but unfortunately the mesh is held down with regularly spaced battens, so you end up spending more time looking at where you place your feet than at the beautiful forest around you. It's worth taking your time and spending a couple of hours in the forest areas around the cave.

Clearwater Cave & Wind Cave

The Clearwater Cave is 51 km long (the longest cave passage in South-East Asia) and 355 metres deep. The cave is lit, though it is a good idea to take a strong torch to see the finer details of its various features and limestone formations. There is a wooden plankwalk through the cave.

To get to the Clearwater system, you must hire a boat to take you up the Melinau River about 10 minutes from the park HQ. The usual tour involves stopping at the Wind Cave, which is the starting point for some of the longest tunnels and is part of the Clearwater Cave system. The cave has a plankwalk throughout, and the Wind Cave has some impressive caverns and limestone formations, though the main Clearwater Cave with its river running through is more interesting.

There is a swimming hole at the entrance to the Clearwater Cave where you can spend an enjoyable afternoon.

Boat hire is RM85, or RM20 per person for five or more people. A guide costs RM20 per cave. You can also include a visit to the Batu Bungan Penan settlement on the way to the caves.

Other Caves

According to the tourist literature, the Sarawak Chamber is the largest cave in the world and is 'about the size of 16 football fields'. It can be visited on an adventure caving expedition. There are several other caves in the park. It is estimated that the number of caves already explored represents only about 40% of the total number present in Gunung Mulu National Park.

Adventure Caving

It is possible to explore the nooks and crannies of the caves away from the pedestrian plankwalks. The national park has adventure caving expeditions allowing you to crawl, climb and swim your way through the many passages of the caves. The Sarawak Chamber is the most frequently visited and it costs RM80 for a guide to explore the chamber and two side caves. Equipment is provided. Most adventure caving expeditions are organised by the private tour operators and they explore a number of caves.

The Pinnacles

Gunung Api is the highest limestone mountain in Malaysia and its great attraction is the towering limestone Pinnacles – an incredible stone forest standing 45 metres high, halfway up the side of the mountain. If you want to see the Pinnacles – unless you're part of a small group – you're in for a very expensive three day trek by boat and foot. However, you will see some spectacular scenery.

The trek to the Pinnacles starts with a three to four hour boat trip (depending on the level of the river) from park HQ to Long Berar. From here it is an eight km trek to Camp 5 by the Melinau River. You sleep overnight in the wooden hut at this picturesque spot before climbing Gunung Api.

The ascent is very steep in parts and it takes at least three to four hours to reach the Pinnacles. You must bring water with you. It's best to start out early in the morning, as it's a lot cooler then, and it's more likely that you'll see interesting animals and birds along the way. The ultimate destination is a small viewing point that looks out over the Pinnacles. It is possible to camp here, but the Pinnacles are usually done in one day and most trekkers return to Camp 5 – or if you start early it is possible to continue back to park HQ.

From Camp 5 you can walk north to Lubang Cina on the Terikan River. From the Terikan River it is possible to continue right down to Limbang on the coast via the Medalam River, though this journey is usually done in reverse.

Guides' fees are RM80 for a three-day/two-night trek; each extra day costs RM20 plus RM10 allowance for each night. The national park rate for boat hire to Long Berar is RM350 return for one to four people, or RM85 per person for five or more people. One way costs RM200 for up to four people, or RM45 per person for five or more.

The Gunung Mulu Trail

The climb to the summit of this 2377 metre mountain is normally done as a four day trek and is the highlight of many a traveller's visit to the national park.

If you are reasonably fit and healthy, the ascent and descent of Gunung Mulu can be done in three days, or even two for any star athletes pressed for time. A guide costs RM110 for the four-day/three-night trek, but a shorter trek still costs the same amount.

You should carry enough food for the entire trip, as well as your own cooking utensils and a sleeping bag (it gets quite cold at night). It's not unusual for it to rain every day, and you'll often find yourself wallowing knee-deep in mud – nothing will save you from the leeches there! Take something to keep out the rain and wear good walking shoes. Leech socks are useful.

There are several camps along the trail. Most consist of very basic wooden huts. Camp 1, Camp 3 and Camp 4 are the ones favoured for an overnight stop. The choice of shelters varies, though the most common schedule involves an easy first day and overnight at Camp 1, then a long, hard day two to Camp 4, followed by the ascent to the summit and return to Camp 1 on day three, finally returning to the park HQ on day four.

The trek can also be done in three days, which evens out the exertion more. If you leave park HQ very early in the morning, you can reach Camp 1 in about three hours – plenty of leeches for company. This camp is beside a beautiful river. A further four to five hours' walk will take you as far as Camp 3, which is where most people sleep overnight.

On the second day, you're faced with an extremely steep climb from this camp to Camp 4. The walk to Camp 4 takes four or five hours and there's a shed you can sleep in. If it hasn't rained, there won't be any water at Camp 4, so try to remember to carry some muddy water up from Camp 3.

On the third day, leave your pack at Camp 4 and climb to the summit. You can either sleep at the camp another night, or descend the mountain in the one day. The latter is quite tough on the legs, but at least you can cool down in the river along the way.

Batu Bungan Penan Settlement

Gunung Mulu region is home to the Berawan people, but the government has settled a Penan group in a longhouse on the banks of the Melinau River as part of their campaign to 'civilise' the nomadic Penan. This dirt-poor settlement is used to tourism, and the Penan are very friendly and hospitable people. The women make interesting cane bangles and basketware, and will bring them out for sale.

Batu Bungan is about halfway between the park HQ and Clearwater Cave. A visit to Batu Bungan can be combined with a trip to the caves. It is also possible to walk to Batu Bungan from the airport.

Headhunters' Trail

The backdoor route from Gunung Mulu to Limbang is known as the headhunters' trail by the tour groups which organise this trip. Its name is derived from the Kayan war parties that made their way up the Melinau River from the Baram area to the Melinau Gorge, where they dragged their canoes overland and down to the Terikan River to raid the peoples of the Limbang region. A four-metre-wide road lined with poles was used to move the canoes, and a canal was dug around Batu Rikan.

The trip involves walking from Camp 5, on the way to the Pinnacles, to Lubang Cina on the Terikan River. The journey is then by boat down the Terikan to the Medalam River with an overnight stay at the Bala Losong longhouse. The trip continues downriver the next day to Medamit, on the main road. From here a bus goes to Limbang. The journey is also done in reverse: if you want to arrange this trip yourself, it should be done from Limbang, though it involves expensive boat hire. You may have problems getting a permit from the Gunung Mulu side, as this is another sensitive area, and it is necessary to come by the villages downriver to ensure boat hire.

Places to Stay & Eat

Given the preference for tour groups and the popularity of the park, it can sometimes be difficult to get a booking for accommodation, but private accommodation is available outside the park. If you turn up without a booking, it is unlikely you will be given a bed at the park, even if there is plenty of room available.

The standard of accommodation is very good. There's a 15 bed dorm at the hostel, and a bed in one of these costs RM10 per person. A room in the chalets costs RM60, or it costs RM120 for the whole chalet. There's also a VIP resthouse with a six bed room for RM150. The Annexe has eight five-bed rooms with attached bathroom and fans for RM15 per bed.

The canteen serves reasonable but slightly expensive meals. You can cook your own food, as there are gas stoves and you can use the cutlery, crockery, pots and pans. There is a small store at park HQ selling basic tinned foods, bread, milk, eggs and margarine.

Outside the park, the place to head for is the *Melinau Canteen* (☎ 011-291641 or 085-657884 in Miri). It is just a few hundred metres downriver from the jetty at the park HQ, around the bend on the other side of the river. This Berawan-owned place costs RM10 per person in bunk rooms. Tour groups occasionally fill the place up, but usually you will have no problem getting a room to yourself. Meals are available, and a provisions shop sells tinned goods, snacks, beer etc, but prices are high because of the cost of transport.

Further downriver at Long Pala are more guesthouses owned by the tour companies, such as Tropical Adventure, Seridan Mulu and Alo Doda. It is possible to stay here for around RM15 upwards per night if they are not full, though they are a long way from the park HQ.

Finally, the *Royal Mulu Resort* (☎ 085-421122; fax 085-421088) is a luxury hotel with rooms built along massive wooden walkways above the river. This place miraculously has the lot: swimming pool, satellite TV and international cuisine at the coffee shop/restaurant. Standard rooms cost RM165 to RM250, and suites are RM500 to RM2000. Discounts are often available. A new road runs from the resort to the airport.

Getting There & Away

Air Flights to Gunung Mulu go from Miri (three daily, RM69), Marudi (two weekly, RM40) and Limbang (two daily, RM40). The flight from Miri works out to be RM1.90, more expensive than going by bus and boat. Many visitors to the park fly up and take the boat back to experience river travel. The pilot will, upon request, fly in low between the peaks before circling back to land – a breathtaking experience.

The airport is on the opposite side of the river from the park HQ. A boat to the park or the Melinau Canteen costs RM5. The airport road runs to Long Pala and the Royal Mulu Resort. It is about a 10 to 15 minute walk along this road to the Melinau Canteen. Boats to Long Pala cost RM10.

Bus/Boat With the introduction of regular flights between Miri and Gunung Muru, the overland route by combination of bus and boat has become very hit and miss. It's by no means impossible, but it can be both time-consuming and expensive – there's no certainty that you will do the trip cheaper this way than you would by flying.

From Miri take a bus to Kuala Baram for RM2.20. Buses depart Miri regularly, but if you want to try and get to the national park in one day, take the 6 am bus. Alternatively, you can stay in Marudi for the night.

From Kuala Baram there are express boats to Marudi for RM15; the first departure is at 7.15 am and they leave at least hourly until 3 pm. The trip takes about three hours. From Marudi, the next stage is Long Terawan. Launches make the journey when they have enough passengers, and if the water is high enough they go all the way through. If not, you will have to change boats at Long Apoh. Marudi to Long Terawan costs RM20.

Travel onwards to the national park from Long Terawan is via charter boat. The official rate is RM150 or RM35 per person if there are more than five of you. In practice, however, few local boat owners are willing to do the trip for RM150 and you may end up paying more or waiting until more people turn up. The journey takes around two hours.

For the return trip from the park you need to be up at 5 am to get the boat to Long Terawan (or Kuala Apoh/Long Panai) in time to get the connecting boat to Marudi.

BARIO

Bario sits on a beautiful high valley floor in the Kelabit Highlands, close to the Indonesian border. It makes an ideal base for treks in the highlands. A permit is required from the Resident's Office in Miri. On arrival you may be asked for your permit, but it's not a problem to go straight out to one of the nearby Kenyah or Kelabit longhouses.

Bario has shops where you can stock up on supplies and gifts to take to the longhouses, as does Ba Kelalan.

The Malaysia Airlines agent is the Bario Co-operative Society.

Places to Stay

Tarawe's is the place to head for. It's run by a local and his English wife. The cost is RM25 per person, and they welcome travellers and provide good trekking information.

Getting There & Away

MAS flies Twin Otters from Bario to Miri daily (RM70), usually via Marudi (RM55). The flights are very much dependent on the weather and it's not uncommon for flights to be cancelled, so make sure your schedule is not too tight. These flights are also fully booked well in advance during school holidays.

TREKS AROUND BARIO

There are many trekking possibilities around Bario. Of the longhouses close to town, you can walk east to Pa Umor (about one hour) and nearby Pa Ukat. The trail then continues on to Pa Lungan. A Kelabit burial ground is close to town on the way to Pa Ramapuh, about a 1½ hour walk. There is a waterfall about an hour beyond Pa Ramapuh. Another day walk is to Pa Berang, a Penan settlement three hours from Bario.

The most popular walk is the two day walk to Ba Kelalan and then a flight out, but it is also possible to walk to Long Lellang from where MAS also has a flight. To Long Lellang is a four to six day trek via the Penan settlement of Pa Tik. Expect rain, mud, leeches and some regrets, because jungle walking is no Sunday stroll, but if you are prepared for the hardship the experience is unforgettable. Guides are recommended, and essential for longer walks away from inhabited areas.

Bario-Pa Lungan-Gunung Murud

A four hour walk on a wide trail takes you to Pa Lungan, a friendly longhouse with a pleasant river to swim in. The chief has a room for visitors with mats, blankets, pillows and mosquito net.

From there you can hire guides and bearers to climb Gunung Murud, at 2423 metres (7946 feet) the highest peak in Sarawak. It is a two day walk to Gunung Murud.

Bario-Ba Kelalan-Long Semado

Another possibility is to walk to Ba Kelalan, a day's walk beyond Pa Lungan, and then fly to Lawas (daily flights, RM46), or continue walking to Long Semado, which is also connected to Lawas by Twin Otter flights (twice weekly, RM40). Walks in this area are not a picnic – you need to be self-sufficient in food and shelter, and to be prepared for some hard walking. It's a very good idea to hire a local guide. This costs around RM40 per day and they can usually carry some of your gear. As well as a guide, in theory you also need a Border Permit from the army in Bario, as the route takes you into Kalimantan via Pa Rupai.

Bario-Lio Matoh

You can also walk to Lio Matoh. This takes seven to nine days, depending on how fast you go. It's a great trek, as you stay in longhouses most nights (in basic jungle huts the others), but you must take a guide.

The nightly stops and walking times on a nine day walk are as follows:

Day 1	Long Danau	9 hours
Day 2	Ramudi	5 hours
Days 3, 4, 5	Jungle Huts	15 hours total
Day 6	Long Palawan	7 hours
Day 7	Long Banga	3 hours
Day 8	Jungle hut	6 hours
Day 9	Lio Matoh	7 hours

The guest books in the longhouses are full of good information. Lots of the Kelabits are hard-core Christians and don't smoke, so bring sugar, seeds, tea, kerosene or anything imaginative for the chief.

LIMBANG

This town is the divisional HQ of the Limbang District, sandwiched between Brunei and Sabah. There is little of interest in the town itself, but you may well find yourself coming through on the way to or from Brunei or Gunung Mulu. Limbang is the starting or ending point for the 'headhunters' trail' between Gunung Mulu and Limbang (see under Gunung Mulu National Park).

The town centres on a massive blue-roofed market. On Friday the weekly *tamu* is held in the car park out front and is attended by villagers from the surrounding district.

Limbang's small museum is well worth a look. The **Muzium Wilayah** is dedicated to the crafts, traditions and culture of the region. Follow the river road eastwards past the police station and then take the shaded footpath along the riverbank. The museum is open from 9 am to 6 pm, every day except Monday; admission is RM2.

Willing Travel (☎ 085-21323), on the main street opposite the wharf, can book

MAS tickets and express boat tickets to Labuan and Lawas.

Places to Stay

Like Miri, Limbang has been turned into a sin centre by Brunei's religious police, and some of the cheap-looking places on and around the main street opposite the wharf are decidedly sleazy. The decent places are mostly mid-range air-con hotels. The best cheap option, if you can get in, is the *Government Resthouse* (☎ 085-211301), which has tatty but clean rooms with fan for RM15 or air-con rooms for RM45. The *Muhibbah Inn* (☎ 085-212488) has air-con rooms from RM52, and the fairly new but already battered *Centre Point Hotel* (☎ 085-212922) has air-con rooms with bath, TV and in-house movies for RM58. The best deal in town is the *Metro* (☎ 085-211133) near the central market. Air-con rooms with shower, TV and minibar cost RM46 up to RM138 for the suite.

Places to Eat

For food stalls, go to the 1st floor of the market or try those at the bus station. Limbang has plenty of coffee shops, including *Maggie's* next to the National Inn on the riverside to the west of the centre. Excellent grilled fish and cold beer is served at tables overlooking the river. A little further along, the *Tong Lok* is a smart, air-con Chinese restaurant. The *Bamboo Seafood Restaurant* in the Limbang Recreation Club near the museum is another place for good seafood at outdoor tables.

Getting There & Away

Air MAS has seven daily Twin Otter flights to Miri (RM45), weekly flights to Labuan (RM30), twice-daily flights to Mulu (RM40), daily flights to Lawas (RM25) and twice-weekly flights to Kota Kinabalu (RM60). The airport is four km from the town centre, and a taxi costs RM4 per person.

Road There is a local road network, and it is possible to go by car between the two halves of Brunei via Limbang, but there are no buses. It is difficult and expensive to go from Limbang to the western half of Brunei, but taxis regularly make the trip for RM10 to the eastern Brunei border, from where it is easy to get another taxi for B$5 to Bangar. From Bangar it is possible to go overland to Lawas and on to Sabah, but this involves expensive taxis and a walk across the border (see under Lawas for details).

Regular buses to other parts of Limbang district go to Pandaruan, Buagsiol, Batu Danau, Kubong, Ukong, Tedungan and Medamit. Medamit buses leave from 5 am to 3.30 pm for the back-door route to Gunung Mulu (see under Gunung Mulu National Park).

Boat There are plenty of boats daily to Bandar Seri Begawan, the capital of Brunei. The trip takes about 30 minutes and costs RM15 from Limbang, B$10 from Brunei. Boats go when they have a full load of 12 passengers, but this route has a lot of traffic and you shouldn't have to wait long. The last boat leaves at around 4.30 pm.

An express boat goes to Lawas every morning at 8 am for RM15. The express boat to Labuan leaves at 7.15 am and costs RM20. From Labuan to Limbang the boat leaves at 12.30 pm. Book at Willing Travel (☎ 085-21323).

LAWAS

Lawas is a busy little town on the banks of the Batang Lawas. Like Limbang, it is essentially a transit town and you may find yourself here while en route to or from Brunei, on your way up to Bario in the Kelabit Highlands and Ba Kelalan, or in order to take the short flight to Miri skipping clean over Brunei. Logging is the big industry in this part of Sarawak, and a logging road goes all the way from Lawas to Long Semado.

The MAS agent is the Eng Huat Travel Agency (☎ 085-855570).

Places to Stay & Eat

Most hotels are air-conditioned and expensive, but a good cheap hotel is the friendly *Hup Guan Lodging House* (☎ 085-85362) above a pool hall opposite the town park.

EAST MALAYSIA

Large, clean rooms with fan cost RM15/20 for singles/doubles, or the one air-con room costs RM28. The only drawback is that the rooms are very hot during the day.

For an air-con room with attached bath, *Hotel Muhibbah* (☎ 085-85509) costs RM35/40. The *Hotel Million* (☎ 085-85088) has better rooms with TV for RM35 to RM45, but the cheaper rooms are very small. The two best places in town are the flash *Gaya Inn* (☎ 085-85522), which costs RM45/55 up to RM80, and the *Soon Seng* (☎ 085-85871), which is better value with good rooms for RM45.

Lawas has a few food-stall areas – the stalls opposite the new market are good. Of the coffee shops around town, the best ones are in the block between the Gaya Inn and the Soon Seng. The one under the Soon Seng is the most popular, and has a host of rag-toting staff to wipe down your table at every instant. The food is very good: you can get a small grilled fish in the sauce of your choice for RM5.

Getting There & Away

Air Lawas is well served by MAS Twin Otters. There are weekly flights to Kota Kinabalu (RM47), three flights daily to Miri (RM59), two flights daily to Limbang (RM25), daily flights to Ba Kelalan (RM46), two flights weekly to Long Semado (RM40) and weekly flights to Labuan (RM31) and Long Pasia (RM30).

Bus The bus to Kota Kinabalu (and towns en route) leaves at 7.30 am and costs RM20. Otherwise catch a bus to Merapok, on the Sarawak/Sabah border, for RM5, and from there you can catch a bus to Sipitang. The road from Lawas to Sipitang is very good and is sealed virtually all the way.

If you miss the boats to Brunei, it is possible, though expensive, to travel overland to Bangar in Brunei and then get a boat to Bandar Seri Begawan. Clear Malaysian immigration in Lawas at the ferry wharf, and then from Lawas take a bus to Trusan (half an hour along a bad road) for RM3, or a taxi for RM30. Then cross the river for 50 sen; taxis on the other side to the Brunei border cost RM15. The road stops at the border and you have to walk over the hill to Brunei. There is no border post here. On the other side, taxis are waiting to take you to Bangar. Ask the taxi driver to take you to immigration, past the centre on the other side of Bangar, and then bring you back to the wharf. All up it takes about 40 minutes and the taxi should cost B$20. From Bangar regular boats go to Bandar Seri Begawan for B$7.

Boat For Brunei, the only boat goes at 7.30 am and costs RM20. One boat a day goes to Labuan at 7.30 am for RM20 – book at the Bee Hiong Restaurant (☎ 085-85137) underneath the Hotel Million. The boat to Limbang goes at 9 am and costs RM15.

MERAPOK

Merapok is a strange one-street hamlet in the middle of nowhere, but it does have a pool hall where you can pot a few balls while you wait for a bus. The Sabah/Sarawak border and police checkpost is a few hundred metres out of town. Both states have their immigration posts on their respective sides of the border, and you have to report to both. They close at 6 pm, but the police checkpost will handle immigration formalities outside office hours.

Getting There & Away

Buses go to Lawas and Sipitang, though you may be in for a wait. You can also catch the Kota Kinabalu-Lawas bus on the highway. For hitching, traffic is regular but light.

Sabah

The chief attractions of Sabah are Mt Kinabalu, the turtle islands, diving at Sipadan and the opportunity to see wildlife in the national and state parks. Budget travellers will generally find Sabah more expensive than Peninsular Malaysia, but it is still possible to keep costs to a minimum if you stick to the beaten trail – most of the major attractions have inexpensive accommodation and cheap eats. Mid-range travellers, on the other hand, will generally find Sabah provides good value for money.

Full Name: Sabah Negeri di Bawah Bayu
Area: 73,620 sq km
Capital: Kota Kinabalu
Population: 1.8 million

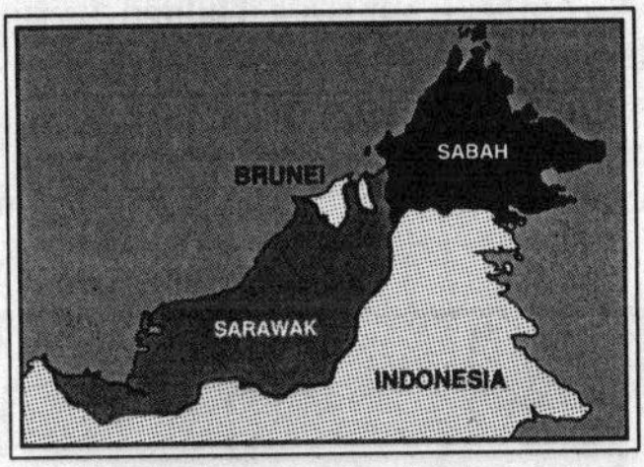

History

Prior to independence, Sabah was known as North Borneo and operated by the British North Borneo Company. After WWII Sabah and Sarawak (which had been ruled by the Brooke family) were handed over to the British government, and they both finally gained their independence when they merged with the peninsular states to form the new nation of Malaysia in 1963.

There was some trouble after independence, as Sabah's existence was disputed not only by Indonesia but also by the Philippines. There are close cultural ties between the people of the Sulu Archipelago of the Philippines' Mindanao province and the neighbouring people of Sabah. To this day there is a busy smuggling trade operating from Sabah into Mindanao, and Mindanao's Muslim rebels often retreat down towards Sabah when pursued by government forces.

After independence, Sabah was governed for a time by Tun Mustapha, who ran the state almost as a private fiefdom and was often at odds with the central government in Kuala Lumpur. In 1967 he even threatened secession. He disappeared from view in 1975. In 1985 the Kadazan-controlled Sabah United Party (Parti Bersatu Sabah – PBS) came into power and joined the National Front Alliance.

Tensions with the federal government, however, were rife. In 1990 the PBS pulled out of the alliance with the National Front just days before general elections. The PBS claimed that the federal government was not equitably returning the wealth that the state generates, and in 1993 it banned the export of logs from Sabah, largely to reinforce this point. The federal government used its powers to overturn the state decision.

Partly as a result of the state's bad relations with the federal government, Sabah is currently the poorest of Malaysia's states. It may be rich in natural resources, but a third of the population lives below the poverty line.

Today the National Front is back at the helm in Sabah. No sooner had they been elected into power than RM$185 million was allocated for social and economic redevelopment of the state. New roads, power plants and schools are planned. Sabah's chief minister, Salleh Tun Said, plans to eliminate poverty and turn Sabah into an economic hub by the year 2000. A tall order, but then if there's anywhere in Malaysia that needs a kickstart it's Sabah.

Visas & Permits

Sabah is semi-autonomous and, like Sarawak, has its own immigration controls. On arrival you are likely to be given a month's stay permit and it's rare to be asked to show money or onward tickets.

Permits can be renewed at immigration offices, which can be found at most points of arrival, even at small riverine places like Merapok near Beaufort. If you miss them it's no problem – you simply report to another immigration office, even several days later, and explain the situation.

No further permits are required to visit the interior.

General Costs

Sabah is an expensive place to travel around. Only at Kinabalu National Park and Poring Hot Springs will you find accommodation that could be classed as 'budget'. Elsewhere it's the familiar story of at least RM20 per night and often much more.

Lodging is also complicated by the fact that virtually all of the cheaper places are brothels, which means you may have to stay in places which would normally be outside the range of budget travel.

Sabah also has a series of government resthouses, which were a good accommodation option until the price for non-government guests was raised to RM40 per person

per night. Still, they offer good mid-range accommodation and sometimes are the only option. There are resthouses in Keningau, Kota Belud, Kota Marudu, Kuala Penyuh, Kudat, Kunak, Lahad Datu, Papar, Ranau, Semporna, Sipitang, Tambunan, Tenom and Tuaran. Generally, the resthouses are for government officials and their families, but if a place is not full, travellers are *sometimes* permitted to stay. Bookings are made through the district officer of the appropriate town, and there are listings in the government pages of the telephone directory.

Getting Around

Road Sabah has an excellent road system, and almost all the major roads are sealed. The exceptions are the road to Lawas in Sarawak, where the 47 km stretch between Beaufort and Sipitang is still unsealed, and a small section on the Sandakan-Lahad Datu highway before the Kinabatangan River. The Kota Kinabalu-Sandakan highway is now sealed all the way. However, all highways are subject to the occasional km or two under repair, usually the result of being washed away, and these stretches are invariably filling-rattlers.

Hitching is possible in Sabah, although traffic is usually light. In this chapter we've indicated where hitching is feasible. However, hitching is never entirely safe and travellers who decide to hitch should understand that they are taking a small but potentially serious risk. People who do choose to hitch will be safer if they travel in pairs and let someone know where they are planning to go.

Bus While some big air-con buses do the major runs, notably Kota Kinabalu-Sandakan, most travel is by minibus. The minibuses are quick and efficient. There are usually frequent departures until around noon, but afternoon departures can be scarce on the longer runs.

Rail There is a railway between Kota Kinabalu and Tenom. For details, see Getting There & Away in the Kota Kinabalu, Tenom and Beaufort sections in this chapter.

Kota Kinabalu

Known as Jesselton until 1963, Kota Kinabalu was razed during WWII to prevent the Japanese using it as a base. Today it's a modern city of wide avenues and tall buildings, with little in the way of historical charm. All the same, KK, as everyone calls it, is not an unpleasant city. It is a pity, however, that local authorities have not capitalised on KK's seaside views and developed the waterfront as has been done in Kuching.

One of Asia's fastest growing cities, with a population of around 200,000, KK is an interesting blend of European, Malay and Chinese culture. It's worth spending a few days in KK if only to sample the excellent variety of cuisines – something which is sadly lacking elsewhere in the state. You must also go to KK to book accommodation for the trip to Mt Kinabalu, Sabah's number one attraction.

Orientation

Although the city sprawls for many km along the coast from the international airport at Tanjung Aru to Likas, the centre itself is quite small and most places are within easy walking distance of each other. This includes the bulk of the hotels and restaurants, banks, travel agents, tourist offices, the national parks office and the GPO.

There is no bus station as such in town, but there are two or three areas in central KK where you can find the bus you want, or at least be directed to the right area by the runners who accost you as you walk along. Taxis are all over town, but seem to congregate in the area between the GPO and the council offices.

Kota Kinabalu has plenty of shopping complexes. The older-style centres such as Segama and Sinsuran are grid-like blocks of two or three storey shophouses, while the newer malls like Centre Point and Wisma Merdeka offer some of the best shopping possibilities.

Information

Tourist Offices Kota Kinabalu has two excellent tourist offices. Tourism Malaysia (☎ 088-211732) is on the ground floor of the Wing Onn Life building on Jalan Segunting at the northern end of the city centre. The staff are knowledgeable and helpful, and it is open Monday to Thursday from 8 am to 4.15 pm, Friday from 8 to 11.30 am and 2 pm to 4.15 pm, and on Saturday from 8 am to 12.45 pm.

The Sabah Tourism Promotion Corporation (☎ 088-218620), 51 Jalan Gaya, is housed in a historic building. It can answer most queries and produces good brochures, including an excellent map of Kota Kinabalu and Sabah. It also has an office on Level 1 of the airport building.

Sabah Parks Office The Sabah Parks office (☎ 088-211585) is very conveniently situated in Block K of the Sinsuran Kompleks located on Jalan Tun Fuad Stephens. It handles reservations for accommodation for Mt Kinabalu, Tunku Abdul Rahman National Park, Poring Hot Springs, Pulau Tiga, Turtle Islands National Park and Tawau Hills Park.

The further ahead you make reservations, the better chance you have of being able to go when you want to. Mt Kinabalu is a very popular place, with both overseas visitors and locals, and accommodation at the park HQ is often booked up a week in advance. Book as early as possible.

The office is open Monday to Thursday from 8.30 am to 4.15 pm, Friday from 8 to 11.30 am and 2 to 4.15 pm and Saturday from 8.30 am to noon. The staff are helpful, and in addition to handling reservations they stock a range of guidebooks and information pamphlets on Kinabalu National Park and Tunku Abdul Rahman National Park. They also sell postcards and T-shirts.

Other Offices The immigration office (☎ 088-216711) is on the 4th floor of the tall government building, near Jalan Tunku Abdul Rahman, around the corner from the Diamond Inn.

Bookings for the Borneo Rainforest Lodge at the Danum Valley can be made at the Innoprise Jungle Lodge office (☎ 088-243245; fax 088-254227) in the Sadong Jaya Kompleks, though bookings can also be easily made at the office in Lahad Datu.

Foreign Embassies The Indonesian consulate (☎ 088-219110) is on Jalan Karamunsing, south of the city centre. Visas can be issued here without fuss, and there is also a consulate in Tawau if you are heading to Kalimantan via Tarakan.

There is a Japanese consulate (☎ 088-254695) on the 5th floor of Wismah Yahim.

Money If you're staying in the Sinsuran Kompleks, the most convenient bank is the branch of the Sabah Bank right next door to the Sabah Parks office. There are plenty of others around the central town area. You'll find moneychangers on the ground floor of Centre Point and Wisma Merdeka.

Post & Communications The post office is right in the centre of town and has an efficient poste restante counter.

For international calls, most public phone booths are Uniphone but if you have a Telekom card you can use the Telekom booths behind the post office and at the Telekom office on Jalan Tunku Abdul Rahman, about 15 minutes' walk south of the centre of town, where international telephone booths are also available.

Travel Agencies There are plenty of travel agencies in KK, all of them expensive. For scuba diving, Borneo Divers & Sea Sports (☎ 088-222226) has a dive shop on the ground floor of Wisma Sabah, and the main office is upstairs on the 4th floor. They can arrange a dive to just about anywhere, offer dive courses and have a place on Sipadan Island. Borneo Sea Adventures (☎ 088-218216), 1st floor, 8A Karamunsing Warehouse, is another dive company that has accommodation on Sipadan.

For white-water rafting, try Api Tours (☎ 088-221233) in Wisma Sabah. A rafting day trip from KK, which involves taking the Tenom train part of the way and then rafting

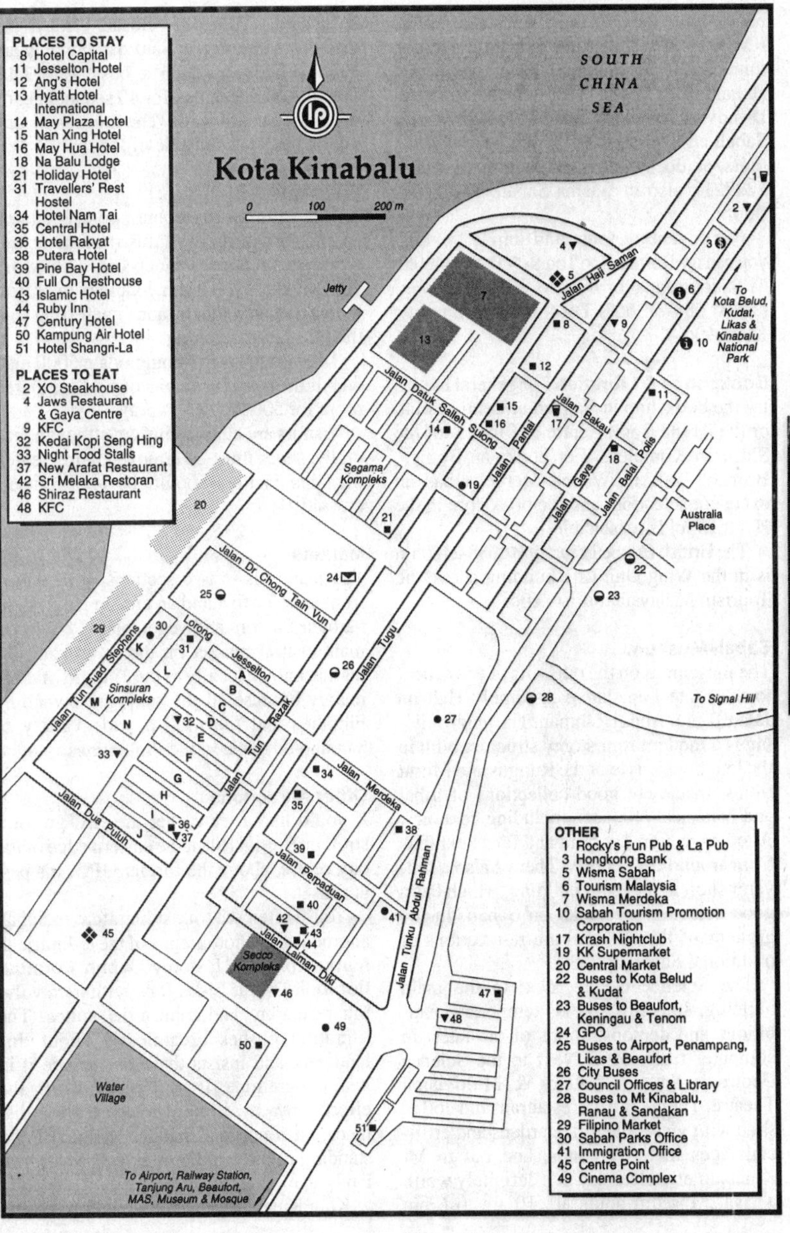

EAST MALAYSIA

back along the Padas River, costs around RM180, but with travelling and preparation time you'll be lucky to have two hours' actual rafting. Longer trips can be arranged. Discovery Tours (☎ 088-221244) in Wisma Sabah also offers rafting trips, among other tours, as does Borneo Expeditions (☎ 088-222721), also in Wisma Sabah, on the 3rd floor.

For adventure tours and jungle trekking you can try Borneo Eco Tours (☎ 088-234005), 6J Sadong Jaya; or Borneo Wildlife Adventure (☎ 088-213668), Lot 4, Block L, Sinsuran Kompleks.

Bookshops & Libraries For general books, try the bookshop in Yaohan at Centre Point, or the Arena Book Centre in Block L of the Sinsuran Kompleks. For books on Borneo, Borneo Craft in Wisma Merdeka has an excellent selection, and the bookstore in the Hyatt Hotel is reasonable.

The British Council Library (☎ 088-248055) is in the Wing Onn Life building above the Tourism Malaysia tourist office.

Sabah Museum

The museum is on the outskirts of town, next to the State Legislative Assembly Hall on Jalan Tunku Abdul Rahman. The main building is a modern four storey structure built in the longhouse style of the Rungus and Murut tribes. Inside are good collections of tribal and historical artefacts, including ceramics. Another section has flora and fauna exhibits from around the country. There's also a souvenir shop in the main building, which has a good selection of books on Sabah. In the grounds of the museum are re-creations of traditional Sabah houses.

The Science Centre, next to the main building, sometimes holds temporary exhibitions and demonstrations of the latest in computer technology. Next to the Science Centre is the Art Gallery & Multivision Theatre. There is also a restaurant and coffee shop with views over the gardens and artificial lakes in the grounds, and out to Mt Kinabalu on a clear day. It's definitely worth a visit. Museum hours are 10 am to 6 pm Monday to Thursday; closed Friday; and from 9 am to 6 pm on Saturday, Sunday and public holidays. Catch a bus along Jalan Tunku Abdul Rahman for 40 sen and get off just before the mosque. The museum is on a hill on the left-hand side of the road.

State Mosque

As an example of contemporary Islamic architecture at its best, this mosque is well worth a visit. It's on the outskirts of town and you'll see it if you're on your way to or from the airport. It's much more interesting than the mosque at Kuching.

The mosque can accommodate 5000 male worshippers and has a balcony where there's room for 500 women to pray.

Visitors are allowed inside, although, naturally, shoes must be removed before entering, and visitors should be appropriately dressed.

Markets

The market is in two sections – the waterfront area for fish and an area in front of the harbour for fruit and vegetables. Next to the main central market on the waterfront is a market known locally as the Filipino Market, mainly because all the stalls are owned by Filipinos and they sell a wide variety of handicrafts made in the Philippines.

Other Attractions

If you'd like a view over the city, go for a stroll up **Signal Hill** at the eastern edge of the city centre, above the former GPO. It's best at sunset.

You'll often see tourist literature in Sabah adorned with photographs of the cylindrical, mirror-fronted, 31 storey **Sabah Foundation building** at Likas Bay, with its revolving restaurant and ministerial suites. The literature gushes breathlessly about this landmark and insists that you include it in your programme. It isn't really worth the effort. Anyway, it can be seen from a distance, en route to Kinabalu National Park, standing in the middle of a vast, devastated landscape.

Kota Kinabalu has its own **water village**

of stilt houses, just south of the city area and Centre Point, though much of Kampung Air has already been reclaimed.

Places to Stay – bottom end

There are three popular travellers' hang-outs in the centre of town and a couple more on the outskirts of town. Otherwise, you'll sometimes find mid-range hotels with cheaper fan-cooled rooms on the higher floors – it's worth asking.

The *Traveller's Rest Hostel* (☎ 088-224264) is the most popular travellers' place and is centrally located on the 3rd floor in Block L of the Sinsuran Kompleks. It can get crowded but it is a friendly place and the dorm beds at RM13 including breakfast are good value. Other rooms available include singles with fan at RM25 and doubles with air-con and bath at RM45. The hostel also has travel information, a laundry service, and a travel service that provides inexpensive tours to destinations around Sabah.

Next door is the *Borneo Wildlife Youth Hostel* (☎ 088-213668). It has basic but clean dorm rooms at RM12 per bed. Another good option, in altogether more pleasant surroundings, is *Na Balu Lodge* (☎ 088-262281). It's above YBJ Antiques, a block south-west of the Jesselton Hotel. Dorm beds with mosquito nets and fans cost RM20 with breakfast. There's a dining room and kitchen, and a travel service with a wide range of tours.

Jack's Bed & Breakfast (☎ 088-232367), 17 Block B, 1st floor, Jalan Karamunsing, is a little further out, but it is spotlessly clean and well run. It costs RM18 for a dorm bed and breakfast and has a variety of dorm rooms. It's out towards the state mosque, about one km past the cinema complexes on Jalan Tunku Abdul Rahman. Catch a bus to the Kompleks Kuwasa, a large office block containing many of the airline offices, and Jack's is a couple of blocks behind.

Farida's Bed & Breakfast (☎ 088-35733), 413 Jalan Saga in Likas, is six km north of the centre of town. It is a long way from anywhere, but it is the best of the travellers' hostels around. Set in a large, quiet, suburban house, it costs RM18 per person for a double room including a great breakfast, or RM12 per person for a bed only. To get there, take any minibus that goes along Jalan Tuaran and get off at the Likas Baptist Church. Walk 100 metres down Jalan Likas and then turn right into Jalan Saga – Farida's is 200 metres on the left.

The *Seaside Travellers Inn* (☎ 088-750313), H 30 Gaya Park, Jalan Penampang, is 20 km from town past the airport towards Papar. It is not the place to stay if you want to explore KK, but may be ideal if you want a day or two on the beach and you are leaving from the airport. Accommodation ranges from a dorm bed for RM20 and single/double rooms for RM40/50 up to bungalows for RM80 to RM90, all with a continental breakfast. The beach won't win any awards, but it is pleasant and the accommodation is good. Take a Papar minibus and get off near the Km 20 mark – the inn is a short walk from the school, not far from where the airport road meets the Penampang-Papar highway.

The travellers' hostels provide better value for money than KK's budget hotels, many of which tend to be noisy and slightly seedy. The *Islamic Hotel*, above the restaurant of the same name at 8 Jalan Perpaduan, has fan rooms and common bath for RM27.

The *Putera Hotel* (☎ 088-512814) on Jalan Merdeka, near the corner of Jalan Tunku Abdul Rahman, is a fairly clean Chinese hotel with large single/double rooms for RM20/25 with fan, or RM35 to RM45 for a double with air-con.

For just a little more, the *Hotel Rakyat* (☎ 088-211100), in Block I of the Sinsuran Kompleks, is very good value. Rooms in this clean, friendly, Muslim-run hotel cost RM30/35 for singles/doubles with fan and bath, and RM35 up to RM55 with air-con and bath.

If the above are full, the *Central Hotel* (☎ 088-513522), 5 Jalan Tugu, has air-con rooms with attached bath for RM40/48. Nearby on Jalan Merdeka, you'll find the *Hotel Nam Tai* (☎ 088-514803). It's fairly clean and has double rooms for RM35 to RM45.

Places to Stay – middle

Kota Kinabalu has dozens of mid-range hotels, though a room that would cost RM40 elsewhere in Malaysia costs RM60 and upwards in KK.

The *Full On Resthouse* (☎ 088-219321), adjacent to the Islamic Hotel, has reasonable rooms for RM44/48, all with air-con and bath attached. The *Full Hua* (☎ 088-234950), at 14 Jalan Tugu near the Central Hotel, is one of the best buys in this range and has very good singles/doubles with air-con, attached bath and TV for RM52/62, though planned renovations will probably push prices up. The *Diamond Inn* (☎ 088-261222), on Jalan Haji Yakub, has standard singles at RM60 and comfortable doubles at RM75/85. The *Ruby Inn* (☎ 088-213222), Jalan Laiman Diki, is run by the same people and costs RM85/95 with the same facilities.

The best mid-range accommodation is up in the fashionable northern end of town. Close to the Hilton, on Jalan Haji Saman, is the *Wah May Hotel* (☎ 088-266118), a well run and popular hotel with standard twins at RM85 and deluxe twins at RM98. If it's full, the nearby *Nan Xing Hotel* has slightly cheaper rates and is also a good place to stay. *Ang's Hotel* (☎ 088-55433) is a little further along. Once a good hotel, its rooms are looking the worse for wear and cost from RM52/62 up to RM70/82 for 'superior' rooms. The *May Plaza Hotel* (☎ 088-215417) is another faded hotel, but it's not without charm. The rooms cost from RM78 – avoid the ones overlooking the street below as they tend to be noisy. Further down Jalan Tun Razak, the *Holiday Hotel* (☎ 088-213116) is a good option, with rooms from RM66/77 to RM88/99.

Places to Stay – top end

KK has hotels with prices right up there with the leading hotels in Singapore, Kuala Lumpur and Penang, but it also has some three star hotels offering discounts and good rooms for around RM100. The *Century Hotel* (☎ 088-242222), Lot 12 Jalan Masjid Lama, is a new hotel with very good rooms for RM110/120 plus 15%. The *Hotel Capital* (☎ 088-231999), 23 Jalan Haji Saman, is a more upmarket option right in the centre of town. It has a good coffee shop, and rooms start at RM160/170 for standard singles/doubles.

Going up a notch in quality, the *Hotel Shangri-La* (☎ 088-212800), 75 Bandaran Berjaya, has rooms from RM175/185. Across the main road from the Shangri-La is the new *Kampung Air Hotel* (☎ 088-256622), which provides upmarket comforts at reasonable rates. Singles/doubles start at RM120/140 plus taxes.

The *Jesselton* (☎ 088-223333; fax 088-240401), 69 Jalan Gaya, takes first prize in the colonial-charm stakes. It is the oldest of KK's many hotels but has been tastefully refurbished. It has just 33 rooms and rates are RM220 for a standard, RM280 for a superior and RM310 for a deluxe.

The only international-standard hotel in the centre of town is the *Hyatt Kinabalu International* (☎ 088-221234; fax 088-218909), Jalan Datuk Salleh Sulong, opposite the waterfront. It has a swimming pool, restaurants, business facilities etc, and charges from RM310 for standard rooms.

The other big international hotel is the *Shangri-La Tanjung Aru Resort* (☎ 088-225800), on the beach at Tanjung Aru near the airport. It has an impressive array of facilities, and rates from RM360/395 for singles/doubles.

Places to Eat

For the variety of restaurants and the quality of food available, KK is probably the best city in Borneo. There are Chinese, Indian, Malay, Indonesian, Spanish, Filipino, Japanese, Korean and western restaurants right in the centre of town.

The best night market in town is at the Sedco Kompleks. The speciality is seafood, but other dishes are also available. The stall owners have an uncanny instinct for the arrival of rain and can have the whole area covered in minutes. For hawker food, there's another night market which sets up in the evenings in the vacant lot at the southern end of the Sinsuran Kompleks. Many of the stalls sell second-hand clothes and are run by Filipinos, but there's a good variety of food stalls; you can even get that Indonesian delicacy coto Makassar (buffalo-gut soup) if you're feeling adventurous. The top floor of the central market also has good food stalls.

KK's shopping malls are good hunting grounds for cheap fare. *Centre Point* has a whole collection of moderately priced eating places in the basement, serving Malay and Chinese food as well as western fast food at *Pizza Hut* and *KFC*; there's also a *Burger King* on the ground floor. On the 2nd floor of the Yaohan department store are some slightly expensive food stalls in squeaky-clean air-con surroundings. *Wisma Merdeka* has a small but good food centre on the 2nd floor overlooking the sea, as well as *Sate Ria* and *KFC* outlets, among others.

For Indian Muslim food, try the *New Arafat Restaurant* in Block I of the Sinsuran Kompleks. This 24 hour place is run by very friendly Indians and serves excellent curries, rotis and murtabaks.

In Block E of the Sinsuran Kompleks is the *Kedai Kopi Seng Hing*, an unremarkable Chinese cafe which serves remarkable prawn mee soup at lunchtime – recommended.

Further out of town at the Kompleks Kuwasa in Block B, the *Gardenia Atrium Lounge* has good coffee and pastries. In Block D of the same complex is the *Avasi Cafeteria*, a very popular lunchtime hang-out for local office workers.

Don't be put off by the smoked glass windows and credit-card signs at the *Sri Melaka*, 9 Jalan Laiman Diki. It has excellent local dishes for around RM6 to RM8 for mains. The *Shiraz Restaurant* in the Sedco Kompleks serves north Indian food.

The *Wishbone Cafe & Restaurant* on Jalan Gaya is not bad – it's downstairs in the Jesselton and serves both western and Asian food. The *Tivoli Restaurant* in the Hotel Shangri-La has a good evening Malay buffet. The *Sri Kapitol Coffee House* in the Hotel Capital is an excellent coffee shop on the ground floor, serving moderately priced Malay specialities and some western dishes. The *Pool Side* cafe at the Hyatt is the most salubrious hawker centre in town, and they do a good job of old favourites such as laksa at reasonable prices (that is, until you add on the service charge, tax and the price of drinks).

For something a little more upmarket there's the *XO Steakhouse* at 54 Jalan Gaya at the northern end of town. It serves excellent 'air-chilled' steaks which have been flown in from Australia and the USA. You can expect to pay around RM20 for an Australian steak, or RM30 to RM40 for an American one. However, a better steak deal is available just a few doors away at *Rocky's Fun Pub*. For RM13 you get a three course meal with coffee – lunchtime courses are RM9.50.

For upmarket Chinese cuisine, *Jaws Restaurant* is rated as one of the best in town. It's on the 4th floor of the Gaya Centre, behind the Hilton. The emphasis is on seafood, but dim sum is also available in the mornings.

Entertainment

As is the case elsewhere in Borneo, KK's nightlife doesn't really start happening until very late. *Shenanigans* at the Hilton is probably the most popular place in town. There is live music, and the place gets packed out on the weekends. Entry is free, but drinks are very expensive – RM13 per beer.

Rocky's Fun Pub is a bar until 10.30 pm and then transforms into a disco. A few doors down is the *LA Pub*, a very similar set-up that attracts a slightly younger crowd. *Krash*, on the ground floor of the New Sabah Inn, has the hippest deejays in town, but again the place will be deserted before 10.30 pm. Don't arrange any morning activities for the next day if you are planning a night out in KK.

A final entertainment option is the *MTV parlours* that litter the streets of KK. These places have laser-disc movies that you can rent and watch on plush sofas in rooms provided – costs range from RM20 to RM30 per movie.

Things to Buy

Though a major centre, KK isn't a great place for handicrafts. Centre Point has a few shops, of which Borneo Handicraft has the most interesting selection. In Wisma Merdeka,

Borneo Craft has a few souvenirs and the best Borneo book collection. Borneo Gifts in Wisma Sabah has mostly souvenirs. You can also try the shop in the Sabah Tourism Promotion Corporation building. There is a small shop in the Tanjung Aru Beach Hotel which has some fairly expensive handicrafts and souvenirs for sale.

You can buy Filipino crafts in the market and at the night markets around town.

Getting There & Away

Air The Malaysia Airlines office (☎ 088-213555) is in the Kompleks Karamunsing, about five minutes' walk south of the Hotel Shangri-La along Jalan Tunku Abdul Rahman, and off to the left at the huge roundabout. It is open Monday to Friday from 8.30 am to 5.30 pm, Saturday from 8.30 am to 3.30 pm and Sunday from 9 am to 1 pm.

It also has an office at the airport which is open from 5 am to 7 pm daily. Travel agents closer to town can book MAS flights and all charge the same price. Philippine Airlines (☎ 088-239600) is also in the Kompleks Karamunsing.

Over the other side of Jalan Tunku Abdul Rahman is the KWSP building, which also contains a number of airline offices, including Dragon Air (also Cathay Pacific) (☎ 088-254733), Royal Brunei Airlines (☎ 088-242193), Singapore Airlines (☎ 088-255444) and Thai Airways (☎ 088-232896).

Peninsular Malaysia & Singapore The cheapest way of getting from Peninsular Malaysia to KK is by purchasing a 14 day advance-purchase ticket from Johor Bahru for RM295; the regular fare is RM347. There are also economy night flights from Kuala Lumpur for RM306; advance-purchase fares for RM372; or the regular fare of RM437. Advance-purchase tickets must be paid for 14 days in advance, while the night fares only apply to certain flights.

The KK-Singapore fare is RM514 (S$391 from Singapore), so it is cheaper to take the flights to or from Johor Bahru and cross the Causeway on the MAS bus which takes you right into Singapore for RM10.

Hong Kong Malaysia Airlines and Cathay Pacific each have three flights weekly between KK and Hong Kong. The flight time is a little under four hours. Direct flights are frequently fully booked, making a change in Singapore necessary, though this is around RM100 more expensive.

The Philippines MAS flies to Manila five times a week. Philippine Airlines also operates on this route. Flight time is just under two hours.

Around Sabah & Sarawak KK is the hub of the MAS network in Sabah and there are regular flights to Bintulu (two daily, RM127), Brunei (three times weekly, RM117), Kuching (seven daily, RM228), Labuan (five daily, RM52), Lahad Datu (four daily, RM106), Miri (six daily, RM82), Sandakan (five daily, RM83) and Tawau (five daily, RM96).

There are also 12 seater Twin Otter flights from KK to Limbang (twice weekly, RM60), Lawas (weekly, RM47) and Kudat (twice weekly, RM50).

Bus There is no main bus station in KK; instead, there are a few places from where buses, minibuses and taxis depart. Most of the long-distance buses leave from the open area south-east of the council offices along Jalan Tunku Abdul Rahman.

The large open plot of land behind the GPO is a very busy minibus park that services the market. Most buses from here are local but also go to centres around KK, such as Penampang, Papar and Tuaran.

As you approach the long-distance minibus area you'll be accosted by touts drumming up business. Don't commit yourself to any minibus until you get there and see how many people they have; there'll often be more than one minibus going and the one you're getting on may be empty, in which case it will be a long wait while it fills up. If you get to the bus stand and there isn't a minibus with even one passenger going your way, hang back for a few minutes; chances are there's one nearly full doing a lap of the town trying to fill the last couple of seats.

All minibuses leave when full, and there are frequent early-morning departures. There are fewer departures later in the day, and don't count on departures for long-haul destinations in the afternoon. The general rule is travel early, and the further you travel the earlier you should leave. Some examples of minibus fares from KK are:

Beaufort (97 km), regular departures until about 5 pm, two hours on a very good road, RM5
Keningau (128 km), regular departures to about 1 pm, about 2½ hours on a road which is surfaced all the way, RM10
Kota Belud (77 km), departures until 5 pm, two hours, RM10
Kudat (190 km), departures until about 5 pm, three hours, RM12
Lawas (195 km), buses depart at 7.30 am and 1.30 pm, five hours on a paved road except for the 47 km stretch between Beaufort and Sipitang, RM25-30
Papar (50 km), departures until 4 pm, one hour, RM2.50
Ranau (156 km), early-morning departures, the last bus leaves at 6 pm and takes about two hours (all buses pass Kinabalu National Park), RM10
Sandakan (386 km), minibus departures early morning only, about six hours, RM35. The big air-con buses, operated by Mizume Enterprise, Lim Sim Siau and Tong Ma, depart at 7 am and are the most comfortable way to do this trip. Fares hover between RM20 and RM25, and it's advisable to book ahead. The road is sealed all the way, except where the new road is already starting to deteriorate.
Tenom, regular departures on a good sealed road, RM25 by taxi, RM20 by minibus
Tuaran (35 km), departures throughout the day, 45 minutes, RM2

If you're heading for Kinabalu National Park from KK, you can get there by taking the minibuses for Ranau or Sandakan and getting off at the park HQ, which is right by the side of the road. Ask the driver to drop you off there. The fare to the park HQ costs RM10 and takes about 1½ hours.

Train The railway station is five km south of the city centre at Tanjung Aru, close to the airport. There are daily trains to Beaufort and Tenom at 8 and 11 am. The 8 am train is a goods train, which arrives in Beaufort at 11.15 am and Tenom at 2.44 pm; and the 11 am diesel train arrives in Beaufort at 1.37 pm and Tenom at 3.55 pm. Bookings can be made by contacting the Tanjung Aru station (☎ 088-254611) or the Beaufort station (☎ 087-211518). Although the stretch between Beaufort and Tenom is very spectacular and well worth the ride, it is easier and quicker to get to Beaufort or Tenom from KK by road.

Taxi Besides the minibuses, there are share-taxis to most places. They also go when full and their fares are at least 25% higher than the minibuses. Their big advantage is that they are much quicker and more comfortable.

Boat There are three daily boats to Labuan from the jetty behind the Hyatt Hotel. The *Rezeki Murni* and the *Labuan Express* leave at 8 and 10 am and 1.30 and 3 pm. The fare is RM28 in economy class and RM33 in 1st class. There's usually no need to book in advance, but if you want to you can contact Rezeli Murni (☎ 088-236835), Lot 3, 1st floor, Block D, Segama Kompleks.

The other boat is the *Kinabalu Express* (☎ 088-219810), which leaves at 8 and 10 am and 1.30 pm. Economy seats are RM28, 1st class RM32.

Getting Around

The Airport One of the few times you'll need to use local public transport is when going to the airport at Tanjung Aru, south-west of the centre. To get there take a 15 minute taxi ride for RM11, or a red Putatan bus for 65 sen from Jalan Tunku Abdul Rahman, and ask to be dropped at the airport. This bus stops opposite the road which leads to the airport, and from there it's a 10 minute walk to the terminal.

Heading into town from the airport, there's a bus stop to the right as you leave the airport. Taxis operate on a coupon system and it costs RM10.20 for a fare into town.

The airport is new and modern, with an efficient MAS office, a post office, a Telekom office, a bank, a small bookshop and a cafe and an overpriced restaurant upstairs.

Taxi Local taxis are plentiful in the extreme. They are not metered, so it's a matter of negotiating the fare before you set off. Taxi stands are all over town, but most can be found in the large area between the council offices and the GPO.

Car There are a number of car rental operators, including:

Adaras Rent a Car
Lot G07, Ground floor, Wisma Sabah
(☎ 088-222137)
Ais (no, not Avis)
1st floor, Lot 5, Block A, Asia City
(☎ 088-238954)
Kinabalu Rent a Car
Hyatt Kinabalu International (☎ 088-221234)

Other car rental agencies can be found in Wisma Sabah. Car hire is very expensive but competition is brisk and you should be able to get a better deal for longer rental. The going rate for a Proton Saga is RM130 per day, while a Toyota Land Cruiser will cost around RM350 per day.

AROUND KOTA KINABALU

Tunku Abdul Rahman National Park

This park has a total area of nearly 4929 hectares and is made up of the offshore islands of Gaya, Mamutik, Manukan, Sapi and Sulug. Only a short boat ride from the centre of the city, they offer some of the best beaches in Borneo, crystal-clear waters and a wealth of tropical corals and marine life.

Accommodation on the islands is booked through the Sabah Parks office in KK (see Information in the Kota Kinabalu section above). There are chalets in Manukan and Mamutik and it is also possible to camp on Gaya, Sulug, Mamutik and Sapi for RM5 per person, if you bring your own tent and apply for permission in writing from the Sabah Parks office – officially, you must do this 'well in advance'.

Pulau Manukan You'll find the park HQ on Pulau Manukan, the second-largest island of the park. With an area of 20 hectares, the island offers good beaches with coral reefs on the southern and eastern coasts, and there are walking trails around the perimeter.

This island has also undergone extensive development with the construction of chalets, a restaurant, a jetty, a swimming pool and squash courts. With its well-developed facilities, it is the most popular with KK residents. There are 20 chalets (each with two rooms) which are fully furnished but don't have cooking facilities. The cost of the chalets is RM200 per night for weekends and public holidays, or RM140 for weekdays.

Pulau Gaya With an area of about 1465 hectares, Pulau Gaya is by far the largest island in the park and is the one just offshore from Kota Kinabalu.

This island is inhabited by about 500 Malaysians and 4700 Filipino refugees, who live in stilt villages on the water. The water village, actually outside the park boundaries, is quite interesting (though you won't exactly be welcomed), but as there are few walkways you may have to take one of the local boats which ferry people about.

There are about 20 km of marked hiking trails and the well-known Police Beach at Bulijong Bay. If you're lucky, you may see monkeys, pangolins or even what's known as the bearded pig.

Pulau Sapi Pulau Sapi (Cow Island) lies just off the south-western tip of Pulau Gaya and is the most visited island in the park. With an area of just 10 hectares, the island has good beaches and trails and day-use facilities. There's a three km nature trail on the island. The monkeys that live in the forest sometimes go down to the beach to swim and look for crabs. You may also see the white-bellied sea eagle around this island.

While there is no accommodation, there are shelters, changing rooms, toilets and barbecue pits. Snorkelling equipment can be hired at RM15 for a snorkel and mask.

Pulau Mamutik This is the smallest island in the park, with an area of just six hectares.

There are good beaches right around the island and some good coral reefs, particularly on the eastern side.

There is a three bedroom resthouse for up

to eight people on the island. It costs RM250 per night on weekends and public holidays, or RM180 on weekdays.

Pulau Sulug This island, covering eight hectares, is the least visited island of this group, probably because it's the furthest away from KK, and is being pushed as a 'Robinson Crusoe experience'. It has some beautiful coral reefs and tropical fish, but only one beach, on the eastern shore.

Getting There & Away Coral Island Tours (☎ 088-223490) has boats from behind KK's Hyatt Hotel to the islands at 10 am and 12.30 pm, returning at 1.30 pm and 3.30 pm, daily. The cost is RM16 return to any of the islands for a minimum of four people, and you will also have to pay a RM2 parks fee, which is good for all the islands. Coral Island Tours has an office in the lobby of the Hyatt Hotel.

Sea Quest (☎ 088-230943), B207 Wisma Merdeka in KK, is another operator that has ferry services to Manukan, Sapi, Mamutik and Gaya for RM15, or to Police Beach for RM20. Boats leave at 9 am and return at 4.30 pm, but they depend on getting enough people. Book in advance.

If you just want to go across to Pulau Gaya's water village, boats shuttle back and forth from the Filipino Market and from near the Hyatt. Private boats and operators can also be hired from the area next to the Hyatt. The charge is very much open to negotiation, but a boat to any of the islands should cost about RM40 to RM50.

Tanjung Aru Beach

Several km south-west of central KK is Tanjung Aru Beach, adjacent to Prince Philip Park and close to the international airport. It's not bad, as beaches go, and the area is dotted with open-air food and drink stalls and the occasional pile of rubbish.

To get to Tanjung Aru Beach, take a red bus displaying 'Beach' from Jalan Tunku Abdul Rahman. It costs 60 sen and will drop you near the yacht club, a pleasant 500 metres from the Shangri-La hotel at the other end of the beach.

South of Kota Kinabalu

RAFFLESIA FOREST RESERVE

The highway from Kota Kinabalu to Tambunan and the central valley region crosses the forested Crocker Range. Logging has taken a devastating toll on most of Sabah, but the Crocker still has areas of forest left, and the mountain views are superb. Much of the range south of the highway, and some to the north, is now part of the Crocker Range National Park.

Near the top of the range on the highway is the Rafflesia Forest Reserve, devoted to the world's largest flower. The rafflesia is a parasitic plant that is hidden within its host, the stems of jungle vines, until it bursts into bloom. The large bulbous flowers are up to one metre in diameter. The species unique to Sabah is the *Rafflesia pricei*, a slightly smaller variety than that found in Sumatra.

The Rafflesia Information Centre (☎ 087-774691), on the highway 59 km from Kota

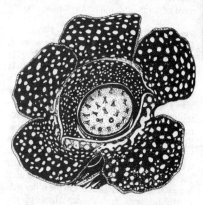

The rafflesia is the world's largest flower. Unique to Sabah is the *Rafflesia pricei*, a slightly smaller variety than the largest of its species, the *Rafflesia amoldi*, found in Sumatra. For much of its life the rafflesia lies hidden in the base of jungle vines, until the hard bud bursts through the host plant and develops into a huge cauldron flower. Pollinated by flies, it is a carrion plant, preying on insects.

Kinabalu, has interesting displays and information devoted to the rafflesia. It is open Monday to Friday from 8 am to 12.45 pm and 2 to 5 pm, and on weekends from 8 am to 5 pm. From the centre, trails lead into the forest where the rafflesias can be found. Whether you will find one in bloom is very much a matter of luck, though the staff at the centre can tell you of the latest sightings. The flowers may be close to the centre or involve a walk deep into the forest. In theory, guides are available to take you to the flowers at fixed times, but in fact staff are rarely available.

Even if there are no rafflesias, there are pleasant walks to be had. There is also a good walk to Air Terjun Sensuron, a waterfall just off the highway, four km from the Rafflesia Information Centre towards KK. It is a 45 minute walk down to the falls from the highway, and near the starting point on the other side of the road is a lookout point and picnic tables. Seven km from the park towards KK is the Gunung Emas Highlands Resort. This is a popular place to stop for a meal or drink, and it also has a mini-zoo.

Places to Stay & Eat

There is no accommodation at the reserve, but *Gunung Emas Highlands Resort* (☎ 011-811562), Km 52, KK-Tambunan Rd, is perched on the side of the mountain only seven km from the information centre. The views are superb and the climate refreshingly mild, if not downright cold. This mid-range resort has a variety of accommodation. Simple but comfortable rooms in the main building annex are RM42 per double, or there are four-bed bunk rooms at RM21 per person. The VIP suite, which is popular with honeymooners, is RM210. On the other side of the highway and a steep climb up the mountain are the hilltop cabins built around tree trunks. These tree-houses are cute, but small and very rustic for RM63. It is an almost vertical walk up to the shower blocks near the cabins and down to the restaurant on the highway.

The restaurant at the resort serves good local fare. It is overrun with day-trippers on weekends, when the cars and noise from the video games destroy the tranquil atmosphere. The resort also owns the nearby *Goldenhill Motel*, which also has a restaurant and singles/doubles for RM40/70.

Getting There & Away

Take a Tambunan or Keningau minibus to the reserve or the resort for RM8. From Tambunan the cost is RM3.

TAMBUNAN

Across the Crocker Range from Penampang, Tambunan is a small agricultural service town about 81 km from KK. This was the stamping ground of Mat Salleh, who rebelled against the British late last century. His gravestone is in a run-down graveyard just off the main road, 750 metres out of town towards Ranau.

The only thing of interest in the town is the Tambunan Village Resort Centre, which is built totally out of bamboo. In the centre of town there is a tourist information office, open from 9.30 am to 4.15 pm Monday to Friday and 9.30 am to 12.45 pm on Saturday. There's also a main stage where cultural performances are held irregularly, but for the most part there is nothing happening in Tambunan.

If you have your own 4WD vehicle, or are well equipped for trekking, some interesting side trips can be done from Tambunan. **Mawar Falls** is a pretty waterfall in the Crocker Range, though it requires something of an expedition. From Tambunan head towards Ranau; 7.5 km past the turn-off to KK there is a small shop and the very difficult-to-see sign to 'Air Terjun Mawar'. Turn left and keep going past rural areas and new Murut settlements, high up into the mountains. It is beautiful countryside, though the road is long and tortuous and involves fording a small river.

Places to Stay

The *Tambunan Village Resort Centre* (☎ 087-774076; fax 087-774197) is off the road about one km away from the shopping centre towards Ranau. It has been treated to a face-lift over the last couple of years, which means it is not quite the bargain it once was. Comfortable chalets cost RM70, two-bedroom chalets are RM80. Cheaper accommodation is available at the nearby (five minutes' walk) Tandarson Park area. Basic rooms in three-bedroom chalets here cost RM30. A camping ground is also available for those with their own equipment – a spot to camp on costs RM3.50.

The other alternative is the good *Government Resthouse* (☎ 087-774339), near the mosque and 500 metres behind the shopping centre, which costs RM40 per person.

Getting There & Away

There are regular minibuses plying the roads between Tambunan and KK, Ranau, Keningau and Tenom.

MT TRUS MADI

On the other side of the highway from the Tambunan town shopping area, a road leads to Mt Trus Madi, Sabah's second-highest peak at 2649 metres. Though it is surrounded by logging concessions, there are hopeful plans afoot to turn this wild, jungle-clad mountain into a wilderness reserve. To get to the mountain, take the road towards Kaingaran, and past Kampong Batu Lapan take the road to the right which leads to a network of logging roads. With good maps or a guide, it is possible to go by 4WD up to about 1500 metres, from where it is a five to seven hour climb to the top of Trus Madi. There are a couple of trails, both mud-soaked and treacherous in parts.

Some tour operators from KK have treks to Trus Madi for those who find Mt Kinabalu a little too pedestrian. For independent trekkers, it is very wise to take a guide or at least get maps and assistance from the forestry department before setting off. You must be well equipped and take all food and water up the mountain. Contact the Forestry Department (Jabatan Perhutanan; ☎ 087-774691) at the District Office in Tambunan; they might also be able to arrange transport for the 1½ hour trip up to the trails. From Tambunan it is a 28 km walk along the pleasant valley road then up through the logging roads.

KENINGAU

The only reason to stop in Keningau is to see the large *tamu* (weekly market) that takes place on Thursdays. Otherwise, it is a mini lumber and agricultural boomtown deep in the heart of Murut country with little to recommend itself to the traveller. It is the provincial capital of the Interior Residency, though it's most unlikely you'll see anyone dressed in traditional tribal wear. Attracted by the prospects of well-paid employment, migrants have flocked here from neighbouring districts, and the town's population has more than doubled since the 1960s.

Places to Stay

In the unlikely event you are forced to overnight in Keningau, there are plenty of hotels. Prices tend to be high, however, and the cheaper places are very seedy.

Merdeka Lodging House is about the cheapest non-brothel you'll find. A windowless room with fan costs RM28, or an air-con room costs RM35. It is on the main road opposite the BP station; the entrance is around the back. If you don't mind forking out a little more for some comfort, the *Tai Wah Hotel* (☎ 087-332092), which is close to the central square where buses and taxis congregate, is a good choice. Air-con rooms range from RM40 to RM50.

About one km from the town centre towards Tambunan, next to the sports complex (which has a good swimming pool), is the *Rumah Annex Keningau*, Keningau's government resthouse. It costs RM40 per person for an excellent room, but you'll have to do some fancy talking at the District Office (☎ 087-331535) to get in. Across the road is the *Hotel Perkasa Keningau* (☎ 089-331044), the best hotel in town, where rooms start at RM110.

Getting There & Away

Share-taxis and minibuses are the only transport available and can be found around the central square by the market. The cheapest way to travel between Keningau and KK is to go by minibus for RM10. The journey takes about 2½ hours. Taxis make the same trip but charge RM20.

Keningau to Tenom costs RM5 by taxi or minibus and takes about one hour along a good bitumen road through forest and rubber plantations. There are also taxis and minibuses to Tambunan and Ranau. From Ranau you can go to either Sandakan or Kinabalu National Park.

A rugged and spectacular logging road runs from Keningau towards the coast, crossing the Crocker Range and linking up with the Papar-Beaufort road. It is only recommended for 4WD vehicles – and remember that logging trucks always have right of way.

Tamus

The local weekly markets (known as *tamus*) held at small towns all over Sabah are a colourful local attraction. Tamu days are:

Town	*Tamu Day*
Babagon	Saturday
Beaufort	Saturday
Keningau	Thursday
Kinarut	Saturday
Kiulu	Tuesday
Kota Belud	Sunday
Kota Kinabalu	Sunday
Kuala Penyu	1st Wednesday of the month
Kundasang	20th of the month
Manggis	Thursday
Matunggong	Saturday
Membakut	Sunday
Mesapol	Friday
Papar	Sunday
Penampang	Saturday
Putatan	Sunday
Ranau	1st of the month
Sikuati	Sunday
Simpangan	Thursday
Sindumin	Saturday
Sinsuran	Friday
Sipitang	Thursday
Tambunan	Thursday
Tamparuli	Wednesday
Tandek	Monday
Telipok	Thursday
Tenghilan	Thursday
Tenom	Sunday
Tinnopok	15th & 30th of the month
Toboh	Sunday
Topokon	Tuesday
Tuaran	Sunday
Weston	Friday

TENOM

Tenom is the home of the friendly Murut people, most of whom are farmers. Soya beans, maize and a variety of vegetables are grown in this fertile area, and there are several cocoa plantations.

It's a very pleasant rural town, with much more old-world charm than Beaufort, and is also the end of the railway line from Tanjung Aru (KK).

Despite the peaceful setting, there's absolutely nothing to do in the town itself – except play snooker or get assaulted by the horrendous cacophony in one of the video-game parlours, a pastime which has really taken off in a big way in Sabah.

Just outside of town, however, the Tenom Agricultural Research Station makes an interesting diversion, and the train trip to Beaufort is highly recommended.

Information

Tenom is a compact little place and it's very easy to find your way around. Minibuses tend to cruise up and down the main street, while taxis hang out in front of the Yun Lee Restaurant.

Murut Longhouses

There are some interesting longhouses around Tenom, but they can be a bit difficult to reach. The best longhouses are along the Padas River towards Sarawak, as far as Tomani and beyond.

There are buses going from Tenom to Tomani for around RM4, or you may be able to get a boat there.

Agricultural Research Station

This research station run by the Department of Agriculture is at Lagud Sebrang, about 15 km north-east of Tenom. There are ongoing research programmes into cocoa, food crops, coffee, fruit trees and apiculture (bees).

The main point of interest for the casual visitor is the Orchid Centre, which has been established over a period of years by a British man, Anthony Lamb, who has spent many years in Borneo. The Orchid Centre is open to visitors from 8 am to 1 pm, Monday to Friday.

If you want a meal while you're out there, there's a canteen opposite the sports field that sells basic rice and mee meals. The centre also has a resthouse for officials where visitors can stay, but it is three km down a track from the administration area. If you have a deeper interest and want to make a more formal visit, ring the office (☎ 087-735661) in advance.

To reach the centre, take a Lagud Sebrang minibus from beside the sports field in Tenom. They run about every hour or so throughout the morning (RM2), but things dry up in the early afternoon, so go early to avoid getting stranded out there (although it is possible to hitch). Taxis do the return trip for RM20.

Places to Stay

Look out for the *Hotel Syn Nam Tai* on the main street. It's a basic Chinese hotel and has fan rooms for RM17/22 with common bath. A little bargaining may be required. The Indian-run *Sabah Hotel* (087-735534) is definitely a step up from the Syn Nam Tai. Good, clean fan rooms cost RM22, or air-con rooms are RM37. The *Hotel Kim San* (☎ 087-735485), set back from the main road, has run-down air-con rooms for RM28 a double.

For something slightly more upmarket, the *Hotel Sri Jaya* (☎ 087-735669, on the main street, is a newer hotel and the best mid-range place. Singles/doubles with air-con, TV and attached bath cost from RM35.

At the top of the scale is the *Hotel Perkasa Tenom* (☎ 087-735811), situated high on a hill overlooking the town and the surrounding district. With 70-odd fully air-con rooms it seems totally over the top for sleepy Tenom, and in fact it has very low occupancy rates. Rooms cost from RM80 though discounts may be available. If you want to check in or you have a reservation, ring from the town and someone will come down to collect you; otherwise take a taxi for RM2.

Places to Eat

As usual there are plenty of Chinese kedai kopis all over town selling basic Chinese food. The *Yun Lee Restaurant* on the main street is popular with the locals, but it closes very early in the evening. One place that is

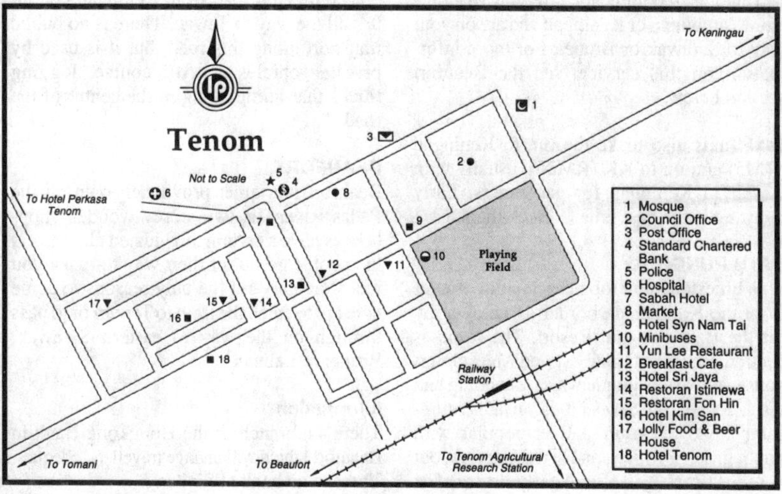

open in the evening is the *Restoran Fon Hin*, not far from the Hotel Kim San.

For good Indian food, rotis and murtabak, try the *Bismillah Restaurant* in the Sabah Hotel, or the *Restoran Istimewa*, which sets up tables outside in the evenings. The more upmarket *Jolly Food & Beer House* also offers al fresco dining in the evenings, or you can try the air-con bar section inside. The *Hotel Perkasa Tenom* has a *malam kampung* (village night) on Saturday nights until midnight on the lawns overlooking the town and surrounding areas. Hawker-style stalls sell local favourites at moderate prices, and the setting is the best in town.

Getting There & Away

Bus There are dozens of minibuses which cruise up and down the main street trying to drum up business. Most are going to Keningau (RM5), but some also go to KK. There are also a few minibuses which head south to Tomani (RM4).

Train Although the railway line goes as far as Melalap, which is further up the valley, Tenom is the railhead as far as passenger trains are concerned. The 46 km journey to Beaufort is the most spectacular part of the trip and is recommended if you've come from Tambunan or Keningau and are on your way to Sarawak or Brunei. For more information on this service, see the Beaufort section below.

Taxi Taxis also make the run to Keningau (RM5) and on to KK (RM25), usually with a wait in Keningau for passengers. Early morning is the best time to catch them.

BATU PUNGGUL

This limestone outcrop near Sapulut, not far from the Kalimantan border, is noteworthy for the Batu Punggul Resort. The resort is centred on a traditionally styled Murut longhouse, and offers jungle walks, canoeing and visits to nearby caves. It is an adventure-camp style of resort and is popular with youth groups, which can fill the place up, but at other times it is often nearly empty. The journey there involves travel by boat along the Sapulut River, and the area is home to many Murut longhouses.

Places to Stay & Eat

Accommodation at the resort can be booked through the Rural Development Corporation (☎ 088-426051), Km 9, Tuaran Rd, Kota Kinabalu. A dorm bed on the longhouse floor costs RM6, and four-bed rooms cost RM32. There is also a resthouse with a four bed 'master bedroom' (with attached bathroom) for RM150, and basic doubles for RM30. Camping costs RM2 per day, and tents start at RM6 for a two person tent. Meals and provisions are available at the canteen, and kitchen facilities can be hired.

Getting There & Away

Getting to the resort by yourself is very expensive, and it is best to arrange accommodation and bookings through the Rural Development Corporation. Guests at the resort normally go by road from Keningau to Sapulut and then take a longboat up the river to the resort. Minibuses go from Keningau to Sapulut in the morning. A boat from Sapulut to Batu Punggul and back costs RM250 and can take up to six people.

The logging road from Keningau continues all the way to Tawau. There is no public transport along this road, but it is used by private vehicles and, of course, logging trucks that hurtle along in the centre of the road.

BEAUFORT

Beaufort is a quiet provincial town on the Padas River. Its two storey wooden shophouses have a certain dilapidated charm, and the people go out of their way to make you feel welcome, but the only reasons to come here are to catch the train to Tenom or to pass through on the way to eastern Sarawak, Brunei or Labuan.

Information

There's a branch of the Hongkong Bank in Beaufort which will change travellers' cheques. There is no bank at Sipitang.

Places to Stay

If you miss the train to Tenom, you will have to spend a night in Beaufort. If you are heading to Sarawak, you are better off continuing to Lawas, which has cheaper accommodation.

The three hotels in town are of the same standard and have air-con rooms with TV and attached bathrooms. They show a surprising lack of competitive spirit and all charge RM30/36 for singles/doubles. The *Hotel Beaufort* (☎ 087-211911) and the *Beaufort Inn* (☎ 097-211232), 100 metres east, are near each other in town, while the *Mandarin Inn* (☎ 087-212800) is over the bridge across the river. The Hotel Beaufort wins by a nose for position.

Places to Eat

Beaufort has numerous coffee shops offering the standard rice and mee dishes. The *Restoran Kim Wah*, underneath the Hotel Beaufort, does good Chinese food and has an air-conditioned section around the corner from the coffee shop. *Kedai Kopi Taman* serves both Chinese and good Malay food. The *Kedai Teck Loong* near the Beaufort Inn has a wide range of fruit juices. For cakes, buns and other pastries the *Beaufort Baker* has a good selection.

Getting There & Away

Bus The minibuses gather near the Hotel Beaufort, but there's absolutely no way you'll miss them as they cruise around town honking hopefully at pedestrians. There are frequent departures for Kota Kinabalu (two hours, RM5), and less frequent departures for Sipitang (1½ hours, RM5).

To Menumbok (for Labuan) there are plenty of minibuses until early afternoon. The trip, along a reasonable gravel road, takes one hour at a cost of RM9. The express bus for Lawas passes through Beaufort from KK at around 9.30 am.

Train Sabah is the only place in East Malaysia where you will find a railway, and even here there's only one line. The 154 km track

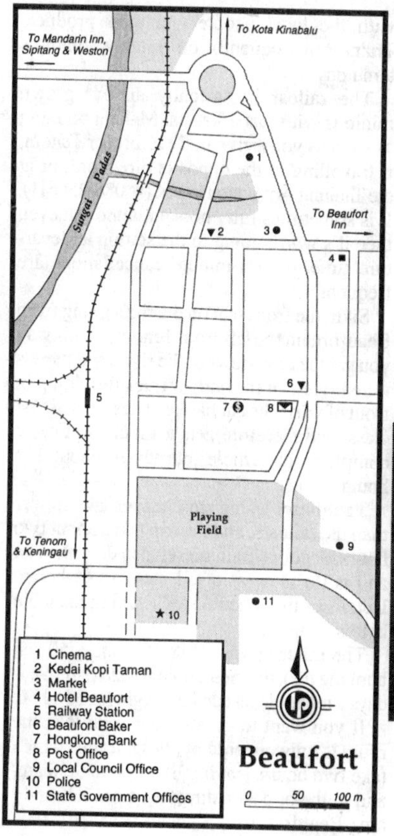

connects Tenom to KK (Tanjung Aru) via Beaufort.

It's a spectacular trip between Beaufort and Tenom, where the train follows the Padas River through steamy jungle. At times the dense jungle forms a bridge over the narrow track. The trip from Beaufort to KK is not so exciting and takes too long to be convenient or worthwhile.

There are two types of passenger trains available. The railcars are the best for comfort, speed and views, and the ordinary diesel trains are the ones to take if you want a slower, more colourful journey, packed in with the local people and their produce. Trains run frequently on Sunday, Tenom's tamu day.

The railcar is basically an overgrown minibus with just 13 seats. Make a booking as soon as you arrive in Beaufort (or Tenom, if travelling in the opposite direction), or at the Tanjung Aru station in KK (☎ 088-254611). It is sometimes fully booked, although even then it's worth going to the station at departure time, as last-minute cancellations are frequent

Sit in the front seat on the right going from Beaufort, on the left from Tenom, as this way you get the best views of the river, and there's a clear view of the narrow track unfolding in front of you. The car has been designated '1st class' and therefore gets a 1st class price; it completes the whole journey in about 1½ hours.

The diesel trains are cheaper and slower than the railcars, and the trip takes about two hours. A goods train diesel also does the run and is the slowest of all, taking 2¾ hours. Details of the schedule are listed in the table below.

The railcar costs RM8.35 (plus a 50 sen booking fee), the diesel train RM2.75; on Sundays a return ticket can be bought for RM4.50.

If you want to go all the way to KK, the route is only covered by diesel trains, which take five hours, leaving Beaufort at 9.50 am, and in the opposite direction from KK at 11 am. Beaufort to KK costs RM4.80. The goods train leaves Tanjung Aru at 8 am, arriving in Beaufort at 11.15 am and Tenom at 2.44 pm. In the other direction it leaves Tenom at 8 am, arrives in Beaufort at 10.45 am and KK at 2.37 pm.

PAPAR

Situated 38 km south of KK, this is a coastal Kadazan town where coconut wine is made. There's a beach at Papar, outside of town, and the Papar River where you can take a boat ride. It's worth going on a Sunday so you can experience the weekly tamu. To get there, take a minibus for RM2.50 from the area near the market in KK.

KUALA PENYUH

Kuala Penyuh is at the northern end of a flat swampy peninsula dotted with water buffalo. This is the place to get to Pulau Tiga State Park. The town itself is unremarkable, but there are some very good beaches nearby, the best being around the headland from the estuary, eight km from town. The beach has picnic tables and toilets, but no other facilities.

Places to Stay

Beachcombers Resort (☎ 011-888326) is a new downmarket resort on the beach. It caters mostly for KK weekenders with two-day packages for RM150, including all meals. It also offers horse riding (RM10 per hour) and tours to Pulau Tiga (RM50 for a minimum of five people). Contact Popeye Tours & Travel (☎ 088-218669), 2nd floor, Lot 2, Block N, Sinsuran Kompleks, in KK.

Getting There & Away

Take a minibus from near the market in KK for RM10. From Menumbok a minibus costs

Train Schedule

Beaufort-Tenom		
	Mon-Sat	8.25 (R), 10.50 am (D), noon (G), 1.55 (D), 3.50 pm (R)
	Sun	6.45 (D), 10.50 am (D), 2.30 (D), 4.05 pm (R)
Tenom-Beaufort		
	Mon-Sat	6.40 (R), 7.30 (D), 8 am (G), 1.40 (D), 4 pm (R)
	Sun	7.20 (R), 7.55 am (D), 12.10 (D), 3.05 pm (D)

R = Railcar, D= Diesel, G = Goods Train

EAST MALAYSIA

RM10. From Beaufort take a Menumbok minibus and get off at the junction to Kuala Penyuh, where minibuses or taxis are usually waiting. It is a long, dusty road from Beaufort. The quickest way from KK is via the turn-off just before Membakut on the main highway. The road ends at the river on the other side of the town – a car ferry shuttles across from 6 am to 6 pm.

PULAU TIGA STATE PARK

Off coastal Kuala Penyuh is the Pulau Tiga State Park, with an area of nearly 15,864 hectares. There is still volcanic activity in the form of bubbling mud and methane gas. There are trails across the island for walking, and good snorkelling around the island. The walks provide an opportunity to see macaque monkeys and native birdlife.

Accommodation is available through the Sabah Parks office in KK. Beds in basic four-bed dorms cost RM10, while more comfortable doubles (there are only two) cost RM60. The islands are expensive to get to – boats cost around RM120 from Kuala Penyuh, or try Beachcombers Resort in Kuala Penyuh.

SIPITANG

Sipitang is the closest Sabah town to the Sabah/Sarawak border. Located on a wide, shallow bay, it is pleasant enough, though the only reason to stop here is to get bus connections. If you are heading to Lawas for boat connections to Brunei or Limbang, spend the night in Lawas or you'll miss the early-morning departures.

Places to Stay & Eat

Sipitang has a few reasonable hotels to choose from if you have to stay the night. The *Hotel Asinol* is the cheapest in town. Small singles with fan cost RM20, doubles RM25 and air-con rooms RM35. The *Hotel Lian Hin* has air-con singles/doubles with attached bath for RM30/35. Top of the range, but only just, are the *Shangson Hotel* (☎ 087-821809) and the *Motel Ho Hin Chan* (☎ 087-821716), a little further out of town. Both have air-con rooms with attached bath and TV for RM35/40.

Sipitang has a number of coffee shops, and food stalls on the main street. *Restoran Anda* has basic Malay fare, and at the back of the restaurant you can sit over the ocean and enjoy the sea breezes.

Getting There & Away

Minibuses ply between Beaufort and Sipitang throughout the day and cost RM5, and buses go to Merapok for RM3. From Beaufort there are buses, taxis and trains to KK or Tenom. The 47 km road to Beaufort is a dusty bone-cruncher. In contrast, the good road south to Merapok and Lawas is paved and very scenic in parts as it runs parallel to jungle-clad mountains.

The boat to Labuan leaves at 7.30 am for the one hour trip and costs RM20.

PULAU LABUAN

Off the coast from Menumbok, Labuan is a Federal Territory governed directly from Kuala Lumpur. As a duty-free centre, it attracts alcohol-starved hordes from nearby Brunei, but its tax-free status is mainly to attract offshore banking. Labuan also has major petroleum gas installations.

Bandar Labuan is the main town and the place where the ferries tie in. The main attraction is the duty-free shopping, which amounts to booze and cigarettes. There's nothing else to do. Given that there is not even anywhere pleasant to enjoy your cheap drinks, the sensible thing to do is to avoid Labuan altogether or spend as little time there as possible.

Information

Labuan has a small tourist information office (☎ 087-423445) on the corner of Jalan Dewan and Jalan Berjaya, just up from the post office.

There are numerous banks around town – the Hongkong Bank is the best for changing travellers' cheques. Moneychangers around town will change cash and travellers' cheques at good rates; try Syarikat K Abdul Kader at 90 Jalan OKK Awang Besar.

Syarikat Aifas is a book and gift store in the lobby of the Hotel Labuan with a reasonable selection of books on Borneo and general books in English.

Borneo Divers (☎ 087-415867) has an office at the Waterfront Financial Hotel. They have dives to some shipwrecks to the south-west of Labuan for US$40 for one dive or US$70 for two. See the section on wreck diving below for more information.

Things to See & Do

In the town itself, Bandar Labuan has an active **market**, and water-taxis carry passengers to the **stilt villages**, Kampong Patau-Patau Satu and Kampong Patau-Patau Dua, built on the water around the bay. A 15 minute walk from the ferry jetty is the mosque, **Masjid Negeri**, an impressive piece of Star Wars-meets-Arabia architecture.

Labuan is where the Japanese forces in North Borneo surrendered at the end of WWII. The **Labuan War Cemetery** has row upon row of headstones dedicated to the Commonwealth servicemen, mostly Australian and British, who lost their lives in Borneo. The cemetery is near the golf course, two km east of town along Jalan Tanjung

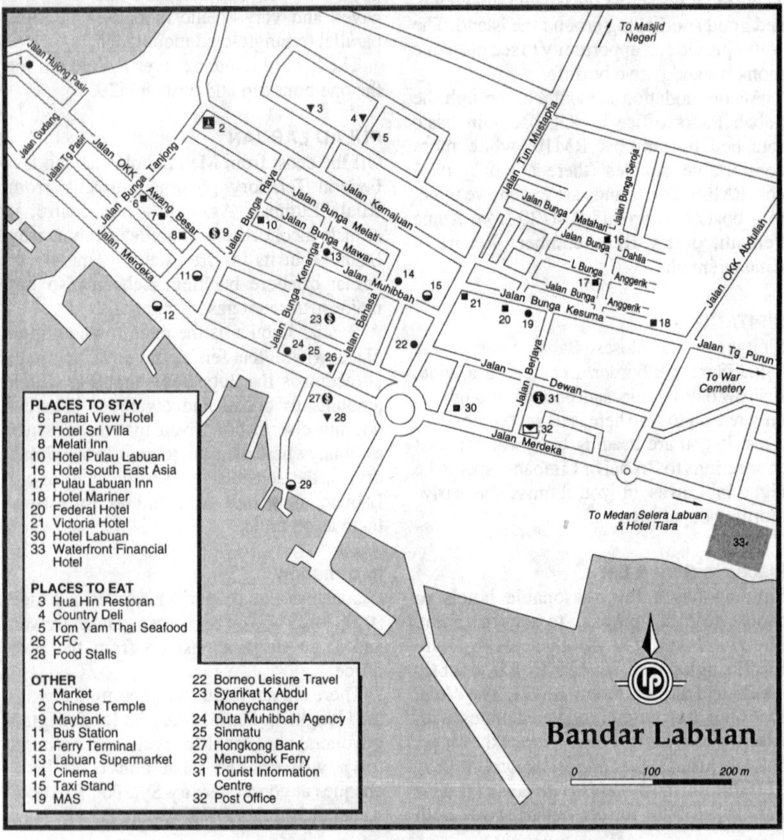

PETER TURNER

SIMON ROWE

SIMON ROWE

PETER TURNER

PETER TURNER

Mt Kinabalu, Sabah

Top: The jagged granite peaks of Mt Kinabalu
Left: Low's Peak
Right Top: A mountain guide
Right Middle: Sunrise
Right Bottom: The summit

ALL PHOTOS BY GLENN BEANLAND

Sabah

Top: Children on the roof of a fishing boat
Middle: Fishing boats at the port town of Kudat
Bottom: The landing field at Kudat

Purun. **Peace Park** on the west of the island at Layang Layangan commemorates the place of surrender and has a Japanese war memorial. It was also in Labuan that the Japanese officers responsible for the 'death marches' from Sandakan were tried by an Australian War Crimes Court.

Labuan has some good **beaches** along the west coast, at Pohon Batu and south from Layang Layangan, but swimming can be perilous because of stingrays and box jellyfish. **The Chimney**, the remains of an old factory on the north of the island, is cited as a tourist attraction – it's not, but there are good views along the coast from here.

Pulau Keraman, Pulau Rusukan Kecil and Pulau Rusukan Besar are uninhabited **islands** lying just to the south-west of Labuan and are to be gazetted as a marine park. The beaches are pristine, but dynamite fishing has destroyed much of the coral reefs. Pulau Papan is just five km from Bandar Labuan. It is being developed as an agricultural park and day-trip destination. Chalets and a regular boat service are planned.

Wreck Diving

Unless you live in Brunei and are in need of a good stiff drink, the only compelling reason to go to Labuan is to enjoy some of the best commercial wreck diving in Asia. Four wrecks have been discovered off Labuan. Two were sunk during WWII, and two sank in the 1980s.

The wrecks are known by local names. The 'American Wreck' is the USS *Salute*, a minesweeper built in late 1943 and sunk (by a mine) less than two years later in 1945. The 'Australian Wreck', on the other hand, is not Australian at all. Its identity is still uncertain, but it was built in Rotterdam in 1900 and captured by the Japanese in 1942. It was sunk by the Royal Australian Air Force (hence the name) in 1945. The 'Cement Wreck' is the MV *Tung Huang*, which hit a sandbank while carrying cement for the construction of the sultan of Brunei's new palace in September 1980. The 'Blue Water Wreck' is the Philippine MV *Mabini Padre*, a fishing trawler that sank in November 1981.

Of all the wrecks, the Cement Wreck is the easiest to dive and is suitable for wreck-dive training. The American Wreck and the Blue Water Wreck are only for experienced wreck divers. Dives are organised by Borneo Divers – see the Information entry above for local details or the Kota Kinabalu section for details of the company's head office.

Places to Stay – bottom end

Budget accommodation in Bandar Labuan is very limited. On weekdays there is some latitude for bargaining, but on weekends and public holidays you'll probably have to take whatever is going.

The *Pantai View Hotel* (☎ 087-411339) on Jalan Bunga Tanjong is a decent hotel with large fan rooms on the top floor that are the best value around at RM25 – you will be very lucky to get one of these, however. Most rooms are air-con with attached bath and TV and cost from RM40 to RM50.

Around the corner on Jalan OKK Awang Besar, *Hotel Sri Villa* (☎ 087-416369) has large fan rooms for RM38, or you might be able to get a smaller room for RM33. Air-con rooms range from RM42 without bath to RM58 with attached bath and TV. The nearby *Melati Inn* (☎ 087-416307) has small air-con rooms with common bathroom for RM35, but most rooms have attached bathroom and cost from RM45 to RM50.

Places to Stay – middle

The *Hotel South East Asia* (☎ 087-415140) on Jalan Bunga Seroja has rooms with air-con for RM41 or more expensive rooms ranging up to RM58.

The other mid-range hotels are a noticeable jump up in quality and price. The *Victoria Hotel* (☎ 087-412411) on Jalan Tun Mustapha charges RM69/92 for singles/doubles or RM76/98 for larger rooms with minibars. Close by on Jalan Bunga Kesuma, the *Federal Hotel* (☎ 087-411711) is slightly cheaper with singles for RM66 and doubles at RM88. The *Hotel Pulau Labuan* (☎ 087-416288) on Jalan Bunga Raya is better, with rooms for RM79/95 after discount. They also run the smaller, new *Pulau Labuan Inn*

(☎ 087-411750), which has very good rooms for RM68/78, making it a good alternative to the more expensive hotels.

Places to Stay – top end

Most of these hotels add a 10% service charge, but in tax-free Labuan hotels do not charge the usual 5% government tax.

The *Hotel Labuan* (☎ 087-412502) has a central location and costs RM130 for superior rooms and RM150 for deluxe rooms. The *Hotel Mariner* (☎ 087-418822) on Jalan Bunga Kesuma is smaller and, unless a promotional discount applies, very bad value at RM148 for a single and RM192 for a double. At the time of writing, 40% discounts were being offered.

The *Waterfront Financial Hotel* (☎ 087-418111) is the best in town and popular with businesspeople. Rates range from RM330 to RM530. The *Hotel Tiara* (☎ 087-414300) is out on Jalan Tanjung Batu, towards the Labuan War Cemetery. It has large suites from RM260, but discounts are often available.

Places to Eat

Food stalls can be found on Jalan Muhibbah between the Labuan Supermarket and the cinema, and a small food centre is behind the Hongkong Bank. The area north of the Hotel Pulau Labuan is a good area for restaurants. Look out for the *Tom Yam Thai Seafood* restaurant and the *Country Deli*. There is also an expensive Korean restaurant in this area.

Bandar Labuan has plenty of Chinese coffee shops. A cut above the rest is the *Hua Hin*, which sets up tables on the pavement in the evenings and will serve you whatever you want at reasonable prices. They also have more expensive fresh seafood. Waitresses representing the breweries compete with each other to fill up your glass with their brand of beer, which costs RM3 for a big bottle. The *Wong Kee* next to the Hotel South East Asia is another good open-air Chinese restaurant.

The *Sri Villa*, underneath the hotel of the same name, is a good Indian restaurant with cheap fare and roti canai for breakfast.

Opposite the Hotel Tiara, the more upmarket *Labuan Beach Restaurant* is right on the beach and you can dine outside on the veranda. It has a variety of dishes, including seafood and western food.

Things to Buy

Despite its much-touted duty-free status, Labuan doesn't have a lot to offer shoppers. Most of the duty-free shops around town sell alcohol and cigarettes but not much else. Cans of beer cost as little as RM1.20, and if you intend visiting an Iban longhouse in Sarawak, you will make a hit with a bottle of whisky – Johnny Walker Red RM30; Glenfiddich RM46. Monegain Duty Free, near the Duta Muhibbah office, has the best selection and good prices.

A few shops sell electronic goods, but the selection is limited and not particularly cheap. A couple of more upmarket duty-free shops, such as the one at the ferry terminal, sell perfume, leather goods and watches. For everyday shopping the best place to go is the large Labuan Supermarket on Jalan Bunga Kenanga, which has a department store upstairs.

Getting There & Away

Air Labuan is well served on the Malaysia Airlines domestic network. There are regular flights to Kota Kinabalu (six daily, RM52), Kuala Lumpur (daily, RM372), Kuching (daily, RM199) and Miri (twice daily, RM66). A taxi to the airport should not cost more than RM5 from Bandar Labuan.

There are also weekly Twin Otter flights between Labuan and Lawas (RM31) and Limbang (RM30).

Boat – Brunei Boats to Bandar Seri Begawan in Brunei depart at 8 am, noon and either 2 or 3 pm. Tickets can be bought at the small kiosk outside the ferry terminal building before departure, but it is best to book in advance, especially on weekends. The main agent is the Duta Muhibbah Agency (☎ 087-413827), 52 Jalan Merdeka, which sells tickets for the 8 am boats – the *Duta Muhibbah* (RM24 or RM32 1st class) and the *Rajawali* (RM22, RM28 1st class) – as well as the *Ratu*

Samudra (RM24, RM32 1st class), which departs in the afternoon. Borneo Leisure Travel is the agent for the *Ratu Samudra* and the *Mutiara Laut* (RM24). These more modern ships alternate and leave at either 2 or 3 pm. The older *Sri Labuan Tiga* (RM22) leaves at noon and can be booked at Sinmatu (☎ 087-412261) on Jalan Merdeka.

You should arrive at the wharf at least half an hour before departure. The journey takes 1½ to two hours.

Boat – Sabah Boats leave from Bandar Labuan to Menumbok, Sipitang and Kota Kinabalu.

The cheapest option is the slow car ferry to Menumbok, which leaves at 8 am and 1 pm, costs RM5 for passengers and takes around 1½ hours. Tickets and departures are from the wharf behind the Hongkong Bank. The alternative is the frequent small launches which shuttle back and forth between Bandar Labuan and Menumbok, which is really nothing more than a jetty, a restaurant and a few houses. The crossing takes about 30 minutes and costs RM10. Boats leave when full (you shouldn't have to wait more than half an hour) from the main ferry terminal between 7.30 am and 5 pm. From Menumbok there are frequent minibuses to Beaufort (one hour, RM9) and Kota Kinabalu (two hours, RM15).

The small launches also connect Labuan and Sipitang. They operate from 10 am to noon and go when full (about one hour, RM20).

Three launches also connect Labuan and Kota Kinabalu. Tickets can be bought just before departure, or you can book in advance. The *Duta Muhibbah Dua* (RM28, RM33 1st class) leaves Labuan at 8.30 am, and the *Labuan Express Dua* (RM28) departs at 1 pm. These boats can be booked through Sinmatu. *Express Kinabalu* leaves Labuan at 3 pm and can be booked at the Duta Muhibbah Agency. The fare is RM28.

Boat – Sarawak Two boats per day go to Limbang at 12.30 pm and cost RM20. One boat per day goes to Lawas at 1 pm and also costs RM20. Buy your ticket at the ferry terminal on the morning of departure.

Getting Around

Labuan has a good minibus network. Buses go regularly and fares range from 50 sen for a short trip to RM2 for a bus to the top of the island. The destinations are displayed on the side of the buses.

Taxis are mostly private cars and leave from the stand in front of the cinema. The standard fare for a journey of up to a few km is RM5, but you shouldn't have to pay more than RM15 for a taxi from one end of the island to the other. A taxi to the airport should not cost more than RM5.

North of Kota Kinabalu

TUARAN

Tuaran, 33 km from KK, is a bustling little town with tree-lined streets. Tamu day is Sunday (if you aren't tamued out after Kota Belud), and the town has a few points of interest nearby.

As you come from KK, **Telipok** is 10 km before Tuaran. Much of the pottery you see in the souvenir shops in KK comes from here. Sinar Pottery, at the Km 12 mark, and Grace Dynamic, at Km 11, both have big shops selling all manner of pots. Soon Yi Song, at Km 8, fires pots in traditional kilns.

Two km before Tuaran is the turn-off to **Mengkabong Water Village**. In this Bajau village, on an estuary near the sea, canoes and sampans are the main form of transport to the houses built on stilts over the water. Once a very picturesque spot, it has been modernised in recent years and is now of little interest.

Mimpian Jadi Resort, nine km from Tuaran, is a popular day trip for KK residents on weekends and holidays. The resort and the wide, white-sand beach are pleasant enough, but it is not worth a special trip. Entry is RM3 if you enter the beach by the resort.

Places to Stay

Mimpian Jadi Resort (☎ 011-812634) is Taiwanese owned and pitched mostly at Taiwanese tour groups. It's overpriced, with semi-detached cabins from RM260, and simple rooms with common facilities an astonishing RM110.

Also nearby is the new *Sabandar Bay Resort* (☎ 088-251622), a sprawling place with a swimming pool, water slides, a conference centre and disco. Rooms start at RM160, semi-detached chalets cost RM300 and detached chalets RM400.

Tuaran is best done as a day trip, but the town has a *Government Rest House* (☎ 088-788363) and also the *Orchard Motel* (☎ 088-787445), which has expensive fan rooms for RM30 and air-con rooms for RM50.

Getting There & Away

Minibuses go regularly from Kota Kinabalu to Tuaran for RM2. Minibuses to Mengkabong are less frequent and cost 60 sen. Regular minibuses go from Tuaran to Kota Belud.

Minibuses go to the villages near the resort and will continue on for RM3.60, but they are not very frequent. Hitching is a good bet on weekends.

KOTA BELUD

Kota Belud is the venue of one of Sabah's largest tamus, which takes place every Sunday – get there as early as possible.

Tamus are not simply open-air markets where village people gather to sell their farm products of fruit and vegetables and to buy manufactured goods from the Chinese and Indian traders; they are also social occasions when news and stories are exchanged.

The weekly tamu at Kota Belud attracts all manner of traders, from quasi-medical commercial travellers selling herbal remedies and magic pills to water-buffalo owners who haggle all morning over the price of a cow or a calf. The Bajau also sell their horses, but they don't put on their traditional dress, unless perhaps a tour bus is in town.

Unfortunately, those looking for tribal handicrafts will be disappointed. You may have more luck in that department at the Sunday tamu at Sikuati, 23 km from Kudat, which is attended by the Rungus people who live in longhouses in the surrounding area.

Kota Belud itself is just a small, sleepy rural town. The biggest building is the new *pasar besar*, the meat and vegetable market. Everything closes down early and the only nightlife is enjoyed by the cows, horses and dogs that roam the streets foraging through the garbage.

About 20 km out of Kota Belud on the way to Kudat is a marsh and coastal scrub area that is home to dozens of bird species and is a favourite spot for bird-watchers.

Places to Stay

Most people visit Kota Belud as a day trip from KK. The only hotel in town is the *Hotel Kota Belud* (☎ 088-976576), above a pool hall. Clean air-con singles/doubles cost RM32/38 with common bathroom, but it's no bargain.

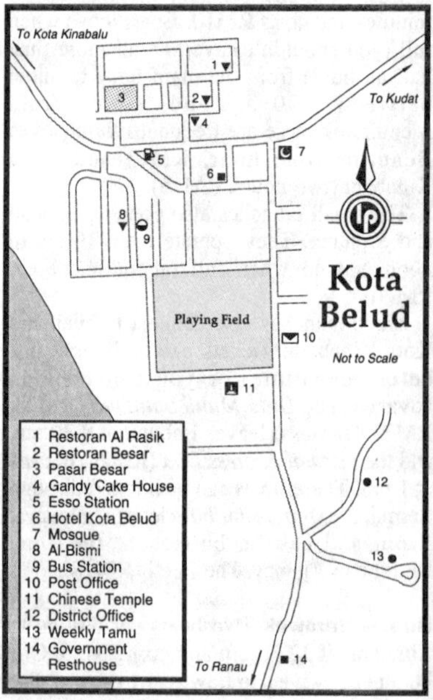

Places to Eat
Kota Belud is not a gastronome's delight, but the Sunday market has plenty of tasty snacks. Fortunately the town has some good Indian restaurants, such as *Restoran Al-Ameen* and the *Al-Bismi* opposite the bus station. *Restoran Al Rasik* has standard Malay fare at cheap prices. Kota Belud has a few Chinese coffee shops but they tend to close very early in the evening. *Gandy Cake House* is a good bakery for cakes and pastries.

Getting There & Away
The main area for minibuses and share-taxis is at the bus station in front of the old market. Most of these serve the Kota Belud-Kota Kinabalu route, which costs RM10 and takes about two hours. The road is sealed all the way. On Sunday, tamu day, the number of minibuses and taxis has to be seen to be believed. On other days it's much quieter.

Minibuses to Kudat cost RM5 and take about two hours.

To get to Kinabalu National Park, take any of the minibuses or share-taxis which are going to Kota Kinabalu and get off at Tamparuli, about halfway there. The trip takes about half an hour and costs RM4. From Tamparuli there are several minibuses and taxis to Ranau every day up to about 2 pm. The taxis cost RM12 and the minibuses RM6. The journey to the national park HQ takes about an hour along a good sealed road. Tell the driver to drop you off there. The direct road from Kota Belud to Ranau is very rough and not used by minibuses.

KUDAT
Kudat is a fairly large but sleepy port town in the very north of Sabah, 238 km from Kota Kinabalu. Kudat has a noticeable Filipino influence, as much of the trade here is with the Philippines, and the Kudat area is also the home of the Rungus people, tribal cousins of the Kadazans.

Kudat itself has little of interest and few travellers make it this far north. The area around Kudat has fine beaches and Rungus longhouses, though it is difficult to get around without your own transport.

Places to Stay
The best buy is the *Restoran dan Hotel Islamik*. Large, clean rooms with fan cost RM15/20 for singles/doubles. The management is friendly, and the restaurant downstairs does decent roti and murtabak. It is on the edge of the central shopping area – a block further away from the bus station than the Hotel Sunrise.

All the other hotels are mid-range air-con places. The *Hotel Sunrise* (☎ 088-613517) is of a good standard and has a few rooms for RM30 without bath, but most have bath and TV and cost from RM40 upwards. The *Hotel Kinabalu* (☎ 088-613888), in the new section of town near the golf course and the *pasar besar* (big market), is a good option. Singles/doubles with air-con, TV and attached bath cost RM36/48, though some of the singles are windowless. *Hotel Greenland* (☎ 088-613211), in the same street, is similar but not as good value. Rooms without bath cost RM35, but most with attached bath cost RM49/56.

Getting There & Away
Air There are MAS Twin Otter flights from Kudat to Sandakan (six weekly, RM54) and Kota Kinabalu (twice weekly, RM50).

Bus Several minibuses a day make the three to four hour trip from Kota Kinabalu for RM12.

AROUND KUDAT
You'll find some of the best beaches in Sabah around Kudat. **Bak Bak** is the town beach, about 11 km from Kudat. It has beautiful clear water, picnic and toilet facilities and food stalls on weekends, though the beach itself is only a narrow strip of sand against a retaining wall. The fishing villages further north of Bak Bak have some superb white-sand beaches with crystal-clear water, but there is no accommodation.

More and more Rungus people are building their own houses in preference to living in traditional longhouses, but there are still some interesting longhouses around Kudat. If you visit one, it's polite to take a few small gifts of food or cigarettes. The best known of these longhouses is **Matunggung**, on the highway south of Kudat, as it is visited by tour groups, but other longhouses can be found further inland from the highway. Matunggung is a traditional thatched-roof longhouse with enclosed bamboo-slatted sides. Within the longhouse, each family's living quarters, called a *valai*, is composed of sleeping, dining and living areas and an attic.

The traditional dress for Rungus women is black sarungs and colourful, beaded necklaces. On festive occasions, heavy brass bracelets are worn as well. The Rungus tribes produce some excellent, elaborate beadwork and you can sometimes buy their handicrafts at the Sunday tamu held at **Sikuati**, a town 23 km from Kudat. Sikuati is on the highway, a km from the coast where there is an excellent beach. Sikuati Bay has a long, sweeping white-sand beach, though the water can be choppy and it is not as clear as that around Bak Bak.

Getting There & Away

Bak Bak is difficult to get to without your own transport – count on RM6 for a taxi out there, RM12 to be picked up. Sikuati and Matunggung are both on the highway and the minibuses will drop you off there.

MT KINABALU

Towering 4101 metres above the lush tropical jungles of North Borneo, and the centrepiece of the vast 750 sq km Kinabalu National Park, Mt Kinabalu is the major attraction in Sabah. It is the highest mountain between the snow-capped peaks of the Himalayas and those of New Guinea. Although 50 km inland, its jagged granite peaks are visible most mornings from many places along the coast.

Despite its height, it is one of the easiest mountains in the world to climb, and thousands of people of all age groups and fitness levels climb the mountain every year. No special skills or equipment are required. All you need is a little stamina, and gear to protect you from the elements – it can get very cold and wet up there.

However, the walk is no Sunday picnic stroll. Not everyone is willing or able to tackle the relentless climb to the top, but those who persevere will be rewarded with a memorable experience. The views – even before you get to the top – are magnificent and the sunsets equally incredible. Where else could you see the rays of the setting sun shining *up* through the clouds below you?

While the climb is the main reason most visitors come to the park, the park itself is a beautiful spot, and some visitors come just to savour the hill-station atmosphere. There are interesting walks at the base of the mountain, the climate is agreeably cool, even cold at night, and the accommodation is excellent.

History

The first recorded ascent of the mountain was made in 1851 by Sir Hugh Low, the British colonial secretary on the island of Labuan. The highest peak is named after him, as is the mile-deep 'gully' on the other side of the mountain.

In those days the difficulty of climbing Mt Kinabalu lay not in the ascent itself, but in getting to the base of it through the trackless jungles and finding local porters willing to go there. None of the Dusun (now called Kadazan) tribespeople who accompanied Low had ever climbed the mountain before, believing it to be the dwelling place of the spirits of their dead.

Low was therefore obliged to take along with him a guide armed with a large basket of quartz crystals and teeth to protect the party. The ceremonies performed by the guides to appease the spirits on reaching the summit became more elaborate as time went on, so that by the 1920s they had come to include the sacrifice of seven eggs and seven white chickens, loud prayers and gunshots. In recent times, however, the custom appears to have died out.

These days you won't have to hack through the jungle for several days to get to the foot of the mountain, like the early explorers did, as there's a sealed road all the way from Kota Kinabalu to the park HQ.

The Legend of Mt Kinabalu

There's a colourful local Kadazan legend as to how Mt Kinabalu got its name. Many years ago, it is said, the emperor of China heard that on this mountain there was a fabulous pearl, guarded by a dragon. He told his three sons that whichever one of them could bring him the pearl would be the next emperor.

Two sons tried and failed; the third son managed to snatch the pearl, but just as he was sneaking away the dragon woke and gave chase. The prince managed to hide in the jungle, with the pearl, while the rest of his party went on, with the dragon in hot pursuit. They jumped back into their boat and hightailed it for China. The dragon still followed, so they fired their cannons at it, and it eventually drowned, having swallowed numerous cannonballs, thinking that they were the pearl.

Meanwhile, back in the jungle, the prince took a local wife and raised a family, but after some years decided that it was time to return to China and claim the throne. He promised his wife that he would come back to fetch her, but of course he never showed up. In despair she climbed to the top of the mountain to pray for his return, and died in the process. Hence *Kina*, meaning China, and *balu*, widow. ■

Geology

From its immense size you might imagine that Mt Kinabalu is the ancient core of the island of Borneo, but in fact the mountain is a relatively recent arrival. Its origins go back a mere nine million years to when a solidified core of volcanic rock began swelling up from the depths below, pushing its way through the overlying rock. This upward movement is apparently still going on, and a team of Japanese geologists has estimated that the mountain continues to grow at the rate of about five mm per year.

On account of its youth, very little erosion has occurred on the exposed granite rockfaces around the summit, though the effects of glaciers which used to cover much of Kinabalu can be picked out by the trained eye. The glaciers have disappeared but, at times, ice forms in the rockpools near the summit – it gets pretty cold up there at night, so you need warm clothing to make the final ascent.

Flora

Exhilarating though it undoubtedly is, merely being able to climb to the top of this mountain isn't the only experience that awaits you. Mt Kinabalu is a botanical paradise stocked with a phenomenal number of different plants, many of which are unique to the area.

Some of the more spectacular flowers belonging to the orchid family are found there – almost 1000 species have been discovered so far, with many more blooming unnamed among still-unexplored gullies and ridges. There are many unusual rhododendrons and the giant red blossoms of the rafflesia, which, at more than 70 cm in diameter, is the largest flower in the world.

Even if you don't manage to catch sight of a rafflesia you will certainly see one or more of the many types of insectivorous pitcher plants which grow in profusion there. You may well come across them elsewhere in Borneo – particularly in Gunung Mulu National Park, Sarawak – but there's nowhere else they grow in such numbers.

They come in all manner of elaborate shapes, sizes and colours, although you probably won't be as lucky as the 19th century botanist, Spencer St John, who found one that was 30 cm in diameter. He reported finding a *Nepenthes rajah* pitcher of this size which contained 2½ litres of watery fluid and a drowned rat!

Most plants, however, are only large enough to catch unwary insects which are attracted to nectar which the plants secrete, but then find themselves unable to escape up the slippery inner surface of the pitcher. While on your way to the summit, try exploring a few metres in the undergrowth on either side of the trail – you're bound to come across a pitcher plant sooner or later.

Further Reading

Before you go to the park you might like to read a little about what's in store for you on

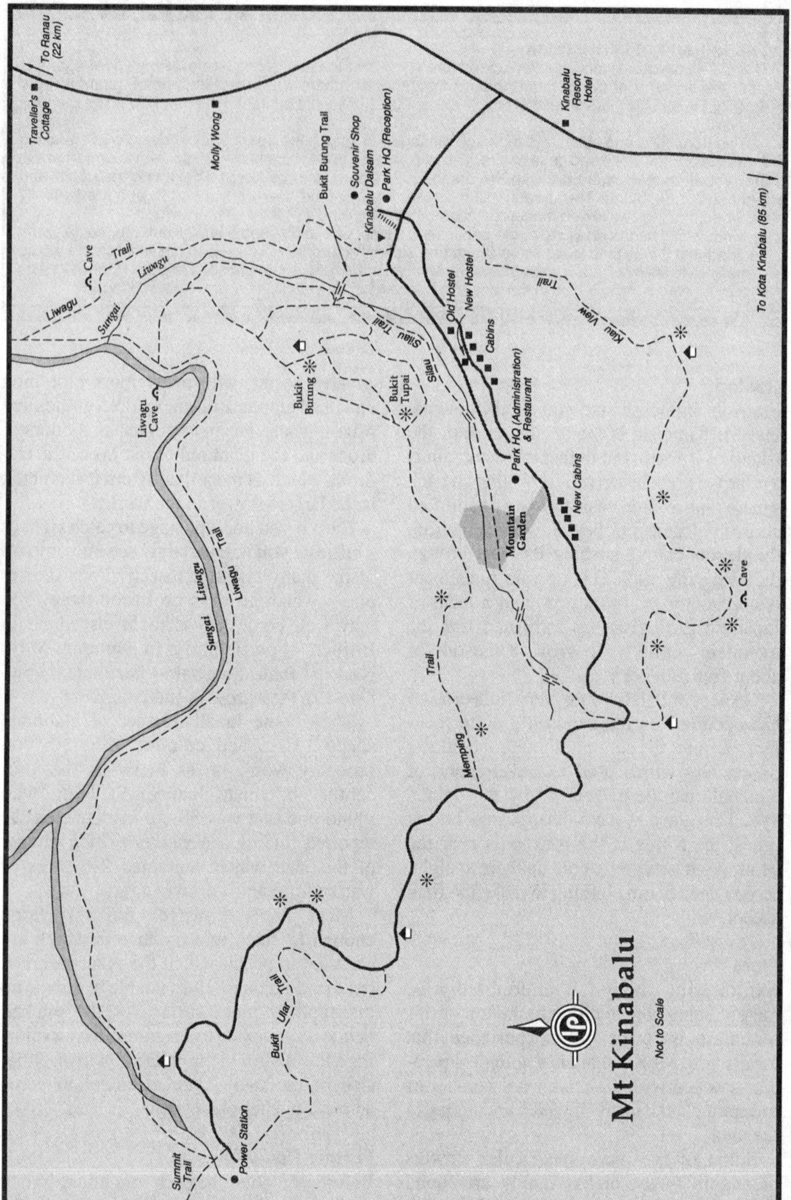
To Ranau (22 km)
Traveller's Cottage
Molly Wong
Bukit Burung Trail
Souvenir Shop
Park HQ (Reception)
Kinabalu Dalsam
Kinabalu Resort Hotel
To Kota Kinabalu (85 km)
Liwagu Trail
Cave
Sungai Liwagu
Old Hostel
New Hostel
Cabins
Silau Silau Trail
Kiau View Trail
Bukit Burung
Bukit Tupai
Liwagu Cave
Park HQ (Administration) & Restaurant
New Cabins
Mountain Garden
Sungai Liwagu
Liwagu Trail
Cave
Memping Trail
Bukit Ular Trail
Summit Trail
Power Station
Mt Kinabalu
Not to Scale

the mountain by purchasing a copy of the national parks publication, *A Guide to Kinabalu National Park* by Susan Kay Jacobson, which is on sale at the office in Kota Kinabalu and at the gift shop at the park.

Another book which is worth reading even if you're not a botanist is *Nepenthes of Mount Kinabalu* by Shigeo Kurata. (*Nepenthes* is the botanical name for pitcher plants.)

Hugh Low's experiences on the mountain are recounted in a book called *Experiences in the Forests of East Asia*, written by Spencer St John. It was originally published in London in 1864, but a reproduction paperback is available locally.

Park Headquarters

Accommodation and catering at park headquarters are excellent and well organised. The headquarters are built in a beautiful setting with a magnificent view of Mt Kinabalu when the clouds are not obscuring the slopes and summits.

Make advance reservations for accommodation at the Sabah Parks office in Kota Kinabalu. Accommodation at the park HQ can be tight, and it is even tighter on the mountain. However, if you arrive without a booking and all the beds are taken, it's highly unlikely that you will be turned away. On arrival, check in at the reception centre and, if staying overnight, present your reservation slip from Kota Kinabalu and you'll be allocated your bed or room. Valuables can be deposited in the safe at reception and any excess baggage can be stored there until you return from the mountain. A small selection of crafts and books is also available. Prices compare well with those elsewhere.

All the hostels and resthouses are within walking distance of the reception, and just beyond them is the administration building. The slide and video show presented here from Friday to Monday at 7.30 pm gives an excellent introduction to the mountain. Also shown here is a whiz-bang 15 minute 'multivision' slide show (using 14 projectors!) which introduces Sabah's national parks. It is shown daily at 1.30 pm and admission costs RM1.

The Mountain Garden behind the administration building is well worth a look. It has exhibits of many of the plants found on the mountain.

Walking Trails

It's well worth spending a day exploring the well-marked trails around park HQ. There's a rough map available at the reception desk which shows all the trails and points of interest.

All the trails link up with others at some stage, so you can spend the whole day, or indeed days, walking at a leisurely pace through the beautiful forest. Some interesting plants and, if you're lucky, the occasional animal can be seen along the Liwagu Trail, which follows the river of the same name. When it rains, watch out for slippery paths and armies of leeches.

At 11.15 am each day there is a guided walk which starts from the administration building and lasts for one to two hours. It's well worth taking and follows an easy path. The knowledgeable guide points out flowers, plants and insects along the way. If you set out from KK early it's possible to arrive at the park in time for the guided walk.

Hiring Guides & Porters

Hiring a guide is compulsory, but porters are optional. The guides and porters are usually members of the Kadazan tribe from the local area, and are not employees of the national park as such.

A guide's fee is a minimum of RM25 per day for one to three people, RM28 for four to six people or RM30 for seven to eight (the maximum).

A porter's fee is RM25 per day for a maximum load of 11 kg up to the Panar Laban huts and RM1 for every extra half kg. For the second segment up to the Sayat-Sayat hut it's RM28 per day and RM1.20 for every half kg over 11 kg.

On arrival at the park HQ, you will be told to come to the park office on the morning of your climb and a guide will be assigned to you. On the morning of any given day, there is usually a throng of people waiting to obtain a guide – the earlier you start, the better. The park staff will try to attach individual travellers to a group so that guide fees can be shared. Couples can expect to be given their own guide.

There are many conflicting opinions about the use of guides. The national parks organisation says they're compulsory because climbers can 'easily lose their way on the rock surface when the fog and mist start covering the upper part of the mountain', which is probably true at 4 am in the dark if no else is climbing the mountain. Another theory is that, with compulsory guides, the chances of people stealing pitcher plants and smuggling them out of the country are drastically reduced.

It's an expensive nuisance if you can't share the cost of a guide with other people. The best compromise you can make is to tell the Sabah Parks office that you intend to share a guide with other people when you get there – this is no problem. A guide is not compulsory if you want to walk the trail only as far as Laban Rata, below the rock-face.

Permits

A climbing permit is required for Mt Kinabalu. The cost is RM10, RM2 for students and free for children under 13. It is payable when you pay for your guide at the park HQ.

All climbers are also required to take out Climber's Personal Accident Insurance at the HQ. The cost is RM3.50 per person per journey and it provides you with RM50,000 for death by accident or permanent disablement as a result of accident (you won't get anything if you do it on purpose), RM5000 for expenses related to accidental injury and (ominously) RM2000 for 'repatriation of remains'.

The Summit Trail

While Mt Kinabalu is an easy mountain to climb, it shouldn't be underestimated. You'll see why when you arrive at the park HQ and look up at the summit towering above you. The climb is relentless and gets steeper as you get closer to the summit. The secret to climbing Mt Kinabalu is stamina. Take it slowly, very slowly if you are tired and out of breath. No prizes are awarded for racing up the mountain, unless you do it in under three hours (there and back!) as they do in the annual climbathon, dominated by Gurkhas. Many people start off briskly and have to take frequent and increasingly longer rest breaks, while the old hands just keep trudging along. Take it easy and walk at a comfortable pace. Those with heart conditions should not attempt the climb.

Warm clothes, raincoat and torch are needed. Bring snacks for the climb, and food if you intend to do your own cooking. A few provisions are sold at the Laban Rata resthouse, but there is little in the way of substantial food for cooking. Water bottles can be filled at tanks along the trail, except between Laban Rata and the summit.

It is wise to stay overnight at the park HQ at least the night before the climb. This will allow you to make an early start and to acclimatise a bit – Mt Kinabalu is quite high enough for altitude sickness problems to occur. The climb is normally done in two days. Most people climb to Laban Rata or the nearby huts, where they stay overnight, then climb to the summit at dawn, returning to the park HQ on the same day.

Visitors usually shorten the walk by well over an hour by taking the minibus from the park HQ up as far as the power station. It shuttles back and forward every morning and takes only about 15 minutes. It costs RM2. It is not much fun walking along the road, though the Liwagu Trail to the power station is a beautiful alternative for those who can afford to add an extra three hours or so to the climb.

Shelters with signboards showing your progress are regularly spaced along the trail, and drinking water is available from tanks at each of these rest stops. The walk starts off through tall oak forest, then rhododendron trees are noticeable. The higher the climb, the more stunted and mossy the growth becomes. Ask your guide to point out the pitcher plants, which can be found on side trails along the way. A detour can be made to

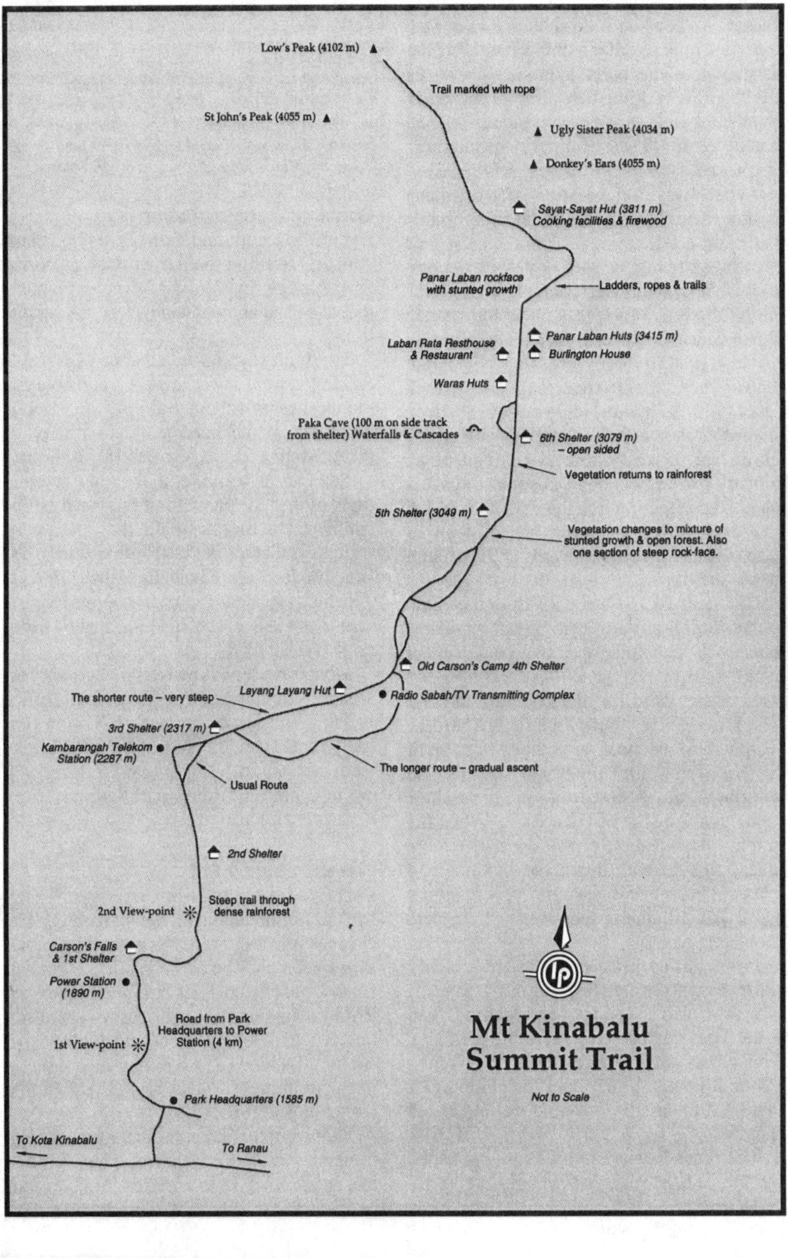
Low's Peak (4102 m)
Trail marked with rope
St John's Peak (4055 m)
Ugly Sister Peak (4034 m)
Donkey's Ears (4055 m)
Sayat-Sayat Hut (3811 m)
Cooking facilities & firewood
Panar Laban rockface with stunted growth
Ladders, ropes & trails
Panar Laban Huts (3415 m)
Laban Rata Resthouse & Restaurant
Burlington House
Waras Huts
Paka Cave (100 m on side track from shelter) Waterfalls & Cascades
6th Shelter (3079 m) – open sided
Vegetation returns to rainforest
5th Shelter (3049 m)
Vegetation changes to mixture of stunted growth & open forest. Also one section of steep rock-face.
Old Carson's Camp 4th Shelter
Layang Layang Hut
Radio Sabah/TV Transmitting Complex
The shorter route – very steep
3rd Shelter (2317 m)
Kambarangah Telekom Station (2287 m)
The longer route – gradual ascent
Usual Route
2nd Shelter
Steep trail through dense rainforest
2nd View-point
Carson's Falls & 1st Shelter
Power Station (1890 m)
Road from Park Headquarters to Power Station (4 km)
1st View-point
Park Headquarters (1585 m)
To Kota Kinabalu
To Ranau
Mt Kinabalu Summit Trail
Not to Scale

EAST MALAYSIA

Paka Cave near the sixth shelter. It is, in fact, merely a rock overhang with a bamboo platform where the early explorers spent the night before tackling the summit. This poor-man's Laban Rata is not that interesting and can be left for the descent when the lungs are less taxed.

Laban Rata is the resting spot for many people. It has heating, hot water, comfortable beds and a restaurant with fine views. This is the place to rest, commiserate with or boast to your fellow climbers, and settle in for the night, though some press on to the spartan Sayat-Sayat hut after a meal. The climb to Sayat-Sayat involves crossing the Panar Laban rock-face, a sheer expanse of rock laced with ropes to help you up the steep incline. It is one of the toughest parts of the climb and a hard chore at the end of an already hard day, though in some ways it is easier than tackling it in the dark and cold of a 3 or 4 am climb, when the residents of Laban Rata are urged onwards to the summit to see the dawn.

The steepest and hardest part of the climb is saved till last. Past Sayat-Sayat, more desolate rock-faces and ropes await the string of climbers stretched out in the dark, trying to keep warm, hold ropes and juggle torches. The summit is beyond a final stretch of rock-face, and at the small area that is the top of Mt Kinabalu, climbers crowd together and huddle against the cold, priming their cameras for a shot of the sunrise. When the sun has risen and the photos are taken, there is a quick exodus down the mountain to Laban Rata, while the late risers, perhaps the wisest of all, make their way to the less crowded summit.

First-class certificates are issued for RM1 for those who complete the climb, but certificates are also issued for making it to Laban Rata. They can be collected at the park HQ. The climb down takes about five hours. While it is a lot easier than the climb up, it can be a lot more damaging on underused muscles.

The times listed here are those published by the Sabah Parks office and are fairly conservative.

Path	*Time Required*
Park HQ to Power Station (15 minutes' drive)	1 hour
Power Station to Layang Layang	3 hours
Layang Layang to Paka Cave	1¾ hours
Paka Cave to Laban Rata	1½ hours
Laban Rata to Sayat-Sayat	1½ hours
Sayat-Sayat to Summit	1½ hours

Booking Accommodation

Overnight accommodation is provided at the park HQ itself on the Ranau road, at Poring Hot Springs, in the new resthouse on the mountain and in mountain huts on the summit trail.

Try to book as far in advance as possible (at least several days to a week), and note that on weekends, school holidays and public holidays all the accommodation may be taken. Mountain huts also need to be booked.

You can, if you like, make your reservations by post or phone, but they will not be confirmed until fully paid for. The postal address is Sabah Parks (Reservations), PO Box 10626, Kota Kinabalu, Sabah. In Kota Kinabalu you can contact the reservation clerk on ☎ 088-211585 and the general office on ☎ 088-221001.

Most travellers, however, make their reservations by calling at the Sabah Parks office in Jalan Tun Fuad Stephens, KK. It is centrally located and is open Monday to Friday from 8.30 am to 4.15 pm (closed from11.30 am to 2 pm on Friday) and Saturday from 8.30 am to noon.

Places to Stay & Eat

Park Headquarters There's a variety of excellent accommodation at the park HQ. The cheapest places are the 46 bed *Old Fellowship Hostel* and the 52 bed *New Fellowship Hostel*, which cost RM10 per person, or RM5 for anyone under 18 years of age. Both hostels are clean and comfortable, have cooking facilities and a dining area with an open fireplace. The Old Hostel tends to be less cramped.

The rest of the accommodation at park HQ is very good but expensive. The twin-bed cabins are RM50 and annexes for up to four people are RM100. On weekends and during school holidays these rates jump to RM80 and RM160 respectively. There are two-bedroom chalets which can sleep up to six people and they cost RM150 per night (RM200 at weekends/holidays). Then there are the deluxe cabins, single storey for five people and double storey for seven people, costing RM150 (RM200) and RM180 (RM250) respectively.

At the top of the range there's the *Kinabalu Lodge*, where one unit costs RM270 (RM350) per night and sleeps eight people.

There are two places where you can buy meals at park HQ. The cheaper and more popular of the two is the restaurant known as *Kinabalu Dalsam*, down below reception, which offers Malay, Chinese and western food at reasonable prices. There's also a small shop which sells a limited range of tinned foods, chocolate, beer, spirits, cigarettes, T-shirts, bread, eggs and margarine.

The other restaurant is in the main administration building, just past the hostels. It's more expensive than the Dalsam, but the food is very good. Both restaurants are open from 7 am to 9 pm.

On the Mountain On your way up to the summit you will have to stay overnight at one of the mountain huts at 3300 metres or the 54 bed *Laban Rata Rest House*, which costs RM25 per person in four-bed rooms. It has heating, hot water and a restaurant, and is, not surprisingly, the most comfortable overnight stop on the mountain. It also has one double room with bathroom for RM100 and a four bed suite for RM200.

Nearby, the 12 bed *Waras* and *Panar Laban* huts, and the 44 bed *Guntin Lagadan Hut* are cheaper at RM10 per person, or RM5 for those under 18. They are more spartan and unheated, but a sleeping bag is provided and the huts are within walking distance of the restaurant, which is not only open for regular meals but also opens from 2 to 3 am so you can grab some breakfast before attempting the summit. The huts have cooking facilities which you can use if you bring your own food.

The eight bed *Sayat-Sayat* hut is closer to the summit, but it is the most primitive of all the huts. It is a tin shed with a few bunks and cooking facilities. There is no electricity, and water has to be carried up (or you can boil rather muddy water from a nearby stream). It also costs RM10, or RM5 for those under 18. For most climbers the huts around Laban Rata are quite far enough to walk in one day, but on the other hand, if you stay overnight in the Sayat-Sayat hut you don't have to get up in the middle of the night in order to reach the summit by dawn. Collect sleeping bags at Laban Rata on the way through if you intend staying at Sayat-Sayat.

As far as sleep is concerned, it doesn't make much difference where you stay; you may sleep quite fitfully – the air is rather thin up there. It's *very* cold in the early morning (around 0°C!), so take warm clothing with you.

Outside the Park It is certainly much better to stay in the park itself, but if for some reason the park is full there are a number of places with mountain views spread out on the main road.

Right near the entrance to the park is the *Kinabalu Resort Hotel* (☎ 011-810781), which has comfortable but overpriced rooms for RM70 with attached bath and TV, or RM90 for family rooms. The Cantonese restaurant here is good. *Molly Wong* (☎ 088-214903), further along the road towards Ranau, has simple rooms with attached bath at RM60/50 for triples/doubles.

The best choice is the *Traveller's Cottage* (☎ 088-750313) further along from the park towards Ranau. Dorm beds cost RM25, basic economy doubles RM38 and standard doubles RM56/67, while excellent self-contained cottages with two bedrooms, kitchen and large lounge cost RM99 per bedroom. Bring your own food.

Further along again towards Ranau is *Kinabalu Rose Cabin* (☎ 088-889233), a new resort which has rooms for RM100 (RM130 on weekends) and suites for RM180 (RM230). The rooms are good, but not as attractive or as good value as the Traveller's Cottage. Opposite is the new *Merlin Resort* (☎ 088-889085) with similar rates. Also close by is the *Mountain View Motel* (☎ 088-889085), where basic singles/doubles cost from RM39/49 and triples with attached bathroom cost RM69.

Kundasang is at the bottom of the mountain, halfway to Ranau, and has a grotty market that straggles along the roadside. Perched high on a hill outside of town is the *Hotel Perkasa Mt Kinabalu* (☎ 088-214142), the most luxurious accommodation outside the park. Rooms cost RM130/160 and suites cost RM250. The best thing about the hotel is the panoramic 360-degree views.

Getting There & Away

Bus There are several minibus routes to Renau.

Kota Kinabalu There are several minibuses daily from KK to Ranau which depart up to about 1 pm. The 85 km trip as far as the park HQ takes about 1½ to two hours and the fare is around RM10.

If you're heading back towards KK, minibuses pass the park HQ until the afternoon, but the best time to catch one is between 8 am and noon. Stand by the side of the main road and wave them down. If you can't be bothered waiting, hitching is quite easy.

Kota Belud & Tamparuli Tamparuli is where the road up the coast to Kudat branches for Kota Belud and Ranau. If you've been visiting Mengkabong Water Village or Kota Belud and are heading for Kinabalu National Park, then first go to Tamparuli.

From Tamparuli there are several minibuses and share-taxis daily to Ranau which, like the ones from KK, pass right by the park HQ. The minibuses cost RM5, while a taxi will cost you at least double that. The journey to the park HQ takes about two hours from Kota Belud, one hour from Tamparuli.

Ranau & Sandakan To get from the park HQ to Ranau, wait at the side of the main road for a minibus going to Ranau or Sandakan, or hitch. There is a large bus to Sandakan which passes park HQ around 9 am, and there are other minibuses which pass Kinabalu National Park on their way to Ranau, but the last one goes by before 2 pm.

The 22 km journey to Ranau takes about half an hour and costs RM3, while the trip to Sandakan takes at least four hours and costs RM27.

RANAU

Ranau is just a small provincial town halfway between Kota Kinabalu and Sandakan. Nothing much ever happens there, but it has some remarkably friendly people. Although it's usually quiet, Ranau does have a very colourful and busy tamu on the 1st of each month. Few travellers stay overnight since the big attraction is Poring Hot Springs about 19 km north of the town. It is primarily a place to get a bus connection to or from Poring Hot Springs, or from Kinabalu National Park.

Places to Stay & Eat

If you get stuck, Ranau has a couple of pricey mid-range hotels to choose from. *Hotel*

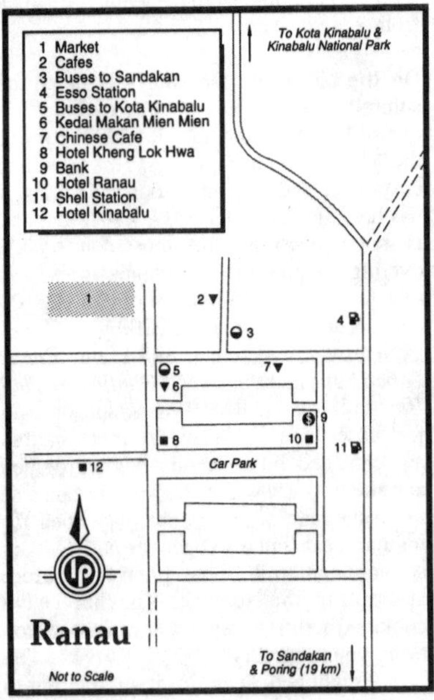

Ranau (☎ 088-875351) is the first place you see when entering the town and is opposite the petrol stations. Singles/doubles with fan cost RM30/45 and range up to RM60 with air-con, TV and bath. *Hotel Kinabalu* (☎ 089-876028) has similar rooms for the same price and suites for RM80. Both are of a good standard, but the Hotel Kinabalu is fairly new and a tad better.

Ranau has plenty of coffee shops, mostly Chinese. *Kedai Makan Mien Mien* has a variety of dishes, including an excellent chicken curry in thick coconut gravy. Rice, vegetables and a meat dish will cost you around RM3.

Getting There & Away

Bus – Kota Kinabalu Minibuses and taxis depart daily up to about 4 pm, sometimes later, and cost RM10 and take about three hours. It is best to catch them in the morning, as the afternoon services are less reliable.

Bus – Sandakan The large air-con buses are the best bet. They leave Ranau for Sandakan from around 7.30 am until noon and cost RM25. The road is good, sealed almost all the way, and the journey takes around 3½ hours. Minibuses go throughout the day but can take a while to fill up, especially in the afternoon.

Bus – Poring Hot Springs On weekends it's easy and cheap to get to the hot springs from Ranau. Drivers in pick-ups cruise around the blocks, shouting 'Poring, Poring!'. The price is RM3 per person and the transport leaves when it's full (which doesn't take long, as many Ranau people go there for the afternoon and return in the evening).

On weekdays it isn't quite so easy, especially if you arrive in Ranau during the afternoon. If this happens you'll have to ask around the cafes and shops to see if anyone is going there and you can share the cost.

When leaving the park, transport is available from the shops opposite for RM5. The national park staff can arrange this for you. There is a regular departure at 6.30 am, and then roughly at 10 am and 2 pm, depending on demand. Otherwise it is a case of waiting for a minibus that is dropping someone off.

Taxi Taxis *are* available – and the drivers will approach you, muttering 'charter, charter', but they will ask a high price for taking you. It will require some hard bargaining – RM15 is a good price, and is a better alternative than spending the night in Ranau.

PORING HOT SPRINGS

The Poring Hot Springs are also part of the Kinabalu National Park but are 43 km away from the park HQ and 19 km north of Ranau.

The springs were developed by the Japanese during WWII. Steaming, sulphurous water is channelled into pools and tubs in which visitors can relax their tired muscles after the trek to the summit of Mt Kinabalu. The pools are in a pretty garden setting of hibiscus and other flowers, trees and hordes of butterflies.

The outdoor tubs are of varying sizes and can fit a couple of people. They have hot and cold water taps, so you can mix your ideal temperature. The water from the springs is very hot, and you can boil eggs for breakfast in it – but, as the sign indicates, only inside a plastic bag. The baths are open from 7 am to 6 pm daily.

Some quite luxurious private cabin baths are also available. A standard cabin costs RM15 for the first hour or part thereof, then RM25 for every additional hour, and they have large baths capable of accommodating eight people. The deluxe cabins have lounge areas and jacuzzis and cost RM20 for the first hour, then RM30 for each additional hour.

After a hot bath you can take a cooling dip in the rockpool.

As at Kinabalu park HQ, there are several km of forest trails around the springs. The Kipungit Falls are only about 10 minutes' walk away, and you can swim at their base. Follow the trail further up the hill, and after 15 minutes you reach the bat caves, large boulder overhangs housing bats. Langanan Falls is a further 1¼ hours away.

Another very worthwhile and unusual attraction is the **Jungle Canopy Walkway**.

It consists of a series of rope walkways suspended in the trees well above the jungle floor (up to 30 metres high), and it offers a unique monkey's-eye view of the surrounding forest. The springy walkways are not for the faint-hearted. As you bounce up and down high above the ground, it's like bungy-jumping without the jump. It's quite safe and great fun – well worth the RM2 entry fee. There is also a fee of RM5 for cameras and a hefty RM30 for video cameras, but they don't worry too much about it unless you have a camera obviously dangling around your neck. The walkway is open from 10 am to 4 pm, so the best times for seeing some jungle wildlife are missed. Night walks are supposedly available from 6 to 10 pm, for RM30 for a group of up to three people, but it will take a lot of insistence to get one.

A new HQ and information centre has been built at Poring, and a rafflesia centre, orchid centre, tropical garden and butterfly farm will open in the future.

As is the case at Mt Kinabalu, if you intend to stay overnight it is important to reserve accommodation at the Sabah Parks office in Kota Kinabalu in advance. This is especially true on weekends; during the week it's not usually a problem to roll up without a booking, though the parks people certainly don't like it. See the Mt Kinabalu section for full reservation details.

Places to Stay & Eat

The *Poring Hostel* has two units – one with 24 beds and one with 40 beds. Costs are RM10 per person (RM5 if you are under 18 years of age), and blankets and pillows are provided free of charge. There is a clean, spacious kitchen with gas cookers. A camping ground is also available for RM5 per tent, though you will have to bring your own. Pillows and blankets can be hired for 50 sen each.

Other Poring accommodation comes in the form of cabins with two bedrooms and cabins with three bedrooms. Both kinds have shared facilities. The three-bedroom cabins sleep six people and cost RM75 per cabin on weekdays, RM100 on weekends. The two-bedroom cabins sleep four people and cost RM60 on weekdays, RM80 on weekends. The mosquitoes at Poring are vicious, but thankfully all the rooms have netting.

There are cooking facilities at Poring, but there are also three inexpensive eating places right opposite the park gate. You can buy food for cooking here as well, though it is cheaper if you bring your own.

Getting There & Away

Access is by minibus, taxi or hitching the 19 km along the bitumen road from Ranau – see Getting There & Away in the Ranau section for details.

Eastern Sabah

SANDAKAN

The former capital city of Sabah, Sandakan is today a major commercial centre where the products of the interior – rattan, timber, rubber, copra, palm oil and even birds' nests from the Gomantong Caves – are brought to be loaded onto boats for export.

The city lies at the entrance to a huge bay, and its docks sprawl along the waterfront for many km. The bay itself is dotted with islands, some of which have excellent beaches.

Sandakan itself, however, is a bit of a dump, and the real attractions lie outside the city. One of the world's four orang-utan sanctuaries is at Sepilok (the others are in Sumatra, west of Medan; at Semenggok in Sarawak; and in Tanjung Puting National Park in Kalimantan). Gomantong Caves, on the other side of the bay, is another worthwhile attraction. Edible birds' nests are collected there for the famous Chinese soup, and offshore there's one of the world's few turtle sanctuaries, where giant turtles come to lay their eggs.

History

In the 18th century, Sandakan came under the suzerainty of the sultan of Sulu, the southern islands of present-day Philippines. In the 19th century, British traders came to the region, but the first foreign settlement was mainly a German one on Pulau Timbang in Sandakan Bay in the 1870s. In 1878 Baron von Overbeck, an Austrian, acquired a lease from the sultan of Sulu for much of eastern Sabah, and this was later sold to Alfred Dent, the well-known Hong Kong-based publisher. Sandakan was established by the Resident, William Pryer, and the city boomed. In 1884 Sandakan became the capital of British North Borneo, and it remained the capital until the Japanese invasion and subsequent Allied bombing in 1945 virtually destroyed the town. In 1946 the capital was moved to Jesselton, now Kota Kinabalu.

Orientation

The centre of Sandakan is very compact and consists of three main blocks built between the seafront and the wooded hills on which the governor's residence sits. In these blocks you'll find many of the hotels and restaurants, banks, MAS office, the local bus stand and the long-distance minibus stands. Confusion arises when you are trying to find a certain address here though, because street signs are virtually nonexistent, the sequential order for naming streets (Jalan Dua, Jalan Tiga, Lebuh Empat – First, Second and Third Street – etc) defies logic and 'Jalan' and 'Lebuh' are used interchangeably.

The minibus stand for local blue buses (Labuk Bus Co) is squashed in by the waterfront. All other local minibuses leave from the stand just past the old Port Authority building. The long-distance minibuses go from the bus stand just by the Sandakan Community Centre at the western end of the centre.

The Sabah Parks office is in the central area, but the immigration and forestry departments are close to the airport, about 11 km from the centre along the Ranau road.

Information

The post office is on Jalan Leila at the western end of town, just past the Shop & Save Supermarket. The immigration office is in the secretariat building, just past the roundabout at Batu 7 on the Ranau road, 11 km from the centre of town. Take any Batu 7 or higher bus (Batu 8, 12, 19, 30 etc).

Bookings & Permits The Sabah Parks office (☎ 089-273453) is on the 9th floor of Wisma Khoo Siak Chiew at the end of Jalan Tiga. This is where you need to come to make a reservation to visit the Turtle Islands National Park (Taman Pulau Penya). The staff are helpful and can arrange transport at reasonable prices. The office is open Monday to Thursday from 8 am to 12.45 pm and 2 to 4.15 pm, Friday from 8 to 11.30 am

The Sandakan Death Marches

Sandakan was the site of a Japanese POW camp during WWII, and in September 1944 there were 1800 Australian and 600 British troops interned here. What is probably not widely known is that more Australians died here than during the building of the infamous Burma Railway.

Early in the war, food and conditions were not too bad, and the death rate was around three per month, but as it became clearer to the Japanese officers that they didn't have enough staff to guard against any rebellion in the camps, and that the Allies were closing in, they decided to cut the prisoners' rations to weaken them. The death rate started to rise and disease spread.

It was also decided to move the prisoners inland, 250 km through the jungle to Ranau. On 28 January 1945, 470 prisoners set off; 313 made it to Ranau. On the second march, 570 started from Sandakan; just 118 reached Ranau. The third march consisted of the last men in the camp and numbered 537. Conditions on the marches were deplorable: many men had no boots, rations were less than minimal and many men fell by the wayside. Those who couldn't walk when the camp was evacuated by the Japanese were disposed of.

Once in Ranau, the surviving prisoners were put to work carrying 20-kg sacks of rice over hilly country 40 km to Paginatan. Disease and starvation took a horrendous toll, and by the end of July 1945 there were no prisoners left in Ranau; the only survivors from the 2400 at Sandakan were six Australians who had escaped either from Ranau or during the marches. ■

and 2 to 4.15 pm and Saturday from 8 am to 12.45 pm.

For a permit for the Gomantong Caves, you need to pay a visit to the Wildlife office (☎ 089-666550) of the Ministry of Tourism & Environment, housed in a flash new building at Batu 7, about 500 metres past the 11 km peg on the Ranau road. While you're out there, pay a visit to the Forestry Department museum in the same building.

Things to See & Do

The town doesn't have any 'must see' attractions, but there are a few points of interest if you have nothing else to do. The **waterfront** is a good place for boat spotting (fishing boats, barges, ferries and ocean-going container ships), and also has a vegetable and a fish market – though these get a bit fetid in the heat of the day.

The new **Puu Jih Shih Temple**, four km west of the centre, is a large Buddhist temple, from which there are good views over Sandakan Bay. Take a bus to Tanah Merah and ask for the temple. Near the temple on the coast road is **Pasir Putih Beach**, which has good seafood dining on weekends. Closer to town, the interesting **Sam Sing Kung Temple** dates from 1887 and fronts the Padang.

Other buildings of note are **St Michael's & All Saints Church**, built in the 19th century and one of the few stone buildings in East Malaysia, and the futuristic **Sandakan Mosque** at Sim Sim, one km east of town along the coast. Sim Sim is an interesting stilt village where you can wander around between the houses.

For a fine view over the town, head up the hill towards the Sandakan Renaissance Hotel and turn right at Jalan Istana near the roundabout. The **observation pavilion** is one km or so along and offers views right across the town and the bay. Just behind is **Agnes Keith's House**, an old two storey wooden villa. Agnes Keith, an American, came to Sanda-

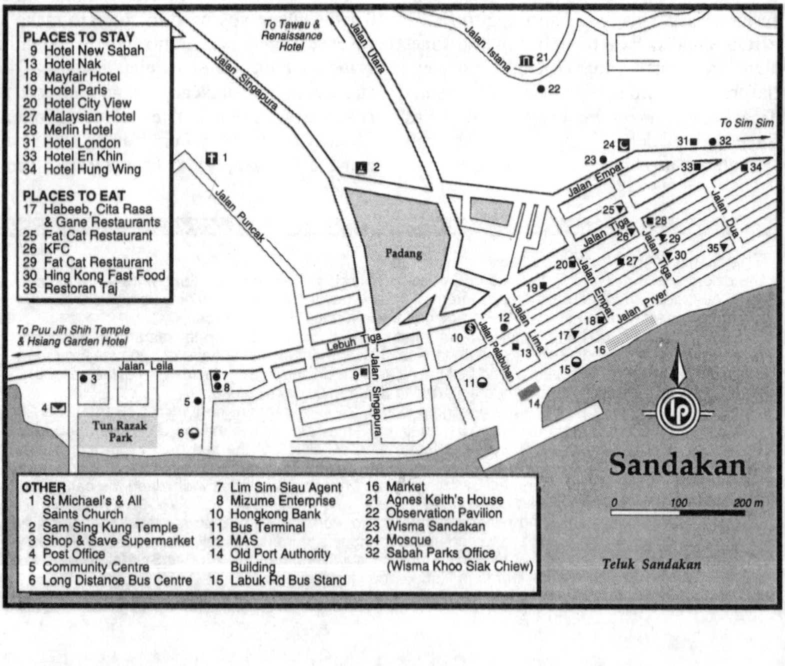

kan in the 1930s with her husband, who was the Conservator of Forests, and wrote about her experiences in three books, spanning her time in Sabah until 1952.

Organised Tours

For tours, try Wildlife Tours (☎ 088-24600), 9th floor, Wisma Khoo Siak Chiew, and also at the Sandakan Renaissance Hotel (☎ 089-273093); Api Tours (☎ 089219958), Ground floor, C1, Block 50, Jalan Leila; or Discovery Tours (☎ 089-274106), 10th floor, Wisma Khoo Siak Chiew. A city tour costs around RM40, Sepilok RM60 and turtle islands from RM250 (one night) to RM450 (two nights). Gomantong Caves and the Kinabatangan River costs RM200 for a day tour or RM400 for two days/one night. The best value tours in Borneo are operated by Uncle Tan (see Places to Stay below). A turtle islands tour costs RM80 and RM30 for each night. Transport to Uncle Tan's jungle camp on the Kinabatangan River costs RM130, but accommodation including meals is only RM15 per night. Uncle Tan also has accommodation at Tanjung Aru fishing village. Tan's tours are not for those travellers who want Swiss-watch schedules and four star accommodation, but for budget travellers his tours are the best option for exploring eastern Sabah.

Places to Stay – bottom end

Many travellers head for *Uncle Tan's* (☎ 089-531917), Batu 17½, Labuk Rd, 29 km from town on the main highway. All the bus drivers know this place, so ask to be dropped off there on the way into Sandakan. Coming from town, take a Labuk Road bus going to Batu 19 or beyond for RM1.70. Tan charges RM20 for a dorm bed, including breakfast, and free tea and coffee throughout the day. Mountain bikes are available for RM2 per day – a good way to visit Sepilok. Uncle Tan also runs very cheap, low-key tours to both the turtle islands and to a jungle camp he has on the lower Kinabatangan River. He also has tours to Tanjung Aru, where you can stay in the stilt village.

The other popular travellers' haunt is the *Travellers' Rest Hostel* (☎ 089-216454), 2nd floor, Block E, Bandar Ramai-Ramai, over in the west of town. It's a friendly place with dorm beds at RM13 and a couple of simple doubles for RM25. Like Uncle Tan's, the Rest Hostel runs tours to the turtle islands and other attractions.

Borneo Bed & Breakfast (☎ 089-216381), 2nd floor, Lot 12, Block E, Bandar Kim Fung, Mile 4, Jalan Labuk, is around seven km from town, two blocks behind the big Capital Supermarket on the main road into Sandakan. There are only three spotlessly clean, spacious rooms with fans – two with twin beds and one with a double bed – and there is a good communal area. It is good value at RM15 per person (RM20 with breakfast), or a double for a couple is RM25 (RM35 with breakfast).

All the other so-called cheap accommodation is in the centre of town and these are no great bargains. The *Hotel Hung Wing* (☎ 089-218895) on Jalan Tiga is a mid-range hotel with some cheaper rooms which are good value. Generally, the higher the floor, the cheaper the room. If you're willing to climb to the 6th floor, you'll find clean, spacious rooms with attached bathroom and fan for RM25/30. Other air-con rooms range from RM44 to RM65.

Also on Jalan Tiga is the *Hotel Paris* (☎ 089-218488), which has clean rooms from RM25/30 with fan and bath, or RM38/48 with air-con and bath. The *Mayfair Hotel* (☎ 089-219855) at 24 Jalan Pryer is the best bet for an air-con room with attached bath, costing RM32/40. This is a good value mid-range hotel.

Places to Stay – middle

The mid-range hotels are all similar in standard and their cheaper rooms go quickly. The *Hotel New Sabah* (☎ 089-218711) on Jalan Singapura has good rooms with air-con, TV and attached bathroom for RM44 to RM55. The *Hotel En Khin* (☎ 089-217377) at 50 Jalan Tiga, almost opposite the Hung Wing, is a good, cheap Chinese place and costs RM40/50.

The *Hotel London* (☎ 089-216371) on Jalan Empat is a very clean, well-run hotel and probably the best in this price range. Rooms cost RM40/50 with attached bath.

Places to Stay – top end

The *Hotel Nak* (☎ 089-272988), on Jalan Edinburgh, is a large hotel that was once Sandakan's best. It's now looking very much the worse for wear. Rooms cost from RM57 to RM86 for big rooms facing the sea.

The *Hotel City View* (☎ 089-271122), on Jalan Tiga, is a little newer and a touch better appointed. Rooms cost RM140/70 to RM190/210 for deluxe rooms, though discounts are sometimes available. The *Hsiang Garden Hotel* (☎ 089-273122) is two km west of town, just off Jalan Leila in Hsiang Garden Estate, a new shopping/industrial area. Very good rooms range from RM90 to RM140.

The only international-standard hotel, and a favourite of the Sepilok tour groups, is the *Sandakan Renaissance Hotel* (☎ 089-213299), about a km up the hill from the main roundabout in town. It has a swimming pool, sporting facilities, restaurants etc. Most rooms are RM285 or RM315, and prices range up to RM1500 for suites.

Places to Eat

Sandakan is full of cheap Chinese restaurants and coffee houses serving the standard rice or noodles with fried vegetables, so if that's what you're after you'll be well satisfied.

For good Malay food try the *Habeeb Restoran* on Jalan Pryer. They do excellent murtabak, and also have an air-con room upstairs. There are a couple of similar places close by, including the *Cita Rasa* and *Restoran Gane*.

For a western breakfast or snack there are a few choices. The best is probably *Fat Cat* on Jalan Tiga. Nearby, the *Superman Ice Cream Parlour* on Jalan Tiga serves very good ice creams and juices. There is a *KFC* on the opposite corner. Another possibility is the *Apple Fast Food* restaurant on the ground floor of the Hotel Nak on Jalan Edinburgh. Wisma Sandakan is the multistorey peach-coloured office block which backs onto the hill behind town. On the 2nd floor there are a few fast-food possibilities, including another *Fat Cat Restaurant*, *Satay Ria* and the *Restoran Gili Padi*, which serves good local dishes.

For absolutely no-frills food, try one of the stalls upstairs in the central market. A couple of ringgit will get you a decent meal – but choose your stall carefully, as the hygiene standards are a bit rough. There's more market food at the night market which sets up outside the post office each evening.

For more expensive dining possibilities, the *Ming Restaurant* in the Sandakan Renaissance Hotel has Cantonese and Sichuan food and dim sum breakfast and lunch. The *Jaiman Restaurant* on the 1st floor of Wisma Khoo Siak Chiew has good local specialities at moderate prices. Hsiang Garden Estate, two km west of the city centre along Jalan Leila, is a newer shopping and industrial area with a number of more expensive restaurants. Here you'll find the *Korean Restaurant*, the *Japanese Corner* in the Hsiang Garden Hotel's restaurant and the *XO Steak House*.

Getting There & Away

Air Sandakan is on the Malaysia Airlines domestic network and there are regular flights to: Kota Kinabalu (five daily, RM83), Kudat (daily, RM54), Lahad Datu (daily, RM48), Semporna (three weekly, RM50) and Tawau (two daily, RM61).

The MAS office (☎ 089-273966) is on the ground floor of the Sabah building, right in the centre of town. It is open Monday to Friday from 8 am to 4.30 pm, Saturday from 8 am to 3 pm and Sunday from 8 am to noon.

Bus The long-distance bus station is next to the community centre, out towards the post office. All the long-distance minibuses, Land Cruisers and big air-con buses to KK congregate here. Most buses go early in the morning, though a few minibuses and Land Cruisers go in the afternoon.

Buses to Kota Kinabalu cost RM35, though price wars have seen tickets drop to as low as RM20. Most buses leave at 6.30 and 7 am and take around six hours. The last buses to KK usually leave at around 10 or 11 am. The big air-con buses are operated by

Mizume Enterprise (☎ 011-887787), which has an office near the bus station, and Lim Sim Siau (☎ 011-887376), which has a desk in the Sandakan Milk Bar around the corner.

You can take the same transport to Kinabalu National Park HQ for RM25. Minibuses to Ranau cost RM20 and the journey takes about four hours.

There is one large Bungaraya Co bus which departs Sandakan for Lahad Datu and Tawau daily at 5.30 am, but there are also many minibuses which depart throughout the morning for Lahad Datu, some going on to Tawau. The trip to Lahad Datu takes about three hours and costs RM15. Occasional minibuses also go all the way to Keningau for RM35.

If staying at Uncle Tan's, you can hail long-distance buses on the highway, but it can be difficult finding one that has a seat free. You have a better chance early in the morning, otherwise you may have to take a bus into town and then out again from the bus station.

Getting Around

If you're arriving or leaving by air, the airport is about 11 km from the city. A taxi costs RM15. The Batu 7 Airport bus runs by the airport but does not enter the terminal. It stops on the main road about 500 metres from the terminal. The fare to/from the city centre is 70 sen.

AROUND SANDAKAN

Australian War Memorial

The Australian War Memorial is in a quiet park just past the government buildings at Batu 8 (Km 12) on the road to Ranau. This was the site of the Japanese POW camp and the starting point for the 'death marches' to Ranau. There's just a couple of bits of rusting machinery around, but the place has an eerie air, and local ghost stories abound.

To get there, take any Batu 8 or higher bus and get off at the Esso station about one km on the right past the government buildings at the airport roundabout. Walk along Jalan Rimba for about 10 minutes; the camp is on the right about 100 metres after the road turns to gravel.

Crocodile Farm

At Batu 8 on Labuk Rd near the war memorial there is a crocodile farm, a depressing place with a couple of thousand crocodiles in concrete tanks.

Sepilok Orang-Utan Rehabilitation Centre

Located at Sepilok, about 25 km from Sandakan, this is one of only four orang-utan sanctuaries in the world. It was established in 1964 and now covers 4000 hectares.

Apes are brought here to be rehabilitated to forest life, and so far the centre has handled about 80 of them, but only about 20 still return regularly to be fed. It's unlikely you'll see anywhere near this number at feeding time – three or four is a more likely number.

The apes are fed from two platforms, one in the middle of the forest about 30 minutes' walk from the centre (platform B), and the other close to the HQ (platform A). The latter platform is for the juvenile orang-utans, which are fed daily, usually at 10 am and 2 pm. At platform B the adolescent apes which have been returned to the forest are fed daily at 11 am. They are just fed milk and bananas, and there's no guarantee they'll show up, as this feeding is purely supplementary to what they can find for themselves in the jungle. For this feeding the rangers leave from outside the Nature Education Centre at 10.30 am daily.

Of the ones which have returned to the wild, females often come back to the feeding platforms when they're pregnant and stay near the sanctuary centre until they've given birth, after which time they go back to the forest.

The schedule can change, and the daily programmes (morning and afternoon) are posted at the Visitor Reception Centre, where there is a souvenir shop and a cafeteria nearby. At the Visitor Information Centre next door, video shows are included as part of the daily programme, usually at 11 am and 3 pm. The reserve also has a Nature Education Centre, which displays interesting information about the animals of the reserve, and includes some bad examples of taxidermy.

As well as the orang-utans, there are a couple of Sumatran rhinos and other animals at the centre.

As one of Sabah's prime tourist attractions, Sepilok is very well organised and professionally managed. The only problem is that it can resemble a zoo, especially at the crowded, camera-snapping feeding sessions at platform A, and the 'close-encounter' sessions, where the young orang-utans are brought out for visitors to cuddle. Don't let this put you off, though. A lot of good work is done here, and the reserve is well worth a visit. If you want to avoid the more touristed programme, go to platform B or simply wander through the reserve, which offers some fine walks and plenty of wildlife, and you may see orang-utans anyway.

You are allowed to wander through the forest at your own pace – and at your own risk. Although the orang-utans are not aggressive animals, one of the males, Raja, can be very inquisitive, to say the least. He made headlines when he confronted a French tourist and then stripped him naked. The proboscis monkeys can be aggressive, and it is not uncommon to see snakes and lizards in the forest.

Two walking trails branch off from the Nature Education Centre. The waterfall trail takes about an hour. The main mangrove trail is a 1½ to two hour walk and leads right down to the sea estuaries in the reserve. This is a favourite trail for bird-watchers and many species can be found at Sepilok, including the rare Bornean bristlehead. Ask at the reception centre for pamphlets. Wear hiking boots, take water and expect to find leeches and plenty of mosquitos. There are dilapidated huts near the end of the trail.

Don't be in so much of a hurry to see the orang-utans that you miss the forest. If you're taking photographs you'll need ASA 400 film (it's quite dark in the forest).

Visiting hours at the centre are Saturday to Thursday from 9 am to noon and 2 to 4 pm; and Friday from 9 to 11.30 am and 2 to 4 pm. To see all the programme, you should arrive at 9 am or 2 pm. Arrive in the morning if you want to do the walks and explore the forest, and you can stay all day. Admission is RM10 (RM1 for Malaysians).

About 500 metres before the rehabilitation centre is a Forest Research Centre, which has, among other things, a good library and entomology museum, though it isn't open to the general public.

Getting There & Away To get to the centre take the blue Labuk bus marked 'Sepilok Batu 14' from the local bus stand next to the central market on the waterfront at Sandakan. The fare is RM1.50 and the journey takes about 45 minutes. There are departures at 9.20 and 11.20 am, and 1 and 3 pm. There are also other minibuses which make the trip every hour or so.

Islands

Berhala Island is at the entrance to Sandakan Bay and was used by the Japanese as a POW camp. It has impressive vertical cliffs, and much of the island is a forest reserve. There is a small beach with picnic facilities, and a village on the other side of the island.

Libaran Island, further north near the Turtle Islands National Park, is a low rocky island inhabited by Cagayan people, originally from the Philippines.

Another interesting place is the floating village of Tanjung Aru, on an island in Sandakan Bay. To get there, charter a boat from the wharf behind the bus stand for around RM12, or hitch a ride on a fishing boat for a couple of ringgit. Uncle Tan can arrange tours here.

TURTLE ISLANDS NATIONAL PARK

The Pulau Penyu National Park comprises three small islands which lie 40 km north of Sandakan, within swimming distance of the nearby islands of the Philippines. Pulau Selingan, Pulau Bakungan Kecil and Pulau Gulisan are visited by marine turtles which come ashore to lay their eggs. The main season for the green turtles is from July to October, and for hawksbill turtles from February to April.

The green turtle is a strong, slow-moving creature, commonly found on Pulau Selingan

EAST MALAYSIA

and Pulau Bakungan Kecil. It weighs between 50 and 90 kg and lays around 180 eggs. The hawksbill turtle lays its eggs on Pulau Gulisan. It's much smaller than the green turtle, weighing between 25 and 55 kg.

Pulau Selingan has a park information centre and three chalets. As well as providing a chance to see the turtles, the islands have beautiful white-sand beaches and clear water.

Places to Stay & Eat

It's not possible to visit the turtle islands on a day trip, so any excursion involves staying overnight. The only accommodation is at the *Sabah Parks Chalet* on Pulau Selingan, which costs RM30 per person per night or RM150 for a two person chalet. The chalets are fully furnished and have cooking facilities, and a cafeteria on the island serves meals. Bookings must be made in advance at the Sabah Parks office (☎ 089-273453) in Sandakan as facilities are limited and tour companies often take bulk bookings.

Uncle Tan's all-inclusive tours to the turtle islands for RM180 includes accommodation at nearby Pulau Libaran.

Getting There & Away

The Sabah Parks office can arrange transport to the islands and will try to put individuals in with a group. The cost is around RM85 per person. If you have to charter a boat, expect to pay RM350 or more for the return journey. Uncle Tan in Sandakan organises cheap trips out to the islands, but accommodation is outside the park. Travel agent prices are much higher.

GOMANTONG CAVES

These caves are over on the opposite side of the bay from Sandakan and about 20 km inland. They are famous as a source of swiftlets' nests, which are the raw material for that famous Chinese delicacy, bird's-nest soup. Permits are required to visit the caves and need to be obtained in advance from the Wildlife office in Sandakan. It is possible to arrange accommodation, though it is not encouraged.

The caves are a 10 minute walk along the trail from the new information centre and office. The trail to the caves forks not far from the office. Continue to the right for the main cave, Simud Hitam, or 'Black Cave', and along the way you pass the living quarters of the nest collectors. You can venture into the caves, though exploring inside involves wading through ankle-deep guano alive with insects. In the season, you can watch the nests being collected from the roof of the cave, as they are at Niah in Sarawak, by men climbing long, precariously placed bamboo poles.

The left-hand trail from the office leads to the top of the mountain. After a few metres, the trail forks again. The right-hand trail is a 15 minute walk to a top entrance of the cave, while the left-hand trail continues for 30 minutes and leads high up the mountain and to the Simud Putih, or 'White Cave'. The White Cave contains the more valuable white birds' nests. Both trails are steep and involve some rock climbing.

The area has plenty of wildlife, especially birds, and the walks are worthwhile, but the caves are difficult to reach. Certainly the Niah Caves in Sarawak are more spectacular and easier to visit, and the Madai Caves near Lahad Datu are interesting and more accessible.

Getting There & Away

It is possible to visit the caves using public transport, but it takes at least two hours from Sandakan and may involve a lot of walking. First, take any Lahad Datu minibus and ask for the Sukau turn-off. At the turn-off is a small coffee shop in the middle of nowhere, and from here buses go infrequently to Sukau past the park turn-off, 20 km away. Traffic is light for hitching, but the chances of a lift are good. From the turn-off it is 4.5 km to the park HQ. Be prepared to walk.

Another way to get there is to take a boat from behind the Sandakan market to Suan Lamba, on the other side of Sandakan Bay and upriver, for RM3. Then it is eight km to the park turn-off by road (this may involve Land Cruiser hire), then the 4.5 km to the HQ.

KINABATANGAN RIVER

The Kinabatangan River is the largest river in Sabah and flows east from the ranges on the western side of the state and then north-east to enter the sea east of Sandakan. Although logging is widespread along the upper reaches of the river, downriver from the Sandakan-Lahad Datu highway some primary forest remains and the forest is home to high concentrations of wildlife. It is an ideal place to observe the wildlife of Borneo, and sightings of the native proboscis monkeys are common along the banks in the morning and evening. Orang-utans and gibbons are also seen from time to time.

This area is virtually inaccessible, but Uncle Tan (see the Sandakan section) has a jungle camp about an hour downstream from the Sandakan-Lahad Datu road, and while it is extremely basic, it does give travellers an opportunity to get out of the towns and stay in the jungle. Tan charges RM15 per person per day for accommodation and meals. Transport there is by bus to where the highway crosses the river, and then by boat to the camp. The charge is RM130 for transport, so obviously it's better if you stay a few days.

Many travellers come to the camp with the intention of staying a couple of days, and stay much longer. Seeing wildlife is always a matter of luck, but your chances are as high here as anywhere in Borneo.

Travel agents also have more expensive trips on the Kinabatangan, and they have more salubrious camps at Sukau. Sukau is the main settlement on the lower Kinabatangan, 25 km along the road past the Gomantong Caves.

Batu Putih (also called Batu Tulug), one km from where the highway crosses the river, is a limestone outcrop containing caves. Burial remains have been found in the caves, as they have in many of the caves along the Kinabatangan.

LAHAD DATU

Lahad Datu is a busy little plantation and timber service town of 20,000 people. There are very few tourists and the only reason for visiting is if you are en route to or from the Danum Valley, 80 km west of Lahad Datu. Given that the only accommodation at the valley now is in the form of an expensive resort, Lahad Datu will probably fall off the travellers' map entirely.

The town is full of Filipino and Indonesian migrants/refugees, and the streets are full of women trying to make a few ringgit selling cigarettes. This area of eastern Sabah around the Celebes Sea is also known for its pirates, equipped with the essentials of modern piracy – machine guns and speed boats. Don't think about trying to catch a boat from here. Pirate raids on ships and coastal villages are common, and raids on buses have also been reported on the back roads.

Information

Bookings for Danum Valley Borneo Rainforest Lodge can be made at Innoprise Corporation (☎ 089-881092), Block 3, Ground floor, Fajar Centre. You can also book in KK. The office in Lahad Datu is open normal office hours.

The MAS office (☎ 089-81707) is on the ground floor of the Hotel Mido on the main street.

For changing money, try the Standard Chartered Bank opposite the Hotel Mido on the main street, or the Sabah Bank around the corner, which has good rates and low fees for travellers' cheques.

Places to Stay

Try not to get marooned here; budget accommodation is virtually nonexistent and Lahad Datu has little to offer visitors.

The cheap places to stay are found around the main street, particularly in the side street opposite the Esso station. Try the *Rumah Tumpangan Malaysia* (☎ 089-83358), between the Ocean Hotel and the cinema, where rooms with fan and common bath cost RM20 to RM30 or the *Hotel Venus* (☎ 089-81900), on the same street, where fan rooms cost RM25 and air-con rooms are RM33.

The *Ocean Hotel* (☎ 089-81700), on the main street opposite the Hap Seng building, provides more luxury with air-con and attached bath for RM38/48. The nearby *Hotel Perdama* (☎ 089-81400) is similar and only slightly more expensive at RM44/55.

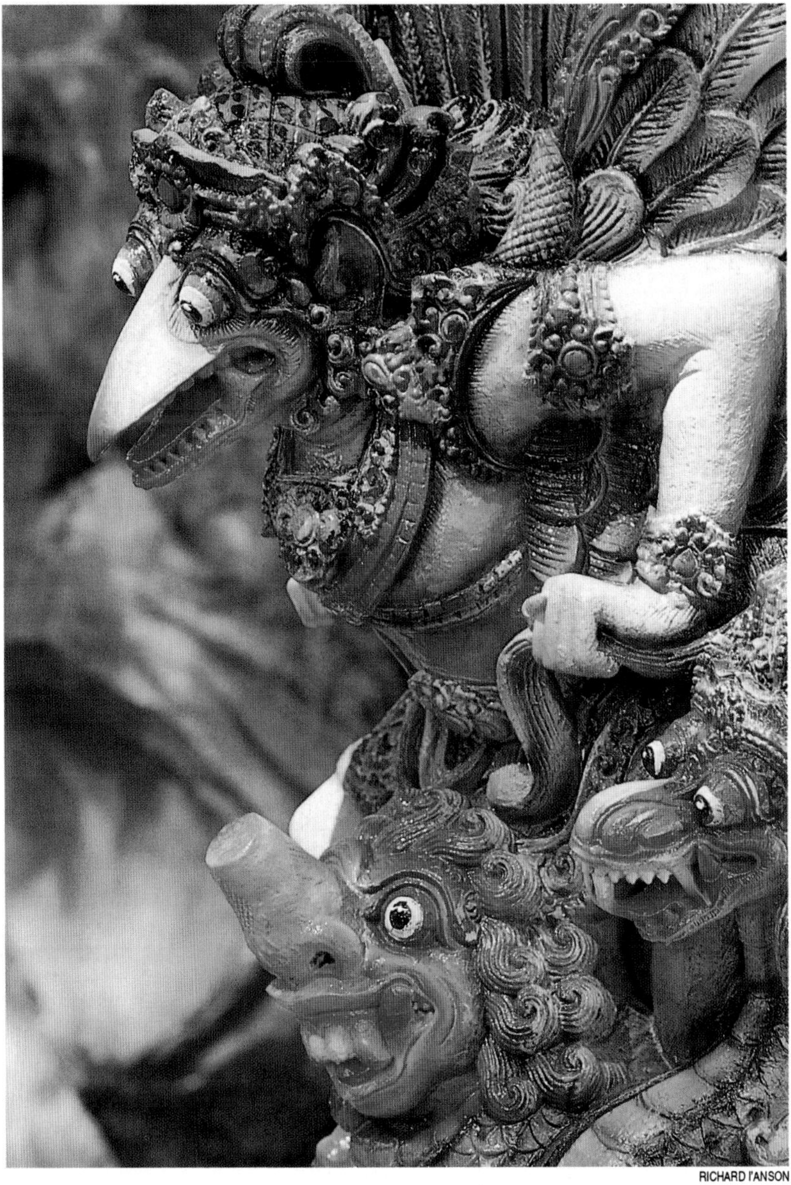

RICHARD I'ANSON

Singapore
The original Tiger Balm Gardens, with its grotesque statues, has been turned into a Chinese mythological theme park, now called Haw Par Villa.

RICHARD I'ANSON

PETER TURNER

PETER TURNER

RICHARD I'ANSON

Singapore

Top Left: The Singapore skyline
Top Right: An ornate terrace house
Bottom Left: The colourful Thian Hock Keng Temple is the oldest Chinese temple in Singapore.
Bottom Right: Chinatown, Singapore's cultural heart

Places to Eat

The food stalls next to the Chinese temple, behind the cheap hotels, are good and specialise in Filipino food. In the evenings the hawkers set up their stalls in the area behind the Hotel Mido. A couple of ringgit will get you a decent feed.

One of the best places for Muslim Malay food is the *Restoran Kabir* near the minibuses. They serve excellent curries, rotis and murtabak, and there is an air-con room upstairs. *Azura Restoran* is another good place for roti and murtabak, and *Restoran Kim Loong* has standard Chinese fare.

The *Sentosa Coffee House* in the Hotel Mido has western breakfasts and cheap meals in its air-con restaurant. Most mains cost RM4 to RM6, or the three-course set lunch is good value at RM10.

Getting There & Away

Air MAS operates services between Lahad Datu and Kota Kinabalu (three daily, RM106), Sandakan (daily, RM48) and Tawau (weekly, RM40). The airport is only a couple of km from town on the highway. A taxi to town costs RM3.

Bus The long-distance minibuses leave from the vacant lot near the waterfront. There are frequent departures for Sandakan (3½ hours, RM15), Semporna (2½ hours, RM8) and Tawau (2½ hours, RM8). There are plenty of departures to all places until around 3 pm. The road to Semporna and Tawau is one of the best in the state.

AROUND LAHAD DATU

Danum Valley Conservation Area

Located on the Segama River 85 km west of Lahad Datu, the Danum Valley Conservation Area has a field centre that has been set up by the Sabah Foundation and the Royal Society in conjunction with a number of private companies to provide facilities for research, education and recreation in a rainforest area. Many of the private sponsors are involved in logging in Sabah, and one of the main areas of study is forest regeneration. The field centre is an area of established secondary rainforest, and is at the centre of a large logging area, which might explain why there are such high concentrations of wildlife in the refuge of the field centre. It is no longer possible to stay at the field centre, but it can be visited as a day trip.

Most of Borneo's mammals are represented at Danum Valley, and 240 species of birds have been recorded. Some of the rarer animals sighted include Sumatran rhinos, elephants, bantengs and clouded leopards. While you have to be lucky to see wildlife in the jungle, in one day at Danum Valley I saw elephants, orang-utans, gibbons, hornbills and tortoises, as well as countless birds and insects. Danum Valley's birdlife attracts bird-watchers from all over the world.

A number of walks can be done along more than 50 km of walking trails. The staff at the Field Centre may be able to tell you of the areas where the latest wildlife sightings have occurred, but day-trippers will have little time for long excursions. Leeches are common; jungle boots and leech socks, which are usually not available at the centre despite what the brochures say, are recommended.

It's necessary to get an entry permit and make bookings in advance at the Innoprise Corporation office in Kota Kinabalu or at the office in Lahad Datu. There is a checkpoint at the start of the logging concession, and you will not be allowed entry without a permit. Entry permits for foreign visitors cost RM10 for day visitors. Guests of the Borneo Rainforest Lodge do not need to apply for permits. Access is only by the centre's transport, by the lodge's transport or by private vehicle.

Places to Stay & Eat The Borneo Rainforest Lodge is marketed in conjunction with Tiger Tops of Nepal. The emphasis is on an educational stay, with tours of the rainforest and visits to the field centre. Costs are all-inclusive of activities and full board. Accommodation is on a share basis in twin rooms in chalets. One night costs RM350, two nights RM500, three nights RM720 and all additional nights an extra RM200.

Bookings should be made through Innoprise Jungle Lodge (☎ 088-243245; fax 088-243244), 3rd floor, Block D, Lot 10, Sadong Jaya Kompleks, KK, or at the Lahad Datu booking office (see the Lahad Datu entry above).

Getting There & Away A Sabah Foundation vehicle leaves the centre on Monday, Wednesday and Friday at 9 am, and returns from Lahad Datu on the same days at around 3 pm; the one-way cost is RM30. If you are flying in from KK on those days, you can be met at the airport. The centre is 70 km from the highway along an unsealed but good logging road.

Guests of the Rainforest Lodge will have their transport included. The lodge is 97 km from Lahad Datu.

MADAI CAVES

These limestone caves, like the Gomantong Caves, are famed for their birds' nests. At the entrance to the cave is a sprawling kampung of wooden shanties, which are empty for most of the year except when the birds' nests are in season. Then the collectors climb to the top of the caves on precarious bamboo poles in their search for the valuable white birds' nests worth RM750 or more a kg.

The caves are near the Lahad Datu-Tawau highway. The turn-off is 69 km from Lahad Datu, and then it is 3.5 km to the caves. In the season you may be asked to show a permit from the Wildlife office in Lahad Datu, but otherwise just make yourself known at the village. Foreign visitors are unlikely to be poachers – and anyway, guards are permanently posted inside the caves.

A small river runs through the caves and emerges at the entrance. A torch is necessary to explore the caves, and a guide is needed to go far inside. To get to the back of the main cave, it is necessary to cross the river – thigh-deep in places – and walk through ankle-deep guano seething with beetles. It is possible to walk right through the cave and exit at the top, but this involves clambering over slippery rocks. It is easier to take the trail outside to the top entrance of the caves. A guide and torch can be hired in the village for around RM5.

The Madai area is rarely visited by tourists, and it is difficult to explore without your own transport, but it does have a few points of interest. The large Madai Waterfall is right next to the highway, 58 km from Lahad Datu. The small Hutan Rekreasi Madai is a forest reserve around the falls with picnic facilities and food stalls. The reserve office has a good map of the surrounding area and is the place to get information on the forests and walks nearby. Just opposite the falls is the Kletus Muyuk Trail, a 45 km walking trail which leads to Gua Madai and the Madai-Baturong Forest Reserve, further inland from the caves. The Baturong Caves and the hot spring at Kampung Air Panas are other points of interest in the area.

Places to Stay

The only accommodation is at Kunak, an unremarkable town off the main highway, 18 km from the caves. The *Dreamland Hotel* (☎ 089-851322) is an expensive, unimpressive mid-range place with air-con rooms with attached bath and TV starting at RM52/62 for singles/doubles. You could always ask at the village by the caves – outside the collecting season there are dozens of empty shacks.

Getting There & Away

All buses from Lahad Datu to Semporna or Tawau pass by the caves. Buses run to the caves from Kunak for RM2, but you could be in for a long wait. Traffic on the road to the caves is light.

SEMPORNA

At Semporna, between Lahad Datu and Tawau, there is a large stilt village, and a cultured pearl farm off the coast. Semporna has a beautiful setting around a small bay, with picturesque islands not far offshore, but about the only time you're likely to come through here is if you are on an organised diving trip to Sipadan Island, off the coast to the south-east.

The Semporna Ocean Tourism Centre is a large development built on stilts over the water. It has a hotel, restaurant and a pathetic aquarium at the end of the pier.

Places to Stay & Eat
The main hotel in Semporna is the *Dragon Inn Hotel* (☎ 089-781088). It is part of the Semporna Ocean Tourism Centre, built in traditional floating-village-style over the water. The bamboo and thatch rooms cost RM68/78 for a room with bath, air-con and TV. Family rooms cost RM105 and VIP suites are RM157. The hotel is about 100 metres out in the bay, and is connected to the shore by a causeway which leads to the small port.

In the town, *Hotel Semporna* (☎ 089-781378) is cheaper but poor value. Air-con rooms cost RM45 with shared bathroom, or RM55 with attached bathroom.

The *Pearl City Chinese Restoran* forms the other part of the Semporna Ocean Tourism Centre. The food is excellent, but this is definitely not a cheap restaurant. A cheaper option is the *Floating Restoran & Bar*, halfway along the short causeway which connects the town to the Semporna Ocean Tourism Centre. For RM7 you can get an excellent meal of local fish.

In the town itself there are numerous Chinese kedai kopis as well as the popular *Restoran Kinabalu*, which serves good Malay food.

Getting There & Away
Air MAS operates Twin Otter flights between Semporna and Sandakan (thrice weekly, RM50), Tawau (twice weekly, RM40) and Tomanggong (twice weekly, RM40). The MAS agent is Today Travel Services (☎ 089-781077).

Bus There are plenty of minibuses between Semporna and Lahad Datu (2½ hours, 160 km, RM8) and Tawau (1½ hours, 110 km, RM4). There are also taxis to Tawau for RM10.

SIPADAN ISLAND
This small island 36 km off the south-east coast of Sabah offers excellent diving, mainly because it is an oceanic island, ie it is the tip of a limestone pinnacle which rises from the ocean floor. This means that on the eastern side of the island, you walk out from the beach and it drops almost vertically to around 600 metres and you are diving on the 'wall'. The sea is teeming with marine life, including large tuna, whalesharks, manta rays and turtles, and the island is billed as one of the world's great diving destinations. There are plans to make Sipadan part of a marine park before development has adverse effects, but the ownership of the island has not been fully resolved, as Indonesia also has claims on Sipadan.

As far as tropical paradises go, Sipadan has beautiful white-sand beaches and dense forest, but no swaying coconut palms. It is a beautiful spot, but unless you are a diver it is hard to justify the cost of visiting the island. Sipadan has already seen three resorts pop up since 1989 offering dive packages, though discounts are offered for non-divers. Unless you go with a dive company or as a group, it can be very expensive to get to Sipadan.

Places to Stay & Eat
Accommodation on the island is comfortable but not five star by any means. Meals are provided by the resorts. The dive centres on Sipadan have offices on the wharf in Semporna, and you can get better deals there than in KK, but it may be difficult to get accommodation on Sipadan at the last moment.

Borneo Divers (☎ 088-222226), on the 4th floor of Wisma Sabah in Kota Kinabalu, are the original operators on Sipadan and offer all-inclusive trips costing US$605 per person for a two day trip ex-KK, up to US$965 for a five day trip. These prices are all inclusive – transport, diving equipment, unlimited beach diving, boat dives, food and drinks and beach-hut accommodation. Borneo Divers also have a hyperbaric (decompression) chamber installed on the island. Non-divers only get a 10% discount.

According to Borneo Divers the other resort operations on Sipadan are illegal, and at the time of writing efforts were being made to have them removed. If the actions are successful, Borneo Divers will be the only operators on the island.

Sipadan Dive Centre (☎ 088-240584), A1004, Wisma Merdeka, Jalan Tun Tazak, Kota Kinabalu, has two-day trips ex-KK for RM1275 (RM965 for non-divers) up to

RM1900 (RM1520 non-divers) for five-day trips. A good deal is available on packages from Semporna for RM400 for two days/one night (RM300 for non-divers).

The third resort operator is Pulau Sipadan Resort (☎ 089-765201), 1st floor, 484 Bandu Sabindo, Tawau. Divers' packages start at RM1250 for three days/two nights from Tawau, and discounts are available for non-divers.

Getting There & Away

Most visitors to Sipadan go on a tour, and getting there under your own steam is expensive. To hire a boat for a day trip to Sipadan from Semporna costs around RM250 for the slower fishing boats that can take up to 15 people. The dive centres will ask around RM400 for their speedboats.

The truly decadent can take a helicopter to Sipadan from Tawau for RM473 one-way or RM715 return. Flights are operated by Sabah Air (☎ 088-56733) in KK.

TAWAU

A mini-boomtown on the very south-east corner of Sabah close to the Indonesian border, Tawau is a provincial capital and a centre for export of the products of the interior – timber, rubber, manila hemp, cocoa, copra and tobacco.

There's precious little to do or see in Tawau – it's just a town you pass through on the way to or from Tarakan in Kalimantan. Like Lahad Datu, Tawau has large numbers of Filipino and Indonesian refugees and immigrants.

The biggest attraction outside the town is the **Tawau Hills Park,** with its volcanic peaks and ridges and dipterocarp rainforest. The waterfall in the park is a popular excursion, but you need your own transport to get out there.

Tawau is still a small, compact town with virtually everything in or near the centre. The only time you may need to use public transport is to get to the airport, which is a km out of town.

Information

The MAS office (☎ 089-765533) is in the Wisma SASCO, close to the centre of town. It is open Monday to Friday from 8 am to 4.30 pm; Saturday from 8 am to 3 pm; and Sunday from 8 am to noon. Bouraq, the Indonesian feeder airline, uses Merdeka Travel (☎ 089-771927) at 41 Jalan Dunlop as its agent. The Indonesian consulate (☎ 089-772052) is on Jalan Apas, some distance from the centre on the main road coming into town.

Places to Stay – bottom end

So-called budget hotels in Tawau are, like those elsewhere in Sabah, poor value for money.

For rock-bottom accommodation, Tawau has a couple of very basic lodging houses that aren't brothels, but they are not recommended for women travellers. The cheapest is the *Penginapan Kinabalu Lodging House*, with basic rooms for RM15/20 with a bit of bargaining. The *Hotel Malaysia* is similar and bare, but clean rooms with fan cost RM20 and air-con rooms cost RM30.

Much better is the very clean, well-run *Hotel Soon Yee* (☎ 089-772447). A fan room costs RM20, and air-con rooms with bath start at RM30. The *Ambassador Hotel* (☎ 089-772700) at 1872 Jalan Paya, just out of the centre, has large rooms with air-con and bath attached for RM25 – for one, two or three people – though even this otherwise good hotel has resident working girls.

Places to Stay – middle

The *Loong Hotel* (☎ 089-765308), 3868 Jalan Wing Lok, is the best bet for good mid-range facilities. Spotlessly clean air-con rooms with attached bathroom and TV are RM35/45 for singles/doubles. The *Hotel Tawau* (☎ 089-771100) at 73 Jalan Chester has basic fan rooms for RM27 or air-con rooms with attached bath for RM38.50/ 47.50, but the Loong is better. The *Oriental Hotel* (☎ 089-761601) has large but scruffy rooms for RM37/45.

The *Hotel Royal* (☎ 089-773100), near the Empire Cinema, has single/double rooms for RM55/65, all with air-con, bath, TV and in-house video, but this place has seen better days. The *Hotel Emas* (☎ 089-762000) on Jalan Utara is a good hotel and the best by far in this range. Singles/doubles cost RM75/85 and

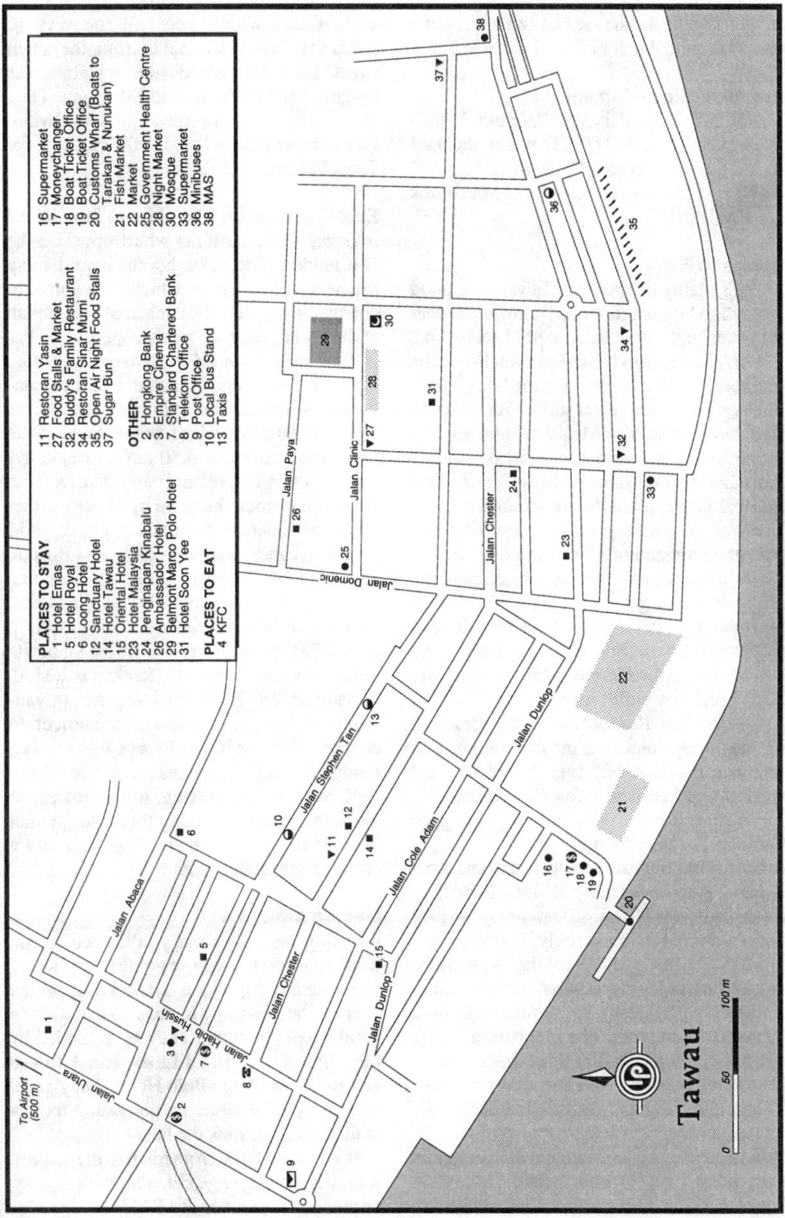
Tawau
PLACES TO STAY
1 Hotel Emas
5 Hotel Royal
6 Loong Hotel
12 Sanctuary Hotel
14 Hotel Tawau
15 Oriental Hotel
23 Hotel Malaysia
24 Penginapan Kinabalu
26 Ambassador Hotel
29 Belmont Marco Polo Hotel
31 Hotel Soon Yee
PLACES TO EAT
4 KFC
11 Restoran Yasin
27 Food Stalls & Market
32 Buddy's Family Restaurant
34 Restoran Sinar Murni
35 Open Air Night Food Stalls
37 Sugar Bun
OTHER
2 Hongkong Bank
3 Empire Cinema
7 Standard Chartered Bank
8 Telekom Office
9 Post Office
10 Local Bus Stand
13 Taxis
16 Supermarket
17 Moneychanger
18 Boat Ticket Office
19 Boat Ticket Office
20 Customs Wharf (Boats to Tarakan & Nunukan)
21 Fish Market
22 Market
25 Government Health Centre
28 Night Market
30 Mosque
33 Supermarket
36 Minibuses
38 MAS
To Airport (500 m)
Jalan Utara
Jalan Abaca
Jalan Habib Hussin
Jalan Chester
Jalan Stephen Tan
Jalan Cole Adam
Jalan Dunlop
Jalan Domenic
Jalan Paya
Jalan Clinic
0
50
100 m

are good value for the facilities on offer; some suites are available for RM170 and RM200.

Places to Stay – top end

Tawau's top hotel is the *Belmont Marco Polo Hotel* (☎ 089-777988), where standard rooms go for RM115/145 on weekdays and RM105/ 115 on weekends. Superior rooms are RM135/145.

Places to Eat

There's plenty of choice in Tawau. For good Malay food try the *Restoran Sinar Murni* near the waterfront – the chicken curry here is good.

For hawker food, there are stalls in the market. Next to the mosque on Jalan Clinic is a lively area of hawker stalls with inexpensive Indonesian and Malay favourites. For Indian food, the *Restoran Yasin* does good murtabak and curries. *Buddy's Family Restaurant* is the place for western fast food. There are also a couple of branches of *Sugar Bun* and a branch of *KFC* around town.

For a bit of a splurge, the restaurant in the *Hotel Emas* is good and sometimes has a steamboat buffet in the evenings. It also offers a western breakfast for RM9. The coffee shop in the *Belmont Marco Polo Hotel* has a breakfast buffet for RM14.

The *Kublai Restaurant* in the Belmont Marco Polo Hotel is a major splurge. The lobby coffee shop, however, has some good western food at more affordable prices.

Getting There & Away

Air MAS has flights between Tawau and Kota Kinabalu (six times daily, RM96), Sandakan (twice daily, RM74), Lahad Datu (daily, RM40) and Semporna (twice weekly, RM40).

MAS also has international flights (on Monday and Saturday) to Tarakan in Kalimantan (Indonesia). It's just a 35 minute flight on a 12 seater Twin Otter. The Indonesian feeder airline, Bouraq, also flies three times weekly (Tuesday, Thursday and Saturday) between Tawau and Tarakan. The fare is RM200.

Bus There are frequent minibuses to Semporna (1½ hours, RM4) and Lahad Datu (2½ hours, RM15). There's also a large bus daily at 5.30 am which goes all the way to Sandakan. They all leave from the main street. Land Cruisers do the run along the logging road all the way to Keningau. They leave early in the morning and cost RM50. Land Cruisers leave through the morning for Sandakan and cost RM25.

Boat – Indonesia The place to buy tickets is down at the customs wharf opposite the fish market. The ticket booths here display the next sailing times, which are subject to change. Ringgit can be exchanged for rupiah at the moneychanger nearby.

The KM *Samudra Express* operates between Tawau and Nunukan and then continues to Tarakan in Kalimantan. It leaves from the customs wharf at the back of the large supermarket at 8.30 am on weekdays (confirm this beforehand) and returns from Nunukan at noon (be there by 11 am). Other boats that operate to Nunukan are the KM *Samudrah Indah*, leaving daily at 4.30 pm, and the KM *Harapan Mulia*. It takes one hour to Nunukan and three hours to Tarakan. The cost to Nunukan is RM25 (or 11,000 rp plus 1000 rp departure tax in the opposite direction), and the cost to Tarakan is RM60. Schedules are haphazard on the Tawau-Nunukan run, and constantly subject to change, but there is usually a boat every day, though Sunday departures are less reliable.

If you are travelling to Nunukan or Tarakan, it's worth noting that visas cannot be issued on arrival; you must get one before crossing into Indonesia.

Getting Around

Probably the only time you'll need to use local transport is if you're going to or coming from the airport, which is one km from the centre. The best thing to do is take one of the hotel buses into town. They are provided by the Hotel Royal, Hotel Emas, Hotel Tawau and Belmont Marco Polo Hotel. They're all free and you're under no obligation to stay at the hotel that runs the bus.

If you want to go from town to the airport, it may not be so easy. Hitching is very easy, or you can take a taxi for RM3.

Singapore

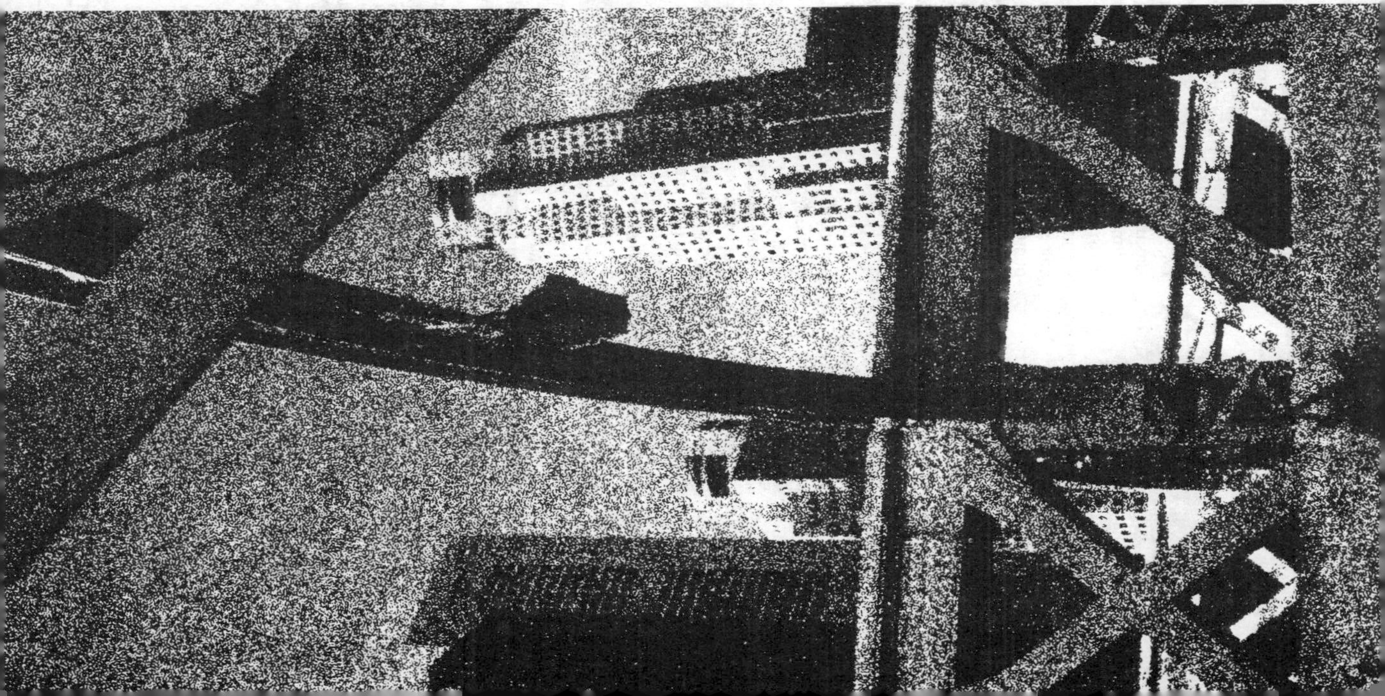

Facts about Singapore

HISTORY

Today, Singapore is one of the great modern city-states, yet in the 14th century Chinese traders described Singapore, or Temasek as it was then known, as a barren, pirate-infested island.

According to Malay legend, a Sumatran prince encountered a lion on Temasek and this good omen prompted him to found Singapura, or Lion City. Although lions have never inhabited Singapore and there is little evidence of any early city, it was likely that Singapore was a small trading outpost of the powerful Sumatran Sriwijaya empire before it became a vassal state of the Javanese Majapahit empire in the mid-13th century.

In the early 1390s, Parameswara, a prince from Palembang, threw off allegiance to the Majapahit empire and fled to Temasek. Although Parameswara and his party were well received, they promptly murdered their host and used the island as a pirate base. In 1398 the Thais attacked Temasek, and Parameswara fled to Malacca (now called Melaka). It was a propitious move, for he went on to found one of the great trading ports of the east, while Singapore again became a quiet backwater.

The Arrival of Raffles

The interest in the spice and China trades brought the Portuguese, Dutch and then the British to the Straits of Melaka. The trade passed Singapore by until Sir Stamford Raffles arrived on the scene. After Holland had fallen to France during the Napoleonic wars, the British ruled Java, where Raffles was governor-general, from 1811 to 1816. With the defeat of France, Britain returned Dutch territories. Raffles, fearing a resurgence of the Dutch trading monopoly, set forth to establish a settlement in Riau (Sumatra) with Colonel William Farquhar, the former British Resident of Melaka.

On 29 January 1819 Raffles landed on the island of Singapore. He reached agreement to found a settlement with the local ruler, the *temenggong*, and with Sultan Hussein, a contender to the fragmented Malay court.

Raffles promptly left to rule the British colony of Bencoolen on Sumatra while Farquhar quickly set about establishing a trading post, free of tariffs. Singapore thrived and by 1821 the population had grown to 5000, including 1000 Chinese.

Raffles, who had little direct involvement in Singapore's early development, returned in 1822 and set about running Singapore. He moved the commercial district across the river to its present site and levelled a hill to form Raffles Place. The government area was allocated around Forbidden Hill (now Fort Canning Hill) and the east bank of the river. Chinatown was divided among the various Chinese groups, and Raffles himself moved to Forbidden Hill.

Statue of Stamford Raffles, who laid the foundations of Singapore

By the time Raffles left in 1823 he had laid the foundations of the city, but more importantly he had firmly established Singapore as a free port – something that Singapore traders have vehemently fought for ever since.

Early Years

In 1826 Singapore became part of the Straits Settlements with Penang and Melaka. The Straits Settlements came under the authority of Calcutta, which allocated them few funds. While commerce boomed, the judiciary and bureaucracy were hopelessly underfunded and social services were nonexistent.

By all accounts, Singapore was a fetid, stinking, disease-ridden colony. Piracy remained a problem and was not eliminated until the 1870s. Despite Singapore's problems, free trade flourished and migrants came in their thousands. Singapore became the major port in the region, and its population – Bugis, Javanese, Arab, Indian and Chinese – reflected its trade. The Chinese, who were soon the largest group, were mainly immigrants from the southern provinces – Hokkien, Teochew, Cantonese and Hakka.

Singapore's trade went through boom and bust periods in the early days and depended on uncertain entrepôt trade, but *laissez-faire* Singapore continued to grow. By the 1860s Calcutta provided more funds to the increasingly important settlement and many of Singapore's grand colonial buildings date from this period.

A Thriving Colony

On 1 April 1867 the Straits Settlements became a fully fledged crown colony, run from Singapore. Singapore was a key link in the chain of British ports, especially with the opening of the Suez Canal.

Chinese migration continued and in the 1870s massive numbers came to Singapore. Many of the Chinese were now wealthy in their own right and owned trading houses. Indian migration had also increased steadily from the mid-19th century.

Peninsular trade, most of which was exported through Singapore, grew dramatically at the end of the 19th century. Singapore prospered and took on the appearance of a cosmopolitan city. The manually drawn rickshaw was imported into Singapore in 1880, the first car arrived in 1896 and the main building of Raffles Hotel was opened in 1899.

Singapore was soon established as the major port of the region and continued to grow. The Chinese were by far the greatest immigrant group and Chinese immigration peaked in 1930, when 250,000 Chinese came to Singapore. The period also witnessed secret society warfare, and the upheavals in China were played out in Singapore with the establishment of the Kuomintang Party, which had a very active Communist faction. The colonial government sought to restrict Chinese immigration, but by the 1930s Singapore was undeniably and irrevocably a Chinese city.

Though the Malayan Communist Party was well established and the seeds of independence grew in the community, the colonial government was firmly ensconced, convinced of its right to rule and looking forward to a long and prosperous reign.

Japanese Invasion

On 7 December 1941 the Japanese bombed Pearl Harbor and invaded the Malay peninsula. In less than two months, they stormed down the peninsula, conquering all before them. The Japanese invaded Singapore from the north-west on 8 February 1942. They met fierce resistance but over the next week they slowly advanced towards the city. Churchill sent word to hold Singapore at all cost, but the pessimistic military command led by Lieutenant-General Arthur Percival feared a bloodbath of Singapore's citizens.

On 15 February, with the city in range of Japanese artillery, Percival surrendered. It was one of the worst defeats in the history of the British empire. The European population was herded onto the Padang and then marched away for internment, many of them at the infamous Changi Prison.

Singapore was renamed Syonan (Light of the South) and the Japanese quickly set about establishing control. Communists and

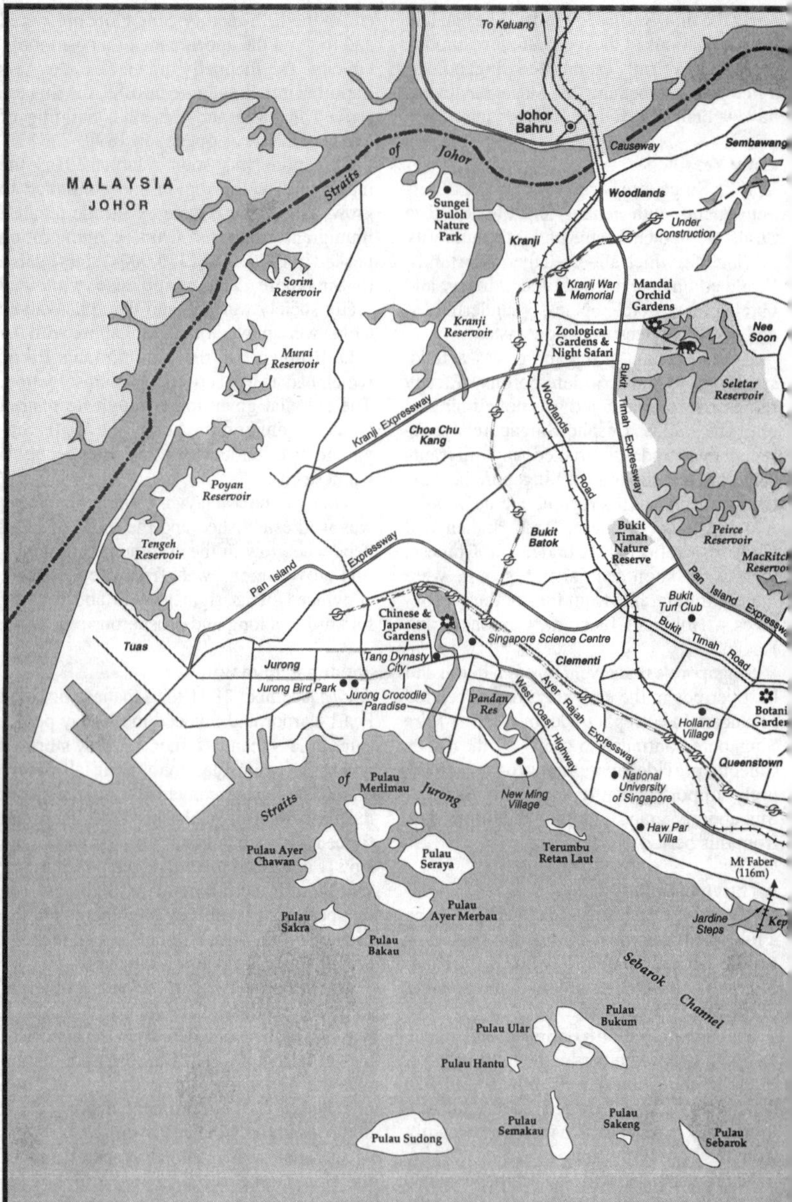
To Keluang
Johor Bahru
Causeway
Sembawang
MALAYSIA
JOHOR
Straits of Johor
Sungei Buloh Nature Park
Woodlands
Under Construction
Kranji
Sorim Reservoir
Kranji War Memorial
Mandai Orchid Gardens
Kranji Reservoir
Zoological Gardens & Night Safari
Nee Soon
Murai Reservoir
Seletar Reservoir
Kranji Expressway
Woodlands Road
Bukit Timah Expressway
Choa Chu Kang
Poyan Reservoir
Bukit Timah Nature Reserve
Peirce Reservoir
Bukit Batok
Tengeh Reservoir
Pan Island Expressway
Bukit Turf Club
Bukit Timah Road
Chinese & Japanese Gardens
Singapore Science Centre
Tuas
Tang Dynasty City
Jurong
Clementi
Jurong Bird Park
Jurong Crocodile Paradise
Pandan Res
West Coast Highway
Ayer Rajah Expressway
Holland Village
Queenstown
New Ming Village
National University of Singapore
Straits of Jurong
Pulau Merlimau
Haw Par Villa
Pulau Ayer Chawan
Pulau Seraya
Terumbu Retan Laut
Mt Faber (116m)
Pulau Sakra
Pulau Ayer Merbau
Jardine Steps
Pulau Bakau
Sebarok Channel
Pulau Ular
Pulau Bukum
Pulau Hantu
Pulau Semakau
Pulau Sakeng
Pulau Sudong
Pulau Sebarok

SINGAPORE

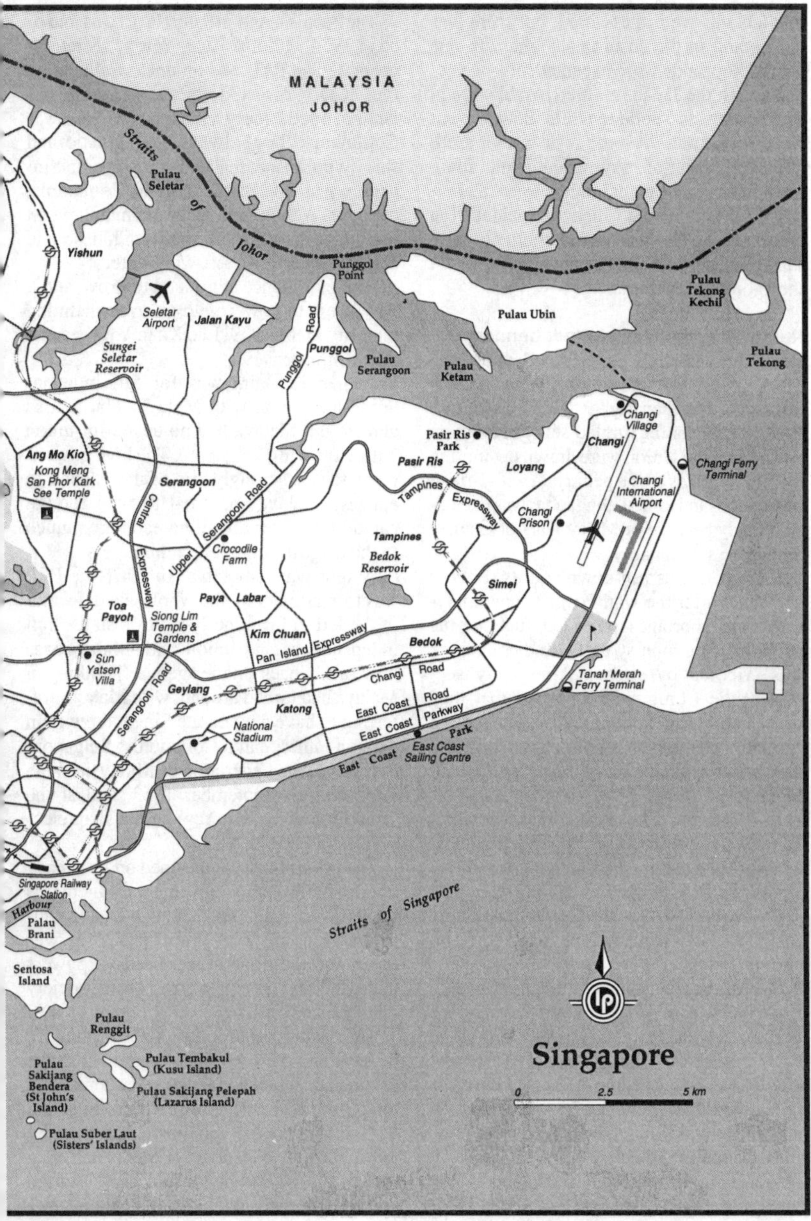
MALAYSIA
JOHOR
Straits of Johor
Pulau Seletar
Yishun
Seletar Airport
Jalan Kayu
Sungei Seletar Reservoir
Punggol Point
Punggol Road
Punggol
Pulau Serangoon
Pulau Ketam
Pulau Ubin
Pulau Tekong Kechil
Pulau Tekong
Changi Village
Changi
Pasir Ris Park
Pasir Ris
Loyang
Changi Ferry Terminal
Changi International Airport
Changi Prison
Tampines Expressway
Tampines
Bedok Reservoir
Simei
Ang Mo Kio
Kong Meng San Phor Kark See Temple
Serangoon
Central Expressway
Upper Serangoon Road
Crocodile Farm
Paya Labar
Toa Payoh
Siong Lim Temple & Gardens
Kim Chuan
Pan Island Expressway
Bedok
Sun Yatsen Villa
Serangoon Road
Geylang
Changi Road
East Coast Road
Katong
East Coast Parkway
National Stadium
East Coast Park
East Coast Sailing Centre
Tanah Merah Ferry Terminal
Singapore Railway Station
Harbour
Pulau Brani
Sentosa Island
Straits of Singapore
Pulau Renggit
Pulau Tembakul (Kusu Island)
Pulau Sakijang Bendera (St John's Island)
Pulau Sakijang Pelepah (Lazarus Island)
Pulau Suber Laut (Sisters' Islands)
Singapore
0
2.5
5 km

intellectuals were massacred, but there was no method in the ensuing slaughter. In one week, thousands were executed.

Though the Japanese ruled harshly, life in Singapore was tolerable while the war went well for Japan. As the war progressed, however, inflation skyrocketed and food, medicines and other essentials were in short supply. Many people died of malnutrition and disease. The war ended suddenly with Japan's surrender, and Singapore was spared the agony of recapture.

Post War & the Road to Independence

After the suffering experienced under the Japanese, the British were welcomed back to Singapore but their right to rule was now in question. Plans for limited self-government and a Malayan Union were drawn up, uniting the Malay states of the peninsula with British possessions in Borneo. Singapore was excluded, largely because of Malay fears of Chinese Singapore's dominance.

Singapore was run-down and its services neglected after the war. Poverty, unemployment and shortages provided fuel for the Malayan Communist Party, and Singapore was crippled by strikes. After early successes, the Communists realised that they were not going to gain power under the colonial government's political agenda and they began a campaign of armed struggle in Malaya.

In 1948 the Emergency was declared. There was no fighting in Singapore but left-wing politics languished under the political repression of Emergency regulations.

By the early 1950s the Communist threat waned and left-wing activity again surfaced into the open.

One of the rising stars of this era was Lee Kuan Yew, a third generation Straits-born Chinese who had studied law at Cambridge. After flirting with the conservative Progressive Party, Lee became a legal adviser to several unions, where he became acquainted with the left and union politics. Most importantly, he realised the need to be aligned with the forces that appealed to the Chinese-educated majority.

The People's Action Party (PAP) was founded in 1954 with Lee Kuan Yew as secretary-general. The PAP was an uneasy alliance – Lee Kuan Yew led the non-Communist faction, but the party's main power base was Communist. Lee, always a pragmatic and shrewd politician, realised that power in Singapore was impossible without Communist support. Although a noncommunal party, PAP appealed to the majority Chinese and attracted the strong left-wing vote.

PAP's influence continued to grow, and it was swept to power with an overwhelming majority in the 1959. Lee Kuan Yew became prime minister.

Singapore's aim was for full independence and union with Malaya. The British agreed, but Malaya had no desire for union with a left-wing Singapore. The PAP government took a strongly pro-Malay stance to appease Malaya and tried to woo foreign capital to bolster the ailing economy, much to the disgust of the left faction.

A split was inevitable. In 1961 the PAP was torn asunder by the wholesale defection of the left to form the Barisan Sosialis. Full independence and union with Malaya was now firmly back on the agenda. Thinking in Malaya had turned around, with Malaya preferring to have a moderate Singapore within a union rather than a Communist Singapore outside it. The Federation of Malaysia came into being in September 1963, and at the same time Lee Kuan Yew held a snap election.

The government campaigned on its already impressive list of achievements – increases in public housing, health standards and education spending were dramatic. Crime was down and the government used its powers under the Emergency to arrest secret-society members.

The Malaysian union was never going to be easy and the PAP made a grave mistake in contesting the 1964 federal elections, even though it had earlier promised not to stand. Its social democrat platform was soundly rejected by the conservative Malaysian electorate, and its campaign had only aroused suspicions of a Singaporean takeover.

Tension mounted when Singapore refused to extend the privileged position held by Malays in Malaya to the Malays in Singapore. Communal violence broke out in the Malay Geylang district of Singapore in 1964 and more than 20 people were killed.

By 1965 Singapore was expelled and the union was over. A tearful Lee Kuan Yew likened Singapore to a head without a body and feared that Singapore, with no natural resources, would not survive.

Republic of Singapore

Singapore became independent on 9 August 1965. Lee's fears proved to be unfounded, and Singapore boomed and became the economic success story of the region. Rapid industrialisation and large foreign investment helped give Singapore full employment and a rising standard of living.

Stable government, industrial calm and previously unknown political quiet prompted further foreign investment. Lee Kuan Yew presided over an economic miracle and Singapore's international standing grew.

Singapore's government was talented and relatively free of corruption and it enjoyed popular support. However, opposition to the government was dealt with harshly. Media crackdowns and government control over student groups and labour organisations increased.

The PAP believed its benign dictatorship was the only way to secure peace and prosperity for Singapore, and Lee Kuan Yew remains staunchly unrepentant, convinced that his tough measures were necessary to develop Singapore. By the 1970s Singapore was the wealthiest country in Asia behind Japan.

The PAP won every seat in each election held until 1981, when JB Jeyaretnam of the Workers' Party won a seat at a by-election. The government was shocked and undertook even greater control of the press, and Lee Kuan Yew mounted a vitriolic campaign against Jeyaretnam, who was convicted of failing to correctly declare party funds in 1986, resulting in his being barred from parliament for five years.

By the 1980s the second tier of PAP leaders came to the fore and Lee Kuan Yew handed over greater responsibility to his juniors. Goh Chok Tong became deputy prime minister and Lee Kuan Yew's designated successor. Lee Hsien Loong, Lee Kuan Yew's son, was also elected to parliament and rapidly became a rising star in cabinet. Singapore's economic miracle continued, and the country possessed a diversified economic base and a literate, skilled population.

Lee Kuan Yew resigned as prime minister in November 1990 and Goh Chok Tong took over. Though Lee has detractors, his achievements are undeniable. He transformed Singapore from a poverty-stricken, run-down city with no natural resources and an uncertain future to a great city-state where its citizens enjoy a safe and prosperous existence. A shrewd politician, brilliant orator and astute leader, he is the father of modern Singapore.

Lee Kuan Yew remains a constant in the public eye as Special Minister, acting as a guardian figure at home and envoy for Singapore abroad. Goh Chok Tong has shown a desire to create a kinder, gentler government, more inclined to consultation and liberal values. Goh's social reforms saw a relaxation of censorship laws, a flourishing in the arts and a greater awareness of the quality-of-life issues that concern most modern, industrialised nations. Yet despite a change in style away from Lee Kuan Yew's aggressively paternalistic rule, few real steps have been made towards democratisation.

GEOGRAPHY

Singapore consists of the main, low-lying Singapore Island and 58 much smaller islands within its territorial waters. It is situated just above 1° N in latitude, a mere 137 km north of the equator. Singapore Island is 42 km in length and 23 km in breadth, and together with the other islands, the republic has a total landmass of 646 sq km (and growing through land reclamation). The other main islands are Pulau Tekong (24.4 sq km), which is gazetted as a military area but planned to be semi-residential eventually;

Pulau Ubin (10.2 sq km), which is a rural haven from downtown Singapore; and Sentosa Island (3.3 sq km), Singapore's fun park. Built-up urban areas comprise around 50% of the land area, while parkland, reservoirs, plantations and open military areas occupy 40%. Remaining forest accounts for only 4%.

Bukit Timah (Hill of Tin), in the central hills, is the highest point on Singapore Island at an altitude of 162 metres. The central area of the island is an igneous outcrop, containing most of Singapore's remaining forest and open areas. The western part of the island is a sedimentary area of low-lying hills and valleys, while the south-east is mostly flat and sandy.

Singapore is connected with Peninsular Malaysia by a km-long causeway. To relieve congestion, a second causeway is planned for the west of the island. Under current plans, further land reclamation and housing developments will dramatically change Singapore's geography. The Mass Rapid Transit (MRT) will be extended to the north and east, where new housing developments will occur, and massive land reclamation will create new islands along the south-east coast.

CLIMATE

Singapore has a typically tropical climate. It's hot and humid year-round, and initially it can be very uncomfortable. Once you are used to the tropics, however, it never strikes you as too uncomfortable. The temperature almost never drops below 20°C (68°F), even at night, and usually climbs to 30°C (86°F) or more during the day. Humidity tends to hover around the 75% mark.

Rain, when it comes, tends to be short and sharp. You may be unlucky and strike rain on every day of your visit, but don't believe local legend about it raining every day for months on end. Only about half the days of the year receive rain. Singapore is at its wettest from November to January and at its driest from May to July, but the difference between these two periods is not dramatic and Singapore gets an abundance of rainfall in every month.

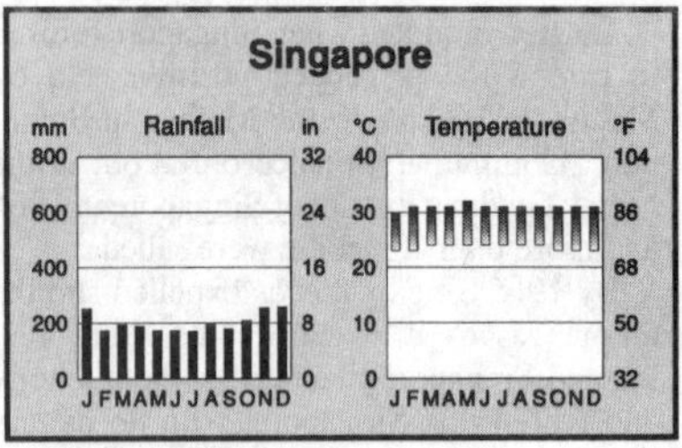

Being almost right on the equator, Singapore receives a steady supply of 12 hours' daylight every day. The sun shines for about half of the day on average (less from November to January). Much of the sunshine is filtered through thin cloud but can be intense, nonetheless.

GOVERNMENT & POLITICS

Singapore's government is based on the Westminster system. The unicameral parliament has 81 elected members representing 52 electoral divisions. Voting is compulsory, and governments are elected for five years, but a ruling government can dissolve parliament and call for an election at any time.

As well as elected members the government has instituted a system that allows it to appoint an opposition. This allows Singapore to have an opposition without having to vote for it.

Singapore also has a president, who is elected to the position. The position is largely ceremonial and real power lies with the prime minister and his government, though recent legislation increased the president's power of veto over financial bills and government appointments.

The legal system is also based on the British system. The Supreme Court is the ultimate arbitrator and consists of the High Court, the Court of Appeal and the Court of Criminal Appeal. Most cases are heard by the District Courts and Magistrates Courts, except for the most serious criminal or civil hearings.

So in theory Singapore has a democratically elected government and political system similar to many western democracies. The political practice is somewhat different.

The judiciary's independence is enshrined in the constitution, but many judges are appointed on short tenure and their renewal is subject to party approval. Rulings that have gone against the government have seen new laws quickly enacted by parliament to ensure government victory. The old Communist bogey is used to justify Singapore's Internal Security Act, which is still there to detain outspoken critics. Singapore's Internal Security Department has sophisticated databanks with detailed information on Singapore's citizens, and there is widespread fear of losing jobs, promotional opportunities or contracts through criticism of the government. There is little freedom of the press and a tight lid is held on government criticism.

The PAP is becoming increasingly concerned that it may lose power, though to the credit of Goh Chok Tong and his supporters, the government is trying to address, even if in a superficial way, some of the electoral concerns that have seen a decline in PAP support. Rather than repress opposition, there is seen to be a need to listen to it.

The main opposition party is the Singapore Democratic Party (SDP), and the combined opposition parties attract around 40% of the vote. The PAP has seen the opposition as mainly nontraditional Chinese, ie Malay, Indian and the English-educated Chinese middle class. However, the evidence and size of the vote also shows that the Chinese-educated Chinese working class, traditionally the backbone of PAP support, is also turning away.

However, the chances of the opposition gaining power are very remote. The PAP undeniably has popular support, and as long as the government can keep the economy and personal wealth growing, the opposition is unlikely to gain the huge increase in its vote required to attain government. Hip pocket issues, like taxation or state-housing waiting lists, are of prime political importance and only economic disaster or a major government scandal is likely to shake the PAP's political dominance.

ECONOMY

Singapore is one of Asia's four 'dragons' – the Asian economic boom countries of Taiwan, Korea, Hong Kong and Singapore. For over 20 years Singapore has recorded phenomenal growth rates, currently running at over 9%. Singapore has a large current account surplus, it is a net creditor, inflation is low and unemployment is virtually nonexistent.

Singapore's economy is based on trade, shipping, banking and tourism, with a growing programme of light industrialisation. It also has a major oil-refining business producing much of the petroleum for the South-East Asian region. Other important industries include ship building and maintenance, and electronics. Singapore's port vies with Hong Kong to be the busiest in the world.

On 1 January 1996 the OECD removed Singapore from its aid list of developing countries, but Singapore is keen to point out that it has not reached developed-nation status. With its strong industrial base and a per capita GDP higher than New Zealand and some other developed countries, Singapore does indeed seem ready to assume developed nation status – but it is not keen to forego the trade benefits such an upgrade would entail.

While tariffs are low or nonexistent and foreign capital is encouraged with minimal restrictions, Singapore is very definitely a managed economy in the Japanese mould. It is the government that provides direction by targeting industries for development and offering tax incentives, or by simply telling them what to do. Unions and the labour market are controlled by the government, and there is tough legislation against strikes.

While the government promotes free trade, it always reserves the right to intervene, as it did in 1985 when it closed the stock exchange for three days after a major Singaporean company, Pan Electric Industries, went into receivership.

Singapore guarantees its citizens decent housing, health care, high standards of education and superannuation, making it a welfare state in comparison with its Asian neighbours. There are no unemployment payments or programmes, but unemployment is negligible and the government insists that anyone who wants work can find it. In fact, Singapore has to import workers from neighbouring countries, particularly to do the hard, dirty work which Singaporeans no longer want any part of.

All workers and their employers make sizeable contributions to the Central Provident Fund (CPF), a form of superannuation that is returned on retirement. Some CPF savings, however, can be used in the purchase of government housing.

POPULATION

Singapore's polyglot population numbers 2.95 million. It's made up of 77.5% Chinese, 14.2% Malay, 7.1% Indian and 1.2% from a variety of races.

Singapore's population density is high but the government waged a particularly successful birth control campaign in the 1970s and early 1980s. In fact, it was so successful that the birth rate dropped off alarmingly, especially in the Chinese community. To reverse the trend and further the government's genetic-engineering programme, tax incentives were introduced for university-educated women who had children, although at the same time rewards of S$10,000 were offered to those willing to undergo sterilisation.

Later policies offered tax rebates of up to S$20,000 for couples who have a third and fourth child. In another move, government-sponsored marriage brokers taught social skills to hard-working Singaporeans so dedicated to their work that they don't know how to woo the opposite sex. Government-sponsored 'love boats' cruised the harbour with potential breeding stock.

PEOPLE

Singapore's character, and the main interest for the visitor, lies in the diversity of its population. Chinatown still has some of the sights, sounds and rituals of a Chinese city, Little India is a microcosm of the subcontinent, and in Arab St the muezzin's call from the mosque still dominates the lives of its inhabitants. But modern Singapore is essentially a Chinese city with strong western influences.

English is the principal language of education, and growing prosperity sees Singaporeans consuming western values along with western goods. For the government, this divergence from traditional values threatens to undermine the spirit – essentially the work-oriented Chinese spirit – that built Singapore. In an attempt to reverse the new ways of the young, the government runs campaigns to develop awareness of traditional culture and values. These include cultural exhibitions and the compulsory study of the mother tongue in schools.

Government policy has always been to promote Singapore as a multicultural nation where the three main racial groups can live in equality and harmony while still maintaining their own cultural identities. The government strives hard to unite Singaporeans and promote equality, though there are imbalances in the distribution of wealth and power among the racial groups. For the most part, the government is successful in promoting racial harmony, a not-always-easy task in multiracial Singapore.

Chinese

The Chinese first settled in the Nanyang, as South-East Asia is known in China, as far back as the 14th century. In the 19th and 20th centuries waves of Chinese migrants in search of a better life poured into Singapore and provided the labour that ran the colony.

The migrants came mostly from the southern provinces: Hokkien Chinese from the vicinity of Amoy in Fujian province; the Teochew from Swatow in eastern Guangdong province; Hakka from Guangdong and Fujian; and Cantonese from Canton. Hokkiens and Teochews enjoyed an affinity in dialect and customs, but the Cantonese and Hakkas may as well have come from opposite ends of the earth. The Chinese settlers soon established their own areas in Singapore, and the divisions along dialect lines still exist to some extent in the older areas of town.

Settlement for the immigrants was made easier by Chinese organisations based on clan, dialect and occupation. Upon arrival, immigrants were taken in by the various communities and given work and housing. The secret societies were particularly prevalent in Singapore in the 19th century; they provided many useful social functions and were more powerful than the colonial government in the life of the Chinese. However, they eventually declined and became nothing more than criminal gangs.

Nowadays, most Chinese are Singaporean-born. The campaign to speak Mandarin has given the Chinese a common dialect, but English is also a unifying tongue. Increasing westernisation and English education for the most part have not undermined traditional Chinese customs and beliefs.

Malays

The Malays are the original inhabitants of Singapore. They are the main racial group throughout the region stretching from the Malay peninsula across Indonesia to the Philippines. Many Malays migrated to Singapore from the peninsula, and large numbers of Javanese and Bugis (from Riau and Sulawesi) also settled in Singapore.

Malays in Singapore are Muslim. Islam provides the major influence in everyday life and is the rallying point of Malay society. The month of Ramadan, when Muslims fast from sunrise to sunset, is the most important month of the Islamic year. Hari Raya Puasa, the end of the fast, is the major Malay celebration.

Islam was brought to the region by Arab and Indian traders and adopted in the 15th century, but traditional Malay culture still shows influences of pre-Islamic Hindu and

The Peranakans

The Peranakans are the descendants of early Chinese immigrants who settled in Melaka and married Malay women. With the formation of the Straits Settlements, many moved to Penang and Singapore. Peranakan means 'half-caste' in Malay, and the Peranakans' culture and language are fascinating hybrids of Chinese and Malay traditions: the Peranakans took the names and religion of their Chinese fathers, but the customs, language and dress of their Malay mothers. Nonya cooking is perhaps the best metaphor for describing Peranakan culture – Chinese dishes with Malay ingredients and flavours.

Baba is the term for a male Peranakan and Nonya for a female, but Peranakans also used the terms 'Straits-born' or 'Straits Chinese' to distinguish themselves from later arrivals from China, whom they looked down upon.

Peranakans were often wealthy traders, allowing them to indulge in their passion for sumptuous furnishings, jewellery and brocades. Peranakan terrace houses were gaily painted, with patterned tiles embedded in the walls for extra decoration, while heavily carved and inlaid baroque-style furniture was favoured. Nonyas wore fabulously embroidered *kasot manek* (slippers) and *kebaya* (blouses worn over sarongs) tied with beautiful *kerasong* brooches, usually of fine filigree gold or silver. Babas assumed western dress in the 19th century, reflecting their wealth and contacts with the British, and their finery was saved for important occasions such as the wedding ceremony, a highly stylised and intricate ritual exhibiting Malay *adat* (traditional custom).

The Peranakan patois is a Malay dialect but contains many Hokkien words, making it largely unintelligible to Malay speakers. It is a dying language, and it is estimated that fewer than 5000 people speak it in Singapore. Western culture is supplanting Peranakan tradition among the young, and the language policies of the government are also helping in its decline. The Peranakans are ethnically Chinese, and Mandarin, which they are required to study at school, is increasingly used as the main language at home, along with English. Many Peranakans marry within the broader Chinese community, resulting in the further decline of Peranakan patois.

Peranakan societies such as the Peranakan Association and the Gunong Sayang Association report growing interest in Peranakan traditions as Singaporeans discover their roots, but when the older generation passes it is likely that Peranakan culture and language will be consigned to history books.

For visitors to Singapore, the Peranakan Place Museum offers a look inside a Nonya and Baba house as it was at the turn of the century, while the Katong district has a number of Peranakan restaurants and the Katong Antique House on East Coast Rd, a repository of Peranakan artefacts. *Mas Sepuloh* by William Gwee is a widely available book on the Peranakan language. ■

animist beliefs. For example, *wayang kulit*, the Malay shadow puppet play, portrays tales from the Hindu epics of the *Ramayana* and *Mahabharata*.

Malays have a strong sense of community and hospitality, and the *kampong*, or village, is at the centre of Malay life. The majority of Malays live in high-rise districts such as Geylang, but in fast-diminishing rural Singapore and the islands to the north, a few Malay kampongs still exist.

Indians

Indian migration dates mostly from the middle of the 19th century when the British recruited labour for the plantations of Malaya. While many Indians arrived in Singapore, most passed through and eventually settled in Malaya.

In Singapore, approximately 60% of the Indian population are Tamil and a further 20% are Malayalis from the southern Indian state of Kerala. The rest come from all over India and include Bengalis, Punjabis and Kashmiris. The majority of Indians are Hindu, but a large number are Muslim and there are also Sikhs, Parsis, Christians and Buddhists.

Major Indian celebrations are Thaipusam and Deepavali.

ARTS

Singapore is a country that is normally associated with business and technology and the arts have tended to take a back seat to economic development. In the liberalised environment under Goh Chok Tong Singapore contemporary arts are starting to flourish, and the more traditional forms of music and dance can still be seen.

Chinese Opera

Chinese drama is a mixture of dialogue, music, song and dance. It is an ancient form of theatre but reached its peak during the Ming Dynasty from the 14th to 17th centuries. It went through a decline in the 19th century but its highest form survived in the Beijing opera, which has enjoyed a comeback in China after the Cultural Revolution. Chinese opera, or *wayang*, in Singapore and Malaysia has come from the Cantonese variety, which is seen as a more music hall, gaudy variety.

What it lacks in literary nuance is made up for by the glaring costumes and crashing music that follows the action. Performances can go for an entire evening, and it is usually easy enough for the uninitiated to follow the gist of the action. The acting is heavy and stylised, and the music can be searing to western ears, but a performance is well worthwhile if you should chance upon one. Street performances are held during important festivals such as Chinese New Year, Festival of the Hungry Ghosts or the Festival of the Nine Emperor Gods.

The band that accompanies the action is usually composed of fiddles, reed pipes and lutes, as well as the drums, bells and cymbals that are most noticeable when the action hots up. The scenery is virtually nonexistent and props rarely consist of more than a table and chairs, but it is the action that is important.

Lion Dance

This dance is accompanied by musicians who bash cymbals and drums to invoke the spirits. The intricate papier-mâché lion's head is worn by the lead performer while another dancer takes the part of the body. At its best it is a spectacular, acrobatic dance with the 'head' jumping on the shoulders of the 'body', climbing poles and performing acrobatic tumbling. The lion may also be accompanied by two clowns who attend it.

The dance is usually performed during Chinese festivals to gain the blessings of the gods, and traditionally a dance troupe would be paid with *ang pow* (red packets of money) held up high to be retrieved with acrobatics. The dragon dance is a variation on the same theme.

Other Performing Arts

Malay and Indian dances sometimes can be seen. *Bangsawan*, or 'Malay opera', was introduced from Persia and is a popular drama form still performed in Singapore.

Singapore's theatre scene is becoming more active and more local plays are being produced. The Substation is an alternative venue, while the Drama Centre, the Victoria Theatre and Kallang Theatre stage local and overseas productions.

The Victoria Concert Hall is the home of the Singapore Symphony Orchestra, and concerts of classical Chinese music are performed by the Singapore Broadcasting Corporation's Chinese Orchestra.

The Singapore Festival of Arts, which features many drama performances, is held every second year around June. Music, art and dance are also represented at the festival, which includes a Fringe Festival featuring plenty of street performances.

Singapore's film industry is definitely still nascent, but the government is keen to develop the film business and attract movie studios to Singapore. Singapore was producing Malay movies back in the 60s and 70s, but the long drought of local production was broken in 1991 with *Medium Rare*, based on a true story about an occult murderer. It was followed by the local box office success, *Bugis Street*, about Singapore's transvestites and notable for getting its nudity and sex scenes past the censors. The latest offering is Eric Khoo's *Mee Pok Man*, a low-budget movie about the doomed romance between a noodle hawker and a prostitute.

To perform the acrobatic lion dance, the lead dancer wears the head while a second dancer takes the body.

SOCIETY

Singapore is a society in transition, most noticeably in the last five years or more. The change of leadership has had some effect, though the real dynamic is the younger generation. The society is moving away from its immigrant-Chinese outlook as Singaporeans keenly examine and redefine their own unique identity.

Singapore is often portrayed by outsiders as a soulless money-making machine, an unkind assessment but not without some basis. Cultural pursuits have taken a back seat to technology and economic progress, but as the population becomes wealthier, more educated and broad-minded, the restrictive focus on economic development alone is fading.

The government itself is keen to define the Singaporean identity, especially in its promotion of 'Asian Values'. Its 'neo-Confucion' ideals are based on traditional subservience to family and society, hard work and the desire to succeed. This dovetails neatly with its authoritarian notions of 'Asian democracy', arguing that western pluralism and democracy are decadent luxuries that Singapore cannot afford. Traditional Chinese culture is stressed, yet Singapore enjoys diverse and growing cultural expression, despite political restrictions.

The widespread use of English and the inheritance of British institutions has meant that Singapore has always been much more western-oriented than other South-East Asian nations. This western orientation, though, has largely been confined to an English-educated elite while the large Chinese-educated working class has traditionally defined Singaporean society. This is changing with a growing middle class and the increasing use of English.

Young Singaporeans have eagerly embraced Levis, Walkmans and western popular culture. But, as in Japan, it is wrong to assume that Singapore is simply aping the west and development will turn it into a European society. Traditional values and customs remain, adapting and blending with the trappings of development. Singaporeans

Kiasu or What?

One of the buzz words of the 1990s in Singapore is *kiasu*. In a recent courtesy campaign (a yearly event to increase social awareness and good manners among Singaporeans), the overseas 'kiasu' Singaporean tourist was targeted. There have been reports of kiasu Singaporeans on holiday piling their plates to overflowing at buffets and then being unable to finish and sneaking out the leftovers. Then there was the excitement among a kiasu tour group when one of its members found a phone that allowed overseas calls at the local rate and the entire group rushed off to the magic booth and spent the rest of the day on the phone to Singapore. Throw in queue jumping, noisy antics in hotels and desperate attempts to avoid entrance fees and the government decided it was time to do something about kiasu Singaporeans.

So what is kiasu? It is best summed up by Mr Kiasu, a Singaporean cartoon hero, whose philosophy from A to Z includes: Always must win, Everything also must grab, Jump queue, Keep coming back for more, Look for discounts, Never mind what they think, Rushing and pushing wins the race and Winner takes it all! all! all!

And are Singaporeans kiasu? At the risk of generalising, it's true that Singaporeans are competitive and that a bargain will never pass a Singaporean by, but would Singapore's economy be so dynamic if Singaporeans were otherwise? It can sometimes be frustrating trying to get out of a lift or MRT train as fellow passengers push to get off while boarding passengers rush to get in, but it is better than trying to board the subway in New York or Tokyo. Singaporeans haven't inherited the British love of queues and, as in most Asian countries, they don't have much time for deferential excesses such as continually saying 'please', 'thank you' and 'sorry', but in a world of plastic smiles and 'have a nice day' the no-nonsense Singaporean approach has something going for it.

Singaporeans have taken the kiasu tag in good humour, as shown by the popularity of Mr Kiasu, and fast-food outlets even offer kiasu burgers. So, when in Singapore, hunt out those bargains, don't pay unless you have to, overindulge at buffets and have a kiasu good time. ■

have a confident vision of themselves as a dynamic Asian nation, even if what it means to be Singaporean is still being defined.

The great icons of Singaporean culture still tend to be food, but chicken-rice or roti prata do not a culture make. Yet the nascent but growing interest in the arts has seen a rush of publications examining Singaporean society and traditions, while in other areas, such as theatre and music, Singaporeans examine their identity as never before. Much of it is retrospective – reminiscences of street hawkers or ponderings on the loss of the kampong life – but modern life is also explored despite the discouragement to question the structure of Singaporean society.

Though the dominant Chinese culture and growing westernisation are the most obvious facets of Singaporean society, of course Malay and Indian traditions have also shaped Singapore. Traditional customs and beliefs among the various ethnic groups are given less importance or have been streamlined by the pace of modern life, but the strength of traditional religious values and the practice of time-honoured ways remains.

For a rundown on Chinese, Malay and Indian customs, see the Society & Conduct section in the Facts about Malaysia chapter.

RELIGION

The variety of religions found in Singapore is a direct reflection of the diversity of races living there. The Chinese are predominantly followers of Buddhism and Shenism (or deity worship), though some are Christians. Malays are overwhelmingly Muslim, and most of Singapore's Indians are Hindus from south India, though a sizeable proportion are Muslim and some are Sikhs.

Despite increasing westernisation and secularism, traditional religious beliefs are still observed by the large majority of Singaporeans. Singaporeans overwhelmingly celebrate the major festivals associated with their religions, though religious worship has declined among the young and the higher educated, particularly the English educated. In the Chinese community, for example, almost everyone will celebrate Chinese New Year, while the figure for those who profess Chinese religion is around 70%.

An interesting reversal of the trend away from religion is the increase in Christianity, primarily among the English-educated Chinese elite, and the charismatic movements in particular are finding converts.

The government is wary of religion and has abolished religious instruction in schools with the stated aim of avoiding religious intolerance and hatred, but it is also interesting to note that religious groups have been at the forefront of political opposition. The government's stated philosophy is Confucian, which is not a religion as such but a moral and social model. Its ideal society is based on the Confucian values of devotion to parents and family, loyalty to friends, and the emphasis is on education, justice and good government. It is a secular, pragmatic society instilled with a healthy dose of materialism.

For an explanation of the major religions of the region, see the Religion section in the Facts about Malaysia chapter.

LANGUAGE

The four official languages of Singapore are Mandarin, Malay, Tamil and English. Chinese dialects are still widely spoken, especially among the older Chinese. The most common dialects are Hokkien, Teochew, Cantonese, Hainanese and Hakka. The government's long-standing campaign to promote Mandarin, the main nondialectal Chinese language, has been very successful and increasing numbers of Chinese now speak Mandarin at home.

Malay is the national language. It was adopted when Singapore was part of Malaysia, but its use is mostly restricted to the Malay community.

Tamil is the main Indian language; others include Malayalam and Hindi.

English is becoming even more widespread. All children are taught their mother tongue (which in the case of the Chinese is Mandarin) at school. This policy is largely designed to unite the various Chinese groups and to make sure Chinese Singaporeans don't lose contact with their traditions.

Singapore has developed its own brand of English, humorously referred to as Singlish. While irate Singaporeans write to the *Straits Times* and complain about the decline in the use of the queen's English, many Singaporeans revel in their own unique patois. It contains borrowed words from Hokkien and Malay, such as *shiok* (delicious) and *kasar* (rough), and is often a clipped form of English, dropping unnecessary prepositions and pronouns. The ever-present 'lah' is an all-purpose word that can be added to the end of sentences for emphasis.

Facts for the Visitor

WHEN TO GO

Anytime. Climate is not a major consideration, as Singapore gets a fairly steady annual rainfall. Your visit may coincide with various festivals – Singapore has something happening every month (see Public Holidays & Special Events later in this chapter). Thaipusam is one of the most spectacular festivals, occurring around February, or if shopping and eating are your major concerns, July is a good month when the Singapore Food Festival and Great Singapore Sale are held.

MAPS

Various good giveaway maps, many in Japanese as well as English, are available at tourist offices, at Changi airport, at most middle and top-end hotels and at some shopping centres.

Of the commercial maps, *Nelles* and *Periplus* are the best. The best reference of all if you plan on spending any length of time in Singapore or want to rent a car is the *Singapore Street Directory*, a bargain at S$9 plus GST, available at most bookshops.

TOURIST OFFICES

The Singapore Tourist Promotion Board (STPB) has two Tourist Information Centres. The first is on the ground floor at its head office at 1 Orchard Spring Rd (☎ 800-738 3778), off Cuscaden Rd in the Orchard Rd area. The other is conveniently located at 02-34 Raffles Hotel Arcade (☎ (800-334 1335) on North Bridge Rd. Both can answer most of your queries and have a good selection of hand-outs. The big hotels and Changi airport also stock a range of tourist leaflets and free tourist maps.

Pick up a copy of the *Singapore Official Guide*, which is updated monthly and has the latest opening hours, prices and bus routes. The STPB also produces other excellent publications, such as food, hotel, nightlife and shopping guides.

If you have access to the Internet and want to get the latest on Singapore before you go, the STPB puts its official guide on an excellent site: http://www.travel.com.sg/sog/

Singapore Tourist Promotion Board

The STPB offices overseas include:

Australia
: Suite 1202, Level 12, Westpac Plaza, 60 Margaret St, Sydney 2000, NSW (☎ (02) 9241-3771)
: 8th floor, St George's Court, 16 St George's Terrace, Perth 6000, WA (☎ (09) 325-8578)

Canada
: Suite 1000, The Standard Life Centre, 121 King St West, Toronto, Ontario M5H 3T9 (☎ (416) 363-8898)

France
: Centre d'Affaires Le Louvre, 2 Place du Palais-Royal, 75044 Paris Cedex 01 (☎ (01) 42.97.16.16)

Germany
: Hochstrasse 35-37, 60313 Frankfurt (☎ (069) 297 8825)

Hong Kong
: Suite 1402, Century Square, 1-3 D'Aguilar St, Central, Hong Kong (☎ 2522 4052)

Japan
: 1st floor, Yamato Seimei Building, 1 Chome, 1-7 Uchisaiwai-cho, Chiyoda-ku, Tokyo 100 (☎ (03) 3593-3388)

Switzerland
: Hochstrasse 48, CH-8044 Zurich (☎ (01) 252 5454)

UK
: 1st floor, Carrington House, 126-130 Regent St, London W1R 5FE (☎ (0171) 437-0033)

USA
: 12th floor, 590 Fifth Ave, New York, NY 10036 (☎ (212) 302-4861)
: Suite 510, 8484 Wilshire Blvd, Beverly Hills, CA 90211 (☎ (213) 852-1901)

VISAS & DOCUMENTS

Most nationalities do not require a visa to visit Singapore. Citizens of British Commonwealth countries (except India) and citizens of the Republic of Ireland, Liechtenstein, Monaco, Netherlands, San Marino, Switzerland and the USA do not require visas for any number of visits. Citizens of Austria, Belgium, Denmark, Finland, France, Germany, Iceland,

SINGAPORE

Italy, Japan, Korea, Luxembourg, Norway, Spain and Sweden do not require visas for social purposes for stays of up to 90 days.

Upon arrival a 14-day or 30-day-stay permit is normally issued depending on your stated length of stay. You can easily extend a 14-day-stay permit for another two weeks but you may be asked to show an air ticket out of Singapore and/or sufficient funds to stay. Further extensions are more difficult but in theory most nationalities can extend for up to 90 days. The Immigration Department (☎ 532 2877) is in the Pidemco Centre, 95 South Bridge Rd, on the corner of Pickering St, south of Boat Quay.

If you will be driving in Singapore, bring your current home licence and an International Driving Permit issued by a motoring association in your country.

Students should bring their international student card if they already have one – it's not of much use, as student discounts are almost invariably for Singaporeans only, but you might be able to bluff a discount at some attractions. A YHA card is not worth acquiring as Singapore has no YHA hostels but, again, bring it if you already have one as flashing it like a student card might bring discounts.

Travel insurance is always a wise investment and should be purchased before you leave home.

EMBASSIES

Singaporean Embassies

Some Singaporean embassies and high commissions overseas include:

Australia
: 17 Forster Crescent, Yarralumla, Canberra 2600, ACT (☎ (06) 273-3944)

France
: 12 Square de l'Avenue Foch, 75116 Paris (☎ (01) 45.00.36.61)

Germany
: Suedstrasse 133, 53175 Bonn 2 (☎ (228) 951 0314)

Hong Kong
: 9th floor, Admiralty Centre Tower I, 18 Harcourt Rd (☎ 2527-2212)

India
: E6 Chandragupta Marg, Chanakyapuri, New Delhi 110021 (☎ (011) 688 6506)

Indonesia
: Jalan H R Rasuna Said, Kuningan, Jakarta 12950 (☎ (021) 520-1489)

Japan
: 12-3 Roppongi, 5 Chome, Minato-ku, Tokyo (☎ (03) 3585-9111)

Malaysia
: 290 Jalan Tun Razak, 50400 Kuala Lumpur (☎ 03-261 6404)

New Zealand
: 17 Kabul St, Khandallah, Wellington (☎ (04) 479-2076)

Philippines
: 6th floor, ODC International Plaza, 219 Salcedo St, Legaspi Village, Makati, Metro Manila (☎ (02) 816-1764)

Thailand
: 129 Sathorn Tai Rd, Bangkok (☎ (02) 286-2111)

UK
: 9 Wilton Crescent, London SW1X 8SA (☎ (0171) 235-8135)

USA
: 3501 International Place NW, Washington, DC 20008 (☎ (202) 537-3100)

Foreign Embassies in Singapore

Many foreign consulates and embassies are conveniently located around Orchard Rd. Addresses for some of them include:

Australia
: 25 Napier Rd (☎ 737 9311)

Austria
: 22-05 Shaw Centre, 1 Scotts Rd (☎ 235 4088)

Belgium
: 09-24 International Plaza, 10 Anson Rd (☎ 220 7677)

Brunei
: 325 Tanglin Rd (☎ 733 9055)

Canada
: 14-00 IBM Towers, 80 Anson Rd (☎ 225 6363)

Denmark
: 13-01 United Square, 101 Thomson Rd (☎ 250 3383)

France
: 5 Gallop Rd (☎ 466 4866)

Germany
: 14-00 Far East Shopping Centre, 545 Orchard Rd (☎ 737 1355)

India
: 31 Grange Rd (☎ 737 6777)

Indonesia
: 7 Chatsworth Rd (☎ 737 7422)

Italy
: 27-02 United Square, 101 Thomson Rd (☎ 250 6022)

Japan
: 34-00 IBM Towers, 80 Anson Rd (☎ 235 8855)

Malaysia
301 Jervois Rd (☎ 235 0111)
Myanmar (Burma)
05-04 BN Building, 133 Middle Rd
(☎ 338 1073)
Netherlands
13-01 Liat Towers, 541 Orchard Rd (☎ 737 1155)
New Zealand
15-06 Ngee Ann City Tower, 391A Orchard Rd
(☎ 235 9966)
Norway
44-01 Hong Leong Building, 16 Raffles Quay
(☎ 220 7122)
Philippines
20 Nassim Rd (☎ 737 3977)
Sri Lanka
13-07 Goldhill Plaza, 51 Newton Rd
(☎ 254 4595)
Sweden
05-08 PUB Building, 111 Somerset Rd
(☎ 734 2771)
Switzerland
1 Swiss Club Link (☎ 468 5788)
Thailand
370 Orchard Rd (☎ 737 2644)
UK
Tanglin Rd (☎ 473 9333)
USA
30 Hill St (☎ 338 0251)

CUSTOMS

Visitors to Singapore are allowed to bring in one litre of wine, beer or spirits duty-free. Electronic goods, cosmetics, watches, cameras, jewellery (but not imitation jewellery), footwear, toys, arts and crafts are not dutiable, and for other items such as clothes the usual duty-free concession for personal effects applies. Singapore does not allow duty-free concessions for cigarettes and tobacco. Importing of chewing gum is banned, but you are most unlikely to have your gum confiscated if it is for personal use.

Duty-free concessions are not available if you come from Malaysia or if you leave Singapore for less than 48 hours (ie you can no longer stock up on duty-free goods on a day trip to Batam in Indonesia).

Drugs, fire crackers, toy coins and currency, obscene or seditious material, gun-shaped cigarette lighters, endangered species of wildlife or their by-products and pirated recordings and publications are prohibited. *The importation or exportation of illegal drugs carries the death penalty* for more than 15 grams of heroin, 30 grams of morphine, 500 grams of cannabis or 200 grams of cannabis resin, or 1.2 kg opium. Trafficking in lesser amounts ranges from a minimum of two years in jail and two strokes of the rotan to 30 years and 15 stokes of the rotan. If you bring in prescription drugs you should have a doctor's letter or prescription confirming that they are necessary.

There is no restriction on the importation of currency.

MONEY

Costs

Singapore is much more expensive than other South-East Asian countries and the strength of the Singapore dollar against most currencies has seen a substantial rise in costs for most visitors.

If you are travelling on a shoestring budget, prices will come as a shock but you can still stay in Singapore without spending too much money. The great temptation is to run amok in the shops and blow your budget on electrical goods or indulge in all the luxuries you may have craved while travelling in less-developed Asian countries.

Expect to pay US$4 per night or more for a dorm bed and from US$15 to US$35 for a double room in a cheap hotel or guesthouse. You can eat well in Singapore for a reasonable price. A good meal at a food centre can cost less than US$3. Transport is cheap in Singapore and many of the island's attractions are free. So it is possible to stay in Singapore for under US$15 per day, though US$20 is a more realistic minimum. You should be prepared to spend a lot more if you want to eat in some restaurants, check out the nightlife or visit a lot of the attractions.

If you have more to spend, then most of your cash will be absorbed in hotel bills and restaurants. Mid-range, second-string hotels cost from US$35 to US$60, though hotels at the top of this range are of a pretty good standard. International-standard hotels cost from US$100 and go way up. Depending on discounts available, top-end hotels may offer good value for the facilities on offer. Restaurants cost US$10 or less for a good meal in an old-style coffee shop or a meal in a fast-food restaurant. For US$10 to US$20 you can eat at a fancier restaurant, and you can dine in top restaurants in this range if set meals, buffets or cheaper lunch menus are on offer. Above US$20 should get you high standards of food and service, though you will generally have to spend US$30 or much more to dine at Singapore's best restaurants. Taxis are quite cheap in Singapore, as are many other nonessentials.

Credit Cards & ATMs

All major credit cards are widely accepted, although you're not going to make yourself too popular after a hard bargaining session for a new camera if you then try to pay for it with your Visa card. The authorities suggest that if shops insist on adding a surcharge you contact the relevant credit company in Singapore.

If your credit card has a personal identification number (PIN) attached, you can make cash withdrawals at most automatic teller machines (ATMs). A credit card is an easy way to carry your money. Of course, you will be charged interest unless you make sure your account is in the black before you leave. It is still a good idea to have some back-up cash, travellers' cheques or another credit card or two, in case something goes wrong with your main credit card account.

Many banks are now connected to international networks, allowing you to withdraw funds from your savings account if you have a card with a PIN attached, eg Singapore banks are networked to the Cirrus, Plus and Star systems. Check with your bank at home before you leave.

Currency

The unit of currency is the Singapore dollar.

Singapore uses 1c, 5c, 10c, 20c, 50c and S$1 coins, while notes are in denominations of S$2, S$5, S$10, S$50, S$100, S$500 and

Fines

'Singapore is a fine country', said the taxi driver. 'In Singapore we have fines for everything.'

In Singapore a number of activities are frowned upon, and the sometimes Draconian methods of dealing with minor transgressions have caused both mirth and dread among visitors. The famous campaign against long hair is a thing of the past, but it wasn't that long ago that immigration inspections included looking at hair length, and long-haired men were turned away on arrival or given a short-back-and-sides on the spot.

Singapore remains tough on a number of other minor issues, however, and the standard way of stamping out un-Singaporean activities is to slap a S$1000 fine on any offender. Actually, it is very rare that anybody does get fined that much, but the severity of the fines is enough to ensure compliance.

Smoking in public places – buses, lifts, cinemas, restaurants, air-conditioned shopping centres and government offices – is hit with a S$500 fine. You can smoke at food stalls and on the street (as long as you dispose of your butt, of course). The move to ban smoking in private cars was eventually quashed because of the difficulty of enforcing it. A few years ago it was fashionable among Singapore subversives to urinate in elevators, but a successful campaign of heavy fines and security cameras has stamped that one out.

Jaywalking is a relatively minor crime – walk across the road within 50 metres of a designated crossing and it could cost you S$50. The successful anti-littering campaign continues, with fines of up to S$1000 for dropping even a cigarette butt on the street. Not surprisingly, Singapore is amazingly clean.

The MRT, Singapore's pride and joy, attracts some particularly heavy fines. Eating, drinking and smoking are forbidden, and watch out if you use the MRT toilet and don't flush it. In fact, the 'flush or fine' campaign applies all over Singapore and has prompted apocryphal reports of flush sensors in the toilets to detect offenders.

The latest frowned-upon activity in Singapore is gum chewing. Anti-social elements were leaving gum deposits on the doors of the MRT, causing disruptions to underground rail services. The sale and importation of chewing gum is now banned and subject to heavy fines, though individual 'possession' is not an offence. ■

S$1000; Singapore also has a S$10,000 note – not that you'll see too many.

Currency Exchange

The following table shows the exchange rates:

Australia	A$1	=	S$1.11
Canada	C$1	=	S$1.03
France	FF10	=	S$2.72
Germany	DM1	=	S$0.92
Hong Kong	HK$10	=	S$1.82
Indonesia	Rp 1000	=	S$0.60
Japan	¥100	=	S$1.29
Malaysia	RM 1	=	S$0.56
New Zealand	NZ$1	=	S$0.95
Thailand	Baht 100	=	S$5.57
UK	UK£1	=	S$2.16
USA	US$1	=	S$1.41

Changing Money

Most of the major banks are in the Central Business District, although there are also a number of banks along Orchard Rd and local banks all over the city. Exchange rates tend to vary from bank to bank and some even have a service charge on each exchange transaction – this is usually S$2 to S$3, so ask first. Banks are open from 9.30 am to 3 pm weekdays and from 9.30 to 11.30 am on Saturday.

Moneychangers do not charge fees, so you will often get a better overall exchange rate for cash and travellers' cheques than at the banks. You will find moneychangers in just about every shopping centre in Singapore. Indeed, most of the shops will accept foreign cash and travellers' cheques at a slightly lower rate than you'd get from a moneychanger.

Apart from changing other currencies to Singapore dollars, moneychangers also offer a wide variety of other currencies for sale and will do amazing multiple-currency transactions in the blink of an eye. You can even get good rates for some restricted currencies.

Tipping & Bargaining

Tipping is not usual in Singapore. The most expensive hotels and restaurants have a 10% service charge, in which case tipping is discouraged. Don't tip at hawker stalls, though the more expensive coffee shops and restaurants that do not add a service charge may expect a tip. Taxi drivers do not expect a tip and may actually round a fare down if it is 10c or 20c above an even dollar, though they may expect you similarly to round it up. Staff in the international hotels, such as the room staff or the doorman who hails your taxis, may expect a tip if they have provided good service.

Bargaining is falling by the wayside in Singapore, but tourists should still expect to haggle for luxury items and souvenirs in some stores. It is unnecessary to bargain for everyday goods or transport, as happens in many Asian countries, though it doesn't hurt to ask about discounts at the more expensive hotels.

Many shops and department stores have fixed prices for clothes and luxury items. A fair number of small shops in the tourist areas, especially electronic shops, don't display prices. In this case bargaining is almost always required, and a request for prices is usually greeted with talk of special offers and the production of a calculator. For antiques, handicrafts and other tourist-oriented items, a price tag doesn't mean you can't bargain, and you usually should.

Some smaller traders put only a small mark-up on goods, while others are very greedy. You need to know prices. With so many large discount stores and fixed-price shops, it hardly seems worth bargaining in Singapore anymore.

Taxes & Service Charges

Singapore's has a 3% GST applied to all goods and services. Visitors purchasing goods worth S$500 or more through a shop participating in the GST Tourist Refund Scheme can apply for a refund of GST. Shops participating in the scheme display a 'tax refund' sticker, and you must fill in a claim form upon presentation of a passport at the shop. The claim form and the goods must then be presented to the relevant counter at Changi or Seletar airports on departure. You then mail the customs-stamped form back to the shop, which will post a cheque for the refund.

In addition to the 3% GST, a 10% service charge and 1% 'cess' (government entertainment tax) is added to the more expensive hotel and restaurant bills, as well as at most nightspots and bars. This is the 'plus-plus-plus' that follows quoted prices, for example, S$120+++. Some of the cheaper establishments don't add taxes but absorb them into the quoted price. This is 'nett' price, eg S$70 nett.

POST & COMMUNICATIONS

Postal Rates

The GPO on Fullerton Rd, close to the Singapore River near Raffles Place, is open 24 hours for basic postal services. The efficient poste restante service is open only during normal business hours. The Comcentre, 31 Exeter Rd, very near the Somerset MRT station on Orchard Rd, is also open 24 hours, and the Changi airport post office is open from 8 am to 8 pm.

An air mail letter to most Asia-Pacific countries costs 60c or 70c for the first 20 grams and 25c or 30c for each additional 10 grams; to Europe and the Americas the cost is S$1 for the first 20 grams and 35c for each additional 10 grams. Postcards are 50c.

Parcel rates by surface mail to countries outside the region cost around S$14 to S$19 for the first kg, around S$25 to S$30 for up to five kg. For up to 10 kg the cost is around S$35 to S$40, the main exception being the USA, where heavier parcels are about double the rate to any other destination.

Telephone

From telephone booths, the cost of a call is 10c for three minutes. Local calls from inside the terminal at Changi airport are free. A few hotels have free local calls, though most charge around 50c per call and some charge by the minute. The going surcharge on international calls is 25%.

Overseas telephone calls can be made 24 hours a day and the service is very efficient. As well as at hotels, you can make international phone calls at a Telecom centre, such as the ones at 15 Hill St (near Fort Canning Park) or 71 Robinson Rd (near Raffles Quay), or at selected post offices, such as the GPO.

The easiest way to make an international phone call is to dial it yourself from a public pay phone, but you'll need a phone card and a phone which accepts these cards (many pay phones will now operate only with phone cards – not coins). Phone cards, which come in denominations of S$2 to S$50, are available at Telecom centres, post offices and a number of retail outlets such as newsagents and some supermarkets.

Credit-card phones are also available (just swipe your Amex, Diners, MasterCard or Visa card through the slot). At the phone centres, there are also Home Country Direct phones – press a country button to contact the operator, then reverse the charges or have the call charged to your international telephone card. The Home Country Direct service is available from any phone by dialling the appropriate code, listed in the front pages of the phone book.

For directory information call 03; the police emergency number is 999.

The country code for calling Singapore is 65.

BOOKS

Lonely Planet

Lonely Planet publishes the *Singapore city guide* and a *Malay phrasebook* and a *Mandarin phrasebook*. LP's *South-East Asia on a shoestring* is our overall guidebook to the region. There are also individual guides to all South-East and North-East Asian countries.

Guidebooks

Living in Singapore by the American Association of Singapore is handy for westerners planning to set up house in Singapore. This is a useful introduction to life in the tropical city-state.

The *1907 Handbook to Singapore* by GM Reith is a reprint by the Oxford University Press of a British colonial guide that describes the sights of old Singapore. It concentrates on the public buildings, gardens and clubs, many of which have hardly changed. It comes with the attitudes of the times, eg Malay is called a 'primitive language', but largely avoids reference to Asian cultures. It is a good insight into the interests of the British colonial, and the photographs, old map and advertisements are interesting.

History

There are a great number of books dealing with various events in Singapore's history.

A History of Singapore by CM Turnball is the best choice for a detailed overview of Singapore's history from prehistory to the present. It is an excellent scholarly work which is also very readable and a mine of interesting information. The author has also written *A Short History of Malaysia, Singapore & Brunei*.

Singapore: Its Past, Present and Future by Alex Josey deals mostly with Singapore's later history and is very pro-People's Action Party.

Raffles by Maurice Collins is the straightforward story of the man who founded Singapore.

Politics

Lee Kuan Yew – The Struggle for Singapore by Alex Josey covers all the twists and turns of Lee Kuan Yew's rise to power and the successful path along which his People's Action Party has piloted Singapore.

Governing Singapore by Raj Vasil is widely available in Singapore and is as close as you'll get to the official PAP line. It includes interviews with Lee Kuan Yew and Goh Chok Tong.

No Man Is an Island by James Minchin is hard to find in Singapore. For an insight into both sides of the PAP story, this warts-and-all portrait of Lee Kuan Yew is one of the best.

Chee Soon Juan, the leader of the Singapore Democratic Party, is a thorn in the side of the government. After standing in the 1992 elections against Goh Chok Tong, he was sacked from his academic post for allegedly misusing postage funds and then sued for S$1 million for claiming that his dismissal was politically motivated. His book *Dare to Change: an Alternative Vision for Singapore* (1994) roundly criticises the government and offers social-democrat alternatives. It was such a local success that it has been followed by *Singapore: My Home Too* (1995).

Another thorn in the side of the government, and also a former academic at the National University of Singapore, is Christopher Lingle. His article in the *International Herald Tribute*, questioning the independence of the judiciary, resulted in yet another defamation suit in the government's favour. Dr Lingle fled the country and continues the battle in *Singapore's Authoritarian Capitalism* (1996), a damning study of political repression and the 'Asian Values' professed by the government.

People & Society

Tales of Chinatown by Sit Yin Fong is a readable and informative piece on Chinese life. Fong was a journalist in Singapore for many years and writes anecdotal short stories about Chinese customs and beliefs.

Son of Singapore by Tan Kok Seng is the fascinating autobiography of a labourer who grew up in Singapore in the 1950s.

The Babas Revisited by Felix Chia is a classic study of the history, culture and language of the Straits Chinese.

Culture Shock: Singapore by Jo Ann Craig, one of a popular series, explains the customs, cultures and lifestyles of Singapore's polyglot population primarily to expatriates working there.

Fiction

Singapore and Malaysia have always provided a fertile setting for novelists, and Joseph Conrad's *The Shadow Line* and *Lord Jim* both use the region as a backdrop. Somerset Maugham spent time in Singapore writing his classic short stories, many of which were set in Malaya – look for the *Borneo Stories*.

Singapore has recently experienced a literary boom and many young novelists are hard at work writing in English about Singapore. Of the old guard, Goh Sin Tub is a respected writer who has written many books. *Goh's 12 Best Singapore Stories* is widely available. *Juniper Loa* by Lin Yutang is set mostly in the 1920s and is typical of earlier literature looking back at the mother land and the immigrant experience. It is about a young man who leaves China for Singapore and Juniper Loa is the woman he leaves behind.

Of the recent novelists, Philip Jeyaretnem is one of the leading lights and his *Raffles Place Ragtime* is a Singaporean best-seller. *A Candle or the Sun* by Gopal Baratham was published in 1991, after years of rejection by skittish Singaporean publishers. It is about a Christian group that runs foul of the authorities by questioning the government's authoritarianism. *Fistful of Colours* by Suchen Christine Lim, a winner of the Singapore Literature Prize, contrasts the difference and tensions between the modern and traditional, the old and the young in Singapore's ethnic communities. Catherine Lim is another highly regarded woman writer. Her books, such as *Little Ironies – Stories of Singapore*, are mostly about relationships with Singapore as a backdrop.

General

Portraits of Places (1995) by Brenda SA Yeoh and Luly Kong is an interesting sociological study of changing Singapore, examining selected areas from the Orchard Rd to Kampung Wak Selat, the 'last village in Singapore', near Kranji.

David Brazil's *Street Smart Singapore* is a lively look at the Lion City stacked with interesting titbits on its history and culture.

The *Mr Kiasu* comic books portray the 'kiasu' (ie selfish, pushy, always-on-the-lookout-for-a-bargain) Singaporean. The Singlish-speaking, nonconformist, 'everything also must grab' Mr Kiasu has reached celebrity status in Singapore. These original and distinctly Singaporean cartoons are proof that Singaporeans can laugh at themselves.

Bookshops

Singapore's main bookshop chains are MPH and Times, with a huge range of books in English. In the Orchard Rd area, Centrepoint and Plaza Singapura shopping centres have a good selection of bookshops.

MPH's main shop at 71-77 Stamford Rd in the colonial district has been extensively renovated and is probably the best general bookshop in the region. It is also the most salubrious, and has a coffee shop and a record store. MPH also has other stores on the 4th floor of Centrepoint on Orchard Rd, on Robinson Rd and at Changi airport.

Times also has a large bookstore on the 4th floor of Centrepoint on Orchard Rd, and at Lucky Plaza and Plaza Singapura on Orchard Rd, Holland Village, Changi airport, Marina Square and a large store at Raffles City.

Select Books on the 3rd floor of the Tanglin shopping centre at 19 Tanglin Rd, north of the Orchard Rd area, specialises in general and academic books on Asia and is the best in Singapore for books on South-East Asia.

NEWSPAPERS & MAGAZINES

Singapore has three Chinese daily newspapers with a combined daily circulation of over 450,000 and three English newspapers with a slightly higher circulation. There is also a Malay daily and a Tamil daily. The major newspapers come under the umbrella of the gigantic Singapore Press Holdings.

The English daily newspapers are the establishment *Straits Times*, the *Business Times* and the *New Paper*, an evening tabloid. The *Straits Times* has good regional and foreign news and some good feature articles. The best independent views on Singaporean politics are found in the readers' letters.

The *New Paper* is a long way behind the *Straits Times* in circulation and is seen as the fun alternative. It is a more staid version of an English tabloid and comes up with some amazingly trite, attention-grabbing headlines. It contains very little news. *Time*, *Newsweek* and many other foreign magazines are readily available.

The press in Singapore knows its limits and you will find very little criticism of the government. The foreign media sometimes doesn't know its limits, and the government has brought pressure to bear on, or restricted the circulation of, foreign publications that do not report to its liking, as the *Far Eastern Economic Review* and others have found out.

RADIO & TV

The government-run Singapore Broadcasting Corporation was corporatised in 1994, which has seen a slight relaxation of government controls on broadcasting although television censorship is still fairly strict.

The Radio Corporation of Singapore controls most of the radio stations, with 10 stations transmitting in four languages – Malay, Mandarin, Tamil and English – on the AM, FM and short-wave bands. The BBC transmits in Singapore on 88.9 FM.

Singapore has three TV channels: 5, 8 and 12, broadcasting in English, Mandarin, Malay and Tamil, and cable television is on the way. Singaporeans can also pick up Malaysian television – TV1 and TV2.

Channel 8 carries mostly local productions, a booming area. Singapore has been making local news shows, game shows and fairly amateurish dramatic productions for years, but local production is looking healthy and starting to out-rate the many American imports. *Under One Roof* is an enormously popular Singaporean sit-com that has already inspired two offshoots.

PHOTOGRAPHY

It is, of course, polite to ask permission before photographing people or taking pictures in mosques or temples. There is usually no objection to taking photographs in places of worship; in Chinese temples virtually anything goes.

Film is cheap and readily available in Singapore. Processing is also reasonably priced.

TIME

Singapore is 16 hours ahead of US Pacific Standard Time (San Francisco and Los Angeles), 13 hours ahead of US Eastern Standard Time (New York), eight hours ahead of GMT/UTC (London) and two hours behind Australian Eastern Standard Time (Sydney and Melbourne). Thus, when it is noon in Singapore, it is 8 pm in Los Angeles and 11 pm in New York (the previous day), 4 am in London and 2 pm in Sydney and Melbourne.

ELECTRICITY

Electricity supplies are dependable and run at 220-240V and 50 cycles. Plugs are of the three-square-pin type, as used in the UK.

WEIGHTS & MEASURES

Singapore uses the metric system, though you may occasionally come across references to odd measurements such as the *thola*, an Indian weight, or *batu*, the Malay word for mile (literally meaning stone).

LAUNDRY

Singapore has plenty of laundries, such as the Laundryland chain (check the phone book). There is a Laundryland at 01-06 Orchard Towers on Orchard Rd. A large load, including drying and folding, costs around S$10. All major hotels offer a laundry service, which can set you back a small fortune, and even most cheap hotels do laundry at more moderate rates.

HEALTH

In Singapore you can eat virtually anywhere and not worry, and the tap water is safe to drink. Vaccinations are required only if you come from a yellow fever area, and Singapore is not a malarial area. The main health concern is the heat; it is important to avoid dehydration by drinking plenty of fluids.

Dehydration or salt deficiency can cause heat exhaustion. Take time to acclimatise to high temperatures and make sure you get sufficient liquids. Salt deficiency is characterised by fatigue, lethargy, headaches, giddiness and muscle cramps, and in this case salt tablets may help.

Medical facilities are of a high standard and readily available. A visit to a general practitioner costs around S$30. Singapore's public hospitals will accept self-referred patients. Singapore General Hospital (☎ 222 3322) is on Outram Rd, near Chinatown and the Outram Park MRT station.

WOMEN TRAVELLERS

Singapore is probably the safest Asian country to travel in and sexual harassment is very rare. Women are not cloistered in Singaporean society and enjoy much more freedom and equality than in the rest of Asia. Government policy favours sexual equality, and abortion is available on request, although not for 'foreign' pregnancies.

DANGERS & ANNOYANCES

Singapore is a very safe country with low crime rates. The usual precautions apply and pickpockets are not unknown, but in general crime is not a problem. This is not surprising given the harsh penalties meted out to offenders and the fact that hundreds of suspected criminals are held in jail without trial because the government does not have enough evidence to ensure conviction.

The importation of drugs carries the death penalty and, quite simply, drugs in Singapore should be avoided at all costs, not that you are likely to come across them. In case you think the government is bluffing, the tally of executions for drug convictions stands at over 40 so far, an astonishing number given the size of Singapore's population.

BUSINESS HOURS

In Singapore government offices are usually open from Monday to Friday and Saturday morning. Hours vary, starting around 7.30 to 9.30 am and closing between 4 and 6 pm. On Saturday, closing time is between 11.30 am and 1 pm.

Shop hours are also variable. Small shops are generally open Monday to Saturday from 10 am to 6 pm, while department stores and large shopping centres are open from 10 am to 9 or 9.30 pm, seven days a week. Most small shops in Chinatown and Arab St close on Sunday, though Sunday is the big day in Little India.

PUBLIC HOLIDAYS & SPECIAL EVENTS

The following days are public holidays in Singapore. For those days not based on the western calendar, the months they are likely to fall in are given:

New Year's Day
  1 January
Chinese New Year
  January or February – two days
Hari Raya Puasa
  January or February
Good Friday
  April
Hari Raya Haji
  April
Labour Day
  1 May
Vesak Day
  May
National Day
  9 August
Deepavali
  November
Christmas Day
  25 December

With so many cultures and religions, there is an amazing number of celebrations in Singapore. Many of the religious events are the same as those celebrated in Malaysia. The tourist office puts out a *Festivals & Events* brochure each year, and the *Singapore Official Guide* has more specific and detailed listings for each month.

Chinese New Year is the major holiday and the streets have plenty of life, and the dramatic Thaipusam Hindu festival is also celebrated in Singapore with masochistic feats.

The Singapore Festival of Arts is a biennial event held every even year, featuring a programme of art, dance, drama and music. The innovative Fringe Festival puts on free performances. It alternates with a Festival of Asian Performing Arts held every odd year.

In July, the Singapore Food Festival celebrates the national passion, with special offerings at everything from hawker centres to gourmet restaurants.

During the Great Singapore Sale, Orchard Rd is decked out with banners and merchants are encouraged by the government to drop prices in an effort to boost Singapore's image as a shopping destination. It is held for one month around July and usually overlaps with the Food Festival for a couple of weeks.

Singapore National Day is held on 9 August, when a series of military and civilian processions and an evening firework display celebrate Singapore's independence in 1965.

The Pilgrimage to Kusu Island, held around November, honours Tua Pek Kong, the Taoist God of Prosperity.

Singapore 'light-ups', when the streets are decked with lights, are a speciality. During Deepavali, Little India is ablaze with lights for a month to celebrate the most important Hindu festival. At Christmas, Orchard Rd celebrates with shopfront displays and the Christmas light-up.

FOOD & DRINKS

Food is the national pastime in Singapore, and the variety of places to try it is simply astonishing. Hawker centres are everywhere, and Singapore's restaurants serve every type of cuisine imaginable.

For the most part, the traditional Chinese, Indian and Malay dishes found in Malaysia are the same as those found in Singapore – see the Malaysia Food section for details. If Singapore has a national dish it is Hokkien fried mee, which Singaporeans have adopted as their own and call 'Singapore fried noodles'.

Singapore has all the favourite regional drinks you'll find in Malaysia, and there are no dry areas in Singapore!

Getting There & Away

AIR

Along with Bangkok, Singapore is a major travel hub in Asia and a good place to buy air tickets. The overwhelming bulk of international air traffic goes through Changi airport (see the Getting Around chapter), while small Seletar airport services only a handful of short regional flights.

Travel Agencies in Singapore

Singapore is a good place to look for cheap plane tickets, and it competes with Bangkok and Penang to be the discount flight centre of the region.

For good travel agents, STA Travel (☎ 734 5681) in the Orchard Parade Hotel, 1 Tanglin Rd, is part of the international budget travel chain and it also has an office (more a booth) at 127 Bencoolen St under the Why Not Homestay in the colonial district. Also on Bencoolen St at 171-C in the same building as Hawaii Hostel is Harharah Travel (☎ 337 2633). All these travel agents sell air, bus and train tickets. Airpower Travel (☎ 337 1392) at B1-07 Selegie Centre, 189 Selegie Rd, north of Fort Canning Park, and at 26 Sultan Gate (☎ 294 5664), near Arab St, is recommended by many travellers.

Otherwise Singapore has hundreds of travel agents all over town for checking prices on flights. Chinatown Point on New Bridge Rd in Chinatown has a good selection of large travel agents upstairs for one-stop shopping for tickets and tours.

Fares vary with when you want to fly and with whom you want to fly. The cheapest fares are likely to be with the least loved airlines (various Eastern European ones, Bangladesh Biman etc), via inconvenient routes (you're forced to make stopovers on the way) at awkward times (they only fly every other Tuesday at 3 am).

Some typical rock-bottom discount fares being quoted in Singapore include South-East Asian destinations like Bangkok from S$200 one-way, Denpasar from S$220 one-way or S$370 excursion return and Jakarta S$120 one-way or S$200 return. To the subcontinent, you can fly to Delhi or Kathmandu for S$450 one-way, Madras for S$400.

Fares to Australia include Sydney or Melbourne for S$500 one-way or S$600 excursion return and Perth from $400 one-way or S$500 return. London, or other European destinations, costs from S$550 one-way with the Eastern European airlines and from S$620 one-way with the better airlines.

One-way fares to the US west coast are around S$650 direct or with a stop in Manila.

There are always some special multistop deals on offer, such as Singapore-Jakarta-Sydney-Noumea-Auckland-Papeete-Los Angeles for S$1600.

USA

Tickets to Singapore in the low season start from as little US$750 return from the US west coast, US$1000 return from the east coast. High season prices from June through August can jump to US$1100 from the west coast, US$1300 from New York.

Singapore Airlines (SIA) and others have direct flights but it is usually cheaper to fly via another port, such as with China Airlines via Taipei or Cathay Pacific via Hong Kong.

It is also worth looking into circle Pacific flights. From Los Angeles or San Francisco you can fly Honolulu-Denpasar-Singapore, then overland to Bangkok, flying on to Hong Kong or Taipei, and then return to the USA for around US$1250. For US$1500, you go via Auckland and the South Pacific. Add another US$200 to include Australia.

The *New York Times*, the *LA Times*, the *Chicago Tribune* and the *San Francisco Examiner* all produce weekly travel sections in which you'll find any number of travel agents' ads. Council Travel and STA Travel have offices in major cities nationwide.

The magazine *Travel Unlimited* (PO Box 1058, Allston, MA 02134) publishes details of the cheapest air fares and courier possibilities for destinations all over the world from the USA.

Australia

Advance-purchase return fares from the Australian east coast to Singapore vary from around A$750 to A$1000 return, depending on the season of travel and the length of stay. From Perth fares are around A$650 to A$950. The 30-day or 45-day excursion fares are the cheapest, while the most expensive is a return ticket valid for over 60 days in the high season, generally from 15 November to 31 January.

Many of the airlines that fly from Australia to Asia, the Middle East and Europe stopover in Singapore. Two of the cheapest are Gulf Air and Lauda Air. Gulf Air flights for around A$750 are the cheapest on offer and bookings should be made well in advance. Singapore Airlines and Qantas are the main carriers. Both have cheap package tours and good stopover accommodation deals, as does Malaysia Airlines (MAS). MAS sometimes has cheap flights to Singapore via Kuala Lumpur.

For cheap tickets, STA Travel has competitive prices for Asian air fares, as does the Flight Centre, another Australia-wide chain which can also offer good accommodation discounts, but shop around.

New Zealand

A number of airlines fly from Auckland to Singapore. Return tickets range from around NZ$1100 in the off season to NZ$1400 in the high season. The high season is generally December and January. Air France was offering some of the lowest off-season fares. British Airways, Air New Zealand, Singapore Airlines, Qantas and Garuda all fly direct to Singapore, or stopovers are possible in Indonesia and Australia.

Flight Centre and STA Travel are two large discount travel agents with offices throughout the country.

UK

London has the best deals for flights to Singapore, serviced by a host of airlines. Singapore Airlines, British Airways and Qantas are major carriers, but cheaper tickets are usually with less loved airlines such as Aeroflot via Moscow or Pakistan International Airlines via Karachi for as little as UK£220 one-way, UK£415 return. Finnair via Helsinki and some of the Arab airlines such as Royal Jordanian and Emirates are other discounters.

Prices for direct flights with Singapore Airlines or Qantas start from around UK£500.

For information on travel agents and special deals, check the Sunday papers and weekly listings magazines such as *Time Out*. London's 'bucket' shops can offer some great deals, but some of these places are fly-by-night operations. Most British agents are registered with the Association of British Travel Agents (ABTA), which guarantees tickets booked with member agents.

Popular and reliable British agents are Campus Travel (☎ (0171) 730 8111), with 41 branches nationwide; STA Travel (☎ (0171) 361 6262); Trailfinders (☎ (0171) 938 3366), with branches in London, Birmingham, Bristol, Glasgow and Manchester; and Crusader Travel (☎ (0181) 744 0474).

Continental Europe

Special round-trip fares to Singapore from Amsterdam have recently ranged from Dfl 2409 to Dfl 7486 and from Paris from FF 9270 to FF 14,440.

Malaysia

The shuttle service operated by Malaysia Airlines and Singapore Airlines has frequent flights between Kuala Lumpur and Singapore for RM119 (S$111 from Singapore); seats are available on a first-come, first-served basis. Booked seats cost RM159 (S$147). MAS also connects Singapore to Kuantan (RM146, S$136), Langkawi (RM218, S$204) and Penang (RM182, S$170) in Peninsular Malaysia, and Kuching (RM205, S$193) and Kota Kinabalu (RM418, S$391) in East Malaysia. First class fares are around 40% extra.

Pelangi Air has daily direct flights from Singapore's Changi airport to Melaka (RM118,

S$110); from Seletar airport, Pelangi has daily flights to/from Tioman Island (RM112, S$99).

Silk Air also has daily flights to/from Tioman (RM112, S$99), and flights to/from Kuantan (RM146, S$136) and Langkawi (RM$180, S$170).

Return fares are double the single fares quoted here. Fares from Singapore to Malaysia are almost the same price as Malaysia to Singapore, but in Singapore dollars not Malaysian ringgit. With the considerable difference in the exchange rate it is much cheaper to buy tickets in Malaysia, eg rather than a return fare to Kuala Lumpur from Singapore, buy a one-way ticket and the return leg in Kuala Lumpur.

Going to Malaysia, you can save quite a few dollars if you fly from Johor Bahru rather than Singapore. For example, to Kota Kinabalu the fares are RM418 from Johor Bahru but S$391 from Singapore. To persuade travellers to take advantage of these lower fares, the SPS (☎ 250 3333) bus service operated by Malaysia Airlines runs directly from the Novotel Orchid, 214 Dunearn Rd, to the Johor Bahru airport. It costs S$10 and takes about two hours. In Singapore, tickets for internal flights originating in Malaysia are only sold by Malaysia Airlines (☎ 336 6777), 02-09 Singapore Shopping Centre, 190 Clemenceau Ave.

Indonesia

A number of airlines fly from Singapore to Jakarta for as low as S$120 one-way and around S$200 return. To Bali costs from S$220 one-way. Garuda is the main carrier, though Air France has been offering the lowest prices. Garuda also has direct flights between Singapore and Medan, Padang, Palembang, Pekanbaru, Pontianak and Surabaya.

Internal flights are cheaper if tickets are bought in Indonesia. For Pontianak in Kalimantan and some destinations in Sumatra, such as Pekanbaru, it is cheaper to take the ferry to Batam and then an internal flight from there. Garuda offers an internal air pass costing US$300 for three flights, but this is only economical for very long distances.

From Jakarta to Singapore, flights cost from as little as US$65 (Air India is currently one of the cheapest). For international flights, the travel agencies on Jalan Jaksa, the budget accommodation area, are convenient places to start looking. Indo Shangrila Travel (☎ 625 6080), Jalan Gajah Mada 219G, is a large ticketing agent and often has some good deals.

Departure Tax

From Singapore, the air departure tax is S$15.

LAND

Malaysia

Bus For Johor Bahru, the air-con express bus operated by Singapore-Johor Express Ltd (☎ 292 8149) departs every 15 minutes between 6.30 am and midnight from the Ban San terminal on the corner of Queen and Arab Sts. It costs S$1.80. Alternatively, the public SBS bus No 170 also leaves from the Ban San terminal and costs 90c; the Bugis MRT station is within walking distance. Bus No 170 can be hailed anywhere along the way, such as on Rochor, Rochor Canal or Bukit Timah Rds.

The bus stops at the Singapore checkpoint, but don't worry if it leaves while you clear immigration – keep your ticket and you can just hop on the next one that comes along. The bus then stops at Malaysian immigration and customs at the other end of the Causeway, one km away. After clearing the Malaysian checkpoint, you can then catch the bus again (your ticket is still valid) to the Johor Bahru bus terminus on the outskirts of town, or you can walk to town from the Causeway. Moneychangers, whose first offer will usually be less than the going rate, will approach you or there are plenty of banks and official moneychangers in Johor Bahru.

If you are travelling beyond Johor Bahru, it is easier to catch a long-distance bus straight from Singapore, but there is a greater variety of bus services from Johor Bahru and the fares are cheaper.

In Singapore, long-distance buses to Melaka and the east coast of Malaysia leave from and arrive at the bus terminal on the corner of Lavender St and Kallang Bahru, opposite the large Kallang Bahru complex. It is to the north-east of Bencoolen St, near the top end of Jalan Besar. Take the MRT to the Lavender station, then bus No 5 or 61; otherwise it's a half km walk.

Pan Malaysia Express (☎ 294 7034) has buses to Kuala Lumpur (S$17.80) at 9 am and 9 pm, Mersing (S$13.10) at 8, 9, 10 am and 10 pm, Kuantan (S$16.50) at 9 and 10 am and 10 pm, and Kota Bharu (S$30.10) at 7.30 pm. Also at the bus station, Hasry (☎ 294 9306) has buses to Kuala Lumpur (S$17) at 8 and 9 am and 3, 9.30 and 11 pm; Melaka at 8.30 am and 2.30 pm. Melaka-Singapore Express (☎ 293 5915) has buses to Melaka at 8, 9, 10, 11 am and 1, 2, 3, 4 and 5 pm. The fare is S$11 for an air-con bus and the trip takes 4½ hours. Most take the Lebuh Raya, the main north-south expressway, but a few take the old highway via Muar (S$9). It is preferable to buy your tickets the day before departure. Many travel agents also sell bus tickets to Malaysia.

For destinations north of Kuala Lumpur, most buses leave from the Golden Mile Complex, 5001 Beach Rd, at the north-east end near Arab St. The Lavender MRT station is about 0.5 km away. This terminal handles all the buses to Thailand and northern destinations on the way, such as Ipoh, Butterworth, Penang and Alor Setar. It costs around S$35 to Penang and most buses leave in the afternoon and evening. Bus agents line the outside the building. Kway Chow Travel (☎ 293 8977) and Gunung Raya (☎ 294 7711) are two of the bigger agents for Malaysian west coast destinations.

Morning Star Travel (☎ 292 9009) is another agent right at the Lavender MRT station. It has buses to Kuala Lumpur (S$17) at 9.30 am and 9.30 pm, Penang (S$35) at 8 pm, Alor Setar (S$36) at 6 pm and Melaka (S$11) at 8.30 am. All buses leave from next to the MRT station, except for the Melaka bus, which leaves from the Kallang Bharu terminal.

You can also catch buses to Kuala Lumpur from the Ban San terminal on the corner of Queen and Arab Sts. Kuala Lumpur-Singapore Express (☎ 292 8254) has buses to Kuala Lumpur at 9 am and 1 and 10 pm for S$17.30 or S$22 VIP.

Most of the buses are new and in immaculate condition with mod-cons such as radio, TV, toilet and freezing air-conditioning. To Kuala Lumpur takes about seven hours along the Lebuh Raya expressway. There's also a lunch and snack break on the way. Hitchhikers to Malaysia should go to Johor Bahru before starting.

Train Singapore is the southern termination point for the Malaysian railway system. Malaysia has two main rail lines: the primary line going from Singapore to Kuala Lumpur, Butterworth, Alor Star and then into Thailand; and a second line branching off at Gemas and going right up through the centre of the country to Tumpat, near Kota Bharu on the east coast.

The Singapore railway station (☎ 222 5165 for fare and schedule information) is on Keppel Rd, south-west of Chinatown, about one km from the Tanjong Pagar MRT station. The booking office is open 8.30 am to 2 pm and 3 to 7 pm.

Four trains go every day to Kuala Lumpur. The *Ekspres Rakyat* leaves at 7.30 am (arrives 1.50 pm), the *Ekspres Sinaran Pagi* at 2.25 pm (arrives 8.55 pm), a limited express train at 8 pm (arrives 5.10 am) and the *Sinandung Malam* at 10.30 pm (arrives 6.05 am).

All trains are efficient, well maintained and comfortable, but ordinary and mail trains stop at all stations and are slow. The express trains are well worth the extra money, and the *Ekspres Rakyat* continues on to Butterworth, arriving at 10.35 pm. There is also an express train to Tumpat (in the very north-east of Malaysia) at 11.30 pm, which reaches Jerantut at 4 am for Taman Negara National Park. Nonexpress train fares from Singapore to Malaysia include:

Destination		*Fare*	
	1st (S$)	*2nd (S$)*	*3rd (S$)*
Johor Bahru	4.20	1.90	1.10
Kuala Lumpur	60.00	26.00	14.80
Ipoh	91.50	39.70	22.60
Butterworth	118.50	51.40	29.20
Jerantut	60.00	26.00	14.80
Wakaf Baru	111.00	48.10	27.40

Express train fares from Singapore include:

Destination		*Fare*	
	1st (S$)	*2nd (S$)*	*3rd (S$)*
Johor Bahru	13	10	6
Kuala Lumpur	68	34	19
Ipoh	100	48	27
Butterworth	127	60	34
Jerantut	68	34	19
Wakaf Baru	119	57	32

While there is a noticeable jump in comfort from 3rd to 2nd class, 1st class is not much better than 2nd class and considerably more expensive.

You can buy a 30 day rail pass allowing unlimited travel in Malaysia for US$120, or a 10 day pass for US$55. The pass entitles you to travel on any class of train, but does not include sleeping berth charges. Rail passes are only available to foreign tourists and can be purchased at a number of main railway stations.

From Singapore, there is also a *relbas* service to Kulai, just past Johor Bahru. This train is a different way to get to Johor Bahru, but you should allow up to an hour to buy your ticket and clear customs. The buses are much quicker and more convenient. Trains leave at 8.30 and 11.40 am and 5.15 and 8 pm.

Taxi Malaysia has a cheap, well-developed, long-distance taxi system that makes Malaysian travel a real breeze. A long-distance taxi plies between set destinations, and as soon as a full complement of four passengers turns up, off you go. From Singapore, the best bet is to go to Johor Bahru and then take a taxi from there – it's cheaper and there are many more services – but Singapore also has such taxis to destinations in Malaysia.

For Johor Bahru, taxis leave from the Ban San terminal on the corner of Queen and Arab Sts. They cost S$6 per person, and an extra S$1 if there are long delays at the Causeway. Foreigners are likely to have to pay more or hire a whole taxi for S$24 since they take longer to clear the border than Singaporeans or Malaysians.

Crossing the Causeway The Causeway is that one-km link between Singapore and the mainland. An impressive piece of engineering in its day, it has difficulty coping with the amount of traffic on weekends and especially on long weekends and public holidays. If you're travelling by private vehicle or taxi, try to avoid these times. Take a bus, as buses sail on past in the express lane while the cars are stuck in the interminable queues.

Singapore has all sorts of future plans for improving cross-border traffic to Malaysia. A new bridge is planned between Geylang Patah in Malaysia and Tuas on the western side of Singapore Island. The MRT is being extended out to Woodlands and a new checkpoint will be built.

Thailand

If you want to go direct from Singapore to Thailand overland, the quickest and cheapest way is by bus.

Bus The main terminal for buses to and from Thailand is at the Golden Mile Complex, 5001 Beach Rd. It's at the north-eastern end of Beach Rd, where it meets Crawford St; the Lavender MRT station is within walking distance. A number of travel agents specialising in buses and tours to Thailand operate from there. Grassland Express (☎ 292 1166) has buses at 7 and 8.30 pm to Hat Yai. Phya Travel (☎ 293 6692) has buses to Hat Yai and Bangkok at 3.30 and 7 pm, with connections to Phuket and Suratthani from Hat Yai. Kwang Chow Travel (☎ 293 8977) has a bus to Hat Yai and Bangkok at 7.30 pm, or there are many other agents. Most leave in the afternoon and travel overnight.

Fares cost around S$35 to S$45, reflecting the difference in the buses, though all buses are air-con. The S$45 VIP coaches have videos and include a free meal. Most of these buses also stop in Butterworth.

Train The rail route into Thailand is on the Butterworth-Alor Setar-Hat Yai route, which crosses into Thailand at Padang Besar. From Butterworth trains go to/from Singapore. You can take the *International Express* from Butterworth in Malaysia all the way to Bangkok with connections from Singapore. The *International Express* leaves Butterworth at 1.40 pm, arrives in Hat Yai at 4.40 pm and in Bangkok at 8.35 am the following morning. From Singapore to Bangkok costs S$91.70 (2nd class).

A variation on the *International Express* is the *Eastern & Oriental Express*, which departs on alternate Fridays, Wednesdays, and Sundays. The train caters to the well heeled and is done out in antique opulence, South-East Asia's answer to the *Oriental Express*. It takes 42 hours to do the 2000 km journey from Singapore to Bangkok. Don your linen suit, sip a gin and tonic and dig deep for the fare: S$1920 per person in a double compartment, up to S$4990 in the presidential suite. You can also take the train just to Kuala Lumpur or Butterworth for less.

SEA

Singapore has a number of ferry connections to Malaysia and the Indonesian islands of the Riau Archipelago. Cruise trips in the region have also become very popular with Singaporeans.

The big cruise centre at the World Trade Centre, south-west of the railway station, is the main departure point for ferries and cruises. The World Trade Centre is a mini Changi airport with duty-free and other shops. A host of agents handle bookings for the ferries, cruises and resorts. To get to the World Trade Centre, take the MRT to Tanjong Pagar, then bus No 10, 97, 100 or 131. Buses Nos 65 and 143 go from Orchard Rd to the WTC. From the colonial district buses Nos 97 and 167 go from Bencoolen St or No 100 goes from Beach Rd.

The new Tanah Merah ferry terminal to the east near Changi airport also handles ferries to the Indonesian island of Bintan, and may handle other services in the future. Changi, at the far eastern tip of the island, also has ferries to Malaysia.

Malaysia

Tanjung Belungkor A ferry operates from Changi Village to Tanjung Belungkor, east of Johor Bahru. It is primarily a service for Singaporeans going to Desaru in Malaysia. The 11 km journey takes 45 minutes and costs S$15/24 (RM15/27) one-way/return for adults and S$9/15 (RM13/24) for children aged under 12 years. Cars cost S$20/32 (RM20/36) and bicycles $S4/7 (RM4/7). Ferries leave Singapore at 8.15 and 11.15 am and 12.15 and 5.15 pm; from Tanjung Belungkor departures are at 9.45 am and 12.45, 3.45 and 6.45 pm. From the Tanjung Belungkor jetty buses operate to Desaru and Kota Tinggi.

To get to the Changi terminal, take bus No 2 to Changi Village and then a taxi. The ferry terminal is behind Changi airport just off Changi Coast Rd.

Pengerang From Changi Village, ferries also go to Pengerang across the strait in Malaysia. This is an interesting back-door route into Malaysia. Ferries don't have a fixed schedule, which is most unlike Singapore, and leave throughout the day when a full quota of 12 people is reached. The cost is S$5 per person or S$60 for the whole boat. The best time to catch one is early in the morning before 8 am. Clear Singapore immigration at the small post on the Changi River dock.

Tioman Island To Tioman Island, Kalpin Tours (☎ 271 4866), 02-40 World Trade Centre, is the agent for the high-speed catamaran that does the trip in 4½ hours. Departures are at 7.55 am from the World Trade Centre and the fare is S$79/140 one-way/return. Sailings usually don't run in the monsoon season from October/November to March 1.

Kukup Kalpin Tours has ferries from the World Trade Centre to the fishing village of

Kukup in Johor, a popular weekend trip for Singaporeans. Ferries leaves at 7.55 am and 3 pm on Saturday and Sunday, returning at 10 am and 5 pm. The cost is S$26/36 one-way/return.

Indonesia

Curiously, no direct shipping services run between the main ports in Indonesia and near-neighbour Singapore but it is possible to travel between the two nations via the islands of the Riau Archipelago.

The Riau Archipelago is the cluster of Indonesian islands immediately south of Singapore. The two most visited islands are Batam and Bintan, both of which can be reached by ferry from Singapore. Most nationalities are issued a tourist pass, valid for 60 days, upon arrival and do not require a visa. The ferries are modern, fast and air-conditioned and show movies. From Batam boats go to Sumatra, a popular way to enter Indonesia.

Batam Batam Island is a resort and industrial park. From Singapore it only takes half an hour to reach Sekupang or 45 minutes to Batu Ampar, both on Batam Island.

Departures are from the World Trade Centre. The main agents to Batam are Kalpin Tours/Auto Batam (☎ 271 4866), Dino Shipping (☎ 270 2228) and Sin Ka Pin Marine (☎ 272 7540). Between them they have dozens of departures every day to Batam, at least every half hour from 7.35 am to 9.15 pm. Tickets cost S$16/26 one-way/return. Ferries dock at Sekupang, which has boats to Tanjung Buton on the Sumatran mainland, from where it is a three hour bus ride to Palembang. This a popular travellers' route to Sumatra.

Ferries also go to Batu Ampar on Batam, which is close to the main town of Nagoya, roughly every hour from 7.30 am to 8.30 pm. Dino Shipping also has two ferries a day at 9.35 am and 4.45 pm to Nongsapura in the north of the island.

Bintan The same companies that operate ferries to Batam also have ferries to Bintan from the World Trade Centre. Ferries go to Tanjung Pinang, the main city on the island, at 9, 9.50 and 10.10 am and 1.30, 3 and 5.10 pm. Tickets cost S$51/68 one-way/return. The journey takes about 1½ hours.

A new Tanah Merah ferry terminal has opened at the eastern end of Singapore on Tanah Merah Ferry Rd, off East Coast Parkway just before Changi airport. This terminal handles ferries to the big Bintan Resort in the north-west of Bintan. Departures are at 9 am, noon and 3.30 pm Monday to Thursday, returning at 10.45 am and 2.15 and 6.15 pm. Friday to Sunday, ferries leave at 9 am and 2.30 and 7 pm, returning at 2.15, 5.45 and 9 pm. Fares are S$30/49 one-way/return (S$16/27 for children) and the trip takes one hour. Book with Bintan Resort Ferries (☎ 345 1210). Kalpin Tours also has boats to Lobam in the west of Bintan at 8.45 am and 1.30 pm. To get the Tanah Merah ferry terminal, take the MRT to Bedok and then bus No 35. Taxi fare from the city is around S$12 to S$15.

Karimun From the World Trade Centre, Kalpin Tours and Dino Shipping have at least four ferries daily to Tanjung Balai, the main port on Pulau Karimun, another Riau resort island of minor note. The cost is S$27/47 one-way/return.

Cruises

There is no shortage of cruises operating from Singapore or including Singapore in their itineraries. Plenty of cruises around Asia depart from Singapore (especially to Indonesia, Malaysia and Thailand), Australia, India, Kenya, Europe and other destinations. International companies such as P&O, Seven Seas, CTC and Winstar operate services, but the best deals are with the Singaporean operators that offer cheap cruises departing from the World Trade Centre. These have become very popular with Singaporeans.

Cruises range from an overnight ocean cruise for S$199 twin share to longer cruises to Phuket or Manila. Three-day/two-night cruises to Penang are very popular and start from as little as S$400 for two people. The best deals are advertised in the newspaper travel sections, but check for 'administration fees' and 'holiday surcharges'.

The main operator is Star Cruise (☎ 733 6988), 13-01 Ngee Ann City Tower B, 391 Orchard Rd, which operates a number of liners. Vessels range from the large and somewhat crowded *Star Aquarius* to the more luxurious Megastar ships. Morning Star Travel (☎ 735 9009) is a major agent with offices all over Singapore.

New Century Tours (☎ 275 2866) operates the *Leisure World* liner with an emphasis on youth and Chinese pop music.

Getting Around

Singapore is undoubtedly the easiest city in Asia to get around and has an excellent public transport system. While other cities like Bangkok, Jakarta and Kuala Lumpur are choked by massive traffic jams and attempt to solve their problems with stop gap, privately funded public transport systems, Singapore has bitten the bullet and invested huge amounts in transport infrastructure.

With a typical mixture of far-sighted social planning and authoritarianism, the government has built a magnificent rail system and controls private cars by a restrictive licensing system and prohibitive import duties that make owning a car primarily a preserve for the rich. The island has excellent roads and an efficient expressway system, and cars entering the central business district (CBD) have to buy special licences.

Singapore also has an extensive bus network and cheap taxis, making getting around Singapore a breeze.

The *TransitLink Guide*, S$1.20 from bookshops, is a good investment if you will be using a lot of public transport. The guide lists all bus routes and the Mass Rapid Transit (MRT) rail network in a convenient pocket-size format. Maps show the surrounding areas for all MRT stations, including bus stops. The *TransitLink Map* (S$5) maps the whole island with numbered bus routes and MRT stations, but while it's good for outlying districts it doesn't show bus stops in the central city area. The *Singapore Official Guide*, a free handout from the tourist office, lists Singapore's major attractions and how to reach them by bus and MRT.

THE AIRPORT

Singapore's ultramodern Changi International Airport is another of those miracles that Singapore specialises in. It's vast, efficient and organised and was built in record time. It has banking and money-changing facilities, a post office and telephone facilities (open 24 hours), free hotel reservation counters (open from 8 am to 11 pm), left luggage facilities (S$3 per bag for the first day and S$4 per day thereafter), nearly 100 shops, restaurants, day rooms, fitness centres, saunas and business centres. There are free films, audio/visual shows, bars with entertainment, hairdressers, medical facilities, a swimming pool, a mini Science Discovery Museum (in Terminal 2) etc, etc. In fact, Changi has just about everything, so you can book into a hotel room in the terminal, pig out on Singapore's food, take a free city tour and you've done Singapore!

Changi is not really one airport but two – Terminal 1 and the newer, even more impressive Terminal 2 – each in themselves international airports to match the world's best. They are connected by the Changi Skytrain, a monorail that shuttles between the two. Terminal 2 is expected to handle Singapore's increasing air traffic well into the 21st century, but Terminal 1 still handles most of the airlines. The following airlines use Terminal 2: Air France, Delta, Finnair, Malaysia Airlines, Myanmar Airways, Philippine Airlines, Royal Brunei Airlines, Silk Air, Singapore Airlines and Swiss Air. All other airlines use Terminal 1.

Singapore does have another 'international' airport – forgotten Seletar, which handles a few services for the smaller regional airlines, such as Pelangi flights to Tioman Island in Malaysia. It is in the north of the island, and the easiest way to get there is to take a taxi; the nearest MRT station is Yio Chu Kang.

On your way through the arrivals concourse at Changi, pick up the free booklets, maps and other guides available from stands. They give you a lot of useful information and good-quality colour maps of Singapore Island and the city centre. There are even guides to the airport and the glossy monthly travel rag *Changi*.

Well-appointed day rooms at the airport cost from S$50 to S$80 per six hours in

Terminal 1 or S$42/48 for single/double rooms in Terminal 2. The Transit Hotel in Terminal 1 has a rooftop swimming pool and jacuzzi, which non-guests can use for S$15. The hotels are on the departure side of immigration and you must stay at the terminal you depart from. Or, if you just need a shower, you can have one for S$10, including towel and soap.

If you are one of the millions of air travellers fed up with overpriced and terrible food at airports, then Changi airport has a variety of restaurants serving a whole range of cuisines at normal prices. Terminal 2 just pips Terminal 1 for the silver fork award in dining excellence. To find even cheaper food, go to the hawker-food centre in the upstairs level of the car park just outside Terminal 2. The elevator beside McDonald's on the arrival level in Terminal 1 will take you to the Basement 1 Food Centre. It's actually the staff cafeteria but the public can eat there.

Changi airport continues to poll in the various travel-trade magazines as the best airport in the world. You'll understand why when you arrive and are whisked through immigration to find your bags waiting on the other side.

The airport tax (Passenger Service Charge) from Changi is S$15, payable at check-in or you can purchase PSC coupons in advance at airline offices, travel agencies and major hotels.

SINGAPORE

To/From the Airport

Singapore's Changi International Airport is at the extreme eastern end of the island, about 20 km from the city centre. Airport buses and public buses (catch them in the basement), taxis and the more expensive limousine services run along the expressway into the city centre.

The most convenient bus is the Airbus (☎ 542 1721), running roughly every 20 minutes from 6 am to midnight. Three routes service all the main hotels in the colonial district (it also drops off on Bencoolen St), as well as the hotels along Orchard, Tanglin and Scotts Rds. The cost is S$5 (children S$3).

Public bus Nos 16 and 16 E (express) operate every eight to 12 minutes from 6 am to 8 pm and take about half an hour to reach the city. The cost is S$1.30 but bus drivers don't give change so make sure you get some coins when you change money. As this bus approaches the city, it comes off the flyover into Raffles Blvd and then Stamford Rd. For Beach Rd, get off when you see the round towers of the Raffles City skyscraper on your right, just past the open playing fields of the Padang on your left. A half km further along is the National Museum and the stop for Bencoolen St. The bus then continues up Penang Rd, Somerset Rd and Orchard Blvd (which all run parallel to Orchard Rd). When heading out to the airport, catch these buses on Orchard or Bras Basah Rds.

An alternative is to take the No 27 bus (80c, 20 minutes) to the Tampines Interchange, then hop on the MRT. From Tampines to City Hall costs $1.20 and takes 25 minutes.

Taxis from the airport are subject to a S$3 supplementary charge on top of the meter fare, which is around S$12 to most places downtown. This supplementary charge only applies to taxis from the airport, not from the city.

MASS RAPID TRANSIT

Singapore's ultramodern Mass Rapid Transit (MRT) subway system is the easiest, quickest and most comfortable way of getting around Singapore, and it can transport you across town in air-conditioned comfort in minutes.

The MRT was primarily designed to provide a cheap, reliable rail service from the housing estates to the city and industrial estates. Most of the 44 km of underground track is in the inner-city area, but out towards the housing estates the MRT runs above ground. Not content with this most impressive system, the government has new lines planned, and the line linking Choa Chu Kang and Yishun, via Woodlands near the Causeway, is nearing completion. Another line is planned to eventually run to Punggol in the north-east.

The Orchard Rd area is well serviced by the Somerset, Orchard and Newton MRT stations. In the colonial district, the Dhoby Ghaut station is close to Bencoolen St, while the Beach Rd accommodation area is between the City Hall and Bugis stations. The Raffles Place MRT station is right in the heart of the Central Business District and the Outram Park and Tanjong Pagar stations are on the edge of Chinatown.

Using the subway system is extremely simple. You check the map showing fares from your station, put money in the slot and press the button for the fare you want. You can get a single-trip ticket or a stored-value card that is valid until you've used up the value of the ticket. You insert the ticket into the entry gate to enter and on departure the ticket is retained by the exit gate unless it still has 'stored value'.

Single-trip tickets cost from 60c to S$1.50. Ticket machines take 10c, 20c, 50c and S$1 coins; they also give change. Note-changing machines change S$2 notes. Stored-value cards, which can be used on buses as well as the MRT, cost S$10 (plus S$2 deposit) and are purchased from the TransitLink sales offices at MRT stations and the main bus interchanges.

The trains run from around 6 am to midnight. At peak times, trains run every three to four minutes, and at off-peak periods every six to eight minutes.

BUS

Singapore has an extremely frequent and comprehensive bus network. While the MRT is easy and convenient to use, for door-to-door public transport it is hard to beat the buses. You rarely have to wait more than a few minutes for a bus and they will get you almost anywhere you want to go.

Bus fares start from 50c (60c for air-con buses) for the first 3.2 km and go up in 10c increments for every 2.4 km to a maximum of S$1 (S$1.30 air-con). There are also a few

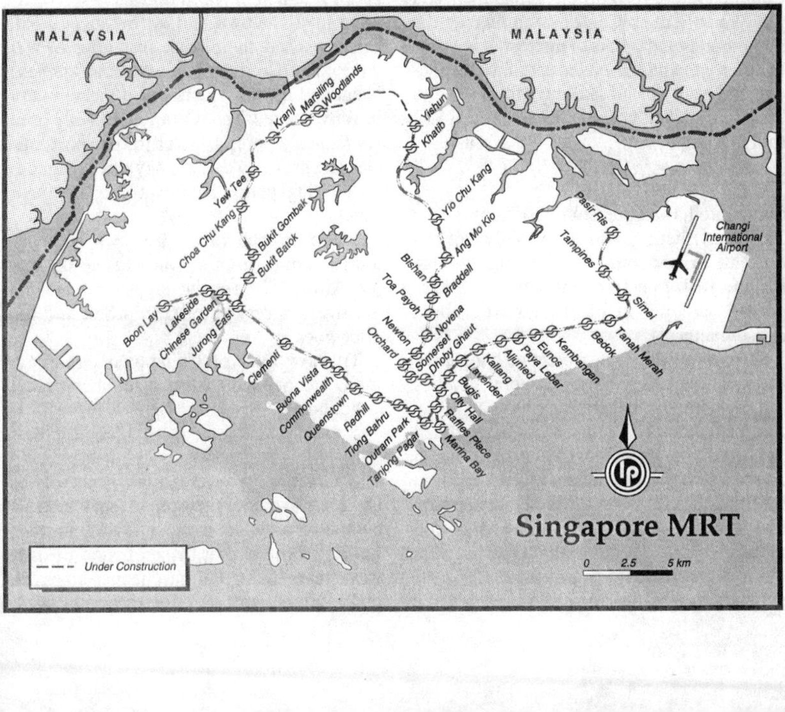

flat-rate buses. When you board the bus drop the exact fare into the change box. No change is given.

The TransitLink farecard is a stored-value card that can be used on the MRT and on buses that have validator ticket machines. Put the card in the validator and select the correct fare. Farecards can be bought at MRT stations and bus interchanges for S$12 – S$2 deposit and S$10 of value – and are valid for six months.

Singapore Explorer tickets cost S$5 for one day and S$12 for three days of unlimited travel on the buses. A map of the major tourist attractions is included. These maps are available from many hotels, including the YMCAs, and travel agents, or phone ☎ 800-287 2727 for more details.

Tourist Bus

The Singapore Trolley is a grotesque bus made to look like an old-fashioned tram and it runs from the Botanic Gardens to the Orchard Rd area, the colonial district, Central Business District, Chinatown and the World Trade Centre, stopping at the major hotels and points of interest. It is a very handy route and the bus is certainly distinctive and easy to find. All-day (from 9 am to 10.30 pm) tickets cost S$9 for adults and S$7 for children.

TAXI

Singapore has a good supply of taxis – over 10,000 of them – and it's usually not too difficult to find one. The exceptions may include rush hours or meal times (Singaporeans are not at all enthusiastic about missing a meal).

It is quite easy to recognise Singapore taxis, although they come in several varieties – most common being black with a yellow roof or pale blue. Taxis are all metered and the meters are used – unlike in some Asian countries where the meters always seem to be 'broken'. Taxis cost S$2.40 for the first one km, then 10c for each additional 240 metres.

From midnight to 6 am, there is a 50% surcharge over the meter fare. From the airport, there is a surcharge of S$3 for each journey – but not *to* the airport. Radio bookings cost an additional S$2.20, or S$3.20 if booked 30 minutes or more in advance. There is also a S$1 surcharge on all trips from the Central Business District between 4 and 7 pm on weekdays and from noon to 3 pm on Saturday. You may also have to pay the S$3 restricted area licence (see the following Restricted Zone & Car Parking section) if you are the first passenger of the day to take the taxi into the Central Business District during restricted hours.

Singapore taxi drivers are generally refreshingly courteous and efficient, plus the cars themselves are super-clean since drivers can be fined for driving a dirty cab. Some taxis also accept Visa cards. There are many taxi companies; for radio bookings 24 hours, NTUC (☎ 452 5555) is one of the biggest companies.

TRISHAW

Singapore's bicycle rickshaws are fast disappearing, although you'll find a few still operating in Chinatown and off Serangoon Rd. Trishaws had their peak just after WWII when motorised transport was almost nonexistent and trishaw riders could make a very healthy income. Today, they are mainly used for local shopping trips or to transport articles too heavy to carry. They rarely venture on to Singapore's heavily trafficked main streets.

There are, however, trishaws at many tourist centres in case you want to try one out. Always agree on the fare beforehand. On the street, a very short ride is S$2 and the price goes up from there.

Trishaw tours of Chinatown and Little India are operated from a number of the larger hotels.

CAR

Singaporeans drive on the left-hand side of the road and the wearing of seat belts is compulsory. Unlike in most Asian countries, traffic is orderly, but the profusion of one-way streets and streets that change names can make driving difficult for the uninitiated.

The *Singapore Street Directory* is essential for negotiating Singapore's streets.

Rental

Singapore has branches of the three major regional rent-a-car operators – Sintat, Hertz and Avis. There are also a large number of small, local operators. If you want a car just for local driving, many of the smaller operators quote rental rates that are slightly cheaper than the major companies. Rental rates are higher than in Malaysia and there are expensive surcharges to take a Singapore rent-a-car into Malaysia. If you intend renting a car to drive in Malaysia for any length of time, it is much better to rent a car in Johor Bahru or elsewhere in Malaysia.

Rates start from S$100 a day, while collision damage waver will cost about S$20 per day, for a small car such as a Toyota Corolla or Mistubishi Lancer. Special deals, especially for longer term rental, may be available. There are hire booths at Changi airport and in the city; addresses of some of the main operators are:

Avis
  Boulevard Hotel, Cuscaden Rd (☎ 737 1668)
Budget
  26-01A Clifford Centre, 24 Raffles Place (☎ 532 4442)
Hertz Rent-a-Car
  125 Tanglin Rd (☎ 734 4646)
Ken-Air Rent-a-Car
  01-41 Specialists Centre, 227 Orchard Rd (☎ 737 8282)
Sintat
  60 Bendemeer Road (☎ 295 2211)

Restricted Zone & Car Parking

From 7.30 am to 6.30 pm from Monday to Friday, and from 10.15 am to 2 pm on Saturday, the area encompassing the Central Business District, Chinatown and Orchard Rd is a restricted zone where cars may only enter with an area licence sticker. A licence costs S$3 per whole day or S$60 per month – not surprisingly this has dramatically reduced traffic problems in the rush hour! The licence requirement also applies to taxis, so if you want to take a taxi into the central business district during these hours you must pay for the taxi licence, which costs S$3 – unless somebody else has already done so, of course. The licence stickers are sold at booths just outside the district boundaries, or you can buy them at post offices, 7-Eleven stores and some petrol stations up to three days in advance.

And if you should carelessly enter the CBD without a licence? There may well be inspectors standing by the roadside noting down the number plates of unlicensed cars as they enter the CBD. A fine will soon arrive at the car owner's address.

Parking in many places in Singapore is operated by a coupon system. You can buy a booklet of coupons at parking kiosks and post offices. You must display a coupon in your car window with holes punched out to indicate the time, day and date your car was parked.

BICYCLE

Singapore's fast moving traffic and good public transport system does not make bicycling such an attractive proposition. Bicycles can be hired at a number of places on the East Coast Parkway, but they are intended mostly for weekend jaunts along the foreshore. Mountain bikes, racers and tandems are available for around S$3 to S$5 per hour. See the East Coast section in Things to See & Do for details. Bikes can also be rented at Sentosa Island.

WALKING

Getting around the old areas of Singapore on foot has one small problem – apart from the heat and humidity that is. The problem is the 'five-foot ways' instead of sidewalks or pavements. A five-foot way, which takes its name from the fact that it is roughly five feet wide, is a walkway at the front of the traditional Chinese shophouses, but enclosed, veranda-like, in the front of the building.

The difficulty with them is that every shop's walkway is individual. It may well be higher or lower than the shop next door or closer to or further from the street. Walking thus becomes a constant up and down and side to side, further complicated by the fact that half the shops seem to overflow right across the walkway, forcing you to venture into the street, and bikes or motorcycles are parked across them.

Even newer areas like Orchard Rd suffer from the five-foot-way syndrome in places with shopping centres on different levels. The hazards are complicated by the flash, but very slippery, tiles out the front that are an essential part of shopping-centre architecture. After a rainstorm on Orchard Rd, count the tourists falling.

BOAT

You can charter a bumboat (motorised sampan) to take a tour up the Singapore River or to go to the islands around Singapore. There are regular ferry services from the World Trade Centre to Sentosa and the other southern islands, and from Changi Village to Pulau Ubin. Or you can take river tours or boat tours around the harbour.

ORGANISED TOURS

A wide variety of tours are available in Singapore. They can be booked at the desks of the big hotels or through the operators. The *Singapore Official Guide* lists tours and the operators. Any of Singapore's travel agents can also book tours for you, or you could contact the tourist office.

Tours include morning or afternoon trips around the city or to Jurong Bird Park, the east coast or the various parks and gardens in Singapore. Most tours go for around 3½ hours, though full-day tours are offered. Tours vary in price, depending on how long they last and the cost of admission to the attractions covered, but most half-day tours cost between S$20 and S$40, while full-day tours can range up to S$70.

There are city tours, which vary but generally take in the colonial district and the CBD, Chinatown, Orchard Rd, Mount Faber, Little India or the Botanic Gardens and possibly a handicraft shop (take the 'very good discounts' with a grain of salt).

Historical tours cover some of the same areas as city tours but focus on the founding of Singapore. War tours cover the battlefields, Changi prison, war memorials, armed services bases etc. There are tours of Chinatown, Little India and Arab St, some involving touring by bicycle rickshaw.

Jurong Bird Park is covered by many operators and extended tours of Jurong also include Crocodile Paradise, Chinese Garden, Ming Village or a visit to the Tiger Brewery.

Other tours include the zoo, Tang Dynasty City, Sentosa, the east coast, horse racing and the Singapore Science Centre. Nature tours that take in Bukit Timah, Pulau Ubin and the like are currently very popular. In fact, tours cover just about all of Singapore, so it is just a matter of finding one that covers your particular interests.

The Singapore Trolley (see the Bus section above) allows you to put together your own tour of Central Singapore. It plies a set route and you can get on and off where you like. Helicopter tours are also available for a view of the city that even the Westin Stamford can't match. A half-hour from Seletar airport costs S$150 for adults and S$75 for children.

Don't forget the free city tour for transit passengers from Changi airport who have four hours to spare. Two-hour tours go at 10 am, and then on the hour from 1 to 7 pm. You can tour the city in sealed no-man's land, at least in theory. You don't clear customs and the interior of the bus could be classed as international territory.

Cruises

River Cruises One of the best ways to get a feel for central Singapore and its history is to take a river cruise. Singapore River Boat (☎ 227 0802) operates a half-hour river tour for S$7 per adult and S$3 per child. It leaves from the Clarke Quay jetty, just south-west of Fort Canning Park. You can buy tickets at the booth there, and tours leave on the hour from 9 am to 11 pm. The tour goes downriver to the harbour and Clifford Pier and then returns. A taped commentary, complete with weak jokes, gives a good rundown on the history of the buildings along the river.

Harbour Cruises A whole host of operators have harbour cruises departing from Clifford Pier, just east of Raffles Place. There is no shortage of touts trying to sell you tickets, or you can buy them at the Clifford Pier booking offices. Companies offer *tongkang* (Chinese junk) cruises as well as a number of lunch and dinner cruises. Most of them do the rounds of the harbour, which involves a lot of time passing oil refineries, then take a look at Sentosa and the southern islands of St John's, Lazarus and Kusu. The short stop at Kusu is worthwhile and you will get some good views of the city and harbour.

Fairwind (☎ 533 3432) has 2½ hour tours at 10.30 am and 3 pm that cost S$20 for adults and S$10 for children. Its 1½ hour tour at 4 pm costs the same but doesn't stop at Kusu. Watertours (☎ 533 9811) operates tours at the same times for S$24 (morning) and S$29 (afternoon, including tea). Its gaudy Chinese junks look like refugees from Haw Par Villa, but it is a comfortable option.

J&N Cruise (☎ 223 8217) covers much the same route in a catamaran from the World Trade Centre. The 1½ hour luncheon cruise at 12.30 pm costs S$35 for adults and S$20 for children, and the two hour cruise at 3 pm costs S$30 for adults and S$17 for children. All prices exclude 3% GST.

All these companies also operate dinner and/or evening cruises, as does Resort Cruises (☎ 278 4677). Dinner cruises range from around S$34 to S$80.

It is also possible to charter boats – the Singapore Tourist Promotion Board (☎ 339 6622) can put you in touch with charter-boat operators.

Singapore

Things to See & Do

Singapore's greatest attraction is its ability to offer a taste of Asian culture in a small, easy-to-get-around package. Minutes from the modern business centre and its towering air-conditioned office blocks are the narrow streets of Chinatown, while across the river is Little India (Serangoon Rd) and the Muslim centre of Arab St.

Further out of the city, the Jurong area has a number of gardens, theme parks and other attractions. The central hills to the north of the city are Singapore's green belt, containing some fine parks and the zoo. Sentosa is Singapore's most famous fun-park island, though quieter islands are scattered around Singapore.

HIGHLIGHTS

The best way to get a feel for Singapore is to wander around its inner city. Though the ethnic areas are quickly becoming dining and drinking venues rather than repositories of traditional culture, **Chinatown**, **Little India** and **Arab St** are still fascinating areas to wander around.

One of the most successful redevelopment projects is along the **Singapore River**, worth a wander at any time but it really comes alive in the evening when the restaurants and bars are packed. Boat Quay is now Singapore's premier nightspot, while Clarke Quay is more family oriented, and also has shopping, children's rides and open-air entertainment. A river boat tour is an excellent way to view this historic artery of Singapore.

Further afield, **Sentosa** is Singapore's answer to Disneyland, though the comparison is a loose one. This theme park island has plenty of rides, family attractions and even beaches, while Fort Siloso, Pioneers of Singapore and Underwater World provide more educational entertainment.

The **Singapore Zoo** is one of Singapore's most popular attractions. Even if you normally avoid zoos like the plague, the spacious and well-designed enclosures make it seem like an animal resort compared with most zoos. Highly recommended is the **Night Safari** next to the zoo, which allows you to view animals along jungle paths at night. The **Jurong Bird Park** is another attraction with beautifully landscaped gardens, a huge variety of birdlife and well-tended enclosures.

Green and clean Singapore also has plenty of gardens to visit. The pick of them is the **Botanic Gardens**, or if you want to walk in the jungle **Bukit Timah Nature Reserve** is about as far away from the city as you can get.

Last but not least, every visitor ends up at **Orchard Rd**, and some never get beyond it. It is a dazzling strip of modern delights, with shopping centres, luxury hotels, hundreds of restaurants and a profusion of nightspots strung out along its length.

Singapore has plenty of other attractions: less-visited traditional areas, themes parks, gardens, historic buildings, temples, museums and other islands. Everywhere you go Singapore's wonderful food attracts a stop, and shopping and nightlife opportunities abound. Singapore has more than enough to keep you amused from a one-day stopover to a week's exploration.

COLONIAL SINGAPORE

The mark of Stamford Raffles is indelibly stamped on central Singapore. His early city plans moved the business district south of the river and made the area north of the river the administrative area. This early framework remained the plan for central Singapore through generations of colonial rule and the republican years of independence. While Singapore is now a modern city, many reminders of old Singapore remain.

North of the river is colonial Singapore, where you'll still find the imposing monuments of British rule – the stone grey edifices of the town hall, parliament and museum, the churches and Victorian architecture. Many of these buildings still serve their original purpose. The Central Business District is the commercial heart of Singapore, though its monuments are now the skyscrapers of modern finance. Dividing these two areas is the Singapore River, which has always been the centre of Singapore. It was the site of the first British arrivals and for a long time the main artery of Singapore's trade.

The colonial district is easily reached by Mass Rapid Transit (MRT); get off at either the City Hall or Raffles Place stations. From the Raffles Place MRT station it is a short walk to Cavenagh Bridge and the Singapore River, a good starting point for a tour of the area.

The half-lion, half-fish Merlion stands guard at the mouth of the Singapore River.

Singapore River

The river was once the thriving heart of Singapore but is now a quiet pedestrian precinct – an escape for lunchtime office workers, the spot to cast a line for fish, a weekend haunt for wedding photography sessions, or the place to dine in one of the renovated terraces or godowns next to the river. The bustling activity of sampans, bumboats, cranes, and yelling, sweating labourers have all gone and the new riverfront is a recreational stretch of photo opportunities and colonial restoration.

At the mouth of the river stands Singapore's symbol of tourism, the **Merlion**, a much photographed water-spouting, half-lion/half-fish statue. The small park around it is open from 7 am to 10 pm daily. Heading upstream, **Anderson Bridge** is the first of the old bridges that span the river. The next along is **Cavenagh Bridge**, built in 1869, now for pedestrians only. It provides good access to **Empress Place**. Named in honour of Queen Victoria, Empress Place is Singapore's oldest pedestrian area, and is surrounded by many reminders of British rule. The **Empress Place building**, built in 1865, is an imposing Georgian structure that was once a court house and later housed a number of government offices. Its most recent function was as a museum, but it is currently undergoing further refurbishment.

Nearby, next to the river at Raffles Landing Site, is **Raffles' Statue**, standing imperiously by the water. It's approximately in the place where Stamford Raffles first set foot on the island of Singapore.

Naturally, there are plenty of places to eat along the river. A busy hawker centre popular with lunchtime crowds is on the northern bank of the river near Cavenagh Bridge. On the south bank, **Boat Quay** is a picturesque area of restored old shops with soaring office buildings right behind. The stretch of renovated terraces along to South Bridge Rd and Elgin Bridge is one of Singapore's most popular restaurant and nightlife strips and is abuzz until the early hours of the morning.

Crossing over, North Boat Quay leads upriver to **Clarke Quay**. From the landing at the eastern end of Boat Quay take the Clarke Quay River Taxi, a cheap bumboat tour, costing S$1 (S$2 in the evening).

The old Clarke Quay godowns on this bend of the river have been completely rebuilt in

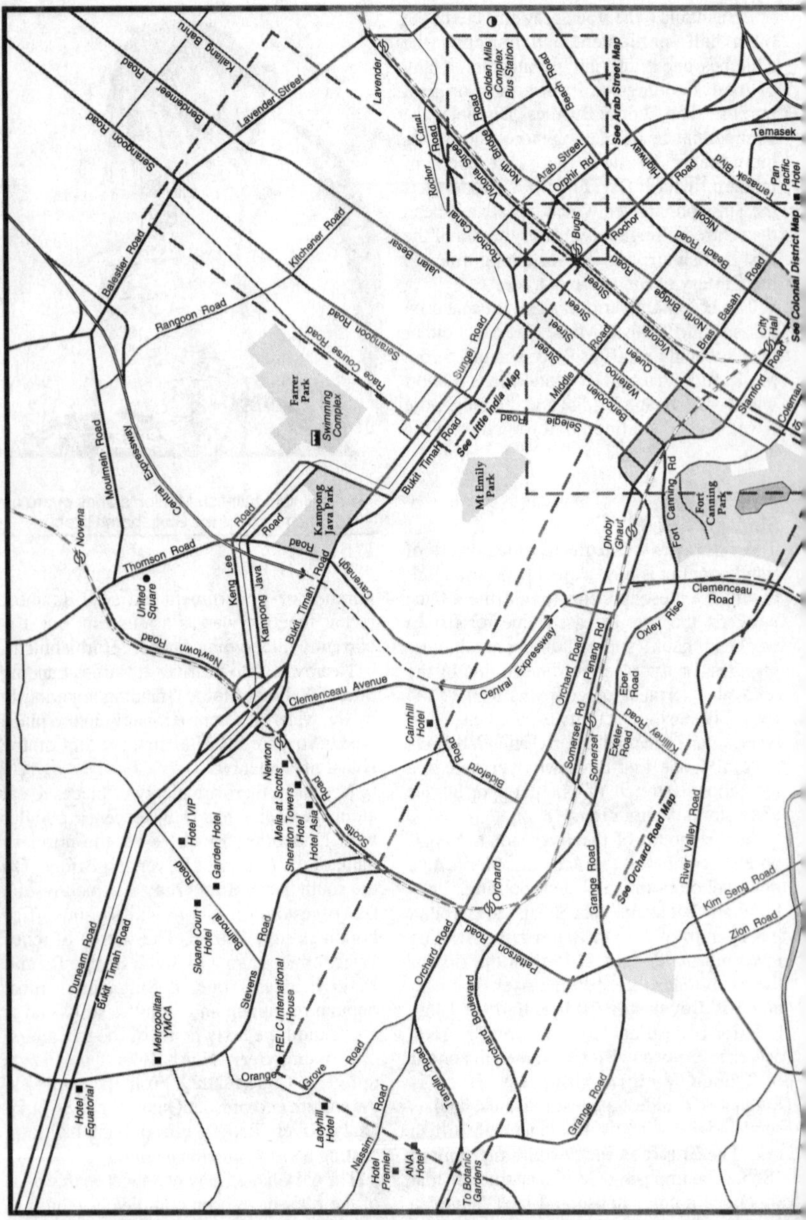
Kallang Bahru
Bendemeer Road
Serangoon Road
Lavender Street
Lavender
Golden Mile Complex Bus Station
Beach Road
See Arab Street Map
Canal Road
Rochor Canal Road
Victoria Street
North Bridge Road
Arab Street
Ophir Rd
Highway
Temasek
Temasek Blvd
Pan Pacific Hotel
Road
Nicoll
Rochor
Beach Road
Bugis
Rochor Road
Jalan Besar
Kitchener Road
Balestier Road
Rangoon Road
Serangoon Road
Race Course Road
Farrer Park
Swimming Complex
Sungei Road
Street
Street
Street
Street
Middle Road
Queen
Victoria
North Bridge
Bras Basah
Road
City Hall
Road
See Colonial District Map
Waterloo
Bencoolen
Selegie Road
Stamford
Coleman
See Little India Map
Bukit Timah Road
Mt Emily Park
Fort Canning Rd
Fort Canning Park
Moulmein Road
Central Expressway
Novena
Thomson Road
United Square
Keng Lee Road
Kampong Java Road
Kampong Java Park
Road
Bukit Timah Road
Cavenagh
Dhoby Ghaut
Clemenceau Road
Oxley Rise
Penang Rd
Orchard Road
Central Expressway
Newtown Road
Clemenceau Avenue
Cairnhill Hotel
Eber Road
Killiney Road
Exeter Road
Somerset Rd
Somerset
Bideford Road
Newton
Melia at Scotts
Sheraton Towers Hotel
Hotel Asia
Scotts Road
Hotel VIP
Garden Hotel
Sloane Court Hotel
Balmoral Road
River Valley Road
Grange Road
See Orchard Road Map
Orchard
Kim Seng Road
Zion Road
Paterson Road
Orchard Road
Stevens Road
Dunearn Road
Bukit Timah Road
Metropolitan YMCA
RELC International House
Orchard Boulevard
Grange Road
Orange Grove Road
Tanglin Road
Hotel Equatorial
Ladyhill Hotel
Nassim Road
Hotel Premier
ANA Hotel
To Botanic Gardens

SINGAPORE

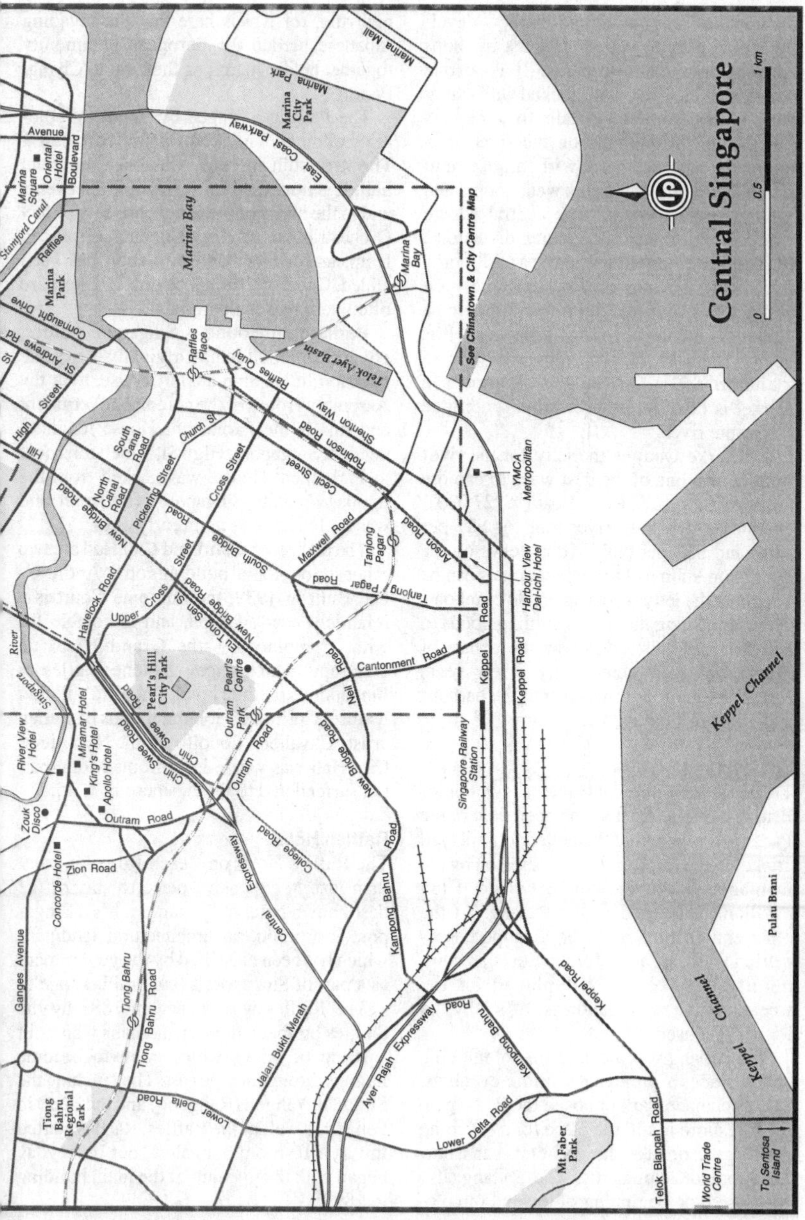

Central Singapore
0
0.5
1 km
See Chinatown & City Centre Map
Marina Bay
Marina City Park
Marina Park
Marina Mall
East Coast Parkway
Marina Square
Oriental Hotel
Boulevard
Avenue
Stamford Canal
Raffles
Connaught Drive
St Andrews Rd
High Street
Hill St
Raffles Place
Raffles Quay
Telok Ayer Basin
Shenton Way
Robinson Road
Cecil Street
Church St
South Canal Road
North Canal Road
Pickering Street
Cross Street
New Bridge Road
Havelock Road
Upper Cross Street
South Bridge Road
Maxwell Road
Tanjong Pagar
Tanjong Pagar Road
Anson Road
YMCA Metropolitan
Harbour View Dai-Ichi Hotel
Keppel Road
Eu Tong Sen St
Cantonment Road
Neil Road
Pearl's Centre
Outram Park
Outram Road
Pearl's Hill City Park
Chin Swee Road
Singapore River
River View Hotel
Miramar Hotel
King's Hotel
Apollo Hotel
Zouk Disco
Concorde Hotel
Zion Road
Singapore Railway Station
Central Expressway
College Road
Kampong Bahru Road
Jalan Bukit Merah
Ayer Rajah Expressway
Tiong Bahru
Tiong Bahru Road
Ganges Avenue
Tiong Bahru Regional Park
Lower Delta Road
Mt Faber Park
Telok Blangah Road
World Trade Centre
To Sentosa Island
Keppel Channel
Pulau Brani

SINGAPORE

the name of restoration and the new development is a more varied complex of shops and children's amusements. It is also a popular dining spot, well stocked with eating possibilities from satay stalls to wine bars and floating restaurants on the river. It is fairly family oriented with amusement arcades, toy and children's wear shops, and a playground upstairs. The central square regularly has music and other diversions. **Clarke Quay Adventure** here is a fairly corny river-boat ride attraction which takes you past alcoves with wax dummies portraying a dubious, raucous history of Singapore. It is open 11 am to 11 pm; admission is S$5 (children S$3). On Sunday afternoons a market is held on the pedestrian footbridge across the river.

At Clarke Quay is the jetty for the **river boat tours**, one of the best ways to explore the river. Singapore River Boat (☎ 227 0802) operates a half-hour river tour for S$7 per adult and S$3 per child. Tours leave on the hour from 9 am to 11 pm, and tickets can be bought at the jetty. Tours are in old bumboats that used to clog the river, shuttling goods to and fro when the river was the centre of Singapore's commerce, only a few years ago. The tour goes downriver to the harbour and Clifford Pier and then returns.

The Padang

There is no more quizzical a symbol of British colonialism than the open field of the Padang. It is here that flannelled fools played cricket in the tropical heat, cheered on by the members in the Singapore Cricket Club pavilion at one end of the Padang. At the other end of the field is the Singapore Recreation Club, set aside for the Eurasian community. Cricket is still played on the weekends but segregation is, officially, no longer practised.

The Padang was a centre for colonial life and a place to promenade in the evenings. The Esplanade Park opposite the Padang on the foreshore is still the place for an evening stroll, give or take the odd crane and new foreshore developments. The Padang also witnessed the beginning of the end of colonial rule, for it was here that the invading Japanese herded the European community together before marching them off to Changi Prison.

The Padang is ringed by imposing colonial buildings. The **Victoria Concert Hall & Theatre**, built in 1862, was once the town hall. It is now used for many cultural events and is the home of the Singapore Symphony Orchestra. A new refurbishment has spruced it up, and a merchandising shop has been added. Check performance times; tickets are often very reasonably priced.

Parliament House is Singapore's oldest government building. Originally a private mansion, it became a court house, then the Assembly House of the colonial government and finally the Parliament House for independent Singapore. High St, which runs next to Parliament House, was hacked from the jungle to become Singapore's first street, and was an Indian area in its early days.

The **Supreme Court** and **City Hall** are two other stoic colonial buildings on St Andrew's Rd. Built in 1939, the Supreme Court is a relatively new addition, and is notable for what it replaced – the Grand Hotel de L'Europe, which once outshone Raffles as Singapore's premier hotel. This fine building features Corinthian column murals by Italian artist, Cavaliere Rodolfo Nolli. Next door, City Hall was where Lord Louis Mountbatten surrendered to the Japanese in 1945.

Raffles Hotel

The Raffles Hotel on Beach Rd is far more than just an expensive place to stay or the best known hotel in Singapore. It's a Singapore institution, an architectural landmark which has been classified by the government as a part of Singapore's 'cultural heritage'.

The Raffles was opened in 1887 by the Sarkies brothers, three Armenians who built a string of hotels which were to become famous throughout the east. They include the Strand in Yangon (Rangoon) and the E&O in Penang as well as the Raffles. Raffles started life as a 10 room bungalow, but its heyday began with the opening of the main building in 1899.

The Raffles soon became a byword for oriental luxury and featured in novels by Joseph Conrad and Somerset Maugham. Rudyard Kipling recommended it as the place to 'feed at' when in Singapore (but stay elsewhere he added!), and in its Long Bar, Ngiam Tong Boon created the Singapore Sling in 1915.

More recently, the Raffles underwent extensive renovations and extensions; it had fallen from grace and could no longer compete with Singapore's modern hotels. It reopened in 1991, once again a top hotel, though for some it wasn't the same old Raffles. While it is true that the Raffles is now a slick exercise in tourism marketing, for many it still oozes the old-fashioned atmosphere of the east as Somerset Maugham would have known it.

The **lobby** of the restored main building is open to the public (dress standards apply) and high tea is served in the Tiffin Room, though the Writers' Bar next door is little more than an alcove. In the other wings, the **Long Bar** or the **Bar & Billiard Room** are the places to sip a Singapore Sling at S$16 a pop.

The Raffles Hotel Arcade is a collection of expensive shops, and hidden away on the 3rd floor is the **Raffles Hotel Museum**. It is well worth a look, especially the old postcards. Admission is free and it is open from 10 am to 9 pm. Raffles memorabilia are on sale at the museum shop, including the hotel crockery. Next to the museum, Jubilee Hall theatre puts on *Raffles Revisited*, a multimedia presentation on the history of the Raffles Hotel. Viewing times are at 10 and 11 am and 12.30 and 1 pm, and admission is S$5 for adults, S$3 for children.

Churches

The most imposing examples of colonial architecture between Bras Basah Rd and Coleman St are the churches.

St Andrew's Cathedral is Singapore's Anglican cathedral, built in Gothic style between 1856 and 1863. It's in the block surrounded by North Bridge Rd, Coleman St, Stamford Rd and St Andrew's Rd. The Catholic **Cathedral of the Good Shepherd** on Queen St is a stolid neoclassical edifice built between 1843 and 1846 and is a Singapore historic monument.

The churches draw a thriving crowd of well-to-do Singaporeans on a Sunday, though many of the other churches and religious buildings are being transformed into new uses under the auspices of the Urban Redevelopment Authority. The magnificent St Joseph's Institution, a former Catholic boy's school, is now the Singapore Art Museum (see below). On the corner of Bras Basah Rd and Victoria St, the equally impressive Convent of the Holy Infant Jesus is undergoing an ironic refurbishment that will turn it into a shopping centre.

The oldest church in Singapore is the Armenian **Church of St Gregory the Illuminator** on Hill St, which is no longer used for services.

Singapore Art Museum

One of Singapore's finest colonial buildings, St Joseph's Institution, near the corner of Bras Basah Rd and Queen St, has been restored and converted into this fine arts museum.

Rotating exhibits showcase modern art from Singapore and South-East Asia. Even if the art is not your cup of tea, the building is worth a look and the museum has a good cafe facing Queen St.

The museum is open from 9 am to 5.30 pm, closed Monday. Entry costs $3 (children S$1).

Fort Canning

If you continue north-west up Coleman St from the Padang, you pass the Armenian Church and come to Fort Canning Hill, a good viewpoint over Singapore. Once known as Forbidden Hill, it contains the shrine of Sultan Iskander Shah, the last ruler of the ancient kingdom of Singapura. Archaeological digs in the park have uncovered Javanese artefacts from the 14th century Majapahit empire.

When Stamford Raffles arrived, the only reminder of any greatness that the island may

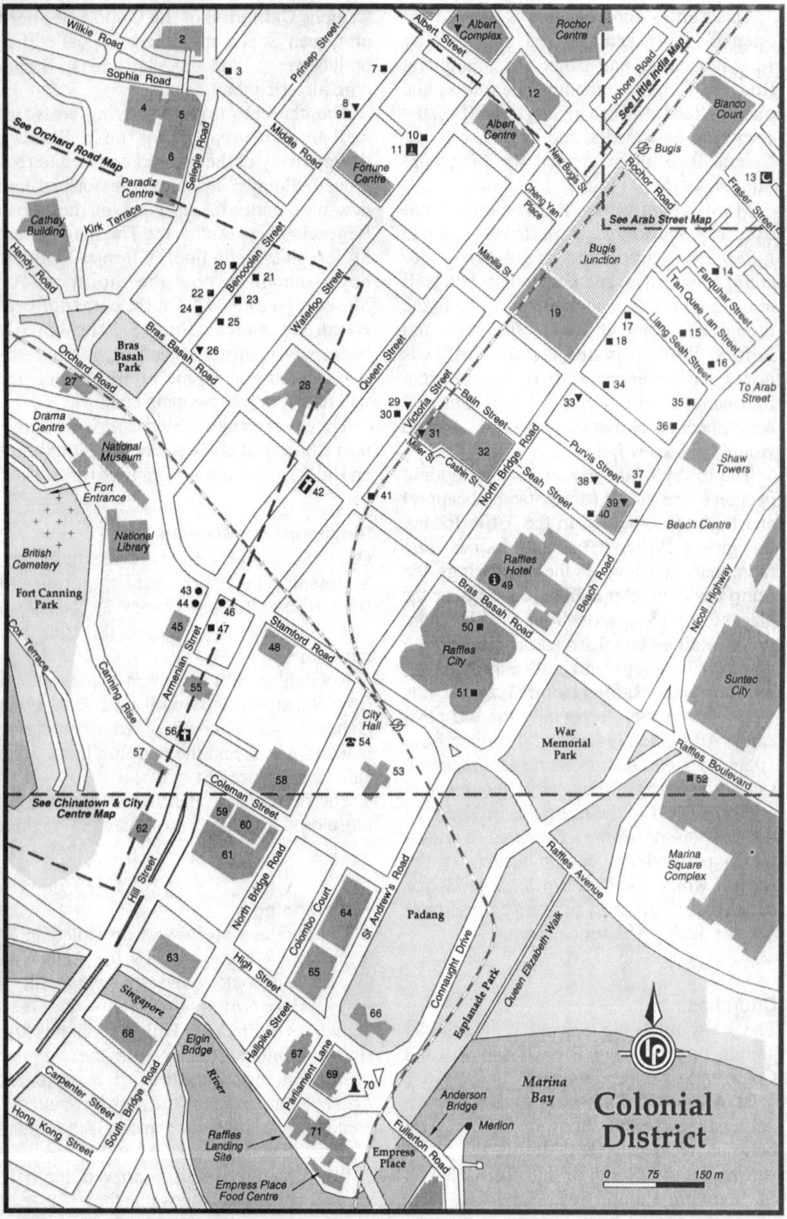
Colonial District
Wilkie Road
Sophia Road
Selegie Road
Prinsep Street
Middle Road
Albert Street
Albert Complex
Rochor Centre
Albert Centre
Fortune Centre
New Bugis St
Johore Road
See Little India Map
Blanco Court
Bugis
Rochor Road
Fraser Street
See Orchard Road Map
Paradiz Centre
Cathay Building
Kirk Terrace
Handy Road
Cheng Yan Place
See Arab Street Map
Bugis Junction
Manila St
Bencoolen Street
Waterloo Street
Queen Street
Farquhar Street
Tan Quee Lan Street
Liang Seah Street
To Arab Street
Bras Basah Park
Bras Basah Road
Orchard Road
Victoria Street
Bain Street
Purvis Street
Shaw Towers
Drama Centre
National Museum
Fort Entrance
Miller St
Cashin St
North Bridge Road
Seah Street
Beach Centre
British Cemetery
National Library
Raffles Hotel
Fort Canning Park
Beach Road
Nicoll Highway
Stamford Road
Armenian Street
Raffles City
Cox Terrace
Canning Rise
Suntec City
City Hall
War Memorial Park
Raffles Boulevard
See Chinatown & City Centre Map
Coleman Street
Hill Street
Raffles Avenue
Marina Square Complex
North Bridge Road
Colombo Court
St Andrew's Road
Padang
Connaught Drive
Queen Elizabeth Walk
High Street
Esplanade Park
Singapore
Hallpike Street
Elgin Bridge
River
Parliament Lane
Marina Bay
Anderson Bridge
Merlion
Carpenter Street
South Bridge Road
Hong Kong Street
Raffles Landing Site
Fullerton Road
Empress Place
Empress Place Food Centre
0
75
150 m

SINGAPORE

once have claimed was an earthen wall that stretched from the sea to the top of Fort Canning Hill. Raffles built his house on the top of the hill and it became Government House until the military built Fort Canning in 1860. There is little left of the historic buildings that were once on the hill, but it is a pleasant park and you can wander around the old Christian cemetery and see the many gravestones with their poignant tales of hopeful settlers who died young. On the top of the hill is the Fort Canning Centre, a former barracks which now houses the Singapore Dance Theatre.

National Museum

The National Museum on Stamford Rd traces its ancestry back to Raffles himself, who first brought up the idea of a museum for Singapore in 1823. The original museum opened in 1849, then moved to another location in 1862 before being rehoused at the present building in 1887.

The museum is not extensive but has substantial collections focusing on regional cultures, history, crafts etc. Exhibits include archaeological finds from the Asian region, articles relating to Chinese trade and settlement in the region, Malaysian and Indonesian arts and crafts, Peranakan artefacts and a wide collection of items relating to Stamford Raffles. The museum also has a superb jade collection donated by the Aw brothers, of Tiger Balm fame. The family amassed not only this priceless collection of jade pieces but also a variety of other valuable pieces of art.

The trouble with the National Museum has always been that only a fraction of its collection is on show, and as the exhibits are rotating, it is potluck as to what you see. However, the collections are being dispersed into the many new museums popping up

PLACES TO STAY

3 Sun Sun Hotel
7 Goh's Homestay & Hawaii Hostel
9 Why Not Homestay
10 South-East Asia Hotel
14 New 7th Storey Hotel
15 New Backpackers Lodge
16 Backpackers' Cozy Corner
17 Ah Chew Hotel
18 Waffles Home Stay
19 Hotel Inter-Continental
20 Hotel Bencoolen
21 Lee Boarding House, Peony Mansions & Latin House
22 Bencoolen House
23 San Wah Hotel
24 Strand Hotel
25 Bayview Inn
27 YMCA International House
30 Allson Hotel
34 Lido Hotel
35 Das Travellers' Inn
36 Lee Travellers' Club & Willy's Guest House
37 Shang Onn Hotel
40 Metropole Hotel
41 Carlton Hotel
47 Mayfair City Hotel
50 Westin Plaza Hotel
51 Westin Stamford Hotel
52 Marina Mandarin Hotel
59 Excelsior Hotel
60 Peninsula Hotel

PLACES TO EAT

1 Fatty's Wing Seong Restaurant
8 Sahib Restaurant
26 Regency Palace
29 Koh Fong Restaurant
31 Xiang Man Lou Food Court
33 Swee Kee Restaurant
38 Yet Con Restaurant
39 Tropical Makan Palace Food Stalls
62 Hill Street Food Centre

OTHER

2 Selegie Complex
4 Peace Mission
5 Peace Centre
6 Parklane Shopping Mall
11 Kuan Yin Temple
12 Fu Lou Shou Complex
13 Mosque
28 Singapore Art Museum
32 Bras Basah Complex
42 Cathedral of the Good Shepherd
43 National Museum Shop
44 Substation
45 Asian Civilisations Museum
46 MPH Bookstore
48 Stamford House
49 Singapore Tourist Promotion Board Office
53 St Andrew's Cathedral
54 Telecom
55 US Embassy
56 Church of St Gregory the Illuminator
57 Singapore Philatelic Museum
58 Peninsula Plaza
61 Funan Centre
63 High Street Centre
64 City Hall
65 Supreme Court
66 Singapore Cricket Club
67 Parliament House
68 Riverwalk Galleria
69 Victoria Concert Hall & Theatre
70 Raffles' Statue
71 Empress Place Building

around the city, such as the Singapore Art Museum and the Asian Civilisations Museum, still under construction just around the corner on Armenian St.

The museum is open from 9 am to 5.30 pm, except Monday, when it is closed. Admission is S$2. Tours of the museum for groups of 10 to 12 are available (☎ 338 0000). The National Museum Shop, a short walk away on Armenian St, has publications and an attractive array of gifts.

Singapore Philatelic Museum

Yet another new museum, this philatelic museum is housed in a colonial building dating from 1908. Stamp collectors will find it interesting and it is well presented with rare and not-so-rare stamps from Singapore and around the world, and the stamp-making process is traced from artwork through to printing. An audio-visual theatre and interactive games provide a high-tech touch.

The museum is open from 9 am to 4.30 pm; closed Mondays and public holidays. Entry is S$2 (children S$1). Free guided tours start at 11 am and 2 pm.

New Bugis St

For years Bugis St was famous as Singapore's raucous transvestite playground. In a country that banned jukeboxes and long hair, Bugis St was proof that Singapore dared to be daring. Bugis St was never, officially, more than another food-stall centre but, in practice, at the witching hour certain young men turned into something more exotic than pumpkins. It was the place to be until the early hours of the morning, to join the crowds and watch the goings on – that is until Bugis St was totally demolished during the building of the MRT. As is the case with so many of Singapore's attractions, the answer was to rebuild it, to make it newer and better than ever.

So now Singapore has a New Bugis St, just south-west of the MRT station, complete with new terrace look-alikes and new lock-up wooden stalls with new canvas walkway overhangs. Transvestites are not allowed, and of course New Bugis St is a pale shadow of its former self. Nonetheless it is a pleasant, even if much quieter, place to hang out in the evenings. Some of the open-air restaurants and bars stay open until 3 am or until the last customers go home. There are fruit and food stalls, and you can pick up a copy watch or a T-shirt. The Bugis MRT station is right across the way, and the large and very popular Bugis Junction shopping centre continues the neo-colonial architecture theme.

Kuan Yin Temple

This temple on Waterloo St is one of the most popular Chinese temples – after all, Kuan Yin is one of the most popular goddesses. This temple was rebuilt in 1982, but the flower sellers and fortune tellers out front make it one of the liveliest temples in Singapore. A few doors away is the **Sri Krishnan Temple**, which also attracts worshippers from the Kuan Yin Temple, who show a great deal of religious pragmatism by also burning joss sticks and offering prayers at this Hindu temple.

Central Business District

Once the vibrant heart of Singapore, **Raffles Place** is now a rather barren patch of grass above the MRT station surrounded by the giant high-rise buildings of the Central Business District. There are a few shopping possibilities nearby, including Aerial Plaza, a collection of small shops and aggressive Indian tailors, from where you can cross Collyer Quay to **Clifford Pier**, the place to hire a boat or catch a harbour tour (see Organised Tours in the Singapore Getting Around chapter). Singapore's harbour is one of the busiest in the world; there are always boats anchored offshore, with one arriving or departing at least every 15 minutes.

Further south along the waterfront, you'll find large office blocks, airline offices, more shops and the **Lau Pa Sat** festival market housed in the Telok Ayer Centre, a fine piece of cast-iron Victoriana that was once a market. It was pulled down during the construction of the MRT but has been restored and now stands on its original site. It has a wide selection of eating places and craft stalls, and cultural performances are occa-

SINGAPORE

sionally held here. It is lively in the evenings, when adjoining Boon Tat St is closed off and hawker carts are set up. Singapore's disappearing Chinatown is inland from this modern city centre.

CHINATOWN

Singapore's cultural heart is Chinatown, providing a glimpse of the old ways – the ways of the Chinese immigrants that shaped and built modern Singapore.

Much of Chinatown has been torn down and redeveloped over the last 30 years, though the greatest changes have occurred since around 1990. Many of the old colonial shop fronts, which are synonymous with the Chinese on the Malay peninsula, have been restored, or rather ripped down and rebuilt in the same style, under the direction of the Urban Redevelopment Authority.

The redevelopments are faithful to the original, and it is wonderful to see the spirit of the old buildings winning out over the concrete high-rises, but the re-creations are now desirable properties commanding high rents for businesses, shops and restaurants. Many of the traditional businesses have moved out and a new gentrified Chinatown has taken its place. Much of the old Chinatown is now fashionable restaurants and expensive shops.

Chinatown is still a good place to wander around. Though many of the traditional crafts and businesses have gone, it contains some of Singapore's most notable temples and there are plenty of eating and shopping possibilities. Chinatown is roughly bounded by the Singapore River to the north, New Bridge Rd to the west, Maxwell and Kreta Ayer Rds to the south and Cecil St to the east.

Walking Tour

You can start a Chinatown walking tour from the Raffles Place MRT station in the Central Business District. From the station, wander west along Chulia St and south down Philip St to the Wak Hai Cheng Bio Temple. This Teochew Taoist temple is quite run-down but has some interesting scenes depicted under, and on top of, the roof of the main temple.

Continue down Philip St and over Church St to Telok Ayer St. Up until only a couple of years ago, this was a clamouring district of traditional business, but the blocks around Pekin and Cross St are now deserted, awaiting redevelopment. It's amazing how on many of these old Chinese houses, bushes and even large trees seem to sprout straight out of the walls – an indication of the amazing fertility which Singapore's steamy climate seems to engender.

At the junction with Boon Tat St, you'll find the **Nagore Durgha Shrine**, an old mosque built by Muslims from south India during 1829 and 1830. It's not that interesting, but just a little south-west down the street is the Chinese **Thian Hock Keng Temple**, or Temple of Heavenly Happiness, one of the most interesting temples in Singapore (see below).

Continue walking along Telok Ayer St and you'll soon come to the **Al-Abrar Mosque**, which was originally built in 1827 and rebuilt in its present form from 1850 to 1855. A right turn and then another right turn will bring you into Amoy St, a Hokkien area that once catered to sailors and the sea trade. This street has almost been totally modernised, and represents the first look at the new Chinatown.

Continue up Amoy St over Cross St, and then turn left (north-west) up Cross St to Club St. A **thieves' market** is held every afternoon in the vacant lot near the corner here. The quiet area around Club St, Ann Siang Rd and Ann Siang Hill was a clove and nutmeg plantation until it became a prime residential area for Hokkien merchants. This area was noted for its highly decorated terraces, a number of which housed the old Chinese guilds, though only a few remain now. Ann Siang Hill in particular has some fine terrace houses, both restored and unrestored.

South-west down South Bridge Rd is the **Tanjong Pagar** conservation area, wedged between Neil and Tanjong Pagar Rds. This was the first major restoration project in Chinatown. The beautifully restored terraces accommodate a variety of restaurants and bars. The old Jinrikisha station on the corner

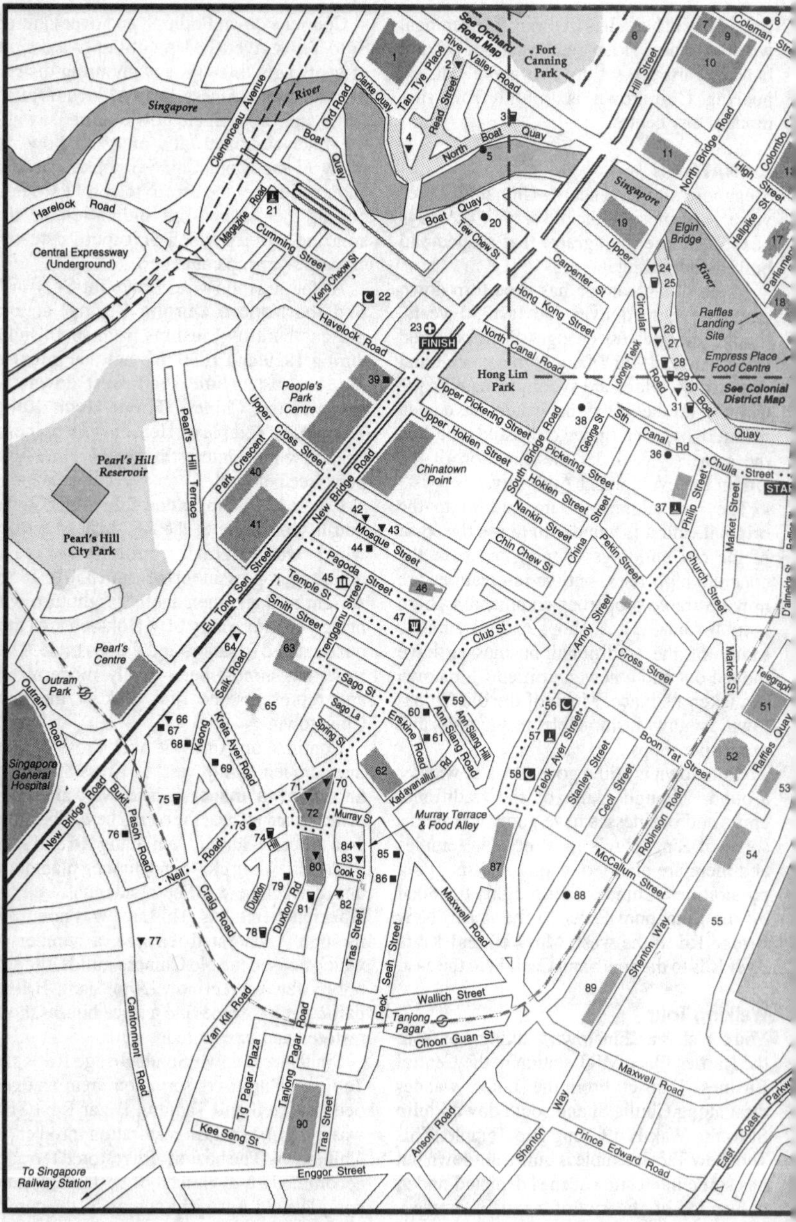
See Orchard Road Map
Fort Canning Park
Coleman Street
Singapore River
Clemenceau Avenue
Ord Road
Clarke Quay
Tan Tye Place
River Valley Road
Read Street
Boat Quay
North Boat Quay
Hill Street
North Bridge Road
High Street
Colombo Ct
Harelock Road
Magazine Road
Cumming Street
Tew Chew St
Boat Quay
Central Expressway (Underground)
Keng Cheow St
Carpenter St
Upper
Elgin Bridge
Hallpike St
Parliament
Hong Kong Street
Circular Road
Havelock Road
FINISH
North Canal Road
Raffles Landing Site
Lorong Telok
Empress Place Food Centre
People's Park Centre
Hong Lim Park
See Colonial District Map
Upper Pickering Street
Upper Cross Street
Upper Hokien Street
South Bridge Road
George St
Sth Canal Rd
Boat Quay
Pearl's Hill Terrace
Park Crescent
New Bridge Road
Chinatown Point
Pickering Street
Chulia Street
START
Pearl's Hill Reservoir
Hokien Street
Philip Street
Market Street
Nankin Street
China Street
Mosque Street
Pearl's Hill City Park
Chin Chew St
Pekin Street
Church Street
Eu Tong Sen Street
Pagoda Street
Temple St
Smith Street
Trengganu Street
D'almeida St
Club St
Amoy Street
Pearl's Centre
Salk Road
Cross Street
Market St
Telegraph
Outram Park
Sago St
Sago La
Ann Siang Hill
Ann Siang Road
Quay
Outram Road
Keong
Kreta Ayer Road
Spring St
Erskine Road
Telok Ayer Street
Boon Tat Street
Raffles
Singapore General Hospital
Kadayanallur Rd
Stanley Street
Cecil Street
Robinson Road
Bukit Pasoh Road
New Bridge Road
Murray St
Murray Terrace & Food Alley
Neil Road
Hill
Duxton
Duxton Rd
Cook St
McCallum Street
Craig Road
Tras Street
Maxwell Road
Shenton Way
Peck Seah Street
Cantonment Road
Yan Kit Road
Wallich Street
Tanjong Pagar
Choon Guan St
Tg Pagar Plaza
Tanjong Pagar Road
Maxwell Road
Parkway
East Coast
Kee Seng St
Tras Street
Anson Road
Shenton Way
Prince Edward Road
To Singapore Railway Station
Enggor Street

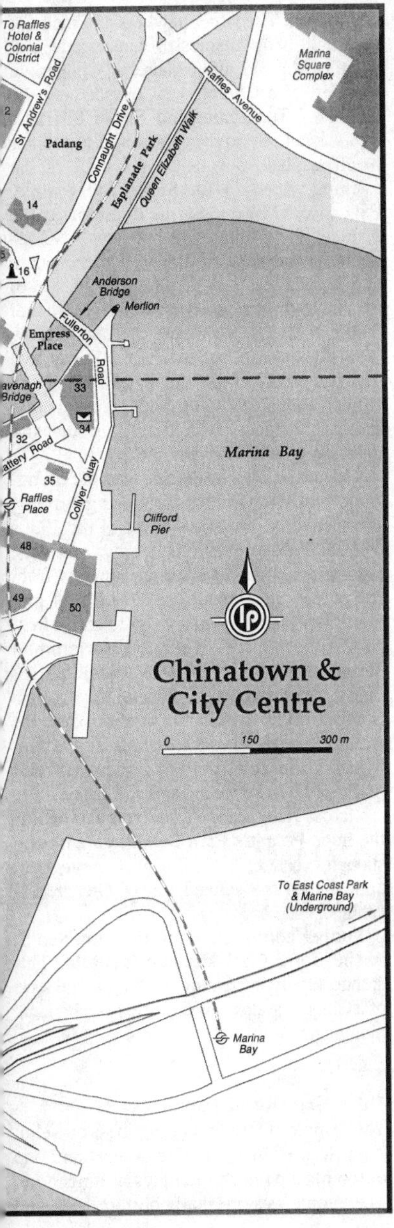

PLACES TO STAY

1 New Otani Hotel & Liang Court
7 Excelsior Hotel
9 Peninsula Hotel
39 Furama Hotel
44 Dragon Cityview Hotel
60 Damenlou Hotel
61 Inn of the Sixth Happiness
67 Chinatown Guest House
68 Royal Peacock Hotel
69 Chinatown Hotel
76 Majestic Hotel
79 Duxton Hotel
85 New Asia Hotel
86 Air View Hotel
90 Amara Hotel

PLACES TO EAT

2 Satay Club
4 JP Bastiani Wine Bar
6 Hill Street Food Centre
24 cafe@boatquay
26 Izumi
27 Maharajah
30 Pasta Fresca
32 Boat Quay Food Centre
40 People's Park Food Centre
42 Chui Wah Lin
43 Teo Hiang Hin
59 La Cascade
62 Maxwell Food Centre
63 Chinatown Complex (Market & Food Place)
64 Tiong Shan Restaurant
66 Tasree Restaurant
70 Jinrikisha Station
71 Tea Chapter
77 Hillman Restaurant
80 Goldleaf Restaurant
82 CyberNet Cafe
83 Beng Hiang Restaurant
84 Moti Mahal Restaurant
87 Amoy St Food Centre

OTHER

3 Crazy Elephant
5 Boat Tour Jetty
8 Peninsula Plaza
10 Funan Centre
11 High Street Centre
12 City Hall
13 Supreme Court
14 Singapore Cricket Club
15 Victoria Concert Hall & Theatre
16 Raffles' Statue
17 Parliament House
18 Empress Place Building
19 Riverwalk Galleria
20 Ellenborough Street Market
21 Tan Si Chong Su Temple
22 Melaka Mosque
23 Tong Chai Medical Institute
25 Riverbank

Continued over page

28	Molly Malone's
29	Escobar
31	Harry's
33	Fullerton Building
34	Post Office
35	Hongkong Bank Building
36	OCBC Centre
37	Wak Hai Cheng Bio Temple
38	Pidemco Centre
41	People's Park Complex
45	Chinaman Scholars Gallery
46	Jamae Mosque
47	Sri Mariamman Temple
48	Clifford Centre
49	Ocean Building
50	Overseas Union Shopping Centre
51	Hong Leong Building
52	Lau Pa Sat (Telok Ayer Centre)
53	Telok Ayer Transit Centre
54	Shenton House
55	UIC Building
56	Nagore Durgha Shrine
57	Thian Hock Keng Temple
58	Al-Abrar Mosque
65	Kreta Ayer People's Theatre
72	Tanjong Pagar
73	51 Neil Road Complex
74	Elvis' Place
75	Butterfly Bar & Cafe
78	JJ Mahoney Pub
81	Moon
88	Silk Air
89	DBS Building

of Neil and Tanjong Pagar Rds, now a restaurant, is an interesting triangular building that was once the depot for the hand-pulled rickshaws. The **Tanjong Pagar Heritage Exhibition** in the 51 Neil Rd complex is a small, interesting exhibition with old photographs that shows what Chinatown used to be like. It is open from 11 am to 9 pm. Admission is free.

Near Tanjong Pagar, the **Bukit Pasoh area** is a traditional part of Chinatown. Bukit Pasoh Rd, where you'll find the Majestic Hotel, is known as the street of the clans because of the many clan association houses here. Keong Saik Rd is a curving street of old terraces with coffee shops, clan houses and clubs. This street is a hive of new building work, and new hotels and bars are replacing the traditional businesses.

Heading back to the centre of Chinatown, north-east up to South Bridge Rd, you enter the **Kreta Ayer district**, the real heart of Chinatown. The street hawkers and many of the traditional businesses have gone, but some of the old atmosphere of Chinatown remains. The Chinatown Complex, on the corner of Trengganu and Smith Sts, is a lively local shopping centre and a popular meeting place outside in the cool of the evening. Along with Smith St, Temple, Pagoda and Mosque Sts are traditionally the heart of old Chinatown, but new developments have destroyed a lot of the atmosphere and Pagoda St is a mess of renovation. Smith St has gold, jade, souvenirs and traditional medicine shops. Mosque St has a good row of old-fashioned coffee shops. The whole area has plenty of old and new souvenir and trinket shops selling masks, reproduction bronzes, bamboo ware, carvings and silk dressing gowns. Bargain hard.

Upstairs at 14B Trengganu St is the **Chinaman Scholars Gallery**. This living museum is styled as a Cantonese house of the 1930s and includes furniture, clothing, artefacts, photographs and musical instruments from the period. It is open from 9 am to 4 pm; admission is S$4 for adults, S$2 for children.

Also in this area is the **Sri Mariamman Temple**, Singapore's oldest Hindu temple (see below). The **Jamae (or Chulia) Mosque** on South Bridge Rd is only a short distance from the Sri Mariamman Temple. It was built by Indian Muslims from the Coromandel Coast of Tamil Nadu between 1830 and 1855.

Across New Bridge Rd from Pagoda St is the huge **People's Park Complex** – a modern shopping centre, but with much more local appeal than the general run of Orchard Rd centres.

Further north-east along Eu Tong Sen St is the **Tong Chai Medical Institute**. This architecturally interesting building in the style of a Chinese godown is classified as a national monument.

Thian Hock Keng Temple

The Temple of Heavenly Happiness on Telok Ayer St in Chinatown is the oldest and one of the most colourful temples in Singapore. The temple was originally built in 1840 and dedicated to Ma-Cho-Po, the queen of heaven and protector of sailors.

At that time it was on the waterfront and, since many Chinese settlers were arriving by sea, it was inevitable that a joss house be built where they could offer thanks for a safe voyage. As you wander through the courtyards of the temple, look for the rooftop dragons, the intricately decorated beams, the burning joss sticks, the gold-leafed panels and, best of all, the beautifully painted doors.

Sri Mariamman Temple

The Sri Mariamman Temple on South Bridge Rd, right in the heart of Chinatown, is the oldest Hindu temple in Singapore. It was built in 1827 but rebuilt in 1862. With its colourful *gopuram*, or tower, over the entrance gate, this is clearly a temple in the south Indian Dravidian style. A superb collection of colourfully painted Hindu figures decorate the *gopuram*.

Around October each year, the temple is the scene for the Thimithi festival, during which devotees walk barefoot over burning coals – supposedly feeling no pain, although spectators report that quite a few hotfoot it over the final few steps!

LITTLE INDIA

Although Singapore is a predominantly Chinese city, it does have its minority groups and the Indians are probably the most visible, particularly in the colourful streets of Little India along Serangoon Rd. This is another area, like Chinatown, in which you can simply wander around and take in the flavours. Indeed, around Serangoon Rd it can be very much a case of following your nose because the heady aroma of Indian spices and cooking seems to be everywhere.

If you want a new sari, a pair of Indian sandals, a recent issue of *India Today* or the *Indian Movie News*, a tape of Indian music or a framed portrait of your favourite Hindu god, then Little India is the place to go.

It's also, not surprisingly, a good place to eat. Since many of Singapore's Indians are Hindu Tamils from the south of India, Little India has many vegetarian restaurants, and there are some superb places to eat vegetarian food.

Walking Tour

Little India is not very extensive, and you can sample its sights, scents and sounds in an hour or two. Little India is roughly the area bounded by Bukit Timah Rd to the south, Lavender St to the north, Race Course Rd to the west and Jalan Besar to the east. The real centre of Little India is at the southern end of Serangoon Rd and the small streets that run off it. Here, the shops are wall-to-wall Indian, but only a hundred metres or so away the Chinese influence reappears.

Unfortunately, much of the western side of Serangoon Rd has been flattened and consists of open fields, but there are interesting temples further north. Race Course Rd has a few shops and some good restaurants down its southern end, but the housing estates have made an unmistakable contribution to its atmosphere. Sunday is the big day in Little India, when the temples are buzzing and hundreds of Indian men, Bangladeshi immigrant workers, come out to socialise, milling around the streets arm-in-arm or squatting by the side of the road to chat.

The **Zhujiao Centre** on Serangoon Rd near Buffalo Rd is Little India's market. It was known as the KK market (Kandang Kerbau, meaning 'cattle pens', as this was once a cattle-holding area) before it was rehoused in this modern building. Downstairs is a 'wet market', the Singaporean term for a produce market, and it is one of the liveliest local markets in Singapore, selling all types of fruit and vegetables as well as meat and fish. The hawker centre here has plenty of Indian food stalls. Upstairs, stalls sell a variety of clothes and everyday goods and you can also buy brassware and Indian textiles.

Across Serangoon Rd is the **Little India Arcade**, presenting the new face of Little India. This block of renovated shophouses has its fair share of tourist-oriented souvenir shops, but manages to maintain the traditional atmosphere of Little India with Indian textile, grocery and flower shops, making it

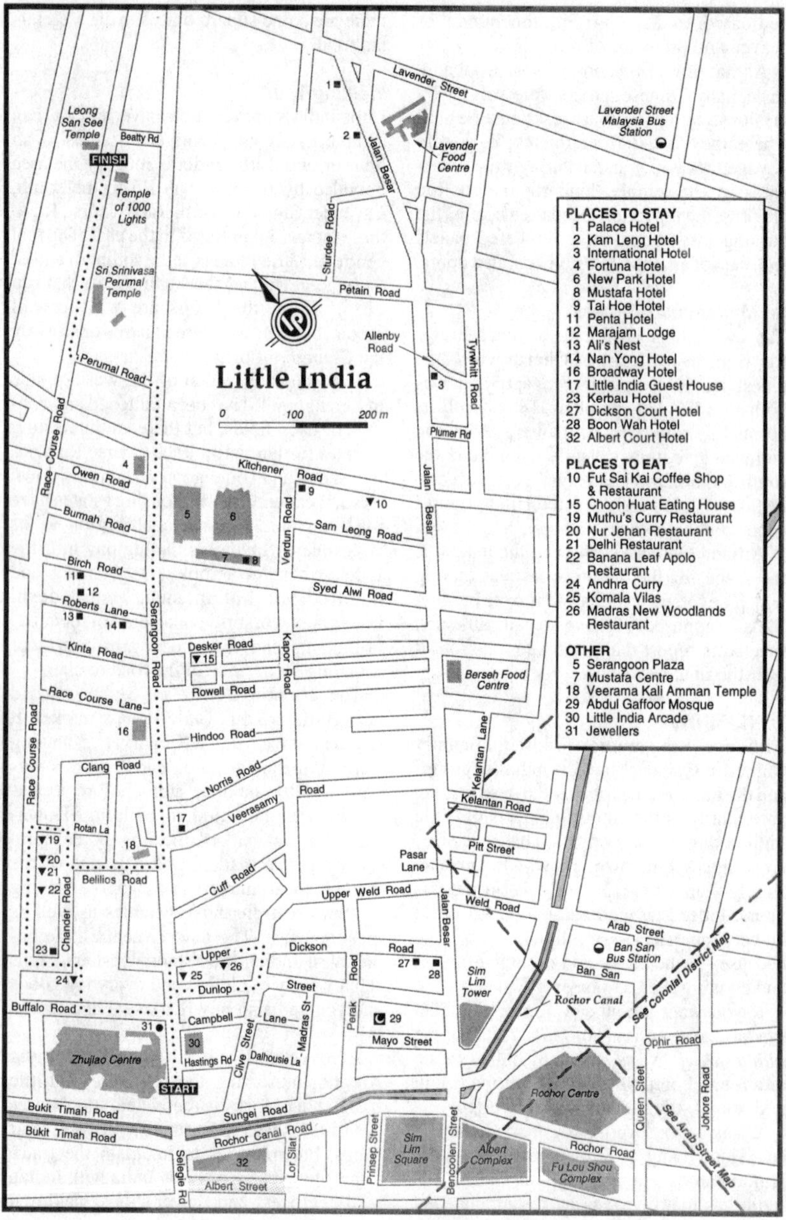
Little India
0
100
200 m
PLACES TO STAY
1 Palace Hotel
2 Kam Leng Hotel
3 International Hotel
4 Fortuna Hotel
6 New Park Hotel
8 Mustafa Hotel
9 Tai Hoe Hotel
11 Penta Hotel
12 Marajam Lodge
13 Ali's Nest
14 Nan Yong Hotel
16 Broadway Hotel
17 Little India Guest House
23 Kerbau Hotel
27 Dickson Court Hotel
28 Boon Wah Hotel
32 Albert Court Hotel
PLACES TO EAT
10 Fut Sai Kai Coffee Shop & Restaurant
15 Choon Huat Eating House
19 Muthu's Curry Restaurant
20 Nur Jehan Restaurant
21 Delhi Restaurant
22 Banana Leaf Apolo Restaurant
24 Andhra Curry
25 Komala Vilas
26 Madras New Woodlands Restaurant
OTHER
5 Serangoon Plaza
7 Mustafa Centre
18 Veerama Kali Amman Temple
29 Abdul Gaffoor Mosque
30 Little India Arcade
31 Jewellers
Lavender Street
Lavender Street Malaysia Bus Station
Lavender Food Centre
Jalan Besar
Leong San See Temple
Beatty Rd
FINISH
Temple of 1000 Lights
Sturdee Road
Sri Srinivasa Perumal Temple
Petain Road
Allenby Road
Tyrwhitt Road
Perumal Road
Plumer Rd
Race Course Road
Owen Road
Kitchener Road
Burmah Road
Verdun Road
Sam Leong Road
Birch Road
Roberts Lane
Syed Alwi Road
Serangoon Road
Kinta Road
Desker Road
Kapor Road
Rowell Road
Berseh Food Centre
Race Course Lane
Hindoo Road
Kelantan Lane
Clang Road
Norris Road
Road
Veerasamy
Kelantan Road
Rotan La
Pitt Street
Pasar Lane
Belilios Road
Cuff Road
Upper Weld Road
Weld Road
Chander Road
Arab Street
Ban San Bus Station
Upper
Dickson
Road
Dunlop
Street
Ban San
Sim Lim Tower
Rochor Canal
See Colonial District Map
Buffalo Road
Campbell
Lane
Madras St
Perak Road
Mayo Street
Clive Street
Zhujiao Centre
Hastings Rd
Dalhousie La
Ophir Road
START
Rochor Centre
Bukit Timah Road
Sungei Road
Queen Street
Johore Road
Rochor Canal Road
Bencoolen Street
Prinsep Street
Lor Silat
Sim Lim Square
Albert Complex
Rochor Road
Fu Lou Shou Complex
See Arab Street Map
Selegie Rd
Albert Street

SINGAPORE

a more successful project than in many parts of Chinatown. From here wander around the backstreets with the names of imperial India such as Clive, Hastings and Campbell. This is the heart of Little India with a variety of shops selling spices, Indian music cassettes, saris, religious artefacts and everyday goods for the Indian household. Dunlop St in particular maintains much of its old-fashioned charm. This is also a restaurant area and the best place to sample south Indian vegetarian food. At 76 Serangoon Rd is the famous Komala Vilas restaurant and around the corner in Upper Dickson Rd is the equally good Madras New Woodlands restaurant.

Apart from the ubiquitous gold shops, there are a few interesting **jewellers** on Serangoon and Buffalo Rds that make jewellery crafted with traditional designs.

The southern end of Race Course Rd has the best collection of non-vegetarian restaurants in Singapore, from the tandoori food of north India to Singapore's famous fish-head curry (sounds and looks terrible, tastes delicious).

On the corner of Belilios and Serangoon Rds is the **Veerama Kali Amman Temple**, a Shivaite temple dedicated to Kali. It is always popular with worshippers, especially at dusk.

Further north-east along Serangoon Rd is the **Serangoon Plaza**. Architecturally, historically and culturally it's a write-off, but the department stores here are good places for bargains. The range may not be extensive, but the fixed prices for electrical goods and other household items are usually as good as you'll find anywhere in Singapore. The Mustafa Centre around the corner is a new, larger offshoot crammed with places for bargain hunters.

Also in this area, in the alleyways behind Desker Rd, are the infamous brothels. Rows of blockhouse rooms line the alley and a constant parade of men wander up and down. It is fairly seedy but very lively, and the coffee shops with outdoor tables here do a roaring trade. This area is the successor to old Bugis St, without the tourists and carnival atmosphere, and later in the evenings the transvestites strut their stuff.

In complete contrast, the **Sri Srinivasa Perumal Temple** is a large temple dedicated to Vishnu. The temple dates from 1855 but the impressive gopuram is a relatively recent addition, built in 1966. Inside the temple, you will find a statue of Perumal, or Vishnu, and his consorts Lakshmi and Andal, as well as his bird-mount Garuda. This temple is the starting point for devotees who make the walk to the Chettiar Hindu Temple during the Thaipusam festival.

Not far from the Sri Srinivasa Perumal Temple is the Sakaya Muni Buddha Gaya Temple, better known as the **Temple of 1000 Lights** (see below). It's a glitzy, slightly tacky Thai-influenced temple, but one of Singapore's best known, and it welcomes visitors. A more beautiful temple is the **Leong San See Temple** over the road. This Buddhist and Taoist temple has some fine ceramic carvings inside.

From Little India, you can wander across to **Jalan Besar**. The Indian influence is not so noticeable here; the fine old pastel-coloured terraces with intricate stucco and tiles are Peranakan in style. Of particular note are the terraces on Petain Rd, and those on the corner of Plumer Rd and Jalan Besar.

A number of traditional businesses are on and around Jalan Besar, and the area around Kelantan Lane and Pasar Lane is a place to look for antiques. On Sundays a flea market operates, selling everything from old shoes and computer chips to motorcycle parts, and if you rummage around you can find old coins, porcelain and brassware.

Just off Jalan Besar on Dunlop St, down towards Rochor Canal Rd, is the **Abdul Gaffoor Mosque**. It's an intriguing fairytale blend of Arab and Victorian architecture.

Temple of 1000 Lights

Towards the north-eastern end of Race Course Rd at No 366, close to the corner of Serangoon and Beatty Rds, is the Sakaya Muni Buddha Gaya Temple, or the Temple of 1000 Lights. This Buddhist temple is dominated by a brightly painted 15-metre-high seated figure of the Buddha. The temple was inspired by a Thai monk named

Vutthisasara. Although it is a Thai-style temple, it's actually very Chinese in its technicolour decoration.

Apart from the huge Buddha image, the temple includes oddities like a wax model of Gandhi and a figure of Ganesh, the elephant-headed Hindu god. A huge mother-of-pearl footprint, complete with the 108 auspicious marks which distinguish a Buddha foot from any other two-metre-long foot, is said to be a replica of the footprint on top of Adam's Peak in Sri Lanka.

Behind and inside the giant statue is a smaller image of the reclining Buddha in the act of entering nirvana. Around the base, models tell the story of the Buddha's life, and, of course, there are the 1000 electric lights, which give the temple its name.

Any bus going north-east along Serangoon Rd will take you to the temple.

ARAB ST

While Chinatown provides Singapore with a Chinese flavour and Serangoon Rd is where you head to for the tastes and smells of India, Arab St is the Muslim centre. Along this street, and especially along North Bridge Rd and along side streets with Malay names like Pahang St, Aliwal St, Jalan Pisang and Jalan Sultan, you'll find batiks from Indonesia and sarongs, hookahs, rosaries, flower essences, hajj caps, songkok hats, basketware and rattan goods.

Walking Tour

The easiest way to begin a tour of the Arab St area is to take the MRT to the Bugis station and walk up Victoria St to Arab St.

Arab St is traditionally a textile district, and while the big merchants inhabit the textile centre on Jalan Sultan, Arab St is still alive with textile shops selling batiks, silks and more mundane cloth for a sarong or shirt. A number of craft shops sell leather bags and souvenirs, and up the end of Arab St near Beach Rd are the caneware shops. Negotiate the five-foot-ways and haggle for the wares.

Sultan Mosque (see below), the focus for Singapore's Muslim community, is on the corner of Arab St and North Bridge Rd. It is the largest mosque in Singapore and the most lively. You'll also find good Indian Muslim food at restaurants across the street on North Bridge Rd. One street back towards the city is **Haji Lane**, a narrow picturesque lane lined with two-storey shophouses that contain a number of textile and other local businesses. Kazura, at No 51, is a traditional perfume business with rows of decanters containing perfumes such as 'Ramadan' and 'Aidal Fitri' for the faithful. At the end of Haji Lane turn left into Beach Rd.

If you have time for a detour north-east along Beach Rd, the **Hajjah Fatimah Mosque** is interesting. A national monument, it was built by a Melakan-born Malay woman, Hajjah Fatimah, on the site of her home around 1845. The architecture shows colonial influences.

Otherwise, turn back up Arab St. Heading north-east up Baghdad St from Arab St, you find more batik and craft shops and then you cross **Bussorah St**. During the month of Ramadan, when Muslims fast from sunrise to sunset, the area is alive with food stalls, especially in Bussorah St, where the faithful come to buy food at dusk. Bussorah St is destined to become the new yuppie Arab St. The old terraces are being renovated and palm trees have been planted to give that Middle Eastern 'oasis look'.

At 24 Baghdad St you'll find **stone carvers** crafting the small headstones for Muslim graves, and further along between Sultan Gate and Aliwal St are other stone carvers that also produce carvings for Chinese temples and graves.

If you turn left into Sultan Gate you come to the historic gates that lead to the **Istana Kampong Glam**. The *istana* (palace) was the residence of Sultan Ali Iskander Shah and was built around 1840. The Kampong Glam area is the historic seat of the Malay royalty, resident here before the arrival of Stamford Raffles. In the early days of Singapore, it was allocated not only to the original Malays but also to Javanese, Bugis and Arab merchants and residents.

The palace isn't open to visitors, but if you walk through the gateway and around to the left a doorway in the palace wall leads you to Kandahar St, behind the Sultan Mosque. Muscat St winds behind the mosque back to Arab St, or you can continue up Kandahar St to North Bridge Rd. Cross over North Bridge Rd and you'll find a number of venerable Indian Muslim restaurants selling roti prata and biryani.

On the corner of Jalan Sultan and Victoria St is **Malabar Muslim Jama-Ath Mosque**, a beautiful little mosque covered in blue tiles that is at its fairy-tale best when lit up in the evenings during Ramadan. Behind it is the old **Kampong Glam cemetery**, where it is said that the Malay royalty is buried among the frangipani trees and coconut palms. Many of the graves have fallen into ruin and are overgrown, but more recent graves are tended, as is evidenced by the cloths placed over the headstones.

Sultan Mosque

The Sultan Mosque on North Bridge Rd near Arab St is the biggest mosque in Singapore. It was originally built in 1825 with the aid of a grant from Stamford Raffles and the East India Company as a result of Raffles' treaty with the sultan of Johor. A hundred years later, the original mosque was replaced by a magnificent gold-domed building. The mosque is open to visitors from 5 am to 8.30 pm daily; if you can manage it, the best time to visit is during a religious ceremony.

ORCHARD RD

Singapore's international tourists and its wealthy residents also have whole areas of Singapore to themselves. Orchard Rd is where the high-class hotels predominate, and beyond it you enter the area of the Singapore elite. Prior to independence, the mansions of the colonial rulers were built there, and today the wealthy of Singapore, as well as many expatriates, live in these fine old houses.

Orchard Rd itself is mostly a place to shop, eat and stay. Its rows of modern shopping

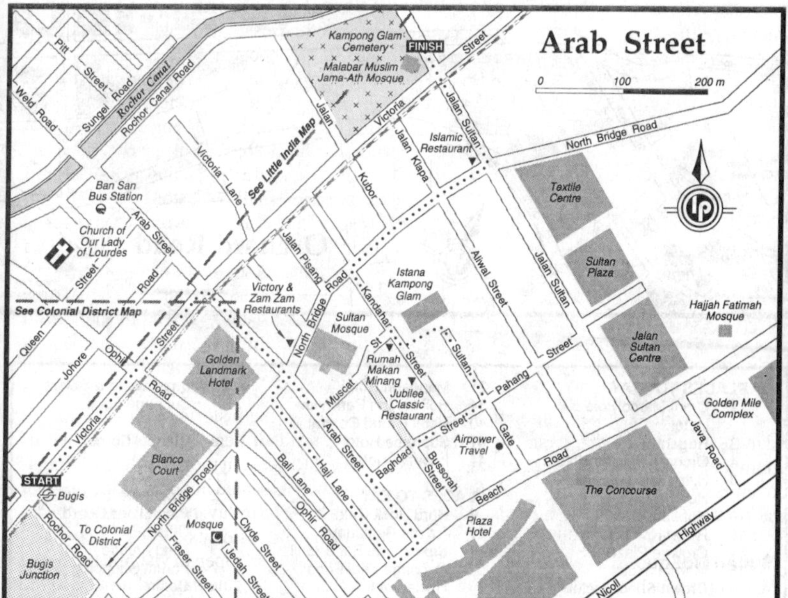

centres hold a variety of stores selling everything from the latest in Japanese gadgetry to the antiques of the east. Here you'll also find the majority of Singapore's international hotels, many of Singapore's nightspots and a whole host of restaurants, bars and lounges. This area is a showcase for modern Singapore and the delights of capitalism, but it also has a few points of cultural interest where you don't need your credit card.

Peranakan Place

Among the glass and chrome is Peranakan Place, a complex of old Baba-Nonya shophouses on the corner of Orchard and Emerald Hill Rds.

Peranakan culture is that of the Straits-born Chinese who spoke a Malay dialect and developed their own customs that are a fascinating hybrid of Chinese and Malay. 'Nonya' is the word for an adult Peranakan woman, 'Baba' her male counterpart. The **Peranakan Showhouse Museum** is one shophouse decorated with Peranakan artefacts, furniture and clothing. If traditional Straits Chinese culture interests you, you shouldn't miss this one. The museum is in a terrace house a few doors back from Orchard Rd. Interesting tours of the museum are available on demand and cost S$4 for adults and S$2 for children. The museum is open from 10.30 am to 12.30 pm and 2 to 3.30 pm, Monday to Friday.

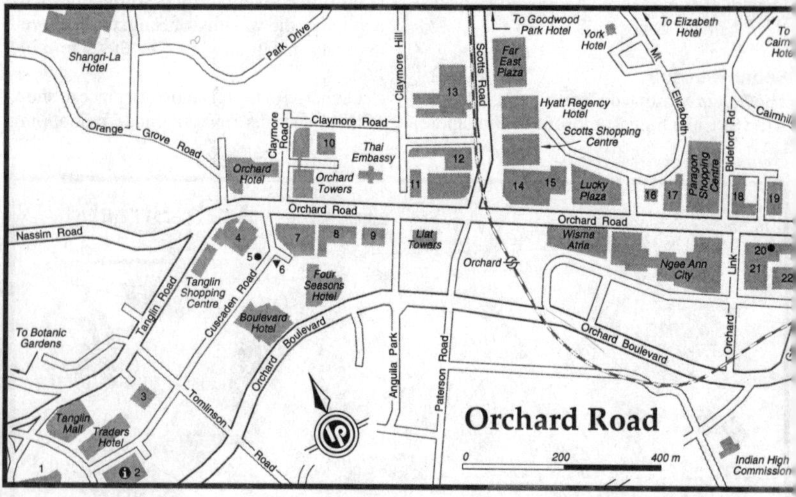

PLACES TO STAY
- 1 Omni Marco Polo Hotel
- 3 Regent Hotel
- 4 Orchard Parade Hotel
- 8 Hilton International Hotel
- 10 Hotel Negara
- 13 Royal Holiday Inn Crowne Plaza
- 15 Marriott Hotel
- 18 Crown Prince Hotel
- 21 Mandarin Hotel
- 34 Holiday Inn Park View
- 40 Hotel Grand Central
- 41 Supreme Hotel
- 44 Imperial Hotel

PLACES TO EAT
- 6 Hard Rock Cafe
- 27 Azizas Restaurant
- 31 Saxophone Bar & Grill
- 32 Cuppage Thai Food Restaurant
- 38 Snackworld & Selera Cuppage Food Centre
- 39 Istanbul Corner

OTHER
- 2 Singapore Tourist Promotions Board Office
- 5 Ming Arcade
- 7 Forum Shopping Centre

From Peranakan Place, wander north up Emerald Hill Rd, where some fine terrace houses remain. This whole area was once a nutmeg plantation owned by William Cuppage, an early Singapore settler. At the turn of the century, much of it was subdivided and it became a fashionable residential area for Peranakan and Straits-born Chinese merchants. Today it is a fashionable drinking spot with some good bars along the street.

Peranakan Place is just north of the Somerset MRT station.

Istana

The Istana (palace) is the home of Singapore's president and is also used by the prime minister for ceremonial occasions. Formerly Government House, the Istana is set about 750 metres back from the road in large grounds. The closest you are likely to get to it are the well-guarded gates on Orchard Rd, but the Istana is open to the public on selected public holidays, such as New Year's Day. If you are lucky enough to be in Singapore on one of these days, take your passport and join the queues to get in.

House of Tan Yeok Nee

On the corner of Clemenceau Ave and Penang Rd, near Orchard Rd, the House of Tan Yeok Nee was built in 1885 as the townhouse of a prosperous merchant in a style

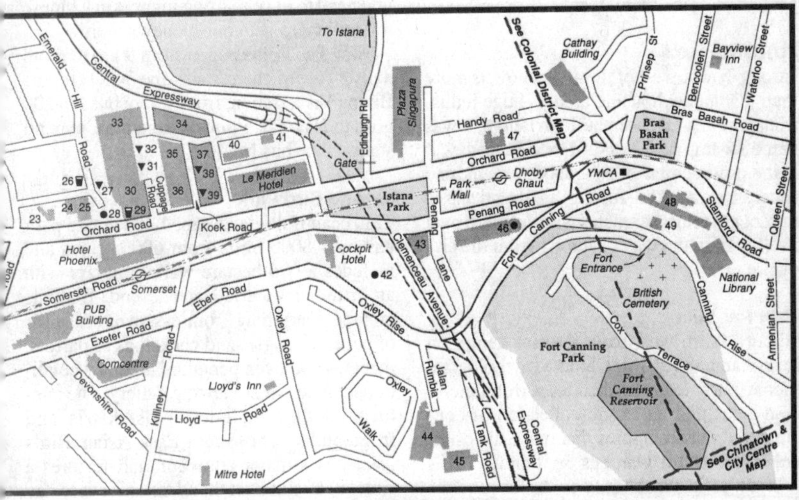

9 Far East Shopping Centre
11 International Building
12 Shaw Centre
14 Tang's
16 Tang Building
17 The Promenade Shopping Centre
19 Yen San Building
20 Singapore Airlines
22 Orchard Theatre
23 Faber House
24 Midpoint Orchard
25 Orchard Emerald
26 No 5, Que Pasa & The Den
28 Peranakan Place
29 Papa Joe's
30 Centrepoint
33 Cuppage Centre
35 Cuppage Plaza
36 Orchard Point
37 Orchard Plaza
42 House of Tan Yeok Nee
43 Singapore Shopping Centre
45 Chettiar Hindu Temple
46 Supreme House
47 MacDonald House
48 National Museum
49 Drama Centre

then common in the south of China. This national monument was the Salvation Army headquarters for many years, but it has recently changed hands and is now closed to the public.

Chettiar Hindu Temple

On Tank Rd at the intersection of River Valley Rd, not far from Orchard Rd, this temple was completed in 1984 and replaces a much earlier temple built by Indian *chettiars*, or money lenders. It is a Shivaite temple dedicated to the six-headed Lord Subramaniam and is at its most active during the festival of Thaipusam, when the procession ends here. Worshippers make offerings of coconuts, which are smashed on the ground to crack them open.

JURONG

Jurong Town, west of the city centre, is more than just a new housing area. A huge industrial complex has been built on land that was still a swamp at the end of WWII. Today, it is the powerhouse of Singapore's economic success story. The Jurong area also has a number of tourist attractions, in Jurong Town itself and on the way to Jurong from the city centre.

Haw Par Villa

About 10 km west from the city centre on Pasir Panjang Rd, this Chinese mythological theme park features theatre performances, boat rides and an exotic collection of concrete and plaster figures that made the original Tiger Balm Gardens so famous. This hillside park was built with the fortune the Aw brothers made from their miracle cure-all Tiger Balm, and featured a gaudy grotesquerie of statues illustrating scenes from Chinese legends and the pleasures and punishments of this life and the next.

Renovations and high-tech additions have changed the face of this long-popular monument to bad taste, but the surviving statuary remains its major attraction. Favourite displays include the Ten Courts of Hell, where sinners get their gory comeuppance in the afterlife, and the 'moral lessons' aisle, where sloth, indulgence, gambling and even wine, women and song lead to their inevitable unhappy endings.

New additions include a heart-in-the-mouth roller-coaster boat ride and theatres where the inevitable 'multimedia' displays narrate Chinese myths and legends. The large, covered amphitheatre has live performances popular with children, and new schedules advertise daily performances such as lion dances and performers on stilts.

Haw Par Villa is popular with Singaporean families – it's fun for the kids and teaches them Chinese mythology and the moral tales scare the bejesus out of them if they misbehave. It costs S$16.50 for adults and S$10.50 for children – needless to say, you need to have a strong interest in Chinese mythology to get your money's worth.

Haw Par Villa is open from 9 am to 6 pm daily. To get there, take the MRT to the Buona Vista station, from where bus No 200 goes to Haw Par Villa; or from the Clementi station take bus No 10.

Jurong Bird Park

This beautifully landscaped 20 hectare park has over 8000 birds from 600 species and includes a two hectare walk-in aviary with an artificial waterfall at one end. Exhibits include everything from cassowaries, birds of paradise, eagles and cockatoos to parrots, macaws and even penguins in an air-conditioned underwater viewing gallery. The nocturnal house includes owls, kiwis and frogmouths. The South-East Asian Birds Aviary is a major attraction and features a simulated rainforest thunderstorm every day at noon. The park also has one of the world's largest collections of hornbills, as well as a new walk-through parrot aviary.

A number of other shows are held throughout the day, including the World of Hawks at 10 am, Hornbill Chit Chat at 11.45 am, the Wonderful World of Birds at noon, 1 and 2 pm, and King of the Skies at 4 pm. Breakfast with the Birds is the park's answer to bird-singing contests, and the S$12.36 buffet breakfast from 9 to 11 am is a pleasant way to start the day.

You can walk around the park or take the Panorail service – an air-con monorail that does a tour of the park, stopping at the Waterfall Aviary. The Panorail costs S$2.06 for adults, S$1.03 for children.

Admission to the park is S$9.27 for adults and S$3.09 for children. The park is open from 9 am to 6 pm, Monday to Friday, and 8 am to 6 pm on weekends and public holidays. To get there, take the MRT to the Boon Lay station and then bus Nos 194 or 251. The bird park is on Jalan Ahmad Ibrahim. You can climb up Jurong Hill, beside the park, from where there is a good view over Jurong.

Jurong Crocodile Paradise

Singapore's crocodile farms have spawned quite an industry in crocodile skin products and crocodile parks like this one. Right next to Jurong Bird Park, this is the largest of the parks with the best set-up for tourists. It has crocodiles of all ages, alligators, a shop selling crocodile products, crocodile wrestling performances and even a seafood restaurant that has crocodile on the menu. The crocodile wrestling performances at 10.45 and 11.45 am, and 2 and 3 pm are not for nature lovers. It is open from 9 am to 6 pm daily and costs S$6 for adults and S$3 for children. It is easily combined with a trip to Jurong Bird Park.

Chinese & Japanese Gardens

Off Yuan Ching Rd, the Chinese and Japanese gardens adjoining Jurong Bird Park each cover 13.5 hectares. The Chinese Garden, which occupies an island on Jurong Lake, is colourful and has a number of Chinese-style pavilions. The main attraction is the extensive *penjing* (Chinese bonsai) display. Linked by a bridge, the less interesting Japanese Garden has large grassed areas and a few buildings. Garden lovers will find Singapore's Botanic Gardens of more interest, but the Chinese Garden is very pleasant and a must for bonsai enthusiasts.

The gardens are open from 9 am to 7 pm Monday to Saturday and from 8.30 am to 7 pm on Sundays and holidays. Admission to both gardens is S$4.50 for adults and S$2 for children. The Chinese Garden MRT station is right by Jurong Lake and a five minute walk away from the Chinese Garden.

Singapore Science Centre

On Science Centre Rd, off Jurong Town Hall Rd, the Science Centre is great fun. It attempts to make science come alive by providing countless opportunities to try things out for yourself. There are handles to crank, buttons to push, levers to pull, microscopes to look through and films to watch. The centre is primarily designed to encourage an interest in science among Singapore's school children, but it is amazing how many adults compete with the kids to have a go on the hands-on exhibits. The centre is open from 10 am to 6 pm Tuesday to Sunday and admission is S$3 (children S$1.50). Changi airport also has a free mini science centre in Terminal 2.

One of the main attractions is the Omni Theatre, next to the main science centre building, with full-blown, three-dimensional whiz-bang movies covering topics from space flights to journeys inside the atom. There is also a planetarium at the centre.

The easiest way to get there is to take the MRT to the Jurong East station and then walk 0.5 km west or take bus No 66 or 335 from the station.

Tang Dynasty City

This multimillion-dollar theme park is a re-creation of old Chang'an (modern-day Xian), the Tang dynasty capital, which was the centre of China's golden age from the 6th to 8th centuries AD. Behind the massive 10-metre-high walls, Tang Dynasty City's main street features a courthouse, geisha house and shops, and there are temples, restaurants and theatres, all built in Chinese style and attempting to re-create the period. 'Silk Road' camel rides, craft demonstrations, performances and antique displays, such as a jade suit and the reproduction of the life-size Xian terracotta army, are all part of the experience.

Like most theme parks it is just a little artificial, but the size and style of the buildings are impressive and Tang Dynasty City makes an interesting diversion. The park also has shops selling tea, wine and antiques, a wax museum with a talking Mao and other notables from Chinese history, and kungfu and other street performers.

Tang Dynasty City is open every day from 9.30 am to 6.30 pm. Admission is S$15.45 (S$10.30 for children). Buffet lunch shows, featuring acrobatic troupes from China, are also held.

Tang Dynasty City is on the corner of Yuan Ching Rd and Jalan Ahmad Ibrahim, near the Chinese and Japanese gardens. Take the MRT to the Lakeside station and then bus No 154 or 240, or it is a two km taxi ride from the station.

New Ming Village & Pewter Museum

This pottery workshop at 32 Pandan Rd produces reproduction porcelain from the Ming and Qing dynasties. You can see the craftspeople create their pottery and, of course, you can buy their works. It is open every day from 8.30 am to 5.30 pm. Admission is free. The complete production process is done on the premises and guided tours are available on demand for groups.

Ming Village is owned by Royal Selangor Pewter. Consequently the village also has a small pewter museum with some interesting pieces, and the showroom sells an extensive selection of pewter as well as pottery. The pewter is made in Malaysia, but the polishing and hand-beaten designs are demonstrated at the village.

To get there, take the MRT to Clementi and then bus No 78 to Pandan Rd.

Singapore Mint Coin Gallery

This gallery, at Singapore's mint on Jalan Boon Lay just east of the Boon Lay MRT station, exhibits coins and medals from Singapore and a few coins from around the world. This place is essentially an outlet for the gold medallions that the mint sells, but a few mint sets of Singapore coins are also for sale. Only dedicated coin enthusiasts would want to make the trip out here. It is open Monday to Friday from 9 am to 4 pm.

EAST COAST & CHANGI

East Coast Park is a popular recreational haunt for Singaporeans. It is the place to swim, windsurf, lie on the sand, rent a bike or, of course, eat. The stretch of beach along the east coast, south of the East Coast Parkway expressway, was born of reclaimed land and won't win any awards as a tropical paradise, but it is by far Singapore's most popular beach and has good recreational facilities.

Further inland are the interesting areas of Geyland and Katong, largely Malay districts, which are rarely frequented by foreign visitors. Geylang is as close to a 'Little Malaysia' as you'll find; and Katong, centred on East Coast Rd, has Peranakan influences and interesting dining possibilities.

Changi is known for its renowned airport and infamous prison, both attractions in their own right, while further out is Changi Village and its nearby beach.

Geylang

If you want to experience Malaysia, the real thing is just across the Causeway. However, there are Malay areas in Singapore, though Malay culture is not so obvious nor easily marketed as a tourist attraction.

Geylang Serai is a Malay residential area, though you are not going to see traditional *atap* houses and sarong-clad cottage industry workers. The area has plenty of high-rise buildings, though there are some older buildings around, especially in the *lorong* (alleys) that run off Geylang Rd. The lorongs house one of Singapore's most active red-light districts.

Geylang Serai is easily reached by taking the MRT to the Paya Lebar station. From here it is a short walk down Tanjong Katong Rd to Geylang Rd, the main shopping street.

A short walk east along Geylang Rd will bring you to the **Malay Cultural Village**. This complex of traditional Malay-style houses was built as a showpiece of Malay culture, though it hasn't really taken off as a tourist attraction. On weekends it attracts Singaporean families desperately seeking *kampong* (village) nostalgia, but is very quiet during the week. Admission is free to wander around the craft shops and bird market or to eat at the satay stalls and restaurants. For S$10 (children S$7), you can visit the Kampung Days museum and the Legenda Fantasi show. The museum has kampong buildings with waxworks figures, a few artefacts and interesting videos on Malay weddings, games and kampong life. The Legenda Fantasi is a good, whiz-bang show for the kids with laser effects and a booming sound system telling Ali Baba stories with a Singaporean slant. The best time to go is on the weekend when free dance performances are held from 7 to 9 pm.

Just next door to the cultural centre is the **Geylang Serai Market**. It's hidden behind some older-style housing blocks on Geylang Rd, and entrance is through a small laneway that leads to a crowded, traditional Asian market that hasn't yet been rebuilt as a concrete box. It is a good place to browse and much more interesting than most of Singapore's new markets. It reaches its peak of activity during Ramadan, when the whole area is alive with market stalls that set up in the evenings for the faithful after a long day of fasting.

Katong

From the Geylang Serai Market you can head down Joo Chiat Rd to the East Coast Rd and explore the Katong district. **Joo Chiat Rd** has a host of local businesses operating during the day, and at night the restaurants and music lounges are popular. Despite some restoration the streetscape has largely escaped the developer; some fine Peranakan-style terraces and some of the atmosphere of old Singapore remain.

Stop in at Amoy Tea at 331 Joo Chiat Rd, a traditional shop selling a variety of Chinese tea and some superbly crafted tea sets. Nearby are some antique shops, such as Dragon Arts & Crafts at No 341. Guan Hoe Soon at No 214 has Peranakan/Chinese food and Casa Bom Vento at No 467 is an interesting Eurasian restaurant.

On Koon Seng Rd, just west around the corner from Joo Chiat Rd, are some of the finest terrace houses in Singapore. They exhibit the typical Peranakan love of ornate design and are decorated with plaster stucco dragons, birds, crabs and brilliantly glazed tiles. *Pintu pagar* (saloon doors) at the front of the house are another typical feature that lets in the breeze while retaining privacy.

Further south, Joo Chiat Rd runs into **East Coast Rd**, a well-to-do, 'village' shopping stretch that is the centre of Katong. Before land reclamation moved the beach, Katong was a quiet village by the sea. Now East Coast Rd bustles with city traffic and Singapore's modern developments have engulfed the east coast. Despite this, Katong still retains its delightful village atmosphere. East Coast Rd is noted for its Peranakan influence, mostly because of the opportunity to sample Peranakan food and view the fascinating collection of Peranakan antiques at the Katong Antique House at No 208. The intricately hand-embroidered Nonya slippers are hard to resist, though opening hours are haphazard. Also on the itinerary for a tour of Katong is a visit to Katong Bakery & Confectionery, 75 East Coast Rd. Nonya cakes and pastries are served in this relic from pre-war Singapore.

It is also worth wandering the backstreets of Katong around Joo Chiat and East Coast Rds where you'll find more terraces, coffee shops and temples. Just off East Coast Rd in Ceylon Rd is the Hindu Senpaga Vinayagar Temple, and about a km away in Wilkinson St is a Sikh temple, Sri Guru Nanak Sat Sangh Sabha.

East Coast Rd changes its name to Mountbatten Rd as it heads into the city and crosses Tanjong Katong Rd, which leads back to Geylang and the Paya Lebar MRT station. This area contains a number of grand old villas, such as the Villa Dolce at 164 Tanjong Katong Rd. Mountbatten Rd also has some fine old houses.

Parkway Parade is a huge shopping centre on Marine Parade near the end of Joo Chiat Rd. The East Coast Park and seaside is just behind it, but you have to cross the East Coast Parkway expressway – take a taxi.

From East Coast Rd, bus Nos 12 and 32 head into the city along North Bridge Rd in the colonial district, while bus No 14 goes down Stamford Rd and then Orchard Rd. Coming from the city, bus No 16 can be boarded in Orchard and Bras Basah Rds, and goes along Joo Chiat Rd, crossing East Coast Rd.

East Coast Park

Stretching along Singapore's east coast on reclaimed land, East Coast Park comes alive on weekends with Singaporeans relaxing by the beach, eating at the seafood outlets or indulging in more strenuous sporting activities. The foreshore parkland has a track running right along the coast for bicycling, jogging or rollerblading, and you can hire bicycles, canoes and sailboards. The beach is reasonable, with a continuous sandy stretch and calm waters, though like all of Singapore's beaches the water is hardly crystal clear.

The **Singapore Crocodilarium** is at 730 East Coast Parkway and has a large number of crocodiles crammed into concrete tanks. A shop also sells croc products. It's open daily from 9 am to 5 pm and admission is S$2 for adults and $1 for children.

Big Splash, 902 East Coast Parkway, is a water fun park with swimming pools and a huge water slide. It has been superseded by Fantasy Island at Sentosa and is currently closed undergoing works.

The **East Coast Recreation Centre** is the big place in East Coast Park with bowling, squash, crazy golf, fun rides, a selection of restaurants and food stalls, and canoe and bicycle hire. As well as racers (S$3 per hour) and mountain bikes (S$4 per hour), tandems can be also be hired.

One km further away from the city is the **East Coast Lagoon**, noted for its seafood. The UDMC Seafood Centre has a number of restaurants. Also here is the East Coast Sailing Centre (☎ 449 5118), a private club which rents sailboards to the public for S$20 for the first two hours and S$10 for each subsequent hour. Bicycles and canoes can also be hired at the kiosk near the food centre.

The only bus is No 401, operating from the Bedok MRT station along the service road in the park on Sundays and public holidays. All other buses whiz by on the East Coast Parkway expressway so you'll have to catch a taxi.

Changi Prison Museum

Changi is still used as a prison but next to the main gate is a museum with a bookshop and a poignant replica of the simple thatched prison chapel built and used by Allied prisoners of war during their horrendous internment at the hands of the Japanese during WWII. Pinned to the chapel are notes from those who lost loved ones in Changi. The small museum features drawings made by the prisoners depicting life in Changi, as well as photographs and other exhibits providing an overview of the war in Asia. The museum is open Monday to Saturday from 9.30 am to 4.30 pm, though you can visit the chapel outside these hours. A service is held at the chapel from 5.30 to 6.30 pm.

Changi Prison is on Upper Changi Rd near the airport and can be reached by bus No 2 from Victoria St in the colonial district.

Changi Village

Changi, on the east coast of Singapore, is an escape from the hubbub of downtown Singapore. Don't expect to find traditional kampong houses – the buildings are modern – but Changi does have a village atmosphere. Changi's beach is not exactly a tropical paradise but it has a good stretch of sand and offers safe swimming. It's popular on weekends but almost deserted during the week. The food in Changi is an attraction, and there are some good seafood restaurants and food stalls near the beach.

From Changi, you can catch ferries to Pulau Ubin (see the Other Islands section later in this chapter). Ferries also go to Pengerang across the strait in Malaysia (see the Singapore Getting There & Away chapter).

You can reach Changi on bus No 2 from Victoria St in the colonial district; it also passes Changi Prison.

SENTOSA ISLAND

Sentosa Island, just off the south coast of Singapore, is the granddaddy of all Singapore's fun parks. It is Singapore's most

TONY WHEELER

TONY WHEELER

RICHARD I'ANSON

Singapore

Top Left & Right: The gaudy statues illustrating scenes from Chinese legends are the major attraction of Haw Par Villa.

Bottom: A mural on Orchard Rd

PETER TURNER

RICHARD NEBESKY

Singapore
Left: The gold-domed Sultan Mosque near Arab St
Right: The water-spouting Merlion, Singapore's symbol of tourism

visited attraction, especially popular with locals who flock here on weekends. A host of activities are spread around this landscaped island, and while, like its beaches of imported sand, it is a synthetic attraction, Sentosa is a good place for children and there is enough to keep adults occupied. Sentosa has museums, aquariums, beaches, sporting facilities, walks, rides and food centres. It is easy to spend a day at Sentosa but if that isn't enough there's a campground, a hostel and two luxury hotels.

Sentosa is open daily from 7.30 am until around 11 pm, an hour or so later on weekends. Many of the attractions close at 7 pm but cultural shows, plays and bands are sometimes held in the evenings – check with the tourist office or ring the Sentosa Information Office (☎ 275 0388).

Basic admission to Sentosa is S$5 for adults (S$3 after 6.30 pm) and S$3 for children under 12. This covers entry and all transport on the monorail and buses around Sentosa. Most of the attractions cost extra, and can really add up if you want to see them all.

The free bus service runs around the island roads with departures every 10 minutes. The free monorail loop service is the most scenic but slowest way to get around the island. You can get around Sentosa by bicycle – rent a bike from the hire kiosk by the ferry terminal.

Underwater World

This spectacular aquarium is one of Sentosa's most popular attractions. Displays include the turtle pool, moray eel enclosure, reef enclosures with live coral, a theatre showing continuous films and a touch pool where visitors are invited to dip their digits into the pool and fondle the sealife. These exhibits are just mere entrées to Underwater World's 'travellator', an acrylic tunnel that takes spectators through the main tanks as all manner of fish swim around you in all their natural technicolour glory. There is nothing quite like the sight of a huge manta ray, 60 kg grouper, or shark swimming up to you and then passing overhead.

Underwater World is open daily from 9 am to 9 pm and costs S$12 for adults and S$6 for children.

Pioneers of Singapore, Surrender Chamber & Festivals of Singapore

The Pioneers of Singapore waxwork museum relives history and re-creates life in old Singapore. It gives an excellent account of Singapore's past and focuses on the traditional cultures of Singapore's main communities. The adjoining Surrender Chamber exhibit traces the history of Singapore's occupation during WWII up to the formal surrender by the Japanese forces in 1945. These days it is surprisingly popular with Japanese tour groups.

A new addition is Festivals of Singapore, which has wax dummy exhibits and explanations of Singapore's many festivals.

This museum is well done, in an old-fashioned sort of way – perhaps this means it will eventually be renovated with multimedia displays, robotic figures and high-tech lighting effects.

Admission is S$5 for adults and S$3 for children. It is open from 9 am to 11 pm.

Fort Siloso

Once used as a military base, the gun emplacements and underground tunnels of Fort Siloso, which date from the late 19th century, can be explored. The guns were all pointing in the wrong direction when the Japanese invaded in WWII and the island was then used by the victorious Japanese as a prisoner-of-war camp.

From 1989 until 1993, Fort Siloso housed Sentosa's most unusual attraction, political prisoner Chia Thye Poh. Chia, arrested in 1966 under the Internal Security Act for allegedly being a Communist, served 23 years in jail before being banished to complete his bizarre sentence among the holiday delights of Sentosa Island.

A guided walk leads around the gun emplacements, tunnels and buildings, with waxwork recreations of life in a colonial barracks. A mini sound-and-light show relives the period immediately before the

SINGAPORE

Japanese invasion, and a 'Behind Bars' exhibit focuses on prison life for the POWs under the Japanese. It is a pleasant walk with good views and, though not wildly exciting, it is one of Sentosa's more interesting attractions for the money.

Fort Siloso is open from 9 am to 7 pm and costs S$3 for adults and S$2 for children.

Fantasy Island

This is a huge water theme park with swimming pools, 13 different water rides and 32 slides. Rides range from 'river rafting' to the more terrifying Gang of Four, Blackhole and Kyag slides. The park also has an Entertainment Mall with electronic games at the entrance.

It's great for the kids – bad for the wallet. Entrance costs S$16 (children S$12), lockers are S$1 and floats are S$3 and S$4. Fantasy Island is open from 10.30 am to 7 pm, from 10 am on weekends and public holidays.

Volcanoland

Based on a Mayan city and dominated by a giant, concrete volcano, Volcanoland is Sentosa's tackiest attraction. Singaporean 'Mayan' Indians put on dances and drape snakes around tourist necks for photos. The show inside the volcano is held every half hour and takes you through an explorer's tunnel and mock mine-elevator trip to a theatre where even the booming sound effects cannot enliven the dull movie on the evolution of life. The eruption finale is a fizzer and when the exit doors open to reveal the gift shop it is almost a relief. Save your S$10. The volcano 'erupts' every half hour with a bang and a puff of smoke – you can see it from outside.

Butterfly Park & Insect Kingdom Museum

At the Butterfly Park, you can walk among live butterflies of over 50 species. In the museum there are thousands of mounted butterfly specimens, rhino beetles, *Dynastes hercules* (the world's largest beetles), and scorpions, among other insects. The walk through the butterfly house is the highlight.

It is open from 9.30 am to 5.30 pm Monday to Friday, and 9.30 am to 6.30 pm weekends and public holidays. Entry costs S$5 for adults and S$3 for children.

Asian Village

This collection of craft shops and food outlets reflect Asia's various cultures: Japan, China, India, Thailand, Philippines, Malaysia and Indonesia. The theme park buildings are vaguely styled after traditional houses, and the entertainment park rides are popular. Entry is free, though the rides cost extra. It is open from 10 am to 9 pm.

Other Attractions

The **Maritime Museum** (open 10 am to 7 pm; adults S$2, children 50c) has exhibits recording the history of Singapore's port and shipping, as well as fishing tools and primitive craft. **Sentosa Orchid Gardens** (open 9.30 am to 6.30 pm; adults S$3, children S$1) is an orchid garden with a Japanese theme.

Of the free attractions, the **Nature Walk** is in a more natural environment, except for the Dragon Trail section, which has dragons and fossils to liven things up. Long-tailed macaques are common, but hide your food from these aggressive monkeys. You can also wander around the impressive ferry terminal, Fountain Gardens and Flower Terrace.

At night, the **Musical Fountain** spurts water to music and flashing, coloured lights, while the **Pasar Malam** (night market) stalls sell souvenirs. Nearby is the **Rasa Sentosa Food Centre** – naturally Sentosa has a hawker centre – and the ferry terminal also has some dining possibilities.

Other newly completed attractions are an adventure golf theme park and the Merlion Tower, a huge Merlion with good views from the top.

Beaches & Recreational Facilities

Sentosa's southern coastline is devoted to beaches: Siloso Beach at the western end, Central Beach and Tanjong Beach at the eastern end. As a tropical paradise, Sentosa has a long way to go to match the islands of Malaysia or Indonesia, but in a case of 'if

Mohammed won't come to the mountain' Singapore has imported its beach from Indonesia and planted coconut palms to give it a tropical ambience. The imported sand does make for a good beach, probably Singapore's best.

The beaches have shelters and four rest stations with kiosks, changing facilities, deck chairs and umbrellas. Pedal cats, aquabikes, fun bugs, canoes and surf boards are all available for hire.

Sentosa has a 5.7-km-long bicycle track that loops the island and takes in most of the attractions. Bicycles can be hired at bicycle stations on the track, such as the kiosk at Siloso Beach or at the ferry terminal, and cost from S$2 to S$5 per hour.

Sentosa also has a roller-skating rink, which costs S$2 entry. There are two 18-hole golf courses: Serapong, for members only, and Tanjong, which is open to the public and costs S$80 for a round on weekdays or S$120 on weekends.

Getting There & Away

Take SBS bus No 65 or 143 from Orchard Rd, or 61, 84, 143, 145 or 166 from Chinatown to the World Trade Centre (WTC), south-west of the railway station. Tourist buses, such as the Singapore Trolley, also run to the WTC. Then from the bus terminal across from the WTC take Sentosa Bus Service A. Alternatively, take the MRT to the Tiong Bahru station and then Sentosa Bus Service B or C. Services A & C run from around 7 am to 11.30 pm, Service B only on weekends and holidays. The cost for any of these buses is $6 (children $4), including admission to Sentosa.

From Orchard and Bras Basah Rds, Service E runs all the way to Sentosa every 10 or 15 minutes from 10 am to 7.30 pm. The last bus returns from Sentosa at 8.30 pm. The bus costs S$7 (children S$5), including admission.

The other alternatives are to take the ferry from the World Trade Centre or the cable car.

The ferry used to be the main access to the island before the bridge was built. It is still one of the most pleasant ways to reach Sentosa and costs 80c one way, S$1.30 return. Ferries operate from 9.30 am to 9 pm.

The cable car leaves from the top of Mt Faber from 8.30 am to 9 pm, or you can board it at the World Trade Centre. The fare is S$5.50 (children S$3), and you can buy tickets for separate stages. The cable-car ride, with its spectacular views, is one of the best parts of a visit to Sentosa. Take the ferry across and then the cable car back to Mt Faber – it is easier walking down Mt Faber than up.

OTHER ISLANDS

Singapore's other islands include Kusu and St John's, Pulau Sakeng, the Sisters' Islands (all south of Singapore), and islands such as Pulau Bukum, which are used as refineries and for other commercial purposes. Further south of Singapore's southern islands are many more islands – the scattered Indonesian islands of the Riau Archipelago. There are other islands to the north-east between Singapore and Malaysia.

You don't have to leave the island of Singapore to find beaches and indulge in water sports. Although the construction of Changi International Airport destroyed one of Singapore's favourite stretches of beach, there is still the East Coast Park on the East Coast Parkway. Scuba diving enthusiasts will find coral reefs at Sisters' Islands and Pulau Semakau.

St John's & Kusu Islands

Although Sentosa is Singapore's best known island, there are two others which are also popular with locals as a city escape. On weekends, they can become rather crowded but during the week you'll find St John's and Kusu fairly quiet and good places for a peaceful swim. Both islands have changing rooms, toilet facilities, grassy picnic spots and swimming areas.

St John's Island is much bigger than Kusu and has better beaches for swimming, though Kusu is the more interesting. Kusu has a Chinese temple, the Tua Pek Kong Temple near the ferry jetty, and a Malay shrine *(kramat)* up a steep flight of steps to the top of a hill at the end of the island.

Kramat Kusu is dedicated to Sahed Abdul Rahman, his mother Nanek Ghalib and his sister Puteri Fatimah. Though kramat worship is frowned upon by the Islamic clergy, this is Singapore's most popular shrine, especially for childless couples who pray for children, as evidenced by the pieces of cloth tied around trees on the way up to the shrine. Kusu is the site of an important annual pilgrimage, honoured by Taoists.

Most of the harbour tours pass St John's Island and stop at Kusu for 20 minutes or so (see Organised Tours in the Singapore Getting Around chapter). You can walk around Kusu in 20 minutes.

To get to these islands, take a ferry from the World Trade Centre. It costs S$6.20 (children S$3.10) for the round trip and takes 30 minutes to reach Kusu before continuing on to St John's.

Monday to Saturday

WTC	Kusu	St John's
10.00 am	10.45 am	11.15 am
1.30 pm	2.15 pm	2.45 pm

Sundays & Public Holidays

WTC	Kusu	St John's
9.45 am	10.30 am	11.00 am
11.15 am	noon	12.30 pm
12.45 pm	1.30 pm	2.00 pm
2.15 pm	3.00 pm	3.30 pm
3.45 pm	4.30 pm	5.00 pm
5.15 pm	6.00 pm	6.30 pm

Other Southern Islands

Many of the islands on Singapore's southern shore accommodate the refineries that provide much of Singapore's export income. Others, such as Salu, Senang, Rawai and Sudong, are live firing ranges. However, there are a few off-the-beaten-track islands where you can find a quiet beach. Pulau Sakeng has a village and many inhabitants work at nearby Pulau Bukum, where the Shell refinery is located.

The Sisters' Islands are popular for swimming and diving, with coral reefs nearby. Pulau Hantu is also popular. Other islands include Lazarus Island (Pulau Sakijang Pelepah), Buran Darat, Terumbu Retan Laut and Pulau Renggit.

To reach these islands, you must rent a motorised bumboat from Clifford Pier or Jardine Steps at the World Trade Centre. Expect to pay around S$50 per hour. The boats will take six to 12 people. You can ask individual boat owners or contact the Singapore Motor Launch Owners' Association on the 2nd floor at Clifford Pier, just east of the Raffles Place MRT station.

Northern Islands

The easiest northern island to visit is Pulau Ubin, which makes a pleasant day trip and is reached by boat from Changi Village. Pulau Tekong, Singapore's largest island, tends to be forgotten because it is often cut off the eastern edge of Singapore maps (including the one in this book). It is now off limits since the military took it over in the early 90s.

Pulau Ubin From Changi Village, you can wander down to the ferry jetty and wait for a bumboat to take you across to Pulau Ubin. You can tell that this is a different side of Singapore as you wait for the ferry to fill up – they go when a quota of 12 people is reached and there is no fixed schedule. Pulau Ubin has quiet beaches, a kampong atmosphere and popular seafood restaurants. This rural island is as unlike 'Singapore' as you will find in Singapore. It is also a natural haven for many species of birds that inhabit the mangroves and forest areas.

The best way to explore the island is by bicycle, which can be hired for S$5 an hour near the jetty. They have maps of the island, though the island is small enough to explore without getting lost. You can visit a spectacular disused quarry with granite walls and a number of temples, including a Thai Buddhist temple and one reached via the beach only at low tide. It is a peaceful rural scene of fish farms, coconut palms and a few houses. The island's most popular seafood restaurant is the Ubin Restaurant.

The old bumboat ferries to Pulau Ubin cost S$2 and run between 6 am and 10 pm, but you may be in for a wait if there are no other passengers – often the case during the week.

NORTHERN & CENTRAL SINGAPORE

Singapore has been dubbed the 'Garden City' and with good reason – it's green and lush, and parks and gardens are scattered everywhere. In part, this fertility is a factor of the climate; you only have to stick a twig in the ground for it to become a tree in weeks! The government has backed up this natural advantage with a concentrated programme that has even turned the dividing strip on highways into flourishing gardens – you notice it as you drive into Singapore from the Causeway.

Despite the never-ending construction, land reclamation and burgeoning HDB (Housing & Development Board) estates, Singapore has large areas of parkland and even natural forest. These areas are mostly found to the north of the city in the centre of Singapore Island.

Botanic Gardens

Singapore's 127-year-old Botanic Gardens are on the corner of Cluny and Holland Rds, not far from Orchard Rd. They are a popular and peaceful retreat for Singaporeans.

The Botanic Gardens contain an enormous number of species of plants, in both a manicured garden setting and in four hectares of primary jungle. The gardens also house the herbarium, where much work has been done on breeding the orchids for which Singapore is famous. The orchid enclosure contains over 12,000 orchids representing 2000 species and hybrids in all. In an earlier era, Henry Ridley, director of the gardens, successfully propagated rubber tree seeds sent from Kew Gardens in 1877, after they were smuggled out of Brazil. The Singapore Botanic Gardens pioneered the Malayan rubber boom.

The 54 hectare gardens are open from 5 am to midnight; admission is free. Early in the morning, you'll see hundreds of Singaporeans jogging there.

The gardens can be reached on bus No 7 or 174, which run along Stamford Rd and Orchard Blvd. Bus No 106 runs along Bencoolen St and Orchard Blvd to the gardens.

Sunday Morning Bird Singing

One of the nicest things to do on a Sunday morning in Singapore is to go and hear the birds sing. The Chinese love caged birds, as their beautifully ornate birdcages indicate. The birds – thrushes, *merboks, sharmas* and *mata putehs* – are treasured for their singing ability. To ensure the quality of their song, the doting owner will feed the bird a carefully prepared diet and once a week crowds of bird fanciers get together for a bird song session.

The birdcages are hung up on wires strung between trees or under verandas. They're not mixed indiscriminately – sharmas sing with sharmas, merboks with merboks – and each type of bird has its own design of cage. Tall and pointy ones for tall pointy birds, short and squat ones for short squat birds.

Having assembled the birds, the proud owners then congregate around tables, sip coffee and listen to their birds go through their paces. It's a delightful scene both musically and visually.

The main bird-concert venue is on Sunday mornings from around 8 to 11 am at the junction of Tiong Bahru and Seng Poh Rds, only a few hundred metres from the Havelock Rd hotel enclave. The coffee shop here is always well patronised on Sunday mornings.

To get there take the MRT to the Tiong Bahru station, then walk east 0.5 km. By bus, take No 123 from Orchard Rd.

Zoological Gardens

Located at 80 Mandai Lake Rd in the north of the island, Singapore's world-class zoo has over 2000 animals representing 240 species on display in almost natural conditions. Wherever possible, moats replace bars and the zoo is spread out over 90 hectares of lush greenery. Exhibits of particular interest are the pygmy hippos, Primate Kingdom, Wild Africa and Children's World. As well as providing a play area, Children's World includes a domesticated animals section where children can touch the animals, see Friesian cow milking demonstrations and sheep dogs in action at the sheep roundup show.

There is a breakfast programme at 9 am and high tea at 4 pm, where you are joined by one of the orang-utans! There are also elephant rides and work performances. At most times of the day, you have a good chance of seeing one of the animal performances or one of the practice sessions in the zoo's outdoor theatre. Primates & Reptiles shows are held at 10.30 am and 2.30 pm, Elephants & Sealions at 11.30 am and 3.30 pm.

The Komodo dragons are another popular attraction and you can see their feeding frenzy on Sunday afternoons, though in fact they are not all that ferocious.

The zoo is open daily from 8.30 am to 6 pm daily. Admission is S$9.27 (children S$4.12). There is a zoo tram which runs from the main gate and costs S$2 for adults and S$1 for children.

To get to the zoo, take the MRT to the Ang Mo Kio station, and then bus No 138.

Night Safari Not content with having an excellent zoo, Singapore also opened the impressive Night Safari on a 40 hectare site next to the zoo in secondary forest. Open 7.30 pm to midnight daily, walking trails crisscross the park and allow a unique opportunity to view nocturnal animals. The park is divided into a number of habitats, focusing mostly on Asian wildlife, and special lighting picks out the animals. With 1000 animals representing 100 species, the Night Safari is not as diverse as the zoo, but wandering the trails at night is a recommended experience.

There is also a tram ride (including commentary) which loops through the park and stops near the East Lodge restaurant at the far side of the park. Noisy, camera flashing passengers can spoil the ride, despite being exhorted to keep quiet and avoid flash photography. The western side of the park is only accessible by tram. To explore all the park, it is best to do a complete loop and then walk the trails. The complete East Loop walking trail is 2.8 km in length and takes about an hour.

The Night Safari costs S$15.45 or $10.30 for children under 12 years. The tram ride costs an extra S$3 (children S$2). The entrance is directly opposite the zoo entrance, a few hundred metres away.

Getting to the Night Safari is the same as for the zoo. In addition, the Bus Plus Zoo service (S$5, children S$3) picks up on Orchard, Bras Basah and Scotts Rds from 6.30 to 8.30 pm. The return buses run until 11 pm.

Mandai Orchid Gardens

Singapore has a major business in cultivating orchids and the Mandai Orchid Gardens, beside the zoo on Mandai Lake Rd, is the best place to see them – four solid hectares of orchids! The gardens are open daily from 8.30 am to 5.30 pm and admission is S$2 for adults, 50c for children.

Bukit Timah Nature Reserve

Singapore is not normally associated with nature walks and jungle treks, but they can be enjoyed at this 81 hectare nature reserve. It is the only large area of primary forest left in Singapore and is a haven for Singapore's wildlife. On Upper Bukit Timah Rd, 12 km from the city, the reserve also boasts the highest point in Singapore, 162 metre Bukit Timah.

The reserve is run by the National Parks Board and at the entrance to the reserve is an exhibition hall with interesting displays on Singapore's natural history. Adjoining the hall are changing rooms and showers. Oddly enough, the other national parks run by the board are the much more urban Fort Canning Park and Singapore Botanic Gardens.

Of the walks in the park, the most popular is the summit walk along a paved road to the top of Bukit Timah. Even during the week it attracts a number of walkers, though few venture off the pavement to explore the side trails. The road cuts a swathe through dense forest and near the top there are panoramic views across Pierce Reservoir.

The best trails to explore the forest and see the wildlife run off the summit road. Try the North View, South View or Fern Valley paths, where it is hard to believe that you are in Singapore. These paths involve some scrambling over rocks in parts, but are easily negotiated.

The park has over 800 species of native plants, including giant trees, ferns and native flowers. Wildlife is difficult to see, though long-tailed macaques and squirrels are in abundance. Flying lemurs, reticulated pythons and birds such as the racquet-tailed drongo and white-bellied sea eagle inhabit the reserve. Try to pick up either one of the two editions of *A Guide to the Bukit Timah Nature Reserve* explaining the reserve's flora and fauna (available at Mobil and BP service stations and some bookshops).

The exhibition hall is open from 8.30 am to 6 pm. Entry is free. It is a good idea to bring a water bottle if you intend going on some extended walks. A towel and even a change of clothes are also worth bringing as the walks are strenuous in parts and the conditions are hot and very humid.

To get to Bukit Timah, take bus No 171 or 182, which both run along Orchard and Stamford Rds in the colonial district and pass the Newton MRT station. Get off just past the 12 km mark at the large, yellow Courts Mammoth Super Store on Upper Bukit Timah Rd. The entrance to the park is on the other side, about one km along Hindhede Drive.

Sungei Buloh Nature Park

This 87 hectare wetland nature reserve is home to 140 species of birds, most migratory. From the visitor centre with its well-presented displays, trails lead around ponds and mangrove swamps to hides for observing the birds. The birdlife, rather than the walks, is the main reason to visit as the area is mostly former orchard and fish ponds.

Sungei Buloh is open from 7 am to 7 pm on weekends and holidays. Admission is S$1 for adults (children 50c) and audio-visual shows on the park's flora and fauna are held at 9 and 11 am and 1 and 3 pm. Guided walks are also held at 9.30 am and 4 pm, weather permitting.

The park is in the north-west of the island, overlooking the Straits of Johor. Take the MRT to the Choa Chu Kang station, then bus No SS7 to Woodlands Interchange, then bus No 925.

Other Parks

Despite Singapore's dense population, there are many small parks and gardens.

MacRitchie Reservoir has a 12 hectare park area with a jogging track, exercise area, playground and tea kiosk. It is a pleasant retreat from the city, and popular with joggers. A band often plays on Sundays (check the newspapers). To the north of MacRitchie Reservoir is **Upper Seletar Reservoir**, where paddle boating is possible, and further east is **Lower Seletar Reservoir**, where you can go fishing. For MacRitchie Reservoir take bus No 167 from Stamford Rd, No 132 from Orchard Rd or No 156 from the Bishan MRT station. For Upper Seletar take bus No 138 from the Ang Mo Kio MRT station. For Lower Seletar, take the MRT to Yishun, then bus No 851, 852, 853, 854 or 855.

Off Kampong Bahru Rd, the 116-metre-high **Mt Faber** is a pleasant park with fine views over the harbour and the city. To get there, take the cable car up from the World Trade Centre. Mt Faber can conveniently be visited in conjunction with a trip to Sentosa Island.

Pasir Ris Park on the north-east coast is for the most part a manicured park with a narrow stretch of beach. The park also has a wooden walkway that goes through a mangrove swamp area that is good for bird-watching. The park is often empty during the week, but comes alive on weekends and holidays, when the nearby trade-union-run NTUC Pasir Ris Resort fills up. To get there take the MRT to the Pasir Ris station and then bus No 350 to the resort, only a short walk from the beach.

Bukit Batok, also known as Little Guilin, is a former quarry, now a park, that is compared to the spectacular limestone formations and lakes of Guilin in southern China, hence the name. This pleasant park is built around a hilly outcrop and lake, but it is a poor imitation of Guilin. It is near the Bukit Gombok MRT station, 14 km to the north-west of the city.

Bukit Turf Club

The horse-racing calendar is part of the Malaysian circuit and races are held in

Singapore once a month at the Bukit Turf Club on Bukit Timah Rd. At other times, races are broadcast on the huge video screen. The race course is to be redeveloped for housing and is slated to move to Woodlands in the future.

The races are usually held on weekends and admission is S$5.15, or S$10.30 under the fans in the stand. If you are going to blow your dough at the races then you might as well spend S$15.45 for a seat in the air-conditioned members' stand – it gets very hot in the ordinary section on a crowded race day. Show your passport and buy a ticket to the members at the tourist information booth outside. The only drawback is that you cannot get down to view the horses from the sealed-off members' stand.

The Bukit Turf Club produces a racing calendar, which is available at the STPB (Singapore Tourist Promotion Board) offices; or ring ☎ 469 3611 for information. All betting is government-controlled, and the minimum win or place bet is S$5. A lot of money passes through the windows on race days, which regularly attract about 30,000 punters. Despite government crackdowns, race fixing is growing with the popularity of the sport.

Be sure to dress properly – no shorts, sandals or T-shirts are allowed. The turf club also has a good hawker centre.

SINGAPORE

Holland Village

If you're wondering what the life of an expatriate is like, head for Holland Village. It's on Holland Rd, a westerly continuation of Orchard Rd, and services the garden-belt suburbs of the well-to-do.

Holland Village is, in fact, just a suburban shopping centre where foreigners can shop, sip coffee and feel at home, but it has a definite village community atmosphere. It is best known for its host of fashionable restaurants and watering holes, concentrated on Lorong Mambong, just back from the main road. The Holland Shopping Centre is a modern complex and a good place to shop for antiques, furnishings and crafts such as porcelain ware, batik, wood carvings etc.

The nearest MRT station is Buona Vista, about a 15 minute walk along Buona Vista Rd from Holland Village. Or take bus No 7, 105 or 106 from Penang Rd/Orchard Blvd.

Temples

The central city areas of Singapore provide plenty of opportunities to experience Singapore's colourful temples, but a couple of temples of note are found in the outer areas.

Siong Lim Temple This is one of the largest temples in Singapore and includes a Chinese rock garden. It was built in 1908 but includes more recent additions. It features Thai Buddha statues and 2000 kg incense burners. There is a monastery next to the main temple, and next to the monastery is another temple featuring a gigantic Buddha statue. It's at 184E Jalan Toa Payoh, north of the city centre, about one km east from the Toa Payoh MRT station.

Kong Meng San Phor Kark See Temple This is the largest temple in Singapore and covers 12 hectares. A modern temple, it is impressive in its size and design, though its main function is as a crematorium: funerals, complete with paper effigies, are frequent. The attached old people's home is reminiscent of the old 'death houses' that used to exist in Chinatown's Sago St. Old folk were once packed off to death houses towards the end of their lives, thus avoiding the possible bad luck of a death in the home. The temple is on Bright Hill Drive, about 1.5 km west of the Bishan MRT station.

Kranji War Memorial

Near the Causeway off Woodlands Rd, the Kranji War Memorial includes the graves of thousands of Allied troops who died in the region during WWII. The walls are inscribed with the names of those who died and a register is available for inspection. It can be reached by bus No 182 from Somerset Rd.

Housing Estates

Still another side of Singapore is found in the modern HDB (Housing & Development Board) satellite cities like Toa Payoh, Pasir Ris, Tampines and Bukit Panjang. Nearly 90% of Singaporeans live in these government housing blocks and once again it's a programme that Singapore manages to make work.

While high-rise housing has become a dirty word in many countries, in Singapore it's almost universally popular. Many of the residents own their own flats, with subsidised interest rates provided by the HDB.

The MRT makes it simple to visit HDB areas. Just jump on a train and pop up somewhere like Toa Payoh, or Tampines, where you'll find the big new Century Park shopping mall. True, you won't see stunning architecture and breathtaking landscapes, you won't be spellbound by exotic ritual, but you will get a glimpse of what life is like for the overwhelming majority of Singaporeans. The estates are often good places to shop – straightforward, cheap and without the inflated prices and haggling that often go with the more popular tourist areas – and of course they have plenty of places to eat. You may find the best *ah balling* or the cheapest chicken-rice in Singapore.

Kampongs

Recently the Singapore press announced that the last kampong in Singapore was due to be torn down, sparking a debate about whether or not it should be preserved and turned into a tourist attraction. There are in fact still a few kampongs in Singapore, though they may have iron roofs, electricity and a car parked next to the house. The government has met strong resistance in the past from the Malay community when villages have been torn down to make way for HDB estates.

In the north-east of the island, for example near the coast between Sembawang and Punggol, you can still come across rural scenes, and you can still find kampongs. Some of the islands such as Pulau Ubin are also rural and very Malay in character, and they have kampongs that have so far escaped the ravages of development.

Sun Yatsen Villa

This old villa was Sun Yatsen's residence in Singapore before the overthrow of the Qing (or Manchu) dynasty that saw an end to imperial China and Dr San Yatsen's promotion to president of the new republic in 1912. His time in Singapore was largely spent organising secret societies and fund-raising for the overthrow of the Qing dynasty. The house is a fine example of an old villa and inside are personal items and photographs of the Chinese revolutionary, while upstairs is a Chinese library.

The villa is on Ah Hood Rd, about 0.5 km south of the Toa Payoh MRT station. Bus No 145 goes from Balestier Rd – get off at Ah Hood Rd.

SPORTS

Singapore's private clubs and country clubs have excellent sporting facilities but there are also fine public facilities, such as those

Kelongs

To the north-east of Singapore in the Johor Strait, particularly around Ponggul and Changi, are the *kelongs*, long arrow-shaped fences erected to trap fish. The kelongs consist of *lawa*, or fishing stakes, that intercept the fish as they come inshore at night on the tidal currents and direct them down a shaft into a netted chamber, the *bunoh mati*, or 'death chamber'. The lawa are made from a palm that gives off a fluorescent glow, which helps direct the fish down into the nets. Powerful lights are used earlier in the evening to attract small fish and plankton into the chambers, which then attract larger fish. Once the large fish are in the bunoh mati, the kelong operators drag them out with nets.

Kelongs are a Malay invention, but the majority of kelong operators are Teochow Chinese, who built larger kelongs with living quarters to make them commercially viable. These fascinating fishing-traps are another disappearing sight, as the Singapore government doesn't want any of these untidy things in the water and favours fish farms instead. Permits for kelongs are not being renewed once they expire, and the remaining kelongs number around 30. ■

at Farrer Park near Little India, and a host of commercial ventures.

Archery

Contact the Archery Club of Singapore (☎ 258 1140) at 5 Bintang Walk.

Badminton

Badminton is popular in South-East Asia and the region has produced world champions in this sport. Courts at the Singapore Badminton Hall (☎ 344 1773), 102 Guillemard Rd, are open from 8 am to 11 pm; bookings are essential.

Bicycling

Recreational bicycling ranges from a leisurely peddle along the foreshore of the east coast to mountain biking at Ulu Pandan.

The easiest riding possibilities are the east coast, Sentosa and Pulau Ubin. Bikes can also be hired at these places.

Bukit Timah has two mountain bike trails, seven km in all, running around the edge of the nature reserve between Chestnut Ave and Rifle Range Rd. The trails cut though jungle and abandoned quarry sites and, though hilly in parts, are well surfaced.

The Ulu Pandan Boy's Brigade Mountain Bike Track is a more challenging, unpaved four km trail for jungle and mud adventure. It is opposite the Singapore Polytechnic on Dover Rd.

Bowling

Tenpin bowling is very popular in Singapore. The cost per game is around S$3 to S$3.80; shoe hire is around 50c. Some alleys are:

Singapore Tenpin Bowling Congress
    01-01 Balestier Plaza, 400 Balestier Rd
    (☎ 355 0136)
Superbowl
    15 Marina Grove, Marina South (☎ 221 1010)

Cricket

The Singapore Cricket Club holds matches every weekend on the Padang from March to October. The club is for members only but spectators are welcome.

Golf

Singapore has plenty of golf courses, though some are for members only or do not allow visitors to play on weekends. A game of golf costs around S$90 on weekdays, and from S$100 to S$220 on weekends. Club hire is expensive. The following courses have 18 holes, except for Changi, Seletar and Warren, which are nine-hole courses:

Changi Golf Club
    Netheravon Rd (☎ 545 5133)
Jurong County Club
    9 Science Centre Rd (☎ 560 5655)
Keppel Club
    Bukit Chermin (☎ 273 5522)
Marina Bay Golf & Country Club
    6 Marina Green (☎ 221 2811)
Raffles Country Club
    450 Jalan Ahmad Ibrahim (☎ 861 7655)
Seletar Country Club
    Seletar Airbase (☎ 481 4745)
Sembawang Country Club
    Sembawang Rd (☎ 257 0642)
Sentosa Golf Course
    Sentosa Island (☎ 275 0022)
Singapore Island Country Club
    Upper Thomson Rd (☎ 459 2222)
Warren Golf Course
    Folkestone Rd (☎ 777 6533)

Singapore has driving ranges at the Parkland Golf Driving Range (☎ 440 6726), 920 East Coast Parkway, and Green Fairways (☎ 468 8409), Bukit Turf Club, Fairways Drive.

Squash

Most of the country clubs listed above have squash courts. Some of the public courts are:

East Coast Recreation Centre
    East Coast Parkway (☎ 449 0541)
National Stadium
    Kallang (☎ 440 6839)

Swimming

Singapore has a number of beaches for swimming – try East Coast Park, Changi Village, Sentosa or the other islands. Singapore has plenty of public swimming pools; admission is S$1. The Farrer Park Swimming Complex in Dorset Rd is the closest to the Bencoolen St and Orchard Rd areas.

Tennis

Tennis courts cost from S$3 to S$6 per hour. Courts available for hire include:

Farrer Park Tennis Courts
Rutland Rd (☎ 299 4166)
Singapore Tennis Centre
1020 East Coast Parkway (☎ 442 5966)

Water Sports

The East Coast Sailing Centre (☎ 449 5118), 1210 East Coast Parkway, is the place to go for windsurfing and sailing. Sailboards cost S$20 for two hours hire; lessons are available. They also rent Laser-class boats for $20 per hour. Sailboards and aquabikes are also available for hire on Sentosa Island.

For water-skiing, William Water Sports (☎ 282 6879), at Ponggol Point in the north of the island, rents boats, a driver and gear for S$65 per hour. Cowabunga Ski Centre (☎ 344 8813), 10 Stadium Walk, Kallang, is the home of the Singapore Water Ski Federation and offers lessons and equipment.

Places to Stay

Singapore has a wide variety of accommodation in all price categories – you can get a dormitory bed in a guesthouse for S$7, a room in a cheap Chinese hotel for around S$30, pay over S$300 for a room in an 'international standard' hotel, or over S$6000 for the best suite at the Raffles. Hotel standards are usually high but so are prices, making Singapore the most expensive city in South-East Asia for hotels and up there with other expensive cities around the world.

In the major hotels, a 3% GST, 1% government tax and 10% service charge are added to your bill. This is the dreaded 'plus-plus-plus' which follows the quoted price (eg S$140+++), while 'nett' means that price includes tax and service charge. The hotels stipulate that you should not tip when a service charge applies. The 4% taxes (ie GST and government taxes) also apply to the cheaper hotels but they are usually included in the quoted price.

PLACES TO STAY – BOTTOM END

The budget accommodation is to be found in the guesthouses and ever-shrinking number of cheap Chinese hotels.

Singapore's guesthouses are just residential flats or office space broken up into dormitories and cubicle-like rooms. The trouble with them is that overcrowding tends to stretch the limited facilities, and the rooms really are small. In addition, everybody else there will be a traveller, just like yourself. On the other hand, they're good sources of information and good places to meet people and you won't find any cheaper accommodation in Singapore.

New guesthouses are constantly opening up, and the services they provide are improving. Dormitory beds cost from S$7 and rooms from S$15, though most rooms go for around S$20 and range up to S$50 for hotel-standard rooms with air-con, attached bath and TV. Cheap rooms are often small spartan boxes with a fan. Free tea and coffee are standard offerings and a basic breakfast is usually thrown in. Singapore does not have an official youth hostel.

The other main budget accommodation option is the cheap Chinese hotels. Most of the cheap hotels have seen better days, but they do have more character than the guesthouses. They appear to be resigned to redevelopment and are, sadly, deteriorating each year. Rooms range from around S$25 to S$60. Singapore also has three YMCAs, though these are more mid-range options, and two inconveniently located campgrounds.

The main area for budget accommodation is in the colonial district bounded by Bras Basah, Rochor, Beach and Selegie Rds. Bencoolen St and Beach Rd have a number of guesthouses. Other cheap possibilities are found further north in Little India and nearby Jalan Besar, and in Chinatown. A number of cheap hotels can also be found out in the lorongs (alleys) of Geylang, east of the city, but most travellers find them far too inconvenient.

Bencoolen St Area

Bencoolen St has traditionally been the budget accommodation centre, and at almost any time of the night or day you can see travellers with backpacks seeking out a cheap hotel or guesthouse. Bencoolen St itself has very little character left but it's within walking distance of the city centre, Orchard Rd and Little India.

From Changi International Airport, public bus No 16 or 16E will drop you on Stamford Rd. Get off near the National Museum, cross Stamford Rd and walk north through the small park to Bras Basah Rd and Bencoolen St. From the Singapore railway station, bus No 97 also stops on Stamford Rd. From the Lavender St bus station, almost all buses that run along Jalan Besar also go down Bencoolen St. The nearest MRT station is Dhoby Ghaut, about 10 minutes' walk from Bencoolen St.

Guesthouses Singapore's original backpackers' centre is at 46-52 Bencoolen St. There's no sign at all; go around the back and take the lift. Almost the entire building is devoted to guesthouses, some of which have been running for almost 20 years. The place looks like it – filthy stairwells and graffiti-adorned lift – though some of the places offer reasonable rooms.

At the top, at least in elevation, *Lee Boarding House* (☎ 338 3149) has its reception at Room 52 on the 7th floor but they have rooms on other floors. It's a large place with dorm beds for S$8 or beds in less crowded air-con dorms for S$9. Rooms range from standard fan singles/doubles for S$19/29 to air-con rooms for S$29/35, right up to good hotel-style rooms with air-con and bathroom for S$45 to S$70. *Peony Mansions* (☎ 338 5638), one of the original guesthouses, is on the 4th floor. Dormitory beds cost S$8, single rooms cost from S$20 and doubles from S$30 to S$45. The dorms aren't great but the rooms are reasonable and many have been upgraded. There are other guesthouses in the block, such as *Latin House* (☎ 339 6308) on the 3rd floor at No 46, which is an anonymous place with run-down rooms.

On the other side of Bencoolen St, between the Strand and Bencoolen hotels, is *Bencoolen House* (☎ 338 1206) at No 27. The reception area is on the 7th floor. Dorm beds cost S$7, a few singles cost S$20, but most rooms cost from S$25 up to S$45 for an air-con room. It's a bit run-down but OK.

In the thick of things, the *Why Not Homestay* (☎ 338 8838), 127 Bencoolen St, is a popular place with an excellent 24 hour Indian coffee shop downstairs. It has a variety of reasonable rooms from S$25 for a fan room with two bunk beds to S$50 for a room with air-con and shower. *Green Curtains* (☎ 334 8597), next door at No 131A, is an offshoot of Peony Mansions with well-maintained rooms. The S$20 fan rooms are fairly small and dark but better rooms range up to S$45.

At 171 Bencoolen St is another centre for guesthouses. *Goh's Homestay* (☎ 339 6561), up a long flight of stairs to the 3rd floor at 171A, has an eating/meeting area where you can get breakfast, snacks and drinks. The rooms are clean but small, without windows and expensive at S$34/44 for singles/doubles; dorm beds cost S$12. *Hawaii Hostel* (☎ 338 4187) on the 2nd floor at 171B is an impersonal place with eight-bed dorms for S$10, pokey singles for S$25 and better air-con doubles for S$35. Breakfast is not included.

Hotels Redevelopment in the area has seen the demise of most of the old hotels. The *San Wah* (☎ 336 2428) at 36 Bencoolen St is a little better than the cheapest Chinese hotels and many of the rooms are air-conditioned. It has a pleasant courtyard area set back from the street. Singles/doubles cost S$45/50, S$5 more with air-con.

At 260-262 Middle Rd, near the corner of Selegie Rd, is the good, spotlessly clean *Sun Sun Hotel* (☎ 338 4911). It's a cut above the other traditional Chinese hotels and some rooms have their own balconies. There's also a restaurant and bar downstairs. Singles/doubles/triples cost S$40/48/58, or air-con doubles cost S$54.

SINGAPORE

Beach Rd Area

Beach Rd, a few blocks from Bencoolen St towards the (ever-receding) waterfront, is another centre for cheap hotels. If you aspire to the Raffles but can't afford it, at least you can stay nearby. From Changi airport, bus No 16 or 16E can drop you near the towering Raffles City complex, opposite the Padang, from where it's a short walk to Beach Rd. From the railway station and the World Trade Centre take bus No 100. Bus Nos 82 and 107 run down Beach Rd from the Lavender St Malaysia bus station, and pass the Golden Mile Complex bus station on Beach Rd only a 10 minute walk from the cheap hotels. The Beach Rd area is about halfway between the City Hall and Bugis MRT stations.

Guesthouses *Lee Traveller's Club* (☎ 339 5490) is on the 6th floor of the Fu Yeun building at 75 Beach Rd and they have more rooms on the other floors. It is a large place and popular, though not as cramped as some others. It costs $8 in an eight-bed, air-con dorm and singles start at S$15, though most rooms are air-con doubles for S$30 and S$35. It is one of the better guesthouses and has a small kitchen for guests' use. *Willy's* (☎ 337 0916) is in the same building on the 3rd floor. It is a reasonable if cramped place with a rabbit warren of rooms: it's S$7 for a bed in a small dorm, tiny windowless singles go for S$20 and better air-con doubles are S$28 and S$30. It also has a small kitchen.

Waffles Home Stay (☎ 334 1608) on the 3rd floor, 490 North Bridge Rd, is on the top floor of an old Chinese shop. Enter through the shop or from the lane at the rear after hours. It is a friendly place with dorms for S$8 and S$10 and a few basic double rooms for $26.

Liang Seah St, which runs into Beach Rd, has a couple of guesthouses that are holding on in the face of all the redevelopment along this street. The popular *New Backpackers Lodge* (☎ 334 8042) at No 18A is in an old terrace which has been chopped in half. The Chinese hotel-style rooms have little furniture. It has lost a bit of its shine and can be crowded. A dorm bed costs S$8 and most rooms go for S$25. *Backpackers' Cozy Corner* (☎ 296 8005) at No 2A, nearer to Beach Rd, is a good, new place that tries harder and offers a slightly better standard of rooms. Dorm beds cost S$7 and rooms range from S$15 to S$28 with fan and S$32 to S$40 with air-con and attached bathroom.

Hotels The hotels here are all of a similar basic standard: traditional Chinese hotels with wire-topped walls, shuttered windows, a few pieces of furniture and a basin with running water. They are run-down but good for the price.

The *Shang Onn* (☎ 338 4153) at 37 Beach Rd on the corner of Purvis St is a little more expensive than the other places. Single/double/triple rooms will cost you S$30/34/45. The rooms are very clean and have character but not much else. At 54 Middle Rd, the *Lido* (☎ 337 1872) is a rickety, old wooden hotel but immaculately kept. Large singles/doubles at S$24/28 are good value, but the management is less than welcoming.

At the corner of Liang Seah St and North Bridge Rd is the *Ah Chew Hotel* (☎ 336 3563), a very traditional old Chinese hotel. The S$30 rooms are basic, but at least the eyeball-sized holes in some of the rooms have been taped over. The old guys who run the place are very friendly and the shared bathrooms are spotless.

Chinatown

Chinatown, an interesting area to stay, has a few cheap hotels, most of which are within walking distance of the railway station and the Outram Park and Tanjong Pagar MRT stations.

Guesthouses The friendly *Chinatown Guest House* (☎ 220 0671), 5th floor, 325D New Bridge Rd, opposite Pearl's Centre, has dorm beds for S$10 and reasonable rooms for S$30 and up to S$45 with air-con. It's about the cheapest option in Chinatown and handy to the Outram Park MRT station.

Hotels One of the better cheap hotels in Singapore is the *Majestic Hotel* (☎ 222 3377) at

31 Bukit Pasoh Rd on the south-western edge of Chinatown. It's a quiet street in an interesting area, right near the Outram Park MRT station. Air-con singles/doubles are S$47/55 without bath, S$59/69 with bath. The rooms without bathroom are the most pleasant, as they face the street and have balconies. Though looking a little spotty, an upgrade is planned but prices may rise. This popular hotel is often full.

Not far away on Peck Seah St are a couple of carpeted, air-con hotels. The *New Asia* (☎ 221 1861) is on Maxwell Rd at the corner of Peck Seah St. Most rooms are small but reasonable value for S$45/55 for singles/doubles or S$5 extra with TV. A couple of doors down at 10 Peck Seah St, the *Air View Hotel* (☎ 225 7788) is a bit better than the New Asia and costs $60 for doubles or S$75 with two double beds. All rooms have a shower cubicle and TV.

Little India & Jalan Besar

Little India and Jalan Besar, near the Lavender St Malaysia bus station, also have a number of cheap hotels. It is not as convenient as the other areas, but it is close to the Lavender St bus station if you arrive by long-distance bus from Malaysia, and it is handy for exploring Little India and Arab St.

See the Little India map for the location of places to stay in this area.

Guesthouses A couple of good guesthouses have sprung up in Little India, both on Roberts Lane. The popular *Ali's Nest* (☎ 291 2938) at No 23 is run by the friendly Ali, who lived in Holland and speaks Dutch. Beds in dorms containing four to eight beds are S$7. A few small singles go for S$15, or better doubles cost S$25.

Marajam Lodge (☎ 293 5251) at No 30 is a bigger place with a variety of rooms scattered around for S$15 to S$25, S$30 with air-con. The hallway dorm costs S$7, or a two-bed shared room costs S$11 per person. Both guesthouses provide a free breakfast.

Hotels The *Little India Guest House* (☎ 294 2866) is just off Serangoon Rd in the heart of Little India at 3 Veerasamy Rd. It is more a small hotel than a guesthouse. Small, well-appointed rooms with shared bathrooms cost S$38/50/62 for singles/doubles/triples.

Jalan Besar has a few cheap hotels, but this is not a convenient location unless perhaps you arrive at the Malaysia bus station on Lavender St and can't be bothered looking further. The pick of the bunch is the spotlessly clean *Palace Hotel* (☎ 298 3108) at 407A-B Jalan Besar, only a short walk from the Malaysia bus station. Large, balconied double rooms for S$25 are good value. Further south down Jalan Besar at No 383, the *Kam Leng* (☎ 298 2289) is a run-down old hotel with rooms at S$28 for a fan room and S$35 with air-con. At No 290A, the architecturally interesting *International Hotel* (☎ 293 9238) has large doubles for S$40 or S$48 with bath, and most have balconies.

Other Areas

Hotels The *Mayfair City Hotel* (☎ 337 4542) is at 40-44 Armenian St near Orchard Rd, behind the National Museum in the colonial district. It's in one of Singapore's oldest streets and within walking distance of many attractions. Good rooms with air-con, shower and TV cost S$60/70 for singles/doubles.

The *Mitre Hotel* (☎ 737 3811), 145 Killiney Rd, is the cheapest hotel anywhere near Orchard Rd (half a km to the north). It would have to be the most dilapidated fleapit in Singapore, but that said it does have a good deal of character. It is in an old villa with large grounds set back off the street. The dingy bar on the ground floor is popular with the oil-rig workers who stay here. Rooms range from S$24 for a rough single with fan to S$36 for a passable double with air-con and attached bath.

The Ys Singapore has three YMCAs, which take men, women and couples. They provide good mid-range accommodation and, though not the bargain they used to be, are still very popular. Advance bookings in writing with one night's deposit are usually essential. Book at least six weeks in advance for the YMCA International and around three weeks in advance for the others. Non-YMCA members must pay a small charge for temporary membership.

The *YMCA International House* (☎ 336 6000) is at 1 Orchard Rd in a handy position with good facilities including a fitness centre, roof-top swimming pool, squash and badminton courts and a billiards room. There's also a restaurant which offers a cheap daily set meal and a McDonald's. All rooms have air-con, TV, telephone and attached bathroom but are of a fairly average mid-range standard and becoming expensive at S$80 single, S$90 double, S$105 family and S$115 superior room, plus 13% tax and service charge. A bed in a four-bed dorm costs S$25. Despite the high rates, it is often booked well in advance.

The *Metropolitan YMCA* (☎ 737 7755), 60 Stevens Rd, also has well-appointed rooms, a pool and a cafe. It is a good 15 minute walk north of Orchard and Tanglin Rds and less conveniently located than the Orchard Rd YMCA. Singles/doubles/triples with bathroom, TV and air-con range from S$78/87/100 to S$91/100/118 for a 'pool view' room.

The *Metropolitan YMCA International Centre* (☎ 222 4666) is at 70 Palmer Rd. Though a little far out, it is close to Chinatown, the railway station and the Tanjong Pagar MRT station. Singles with common shower are S$34, but these are for men only. Doubles/triples with attached bathrooms are S$71/80. All rooms have air-conditioning. The facilities are good and there is a cafe.

Camping The best place for camping is at Sentosa Island, where pre-erected four-person tents cost S$12 per night plus 3% tax. Camp beds cost an extra 50c each. They cater primarily for groups, but individuals can stay by booking in advance through the Sentosa Information Centre (☎ 270 7888). The nearby youth hostel is only open to organised groups and an air-con bunk room for up to 12 people costs $120.

There's also the good *East Coast Campsite* on East Coast Parkway, at the five km marker, but officially you must book three months in advance and obtain a permit from the People's Association (☎ 340 5113) on Stadium Link, opposite the National Stadium.

PLACES TO STAY – MIDDLE

Singapore is experiencing a mini boom in mid-range accommodation. New hotels are springing up in Chinatown, Little India and the colonial district to cater for independent visitors who want a little luxury but not the price tag of the five-star hotels. Most of the new hotels have well-appointed rooms with attached bathroom, hot water, air-con, phone and TV but forego the trimmings of the big hotels and offer rooms only.

The cheaper hotels listed here are mostly the second-string, older places which have comfortable rooms but could do with a facelift.

Colonial District

The *New 7th Storey Hotel* (☎ 337 0251) at 229 Rochor Rd, at the northern end of the colonial district, is an older, upmarket cheapie. Reasonable budget rooms with air-con, TV, telephone and carpeting go for S$59, S$75 with attached bathroom. It is close to the MRT but the immediate area is deserted and awaiting renovation.

The *South-East Asia Hotel* (☎ 338 2394) at 190 Waterloo St is quiet and good for the money. All rooms have air-con, attached bathroom, TV and phone. Doubles cost S$63, or S$79 with two double beds.

Waterloo Hostel (☎ 336 6555), 55 Waterloo St, is not your average hostel and offers very good air-con rooms with TV, phone and fridge. Part of the Catholic Centre, it is quiet and well run with singles/doubles for S$63/73, S$73/83 with attached bath. The tariff includes breakfast.

Modern-style hotels with air-con and bathrooms include the *Hotel Bencoolen* (☎ 336 0822), 47 Bencoolen St, situated among the rock-bottom guesthouses. Rooms are comfortable but cheaply put together and faded. Doubles cost S$88, or S$93 with fridge. Much better is the *Strand Hotel* (☎ 338 1866), 25 Bencoolen St, practically next door to the

Hotel Bencoolen. Excellent, upgraded rooms are a good alternative to the top-end hotels and cost S$95 for a double. The hotel has a coffee shop and bar.

The *Metropole Hotel* (☎ 336 3611) on Seah St behind the Raffles is an older three-star hotel that has lost its shine, but it has a good coffee shop and restaurant. Rooms have had a minor face-lift and start at S$100/115 plus 14% for singles/doubles.

The *Beach Hotel* (☎ 336 7712), 95 Beach Rd, is a new hotel with double rooms for $95, $105 and S$120. The rooms are well appointed and many of the attached bathrooms have baths, but the hotel has no coffee shop or other facilities.

Little India

Little India is experiencing a boom in mid-range accommodation, as new hotels spring up because of the renovations in the area. Though Little India is a less convenient area for visiting Singapore's attractions, the hotels here are currently the best buys in this range.

The *Boon Wah Hotel* (☎ 299 1466), at 43A Jalan Besar on the corner of Upper Dickson Rd, has reasonable rooms with air-con, TV and attached bathroom for S$70 a double.

Close to Serangoon Rd, the *Tai Hoe Hotel* (☎ 293 9122) at 163 Kitchener Rd is a former old fleapit which has been torn down and completely rebuilt. It now offers excellent modern rooms with attached bathroom, TV, phone and bar fridge. Opening rates of S$68/78 for singles/doubles make it one of the best mid-range buys in Singapore, but prices may rise.

The small *Kerbau Hotel* (☎ 297 6668) on Chander Rd is another new hotel. Spotless rooms with attached bathroom, phone and TV cost S$70/80/90 for singles/doubles/triples. Rooms are on the small side and those on the ground floor are windowless, but the more expensive upstairs rooms are better.

The multistorey *Broadway Hotel* (☎ 292 4661), 195 Serangoon Rd, is one of the oldest of the hotels in Little India but well maintained. The rooms have air-con, TV and attached bathrooms and cost S$80/90, S$90/100 for superior rooms, plus 4% tax. The hotel has a good, cheap Indian coffee shop.

The *Mustafa Hotel* (☎ 295 5855), 145 Syed Alwi Rd, is the hotel for shoppers. It is upstairs above the Mustafa Centre, a large department store bustling with bargain hunters. New, quite luxurious rooms are good value. Prices range from $90/110 to S$180 for large triples.

Other new hotels include the large *Fortuna Hotel* (☎ 295 3577), 2 Owen Rd, with some of the best rooms in the middle range starting at S$110, and the smaller *Penta Hotel* (☎ 299 6311), with well-appointed rooms from S$108/125. Both regularly offer discounts, making them a good option.

Also at the top of this range, over near Jalan Besar, the *Dickson Court Hotel* (☎ 297 7811), 1 Upper Dickson Rd, is a new boutique hotel with 51 well-appointed rooms from S$105 to S$155 plus 14%. Designed around new shophouses, it has some style but some of the rooms are small and dark. It has a restaurant and bar.

Orchard Rd Area

You can find a few reasonably priced hotels around Orchard Rd. At Kramat Rd, one block north of Orchard Rd, the *Supreme Hotel* (☎ 737 8333) is central and a good buy for the position. It is a good mid-range hotel and costs S$85 nett a double.

Lloyd's Inn (☎ 737 7309), 2 Lloyd Rd, is a small but modern hotel less than a 10 minute walk from Orchard Rd. It is in a quiet street among the old villas of Singapore and the rooms are spread out, motel style, around the reception building. The well-appointed rooms for S$85 a double or S$95 a double with fridge are good value. Bookings are advisable.

In the quiet residential area to the north of Orchard and Tanglin Rds are some good hotels, but they are a little out of the way. The *Sloane Court Hotel* (☎ 235 3311), 17 Balmoral Rd, is a pleasant Tudor-style hotel in a garden setting with an English pub. The rooms are comfortable but nothing special and cost S$80/90, plus 14%, for singles/doubles. A few hundred metres away is the *Hotel VIP* (☎ 235 4277) at 5 Balmoral Crescent. The rooms are a little run-down, but the hotel has a swimming pool and rooms are reasonable value at S$99.

Next to the Shangri-La Hotel, the *RELC International House* (☎ 737 9044), 30 Orange Grove Rd, has large well-appointed doubles with balcony and fridge from S$110, after discount, making them good value. RELC stands for Regional English Language Centre, and the bottom floors are devoted to conference rooms and teaching facilities while the top floors are occupied by a good standard hotel.

Chinatown

Chinatown's renovated terraces are also home to a number of mid-range hotels offering rooms with character, but because of the terrace design, the cheaper rooms are often windowless. Prices are high in these small hotels, and given that some are charging close to top-end hotel rates but have limited facilities, expect discounts.

Dragon Cityview Hotel (☎ 223 9228), 18 Mosque St in Chinatown, is in a row of renovated shophouses and the rooms are well appointed with air-con, attached bathroom and TV. Small singles for S$65 are dark and many are located around the noisy air-con shaft. Doubles are much better at S$98 or S$118 for larger rooms with bar fridge.

The small *A&G Chinatown Hotel* (☎ 222 1218) is in the thick of things at 68A Smith St. Rooms with minibar are very comfortable but simple and cost S$95/105 for singles/doubles. The cute *Damenlou Hotel* (☎ 221 1900), 12 Ann Siang Rd, has more character and a good cafe. Well-appointed rooms cost S$100/120, but some are better than others so it pays to look at a few.

Two new hotels are at the southern edge of Chinatown near the Outram Park MRT station. The *Chinatown Hotel* (☎ 225 5166) is a good small hotel with a guesthouse feel. After discount, singles/doubles are S$93/108 including breakfast in the lobby dining area. The larger *Royal Peacock* (☎ 223 3522), 55 Keong Saik Rd, is more luxurious and has a stylish bar/cafe. All rooms have minibars and VCRs and cost from S$125/135 to S$175/185 for singles/doubles, but the cheapest rooms are dark.

The *Inn of the Sixth Happiness* (☎ 223 3266), 33 Erskine Rd, is one of the first and still one of the best of the terrace hotels. Standard rooms on the ground floor cost S$130 and run off a winding passageway with attractive open courtyard areas, but the rooms are small and windowless. The superior rooms for S$180 and deluxe rooms for S$220 upstairs are much better. Suites are also available. Add 14% tax and service to the rates, but large discounts of around 40% are usually on offer.

PLACES TO STAY – TOP END

The rates for Singapore's international standard hotels constantly change as they ride the roller coaster of supply and demand. Discounts are not usually available if you walk in off the street, but it is always worth asking. Travel agents overseas should be able to secure good deals on accommodation.

The Singapore Hotels Association (☎ 542 6955) operates an outlet at Changi International Airport and keeps an up-to-the-minute list of available rooms. You don't pay extra for the service, and you will be quoted the current discount rates.

All these hotels will be air-conditioned, all rooms will have bathrooms, TV and minibar and in almost all cases there will be a swimming pool and a variety of restaurants, coffee shops and bars. They are all of international standard and often there is little to distinguish one from the other – the choice boils down to price and where you want to stay.

The hotels at the bottom end of this range are of a good standard but are either getting a little old or lack the extensive facilities of the larger hotels.

For addresses and telephone numbers of the hotels listed in this section, see the Top-End Details section below.

Orchard Rd Area

Orchard Rd is where everyone wants to stay, and consequently hotels tend to be a little more expensive than those in other areas. However, Orchard Rd has some moderately priced hotels of a high standard.

The *Cockpit Hotel* is looking a little weary and the facilities are limited but it is well located and moderately priced. The *Hotel Grand Central* is indeed central to Orchard Rd and has good facilities, though it is not particularly grand.

Other cheaper hotels are at the end of Orchard Rd, near Scotts and Tanglin Rds. Most are smaller hotels just beyond an easy walk to the action. The *Hotel Premier* is used as a training centre for hotel and catering staff. The standards of service tend to be potluck, and the hotel needs maintenance, but the rates are always reasonable. Nearby on Lady Hill Rd, the *Ladyhill Hotel* is a slightly more expensive low-rise hotel in an attractive garden setting. The *Garden Hotel* on Balmoral Rd is another smaller hotel with a courtyard pool. The *Hotel Asia* is more expensive but it lacks the facilities of most other big hotels on Scotts Rd.

The centrally located hotels in Orchard Rd are more popular and generally more expensive. These include the *Orchard Parade*, *Boulevard*, *Four Seasons* and the *Orchard* hotels. The *Cairnhill Hotel* on Cairnhill Circle is a notch below most of the other hotels but reasonably priced. The relatively small *Holiday Inn Park View* is well positioned and has good discounted rates. Further down Orchard Rd is the French-run *Le Meridien* and, on Penang Rd, *Hotel Phoenix* is at the lower end of the range for the Orchard Rd area. The *Imperial Hotel* on Jalan Rumbia enjoys a hill-top location near River Valley Rd and is within walking distance of the city end of Orchard Rd. It is also cheaper.

Most of the top hotels are at the top end of Orchard Rd around Scotts and Tanglin Rds. These include the *Omni Marco Polo* and the impressive *Regent*. In between the two is the *Traders' Hotel*, a new hotel but without the usual profusion of facilities. The super-luxury *Shangri-La* is set in five hectares of garden on Orange Grove Rd.

The *Marriott Hotel* has had a complete makeover and its well-appointed opulence is priced accordingly. In restrained oriental style, the *Mandarin* is one of Singapore's best.

Other international hotel chains are well represented. The *Hilton* is on Orchard Rd, and the *Royal Holiday Inn Crowne Plaza*, *Hyatt Regency* and *Sheraton Towers* are all on Scotts Rd.

Next to the Sheraton Towers, *Melia at Scotts* is popular with tour groups. Other hotels around Scotts Rd include the renovated *York Hotel* on Mt Elizabeth Rd, and in the same street the newer *Elizabeth Hotel*.

The beautiful, old-fashioned *Goodwood Park Hotel* on Scotts Rd was designed by the same architect who designed the Raffles. Its architecture is more ornate and, if anything, even more delightful than the Raffles. It is set on six hectares, and is one of Singapore's most expensive hotels.

Colonial District

The colonial district also has a good selection of luxury hotels. The real estate may not be as prestigious as Orchard Rd, but if anything these hotels are more conveniently located for most of Singapore's attractions.

The *Bayview Inn* is a good three-star hotel in Bencoolen St among the backpackers' guesthouses. Regular discounts make it a good buy.

The *Hotel Inter-Continental* is a new hotel in the Bugis Junction complex. Shophouse rooms out the front re-create the style of the complex, and high-rise rooms are also done in period style. It has plenty of class and all the trimmings of a top hotel.

On Coleman St, over towards the business centre of Singapore, the *Peninsula Hotel* and its sister hotel, the *Excelsior*, are moderately priced hotels.

The *Carlton* on Bras Basah Rd has good facilities, and the *Allson Hotel* on Victoria St is another, slightly cheaper, tourist hotel.

On top of the Raffles City shopping centre and City Hall MRT station is the tallest hotel in the world, the 73 storey *Westin Stamford*

Hotel, and its sister hotel, the *Westin Plaza Hotel*, with its countless restaurants and lounges, and two roof-top swimming pools.

Nearby on the edge of the colonial district, the massive Marina Square complex is testament to the rampant capitalism that has risen from the wasteland of reclamation. Here you'll find the *Marina Mandarin*, *Oriental* and *Pan Pacific*, with competing lobbies that owe their inspiration to Hollywood special effects movies. To match this trio, the *Ritz Carlton Millenia* next door is another new luxury hotel.

At the junction of Bras Basah and Beach Rds, the venerable *Raffles* is as much a superb tourist attraction as it is a fine old hotel. What other hotel can claim that a tiger was once shot in the billiards room? The limited number of beautiful antique-decorated rooms are only for those with money to burn. Don't expect discounts at the Raffles.

Chinatown

If you want to experience the atmosphere of Chinatown, the futuristic *Furama Hotel* on Eu Tong Sen St is right in the centre of things. The *Amara Hotel* and *Harbour View Dai-Ichi* are well-appointed business hotels on the edge of Chinatown.

The *Duxton Hotel* in the Tanjong Pagar area is a boutique hotel which has taken up residency in the renovated terraces of Chinatown. Rooms are furnished in opulent, antique style. It does not have a pool.

Havelock Rd Area

Over on Havelock Rd, south of Orchard Rd, is another hotel enclave. Chinatown is within walking distance and the Singapore Explorer shuttle operates from the hotels to Orchard Rd, but basically these hotels are in the middle of nowhere. Consequently they tend to be cheaper and are generally good value. While not superluxury hotels they are all of a good standard and include the *Apollo*, *King's*, *Miramar*, *River View* and *Concorde* hotels. The pick of these are the River View, right on the Singapore River, and the Concorde, with its impressive lobby and superior facilities.

Other Areas

In Little India and Arab St are a few good hotels that are reasonably priced. The *New Park Hotel*, on Kitchener Rd in Little India, is popular with tour groups and close to good shopping. The *Albert Court Hotel*, on Albert St at the southern edge of Little India, is another boutique hotel in a new shophouse redevelopment. It is smaller than most and without many of the big hotel extras. It doesn't have a pool.

The *Golden Landmark Hotel*, on the corner of Victoria and Arab Sts, has Middle Eastern-inspired architecture to match its location. The rates are very competitive. At the end of Arab St on Beach Rd is the *Plaza Hotel*.

Sentosa Island has two luxury hotels if you want to get away from it all: the *Beaufort* and the *Rasa Sentosa Beach Resort*.

If you are just in transit, the *Airport Transit Hotel* offers rooms in six-hour blocks to freshen up and get some shut-eye before your next flight. The other nearest hotel to the airport is the *Le Meridien Changi*, eight km from the airport in quiet Changi Village.

Top-End Details

The following list contains details of all top-end hotels. Unless otherwise stated, all prices are '+++', ie add the 10% service charge, 3% GST and 1% government tax. The rate quoted is the published rate for a standard single/double room. These prices should be used as a guide only, as Singapore hotel rates are subject to large variations. Discount rates of 20% or more (sometimes much more) on the published rates are often available.

Airport Transit Hotel, Terminals 1 & 2, Changi International Airport
(☎ 543 0911; fax 545 8365). S$50/56 for six hours in Terminal 1; S$42/48 for six hours in Terminal 2.

Albert Court Hotel, 180 Albert St
(☎ 339 3939; fax 339 3252). S$170/190.

Allson Hotel, 101 Victoria St
(☎ 336 0811; fax 339 7019). S$220/240.

SINGAPORE

Amara Hotel, 165 Tanjong Pagar Rd (☎ 224 4488; fax 224 3910). S$230/250.
ANA Hotel, 16 Nassim Hill (☎ 732 1222; fax 235 1516). S$270/300.
Apollo Hotel, 405 Havelock Rd (☎ 733 2081; fax 733 1588). S$200/210.
Hotel Asia, 37 Scotts Rd (☎ 737 8388; fax 733 3563). S$120/140.
Bayview Inn, 30 Bencoolen St (☎ 337 2882; fax 338 2880). S$115/125.
Beaufort Hotel, Bukit Manis Rd, Sentosa (☎ 275 0331; fax 275 0228). S$305/310.
Boulevard Hotel, 200 Orchard Blvd (☎ 737 2911; fax 737 8449). S$220/280.
Cairnhill Hotel, 19 Cairnhill Circle (☎ 734 6622; fax 235 5598). S$140/160.
Carlton Hotel, 76 Bras Basah Rd (☎ 338 8333; fax 339 6866). S$195/205.
Cockpit Hotel, 115 Penang Rd (☎ 737 9111; fax 737 3105). S$165/220.
Concorde Hotel, 317 Outram Rd (☎ 733 0188; fax 733 0989). S$170/190.
Crown Prince Hotel, 270 Orchard Rd (☎ 732 1111; fax 732 7018). S$260/290.
Duxton Hotel, 83 Duxton Rd (☎ 227 7678; fax 227 1232). S$280/310.
Elizabeth Hotel, 24 Mt Elizabeth Rd (☎ 738 1188; fax 732 3866). S$260/300.
Hotel Equatorial, 429 Bukit Timah Rd (☎ 732 0431; fax 737 9426). S$190 single or double.
Excelsior, 5 Coleman St (☎ 338 7733; fax 339 3847). S$220/240.
Four Seasons Hotel, 190 Orchard Blvd (☎ 734 1110; fax 733 0682). S$395/435.
Furama Hotel, 60 Eu Tong Sen St (☎ 533 3888; fax 534 1489). S$200/220.
Garden Hotel, 14 Balmoral Rd (☎ 235 3344; fax 235 9730). S$170/240.
Golden Landmark Hotel, 390 Victoria St (☎ 297 2828; fax 298 2038). S$170/190.
Goodwood Park Hotel, 22 Scotts Rd (☎ 737 7411; fax 732 8558). S$355 single or double.
Hotel Grand Central, Kramat Lane & Cavenagh Rd (☎ 737 9944; fax 733 3175). S$190/210.
Harbour View Dai-Ichi, 81 Anson Rd (☎ 224 1133; fax 222 0749). S$240/260.
Hilton International Hotel, 581 Orchard Rd (☎ 737 2233; fax 732 2917). S$298 single or double.
Holiday Inn Park View, 11 Cavenagh Rd (☎ 733 8333; fax 734 4593). S$290/320.
Hyatt Regency Hotel, 10-12 Scotts Rd (☎ 733 1188; fax 732 1696). S$410 single or double.
Imperial Hotel, 1 Jalan Rumbia (☎ 737 1666; fax 737 4761). S$330/350.
Hotel Inter-Continental, 80 Middle Rd (☎ 338 7600; fax 338 7366). S$300 single or double.
King's Hotel, Havelock Rd (☎ 733 0011; fax 732 5764). S$180/200.
Ladyhill Hotel, 1 Lady Hill Rd (☎ 733 0011; fax 732 5764). S$170/190.
Le Meridien Changi Hotel, 1 Netheravon Rd (☎ 542 7700; fax 542 5295). S$200/210.
Le Meridien Singapore Hotel, 100 Orchard Rd (☎ 733 8855; fax 732 7668). S$300/330.
Mandarin Hotel, 333 Orchard Rd (☎ 737 4411; fax 732 2361). S$320/360.
Marina Mandarin Hotel, 6 Raffles Blvd (☎ 338 3388; fax 339 4977). S$330/370.
Marriott Hotel, 320 Orchard Rd (☎ 735 5800; fax 735 9800). S$300/340.
Melia at Scotts, 45 Scotts Rd (☎ 732 5885; fax 732 1332). S$260/290.
Hotel Miramar, 401 Havelock Rd (☎ 733 0222; fax 733 4027). S$190/210.
Hotel Negara, 10 Claymore Drive (☎ 737 0811; fax 737 9075). S$280/360.
Hotel New Otani, 117A River Valley Rd (☎ 338 3333; fax 339 2854). S$260/280.
New Park Hotel, 181 Kitchener Rd (☎ 291 5533; fax 297 2827). S$200/220.
Novotel Orchid Hotel, 214 Dunearn Rd (☎ 250 3322; fax 250 9292). S$220/240.
Omni Marco Polo Hotel, 247 Tanglin Rd (☎ 474 7141; fax 471 0521). S$300 single or double.
Orchard Hotel, 442 Orchard Rd (☎ 734 7766; fax 733 5482). S$280/310.
Orchard Parade Hotel, 1 Tanglin Rd (☎ 737 1133; fax 733 0242). S$260/280.
Oriental Hotel, Marina Square, 5 Raffles Ave (☎ 338 0066; fax 339 9537). S$360/380.
Pan Pacific Hotel, Marina Square, 7 Raffles Blvd (☎ 336 8111; fax 339 1861). S$280/320.
Peninsula Hotel, 5 Coleman St (☎ 337 8080; fax 339 6236). S$185/200.
Hotel Phoenix, 277 Orchard Rd (☎ 737 8666; fax 732 2024). S$220/240.
Plaza Hotel, 7500A Beach Rd (☎ 298 0011; fax 296 3600). S$210/230.
Hotel Premier, 22 Nassim Hill (☎ 733 9811; fax 733 5595). S$120 single or double.
Raffles Hotel, 1 Beach Rd (☎ 337 1886; fax 339 7650). S$650 single or double.
Rasa Sentosa Beach Resort, 101 Siloso Rd, Sentosa (☎ 275 0100; fax 275 0355). S$220/260.
Regent Singapore, 1 Cuscaden Rd (☎ 733 8888; fax 732 8838). S$350 single or double.
Ritz Carlton Millenia, 7 Raffles Ave (☎ 337 8888; fax 338 0001). S$430 single or double.
River View Hotel, 382 Havelock Rd (☎ 732 9922; fax 732 1034). S$180/200.
Royal Holiday Inn Crowne Plaza, 25 Scotts Rd (☎ 737 7966; fax 737 6646). S$300/340.
Shangri-La Hotel, 22 Orange Grove Rd (☎ 737 3644; fax 733 7220). S$300/330.
Sheraton Towers, 39 Scotts Rd (☎ 737 6888; fax 737 1072). S$345 single or double.

Traders' Hotel, 1A Cuscaden Rd
(☎ 831 4314; fax 831 4314). S$212/265.
Westin Plaza Hotel, 2 Stamford Rd
(☎ 338 8585; fax 338 2862). S$315 single or double.
Westin Stamford Hotel, 2 Stamford Rd
(☎ 338 8585; fax 337 1554). S$300/315.
York Hotel, 21 Mt Elizabeth
(☎ 737 0511; fax 732 1217). S$230/255.

Places to Eat

Singapore is far and away the food capital of Asia. When it comes to superb Chinese food, Hong Kong may be a step ahead but it's Singapore's sheer variety and low prices which make it so good. Equally important, Singapore's food is accessible – you haven't got to search out obscure places, you don't face communication problems and you don't need a lot of money.

Alternatively, if you want to make gastronomic discoveries, there are lots of out-of-the-way little places where you'll find marvellous food that few visitors know about. The Singaporean enthusiasm for food (and economical food at that) is amply illustrated by newspaper and magazine articles on the best hawker stalls in the city. Everyone has their favourite chicken-rice or roti prata stall tucked away in one of the hundreds of hawker centres that dot the city.

To get to grips with food in Singapore, you firstly have to know what types of food are available and then where to find them. The STPB's *Singapore Official Guide* and the *Eating Out in Singapore* booklets are good introductions to Singaporean food with restaurant recommendations. The annual *Singapore's Best Restaurants* is a selection of fine restaurants, chosen by a survey of *Singapore Tattler* magazine subscribers, a decidedly well-to-do bunch. Moderately priced restaurants are increasingly included. Other publications come and go, but every newspaper and magazine has a food section listing the latest gastronomic discoveries and promotional offers.

Dining possibilities range from streetside hawker stalls to fancy five-star hotel restaurants, with a whole gamut of possibilities in between. In a hawker centre you can eat excellent food for under S$5. This is the real Singaporean dining experience, not to be missed.

Next up the scale are the coffee shops, or *kopi tiam* (kopi is Malay for 'coffee' and tiam is Hokkien for 'shop'). These spartan, open-fronted restaurants with marble-topped tables often have similar food to the hawker centres and within each coffee shop you may find two or three different stalls serving their own specialities. Other coffee shops are more restaurant-like and the menus are more extensive; the food may be as good as a top restaurant and cost a fraction of the price. The old coffee shops, typically housed in a terrace or under an old hotel, are a dying breed.

Restaurants run the full range from glorified coffee shops to luxury restaurants. The price increases with the quality of the decor and the efficiency of the service. Unlike most Asian cities, where western chain food is a luxury item, Singapore's Asian and western chain restaurants are reasonably priced.

All the luxury hotels have a selection of restaurants, and they house most of Singapore's fine dining establishments, though they are facing increasing competition from new restaurants springing up all over town. It may be sacrilegious to say so, but Singapore has too many restaurants and many will not survive the current boom. In the meantime, stiff competition will keep the already high prices down; already many restaurants offer good buffet and special promotional deals.

Mid-range and expensive restaurants will normally add a 10% service charge and 4% tax. Many restaurants offer good-value set lunches and more expensive set dinners. Keep an eye out for buffets, which allow you to try a number of dishes as you stuff yourself to the eyeballs at very reasonable prices. Many restaurants have lunch and dinner buffets, but the big hotels are the traditional buffet specialists.

See the colour section Food in Singapore & Malaysia in the Malaysia Facts for the Visitor chapter.

HAWKER FOOD

Traditionally, hawkers had mobile food stalls (pushcarts), set up their tables and stools around them and sold their food right on the streets. Real, mobile, on-the-street hawkers have now been replaced by hawker centres, where a large number of stationary hawkers can be found under the one roof. These centres are the baseline for Singapore food, where the prices are lowest and the eating is the most interesting.

Scattered among the hawkers are tables and stools, and you can sit and eat in any area you choose – none of them belong to a specific stall. A group of you can sit at one table and all eat and drink from different stalls.

One of the wonders of food-centre eating is how the various operators keep track of their plates and utensils – and how they manage to chase you up with the bill. The real joy of these food centres is the sheer variety; while you're having Chinese food, your companion can be eating a biryani and across the table somebody else can be trying the satay. As a rough guide, most one-dish meals cost from S$2 to S$3, but the price is higher for more elaborate dishes.

There are hundreds of hawker centres all over Singapore, and many new shopping complexes and housing blocks set aside areas for the hawkers. Even Changi International Airport has good food centres. A variation on the hawker centres are the food courts, essentially the same thing but air-conditioned and more like cafeterias with slightly higher prices. All centres are government-licensed and subject to health department regulations.

City Centre

In the business centre, *Empress Place* beside the Singapore River is a pleasant place to sit beside the river and have a meal. It is very busy at lunchtime.

Near the waterfront towards Chinatown is *Lau Pa Sat*, on Raffles Quay near the Raffles City MRT station. It is housed in the renovated Telok Ayer market building, a wonderful example of intricate Victorian cast-iron architecture in the railway-station mould. It has some souvenir stalls and occasionally stages cultural exhibits, but the main emphasis is on the favourite Singaporean pastime – food. Hawkers inside serve Nonya, Korean and western food, as well as the more usual fare; and the famous Zam Zam restaurant has also opened a very popular Indian Muslim

SINGAPORE

The Hawkers' Variety

Some typical hawker food you may come across includes carrot cake, or *chye tow kway*, usually sold for S$2 to S$3. Also known as radish cake, it's a vegetable and egg dish, tasting something like potato omelette, and totally unlike the western health-food idea of carrot cake.

Indian biryanis cost around S$3 or you can have a murtabak for around S$2. Naturally, chicken-rice and *char siew*, or roast pork, will always be available in food centres (S$2 to S$3). All the usual Cantonese dishes like fried rice (S$1.50 to S$3), fried vegetables (S$3), beef & vegetables (S$5) and sweet & sour pork (S$3 to S$5) are available, plus other dishes like fish heads with black beans & chilli from S$3 to S$5.

There will often be Malay or Indonesian stalls with satay from 30c to 35c a stick, *mee rebus* for S$2 and *mee soto* at similar prices. *Won ton mee*, a substantial soup dish with shredded chicken or braised beef, costs from S$2 to S$3. You could try a *chee chong fun*, a type of stuffed noodle, which costs from S$2 to S$4 or more, depending on whether you want the noodles with prawns, mushrooms, chicken or pork. *Hokkien fried prawn mee* costs around S$2 to S$4, as does *prawn mee soup. Popiah* (spring rolls) and *laksa* (a spicy coconut-based soup) are other regulars, but there's also a whole variety of other dishes and soups.

Or, you can even opt for western food like sausages, egg & chips, burgers or fish & chips. Drinks include a large bottle of beer for S$8, soft drinks from 80c, *ais kacang* for 80c or sugar-cane juice from 50c to S$1, depending on the size. Fruit juices such as melon, papaya, pineapple, apple, orange or starfruit range from 80c to S$2. To finish up you might try a fruit salad for S$2 or a *pisang goreng* (fried banana) for 50c. ■

stall. Restaurants with bars are also found here. Lau Pa Sat is more sanitised and expensive than the usual hawker centres, but as part of the re-creation of old Singapore, quasi-mobile hawkers set up in the evenings on Boon Tat St, where the dining is cheaper and cooler than inside.

A more traditional hawker centre, the *Telok Ayer Transit Centre*, is hidden behind a park just on the other side of Raffles Quay and houses the original hawkers of the Telok Ayer centre before it was dismantled. It is famous for its Teochew rice porridge and stalls stay open 24 hours. It is noisy, busy and just a little grotty (at least for Singapore). Stalls stay open 24 hours, though it's best after midnight.

Orchard Rd

Newton Circus Hawker Centre is at the top (north-eastern) end of Scotts Rd, right near the Newton MRT station. It is very popular with tourists and therefore tends to be a little more expensive, but it is lively and open 24 hours. Eat there while you can – it is destined for redevelopment in the near future.

South-east down Orchard Rd is another popular food centre upstairs in the *Cuppage Centre*. The downstairs section is a vegetable and produce market with a wonderful selection of fruit. It is mainly a daytime centre and closes around 8 pm.

The *Scotts Picnic Food Court* in the Scotts Shopping Centre on Scotts Rd, just off Orchard Rd by the Hyatt Regency Hotel, is a glossy food court, and the stalls offer a variety of international Asian cuisine including Thai and Japanese.

Orchard Rd has a number of other food courts. *Orchard Emerald Food Court* in the basement of the Orchard Emerald shopping centre has a varied selection of Asian food. In the same vein are the food stalls downstairs in *Orchard Towers*, on the corner of Orchard and Claymore Rds, and the *Food Life Food Court* on the 4th floor of the Wisma Atria. The latter is small but has a good selection of local dishes and 'moderne' decor from the 50s. The busy hawker centre on the 6th floor of *Lucky Plaza* has a good range of local hawker favourites and is as cheap as you'll find anywhere.

Colonial District

The *Albert Centre* on Albert Rd between Waterloo and Queen Sts is an extremely good, busy and very popular centre which has all types of food at low prices. On the corner of Bencoolen and Albert Sts, in the basement of the Sim Lim Square complex, is the *Tenco Food Centre*, a very clean establishment.

Victoria St has a good selection of hawker centres. *Victoria St Food Court*, near the Allson Hotel, is a notch up from most food centres. It has an air-con section at the back and a bar with draught beer. The food is cheap and good, and you can get western-style breakfasts here. A few doors away, the *Koh Fong Restaurant* is not a restaurant but a grouping of food stalls around open-air tables. Across the road in the Bras Basah Complex, the *Xiang Man Lou Food Court* is a small, new, air-con food court with Malay and Indian tandoori stalls, which also offer some Chinese favourites. It is open 24 hours.

The new *Bugis Junction* shopping centre on North Bridge Rd has an excellent food court in the basement, right near the entrance to the Bugis MRT station. It is more expensive than most, but has a good range and is great for Japanese food.

Food Paradiz, in the basement of the Paradiz Centre on Selegie Rd, is another good air-con food court.

The *Tropical Makan Palace* in the basement of the Beach Centre, 15 Beach Rd, is close to the Raffles and the budget accommodation area. It has food stalls in the air-conditioned section or you can eat outside.

Just north of the river on Hill St, the large *Hill St Food Centre* is popular, and across the road the *Funan Centre* has a very good air-con food court on the 7th floor.

Little India

On Serangoon Rd at the start of Little India, the large *Zhujiao Centre* is a market with a number of food stalls. As you would expect, Indian food dominates. Opposite the market, the new, air-con *Hastings Food Court* in the Little India Arcade has vegetarian and non-vegetarian food, as well as Kerala specialities and north Indian tandoori food.

Over on Jalan Besar are two food centres, the *Berseh Food Centre* halfway down on the corner of Jalan Berseh and the lively *Lavender Food Centre* at the end of Jalan Besar near Lavender St, which is good for seafood and stays open until the early hours of the morning.

Chinatown

The Chinatown area has a number of excellent food centres. The *People's Park Complex* has a good, large food centre, and the *Maxwell Food Centre* is an old-fashioned centre on the corner of South Bridge and Maxwell Rds. The pig's trotters in black bean sauce is a speciality.

Some of the best Chinese food stalls in town are on the 2nd floor at the *Chinatown Complex* on the corner of Sago and Trengganu Sts, where there is also a market. Try the *Fu Ji Crayfish*, stall No 02-221, where crayfish hor fun costs only S$3, or a superb crayfish (actually scampi) or prawn claypot with vegetables and rice costs around S$5.

The *Fountain Food Court* at 51 Craig Rd is a different type of food centre in keeping with the new Chinatown. You can dine in air-con comfort, and the nouveau decor includes sand-blasted and bag-painted walls. The food is good, but some dishes are at restaurant prices. They have satay and other Malay food, popiah and kueh (cakes), and good (and cheap) congee.

Other hawker centres can be found alongside the *Tanjong Market*, not far from the railway station, and at the *Amoy St Food Centre*, where Amoy St meets Telok Ayer St.

The famous *Satay Club* has finally fallen into the hand of the redevelopers, but many of the vendors have relocated from opposite the Padang to Clarke Quay, where over a dozen vendors fan their charcoal grills. The satay here is still the best in Singapore; just make sure you specify how many sticks (35c a time) you want or they'll assume your appetite is much larger than it actually is. It is at its liveliest in the evening. Clarke Quay also has an air-con food court.

Other Areas

The *Taman Serasi Food Centre* has one of the best settings – it is next to the Botanic Gardens north-west of the city centre on Cluny Rd, just off Napier Rd. The stalls are predominantly Malay. Try the Roti John, a type of fried sandwich with chilli, washed down with the fabulous soursop fruit juice.

The *Rasa Singapura Food Court* is a collection of hawkers selected in a special competition to find the best stalls for each dish. It used to be on Tanglin Rd but most of the hawkers have moved to the Bukit Turf Club on Turf Club Rd and they have taken the name with them. During the week, it's open for lunch and dinner until 11 pm. On weekends, it's open all day until midnight but you have to pay entry to the races until 6 pm.

CHINESE FOOD

Singapore has plenty of restaurants serving everything from a south Indian rice plate to an all-American hamburger, but naturally it's Chinese restaurants that predominate. Many Chinese restaurants cater for family and work groups and offer banquets for eight or more people. For groups they offer a wonderful opportunity to try a whole range of dishes at a reasonable price. Even at the à la carte restaurants, dishes are meant to be shared, and restaurants offer small, medium and large servings to cater for different size groups. The prices of dishes quoted here are for small servings.

Cantonese

The famous *Fatty's Wing Seong Restaurant* (☎ 338 1087), at 01-33 Albert Complex on Albert St, near the corner of Bencoolen St, has been popular with westerners ever since Fatty became a favourite with British troops stationed in Singapore during the Emergency. The food is consistently good and moderately priced. Most dishes cost around S$5 to S$8, but can go up to S$20 or more for crab. The restaurant is always crowded, but the

SINGAPORE

ever-busy staff turn the tables around quickly so you shouldn't have to wait long.

The *Hillman* (☎ 221 5073) at 159 Cantonment Rd, near the Outram Park MRT station at the edge of Chinatown, is a straightforward open-fronted restaurant where you can have a good meal for under S$15 per person, though seafood and the more exotic dishes such as shark's fin will cost more. The picture of Paul Bocuse, signed with a glowing recommendation from the master chef, is now faded but the food is fresh and still good.

The *Esquire Kitchen* (☎ 336 1802), 02-01 Bras Basah Complex in the colonial district, is a moderately priced air-con place with typical red Chinese decor and good food. They do excellent-value set lunches and dinners – three dishes and dessert costs S$18 for two people. More expensive banquets are also available.

Grand City (☎ 338 3622), 07-04 Cathay building, is a more expensive restaurant and has a varied menu with good seafood and chicken dishes. Set menus start at around S$40 for two. It is near the Dhoby Ghaut MRT station, right at the start of Orchard Rd.

Tsui Hang Village (☎ 338 6668), 02-142 Marina Square, 6 Raffles Blvd, is a popular Hong Kong-style restaurant. You can fill yourself on a good set lunch for around S$40 for two, or the set dinners start at S$60; à la carte meals are available. They also have a branch at the Asia Hotel, 37 Scotts Rd, near Orchard Rd

For dim sum a good bet is the *Tiong Shan Restaurant*, an old-fashioned coffee shop on the corner of New Bridge and Keong Saik Rds in Chinatown. A plate of dim sum is around S$1.50, and as good as you'll find anywhere. They have other dishes here as well.

More expensive dim sum can be had in more luxurious air-con surroundings at the *Regency Palace* (☎ 338 3281) in the Plaza by the Park, 51 Bras Basah Rd, in the colonial district. The prices are reasonable and most plates cost about S$2 to S$4. Many of the big restaurants offer dim sum, but remember that dim sum is a lunchtime or Sunday breakfast dish – in the evening these restaurants change to other menus.

On Orchard Rd, the small pedestrian street of Koek Rd between Centrepoint and Cuppage Plaza is a good little restaurant strip for cheap eats. A variety of restaurants are scattered around here, but the eastern side is lined with various Chinese coffee shops, such as the *Selera Cuppage Food Centre* and *Snackworld*, with tables on the pavement. Steamboats from S$15 are a speciality, though most dishes cost S$4 to S$8.

Teochew

Teochew food is a widely available cuisine. Among the many coffee shops in Chinatown's Mosque St you'll find a good selection of Teochew food. These very traditional restaurants are good places to sample simple Teochew food in the atmosphere of old Chinatown. Menus are hard to come by but a request for suggestions and prices will be readily answered, and the prices are low. The *Chui Wah Lin* (☎ 221 3305) at 49 Mosque St has very good porridge – try the duck porridge for S$3. *Teo Hiang Hing* (☎ 224 7058) at 47 Mosque St is another good Teochew eatery. The Ellenborough St market, near Boat Quay in Chinatown, is also noted for its Teochew food stalls.

For moderately priced Teochew food in more luxurious surroundings, try the *Teochow City Seafood Restaurant* (☎ 733 3338), 05-16 Centrepoint, 176 Orchard Rd.

Hainanese

Chicken-rice is a common and popular dish all over town. Originally from Hainan in China, chicken-rice is a dish of elegant simplicity, and in Singapore they do it better than anywhere else. *Swee Kee* (☎ 337 0314) at 51 Middle Rd, close to the Raffles Hotel, is a long-running specialist with a very good reputation. Chicken-rice served with chilli, ginger and thick soya sauce is S$3.50. They also do steamboats; a S$20 version has a stock enriched by various Chinese herbs and Mao Tai wine.

A stone's throw from Swee Kee, at 25 Purvis St, you'll find *Yet Con* (☎ 337 6819), which some claim is the best of all Singapore's chicken-rice places. This area west of

Beach Rd is something of a Hainanese stronghold.

Hokkien

Hokkien food is not all that popular despite the large number of Hokkiens in Singapore, but *Beng Hiang* (☎ 221 6684) in Chinatown is renown for its Hokkien food.

Beng Thin Hoon Kee (☎ 553 7708) is on the 5th floor of the OCBC Centre on Chulia St; it is a short walk from the Raffles Place MRT station and has moderately priced dishes, including Hokkien seafood.

Sichuan

Sichuan, or Szechuan, restaurants are fairly common though usually expensive; this spicy food is popular with Singaporeans. *Chinatown* (☎ 737 1666) in the Imperial Hotel, 1 Jalan Rumba, just to the west of Fort Canning Park, has an extensive à la carte menu and you can eat for around S$40 per head, or choose from their set meals for S$25. The *Golden Phoenix* (☎ 732 0431) in the Hotel Equatorial, 429 Bukit Timah Rd, is a long-running restaurant with consistently good food but it's very expensive.

Vegetarian

On Bencoolen St in the colonial district, the Fortune Centre is a good place for cheap vegetarian food. On the ground floor you'll find the *ABC Eating House* and *Yi Song* food stalls, which have cheap vegetarian food in air-con surroundings. Upstairs on the 4th floor is the *Eastern Vegetarian Food* coffee shop, offering rice or noodles with three selections from S$2. It is open on Sundays and public holidays.

At 143, 147 and 153 Kitchener Rd in Little India, the *Fut Sai Kai* (☎ 298 0336), which translates as 'monk's world', is a spartan old coffee shop and an air-con restaurant next door. Most main dishes cost around S$8 to S$10. Similarly priced is the *Kwan Yim* (☎ 338 2394), another traditional, long-running vegetarian restaurant. It's at 190 Waterloo St in the South-East Asia Hotel in the colonial district.

Chinatown has some moderately priced vegetarian restaurants, including the *Happy Realm* (☎ 222 6141) on the 3rd floor of Pearl's Centre on Eu Tong Sen St, one of the best around. Main dishes cost around S$5 to S$6 and they have good claypot dishes. *Loke Woh Yeun* (☎ 221 2912), 20 Tanjong Pagar Rd, is another in Chinatown where you can have a meal for under S$15. While it is mostly vegetarian they also have chicken and prawn dishes.

Seafood

Singapore has another variation on Chinese food. Seafood in Singapore is simply superb, whether it's prawns or abalone, fish-head curry or chilli crabs. Most of the specialists are some distance out from the city centre but the trip is worthwhile. Seafood isn't cheap, and a whole fish, crab or prawns start at just under S$20 per dish. Many places don't have set prices, but base them on 'market price' and the size of the fish. Make sure you check the price first.

The *UDMC Seafood Centre*, at the beach on East Coast Parkway, has a number of seafood restaurants and is very popular in the evenings. The food and the setting are good, but they tend to hustle a bit at some of these places, so definitely check the prices first. *Ponggol Seafood* is one of the better known restaurants here, having had a loyal following for years at its rural location at Ponggol on the north-east coast before housing developments forced it to move. The food is still excellent, though slightly more expensive at around S$30 a head.

Long Beach Seafood Restaurant (☎ 445 8833), 1018 East Coast Parkway, is one of Singapore's best known seafood restaurants. It is famous for its black pepper crabs and 'live drunken prawns' (soaked in brandy). It is a casual, huge restaurant next to the Singapore Tennis Centre, and they also have a branch at UDMC.

The Bugis St area in the colonial district also has a couple of hustling seafood places, but it is a pleasant place to dine under the stars and people-watch. Other, cheaper dishes at fixed prices are available from the menus.

Although not cheap, seafood in Singapore is superb.

Something Different

Tanjong Pagar, to the south of Chinatown, has a number of Chinese tea houses, where the emphasis is on the art and presentation of tea drinking. Take your shoes off at the door, and as you sit on cushions on the floor the waitress will bring you a tea set (complete with burner and kettle of boiling water) and demonstrate the art of tea preparation.

Tea Chapter (☎ 226 1175), 9A Neil Rd, boasts Queen Elizabeth and Prince Philip among the clientele. Dim sum snacks are served for around S$2 per plate, and the extensive range of Chinese teas costs from S$6 to S$15. It is open from 11 am till 11 pm. A few doors away at No 23, *Yixing Yuan* offers a small dim sum lunch for around S$7, or otherwise you can have dim sum for around S$2 to S$3 per plate, washed down with the tea of your choice. Both tea houses have shops that sell expensive tea and tea paraphernalia.

Snackworld (☎ 732 6921), 01-12/13 Cuppage Plaza, including the annexe outside on Cuppage Terrace off Orchard Rd, has crocodile on the menu, starting at S$25 a plate. If you can stomach the thought of eating the wildlife (actually it is farmed and, of course, it is supposed to taste like chicken), they have a wide range of dishes at some of the best prices in town.

The *Imperial Herbal Restaurant* (☎ 337 0491) in the Metropole Hotel, 41 Seah St, near the Raffles Hotel in the colonial district, is an unusual restaurant with an extensive range of dishes cooked with medicinal herbs. You can order dishes recommended by the resident herbalist and sample weird and wonderful things like scorpions and deer penis. Expect to pay about S$40 per person.

INDIAN FOOD

There are three types of Indian food in Singapore: south Indian, Indian Muslim and north Indian.

South Indian food is mostly vegetarian and Little India is the main centre for it. You can get a thali, an all-you-can-eat rice plate with a mixture of vegetable curries, for less than S$5.

Indian Muslim food is something of a hybrid. It is the simpler south Indian version of what is basically north Indian food. Typical dishes are biryani, served with chicken or mutton curry, roti and murtabak. It can be found all over Singapore but the main centre is in North Bridge Rd opposite the Sultan Mosque. Indian Muslim food is also well represented in the hawker centres; you can have a superb chicken biryani from just S$2.50 to S$3.50.

For the rich north Indian curries and tandoori food, you have to go to more expensive restaurants. They can be found all around Singapore, but Little India has a concentrated selection of very good restaurants on Race Course Rd where you'll pay considerably less than Indian restaurants in the more fashionable areas.

To sample eat-with-your-fingers south Indian vegetarian food, the place to go is the Little India district off Serangoon Rd. The famous and very popular *Komala Vilas* (☎ 293 6980) at 76 Serangoon Rd was established soon after the war and has an open downstairs area where you can have masala dosa (S$1.50) and other snacks. The upstairs section is air-conditioned and you can have their all-you-can-eat rice meal for S$4.50. Remember to wash your hands before you start, use your right hand and ask for eating utensils only if you really have to! On your way out, try an Indian sweet from the showcase downstairs.

Two other rice-plate specialists are *Sri Krishna Vilas* at 229 Selegie Rd and *Ananda Bhavan* at 219-221 Selegie Rd (the southern extension of Serangoon Rd). There are several other Indian eateries on and off Serangoon Rd and a main contender in the local competition for the best south Indian food is the *Madras New Woodlands Restaurant* (☎ 297 1594) at 14 Upper Dickson Rd off Serangoon Rd, around the corner from Komala Vilas. A branch of the well-known Woodlands chain in India, New Woodlands serves freshly prepared vegetarian food in very clean air-conditioned rooms. The yoghurt is particularly good. Prices are about the same as at Komala Vilas.

Race Course Rd, a block north-west from Serangoon Rd, is the best area in Singapore for non-vegetarian curry. Try the *Banana Leaf Apolo Restaurant* (☎ 293 8682) at 56 Race Course Rd for superb Indian food, including Singapore's classic fish-head curry. It is newly renovated with gleaming granite and air-con luxury but prices are still cheap with set meals at S$4.50 for vegetarian, S$6 for non-vegetarian, more for fish-head curry. The very popular *Muthu's Curry Restaurant* (☎ 293 7029) at 78 Race Course Rd also specialises in fish-head curry and other seafood dishes. Rice plates vary from S$4 to S$6 depending on what you choose from the counter, or fish-head curry starts at S$15 for a serve to be shared among a table of diners.

In the same block of Race Course Rd are good north Indian restaurants with typically dark decor. They serve the cheapest, and some of the best, Indian tandoori food in Singapore. *Delhi Restaurant* (☎ 296 4585) at 60 Race Course Rd has Mughlai and Kashmiri food, with curries from S$7 to S$10. Expect to pay around $20 per person for a substantial meal with bread and side dishes. The food is excellent and this restaurant is always popular. If it is full, the sister restaurant a few doors down at No 48, *D' Deli Pubb & Restaurant* (☎ 294 5276), has the same fare with a bar at the front. *Nur Jehan* (☎ 292 8033) at 66 Race Course Rd is slightly cheaper and also has good tandoori and other north Indian food. *Maharajah's Tandoor* (☎ 293 0865), 70 Race Course Rd, offers similar prices and range of food as the others.

Just around the corner is *Andhra Curry* (☎ 293 3935) at 41 Kerbau Rd, with tasteful decor in a renovated Peranakan terrace. Cheap vegetarian and non-vegetarian set meals are offered for lunch and dinner, but the most popular part of the restaurant is the food-stall area in a beer garden setting out the front.

Another cheap north Indian restaurant in Little India is the small *Bombay Restaurant*, in the Broadway Hotel at 195 Serangoon Rd. It has curries and kormas for around S$6 and breads such as naan.

For Indian Muslim food (chicken biryani for S$3.50, as well as murtabak and fish-head curry), there are a couple of cheap, venerable establishments on North Bridge Rd in the Arab St area, opposite the Sultan Mosque. Each of them has the year of founding proudly displayed on their signs out front. The *Victory* (established 1910) is at 701 North Bridge Rd, the *Zam Zam* (established 1908) is at 699 and newly renovated and further along at 791-797 is the *Islamic*. Slightly more upmarket in renovated and air-conditioned surrounds, the *Jubilee Classic Restaurant*, 28 Kandahar St, has the same Muslim dishes and a few more at very reasonable prices.

There's a small, basic Indian Muslim place called *Sahib Restaurant* under the backpackers' guesthouses at 129 Bencoolen St near Middle Rd, across from the Fortune Centre, in the colonial district. They have very good food and specialise in fish dishes, including fish-head curry, but have chicken and vegetable items too. Meals are around S$4 and they are open 24 hours. In Chinatown a similarly lively and cheap 24 hour restaurant is the *Tasree Restaurant*, 323 New Bridge Rd opposite the Pearl's Centre.

In the Orchard Rd area, *Maharani* (☎ 235 8840) is on the 5th floor of the Far East Plaza, 14 Scotts Rd. The north Indian food and the service are good in this casual restaurant. You can eat well for S$20 per person and lunch buffets are offered on weekends. The Orchard Rd area also has a vegetarian Woodlands restaurant, the *Bombay Woodlands Restaurant* (☎ 235 2712), B1-01 Tanglin Shopping Centre, 19 Tanglin Rd. The decor is very Orchard Rd and the prices are about three times what you pay in Little India but the buffet lunches for S$10 are still reasonable value.

Boat Quay near Chinatown has a good selection of more expensive north Indian restaurants for dining inside or overlooking the river. *Maharajah* (☎ 535 0122) at No 41 is one of the cheaper options with curries for around S$8 to S$14. A good meal costs S$25 or less per person. The fashionable *Royal Bengal* at 72 Boat Quay is lavishly decorated in colonial style, as are the staff. The food is not just Bengali, and a meal will cost around S$35. The marginally cheaper *Hazara* is a small 'north Indian frontier' restaurant at No 57 with Indian antiques and efficient service. The food is very good though the serves are small. This is an offshoot of their original restaurant at 24 Lorong Mambong in Holland Village, west of the city.

MALAY & INDONESIAN FOOD

Though Malay food is scattered throughout Singapore, Malay restaurants are not too abundant. The occasional stall or two at some of the food centres serve Malay food, and satay is especially easily found. Indonesian food shares many similarities with Malay cuisine, though some dishes such as gado gado are uniquely Indonesian.

The Orchard Rd area has a number of good restaurants. *Bintang Timur* (☎ 235 4539), 02-13 Far East Plaza, 14 Scotts Rd, has excellent Malay food at excellent prices. You can try a good range of dishes and eat your fill for S$20 or less. *Tambuah Mas* (☎ 733 3333), 04-10/13 Tanglin Shopping Centre, 19 Tanglin Rd, is a cheap Indonesian restaurant with a good selection of seafood dishes and Indonesian favourites such as rendang, gado gado and cendol. Another good Indonesian restaurant is *Sanur* (☎ 734 2192), 04-17/18 Centrepoint, 176 Orchard Rd. Most mains are S$7 to S$10 and range up to S$20 for whole fish. More expensive is *Azizas Restaurant* (☎ 235 1130), 36 Emerald Hill Rd, at Peranakan Place. It serves authentic Malay meals and is regarded as one of Singapore's top Malay restaurants.

Pancha Sari (☎ 338 1032), 03-239 Marina Square, is a reasonably priced Indonesian restaurant in the colonial district. Most mains cost S$6 to S$10 and you can eat well for under S$20. The small lunch set menu is S$6.50.

If you like the fiery food of north Sumatra, there are a few nasi padang specialists, the best known being *Rendezvouz*, 02-19 in the Raffles City shopping centre on Bras Basah Rd in the colonial district. The good and cheap *Rumah Makan Minang* is on the corner of Muscat and Kandahar Sts, behind the Sultan Mosque on Arab St, in a renovated shophouse.

House of Sundanese Food (☎ 345 5020), 218 East Coast Rd, east of the city towards Katong, specialises in the cuisine from West Java. Try a number of dishes, nasi padang style, many of which cost around S$4. The chicken dishes are particularly good, or try the charcoal-grilled whole fish for around S$20. They also have a branch at 55 Boat Quay, but it is not as good as the one at East Coast Rd.

The Geylang district in the east coast area has plenty of Malay eateries. For Malay food stalls during the day, go to the *Geylang Serai Market* on Changi Rd. This is the predominantly Malay area in Singapore, and it's worth a visit just to see the market, which is more traditional than the new complexes. To get there, take the MRT to the Paya Lebar station and walk east along Sims Ave to Geylang Serai.

About one km from Geylang Serai Market, *Casa Bom Vento*, 467 Joo Chiat Rd, is an interesting restaurant serving Eurasian food, which is a mixed cuisine, basically Malay in origin with a Portuguese bent. Try the beef smor (pepper steak) or the debal (devil curry), a traditional post-Christmas dish of leftover meats and vegetables cooked up in a fiery curry. Mains cost around S$6 to S$10.

NONYA FOOD

Nonya & Baba Restaurant (☎ 734 1382) is one of the best restaurants to try Nonya food at reasonable prices. Most mains cost around S$6 for small claypots, or up to S$15 for large serves. A variety of snacks and sweets are also available. It is at 262-264 River Valley Rd, near the corner of Tank Rd and directly behind the Imperial Hotel, west of Fort Canning Park. The Dhoby Ghaut MRT station at the start of Orchard Rd is a 15 minute walk away.

There are Nonya buffets at the *King's* and *Apollo* hotels in Havelock Rd (north-west of Pearl's Hill City Park), and the *Bayview Inn* in Bencoolen St in the colonial district has a good lunchtime buffet for S$13.80 on Wednesdays, Saturdays and Sundays. In Holland Village, west of the city, the *Baba Cafe* (☎ 468 9859) at 25B Lorong Liput has good-value food in an attractive setting. In the basement of Plaza Singapura on Orchard Rd, the food plaza has a good selection of Nonya cakes and savoury pastries for take-away snacks.

One of the best places to go for Nonya food is east of the city in the Geylang and Katong districts. Along (and just off) Joo Chiat Rd, between East Coast and Geylang Rds in particular, is a good hunting grounds for all kinds of Asian foods. *Guan Hoe Soon* (☎ 344 2761), 214 Joo Chiat Rd, is a long-running, moderately priced restaurant noted for its Nonya dishes. Though air-conditioned it's really just a glorified coffee shop.

East Coast Rd in Katong is a great place to try Nonya food. The *Peranakan Inn* (☎ 440 6194), 210 East Coast Rd, is one of the cheapest places in Singapore to eat Nonya food in an air-con setting. Most dishes cost S$4 to S$6, and more expensive seafood dishes are around S$15. On the corner of East Coast and Ceylon Rds, the *Hok Tong Hin Restaurant* is a hawker-style coffee shop where you can get superb laksa for only S$2. The *Carlton Restaurant*, on the corner of East Coast Rd and Lorong Stangee, is similar. During the day, try the Nonya kueh and curry puffs at the *Katong Bakery & Confectionary* (☎ 344 8948), 75 East Coast Rd. This wonderful, old-fashioned cake shop is a throwback to the Singapore of yesteryear. If you prefer more sanitised surroundings, East Coast Rd also has plenty of new cake shops for take-aways. The best bus for East Coast Rd is No 14, which goes along Orchard and Bras Basah Rds in the colonial district. Bus Nos 10, 12 and 40 will also get you there from the colonial district.

OTHER ASIAN FOOD

Thai

The Golden Mile Complex at 5001 Beach Rd, just north-east of Arab St, is a modern shopping centre catering to Singapore's Thai community where you'll find a number of small coffee shops serving Thai food and Singha beer. Prices are cheap – you can get a good meal for S$4 or S$5. Here you'll also find the *Pornping Thai Seafood Restaurant* (☎ 298 5016), which is a notch up in quality, and has a bar and an extensive Thai menu.

Parkway Thai (☎ 737 8080) in Centrepoint, 176 Orchard Rd, has an extensive menu – small mains range from S$8 up to $15 for seafood. *Cuppage Thai Food Restaurant* (☎ 734 1116), 49 Cuppage Rd, is not the greatest Thai restaurant but it has set dinners for two at S$28 and S$38, and a pleasant al fresco setting just off Orchard Rd.

Baan Thai (☎ 735 5562), 04-23 Ngee Ann City, Orchard Rd, is one of the best Thai restaurants in Singapore with good sized mains for around S$14 to S$20.

Japanese

Singapore has experienced a Japanese restaurant boom, which reflects the Japanese tourist boom. While you can spend a small

SINGAPORE

fortune at a Japanese restaurant, you can also find food at moderate prices.

The Cold Storage supermarket in the *Takashimaya department store* at Ngee Ann City, Orchard Rd, has a great take-away bar for sushi and sashimi at very low prices. Also at Takashimaya, *Nogawa* (☎ 735 9918) on the 4th floor is a reasonably priced Japanese restaurant with sushi from S$4 and mains for around S$15 to S$18.

A few food courts also have teppanyaki grills with a dining bar. There's one in the basement at Bugis Junction shopping centre on North Bridge Rd in the colonial district, with grill for around S$6 to S$10, and S$15 set meals. *Teppanyaki Place* in the Tanglin Mall Food Court on Tanglin Rd, at the northern end of Orchard Rd, has grills at S$16 for two.

Small Japanese restaurants displaying their plastic-glazed meals in the window can be found all around Singapore. *Restaurant Hoshigaoka* is a chain of Japanese restaurants, with branches at 03-45 Centrepoint and 01-18 Wisma Atria on Orchard Rd, and 03-237 Marina Square, east of the Padang. Small set meals, such as tempura and sushi meals, are around S$20.

Izumi (☎ 534 3390) at 48 Boat Quay is more expensive but worth it. Cheaper set dinners for S$30 are available.

For top-of-the-range Japanese food, try the *Keyaki* (☎ 336 8111), in the Pan Pacific Hotel on Raffles Blvd, east of the Padang.

Korean

Seoul Garden is a Korean chain with branches at 05-01 Shaw Centre, 1 Scotts Rd in the Orchard Rd area and 03-119 Marina Square, 6 Raffles Blvd, among others. The Korean BBQ set lunches for around S$12 and the slightly more expensive set dinners are excellent value. Tanjong Pagar Rd in Chinatown also has a number of Korean restaurants, and Clarke Quay has riverside Korean BBQ stalls. The Clarke Quay *towkangs*, refurbished Chinese junks moored on the Singapore River, also have Korean and other BBQs. A good feed with beer will cost around S$20.

Taiwanese

Try the reasonably priced *Goldleaf* at 24-24A Tanjong Pagar Rd in Chinatown. A speciality is chicken covered in whole fried chillies. You can eat very well for less than S$20.

WESTERN FOOD

Fast Food

Yes, you can get western food in Singapore too. There are over 50 *McDonald's*, found all over town. It's good to see that the corporate smile and 'have a nice day' haven't really caught on in Singapore – you can be served with the same brusque efficiency as you would find in any Singaporean coffee shop.

There are also *A&W, KFC, Burger King, Dunkin' Donuts, Denny's, Pizza Hut, Baskin Robbins* and *Swensen's Ice Cream* outlets – obviously there's no shortage of western fast food.

Italian

Gone are the days when Italian food was only available at a few super expensive restaurants or chain stores serving soggy pizza and insipid pasta. Italian is 'in' and Italian restaurants are sprouting up everywhere.

Boat Quay near Chinatown has its fair share of Italian restaurants. One of the best for the money is *Pasta Fresca* (☎ 469 4920) at 30 Boat Quay; it has a huge range of authentic pastas from S$10 and small pizzas from S$12 to S$15. Round off a meal with tiramisu, the most fashionable Italian dessert in Singapore. It is open 24 hours. This restaurant is part of chain and they also have an outlet on the 4th floor of Shaw House, 350 Orchard Rd on the corner of Scotts Rd.

At 31 Boat Quay, *Luna Luna* (☎ 538 2030) specialises in seafood. It is enormously popular, as much due to the Boat Quay location as the good food. A meal will set you back at least S$35, but cheaper set lunches and dinners are available. *Al Dente Trattoria* (☎ 536 5366) at 70 Boat Quay is another restaurant serving primarily pasta and pizza.

Pete's Place (☎ 733 1188) in the Hyatt Regency on Scotts Rd in the Orchard Rd area has good Italian food in a rustic setting with a salad bar. Most pasta dishes cost around S$15 and the pizzas are particularly good. The antipasto buffet is S$24.50.

Ristorante Bologna (☎ 338 3388) in the Marina Mandarin Hotel in the Marina Square complex, on the edge of the colonial district, is one of the best and most expensive Italian restaurants in town.

French

A number of restaurants do a pretty good job of convincing you that you're in France, even though you're almost on the equator.

La Cascade, 7 Ann Siang Hill Rd in Chinatown, is one of the cheaper French restaurants with set meals for around S$45.

Le Restaurant de France (☎ 733 8855) in the Le Meridien Hotel, 100 Orchard Rd, is one of the better French restaurants in Singapore. Or you may like to take a credit card or two to *Maxim's de Paris* in the Regent Hotel, 1 Cuscaden Rd, in the Orchard Rd area. The best value is the dinner buffet for S$95.

Other International Food

Hard Rock Cafe (☎ 235 5232), 50 Cuscaden Rd, near the corner of Orchard and Tanglin Rds, is popular for American-style steaks, BBQ grills and ribs. Main meals cost around S$20, and snacks such as burgers cost around S$8. The restaurant finishes around 10.30 pm when the bands start, but there is a small snack bar that stays open.

Bob's Tavern (☎ 467 2419), 17A Lorong Liput, Holland Village, to the west of the city, is an English-style pub popular with expats who for some reason miss English food. It does good steaks, fish & chips etc. Main meals cost around S$20. You can drink at the bar, or dine outside on the verandah.

Singapore steak houses are mostly run by chains such as the *Ponderosa* (☎ 336 0139) in the 02-13 Plaza Singapura, 68 Orchard Rd; 02-232 Marina Square; and 02-20 Raffles City shopping centre in the colonial district. A steak and a salad bar serving costs around S$20. The *Sizzler* chain is also moving into Singapore, but the biggest chain is *Jack's Place* with restaurants all over town, including 03-18/19 Wisma Atria, 435 Orchard Rd, and 01-01 Bras Basah Complex in the colonial district. Grills cost S$16 to S$22, while pasta and chicken dishes cost around S$12.

Many other cuisines are represented in Singapore. For German food, there is the *Brauhaus Restaurant & Pub* (☎ 250 3116), United Square, 101 Thomson Rd, to the north of the city centre. The *Treffpunct Cafe*, B2-09 Tanglin Shopping Centre in the Orchard Rd area, is a small deli serving German sausages and the like.

Istanbul Corner, 01-11 Cuppage Plaza, 5 Koek Rd, right near the corner of Orchard Rd, is one of the few Middle Eastern restaurants and is pretty cheap.

El Felipes Cantina (☎ 468 1520), 34 Lorong Mambong in Holland Village, is an old favourite that has large serves and moderate prices. Tex-Mex dishes cost around S$12 to S$15, and innovative mains with a Spanish touch are slightly more expensive. Next door, the similar *Cha Cha Cha* (☎ 462 1650), 32 Lorong Mambong in Holland Village, is the most popular Mexican restaurant in town, as much for the margaritas as the good food. *Chili's Bar & Grill*, 75 Boat Quay near Chinatown, has American grills with overtones of Tex-Mex and is moderately priced.

Saxophone Bar & Grill (☎ 235 8385), 23 Cuppage Terrace just off Orchard Rd, is a pleasant place to dine al fresco and listen to the music coming from inside. The food is French/continental and expensive.

Bastiani's (☎ 339 0392), 01-13 Clarke Quay, is a wine merchants with a very chic wine bar where high fliers like to be seen. Their wine buffet on Thursday and Friday nights for S$45 has cheese, antipasto, meats and a number of varieties of wine included in the price.

Alkaff Mansions (☎ 278 6979), west of the city at 10 Telok Blangah Green, has ambience plus-plus-plus. This restored old mansion offers Dutch rijsttafel (buffet 'rice table') with an endless parade of dishes served with a touch of colonial theatre for a whopping S$65 – this is popular with tour groups. Much cheaper but still allowing you

PETER TURNER

PETER TURNER

Brunei

Top & Bottom: Two views of the stunning Omar Ali Saifuddin Mosque, one of the most impressive structures in the east

HUGH FINLAY

SUE TAN

PETER TURNER

Brunei

Top: Chinese opera is performed at the Chinese Temple in Bandar Seri Begawan.
Bottom Left: The Chinese Temple has colourful tilework and carved wood.
Bottom Right: Kampung Ayer is a village on stilts on the Brunei River in BSB.

to take in the serene surroundings and the graciousness of the mansion are the western and Asian buffets for S$28 for lunch and S$35 for dinner.

BREAKFAST, SNACKS & DELIS

The big international hotels have their large international breakfast buffets of course (around S$20 to S$25) but there are still a few old coffee shops which do cheap Chinese and Indian breakfasts – take your pick of dosa and curry or *yu-tiao* and hot soy milk.

Roti chanai with a mild curry dip is a delicious and economical breakfast available at *Sahib Restaurant*, 129 Bencoolen St, in the cheap hotel area. Most of the old coffee shops will rustle you up toast and kaya (egg and coconut jam) without too much difficulty.

There are many places which do a fixed-price breakfast – continental or American. Try the *Silver Spoon Coffee House* at B1-05 Park Mall, 9 Penang Rd, off Orchard Rd. *McDonald's* and *A&W* do fast-food breakfasts: you can have a McDonald's 'big breakfast' for S$3.90. In Bencoolen St, the *Golden Dragon Inn* is a Chinese coffee shop on the 2nd floor of the Fortune Centre that does a reasonable job of western grills. If you crave cholesterol for breakfast, ham and eggs costs only S$3, and later in the day steak or prawns with chips and eggs served on a sizzler costs S$6.

Of the hotel buffet breakfasts, *Coleman's Cafe* (S$13.50) in the Peninsula Hotel and *Cafe Victoria* (S$18) in the Carlton Hotel are two good places in the colonial district.

One of the nicest breakfasts is undoubtedly *Breakfast with the Birds* (☎ 265 0022) at Jurong Bird Park. The buffet breakfast costs S$12.36 (admission is extra), the waffles are great and the birds will tell your fortune for free.

For western-style pastries, head for the *Café d'Orient de Delifrance* at Peranakan Place on Orchard Rd – the croissants and coffee are hard to beat for breakfast. This is the original store with the best setting, but you can find branches everywhere in Singapore.

Old Chang Kee is a chain that specialises in that old favourite – curry puffs. There is one at Lau Pa Sat, on Raffles Quay, and at the corner of McKenzie and Niven Rds, near Selegie Rd in the colonial district. On the opposite corner, the *Selera Restaurant*, 15 McKenzie Rd, is the best place in town for curry puffs. Try their range, washed down with coffee in an old-style kopi tiam. The small *L E Cafe* at 264 Middle Rd, under the Sun Sun Hotel almost at Selegie Rd, is an old-fashioned place with European and oriental cakes and pastries for take-aways.

Singapore has plenty of delis that cater for lunching office workers and snacking shoppers. In the Orchard Rd area, *Aroma's Deli*, 01-05 Tanglin Shopping Centre on Tanglin Rd, has good coffee and a changing deli menu. *Seah Street Deli* in the Raffles Hotel is slightly misnamed. This is Singapore's answer to a New York deli – pastrami, bagels and rye at higher than average prices but still excellent.

HIGH TEA

Most of the coffee shops in the big hotels do 'high tea', featuring local cakes and snacks and all the tea or coffee you can drink. They are usually buffet affairs held in the afternoon, around 4 pm of course, and are good value and delightful eating experiences. Add 14% to all the following prices.

Cafe Oriental in the Amara Hotel near Chinatown has a Nonya buffet, one of the most popular cuisines for high tea, for S$10 from 3 to 6 pm during the week.

The *Coffee Lounge* at the exclusive Goodwood Park Hotel in the Orchard Rd area has a good Nonya kueh buffet from 3 to 5.30 pm for S$13.80. The *Cafe Espresso* at the Goodwood Park has an English high tea for S$18.50.

The *Bar & Billiard Room* at the Raffles Hotel has high tea from 3.30 to 5 pm featuring Asian and continental food. Though expensive at S$21, it is one of the most affordable things you can do at the Raffles.

Coleman's Cafe in the Peninsula Hotel, just west of the Padang, is particularly good value at S$7.50 for a range of savoury hawker favourites, but only on Saturdays from 3.15 to 6 pm.

The *Kaspia Bar* at the Hilton does a good English high tea from 3 to 6 pm on weekdays. Buttered crumpets, scones with jam and cream, sandwiches and cheeses are featured. It costs S$16.50.

The *Melting Pot Cafe* at the Concorde Hotel, west of Chinatown, has the longest high tea in town – from noon to 5 pm on weekends – for an afternoon of decadence costing S$13.80.

CYBERCAFES

High-tech Singapore is jumping on the Internet bandwagon as the government exhorts the nation to surf the net and look for new business opportunities. Cybercafes seem to be springing up everywhere, though food definitely takes a back seat to the information superhighway.

The *CyberNet Cafe* (☎ 324 4361), 57 Tanjong Pagar Rd in Chinatown, has a bank of terminals for S$10 per hour plus S$2 registration fee. A tutorial session for beginners costs S$15 per hour. Coffee, soft drinks and a very limited selection of snacks are available. It is open 11 am to 9 pm Monday to Saturday, 2 to 7 pm on Sundays.

The *cafe@boatquay* (☎ 230 0140), 82 Boat Quay at the North Bridge Rd end, is a geek escape in the liveliest restaurant and bar strip in Singapore. It is open daily from 8 am to midnight and connection time is S$10/hour. A wide variety of sandwiches, pastries, desserts and drinks, including beer, are served. Everything attracts a 14% tax and service charge.

SUPERMARKETS

Singapore has plenty of supermarkets with everything from French wine and Australian beer to yoghurt, muesli, cheese and ice cream. *Cold Storage* is one of largest supermarket chains and they have well-stocked supermarkets in the basements of Takashimaya at Ngee Ann City and Centrepoint, both on Orchard Rd. Another is at Bugis Junction on Victoria St in the colonial district.

For late night groceries, *Smart*, on the northern side of the Marina Square complex, just west of the Padang, is open 24 hours. 7-Eleven stores are found all over town. In the colonial district you'll find one at 75 Victoria St, and on Orchard Rd in the Centrepoint complex.

Entertainment

Singapore's nightlife is burgeoning, as the young middle class spends its increasing wealth on entertainment. It's not of the Bangkok sex and sin variety, nor does a wild club scene exist, but the huge number of bars and discos are becoming increasingly sophisticated.

Many of the casual, smaller bars springing up everywhere have live music. Boat Quay is packed nightly until the early hours of the morning, but Orchard Rd and Chinatown also have their fair share of good bars. Smoking is permitted in bars, though if food is also served smoking is restricted until after meal hours. For better bands, you have to go to the clubs and discos, where a cover charge normally applies, dress is smart casual, drinks are expensive and the bands mostly play covers. Almost every four-star hotel has a Filipino band playing in the lobby, every five-star hotel has a jazz band in the lobby, while even many three-star hotels can muster up a piano bar.

Highbrow entertainment in the form of classical music, ballet and theatre can be enjoyed in Singapore, as well as Chinese opera and tourist-oriented cultural shows.

The free tourist magazines and the local newspapers have limited entertainment sections. The *Straits Times* is good for cultural and special events happening in Singapore. *Eight Days*, the weekly television and entertainment magazine, has the best listings. For nightlife look out for the free *I-S Magazine*.

BARS, BANDS & DISCOS

The time to drink is during the happy hours, usually around 5 to 8 pm, when drinks are as cheap as half price. Though most of the bars also serve food, the serious drinking is done outside meals times – you can grab a stool at the bar anytime.

Many bars feature bands. Imports still dominate – mostly Filipino bands and occasionally western musicians – playing jazz, pop covers, old favourites or even something more risqué like the blues. Singapore has hardcore bands like Stompin' Ground, but they won't be playing in Orchard Rd. It is difficult to see original Singaporean performers singing about life in the HDB estates, or dissatisfaction with the oppressive nature of Singaporean society, but they do exist and Singaporean music is developing its own identity. *Substation* in Armenian St in the colonial district occasionally puts on concerts of original local performers. Popular artists such as Dick Lee and Kopi Kat Klan laid the foundation for local performers singing songs with Asian themes and a Singaporean voice. The local recording scene is expanding but still nascent.

Singapore has no shortage of discos. They tend to be big on decor and are yuppie hangouts with strict dress codes. A few dance party clubs exit but they are fairly tame. A cover charge of around S$15 to S$20 applies on weekdays and S$20 to S$30 on weekends, but this usually includes the first drink. Women often pay less.

Some venues don't have a cover charge, but drinks are expensive and you can expect to pay around S$8 for a glass of beer. Those that do have a cover charge usually provide the first drink free. For most venues, a 10% service charge and 4% government tax are added to the drinks and the cover charge. Most have happy hours until around 8 pm, when the beers are up to half price, but the music doesn't start until later.

Orchard Rd

The Orchard Rd area is still the main centre for nightlife, with a host of bars and pubs mainly in the hotels and hidden away in the shopping centres.

One of the biggest discos, *Fire*, 04-19 Orchard Plaza, 150 Orchard Rd, is teenage techno heaven. The cover charge is S$12 for girls (S$21 on weekends), S$15 for boys (S$24 on weekends). Under the same management and the favourite in Singapore at the moment is *Sparks*, Level 7, Ngee Ann City. The dance floor jumps to the biggest music system in town, and everything stops for the dazzling laser show. For something quieter, other bars here include the *Jazz Evergreen*. The *World Music Bar* also gets some interesting bands. Cover charges range from $15 during the week to $25 on weekends.

The Gate at the Orchard Hotel is an attempted copy of a London club and attracts a moneyed crowd. The price of the drinks almost matches that of the clientele's designer clothes. Under 23s are discouraged and cover charges range from $15 to $25 for Saturday entry.

Other discos are *Chinoiserie* in the Hyatt Regency and *Xanadu* in the Shangri-La Hotel, both upmarket places that attract a wealthy clientele.

Orchard Towers at 400 Orchard Rd has a concentration of venues. It has been tagged the 'Four Floors of Whores', which, though there are a few bar girls, makes it sound more risqué than it is. *Top Ten* on the 4th floor is a large barn of a place with Manhattan skyline decor and an affluent clientele. It is primarily a disco but a band alternates brackets. Entry costs S$22 for the first drink on Fridays, S$28 on Saturdays and S$17 for the rest of the week. *Ginivy*, on the 2nd floor of Orchard Towers, has two types of music – country and western. It's a casual place with middle-aged cowboys and a smattering of bar girls. In a similar vein but smaller and quieter is *FB's* on the 3rd floor, featuring football and Fosters.

Anywhere, 04-08 Tanglin Shopping Centre, 19 Tanglin Rd, is a long-running rock'n'roll place. The band, Tania, has been playing here for over 15 years and features a cross-dressing lead singer. The band has a regular following of mostly expats and can belt out a song when they try. This place has a casual, convivial atmosphere and no cover charge.

Hard Rock Cafe, 50 Cuscaden Rd, has the usual rock memorabilia and good atmosphere. It has better bands than most venues, and occasionally imports some big names from overseas. The music and cover charge starts, and the ash trays come out, after 10.30 pm when the dining stops. Entry is S$15, except Sundays – otherwise get there early. It stays open until around 2 or 3 pm.

Opposite the Hard Rock Cafe in the basement of the Ming Arcade, *Cave Man* is a cool little bar with graffiti everywhere and modern music on the jukebox. Not a lot happens, but it's a casual bar for conversation. For something completely different, the *Fame Party Pub* on the 7th floor is a large Indian disco with Hindi pop tunes.

Brannigan's in the Hyatt Regency is a popular, casual pick-up spot, with a mixed clientele and its fair share of bar girls. Good bands play until 1 or 2 pm, and happy hours are from 5 to 8 pm. It is packed on weekends.

Emerald Hill Rd has a collection of bars in the renovated terraces just up from Orchard Rd. *No 5* at, you guessed it, 5 Emerald Hill Rd, is very popular with a largely tourist clientele. Though the bar is crowded, you can choose to drink at the tables outside, while acoustic music plays upstairs. Next door at No 7, *Que Pasa* is a popular tapas bar with a Spanish theme, while next along at No 9, *The Den* has a Movie House bar upstairs. Upstairs at Peranakan Place on the corner of Emerald Hill and Orchard Rds, *Papa Joe's* is another popular place with a covers band on the weekend and a first drink cover charge.

Nearby, the *Saxophone Bar & Grill*, 23 Cuppage Terrace near the corner of Orchard Rd, is a small place with some good blues, jazz and funk music. It's so small that the band has to play on a platform behind the bar, but you can sit outside and listen to the music after the dining finishes. There is no cover charge.

The *Tapas Bar* at the Omni Marco Polo Hotel, 247 Tanglin Rd, is another very popular bar with a Latin theme and a lively dance floor. The band has salsa and flamenco rhythms, and the tapas buffet for S$5 is good, though not exactly Spanish.

Fabrice's World Music Bar at the Marriott Hotel, 320 Orchard Rd, is home to some interesting bands with music ranging from reggae and African to Latin American.

The River

The renovated banks of the Singapore River in the centre of town are the happening place in Singapore, especially Boat Quay. Further along the river, Clarke Quay is less frenetic but also has its fair share of watering holes that are popular on the weekend.

Boat Quay Is there life after Boat Quay? This place has become so incredibly popular that the rest of Singapore seems dead in comparison. The crowds start coming around 6 pm for a quiet drink or a meal, and keep growing through the night. Weekends are very busy until 2 or 3 am, while weekdays are marginally quieter and most bars close by 1 am. Boat Quay attracts everyone from the rich and famous to young Singaporean kids vomiting into the gutter after a night of over-indulgence.

Boat Quay has so many bars that you can just wander along until one takes your fancy. At the eastern end, *Harry's* at No 28 gets going early in the evening as city workers flock for happy hour until 8 pm. Corporate high fliers and wannabees, mostly expat, meet over beers and are joined later in the evening by a mixed, upmarket crowd who come for the jazz bands. Singapore cocktail barmen haven't yet invented the Nick Leeson Slammer, but if they did it would be at Harry's or *Escobar* a few doors down at No 37. These places finish up around midnight.

Just around the corner, *Molly Malone's*, 42 Circular Rd, is an Irish pub and a good place for a change of pace. It has a real pub atmosphere with Guinness on tap and traditional Irish bands upstairs. It closes at midnight, and on Sundays.

Back on Boat Quay, *Culture Club* at No 38 sometimes has decent bands, as does the faster paced *Zappa Rock Bar* at No 45. *Exclusiv 56* at No 56 is a quieter bar with an older clientele and jazz on the jukebox.

Rootz at No 60 is popular with young Malays and has reggae and hip-hop music.

Further along are the *Riverbank* at No 69 and *Shoreline*, very popular with young Singaporeans. They stay open until 2 pm during the week and 3 pm on weekends when everything else is closed.

Right at the end of Boat Quay near the bridge, *cafe@boatquay* at No 82 is a cybercafe with banks of terminals for surfing the net. It closes at midnight.

Clarke Quay Though the quieter cousin of Boat Quay, Clarke Quay has a good selection of places for a beer. The bars are not so overwhelmed by crowds and they tend to be more convivial.

The *Crazy Elephant*, right next to the river at Trader's Market, is the most happening bar at Clarke Quay. It has some decent rock bands and plenty of room on the pavement outside for chatting. The *Wild West Tavern* upstairs is decked out like a saloon and is popular for country music of sorts, though the band seems more intent to play old pop covers. Also upstairs, the quieter *Charleston* has rockabilly, jazz and Irish music from mostly local bands. It's a low-key pub with a pool table and cheap beers. It's also a reasonable place to escape the yuppie crowds, which tend to head to *JP Bastiani*, a chic wine bar nearby.

The towkangs moored on the river at Boat Quay house moderately priced restaurants with bars that sometimes have acoustic music. Music also plays at the central square near the Satay Club.

Chinatown

The Tanjong Pagar area in Chinatown has a number of pubs in the renovated terraces, though they have dropped in popularity and Boat Quay has grabbed much of the clientele. Tanjong Pagar Rd, Duxton Rd and Duxton Hill all have a number of bars, and the beers are a little cheaper than elsewhere.

Duxton Hill has a string of bars that are pleasant, if relatively quiet places to have a drink. *Elvis' Place*, 1A Duxton Hill, is lined with Elvis memorabilia, though they have foregone the 50s music and it is much like any other bar. The *Cable Car* at No 2 is done out like a San Francisco cable car, while further along at No 6, *Duxton's Chicago Bar* is another drinking hole that occasionally has bands. The *Flag & Whistle* at No 10 is an English-style pub which is great for conversation – you could hear a pin drop.

The pick of the pubs in this area is the *JJ Mahoney Pub* at 58 Duxton Rd. It has a big range of beers, including Bass on tap, a band on the ground floor, a games room bar on the 2nd floor and karaoke on the 3rd.

The liveliest nightspot in Tanjong Pagar is *Moon*, 62 Tanjong Pagar Rd, a small but happening place with a lively dance floor and a club atmosphere. It is open until 2 am Monday to Thursday, and until 3 am on Fridays and Saturdays when a S$23 cover charge will buy you entry and two drinks.

Closer to the Outram Park MRT station, the *Butterfly Bar & Cafe*, 55 Keong Saik Rd, is a funky little place with post-modern decor and happy hours until 8 pm.

Colonial District

Of course you can have a drink at the *Raffles*, at the Long Bar or the Bar & Billiard Room, where that infamous tiger was supposedly shot. One of the favourite pastimes in the elegant Long Bar is throwing peanut shells on the floor – swinging stuff. The billiard room is laid back, and you can recline in the wicker chairs, tickle the ivories or chug-a-lug outside on the patio. In the evenings both bars have light jazz from 7.30 pm, and serve food. Sip your expensive drinks – there are no happy hours.

The *Compass Rose* on the 70th floor of the Westin Stamford Hotel, 2 Stamford Rd, has stunning views and prices to match. After 8.30 pm a minimum charge of S$15 applies. This is not the place to don jeans. *Somerset's*, in the Western Plaza next door, is a jazz venue.

The bar in the lobby at the *Marina Mandarin* has jazz in the evenings in salubrious and impressive surroundings. Nearby, the new Millenia Walk complex at the Ritz Carlton Hotel is set to house a branch of the *Planet Hollywood* chain.

A less pretentious and much cheaper place to drink is at New Bugis St. You can have a beer at the food stalls under the stars in the evening until 3 am, or whenever everyone goes home. If you want to pay more, there are a couple of places that have karaoke and bad Filipino bands. For something different, the *Boom Boom Room* (☎ 339 8187), 3 New Bugis St, is a supper club affair with a cabaret and Singapore's only regular stand-up comic. It's different and the cover charge is S$17.

Other Areas

Zouk, 17-21 Jiak Kim St, near the Havelock Rd hotels, is a legendary dance club. Housed in an old godown by the Singapore River, it has the dubious honour of being busted and closed for drugs, but has reopened and is as popular as ever. A cover charge of around S$25 applies on weekends, S$15 on weekdays.

Not far from Arab St on Beach Rd, The Concourse shopping centre is home to a couple of retrospective theme pubs on the basement level – the 50s *Elvis at The Concourse* and the *Pyschedelic Cafe Pub*, decked out with 60s memorabilia.

Wala Wala Bar & Grill, on Lorong Mambong out in Holland Village to the west of the city, has one of those sin machines that were banned for many years in Singapore – a jukebox. It is an American-style restaurant and bar popular with expats. Happy hours are from 4 to 9 pm. *Chaplin's* is another on Lorong Liput, the continuation of Lorong Mambong, if you are looking to kick on after a meal at one of the many restaurants here, though the restaurants themselves, such as *Cha Cha Cha* are popular watering holes. For a quiet drink in English pub ambience, try *Bob's Tavern*, 17A Lorong Liput.

CINEMA

There are plenty of cinemas in Singapore, with the main fare being Hollywood hits. Chinese kungfu films and all-singing, all-dancing Indian movies are also popular. Recently, alternative cinema has found an outlet in Singapore: the Cathay Cinema's *Picture House*, 6 Handy Rd, at the city end of Orchard Rd, regularly shows art house movies, as does *Jade Classics* in Shaw Towers, 100 Beach Rd. Multi-theatre cineplexes are at Shaw Towers on Beach Rd, and at the Shaw Centre on Scotts Rd, near the corner of Orchard Rd. *United Artists Theatre* is a four theatre cineplex at Bugis Junction on Victoria St.

Singapore has an annual film festival and the various expatriate clubs also show movies. The Alliance Française often has movies open to the public, some with English subtitles.

THEATRE

Singapore's nascent theatre scene is starting to come of age as Singaporeans become more interested in expressing, and discovering, their identity. More local plays are being produced, and alternative theatre venues such as the *Substation* (☎ 337 7800), 45 Armenian St in the colonial district, are helping to foster an interest in theatre. Plays, workshops, poetry readings and visual art exhibits are held here, and at the back the Garden has craft and art works for sale.

The main venues for theatre are the *Drama Centre* (☎ 336 0005) on Canning Rise (northwest of Fort Canning Park), the *Victoria Theatre* (☎ 336 2151), Empress Place (opposite Boat Quay) and *Kallang Theatre* (☎ 345 8488), opposite the National Stadium on Stadium Rd. Performances range from local and overseas plays performed by a variety of local theatre companies, to the blockbusters such as *Phantom of the Opera* and *Les Misérables*. Some of the hotels, such as the Hilton and Raffles, also stage theatre shows from time to time.

The Singapore Festival of Arts, which features many drama performances, is held every second year around June. Music, art and dance are also represented at the festival, which includes a Fringe Festival featuring plenty of street performances.

CHINESE OPERA

In Chinatown or in the older streets of Serangoon Rd and Jalan Besar, you may chance upon a *wayang* – a brilliantly costumed Chinese street opera. In these noisy and colourful extravaganzas, overacting is very important; there's nothing subtle about it at all. The best time of year to see one is around September during the Festival of Hungry Ghosts. They are often listed in the 'What's On' section of the *Straits Times*.

CLASSICAL MUSIC

Highbrow entertainment of the western kind can be found at the *Victoria Concert Hall* (☎ 338 1230), the home of the Singapore Symphony Orchestra opposite the Padang. Tickets are very reasonably priced starting at S$5, or more depending on the visiting musicians.

CULTURAL SHOWS

At the Mandarin Hotel on Orchard Rd there is an ASEAN night every night at 8 pm. It features dancing and music from all over the region. The show costs S$24 for adults and S$15 for children; including dinner it is S$48 for adults and S$26 for children.

OTHER ENTERTAINMENT

The big hotels have cocktail lounges and there are some Chinese nightclubs scattered around the city. The *Neptune Theatre Restaurant*, Collyer Quay in the city centre, has a Chinese cabaret, Cantonese food and hostesses. It is glitzy but just this side of seedy and the shows are as risqué as Singapore will allow. The *Red Lantern Beer Garden* downstairs is definitely seedy and has a band in the evening, and cheap meals, good prices for beer and a band at lunchtime. *Lido Palace* in the Concorde Hotel on Outram Rd also has a Chinese cabaret and dance hostesses. In the same vein is *Golden Million Nite-Club* in the Peninsula Hotel on Coleman St, just north of the river.

If you're worried that Singapore is simply too squeaky clean for belief, you may be relieved to hear that there's a real locals-only, low-class, red-light district stretching along the laneway behind Desker Rd between Jalan Besar and Serangoon Rd in Little India. Rows of blockhouse rooms have women standing in doorways while a constant stream of men wander past. Outside, hawkers sell condoms and potency pills, and makeshift tables are set up with card games to gamble on.

Desker Rd is also the successor to Bugis St and late in the evenings transvestites strut their stuff. It doesn't have the atmosphere of old Bugis St, but it is lively and the coffee shops here, such as the *Choon Huat* at 2 Desker Rd and the *Hong Fa* nearby, are interesting places to sit out on the pavement for noodles or a beer.

The predominantly Malay district of Geylang, east of the city, is full of houses and bars operated by organised Chinese gangs who 'employ' women of all nationalities, including Indonesians, Indians and the occasional Caucasian. They are found in the *lorongs* off Sims Ave. Of course, Singapore caters to business needs, and there is no shortage of 'health centres' and escort services.

Shopping

One of Singapore's major attractions is shopping. The sheer range is impressive and prices for many goods are still competitive with other discount centres, but these days, with tariffs dropping everywhere around the world, Singapore is not the bargain centre it once was. 'Duty free' and 'free port' are somewhat throwaway terms. Remember that not everything is loaded down with import duty in your own country, and Singapore also has some local industries to protect.

Before you leap on anything as a great bargain, it pays to know prices at home. Depending on your country of residence, Singapore may have few bargains to offer. Americans, for example, will find cheaper prices at home for many goods.

Shop around to find out what the 'real' price is. In Singapore, fixed price shops are increasingly becoming the norm but bargaining is still often required, especially in the tourist areas. Many of the small shops, such as electronic and souvenir shops, don't display prices and you should bargain at these outlets. Even when prices are displayed it doesn't always mean that prices are fixed. If you are unsure, ask if the price is the 'best price'.

Shop around and compare prices. Try the big fixed-price department stores where the price is unlikely to be rock bottom, but most likely in the ball park.

Given the existence of larger discount stores offering fixed prices, if you are not practised at bargaining and don't know prices it is better to frequent those outlets. Except for antiques, handicrafts and souvenirs, where bargaining is almost always required, good deals can be found without having to haggle.

Singapore has consumer laws and the government wants to promote the island as a good place to shop, however, you should be wary when buying. Make sure you get exactly what you want before you leave the store.

Guarantees are an important consideration if you're buying electronic gear, watches, cameras or the like. Make sure the guarantee is international and that it is filled out correctly with the shop's name and the serial number of the item written down.

Check for the right voltage and cycle when you buy electrical goods. Singapore, Australia, New Zealand, Hong Kong and the UK use 220 to 240 volts at 50 cycles while the US, Canada and Japan use 110V to 120V at 60 cycles. Check the plug – most shops will fit the correct plug for your country.

If you have any problems take your purchases back to the store, though many shops, particularly the small ones, are not noted for after-sales service. Otherwise contact the Consumers' Association of Singapore (☎ 270 5433) or the Singapore Tourist Promotion Board. The STPB's *Singapore Official Guide* lists 'errant traders' that have been found guilty of tourist rip-offs. Traders in Lucky Plaza on Orchard Rd and Sim Lim Tower in the colonial district seem to figure regularly.

WHERE TO SHOP

Singapore is almost wall-to-wall with shops, and while there are certain places worth heading to for certain items, shopping centres usually have a mixture of stores selling electronics, clothes, sporting goods etc. Shopping centres are found all over town, but of course Orchard Rd is famous for its profusion of shopping possibilities.

Orchard Rd

The major shopping complexes on and around Orchard Rd have a mind-boggling array of department stores and shops selling whatever you want. The prices aren't necessarily the best, but the range of goods is superb, and this is certainly a good place for high-quality, brand-name items.

Plaza Singapura on Orchard Rd is good for golfing gear and musical instruments. Orchard Point, Orchard Plaza and Cuppage Plaza are clustered together and have a variety of shops and food outlets. Centrepoint is one of the liveliest shopping centres, with good bookshops on the 4th floor, and Marks & Spencer and Robinson's department stores.

On the corner of Orchard Rd and Orchard Link is the Ngee Ann City, which houses the large Takashimaya department store. The basement is great for food, especially Japanese food, while the individual shops are dominated by exclusive outlets. Paragon and the Promenade are two other up-market shopping centres with many designer boutiques.

Further along and much more downmarket is Lucky Plaza. It is a bustling, hustling place with dozens of shops crammed together. It is good for cheap clothes, bags and shoes, but bargain hard and shake off the touts and pesky tailors. Opposite Lucky Plaza is Wisma Atria, which has an Isetan department store and boutiques. On the corner of Scotts and Orchard Rds is Tang's, one of Singapore's oldest, establishment department stores.

Scotts Rd is another good place to shop. The Shaw Centre has the large Isetan department shore. Also on Scotts Rd, the Scotts Shopping Centre has plenty of boutiques and an excellent food court in the basement. The Far East Plaza is a big centre with electronics and a bit of everything.

At the top of Orchard Rd, the Far East Shopping Centre has some sporting stores that are good for golfing needs and bicycles. The Forum Galleria is good for toys and children's gear.

Tanglin Rd is quieter, and the main shopping centre is the Tanglin Shopping Centre, which has a good selection of expensive Asian arts and antiques. Well worth a browse but bargain if you want to buy.

Colonial District

In the colonial district, Raffles City is architecturally one of the most impressive shopping centres, and has some interesting small shops. Sogo department store is here. Nearby, Marina Square has a huge array of shops in a massive complex which includes three hotels and plenty of restaurants.

Bugis Junction is a new shopping centre on Victoria St that has breathed some life into the area. Built on the old Bugis St above the Bugis MRT station, it comprises shophouse recreations covered by an atrium, the large Seiyu department store and the Hotel Inter-Continental.

On Bencoolen St in the Little India area, Sim Lim Square is renown for computers and electronic goods. Sim Lim Tower across Rochor Canal Rd is a big electronic centre with everything from capacitors to audio and video gear. They are popular with tourists looking for bargains so the first asking price is often higher than elsewhere.

Chinatown

Chinatown is a popular shopping area with more local flavour. The People's Park Complex and the People's Park Centre are good places to shop. They form a large complex with plenty of electronics, clothing and department stores. The electronics are only as cheap as you make them. The Chinatown Complex has an interesting market for everyday goods and cheap shops.

Chinatown Point specialises in craft shops and the quiet Riverwalk Galleria has some more arts and craft stores. Smith St has some craft and souvenir shops.

Other Areas

Little India has lots of oddities, and the Serangoon Plaza department stores have electrical and everyday goods at honest prices. They have proved so popular for cheap electronics, clothes and household goods, that the large Mustafa Centre department store has opened around the corner on Syed Alwi Rd.

Arab St is good for textiles, basketware and South-East Asian crafts.

Housing estate areas have plenty of shopping for cheaper clothes and household items and bargaining is the exception rather than the rule. Try Ang Mo Kio, Bedok, Clementi, Toa Payoh, Geylang – all easily reached by the MRT. Tampines has the big Century Park shopping mall.

WHAT TO BUY

From clothes irons to luggage and from oriental rugs to model aeroplanes, Singapore's shops have whatever you want. The following information, only a sample of Singapore's shopping possibilities, suggests places to start looking.

Arts, Crafts & Antiques

Singapore has no shortage of arts and antiques, mostly Chinese but also from all over Asia.

Tanglin Shopping Centre on Tanglin Rd in the Orchard Rd area is good for quality but expensive arts and antiques. The Singapore Handicraft Centre in Chinatown Point has dozens of shops selling Chinese lacquerware, pottery, jewellery etc, but there are some Indonesian and other Asian crafts as well.

Arab St is a good place for South-East Asian crafts such as caneware, batik and leather goods. In Chinatown around Smith St, small shops sell goods ranging from trinkets and souvenirs, basketware, fans and silk dressing gowns, to more expensive curios and antique pottery.

Cameras & Film

Cameras are available throughout the city. Camera equipment is not such a bargain these days as camera prices are often as heavily discounted in the west as in Singapore or Hong Kong.

When buying film, bargain for lower prices if you're buying in bulk – 10 films cost less than 10 times one film. Developing is cheap all over Singapore, eg a roll of print film costs about S$2 for developing and 20c to 40c per print. Developing and mounting for a 36-exposure slide film costs around S$12.

Clothes & Shoes

Clothes and shoes – imported, locally made and made to measure – are widely available. Singapore is not as cheap as most other Asian countries, but the range is excellent, especially for brand-name items.

Many of the department stores have reasonably priced clothes. Nison in the People's Park Complex in Chinatown has cheap clothes. Lucky Plaza on Orchard Rd is a good centre for cheap clothes and shoes, but bargain hard for everything. The Peninsula Shopping Centre is good for men's shoes.

Wisma Atria, Orchard C&E and OG department store are good places on Orchard Rd for clothes.

Computers

Singapore is enforcing international copyright laws, so cheap software and software manuals are not so openly on display as in other Asian countries. The Funan Centre on North Bridge Rd, just east of Fort Canning Park, is the main computer centre, with dozens of computer shops on the top floors, as well as a large Challenger Superstore. The top floors of Sim Lim Square, on the corner of Bencoolen St and Rochor Canal Rd, are good for cheap computers and peripherals.

Electronic Goods

Sim Lim Square, on the corner of Bencoolen St and Rochor Canal Rd, has a concentrated range of electronics shops, and Sim Lim Tower, nearby on Jalan Besar, has everything from cassette players to capacitors, but be wary and be prepared to bargain hard. Plaza Singapura on Orchard Rd also has a number of shops selling electronic goods, but really you can buy electronic goods everywhere in Singapore.

Other

Guitars, keyboards, flutes, drums, electronic instruments, recording equipment etc are all good buys, though not necessarily as cheap as the country of origin. Good shops to try include: Swee Lee Company, No 03-09 Plaza Singapura, 68 Orchard Rd, and City Music, No 02-12 Peace Centre, 1 Sophia Rd, on the corner of Selegie Rd. Yamaha has a number of showrooms, including one on the 7th floor of Plaza Singapura in Orchard Rd.

Cheap pirated tapes are things of the past but legitimate tapes and CDs are reasonably priced. Tower Records on the 4th floor of the Pacific Plaza, 9 Scotts Rd near the corner of Orchard Rd, has the biggest and best selection at higher prices. MPH bookstore at 71-77 Stamford Rd in the colonial district has a good CD section upstairs.

For sporting goods, most of the department stores also have well-stocked sports sections. For general sports stores, try the Far East Shopping Centre and Plaza Singapura on Orchard Rd. Lucky Plaza on Orchard Rd also has sports shops including diving shops. For brand-name bicycles and components, try Soon Watt & Co, 482 Changi Rd.

Brunei

Brunei Darussalam

Brunei is a tiny Islamic sultanate lying in the north-eastern corner of Sarawak. Indeed, at just 5765 sq km, Brunei is one of the smallest countries in the world. It is also one of the wealthiest. And if this is not enough to pique your interest, Brunei becomes even more intriguing when you consider that this small strip of territory wedged in against the South China Sea by the sprawling landmass of Sarawak is all that remains of an empire that in the 16th century controlled all of Borneo.

The country's full name is Negara Brunei Darussalam, which is usually translated by the local tourist authorities as 'Brunei – the abode of peace'. Peaceful it certainly is. With alcohol virtually unobtainable, no nightlife to speak of, a political culture of quiet acquiescence to the edicts of the sultan and Islamic laws that, among other things, forbid boys and girls holding hands, about the only thing that cannot be counted on to be dull in Brunei is the weather.

In short, the 'abode of peace' is a little slice of contrived heaven – an Islamic Disneyland. And presiding over it all is the sultan. Most Bruneians seem to find this a satisfactory arrangement. God in this neck of the woods is less fire and brimstone than a benevolent despot, intolerant of political dissent perhaps, but free with his largesse and happy as long as he has the means to lavishly indulge his interests. These include a US$350 million palace; fleets of Italian exoticars and private aircraft; and his grand passion – a fabulous polo farm with 200 Argentine ponies, some enjoying air-conditioned stalls.

Fortune magazine has estimated the sultan's personal fortune at a shade over US$37 billion – making him one of the richest people in the world.

The money comes from oil, and the oil comes mainly from offshore wells at Seria and Muara. And to be fair, *everyone* in Brunei benefits from oil money. There are no taxes, there are pensions for all, free medical care, free schooling, free sport and leisure centres, cheap loans, subsidies for many purchases (including cars) and the highest minimum wages in the region.

Facts about Brunei

HISTORY

In the 15th and 16th centuries Brunei Darussalam, as it's formally known, was a considerable power in the area, and its rule extended throughout Borneo and into the Philippines.

The Spanish and the Portuguese were the first European visitors, arriving in the 16th century. The Spanish actually made a bid to take over but were soon ousted.

The arrival of the British in the guise of James Brooke, the first white raja of Sarawak, in the early 19th century, spelt the end of Brunei's power.

A series of 'treaties' was forced onto the sultan as James Brooke consolidated his hold over Kuching with the aim of developing commercial relationships and suppressing piracy, a favourite Bruneian and Dayak occupation (piracy was a favourite excuse for justifying European land grabs). The country was gradually whittled away until, with a final dash of absurdity, Limbang was ceded to Sarawak in 1890, thus dividing the country into two parts.

In 1929, just as Brunei was about to be swallowed up entirely, oil was discovered. The present sultan's father, who abdicated in 1967, kept Brunei out of the Malayan confederacy, preferring that the country remain a British protectorate, which it had been since 1888.

In 1962, in the lead-up to amalgamation with Malaysia, the British pressured Sultan Omar Saifuddin to hold elections. The opposition Ra'ayat Party, led by AM Azahari, which wanted to keep Brunei independent and make the sultan a constitutional monarch within a democracy, won an overwhelming victory. As the sultan's plans to take Brunei into union with Malaysia became clear, Azahari fled to the Philippines, from where he directed an armed rebellion with the support of Indonesia. The rebellion was quickly crushed with British military backing and the sultan later opted for independence from Malaysia, but the country has been under emergency laws ever since, though you'll see little evidence of this.

In early 1984 the popular sultan and *yang di-pertuan* (king), His Majesty Paduka Seri Beginda Sultan Haji Hassanal Bolkiah Mu'izzaddin Waddaulah, the 29th of his line, led his tightly ruled country somewhat reluctantly into complete independence from Britain. The 37-year-old leader rather enjoyed the English umbrella and colonial status, and independence was almost unwanted.

Since independence, Brunei has shown an increasing trend towards Islamic fundamentalism and is keen to counter growing modernisation and accompanying western values. Melayu Islam Beraja (MIB) is the national ideology, stressing Malay culture, Islam and monarchy, and is promulgated through the ministries of education, religious affairs and information. In 1991 the sale of alcohol was banned, stricter dress codes have been introduced and in 1992 MIB became a compulsory subject in schools.

At the same time, however, some commentators see a loosening of the sultan's autocratic grip on the country. Although the sultan once again renewed the emergency laws in 1995, in February of the same year he also allowed the Brunei Solidarity National Party to hold an inaugural assembly. Meanwhile, a government-appointed committee has recommended constitutional changes to allow for an elected parliament. This hardly amounts to a gathering tide of democratic reform, but it does indicate that the sultan perhaps is aware that, as an absolute Islamic monarchy, Brunei is out of step with its ASEAN neighbours and that in the long run reform of some kind is a necessity.

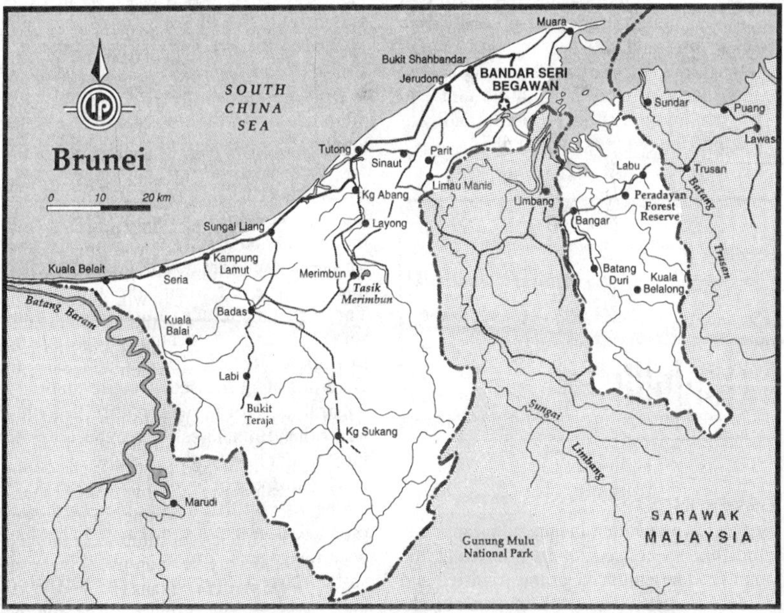

GEOGRAPHY

Brunei consists of two separate areas, bordered by the South China Sea to the north and bounded on all other sides by Sarawak. The western part of Brunei is divided into the three districts of Muara, around Bandar Seri Begawan, Tutong in the centre and Belait in the south-west. The terrain is hilly lowland, rising to around 300 metres in the interior. The eastern part of the country is Temburong district, consisting of a coastal plain rising to a height of 1841 metres at Bukit Pagon, the highest peak in the country. Four main rivers drain the country: the Belait, Tutong, Brunei and Temburong.

Brunei covers an area of 5765 sq km and the main towns are the capital, Bandar Seri Begawan, the oil town of Seria and the commercial town of Kuala Belait. Brunei is mainly jungle, and approximately 75% of the country is covered by forest.

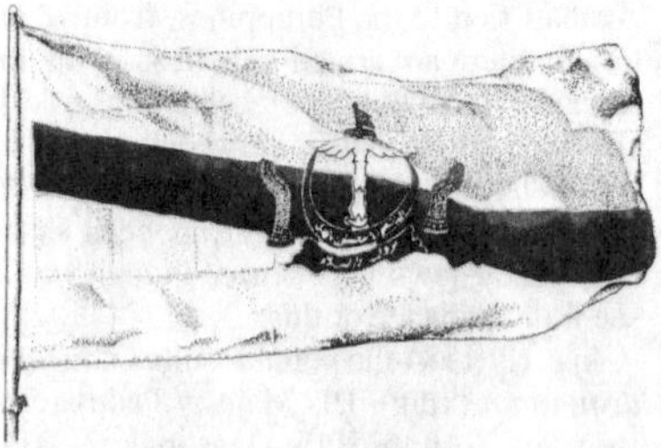

The national flag of Brunei

CLIMATE

The heaviest rainfall periods are from September to January, during the north-east monsoon, though Brunei doesn't really have marked wet and dry seasons and rainfall occurs throughout the year. Temperatures are consistently around 24°C minimum and 31°C maximum with an average humidity of 79%, making it a pretty warm place.

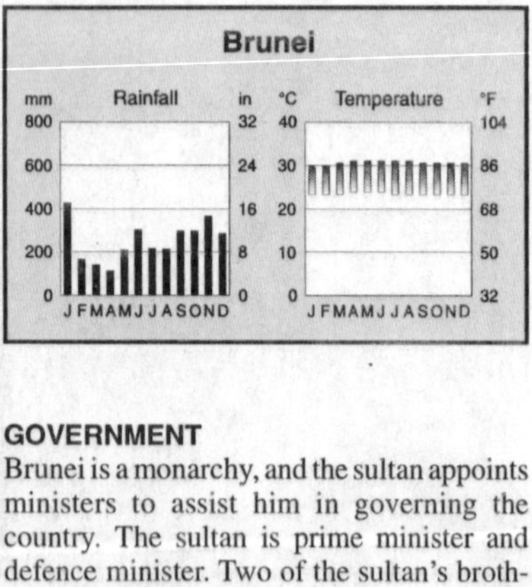

GOVERNMENT

Brunei is a monarchy, and the sultan appoints ministers to assist him in governing the country. The sultan is prime minister and defence minister. Two of the sultan's brothers are also ministers. Democracy is not on the government's agenda, and the only democratic elections ever held were in 1962.

Judicial power is vested in the Supreme Court – comprising the Court of Appeal and the High Court – and the Magistrate's Court. Islamic, or *syariah*, courts deal with offences against Islam committed by Muslims. The judicial system is loosely based on the British system, but the philosophy of MIB is being applied to the law and the appointment of British Hong Kong judges is being phased out.

Brunei is a member of ASEAN and enjoys close relations with both Malaysia and Singapore.

ECONOMY

Oil! The country is virtually dependent on the stuff, although some diversification plans for the economy are now being instituted for that fearsome day when the pump runs dry. These plans include more rice-farming, some forestry and eventual self-sufficiency in beef production. To this latter end, the government purchased a cattle station in Australia's Northern Territory, which is larger than Brunei itself! Fresh beef is flown into Bandar Seri Begawan daily.

The prospect of an oil-less Brunei is still a long way off. Brunei has increased its oil production in the 90s, and new fields have been discovered. Brunei is also one of the world's largest exporters of liquefied natural gas. A small amount of rubber is also exported.

The government, with Brunei Shell Petroleum (the only oil company there in any substantial way), is by far the country's largest employer. All government workers get subsidised holidays and trips to Mecca – which is probably not too bad providing you can organise a stopover in Bangkok en route.

The traditional pattern of agriculture in Brunei is that of shifting cultivation, which continues in the more remote areas. Farming is largely a part-time occupation and there are no large estates. About 80% of the country's food has to be imported.

POPULATION & PEOPLE

The total population of Brunei is about 260,000 and is composed of Malays (69%), Chinese (18%), Indians and around 14,000 Iban, Lun Bawang and other tribal people of the interior. There are also around 20,000 expatriate workers from Europe and elsewhere in Asia.

ARTS

During the height of the Brunei sultanates, brass and silver artisans produced work of fine design and great beauty. Brass gongs, cannons and household vessels, such as kettles and betel containers, were prized throughout Borneo and beyond. They were often embossed with designs of serpents and animals or verses from the Koran, and prized pieces were believed to have special powers. Cannons, in particular, were used not only for war but for paying dowries and for ceremonial purposes. Today they are family heirlooms and can be found in Malay homes or remote Dayak villages, where they have been given spiritual significance. The best collection of cannons can be seen in the Brunei Museum.

Artisans used the lost wax technique to cast brass, a method believed to have been introduced during the reign of Sultan Bolkiah, at the end of the 15th century. It declined with the fortunes of the Brunei sultanate, and the great brassware of Brunei is now a lost art.

Silverware was probably introduced from Java about the same time as brass casting, and the Portuguese explorer Pigafetta commented on the silver and gold vessels he found in Brunei in 1521. Silver smithing, like brass casting, was an inherited art and passed down through families and guilds located in Kampung Ayer. The exponents of silverwork these days are to be found at the Handicraft Centre, set up to preserve the dying crafts of Brunei.

The weaving art of *jong sarat* has survived, and jong sarat sarungs are still prized for ceremonial occasions. Jong sarat uses gold thread and coloured cotton woven on a loom in stylised floral designs known as *sukma-indera*. Bright colours are used, but sparingly, and the designs are restrained.

SOCIETY & CONDUCT

Bruneians are mostly Malay, and customs, beliefs and pastimes are very similar if not identical to those of the Malays of Peninsular Malaysia. *Adat*, or customary law, governs many of the ceremonies in Brunei, particularly royal ceremonies and state occasions. There is even a government department of *adat istiadat*, which is responsible for preserving ceremony and advising on protocol, dress and heraldry.

The usual Asian customs apply: only the right hand should be used for offering or passing something; pointing with the forefinger is rude and should be done with the thumb; beckoning someone is done with an open hand with the fingers waving downwards. Offering pork or alcohol to Muslims not only may cause offence – it is tempting them to break the law. Smoking and eating shellfish are tolerated but not considered the done thing. When entering a mosque or a house, remove your shoes first.

RELIGION

Brunei is quite a strict Muslim country, and a Ministry of Religious Affairs has been set up to foster and promote Islam. The ministry also has special officers who investigate breaches of Islamic law by Muslims, and apparently government men prowl the streets after dark looking for unmarried couples standing or sitting too close to each other. Getting nailed for this crime, known as *khalwat*, can mean imprisonment and a fine. The sale of alcohol is banned and non-Islamic restaurants (eg Chinese restaurants) display signs stating that they are not suitable for Muslims.

The constitution does allow other religions to be practised in the country in peace and harmony, and non-Muslim visitors need not worry about being spat upon and abused for being infidels. Bruneians are very friendly and hospital people, and not all are as zealous as the government.

LANGUAGE

The official language is Malay but English is widely spoken. Jawi, Malay written in Arabic script, is taught in schools, and most signs in the country are written in both Jawi and the Roman script.

Facts for the Visitor

HIGHLIGHTS

Most of the highlights of Brunei are in or close to Bandar Seri Begawan, the capital. The most impressive of Bandar's sights is the Omar Ali Saifuddin Mosque, a massive tribute to both Brunei's wealth and its devotion to Islam. Kampung Ayer, on the other hand, is a reminder of the days before Brunei struck it rich with oil money: a photogenic collection of villages on stilts on the Brunei River.

The pick of Brunei's museums is the Brunei Museum and the nearby Malay Technology Museum. Both are excellent, the first focussing on things Bruneian, the second on traditional Malay culture.

Attractions outside Bandar are minimal, but if you have time it's worth heading out to Jerudong, which has a massive amusement park (Jerudong Playground) and Jerudong Beach. Temburong, the eastern part of Brunei surrounded by Sarawak, makes for a good day trip from Bandar – the boat trip in itself is an attraction. There are jungle walks and an Iban longhouse at Temburong.

TOURIST OFFICES

There is an information desk at the airport, but the only decent publication available is the *Explore Brunei* booklet, which has a good map and useful information on sights and accommodation around Brunei.

VISAS

For visits of up to 14 days, visas are not necessary for citizens of New Zealand, Norway, France, Switzerland, Canada, Japan, Thailand, the Philippines, Indonesia, the Netherlands, Luxembourg, Belgium, Germany, Sweden, South Korea and the Republic of the Maldives. British, Malaysian and Singaporean citizens do not require visas for visits of 30 days or less.

All other nationalities, including British overseas citizens and British dependent territories citizens, must have visas to visit Brunei. Brunei embassies overseas have been known to give incorrect advice, so you should double-check if your nationality is not listed above and you are told that you do not require a visa to enter the country.

If entering from Sarawak or Sabah, there's no fuss on arrival – no money-showing, no requirement for an onward ticket, and it's unlikely your bags will even be looked at – and a one-week-stay permit is more or less automatic. If you ask you can usually get two weeks – it might be useful, you never know.

Transit passengers do not require visas if arriving and leaving by air, provided they do not leave the airport.

EMBASSIES

Brunei Embassies

Brunei has diplomatic offices in the following countries:

Australia
: 16 Bulwarra Close, O'Malley, ACT 2606
(☎ (06) 290-1801)

France
: No 4, Rue Logelbach, Paris 75017
(☎ (01) 44.42.67.47)

Germany
: No 18 Kaiser Karl Rinc, 5300, Bonn
(☎ (0228) 67 20 44)

BRUNEI

Indonesia
: Bank Central Asia Building, Jalan Jenderal Sudirman, Jakarta (☎ (021) 571-2124)

Japan
: 5-2 Kitashinagawa 6-Chome, Shinagawa-ku, Tokyo 141 (☎ (03) 3447-7997)

Malaysia
: 8th & 9th floors, Wisma SHL, Jalan Tun Razak, Kuala Lumpur (☎ 03-261-2800)

Philippines
: Bank of Philippine Islands Building, Ayala Ave, Paseo de Roxas, Makati, Manila (☎ (02) 816-2836 ext 38)

Singapore
: 325 Tanglin Rd, Singapore (☎ 733-9055)

Switzerland
: 46 Avenue Blanc, Geneva (☎ (022) 738-1144)

Thailand
: No 154, Soi 14, Ekamai, Sukhumvit 63, Bangkok 10500 (☎ (02) 391-6017)

UK
: 19/20 Belgrave Square, London SW1X 8PG (☎ (0171) 581-0521)

USA
: Watergate, Suite 300, 2600 Virginia Ave NW, Washington, DC 20037 (☎ (202) 342-0159)

Foreign Embassies in Brunei

Countries with diplomatic representation in Brunei include:

Australia
: 4th floor, Teck Guan Plaza (☎ 02-229435)

France
: 301-306, Kompleks Jalan Sultan, Jalan Sultan (☎ 02-220960)

Germany
: 6th floor, UNF Building, Jalan Sultan (☎ 02-225547)

Indonesia
: Lot 4498, Sungai Hanching Baru, Jalan Muara (☎ 02-330180)

Japan
: 1-3 Jalan Jawatan Dalam, Kampong Mabohai (☎ 229265)

Malaysia
: 437 Kampong Pelambayan, Jalan Kota Batu (☎ 02-228410)

Philippines
: Badiah Complex, Jalan Tutong (☎ 02-241465)

UK
: Hongkong Bank Building, Jalan Sultan (☎ 02-229435)

USA
: 3rd floor, Teck Guan Plaza, Jalan Sultan (☎ 02-229670)

CUSTOMS

Persons over 17 years of age may bring in 200 cigarettes or 250 grams of tobacco duty-free, and non-Muslims may import two bottles of liquor and 12 cans of beer, which must be declared upon arrival.

The importation of drugs carries the death penalty.

MONEY

Costs

Brunei's accommodation can be fiercely expensive. There is only one budget accommodation option in the country, but it cannot always be relied upon for a bed. Mid-range accommodation is a bit of a disaster, though some top-end hotels are not that much more expensive than the equivalent in Malaysia. Transport within the country and food are comparable to prices in the rest of East Malaysia, ie more expensive than Peninsular Malaysia but not outrageously expensive.

Currency

The official currency is the Brunei dollar (B$), but Singapore dollars are equally exchanged and can be used. There's about a 40% difference between the Brunei dollar and the Malaysian ringgit. Banks give around 10% less for cash than they do for travellers' cheques.

Brunei uses 1c, 5c, 20c and 50c coins, and notes in denominations of B$1, B$5, B$10, B$50, B$100, B$500 and B$1000.

Currency Exchange

The following table shows the exchange rates:

Australia	A$1	=	B$1.11
Canada	C$1	=	B$1.03
France	FF10	=	B$2.71
Germany	DM1	=	B$0.92
Hong Kong	HK$10	=	B$1.82
Indonesia	Rp 1000	=	B$0.60
Japan	¥100	=	B$1.29
Malaysia	RM1	=	B$0.56
New Zealand	NZ$1	=	B$0.95
Singapore	S$1	=	B$0.99
Thailand	Baht 100	=	B$5.57
UK	UK£1	=	B$2.16
USA	US$1	=	B$1.40

POST & COMMUNICATIONS

Post offices are open 7.45 am to 4.30 pm daily, except Friday and Sunday. Friday opening hours are 8 to 11 am and 2 to 4.30 pm. Air mail postcards to Malaysia and Singapore cost 30c; to all other countries 60c.

Telecom offices sell phone cards in denominations of B$10, B$20, B$50 and B$100, and these can be used in public booths to make international calls. Faxes can be sent from the Telecom office or from the big hotels, such as the Sheraton, which has a good business centre.

Area codes in Brunei include BSB/Muara (2), Temburong district (5) and Belait district (3).

To call Brunei from outside the country, the country code is 673.

BOOKS

Books on Brunei are few and far between, and you are as likely to find books on Argentine topiary in your local bookshop as titles about Brunei. What is available – usually coffee-table pictorials celebrating the wonders of the Abode of Peace – can be found in Brunei bookshops.

By God's Will – A Portrait of the Sultan of Brunei by Lord Chalfont is a measured look at the sultan and Brunei.

Brunei Darussalam, A Guide is an excellent glossy publication produced by Brunei Shell. It was designed for the expat community and outlines a host of day trips and sights to be found around the country. Many of the excursions are of limited interest to international visitors, but if you will be spending any length of time in Brunei, this is your guide. It is available to the public and costs B$15, though very few bookshops stock it. It can be bought from the publications office of Brunei Shell in Bandar Seri Begawan, opposite the Hongkong Bank. *Explore Brunei* is the government tourist guide, which has a good map of Bandar Seri Begawan.

The government produces a number of publications about Brunei. If you want an exhaustive analysis of everything to do with Brunei, including statistics on just about everything, the glossy government publication entitled *Brunei Darussalam in Profile* is available on request from Brunei diplomatic missions. *Brunei Darussalam in Brief* and *Selamat Datang* are other useful publications.

NEWSPAPERS

The *Borneo Bulletin*, published in Kuala Belait, is the country's only daily newspaper. Malaysian and Singaporean newspapers are available, as are some foreign magazines. The government publishes *Pelita Brunei*, a weekly newspaper in Malay, and the *Brunei Darussalam Newsletter*, a fortnightly newsletter in English which is mainly concerned with the sultan's latest official opening ceremonies or public utterances.

RADIO & TV

Brunei has two radio channels transmitting on both the medium wave and FM bands. One is a Malay channel, while the other transmits in English, Chinese and Gurkhali. English transmission times are from 6.30 to 8.30 am, 11 am to 2 pm and 8 to 10 pm. Five times a day, during Muslim prayer times, the radio and TV transmit the muezzin's call nationally.

Brunei is very proud of the fact that it was the first country in the region to introduce colour TV in 1975. TV is broadcast on channel 5 for most of the country, while Belait district receives transmission on channel 8. Malaysian TV can also be received.

TIME

Brunei, in common with Malaysia and Singapore, is 16 hours ahead of US Pacific Standard Time (San Francisco and Los Angeles), 13 hours ahead of US Eastern Standard Time (New York), eight hours ahead of GMT/UTC (London) and two hours behind Australian Eastern Standard Time (Sydney and Melbourne). Thus, when it is noon in Brunei, it is 8 pm in Los Angeles and 11 pm in New York (the previous day), 4 am in London and 2 pm in Sydney and Melbourne.

ELECTRICITY

Electricity supplies are dependable and run at 220-240V and 50 cycles. Plugs are of the three-square-pin type, as used in Malaysia and Singapore.

WEIGHTS & MEASURES

Like almost everywhere in the world, Brunei uses the metric system.

HEALTH

Brunei is generally a very healthy country with high standards of hygiene, and the tap water is safe to drink. Malaria has been eliminated from Brunei. The usual health precautions should be taken, especially in regards to heat exhaustion and dehydration – see the Health section under Malaysia.

The Hart Medical Clinic (☎ 02-225531) at 47 Jalan Sultan is a clinic close to the centre of Bandar Seri Begawan. The RIPAS hospital just north of Jalan Tutong is a fully equipped, modern hospital.

WOMEN TRAVELLERS

Brunei is a very safe country to travel in. Muslim women are required to cover up from head to toe, with only the face and hands exposed, but Bruneian women are less cloistered than those in other Islamic societies, and Bruneian men are generally more tolerant and less repressed than their government. Allowances are made for non-Muslim women, and because of the large expat population, many Bruneians are used to western ways. Nevertheless, dress should be conservative and not revealing. Bare shoulders and short dresses are inappropriate, and while it is good form to have elbows and knees covered, it is not necessary to wear a scarf, unless you really want to impress a pious host.

BUSINESS HOURS

Government offices are open from 7.45 am to 12.15 pm and 1.30 to 4.30 pm, Monday to Thursday and Saturday. Private offices are generally open from 9 am to 5 pm Monday to Friday and from 9 am to noon on Saturday, while banks are open from 9 am to 3 pm during the week and from 9 to 11 am on Saturday. Shops open around 9 am, and in the big shopping areas, such as Jalan Tutong and Gadong, shops stay open until 9 or 9.30 pm. Most shops in the downtown area are closed by 6 pm.

PUBLIC HOLIDAYS

Holidays and festivals in Brunei are mostly religious celebrations or festivities which mark the anniversaries of important events in the history of the country.

As in Malaysia and Singapore, the dates of most religious festivals are not fixed, as they are based on the Islamic calendar.

Fixed holidays are:

New Year's Day
    1 January
National Day
    23 February
Anniversary of the Royal Brunei Armed Forces
    31 May
Sultan's Birthday
    15 July
Christmas Day
    25 December

Variable holidays include:

Chinese New Year
    January or February
Isra Dan Mi'Raj
    February
Awal Ramadan (1st day of Ramadan)
    March
Anniversary of the Revelation of the Koran
    April
Hari Raya Aidilfitri (end of Ramadan)
    April
Hari Raya Haji
    June
First Day of Hijrah
    July
Hari Moulud (Prophet's Birthday)
    July or August

Getting There & Away

AIR

Royal Brunei Airlines has direct flights from Bandar Seri Begawan to Darwin, Perth, Bali, Jakarta, Singapore, Kuala Lumpur, Kuching,

Manila, Taipei, Hong Kong and Abu Dhabi. Malaysia Airlines, Singapore Airlines, Thai Airways International and Philippine Airlines also cover the routes to their home countries. Royal Brunei Airlines has flights continuing on to London, Frankfurt and Jeddah. Being a Muslim airline, Royal Brunei does not serve alcohol on its flights.

Departure tax is B$5 to Malaysia and Singapore and B$12 to all other destinations.

Malaysia & Singapore

To Kuching the air fare is B$236 (RM250 from Kuching), Kota Kinabalu B$78 (RM83 from KK) and Kuala Lumpur B$399 (RM441 from KL). Because of the difference in exchange rates it is around 40% cheaper to fly to Brunei from Malaysia than vice versa. The standard economy fare to Singapore is B$377 one-way (S$377 from Singapore) or 30-day excursion fares are available for B$514 (S$514). Discounts are not usually available on these flights.

Rest of Asia

Published one-way fares to other Asian destinations are Bali (B$457), Jakarta (B$574), Manila (B$444), Taipei (B$740) and Hong Kong (B$666). On flights where Royal Brunei has competition, discounting of up to 20% is available if tickets are bought through a travel agent. To Bangkok the discounted fare is around B$380 and to Manila B$360. From Bangkok to Perth or Darwin some of the cheapest flights go via Brunei. Expect to pay about US$350 with a Brunei stopover.

Australia

The cheapest flights from Darwin or Perth to Brunei cost around A$420 one-way or A$660 return. Royal Brunei is the only carrier and has two flights per week to each city. From the east coast of Australia, it is usually cheaper to fly via Singapore or Kuala Lumpur.

LAND

The main overland route is via bus from Miri in Sarawak. See the Bandar Seri Begawan Getting There & Away section for details. It is relatively easy to travel overland between Limbang in Sarawak and Bangar in the eastern part of Brunei, though boat to Bandar Seri Begawan is the usual method. Overland travel between Lawas and Bangar is difficult and expensive. See under Limbang and Lawas in the Sarawak chapter for details on these border crossings.

SEA

Boats connect Bandar Seri Begawan to Lawas and Limbang in Sarawak, and Labuan Island, from where boats go to Sabah. See the Bandar Seri Begawan Getting There & Away section for details.

Getting Around

Transport around Brunei, for those poor unfortunates who don't have a Volvo or a BMW, is by bus or minibus. The public transport system is infrequent and unreliable – there are no fixed schedules and buses leave when full. Buses on the main highway between Bandar Seri Begawan and Kuala Belait are fairly regular, but you may be in for a long wait on other routes. The bus network is not very extensive and most buses stop operating by 4 pm.

Hitchhiking is another option. In Brunei, hitchhikers are such a novelty that the chances of getting a lift are good. Cars hurtle along the main highway and are less inclined to stop on long stretches. Keep in mind that, while Brunei is generally a very safe place to travel, hitchhiking is never entirely safe in any country in the world, and we don't recommend it. Travellers who decide to hitchhike should understand that they are taking a small but potentially serious risk. People who do choose to hitch will be safer if they travel in pairs and let someone know where they are planning to go.

Regular boats connect Bangar in the Temburong district with Bandar Seri Begawan. Taxis are the only transport around Temburong.

Bandar Seri Begawan

The capital, Bandar Seri Begawan (abbreviated to BSB or Bandar), is the only town of any size and really one of the few places to go in the country. It's a neat, very clean and modern city – you won't see any bicycles, trishaws or even motorcycles. Private air-conditioned cars are the preferred mode of transportation, and by Asian standards even taxis are thin on the ground.

Islam and oil money are BSB's defining characteristics. Arabic script graces the street-signs, domes and minarets dot the skyline. The sprawling public buildings, stadiums and mosques, culminating conspicuously in the splendour of the sultan's palace, belie the fact that this is a city of just 60,000 people. But then, what the heck, Brunei can afford it.

In contrast to the impressive modern architecture, the traditional water villages surrounding the city are an interesting reminder that Brunei has only recently been jump-started into the 20th century. The city also has some worthwhile museums. BSB's nightlife, on the other hand, makes the city odds-on favourite for the coveted title of 'most boring city in the world': there is no nightlife, no alcohol, and the streets are almost deserted by 9 pm. For entertainment, Bruneians get married – music is allowed at weddings.

Most visitors are scratching around for something to do after a couple of days, but the city has its own unique character and Bruneians are some of the friendliest people you'll meet anywhere.

Information

Tourist Offices The tourist information booth at the airport is next to useless but can give you a copy of *Explore Brunei*, a glossy free guide with a good map to Brunei's attractions. Some travel agents and hotels also stock this guide.

Post & Communications The post office is on the corner of Jalan Sultan and Jalan Elizabeth Dua. It is open from 7.45 am to 4.30 pm, except Friday and Sunday. It is best avoided at lunchtimes, when it is understaffed.

Next to the post office is a telephone office, open from 8 am to midnight, where you can send telegrams or faxes, or make expensive international calls at the booths inside. They sell phone cards in denominations of B$10, B$20, B$50 and B$100. International calls can also be made from public phones (they only accept phone cards), which are few and far between. The telephone office only has one, or there are a couple opposite Wisma Jaya.

Cultural Centres The British Council is on the 5th floor of the Hongkong Bank building. It is open Monday to Thursday from 8 am to 12.15 pm and 1.45 to 4.30 pm, on Friday and Saturday from 8 am to 12.30 pm.

Bookshops For books and magazines try the Best Eastern on the ground floor of the Teck Guan Plaza, on the corner of Jalan Sultan and Jalan McArthur. They also have a store in Plaza Athirah near the Yaohan department store. STP distributors has a book and stationery store on Jalan Pemancha next to the Hongkong Bank. Booker International is a good bookshop at Gadong.

Travel Agents The Teck Guan Plaza has a few travel agents, including Ken Travel (☎ 02-223127) on the 1st floor, which acts as the American Express agent. Zura Travel Service (☎ 02-225812), on Jalan Sungai Kianggeh next to the Chinese Temple, has afternoon city tours for B$40 (B$20 for children) and morning countryside tours for B$55 (B$25 for children).

Omar Ali Saifuddin Mosque

Named after the 28th sultan of Brunei, the mosque was built in 1958 at a cost of about US$5 million. Designed by a Kuala Lumpur architectural firm, the golden-domed structure stands close to the Brunei River in its own artificial lagoon and is one of the tallest buildings in BSB. It's also one of the most impressive structures in the east.

As is customary, the interior is simple but tasteful, although certainly no match for the stunning exterior; but which other mosque anywhere has an elevator and an escalator?

The floor and walls of the mosque are made from the finest Italian marble, the stained-glass windows were handcrafted in England and the luxurious carpets were flown in from Saudi Arabia. The small pools and quadrants surrounding the main building are beautiful. The ceremonial stone boat sitting in the lagoon/moat is used for special occasions.

You can sometimes take the elevator to the top of the 44 metre minaret or walk up the long, winding staircase without charge. The view over the city and nearby Kampung Ayer is excellent.

The mosque is closed to non-Muslims on Thursday, and on Friday it is open only from 4.30 to 5.30 pm. From Saturday to Wednesday you may enter the mosque between the hours of 8 am and noon, 1 and 3 pm and 4.30 and 5.30 pm (ie outside of prayer times). Remember to dress appropriately and to remove your shoes before entering. Muslim travellers can enter the mosque to pray at any time.

Kampung Ayer

This collection of 28 water villages, built on stilts out in the Brunei River, has been there for centuries and at present houses a population of around 30,000 people. It's a strange mixture of ancient and modern; old traditions and ways of life are side by side with modern plumbing, electricity and colour TVs. A visit to one of the villages is probably the most rewarding experience you'll have in Brunei, though the garbage which floats around them has to be seen to be believed. The villages are at their best at high tide.

To get there, take the paths from behind the Omar Ali Saifuddin Mosque or from the fish market near the customs wharf. One of the many outboard launches, which act as water taxis and shuttle people back and forth between early morning and late evening, can be taken from the area next to the customs wharf. The fare across the river should be 50c, but expect to pay B$1 or more.

All the houses in each area are connected by a maze of wooden planks, and once there you can just wander at random. It's fascinating to wander around for an hour or so – even if you do keep finding yourself in the middle of someone's kitchen.

When Bandar Seri Begawan was being modernised, it was suggested that the people from the water villages be relocated to the mainland. These people refused to move and in enlightened fashion were permitted to stay. Schools and hospitals, of cement rather than wood, were then built on the water for the villagers.

There are all sorts of shops and businesses among the houses in Kampung Ayer. If you're lucky, you might come across handicraft shops selling silverware, brass, woven cloth and baskets. If not, you can always ask the boat operators to take you to these places.

A boat trip right around Kampung Ayer takes at least 30 minutes, and the boat operators will probably ask B$30 for their efforts. Bargain hard – B$10 is more like what it should be.

Brunei Museum

Located at Kota Batu, six km from the centre of Bandar Seri Begawan, the museum is housed in a beautifully constructed building on the banks of the Brunei River. When combined with a visit to the Malay Technology Museum on the river bank below, it's well worth the short trip out of town.

The museum has a collection of historical treasures from the 15th century, together with artefacts representing the cultural heritage of Brunei. There is also a natural history section with exhibits of stuffed and mounted animals, birds and insects.

There is an extensive section on oil, with an amusing vignette showing local life with and without the 'benefits' that oil brings. Best is the ethnography section with good examples of musical instruments, baskets and brassware. Also check the coffins of the Kenyah people's chiefs. There is a large collection of Chinese ceramics from 1000 AD to more recent times. The museum is open

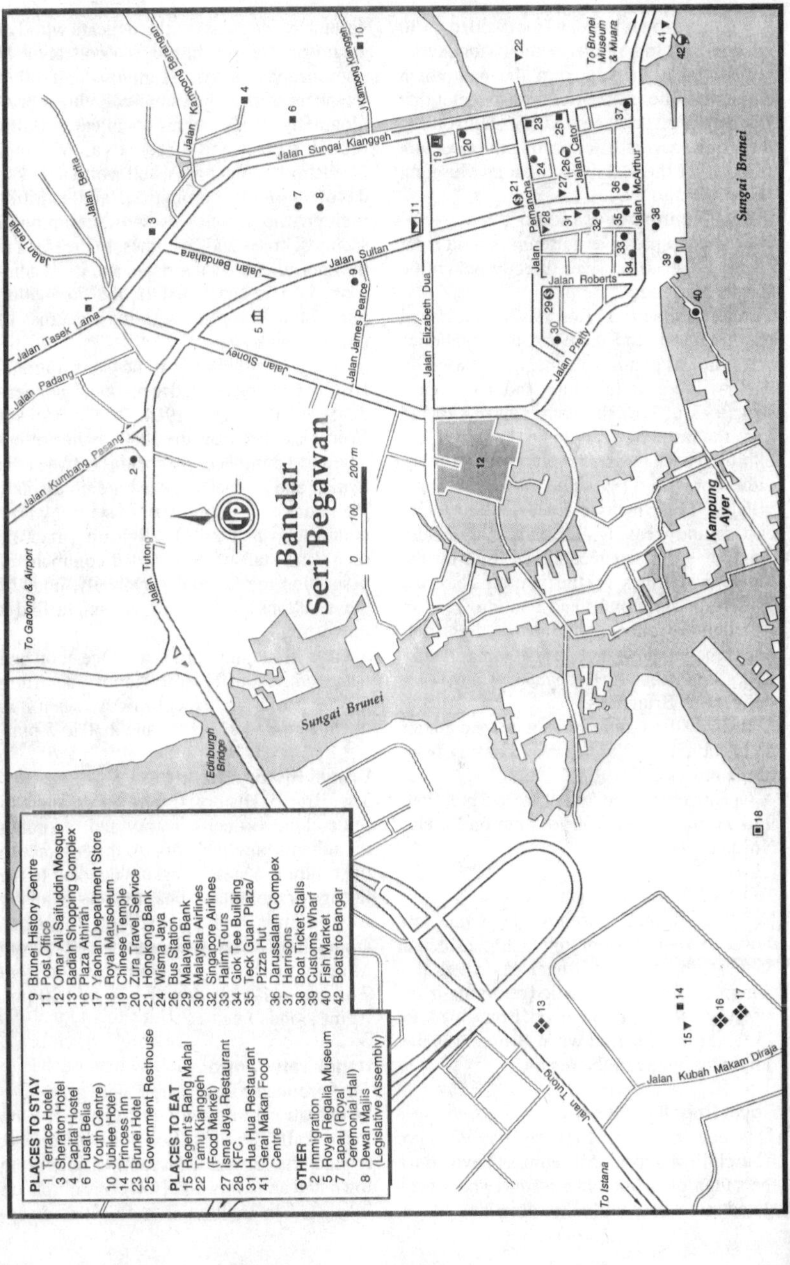
Bandar Seri Begawan
0 100 200 m
To Gadong & Airport
Jalan Tasek Lama
Jalan Padang
Jalan Kumbang Pasang
Jalan Teraja
Jalan Berita
Jalan Kampong Berangan
Jalan Kampong Kianggeh
Jalan Sungai Kianggeh
Jalan Bendahara
Jalan Stoney
Jalan Sultan
Jalan James Pearce
Jalan Elizabeth Dua
Jalan Pemancha
Jalan Cator
Jalan McArthur
Jalan Roberts
Jalan Pretty
To Brunei Museum & Muara
Jalan Tutong
Edinburgh Bridge
Sungai Brunei
Kampung Ayer
Jalan Kubah Makam Diraja
To Istana
PLACES TO STAY
1 Terrace Hotel
3 Sheraton Hotel
4 Capital Hostel
6 Pusat Belia (Youth Centre)
10 Jubilee Hotel
14 Princess Inn
23 Brunei Hotel
25 Government Resthouse
PLACES TO EAT
15 Regent's Rang Mahal
22 Tamu Kianggeh (Food Market)
27 Isma Jaya Restaurant
28 KFC
31 Hua Hua Restaurant
41 Gerai Makan Food Centre
OTHER
2 Immigration
5 Royal Regalia Museum
7 Lapau (Royal Ceremonial Hall)
8 Dewan Majlis (Legislative Assembly)
9 Brunei History Centre
11 Post Office
12 Omar Ali Saifuddin Mosque
13 Badiah Shopping Complex
16 Plaza Athirah
17 Yaohan Department Store
18 Royal Mausoleum
19 Chinese Temple
20 Zura Travel Service
21 Hongkong Bank
24 Wisma Jaya
26 Bus Station
29 Malayan Bank
30 Malaysia Airlines
32 Singapore Airlines
33 Halim Tours
34 Giok Tee Building
35 Teck Guan Plaza/ Pizza Hut
36 Darussalam Complex
37 Harrisons
38 Boat Ticket Stalls
39 Customs Wharf
40 Fish Market
42 Boats to Bangar

from 9 am to 5 pm; Friday from 9.30 to 11.30 am and 2.30 to 5 pm; closed on Monday.

City buses depart from the downtown depot; the fare is 50c, but buses are not that frequent. Taxis cost around B$6, but you can hitch quite easily. After visiting the museum, you can see the Malay Technology Museum.

Malay Technology Museum

This very impressive museum is built right on the edge of the river directly below the Brunei Museum.

A lot of time and effort has been lavished on this place, and there are three galleries with various exhibits. Gallery 1 is based on water-village architecture and has reconstructions of how the houses have evolved over the last 150 years or so. Gallery 2 has exhibits of handicrafts and fishing techniques practised by the people of the water villages. These include silver smithing, brass casting and weaving. The theme of Gallery 3 is the tools and techniques used by the indigenous tribes of the interior for food gathering, agriculture and hunting. It is an excellent display, although the light-coloured mannequins in striped pyjamas hardly look like Penans or Kedayans, or any other indigenous Bruneians.

Brunei's first gunboat is on display under a traditional roof by the river bank in front of the museum.

Opening hours are from 9 am to 5 pm; from 9 to 11.30 am and 2.30 to 5 pm on Friday; closed on Tuesday.

Tomb of Sultan Bolkiah

Near the Brunei Museum, about one km closer to town, is the tomb and mausoleum of the fifth sultan of Brunei, known as the 'Singing Admiral', who died returning from a voyage to Java. He lived from 1473 to 1521, during a period when Brunei was the dominant power in the region.

Royal Regalia Museum

This new museum, formerly the Winston Churchill Memorial Museum, is devoted to the sultan of Brunei. It is a somewhat overstated structure that looks something like a vast tub of ice cream with a delicate whorl of cream on the top. Inside is a collection of photographs of His Highness and other members of the royal family, giving a brief biography of the sultan complete with his report from Sandhurst Royal Military Academy. Another area well worth a look is devoted to the coronation, and exhibits include the throne, crowns, ceremonial sceptres, krises and costumes. In the foyer is the enormous royal carriage, and in an anteroom is a re-enactment of the coronation procession, complete with the costumes of the attendants.

Also in this building is the Constitutional History Gallery, created to mark the independence of Brunei in 1984. The history of Brunei is traced from the 1800s to the present day, and a number of the treaties between the British and Brunei's sultans are on display. There are even action scenes set up, where buttons may be pressed to light up part of the scene and start off a recorded commentary describing the 'action' – typically, none of these buttons work. Historians might find it interesting.

Next to the museum is a coffee shop and a souvenir shop. The museum is open from 8.30 am to 5 pm, except Friday, when it is open from 9 to 11.30 am and 2.30 to 5 pm.

Brunei History Centre

The Brunei History Centre is devoted to researching Brunei's history and recording the sultan's family history. At the entrance to the centre is a small museum devoted to the lineage of the sultan. It has replicas of all the royal tombs and shows their locations around Bandar Seri Begawan. It is open from Monday to Thursday and on Saturday from 7.45 am to 12.15 pm and 1.30 to 4.30 pm. Admission is free.

Handicraft Centre

The preposterously large and grandiose handicraft centre was built to help develop local craftwork. It's along the waterfront toward the Brunei Museum, visible from town and an easy walk. However, if you are interested in traditional crafts, it is disappointing. Only new silverwork and weaving produced by the students are available, and everything is very expensive; you can pay hundreds of dollars for some pieces. Upstairs workshops are open to visitors. The centre is open from 7.45 am to 12.15 pm and 1.30 to 4.30 pm; 8.30 am to 2 pm on Friday and Sunday.

Taman Peranginan Tasek

This park is a pleasant retreat from the city. It has picnic areas, and there are peaceful walks through the park to a small waterfall and a water reservoir.

The park is a short walk from town. Go along Jalan Tasek Lama away from the town centre past the Terrace Hotel, and after two sets of traffic lights take the next right turn. From the entrance gates by the parking lot it is a 15 minute walk to the falls – continue past the flowers and picnic tables, and then follow the stream to the falls. They are best in the wet season, when the water is deeper; you can swim there. Another road by the gate leads to a 15 minute walk uphill to a view over the water reservoir.

The Sheraton Hotel has 'jogging maps' which can also be used for walks.

Chinese Temple

There is a Chinese temple on the corner of Jalan Elizabeth Dua and Jalan Sungai Kianggeh with some colourful, pictorial tilework and plenty of carved, gilded wood. It's a busy place on Saturday evening, and *wayang* (Chinese opera) is sometimes held here.

Lapau & Dewan Majlis

All over town you'll notice uniquely designed, oversized federal buildings that seem to serve no other purpose than to attest to Brunei's wealth and glorify the reign of HRH. The Royal Ceremonial Hall (Lapau) & Legislative Assembly (Dewan Majlis) complex, opposite the youth centre, was the coronation hall for the sultan in 1968. Royal ceremonies are occasionally held here, but it is closed and lies empty most of the time.

Jame'Asr Hassanil Bolkiah Mosque

This is the latest minaretted and domed addition to the Bruneian skyline. It is the largest mosque in the country, constructed at great expense, and as the local tourist literature trumpets, 'a symbol of Islam's firm hold in the country'. It's quite a fabulous sight. It's in Gadong, just a few km from town.

Istana Nurul Iman

The Istana Nurul Iman, the magnificent sultan's palace, is an impressive sight, especially when illuminated at night. It is larger than the Vatican Palace, and you can be sure no expense has been spared in its construction. Unfortunately, the *istana* is open to the public only during Hari Raya Aidilfitri, the end of the fasting month of Ramadan.

The istana is four km out of town on the Tutong road, and the grounds back on to the river. You can either spend a leisurely hour walking to it or try hitching. The Tutong and Seria buses pass the istana, but they run infrequently. It is possible to charter a water taxi and then walk to the front of the palace. On the hill opposite the istana are homes belonging to other members of the royal family.

Royal Mausoleum

The Royal Mausoleum (Makam Diraja) is the burial place of the last four sultans, and other members of the royal family are buried in the grounds. The main pavilion is surprisingly small by Brunei standards. Unless you have transport, it isn't worth the effort. The mausoleum is on the river about half a km from the Yaohan department store.

Other Attractions

The food market, **Tamu Kianggeh**, is on the canal, and water taxis hurtle up and down the canal as they transport passengers to and from the market. The market is not very extensive but has plenty of local colour. The **fish market** near the customs wharf is another traditional market.

In the middle of the river near the Istana Nurul Iman, **Pulau Ranggu** is home to a large colony of proboscis monkeys. Macaques also inhabit the island. If you take a water taxi along the river around sunset you may get a glimpse of the monkeys. Nearby on the river bank, the **Persiaran Damuan** is a landscaped park, accessed from Jalan Tutong, which affords good views of the istana.

Other impressive public buildings in BSB include the **Hassanal Bolkiah National Stadium**, five km from town. The stadium is of Olympic proportions and includes a track and field complex, tennis centre and swimming complex. It is open to the public from 8 am to noon and 1.30 to 4.30 pm, and the swimming pool is often nearly deserted.

Activities

A good way to meet some of the resident expat population is to take part in one of the Hash House Harrier runs. Ask at the British Council for details, or any expats you see in the streets should be able to help – they're generally a friendly bunch. For more details, see Hash House Harriers in the Kuala Lumpur chapter.

Places to Stay – bottom end

Pusat Belia (☎ 02-229423), the youth centre on Jalan Sungai Kianggeh, is a short walk from the town centre. It is the only budget option and one of the best buys you'll find anywhere. A bed in an air-conditioned four-bed dorm costs B$10 for one to three nights and B$5 for each subsequent night. The centre has a swimming pool (entry B$1) and a cafe with a very limited menu. The place is often empty but it can sometimes be full with visiting sporting groups. Officially you need a youth hostel or student card to stay. Entry without a card is at the discretion of the manager, who may make things difficult and will probably tell you to come back in a few hours if he doesn't like the look of you. Some males with long hair have been turned away. There are no budget alternatives.

The *Bradoo Inn* (☎ 02-336723), Simpang 130, Jalan Sungai Akar, has much better rooms for B$50 or B$60/70 for singles/doubles with attached bath. It is out near the airport and a long way from anywhere, but if you are flying into Brunei and out again the next day it is worth considering. Ring them and they will pick you up from the airport, which will save you an expensive cab fare.

If you draw a blank at these places and can't afford the mid-range places, you are really in trouble. Travellers have resorted to sleeping out in the parks when the youth centre has been full, but this is not appreciated by the authorities and you run the risk of having your slumber disturbed by the boys in blue. Showers are available at least in the changing rooms of the youth centre pool for B$1.

Places to Stay – middle

There is a large jump in price from bottom to middle-range accommodation.

The *Capital Hostel* (☎ 02-223561), off Jalan Tasek Lama just behind the Pusat Belia, has faded rooms costing from B$70 to B$138 for rooms with air-con, TV and fridge. The restaurant and bar downstairs serve reasonably priced meals and western breakfasts.

The *Terrace Hotel* (☎ 02-243554), on Jalan Tasek Lama, was formerly known as Ang's Hotel, and by Bruneian standards is an economical mid-range option. Discounts are frequently available; posted rates are B$82/92 for singles/doubles. Deluxe rooms range up to B$138. A 10% service charge applies. The hotel has its own restaurant and is fully air-conditioned.

The *Princess Inn* (☎ 02-221128), Km 2 Jalan Tutong, is out of the town centre, across the Brunei River near the Yaohan department store. It's not particularly well located and the Terrace is better value. Rates range from B$80 to B$154, plus 10%.

Places to Stay – top end

Brunei has a good selection of top-end hotels, and most offer discounts. A 10% service charge applies in all these hotels.

The new *Jubilee Hotel* (☎ 02-228070), Jalan Kampong Kianggeh, has well-appointed singles/doubles for B$125/135 and suites ranging from B$180/200 to B$450. Discounts of up to 30% make this hotel a good deal by Brunei standards.

On the corner of Jalan Sungai Kianggeh and Jalan Pemancha is the *Brunei Hotel* (☎ 02-242372). Each room has air-con, a private bath and TV, and the hotel has a restaurant and alcohol-free bar. Room rates range from B$160/180 to B$180/200, and suites are available. Discounts of around 20% are on offer.

The *Riverview Hotel* (☎ 02-238238), Km 1 Jalan Gadong, is one of Brunei's best. It is to the north of town on the way to the airport and Gadong. Some standard singles are available for B$110, but most rooms cost B$150/170 and suites start at B$210/230.

The *Sheraton Hotel* (☎ 02-244272), along with the Centrepoint in Gadong, is the country's top hotel and has all the modern amenities, including a pool. It is centrally located on Jalan Tasek Lama. There are 170 rooms, with standard singles/doubles from B$240/260 to B$250/270 and suites costing up to B$1480.

The *Centrepoint Hotel* (☎ 02-241536) is Brunei's newest hotel, with a swimming pool, sports centre, private dining rooms and the Yaohan Megamart downstairs – what more could you want (besides a stiff drink)? Room rates start slightly lower than the Sheraton at B$195 and climb up to B$1500.

Places to Eat

All the hotels and the youth centre have their own restaurants. There's not much of a menu at the canteen in the youth centre; basically, what you see is what you get, and the choice is very limited.

The *Gerai Makan* food centre on the riverfront just over the canal from the customs wharf is a good place to eat, although, as is the case all over BSB, not much happens in the evening.

Another place to head for is the food stalls at the *Tamu Kianggeh* market by the river, across the footbridge near the intersection of Jalan Sungai Kianggeh and Jalan Pemancha. In the evening only, another group of stalls springs up in the car park behind the Chinese temple, opposite the post office. You can get excellent food of all descriptions here, including satay, barbecued fish, chicken wings and kueh melayu (sweet pancakes filled with peanut, raisins and sugar). The only trouble with both these sets of food stalls is that they are take-away only, so you have to find somewhere to sit down and eat your food.

The main street, Jalan Sultan, is the best place to look for cheap restaurants. *Isma Jaya Restaurant* has rice and curry meals for around B$3, and a few doors down the *Sin Tai Pong* has chicken-rice for B$2.50. The *Hua Hua Restaurant* nearby is a little more expensive, but the food is very good and it has a wide range of dishes. Ask to see the menu and check the prices. The Hua Hua and the Isma Jaya stay open until 9 pm, a rarity in downtown Bandar.

On Jalan McArthur the *Sri Indah Restoran* has decent roti and murtabak, good for grabbing a quick breakfast before catching a boat.

Bandar Seri Begawan has some good bakeries. On the corner of Jalan McArthur and Jalan Sultan there's the *Carnation Country Bake Corner*, and in the Wisma Jaya next to the Brunei Hotel on Jalan Pemancha is *Mr Brumby Bake House*. The shopping centres in the central part of town also have cheap air-con restaurants serving Malay and Chinese food, such as the *Wisma Delima* in the Wisma Jaya.

Western fast food is not particularly cheap in Brunei. There are branches of *KFC* and *Pizza Hut* (take-away only) in the city centre, but the real fast-food centre is in Gadong, five km out of the city, where you'll find a *McDonald's*, *Pizza Hut*, *Swenson's* and a *Sugar Bun*. The Pizza Hut has a good salad bar and Swenson's is the pick of these for a good meal.

Gadong also has a number of other restaurants, including some good Indian restaurants, such as *Fathul Razak Restaurant*, where you can get an enormous murtabak for just B$4.

Also out in the Gadong district is *AZ-Fast Food* (☎ 449737), 1 Bangunan Azahri, Simpang 5, Jalan Gadong. They don't serve fast food but they have a varied menu, with mostly Chinese dishes, and seafood is the speciality. The food is moderately priced (around B$6 for main dishes, more for seafood), but the best thing about this place is the location on stilts over the river. It is off Jalan Gadong. As you come from the centre past the Riverview Hotel, cross the bridge and the restaurant is on the left by the river in a quiet side street.

The shopping area on Jalan Tutong around the Yaohan department store has a number of restaurants, mostly moderately priced Chinese coffee shops, some of which stay open until 10 pm or even later! For western fast food there is a *Jollibee* in the Utama bowling alley next to Yaohan and a *KFC* in the Plaza Athirah. *Regent's Rang Mahal*, near the Princess Inn, is an air-con Indian restaurant with a wide selection of vegetarian and non-vegetarian Indian dishes including dosai and tandoori breads. It does a reasonable job of north Indian curries, most of which cost around B$3. You can stuff yourself for B$10 and still have change, and it has good buffet lunches for B$6.

The meals at the *Capital Hostel* are pretty good and quite cheap. You can get tasty Hokkien noodles and other noodle dishes for around B$5. The *Terrace Hotel* has an excellent restaurant on the ground floor with a good selection of both western (expensive) and Chinese/Malay (cheaper) dishes.

Things to Buy

The centre of town has a few small shopping plazas that close early, such as the Teck Guan and Darussalam complexes and the Wisma Jaya, but if you are wondering where Bruneians spend all their excess oil-soaked dollars, head across the bridge on Jalan Tutong to the huge Yaohan department store. As well as clothes, electrical goods, books etc, the supermarket in the basement is stocked with imported foodstuffs flown in from around the world.

Nearby are a number of shopping plazas, such as Plaza Athirah, Mohamad Yossof and Badiah. The quickest way to walk to the Yaohan department store from the centre (about 20 minutes) is via Kampung Ayer, the water villages, starting from the back of Omar Ali Saifuddin Mosque or from the fish market near the customs wharf – just ask for 'Yaohan' if you get lost.

The other big shopping centre is at Gadong, about five km from the city centre. Gadong has plenty of supermarkets and department stores, a couple of decent bookstores, a number of restaurants and the Yaohan Megamart all collected together in the Centrepoint shopping centre, a massive air-con mall development. If you are contemplating buying a new BMW or Volvo, all the big car-dealers are on Jalan Gadong before you reach the main shopping area.

Getting There & Away

Air Airlines which fly into Brunei include Royal Brunei Airlines, Malaysia Airlines, Singapore Airlines, Thai Airways International and Philippine Airlines. Tickets to Malaysia and Singapore are at a fixed rate, but other international tickets are up to 20% cheaper if bought through travel agents rather than the airlines. Royal Brunei Airlines has a Travel Shop selling discounted fares in the same building as their office.

Airline offices or general sales agents in BSB include:

British Airways
: Harrisons (GSA), corner Jalan Kianggeh & Jalan McArthur (☎ 02-243911)

Malaysia Airlines
: 144 Jalan Pemancha (☎ 02-224141)

Philippine Airlines
: 1st floor, Wisma Hajjah Fatimah Building, Jalan Sultan (☎ 02-222970)

Royal Brunei Airlines
: RBA Plaza, Jalan Sultan (☎ 02-242222)

Singapore Airlines
: 49-50 Jalan Sultan (☎ 02-227253)

Thai Airways International
: 51 Jalan Sultan (☎ 02-242991)

Bus The main highway in Brunei links Bandar Seri Begawan to Seria, Kuala Belait and the Sarawak border near Kuala Baram. It is possible, though difficult, to reach Limbang by road; and you can travel overland to Lawas, but the road stops at the border and you have to walk over a hill. Boat is the only real option. It has been said that the government deliberately keeps the roads out of Brunei in such miserable condition to make any invasion by land difficult!

The bus station in BSB is on Jalan Cator, beneath the Multistorey Carpark (that's what it's officially known as). Buses are infrequent, don't operate to a fixed schedule and go when full. Buses display departure times on the front, but it is wise to be on the bus 15 minutes or more before departure. Minibuses ply many of the routes, as well as the large, older buses, but there is no difference in fares between the two.

For Miri there are two options: private minibuses or the public buses to Seria, then to Kuala Belait and from there to Miri. If you want to reach Miri in one day from Bandar Seri Begawan, start out early in the day.

The private minibuses will pick you up from your hotel in Bandar Seri Begawan and leave very early in the morning to avoid congestion at the ferry crossings. Mr Wong (☎ 02-228392 or 02-225643) lives in the apartment block next to the Pusat Belia on Jalan Kampong Kianggeh and starts picking up passengers for the trip at 5 am. Another operator is the Miri-Sibu Express driver (☎ 02-225002). The fare is B$25.

There are many buses every day to Seria until around 3 pm. The fare is B$4 and the journey takes 1½ to two hours.

From Seria to Kuala Belait there are frequent buses daily, the fare is B$1 and the journey takes about 30 minutes. It's very easy to hitch from Bandar Seri Begawan to Seria or Kuala Belait, because there are plenty of air-conditioned cars and very few hitchhikers. Alongside the road around Seria, and right in the middle of the town itself, you'll see plenty of the 'nodding donkey' oil wells.

There are five buses daily from Kuala Belait to Miri, leaving at 7.30, 9.30 and 11 am and 1.30 and 3.30 pm. These are operated by the Belait United Traction Company. The fare is B$9 and the journey takes about 2½ hours and involves river crossings.

From Kuala Belait it's a five minute bus ride (20 minutes' walk) to the Belait River, where the car ferry plies back and forth. Although the queue for cars can be incredibly long here, especially on weekends, bus passengers and the driver cross the river on the ferry and pick up another bus parked on the other side, thus avoiding the queues.

Once you cross the river it's a short ride to the Brunei immigration checkpoint. After going through Brunei customs you board a Malaysian bus which takes you to the Malaysian immigration checkpoint. From there it's a very short ride to the queue at the next river which usually takes 15 to 30 minutes to cross.

From Kuala Baram to Miri, the road is sealed all the way and is in fairly good condition.

Car Hire car rates start at B$90 per day, and surcharges apply if the car is taken into Sarawak. Companies that rent cars include:

Avis
  Block 4, Hasbullah Building (☎ 02-242284)
Budget U-Drive
  E17, 4th floor, Bangunan GPI, Jalan Gadong (☎ 02-445847)
National Car Systems
  2, 1st floor, Hasbullah 4, Jalan Gadong (☎ 02-224921)

Boat Unless you are going to fly to Labuan or Kota Kinabalu, the only way to get to Sabah or the isolated eastern Sarawak outposts of Limbang or Lawas is to use launches or launch/taxi combinations.

All international boats leave from the dock at the end of Jalan Roberts, where Brunei immigration formalities are taken care of.

Limbang Private *ekspres* boats do this run throughout the day and depart when full. Buy your ticket at the ticket stalls on Jalan McArthur near the customs wharf. The fare is B$10 and the trip takes about 30 minutes.

There isn't much to see or do in Limbang, but the town has a bit of a reputation as a sin spot. You can either stay at Limbang overnight, or fly to Mulu, Miri, Lawas or Kota

Kinabalu. See the Limbang section in the Sarawak chapter for further details.

Labuan Labuan is a duty-free island off Brunei from which you can get ferries to Sabah and then a bus into Kota Kinabalu, ferries direct to Kota Kinabalu, or flights to Sabah, Sarawak or Peninsular Malaysia. For more details, see the Pulau Labuan Getting There & Away section in the Sabah chapter.

From BSB there are four or five daily services to Labuan. Tickets can be bought before departure at the ticket stalls on Jalan McArthur, but it is best to book a day or so in advance, especially for weekends and public holidays. The main ticketing agent is the Ratu Samudra Ticketing office (☎ 02-243057), 201-213 Giok Tee building, Jalan McArthur. They have departures at 8 am from Monday to Thursday and at 8 am and 8.30 am from Friday to Sunday. The more comfortable boat is the air-con *Ratu Samudra*, which takes 1½ hours. Tickets cost B$20 (economy class) and B$25 (1st class). Economy class is perfectly adequate.

On the return journey it leaves Labuan at 2 pm. Other boats include the *Duta Muhibbah* (☎ 02-24803), which departs at 1 pm, and the *Sri Labuan Tiga*, which departs at 3 pm. The *Sri Labuan Tiga* can be booked at Halim Tours (☎ 02-226688), 61 Jalan McArthur; the office is in the laneway opposite the boat ticket stalls. Other Labuan services with the same ticket prices are the *Suria Ekspress* (8.30 am departure) and the *Raja Walit* (1 pm departure).

Lawas One express boat daily goes from BSB to Lawas at 11.30 am. It costs B$15 and takes about two hours. It can be booked at Halim Tours (☎ 02-226688).

See the Lawas Getting There & Away section in the Sarawak chapter for details of onward transport to Sabah and Labuan and flights in Sarawak.

Bangar Regular launches ply between BSB and Bangar in Temburong; they go when full. The first departure is around 6.30 am and the last at 4.30 pm. Launches leave from the jetty near the Gerai Makan food centre, and the trip costs B$7.

Getting Around

The Airport Minibuses to the airport leave from the bus station and display the words 'Lapangan Terbang Antarabangsa' (International Airport). They cost B$1 and operate every 15 minutes (in theory at least) – you may end up waiting 20 to 30 minutes, but no longer.

Taxis cost around B$20 (welcome to Brunei!) The big, modern airport is only eight km from the city.

Bus Local bus services are hit or miss. Generally they leave only when they are full, which often means a long wait. The bus station is beneath the Multistorey Carpark on Jalan Cator.

To get to the museums take a Muara or Kota Batu bus (50c).

Taxi Taxis are metered, expensive and hard to find. Flagfall is B$3, a surcharge of B$5 applies for trips to and from the airport and the meters tick over very quickly. Between 9 pm and 6 am a night-time surcharge of 50% of the metered fare is effective. There is also a B$1 charge for each item of luggage placed in the boot. The best places to look for a taxi are at the bus station on Jalan Cator and the Sheraton, or taxis can be booked by telephone (☎ 02-222214 or 02-226853). There is a booking charge of B$3.

Water Taxi Water taxis, popularly known as flying coffins, are longboats with powerful outboard motors that hurtle up and down the Brunei River transporting passengers to and from the villages of Kampung Ayer. They are most easily caught near the customs and immigration post or the Tamu Kianggeh food market. Fares start at 50c and range up to B$2, but expect to pay much higher charter rates. To charter a boat for a tour of Kampung Ayer and the river shouldn't cost more than B$20 per hour, or less if you bargain hard.

ɿround Bandar Seri ʒegawan

he main landmass of Brunei in the western art of the country is quite small, and any estination is only a few hours' drive from e capital. The countryside has a lot of ristine forest, with waterfalls and reserves at make pleasant day trips, but a car is ssential to reach most of them. There are a ew other points of interest – decent beaches, ome more impressive istanas, longhouses tc – but the only problem is getting to them, ecause of the unreliability of the buses. The nly accommodation outside BSB is at Seria nd Kuala Belait, neither of which has much o offer.

ɅUARA

ɅIuara is a small town north of Bandar Seri ʒegawan at the top of the peninsula. It's a container port of no interest to travellers, but Muara Beach, two km from town, is a popular veekend retreat. The white-sand beach is lean, but like many beaches in Borneo it is lotted with driftwood and the debris of ogging. It is quiet during the week and has ood stalls, picnic tables and a children's playground.

Other beaches around Muara include Meragang Beach and Serasa Beach.

Getting There & Away

The bus from Bandar Seri Begawan to Muara town takes about 40 minutes and costs B$2. You can also try hitching. The road to Muara Beach is to the left at the roundabout before you enter Muara town. Proceed one km or so along this road, and the turn-off to the beach is opposite the Shell operations depot, before the army camp.

BUKIT SHAHBANDAR FOREST RECREATION PARK

This 70 hectare park is on the Muara-Tutong Highway, 15 km from BSB. An information booth run by the Forestry Department is at the entrance to the park, and maps and pamphlets showing the trails are available. Roads run throughout much of the park, and walking trails lead off from the roads. The main trail leads to Triangle Point, a hill with views across the sea and coastline. The forest has some secondary jungle, though most of it is planted with pine and acacia. This park is one of the most popular picnic spots, and there is a small artificial lake, toilets and picnic shelters. It is a pleasant spot, but if you are after jungle walks Temburong is a better bet.

It is possible to camp in the park, but permission must be obtained in advance from the Forestry Department (☎ 02-222687) in BSB.

JERUDONG

Jerudong is the playground of the sultan, where he indulges in his favourite pastime, polo. **Jerudong Park** is a huge complex with a polo stadium and luxurious stables that house polo ponies flown in from around the world, many from Argentina. A golf course and trapshooting and croquet facilities are also at the park. It is very grand and impressive, but uninvited visitors won't be able to tour the complex. If you have your own car, you can avoid the guard post and drive around the back of the stables for a look.

Jerudong's chief attraction is the **Jerudong Playground**, a massive new amusement park. It has a wide range of rides, and is probably a great place to take the kids. At the time of writing, everything was free, but it is likely that charges will have been introduced by the time you have this book in your hands.

Jerudong is just north of the main highway between BSB and Tutong. On the other side of the highway are stud farms with more expensive horseflesh. The Istana Nurul Izzah, home of the sultan's second wife, is nearby on a hill.

Behind Jerudong Park is **Jerudong Beach**. The wide stretch of beach has a number of stalls selling fish, brought in fresh each day by the local fishing boats. There are cliffs to the north of the beach and at the southern end is yet another istana, part of Jerudong Park. The istana is an impressive piece of modern architecture, but the Gurkha guards are unlikely to allow you inside.

Buses to Seria pass the park, but it is a long walk to the beach and you won't be able to see much of the area unless you have a car.

LIMAU MANIS

Limau Manis is a small town 32 km southwest of BSB near the Sarawak border. Brunei has an immigration post here but the Malaysian equivalent is at Limbang. It is possible to go by road from Limau Manis through Sarawak's Limbang district to Temburong, the eastern half of Brunei, but there is no public transport. The best way to reach Limau Manis is by car, or it is possible to hitch. Take Jalan Tutong to Senkurong, and then the turn-off to Limau Manis.

On the way to Limau Manis there are a few points of interest. **Wasai Kandal**, 12 km from BSB, is a forest area with waterfalls and pools. A wide, easy-to-follow path leads past picnic ponds and pools to Air Terjun Tinggi, the most impressive falls, and then a rough track proceeds to another waterfall, Air Terjun Rendah, which has another picnic area. It is about a half-hour walk each way. The trail starts at Kampong Kilanas, which is just off Jalan Tutong before the turn-off to Limau Manis.

Kampong Parit, 26 km from BSB, is a recreational park with a collection of thatched-roof houses re-creating a traditional village. It is a popular picnic spot, and you'll find a playground and food stalls here. The park is right by the road, six km before Limau Manis.

TUTONG

Tutong town, on the main highway halfway between Seria and BSB, is the main town in Tutong district. Seria buses pass the town, but if you want to see the attractions around Tutong you really need to have a hire car – getting anywhere by taxi will cost a small fortune.

Pantai Seri Kenangan (often simply referred to as Pantai Tutong) is a popular beach with picnic tables and a simple restaurant. It is on a spit of land with the ocean on one side and the Tutong River on the other. The white sand, casuarina-lined beach is probably the best in Brunei. The royal family has a surprisingly modest istana at Pantai Seri Kenangan, which is a couple of km off the highway just outside of Tutong town. The turn-off is near the Tamu Tutong, where a market is held daily in the morning. The road to the beach continues for another five km to Kuala Tutong where ferries once crossed the river. The beach at the end of the road is quiet and ideal for camping.

LAKE MERIMBUN

Lake Merimbun, 27 km inland from Tutong is Brunei's largest lake. The picturesque swampy lake has an island in the middle and wooden walkways lead around the lake to picnic pavilions. The wildlife includes monkeys and a wide variety of birds. Unfortunately there is virtually no way of getting out here unless you hire a car.

SERIA

Seria is an oil town on the coast between Tutong and Kuala Belait. The area stretching along the coast between Seria and Kuala Belait is the main centre for oil production in Brunei. Shell Brunei has a number of big installations, the army (including Gurkha and British posts) is there to protect them, and most expatriate workers live here in their suburban enclaves. Seria itself is an unremarkable service town with a few modern blocks of shops and a market. Just outside of town at the beach is the **Billionth Barrel Monument**, commemorating the billionth barrel of oil produced at the Seria field. It looks a little like it was designed by HR Geiger.

Before Seria a road branches off inland to Labi. About halfway to Labi is **Luagan Lalak**, with good views and a lake that fills up in the rainy season. From Labi several **Iban longhouses** can be visited. The main one, called Rumah Panjang Mendaram Besar, is worth visiting. Further along the road is Rumah Panjang Teraja. They are modern wooden longhouses, but in traditional style. There is a road, but as very few cars use it you may have to walk. Take a few small gifts. On the way, you'll pass Rampayoh, where there is a waterfall. At the end of the road past Rumah Panjang Teraja is the Teraja River and a trail to another waterfall and **Bukit Teraja**. Bukit Teraja is the highest hill in the area and affords fine views across Brunei and Sarawak. The main trail to the summit is signposted and starts about six km beyond Rampayoh. The walk goes through primary forest and takes about two hours to the top.

It is also possible to visit Dusun and Punan villages, but this involves hiring a boat (expect to pay around B$200 per day) to take you deep into the interior along the Belait River. The best place to hire a boat is at Kampong Sungai Mau, on the Labi road where it meets the Belait River before Luagan Lalak.

Places to Stay

The *Rumah Tumpangan Seria*, on Jalan Sharif Ali near the market, has fan-cooled rooms for B$35 and air-con rooms for B$40. It is an old, wooden Chinese hotel with spartan rooms, common in Malaysia but unique in Brunei. If you're just passing through Brunei from Sabah to Sarawak, and can't stay in the youth centre in BSB, then it's quite a saving to spend your last Brunei night here rather than at the extremely expensive Bandar Seri Begawan hotels.

Getting There & Away

The road from Bandar Seri Begawan is excellent; there are about 10 buses daily taking two hours and costing B$4. The first bus leaves BSB at 7.30 am and the last one leaves Seria at 2.30 pm. From Seria there are frequent buses to Kuala Belait until 6.30 pm for B$1.

KUALA BELAIT

The last town before Malaysia, Kuala Belait is the main town in Belait district, and the place to get buses for Miri in Sarawak. The town has a lot more charm than Seria, though you won't miss much if you pass it by. It is a well-planned town, with old colonial shophouses in the centre, and the beach is reasonable. The best place to change money is at the Hongkong Bank opposite the bus station.

You can hire a motor launch by the market for trips up the river to **Kuala Balai**, a small river village, once the largest settlement in the district, now almost deserted because the residents have left to find work in the oil industry on the coast. The 45 minute trip (one way) goes by good jungle vegetation at the river's edge. Near Kuala Balai you'll see sago palms growing, and a few sago factories remain. Along the way ask the driver to stop at the wooden case of skulls mounted on stilts, left over from the head-hunting days.

Places to Stay

At the cheap end of the scale there's a *Government Rest House* (☎ 03-334288). Rooms are about B$12 and are generally reserved for government officials; it's very unlikely you will be allowed to stay. It is on the beach, a 10 minute walk along Jalan McKerron from the bus station, and then 200 metres to the right.

Otherwise, there's the *Sentosa Hotel* (☎ 03-334341) at 92 Jalan McKerron, near the bus station, which is fully air-conditioned and has comfortable but ordinary rooms for B$98 (B$103 if you pay by credit card). For the price, it is one of the worst deals you'll find anywhere.

The *Seaview Hotel* (☎ 03-332651), Jalan Maulana, is the best hotel outside BSB, though not quite international standard. It is two km from town on the beach road to Seria, and it has a well-stocked supermarket which is frequented by expats. Singles/doubles cost B$130/155, but the hotel is being renovated and a pool is being built, so prices may rise.

Getting There & Away

For Malaysia there are quite a few buses daily, mostly in the morning, and the fare is B$9 for the 30 minute trip to Miri. Just out of town the road ends and you take a ferry over the Belait River. The road then continues along the coast to the border. At the border you change to a Malaysian bus and head to the Baram River, from where there's another ferry crossing. From there to Miri it's a good road.

Temburong

Temburong district is the eastern slice of Brunei, surrounded by Sarawak. This quiet backwater, rarely visited by travellers, is reached by boat from BSB. The boat trip in itself is worthwhile – the boats go down the Brunei River from BSB and out into the open sea, before negotiating the maze of the mangroves at the mouth of the Temburong River. Temburong has little industry or development, so much of the district is virgin rainforest.

Bangar can be visited in a day trip from BSB, if you start out early in the morning. The Peradayan Forest Reserve is a good outing for a jungle walk, or the Iban longhouse and small zoo at Batang Duri can be visited. For a longer jungle experience, the Kuala Belalong Field Studies Centre accepts visitors.

BANGAR

Bangar is a sleepy town on the banks of the Temburong River. It is the district centre and has a row of shops, government offices and a mosque, but not much else. It is a pleasant town, but there is no accommodation. Bangar has two Chinese coffee shops and the *Hasinah Indian Restaurant,* which is a helpful place for arranging transport. Taxis are the only form of transport around Temburong; they congregate around the boat wharf.

Getting There & Away

Road Temburong has two main roads. One leads south to Batang Duri and the other runs across the district to the east and west borders with Sarawak. Both are very good roads, but traffic is light.

Registered metered taxis are available, as well as private taxis which work out cheaper with some negotiation. For Limbang in Sarawak, taxis go to the border for B$5 and then from the other side of the border a taxi to Limbang costs RM10. The Bangar taxi will take you to the immigration office in Bangar for exiting Brunei, as there is no border post. In Sarawak, report to immigration in Limbang. It is also possible, but expensive, to cross the eastern border into Sarawak to go to Lawas. A taxi to the border costs B$20. See under Lawas in the Sarawak chapter for details of travel from the border into Malaysia.

A private taxi to Batang Duri should cost around B$20 for the return journey, including the wait while you look around the longhouse and the zoo. For the Peradayan Forest Reserve and the walk to Bukit Patoi, taxis also charge B$20 to drop you off and pick you up at an arranged time.

Hitching is possible, though you may be in for a wait, especially at Batang Duri. The chances for a lift on the road to Labu, the town beyond the Peradayan Forest Reserve, are better, but allow plenty of time for the trip back to Bangar if you want to catch the boat back to BSB. The road to Labu is across the bridge from Bangar town.

Boat Regular boats leave from the wharf near the Gerai Makan food centre in BSB and cost B$7. The journey takes about 45 minutes. For the return journey, buy your ticket at one of the two ticket offices at the Bangar wharf. Boats run until around 4 pm, and you shouldn't have to wait more than half an hour.

BATANG DURI

Batang Duri is an Iban longhouse on the Temburong River, 17 km south of Bangar. Boats to the Kuala Belalong Field Studies Centre go from the village jetty. If you visit the longhouse, introduce yourself first, preferably to the *penghulu* (chief), and don't just wander up and down the longhouse veranda, which is akin to walking unannounced into someone's lounge room.

Two km before Batang Duri is the **Taman Batang Duri**, a park and small zoo with civets, monkeys, otters and birds. It is open every day until 6 pm and is worth a quick look. Admission is free.

KUALA BELALONG FIELD STUDIES CENTRE

This scientific research centre is in the Batu Apoi Forest Reserve, a large area of primary rainforest that covers most of southern Temburong. The centre was developed by Brunei Shell and the Universiti Brunei Darussalam to provide facilities for research into tropical rainforest. It is primarily for scientists and school groups, though interested overseas visitors can stay at the centre.

The forest is rich in flora and fauna, and within the reserve the jungle can be explored along walking trails. The main trail is a rugged two day walk to Bukit Belalong. More trails are being developed and visitor facilities are planned, but at present accommodation at the centre is limited. Visitors should not turn up unannounced – bookings must be made through the Biology Department of the Universiti Brunei Darussalam (☎ 02-427001). Accommodation, guides and transport from Bangar can be arranged. A visit to the park is not cheap, and access is by chartered longboat from Batang Duri.

PERADAYAN FOREST RESERVE

This forest reserve contains the peaks of Bukit Patoi and Bukit Peradayan, which can be reached along a walking trail. The dipterocarp rainforest is the most accessible for visitors to Brunei, and the wildlife includes squirrels, treeshrews, moonrat and mouse deer. The chances of spotting the mainly nocturnal wildlife are slim, but the park also contains hornbills, and many sightings have been recorded. Bring water and food for the walk.

The most popular walk is to Bukit Patoi, which starts at the entrance to the park, 15 km from Bangar. The park has toilets and a picnic area at the start of the trail. The trail is steep in parts but well marked, with rest huts along the way. It is about a half-hour walk to Batu Berdinding, a sandstone outcrop, and then another 15 minutes to the summit. All up, the walk shouldn't take more than an hour with plenty of rest stops on the way. At the summit there are fine views to the east across the South China Sea and the Lawas area of Sarawak.

Most walkers descend back along the trail, but it is possible to continue over the other side of the summit and around to Bukit Peradayan. This trail is harder and indistinct in parts, though trees along the trail are marked to show the way. The trail eventually rejoins the road, 12 km from Bangar near the Labu Km 5 marker. Three hours should be allowed for the walk from Bukit Patoi summit to Bukit Peradayan and back to the road.

Glossary

The following is a list of words and phrases which you may come across:

adat – Malay customary law
adat temenggong – Malay law with Indian modifications. Adat temenggong is the law governing the customs and ceremonies of the sultans.
air – water
air terjun – waterfall
alor – groove, furrow, main channel of river
ampang – dam
arrack – distilled fire-water
atap – roof thatching

Baba-Nyonyas – the Straits Chinese, the original Chinese settlers in the Straits Settlements of Melaka, Singapore and Penang, who intermarried with Malays and adopted many Malay customs
bajang – evil spirit (takes the form of a cat)
bandar – a port
batang – stem, tree-trunk, the main branch of a river
batas – boundary wall of a padi field
batu – stone, rock, milepost
belukar – secondary forest
bendahara – chief minister
bendang – irrigated land
bukit – hill
bumiputra – indigenous Malaysians (literally 'sons of the soil')
bunga raya – hibiscus flower (national flower of Malaysia)

dato, datuk – literally 'grandfather', but general male non-royal title of distinction
dusun – small town

genting – mountain pass
gua – cave
gunung – mountain

hilir – lower reaches of a river
hutan – jungle, forest

istana – palace

jalan – road

kali – river
kampung – village
kangkar – Chinese village
kedai kopi – coffee shop
khalwat – 'close proximity', or exhibition of public affection between the sexes
kopi tiam – coffee shop
kota – fort or city
kuala – river mouth, or place where a tributary joins a larger river

labuan – port
laksamana – admiral
laut – sea
Lebuh Raya – expressway or freeway, usually refers to the North-South Highway that runs from Johor Bahru to Bukit Kaya Hitam at the Thai border.
lubuk – deep pool

masjid – mosque
merdeka – independence
muara – river mouth
muezzin – the official of a mosque, who calls the faithful to prayer

negara – country
negeri – state

orang asing – foreigner
Orang Asli – Malaysian aborigines (literally 'original people')
orang laut – indigenous coastal people

padang – open grassy area (usually the city square)
pantai – beach
parit – ditch
pasar – market
pekan – market place or town
penghulu – chief or village head
pengkalan – quay

Peranakan – literally meaning 'half-caste', refers to the Baba-Nyonyas or Straits Chinese
pulau – island
puteri – princess

raja – prince, ruler
rakyat – common people
rantau – straight coastline
rimba – jungle
roti – bread (as in roti canai, flaky Indian bread normally served with a curry sauce)

sebrang – far bank of a river
selat – strait
semenanjung – peninsula
simpang – junction of more than two roads
sungai – river

tamu – weekly market
tanah – land
tanjung – headland
tasik – lake
teluk – bay
temenggong – Malay administrator
tunku – royal prince

ujung – cape
UMNO – United Malays National Organisation

yang di-pertuan – 'he who is lord'
yang di-pertuan agong – Malaysia's head of state, or 'king'
yang di-pertuan besar – head of state in Negeri Sembilan
yang di-pertuan muda – underking
yang di-pertuan negeri – governor

Index

ABBREVIATIONS

Bru – Brunei

Mal – Malaysia

Sin – Singapore

MAP

TEXT

Map references are in **bold** type.

Thanks

Thanks to the many travellers who wrote in with helpful hints, useful advice and interesting and funny stories.

Azmi Hj Abdullah, James Alley, Richard Alvoid, Amanda Aston, F Audet, John Ayers, John Bailey, Chris Bain, M Baker, Stuart Baker, Delia Banks, Jens Baranowski, Rod Baser, Jocelyn Bateman, SJ Bater, M Benjamin, Kate Bielinski, Gavin Biggs, Janice Bomford, John Borich, DC Boyall, Val Braun, Doug Brown, Peter Brown, Jan Buijse, Jean Bureau, Glyn Carre, Jason Carter, Mark Cave, Nam Whue Chin, Ng Yoo Chong, Anders Clausen, Raymond Coe, Andrew Coker, Bruce Cook, Liane Cook, Fenella Cooke, Linda Cummings, Kevin Cunningham

Elsa Dalmasso, Tamatha Darcey, Jay Davidson, Isobel Davie, Robert Davison, Andrew Dean, Esther Dean, A Decalande, Lucien De Prycker, Peter Derrick, N Deschamps, Cynthia Dinowitz, Paul & Sheila Doherty, A Donoghue, Roger Doswell, Pia & Michael Dowling, Susanne Drachmann, Colleen Dulian, Sigi Edwards, T Enbleton, Cathrin Eszbach, Neil & Ruth Evans, Kirsten Evensen, Tim Eyre

Teresa Farrell, Dr Michael Forster, Paul Fowler, Mary Fraser, Mark Fynn, Scott Gilford, Nicky Green, A Griffiths, Paula Guerrein, Paul Gurn, Martin Hadley, Danotty Hall, Stephen Hall, Douglas Hamilton, Bjarne Stig Hansen, Chris Hardy, Robert Harrison, Tom Haslam, Rhonda Hawkins, Gaye Haworth, Toby Helliwell, Sue Henschke, Ruth Heywood, David L Hilburn, Jo'an Hoh, Karl Holmes, Petri Hottola, Paul Hunt, Sharon Isaac, Beverley Jackson, Sven Jensen, T Jey, TP Jeyaram, Chris Jones, Karen Jones, Lloyd Jones, Pernille Jorgensen

Bev & Paul Karlik, Wolfgang Kasper, Jan A Kaulfuhs, George E Kavanagh, Ritchie Kay, Jacqui Kew, John Kirkwood, Hugh Kitchin, Hans Koopman, Susanne Kotner, Doris Kreit, Jean LaForest, Lawrence Lee, Tami Lempert, Sara Lesser, M Lumb, Hugh MacIndoe, Peter & Penny MacKay, Iain MacKenzie, Shan Lyn Ma, Roland Magre, Pat Malone, Angela & Stephen Manthorpo, Goerges Mazzocut, Stephen McElhinney, Venetia McMahon, Maureen Mecozzi, Rachel Mellors, Andy Millard, Julie Miller, Phil Miller, Shaharudin Mohamad, Ishak bin Mokhtar, John Moline, Peter Moran, Bruce & Lorraine Moss, Andrew Mudge

Jerome & Pauline Netter, C Newson, Helle Noach, Karen Nott, Renate Notter, Achim Nuhr, James Ong, Peter O'Reilly, Steffen Owen, Chloe Paine, Rolf Palmberg, Mark Paluch, Allan Pashby, Susan Paterson, Maryanne Patience, Jim Paulin, Frank Peotzki, Isaac Perkins, Guy Petzall, Sarah Price, C Pritchard, BLH Ralph, Jenny Reynolds, Jane Richardson, Murray Robbins, RE Roberts, Lionel Robertson, Jim Ronald, Herb Russell, Sarah Russell, David Thomas Ryyken

William I-Ching Sam, Christine Sauerwein, Mette Schmidt-Hansen, Vreni Schnetzer, Hans Schonockel-Og, R Seger, Chris Sennett, Norman Shepherd, Aidan Siddall, Matthew Siegal, L Simanowitz, Amerjeet Singh, Andrew Smith, Jeffrey Smith, Robyn Smith, Rachel Smyley, L & J Snyder, Jean-C Somer, Hans Sondern, Ben Soo, Marina Starcke, Jennifer Stepanik, Rebecca Stevens, RE Storrar, Paul Sundberg, Ruth Surajudin, Eileen Synnott

G Tan, Helen Tatham, Ali Temara, Albert Teo, Beverly Terry, Dr William L Thomas, Jean Thompson, Charles Tyler, Martin Upham, Eddy van der Ven, Tatiana Visona, Cornelia von Streit, Nick Wagner, U Wajner, Janet Walker, Wai Lun Wan, David & Yvette Wands, Carla Weeman, EJ Weller, Mark Wilkinson, Mike Williams, Bernard Wilson, TA Wong, Sara Wright, JW Zottnick, Hanni & Tony

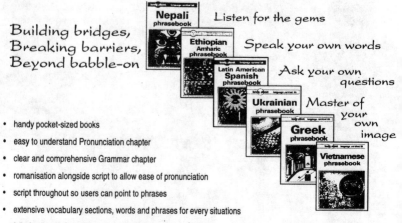

LONELY PLANET JOURNEYS

JOURNEYS is a unique collection of travel writing – published by the company that understands travel better than anyone else. It is a series for anyone who has ever experienced – or dreamed of – the magical moment when they encountered a strange culture or saw a place for the first time. They are tales to read while you're planning a trip, while you're on the road or while you're in an armchair, in front of a fire.

JOURNEYS books catch the spirit of a place, illuminate a culture, recount a crazy adventure, or introduce a fascinating way of life. They always entertain, and always enrich the experience of travel.

ISLANDS IN THE CLOUDS
Travels in the Highlands of New Guinea
Isabella Tree

Isabella Tree's remarkable journey takes us to the heart of the remote and beautiful Highlands of Papua New Guinea and Irian Jaya – one of the most extraordinary and dangerous regions on earth. Funny and tragic by turns, *Islands in the Clouds* is her moving story of the Highland people and the changes transforming their world.

Isabella Tree, who lives in England, has worked as a freelance journalist on a variety of newspapers and magazines, including a stint as senior travel correspondent for the *Evening Standard.* A fellow of the Royal Geographical Society, she has also written a biography of the Victorian ornithologist John Gould.

'One of the most accomplished travel writers to appear on the horizon for many years . . . the dialogue is brilliant' **– Eric Newby**

SEAN & DAVID'S LONG DRIVE
Sean Condon

Sean Condon is young, urban and a connoisseur of hair wax. He can't drive, and he doesn't really travel well. So when Sean and his friend David set out to explore Australia in a 1966 Ford Falcon, the result is a decidedly offbeat look at life on the road. Over 14,000 death-defying kilometres, our heroes check out the re-runs on tv, get fabulously drunk, listen to Neil Young cassettes and wonder why they ever left home.

Sean Condon lives in Melbourne. He played drums in several mediocre bands until he found his way into advertising and an above-average band called Boilersuit. *Sean & David's Long Drive* is his first book.

'Funny, pithy, kitsch and surreal . . . This book will do for Australia what Chernobyl did for Kiev, but hey you'll laugh as the stereotypes go boom'

– Time Out

LONELY PLANET TRAVEL ATLASES

Lonely Planet has long been famous for the number and quality of its guidebook maps. Now we've gone one step further and in conjunction with Steinhart Katzir Publishers produced a handy companion series: Lonely Planet travel atlases – maps of a country produced in book form.

Unlike other maps, which look good but lead travellers astray, our travel atlases have been researched on the road by Lonely Planet's experienced team of writers. All details are carefully checked to ensure the atlas corresponds with the equivalent Lonely Planet guidebook.

The handy atlas format means no holes, wrinkles, torn sections or constant folding and unfolding. These atlases can survive long periods on the road, unlike cumbersome fold-out maps. The comprehensive index ensures easy reference.

- full-colour throughout
- maps researched and checked by Lonely Planet authors
- place names correspond with Lonely Planet guidebooks – no confusing spelling differences
- legend and travelling information in English, French, German, Japanese and Spanish
- size: 230 x 160 mm

Available now:
Chile & Easter Island • Egypt • India & Bangladesh • Israel & the Palestinian Territories •Jordan, Syria & Lebanon • Kenya • Laos • Portugal • South Africa, Lesotho & Swaziland • Thailand • Turkey • Vietnam • Zimbabwe, Botswana & Namibia

---

LONELY PLANET TV SERIES & VIDEOS

Lonely Planet travel guides have been brought to life on television screens around the world. Like our guides, the programmes are based on the joy of independent travel, and look honestly at some of the most exciting, picturesque and frustrating places in the world. Each show is presented by one of three travellers from Australia, England or the USA and combines an innovative mixture of video, Super-8 film, atmospheric soundscapes and original music.

Videos of each episode – containing additional footage not shown on television – are available from good book and video shops, but the availability of individual videos varies with regional screening schedules.

Video destinations include: Alaska • American Rockies • Australia – The South-East • Baja California & the Copper Canyon • Brazil • Central Asia • Chile & Easter Island • Corsica, Sicily & Sardinia – The Mediterranean Islands • East Africa (Tanzania & Zanzibar) • Ecuador & the Galapagos Islands • Greenland & Iceland • Indonesia • Israel & the Sinai Desert • Jamaica • Japan • La Ruta Maya • Morocco • New York • North India • Pacific Islands (Fiji, Solomon Islands & Vanuatu) • South India • South West China • Turkey • Vietnam • West Africa • Zimbabwe, Botswana & Namibia

The Lonely Planet TV series is produced by:
Pilot Productions
The Old Studio
18 Middle Row
London W10 5AT UK

For video availability and ordering information contact your nearest Lonely Planet office.

Music from the TV series is available on CD & cassette.

PLANET TALK

Lonely Planet's FREE quarterly newsletter

We love hearing from you and think you'd like to hear from us.

When... is the right time to see reindeer in Finland?
Where... can you hear the best palm-wine music in Ghana?
How... do you get from Asunción to Areguá by steam train?
What... is the best way to see India?

For the answer to these and many other questions read PLANET TALK.

Every issue is packed with up-to-date travel news and advice including:

- a letter from Lonely Planet co-founders Tony and Maureen Wheeler
- go behind the scenes on the road with a Lonely Planet author
- feature article on an important and topical travel issue
- a selection of recent letters from travellers
- details on forthcoming Lonely Planet promotions
- complete list of Lonely Planet products

To join our mailing list contact any Lonely Planet office.

Also available: Lonely Planet T-shirts. 100% heavyweight cotton.

LONELY PLANET ONLINE

Get the latest travel information before you leave or while you're on the road

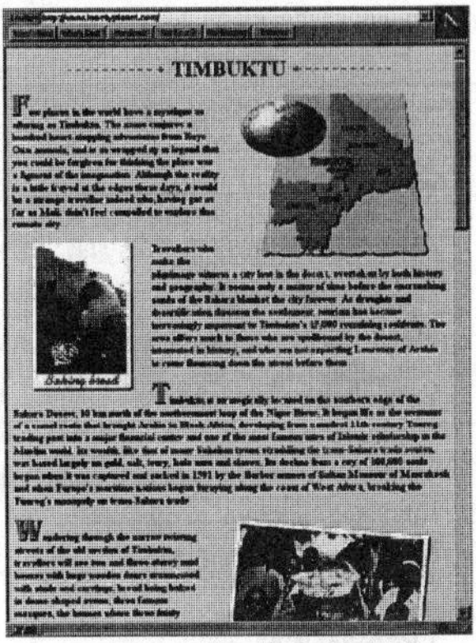

Whether you've just begun planning your next trip, or you're chasing down specific info on currency regulations or visa requirements, check out Lonely Planet Online for up-to-the minute travel information.

As well as travel profiles of your favourite destinations (including maps and photos), you'll find current reports from our researchers and other travellers, updates on health and visas, travel advisories, and discussion of the ecological and political issues you need to be aware of as you travel.

There's also an online travellers' forum where you can share your experience of life on the road, meet travel companions and ask other travellers for their recommendations and advice. We also have plenty of links to other online sites useful to independent travellers.

And of course we have a complete and up-to-date list of all Lonely Planet travel products including guides, phrasebooks, atlases, Journeys and videos and a simple online ordering facility if you can't find the book you want elsewhere.

www.lonelyplanet.com
or
AOL keyword: lp

LONELY PLANET PRODUCTS

Lonely Planet is known worldwide for publishing practical, reliable and no-nonsense trav information in our guides and on our web site. The Lonely Planet list covers just about eve accessible part of the world. Currently there are eight series: *travel guides*, *shoestring guid* *walking guides*, *city guides*, *phrasebooks*, *audio packs*, *travel atlases* and *Journeys* – a uniq collection of travel writing.

EUROPE

Amsterdam • Austria • Baltic States phrasebook • Britain • Central Europe on a shoestring • Central Europe phrasebo Czech & Slovak Republics • Denmark • Dublin • Eastern Europe on a shoestring • Eastern Europe phrasebook • Estor Latvia & Lithuania • Finland • France • Greece • Greek phrasebook • Hungary • Iceland, Greenland & the Faroe Island Ireland • Italy • Mediterranean Europe on a shoestring • Mediterranean Europe phrasebook • Paris • Poland • Portuga Portugal travel atlas • Prague • Russia, Ukraine & Belarus • Russian phrasebook • Scandinavian & Baltic Europe o shoestring • Scandinavian Europe phrasebook • Slovenia • Spain • Spanish phrasebook • St Petersburg • Switzerlan Trekking in Greece • Trekking in Spain • Ukrainian phrasebook • Vienna • Walking in Britain • Walking in Switzerlan Western Europe on a shoestring • Western Europe phrasebook

NORTH AMERICA

Alaska • Backpacking in Alaska • Baja California • California & Nevada • Canada • Florida • Hawaii • Honolulu • Los Angeles • Mexico • Miami • New England • New Orleans • New York, New Jersey & Pennsylvania • Pacific Northwest USA • Rocky Mountain States • San Francisco • Southwest USA • USA phrasebook • Washington, DC & the Capital Region

CENTRAL AMERICA & THE CARIBBEAN

Bermuda • Central America on a shoestring • Costa Rica • Cuba • Eastern Caribbean • Guatemala, Belize & Yucatán: La Ruta Maya • Jamaica

SOUTH AMERICA

Argentina, Uruguay & Paraguay • Bolivia • Brazil • Brazilian phrasebook • Buenos Aires • Chile & Easter Island • Chile & Easter Island travel atlas • Colombia • Ecuador & the Galápagos Islands • Latin American Spanish phrasebook • Peru • Quechua phrasebook • Rio de Janeiro • South America on a shoestring • Trekking in the Patagonian Andes • Venezuela

Travel Literature: Full Circle: A South American Journey

ANTARCTICA

Antarctica

ISLANDS OF THE INDIAN OCEAN

Madagascar & Comoros • Maldives • Mauritius, Réunion & Seychelles

AFRICA

Africa on a shoestring • Arabic (Moroccan) phrasebook • Cape Town • Central Africa • East Africa • Egypt • Egy travel atlas • Ethiopian (Amharic) phrasebook • Kenya Kenya travel atlas • Malawi, Mozambique & Zambia Morocco • North Africa • South Africa, Lesotho Swaziland • South Africa, Lesotho & Swaziland trav atlas • Swahili phrasebook • Trekking in East Africa • We Africa • Zimbabwe, Botswana & Namibia • Zimbabw Botswana & Namibia travel atlas

Travel Literature: The Rainbird: A Central African Journey • Songs to an African Sunset: A Zimbabwean Story

MAIL ORDER

Lonely Planet products are distributed worldwide.They are also available by mail order from Lonely Planet, so if you have difficulty finding a title please write to us. North American and South American residents should write to Embarcadero West, 155 Filbert St, Suite 251, Oakland CA 94607, USA; European and African residents should write to 10 Barley Mow Passage, Chiswick, London W4 4PH; and residents of other countries to PO Box 617, Hawthorn, Victoria 3122, Australia.

NORTH-EAST ASIA

Beijing • Cantonese phrasebook • China • Hong Kong • Hong Kong, Macau & Guangzhou • Japan • Japanese phrasebook • Japanese audio pack • Korea • Korean phrasebook • Mandarin phrasebook • Mongolia • Mongolian phrasebook • North-East Asia on a shoestring • Seoul • Taiwan • Tibet • Tibet phrasebook • Tokyo

Travel Literature: Lost Japan

MIDDLE EAST & CENTRAL ASIA

Arab Gulf States • Arabic (Egyptian) phrasebook • Central Asia • Iran • Israel & the Palestinian Territories • Israel & the Palestinian Territories travel atlas • Istanbul • Jerusalem • Jordan & Syria • Jordan, Syria & Lebanon travel atlas • Middle East • Turkey • Turkish phrasebook • Turkey travel atlas • Yemen

Travel Literature: The Gates of Damascus • Kingdom of the Film Stars: Journey into Jordan

ALSO AVAILABLE:

Travel with Children • Traveller's Tales

INDIAN SUBCONTINENT

Bangladesh • Bengali phrasebook • Delhi • Hindi/Urdu phrasebook • India • India & Bangladesh travel atlas • Indian Himalaya • Karakoram Highway • Nepal • Nepali phrasebook • Pakistan • Rajasthan • Sri Lanka • Sri Lanka phrasebook • Trekking in the Indian Himalaya • Trekking in the Karakoram & Hindukush • Trekking in the Nepal Himalaya

Travel Literature: In Rajasthan • Shopping for Buddhas

SOUTH-EAST ASIA

Bali & Lombok • Bangkok • Burmese phrasebook • Cambodia • Ho Chi Minh City • Indonesia • Indonesian phrasebook • Indonesian audio pack • Jakarta • Java • Laos • Lao phrasebook • Laos travel atlas • Malay phrasebook • Malaysia, Singapore & Brunei • Myanmar (Burma) • Philippines • Pilipino phrasebook • Singapore • South-East Asia on a shoestring • South-East Asia phrasebook • Thailand • Thailand travel atlas • Thai phrasebook • Thai audio pack • Thai Hill Tribes phrasebook • Vietnam • Vietnamese phrasebook • Vietnam travel atlas

AUSTRALIA & THE PACIFIC

Australia • Australian phrasebook • Bushwalking in Australia • Bushwalking in Papua New Guinea • Fiji • Fijian phrasebook • Islands of Australia's Great Barrier Reef • Melbourne • Micronesia • New Caledonia • New South Wales & the ACT • New Zealand • Northern Territory • Outback Australia • Papua New Guinea • Papua New Guinea phrasebook • Queensland • Rarotonga & the Cook Islands • Samoa • Solomon Islands • South Australia • Sydney • Tahiti & French Polynesia • Tasmania • Tonga • Tramping in New Zealand • Vanuatu • Victoria • Western Australia

Travel Literature: Islands in the Clouds • Sean & David's Long Drive

THE LONELY PLANET STORY

Lonely Planet published its first book in 1973 in response to the numerous 'How did you do it?' questions Maureen and Tony Wheeler were asked after driving, bussing, hitching, sailing and railing their way from England to Australia.

Written at a kitchen table and hand collated, trimmed and stapled, *Across Asia on the Cheap* became an instant local bestseller, inspiring thoughts of another book.

Eighteen months in South-East Asia resulted in their second guide, *South-East Asia on a shoestring*, which they put together in a backstreet Chinese hotel in Singapore in 1975. The 'yellow bible', as it quickly became known to backpackers around the world, soon became *the* guide to the region. It has sold well over half a million copies and is now in its 9th edition, still retaining its familiar yellow cover.

Today there are over 240 titles, including travel guides, walking guides, language kits & phrasebooks, travel atlases and travel literature. The company is the largest independent travel publisher in the world. Although Lonely Planet initially specialised in guides to Asia, today there are few corners of the globe that have not been covered.

The emphasis continues to be on travel for independent travellers. Tony and Maureen still travel for several months of each year and play an active part in the writing, updating and quality control of Lonely Planet's guides.

They have been joined by over 70 authors and 170 staff at our offices in Melbourne (Australia), Oakland (USA), London (UK) and Paris (France). Travellers themselves also make a valuable contribution to the guides through the feedback we receive in thousands of letters each year and on our web site.

The people at Lonely Planet strongly believe that travellers can make a positive contribution to the countries they visit, both through their appreciation of the countries' culture, wildlife and natural features, and through the money they spend. In addition, the company makes a direct contribution to the countries and regions it covers. Since 1986 a percentage of the income from each book has been donated to ventures such as famine relief in Africa; aid projects in India; agricultural projects in Central America; Greenpeace's efforts to halt French nuclear testing in the Pacific; and Amnesty International.

'I hope we send people out with the right attitude about travel. You realise when you travel that there are so many different perspectives about the world, so we hope these books will make people more interested in what they see. Guidebooks can't really guide people. All you can do is point them in the right direction.'

– Tony Wheeler

lonely planet

LONELY PLANET PUBLICATIONS

Australia
PO Box 617, Hawthorn 3122, Victoria
tel: (03) 9819 1877 fax: (03) 9819 6459
e-mail: talk2us@lonelyplanet.com.au

USA
Embarcadero West, 155 Filbert St, Suite 251,
Oakland, CA 94607
tel: (510) 893 8555 TOLL FREE: 800 275-8555
fax: (510) 893 8563
e-mail: info@lonelyplanet.com

UK
10 Barley Mow Passage, Chiswick,
London W4 4PH
tel: (0181) 742 3161 fax: (0181) 742 2772
e-mail: 100413.3551@compuserve.com

France:
71 bis rue du Cardinal Lemoine, 75005 Paris
tel: 1 44 32 06 20 fax: 1 46 34 72 55
e-mail: 100560.415@compuserve.com

World Wide Web: http://www.lonelyplanet.com